abled. Plaintiffs primarily used the Rehabilitation Act of 1973 (29 U.S.C.A. § 701 et seq.), the earliest law of this type. But the Rehabilitation Act has a limited scope: it applies only to federally funded workplaces and institutions, and says nothing about those that do not receive government money.

With passage of the ADA in 1990, Congress gave broad protection to people with AIDS who work in the private sector. In general, the ADA is designed to increase access for disabled persons, and it also forbids discrimination in hiring or promotion in companies with fifteen or more employees. Specifically, employers may not discriminate if the person in question is otherwise qualified for the job. Moreover, they cannot use tests to screen out disabled persons, and they must provide reasonable accommodation for disabled workers. The ADA, which took effect in 1992, has quickly emerged as the primary means for bringing AIDS-related discrimination lawsuits.

AIDS and Health Care Closely related to work is the issue of health care. In some cases, the two overlap: health insurance, Social Security, and disability benefits for AIDS victims were often hard to obtain during the 1980s. Insurance was particularly difficult because employers feared rising costs and insurance companies did not want to pay claims. To avoid the costs of AIDS, insurance companies used two traditional industry techniques: they attempted to exclude AIDS coverage from general policies, and they placed caps (limits on benefits payments) on AIDS-related coverage.

In January 1995, the settlement in a lawsuit brought by a Philadelphia construction worker with AIDS illustrated that the ADA can be used to fight caps on coverage. In 1992, the joint union-management fund for the Laborers' District Council placed a $10,000 limit on AIDS benefits, in stark contrast to the $100,000 allowed for other catastrophic illnesses. At that time, the fund said the cap on AIDS benefits was designed to curb all health costs. In 1993, the EEOC ruled that it violated the ADA, and, backed by the AIDS Law Project of Philadelphia, the worker sued. Rather than fight an expensive lawsuit, the insurance fund settled.

AIDS and Education Issues in the field of education include the rights of HIV-positive students to attend class and of HIV-positive teachers to teach, the confidentiality of HIV records, and how best to teach young people about AIDS. A few areas have been settled in court: for instance, the right of students to attend classes was of greater concern in the early years of the epidemic, and no longer remains in dispute.

Certain students with AIDS may assert their right to public education under the Education for All Handicapped Children Act of 1975 (EAHCA), but the law is only relevant in cases

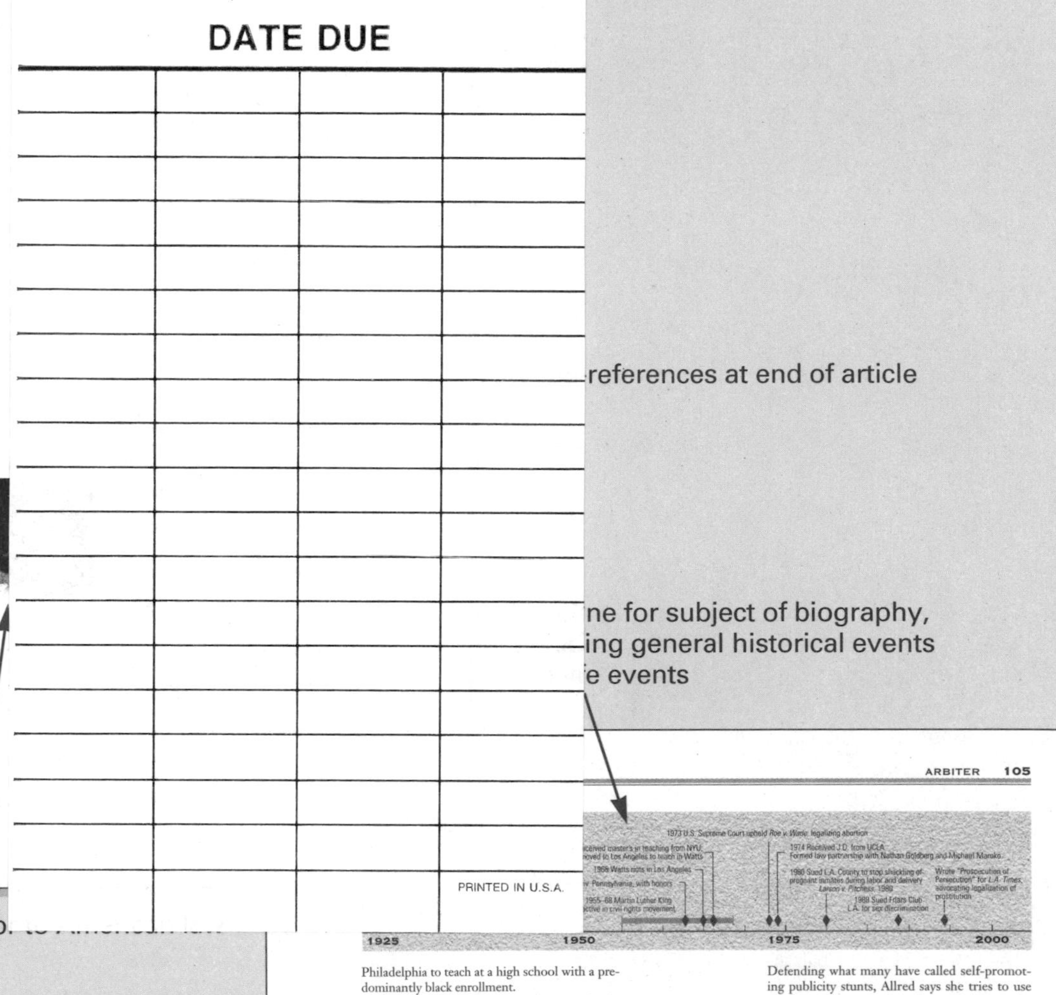

-references at end of article

-ne for subject of biography, -ing general historical events -e events

Biography of contributo...

1925 1950 1975 2000

Philadelphia to teach at a high school with a predominantly black enrollment.

Allred says her interest in the struggle for equal rights arose from personal experiences. While she was in college, she married, gave birth to a daughter, and divorced. Unable to collect CHILD SUPPORT from her former husband, she was forced to return to her parents' home. She also recalls being paid less than a man for what she considered equal work. The reason given was that the man had a family to support, but at the time, Allred was the single mother of an infant.

After moving to California, Allred taught in the turbulent Watts section of Los Angeles and became the first full-time female staff member in United Teachers of Los Angeles, the union representing Los Angeles teachers. The experience stirred her interest in CIVIL RIGHTS and collective bargaining and prompted her to go to law school. She received her law degree, with honors, from Loyola Marymount University, Los Angeles, Law School in 1974. Soon after, she entered a law firm partnership with her classmates Nathan Goldberg and Michael Maroko.

Allred is probably the most flamboyant and well known member of her firm. She has achieved notoriety and name recognition through staged press conferences and demonstrations publicizing and dramatizing the cause she is championing at the time. She also accepts controversial cases that naturally attract media attention. During her years in practice, she has successfully sued Los Angeles County to stop the practice of shackling and chaining pregnant inmates during labor and delivery; put a halt on the city of El Segundo's quizzing job applicants about their sexual histories (*Thorne v. City of El Segundo*, 802 F.2d 1131 [9th Cir. 1986]); represented a client who was turned down for a job as a police officer after a six-hour lie detector exam that included questions about her sex life; and sued a dry cleaning establishment for discrimination because it charged more to launder women's shirts than men's.

Allred relishes confrontation, and her showy tactics have earned her both praise and criticism.

"THERE ARE ENOUGH HIGH HURDLES TO CLIMB, AS ONE TRAVELS THROUGH LIFE, WITHOUT HAVING TO SCALE ARTIFICIAL BARRIERS CREATED BY LAW OR SILLY REGULATIONS."

Defending what many have called self-promoting publicity stunts, Allred says she tries to use the few moments she is in the spotlight to make her point as forcefully as possible. Her detractors say that she wastes her time and energy on trivial issues that do not advance any worthwhile cause and deflect attention away from serious issues. Yet, she points out, she is often stopped on the street by people who recognize her and want to thank her for taking on the small fights that no one else wants.

Some critics say she is all show and no substance. But Allred has many supporters as well. Among them is Justice Joan Dempsey Klein, of the California Court of Appeal, who credits Allred with moving women's issues forward. Klein also points out that Allred saves her dramatics for outside the courtroom and always observes proper decorum when before the bench. According to Klein, Allred is always well-prepared and, for that reason, is quite successful.

Dressed in her trademark reds and electric blues, her striking black hair set off by deep red lipstick, Allred is a potent combination of scholarship and theatrics. Her keen intelligence and shrewd understanding of the power of the media have made her a contemporary success story in the world of law and politics.

ARBITER [*Latin, One who attends something to view it as a spectator or witness.*] Any person who is given an absolute power to judge and rule on a matter in a dispute.

Internal cross references

Quotation from subject of biography

Full cite for case

Definition enclosed in book logos with Latin translation provided

WEST'S ENCYCLOPEDIA *of* AMERICAN LAW

R

WEST'S ENCYCLOPEDIA *of* AMERICAN LAW

Volume 8

WEST GROUP

is the result of efforts by
als and entities from the
ound the United States.
to thank all who made this publication, its quality and content, a priority in their lives.

In addition to the individuals who worked on *West's Encyclopedia of American Law*, West Group recognizes Harold W. Chase (1922–1982) for his contributions to *The Guide to American Law: Everyone's Legal Encyclopedia.*

Printed in the United States of America
05 04 03 02 01 00 99 98   8 7 6 5 4 3 2 1 0
Library of Congress Cataloging in Publication Data
ISBN: 0-314-20161-0 (Hard)

West's encyclopedia of American law.
p. cm.
Includes bibliographical references and indexes.
ISBN 0-314-20161-0 (hard : alk. paper)
1. Law—United States—Encyclopedias.
2. Law—United States—Popular works.
I. West Publishing Company.
KF154.W47 1997
348.73′03—dc20
[347.30803]   96-34350
CIP

PRODUCTION CREDITS
Cover, interior design, and page layout: David J. Farr, ImageSmythe
Composition: Carlisle Communications
Proofreading: Wiest International
Photo research: Elsa Peterson Ltd.
Art research: Nanette E. Bertaut
Editorial research: Pat Lewis
Artwork: Patricia Isaacs, Parrot Graphics
Indexing: Schroeder Indexing Services

This publication is designed to provide information on the subjects covered. It is sold with the understanding that the publisher is not engaged in rendering legal or other professional advice. If legal advice or other professional assistance is required, the services of a competent professional person should be sought.

WEST'S COMMITMENT TO THE ENVIRONMENT

In 1906, West Publishing Company began recycling materials left over from the production of books. This began a tradition of efficient and responsible use of resources. Today, 100 percent of our legal bound volumes are printed on acid-free, recycled paper consisting of 50 percent new paper pulp and 50 percent paper that has undergone a de-inking process. We also use vegetable-based inks to print all of our books. West recycles nearly 27,700,000 pounds of scrap paper annually—the equivalent of 229,300 trees. Since the 1960s, West has devised ways to capture and recycle waste inks, solvents, oils, and vapors created in the printing process. We also recycle plastics of all kinds, wood, glass, corrugated cardboard, and batteries, and have eliminated the use of polystyrene book packaging. We at West are proud of the longevity and the scope of our commitment to the environment.

West pocket parts and advance sheets are printed on recyclable paper and can be collected and recycled with newspapers. Staples do not have to be removed. Bound volumes can be recycled after removing the cover.

Production, printing, and binding by West Group.

PREFACE

The legal system of the United States is admired around the world for the freedoms it allows the individual and the fairness with which it attempts to treat all persons. On the surface, it may seem simple. Yet, those who have delved into it know that this system of federal and state constitutions, statutes, regulations, and common-law decisions is elaborate and complex. It derives from the English common law, but includes principles older than England, and from other lands. Many concepts are still phrased in Latin. The U.S. legal system, like many others, has a language all its own. Too often it is an unfamiliar language.

In 1983, West published *The Guide to American Law: Everyone's Legal Encyclopedia*, in response to a dearth of reference sources weaving the language of the law into the language of everyday life. *West's Encyclopedia of American Law (WEAL)*, developed with generous feedback from users of *The Guide*, replaces that set as an improved and updated legal encyclopedia. *WEAL* is a reference source devoted to the terms and concepts of U.S. law. It also covers a wide variety of persons, entities, and events that have shaped the U.S. legal system. *WEAL* contains thousands of entries, and a number of unique features and visual aids. It is the most complete reference source of its kind.

Main Features of This Set

Entries This encyclopedia contains over 4,000 entries devoted to terms, concepts, events, movements, cases, and persons significant to U.S. law. Entries on legal terms contain a definition of the term, followed by explanatory text if necessary. Entries are arranged alphabetically in standard encyclopedia format for ease of use. A wide variety of additional features, listed later in this preface, provide interesting background and supplemental information.

Definitions Every entry on a legal term is followed by a definition, which begins and ends with the symbol of an open book (📖). The appendix volume includes a glossary containing all the definitions from the *WEAL*.

Cross-References To facilitate research, *WEAL* provides two types of cross-references, within and following entries. Within the entries, terms are set in small capital letters—for example, LIEN—to indicate that they have their own entry in the encyclopedia. At the end of the entries, related entries the reader may wish to explore are listed alphabetically by title.

In Focus Pieces In Focus pieces accompany related entries and provide additional facts, details, and arguments on particularly interesting, important, or controversial issues raised by those entries. The subjects covered include hotly contested issues, such as abortion, capital punishment, and gay rights; detailed processes, such as the Food and Drug Administration's approval process for new drugs; and important historical or social issues, such as debates over the formation of the U.S. Constitution. In Focus pieces are marked by the symbol that appears in the margin.

Sidebars Sidebars provide brief highlights of some interesting facet of accompanying entries. They complement regular entries and In Focus pieces by adding informative details. Sidebar topics include the Million Man March, in Washington, D.C., and the branches of the

U.S. armed services. Sidebars appear at the top of a text page and are set in a blue box.

Biographies WEAL profiles a wide variety of interesting and influential people—including lawyers, judges, government and civic leaders, and historical and modern figures—who have played a part in creating or shaping U.S. law. Each biography includes a time line, which shows important moments in the subject's life as well as important historical events of the period. Biographies appear alphabetically by the subject's last name.

Additional Features of This Set

Milestones in the Law A special section, Milestones in the Law, appearing at the end of selected volumes, allows readers to take a close look at landmark cases in U.S. law. Readers can explore the reasoning of the judges and the arguments of the attorneys that produced major decisions on important legal and social issues. Included in the Milestones section are the opinions of the lower courts; the briefs presented by the parties to the U.S. Supreme Court; and the decision of the Supreme Court, including the majority opinion and all concurring and dissenting opinions for each case.

Enhancements Throughout *WEAL,* readers will find a broad array of photographs, charts, graphs, manuscripts, legal forms, and other visual aids enhancing the ideas presented in the text.

Tables and Indexes *WEAL* features several detailed tables and indexes at the back of each volume, as well as a cumulative index contained in a separate volume.

Appendixes An appendix volume included with *WEAL* contains hundreds of pages of documents, laws, manuscripts, and forms fundamental to and characteristic of U.S. law.

Citations Wherever possible, *WEAL* entries include citations for cases and statutes mentioned in the text. These allow readers wishing to do additional research to find the opinions and statutes cited. Two sample citations, with explanations of common citation terms, can be seen below and opposite.

Bibliography A bibliography is included at the end of each book and in the index volume.

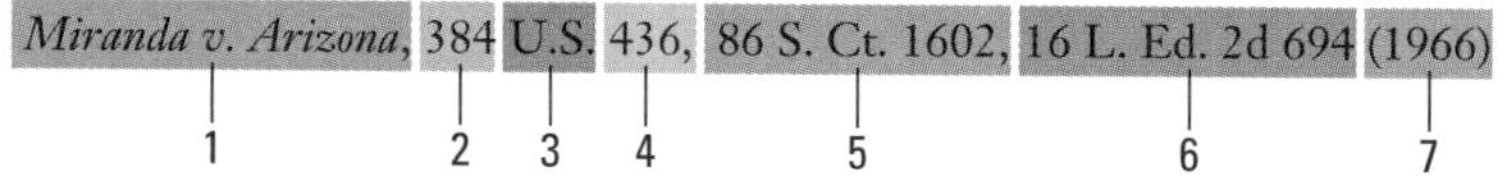

1. *Case title.* The title of the case is set in italics and indicates the names of the parties. The suit in this sample citation was between Ernesto A. Miranda and the state of Arizona.
2. *Reporter volume number.* The number preceding the reporter name indicates the reporter volume containing the case. (The volume number appears on the spine of the reporter, along with the reporter name.)
3. *Reporter name.* The reporter name is abbreviated. The suit in the sample citation is from the reporter, or series of books, called *U.S. Reports,* which contains cases from the U.S. Supreme Court. (Numerous reporters publish cases from the federal and state courts.)
4. *Reporter page.* The number following the reporter name indicates the reporter page on which the case begins.
5. *Additional reporter citation.* Many cases may be found in more than one reporter. The suit in the sample citation also appears in volume 86 of the *Supreme Court Reporter,* beginning on page 1602.
6. *Additional reporter citation.* The suit in the sample citation is also reported in volume 16 of the *Lawyer's Edition,* second series, beginning on page 694.
7. *Year of decision.* The year the court issued its decision in the case appears in parentheses at the end of the cite.

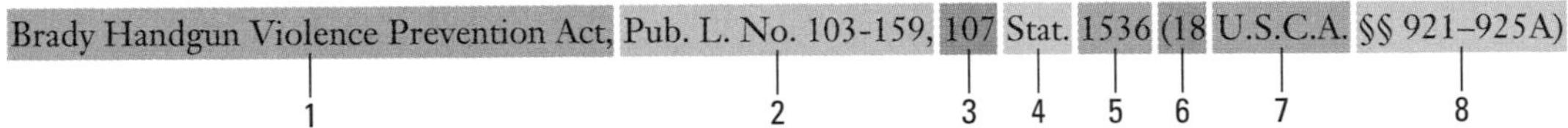

1. *Statute title.*
2. *Public law number.* In the sample citation, the number 103 indicates that this law was passed by the 103d Congress, and the number 159 indicates that it was the 159th law passed by that Congress.
3. *Reporter volume number.* The number preceding the reporter name indicates the reporter volume containing the statute.
4. *Reporter name.* The reporter name is abbreviated. The statute in the sample citation is from *Statutes at Large.*
5. *Reporter page.* The number following the reporter name indicates the reporter page on which the statute begins.
6. *Title number.* Federal laws are divided into major sections with specific titles. The number preceding a reference to the *U.S. Code Annotated* is the title number. Title 18 of the U.S. Code is Crimes and Criminal Procedure.
7. *Additional reporter.* The statute in the sample citation may also be found in the *U.S. Code Annotated.*
8. *Section numbers.* The section numbers following a reference to the *U.S. Code Annotated* indicate where the statute appears in that reporter.

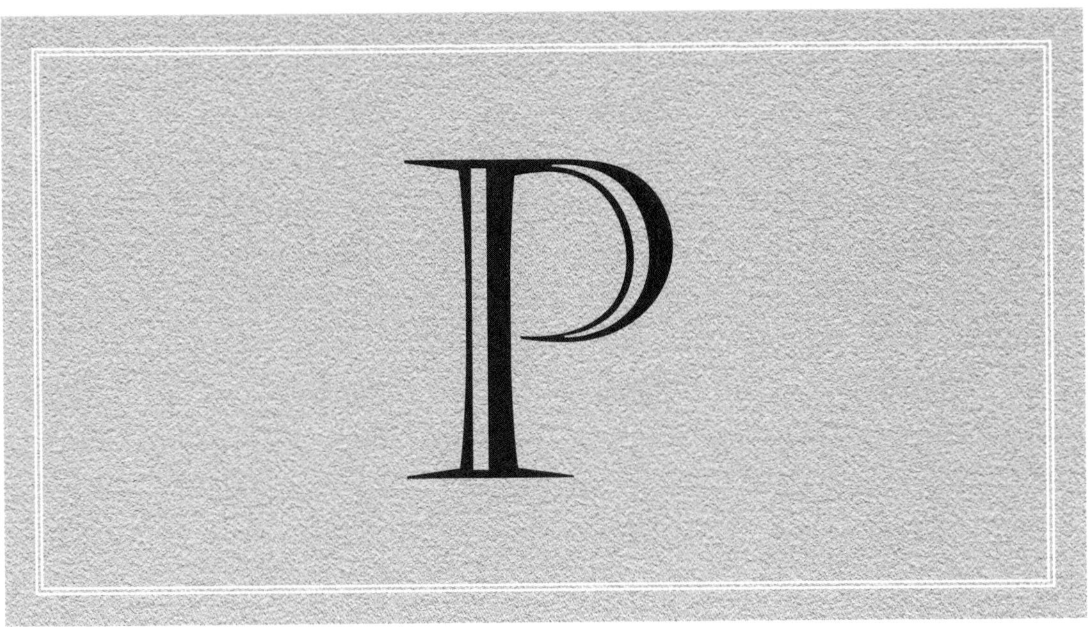

PACIFIC RAILROAD ACT Legislation passed by Congress in 1862 (12 Stat. 489) that authorized the construction of the first transcontinental railway line connecting the east and west coasts.

The need for a transcontinental railway to facilitate transportation of persons and products across the United States became increasingly clear in the 1850s due to the acquisition of California and the resolution of the Oregon boundary dispute. In 1862, before the secession of the South from the Union, the Republican party in Congress was instrumental in enacting legislation that authorized the Union Pacific Railway and the Central Pacific Railroad to construct such a railway. The Union Pacific Railway was to begin construction at Omaha, Nebraska, with the objective of connecting with the Central Pacific Railroad, which was to begin construction at the same time at Sacramento, California. The law provided that after each railroad laid forty miles of track, it was to receive 6,400 acres of public lands and government loans ranging from $16,000 to $48,000 per mile of track completed.

Congress passed additional legislation in 1864 to provide more land and money to complete the project. The two lines finally met at Promontory Point, Utah, in 1869, thereby providing a fast means of access from the Missouri River and the Pacific Ocean by rail.

The Union Pacific Railway and the Central Pacific Railroad were merged into the Union Pacific Railroad in 1900 by Edward Harriman.

See also RAILROADS.

PACIFISM A belief or policy of opposition to WAR or violence as a means of settling disputes.

In the face of unrelenting violence, the practice of pacifism may seem unduly forgiving and weak. The rise of Nazism in the 1930s and the resulting Holocaust is one example of unchecked evil that makes pacifism seem untenable. However, pacifists maintain that unswerving nonviolence can bestow upon people a power greater than that achieved through the use of violent aggression.

Over the years, pacifism has acquired different meanings. As a consequence, it is practiced in a variety of ways. For example, pacifists may make an individual vow of nonviolence. They may also organize and actively pursue nonviolence and peace between nations. They may even assert that some form of support for selective violence is sometimes necessary to achieve worldwide peace.

History The earliest form of recorded pacifism appeared in the teachings of Siddhārtha Gautama, who became known as the Buddha. The Buddha, or the Enlightened One, left his family at a young age and spent his life searching for a release from the human condition. Before dying in northeast India between 500 and 350 B.C., the Buddha taught the paths to elevated existence and inspired a new religion. Buddhism eventually spread from India to central and Southeast Asia, China, Korea, Japan, and the United States.

Buddhism has developed three distinct doctrines: Theravada, Mahayana, and Tantric. The essence of all three involves a search for truth, or dharma. Through meditation, the Buddhist seeks a realization of anatman, or the nonexistence of a soul. This can lead to nirvana, an indescribable state of release, which cannot be achieved without the practice of total nonviolence.

The teachings of Jesus Christ continued the attachment of nonviolence to organized religion. Christ taught, in part, that an appropriate response to violence is to "turn the other cheek" and offer no resistance.

As civilization expanded and distinct states were formed, Christianity was carried to developing areas. It became popularized as the official religion of entire states, the leaders of which sought to retain both Christianity and a stronghold on power. In the third century, the nonresistance aspect of Christianity was reconsidered, and certain passages in the Gospel were interpreted to mean that resistance is an acceptable reaction to evil forces.

Saint Augustine solidified Christianity's break with pure pacifism in the fifth century with a warmly received religious treatise. In *The City of God,* he maintained, in part, that peace could be realized only through the acceptance of Christianity and that the church was to be defended.

More than a millennium passed before the next great pacifist movement was seen. In the fifteenth century, Martin Luther led the Protestant Reformation, which inspired religious creativity. Europeans who were disenchanted with Catholicism broke away from the church, experimented with observations and practices, and founded their own religions. The most pacific of these was Anabaptism. Anabaptists practiced nonviolence and actively supported those suffering from violence.

In the seventeenth century, still more pacific religious groups were established, such as the Mennonites, the Brethren, and the Religious Society of Friends. Of these, the Friends have gathered the largest following in the United States.

Religious Society of Friends In 1652, George Fox founded the Religious Society of Friends in England. Initially, Friends were known as Children of the Light, Publishers of Truth, or Friends of Truth. They held fast to the belief that there exists in all persons a light, which can be understood as the presence of God. With this reverence for other people, nonviolence came naturally. And, since God exists in all people, violence can be avoided by finding and revealing the Light in others.

Friends eventually acquired the nickname Quakers, perhaps from the trembling some experience as they find the Inner Light during meetings. The nickname was originally coined by antagonists and intended as derisive, but many Friends began to use it in their own speech. *Quaker* soon lost its derogative connotation, and it remains the most recognized name for Friends.

A Friend's commitment to pacifism often came with no small dose of activism. Friends interrupted church services and refused to take oaths in seventeenth-century England, arguing that if one always tells the truth, one need not promise to do so. Friends ignored social niceties, refusing, for example, to remove their hat in the presence of royalty. Friends also used the informal *thee* and *thy* in place of the more respectful *you* and *your.* Within four years of the creation of the Society, Friends in England were being imprisoned by the thousands, and they began to seek refuge in the New World.

Ann Austin and Mary Fisher were the first Friends to reach colonial America from England. After their arrival in 1656, Austin and Fisher were imprisoned and deported. Friends who came after them suffered a similar fate. Many of those who stayed moved to Rhode Island, which Roger Williams founded on religious freedom principles.

In 1681, Charles II gave to William Penn, a longtime Friend, the charter to colonial land in America as repayment for a debt owed to Penn's father. In 1682, Penn founded Pennsylvania as a "holy experiment," and many English and European Friends found permanent sanctuary there.

Friends continued their activism in colonial America by obstructing the business of SLAVERY. Many Friends published their opposition to slavery and assisted fugitive slaves. Friends also addressed other social issues, such as the treatment of mentally ill persons and the rights of women. With the onset of the Civil War, many Friends reconsidered their absolute refusal to participate in war and helped the Union forces and slaves. In World Wars I and II, many Friends took an active part in medical and relief work.

The Holy Bible of Christianity is favored by many Friends, but any similarity between the Society and most other Christian religions ends there. The hallmark of Friends is their simplicity. Generally, their service or mass is called a meeting or program and is held at a meetinghouse. Quakers observe long silences, wait for the presence of God, and speak when inspired.

Friends are a fixture in the United States' religious and political landscape and are the most prominent of its pacifists. The American Friends Service Committee, established in 1917, performs relief work for countries ravaged by war, disease, and famine. Friends for a Non-Violent World, another well-known internal organization, exists to promote worldwide peace. Friends in over fifty countries around the world are connected by the Friends of the

World Committee for Consultation, and Friends in the United States and Canada are joined together in the American Friends Fellowship Council.

Mohandas K. Gandhi Mohandas K. Gandhi was the first great modern pacifist. Born October 2, 1869, in Porbandar, India, Gandhi led a high-profile life dedicated to political and social reform through nonviolence.

At age nineteen, Gandhi studied law in London. He made friends at a vegetarian restaurant, and, intrigued by the ethical basis of vegetarianism, he began experiments with diet that would become important in his leadership.

Gandhi returned to India in 1889. Shortly thereafter, he accepted a job as an attorney for a business firm in Pretoria, South Africa. Gandhi suffered discrimination and humiliation en route to Pretoria, but he met the violence directed at him without resistance and lived through the encounters. The experience was cathartic for the sheltered young man. Initially using his status as an attorney, he embarked on a series of creative, successful CIVIL RIGHTS campaigns that lasted fifty-six years.

In South Africa, Gandhi applied political pressure by petitioning the government for action on Indian grievances. He raised issues such as Indian representation in the South African government and the recognition of basic civil rights for Indians, both in South Africa and during return visits to India in 1896 and 1901. Injustice to South African Indians was publicized in the *Indian Opinion*, a weekly established in 1903 and guided by Gandhi beginning in 1904.

In 1906 Gandhi urged South African Indians to submit to arrest and imprisonment rather than comply with unjust laws. Thousands were arrested and imprisoned, including Gandhi, who urged fellow Indians to obey strictly and cheerfully all prison rules except those excessively degrading or offensive to religion.

During the 1900s, Gandhi experimented with various means of resolving conflict. Passive resistance, according to Gandhi, had to be supplemented by an active effort to understand and respect adversaries. In an atmosphere of respect, people could find peaceful, creative solutions. This active campaign for equality was called satyagraha, or "grasping for the truth."

Gandhi led a well-orchestrated political campaign for Indians in South Africa through the early 1900s. The movement reached its pinnacle in November 1913, when Gandhi led Indian miners on the Great March into Transvaal. The march was a profound show of determination, and the South African government opened negotiations with Gandhi shortly thereafter.

Gandhi returned to India in January 1915, withdrew from public sight for a year, and then began a succession of political campaigns. He assisted indigo workers in Bihar and millworkers in Ahmadabad; organized commercial strikes to protest harsh penalties for political violence; led BOYCOTTS of British courts and councils in India; worked for the rights of untouchables, or unorthodox Hindus; promoted peaceful relations between Hindus and Muslims; and orchestrated various protests against English rule of India and taxes oppressive to poor people. Gandhi also held meetings with political leaders, and often fasted to underscore the plight of a particular group.

By promoting a variety of nonviolent activities designed to dramatize and call attention to social injustice, Gandhi won new rights for laborers, members of minorities, and poor people in South Africa and India. In many cases, however, Gandhi was working against centuries of hatred, and success was never absolute.

On January 30, 1948, a Hindu extremist, upset over Gandhi's cooperation with Muslims, shot and killed the leader in New Delhi as he arrived for evening prayers.

APWIDE WORLD PHOTOS

Though better known for challenging injustices in British-ruled India, Mohandas Gandhi spent many years working for the rights of Indian residents of South Africa.

TOPHAM/THE IMAGE WORKS

Martin Luther King, Jr., at a civil rights rally in Washington, D.C., on August 28, 1963, the day he delivered the "I Have a Dream" speech. He would use the phrase in other speeches throughout that summer.

Martin Luther King, Jr., and the Civil Rights Movement Gandhi's campaigns became the inspiration and model for the U.S. civil rights and political movements in the 1950s and 1960s. Among those inspired was MARTIN LUTHER KING, JR. King was born in Atlanta on January 15, 1929, the son of a Baptist preacher. His Baptist upbringing was supplemented by the study of theology at Crozer Theological Seminary in Chester, Pennsylvania, where he received a bachelor of divinity degree in 1951. At Crozer, King was introduced to the nonviolent teachings of Gandhi.

King received a doctor of philosophy degree from Boston University in 1955. In December of the same year, while serving as pastor of the Dexter Avenue Baptist Church, in Montgomery, Alabama, King became involved with the first great pacifist movement in the United States, the African American CIVIL RIGHTS MOVEMENT. He eventually spearheaded that movement.

On December 1, 1955, ROSA PARKS, a black Montgomery resident, refused to surrender her seat on a bus to a white man. Her subsequent arrest for violating segregation laws sparked a boycott of the Montgomery transit system led by King and the black activists of the Montgomery Improvement Association. The boycott lasted over one year, until the Montgomery city government abolished segregation on buses. King's leadership had helped effect political change without the use of violence, and he resolved to build on the success.

In the late 1950s, King organized the SOUTHERN CHRISTIAN LEADERSHIP CONFERENCE (SCLC). The SCLC operated as a network for civil rights work and a platform from which to address the nation and the world. King met with Prime Minister Jawaharlal Nehru of India in February 1959 and discussed, among other topics, the nonviolent legacy of the great Gandhi.

King moved to his native Atlanta in 1960 and became copastor of Ebenezer Baptist Church with his father. For the next eight years, King engaged the United States, especially the Southeast, in much the same way Gandhi had captured India. Armed only with fortitude, the moral rightness of a cause, and an exceptional gift for public speaking, King was able to garner widespread support for a series of popular campaigns that led to the end of official discrimination and segregation in the southern United States.

The influence of Gandhi on King was apparent. At the core of King's philosophy was nonviolence, but this pacifism was buttressed by action. Like Gandhi, King directed much of his energy toward the organization of nonviolent campaigns designed to call attention to social injustice. The campaigns did not always win the hearts and minds of all U.S. citizens. Occasionally, King and fellow civil rights activists were even penalized for the violence of their opponents.

In 1965 King began to focus on the city of Chicago and its treatment of minorities. Marches and demonstrations on the subject of civil rights began to spring up. By the summer of 1966, King and Chicago demonstrators had succeeded in their goal of generating " 'creative tension' " in Chicago (*City of Chicago v. King*, 86 Ill. App. 2d 340, 230 N.E.2d 41 [1967]). Eventually, the demonstrations grew to be too large for the Chicago police to manage.

The Chicago Police Department began in July 1966 to request notice of the time and place of marches. King and other demonstrators offered assurances that adequate notice would be given, but, out of more than two hundred summer demonstrations, only two written notices were received by the police. An assurance by King to the Chicago police on August 4 was followed by several unannounced marches.

On August 16, Chicago demonstrators conducted six separate neighborhood marches without providing notice to the police. The marches disrupted pedestrian and vehicle traffic because at each, the demonstrators were met by several hundred to several thousand counter-demonstrators. The counterdemonstrators hurled rocks, firecrackers, and other objects at the marchers, inflicting injuries and damaging property.

On August 19, the city of Chicago and its superintendent of police filed a COMPLAINT in the Circuit Court of Cook County, Illinois. The city of Chicago sought a court order, or INJUNCTION, to control the number, size, time, and place of marches and demonstrations. Judge Cornelius Harrington granted the injunction, which meant that if any demonstrators defied the order, they could be arrested and jailed for CONTEMPT of court. In addition, the demonstrators faced other criminal charges, such as DISORDERLY CONDUCT and RIOT.

On August 22, Frank Ditto, a demonstration leader, held a press conference at which he declared his intention to violate the court order. Ditto read a prepared statement, which included a request for intervention by the U.S. Department of Justice. Ditto also declared that if Chicago officials were " 'unable to control and maintain law and order during the peaceful process of the democratic system, then Martial Law and not unconstitutional court injunction is required' " (*King*). That night, Ditto, seventeen other adults, and nine children marched along a sidewalk in a Chicago neighborhood from 7:20 P.M. until 8:20 P.M. The next day, the court summoned Ditto to appear before it.

On August 25, Ditto appeared before the court with counsel, and Chicago prosecutors presented the case against him. The hearing was continued to September 6, at which time Ditto argued that the injunction violated his FIRST AMENDMENT rights to free speech and assembly. The court refused to consider the argument because it was not relevant to the question of whether Ditto had violated the order. Ditto was convicted of contempt of court and sentenced to six months in jail.

On appeal, the Fourth Division of the First District Appellate Court of Illinois affirmed Ditto's conviction. According to the court, the constitutionality of the order was beyond the scope of the contempt hearing, and the court cited CASE LAW supporting that legal rule.

Having already spent a "substantial period" of time in jail, Ditto asked for a reduction in his sentence, arguing that he had already endured sufficient punishment. Instead of denying the request with a simple cite of authority, the court took the opportunity to lecture Ditto on proper conduct in civilized society. The court discussed civil disobedience at length, mentioning HENRY DAVID THOREAU and Gandhi, and declared that the "non-materialistic revolutionary doctrines of passive resistance . . . contained no preachment that laws and courts could be defied with impunity."

The court took umbrage at Ditto's request for leniency. "[A]fter urging disrespect for law and the courts in the name of 'civil disobedience,' " the court scolded, "it is then customary to seek the protection of that same judicial arm of government against serious retribution or punishment." The court closed by suggesting that if Ditto changed his attitude "from one of disobedience to one of obedience," he might succeed in reducing his sentence.

Conscientious Objector Status When the United States becomes involved in war, military service may become mandatory, and the status of CONSCIENTIOUS OBJECTOR (CO) is sought by pacifists to avoid military service. To qualify as a CO, one need only show " 'a sincere and meaningful' " objection to all war (*Reiser v. Stone*, 791 F. Supp. 1072 [E.D. Pa. 1992] [quoting *Shaffer v. Schlesinger*, 531 F.2d 124 (3d Cir. 1976)]). This objection need not be grounded in RELIGION. It is legitimate if it results from an " 'intensely personal' " conviction that some might find " 'incomprehensible' " or " 'incorrect' " (*Reiser* [quoting *United States v. Seeger*, 380 U.S. 163, 85 S. Ct. 850, 13 L. Ed. 2d 733 (1965)]).

In *Reiser*, Dr. Lynda Dianne Reiser sought discharge from military service on the grounds of a conscientious objection to war. Reiser had entered the Army in 1983 in the Reserve Officers' Training Corps (ROTC) program at Washington and Jefferson College. After graduating in 1986, she sought and received a deferment of military service in order to attend Temple University Medical School. Upon graduation from medical school in 1990, Reiser sought and received another deferment in order to perform a one-year medical internship. In August 1990, Reiser informed the Army that she was a conscientious objector and that she would refuse the four years of military service required of her in return for the ROTC scholarship.

Although Reiser had possessed moral convictions approaching pacifism before entering the ROTC program, she had envisioned a career in medicine and expected her participation in military service to be minimal. In 1985, serious misgivings over military service began to take hold in Reiser. By 1989, her opposition to military service was firm. After treating a sixteen-year-old shooting victim, Reiser experienced nightmares and attempted to avoid all contact with violence. In April 1990, her beliefs crystallized into complete opposition to violence, war, and military service. Four months later, she applied for CO status.

The Department of the Army Conscientious Objector Review Board (DACORB) denied Reiser's application in September 1990. Despite supporting testimony from Army chaplain Colonel Ronald Miller and Army investigator Lieutenant Colonel Charles Nester, DACORB concluded that Reiser's belief in pacifism was not sincerely held.

Reiser appealed DACORB's decision to the U.S. District Court for the Eastern District of Pennsylvania. After reciting the chronology of the case and the legal standards for CO status, the court conducted a complete review of the record. This included an in-depth examination of Reiser's evolution to pacifism.

In addition to possessing a predisposition to nonviolence, Reiser had undergone a pacific metamorphosis that had not been disproved. Reiser had been deeply affected by the Kurt Vonnegut novel *Slaughterhouse Five* (1969) and had had her growing pacifism affirmed by roommates. She had also experienced a strengthening of her nonviolent convictions as a result of her medical training.

DACORB had ruled that Reiser had failed to prove that she would have "no rest or inner peace" if she were not discharged. This standard had been rejected by the court in an earlier case, which held that conscientious objectors need only show sincerity in their opposition to war (*Masser v. Connolly*, 514 F. Supp. 734, 740 [E.D. Pa. 1981]). According to the *Reiser* court, the "no rest or inner peace" standard was valid, but nothing in the record supported DACORB's conclusion that Reiser would lose no sleep over forced military service.

Because the timing of a CO application alone cannot be used to deny CO status, DACORB took pains to deemphasize the timing of Reiser's application. However, Reiser's application came less than one year before she was scheduled to begin military service, and DACORB was unable to let the issue go untouched. The timing of the application, admitted DACORB, called Reiser's sincerity into question.

DACORB's use of application timing did call Reiser's sincerity into question. What DACORB failed to do, according to the court, was answer the question of Reiser's sincerity. Without additional support for its skepticism, DACORB's use of application timing as a basis for rejecting CO status for Reiser carried no weight. The court ultimately reversed the DACORB decision and relieved Reiser of her obligation to work four years for the U.S. Army.

PACKING The process of exercising unlawful, improper, or deceitful means to obtain a JURY composed of individuals who are favorably disposed to the VERDICT sought.

PACT A bargain, COMPACT, or agreement. An agreement between two or more nations or states that is similar to, but less complex than, a TREATY.

PACTA SUNT SERVANDA [*Latin, Promises must be kept.*] An expression signifying that the agreements and stipulations of the parties to a CONTRACT must be observed.

PACT OF PARIS See KELLOGG-BRIAND PACT.

PACTUM [*Latin, Pact.*] A COMPACT, bargain, or agreement.

Robert Treat Paine

PAINE, ROBERT TREAT Robert Treat Paine was born March 11, 1731, in Boston, Massachusetts. He graduated from Harvard University in 1749 and was admitted to the Massachusetts bar in 1757. After a brief career in the ministry, he became an eminent lawyer, politician, and judge.

Paine first won fame as an associate prosecuting attorney in the Boston Massacre trial. The Boston Massacre, which occurred in 1770, was a violent response to the passing of the TOWNSHEND ACTS by Great Britain. These acts decreed that CUSTOMS DUTIES would be imposed on the importation of tea, lead, glass, paints, and paper. When British troops were sent to Boston to enforce payment of the duties, the colonists harassed them to such an extent that they fired into a crowd, killing five men.

Subsequently Paine served two terms as a member of the Massachusetts Provincial Assembly, from 1773 to 1775 and from 1777 to

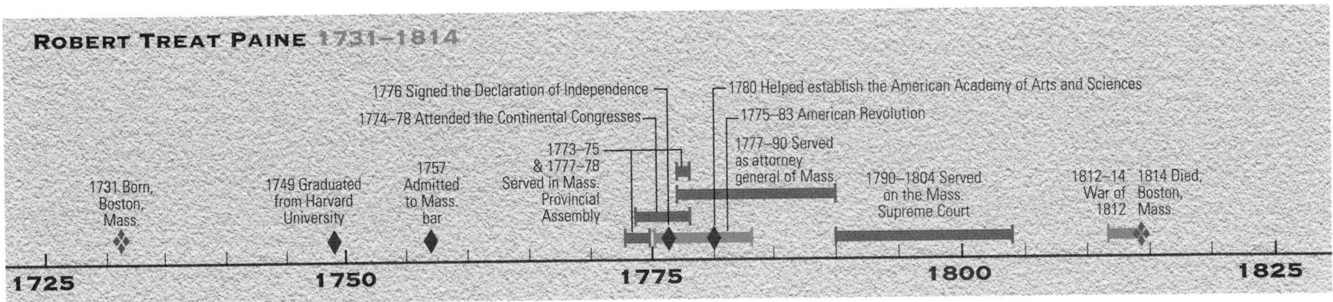

1778, acting as speaker during 1777 and 1778. During the next four years, he was an active member of two congresses: the Provincial Congress, in 1774 and 1775, and the Continental Congress, from 1774 to 1778. In 1776 he signed the DECLARATION OF INDEPENDENCE.

Paine continued to be active in Massachusetts government after the American Revolution. In 1777 he became the first attorney general of Massachusetts and held that office until 1790. From 1778 to 1780, he was involved in the enactment of the Massachusetts constitution and was instrumental in the establishment of the American Academy of Arts and Sciences in 1780.

In 1790, Paine became a justice of the Massachusetts Supreme Court, where he remained until 1804.

Paine died May 12, 1814, in Boston, Massachusetts.

See also BOSTON MASSACRE SOLDIERS; MASSACHUSETTS CONSTITUTION OF 1780.

PAINE, THOMAS Social agitator Thomas Paine was an influential political writer whose support of revolution and republican government emboldened the American colonists to declare independence from England. In 1776, the corset-maker-turned-pamphleteer published the first of a sixteen-part series entitled *The American Crisis.* Paine's tract contained the stirring words "These are the times that try men's souls." Paine wrote the famous pamphlet to lift the spirits of the beleaguered Continental Army.

The effect of Paine's political writing was felt not only in America but also in England and France. After the American Revolution, Paine returned to his native Europe, where he supported the French Revolution. His political opinions ignited a storm in England and landed him in jail in France. During his lifetime, Paine's political views made him both tremendously popular and almost universally despised. In particular, his later writings about organized religion and deism offended many Americans. Shunned and penniless at the end of his life, Paine has only recently found his rightful place in history.

Paine was born into a poor English family on January 29, 1737, in Thetford, Norfolk, England. To help support his Quaker father and Anglican mother, Paine quit school at age thirteen and began training in corset making, his father's trade. Unhappy in his vocation, Paine left home and enlisted as a seaman in the Seven Years' War. Afterward, he traveled to London, where he became interested in science and mechanics. Paine held a variety of jobs, including customs official, preacher, and schoolteacher. At the urging of BENJAMIN FRANKLIN, while Franklin served as a colonial official in England, Paine immigrated to America. Arriving in Philadelphia in 1774, Paine became the managing editor of *Pennsylvania Magazine.*

In January 1776, Paine produced his first important pamphlet, *Common Sense.* A phenomenal success, the publication sold more than five hundred thousand copies. Paine urged the American colonies not only to protest English taxation but to go further and declare independence. He also recommended calling a CONSTITUTIONAL CONVENTION to establish a new government. Paine's tract was extremely influential in convincing the colonists to cut their ties with England; embrace the Revolution; and embark upon a new, republican form of government.

Thomas Paine

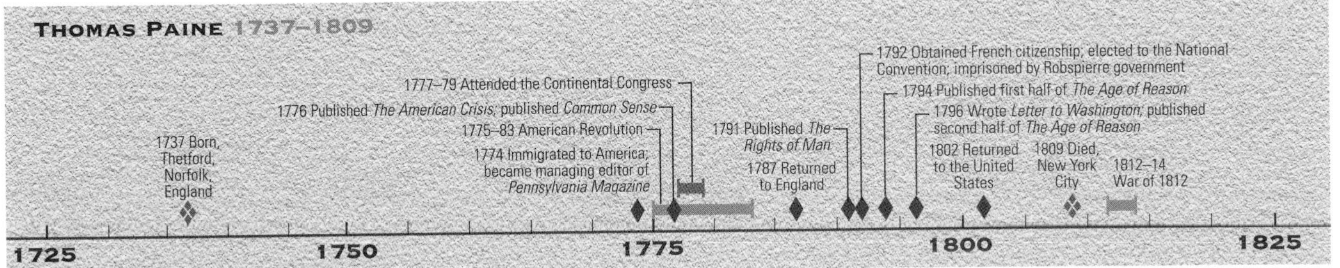

Paine served in the Continental Army and experienced firsthand the miserable conditions of war. To boost the soldiers' morale after a retreat, he wrote the influential series *The American Crisis.* Under orders from General Washington, Paine's pamphlet was read aloud to encourage the troops. *The American Crisis* has been given credit for inspiring the American victory in the Battle of Trenton.

Paine was elected to the Continental Congress in 1777, as secretary of the Committee of Foreign Affairs. He resigned under pressure in 1779 after publishing confidential information about treaty negotiations with France.

After the United States' victory over England, Paine devoted his time to perfecting his inventions. In 1787, he returned to Europe to gather financial support and interest in his ideas for an iron bridge. While in England, Paine became caught up in the debate over the French Revolution. In 1791, he published the first part of *The Rights of Man.* It was a response to EDMUND BURKE's *Reflections on the Revolution in France* (1790), a vigorous denunciation of the events in France. Paine's *The Rights of Man* supported the revolution and upheld the dignity and rights of the common person. Controversial for its time, *The Rights of Man* sold two hundred thousand copies in England but Paine was forced out of that country under an indictment for treason.

Paine moved to France. After obtaining French citizenship, he was elected to the National Convention in 1792. Because Paine protested the execution of Louis XVI, he was arrested and imprisoned by the radical Robespierre government. Barely avoiding the guillotine, he spent ten months in a Luxembourg prison before his release was won by JAMES MONROE, U.S. ambassador to France. Paine wrote *Letter to Washington* in 1796, a critical look at the U.S. president's inability to quickly obtain Paine's freedom.

While in prison, Paine published in 1794 the first half of his most controversial work, *The Age of Reason.* The second half was printed in 1796, after his release. In *The Age of Reason,* Paine criticized organized religion and explained his own deist beliefs. Deism is a religious and philosophical belief that accepts the concept of God but views reason as the key to moral truths. Deism was confused by many of Paine's readers with atheism, the rejection of a belief in God. Because people mistook *The Age of Reason* for an atheist tract, Paine came under attack for his unorthodox religious views.

When Paine arrived in the United States in 1802, he was rejected by many of his former associates. His reputation was damaged by his misinterpreted deist beliefs and by his public criticism of the American hero George Washington.

"SOCIETY IN EVERY STATE IS A BLESSING, BUT GOVERNMENT, EVEN IN ITS BEST STATE, IS BUT A NECESSARY EVIL; IN ITS WORST STATE AN INTOLERABLE ONE."

Paine died June 8, 1809, in New York City, misunderstood and impoverished, with his role in the Revolutionary War downplayed by his detractors. He was buried on his farm in New Rochelle, New York. In 1819, political journalist William Cobbett made arrangements to have Paine reburied in England in a place of honor. Somehow, en route to England, Paine's remains were lost. They were never retrieved.

Paine's reputation as a political philosopher has been largely restored. He is remembered favorably for his rousing call to arms during the American Revolution and for his defense of republicanism and the rights of common people.

PAIRING-OFF In the practice of legislative bodies, a system by which two members, who belong to opposing political parties or are on opposite sides with respect to a certain question, mutually agree that they will both be absent from voting, either for a specified period or when a vote is to be taken on the particular question.

As a result of pairing-off, a vote is neutralized on each side of the question, and the comparative division of the LEGISLATURE remains the same as if both members were present. The practice is said to have originated in the English House of Commons during the time of Oliver Cromwell.

PAIS [*French, The country; the neighborhood.*] A trial *per pais* denotes a trial by the country; that is, trial by JURY.

An ESTOPPEL in pais means that a party is prevented by his or her own conduct from obtaining the enforcement of a right which would operate to the detriment of another who justifiably relied on such conduct. This type of estoppel differs from an estoppel by DEED or by record which, as a result of the language set out in a document, bars the enforcement of a claim against a party who acted in reliance upon those written terms.

PALIMONY See ALIMONY; COHABITATION.

PALMER, ALEXANDER MITCHELL Alexander Mitchell Palmer served as U.S. attorney general from 1919 to 1921. Palmer, who also served as a congressman and federal judge, became a controversial figure for rounding up thousands of ALIENS in 1920 that he considered to be politically subversive. These "Palmer raids" violated basic civil liberties and ultimately discredited Palmer.

BIOGRAPHY

LIBRARY OF CONGRESS

Alexander Mitchell Palmer

Palmer was born May 4, 1872, in Moosehood, Pennsylvania. He graduated from Swarthmore College in 1891 and then studied law at

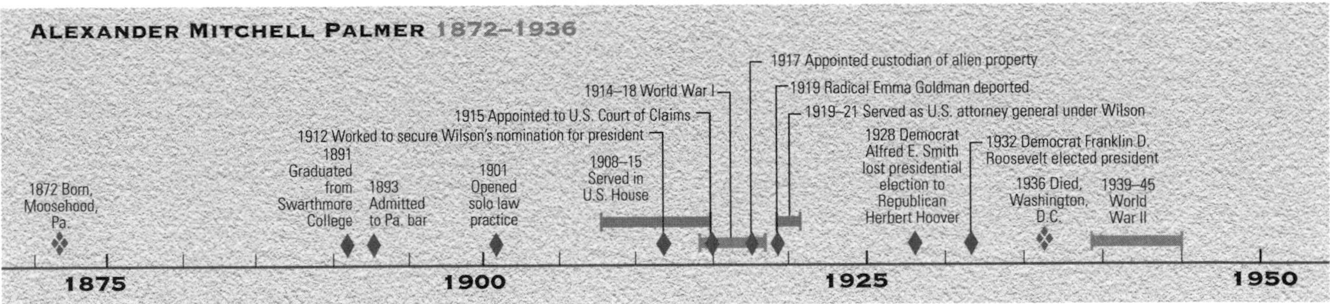

Swarthmore, Lafayette College, and George Washington University. Though he did not earn a law degree, he passed the Pennsylvania bar exam and was admitted to the bar in 1893. He entered a small law firm in Stroudsberg, Pennsylvania, and practiced there until 1901. He then became a solo practitioner.

During the 1890s, Palmer became active in Democratic party politics. He was elected to the U.S. House of Representatives in 1908 where he served until 1915. In 1912 he played a key role in securing the Democratic presidential nomination for New Jersey governor WOODROW WILSON. Following Wilson's victory that fall, Wilson asked Palmer to join his cabinet as secretary of war. Palmer's pacifist Quaker beliefs, however, precluded him from accepting the office.

In 1914 he ran for the U.S. Senate but lost. In April 1915 Wilson appointed him a judge of the United States Court of Claims. It was a brief appointment. He resigned in September and returned to his law practice. He continued his political career, however, serving as a member of the Democratic National Committee during Wilson's eight-year term.

In 1917, after the United States entered World War I, Wilson appointed Palmer custodian of alien property. Palmer's duties included seizing and selling properties belonging to aliens, primarily Germans, and his methods often met with disapproval.

In March 1919 Wilson appointed Palmer U.S. attorney general. Though World War I was over, the Bolshevik Revolution in Russia caused political hysteria in western Europe and the United States. The Communist movement advocated world revolution, and U.S. leaders suspected that left-wing radicals, who were primarily aliens, were plotting to overthrow the government.

Palmer used the Espionage Act of 1917 and the Sedition Act of 1918 to begin a crusade against this perceived threat. He deported the anarchist EMMA GOLDMAN and many other radicals, but these actions were a prelude to his unprecedented dragnets. On January 2, 1920, at Palmer's direction, federal agents in thirty-three cities rounded up six thousand persons suspected of subversive activities. Agents entered and searched homes without warrants, held persons without specific charges for long periods of time, and denied them legal counsel. Hundreds of aliens were deported. Palmer's actions were part of an anti-Communist "RED SCARE" that ignored civil liberties in the pursuit of rooting out allegedly subversive activities. He steadfastly defended the raids in the face of widespread protests.

"FULLY 90 PERCENT OF THE COMMUNIST AND ANARCHIST AGITATION IS TRACEABLE TO ALIENS."

Palmer sought to succeed Wilson as president but lost the Democratic party nomination in 1920. After leaving the office of attorney general in March 1921, Palmer resumed his private law practice and remained active in Democratic party politics, campaigning for presidential candidate Alfred E. Smith in 1928 and FRANKLIN D. ROOSEVELT in 1932.

Palmer died May 11, 1936, in Washington, D.C.

PALM OFF To misrepresent inferior goods of one producer as superior goods made by a reputable, well-regarded competitor in order to gain commercial advantage and promote sales.

The doctrine of palming off is applied to the particular facts of a case in which the defendant is accused of engaging in UNFAIR COMPETITION against the plaintiff.

PALPABLE Easily perceptible, plain, obvious, readily visible, noticeable, PATENT, distinct, manifest.

The term *palpable* usually refers to some type of egregious wrong, such as a governmental error or ABUSE OF POWER.

PALSGRAF v. LONG ISLAND RAILROAD COMPANY The case *Palsgraf v. Long Island Railroad Company*, 248 N.Y. 339, 162 N.E. 99, decided by the New York Court of Appeals in 1928, established the principle in TORT law that one who is negligent is liable only for the harm or the injury that is foreseeable and not for every injury that follows from his or her NEGLIGENCE.

The unique facts of the case created a need for a new application of the generally accepted theory that negligence is the absence of care, according to the circumstances. Mrs. Palsgraf was standing on a railroad platform when she was injured by falling scales. The scales toppled as the result of a shock of an explosion caused by an accident that occurred at the other end of the platform, "many feet away" from Palsgraf.

The accident involved a passenger with a package who was running to catch a departing train. As the passenger jumped to board the train, two railroad employees, one on the train and the other on the platform, reached for and pushed (respectively) him so he would not fall off it. The employees' help caused the passenger to drop the package. The package wrapped in newspaper contained fireworks that exploded upon hitting the tracks. The resulting explosion caused the scales to fall, striking Palsgraf. She sued the railroad for the conduct of its employees that led the passenger to drop his package of fireworks.

Both the trial court and the intermediate appellate court awarded JUDGMENT to the plaintiff, Palsgraf. The Court of Appeals decision, written by BENJAMIN CARDOZO, reversed the judgment. Cardozo stated that negligence is wrongful "because the eye of vigilance perceives the risk of danger . . . The risk reasonably to be perceived defines the duty to be obeyed, and risk imports relation; it is to another or others within the range of apprehension." Given this principle, Cardozo reasoned that "Here, by concession, there was nothing in the situation to suggest to the most cautious mind that the parcel wrapped in newspaper would spread wreckage throughout the station."

The dissenting opinion offered that "Every one owes to the world at large the duty of refraining from those acts that may unreasonably threaten the safety of others . . . Unreasonable risk being taken, its consequences are not confined to those who might probably be hurt." It viewed the concept of PROXIMATE CAUSE as "practical politics," not based on logic. Although it must be ". . . something without which the event would not happen," proximate cause means "that, because of convenience, of public policy, of a rough sense of justice, the law arbitrarily declines to trace a series of events beyond a certain point." The foreseeable or natural results of a negligent act affect a determination of whether the act is a proximate cause of the injuries. The dissenters, therefore, reasoned "given such an explosion as here, it needed no great foresight to predict that the natural result would be to injure one on the platform at no greater distance from its scene than was the plaintiff."

PANDER 🕮 To pimp; to cater to the gratification of the lust of another. To entice or procure a person, by promises, threats, FRAUD, or deception to enter any place in which PROSTITUTION is practiced for the purpose of prostitution. 🕮

Pandering is established when the evidence shows that the accused succeeded in inducing a victim to become an inmate of a house of prostitution. One who solicits for a prostitute is a panderer.

The *pandering of obscenity* refers to the business of purveying, by some form of advertising, pictorial or graphic material that appeals to the prurient interest of customers or potential customers. See also OBSCENE.

PANEL 🕮 A list of jurors to serve in a particular court or for the trial of a designated ACTION. A group of judges of a lesser number than the entire court convened to decide a case, such as when a nine-member APPELLATE COURT divides into three, three-member groups, and each group hears and decides cases. A plan in reference to prepaid legal services. 🕮

The term *open-panel legal services* refers to a plan in which legal services are paid for in advance, usually by insurance, but in which members can select their own lawyers. Under a closed panel, all legal services are rendered by a group of attorneys previously chosen by the insurer, the union, or another entity.

PAPER 🕮 A document that is filed or introduced in evidence in a lawsuit, as in the phrases *papers in the case* and *papers on appeal.*

Any written or printed statement, including letters, memoranda, legal or business documents, and books of account, in the context of the FOURTH AMENDMENT to the U.S. Constitution, which protects the people from unreasonable SEARCHES AND SEIZURES with respect to their "papers" as well as their persons and houses.

In the context of ACCOMMODATION PAPER and COMMERCIAL PAPER, a written or printed evidence of DEBT. 🕮

PAR 🕮 In commercial law, equal; equality. 🕮

The term *par* refers to an equality that exists between the nominal or FACE VALUE of a document—such as a BILL OF EXCHANGE or a share of STOCK—and its actual selling value. When the values are equal, the share is said to be *at par;* if it can be sold for more than its face value, it is *above par;* if it is sold for less than its nominal value, it is *below par.*

PARALEGAL See LEGAL ASSISTANT.

PARALLEL CITATION 🕮 A reference to the same case or statute published in two or more sources. 🕮

For example, *Brown v. Board of Education of Topeka, Kansas,* a landmark decision by the Supreme Court in 1954, can be located in 347 U.S. 483, 74 S. Ct. 686, and 98 L. Ed. 873. These references are parallel CITATIONS to REPORTERS in which Supreme Court decisions are published.

PARAMOUNT TITLE In the law of REAL PROPERTY, ownership that is superior to the ownership with which it is compared, in the sense that the former is the source or the origin of the latter.

The term *paramount title* is, however, frequently used to signify a TITLE that is merely better or stronger than another or will prevail over it. This usage is rarely correct, unless the superiority consists of the seniority of the title referred to as *paramount.*

PARCENER A joint HEIR.

Collectively the joint heirs are called coparceners.

PARDON The action of an executive official of the government that mitigates or sets aside the punishment for a crime.

The granting of a pardon to a person who has committed a crime or who has been convicted of a crime is an act of CLEMENCY, which forgives the wrongdoer and restores the person's CIVIL RIGHTS. At the federal level, the president has the power to grant a pardon, and at the state level the governor or a pardon board made up of high-ranking state officials may grant it.

The power to grant a pardon derives from the English system in which the king had, as one of his royal prerogatives, the right to forgive virtually all forms of crimes against the crown. The Framers of the U.S. Constitution, in Article II, Section 2, Clause 1, provided that the president "shall have Power to grant Reprieves and Pardons for Offences against the United States, except in Cases of Impeachment." Throughout U.S. history the courts have interpreted this clause to give the president virtually unlimited power to issue pardons to individuals or groups and to impose conditions on the forgiveness.

The first major court case on the pardon power, *Ex parte Garland,* 71 U.S. (4 Wall.) 333, 18 L. Ed. 366 (1866), established both the scope of the pardon power and the legal effect on a person who was pardoned. President ANDREW JOHNSON pardoned Arkansas attorney and Confederate sympathizer Alexander Hamilton Garland, who had not been tried, for any offenses he might have committed during the Civil War. Garland sought to practice in FEDERAL COURT, but federal law required that he swear an oath that he never aided the Confederacy. Garland argued that the pardon absolved him of the need to take the oath.

The Supreme Court agreed with Garland. It held that the scope of the pardon power "is unlimited, with the exception stated [IMPEACHMENT]. It extends to every offence known to the law, and may be exercised at any time after its commission, either before legal proceedings are taken, or during their pendency, or after conviction and judgment." The granting of an unconditional pardon fully restores an individual's civil rights forfeited upon conviction of a crime and restores the person's innocence as though he or she had never committed a crime. This means that a recipient of a pardon may regain the right to vote and to hold various positions of public trust.

A president or governor may grant a full pardon or a conditional pardon. A conditional pardon imposes a condition on the offender before it becomes effective. Typically this means the COMMUTATION of a sentence. For example, the president has the power under the Pardon Clause to commute a death sentence on the condition that the accused serve the rest of his or her life in prison without eligibility for parole, even though a life sentence imposed directly by a court would otherwise be subject to parole. In upholding this type of conditional pardon, the Supreme Court in *Schick v. Reed,* 419 U.S. 256, 95 S. Ct. 379, 42 L. Ed. 2d 430 (1974), reasoned that "considerations of public policy and humanitarian impulses support an interpretation of that [pardon] power so as to permit the attachment of any condition which does not otherwise offend the Constitution."

The power to pardon applies only to offenses against the laws of the JURISDICTION of which the pardoning official is the chief executive. Thus the president may only pardon for violations of federal law, and governors may only pardon for violations of the laws of their states.

Unless the pardon expressly states that it is issued because of a determination that the recipient was innocent, a pardon does not imply innocence. It is merely a forgiveness of the offense. It is generally assumed that acceptance of a pardon is an implicit acknowledgment of guilt, for one cannot be pardoned unless one has committed an offense.

The Constitution allows two other pardon powers besides the power of commutation. It expressly speaks about the president's power to grant "reprieves." A REPRIEVE differs from a pardon in that it establishes a temporary delay in the enforcement of the sentence imposed by the court, without changing the sentence or forgiving the crime. A reprieve might be issued for the execution of a prisoner to give time to the prisoner to prove his or her innocence. A related power is the power to grant "amnesty," which is also implicit in the pardon power. AMNESTY is applied to whole classes or communities, instead of individuals. The power to issue an amnesty and the effect of an amnesty are the same as those for a pardon.

The most widely publicized pardons have involved political figures. President GERALD R. FORD's September 1974 pardon of former president RICHARD M. NIXON for all offenses that he had committed or in which he had taken part relieved Nixon from facing criminal prosecution for his role in the WATERGATE scandal. President Ford justified the pardon as a way to restore domestic tranquility to a nation that had spent two years in political turmoil. In 1977 President JIMMY CARTER granted an amnesty to all persons who had unlawfully evaded the military draft during the VIETNAM WAR. Carter too justified his amnesty as a way to end a divisive period in U.S. history. In December 1992 President GEORGE BUSH pardoned six officials of the RONALD REAGAN administration who were implicated in the IRAN-CONTRA scandal. Bush granted the pardons shortly before leaving office. He based the pardons on his belief that the officials had been prosecuted over policy differences rather than for criminal acts.

PARENS PATRIAE [*Latin, Parent of the country.*] A doctrine that grants the inherent power and authority of the state to protect persons who are legally unable to act on their own behalf.

The *parens patriae* doctrine has its roots in English COMMON LAW. In feudal times various obligations and powers, collectively referred to as the "royal prerogative," were reserved to the king. The king exercised these functions in his role of father of the country.

In the United States, the *parens patriae* doctrine has had its greatest application in the treatment of children, mentally ill persons, and other individuals who are legally incompetent to manage their affairs. The state is the supreme guardian of all children within its JURISDICTION, and state courts have the inherent power to intervene to protect the best interests of children whose welfare is jeopardized by controversies between parents. This inherent power is generally supplemented by legislative acts that define the scope of child protection in a state.

The state, acting as *parens patriae*, can make decisions regarding mental health treatment on behalf of one who is mentally incompetent to make the decision on his or her own behalf, but the extent of the state's intrusion is limited to reasonable and necessary treatment.

The doctrine of *parens patriae* has been expanded in the United States to permit the attorney general of a state to commence litigation for the benefit of state residents for federal antitrust violations (15 U.S.C.A. § 15c). This authority is intended to further the public trust, safeguard the general and economic welfare of a state's residents, protect residents from illegal practices, and assure that the benefits of federal law are not denied to the general population.

States may also invoke *parens patriae* to protect interests such as the health, comfort, and welfare of the people, interstate WATER RIGHTS, and the general economy of the state. For a state to have standing to sue under the doctrine, it must be more than a nominal party without a real interest of its own and must articulate an interest apart from the interests of particular private parties.

CROSS-REFERENCES

Antitrust Law; Child Abuse; Children's Rights; Infants.

PARENT AND CHILD The legal relationship between a father or mother and his or her offspring.

The relationship between parent and child is of fundamental importance to U.S. society, because it preserves the safety and provides for the nurture of dependent individuals. For this reason, the parent-child relationship is given special legal consideration. Increasingly, state, local, and federal governments have become more involved in the relationship, especially when a child is abused or neglected. In addition, parental roles have shifted over time, and the law has moved with these changes. Legal rights that were once the sole province of the father are now shared with the mother, and in general, the law seeks to treat parents equally.

The term *child* is used in the limited sense to indicate an individual below the AGE OF MAJORITY. The more precise word for such an individual is *minor*, *juvenile*, or *infant*. The age of majority, which transforms a child legally into an adult, has traditionally been the age of twenty-one years. Many states, however, have reduced the age of majority to eighteen years.

Parent-Child Relationship In its most restricted use, the term *parent* refers only to a mother or father who is related to the child by blood. This is true whether the child is legitimate (the natural parents are married to each other) or illegitimate (the parents are not married to each other). Today, as a result of statutes, adoptive parents have the same rights and responsibilities as natural parents. Other persons standing in the place of natural parents, such as stepparents, are not, however, given such extensive rights and responsibilities. Although in some instances foster parents and foster care agencies have the legal responsibility to nurture a MINOR, they are not entitled to the full status of parent.

A child is the issue or offspring of his parents. A posthumous child is one conceived prior to, and born after, the death of his father. Such a child has the same INHERITANCE rights as a child born while his father is alive. A child is not entitled to full legal rights unless the child is born alive. The law does not ordinarily consider a fetus to be a child.

Various rights and responsibilities that reflect the social goals of nurturing and protecting dependent individuals are attached to the status of parent and child. The PUBLIC POLICY in favor of promoting the protection and care of minors gives rise to the legal PRESUMPTION that the parent-child relationship exists where acknowledged by a parent, or where a parent resides with and raises the child. The relationship continues in the absence of unusual circumstances that mandate intervention by the state. Proper legal procedures must be followed when the state intervenes. Parents or children cannot alter or destroy the relationship either by themselves or merely by agreement.

Ordinarily a parent has the right to the custody and supervision of her child. In addition, a parent has the DUTY to CARE for and nurture her offspring. The child has the right to receive this care and nurture and the obligation to yield to reasonable parental guidance and supervision. The state has a duty to preserve family stability by ensuring proper care of children. The right of the family to PRIVACY limits state regulation of the parent-child relationship to some extent, but modern laws dealing with CHILD ABUSE and NEGLECT give the state greater powers to intervene.

A parent's duties extend beyond the mere providing of daily necessities and financial support. A court may reasonably expect that a parent will provide for the child's education, medical care, and social and religious training, as well as exhibit love and affection for the child. A parent must also discipline the child when necessary.

Constitutional Considerations Statutes governing the parent-child relationship are primarily state laws. These laws must conform to the requirements of the U.S. Constitution and the constitution of the particular state. The U.S. Supreme Court has held that many provisions of the Constitution protect the parent-child relationship, as well as the rights of both parent and child.

The issue of whether to conceive or give birth to a child is governed by Supreme Court decisions involving the right to privacy. With *Griswold v. State of Connecticut*, 381 U.S. 479, 85 S. Ct. 1678, 14 L. Ed. 2d 510 (1965), the Court held that married people have the right to be educated about BIRTH CONTROL methods and to have access to contraceptive devices. The right was extended to unmarried people in *Eisenstadt v. Baird*, 405 U.S. 438, 92 S. Ct. 1029, 31 L. Ed. 2d 349 (1972). In *Roe v. Wade*, 410 U.S. 113, 93 S. Ct. 705, 35 L. Ed. 2d 147 (1973), the Court ruled that a woman has a right to have an ABORTION. Because an established legal principle states that a fetus is not a child, the state cannot interfere arbitrarily with the woman's decision to have an abortion by favoring the welfare of the fetus over her welfare.

Authority of Parents Parents are entitled to the custody of their children. They are free to make all decisions relating to the welfare of their child as they see fit, short of violating laws protecting children from abuse and neglect. Courts will not interfere with REASONABLE directives set forth by parents to discipline their children.

Modern statutes and courts have reconsidered the father's traditional primary role and now give equal powers, rights, and duties to both parents. In the case of DIVORCE or separation, all rights of decision and control over the child go to the parent awarded custody, except when joint custody is awarded. In the case of the death of one parent, the other parent assumes custody.

The parent has the obligation to furnish a home for the child. A parent has the right to use CORPORAL PUNISHMENT, but it must not be so excessive as to constitute child abuse.

A parent's power over his child includes the authority and obligation to oversee medical treatment. A parent will most likely be held guilty of criminal neglect if he disregards the health requirements of his child. In cases where essential medical treatment is not procured for a child, juvenile authorities will start proceedings to provide care for the child and disciplinary action for the parent.

A controversial issue arises when a child is ill and the parents refuse health treatment for religious reasons. In an emergency that would jeopardize the child's life, a court may override the parental consent requirement and authorize treatment. A much greater obstacle exists when the parents, on religious grounds, refuse to provide their child with medical care that is important but not life threatening.

Parents are allowed broad discretion in making decisions regarding their child's education. This freedom, however, is not absolute and is tempered by compulsory state school attendance laws and the right of the state to require that the child be educated. However, most states now allow home schooling, with education provided by a parent.

A parent who is guilty of failure to carry out obligations or of abuse of parental rights is guilty of a crime. A parent who fails to make

CHILDREN'S RIGHTS V. PARENTS' RIGHTS: YOU DON'T OWN ME . . . DO YOU?

IN FOCUS

In 1874 a badly beaten girl known only as Mary Ellen became the first legally recognized victim of child abuse in the United States. Before 1874, society offered little protection for minors. Children were considered the property of their parents, and neither the government nor private individuals intervened when they were injured, overworked, or neglected. Mary Ellen was rescued from unfit parents only after the American Society for the Prevention of Cruelty to Animals (ASPCA) stepped in on her behalf. ASPCA advocates pointed out that if Mary Ellen were a horse or a dog, her mistreatment would be prohibited by statute. A judge agreed that the young girl deserved at least the same protection as an animal.

The status of U.S. children has improved dramatically since Mary Ellen's ordeal. At the turn of the twentieth century, a nationwide child protection movement helped eliminate the long hours, poor wages, and punishing conditions faced by child workers. Child labor laws paved the way for later reforms in compulsory education, foster care, protective services, health care, and criminal justice for juveniles.

Just how far these reforms should go is the subject of debate. A mild uproar over children's rights arose during the 1992 U.S. presidential race between incumbent George Bush (R) and challenger Bill Clinton (D). Scholarly articles written in the early 1970s by Clinton's wife, Hillary Rodham Clinton, were at the heart of the controversy. A former lawyer for the Children's Defense Fund, Clinton questioned the traditional legal presumption of incompetency for children. She believed that children were capable of making many of their own decisions, and thus proposed the elimination of minority status for children and suggested a new presumption of legal competence. Clinton also favored granting children the same substantive and procedural rights enjoyed by adults. And because children's interests are not always the same as their parents', Clinton felt that minors should be allowed to hire their own lawyers.

During the presidential campaign, Clinton's views were attacked by political opponents who claimed she encouraged children to sue their parents. Her critics predicted that Clinton's ideas would lead children to "divorce" their parents over trivial matters such as curfews, homework, allowances, and household chores.

Clinton's views actually were much less extreme than those of so-called child liberationists, who believe that children should be allowed to vote, choose their residence, refuse to attend school, enter into contracts, and take part in activities currently reserved for adults. More radical child advocates maintain that children are just as rational as adults and that the nation's commitment to justice requires equal treatment of all people, regardless of age.

Critics of children's rights believe conferring too many rights on children will erode parental authority and the traditional family. Many conservatives believe that children lack the wisdom to make important decisions and require the guidance of responsible adults. They approve a paternalistic approach to children's welfare, rather than one that empowers young people. Critics also resent the legal system's intrusion into the life of parents, arguing that parents are entitled to the final word in their children's upbringing. Conservatives fear that if children have ready access to attorneys, a rash of frivolous or retaliatory lawsuits will erupt, destroying many fragile families in need of help.

Three well-publicized cases illustrate the philosophical divide over children's and parents' rights.

Kingsley v. Kingsley

In 1992, an eleven-year-old Florida boy went to court to terminate the rights of his biological parents. Gregory Kingsley retained Attorney Jerri Blair to represent him in a proceeding to sever all ties with his natural parents, Rachel and Ralph Kingsley. Kingsley also petitioned for his own adoption by his foster parents, Lizabeth and George Russ. Rachel Kingsley opposed her son's actions; her estranged husband did not.

Kingsley persuaded circuit court judge Thomas Kirk that he had been abandoned by his mother. Most of Kingsley's chaotic, impoverished life had been spent in and out of foster care. His unstable early environment

certain that her child regularly goes to school can be held criminally liable for violating compulsory attendance laws. A number of states have criminal nonsupport and abandonment statutes that make it unlawful for a parent to neglect to provide for her child. Where essential support has been provided by an outside source, such as an agency or an individual, this source can initiate a lawsuit to recoup the expenses of services and supplies. A person who has custody or guardianship of a child can initiate a lawsuit to request that the noncustodial parent pay a suitable amount of money on a regular basis to support the child.

Custody Parents usually have a legal right to custody of their own offspring. The Supreme Court has established that the right to CHILD CUSTODY by a parent is constitutionally protected. The general presumption of the courts is that a child's welfare is protected best when was contrasted with the loving and more affluent home now offered by the Russ family. Kirk determined that Kingsley, a minor, had the capacity to bring the action, and ordered both the parental rights termination and the adoption.

Rachel's attorney, Jane Carey, complained that a child's wish had been declared more important than the preservation of the family. Carey worried that the termination of Rachel's rights sent a message to poor parents that they could never measure up to wealthier families. It also drove a symbolic wedge between U.S. children and their parents. To Gregory's supporters, however, the ruling was an important victory on behalf of neglected, mistreated children.

On appeal, Florida's Fifth District Court of Appeals determined that, as a minor, Kingsley could not initiate a proceeding to terminate his parents' rights (*Kingsley v. Kingsley*, 623 So. 2d 780 [1993]). Only a guardian ad litem, or friend of the court, could do so. Nonetheless, the appeals court upheld the termination of Rachel's parental rights, because clear and convincing evidence proved her abandonment of Kingsley and because Kingsley's foster parents had properly initiated the proceeding by filing separate termination petitions. The court also found that there was no legitimate reason to order Kingsley's adoption at the same time as Rachel's termination of rights. In fact, the simultaneous adoption order was in error because the termination order was subject to appeal.

Although Kingsley's initial triumph was diluted by the appeals court ruling, it challenged traditional notions of parental "ownership" of children.

Mays-Twigg Case

Kimberly Mays of Florida was nine years old when she received shocking news: she had been switched at birth with another baby and raised by parents to whom she was not related. Mays was born in a rural Florida hospital in 1978. She was taken home by Robert Mays and his wife, Barbara Mays, who later died of cancer. The only other Caucasian infant in the hospital at the time was a girl who was taken home and raised by Ernest and Regina Twigg. The switch was discovered after a blood test determined that the Twiggs' daughter, whom they had named Arlena, was not genetically related to them. A review of hospital records and further blood tests established that Mays was actually the Twiggs' biological daughter. After Arlena died of a heart defect in 1988, the Twiggs sought custody of Mays, and failing that, attempted to win visitation rights. Mays requested an end to any contact with the Twiggs, saying visits with them were upsetting.

In August 1993, state circuit judge Stephen Dakan ruled that Mays was not required to meet with her biological parents, because forced visitation was detrimental to her. Dakan reasoned that if a fifteen-year-old minor had the right to an abortion, Mays surely had the right to refuse contact with people who essentially were strangers.

Although Mays was allowed to sever ties with the Twiggs, she later chose to renew them. In a strange twist of events, Mays moved in with the Twiggs in March 1994 because of personal conflicts with Robert Mays.

Although the Mays-Twigg case suggests a weakening in the rights of biological parents, the DeBoer case indicates the opposite.

DeBoer Case

Jessica DeBoer was raised from birth by Jan and Roberta DeBoer, a Michigan couple trying to adopt her. Cara Clausen, DeBoer's unmarried biological mother, terminated her parental rights shortly after DeBoer was born. Dan Schmidt, DeBoer's biological father, did not sign away his parental rights because initially, Clausen named another man as the child's father. Clausen and Schmidt eventually married and decided to reclaim DeBoer. After much legal maneuvering, the Michigan Supreme Court ordered DeBoer, who was now age two, returned to her biological parents in Iowa, saying they had the greater legal claim to her (*DeBoers v. DeBoers*, 442 Mich. 648, 502 N.W.2d 649 [1993]).

Despite expert testimony that it was not in DeBoer's best interests to be separated from the only home and parents she knew, the court ordered the girl turned over to the Schmidts. The DeBoers reluctantly complied with the order after exhausting every avenue of appeal.

Child rights advocates point to this case as an example of how children are still considered the property of their natural parents. At the same time, support groups for birth parents applaud the decision. They believe that Jessica DeBoer—who was renamed Anna Schmidt—belongs with Cara and Dan Schmidt because Dan never relinquished his parental rights and because blood ties have a special social and legal significance.

See also Clinton, Hillary Rodham; Edelman, Marian Wright.

the natural ties of mother and father are preserved. In the absence of clear evidence that a child is in danger, the state must not interfere with the judgment of the parents.

When the two parents do not live together, the issue arises as to where the child will reside. In some cases one parent will agree to relinquish custody to the other parent without giving up any other parental privileges. Although the custodial parent supervises the child's daily care, the noncustodial parent ordinarily has the right to be told about significant occurrences in the child's life. In addition, the noncustodial parent is usually entitled to visit the child at regular intervals. The noncustodial parent may seek a change in custody arrangements if circumstances so mandate.

If separated or divorced parents cannot agree on custody arrangements, the court will intervene. The court considers the circumstances of each case in light of a parent's ability to support and care for the child. In all custodial decisions, the best interests of the child are of paramount importance.

A battle for custody of a child does not always involve the parents. Custody is frequently sought by other relatives, including grandparents, uncles, aunts, or others, such as stepparents or foster parents.

In the event that a child is illegitimate, the unwed mother has a primary custody right that traditionally could not be defeated by the father. However, the Supreme Court has recognized the unwed father's interest in his child and the potential ability to obtain custody or visitation rights (*Lehr v. Robertson*, 463 U.S. 248, 103 S. Ct. 2985, 77 L. Ed. 614 [1983]).

Support Generally a parent is responsible for support of a minor child. This responsibility encompasses the bare essentials of food, clothing, and shelter, as well as education and medical care. A parent who is unable to provide such support is excused. However, that parent must demonstrate an earnest effort to become employed so that he can fulfill his financial responsibility.

At COMMON LAW, the child's father had the primary duty to support the child. The law now recognizes that both parents have an equal responsibility for the support of a child.

Parents are not entitled to use money that belongs to the child (for example, an inheritance) for the child's support. Although a parent is allowed to PETITION the court to release a certain amount of money for the child's expenses, courts are generally unwilling to honor such requests unless warranted by the circumstances. It is, for example, proper to release funds to support a child whose only other means of support would be through public WELFARE.

State and federal governments have become more active in requiring parents to support their children. If parents live apart, whether by reason of divorce or separation, or if they have remained unmarried, various remedies are available to enforce court-issued CHILD SUPPORT orders. State statutes generally provide criminal MISDEMEANOR penalties for a default on support obligations, but courts typically use the contempt power as an enforcement vehicle. Civil CONTEMPT is imposed to encourage payment by jailing for an indeterminate time a parent who is able to pay. The parent is free to leave jail as soon as she makes the payment. Criminal contempt is imposed as punishment for DEFAULT, the sentence being for a specific period.

States have also set up child support collection systems that use stronger enforcement methods to ensure compliance. If a parent fails to pay court-ordered child support his tax refunds and wages can be garnished and his driver's license can be revoked. See also GARNISHMENT.

The federal government has sought to ensure that child support is paid. The Child Support Recovery Act of 1992 (18 U.S.C.A. § 338) makes willful failure to support a child in another state a federal crime. Prosecution is available for unpaid support exceeding $5,000 or for obligations unpaid longer than one year. Penalties range from imprisonment to fines. First offenses are misdemeanors; repeat offenses are FELONIES. In addition, federal courts may make the payment of child support a condition of PROBATION.

The general rule is that no one is obligated to support a child to whom she is not related. A number of states, however, currently require a stepfather to support his wife's children if he lives with them. A child whose natural father does not contribute to her support might be allowed to receive welfare benefits unless she is adopted by the stepfather.

A parent's support obligation does not end merely because the parent is not living with the child. Upon divorce or legal separation, child support agreements arrange for the child's continued support. An identified father must aid in the support of his illegitimate child, even if they have never lived together.

The duty of a parent to support a minor child sometimes continues even when the child becomes a parent, such as the case of a sixteen-year-old girl who has an illegitimate child but continues to live with her parents. The unwed father, however, would have primary responsibility for support of his child provided he acknowledged the child as his or the court orders him to provide support following an action to establish his PATERNITY.

The common-law rule is that a parent has no obligation to support an adult child. Similarly an adult child has no duty to support parents or grandparents. Some states, however, have altered this rule by enacting statutes that impose financial responsibilities upon people for their poverty-stricken relatives. Certain laws require parents to provide support for a child who is incapable of earning a living because of a mental or physical disability, regardless of whether the child has reached the age of majority. Similarly, other statutes require children to support parents who would otherwise be dependent on public welfare.

Child's Earnings and Services At common law, a father had the right to the earnings of a child. State statutes have modified this principle to give either a primary right to a child's earnings to the custodial parent or an equal right to both parents. The right to a child's wages stems from the parental duty of support and therefore can be destroyed if a parent neglects or deserts the child. States, however, also have enacted laws that place a child's earnings in TRUST until the child reaches the age of majority. These laws were originally passed in the 1930s to protect child actors and entertainers who earned large sums of money. Before these laws were passed, some of the parents of these children had squandered their children's incomes.

The issue of the services of a child, which range from performing simple household tasks to working in the family business, ordinarily arises when a child has been injured. A parent may sue the individual who caused the child harm and claim damages for both medical costs and loss of the child's services.

Wrongful Death and Wrongful Life Actions A child is entitled to start a WRONGFUL DEATH action against anyone who causes the death of his parent. Parents may also sue for the wrongful death of children, although at times their economic value to the family is arguable. Parents may recover, however, for the loss of companionship or for their mental pain and suffering upon the loss of the child.

Some state laws prevent parents from recovering for the death of an adult child who is either financially independent or married. Ordinarily the parent who brings suit for wrongful death must be a legal parent, whether natural or adoptive. A parent who has neglected or failed to support a child generally cannot sue for wrongful death.

"WRONGFUL LIFE" cases arise when parents object to the birth of an unwanted or unplanned child. Cases have involved faulty sterilization, failure to diagnose a pregnancy, or, in the case of a pharmacist, dispensing the wrong birth control pills. In a majority of states, the courts refuse to entertain such suits, partly on grounds of public policy and partly on the theory that the benefit of having and keeping the child outweighs any damage. Other courts have allowed recovery, some holding that the probable enjoyment the child will bring must be offset against the cost of having and raising the child. Compensation for the cost of pregnancy and the pain and suffering of pregnancy and childbirth has been upheld.

Emancipation EMANCIPATION is a legal occurrence by which a child acquires the freedom attached to adulthood earlier than at the statutory age. There are no set procedures by which emancipation may be accomplished. Generally, enlistment in the armed forces, MARRIAGE, or becoming self-supporting will effect emancipation. Typically, the inquiry takes place after the fact, and if the child is found to be independent of the parents, emancipation has probably occurred.

An agreement may be made between the parents and the child whereby the child leaves the parents' home and establishes an independent life. Once this happens, the parent relinquishes the right to custody and supervision of the child. Another important meaning of emancipation is that it ends the parental obligation of support.

Another important legal consideration relates to the effect of commercial dealings of persons who, but for emancipation, would have been minors. Once a nearly absolute defense, modern law has significantly restricted the effect of minority as a legal defense to contractual obligations to third parties. Thus, an emancipated sixteen-year-old girl who signs a CONTRACT to buy a car cannot avoid the terms of the contract by later pleading that she was underage and could not legally bind herself.

The issue of emancipation has declined in importance because most states have made eighteen years the age of majority. The most serious questions concerning emancipation involved the age spread from eighteen to twenty-one years.

Responsibility of Parents for Injuries At common law, parents were not responsible for TORTS their children committed against third parties. When they had neglected their duty of supervision, parents could be held liable for their own NEGLIGENCE. This largely remains true, although many state statutes now hold parents vicariously liable for torts committed by their children, for a limited amount.

Another exception to parental IMMUNITY from LIABILITY for their child's torts is the "family purpose doctrine," which allows third parties to recover from parents when they were injured by children driving the family car. This doctrine is based on the idea that the child is acting as the parent's AGENT or authorized representative.

To promote family unity, a number of states have refused to permit lawsuits between parents and children for harm caused by negligence. Some states have rejected this doctrine, however, particularly in the event of AUTOMOBILE accidents. In such cases it was perceived as unjust to allow strangers to obtain insurance benefits when family members were precluded from doing so. A majority of states, however, still regard a parent as immune from legal actions for exercising parental authority and also for injuries stemming from negligent supervision.

In Loco Parentis Persons may act IN LOCO PARENTIS, "in place of the natural parents," in relation to the child in certain situations. Ordinarily, no one is responsible for a child's control or support unless that person is the parent, whether natural or adoptive, or has otherwise agreed to take care of the child. The question of whether a person acting in place of the parent has these responsibilities is contingent upon whether the person intended to undertake them. A college, for example, may act in loco parentis when it houses its students in college-supervised dormitories and imposes rules and regulations on student behavior.

CROSS-REFERENCES

Adoption; Child Care; Child Labor Laws; Children's Defense Fund; Children's Rights; Descent and Distribution; Family Car Doctrine; Family Law; Fetal Rights; Fetal Tissue Research; *In re Gault; Griswold v. Connecticut;* Guardian ad Litem; Guardian and Ward; Health Care Law; Illegitimacy; Infancy; Infants; Juvenile Law; Organ Donation Law *In Focus*: Should Dying Babies Be Organ Donors?; Paternity; Schools and School Districts.

PARENT COMPANY An enterprise, which is also known as a parent CORPORATION, that owns more than 50 percent of the voting shares of its SUBSIDIARY.

PARI CAUSA [*Latin, With equal right.*] Upon an equal footing; having the same rights or claims.

PARI DELICTO [*Latin, In equal fault.*] The doctrine, also known as *in pari delicto*, that provides that courts will not enforce an invalid CONTRACT and that no party can recover in an ACTION where it is necessary to prove the existence of an illegal contract in order to make his or her case.

PARI MATERIA [*Latin, Of the same matter; on the same subject.*] The phrase used in connection with two laws relating to the same subject matter that must be analyzed with each other.

For example, the federal gift tax provisions supplement the federal estate tax provisions. The two are *in pari materia* and must be read together because the gift tax provisions were enacted to prevent the avoidance of estate taxes.

See also ESTATE AND GIFT TAXES.

PARI PASSU [*Latin, By an equal progress; equably; ratably; without preference.*] Used especially to describe CREDITORS who, in marshalling ASSETS, are entitled to receive out of the same fund without any precedence over each other.

PARITY Equality in amount or value. Equivalence of prices of farm products to the prices existing at some former date (the base period) or to the general cost of living; equivalence of prices of goods or services in two different markets. The relationship between two currencies such that they are exchangeable for each other at the PAR or official rate of exchange.

BIOGRAPHY

STEVE ALLEN/GAMMA LIAISON

Rosa Louise McCauley Parks

PARKS, ROSA LOUISE McCAULEY

Rosa Louise McCauley Parks sparked a year-long BOYCOTT of buses in Montgomery, Alabama, by the city's black community, when she refused to give up her seat to a white man on a segregated bus. Her arrest and trial on charges of violating segregation laws led to the U.S. Supreme Court's decision that segregation on the city's buses was unconstitutional, the rise of the Reverend MARTIN LUTHER KING, JR., as a CIVIL RIGHTS leader, and the emergence of the CIVIL RIGHTS MOVEMENT as a national cause.

Parks was born February 4, 1913, in Tuskegee, Alabama. She attended a one-room black school in Pine Level, Alabama. Here, one teacher taught fifty to sixty students, who were separated into rows by age. The students were responsible for cutting wood to heat the school, and occasionally a parent would deliver a load of wood to the school by wagon. Whereas the black community had to heat and even build its own schools, a new brick school for white children was constructed near Parks's home, paid for with public funds, including taxes paid by both blacks and whites, and heated at public

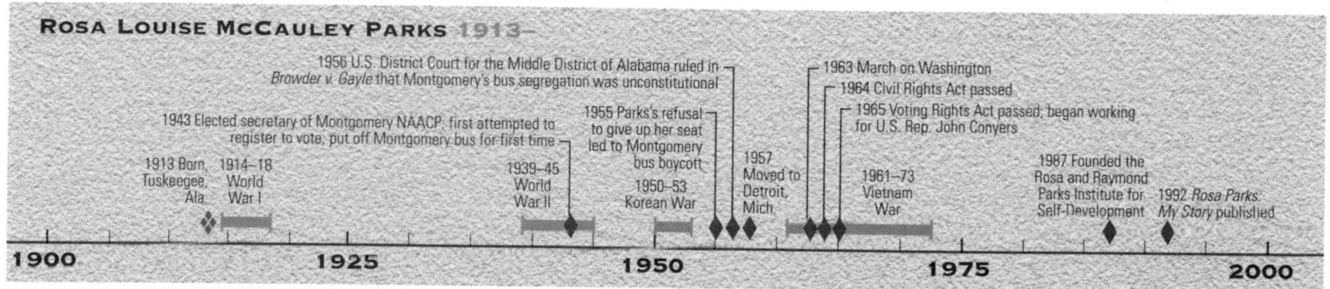

expense. Black children were needed by their families to help plow and plant in the spring and harvest in the fall, so they attended school only five months during the year; white children attended school for nine months.

Because Pine Level offered no schooling to black children beyond the sixth grade, Parks's mother sent her to Montgomery to live with relatives and continue her education. But she was forced to drop out of high school in her junior year to care for first her dying grandmother and later her ailing mother. She finally earned her high school diploma in 1933, at the age of twenty, a year after she had married Raymond Parks.

Her husband was the first activist Parks had met. He was a longtime member of the National Association for the Advancement of Colored People (NAACP). At the time he met Parks, he was working to raise money for the legal defense of nine young black men known as the Scottsboro Boys, who had been arrested for raping a white woman. Although the charges were unsubstantiated, all the men were found guilty and all but one were scheduled to die in the electric chair in 1931. The NAACP and other national organizations were able to file an appeal on the men's behalf with the U.S. Supreme Court, which ordered a new trial. All the defendants were eventually exonerated.

After the Scottsboro defendants were saved from execution, Parks and her husband became involved in voter registration. Parks first attempted to register to vote in 1943. Like most other black persons, she was forced to take a literacy test. Although she believed she had passed the test, she was denied twice. Then, before she could complete her registration, she had to pay an accumulated poll tax of $1.50 a year. Both blacks and whites were subject to the poll tax. However, whites were allowed to register upon turning twenty-one and could simply pay the tax once a year from then on. On the other hand, blacks might not be able to register until they were much older, and they were then forced to pay the tax retroactively to the age of twenty-one. Parks's tax totaled $16.50, a considerable amount of money at that time.

While Parks was making her second attempt to register to vote in 1943, she was put off a Montgomery city bus for the first time. Blacks had to follow certain rules when riding the bus, including stepping in the front door to pay their fare, then stepping off and going around to the back door to board the bus. Blacks were required to sit in the back of the bus, even when the front section reserved for whites was empty. On this occasion, Parks boarded the bus in the front and made her way through the bus to the back. When the driver insisted that she leave the bus and reenter through the back door, she refused. The driver then grabbed her coat sleeve and told her to get off his bus.

"PEOPLE ALWAYS SAY THAT I DIDN'T GIVE UP MY SEAT BECAUSE I WAS TIRED, BUT THAT ISN'T TRUE. I WAS NOT TIRED PHYSICALLY . . . THE ONLY TIRED I WAS, WAS TIRED OF GIVING UP."

By this time, Parks was a member of the NAACP, one of only two women active in the local organization. At the 1943 meeting of the Montgomery branch, she was elected secretary. The Montgomery NAACP had begun to consider filing a lawsuit against the city over bus segregation, but wanted a plaintiff with a strong case.

On the evening of December 1, 1955, Parks left work and boarded the bus home. After she had paid her fare, she realized the bus driver was the same one who had put her off his bus twelve years earlier and whom she had since gone out of her way to avoid. Parks took a vacant seat in the front of the black section of the bus, near three other black persons. As the bus began to fill up, a white man was left standing, and the bus driver demanded that Parks and the other blacks relinquish their seats. The other three people moved back, but Parks refused. The bus driver called the police, who arrested Parks and took her to the city jail. She was soon released on bail, and a trial date was set for the following week. Later that evening, Parks agreed to become the plaintiff the NAACP had been seeking to test the constitutionality of segregation on the buses.

That evening, leaders of the Montgomery Women's Political Caucus began calling for a bus boycott by the black community for December 5, to coincide with Parks's hearing. The eighteen black-owned cab companies in the city agreed to stop at all the bus stops on Monday and charge only ten cents, the same as bus fare.

When Monday came, the Montgomery city buses were nearly empty of black riders, marking the black community's first united protest against segregation. At her court hearing that day, Parks pleaded not guilty. The court ruled that she had violated the state segregation laws, and she was given a suspended sentence and fined.

Earlier that day, several ministers in the city, including the Reverend Ralph D. Abernathy, decided to form a new organization, the Montgomery Improvement Association (MIA), to lead the boycott. The ministers felt that the NAACP did not have a large enough membership in Alabama to assume a leadership role, and they wanted a local group in the forefront so that no one could claim that outside agitators were running the demonstration. The group elected King as its president. King was then pastor of the Dexter Avenue Baptist Church. The group thought he was the best candidate because he was so new to the city and to civil rights work that he had not yet made any strong friends or strong enemies.

The bus boycott lasted more than a year. Many black people lost their job because of their support of the boycott. Parks's husband resigned from his job as a barber at the Maxwell Field Air Force Base when the white shop owner ordered that there was to be no discussion of Parks or the protest in his shop. The city police tried to disrupt the protest by harassing groups of blacks who were waiting at city bus stops for the black-owned cabs, and by threatening to arrest cabdrivers if they did not charge their regular fare.

Once the police actually began arresting the cabdrivers, the community developed a sophisticated private transportation system consisting of twenty cars and fourteen station wagons. Thirty-two pickup and transfer sites were established, and service was scheduled from 5:30 A.M. to 12:30 A.M. Through this system, some thirty thousand people were transported to and from work every day. Although white supporters of the boycott received threatening letters and telephone calls, many white women who were unwilling to go without household help transported their black housekeepers and cooks every day. Blacks were also subjected to violence. King's home and the homes of other boycott leaders were bombed. Drivers of the black car pool were arrested for minor traffic violations, and insurance on the cars in the pool was canceled until King located a black insurance agent in Atlanta who arranged for Lloyd's of London to write a policy for some of the cars.

While the boycott continued, the fight over segregation began in the courts. In February 1956, after the appeal of Parks's conviction was dismissed on a technicality, lawyers filed suit in U.S. district court on behalf of five women, including Parks, who had been mistreated on the buses. The suit claimed that bus segregation was unconstitutional.

At the same time, white lawyers discovered an old state law prohibiting boycotts, and a GRAND JURY issued eighty-nine INDICTMENTS against King, other ministers and leaders of the MIA, and other citizens, including Parks. King was the first to be tried. He was found guilty and was sentenced to pay a $500 fine or serve a year at hard labor. His conviction was successfully appealed, however, and no one else was brought to trial.

In June 1956, a three-judge panel of a U.S. district court in Alabama ruled that Montgomery's bus segregation was unconstitutional (*Browder v. Gayle*, 142 F. Supp. 707[M.D. Ala. 1956]). The city appealed the decision to the U.S. Supreme Court. On November 13, the High Court upheld the district court (352 U.S. 903, 77 S. Ct. 145, 1 L. Ed. 2d 114). The boycotters decided to continue their demonstration until the order was official. On December 20, the Supreme Court's written decision arrived. On the following day, the black community ended the bus boycott.

In the beginning, INTEGRATION of the buses did not go smoothly. Snipers fired at buses, and the city imposed curfews that prevented buses from operating after 5:00 P.M., which kept people who worked until five from riding the buses home.

Because of the boycott, Parks and her husband received hate mail and telephone calls. In 1957 they decided to move to Detroit, where Parks's younger brother, Sylvester, lived. Parks was spending a great deal of time traveling around the country speaking about the bus boycott and the civil rights movement. She often attended meetings of a new organization formed by King and other ministers, the SOUTHERN CHRISTIAN LEADERSHIP CONFERENCE. She also attended the 1963 March on Washington that was organized to push for civil rights legislation. By this time, black people all over the U.S. South were protesting segregation and organizing boycotts.

In 1964 President LYNDON B. JOHNSON signed the CIVIL RIGHTS ACT, 42 U.S.C.A. § 1971, 1975a to 1975d, 2000a to 2000h-6, guaranteeing blacks the right to vote and to use public accommodations. But segregation was still pervasive in the South. In March 1965, King called for a mass march in Alabama from Selma to Montgomery to protest the treatment of civil rights demonstrators in Selma. Parks was invited to join the march for the final eight miles to the capitol in Montgomery.

In 1965 Parks went to work for U.S. Representative John Conyers, whom she had supported in his campaign for the congressional seat from the First District in Michigan. Parks remained as Conyers's receptionist and office assistant until her retirement in 1988.

For a long time, Parks wanted to start an organization to help young people. In 1987 she founded the Rosa and Raymond Parks Institute for Self-Development to offer young people classes in communications skills, health, economics, and political awareness.

CROSS-REFERENCES

Pacifism; *Powell v. Alabama*; Voting Rights.

PARLIAMENTARY LAW The general body of enacted rules and recognized USAGES governing the procedure of legislative assemblies and other deliberative sessions such as meetings of stockholders and DIRECTORS of CORPORATIONS, town meetings, and board meetings. Roberts Rules of Order are an example of such rules.

PAROLE The conditional release of a person convicted of a crime prior to the expiration of that person's term of imprisonment, subject to both the supervision of the correctional authorities during the remainder of the term and a resumption of the imprisonment upon violation of the conditions imposed.

Parole is the early supervised release of a prison inmate. It is usually regulated by statutes, and these provisions vary from state to state. Parole boards created by statute possess the authority to release prisoners from INCARCERATION. Parolees have no constitutional right to representation in parole hearings and parole REVOCATION hearings, but many states provide representation to impoverished inmates and parolees in such hearings.

Parole was first used in the United States in New York in 1876. By the turn of the century, parole was prevalent in the states. In 1910 Congress established the U.S. Parole Commission and gave it the responsibility of evaluating and setting the release date for federal prisoners.

Parole is used for several reasons. It is less expensive to supervise a parolee than incarcerate a prisoner. A person on parole has an opportunity to contribute to society. At the same time, society still receives some protection because the parole is supervised and can be revoked for the most minor of transgressions. Parole is also a method of REHABILITATION, because it gives convicts supervision and guidance during their reentry into society.

Although parole laws vary from state to state, there are some common practices. In many states, the governor is charged with appointing a parole board. The duties of the board are to study the case histories of persons eligible for parole, deliberate on the record, conduct hearings, grant parole, craft the conditions for parole, issue WARRANTS for persons charged with violation of parole, conduct revocation hearings, and grant final discharge to parolees.

States may charge parolees a small monthly fee to offset the costs of supervision. For example, in Kentucky, a person on parole for a FELONY must pay $10 per month while under active supervision, but no more than a total of $2,500; for a MISDEMEANOR parole, the fee is not less than $10 per month and no more than $500 in all. Failure to pay these fees, without a good reason for the failure, may result in revocation of the parole, but revocation may not be based on failure to pay a fee unless the board first has held a hearing on the matter.

For lesser offenses, the determination of eligibility for parole is often left to the parole board. Parole will be ordered only if it serves the best interests of society. Parole is not considered to be a method of reducing sentences or awarding a PARDON.

For more serious offenses, most states limit the discretion of the parole board. Parole statutes in these states generally identify a specified period of imprisonment that must be served before a prisoner is eligible for parole. The time periods are often a percentage of the prison sentence, and they can vary according to the crime for which the prospective parolee was convicted. In Arkansas, for example, persons convicted of first-degree MURDER, KIDNAPPING, aggravated ROBBERY, RAPE, and causing a catastrophe are not eligible for parole until they have served 70 percent of their prison sentence (Ark. Code Ann. § 16-93-611). For lesser felonies, persons must serve at least one-third of their sentence before becoming eligible for parole (Ark. Code Ann. § 16-93-608).

Parole has come under increasing attack since the 1970s. A powerful "truth in sentencing" movement has been successful in many states. Truth in sentencing is a catchphrase used to describe the notion that convicted criminals should serve the entire prison sentence handed down by the court. Many states have abolished parole entirely. In Virginia, for example, a person convicted of a felony that was committed after January 1, 1995, is ineligible for parole (Va. Code Ann. § 53.1-165.1). A felon may have prison time reduced from his sentence for good behavior, but in any case, the felon must serve at least 85 percent of the prison sentence.

On the federal level, Congress abolished parole in the Comprehensive Crime Control Act of 1984 (Pub. L. No. 98-473 § 218(a)(5), 98 Stat. 1837, 2027 [repealing 18 U.S.C.A. § 4201 et seq.]). Federal prisoners may, however, earn a maximum of fifty-four days good time credit per year against their sentence (18 U.S.C.A. § 3624(b)).

See also PROBATION; SENTENCING.

PAROL EVIDENCE *Parol* refers to verbal expressions or words. Verbal EVIDENCE, such as the TESTIMONY of a WITNESS at trial.

In the context of CONTRACTS, DEEDS, WILLS, or other writings, parol evidence refers to extraneous evidence such as an oral AGREEMENT (a parol contract), or even a written agreement, that is not included in the relevant written document. The parol evidence rule is a principle that preserves the integrity of written documents or agreements by prohibiting the parties from attempting to alter the meaning of the written document through the use of prior and contemporaneous oral or written declarations that are not referenced in the document.

Terms of a contract are commonly proposed, discussed, and negotiated before they are included in the final contract. When the parties to the negotiations do put their agreement in writing and acknowledge that the statement is the complete and exclusive declaration of their agreement, they have integrated the contract. The parol evidence rule applies to integrated contracts and provides that when parties put their agreement in writing, all prior and contemporaneous oral or written agreements merge in the writing. Courts do not permit integrated contracts to be modified, altered, amended, or changed in any way by prior or contemporaneous agreements that contradict the terms of the written agreement.

The parol evidence rule applies to written contracts to safeguard the terms of the contract. The courts assume by the parol evidence rule that contracts contain the terms and provisions that the parties specifically intended and lack those provisions that the parties did not want.

The parol evidence rule does not apply to written integrated contracts in some instances. For example, clerical or typographical ERRORS found in the written agreement may be changed because the incorrect term does not represent the true agreement between the parties. Courts will also not apply the parol evidence rule to prohibit contradictory evidence that shows that the contract was entered into under DURESS, MISTAKE, FRAUD, or UNDUE INFLUENCE. Finally, the parol evidence rule will not prevent evidence that shows the existence of a separate agreement between the parties.

The law of sales also involves numerous written and oral contracts to which the parol evidence rule may be applied. However, in sales the court may look to contemporaneous or prior agreements not to contradict a written agreement but to explain or supplement it. The court may examine such evidence based on the parties' course of dealing, usage of trade, course of conduct, or evidence of consistent additional terms. Parties' COURSE OF DEALING refers to a situation where two parties have a history of working together and entering into numerous contracts with each other, and the court can look to that history to clarify or interpret their written expressions. Usage of trade refers to circumstances in which the parties are participants in a particular trade or industry that has established ways of doing business. The courts can examine those established and accepted methods within the industry to help explain a written agreement. Parties' course of conduct refers to the actions of the parties in carrying out the particular contract, such as if a party accepts without objection the continued performance of the other party. It is also permissible for a court to consider supplemental consistent evidence that would generally not be included in the written agreement as long as it does not contradict the terms of the original agreement.

CROSS-REFERENCES

Integrated Agreement; Oral Contract; Sales Law.

BIOGRAPHY

LIBRARY OF CONGRESS

Theophilus Parsons

PARSONS, THEOPHILUS Theophilus Parsons served as chief justice of the Massachusetts Supreme Judicial Court from 1806 to 1813. A man of wide interests and learning, he is recognized for a series of decisions that defined legal principles that have shaped the American business corporation.

Parsons was born February 24, 1750, in Byfield, Massachusetts. He graduated from Harvard University in 1769 and was admitted to the Massachusetts bar in 1774. He established a successful legal practice in the area of Massachusetts that later became Portland, Maine. He gained prominence for his outspoken opinions at the ESSEX JUNTO, a 1778 gathering of merchants and lawyers from New England, the majority of whom resided in Essex County, Massachusetts. This group endorsed a

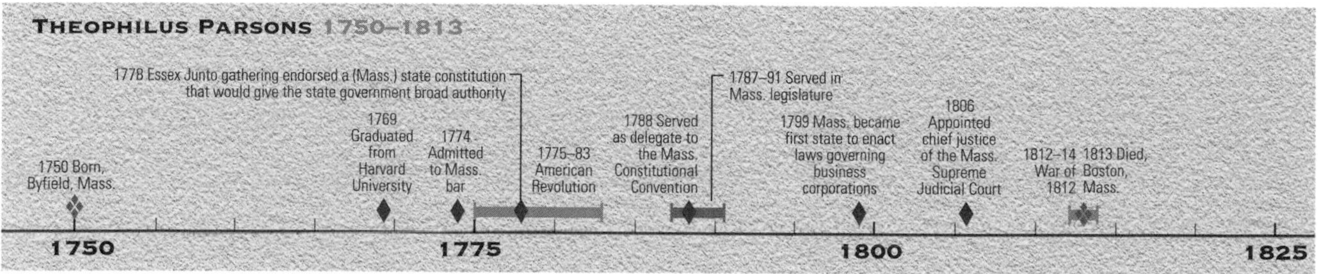

state constitution that gave the state government broad authority.

Parsons strongly supported ratification of the U.S. Constitution. As a delegate to the 1788 Massachusetts Constitutional Convention that ratified the document, Parsons attempted to calm the fears of those delegates who worried about a strong federal government.

From 1787 to 1791, he served in the Massachusetts legislature. He maintained a lucrative commercial law practice and became recognized as a distinguished lawyer. JOHN QUINCY ADAMS, future president of the United States and a member of the prominent Boston Adams family, read the law under Parson's tutelage during this period.

In 1805 Parsons again entered the state legislature, but his tenure was brief. In 1806 he was appointed chief justice of the Massachusetts Supreme Judicial Court, the state's highest court. His commercial law background proved valuable on the court because he decided cases involving shipping and insurance. More importantly, Parsons had the experience and confidence to decide cases involving business CORPORATIONS at a time when very little COMMON LAW was available to guide him.

Much of what became common law in U.S. corporate law was first developed while Parsons served as chief justice. In 1799 Massachusetts became the first state to enact a set of laws governing business corporations. During this period corporations had to obtain their CHARTERS from the legislature. The legislature was liberally granting these charters, and soon the courts were filled with legal issues concerning this new type of private business entity.

The Massachusetts Supreme Judicial Court, under the influence of Parsons, assumed an activist role in defining the rights and responsibilities of corporations. In a series of decisions between 1806 and 1810, the court announced several basic principles. It recognized that a corporation was a private arrangement, closer to a contract than to a municipal government corporation. The court held that a corporation has a duty to be fair to its shareholders and that the shareholders have limited liability for the debts and obligations of the corporation. The court also ruled that a corporation could be sued in TORT. All of these decisions became part of U.S. corporate law in the nineteenth century.

Parsons was a Renaissance man. He studied mathematics and theoretical astronomy and was the author of many scientific studies. He died October 13, 1813, in Boston, Massachusetts.

See also MASSACHUSETTS CONSTITUTION OF 1780.

"THE LOVE OF PRECEDENT AND STABILITY . . . GIVES TO JUDICIAL DECISIONS AN AUTHORITY ALMOST LIKE THAT OF LAW ITSELF."

PARTICULAR AVERAGE LOSS In maritime law, damage sustained by a ship, cargo, or freight that is not recompensed by CONTRIBUTION from all interests in the venture but must be borne by the owner of the damaged property.

Particular average loss is the opposite of general average loss, which denotes contribution by the various interests engaged in a maritime undertaking to recoup the loss of one of them for the voluntary sacrifice of a portion of the ship or cargo in order to save the remaining property and the lives of those on board, or for extraordinary expenses necessarily incurred for the common benefit and safety of all.

See also ADMIRALTY AND MARITIME LAW.

PARTICULARS The details of a claim, or the separate items of an account.

When these are detailed in an orderly form for the purpose of informing a defendant, the statement is called a BILL OF PARTICULARS.

PARTIES The persons who are directly involved or interested in any act, affair, contract, transaction, or legal proceeding; opposing litigants.

Persons who enter into a CONTRACT or other transactions are considered parties to the AGREEMENT. When a dispute results in litigation, the litigants are called parties to the lawsuit. U.S. law has developed principles that govern the rights and duties of parties. In addition, principles such as the standing doctrine determine whether a person is a rightful party to a lawsuit. Also, additional parties may be added to LEGAL PROCEEDINGS once litigation has begun.

Parties in Lawsuits In court proceedings, the parties have common designations. In a civil lawsuit, the person who files the lawsuit is called the PLAINTIFF, and the person being sued is called the DEFENDANT. In criminal proceedings, one party is the government, called the state, commonwealth, or the people of the United States, and the other party is the defendant. If a case is appealed, the person who files the APPEAL is called the APPELLANT, and the other side is called either the RESPONDENT or the APPELLEE. Numerous variations on these basic designations exist, depending on the court and its JURISDICTION. Assigning party designations allows the legal system and its observers to quickly determine the basic status of each party to a lawsuit.

Parties as Adversaries The U.S. legal system is based on the adversarial process, which requires parties to a legal proceeding to contend against each other. From this contest of competing interests, the issues are presented to the court and fully argued. In the end, one of the parties will obtain a favorable result. See also ADVERSARY SYSTEM.

For the adversary process to fulfill its mission of producing justice, it is vital that the issues at stake be argued by persons who have a genuine interest in them. Under the old rules of COMMON-LAW PLEADING, which used to regulate who could bring a lawsuit, only a person who actually held TITLE to disputed property could be a party in a lawsuit concerning the property. This technicality sometimes prevented a person who had the most to gain or lose on the issue from becoming a party and presenting her case. This rule has now been replaced by laws requiring every ACTION to be prosecuted by the real party in interest. This is most important when one person is managing an ASSET for the benefit of another. For example, administrators of a deceased person's ESTATE can sue to protect the estate's interests without having to join the beneficiaries of the estate as parties. This modern rule sharpens the issues so that the decision in a case puts a controversy to rest for all the parties involved.

The U.S. Supreme Court has developed the STANDING doctrine to determine whether the litigants in a federal civil proceeding are the appropriate parties to raise the legal questions in the case. The Court has developed an elaborate body of principles defining the nature and contours of standing. In general, to have standing a party must have a personal stake in the outcome of the case. A plaintiff must have suffered some direct and substantial injury or be likely to suffer such an injury if a particular wrong is not redressed. A defendant must be the party responsible for perpetrating the alleged legal wrong.

A person has standing to challenge a law or policy on constitutional grounds if he can show that the enforcement of the law or implementation of the policy infringes on an individual constitutional right. On the other hand, in most cases a taxpayer does not have standing to challenge policies or programs he is forced to financially support.

Legal Entities That Can Be Parties Only an actual legal entity may initiate a lawsuit. A natural person is a legal entity, for example, and any number of people can be parties on either side of a lawsuit. A CORPORATION is endowed by its CHARTER with existence as a separate legal entity. A business PARTNERSHIP is usually not considered a legal entity, but generally it can sue or be sued in the partnership name or in the names of the individual partners.

Many states permit lawsuits under a common name. This allows a business to be sued in the commonly used business name if it is clear who the owner or owners are. A lawsuit against Family Dry Cleaners, for example, may entitle the plaintiff to collect a JUDGMENT out of the value of the business property. The plaintiff will not be able to touch property that belongs to the owner or owners personally, however, unless they have also been named defendants in the action.

When a group of persons wishes to start a lawsuit, it has several options. If, for example, a group of residential property owners wants to contest the construction of a toxic waste disposal site in its community, it can file a lawsuit listing each property owner as a plaintiff. The group could also select an association name that the court accepts (Citizens Against Toxic Waste) to represent those individuals. A more expensive alternative would be to incorporate the group and file the suit under the corporation's name.

The CLASS ACTION provides another option for bringing parties into a large-scale civil lawsuit. In a class action lawsuit, thousands and even millions of persons can be parties. To obtain a class action designation, the plaintiffs must convince the court that many persons possess similar interests in the subject matter of the lawsuit and that the plaintiffs can act on the group's behalf without specifically identifying every individual member of the group as a party to the litigation. The class action lawsuit can be an economical method of resolving civil claims that involve large numbers of persons with common interests, especially when the amount of each individual CLAIM is too small to warrant independent legal actions by the claimants.

The Capacity to Sue or Be Sued A person must have the requisite legal CAPACITY to be a party to a lawsuit. Some people are considered NON SUI JURIS: they do not possess full civil and social rights under the law. A child is *non sui juris* because the law seeks to protect the child from her improvidence until she reaches the AGE OF MAJORITY. A child who has not reached the age of majority has a legal disability. Others who suffer a similar legal disability include mentally ill persons, mentally retarded persons, and persons who are judged mentally incompetent because of illness, age, or infirmity. Legal disability does not mean, however, that persons in these categories are removed from CIVIL ACTIONS. The claims or defenses of a person who is *non sui juris* usually can be asserted by a legal representative, such as a parent, GUARDIAN, TRUSTEE, or executor.

Prisoners also have limited rights as parties to civil actions. They can appeal their convictions and bring HABEAS CORPUS petitions to challenge the validity of their INCARCERATION. They can file PRISONERS' RIGHTS cases for a violation of their federally protected CIVIL RIGHTS. Some states permit a prisoner to defend himself in an action that threatens him with FORFEITURE of his property, but most states will not permit a prisoner to start a civil lawsuit against any other party during the period of incarceration. Convicted FELONS or prisoners given life sentences may suffer what is called CIVIL DEATH, a total loss of rights, including the right to be a party in a lawsuit.

Joinder of Additional Parties Usually a plaintiff decides when, where, and whom she wants to sue. In some cases a plaintiff may wish to join, or add, other parties after the start of the lawsuit. Proper parties and necessary or indispensable parties may be added while the action is pending.

A proper party is anyone who may be a party in the lawsuit. The JOINDER, or addition, of a proper party in a pending lawsuit is entirely permissible. The court may allow the joinder of an additional party, but the lawsuit does not have to be dismissed if it does not. In some states anyone who has an interest in the subject of the controversy is a proper party in the lawsuit. Some courts encourage joinder of everyone who could be affected by the decision.

Under modern rules of procedure in many states and the federal courts, joinder is not encouraged to the point where a lawsuit becomes unwieldy or cluttered with unrelated parties and claims. Generally, joinder is approved where the claims of the persons sought to be joined arose out of the same transaction or event as the claims of the existing parties, so that all the claims may be settled by answering the same questions of law or fact. The decision to join additional parties is within the discretion of the court. Courts are careful not to exclude parties with an interest in a lawsuit because a failure to join those parties might lead to a series of lawsuits with inconsistent VERDICTS. That could ultimately leave a deserving plaintiff without a REMEDY or force a defendant to pay a certain claim more than once.

Whether a person is potentially necessary or indispensable to an action depends on the character and extent of that person's interest in the subject of the lawsuit. It is fair and equitable to require any person who has an interest that can be affected by the lawsuit to be joined as a party. A person whose interest may be affected by the outcome of the case is considered necessary, and such a person should be joined if possible. A person whose interest is sure to be affected by the outcome of the lawsuit is considered an INDISPENSABLE PARTY, and the case cannot proceed without this person. The case must be dismissed, for example, if a person cannot be joined because she is beyond the jurisdiction of the court. In deciding whether a person should be a party to a lawsuit, the courts carefully weigh the consequences of proceeding without the person and seek a remedy that will give RELIEF to those who are actual parties without doing great harm to a necessary or indispensable party who is missing.

FEDERAL COURTS abandoned this analysis and terminology relating to necessary and indispensable parties in 1966. The Federal Rules of Civil Procedure focus on factors affecting the overall balance of fairness to the parties and potential parties involved rather than on categories of parties. Once a federal court determines that someone absent from the proceedings has an interest that can be affected by the case, the court must order that person to be joined as a party if it is practical to do so. If not, the court must weigh the competing interests of the plaintiff who would like to keep the case in federal court, the defendant who might be exposed to multiple lawsuits on the same issue, and the absent person whose rights may be lost if he does not become a party. The court must also consider how best to avoid wasting judicial time and resources and whether the case before it is the most efficient way to resolve the controversy.

Impleader A defendant who feels that the plaintiff in a lawsuit should have sued someone else on the claim can bring that other person into the case. The procedure for doing this is called IMPLEADER, and the additional party is called a THIRD-PARTY defendant. The original defendant who impleads a third-party defendant is called a third-party plaintiff, but she continues to be a defendant in relation to the plaintiff.

For example, a restaurant patron who becomes ill after eating a ham dinner can sue the restaurant. The patron is the plaintiff, and the restaurant is the defendant. The restaurant may want to implead the meat-packing company that furnished the ham, if it believes that the meat was tainted before it was delivered to the restaurant. The restaurant cannot avoid being a defendant, but it can cover itself by impleading the meat packer and making that company a third-party defendant. If a jury finds that the ham was bad and that the patron is entitled to \$10,000 damages, then the restaurant has an opportunity to show that its employees were not careless in preparing or serving the meat and that the restaurant should not be liable for the damages.

The decision to allow impleading of a third party is within the discretion of the court. The court also decides whether the third-party defendant may file claims against any of the other parties or whether the other parties may make additional claims against the third-party defendant. Permitting all parties to put forward all their claims in one action promotes efficient use of the courts, but a court will not permit additional parties or claims to complicate proceedings, delay resolution of the main controversy, or confuse a jury.

Intervention A person can volunteer to become a party in a lawsuit by a procedure called INTERVENTION. A person might wish to intervene in a lawsuit if he has an interest that will be affected by the outcome of the case and he believes that this interest will not be adequately protected by the other parties.

A court decides whether to permit an intervening party by balancing the interests of the person seeking to intervene with the additional burden imposed on the existing parties if the person is allowed to enter the lawsuit. The court considers whether the INTERVENOR is raising the same issues already present in the case or whether the intervenor is seeking to inject new controversies into the case. The intervenor must demonstrate some practical effect of the outcome of the case on her rights or property. If a person is not allowed to intervene, the person is not bound by the judgment given in the case.

An intervenor must make the request to intervene in a MOTION to the court. Timing is important. If the case has already progressed beyond the preliminary stages, the court is likely to find that the intervenor's intrusion would prejudice the rights of the existing parties, which would be grounds for the court to deny the motion.

PARTITION Any division of REAL PROPERTY or PERSONAL PROPERTY between co-owners, resulting in individual ownership of the interests of each.

The co-ownership of real and personal property can have many benefits to the parties. But when there is discord and the owners cannot agree on the use, improvement, or disposition of the property, all states have laws that permit the remedy of partition.

Most cases of partition involve real property. Persons can own property as tenants in common or joint tenants. As common owners of the property, they have equal rights in the use and enjoyment of the property. Partition statutes allow those who own property in common to sever their interests and take their individual share of the property.

Partition may be either voluntary or compulsory. Voluntary partition is when the cotenants (owners) divide the property themselves, usually by exchanging individual deeds. Each co-owner owns a part of the property and ceases to have an undivided interest in the whole. The parties can also provide for the sale of the property and divide the proceeds among themselves.

When the co-owners cannot agree on the value of the property and their rightful shares, they may select a disinterested third person, such as an arbitrator or an APPRAISER, to divide the property and to allot the shares. A voluntary partition by all the co-owners is legally effective unless there is a contractual challenge to its recognition. These challenges include allegations of FRAUD or unconscionability, or the allegation that the parties are seeking to defraud a third party by agreeing to the partition.

When the co-owners cannot agree to a voluntary partition, a lawsuit to compel partition can be filed to sever property interests. Unless there are exceptional circumstances, a tenant in common or a joint tenant has the absolute right to seek a compulsory partition. Partition must be made even if every other owner objects to it. The motives of the party seeking partition are irrelevant, and the court that hears the lawsuit has no discretion to deny partition. Its main function is to determine the method of executing the partition. Commonly the court will order the property sold and the proceeds divided, instead of ordering a physical partition of the property. If the TITLE to the property is put into issue, most states permit the court to resolve this issue as well as the partition.

Both real and personal property can be subject to compulsory partition. Real property that can be subject to partition includes a building, a story of a building, the land on which a building rests, or the surface of land where there is an oil or gas LEASE.

Similarly, personal property can be subjected to compulsory partition. The fact that the property is owned in unequal shares does not affect the partition. The right has been enforced with respect to a cashier's check payable jointly to those who share a TENANCY IN COMMON, PROMISSORY NOTES, shares of STOCK in a CORPORATION, and stocks of merchandise.

See also JOINT TENANCY.

PARTNERSHIP An association of two or more persons engaged in a business enterprise in which the profits and losses are shared proportionally. The legal definition of a partnership is generally stated as "an association of two or more persons to carry on as co-owners a business for profit" (Revised Uniform Partnership Act § 101 [1994]).

Early English mercantile courts recognized a business form known as the *societas*. The *societas* provided for an accounting between its business partners, an AGENCY relationship between partners in which individual partners could legally bind the partnership, and individual partner LIABILITY for the partnership's DEBTS and OBLIGATIONS. As the regular English courts gradually recognized the *societas*, the business form eventually developed into the COMMON-LAW partnership. England enacted its Partnership Act in 1890, and legal experts in the United States drafted a Uniform Partnership Act (UPA) in 1914. Every state has adopted some form of the UPA as its partnership statute; some states, however, have made revisions to the UPA or have adopted the Revised Uniform Partnership Act (RUPA), which legal scholars issued in 1994.

The authors of the initial UPA debated whether in theory a partnership should be treated as an aggregate of individual partners or as a corporatelike entity separate from its partners. The UPA generally opted for the aggregate theory in which individual partners ("an association") comprised the partnership. Under an aggregate theory, partners are co-owners of the business; the partnership is not a distinct legal entity. This led to the creation of a new property interest known as a "tenancy in partnership," a legal construct by which each partner co-owned partnership property. An aggregate approach nevertheless led to confusion as to whether a partnership could be sued or whether it could sue on its own behalf. Some courts took a technical approach to the aggregate theory and did not allow a partnership to sue on its own behalf. In addition, some courts would not allow a suit to go forward against a partnership unless the claimant named each partner in the complaint or added each partner as an "INDISPENSABLE PARTY."

The RUPA generally adopted the ENTITY approach, which treats the partnership as a separate legal entity that may own property and sue on its own behalf. The RUPA nevertheless treats the partnership in some instances as an aggregate of co-owners; for example, it retains the joint liability of partners for partnership obligations. As a practical matter, therefore, the present-day partnership has both aggregate and entity attributes. The partnership, for instance, is considered an association of co-owners for tax purposes, and each co-owner is taxed on his or her proportional share of the partnership profits.

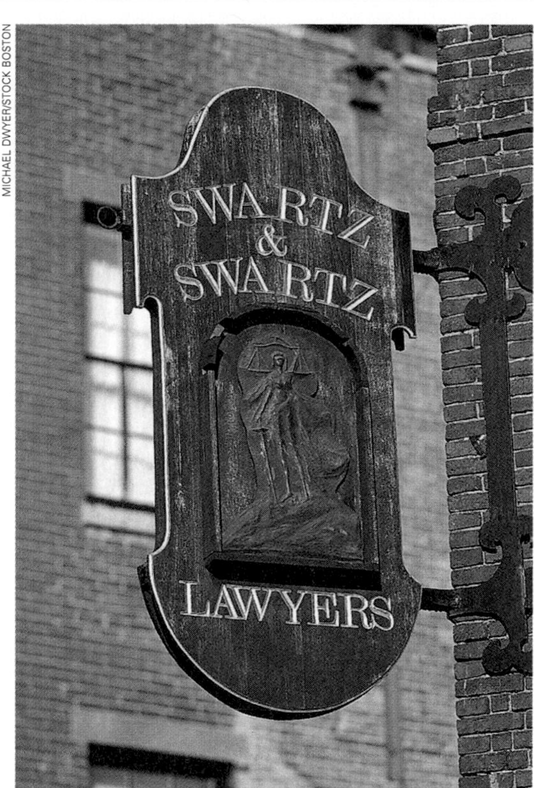

MICHAEL DWYER/STOCK BOSTON

Courts carefully scrutinize business partnerships where partners are also family members.

Formation The formation of a partnership requires a voluntary "association" of persons who "co-own" the business and intend to conduct the business for profit. Persons can form a partnership by written or oral agreement, and a partnership agreement often governs the partners' relations to each other and to the partnership. The term *person* generally includes individuals, CORPORATIONS, and other partnerships and business associations. Accordingly, some partnerships may contain individuals as well as large corporations. Family members may also form and operate a partnership, but courts generally look closely at the structure of a family business before recognizing it as a partnership for the benefit of the firm's creditors.

Certain conduct may lead to the creation of an implied partnership. Generally, if a person receives a portion of the profits from a business enterprise, the receipt of the profits is evidence of a partnership. If, however, a person receives a share of profits as repayment of a DEBT, wages, rent, or an ANNUITY, such transactions are considered "protected relationships" and do not lead to a legal inference that a partnership exists.

Relationship of Partners to Each Other Each partner has a right to share in the profits of the partnership. Unless the partnership agreement states otherwise, partners share profits equally. Conversely, partners must contribute equally to partnership losses unless a

A sample partnership agreement

[*Name*]

PARTNERSHIP AGREEMENT

This agreement, made and entered into as of the [*Date*], by and among [*Names*] (hereinafter collectively sometimes referred to as "Partners").

WITNESSETH:

Whereas, the Parties hereto desire to form a General Partnership (hereinafter referred to as the "Partnership"), for the term and upon the conditions hereinafter set forth;

Now, therefore, in consideration of the mutual covenants hereinafter contained, it is agreed by and among the Parties hereto as follows:

Article I
BASIC STRUCTURE

§ 1.1 Form

The Parties hereby form a General Partnership pursuant to the Laws of [*Name of State*].

§ 1.2 Name

The business of the Partnership shall be conducted under the name of [*Name*].

§ 1.3 Place of Business

The principal office and place of business of the Partnership shall be located at [*Describe*], or such other place as the Partners may from time to time designate.

§ 1.4 Term

The Partnership shall commence on [*Date*], and shall continue for [*Number*] years, unless earlier terminated in the following manner:

(a) By the completion of the purpose intended, or

(b) Pursuant to this Agreement, or

(c) By applicable [*State*] law, or

(d) By death, insanity, bankruptcy, retirement, withdrawal, resignation, expulsion, or disability of all of the then Partners.

§ 1.5 Purpose—General

The purpose for which the Partnership is organized is ________.

Article II
FINANCIAL ARRANGEMENTS

§ 2.1 Initial Contributions of Partners

Each Partner has contributed to the initial capital of the Partnership property in the amount and form indicated on Schedule A attached hereto and made a part hereof. Capital contributions to the Partnership shall not earn interest. An individual capital account shall be maintained for each Partner.

[Portions omitted for purpose of illustration.]

Alternative A

No Partner shall be entitled to receive any compensation from the Partnership, nor shall any Partner receive any drawing account from the Partnership.

Alternative B

The Managing Partners may pay compensation to any Partner as they deem reasonable.

[*continued on page 29*]

A sample partnership agreement (continued)

Article III
MANAGEMENT

§ 3.1 Managing Partners
The Managing Partner(s) shall be [*Names*] [*or* "all partners"].

§ 3.2 Voting
All Managing Partner(s) shall have the right to vote as to the management and conduct of the business of the Partnership according to their then Percentage Share of [*Capital/Income*]. Except as otherwise herein set forth a majority of such [*Captial/Income*] shall control.

Article IV
DISSOLUTION

§ 4.1 Dissolution
In the event that the Partnership shall hereafter be dissolved for any reason whatsoever, a full and general account of its assets, liabilities, and transactions shall at once be taken. Such assets may be sold and turned into cash as soon as possible and all debts and other amounts due the Partnership collected. The proceeds thereof shall thereupon be applied as follows:

(a) To discharge the debts and liabilities of the Partnership and the expenses of liquidation.

(b) To pay each Partner or his legal representative any unpaid salary, drawing account, interest or profits to which he shall then be entitled and in addition, to repay to any Partner his capital contributions in excess of his original capital contribution.

(c) To divide the surplus, if any, among the Partners or their representatives as follows:

(1) First (to the extent of each Partner's then capital account) in proportion to their then capital accounts.

(2) Then according to each Partner's then Percentage Share of *Capital/Income.*

§ 4.2 Right to Demand Property
No Partner shall have the right to demand and receive property in kind for his distribution.

[Portions omitted for purpose of illustration.]

Witnesses	**Partners**
______________________	______________________
______________________	______________________

Dated: ________.

partnership agreement provides for another arrangement. In some JURISDICTIONS a partner is entitled to the return of her or his capital contributions. In jurisdictions that have adopted the RUPA, however, the partner is not entitled to such a return.

In addition to sharing in the profits, each partner also has a right to participate equally in the management of the partnership. In many partnerships a majority vote resolves disputes relating to management of the partnership. Nevertheless, some decisions, such as admitting a new partner or expelling a partner, require the partners' unanimous consent.

Each partner owes a FIDUCIARY duty to the partnership and to copartners. This duty requires that a partner deal with copartners in GOOD FAITH, and it also requires a partner to account to copartners for any benefit that he or she receives while engaged in partnership business. If a partner generates profits for the partnership, for example, that partner must hold the profits as a TRUSTEE for the partnership. Each partner also has a duty of loyalty to the partnership. Unless copartners consent, a partner's duty of loyalty restricts the partner from using partnership property for personal benefit and restricts the partner from competing with the partnership, engaging in SELF-DEALING, or usurping partnership opportunities.

Relationship of Partners to Third Persons A partner is an AGENT of the partnership. When a partner has the apparent or actual authority and acts on behalf of the business, the partner binds the partnership and each of the partners for the resulting obligations. Similarly, a partner's admission concerning the partnership's affairs is considered an admission of the partnership. A partner may only bind the partnership, however, if the partner has the authority to do so and undertakes transactions while conducting the usual partnership business. If a third person, however, knows that the partner is not authorized to act on behalf of the partnership, the partnership is generally not liable for the partner's unauthorized acts. Moreover, a partnership is not responsible for a partner's wrongful acts or omissions committed after the DISSOLUTION of the partnership or after the dissociation of the partner. A partner who is new to the partnership is not liable for the obligations of the partnership that occurred prior to the partner's admission.

Liability Generally, each partner is jointly liable with the partnership for the obligations of the partnership. In many states each partner is jointly and severally liable for the wrongful acts or omissions of a copartner. Although a partner may be sued individually for all the damages associated with a wrongful act, partnership agreements generally provide for indemnification of the partner for the portion of DAMAGES in excess of her or his own proportional share.

Some states that have adopted the RUPA provide that a partner is jointly and severally liable for the debts and obligations of the partnership. Nevertheless, before a partnership's CREDITOR can LEVY a JUDGMENT against an individual partner, certain conditions must be met, including the return of an unsatisfied WRIT of execution against the partnership. A partner may also agree that the creditor need not exhaust partnership ASSETS before proceeding to collect against that partner. Finally, a court may allow a partnership creditor to proceed against an individual partner in an attempt to satisfy the partnership's obligations. See also INDEMNIFY; JOINT AND SEVERAL LIABILITY.

Partnership Property A partner may contribute PERSONAL PROPERTY to the partnership, but the contributed property becomes partnership property unless some other arrangement has been negotiated. Similarly, if the partnership purchases property with partnership assets, such property is presumed to be partnership property and is held in the partnership's name. The partnership may convey or transfer the property but only in the name of the partnership. Without the consent of all the partners, individual partners may not sell or ASSIGN partnership property.

In some jurisdictions the partnership property is considered personal property that each partner owns as a "tenant in partnership," but other jurisdictions expressly state that the partnership may own property. The tenant in partnership concept, which is the approach contained in the UPA, is the result of adopting an aggregate approach to partnerships. Because the aggregate theory is that the partnership is not a separate entity, it was thought that the partnership could not own property but that the individual partners must actually own it. This approach has led to considerable confusion, and the RUPA now expressly states that the partnership may own partnership property.

Partnership Interests A partner's interest in a partnership is considered personal property that may be assigned to other persons. If assigned, however, the person receiving the assigned interest does not become a partner. Rather, the assignee only receives the economic rights of the partner, such as the right to receive partnership profits. In addition, an ASSIGNMENT of the partner's interest does not give the assignee any right to participate in the management of the partnership. Such a right is a separate interest and remains with the partner.

Partnership Books Generally, a partnership maintains separate books of account, which typically include records of the partnership's financial transactions and each partner's capital contributions. The books must be kept at the partnership's principal place of business, and each partner must have access to the books and be allowed to inspect and copy them upon demand. If a partnership denies a partner access to the books, he or she usually has a right to obtain an INJUNCTION from a court to compel the partnership to allow him or her to inspect and copy the books.

Partnership Accounting Under certain circumstances a partner has a right to demand an ACCOUNTING of the partnership's affairs. The partnership agreement, if any, usually sets forth a partner's right to a pre-dissolution accounting. State law also generally allows for an accounting if copartners exclude a partner from the partnership business or if copartners wrongfully possess partnership property. In a court ACTION for an accounting, the partners must provide a report of the partnership business and detail any transactions dealing with partnership property. In addition, the partners who bring a court action for an accounting may examine whether any partners have breached their duties to copartners or the partnership.

Taxation One of the primary reasons to form a partnership is to obtain its favorable tax treatment. Because partnerships are generally considered an association of co-owners, each of the partners is taxed on her or his proportional share of partnership profits. Such taxation is considered "pass-through" taxation in which only the individual partners are taxed. Although a partnership is required to file annual TAX RETURNS, it is not taxed as a separate entity. Rather, the profits of the partnership "pass through" to the individual partners, who must then pay individual taxes on such income.

Dissolution A dissolution of a partnership generally occurs when one of the partners ceases to be a partner in the firm. Dissolution is distinct from the termination of a partnership and the "winding up" of partnership business. Although the term *dissolution* implies termination, dissolution is actually the beginning of the process that ultimately terminates a partnership. It is, in essence, a change in the relationship between the partners. Accordingly, if a partner resigns or if a partnership expels a partner, the partnership is considered legally dissolved. Other causes of a dissolution include the bankruptcy or death of a partner, an agreement of all partners to dissolve, or an event that makes the partnership business illegal. For instance, if a partnership operates a gambling casino and gambling subsequently becomes illegal, the partnership will be considered legally dissolved. In addition, a partner may withdraw from the partnership and thereby cause a dissolution. If, however, the partner withdraws in violation of a partnership agreement, the partner may be liable for damages as a result of the untimely or unauthorized withdrawal.

After dissolution, the remaining partners may carry on the partnership business, but the partnership is legally a new and different partnership. A partnership agreement may provide for a partner to leave the partnership without dissolving the partnership but only if the departing partner's interests are bought by the continuing partnership. Nevertheless, unless the partnership agreement states otherwise, dissolution begins the process whereby the partnership's business will ultimately be wound up and terminated.

Dissociation Under the RUPA, events that would otherwise cause dissolution are instead classified as the dissociation of a partner. The causes of a dissociation are generally the same as those of a dissolution. Thus, dissociation occurs upon receipt of a notice from a partner to withdraw, by expulsion of a partner, or by bankruptcy-related events such as the bankruptcy of a partner. A dissociation does not immediately lead to the winding up of the partnership business. Instead, if the partnership carries on the business and does not dissolve, it must buy back the former partner's interest. If, however, the partnership is dissolved under the RUPA, then its affairs must be wound up and terminated.

Winding Up *Winding up* refers to the procedure followed for distributing or liquidating any remaining partnership assets after dissolution. Winding up also provides a priority-based method for discharging the obligations of the partnership, such as making payments to non-partner creditors or to remaining partners. Only partners who have not wrongfully caused dissolution or have not wrongfully dissociated may participate in winding up the partnership's affairs.

State partnership statutes set the procedure to be used to wind up partnership business. In addition, the partnership agreement may alter the order of payment and the method of liquidating the assets of the partnership. Generally, however, the liquidators of a partnership pay non-partner creditors first, followed by partners who are also creditors of the partnership. If any assets remain after satisfying these obligations, then partners who have contributed capital to the partnership are entitled to their capital contributions. Any remaining assets are then divided among the remaining partners in accordance with their respective share of partnership profits.

Under the RUPA, creditors are paid first, including any partners who are also creditors. Any excess funds are then distributed according to the partnership's distribution of profits and losses. If profits or losses result from a LIQUIDATION, such profits and losses are charged to the partners' capital accounts. Accordingly, if a partner has a negative balance upon winding up the partnership, that partner must pay the amount necessary to bring his or her account to zero.

Limited Partnerships A limited partnership is similar in many respects to a general partnership, with one essential difference. Unlike a general partnership, a limited partnership has one or more partners who cannot participate in the management and control of the partnership's business. A partner who has such limited participation is considered a "limited partner" and does not generally incur personal liability for the partnership's obligations. Generally, the extent of liability for a limited partner is the limited partner's capital contributions to the partnership. For this reason, limited partnerships are often used to provide capital to a partnership through the capital contributions of its limited partners. Limited partnerships are frequently used in REAL ESTATE and entertainment-related transactions.

The limited partnership did not exist at common law. Like a general partnership, however, a limited partnership may govern its affairs according to a limited partnership agreement. Such an agreement, however, will be subject to applicable state law. States have for the most part relied on the Uniform Limited Partnership Act in adopting their limited partnership legislation. The Uniform Limited Partnership Act was revised in 1976 and 1985. Accordingly, a few states have retained the old uniform act, and other states have relied on either revision to the uniform act or even both revisions to the uniform act.

A limited partnership must have one or more general partners who manage the business and who are personally liable for partnership debts. Although one partner may be both a limited and a general partner, at all times there must be at least two different partners in a limited partnership. A limited partner may lose protection against personal liability if she or he participates in the management and control of the partnership, contributes services to the partnership, acts as a general partner, or knowingly allows her or his name to be used in partnership business. However, "safe harbors" exist in which a limited partner will not be found to have participated in the "control" of the partnership business. Safe harbors include consulting with the general partner with respect to partnership business, being a contractor or employee of a general partner, or winding up the limited partnership. If a limited partner is engaged solely in one of the activities defined as a safe harbor, then he or she is not considered a general partner with the accompanying potential liability.

Except where a conflict exists, the law of general partnerships applies equally to limited partnerships. Unlike general partnerships, however, limited partnerships must file a certificate with the appropriate state authority to form and carry on as a limited partnership. Generally, a certificate of limited partnership includes the limited partnership's name, the character of the limited partnership's business, and the names and addresses of general partners and limited partners. In addition, and because the limited partnership has a set term of duration, the certificate must state the date on which the limited partnership will dissolve. The contents of the certificate, however, will vary from state to state, depending on which uniform limited partnership act the state has adopted.

See also LIMITED LIABILITY PARTNERSHIP.

PARTY Any person involved in a transaction or proceeding. A group of voters organized for the purpose of influencing governmental policy, particularly through the nomination and election of candidates for public office.

PLAINTIFFS and DEFENDANTS are parties in lawsuits, for example. They have the right to make claims and defenses, offer proof, and examine and cross-examine witnesses at trials. They can pursue appeals after unsatisfactory JUDGMENTS if they satisfy designated criteria.

In the United States, the Democrats and the Republicans make up the two major national political parties. See also DEMOCRATIC PARTY; REPUBLICAN PARTY.

PARTY OF THE FIRST PART A phrase used in a document to avoid repeating the name of the persons first mentioned in it.

PARTY WALL A partition erected on a property boundary, partly on the land of one owner and partly on the land of another, to provide common support to the structures on both sides of the boundary.

Each person owns as much of a party wall as is situated on her land. The wall is subject to cross-easements—reciprocal rights of use over the property of another—in favor of each owner for the support of her building or for the maintenance of the wall. A party wall can also be owned by adjoining tenants pursuant to a TENANCY IN COMMON, or the wall can belong entirely to one of the adjoining owners, subject to an EASEMENT or a right in the other owner to have it maintained as a dividing wall between the two tenements.

Creation A party wall is ordinarily created by a CONTRACT between the adjoining owners, by statute, or by PRESCRIPTION. ADJOINING LANDOWNERS can enter into a contract to build a party wall. The parties can agree that the wall is to be located on land owned entirely by one of them or that it is to stand partly, usually equally, on both parcels. Under a typical arrangement, one party builds the wall and the other contributes to its construction. The parties can also agree that an existing dividing wall is to become a party wall.

Statutes authorizing the construction of a party wall by one of two adjoining owners when the line between the properties is vacant embody the COMMON LAW and have been upheld as a constitutionally valid exercise of the POLICE

POWER of a state. These statutes are subject to a STRICT CONSTRUCTION since they permit the taking and permanent occupation of a portion of land.

When a wall between adjoining buildings has been continuously and uninterruptedly used as a party wall by the respective owners for a period of time set forth by statute, a prescriptive right to use the wall arises.

A party wall can also be created when the owner of buildings that stand on adjoining lots and share a common wall, which forms a part of each building, conveys the lots to different persons. Each owner acquires TITLE to one-half the wall and an easement for its support as a party wall in the other half. This rule applies even though the DEEDS are silent concerning the rights of the parties in the wall. The result is the same when one of the lots is retained by the original common owner.

Duration A party wall that is constructed without any reference to a time limitation implies permanency. A wall built as a result of an agreement loses its character as a party wall when the parties RESCIND, or cancel, the agreement. Although the title to one-half of such a party wall, which is jointly owned by adjoining landowners, cannot be waived or abandoned, a party wall easement can be extinguished when the party entitled to it renounces his interest.

The easement of support of adjoining buildings by the party wall ends when the wall becomes unfit for its purpose or is so decayed as to need rebuilding from its foundation. When the buildings are accidentally destroyed, the easement ends, even though a portion of the wall, or the whole wall, remains standing.

Manner of Use A party wall is for the mutual benefit and convenience of both owners. Each adjoining owner has the right to its full use as a party wall in the improvement and enjoyment of his property. Neither owner can use the wall in a manner that impairs the other's easement or interferes with his or her PROPERTY RIGHTS.

An adjoining owner is not entitled to extend the front wall or rear wall of his building beyond the center of the party wall. In addition, an adjoining owner cannot extend the beams of her building beyond the center of the wall. Neither party can attach window shutters, exhaust pipes, anchor rods, or other projections or fixtures over the adjoining premises, even if the projection does not actually damage, or interfere with, the rights of the adjoining owner. An easement does not give either owner a right to construct and maintain a roof or cornice that extends beyond the party wall and over the property of the adjoining owner.

DARLENE BORDWELL/THE PICTURE CUBE

These homes share a wall in common, or a party wall. *Whether the wall is owned jointly or wholly by one tenant, each party is entitled by easement to enjoy full use of the wall—on his own side.*

By common USAGE, a party wall has come to mean a solid wall. Unless an agreement exists between the adjoining property owners to the contrary, neither has a right to maintain windows or other openings in the wall unless they are necessary for air and light.

A party wall can be used by the adjoining owners for the construction and maintenance of chimney flues and fireplaces. Both parties are entitled to use a flue built into the middle of the wall, although the lower part of it is located wholly in the other owner's half of the wall.

Neither owner of a party wall has a right to maintain a sign on the other side of the wall, but either has a right to do so on her own side.

Destruction and Rebuilding Ordinarily neither of the adjoining owners has the right to destroy or remove a party wall, but if a fire or other casualty causes the wall to become useless to either owner, it can be removed.

In a number of states, even though a party wall is sufficient to support existing structures, an adjoining owner can replace it with a stronger wall to support a new structure requiring greater reinforcement. The owner must replace the wall within a reasonable time without damaging the property of the adjoining owner.

Either party can replace a party wall that is dangerous to life or property or insufficient for the support of existing buildings. Neither owner has any right to have a dangerous wall bolstered by allowing it to rest upon, or be sustained by, the timbers, walls, or parts of the other's building.

No obligation is imposed upon either owner to erect a new party wall to replace a wall that has been destroyed by some accidental cause, even if the foundation of the wall remains firm and sound. When the adjoining buildings are destroyed and the party wall remains standing, neither adjoining owner is obliged to reconstruct her building as it existed.

Addition, Alteration, and Repair Unless restricted by a CONVEYANCE, transfer, or a party wall agreement, either owner can add to, alter, or repair the wall. In doing so, the owner must not damage the adjoining property or impair the easement to which the owner is entitled.

Either party, for example, may increase the height of the wall, provided the increase does not diminish its strength. Similarly either party may underpin the wall and sink the foundation deeper or increase the thickness of the wall by adding to it on his own land.

Contribution In some JURISDICTIONS, an adjoining landowner who uses a wall built partly on his or her land by the other adjoining landowner has no duty to contribute to the cost of construction of the wall. If there is no evidence of the conditions under which the wall was built, courts presume that each person owns as much of the wall as is situated on his property and has no obligation to contribute to the other's wall.

In some jurisdictions, LIABILITY might be imposed by statute. For example, a statute might authorize one of two adjoining landowners to build a wall partly on the adjoining land and require the other landowner to contribute, if and when she used the wall in the construction and support of an adjoining building; until payment would be made, the wall would be owned exclusively by the builder.

The obligation to contribute can, of course, be a provision in the contract between adjoining landowners, but the agreement need not be express. It can be implied from the conduct of the parties, although a contract cannot be implied from the mere assent by one owner to the construction of a wall standing equally on the land of both.

See also BOUNDARIES.

PASS As a verb, to utter or pronounce, as when the court *passes* sentence upon a prisoner. Also to proceed; to be rendered or given, as when JUDGMENT is said to *pass* for the plaintiff in a suit.

In legislative parlance, a BILL or resolution is said to *pass* when it is agreed to or enacted by the house, or when the body has sanctioned its adoption by the requisite majority of votes; in the same circumstances, the body is said to *pass* the bill or motion.

When an auditor appointed to examine any accounts certifies to their correctness, she is said to *pass* them; i.e., they pass through the examination without being detained or sent back for inaccuracy or imperfection.

The term also means to examine anything and then authoritatively determine the disputed questions that it involves. In this sense a jury is said to *pass upon* the rights or issues in litigation before them.

In the language of conveyancing, the term means to move from one person to another; i.e. to be transferred or conveyed from one owner to another.

To publish; utter; transfer; circulate; impose fraudulently. This is the meaning of the word when referring to the offense of *passing* counterfeit money or a forged paper.

As a noun, permission to pass; a license to go or come; a certificate, emanating from authority, wherein it is declared that a designated person is permitted to go beyond certain boundaries that, without such authority, he could not lawfully pass. Also a ticket issued by a railroad or other transportation company, authorizing a designated person to travel free on its lines, between certain points or for a limited time.

PASSIM [*Latin, Everywhere.*] A term frequently used to indicate a general reference to a book or legal authority.

PASSPORT A document that indicates permission granted by a sovereign to its citizen to travel to foreign countries and return and requests foreign governments to allow that citizen to pass freely and safely.

In 1974, the State Department issued 2,415,003 new passports to U.S. citizens. By 1995, the number had climbed to 5,263,989.

With respect to INTERNATIONAL LAW, a passport is a LICENSE of safe conduct, issued during a WAR, that authorizes an individual to leave a warring nation or to remove his or her effects from that nation to another country; it also

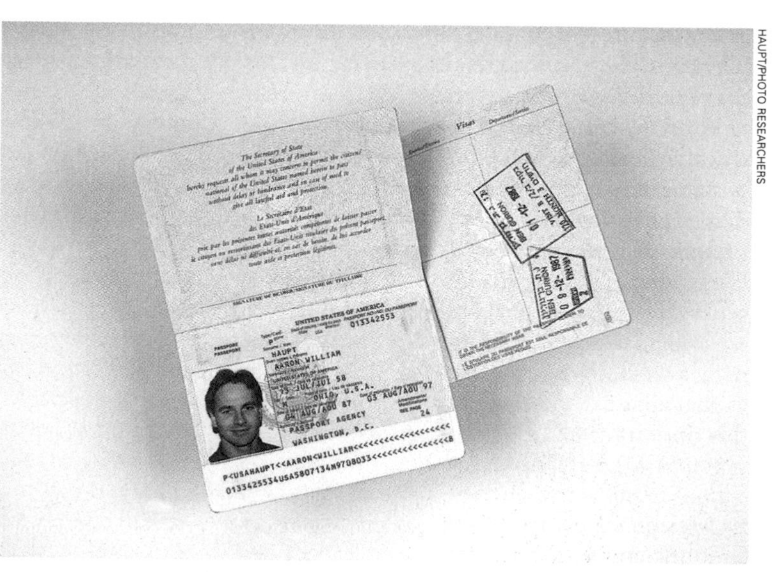

HAUPT/PHOTO RESEARCHERS

authorizes a person to travel from country to country without being subject to arrest or detention because of the war.

In maritime law, a passport is a document issued to a neutral vessel by its own government during a war that is carried on the voyage as evidence of the nationality of the vessel and as protection against the vessels of the warring nations. This paper is also labeled a *pass*, *sea-pass*, *sea-letter*, or *sea-brief*. It usually contains the captain's or master's name and residence; the name, property, description, tonnage, and destination of the ship; the nature and quantity of the cargo; and the government under which it sails.

PATENT Open; manifest; evident.

In the sale of PERSONAL PROPERTY, a *patent defect* is one that is clearly visible or that can be discovered by an inspection made by a person exercising ordinary CARE and prudence.

A patent defect in a legal description is one that cannot be corrected so that a new description must be used.

PATENT AND TRADEMARK OFFICE

The U.S. Patent and Trademark Office (PTO) is a federal agency that grants PATENTS and registers TRADEMARKS to qualified applicants. A division of the Department of Commerce, the PTO was originally named the Patent Office when it was established by Congress in 1836. In 1975 it was renamed the Patent and Trademark Office to reflect its dual function. The PTO is now organized pursuant to 35 U.S.C.A. § 1 et seq.

Under the direction of the secretary of commerce, the PTO is run by the commissioner of patents and trademarks, a deputy commissioner, several assistant commissioners, and a support staff of more than one thousand employees. The primary job of the commissioners is to review the merits of patent and trademark applications. Patents are typically issued upon a showing that a particular applicant has discovered or developed a new and useful process, machine, article of manufacture, chemical composition, or other invention. Trademark protection is typically afforded to applicants who are seeking to identify their commercial goods by means of a distinctive word, name, symbol, or other device.

Trademark applications must be submitted with a drawing of the proposed mark; patent applications must be accompanied by a detailed description of the invention. A filing fee is also required for both patent and trademark applications. Applications are reviewed at the PTO by persons of competent legal knowledge and scientific ability, though such persons need not be scientists or lawyers to qualify for the job. Because the application process often requires a significant amount of technical expertise and legal acumen, many applicants hire INTELLECTUAL PROPERTY attorneys to represent them. The commissioner of patents and trademarks maintains a roster of ATTORNEYS and other AGENTS who are eligible to represent applicants in proceedings before the PTO. Each year the PTO receives hundreds of thousands of patent and trademark applications. However, only a fraction of the applications are approved. During the fiscal year of 1995, the PTO issued 114,000 patents and registered approximately 67,000 trademarks.

When the application process is completed, the PTO attaches its seal of authenticity to all patents and trademarks that have been approved. Additionally, the PTO publishes the *Official Gazette*, a weekly notice of all successful patent and trademark applications. Old editions of the *Gazette* dating back to 1872 are kept at a library in the PTO. The library contains more than thirty million documents, including ownership records for both U.S. and foreign patents and trademarks. The library is open to the public, and the PTO will furnish certified copies of patents, trademarks, and other library records to any interested person.

Patent applicants who are dissatisfied with a decision made by the PTO may appeal to the Board of Patent Appeals and Interferences. The board comprises the commissioner of patents and trademarks, the deputy commissioner, an assistant commissioner for patents, an assistant commissioner for trademarks, and individuals known as examiners-in-chief. Trademark applicants can appeal adverse decisions to the Trademark Trial and Appeal Board, which has a similar composition. Applicants who lose before either the Board of Patent Appeals and Interferences or the Trademark Trial and Appeal Board may appeal directly to the U.S. Court of Appeals for the Federal Circuit, which is vested with JURISDICTION over most intellectual property matters.

In addition to examining the merits of patent and trademark applications, the PTO performs studies regarding the development of intellectual property law at the domestic and international levels. These studies have allowed the PTO to establish a number of programs to recognize, identify, assess, and forecast technological trends and their utility to industry. The PTO has relied on these programs in its efforts to strengthen patent and trademark protection around the world.

PATENTS Rights, granted to inventors by the federal government, pursuant to its power under Article I, Section 8, Clause 8, of the U.S. Constitution, that permit them to exclude others from making, using, or selling an invention for a definite, or restricted, period of time.

The U.S. patent system is designed to encourage inventions that are useful to society by granting inventors the absolute right to exclude all others from using or profiting from their invention for a limited time, in exchange for disclosing the details of the invention to the public. Once a patent has expired, the public then has the right to make, use, or sell the invention.

Once a patent is granted, it is regarded as the PERSONAL PROPERTY of the inventor. An inventor's PROPERTY RIGHTS in an invention itself are freely transferable and assignable. Often employees who invent something in the course and scope of their employment transfer and assign their property rights in the invention to their employer. In addition, a patent holder, or patentee, can grant a LICENSE to another to use the invention in exchange for payment, or a ROYALTY.

Inventors are not required to participate in the patent system and they can elect instead to try to keep their invention a TRADE SECRET. However, if the inventor begins to sell his or her invention or allows the public to use it, others can study the invention and create impostor products. If this happens, the original inventor has no protection because he or she did not obtain a patent.

There are three types of patents: (1) design patents, (2) plant patents, and (3) utility patents. Design patents are granted to protect a unique appearance or design of an article of manufacture, whether it be surface ornamentation or the overall configuration of an object. Plant patents are granted for the invention and asexual reproduction of a new and distinct variety of plant, including mutants and hybrids. Utility patents are perhaps the most familiar, applying to machines, chemicals, and processes.

Governing Laws Patent law in the United States is based upon statutes located in title 35 of the U.S. Code, including the Patent Act of 1952. The rules of the Patent and Trademark Office, found in title 37 of the Code of Federal Regulations, provide secondary authority. In addition, the GENERAL AGREEMENT ON TARIFFS AND TRADE (GATT) has led to significant changes in U.S. patent law that are designed to bring some aspects of U.S. law into conformity with those of the country's trading partners. The GATT Implementation Act was signed into law in 1994, and its provisions that impact U.S. patent law began to take effect in 1995.

Patent Duration One important change in U.S. patent law resulting from GATT is the duration of U.S. patents. Patents were originally given fourteen-year terms from the date of issue, until that was changed in 1861. From 1861 until the implementation of GATT, the term of a patent was seventeen years from the date of issue. Under GATT, all patents issued after June 7, 1995, now have a term of twenty years from the effective filing date. GATT contained a retroactive component which provided that all patents that had been issued, but not yet expired, as of June 7, 1995, would have a term that is the longer of twenty years from its effective filing date or seventeen years from the date of issue. The effective filing date is the date on which the earliest U.S. application is filed under which priority is claimed. In the United States, patent rights begin when the patent is issued.

Upon expiration of the term, the invention becomes public property and is freely available for use, reproduction, or sale. Patents can be extended for up to five years under limited circumstances, including interference proceedings (proceedings to determine the priority of an invention), secrecy orders, and APPELLATE review.

Patentable Inventions The Patent Act provides a broad definition of what can be patented: any new or useful process, machine, manufacture, composition of matter, or any new and useful improvement thereof. Although these categories of patentable subject matter are broad, they are also exclusive, and any item that does not fall into one of them is not patentable.

As defined by the Patent Act, a process is a method of treating certain material to produce a specific physical change in the character or quality of that material. A machine is a device that uses energy to get work done. The term manufacture refers to a process whereby an article is made by the art or industry of people. A composition of matter is a compound produced from the combination of two or more specific ingredients that has properties different from, or in addition to, those separately possessed by each ingredient.

An improvement is any addition to, or alteration in, a known process, machine, manufacture, or composition that produces a useful result. The right to a patent of an improvement is restricted to the improvement itself and does not include the process, machine, or article improved.

Naturally occurring substances, such as a type of bacteria or an element, are not patentable. But a genetically engineered bacterium is patentable. The law of gravity and other laws of nature are not patentable. Other abstract principles, fundamental truths, calculation methods, mathematical algorithms, computer programs, and bookkeeping systems are not patentable. Ideas, mental theories, or plans of action alone, without concrete means to implement them, are not patentable, irrespective of how revolutionary and useful to humanity they might be.

However, a process that uses a NATURAL LAW, fundamental principle, or mathematical equation can be patented. For example, in the 1981 decision of *Diamond v. Diehr,* 450 U.S. 175, 101 S. Ct. 1048, 67 L. Ed. 2d 155, the U.S. Supreme Court decided that an industrial process could be patented in spite of the fact that it depended upon a mathematical equation and involved the use of a computer program.

The *Diamond* ruling upheld a patent to two inventors for an improved process for molding rubber articles. A patent examiner had previously ruled against the inventors, finding that they sought patent protection for a computer program, which the Supreme Court had expressly said could not be patented. The process in question, which was patented, was developed to calculate with greater accuracy the amount of time required to obtain uniform curves in synthetic rubber molds.

As a further requirement for an invention to be patentable, it must meet three criteria: (1) novelty (does not conflict with a prior pending patent application or a previously issued patent); (2) utility (virtually any amount of usefulness suffices); and (3) nonobviousness (to a person of ordinary skill in the art to which the invention pertains).

It is not always easy to determine what is an "ordinary level of skill" or what is "obvious" in deciding whether an invention meets the criterion of nonobviousness. The U.S. Supreme Court decision in *Graham v. John Deere Co.*, 383 U.S. 1, 86 S. Ct. 684, 15 L. Ed. 2d 545, 148 U.S.P.Q. 459 (1966), provides the analytical framework in which to decide whether an invention is nonobvious. Just because all the parts of an invention may be found in a prior art does not necessarily make the invention obvious.

Patents may be rejected for nonutility where their only use is a violation of public morals, such as a tool that can only be used to commit a crime.

Individuals Entitled to Patents To be entitled to a patent, an inventor must be the first and original inventor. Joint inventors can obtain a patent for a joint invention, but none of them can obtain a valid patent as a sole inventor.

APWIDE WORLD PHOTOS

Robert Kearns, the inventor of the intermittent windshield wiper, stands among the thousands of files from his patent infringement cases. The Supreme Court awarded Kearns $21 million in a suit against Chrysler.

U.S. law requires that patent applications be filed in the name of and signed by the actual inventor or inventors. If one of the actual inventors is deceased, then the patent application may proceed in the names of the other inventors, but the application must still properly identify all inventors. If all of the inventors, or the sole inventor, are deceased, another person may file a patent application in their place, but only if the filing individual has a legal right to file (such as through descent of the inventors' personal property) and the inventors are still properly identified.

In the United States, the initial right to file for a patent rests with the actual inventor, even if that is an employee who creates the invention in the course and scope of his or her employment using employer resources. However, it is a regular practice for employees engaged in research leading to patentable inventions to sign written CONTRACTS that specify that they will assign to their employer the exclusive rights under any patent obtained during the course of the employment. The employee may receive a certain percentage of the profits earned by the invention in exchange for the ASSIGNMENT of the patent.

Government employees, other than those employed in the Patent and Trademark Office, are entitled to obtain patents for their inventions or discoveries. During the period of employment and for one year thereafter, anyone who is employed in the Patent and Trademark

Office is ineligible to acquire or take directly or indirectly, except by INHERITANCE or BEQUEST, any rights in a patent that is issued or to be issued by the office.

Procedure for Obtaining a Patent To obtain a valid patent, an inventor must make an application to the Patent and Trademark Office. Before making an application, inventors generally make a preliminary patentability search, a relatively low-cost search of all of the patents issued in the United States, to determine if it is feasible to proceed with an application. Often professional searchers perform these searches and give the results to a patent attorney who provides an opinion as to whether the invention is patentable. Although the preliminary search is not required by law, if it is performed, the inventor is required to provide all information obtained through that search to the Patent and Trademark Office if she ultimately files a patent application.

The application must include specifications and drawings of the proposed invention, an oath signed by the inventor, and the requisite fee. The Patent and Trademark Office keeps patent applications confidential until the patent is granted. The term *letters patent* refers to the document that contains the grant of a patent right.

Specification A specification is a written description of the invention that includes the manner and process of creating, constructing, compounding, and using it. It should also state the practical limits of the operation of the invention. The description must be in complete, clear, concise, and precise terms to make the limits of the patent known, to protect the inventor, and to encourage the inventiveness of others by informing the public of what is still available for patent. Total disclosure of the invention is mandated to allow the public to freely use the invention once the patent has expired. No patent will be granted if the description purposely omits the complete truth about the invention to deceive the public.

The specification concludes with the claims, which explicitly describe both the structure of the invention and what it does. By regulation and time-honored tradition, the patent claims are written in the form of a continuous run-on sentence. The claims give the Patent and Trademark Office and the courts the opportunity to determine whether the subject matter is patentable or whether it has been anticipated by a previous invention. A claim can be either rejected by the Patent and Trademark Office or deemed invalid if it is vague, indefinite, or incomplete. The claim should cover only the actual invention. It can also be rejected if it is so broad as to include what is old and known information in addition to what is new. Each claim must contain only one single and distinct invention, but more than one claim can be included in a single application. The inventor also must disclose in the specification what she considers to be the optimum way of practicing or using the invention.

Drawings Drawings must be included in a patent application only when they are necessary to understand the subject for which a patent is sought. If drawings are omitted, the commissioner of patents can require that they be submitted within two months from the time that the inventor receives notice. Drawings that are submitted after that time cannot be used with the application, and a patent can be denied due to the inadequacy of the specification.

The commissioner can require that the inventor provide a model of the invention. In addition, when the invention involves a composition of matter, the applicant might have to furnish a specimen of it for inspection or experimentation.

Oath and Fee The application for a patent is accompanied by an OATH that the inventor believes herself to be the first and original inventor. The patent laws of the United States do not discriminate on the basis of the citizenship of the inventor. An inventor from another country may apply for a patent on the same basis as a U.S. citizen.

An application for an original patent must be accompanied by a filing fee payable to the Patent and Trademark Office. Fees vary depending upon the type of application and the size of the entity applying for the patent. Small entities pay lower fees. When a patent is issued, the patentee must pay an additional fee. These fees also vary based on the size of the entity to whom the patent is issued. Additional fees are charged for maintaining a patent, which likewise vary with the size of the entity involved in the maintenance of the patent.

Patent and Trademark Office Proceedings Upon receipt of an application for a patent, the commissioner must examine it to determine whether the applicant is entitled to a patent. The Patent and Trademark Office is not restricted to the use of technical evidence in reviewing applications but can act upon anything that establishes the facts with reasonable certainty.

A patent application can be rejected for substantial and reasonable grounds, such as when the alleged invention lacks usefulness or when the invention has been publicly used or

An example of a patent

Source: Reprinted through the courtesy of the U.S. Patent Office.

3,032,012
RETRACTABLE
BALL POINT PEN
Charles K. Lovejoy, Atlanta,
Ga., assignor to Scripto,
Inc., a corporation of Georgia
Filed July 19, 1960, Ser. No.
43,921 2 Claims.
(Cl. 120—42.03)

This invention relates to writing instruments and more particularly to an improved ball point pen having a retractable writing unit wherein the extremity of the writing tip is inclined towards the central longitudinal axis of said pen barrel so as to afford a readily visible writing tip and achieve a near vertical writing angle formed between the axis of the inclined extremity of the writing tip and the writing surface when held by the writer in normal writing position.

In the past ball point pens have utilized angled writing tips, however, such angled tips were not frontally disposed of the central longitudinal axis of the pen barrel, frontally disposed being defined as that side of the writing instrument which the writer sees during writing when the pen is held in normal writing position. The advantage that is achieved by the present invention is that a readily visible writing tip is afforded which provides a near vertical writing angle formed between the axis of the inclined extremity of the writing tip and the writing surface when held by the writer in normal writing position. In addition, the present invention provides a writing instrument that is balanced, the reason for this being that the weight of the writing instrument is stably supported on the writing tip in an underslung fashion when in contact with the writing surface since the writing tip is above or frontally of the central longitudinal axis of the pen barrel which precludes any tendency to rotate in the writer's hand.

These and other features of the present invention are described in further detail below in connection with the accompanying drawings, in which:

FIG.1 is a longitudinal cross section of the writing instrument according to the present invention showing the writing unit at projected position;

FIG. 2 is an enlarged longitudinal cross section of the forward portion of the pen shown in FIG. 1;

FIG. 3 is a transverse cross section taken along the line 3—3 in FIG.2; and

FIG. 4 is a longitudinal cross section of the extremity of the writing tip.

Referring now in detail to the drawings, the writing instrument is generally designated by the reference numeral **10,** and has a retractable ball point writing unit **12** housed within forward barrel portion **14** and rear barrel portion **16** which are normally held together in releasable threaded engagement. The writing unit **12** is longitudinally slidable in inclined relation within the central bore **18** that is formed within forward barrel portion **14** and rear barrel portion **16** and which terminates at its forward end in an aperture **20.** The writing unit **12** is selectively projected or retracted by a projection and retraction mechanism **22** which can be of the type disclosed and claimed in U.S. Patent No. 2.930.354 and which may incorporate the further structural features that are disclosed and claimed in copending application Serial No. 739,545, filed June 3, 1958, now Patent Number 3,007,444. The details of this mechanism are clearly disclosed in the above mentioned issued patent and copending application and hence will not be discussed in detail here, but merely referred to generally by the reference numeral **22** which is recognized to include a latch L and a plunger P. The latch L in response to a depression of plunger P is adapted to engage longitudinally spaced latch shoulders disposed within rear barrel portion **16** for selectively positioning the writing unit at its projected or retracted position. The writing unit is normally urged toward retracted position by spring **24** which is positioned between shoulders **26** and **28** formed in the forward barrel portion **14** and on the writing unit **12,** respectively. Writing unit **12** has a forward metallic tube section **30** of reduced diameter which carries at its forward end writing tip **32.** The writing tip **32** is of general cylindrical shape having a conical extremity **34** formed about an axis **36** that is inclined to the axis **38** of the cylindrical portion of the writ-

An example of a patent (continued)

ing tip **32.** The conical extremity **34** is also formed within the principal diameter that defines the cylindrical configuration of writing tip **32.** A ball **40** is rotatably housed within the angled, conical extremity **34.** The writing unit **12** is prevented from rotating within the central bore **18** by means of key **42,** which is attached to the forward metal tube portion **30,** being slidably disposed in slot **44** which is formed in forward barrel portion **14.** To illustrate the combined advantages of a readily visible writing tip having a near vertical writing angle, it is well to define the axes in question. The longitudinal axis of the writing instrument is shown by reference numeral **46** and it can be readily seen in FIGS. 1 and 2 that the inclined writing extremity **34** is frontally disposed of the longitudinal axis **46** of the writing instrument. By this arrangement the writing extremity is clearly visible to the writer. The writing angle θ is shown as the angle formed between the axis **36** of the angled extremity **34** of writing tip **32** and the writing surface **48.** By referring to FIG. 2 it is readily seen that this angle approaches 90 degrees when held in normal writing position.

The present invention has been described in detail above for purposes of illustrating only and is not intended to be limited by this description or otherwise except as defined in the appended claims.

I claim:

1. In a writing instrument having a barrel formed about a central longitudinal axis with a main central bore and an aperture formed in its forward end, a writing unit including a ball point writing tip at its forward end slidably disposed within said central bore for shifting between projected and retracted positions with respect to said forward barrel end, means normally biasing said writing unit toward retracted position and means for selectively positioning said writing unit at projected and retracted positions, the improvement of said ball point writing tip having a conical portion the axis of which is inclined toward the central longitudinal axis of said barrel, said conical portion terminating in a ball retaining lip which lies in a plane facing the longitudinal axis of said barrel and adapted for disposition through said forward barrel aperture so that said conical portion of the writing tip when projected is frontally disposed of and inclined toward said central longitudinal axis of said barrel to afford a visible writing tip having a near vertical writing angle when brought in contact with a writing surface and to provide a balanced writing instrument that precludes any tendency to rotate about said central longitudinal axis of said pen barrel when held by the writer in normal writing position.

2. In a writing instrument the improvement as defined in claim 1 and further characterized in that said writing unit is keyed against rotation within said barrel.

References Cited in the file of this patent

UNITED STATES PATENTS

2,449,939	Heyberger	Sept. 21, 1948
2,863,421	Rizzo	Dec. 9, 1958
3,000,352	Grube et al.	Sept. 19, 1961

FOREIGN PATENTS

428,021	Italy	Feb. 12, 1947
1,167,185	France	July 7, 1958
1,187,439	France	Mar. 2, 1959

sold previously. If the patent is rejected, the commissioner must notify the applicant of the rejection and the grounds for the rejection. An applicant can request a reexamination of the application and submit evidence to rebut the reasons for rejection. Failure to request a review is considered a waiver of the right to challenge the rejection.

A pending application may be amended until the Patent and Trademark Office ultimately decides the matter, either by issuing the patent or rejecting the patent application. New and enlarged claims can be added by amendment only when they are fairly within the scope of the original claim. An amendment that involves a material departure from the invention described in the original specification or enlarges the scope of the original application is invalid. When made within a reasonable time, amendments relate back to the original date of the application and are treated as if they were included in the original application. This is significant because time determines who will be entitled to the patent when two inventors claim essentially the same invention.

Loss or Denial of a Patent An individual who has invented or discovered a process or object is entitled to a patent if the item or process falls within the specific categories of patentable matter and possesses the necessary attributes of invention, novelty, and utility.

Anticipation A patent will be denied in the event that anticipation occurs, which means that the complete invention was disclosed before the applicant's invention or discovery. This situation might arise when substantially similar elements that produce, or are capable of producing, the same results are found in previously invented machines that are known and commercially used. However, if the two similar inventions accomplish substantially different results or perform totally different functions, they are not deemed to be anticipated, and the second invention will be patentable even if it is essentially identical structurally to the first invention.

For a prior patent to anticipate a later invention, it must disclose the complete and operative invention in such full, clear, and exact terms as to enable a skilled individual involved in the art to practice the invention without the exercise of his or her own inventive skill. A process or instrument used for one purpose might anticipate an invention that uses essentially the same method for a new use if the latter is so comparable to the original invention that it would be apparent to a person experienced in the field. An invention is not anticipated if it has been produced previously due to an accident but is incapable of being repeated because the necessary knowledge to do so is lacking. If the results could be reproduced, however, the invention is considered anticipated.

Previous experimental efforts that are abandoned before the invention achieves actual results do not anticipate the invention. The invention is anticipated, however, if the experiment proves successful.

Statutory Bar Section 102(b) of 35 U.S.C.A. provides a statutory bar to some otherwise meritorious inventions. Under this rule, an inventor is not issued a patent if her invention was described in a book, catalog, magazine article, thesis, or trade publication in the United States or any other country before she invented it or more than a year before she filed the patent application. This statutory bar applies regardless of who made the invention discussed in the prior publication. Thus, if an inventor publishes a description of an invention or places the invention for sale or for public use, a statutory bar can result. Once an invention is placed for sale in the United States, the inventor has just one year in which to file a patent application or the right to patent that invention is forever lost. The clock begins when the invention is placed for sale, even if it is never actually sold. This rule is intended to guarantee that an inventor cannot expand the period of patent protection for the commercial exploitation of her monopoly.

Abandonment and Forfeiture An inventor can lose the right to obtain a patent through ABANDONMENT. An invention is regarded as abandoned when it is subject to free and unrestricted public use.

A recognized exception to this general rule, called the "experimental use exception," is when an invention must be placed in the public use to determine its operability. However this exception is very narrow, and the inventor must be careful to document the invention to support a later claim of experimental use.

An inventor forfeits the right to a patent when she delays making a claim or hides the invention for an extensive period of time because such conduct unduly postpones the time that the public would be entitled to the subsequent free use of the invention. Delay in applying for a patent does not constitute abandonment if the inventor can demonstrate that she never intended to abandon the invention.

Priority When two or more inventors discover or invent the same thing, patent priority can deny a patent to one of the inventors. Patents are generally issued to the first inventor, as determined by certain guidelines. The Patent and Trademark Office commences an interference proceeding to determine the priority of invention between two or more inventors who are claiming substantially the same patentable invention and who each appear to be entitled to the patent, but for the other's application. Such a proceeding examines the dates of conception and reduction to practice and also considers the diligence exercised by the individual who conceived of the invention first but did not reduce it to practice until after the other inventor had done so. The date of conception is the date when the idea, encompassing all the basic and necessary components of the invention, becomes so clearly defined in the mind of the inventor as to be capable of physical expression. Reduction to practice occurs when the way in which the invention works is readily demonstrable.

An inventor who is the first to conceive of an invention and reduce it to practice is entitled to a patent. When an inventor who first conceives of an invention exercises reasonable diligence in reducing it to practice, she will receive a patent, even if the inventor who was second to conceive of the idea was faster in reducing it to practice.

Another general rule is that an individual who actually reduces an invention to practice has priority over one who constructively reduces it to practice. Actual reduction takes place when the invention is put into practical form, whereas constructive reduction occurs when a patent application is filed with the Patent and Trademark Office.

Former U.S. patent law only allowed inventive activity that actually took place within the borders of the country to establish a date of invention. GATT has changed this to allow foreign inventors to prove inventive activity that took place in another country to show a date of invention. Because the United States has a "first to invent" patent system, whereas most other countries have a "first to file" system, the United States had effectively discriminated against foreign inventors because it gave patents to the first inventor to actually make the invention in the United States. GATT addressed this issue that for many years was a disadvantage for U.S. trading partners.

Appeals Applicants for a patent, or for the reissue of a patent, whose claims have twice been rejected can bring an APPEAL from the final decision of the primary examiner to the Patent Office Board of Appeals and Interferences. An applicant who is dissatisfied with the decision of the board of appeals can appeal to the U.S. Court of Appeals for the Federal Circuit or start a CIVIL ACTION against the commissioner in U.S. District Court for the District of Columbia within a specified period of time after the board issues its decision. The applicant is not permitted, however, to institute both a civil lawsuit and an appeal to the U.S. Court of Appeals for the Federal Circuit.

Reissue and Disclaimer A reissued patent is the grant of a new patent that modifies the original invention by the addition of new elements. A reissued patent is essentially an amendment of the original patent effected to rectify some defect or insufficiency in it.

A DISCLAIMER is the voluntary abandonment of some portion of a patent claim that would render it invalid for lack of novelty. It limits the claim to what is new and thereby saves the patentability of the item by circumventing the invalidity that would otherwise defeat the entire claim. An inventor who knows that a patent contains invalid claims should immediately file a disclaimer, because the failure to do so could result in the rejection of the patent.

Assignment and Lease An assignment is a transfer either of the entire patent, encompassing the exclusive right to make, use, and sell the invention, or a specified part thereof, in the United States. The assignment must be in writing and should be recorded in the Patent and Trademark Office. In the event that a patent is assigned but the assignment is not recorded, a later purchaser of the patent can use the purchased patent as if it had never been assigned.

An assignment is different from a license because a license merely provides the licensee with a temporary right to use the patent as agreed. A license need not be in writing. Whether a transfer is an assignment or a license is determined by reference to the contract between the parties. A patent license is personal to the licensee and cannot be transferred unless specifically indicated in the agreement. The licensor, the individual who issued the license to another, ordinarily requires the payment of a royalty for the use of the patent.

Marking Patented Items A patentee or any authorized party who makes or sells any patented item must provide notice to the public that the article is patented by placing the word *patent* and the number given to the patent on the article. If the nature of the article prohibits such a designation, a label that contains the same information should be enclosed in, or marked on, its package. This marking requirement is not applicable to a patent for a process.

Inventors can mark their inventions with the words *patent pending* if they have a patent application on file and pending with the Patent and Trademark Office at the time the products are marked.

Federal law imposes a penalty for various forms of false marking, including marking an unpatented article with the word *patent*, or any term that implies that the article is patented, for the purpose of deceiving the public. If a patent holder fails to mark the patented product as required, he or she may not recover damages for any patent INFRINGEMENT that may take place as a result.

Infringement Infringement is the unauthorized making, using, or selling for practical use or for profit an invention covered by a patent. Effective 1996, GATT also made the offer to sell a patented invention without the permission of the patentee a direct infringement violation.

Although no infringement can occur before a patent is issued, infringement can occur even if the infringer does not have any actual knowledge of the existence of a patent. A direct infringer is one who makes, uses, or sells the patented invention without permission from the patentee. An indirect infringer is one who actively encourages another to make, use, or sell a patented invention without permission. A contributory infringer is one who knowingly sells or supplies a part or component of the patented invention to another, unless the component is a staple article of commerce and is suitable for a substantial noninfringing use.

The definition of an infringement, provided in 35 U.S.C.A. section 271, has been greatly expanded in the late 1980s and 1990s. For example, it is an infringement to apply for federal FOOD AND DRUG ADMINISTRATION approval of a patented drug if the purpose is to obtain approval to manufacture, use, or sell the drug before its patent expires. It is also an infringement to provide a substantial portion of the components of a patented invention to someone outside of the United States so that the components can be assembled outside of the reaches of U.S. patent law. Similarly, it is an infringement to import into the United States a product made by a process covered by a U.S. patent although it was produced outside of the United States.

Remedies The Patent Act provides for several remedies in the event of an infringement, including injunctive relief, compensable damages, TREBLE DAMAGES when appropriate to punish the infringer, payment of attorneys' fees in cases involving knowing infringement, and payment of the costs incurred in bringing the infringement claim in court.

The owner of a patent has a right of action for the unlawful invasion of patent rights by an infringement that has arisen within six years from the date when the lawsuit is initiated.

Injunction Courts frequently grant injunctions to protect property rights in patents. An INJUNCTION is a court decree that orders an infringer to stop illegally making, using, or selling the patented article. An injunction is only granted when an award of monetary DAMAGES will not adequately remedy the situation—for example, when an infringer plans to continue the unlawful acts. If an individual disobeys an injunction and continues to make use of an invention without permission, she will be guilty of CONTEMPT and subject to a fine or imprisonment or both.

Damages In an action for infringement of a patent, compensation for prior infringements can be awarded; however, compensation will be denied for use of the invention before the date the patent was issued. Where there is an infringement, the court will award the patentee actual damages adequate to compensate for the loss in an amount that is equal to a reasonable royalty for the infringing use, together with interest or costs set by the court. If the jury in a trial does not determine the amount of damages, the court will. In either case, the court, under the authority of statute, can increase the damages awarded by the jury up to three times the amount determined, called treble damages. Treble damages are punitive and awarded only in certain instances, such as where the infringer intentionally, in BAD FAITH, infringed the patent.

PATENT WRIT An open court order in earlier times; a WRIT that was not folded and sealed up as a CLOSE WRIT would be.

PATERNITY The state or condition of a father; the relationship of a father.

English and U.S. COMMON LAW have recognized the importance of establishing the paternity of children. In the United States, a child born outside of a legal marriage relationship will lose CHILD SUPPORT and INHERITANCE rights if the fatherhood of the child is not legally established. The father may voluntarily acknowledge paternity in a legal document filed with a court or by agreeing to have his name listed as the father on the child's birth certificate. If the man disputes fatherhood, the mother or the state government may initiate a legal proceeding, known as a paternity action, to adjudicate fatherhood.

The common law also established the "marital paternity presumption," which holds that a child born during a MARRIAGE is the offspring of the husband. Therefore, a child born as a result of the wife's adulterous affair is recognized as a legitimate child of the marriage. This rule recognized that ILLEGITIMACY brought severe economic penalties to a child, including the inability to inherit from the husband, as well as social stigma. By establishing a PRESUMPTION of paternity and therefore legitimacy, the rule promoted family stability and integrity.

This rule was developed at a time when no medical tests existed to prove paternity. In addition, a husband could not testify that he had no access to his wife at the time of conception. A husband could rebut the marital presumption only by proving his impotence or his absence from the country.

By the late nineteenth century, U.S. courts began to allow the defense of impossibility to rebut the marital presumption. The question of paternity became a fact that could be rebutted by clear and convincing evidence that the procreation by the husband was impossible.

The Impossible Heir

In contemporary law the legal determination of paternity generally rests on the results of blood and genetic testing. However, there are times when it can be proved that it was impossible for a husband to be the father of his wife's child because the husband was absent during the period when conception occurred.

In an unusual reversal of modern law on paternity, the Alabama Supreme Court, in *Tierce v. Ellis,* 624 So. 2d 553 (1993), found that Dennis Tierce was the legitimate son of William Tierce, even though William was serving overseas in the armed forces during World War II when Dennis was conceived.

William Tierce returned from the war to Alabama in December 1945 to discover that his wife Irene was six months pregnant. He immediately filed for divorce on the ground of adultery. The divorce was granted in February 1946. On April 4, 1946, Dennis Tierce was born. William Tierce was erroneously listed as the father on the birth certificate, but Tierce never knew of this mistake. He remarried and had five children, including his daughter, Sheila Ellis.

William Tierce died in 1972. When the executors of his estate filed a list of heirs in 1989, they listed Dennis as William's son. Sheila Ellis filed suit, challenging the paternity of Dennis and his status as an heir. The trial court ruled that it was impossible for Dennis to be the biological son of William.

The Alabama Supreme Court reversed, basing its decision on two grounds. First, under the Alabama Uniform Parentage Act (Ala. Code §§ 26-17-1 et seq. [1992 and Supp. 1994]), a husband is presumed to be the father of a child born within three hundred days of a divorce. Dennis was born sixty days after his parents' divorce. Second, the court invoked the common law rule of repose, which requires a prompt disposition of a legal dispute. The court concluded that because William Tierce did not seek a paternity judgment during his divorce proceedings in 1946, his daughter could not now attempt to rebut the marital paternity presumption. Therefore, Dennis Tierce, the impossible heir, could claim a share of the estate of a person he never knew and to whom he was not related.

In 1973 the National Conference of Commissioners on Uniform State Laws proposed the Uniform Parentage Act (UPA), which sought to establish a consistent rule on adjudicating paternity disputes. The UPA, which has been adopted by eighteen states, continued to use the marital paternity presumption. In addition, it presumes a mother's husband to be the natural father of a child if the child is born during the marriage or within three hundred days after the marriage is terminated. The UPA does state, however, that a presumption of paternity may be rebutted by clear and convincing evidence.

Modern science has made the adjudication of paternity issues easier. Modern blood and genetic testing can accurately determine paternity. Human leukocyte antigen tissue typing can provide up to a 98 percent probability that a man was the father of a child. The use of DNA testing provides near-positive paternity identification. Four states that have adopted the UPA have created a presumption of paternity based solely on genetic testing. Some courts have questioned the need for the marital presumption at all because of the certainty produced by testing.

CROSS-REFERENCES

DNA Evidence; Family Law; Paternity Suit.

PATERNITY SUIT A CIVIL ACTION brought against an unwed father by an unmarried mother to obtain support for an illegitimate child and for payment of bills incident to the pregnancy and the birth.

A paternity suit, also known as an AFFILIATION PROCEEDING, is a criminal proceeding in certain states.

Generally the unwed mother initiates a paternity suit; in some JURISDICTIONS, however, if the mother is a MINOR, proceedings must be initiated by a parent or GUARDIAN acting on her behalf.

See also CHILD SUPPORT; ILLEGITIMACY; PARENT AND CHILD.

ARTIST: C. GREGORY STAPKO. COLLECTION OF THE SUPREME COURT OF THE UNITED STATES.

William Paterson

PATERSON, WILLIAM William Paterson was a distinguished public servant during the early years of the Republic of the United States, serving as governor of New Jersey, a Framer of the U.S. Constitution, a U.S. senator, and associate justice of the U.S. Supreme Court. In recognition of his service to New Jersey, the city of Paterson was named for him.

Paterson was born on December 24, 1745, in County Antrim, Ireland. He emigrated with his family to New Jersey in 1747 and graduated from the College of New Jersey (now Princeton University) in 1763. He was admitted to the New Jersey bar in 1768, establishing a law practice in New Bromley, New Jersey.

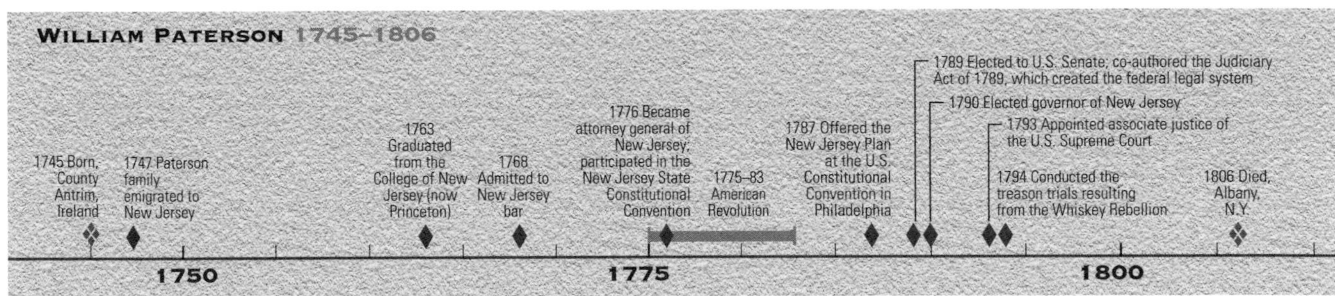

He entered government in 1775, serving in the New Jersey Provincial Congress. He became attorney general of New Jersey in 1776, holding the position for seven years. During this period he briefly served in the New Jersey Senate. He also participated in the New Jersey State Constitutional Convention in 1776.

Paterson played a key role in the U.S. Constitutional Convention, which was held in Philadelphia in 1787. As a delegate from New Jersey, Paterson sought to protect his and other small states from demands by larger states that representation be based on population. Paterson offered an alternative to the large-state proposition, or Virginia Plan. His New Jersey Plan went to the other extreme. He proposed that each state have one vote in Congress. Out of this conflict came the compromise that created two houses of Congress, with the House of Representatives based on population and the Senate on equal representation (two votes per state). The compromise also led to the creation of the Supreme Court in Article III of the U.S. Constitution. Paterson, who signed the Constitution, was a strong supporter of the document and campaigned for its adoption in New Jersey.

He was elected to the Senate in 1789 and was one of the authors of the JUDICIARY ACT OF 1789, which created the federal legal structure of Supreme Court, circuit court, and district court. The act created the office of attorney general and gave the Supreme Court the appellate JURISDICTION to review state court decisions that involved the Constitution, federal laws, and treaties.

Paterson resigned in 1790 to run for governor of New Jersey. Easily elected, he left the governorship in 1793 when President GEORGE WASHINGTON appointed him an associate justice of the U.S. Supreme Court. His tenure on the Court revealed him to be a strong supporter of the federal government and an independent judiciary. His role as a Framer lent credibility to his conclusions as to what was the "original intent" of the drafters of the Constitution.

As a circuit judge (in that period Supreme Court justices also rode circuit), he conducted the TREASON trials of the participants in the WHISKEY REBELLION, a revolt in 1794 against the excise tax on whiskey imposed by Secretary of the Treasury ALEXANDER HAMILTON. He later presided over the trials of prominent Democratic-Republicans who were charged with sedition for criticizing President JOHN ADAMS.

Paterson died on September 9, 1806, in Albany, New York.

See also CONSTITUTION OF THE UNITED STATES.

PATIENTS' RIGHTS The legal interests of persons who submit to medical treatment.

For many years, common medical practice meant that physicians made decisions for their patients. This paternalistic view has gradually been supplanted by one promoting patient autonomy, whereby patients and doctors share the decision-making responsibility. Consequently doctor-patient relationships are very different now than they were just a few decades ago. However, conflicts still abound as the medical community and those it serves struggle to define their respective roles.

Consent Consent, particularly INFORMED CONSENT, is the cornerstone of patients' rights. Consent is based on the inviolability of one's person. It means that doctors do not have the right to touch or treat a patient without that patient's approval, because the patient is the one who must live with the consequences and deal with any discomfort caused by treatment. A doctor can be held liable for committing a BATTERY if the doctor touches the patient without first obtaining the patient's consent.

The shift in doctor-patient relationships seems inevitable in hindsight. In one early consent case, a doctor told a woman he would only be repairing some cervical and rectal tears; instead he performed a hysterectomy. In another case a patient permitted her doctors to examine her under anesthesia but insisted that they not operate; the doctors removed a fibroid tumor during the procedure. In yet another case, a doctor assured a man that a proposed operation was simple and essentially without RISK; the patient's left hand was paralyzed as a result of the surgery.

Tuskegee Syphilis Study

Many patients who suffer from a serious disease agree to participate in medical studies that may lead to a better understanding of the illness and more effective treatment. A fundamental ethical principle regarding these studies requires that patients consent to their participation. The U.S. Public Health Service (PHS) ignored this ethical canon for forty years during its study of the effects of untreated syphilis in more than four hundred African American men living in and near Tuskegee, Alabama. The Tuskegee syphilis study, which was conducted in secret, was flawed by bad science, unethical conduct, and racism.

In 1932 the PHS began researching a popular theory of American health professionals at the time. The theory held that neurological damage from syphilis was more common in white men, whereas black men suffered more cardiovascular damage from the disease. It was also thought that African Americans were affected in other ways by syphilis differently than were whites. To test these ideas, the PHS secured the assistance of the prestigious Tuskegee Institute, located in Macon County, Alabama, to help recruit poor African American male sharecroppers to participate in a study.

More than four hundred infected men were recruited, along with two hundred uninfected men who were a control group. The infected men were not told they had syphilis or that they could transmit the disease through sexual intercourse. Instead they were told they had "bad blood," a local term that referred to a range of illnesses. The men were also deceived into consenting to painful spinal-tap procedures.

The study, which was to last less than a year, proved inconclusive. Some men had received medical treatment for the disease, but the PHS stopped providing medication when it decided to implement a second study. This study monitored the medical conditions of the untreated men over the course of their lives. These men were denied penicillin, an effective weapon against syphilis, when it was introduced in the 1940s. As the men died, their families were provided with burial allowances in return for permitting autopsies to be performed.

The program continued until 1972, when the *Washington Star* exposed the unethical methods used in the study. It is estimated that more than one hundred men died of tertiary syphilis, but it is unknown how many women and children were infected by the study participants. A class action suit against the federal government was settled out of court for $10 million in 1974. Congress responded in 1974 by passing the National Research Act (88 Stat. 342), which requires review boards to approve all studies involving human subjects.

In May 1996 President Bill Clinton made an official apology to the subjects of the study.

Consent must be voluntary, competent, and informed. Voluntary means that, when the patient gives consent, he or she is free from extreme DURESS and is not intoxicated or under the influence of medication, and that the doctor has not coerced the patient into giving consent.

The law presumes that an adult is COMPETENT, but competency may be an issue in numerous instances. Competence is typically only challenged when a patient disagrees with a doctor's recommended treatment or refuses treatment altogether. If an individual understands the information presented regarding treatment, she or he is competent to consent to or refuse treatment.

Consent can be given verbally, in writing, or by one's actions. For example, a person has consented to a vaccination if she stands in line with others who are receiving vaccinations, observes the procedure, and then presents her arm to a health care provider. Consent is inferred in cases of emergency or unanticipated circumstances. For example, if unforeseen serious or life-threatening circumstances develop during surgery for which consent has been given, consent is inferred to allow doctors to take immediate further action to prevent serious injury or death. Consent is also inferred where an adult or child is found unconscious, or where an emergency otherwise necessitates immediate treatment to prevent death or serious harm.

Consent is not valid if the patient does not understand its meaning or if a patient has been misled. Children typically may not give consent; instead a parent or GUARDIAN must consent to medical treatment. Competency issues may arise with mentally ill individuals or those who have diminished mental capacity due to retardation or other problems. However, the fact that someone suffers from a mental illness or diminished mental capacity does not mean that the individual is incompetent. Depending on the type and severity of the disability, the patient may still have the ability to understand a proposed course of treatment. For example, in recent years most JURISDICTIONS have recognized the right of hospitalized mental patients to refuse medication under certain circumstances. Numerous courts have ruled that a mental patient may have the right to refuse antipsychotic drugs, which can produce disturbing side effects.

If a patient is incompetent, technically only a legally appointed guardian can make treatment decisions. Commonly, however, physicians defer to family members on an informal basis, thereby avoiding a lengthy and expensive competency hearing. Consent by a family member demonstrates that the doctor consulted someone who knows the patient well and is likely to be concerned about the patient's well-being. This will probably be sufficient to dissuade a patient from suing for failure to obtain consent should the patient recover.

Legal, moral, and ethical questions arise in competency cases involving medical procedures not primarily for the patient's benefit. These cases typically arise in the context of organ donation from one sibling to another. Many of these cases are approved in the lower courts; the decisions frequently turn on an examination of the relationship between the donor and recipient. If the donor and recipient have a relationship that the donor is aware of, actively participates in, and benefits from, courts generally conclude that the benefits of continuing the relationship outweigh the risks and discomforts of the procedure. For example, one court granted permission for a kidney transplant from a developmentally disabled patient into his brother because the developmentally disabled boy was very dependent on the brother. In another case a court approved a seven-year-old girl's donation of a kidney to her identical twin sister after experts and family testified to the close bond between the two. Conversely, a mother successfully fought to prevent testing of her three-and-a-half-year-old twins for a possible bone marrow transplant for a half brother because the children had only met the boy twice and were unaware that he was their brother.

Married or emancipated minors, including those in the armed services, are capable of giving their own consent. Emancipated means that the MINOR is self-supporting and lives independently of parents and parental control. In addition, under a theory known as the mature minor doctrine, certain minors may consent to treatment without first obtaining parental consent. If the minor is capable of understanding the nature, extent, and consequences of medical treatment, he or she may consent to medical care. Such situations typically involve older minors and treatments for the benefit of the minor (i.e., not organ transplant donors or blood donors) and usually involve relatively low-risk procedures. In recent years, however, some minors have sought the right to make life-or-death decisions. In 1989 a state court first recognized that a minor could make such a grave decision. A seventeen-and-a-half-year-old leukemia patient refused life-saving blood transfusions based on a deeply held, family-shared religious conviction. A psychologist testified that the girl had the maturity of a twenty-two-year-old. Ironically, the young woman won her right to refuse treatment but was alive and healthy when the case was finally decided. She had been transfused before the slow judicial process needed to decide such a difficult question led to a ruling in her favor.

Some state statutes specifically provide that minors may give consent in certain highly charged situations, such as cases of venereal disease, pregnancy, and drug or ALCOHOL abuse. A minor may also overrule parental consent in certain situations. In one case a mother gave consent for an ABORTION for her sixteen-year-old unemancipated daughter, but the girl disagreed. A court upheld the daughter's right to withhold consent.

Courts often reach divergent outcomes when deciding whether to interfere with a parent's refusal to consent to a non-life-threatening procedure. One court refused to override a father's denial of consent for surgery to repair his son's harelip and cleft palate. But a different court permitted an operation on a boy suffering from a severe facial deformity even though his mother objected on religious grounds to the accompanying blood transfusion. In another case a child was ordered to undergo medical treatments after the parents unsuccessfully treated the child's severe burns with herbal remedies.

Courts rarely hesitate to step in where a child's life is in danger. To deny a child a beneficial, life-sustaining treatment constitutes child neglect, and states have a duty to protect children from neglect. One case involved a mother who testified that she did not believe that her child was HIV positive, despite medical evidence to the contrary. The court ordered treatment, including AZT, for the child. Many other cases involve parents who want to treat a serious illness with nontraditional methods or whose religious beliefs forbid blood transfusions. Cases involving religious beliefs raise difficult questions under the FIRST AMENDMENT's Freedom of Expression of Religion Clause, COMMON LAW, statutory rights of a parent in raising a child, and the state's traditional interest in protecting those unable to protect themselves.

Where a child's life is in danger and parental consent is withheld, a hospital seeks a court-appointed guardian for the child. The guardian, often a hospital administrator, then consents to the treatment on behalf of the child. In an emergency case, a judge may make a decision over the telephone. In some cases doctors may choose to act without judicial permission if time constraints do not allow enough time to reach a judge by telephone.

In 1982 a six-day-old infant with Down's syndrome died after a court approved a parental decision to withhold life-saving surgery. The child had a condition that made eating impossible. The baby was medicated but given no nourishment. The public furor over the *Baby Doe* case eventually helped spur the Department of Health and Human Services to create regulations delineating when treatment may be withheld from a disabled infant. Treatment may be withheld if an infant is chronically and irreversibly comatose, if such treatment would merely prolong dying or would otherwise be futile in terms of survival of the infant, or if such treatment would be virtually futile in terms of survival and the treatment would be inhumane under these circumstances.

Although courts overrule parental refusal to allow treatment in many instances, far less common are cases where a court overrides an otherwise competent adult's denial of consent. The cases where courts have compelled treatment of an adult usually fall into two categories: where the patient was so physically weak that the court ruled that the patient could not reflect and make a choice to consent or refuse; or where the patient had minor children, even though the patient was fully competent to refuse consent. The possible civil or criminal LIABILITY of a hospital might also factor into a decision. A court typically will not order a terminally ill patient to undergo treatments to prolong life.

Informed Consent Simply consenting to treatment is not enough. A patient must give *informed consent.* In essence, informed consent means that before a doctor can treat or touch a patient, the patient must be given some basic information about what the doctor proposes to do. Informed consent has been called the most important legal doctrine in patients' rights.

State laws and court decisions vary regarding informed consent, but the trend is clearly toward more disclosure rather than less. Informed consent is required not only in life-or-death situations but also in clinic and outpatient settings as well. A health care provider must first provide information regarding risks, alternatives, and success rates. The information must be presented in language the patient can understand and typically should include the following:

- A description of the recommended treatment or procedure;
- A description of the risks and benefits—particularly exploring the risk of serious bodily disability or death;
- A description of alternative treatments and the risks and benefits of alternatives;
- The probable results if no treatment is undertaken;
- The probability of success and a definition of what the doctor means by success;
- Length and challenges of recuperation; and
- Any other information generally provided to patients in this situation by other qualified physicians.

Only material risks must be disclosed. A material risk is one that might cause a reasonable patient to decide not to undergo a recommended treatment. The magnitude of the risk also factors into the definition of a material risk. For example, one would expect that a one in ten thousand risk of death would always be disclosed, but not a one in ten thousand risk of a two-hour headache.

Plastic surgery and vasectomies illustrate two areas where the probability of success and the meaning of success should be explicitly delineated. For example, a man successfully sued his doctor after the doctor assured him that a vasectomy would be 100 percent effective as birth control; the man's wife later became pregnant. Because the only purpose for having the procedure was complete sterilization, a careful explanation of probability of success was essential.

Occasionally, informed consent is not required. In an emergency situation where immediate treatment is needed to preserve a patient's health or life, a physician may be justified in failing to provide full and complete information to a patient. Moreover, where the risks are minor and well known to the average person, such as in drawing blood, a physician may dispense with full disclosure. In addition, some patients explicitly ask not to be informed of specific risks. In this situation a doctor must only ascertain that the patient understands that there are unspecified risks of death and serious bodily disabilities; the doctor might ask the patient to sign a waiver of informed consent.

Finally, informed consent may be bypassed in rare cases where a physician has objective evidence that informing a patient would render the patient unable to make a rational decision.

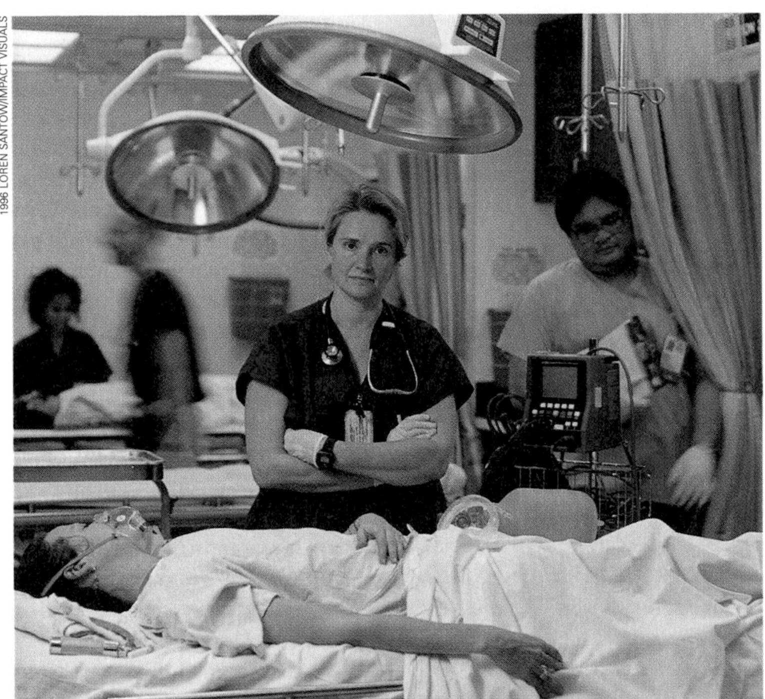

Under the Emergency Medical Treatment and Active Labor Act (1986), hospitals are required to provide emergency treatment until a patient can be discharged or transferred without harm. The Act was intended to curb the practice of "patient dumping."

Under these circumstances a physician must disclose the information to another person designated by the patient.

Informed consent is rarely legally required to be in writing, but this does provide EVIDENCE that consent was in fact obtained. The more specific the consent, the less likely it will be construed against a doctor or a hospital in court. Conversely, blanket consent forms cover almost everything a doctor or hospital might do to a patient without mentioning anything specific and are easily construed against a doctor or hospital. However, blanket forms are frequently used upon admission to a hospital to provide proof of consent to noninvasive routine hospital procedures such as taking blood pressure. A consent form may not contain a clause waiving a patient's right to sue, unless state law provides for binding ARBITRATION upon mutual agreement. Moreover, consent can be predicated upon a certain surgeon doing a surgery. It can also be withdrawn at any time, subject to practical limitations.

Right to Treatment In an emergency situation, a patient has a right to treatment, regardless of ability to pay. If a situation is likely to cause death, serious injury, or disability if not attended to promptly, it is an emergency. Cardiac arrest, heavy bleeding, profound shock, severe head injuries, and acute psychotic states are some examples of emergencies. Less obvious situations can also be emergencies: broken bones, fever, and cuts requiring stitches may also require immediate treatment.

Both public and private hospitals have a duty to administer medical care to a person experiencing an emergency. If a hospital has emergency facilities, it is legally required to provide appropriate treatment to a person experiencing an emergency. If the hospital is unable to provide emergency services, it must provide a referral for appropriate treatment. Hospitals cannot refuse to treat prospective patients on the basis of race, religion, or national origin, or refuse to treat someone with HIV or AIDS.

In 1986 Congress passed the Emergency Medical Treatment and Active Labor Act (EMTALA) (42 U.S.C.A. § 1395dd), which established criteria for emergency services and criteria for safe transfer of patients between hospitals. This statute was designed to prevent "patient dumping," that is, transferring undesirable patients to another facility. The law applies to all hospitals receiving federal funds, such as MEDICARE (almost all do). The law requires hospitals to provide a screening exam to determine if an emergency condition exists, provide stabilizing treatment to any emergency patient or to any woman in active labor before transfer, and continue treatment until a patient can be discharged or transferred without harm. It also delineates strict guidelines for the transfer of a patient who cannot be stabilized. A hospital that negligently or knowingly and willfully violates any of these provisions can be terminated or suspended from Medicare. The physician, the hospital, or both can also be penalized up to $50,000 for each knowing violation of the law.

One of the first cases brought under EMTALA involved a doctor who transferred a woman in active labor to a hospital 170 miles away. The woman delivered a healthy baby during the trip, but the doctor was fined $20,000 for the improper transfer of the woman. In addition to federal laws such as EMTALA, states may also impose by regulation or statute a duty on hospitals to administer emergency care.

There is no universal right to be admitted to a hospital in a nonemergency situation. In nonemergency cases admission rights depend largely on the specific hospital, but basing admission on ability to pay is severely limited by statutes, regulations, and judicial decisions. For example, most hospitals obtained financial assistance from the federal government for construction; these hospitals are required to provide a reasonable volume of services to persons unable to pay. The amount of services to be provided is set by regulation, and the obligation continues for twenty years after construction is completed. Patients must be advised of the hospital's obligation under the law, or the hospital may be foreclosed from suing to collect on the bill. In addition, many states prohibit hospitals from denying admission based solely on inability to pay; some courts have made similar rulings against public hospitals based on hospital charters and PUBLIC POLICY reasons. Hospitals are also prohibited from requiring a deposit from a Medicare or MEDICAID patient.

Once a patient has been duly admitted to a hospital, she or he has a right to leave at any time, or the hospital could be liable for FALSE IMPRISONMENT. This is so even if the patient has not paid the bill or if the patient wants to leave against all medical advice. In rare cases, such as contagious disease cases, public health authorities may have state statutory or regulatory authority to quarantine a patient. In addition, state laws governing involuntary commitment of the mentally ill may be used to prevent a person of unsound mind from leaving the hospital, if a qualified psychiatrist determines that the person is a danger to himself or herself or the lives of others.

A doctor familiar with a patient's condition determines when a patient is ready for discharge and signs a written order to that effect. If the patient disagrees with a decision to discharge, she or he has the right to demand a consultation with a different physician before the order is carried out. The decision to discharge must be based solely on the patient's medical condition and not on nonpayment of medical bills.

In the mid-1990s concern over maternity patients being discharged just a few hours after giving birth prompted legislation at both the state and federal levels. In September 1996 President BILL CLINTON signed a law ensuring a forty-eight-hour hospital stay for a woman who gives birth vaginally and a ninety-six-hour stay for a woman who has a caesarean section, unless the patient and the doctor agree to an earlier discharge. A number of state legislatures have passed similar laws as well.

This patient, suffering chest pains, is clearly not ready to be discharged. If he wished to leave the hospital against the doctor's advice, however, she would have no legal right to stop him.

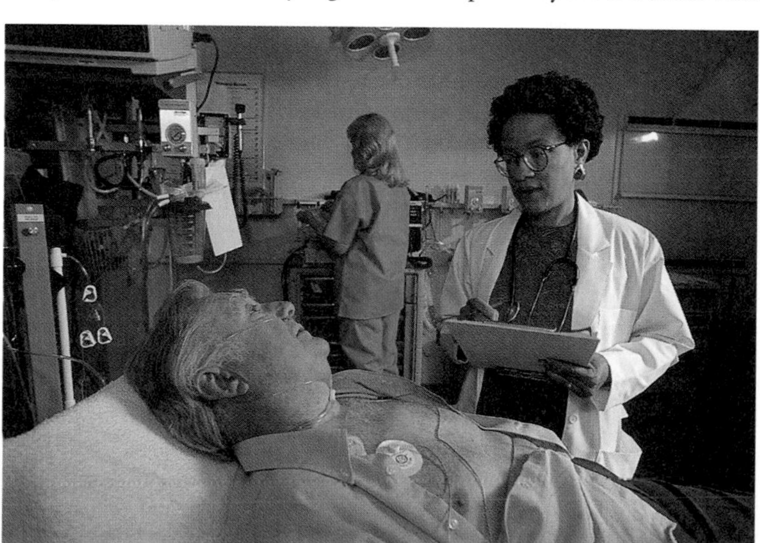
DAEMMRICH/STOCK BOSTON

Medical Experimentation Medical progress and medical experimentation have always gone hand in hand, but patients' rights have sometimes been ignored in the process. Sometimes patients are completely unaware of the experimentation. Experimentation has also taken place in settings where individuals may have extreme difficulty asserting their rights, such as in prisons, mental institutions, the military, and residences for the mentally retarded. Legitimate experimentation requires informed consent, which may be withdrawn at any time.

Some of the more notorious and shameful instances of human experimentation in the United States in the twentieth century include a 1963 study where terminally ill hospital patients were injected with live cancer cells to test their immune response; the "Tuskegee" study, begun before World War II and continuing for forty years, where effective treatment was withheld from poor black males suffering from syphilis so that medical personnel could study the natural course of the disease; and a study where developmentally disabled children were deliberately infected with hepatitis to test potential vaccines.

Failure to obtain informed consent can arise even where consent has ostensibly been obtained. The California Supreme Court ruled in 1990 that a physician must disclose preexisting research and potential economic interests that may affect the doctor's medical judgment (*Moore v. Regents of the University of California*, 51 Cal. 3d 120, 793 P. 2d 479). The case involved excision of a patient's cells pursuant to surgery and other procedures to which the patient had consented. The surgery itself was not experimental; the experimentation took place after the surgery and other procedures. The cells were used in medical research that proved lucrative to the doctor and medical center.

Patients in teaching hospitals are frequently asked to participate in research. Participants do not surrender legal rights simply by agreeing to cooperate and validly obtained consent cannot protect a researcher from NEGLIGENCE.

In hospitals human experimentation is typically monitored by an institutional review board (IRB). Federal regulation requires IRBs in all hospitals receiving federal funding. These boards review proposed research before patients are asked to participate, and approve written consent forms. IRBs are meant to ensure that risks are minimized, the risks are reasonable in relation to anticipated benefits, the selection of subjects is equitable, and informed consent is obtained and properly documented. Federal regulations denominate specific items that must be covered when obtaining informed consent in experimental cases. IRB approval never obligates a patient to participate in research.

Advance Medical Directives Every state has enacted advance medical directive legislation, but the laws vary widely. Advance medical directives are documents that are made at a time when a person has full decision-making capabilities and are used to direct medical care in the future when this capacity is lost. Many statutes are narrowly drawn and specify that they apply only to illnesses where death is imminent rather than illnesses requiring long-term life support, such as in end-stage lung, heart, or kidney failure, multiple sclerosis, paraplegia, and persistent vegetative state.

Patients sometimes use LIVING WILLS to direct future medical care. Most commonly, living wills specify steps a patient does not want taken in cases of life-threatening or debilitating illness, but they may also be used to specify that a patient wants aggressive resuscitation measures used. Studies have shown that living wills often are not honored, despite the fact that federal law requires all hospitals, nursing homes, and other Medicare and Medicaid providers to ask patients on admission whether they have executed an advance directive. Some of the reasons living wills are not honored include medical personnel's fear of liability, the patient's failure to communicate his or her wishes, or misunderstanding or mismanagement by hospital personnel.

Another way individuals attempt to direct medical care is through a durable power of attorney. A durable power of attorney, or proxy decision maker, is a written document wherein a person (the principal) designates another person to perform certain acts or make certain decisions on the principal's behalf. It is called durable because the power continues to be effective even after the principal becomes incompetent or it may only take effect after the principal becomes incompetent. As with a living will, such a document has little power to compel a doctor to follow a patient's desires, but in the very least it serves as valuable evidence of a person's wishes if the matter is brought into court. A durable power of attorney may be used by itself or in conjunction with a living will.

When advance medical directives function as intended and are honored by physicians, they free family members from making extremely difficult decisions. They may also protect physicians. Standard medical care typically requires that a doctor provide maximum care. In essence, a living will can change the standard of care upon which a physician will be judged and may protect a physician from legal or professional repercussions for withholding or withdrawing care.

Right to Die A number of cases have addressed the right to refuse life-sustaining medical treatment. Broadly speaking, under certain circumstances a person may have a right to refuse life-sustaining medical treatment or to have life-sustaining treatment withdrawn. On the one side in these cases is the patient's interest in autonomy, privacy, and bodily integrity. This must be balanced against the state's traditional interests in the preservation of life, prevention of SUICIDE, protection of dependents, and the protection of the integrity of the medical profession.

In *In re Quinlan*, 355 A.2d 647 (1976), the New Jersey Supreme Court permitted withdrawal of life-support measures for a woman in a persistent vegetative state, although her condition was stable and her life expectancy stretched years into the future. Many of the emotional issues the country struggles with today were either a direct result of or were influenced by this case, including living wills and other advance medical directives, the right to refuse unwanted treatment, and physician-assisted suicide.

The first U.S. Supreme Court decision addressing the difficult question regarding the removal of life support was *Cruzan v. Director, Missouri Department of Health*, 497 U.S. 261, 110 S. Ct. 2841, 111 L. Ed. 2d 224 (1990). *Cruzan* involved a young woman rendered permanently comatose after a car accident. Her parents petitioned to have her feeding tube removed. The Supreme Court ruled that the evidence needed to be clear and convincing that the young woman had explicitly authorized the termination of treatment prior to becoming incompetent. The Court ruled that the evidence had not been clear and convincing, but upon remand to the state court the family presented new testimony that was deemed clear and convincing. The young woman died twelve days after her feeding tube was removed.

In June 1997, the Supreme Court decided two right-to-die cases, *Quill v. Vacco*, 80 F.3d 716 (2d Cir. 1996), and *Compassion in Dying v. Washington*, 49 F.3d 586 (9th Cir. 1995). The appellate courts, in New York and Washington, had struck down laws banning physician-assisted suicide as violations of equal protection and due process, respectively. The Supreme Court reversed both decisions, finding no constitutional right to assisted suicide, and upholding states' power to ban the practice.

Privacy and Confidentiality Confidentiality between a doctor and patient means that a doctor has the express or implied duty not to disclose information received from the patient to anyone not directly involved with the patient's care. Confidentiality is important so that health care providers have knowledge of all facts, regardless of how personal or embarrassing, that might have a bearing on a patient's health. Patients must feel that it is safe to communicate such information freely. Although this theory drives doctor-patient confidentiality, the reality is that many people have routine and legitimate access to a patient's records. A hospital patient might have several doctors, nurses and support personnel on every shift, and a patient might also see a therapist, nutritionist, or pharmacologist, to name a few.

The law requires some confidential information to be reported to authorities. For example, birth and death certificates must be filed, CHILD ABUSE cases must be reported, and infectious, contagious, or communicable diseases must be reported. In addition, confidential information may also be disclosed pursuant to a judicial proceeding or to notify a person to whom a patient may pose a danger.

In spite of the numerous exceptions to the contrary, patients legitimately demand and expect confidentiality in many areas of their treatment. Generally speaking, patients must be asked to consent before being photographed or having others unrelated to the case (including medical students) observe a medical procedure; they have the right to refuse to see anyone not connected to a hospital; they have the right to have a person of the patient's own sex present during a physical examination conducted by a member of the opposite sex; they have the right to refuse to see persons connected with the hospital who are not directly involved in the patient's care and treatment (including social workers and chaplains); and they have the right to be protected from having details of their condition made public.

A patient owns the information contained in medical records, but the owner of the paper on which they are written is usually considered the actual owner of the records. The patient's legal interest in the records generally means that the patient has a right to see the records and is entitled to a complete copy of them. The patient's rights are subject to reasonable limitations such as requiring inspection and copying to be done on the doctor's premises during working hours.

CROSS-REFERENCES

Acquired Immune Deficiency Syndrome; Death and Dying; Fetal Rights; Genetic Screening; Health Care Law; Health Insurance; Organ Transplantation; Physicians and Surgeons; Privacy; Privileged Communications; *In re Quinlan.*

PAT. PEND. An abbreviation displayed prominently on an invention for which an application for a patent has been made but has not yet been issued.

The term *Pat. Pend.* provides notice to all that the inventor has applied to the U.S. Patent and Trademark Office for the exclusive right to make, sell, and use his or her invention.

See also PATENTS.

PATRONAGE The practice or custom observed by a political official of filling government positions with qualified employees of his or her own choosing.

When the candidate of a political party wins an ELECTION, the newly elected official has the right to appoint a certain numbers of persons to jobs in the government. This is the essence of the patronage system, also known as the spoils system ("To the victor go the spoils"): appointing persons to government positions on the basis of political support and work rather than on merit, as measured by objective criteria. Though the patronage system exists at all levels of U.S. government, the number of positions that are available through patronage has decreased dramatically since the 1880s.

The patronage system thrived in the U.S. federal government until 1883. In 1820 Congress limited federal administrators to four-year terms, leading to constant turnover. By the 1860s and the Civil War, patronage had led to widespread inefficiency and political corruption. Where patronage had once been confined to the CABINET, department heads, and foreign ambassadorships, by the 1860s low-level government positions were subject to patronage. The loss of a presidential election by a political party signaled wholesale turnover in the federal government. When President BENJAMIN HARRISON took office in 1889, 31,000 federal postmaster positions changed hands.

The ASSASSINATION of President JAMES GARFIELD in 1881 by a disgruntled office seeker who did not receive a political appointment spurred Congress to pass the Civil Service Act, or Pendleton Act of 1883 (5 U.S.C.A. § 1101 et seq.). The act, which at the time only applied to 10 percent of the federal workforce, created a Civil Service Commission and advocated a

MERIT SYSTEM for the selection of government employees. By 1980, 90 percent of federal positions had become part of the civil service system. In addition, the passage in 1939 of the HATCH ACT (53 Stat. 1147) curtailed or restricted most partisan political activities of federal employees.

State and local governments have employed large patronage systems. Big-city political machines in places such as New York, Boston, and Chicago thrived in the late nineteenth century. A patronage system not only rewards political supporters for past support, it also encourages future support, because persons who have a patronage job try to retain it by campaigning for the party at the next election.

Large-scale patronage systems declined steadily during the twentieth century. During the Progressive Era (1900–1920), "good government" reformers overthrew political machines and installed civil service systems. Chicago, under Mayor Richard J. Daley, remained the last bastion of patronage, existing in its purest form until the late 1970s.

Patronage has its defenders. It is a way to maintain a strong political organization by offering campaign workers rewards. More importantly, patronage puts people into government who agree with the political agenda of the victor. Cooperation, loyalty, and trust flow from this arrangement. Finally, patronage guarantees some turnover, bringing new people and new ideas into the system.

Opponents have long agreed that patronage is acceptable at the highest levels of government. Presidents, governors, and mayors are entitled to select their cabinet and department heads. However, history indicates that patronage systems extending far down the organizational chain are susceptible to inefficiency and corruption.

Congress took another look at patronage issues in the Civil Service Reform Act of 1978 (92 Stat. 1121–1131, 5 U.S.C.A. 1201–1209). Concerned that federal bureaucrats were too independent and unresponsive to elected officials, the act replaced the Civil Service Commission with the Office of Personnel Management, under closer control of the president. The act also created the Senior Executive Service, which gives the PRESIDENT greater discretion in reassigning top officials to departments and agencies.

CROSS-REFERENCES

Bureaucracy; Civil Service; Tammany Hall.

BIOGRAPHY

PAUL, ALICE STOKES Alice Stokes Paul was a militant U.S. suffrage leader who is best remembered as the author in 1923 of the EQUAL RIGHTS AMENDMENT. Paul, who for decades played a major role in the National Woman's Party, also successfully lobbied for the inclusion of a ban against SEX DISCRIMINATION in title VII of the CIVIL RIGHTS ACT of 1964 (42 U.S.C.A. § 2000e et seq.).

Paul was born on January 11, 1885, in Moorestown, New Jersey. She graduated from Swarthmore College in 1905 and then went to England to do graduate work. While in England, Paul became involved with the British suffragettes and received three jail sentences for participating in militant actions. She returned to the United States in 1910 and continued her graduate work at the University of Pennsylvania. She earned a Ph.D. degree in social work in 1912.

"IF THE WOMEN OF THE WORLD HAD NOT BEEN EXCLUDED FROM WORLD AFFAIRS, THINGS TODAY MIGHT HAVE BEEN DIFFERENT."

In 1913 Paul formed the Congressional Union for Woman Suffrage, which later became the National Woman's Party (NWP). She advocated a more militant position to publicize the need for an amendment to the U.S. Constitution. Paul organized marches, rallies, and protests outside the White House. As in England, she was jailed three times for organizing and participating in suffrage protests. While in jail she waged hunger strikes, resulting in her hospitalization where she was force-fed.

With the ratification of the NINETEENTH AMENDMENT to the Constitution in 1920, which gave women the vote, Paul shifted her focus to the legal inequality of women. In 1923 she wrote the equal rights amendment, which she called the Lucretia Mott amendment, in honor of the nineteenth-century feminist leader. The

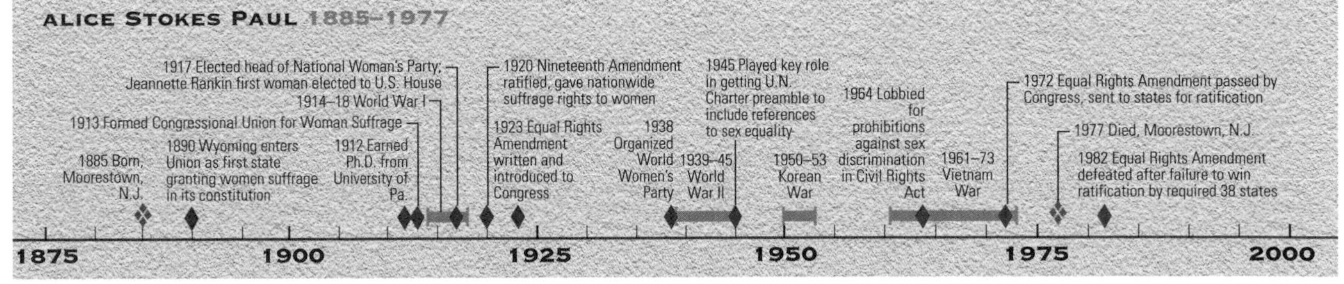

proposed amendment stated that "[e]quality of rights under the law shall not be denied or abridged by the United States or by any State on account of sex" and that "the Congress shall have the power to enforce, by appropriate legislation, the provisions of this article." Paul's proposed amendment was introduced to Congress in 1923, but it would not be approved until March 1972. However, the amendment failed to be ratified by the thirty-eight states required under the Constitution.

Paul continued to lead the NWP, and in 1938 she organized the World Party for Equal Rights for Women, known as the World Woman's Party. She played a key role in seeing that the preamble to the United Nations Charter included references to sex equality. During the debates over the 1964 Civil Rights Act, Paul and the NWP helped lobby for the inclusion of sex discrimination as illegal conduct.

Paul died on July 9, 1977, in Moorestown, New Jersey.

PAUPER An impoverished person who is supported at public expense; an indigent litigant who is permitted to sue or defend without paying costs; an impoverished criminal defendant who has a right to receive legal services without charge.

PAWN To deliver PERSONAL PROPERTY to another as a PLEDGE or as security for a DEBT. A deposit of GOODS with a CREDITOR as security for a sum of money borrowed.

In common USAGE, pawn signifies a pledge of goods, as distinguished from a pledge of intangible personal property, such as a contract right. In a more limited sense, it denotes a deposit of personal property with a PAWNBROKER as security for a loan. A pawned article is retained until the loan is repaid within a certain time. If it is not repaid on time, the pawnbroker may sell the item.

PAWNBROKER A person who engages in the business of lending money, usually in small sums, in exchange for PERSONAL PROPERTY deposited with him or her that can be kept or sold if the borrower fails or refuses to repay the loan.

PAYABLE Justly due; legally enforceable.

A sum of money is said to be payable when a person is under an OBLIGATION to pay it. The term may therefore signify an obligation to pay at a future time, but when used without qualification, it ordinarily means that the debt is due to be paid immediately.

PAYEE The person who is to receive the stated amount of money on a CHECK, BILL, or NOTE.

PAY EQUITY See COMPARABLE WORTH.

PAYMENT The fulfillment of a promise; the performance of an agreement. A delivery of money, or its equivalent in either specific property or services, by a DEBTOR to a CREDITOR.

P.C. An abbreviation for professional corporation, which is a special CORPORATION established by professionals, such as physicians, accountants, or, in some states, attorneys, who practice together.

In most JURISDICTIONS, a professional corporation may be organized by professionals who render a personal service to the public that requires a LICENSE and that, before proper statutory organization, could not be performed by a corporation.

One of the main reasons professionals incorporate is to gain certain tax benefits. Incorporation neither changes professional responsibility nor protects those incorporating from LIABILITY for MALPRACTICE.

PEACE BOND The posting of money in court, as required by a judge or MAGISTRATE, by a person who has threatened to commit a BREACH OF THE PEACE.

PEACE OFFICERS SHERIFFS, CONSTABLES, MARSHALS, city police officers, and other public officials whose duty it is to enforce and preserve the public order.

BIOGRAPHY

ARTIST C. GREGORY STAPKO. COLLECTION OF THE SUPREME COURT OF THE UNITED STATES

Rufus Wheeler Peckham

PECKHAM, RUFUS WHEELER Rufus Wheeler Peckham served as an associate justice of the U.S. Supreme Court from 1895 to 1909. A prominent New York attorney and judge, Peckham was a conservative judge who believed that state and federal government had limited authority to regulate business activity. He expressed this belief most clearly in *Lochner v. New York*, 198 U.S. 45, 25 S. Ct. 539, 49 L. Ed. 937 (1905), a case that is best remembered for the dissent of Justice OLIVER WENDELL HOLMES, JR.

Peckham was born in Albany, New York, on November 8, 1838, into a family of prominent lawyers and judges. He attended private schools and studied abroad as a young man. He read the law in his father's Albany law office and was admitted to the New York bar in 1859, following the lead of his older brother, Wheeler Hazard Peckham. After almost ten years in private practice, he began his career in New York government in 1868 when he became district attorney of Albany County. He served until 1872.

An active participant in New York State Democratic party politics, Peckham and his brother Wheeler were aligned with the upstate wing of the party, which was often in conflict with the New York City faction that was domi-

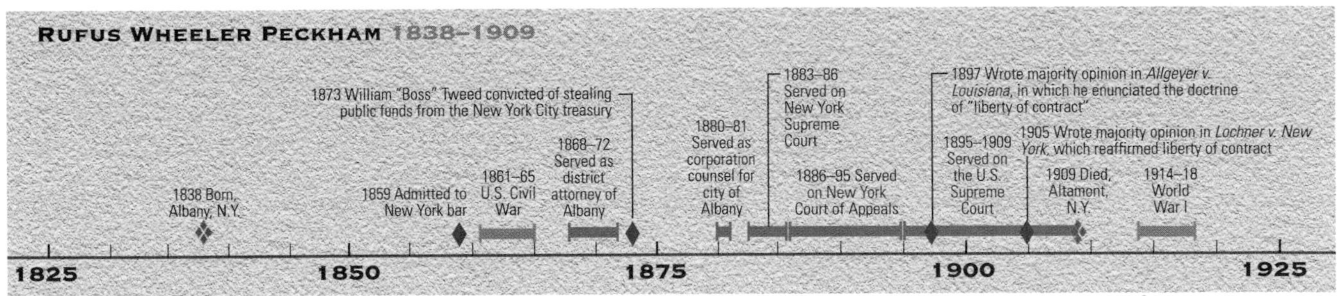

nated by the corrupt TAMMANY HALL regime. Wheeler Peckham was instrumental in the 1873 prosecution of the Tweed Ring, the Tammany machine run by William M. ("Boss") Tweed. His efforts would later hurt his legal career.

From 1880 to 1881, Rufus Peckham served as corporation counsel for the city of Albany. In 1883 he was elected to the New York Supreme Court (the state's trial court), and in 1886 he was appointed to the New York Court of Appeals (the state's highest court). In 1895 President GROVER CLEVELAND nominated Peckham to the U.S. Supreme Court. This followed Cleveland's unsuccessful attempt to appoint Wheeler Peckham to the High Court in 1894. The appointment of Wheeler Peckham failed when New York Senators Edward Murphy, Jr., and David Bennett Hill, both aligned with the New York City Democratic machine, blocked the nomination.

"THE GENERAL RIGHT TO MAKE A CONTRACT IN RELATION TO HIS BUSINESS IS PART OF THE LIBERTY OF THE INDIVIDUAL PROTECTED BY THE FOURTEENTH AMENDMENT . . . THE RIGHT TO PURCHASE OR TO SELL LABOR IS PART OF THE LIBERTY PROTECTED BY THIS AMENDMENT."

Rufus Peckham had little trouble winning confirmation. He joined a Supreme Court that was generally hostile to attempts by state and federal government to regulate business and the economy. Peckham fit right in. In *Allgeyer v. Louisiana*, 165 U.S. 578, 17 S. Ct. 427, 41 L. Ed. 832 (1897), he wrote the majority opinion that struck down a Louisiana insurance law as being a violation of the federal Due Process Clause. He enunciated the doctrine of "liberty of contract" as a limit on state regulation of business. Government could not limit a person from entering "into all contracts which may be proper, necessary, and essential" to the conduct of a person's life.

Peckham reaffirmed liberty of contract in *Lochner*. In his majority opinion, Peckham held that a New York State law that limited bakers to no more than ten hours of work a day violated the "liberty of contract" guaranteed by the FOURTEENTH AMENDMENT, which provided that no state was to "deprive any person of life, liberty or property without DUE PROCESS OF LAW." The state's power to regulate was restricted to matters of health, safety, and welfare. In Peckham's view the restriction of hours did not fit into any of these three areas and therefore the law unconstitutionally interfered with the right of bakers and bakery companies to negotiate work hours and work conditions. Justice Holmes, in his dissent, castigated Peckham and the majority for reading into the Constitution their particular economic theory and for not practicing judicial restraint.

Despite Peckham's opposition to government regulation, he did support ANTITRUST LAWS. This was consistent, in his view, with maintaining individual economic liberty. He articulated his support and helped restore some of the authority of federal antitrust efforts in *United States v. Trans-Missouri Freight Association*, 166 U.S. 290, 17 S. Ct. 540, 41 L. Ed. 1007 (1897), *United States v. Joint-Traffic Association*, 171 U.S. 505, 19 S. Ct. 25, 43 L. Ed. 259 (1898), and *Addyston Pipe & Steel Company v. United States*, 175 U.S. 211, 20 S. Ct. 96, 44 L. Ed. 136 (1899).

Peckham died on October 24, 1909, in Altamont, New York.

See also LABOR LAW; LOCHNER V. NEW YORK.

PECULATION 📖 The unlawful appropriation, by a depositary of public funds, of the government property entrusted to the care of the depository; the FRAUDULENT diversion to an individual's personal use of money or goods entrusted to that person's care. 📖

PECUNIARY 📖 Monetary; relating to money; financial; consisting of money or that which can be valued in money. 📖

PEDERASTY 📖 The criminal offense of unnatural copulation between men. 📖

The term *pederasty* is usually defined as anal intercourse of a man with a boy. Pederasty is a form of SODOMY.

PEERS 📖 Equals; those who are an individual's equals in rank and station. 📖

The traditional phrase *trial by a jury of his peers* means trial by a JURY of citizens.

PENAL 📖 Punishable; inflicting a punishment. 📖

PENALTY 📖 A punitive measure that the law imposes for the performance of an act that is proscribed, or for the failure to perform a required act.

Penalty is a comprehensive term with many different meanings. It entails the concept of punishment—either corporal or pecuniary, civil or criminal—although its meaning is usually confined to pecuniary punishment. The law can impose a penalty, and a private contract can provide for its assessment. Pecuniary penalties are frequently negotiated in construction contracts, in the event that the project is not completed by the specified date.

PENDENTE LITE [*Latin, Pending the litigation.*] During the actual progress of a lawsuit.

PENDENT JURISDICTION The discretionary power of a federal court to permit the assertion of a related state law claim, along with a federal claim between the same parties, properly before the court, provided that the federal claim and the state law claim derive from the same set of facts.

Generally, in the civil law, claims based on federal law are heard in federal court, and claims based on state law are heard in state court. The principle of pendent jurisdiction creates an exception to this general rule by allowing a plaintiff who has filed a claim based on federal law in federal court to add a state law claim to the case. This may be done only if the state law claim arose out of the same transaction or occurrence, or nucleus of facts, that gave rise to the federal claim.

For example, assume that a plaintiff has filed suit in federal court alleging that the respondent has violated her civil rights under the Civil Rights Act of 1964 (42 U.S.C.A. § 2000a et seq.). Assume further that the claim arises from an incident in which the plaintiff was denied service at a public restaurant based on her perceived national origin. If the plaintiff was also physically harmed by the respondent in the incident, she may want to file claims for assault and battery. Assault and battery of a private party are state law claims; no federal laws exist under which the plaintiff could bring such claims. Pendent jurisdiction would give the federal court the authority to hear the assault and battery claims because they arose out of the same incident that gave rise to the federal civil rights claims.

Pendent jurisdiction is a rule of judicial convenience and efficiency. If federal courts could not hear state law claims, many plaintiffs would be forced to present two cases in two courts involving essentially the same matter. Such a rule would be unduly expensive for plaintiffs, would increase the number of cases in the court system, and could lead to seemingly inconsistent results from different courts concerning related matters.

See also jurisdiction.

PENDING Begun, but not yet completed; during; before the conclusion of; prior to the completion of; unsettled; in the process of adjustment.

A lawsuit is said to be pending from its inception until the issuance of a final judgment by a court. The phrase *pending appeal* refers to the time before an appeal is taken, as well as to the period during which an appeal is in progress.

BIOGRAPHY

LIBRARY OF CONGRESS

George Hunt Pendleton

PENDLETON, GEORGE HUNT George Hunt Pendleton was a prominent nineteenth-century lawyer, congressman, senator, and ambassador who played the central role in passing the Civil Service Act, also known as the Pendleton Act of 1883 (5 U.S.C.A. § 1101 et seq.). The Pendleton Act established a federal civil service system that was based on merit rather than on political patronage.

Pendleton was born on July 29, 1825, in Cincinnati, Ohio. After his admission to the Ohio bar in 1847, he established a law practice in Cincinnati. He soon turned his attention toward politics. A lifelong member of the Democratic party, Pendleton was elected to the Ohio Senate in 1853, where he served for two years. In 1857 he was elected to the U.S. House of Representatives, where he served until 1865. During the Civil War, Pendleton gained national prominence for his opposition to President Abraham Lincoln's suspension of habeas corpus and other wartime measures that restricted civil liberties. In 1864 he was the

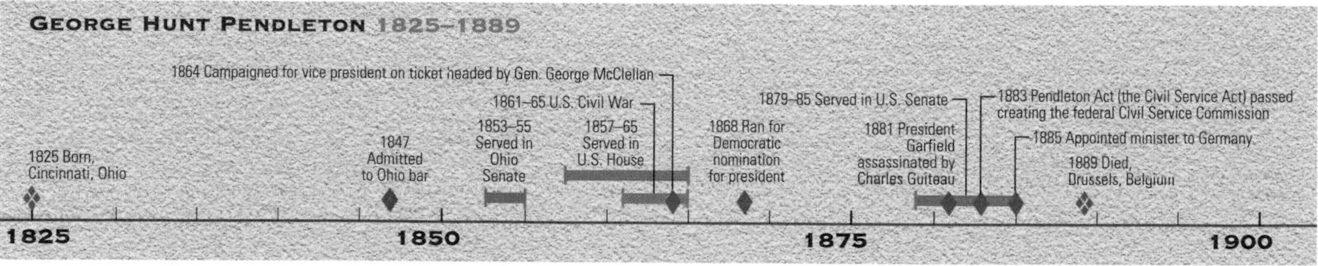

Democratic vice-presidential candidate, campaigning for peace between the North and the South on a ticket headed by Union General George B. McClellan. Lincoln and Vice President ANDREW JOHNSON won reelection.

After the war Pendleton became the leader of the greenbacker movement, which sought to redeem Civil War bonds in paper currency (greenbacks) instead of gold. His advocacy of this cause cost him the 1868 Democratic presidential nomination, because East Coast Democrats disagreed with the scheme.

Pendleton did not reenter national politics until 1879, when he was elected to the U.S. Senate. By 1883 the federal government was plagued by inefficiency and corruption, most of which was attributed to the way federal employees were hired. Under the patronage system (also known as the "spoils system"), federal employees were hired and fired for political reasons. It was understood that presidents were entitled to reward political allies with cabinet posts, judgeships, and diplomatic posts, but the spoils system extended to routine and low-level government workers. This created employee turnover when a president left office and the opposition party came into power.

The 1881 ASSASSINATION of President JAMES GARFIELD by a disappointed office seeker led to the passage of the Pendleton Act in 1883. The act, which created a federal Civil Service Commission that administered a merit-based, open selection process for hiring government employees, began the process of professionalizing the federal government. Politics and factors such as religion and nationality were to have no bearing on the hiring of civil servants. Although the act initially covered only about 10 percent of the jobs, subsequent legislation increased the percentage and it grew steadily.

Pendleton's efforts at patronage reform cost him his Senate seat. Democratic leaders who preferred political patronage prevented his return to the Senate for a second term in 1885. President GROVER CLEVELAND appointed Pendleton minister to Germany in that year. He served in this position until his death on November 24, 1889, in Brussels, Belgium.

PENITENTIARY A PRISON or place of confinement where persons convicted of felonies serve their term of imprisonment.

See also JAIL.

PENNSYLVANIA CONSTITUTION OF 1776 In 1776 Pennsylvania enacted its first state constitution in direct response to the DECLARATION OF INDEPENDENCE and the instructions of the Second CONTINENTAL CONGRESS to the colonies to reject British rule. Dedicated to the idea of placing authority in the hands of the people, and specifying a broad range of rights, the constitution proved to be controversial. Over the next fourteen years, criticism of the document came both from within Pennsylvania and from across the new nation, and the state replaced the constitution in 1790.

With the signing of the Declaration of Independence, the American Revolution had begun. Congress issued two resolutions in May 1776 calling for the colonies to reject British rule and establish governments based on the authority of the people. Pennsylvania had refused to join the rebellion, and Congress hoped to win its support. Instead, revolutionaries in Pennsylvania quickly held public meetings and devoted themselves to electing representatives to a constitutional convention. The noted American statesman and philosopher BENJAMIN FRANKLIN was instrumental in organizing and leading the endeavor. The constitution was debated and revised for four months and was approved on September 28, 1776.

Although five other states also adopted constitutions during this time, the Pennsylvania document was unique. In outlook, the constitution bore the mark of the French philosopher JEAN-JACQUES ROUSSEAU, a critic of representative government who viewed it as a necessary evil. Thus, under the Pennsylvania Constitution, government would aspire to the democratic ideal of maximum participation by citizens while simultaneously ensuring fair, just, and legal representation by politicians.

The constitution pursued this goal in several ways. It created a unicameral legislature—having only one body—a feature unique among American states. Legislators were to be "persons most noted for wisdom and virtue" and were required to swear that they would do nothing "injurious to the people." In an effort to rotate the largest number of people in and out of office, the rules mandated annual elections and limited terms to four out of every seven years. The framers had two goals: to make representatives more responsive to the people, and to allow bad politicians to be removed from office swiftly. To ensure participation by citizens, lawmaking itself was controlled. No bill could be enacted until it had been printed for general reading and, except in rare instances, until a year after its printing.

Strikingly, no provision was made for a state governor. Instead, the executive function fell to an elected twelve-member executive council. These members served staggered three-year terms, making them ineligible for reelection until four years after their terms ended. The framers believed that this approach not only served to train more citizens for political leadership, it also helped to thwart what they most detested: "an inconvenient aristocracy" of politicians. The council and the legislature elected a president and vice president. The president could not exercise any power—whether appointing judges or commanding the state's MILITIA—without the consent of a majority of the council.

Just as the constitution placed restraints on lawmakers, so did it look skeptically at the JUDICIARY. Pennsylvania judges were not given independence. The legislature could revoke judgeships, which lasted seven years, for "misbehavior" at any time. As an additional limitation on the judiciary, the constitution created a special body called the Council of Censors, which met every seven years to review the constitutionality of laws.

The rights granted by the Pennsylvania Constitution were among the most liberal in the United States at that time. The right to vote was based on a minimal property interest; it belonged to free men above the age of twenty-one who had resided in the state for one year and had paid public taxes, as well as to the sons of freeholders. The constitution defended the free exercise of religion, stating that no "man who acknowledges the being of a God, [may] be justly deprived or abridged of any civil right as a citizen" regardless of his "religious sentiments or peculiar mode of religious worship." Other significant liberties included the right to buy one's release from military service, not to be taxed without the consent of lawmakers, and to receive liberal DUE PROCESS in court.

Despite its idealism the Pennsylvania Constitution was neither a success at home nor outside the state. Critics complained about its heavy reliance on a revolving, and extremely powerful, legislature. Influential forces in the state, particularly those in business, attacked the uncertain conditions that it created for commerce. The Federalists, who believed in a strong federal government, detested its independence. Lawyers and judges decried the weakened judiciary. By 1790 the experiment had ended: the state replaced the constitution with one modeled on the U.S. Constitution's SEPARATION OF POWERS and its adherence to the idea of a REPUBLIC.

PENNY STOCKS Inexpensive issues of STOCK, typically selling at less than $1 a share, in companies that often are newly formed or involved in highly speculative ventures.

Penny stocks are usually available for sale over-the-counter, that is, among BROKERS and customers themselves, as opposed to being listed on the American Stock Exchange or the New York Stock Exchange.

PENOLOGY The science of PRISON administration and rehabilitation of criminals.

PEN REGISTER A device that decodes or records electronic impulses, allowing outgoing numbers from a telephone to be identified.

The use of pen registers is governed by a 1986 federal statute, Pen Registers and Trap and Trace Devices (18 U.S.C.A. §§ 3121–3127). The statute also governs the use of trap devices, which are used to identify the originating number from which the wire or electronic communications were transmitted. Neither device enables the listening or recording of the actual communication.

In *Smith v. Maryland*, 442 U.S. 735, 99 S. Ct. 2577, 61 L. Ed. 2d 220 (1979), the U.S. Supreme Court upheld the constitutionality of the use of pen registers, declaring that the use of a pen register is not an invasion of PRIVACY. In the *Smith* case, Patricia McDonough, the victim of a ROBBERY, began receiving threatening and OBSCENE telephone calls from a man identifying himself as the robber. In one instance the man asked her to step out on her porch, and when she did, she identified the car that she had previously described to the police as belonging to the robber. The police traced the license plate number and learned that Smith was the registered owner. With this information the police asked the telephone company to install a pen register at its office to record the numbers dialed from Smith's telephone. The register revealed that a call was placed from Smith's residence to McDonough's telephone, and with this information, along with other evidence, the police obtained a WARRANT to search Smith's residence. During the search the police found Smith's telephone book open to the page where McDonough's name and address appeared. Smith was arrested, and McDonough identified him from a six-man LINEUP as the man who had robbed her.

Smith asserted that the installation of the pen register violated his constitutional rights and that "all fruits derived from the pen register" should be suppressed. The Court of Appeals of Maryland held that no constitutionally protected right of privacy existed in the numbers dialed into a telephone. Therefore, use of the pen register did not violate the FOURTH AMENDMENT, which guarantees the "right of the people to be secure in their persons, house, papers and effects, against unreasonable searches and seizures."

The Supreme Court held that in determining whether a government-initiated ELECTRONIC

SURVEILLANCE constitutes a "search" within the meaning of the Fourth Amendment, it must determine "whether the person invoking the protection can claim a 'justifiable', 'reasonable', or a 'legitimate expectation' of privacy" (*Smith*). The Court examined the government activity that was being challenged and stated that Smith "could not claim that his property was invaded or that the police intruded into a constitutionally protected area" because the pen register was installed on the telephone company's property. The determination as to whether a "search" took place depended on whether Smith had a "legitimate expectation of privacy" regarding the numbers dialed into his telephone.

In its analysis the Court stated that it is doubtful that people expect privacy in the telephone numbers they dial. Not only do people realize that the numbers go through the telephone company once they are dialed but they also realize that the telephone company keeps records for billing purposes of long-distance numbers dialed. Furthermore, most telephone books inform subscribers that the company has the capacity to "identify to the authorities the origin of unwelcome and troublesome calls." The Court held that Smith probably did not have an expectation of privacy in the telephone numbers he dialed but that even if he did, the expectation was not "legitimate." Therefore, the use of the pen register was not a "search" within the Fourth Amendment, and thus a SEARCH WARRANT was not required for its installation.

The dissent in *Smith*, as well as legal commentators, have expressed concern regarding the holding that there is no legitimate right of privacy in the numbers dialed into the telephone. They assert that there is a REASONABLE and legitimate expectation of privacy when the numbers are dialed from a person's residence. Justice POTTER STEWART, in his dissent, stated that using a telephone within a person's home is private conduct and that, without question, this conduct is entitled to Fourth and FOURTEENTH AMENDMENT protection.

Although *Smith* upheld the constitutionality of the installation of a pen register without a warrant, 18 U.S.C.A. § 3123 now requires a court order, based on a law enforcement officer's declaration that the information is relevant to an ongoing investigation, before a pen register may be installed.

Many states have enacted legislation similar to the federal statutes regulating the use of pen registers and trap and trace devices. At the state level, Caller ID and its use of Calling Party Identification has been challenged on several different theories with varying outcomes. Caller ID is a service provided by telephone companies that records each calling party's telephone number, enabling the receiving party to view the number before answering the telephone.

Proponents of Caller ID, primarily telephone companies, believe that it provides additional security to customers because it can detect and prevent obscene and harassing calls and may facilitate emergency response services. The telephone companies also state that customers are able to screen their calls with the service, thus enhancing their privacy.

Opponents of Caller ID argue that the service is an invasion of privacy because some callers may wish to remain anonymous, especially callers with unlisted telephone numbers or users of a confidential crisis hot line. Furthermore, opponents argue that Caller ID is a violation of state and federal trap or trace device statutes.

In determining the legality of Caller ID, states tend to follow either *Barasch v. Pennsylvania Public Utility Commission*, 133 Pa. Cmwlth. 285, 576 A.2d 79 (1990), affirmed 529 Pa. 523, 605 A.2d 1198 (1992), or *Southern Bell Telephone & Telegraph Co. v. Hamm*, 306 S.C. 70, 409 S.E.2d 775 (1991). In *Barasch* the court held that the use of Caller ID was a violation of Pennsylvania's constitutional right of privacy. The court reasoned that people do have a reasonable expectation that the numbers dialed into the telephone are as private as the content of the conversation. In addition, the court held that the Caller ID service violated the state's Wiretapping and Electronic Surveillance Control Act (18 Pa. Cons. Stat. Ann. §§ 5701–5781) (1978) governing the use of trap and trace devices. The statute provides that pen registers and trap and trace devices may not be installed without a court order unless one of the statutory exceptions exists. One of the exceptions provided in section 5771(b)(2) of the act is that if the user of the service consents to the installation of the pen register or trap and trace device, then a court order is not necessary. The Commonwealth Court's decision in *Barasch* held that because both the calling party and the recipient are users of the service, both must give their consent. The Pennsylvania Supreme Court upheld this part of the Commonwealth Court's holding.

Conversely, in *Hamm* the court held that Caller ID was not an invasion of privacy because an individual does not have a legitimate expectation of privacy in the numbers dialed into the telephone. Furthermore, although

South Carolina has a similar exception to the general prohibition of trap and trace devices, the court held that "user of the service" meant only the subscriber and that therefore consent by the calling party is not necessary. The courts that follow the rationale of *Hamm* agree that unless indicated otherwise in the statutes, the purpose of trap or trace device statutes is to protect telephone users from unauthorized third-party or government intrusions and not merely to protect users from one another.

Many states have proposed or have already passed legislation authorizing the use of Caller ID. In addition, telephone companies offering Caller ID also offer per-call and per-line blocking to those individuals who wish to remain anonymous. In per-call blocking, a caller may block the transmission of his or her telephone number by dialing a specified code number before dialing. In per-line blocking, the number is blocked on every call unless the caller dials a specified code number to disable the block for a particular call.

See also SEARCH AND SEIZURE; WIRETAPPING.

PENSION A benefit, usually money, paid regularly to retired employees or their survivors by private businesses and federal, state, and local governments. Employers are not required to establish pension benefits but do so to attract qualified employees.

The first pension plan in the United States was created by the American Express Company in 1875. A few LABOR UNIONS and state and local governments began to offer pension plans shortly thereafter, and by 1935 governments in half the states and many businesses were offering pension plans. In 1997 about half of all U.S. workers had pension plans.

Employers establish pension plans by paying a certain amount of money into a pension fund. The money paid into this fund is not taxed to the employer, and it is not taxed to the employee until the employee retires and begins to collect pension benefits. The employer gives control of the pension fund to a TRUSTEE, who may invest the money in stocks and BONDS and other financial endeavors to increase the fund. Some pension plans require the employee to make a small, periodic contribution to the fund.

The amount of pension that a pensioner receives depends on the type of pension plan. Pension plans generally can be divided into two categories: defined benefit plans and defined contribution plans. A defined benefit plan provides a set amount of benefits to a pensioner. Under a defined contribution plan, the employer places a certain amount of money in the employee's name into the pension fund and makes no promises concerning the level of pension benefits that the employee will receive upon retirement. Employers using defined contribution plans contribute an amount into the pension fund based on the employee's salary. As a result, higher-paid employees receive larger pensions than do lower-paid employees.

The same is true for defined benefit plans: employers tend to offer larger pensions to higher-paid employees. The difference between the two types of plans is that in a defined contribution plan, the employee assumes the risk of investment failure because the funds are not insured by the federal government. Under most defined benefit plans, the employer assumes the risk that pension funds will not be available. Employees assume little risk because most funds are insured by the federal government to a certain limit.

The most important issue to pensioners is the potential loss of their pension benefits. This issue is of less concern when the government is the employer because governments have access to additional funds. Such is not the case with private businesses. Before the 1970s employees did not always receive their promised pension benefits. An employee could lose his or her pension if the employer went out of business and employers could fire long-time employees just before their pensions vested to avoid paying pensions. Citing the profound effect that pension plans have on interstate commerce and the economic security of the country, Congress enacted the EMPLOYEE RETIREMENT INCOME SECURITY ACT of 1974 (ERISA) (29 U.S.C.A. § 1001 et seq.) to regulate pension plans created by private businesses other than religious organizations.

ERISA is a complex collection of federal statutes that take precedence over most state pension laws. The act encourages the creation of pension funds by making employer contributions to pension funds tax free. ERISA also is designed to ensure that pension funds promised to an employee will be available. It establishes rules for the vesting of pensions based on the employee's age and length of employment. Under the law an employer using a pension plan that is not funded by the employees may choose one of several methods for vesting of pensions. An employer may allow all pension benefits to become nonforfeitable once the employee has completed five years of employment. In the alternative, an employee may be guaranteed a percentage of pension funds according to length of service, with the percentage increasing as the length of service increases. An employee with three years of service is guaranteed

20 percent of the derived benefit from the employer contributions to the pension plan. After four years the employee has a right to 40 percent of the benefits; after five years the percentage is 60; after six years the percentage is 80; and an employee who completes seven years of service becomes fully vested. An employee is always entitled to the amount of money she or he has contributed to a pension fund.

Under ERISA, the fiduciaries who control the pension funds must meet certain reporting requirements. The act restricts the kinds of investments that trustees can make using pension funds. It mandates that employers make annual contributions to pension funds, and it devises formulas for setting minimum contribution levels. These formulas are created in actuarial tables based on such factors as the turnover of the participants in the plan, the life expectancy of the participants, the amount of money in pensions promised to employees, and the success of the pension fund's investments. The act authorizes criminal penalties for violators of pension laws and provides CIVIL LAW remedies to victims of pension misuse or abuse.

An employer who is delinquent in making contributions to the pension fund may have to pay penalties. ERISA requires employers to report to pension holders significant facts regarding the pension fund, such as a summary describing in clear language how the plan works, what benefits it provides, and how such benefits can be received. The employer also must report annually to each employee the amount of benefits that have accrued and have vested, and the earliest date on which the employee's pension will VEST as of the date of the report.

ERISA created the Pension Benefit Guaranty Corporation (PBGC) to ensure the payment of certain benefits of pension plans. PBGC is a government corporation within the U.S. Department of Labor that is governed by the secretaries of labor, commerce, and treasury, and funded by PREMIUMS collected from pension plans. If an employer is unable to meet pension obligations, the PBGC may make the payments for the employer. PBGC covers only defined benefit pension plans, with the exception of church-based pension plans. Religious organizations are excepted because courts and legislatures consider church-based pensions to be an ecclesiastical matter beyond the authority of the law.

An employee cannot lose pension benefits by retiring early. Under defined benefit plans, the employee may begin to receive pension benefits upon reaching the normal retirement age of sixty-five years. If an employee retires before reaching age fifty-nine and a half and begins drawing from his pension, his pension payments are taxed at a 10 percent annual rate in addition to any regular income taxes. This excise tax is levied because pension funds are designed to promote security after retirement.

The excise tax does not apply to a pension given to a surviving spouse when the employee dies before the pension is fully paid, even if the employee dies before reaching age fifty-nine and a half. Employees who become disabled before age fifty-nine and a half do not have to pay the excise tax, nor do persons who specifically choose to receive the pension payments as an ANNUITY, or periodically. In addition, the excise tax does not apply to pensions of employees over the age of fifty-five years who have separated from their employer, certain pensions paid for medical expenses, and pension payments made pursuant to certain divorce-related court orders.

ERISA does not regulate pension plans with twenty-five or fewer participants or plans that are solely for business partners or a sole proprietor. Employees of businesses not covered by ERISA may look to state statutes governing pensions that contain regulations and requirements similar to those in ERISA.

Congress refined the tax consequences of pensions in January 1996. Under the Pension Source Act (Pub. L. No. 104-95, amending title 4 of U.S.C.A. § 114), a state that imposes income taxes may not tax pension benefits earned in the state if the pensioner is living in a state that does not impose personal INCOME TAX.

Pensions are an attractive component of employee compensation packages. The money that the employer withholds during the working life of the employee is not taxed, and the money in a pension fund can be increased through investments. When the pensioned employee retires, she or he can ask for the entire pension in one lump sum or can take the pension as an annuity, which is a series of payments that lasts for a specified period of time. If the retiree lives long enough, she or he will receive more money than the employer originally withheld. If the pensioner dies before the pension is fully paid, her or his surviving spouse or another designated survivor may receive the remainder of the pension. A retiree who has worked at several companies may receive several pensions.

Individuals who are self-employed have their own pension options. A self-employed worker may establish a KEOGH PLAN, which is a type of retirement plan for self-employed workers that is comparable to a pension plan. Under a Keogh plan, the worker makes tax-free payments into a fund and receives larger payments upon retirement.

An INDIVIDUAL RETIREMENT ACCOUNT (IRA) is another way to provide for security in retirement. An IRA is a personal retirement account that workers may establish in addition to, or instead of, a pension. Employers may establish similar personal retirement accounts for their employees. These accounts are called 401K plans, after the section of the INTERNAL REVENUE CODE that authorizes them. Under a 401K plan, a worker deposits a portion of his or her gross earnings into the account to avoid income tax on that portion of the earnings. The earnings are subject to TAXATION when the retiring worker receives them. If the worker is in a lower tax bracket by retirement, he or she will end up paying less tax on the portion of the earnings in the IRA.

Pension benefits are distinct from other retirement benefits such as SOCIAL SECURITY and medical assistance. A pension may reduce slightly the amount of Social Security benefits that a government employee receives.

PENTAGON PAPERS See NEW YORK TIMES V. UNITED STATES.

PENT ROAD A street that is closed at its terminal points.

The term *pent*, which means penned or confined, is used to distinguish this type of road from an open HIGHWAY that leads to other thoroughfares. Pent roads are frequently adjacent to the lands of persons who are constructing connecting arteries across their own property to secure needed outlets.

PENUMBRA The rights guaranteed by implication in a constitution or the implied powers of a rule.

The original and literal meaning of *penumbra* is "a space of partial illumination between the perfect shadow . . . on all sides and the full light" (*Merriam Webster's Collegiate Dictionary*, 10th ed., 1996). The term was created and introduced by astronomer Johannes Kepler in 1604 to describe the shadows that occur during eclipses. However, in legal terms penumbra is most often used as a metaphor describing a doctrine that refers to implied powers of the federal government. The doctrine is best known from the Supreme Court decision of *Griswold v. Connecticut*, 381 U.S. 479, 85 S. Ct. 1678, 14 L. Ed. 2d 510 (1965), where Justice WILLIAM O. DOUGLAS used it to describe the concept of an individual's constitutional right of PRIVACY.

The history of the legal use of the penumbra metaphor can be traced to a federal decision written by Justice STEPHEN J. FIELD in the 1871 decision of *Montgomery v. Bevans*, 17 F.Cas. 628 (9th C.C.D. Cal.). (At the time, Field was performing circuit duty while a member of the Supreme Court.) Since the *Montgomery* decision, the penumbra metaphor has not been used often. In fact, more than half of its original uses can be attributed to just four judges: OLIVER

UPI/CORBIS-BETTMANN

The concept of penumbra *involves trying to divine the spirit of a law from its letter. In 1965, Estelle Griswold (left) of Planned Parenthood argued that a Connecticut statute forbidding the distribution of contraceptives to married couples violated a constitutional right to privacy; the U.S. Supreme Court agreed.*

Wendell Holmes, Jr., Learned Hand, Benjamin N. Cardozo, and William O. Douglas.

In an 1873 article on the theory of torts, Justice Holmes used the term penumbra to describe the "gray area where logic and principle falter." In later decisions, Justice Holmes developed the penumbra doctrine as representing the "outer bounds of authority emanating from a law." Justice Holmes usually used the word in an attempt to describe the need to draw arbitrary lines when forming legislation. For instance, in the decision of *Danforth v. Groton Water Co.*, Holmes referred to constitutional rules as lacking mathematical exactness, stating that they, "[l]ike those of the common law, end in a penumbra where the Legislature has a certain freedom in fixing the line, as has been recognized with regard to the police power" (178 Mass. 472, 476–77, 59 N.E. 1033, 1034 [1901]).

Judge Hand expanded the meaning of the word in opinions written between 1915 and 1950 by using it to indicate the vague borders of words or concepts. He used it to emphasize the difficulty in defining and interpreting statutes, contracts, trademarks, or ideas.

Justice Cardozo's use of the penumbra metaphor in opinions written between 1934 and 1941 was similar to Holmes's application, but Justice Douglas took a different approach. Rather than using it to highlight the difficulty of drawing lines or determining the meaning of words or concepts, he used the term when he wanted to refer to a peripheral area or an indistinct boundary of something specific.

Douglas's most famous use of penumbra is in the *Griswold* decision. In the *Griswold* case, appellants Estelle Griswold, executive director of the Planned Parenthood League of Connecticut, and Dr. C. Lee Buxton, a medical professor at Yale Medical School and director of the league's office in New Haven, were convicted for prescribing contraceptive devices and giving contraceptive advice to married persons in violation of a Connecticut statute. They challenged the constitutionality of the statute, which made it unlawful to use any drug or medicinal article for the purpose of preventing conception, on behalf of the married persons with whom they had a professional relationship. The Supreme Court held that the statute was unconstitutional because it was a violation of a person's right to privacy. In his opinion, Douglas stated that the specific guarantees of the Bill of Rights have penumbras "formed by emanations from those guarantees that help give them life and substance," and that the right to privacy exists within this area.

Since *Griswold*, the penumbra doctrine has primarily been used to represent implied powers that emanate from a specific rule, thus extending the meaning of the rule into its periphery or penumbra.

CROSS-REFERENCES

Griswold v. Connecticut; Judicial Review; Jurisprudence.

PEONAGE A condition of enforced servitude by which a person is restrained of his or her liberty and compelled to labor in payment of some debt or obligation.

See also involuntary servitude.

PEOPLE The aggregate of the individuals who comprise a state or a nation.

In a more restricted sense, as generally used in constitutional law, the entire body of those citizens of a state or a nation who are invested with political power for political purposes (the qualified voters).

PER [*Latin, By, through, or by means of.*]

PER CAPITA [*Latin, By the heads or polls.*] A term used in the descent and distribution of the estate of one who dies without a will. It means to share and share alike according to the number of individuals.

In a per capita distribution, an equal share of an estate is given to each heir, all of whom stand in equal degree of relationship from a decedent. For example, a woman died intestate, that is, without a will. Her husband and three children predeceased her, and her only living heirs are her ten grandchildren. These grandchildren will take per capita. In other words, each grandchild will receive one-tenth of the estate.

Per capita differs from per stirpes, where persons do not inherit in their individual capacity but take as part of a group represented by a deceased ancestor closer in line to the decedent.

PERCENTAGE LEASE A rental agreement, usually with respect to a retail business property, whereby a portion of the gross sales or net sales of the tenant is used to determine the rent.

There is generally a provision in a percentage lease that calls for a minimum or base rental. It protects the lessor in the event of poor sales.

PER CURIAM [*Latin, By the court.*] A phrase used to distinguish an opinion of the whole court from an opinion written by any one judge.

Sometimes *per curiam* signifies an opinion written by the chief justice or presiding judge; it can also refer to a brief oral announcement of the disposition of a case by the court that is unaccompanied by a written opinion.

The Constitution is silent on the right of parties to exercise peremptory challenges. In recent years the Supreme Court has forbidden challenges made on the basis of race and gender.

PEREMPTORY CHALLENGE The right to challenge a juror without assigning, or being required to assign, a reason for the challenge.

During the selection of a JURY, both parties to the proceeding may challenge prospective jurors for a lack of impartiality, known as a challenge for cause. A party may challenge an unlimited number of prospective jurors for cause. Parties also may exercise a limited number of peremptory challenges. These challenges permit a party to remove a prospective juror without giving a reason for the removal.

Peremptory challenges provide a more impartial and better qualified jury. Peremptory challenges allow an attorney to reject a potential juror for real or imagined partiality that would be difficult to demonstrate under the challenge for cause category. These challenges, however, have become more difficult to exercise because the U.S. Supreme Court has forbidden peremptory strikes based on race or gender.

Parties do not have a federal constitutional right to exercise peremptory challenges. Peremptory challenges are granted by statute or by CASE LAW. The number of challenges is usually determined by statute, but some JURISDICTIONS allow the TRIAL court to grant additional peremptory challenges. In FEDERAL COURT each side is entitled to three peremptory challenges. If more than two parties are involved in the proceeding, the court may either grant additional challenges or restrict the parties to the minimum number of challenges.

Peremptory challenges came under legal attack in the 1980s. Critics claimed that white prosecutors used their peremptory challenges to remove African Americans from the jury when the criminal defendant was also African American because the prosecutors thought that the potential jurors would be sympathetic to a member of their own race. This constituted racial DISCRIMINATION and a violation of the Fourteenth Amendment's EQUAL PROTECTION Clause.

The U.S. Supreme Court, in *Batson v. Kentucky*, 476 U.S. 79, 106 S. Ct. 1712, 90 L. Ed. 2d 69 (1986), prohibited prosecutors from excluding prospective jurors on the basis of race. Under the *Batson* test, a defendant may object to a prosecutor's preemptory challenge. The PROSECUTOR then must "come forward with a neutral explanation for challenging black jurors." If the prosecutor cannot offer a neutral explanation, the court will not excuse the juror.

The Court extended this holding in criminal proceedings in two later cases. In *Powers v. Ohio*, 499 U.S. 400, 111 S. Ct. 1364, 113 L. Ed. 2d 411 (1991), the Court broadened the *Batson* rule by stating that a defendant need not be of the same race as the excluded juror to successfully challenge the juror's exclusion. In *Georgia v. McCollum*, 505 U.S. 42, 112 S. Ct. 2348, 120 L. Ed. 2d 33 (1992), the Court held that the defense's exercise of peremptory challenges to strike African American jurors on the basis of their race was equally forbidden. Previously, the court had ruled in *Edmonson v. Leesville Concrete Co.*, 500 U.S. 614, 111 S. Ct. 2077, 114 L. Ed. 2d 660 (1991), that in civil trials a private party could not exclude prospective jurors on account of their race by using peremptory challenges. This series of decisions makes any racial exclusion in jury selection constitutionally suspect.

The Supreme Court has also forbidden peremptory challenges based on gender. In *J. E. B. v. Alabama*, 511 U.S. 127, 114 S. Ct. 1419, 128 L. Ed. 2d 89 (1994), the Court ruled that striking jurors on the basis of gender serves to perpetuate stereotypes that were prejudicial and based on historical discrimination. No overriding state interest justified peremptory challenges on the basis of gender. Permitting gender-based strikes could also have undermined the *Batson* holding, because gender might be used as an excuse for racial discrimination.

PEREMPTORY RULING An immediate and absolute decision by the court on some point of law that is rendered without consideration of alternatives.

PERFECT Complete; finished; executed; enforceable; without defect; MERCHANTABLE; marketable.

To perfect a TITLE is to record or register it in the proper place so that one's ownership will be established against all others.

PERFORMANCE The fulfillment or accomplishment of a PROMISE, CONTRACT, or other obligation according to its terms.

Part performance entails the completion of some portion of what either party to a contract has agreed to do. With respect to the sale of GOODS, the payment—or receipt and acceptance of goods—makes an oral sales contract, otherwise unenforceable because of the STATUTE OF FRAUDS, enforceable in regard to goods for which payment has been made and accepted or which have been received and accepted.

SPECIFIC PERFORMANCE is an equitable doctrine that compels a party to execute the agreement according to its terms where monetary DAMAGES would be inadequate compensation for the breach of an agreement, as in the case of a sale of land. In regard to the sale of goods, a court orders specific performance only where the goods are unique or in other proper circumstances.

PERIL The designated contingency, risk, or hazard against which an insured seeks to protect himself or herself when purchasing a policy of INSURANCE.

Among the various types of perils for which insurance coverage is available are fire, theft, illness, and death.

PERJURY A crime that occurs when an individual willfully makes a false statement during a judicial proceeding, after he or she has taken an OATH to speak the truth.

The common-law crime of perjury is now governed by both state and federal laws. In addition, the Model Penal Code, which has been adopted in some form by many states and promulgated by the Commission on Uniform State Laws, also sets forth the following basic elements for the crime of perjury: (1) a false statement is made under oath or equivalent AFFIRMATION during a judicial proceeding; (2) the statement must be material or relevant to the proceeding; and (3) the WITNESS must have the specific intent to deceive.

The punishment for perjury in most states, and under federal law, is the imposition of a fine, imprisonment, or both. Federal law also imposes sentencing enhancements when the court determines that a defendant has falsely testified on her own behalf and is convicted. Under the Federal Sentencing Guidelines, the court is required to automatically increase the defendant's sentence.

Two federal statutes govern the crime of perjury in federal proceedings. Title 18 U.S.C.A. § 1621 codifies the COMMON LAW of perjury and consists of the elements listed above. In 1970, the scope of section 1621 was expanded by the enactment of 18 U.S.C.A. § 1623. Section 1623 changes the definition of intent from willfully offering false TESTIMONY to merely having knowledge that the testimony is false. In addition it adds to the definition of perjury to include the witness's use of information, including any book, paper, document, record, recording, or other material she knows contains a false material declaration, and includes proceedings that are ancillary to any court, such as AFFIDAVITS and DEPOSITIONS, and GRAND JURY proceedings. Section 1623 also contains a RETRACTION defense. If, during the proceeding in which the false statement was made, the person admits to the falsity of the statement before it is evident that the falsity has been or will be exposed, and as long as the falsity does not affect the proceeding substantially, prosecution will be barred under section 1623.

Commentators believe that the existence of these two federal statutes actually frustrates the goals of Congress to encourage truthful statements. The reasoning behind this concern is that when a retraction exists, prosecutors may charge a witness with perjury under section 1621 and when a retraction does not exist, the witness may be charged under section 1623.

Two variations of perjury are SUBORNATION OF PERJURY and false swearing; in many states these two variations are separate offenses. Subornation of perjury is a crime in which the defendant does not actually testify falsely but instead induces, persuades, instigates, or in some way procures another witness to commit perjury. False swearing is a false statement made under oath but not made during an official proceeding. Some states have created a separate offense for false swearing, while others have enacted perjury statutes to include this type of false statement. These crimes also may be punished by the imposition of a fine, imprisonment, or both.

PERKINS, FRANCES At a time when few women achieved prominence in national politics, Frances Perkins distinguished herself as a public official, a respected labor and industry expert, and an adviser to the president of the United States. When Perkins was named secretary of labor by President FRANKLIN D. ROOSEVELT in 1933, she became the first woman in U.S. history to hold a CABINET post. Perkins used her position to help launch the sweeping social and economic reforms of the New Deal.

BIOGRAPHY

Frances Perkins

Perkins was born April 10, 1880, in Boston, and raised in Worcester, Massachusetts. After graduating from Worcester Classical High School, Perkins attended Mount Holyoke College, where she studied physics and chemistry and was class president. As a senior at Mount Holyoke, Perkins was influenced by Jacob A. Riis's 1890 book *How the Other Half Lives* and by a speech given by Florence Kelley, the general secretary of the National Consumers League. Perkins's growing awareness of the plight of underprivileged U.S. citizens would lead to her life's work as a labor activist. After graduating from Mount Holyoke in 1902, Perkins pursued further studies in economics and sociology at the University of Pennsylvania and Columbia University. She earned a master's degree from Columbia in 1910.

After graduate school, Perkins briefly taught biology and physics in a school in Lake Forest, Illinois. In her off-hours, she volunteered at JANE ADDAMS's Hull House, in nearby Chicago, and at other settlement houses. There, Perkins witnessed the poverty and wretched working conditions endured by thousands of U.S. citizens. Determined to help improve the plight of workers, she returned to New York City to work as a lobbyist with her mentor, Kelley, at the New York Consumers League.

Perkins's task was formidable. Throughout the early twentieth century, U.S. businesses were unregulated: workers in sweatshops worked long hours for low pay in unsafe working conditions. There were no building codes to ensure the employees' safety, no regular inspections of equipment and machinery, and no limit to the number of hours employees could work. Children routinely were employed in factories, mills, and mines under the most miserable conditions. Some women worked nineteen hours a day with their children by their side.

An industrial tragedy heightened Perkins's resolve to force changes in the workplace. On March 25, 1911, a fire broke out at the Triangle Shirtwaist Company, in New York City. Perkins happened to be in the neighborhood and watched as employees trapped on the top three floors of the burning ten-story building jumped from windows to their death. The door to the only stairway in the building had been locked by employers, to halt break-ins. One hundred workers perished inside the building, and forty-seven jumped or fell to their death. The owners of the company were later absolved of CRIMINAL NEGLIGENCE for the disaster and collected $64,925 in property damage insurance.

In the fire's aftermath, the New York State Factory Commission was created, with Perkins named as chief investigator. She also became a member of the Committee on Safety of the City of New York and lobbied hard for legislation to make the workplace safer. She toured the state with Alfred E. Smith and ROBERT F. WAGNER and documented the deplorable conditions faced by workers. An exhaustive investigation led to new laws to protect the labor force.

A major success for Perkins was the passage of a bill by the New York Legislature to limit

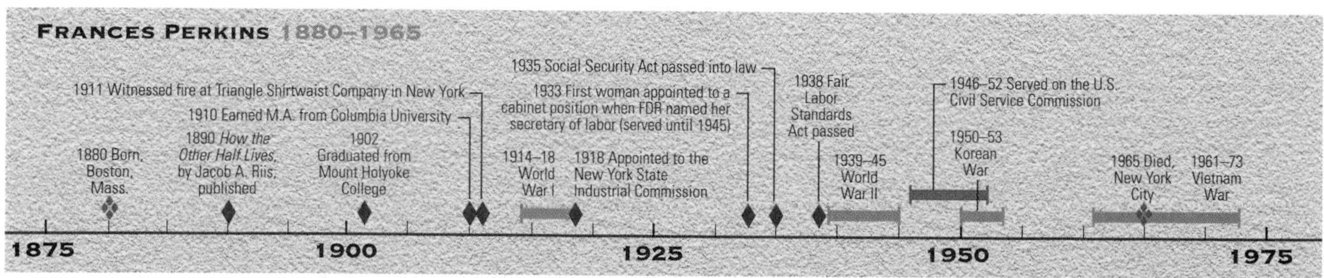

the workweek to fifty-four hours for women and children. The bill was vigorously opposed by the employers of the four hundred thousand female factory workers throughout the state. While lobbying for the bill, Perkins became acquainted with Roosevelt, who was a New York state senator. Although Roosevelt's support of the fifty-four-hour bill was lukewarm, Perkins developed a professional relationship with him that grew stronger as Roosevelt's views on labor and government began to mirror her own.

In 1913 Perkins married Paul Caldwell Wilson and rejected prevailing social convention by retaining her maiden name for professional purposes. In 1918 she was appointed to the New York State Industrial Commission.

Perkins's work with Roosevelt in New York led to a position in the federal government. When Roosevelt was elected president in 1932, he asked Perkins to become secretary of labor. Although she argued that a female trade unionist should be nominated for the post, she eventually accepted the position. Perkins became the only cabinet member to serve during all four of Roosevelt's terms of office.

When Roosevelt took office, the country was in the midst of the Great Depression. About a third of the nation's workforce was unemployed. As labor secretary, Perkins helped shape the Social Security Act (42 U.S.C.A. § 301 et seq.), a key component of Roosevelt's New Deal. Passed by the U.S. Congress in 1935, the act allowed qualified workers in commerce and industry to collect old-age, survivors, and disability insurance benefits. The new program required employers and employees to make contributions to a federal pension fund for aged and disabled persons. In this way, workers and their families were financially protected in the event of unemployment, old age, or the death of a wage earner. Although critics likened the plan to SOCIALISM, SOCIAL SECURITY became a successful federal entitlement program.

Perkins also helped develop the FAIR LABOR STANDARDS ACT of 1938 (29 U.S.C.A. § 201 et seq.), which limited the number of hours employees could work for MINIMUM WAGE. The law also placed restrictions on child labor. It prohibited children under sixteen years of age from working in most jobs, and made hazardous occupations unavailable to workers under eighteen years of age. The Wage and Hour Division of the Department of Labor was also established by the act.

After Roosevelt's death in 1945, Perkins served briefly in the administration of President HARRY S. TRUMAN. She left Truman's cabinet to serve on the U.S. Civil Service Commission from 1946 to 1952. Perkins then taught courses at Cornell University's School of Industrial and Labor Relations. She died in New York City on May 14, 1965, at the age of eighty-five.

"WE ALL TAKE REFUGE IN THE OPTIMISM WHICH IS TYPICAL OF THIS GREAT CREATIVE NATION. EVERY SITUATION HAS FOUND US UNPREPARED."

See also CHILD LABOR LAWS; LABOR LAW.

PERMISSIVE COUNTERCLAIM A CLAIM by a DEFENDANT opposing the claim of the PLAINTIFF and seeking some RELIEF from the plaintiff for the defendant.

Once a plaintiff sues a defendant in a CIVIL ACTION, the defendant has the right to assert a legal claim of her own against the plaintiff. This is known as a COUNTERCLAIM. A counterclaim makes assertions that the defendant *could have made* in a lawsuit if the plaintiff had not already begun an ACTION. A counterclaim is distinct from a mere DEFENSE, which seeks only to defeat the plaintiff's lawsuit, in that it seeks a form of relief. There are two types of counterclaims: compulsory counterclaims and permissive counterclaims. Both are governed in FEDERAL COURT by rule 13 of the Federal Rules of Civil Procedure. The rules in state courts are similar.

The compulsory counterclaim arises from the same transaction or occurrence that forms the basis of the plaintiff's suit. For example, a car accident between two drivers leads to a PERSONAL INJURY lawsuit, but the defendant asserts in a compulsory counterclaim that the plaintiff actually owes him DAMAGES for injuries. A compulsory counterclaim generally must be part of the initial ANSWER to the plaintiff's action and cannot be made later in the suit or in a separate lawsuit.

By contrast, the permissive counterclaim arises from an event unrelated to the matter on which the plaintiff's suit is based. For example, John Smith breaks his leg while visiting the home of Jane Doe. Smith sues Doe, alleging that she negligently left her child's roller skate on her front porch. In a permissive counterclaim, Doe asserts that Smith owes her money. The court will rule separately on plaintiff Smith's and defendant Doe's respective claims; if both claims are permitted to proceed, *Smith v. Doe* will involve the two parties' respective ALLEGATIONS of NEGLIGENCE and a bad DEBT.

Counterclaims are usually valid only if it is possible to make the same claim by starting a lawsuit. Thus, in the example of Smith and Doe, Doe can only make her permissive counterclaim if the STATUTE OF LIMITATIONS on collection of the debt has not expired. Permissive counterclaims need not be made in the initial PLEADING; they can be made at a later time or even in another lawsuit. This flexibility may help the defendant's legal strategy: she can wait and sue in a different court, in order to have another judge hear the case or to avoid arguing the MERITS of separate claims before the same jury.

PERPETRATOR A term commonly used by law enforcement officers to designate a person who actually commits a CRIME.

PERPETUATING TESTIMONY The procedure permitted by federal and state DISCOVERY rules for preserving the ATTESTATION of a WITNESS that might otherwise be lost prior to the trial in which it is intended to be used.

The usual method of perpetuating testimony is by taking a DEPOSITION. It is usually allowed when a witness is aged and infirm or is about to leave the state.

PERPETUATION OF EVIDENCE The procedure employed to assure that proof will be available for possible use at a later trial.

The police, for example, can deposit a murder weapon with the court, prior to the day set for trial of the accused, for purposes of perpetuation of EVIDENCE.

PERPETUITIES See RULE AGAINST PERPETUITIES.

PERQUISITES Fringe benefits or other incidental profits or benefits accompanying an office or position.

The abbreviation *perks* is used in reference to extraordinary benefits afforded to business executives, such as country club memberships or the free use of automobiles.

PER QUOD [*Latin, Whereby.*] With respect to a COMPLAINT in a CIVIL ACTION, a phrase that prefaces the recital of the consequences of certain acts as a ground of special harm to the plaintiff.

At COMMON LAW, this term acquired two meanings in the law of DEFAMATION: with respect to slander, it signified that proof of special DAMAGES was required; in regard to libel, it meant that proof of extrinsic circumstances was required.

Words that are actionable *per quod* do not furnish a basis for a lawsuit upon their face but are only litigable because of extrinsic facts showing the circumstances under which they were uttered or the damages ensuing to the defamed party therefrom.

See also EXTRINSIC EVIDENCE; LIBEL AND SLANDER.

PER SE [*Latin, In itself.*] Simply as such; in its own nature without reference to its relation.

In the law of DEFAMATION, slander *per se* refers to certain language that is actionable as slander in and of itself without proof of special DAMAGES, such as the situation in which a person is falsely accused of having committed a crime. Defamation per se is in contradistinction to defamation PER QUOD, which requires proof of special damages. See also LIBEL AND SLANDER.

PERSON In general usage, a human being; by statute, however, the term can include firms, labor organizations, PARTNERSHIPS, associations, corporations, LEGAL REPRESENTATIVES, TRUSTEES, trustees in BANKRUPTCY, or RECEIVERS.

A corporation is a "person" for purposes of the constitutional guarantees of EQUAL PROTECTION of laws and DUE PROCESS OF LAW.

Foreign governments otherwise eligible to sue in United States courts are "persons" entitled to institute a suit for TREBLE DAMAGES for alleged antitrust violations under the CLAYTON ACT (15 U.S.C.A. § 12 et seq.).

Illegitimate children are "persons" within the meaning of the Equal Protection Clause of the FOURTEENTH AMENDMENT to the U.S. Constitution.

The phrase *interested person* refers to HEIRS, devisees, children, spouses, CREDITORS, beneficiaries, and any others having a PROPERTY RIGHT in, or a claim against, a trust estate or the ESTATE of a DECEDENT, WARD, or protected person. It also refers to PERSONAL REPRESENTATIVES and to FIDUCIARIES.

PERSONAL ACTIONS Lawsuits initiated in order, among other things, to recover DAMAGES for some injury to a plaintiff's personal right or property, for breach of contract, for money owed on a DEBT, or for the recovery of a specific item of PERSONAL PROPERTY.

Under the old COMMON LAW, personal actions were one of the three categories of FORMS OF ACTION, the other two being REAL ACTIONS and MIXED ACTIONS. The right to bring personal actions was an innovation in a day when the only useful property was land. There were few consumer goods and little money in ancient England. From the accession of the Norman kings in 1066, the royal right to supervise ownership and possession of land was seldom questioned. Only when the security of land ownership was seen to depend on the peace of individual persons were personal actions like DEBT, DETINUE, and TRESPASS permitted.

PERSONAL INJURY Any violation of an individual's right, other than his or her rights in property.

The term *personal injury* is not confined to physical injuries, although NEGLIGENCE cases usually do involve bodily injuries.

See also TORTS.

PERSONAL JURISDICTION The power of a court to hear and determine a lawsuit involving a defendant by virtue of the defendant's having some contact with the place where the court is located.

Personal jurisdiction, also known as IN PERSONAM (against the person) jurisdiction, gives a court the authority to make decisions binding on the persons involved in a civil case. Every state has personal jurisdiction over persons within its territory. Conversely, no state can exercise personal jurisdiction and authority over persons outside its territory unless the persons have manifested some contact with the state.

The authority of the court to issue orders to persons present within the territory comes from the sovereign power of the government. The court's authority allows it to reach all residents of a state, including those who are outside the state for a short period and out-of-state residents who enter the state even briefly.

Deciding whether an individual is within the personal jurisdiction of a court has not been difficult to determine. Difficulty has arisen when courts have had to decide whether CORPORATIONS were subject to personal jurisdiction. Corporations have a legal existence and a legal identity but not a TANGIBLE existence. They are subject to lawsuits involving TORT and CONTRACT. As corporations became national economic entities, the courts of a state had difficulty finding personal jurisdiction if the corporation was not located within that state.

Courts established that a corporation is always subject to the JURISDICTION of the courts in the state where it was incorporated. States also require corporations to file written consents to personal jurisdiction before they can conduct business within the state. Other states require that either the corporation designate an AGENT to accept legal process (the legal documents initiating a lawsuit) in the state or that the state attorney general be authorized to accept process for all out-of-state corporations DOING BUSINESS within the state.

In 1945 the U.S. Supreme Court modernized personal jurisdiction requirements when it announced the "MINIMUM CONTACTS" test in *International Shoe Co. v. Washington*, 326 U.S. 310, 66 S. Ct. 154, 90 L. Ed. 95. The Court held that courts could constitutionally exercise jurisdiction over a nonresident defendant if the defendant had sufficient contacts with the state such that forcing the person to litigate in that FORUM did not offend "traditional notions of fair play and substantial justice." Because of the ease of modern communication and transportation, it is usually not unfair to require a party to defend itself in a state in which it conducts business activity.

The threshold of minimum contacts varies. Where the ACTION arises out of or is related to the defendant's contacts with the state, the quantity of contacts necessary to establish personal jurisdiction may be truly minimal. In such cases the nature and quality of the contact are the determining factors. In the case of a nonresident motorist who causes an injury in the forum state (the state of the court asserting jurisdiction), the interest of the state in providing a forum for its residents and regulating its HIGHWAYS, coupled with the defendant's having purposefully entered the state, permits the state to fairly assert personal jurisdiction.

A corporation or individual not physically present in a state may invoke personal jurisdiction by making a single contact with the state by telephone, mail, or facsimile transmission. In *Hanson v. Denckla*, 357 U.S. 235, 78 S. Ct. 1228, 2 L. Ed. 2d 1283 (1958), the Court ruled that even a single transaction can trigger personal jurisdiction when the defendant purposely avails itself of the privilege of conducting activities with the forum state and invokes the benefits and protection of state law.

States quickly took advantage of *International Shoe* by enacting "LONG-ARM STATUTES." These statutes allow the state to reach out and obtain jurisdiction over anyone who is not present in the state but who transacts business within the state, commits a tort within the state, commits a tort outside the state that causes injury within the state, or owns, uses, or possesses REAL PROPERTY within the state.

Personal jurisdiction in the FEDERAL COURTS is governed by rule 4 of the Federal Rules of Civil Procedure. Rule 4 directs each federal district court to follow the law on personal jurisdiction that is in force in the state courts where the federal court is located. Federal courts may use state long-arm statutes to reach defendants beyond the territory of their normal authority. With cases that can only be brought in federal court, such as lawsuits involving federal securities and ANTITRUST LAWS, federal courts may exercise personal jurisdiction over a defendant no matter where the defendant is found.

When a person wishes to challenge personal jurisdiction, he or she must take care in appearing before the court in the forum state. If the defendant makes a GENERAL APPEARANCE, the court will take this to be an unqualified submission to the personal jurisdiction of the court. The defendant waives the right to raise any jurisdictional defects.

To prevent this from happening, a defendant must request a SPECIAL APPEARANCE before the court. A special appearance is made for the limited purpose of challenging the sufficiency of the SERVICE OF PROCESS or the personal jurisdiction of the court. If any other issues are raised, the proceeding becomes a general appearance. The court must then determine whether it has jurisdiction over the defendant. If the defendant is found to be within the personal jurisdiction of the court, the issue may be appealed. Some states permit an immediate APPEAL, whereas others make the defendant raise the issue after the case has been heard on its MERITS in the trial court.

PERSONAL PROPERTY Everything that is the subject of ownership that does not come under the denomination of REAL PROPERTY; any right or interest that an individual has in movable things.

Personal property can be divided into two major categories: (1) CORPOREAL personal property, including such items as animals, merchandise, and jewelry; and (2) INCORPOREAL personal property, comprised of such rights as STOCKS, BONDS, PATENTS, and COPYRIGHTS.

Possession POSSESSION is a PROPERTY interest under which an individual is able to exercise power over something to the exclusion of all others. It is a basic property right that entitles the possessor to (1) the right to continue peaceful possession against everyone except someone having a superior right; (2) the right to recover a CHATTEL that has been wrongfully taken; and (3) the right to recover DAMAGES against wrongdoers.

In order to constitute possession, there must be a degree of actual control over the object, coupled with the intent to possess and exclude others.

The law recognizes two basic types of possession: actual and constructive.

Actual possession exists when an individual knowingly has direct physical control over an object at a given time. For example, an individual wearing a particular piece of valuable jewelry has actual possession of it. *Constructive possession* is the power and intent of an individual to control a particular item, even though it is not physically in that person's control. For example, an individual who has the key to a bank safe deposit box, which contains a valuable piece of jewelry that she owns, is said to be in constructive possession of the jewelry.

Possession of Animals Animals FERAE NATURAE, or wild animals, are those that cannot be completely domesticated. A degree of force or skill is necessary to maintain control over them. Gaining possession is a means of obtaining TITLE to, or ownership of, wild animals.

Generally an owner of land has the right to capture or kill a wild animal on her property and upon doing so, the animal is regarded as belonging to that individual because she owns the soil. The traditional legal principle has been that one who tames a wild animal is regarded as its owner provided it appears to exhibit animus revertendi, or the intent to return to the owner's domicile. Conversely when a captured wild animal escapes and returns to its natural habitat without any apparent intent to return to the captor's domicile, the captor forfeits all personal property right and the animal may be captured by anyone.

Lost, Mislaid, and Abandoned Property Personal property is considered to be *lost* if the owner has involuntarily parted with it and is ignorant of its location. *Mislaid property* is that which an owner intentionally places somewhere with the idea that he will eventually be able to find it again but subsequently forgets where it has been placed. *Abandoned property* is that to which the owner has intentionally relinquished all rights.

Lost or mislaid property continues to be owned by the person who lost or mislaid it. When FINDING LOST GOODS, the finder is entitled to possession against everyone with the exception of the true owner.

The finder of lost articles on land belonging to someone else is entitled to possession against everyone but the true owner, unless the finder is guilty of TRESPASS. The finder of misplaced goods has no right to their possession. The owner of the place where an article is mislaid has a right to the article against everyone but the true owner. Abandoned property can be possessed and owned by the first person who exercises dominion over it with an intent to claim it as his or her own. In any event, between the finder of a lost, mislaid, or abandoned article and the owner of the place where it is found, the law applies to whatever rule will most likely result in the return of the article to its rightful owner.

However tame this lion appears, as a wild animal its status as personal property of the owner depends on its willingness to remain at its owner's domicile.

SANDER/GAMMA LIAISON

Ordinarily when articles are found by an employee during and within the scope of his employment, they are awarded to the employer rather than to the employee-finder.

Treasure trove is any gold or silver in coin, plate, or bullion that is hidden by an unknown owner in the earth or other private place for an extended period. The property is not considered treasure trove unless the identity of the owner cannot be ascertained. Under early COMMON LAW, the finder of a treasure trove took title to it against everyone but the true owner. This doctrine was altered in England by a statute granting title to the crown subject to the claims of the true owner. The U.S. law governing treasure trove has, for the most part, been merged into the law governing lost property. However, certain cases have held that the old treasure trove law has not been combined into the lost property statutes. In some instances, the early common law of England has been held to apply in the absence of a statute governing treasure trove. Regardless of which principles are applied, however, in the absence of contrary statutory provision, the title to treasure trove belongs to the finder against all others with the exception of the true owner. If there is a controversy as to ownership between the true owner and the state, the owner is entitled to treasure trove.

Confusion and Accession CONFUSION and ACCESSION govern the acquisition of, or loss of title to, personal property by virtue of its being blended with, altered by, improved by, or commingled with the property of others. In confusion, the personal property of several different owners is commingled so that it cannot be separated and returned to its rightful owners, but the property retains its original characteristics. Any FUNGIBLE (interchangeable) goods can be the subject of confusion.

In accession, the personal property of one owner is physically integrated with the property of another so that it becomes a constituent part of it, losing any separate identity. Accession can make the personal property of one owner become a substantially more valuable chattel as a result of the work of another person. This occurs when the personal property becomes an entirely new chattel, such as when grapes are made into wine or timber is made into furniture.

Subject to the doctrine of accession, personal property can become real property through its transformation into a FIXTURE. A fixture is a movable item that was originally personalty (personal property) but which has become attached to, and associated with, the land and is, therefore, considered a part of the real property.

Bailments A BAILMENT is the rightful, temporary possession of goods by an individual other than the true owner. The individual who entrusts his property into the hands of another is called the BAILOR; the person who holds such property is the BAILEE. Ordinarily a bailment is effected for a designated purpose upon which the parties have agreed.

The word *bailment* is derived from the French term *bailler*, "to deliver." It is ordinarily regarded as a contractual relationship since the bailor and bailee—either expressly or implicitly—bind themselves to act according to specific terms. The bailee receives only control or possession of the property, and the bailor retains the ownership interests therein. While a bailment exists, the bailee has an interest in the property that is superior to all others, including the bailor, unless she violates some term of the agreement. When the purpose for which the property has been delivered has been accomplished, the property will be returned to the bailor or otherwise disposed of, according to his instructions.

A bailment differs from a SALE, which is an intentional transfer of ownership of personal property in exchange for something of value, because a bailment involves only a transfer of possession or custody not of ownership.

Gifts A GIFT is a voluntary transfer of personalty from one individual to another without compensation or CONSIDERATION or the exchange of something of value. There are two main categories of gifts: INTER VIVOS gifts and CAUSA MORTIS gifts.

A gift *inter vivos* is a voluntary, unconditional transfer of property between two living persons without consideration.

A gift *causa mortis* is one that is made by a donor in anticipation of imminent death.

The three requirements of a valid gift are DELIVERY, DONATIVE intent, and ACCEPTANCE.

Bona Fide Purchasers A basic common-law principle is that an individual cannot pass a better title than she has, and a buyer can acquire no better title than that of the seller. A thief does not have title in stolen goods, so a person who purchases from the thief does not acquire title.

A BONA FIDE purchaser is an individual who has bought property for value with no notice of any defects in the seller's title. If a seller indicates to a buyer that she has ownership or the authority to sell a particular item, the seller is prevented (estopped) from denying such representations if the buyer resells the property to a bona fide purchaser for value without notice of the true owner's rights. At common law, such an ESTOPPEL did not apply when an owner brought an item for services or repairs to a dealer in that type of goods and the dealer wrongfully sold the chattel. The bona fide purchaser, however, is now protected under such circumstances by the UNIFORM COMMERCIAL CODE (UCC).

A buyer who induces a sale through fraudulent representations acquires a VOIDABLE title from the seller. A voidable title is that which may be vacated by the seller, upon discovery of the buyer's FRAUD, at his option. The seller has the authority to transfer a good title to a bona fide purchaser for value without notice of the outstanding equity. The voidable title rule is only applicable in situations where the owner is induced to part with title, not merely with possession, as a result of fraud or deception.

PERSONAL REPRESENTATIVE A person who manages the financial affairs of another person who is unable to do so.

A personal representative is one kind of FIDUCIARY—an individual whom another has trusted to manage her property and money. When a person dies, a personal representative generally is required to settle the decedent's financial affairs. In some instances, a living person may need a personal representative; for example, a MINOR might need a personal representative to make legal decisions for her. Personal representatives can be appointed by a court, nominated by WILL, or selected by the person involved. Their duties are performed under the supervision of PROBATE courts, which are governed by state law.

When someone dies leaving property, a personal representative is required to administer the decedent's ESTATE, which involves resolving any DEBTS and handling the distribution of property. The JURISDICTION, powers, and functions connected with administering the decedent's estate are usually entrusted to special tribunals, known as probate, surrogate, or orphans' courts. These courts supervise the actions of the personal representative.

The choice of a personal representative depends on whether the DECEDENT left a will, the legal document instructing how his estate is to be divided. If the will names a personal representative, that person is called an *executor* (male or female) or *executrix* (female). The court will accept the representative unless he does not meet statutory qualifications. These qualifications vary from state to state but largely concern such factors as age and CONFLICT OF INTEREST. If there is no legally valid will, the decedent is said to have died INTESTATE. In such cases, the court appoints a personal representative for the decedent's estate. The court-appointed representative is called an *administrator* (male or female) or *administratrix* (female).

In special instances, courts appoint one of three types of administrators. They are appointed when (1) an executor cannot or will not serve (*administrator cum testamento annexo*); (2) a prior executor or administrator has not completed the estate (*administrator de bonis non*); or (3) an interim administrator (special administrator), given restricted powers over the estate, is needed until a proper legal representative can be found.

Once approved by the court, personal representatives receive official sanction to fulfill their duties. Executors receive documents called LETTERS TESTAMENTARY—administrators receive LETTERS OF ADMINISTRATION—authorizing the representative to handle the legal affairs of a decedent. Throughout the process of administering an estate, all personal representatives serve as OFFICERS OF THE COURT. They derive their authority from the court and thus serve at the court's pleasure. Their authority can be revoked on various grounds, ranging from NEGLECT to incompetence. Primarily, they must act on behalf of all parties and all interests in the estate. They owe the BENEFICIARIES an absolute duty of loyalty, or fiduciary duty, to administer the estate in their best interest.

In general, the personal representatives' duties are to settle and distribute the estate. This complicated task may require the assistance of an ATTORNEY or a TRUST COMPANY, so-called *coexecutors*. The personal representative's first task is to collect and preserve the ASSETS of the estate. The personal representative also oversees the APPRAISAL of the estate's assets, where necessary. The personal representative must also pay the estate's CREDITORS, as well as any ESTATE AND GIFT TAXES due under federal law. Finally, the representative sees to the distribution of the remaining estate among the decedent's beneficiaries. If there are no beneficiaries, the state usually receives the property.

See also EXECUTORS AND ADMINISTRATORS.

PERSONAL SERVICE The actual delivery of PROCESS to the individual to whom it is directed or to someone authorized to receive it on his or her behalf.

SERVICE OF PROCESS is the delivery of legal NOTICE to a party in a case. Any party who is being sued is entitled to advance notice of the suit. Notice consists of a copy of the COMPLAINT and a SUMMONS to appear in court. If a party does not receive notice of a lawsuit, the court will dismiss the case.

Personal service of the complaint and summons is a form of ACTUAL NOTICE. Actual notice occurs when the summons and complaint are delivered personally to the RESPONDENT. The two other basic forms of process service are SUBSTITUTED SERVICE and CONSTRUCTIVE SERVICE. Substituted service is personal delivery to the residence of the respondent or notice given to an AGENT of the respondent. Constructive service is notice delivered through publication in a newspaper.

If a party cannot be reached in person, substituted service may be made by mailing the summons and complaint by certified or first-class mail. If a party cannot be found, notice may be served by publication in a newspaper.

The U.S. Supreme Court has ruled that service of process should be reasonably calculated to apprise interested parties of the pendency of the ACTION and afford them an opportunity to be heard. The reasonableness of the notice must be considered in light of all the circumstances. For example, if a party receiving notice lives in an apartment building with many children living in the building, one notice left on the front door of the apartment may not be sufficient because it is possible that the children may take the papers (*Greene v. Lindsey*, 456 U.S. 444, 102 S. Ct. 1874, 72 L. Ed. 2d 249 [1982]).

PERSONALTY Goods; CHATTELS; articles; movable property, whether animate or inanimate.

See also PERSONAL PROPERTY.

PER STIRPES [*Latin, By roots or stocks; by representation.*] A term used to denote a method used in dividing the ESTATE of a person. A person who takes per stirpes, sometimes called by right of representation, does not inherit in an individual capacity but as a member of a group.

In a per stirpes distribution, a group represents a deceased ancestor. The group takes the proportional share to which the deceased ancestor would have been entitled if still living.

For example, a man died intestate; his wife predeceased him. He had four children, three of whom are still living at the time of his death. The deceased child had three children, all still living. These three grandchildren will share equally in one-fourth of their grandfather's estate, the share the deceased parent would have taken if still alive. The three living children will also each receive one-fourth of the estate.

Per stirpes differs from PER CAPITA, in which an equal share is given to each of a number of persons who all stand in equal degree of relationship to the deceased.

See also DESCENT AND DISTRIBUTION.

PERSUASIVE AUTHORITY Sources of law, such as related cases or legal encyclopedias, that the court consults in deciding a case, but which, unlike BINDING AUTHORITY, the court need not apply in reaching its conclusion.

PETITION A written application from a person or persons to some governing body or public official asking that some authority be exercised to grant RELIEF, favors, or PRIVILEGES.

A formal application made to a court in writing that requests action on a certain matter.

The FIRST AMENDMENT to the U.S. Constitution guarantees to the people the right to petition the government for the REDRESS of grievances. Petitions are also used to collect signatures to enable a candidate to get on a ballot or put an issue before the electorate. Petitions can serve as a way of pressuring elected officials to adhere to the position expressed by the petitioners.

The right to petition the government for correction of public grievances derives from the English MAGNA CHARTA of 1215 and the English Bill of Rights of 1689. One of the colonists' objections to British rule before the American Revolution was the king's refusal to act on their petitions of redress. The Founders attempted to address this concern with the First Amendment, which affirms the right of the people to petition their government. Almost all states adopted similar guarantees of petition in their own constitutions.

Between 1836 and 1840, abolitionists collected the signatures of two million people on petitions against SLAVERY and sent them to the U.S. House of Representatives. In the early twentieth century, states passed laws allowing INITIATIVE (the proposing of legislation by the people) and RECALL (an election to decide whether an elected official should be removed from office). Both processes start with the collection of a minimum number of signatures on a petition. Small political parties often use petitions to collect signatures to enable their candidates to be placed on the ELECTION ballot.

Petitions are also directed to courts of law and ADMINISTRATIVE AGENCIES and boards. A petition may be made EX PARTE (without the presence of the opposing party) where there are no parties in opposition. For example, the executor of an ESTATE may file a petition with the PROBATE court requesting approval to sell property that belongs to the estate or TRUST.

In contested matters, however, the opposing party must be served with the petition and be given the opportunity to appear in court to argue the MERITS of the issues it contains. A prisoner may file a petition for a WRIT of HABEAS

CORPUS, in which the prisoner requests a HEARING to determine whether he or she is entitled to be released from CUSTODY because of unconstitutional or illegal actions by the government. The prisoner must serve the government office that prosecuted him or her with a copy of the petition. The writ of habeas corpus, like many other types of writs, is discretionary; the court is free to deny the petition.

PETITIONER One who presents a formal, written application to a court, officer, or legislative body that requests action on a certain matter.

In legal proceedings initiated by a PETITION, the RESPONDENT is the person against whom relief is sought, or who opposes the petition. One who APPEALS from a JUDGMENT is a petitioner.

PETITION IN BANKRUPTCY A document filed in a specialized FEDERAL COURT to commence a proceeding to provide a means by which a DEBTOR who is unwilling or financially unable to pay personal DEBTS will satisfy the claims of his or her CREDITORS as they come due.

There are two types of petitions in BANKRUPTCY cases. A voluntary petition is filed by a debtor who wants to make arrangements for the payment of debts and be relieved of LIABILITY for them. An involuntary petition is filed by a statutorily prescribed number of creditors whose aggregate sum of claims exceed a specific amount.

A petition in bankruptcy lists the debtor's ASSETS, liabilities, and debts so that a realistic arrangement for the payment of creditors can be devised.

PETIT JURY The ordinary panel of twelve persons called to issue a VERDICT in a CIVIL ACTION or a criminal prosecution.

Petit JURY is used interchangeably with petty jury.

PETIT LARCENY A form of LARCENY—the stealing of another's PERSONAL PROPERTY—in which the value of the property taken is generally less than $50.

At COMMON LAW, the penalty for the offense was whipping or some other CORPORAL PUNISHMENT. Under modern-day statutes, it is usually a fine, imprisonment, or both.

PETITORY ACTION A legal proceeding by which the plaintiff seeks to establish and enforce his or her TITLE to PROPERTY, as distinguished from a possessory proceeding, where the plaintiff's right to POSSESSION is the issue. Such petitory actions must be based on a claim of LEGAL TITLE to the property, as opposed to a mere equitable interest in it.

In admiralty, suits to try title to property independent of questions concerning possession. See also ADMIRALTY AND MARITIME LAW.

In the CIVIL-LAW jurisdiction of Louisiana, a proceeding instituted by an alleged owner who does not have possession to determine ownership against one in possession.

PETTY OFFENSE A minor CRIME, the maximum punishment for which is generally a fine or a short term in a prison or a house of correction.

In some states, a petty offense is a classification in addition to MISDEMEANOR and FELONY. Under federal law, a petty offense is any misdemeanor, the penalty for which does not exceed imprisonment for a period of six months, a fine of not more than $5,000, or both. Since a petty offense is one that is punishable by no more than a six-month sentence, the accused is not constitutionally entitled to a JURY trial, which would be in order if the accused were charged with a serious offense.

PHARMACIST See DRUGGIST.

PHILADELPHIA LAWYER A colloquial term that was initially a compliment to the legal expertise and competence of an ATTORNEY due to the outstanding reputation of the Philadelphia bar during colonial times. More recently the term has become a disparaging label for an attorney who is skillful in the manipulation of the technicalities and intricacies of the law to the advantage of his or her client, although the spirit of the law might be violated.

For example, an attorney who uses repeated MOTIONS for postponement of an ACTION or excessive DISCOVERY requests as DILATORY tactics primarily for the advantages that inure to his or her client, as opposed to legitimate grounds for such actions, might be regarded as a Philadelphia lawyer.

PHOTO LINEUP A presentation of photographs to a victim or WITNESS of a crime.

A photo lineup, also known as a photo array and or photo display, is a procedure used by law enforcement personnel to discover or confirm the identity of a criminal suspect. Generally a police officer shows a set of photographs to a victim or witness and asks whether he or she recognizes one of the persons in the photographs as the perpetrator. A positive identification of a suspect can be used to place the suspect under arrest, and the act of identification may be used later as EVIDENCE in the prosecution of the defendant.

The Supreme Court has ruled that photo lineups should not be unduly suggestive (*Manson v. Brathwaite*, 432 U.S. 98, 97 S. Ct. 2243, 53 L. Ed. 2d 140 [1977]). That is, a photo lineup should not be conducted in such a way as to highlight the suspect and elicit an identification of the suspect. If a photo lineup is unduly suggestive, any affirmative identification of a suspect may be excluded from her or his subsequent prosecution.

Police officers typically avoid suggestive photo lineups because they are interested in apprehending the right person. Toward this end, they may ask a witness to look at more than one photo lineup containing the suspect to see if the witness can identify the suspect more than once. Each photo lineup may contain as many as six or more photographs of different persons. Furthermore, to be effective, a photo lineup should contain pictures of persons who look similar to the suspect. For example, if police suspect a Caucasian male and a witness remembers seeing a blond, light-skinned male, the photo lineup will not consist of five pictures of dark-haired, dark-skinned males and one picture of the suspect.

For public safety reasons, police officers do not always take the time to arrange a photo lineup to show witnesses. In some cases officers may use only one picture of a suspect. In case of violent crime, for example, police may need to act swiftly and locate a particular suspect. In *Manson*, the Supreme Court ruled that using one photograph for the purpose of identifying a person as a criminal suspect is not unduly suggestive.

The use of photographs in a criminal investigation is just one identification procedure used by police. Other procedures include show-ups and in-person lineups. A show-up is the exhibition of a particular criminal suspect to a victim or witness shortly after the crime occurred. An in-person LINEUP is the live presentation of several persons, including the suspect, to the witness.

Courts examine all the circumstances surrounding an identification. To determine whether any identification is unduly suggestive and therefore inadmissible at trial, courts analyze seven factors, including the opportunity the witness had to view the suspect, the degree of attention the witness paid to the suspect, the accuracy of the witness's description before viewing the suspect or the suspect's photograph, the witness's level of certainty in identifying the suspect, and the length of time that elapsed between the crime and the witness's viewing of the suspect.

A criminal defendant does not have the right to have an attorney present at a photographic lineup until after he or she is indicted or formally charged (*United States v. Ash*, 413 U.S. 300, 93 S. Ct. 2568, 37 L. Ed. 2d 619 [1973]). Nor does a criminal defendant have the right to a hearing, outside the presence of the jury, to make an attempt to block the presentation of photographic identifications (*Watkins v. Sowders*, 449 U.S. 341, 101 S. Ct. 654, 66 L. Ed. 2d 549 [1981]). However, a defendant does have the right to show to the judge and jury any photographic evidence used in the case, to challenge the witnesses on CROSS-EXAMINATION, and to argue to the judge or jury that the photo identification procedure was unduly suggestive and that any identification from it should be disregarded (*United States v. Ash*, 413 U.S. 300, 93 S. Ct. 2568, 37 L. Ed. 2d 619 [1973]).

CROSS-REFERENCES

Criminal Law; Criminal Procedure; Due Process of Law; Right to Counsel.

PHYSICAL FACT In the law of EVIDENCE, an event having a CORPOREAL existence, as distinguished from a mere conception of the mind; one that is visible, audible, or tangible, such as the sound of footsteps or impressions made by human feet on the ground.

PHYSICIAN-PATIENT PRIVILEGE See PHYSICIANS AND SURGEONS; PRIVILEGED COMMUNICATION.

PHYSICIANS AND SURGEONS Physicians and surgeons are medical practitioners who treat illness and injury by prescribing medication, performing diagnostic tests and evaluations, performing surgery, and providing other medical services and advice. Physicians and surgeons are highly trained and duly authorized by law to practice medicine.

The education and focus of chiropractors, dentists, and optometrists differ from those of physicians and surgeons. However, the laws relating to physicians and surgeons generally apply to these medical professionals as well. In addition, these health care providers are subject to laws regulating their specific areas. They are prohibited by law from practicing medicine or surgery.

A physician or surgeon does not have an unqualified right to practice medicine. The state legislature determines who is to be allowed this privilege and exercises its police power to protect the public from deception, FRAUD, and incompetence. A legislature's authority to regulate the practice of medicine is, broadly speaking, only limited by the requirements that the rules be reasonable, bear some relation to the object to be attained, and do not violate any constitutional rights. Legislatures have the power to require a LICENSE or certificate to practice medicine within the state and to

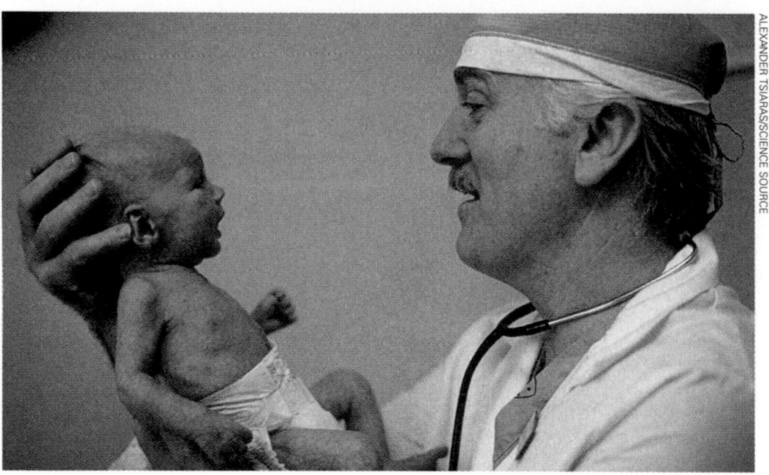

ALEXANDER TSIARAS/SCIENCE SOURCE

States carefully regulate who may use the title "doctor" or obtain a license to practice medicine. Specialists such as pediatricians must typically pass exams beyond the initial licensing exam.

make practicing medicine without a license a criminal offense.

Statutes and regulations carefully regulate who may use the title "doctor." Use of the title or its abbreviation without an indication of the type of degree—D.O., M.D., etc.—is specifically forbidden in many states unless the person holds a physician's and surgeon's certificate.

State statutes delineate requirements for a license to practice medicine. To obtain a license, an applicant must demonstrate requisite education and knowledge. A college degree and graduation from an accredited medical school typically fulfills the education requirement, and passing a state licensing exam demonstrates an applicant's skills. State law determines who may sit for an exam and typically limits the number of tries an applicant has to pass the exam. Specialists, such as cardiologists, ophthalmologists, pediatricians, and neurosurgeons, must usually pass further exams beyond the initial licensing exam.

Applicants typically must also meet certain physical health standards and establish that they are of good moral character. Generally speaking, good moral character means that a person is reliable, trustworthy, and not likely to deceive the public. An applicant who is refused a license because of a lack of good moral character is entitled to receive NOTICE of the reasons and to have a hearing on the issues. State laws typically provide for JUDICIAL REVIEW of a denial, after any administrative APPEALS have been exhausted.

Under certain circumstances physicians licensed in another state may be permitted to waive examination. Commissioned medical officers in the ARMED SERVICES are typically exempt from a state's licensing statute when performing official medical services within the state.

State legislatures have routinely delegated the authority to supervise licensing, exam, and suspension and REVOCATION procedures to a state board of medical examiners. A board's power is limited to the express powers given to it by statute and the implied powers necessary to carry out the express powers.

For action to be taken against a practitioner, a nexus must exist between the acts or omissions and the fitness or competency required to practice medicine. In other words, past isolated incidents unrelated to the profession are generally insufficient by themselves to form a basis for a disciplinary action.

Statutes commonly use words such as *unprofessional, dishonorable,* or *immoral conduct* when describing conduct warranting suspension or revocation. Other terms sometimes used are *gross immorality, willful or wanton misconduct, malpractice, gross violation of one's professional duties, gross misconduct in the practice of the profession,* or *grossly unprofessional conduct of a type likely to deceive or defraud.* These terms are not required to be defined with any particularity. Instead, every case is judged on its own particular facts. Some of the reasons that physicians or surgeons have had their licenses revoked or suspended include failure to keep complete and accurate records of controlled substances, conviction of a crime (particularly one involving MORAL TURPITUDE), drunkenness, abandonment of a patient, deliberate falsification of medical records, fraud in procuring a license, professional incompetency, assisting or aiding another in the unlicensed practice of medicine, and sexual imposition on a patient. A license revocation in one state may be the basis for revocation in another.

State boards are charged with the duty of investigating allegations of professional misconduct. Depending upon the licensing statute, a patient, the state or state licensing board, or any other person may instigate a complaint. During the investigative stage, before a determination has been made to institute formal revocation proceedings, no requirement exists that the physician be informed of the nature of the charges, know the name of the complainant, or participate in selecting any documents. However, a license to practice medicine cannot be revoked without DUE PROCESS OF LAW. Due process means that the physician must receive notice of the intended action and have an opportunity to be heard. The complainant has the burden to establish the facts to justify revocation.

Judicial review of a suspension or revocation is limited to a determination of whether the deciding board abused its discretion. A court will examine whether a sanction is so disproportionate to the offense that it is shocking to a

REASONABLE PERSON's sense of fairness in light of all the circumstances.

Generally speaking, a physician with a license to practice medicine has the unlimited authority to prescribe for and treat the ill and afflicted and may choose to employ any legitimate method of treatment. In some instances state law might permit a physician to practice optometry or dentistry, although the converse is never permitted.

A physician stands in a FIDUCIARY relationship to her patients, meaning that the physician must always exercise the utmost GOOD FAITH and trust when dealing with patients. A confidential relationship exists between the parties: because a patient must feel free to disclose any information that might pertain to treatment and diagnosis, the physician has the professional obligation to keep information confidential absent a patient's consent. But a physician cannot attempt to shield his own incompetence by refusing to disclose information. Moreover, a physician may have a statutory duty to reveal information concerning a patient. Doctors are required to provide authorities with information regarding birth and death, CHILD ABUSE, and contagious or infectious diseases. A physician may also have a duty to disclose confidential information to third parties in other circumstances.

Physicians and their patients have a contractual relationship. A request for an appointment will not suffice to form a doctor-patient relationship, but a telephone call to initiate treatment might. The relationship continues until treatment is completed or upon agreement by the parties. The physician agrees to treat the patient but rarely promises a specific outcome or cure. If a doctor promises a specific outcome but fails to deliver it, the doctor may be liable for breach of CONTRACT. One example would be a surgeon who promises that cosmetic surgery will produce certain results.

A physician's conduct must always meet the standard of care set by the profession, or he may be liable for MALPRACTICE. Physicians and surgeons must possess and exercise the same level of skill and learning ordinarily possessed and exercised by other members of their profession under similar circumstances.

Although not absolute in every instance, some of the responsibilities a physician or surgeon has toward a patient include a duty to

- Fully inform a patient of her condition;
- Notify a patient of the results of a diagnosis or test;
- Inform the patient of the need for different treatment or refer the patient to a specialist or other qualified practitioner;
- Continue medical care until proper termination of the relationship;
- Give proper notice before withdrawal from treatment;
- Not abandon a patient, including making arrangements for treatment during absences;
- Treat nonpaying patients the same as those who pay;
- Use diligence in treatment in providing all necessary care;
- Obtain a patient's INFORMED CONSENT before performing a medical procedure;
- Instruct others as to the care and treatment of a patient;
- Warn others of exposure to communicable and infectious diseases.

A patient has a duty to cooperate with a physician and participate in treatment and diagnosis. For example, a patient does not have a general duty to volunteer unsolicited information but is required to disclose a complete and accurate medical history upon questioning by a physician. A patient also must return for further treatment when required. Failure to cooperate or participate in treatment may result in a limited recovery for a physician's malpractice or completely bar recovery, depending upon the circumstances of the case.

Malpractice occurs when a patient is injured by a physician's bad or unskillful practices. Malpractice is the failure to do something that a reasonably careful physician or surgeon would do, or doing something a reasonably careful physician would not do, under the same circumstances. In other words, malpractice is a deviation from an established standard of practice—a failure to exercise the required degree of skill, care, and diligence or follow accepted rules. It can be willful or due to lack of skill or neglect; it can be a single act or something occurring over the course of treatment.

Ordinarily, in the absence of a special agreement, a physician need not exercise extraordinary skill. Nor must a physician anticipate consequences resulting from peculiar characteristics and conditions of a patient, if the physician has no knowledge of them or would not be expected to reasonably discover them. Not every wrongful act by a physician amounts to malpractice. A physician is ordinarily not liable for injurious consequences if she exercises the required degree of skill and care. A want of skill or care must be the PROXIMATE CAUSE or a substantial factor in the injury or death, but not necessarily the sole cause.

The standard of care was traditionally determined with reference to the geographic locality of the treatment, meaning the level of care

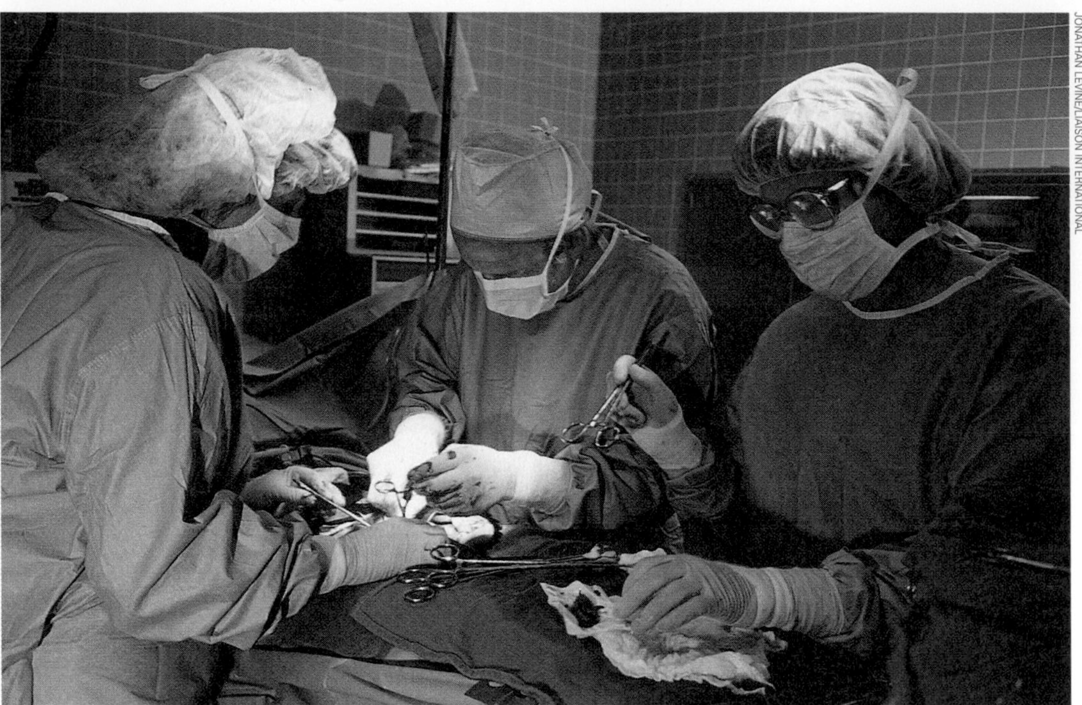

JONATHAN LEVINE/LIAISON INTERNATIONAL

Doctors and patients have a contractual relationship, but a surgeon would rarely promise a specific outcome or cure. If this surgeon promised a specific result for this surgery but failed to deliver, he might be liable for breach of contract or malpractice.

exercised by other physicians or surgeons in good standing in the same general line of practice in the same or similar locality. The locality standard developed when there were significant differences in the opportunities for continuing medical education and vast differences in access to hospitals. However, today's increased ease in dissemination of information, coupled with more uniform methods of treatment, have significantly downgraded the importance of the locality rule. Many JURISDICTIONS now view locality as only one factor to examine rather than a conclusive limit on the degree of skill required. Other authorities have completely abandoned the locality rule in favor of a national standard.

Specialists are held to the standard of care of other specialists in the same field under similar circumstances. This typically means that specialists, because of their advanced training and knowledge, are held to a higher standard than that required of general practitioners. Even though not certified as a specialist, those who hold themselves out to be specialists, or perform procedures normally done by specialists, will be held to a specialist's standard.

A physician must refer a patient or seek a consultation if she knows, or should know, that the treatment of a particular patient is beyond her skill. If a physician fails to make a referral or seek a consultation, she will be held to the standard of care applicable to the appropriate specialty that should have been consulted.

A physician or surgeon is bound to follow the methods that are generally approved and recognized by the profession but is not limited to the most generally accepted treatment methods. Determining whether a treatment is a respected minority treatment can present a difficult question. Nevertheless, a practitioner who otherwise adheres to the applicable standard of care will typically not be held liable for an error in judgment in choosing from different accepted treatments or diagnostic methods. A physician's actions are viewed in terms of the state of medicine at the time of the claimed malpractice, rather than on subsequent medical discoveries or knowledge.

A physician has a nondelegable duty of CARE. This means that the physician is responsible for injury caused by assistants, employees, AGENTS, or APPRENTICES, when that injury is caused by a lack of proper skill or care. For example, a surgeon who retains control over the procedures used by an anesthesiologist may be liable for the negligent actions of the anesthesiologist. Generally, a physician will not be liable for a hospital's NEGLIGENCE or the negligence of others not within his control but may be liable where the negligence is discoverable by the physician in the ordinary course of treatment.

A physician may have an affirmative duty toward a third person who is not the physician's patient where there is a foreseeable risk of harm of the third person by the patient, of which the physician is aware or should be aware. For example, this duty may arise where a psychiatric patient threatens to harm a known victim, or where a patient with a sexually transmitted disease refuses to notify his sexual partners of the illness. At least in the latter case, a physician's duty would generally be limited to those persons readily identified as being in danger. To prevail on such a claim, a third party must demonstrate that she was within the scope of a foreseeable risk of harm and that negligent treatment of the patient was the proximate cause of her injuries.

Only a very few states recognize WRONGFUL LIFE claims. These are actions brought by or on behalf of a disabled child, alleging that the child was born due to a doctor's negligent failure to properly advise the parents, even though the doctor did not cause the disability. The first case to recognize a wrongful life claim was a 1980 California case, where a doctor negligently failed to detect Tay-Sachs disease (*Curlender v. Bio-Science Laboratories*, 106 Cal. App. 3d 811, 165 Cal. Rptr. 477 [Ct. App. 2d Dist. 1980]). The parents had specifically sought prenatal testing for the crippling disease. The severely disabled baby girl had a life expectancy of no more than four years. The court ruled that the serious nature of the harm, coupled with the fact that the disease went undetected because of a lack of due medical attention, sufficed to permit the action.

WRONGFUL BIRTH and wrongful life actions arise out of the same set of circumstances but are brought by different parties. In a wrongful life suit, the child (or someone acting on behalf of the child) is the plaintiff; in the wrongful birth case, the parents bring suit. Often the term *wrongful birth* encompasses two categories: wrongful conception or wrongful pregnancy cases involve a woman who gave birth to an unwanted but healthy child; wrongful birth involves a child who was born with a handicap.

WRONGFUL PREGNANCY cases may arise where the defendant negligently performs a sterilization procedure or otherwise provides ineffective contraception, where a doctor negligently performs an ABORTION, resulting in the birth of a healthy child, or where a physician negligently fails to diagnose a pregnancy and the mother is thereby denied the choice of an abortion at a timely stage. A majority of states recognize a wrongful pregnancy CAUSE OF ACTION. Most, however, limit DAMAGES to the pain associated with the failed procedures. A few jurisdictions permit recovery of child-rearing expenses, but some of those states require that the award be offset by the parents' emotional benefits of raising a healthy child.

Wrongful life claims are permitted in some jurisdictions, but some courts have ruled that the cause of action does not exist in the absence of a statute giving rise to the claim. In addition, the cause of action has been specifically eliminated by statute in some jurisdictions.

In 1989 Congress created the National Practitioner Data Bank (NPDB) to mandate collection of information regarding incompetent practitioners. The NPDB began operation on September 1, 1990; its reporting requirements are not retroactive. The data bank collects information on all malpractice payments of more than one dollar made on behalf of physicians, dentists, and other licensed health care practitioners. The NPDB also collects information regarding disciplinary actions taken by state medical and dental boards. It also monitors professional review actions taken by hospitals and other entities adversely affecting a physician's clinical privileges for more than thirty days and a practitioner's voluntary surrender of clinical privileges during an investigation for incompetence or improper professional conduct. The NPDB also collects information on adverse actions by professional societies against its members.

Insurers, hospitals, medical societies, and boards of medicine must report to the NPDB; plaintiffs or their attorneys may not submit reports. Practitioners receive copies of the reports against them and have an opportunity to dispute the accuracy of the information.

The data bank has been criticized because the current regulations sometimes allow "corporate shielding" to protect practitioners from being reported. Because only individuals, not entities, must be reported, a practitioner would probably not be reported where a malpractice settlement was made on behalf of an incorporated group practice without naming a specific physician. Others criticize the data bank's one-dollar requirement, arguing that "nuisance" claims under a certain amount should not be reported or that different specialties should be given different monetary thresholds before reporting is mandated.

By regulation hospitals must query the NPDB when considering a physician for a medical staff appointment or for clinical privileges. They must also query at least once every two years concerning any physician who is on its medical staff or has clinical privileges at the hospital. Boards of medical examiners, professional societies, other state licensing boards, or other health care entities that are entering an employment or affiliation arrangement with a physician may also request information at any time. In addition, a physician may query the NPDB concerning his own record at any time. Attorneys may have access in very limited circumstances where proof exists that a hospital failed to make a required query.

MEDICAL MALPRACTICE insurers or the public are not allowed access to NPDB information. In 1996 the medical board of Massachusetts launched its own data bank. Information is available by fax, CD-ROM, and the Internet regarding malpractice settlement details, disciplinary action, and the practice and training of physicians.

CROSS-REFERENCES

Acquired Immune Deficiency Syndrome; Birth Control; Death and Dying; Fetal Rights; Fetal Tissue Research; Health Care Law; Health Insurance; Managed Care; Medicaid; Medicare; Patients' Rights; Physician-Patient Privilege; Privileged Communication.

PICKETING The presence at an employer's business of one or more employees and/or other persons who are publicizing a labor dispute, influencing employees or customers to withhold their work or business, respectively, or showing a union's desire to represent employees; picketing is usually accompanied by patrolling with signs.

See also LABOR LAW; LABOR UNION.

PIERCE, FRANKLIN Franklin Pierce served as the fourteenth president of the United States from 1853 to 1857. He was the youngest person to be elected president up to that time. A northern Democrat who sought to preserve southern SLAVERY, Pierce's administration proved a failure because he antagonized the growing abolitionist movement by signing the KANSAS-NEBRASKA ACT of 1854, which gave the two new territories the option of whether to permit slavery. Pierce was unable to win renomination for a second term.

BIOGRAPHY

Franklin Pierce

Pierce was born on November 23, 1804, in Hillsboro, New Hampshire. His parents were Benjamin and Anna Kendrick Pierce. Pierce graduated from Bowdoin College in 1824 and returned home to take over his father's duties as postmaster, after his father entered politics. Pierce studied law with a local attorney and was admitted to the New Hampshire bar in 1827. In that same year his father was elected governor of New Hampshire, which proved helpful to Pierce's own nascent political ambitions.

Pierce was elected as a Democrat to the New Hampshire legislature in 1829 and in 1832 was elected to the U.S. House of Representatives. A strong supporter of President ANDREW JACKSON, Pierce also became associated with the cause of slavery. In 1835 he attacked the flood of abolitionist petitions addressed to the House, which contained the signatures of more than two million people. He joined southern Democrats in imposing a "GAG RULE" that prevented the House from receiving or debating these petitions.

In 1837 Pierce was elected to the U.S. Senate. He resigned in 1842 for personal reasons and returned to Concord, New Hampshire, to become the federal district attorney. Except for a brief tour of duty as an Army officer during the Mexican War (1846–48), Pierce remained out of the political arena until the DEMOCRATIC PARTY national convention in 1852. The three leading candidates for the presidential nomination, Lewis Cass, STEPHEN A. DOUGLAS, and JAMES BUCHANAN, failed to win the necessary votes after forty-eight ballots. The convention turned to Pierce on the forty-ninth ballot as a compromise candidate who, though virtually unknown nationally, enjoyed support from northern and southern Democrats. He easily defeated General Winfield Scott, the Whig party candidate, in November 1852.

Pierce took office in March 1853, at a time when the issue of slavery threatened to divide both the Democratic and Whig parties, as well as the nation itself. Pierce sought to ease tensions by appointing a cabinet that contained a mix of southern and northern officials. Still critical of abolitionism, he enraged the antislavery movement with his signing of the Kansas-Nebraska Act of 1854. The act repealed the MISSOURI COMPROMISE OF 1820, which restricted the boundaries of slavery to the same latitude as the southern boundary of Missouri—36° 30′ north latitude. The new territories of Kansas

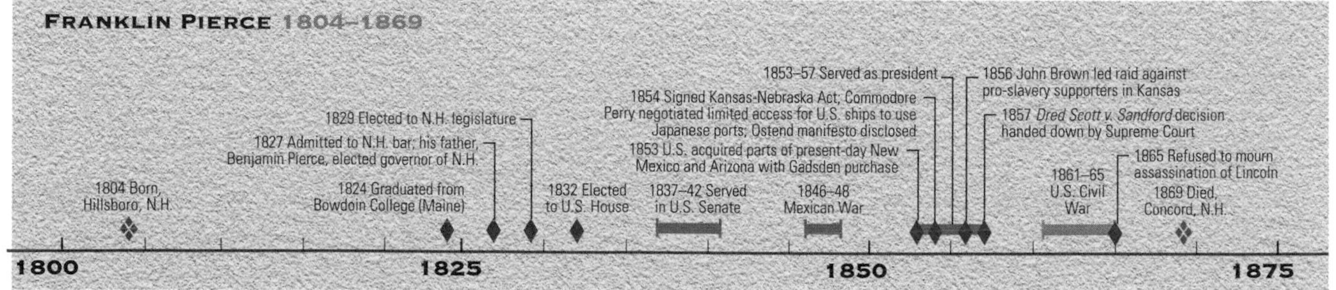

and Nebraska were organized according to the principle of popular sovereignty, which permitted voters to determine for themselves whether slavery would be a legalized institution at the time of the territories' admission as states.

Abolitionists saw the popular sovereignty principle as a means of extending slavery northward and westward. Pierce proved weak and indecisive as violence erupted in Kansas and Nebraska. On May 25, 1856, the militant abolitionist John Brown led a raid against supporters of slavery at Pottawatomie Creek, Kansas, killing five persons. Though appalled at the raid, Pierce said nothing and did little to address the growing violence between abolitionists and supporters of slavery that soon gave the territory the name "Bleeding Kansas." His support of slavery led to defections from the Democratic party and ultimately contributed to the establishment of the antislavery REPUBLICAN PARTY.

Pierce did achieve some success in foreign affairs. In 1854 Pierce received the report of Commodore Matthew C. Perry's expedition to Japan and the news that U.S. ships would have limited access to Japanese ports. His administration acquired a strip of land near the Mexican border for $10 million in the Gadsden Purchase of 1853, negotiated a fishing rights treaty with Canada in 1854, and in 1856 signed a treaty with Great Britain resolving disputes in Central America.

However, Pierce's popularity was damaged by his secret attempt to buy Cuba from Spain. The public disclosure of the October 1854 diplomatic statement called the Ostend Manifesto shocked Congress and the public. The manifesto discussed ways in which the United States might acquire or annex Cuba with or without the willingness of Spain to sell it. Pierce was forced to disclaim responsibility for the plan, but his integrity was placed in doubt.

Pierce was not renominated by the Democratic party in 1856, largely because of his difficulties with the Kansas-Nebraska Act and his ineffective leadership. The party turned to James Buchanan, who was elected but did little to resolve the political and sectional differences over slavery.

Pierce retired from public life in 1857 and returned to Concord, New Hampshire, to practice law. However, he became a vocal critic of President ABRAHAM LINCOLN during the Civil War, attacking the EMANCIPATION PROCLAMATION of 1863. When, in April 1865, he failed to hang a flag in mourning for the assassinated Lincoln, a mob attacked his home.

Pierce died in Concord on October 8, 1869.

PIERCE THE CORPORATE VEIL See CORPORATIONS.

BIOGRAPHY

PIERREPONT, EDWARDS Edwards Pierrepont was a well-known lawyer, judge, and orator before serving as attorney general of the United States under President ULYSSES S. GRANT.

Pierrepont was born on March 4, 1817, in North Haven, Connecticut. He graduated from Yale University in 1837 and Yale Law School in 1840 and then moved to Columbus, Ohio, to open his first law practice. By 1845 he had returned to the East Coast and entered a legal partnership in New York City. Over the next decade, he established a reputation of being a tough trial attorney and gifted courtroom orator.

In 1857 he was elected a judge of the Superior Court of the City of New York; he held the position until 1860 when he resigned to resume the practice of law.

In the years before the Civil War, Pierrepont was said to have had his fingers on the pulse of the nation. He was often asked to speak at civic and political functions, and he privately advised ABRAHAM LINCOLN on issues of the day both before and after Lincoln was elected president. During the war Pierrepont represented the government against prisoners of state confined in U.S. military prisons and forts.

As a Lincoln confidant and supporter, Pierrepont was among those who organized the president's 1864 reelection effort. When the campaign was aborted by an assassin's bullet, the government appointed Pierrepont to handle the prosecution of John H. Surratt for his part in Lincoln's murder.

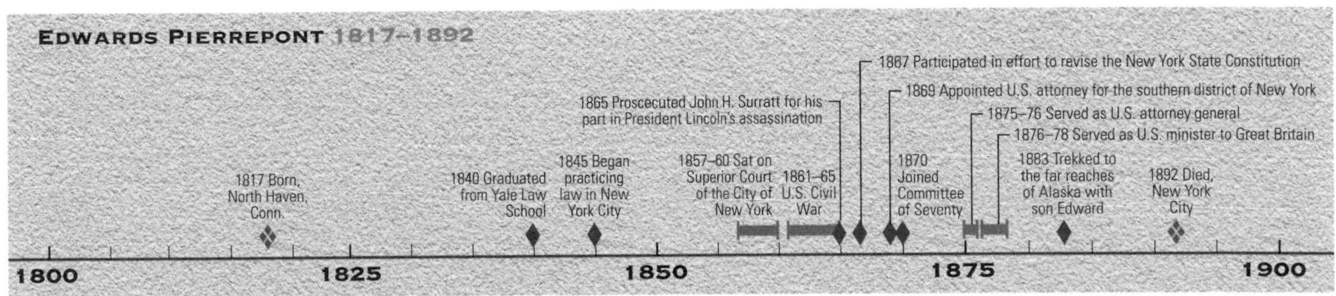

Pierrepont left Washington, D.C., and returned to New York after the war, but he remained in the public eye. As a private attorney, he continued to represent high-profile clients who included railroad barons and postwar industrialists. He also resumed his interest in politics at the state level. In April 1867 he was elected to participate in an effort to revise the state constitution, and he helped to organize local support for the 1868 presidential bid of General Ulysses S. Grant.

In recognition of his efforts, Pierrepont was appointed U.S. attorney for the southern district of New York in 1869, but he resigned just six months later to join the Committee of Seventy established in 1870 to force State Senator William Marcy ("Boss") Tweed from office. (After the Civil War, New York City government was dominated by TAMMANY HALL, a corrupt and abusive Democratic party PATRONAGE organization that operated under Tweed's direction.)

Pierrepont continued to support Grant when he ran for a second term in 1872. Following Grant's reelection, Pierrepont declined a diplomatic post in Russia because he was still involved in the efforts to clean up New York City government. But when Grant offered him a cabinet post in April 1875, Pierrepont was ready to accept.

He served as attorney general of the United States from May 1875 to May 1876. On the domestic front, Pierrepont did not depart significantly from the policies of his predecessor, GEORGE H. WILLIAMS; he maintained Williams's moratorium on CIVIL RIGHTS prosecutions in the South and generally ignored the issues surrounding white violence against blacks. He was more interested in restoring the international economic influence and political clout that the United States had lost during the years following the war.

As attorney general, Pierrepont is most often remembered for his contributions to INTERNATIONAL LAW, including opinions that addressed issues of natural and acquired nationality and grounds for EXTRADITION (15 Op. Att'y Gen. 15 [1875]; 15 Op. Att'y Gen. 500 [1875]).

In May 1876 Pierrepont was named U.S. minister to Great Britain. Before Pierrepont's term of service, the English court rarely gave U.S. presidents and their representatives special treatment. When President Grant visited London in 1877, Pierrepont worked to ensure that Grant would be accorded the same honors and treatment as royal heads of state. Other governments soon followed Great Britain's example in acknowledging the United State's elected leaders.

"A PARDON IS . . . EVIDENCE . . . THAT GUILT HAS ONCE EXISTED, BUT, AT THE SAME TIME, THAT IT HAS BEEN ENTIRELY BLOTTED OUT, SO THAT IN THE EYE OF THE LAW THE OFFENDER IS AS INNOCENT AS IF HE NEVER COMMITTED THE OFFENSE."

During his years in London, Pierrepont devoted much of his time to studying England's financial system. When he returned to the United States in 1878, he published a number of pamphlets on the subject of U.S. and international financial systems, including a controversial 1887 flyer that advocated an international treaty to establish monetary policy, and recommended a common currency based on the value of silver, rather than the gold standard of the day.

In his later years, Pierrepont continued to practice law and edited many of his famous speeches for publication. He received many awards and citations during his long career, including honorary degrees from Yale University, Columbia College in Washington, D.C., and Oxford University in England.

In May 1883, at the age of sixty-six, Pierrepont accompanied his son, Edward Willoughby Pierrepont, to the far reaches of Alaska. Upon their return, father and son published a widely praised paper entitled "From Fifth Avenue to Alaska," for which the son was awarded a fellowship in the Royal Geographical Society of England. Although the rigors of the journey took a toll on the younger man, who died in 1884, the elder Pierrepont lived until 1892. He died March 6, 1892, in New York City.

PILOT In maritime law, a person who assumes responsibility for a vessel at a particular place for the purpose of navigating it through a river or channel, or from or into a port.

The captain, or master, of a large ship has total command in the high seas. However, when a ship enters or leaves a port, or enters a river or channel, the captain turns over navigation to a local pilot. Because of safety and commercial concerns, state and federal maritime law governs the licensing and regulation of pilots.

A docking pilot directs the tugboats that pull a ship from the pier. Once the ship has cleared the pier and is under way in the harbor, the docking pilot leaves the ship and turns navigation over to a harbor pilot. Every ship that enters and leaves a port must have a harbor pilot aboard. Once the ship reaches open water, a small boat picks up the harbor pilot and returns the pilot to port. The captain then resumes full command of the ship.

The harbor pilot must have a thorough knowledge of every channel, sandbar, and other obstacle that could run the ship aground, strike another ship, or cause an accident that would endanger the ship, its crew, its cargo, and any passengers on board. The pilot must also be an experienced sailor who knows how to maneuver a ship through crowded harbors.

Either the state or federal government licenses pilots to ensure that vessels will be properly operated in state and U.S. waters. Federal law requires that federally registered pilots navigate ships on the Great Lakes, and state law regulates the need for pilots in bays, inlets, rivers, harbors, and ports. Where the waters are the boundary between two states, the owner of the ship can hire a pilot who has been licensed by either state to navigate the vessel to and from port.

State and federal laws impose qualifications for a pilot's LICENSE. A pilot must have the highest degree of skill as a sailor and may be tested on that knowledge. The individual may be required to submit written references from persons for whom he or she has served as an apprentice. In addition, the applicant must obtain a reference from a licensed pilot. The pilot may also be required to post a BOND.

Once licensed, the pilot must act in a professional manner. A license can be revoked or suspended for adequate cause, such as when the pilot has operated the ship while intoxicated. The pilot has the right to appeal to a court an administrative body's decision to deny licensure or to impose discipline.

The legal rights and responsibilities of the harbor pilot's action in navigating vessels are well settled. The pilot has primary control of the navigation of the vessel, and the crew must obey any pilot order. The pilot is empowered to issue steering directions and to set the course and speed of the ship and the time, place, and manner of anchoring it. The captain is in command of the ship except for navigation purposes. The captain can properly assume command over the ship when the pilot is obviously incompetent or intoxicated.

The pilot must possess and exercise the ordinary skill and care of one who is an expert in a profession. A pilot can be held personally liable to the owners of the vessel and to other injured parties for DAMAGES resulting from NEGLIGENCE that causes a COLLISION. The pilot will be responsible for damages if his or her handling of the ship was unreasonable, according to persons of nautical experience and good seamanship, at the time of the accident. The negligence of a pilot in the performance of duty is a maritime TORT within the JURISDICTION of a court of admiralty, which deals only with maritime actions.

See also ADMIRALTY AND MARITIME LAW; AIRLINES.

PIMP In feudal England, a type of tenure by which a tenant was permitted to use REAL PROPERTY that belonged to a lord in exchange for the performance of some service, such as providing young women for the use and pleasure of the lord.

An individual who, for a fee, supplies another individual with a prostitute for sexual purposes. To PANDER, or cater to the sexual desires of others in exchange for money.

See also PROSTITUTION.

BIOGRAPHY

Allan Pinkerton

PINKERTON, ALLAN Allan Pinkerton was a famous nineteenth-century detective and founder of the Pinkerton National Detective Agency. Pinkerton served as a spy during the Civil War and was renowned for preventing the ASSASSINATION of President-Elect ABRAHAM LINCOLN in 1861. He became a controversial figure when large companies hired his "Pinkerton men" to break LABOR UNION strikes through the use of intimidation and violence.

Pinkerton was born on August 25, 1819, in Glasgow, Scotland. His father was a police sergeant, but as a young man Pinkerton did not seek a police job. Instead he apprenticed as a cooper and learned to make barrels. In 1842, after he completed his apprenticeship, Pinkerton emigrated to the United States. He settled in Chicago and set up a cooper's shop.

In 1843 Pinkerton moved his business to Dundee, in Kane County, Illinois. In that year he discovered and captured a gang of counterfeiters. The event changed Pinkerton's life. He became involved with police work and was appointed deputy sheriff of Kane County in 1846. He soon shifted to a similar position in Cook County, with headquarters in Chicago.

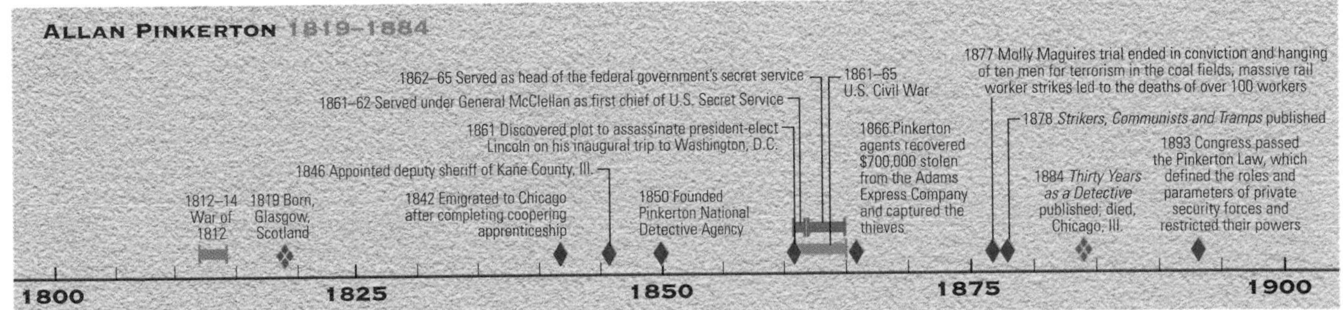

In 1850 he resigned as a deputy and started the Pinkerton National Detective Agency. This private detective agency, which specialized in RAILROAD theft cases, became the most famous organization of its kind. Pinkerton soon opened branches in several cities. In 1866 his agents recovered $700,000 stolen from the Adams Express Company and captured the thieves.

Pinkerton's public image was enhanced by his discovery in 1861 of a plot to assassinate Abraham Lincoln as the president-elect traveled by train from Springfield, Illinois, to Washington, D.C. With the outbreak of the Civil War, Pinkerton entered the Union army as a major. He was commissioned by General George B. McClellan to create a secret service of the U.S. Army to investigate criminal activity, such as payroll thefts and murder. Pinkerton also headed an organization, under the name E. J. Allan, that worked to obtain military information in the Southern states.

Following the Civil War, Pinkerton returned to his detective agency. His agency soon became an integral part in the wars between labor and management that became common in the 1870s. States enacted laws that gave corporations the authority to create their own private police forces or to contract with established police agencies. Pinkerton created groups of armed men known as Pinkerton men, who were contracted out for a daily fee to corporations with labor problems. Their menacing attitudes and use of violence were despised by labor unions and their supporters.

In 1877 the United States was beset by a number of railroad strikes. Pinkerton's agents were used as strikebreakers, and their harsh actions toward the labor unions were criticized. James McParlan, a Pinkerton agent, infiltrated the Molly Maguires, a secret organization of Pennsylvania and West Virginia coal miners. From 1872 to 1876, McParlan became part of the Molly Maguires, who were responsible for terrorism in the coal fields. He later testified in a series of trials that led to the conviction and hanging of ten men for murder.

Pinkerton, an unabashed self-promoter, wrote an account called *The Molly Maguires and the Detectives* (1877). In 1878 he wrote *Strikers, Communists and Tramps* in which he defended the use of his agents as strikebreakers, arguing that he was protecting workers by opposing unionism. He wrote about his role in foiling the Lincoln assassination in *The Spy of the Rebellion* (1883) and his autobiography *Thirty Years as a Detective* (1884).

Pinkerton died on July 1, 1884, in Chicago.

PINKERTON AGENTS The Pinkerton National Detective Agency was founded in 1850 in Chicago by ALLAN PINKERTON. It was one of the first private detective agencies in the United States, and its agents played an important role in law enforcement in the nineteenth and early twentieth century. Pinkerton agents were employed to capture bank robbers, counterfeiters, and forgers, but they also were used to infiltrate LABOR UNIONS and disrupt strikes.

Allan Pinkerton established offices throughout the country. A Pinkerton innovation was photographing criminals after arrest. The "mug shot" soon was adopted by police departments. By the 1870s the Pinkerton agency had the largest collection of mug shots in the world. Agents would clip out newspaper stories about a criminal and include this information in the criminal's file. When a crime was committed in town, the SHERIFF could send descriptions by witnesses to the agency, and the agents would provide a photograph and a detailed description of the suspect to law enforcement agencies in nearby communities.

In the late 1870s, coal mining operators in Pennsylvania hired Pinkerton agents to disrupt union organizing. Some agents infiltrated the Molly Maguires, a secret organization of Pennsylvania and West Virginia coal miners. After a long and highly publicized trial in which Pinkerton agents were WITNESSES, nineteen miners were hanged for crimes committed during the strike.

Pinkerton agents chased bandits across the United States after the Civil War, including the gang led by Jesse and Frank James. Robert Pinkerton, the son of Allan, led the group that followed and captured the Younger Brothers Gang in 1874. Pinkerton agents also pursued, unsuccessfully, Butch Cassidy (Robert Parker) and the Sundance Kid (Harry Longabough) as the pair robbed trains and banks in the southwestern United States in the late 1890s.

The Pinkerton agency remains in existence and has its headquarters in Encino, California. The agency provides investigative services, uniformed security officers, security systems, and other products and services associated with personal and business security.

BIOGRAPHY

LIBRARY OF CONGRESS

William Pinkney

PINKNEY, WILLIAM William Pinkney was a lawyer, statesman, and diplomat before serving as attorney general of the United States under President JAMES MADISON.

Pinkney was born in Annapolis, Maryland, on March 17, 1764. Though his early education was sporadic during the Revolutionary war years, Pinkney was a diligent student. He originally studied medicine, but in 1783 he met

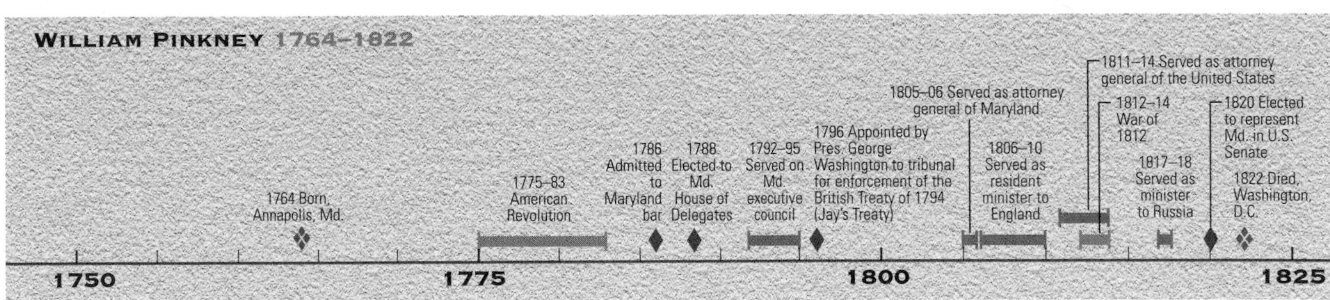

Judge SAMUEL CHASE. Chase thought the young medical student would make a good lawyer and offered to tutor him. For the next three years, Pinkney read law in Chase's Baltimore office. He was admitted to the bar in 1786.

In 1787 Pinkney established a law practice in rural Harford County, Maryland. With encouragement from Chase, he also became active in local politics. In 1788 he was elected to the Maryland House of Delegates, the lower house of the legislative assembly. In the legislature, Pinkney established a reputation as an eloquent speaker and a skillful lawmaker.

By 1792 Pinkney had left his seat in the house of delegates to serve on Maryland's executive council, a body appointed to advise or assist the governor in the execution of official duties. Pinkney lived and practiced law in Annapolis during his term of council service, from 1792 to 1795.

In 1796 President GEORGE WASHINGTON appointed Pinkney to the tribunal responsible for enforcing the British Treaty of 1794 (or Jay's Treaty). This treaty, negotiated by Supreme Court Chief Justice JOHN JAY, established an international commission to arbitrate boundary disputes between the United States and Great Britain, and to settle charges of interference with merchant shipping and trade between the two countries.

Pinkney served on the commission for the next eight years. The experience made him an expert in the fields of admiralty and international law, but his long stay in England took a toll on his personal finances. Unlike other diplomats of his day, Pinkney was not a wealthy man. By 1804 he had decided it was time to capitalize on his acquired expertise. He returned to Maryland and established a legal practice in Baltimore. Before long, he was a familiar and respected figure in Maryland's seaports and courtrooms. In 1805 he served as attorney general of Maryland while continuing to build his private practice.

In 1806 Great Britain renewed its aggression against U.S. ships in international waters. President THOMAS JEFFERSON asked Pinkney to accompany Envoy (and future president) JAMES MONROE to England to negotiate an agreement on the shipping rights of neutrals. Though Pinkney was reluctant to leave a law practice that was just beginning to prosper, he agreed to go. It was not one of his better decisions. Monroe departed England in 1807, leaving Pinkney to serve as resident minister. Pinkney pleaded for a replacement, but Jefferson ignored him. It was four years before Pinkney was relieved of his duties by Jefferson's successor, President Madison.

"THE FREE SPIRIT OF OUR CONSTITUTION AND OF OUR PEOPLE IS NO ASSURANCE AGAINST THE PROPENSION OF UNBRIDLED POWER TO ABUSE."

When Pinkney returned to Baltimore in 1811, he found that his practice had once again been devastated by his absence. In need of income while rebuilding his client base, he ran for, and was elected to, the Maryland state senate. By December of 1811, Pinkney had resigned his seat to accept President Madison's appointment as attorney general of the United States.

In 1811, the attorney general's post was still a part-time position that allowed the officeholder to continue in private practice—and to pursue other interests and commitments. Shortly after taking office, Pinkney chose to demonstrate his support for the War of 1812 by enlisting and serving with a rifle company. This absence, and others required by Pinkney's law practice, contributed to growing sentiment that the country needed a full-time attorney general who resided in Washington, D.C. When Congress instituted a residency requirement in 1814, Pinkney chose to resign rather than put his law practice in jeopardy for a third time. Madison, who had supported the residency requirement, was disappointed with Pinkney's decision.

Even though the residency debate became the defining issue of his term, Pinkney made other contributions while in office. He advised on international trade matters, and worked with Supreme Court Justice JOSEPH STORY to improve the federal criminal code.

Friends and neighbors in Pinkney's home district apparently failed to consider his stand on the residency issue when they drafted him as a candidate for the U.S. House of Representatives in 1815. Members of Congress were not required to live in Washington, D.C., but most of them did while Congress was in session. Pinkney was elected but refused to serve.

It was almost two years before Pinkney reentered the public arena. In 1817 he accepted a diplomatic post as minister to Russia and special envoy to Naples. This time, he served only the designated term abroad.

In 1818 Pinkney returned to Baltimore and the practice of law. For the next two years, he was actively involved in many of the cases heard before the U.S. Supreme Court—including two celebrated confrontations in which he bested lawyer and orator DANIEL WEBSTER (*Trustees of Dartmouth College v. Woodward*, 17 U.S. (4 Wheat.) 518, 4 L. Ed. 629 [1819]; *M'Culloch v. State of Maryland*, 17 U.S. (4 Wheat.) 316, 4 L. Ed. 579 [1819]).

He also made amends for his earlier refusal to serve the people of Maryland in Congress. In 1820 he was elected to the U.S. Senate. He took his seat but did not complete the term. He died in Washington, D.C., on February 25, 1822.

See also MCCULLOCH V. MARYLAND; TRUSTEES OF DARTMOUTH COLLEGE V. WOODWARD.

PIRACY The act of violence or depredation on the high seas; also, the THEFT of INTELLECTUAL PROPERTY, especially in electronic media.

Piracy is a crime with ancient origins. As long as there have been ships at sea, pirates have sought to steal from them. Internationally, laws against piracy have ancient origins, too, but U.S. law developed chiefly in the eighteenth and nineteenth century. The power to criminalize piracy originated in the U.S. Constitution, which was followed by the first federal law in 1790 and crucial revisions over the next sixty years. Additionally, the United States and other nations cooperated to combat piracy in the twentieth century. This resulted in a unique shared view of JURISDICTION: piracy on the high seas can be punished by any nation. In the late twentieth century, the term *piracy* grew to include COPYRIGHT violations of intellectual property such as music, films, and computer software.

In addition to its traditional nautical connotations, piracy has come to refer to copyright violations as well. This clothing was seized by customs officials because it displays copyrighted logos without the permission of the copyright holders.

LISA TERRY/GAMMA LIAISON

The Constitution addresses piracy in Article 1, Section 8. It gives Congress "the Power . . . To define and punish Piracies and Felonies committed on the high Seas, and Offenses against the Law of Nations." Generally, the definition of pirates meant rogue operators at sea—independent criminals who hijacked ships, stole their cargo, or committed violence against their crew. But standards in all areas under the law changed in response to judicial rulings and to historical incidents, forming by the mid-1800s what became the basis for contemporary law.

In 1790 Congress enacted the first substantive antipiracy law, a broad ban on MURDER and ROBBERY at sea that carried the death penalty. In 1818, however, the U.S. Supreme Court ruled that the law was limited to crimes involving U.S. citizens: U.S. jurisdiction did not cover foreigners whose piracy targeted other foreigners (*United States v. Palmer*, 16 U.S. [3 Wheat.] 610). A year later, in 1819, Congress responded by passing an antipiracy law to extend U.S. jurisdiction over pirates of all nationalities.

By the mid-nineteenth century, two other important changes occurred. Penalties for certain piracy crimes—revolt and MUTINY—were reduced and were no longer punishable by death. Then the Mexican War of 1846–48 brought a radical extension of the definition of a pirate. The traditional definition of an independent criminal was broadened to include sailors acting on commissions from foreign nations, if and when their commissions violated U.S. treaties with their government. The Piracy Act of 1847, which established this broader definition, marked the last major change in U.S. piracy law.

Today, the primary source of antipiracy law is title 18, chapter 81, of the United States Code, although numerous other antipiracy provisions are scattered throughout the code. Additionally, international cooperation has shaped a unique form of jurisdictional agreement among nations. Significant in bringing about this cooperation was the Geneva Convention on the High Seas of April 29, 1958 and the

1982 United Nations Convention on the Law of the Sea. The primary effect of such agreements is to allow pirates to be apprehended on the high seas—meaning outside of territorial limits—by the authorities of any nation and punished under its own law. This standard is unique because nations are generally forbidden by INTERNATIONAL LAW from interfering with the vessels of another nation on the high seas. It arose because piracy itself has never vanished; in fact, since the 1970s, it has appeared to have undergone a resurgence.

Apart from its traditional definition, piracy also refers to copyright violations. Committed both in the United States and abroad, this form of piracy includes the unauthorized storage, reproduction, distribution, or sale of intellectual property—for example, music CDs, movie videocassettes, and even fashion designs. The term has been applied, in particular, to the piracy of computer software, which is highly susceptible to theft because of its ease of duplication. Estimates of the cost to copyright holders ranges in the billions of dollars annually. U.S. law protects copyright holders under the Copyright Act (17 U.S.C.S. § 109 [1993]), and a 1992 federal law makes software piracy a FELONY (Pub. L. No. 102-561, 106 Stat. 4233, codified at 18 U.S.C.A. § 2319 [1988 & 1992 Supp.]). Since the 1990s, a number of international treaties and conventions, as well as diplomatic initiatives, have sought to forge greater cooperation among nations to combat such piracy.

See also ADMIRALTY AND MARITIME LAW; COMPUTER CRIME; HIJACKING.

PITNEY, MAHLON Mahlon Pitney served as an associate justice of the U.S. Supreme Court from 1912 to 1922. A lawyer, legislator, and New Jersey Supreme Court judge before his appointment, Pitney was a judicial conservative who believed in "liberty of contract" and who generally opposed efforts to protect the right of workers to join unions.

Pitney was born on February 5, 1858, in Morristown, New Jersey. His father, Henry Pitney, was a lawyer and state supreme court judge. Pitney graduated from Princeton University in 1879 and then studied law with a lawyer instead of attending law school. He was admitted to the New Jersey bar in 1882. He practiced law in Dover, New Jersey, from 1882 to 1889. He returned to Morristown to assume control of his father's firm in 1889, when his father was appointed to the New Jersey Supreme Court.

BIOGRAPHY

ARTIST: ADRIAN LAMB. COLLECTION OF THE SUPREME COURT OF THE UNITED STATES.

Mahlon Pitney

Pitney began a brief political career in the 1890s. He was elected to the U.S. House of Representatives in 1895 as a Republican and served two terms. In 1899 he was elected to the New Jersey Senate, serving as president in 1901. He abandoned the political arena in 1901 when he was appointed to the New Jersey Supreme Court. He served as chancellor, the state's highest judicial post, from 1908 to 1912.

In 1912 President WILLIAM HOWARD TAFT appointed Pitney to the U.S. Supreme Court. During his ten years on the court, Pitney wrote many opinions that dealt with unions and business and their regulation by government. Pitney, an economic conservative, was generally hostile to government interference with employers and employees. During the time Pitney was on the court, U.S. LABOR UNIONS were struggling to survive in a legal environment that favored employers. In *Coppage v. Kansas*, 236 U.S. 1, 35 S. Ct. 240, 59 L. Ed. 441 (1915), Pitney struck down a Kansas statute that prohibited an employer from using force or coercion to prevent employees from joining a union.

Pitney's hostility to unions and government regulation of business was based on his belief in individualism and unrestricted freedom in the marketplace. He subscribed to the liberty of contract theory that commanded widespread support on the Supreme Court. Pitney believed that liberty of contract was guaranteed by the FOURTEENTH AMENDMENT to the U.S. Constitution, which provided that no state was to "deprive any person of life, liberty or property without due process of law." Government regu-

MAHLON PITNEY 1858–1924

1858 Born, Morristown, N.J.

1861–65 U.S. Civil War

1879 Graduated from Princeton University

1882 Admitted to New Jersey bar, began practice in Dover

1889 Took over father's law firm in Morristown when his father was appointed to New Jersey Supreme Court

1895 Elected to U.S. House

1899 Elected to New Jersey Senate

1901 Appointed to New Jersey Supreme Court

1908 Appointed chancellor of New Jersey

1912–22 Served as associate justice of the U.S. Supreme Court

1914–18 World War I

1915 Wrote opinion in *Coppage v. Kansas*, which struck down Kansas statute prohibiting employers from using force to prevent employees from joining unions

1917 Wrote opinion in *New York Central Railroad Co. v. White*, which held employers liable for work-related injuries of their employees

1924 Died, Washington, D.C.

1850 1875 1900 1925

lation of work hours and working conditions was unconstitutional because regulation deprived employer and employee of the liberty to negotiate terms of employment. Likewise, unions hurt individualism by insisting on COLLECTIVE BARGAINING.

Pitney applied these beliefs to business as well. He supported ANTITRUST statutes because monopolies, like unions, distorted the marketplace and reduced the ability of individuals and small companies to compete. Most importantly, Pitney supported state WORKERS' COMPENSATION statutes, which had just been introduced as a way to protect workers hurt on the job. In *New York Central Railroad Co. v. White*, 243 U.S. 188, 37 S. Ct. 247, 61 L. Ed. 667 (1917), and in several subsequent cases, Pitney ruled that employers were liable for the injuries suffered by their workers during the course of employment. Workers' compensation statutes changed the legal landscape for employers and employees. States created administrative systems that quickly and fairly compensated employees for their injuries. Employers were no longer able to invoke COMMON-LAW tort rules to avoid LIABILITY. Without Pitney's leadership on this issue, the laws might not have survived judicial scrutiny.

Pitney suffered a stroke in August 1922 and resigned from the Court in December. He died on December 9, 1924, in Washington, D.C.

"THE CONSTITUTION . . . IMPOSES UPON THE STATES NO OBLIGATION TO CONFER UPON THOSE WITHIN THEIR JURISDICTION EITHER THE RIGHT OF FREE SPEECH OR THE RIGHT OF SILENCE."

P.J. An abbreviation for presiding judge, the individual who directs, controls, or governs a particular tribunal as its chief officer.

PLAGIARISM The act of appropriating the literary composition of another author, or excerpts, ideas, or passages therefrom, and passing the material off as one's own creation.

Plagiarism is THEFT of another person's writings or ideas. Generally, it occurs when someone steals expressions from another author's composition and makes them appear to be his own work. Plagiarism is not a legal term; however, it is often used in lawsuits. Courts recognize acts of plagiarism as violations of COPYRIGHT law, specifically as the theft of another creator's INTELLECTUAL PROPERTY. Because copyright law allows a variety of creative works to be registered as the property of their owners, lawsuits alleging plagiarism can be based on the appropriation of any form of writing, music, and visual images.

Plagiarism can take a broad range of forms. At its simplest and most extreme, plagiarism involves putting one's own name on someone else's work; this is commonly seen in schools when a student submits a paper that someone else has written. Schools, colleges, and universities usually have explicit guidelines for reviewing and punishing plagiarism by students and faculty members. In copyright lawsuits, however, ALLEGATIONS of plagiarism are more often based on partial theft. It is not necessary to exactly duplicate another's work in order to infringe a copyright: it is sufficient to take a substantial portion of the copyrighted material. Thus, for example, plagiarism can include copying language or ideas from another novelist, basing a new song in large part on another's musical composition, or copying another artist's drawing or photograph.

Courts and juries have a difficult time determining when unlawful copying has occurred. One thing the plaintiff must show is that the alleged plagiarist had access to the copyrighted work. Such evidence might include a showing that the plaintiff sent the work to the defendant in an attempt to sell it, or that the work was publicly available and widely disseminated.

Once access is proven, the plaintiff must show that the alleged plagiarism is based on a substantial similarity between the two works. In *Abkco Music, Inc. v. Harrisongs Music, Ltd.*, 722 F.2d 988 (1983), the Second Circuit Court of Appeals found "unconscious" infringement by the musician George Harrison, whose song "My Sweet Lord" was, by his own admission, strikingly similar to the plaintiff's song, "He's So Fine." Establishing a substantial similarity can be quite difficult as it is essentially a subjective process.

Not every unauthorized taking of another's work constitutes plagiarism. Exceptions are made under copyright law for so-called fair use, as in the case of quoting a limited portion of a published work or mimicking it closely for purposes of parody and satire. Furthermore, similarity alone is not proof of plagiarism. Courts recognize that similar creative inspiration may occur simultaneously in two or more people. In Hollywood, for example, where well-established conventions govern filmmaking, this conventionality often leads to similar work. As early as 1942, in *O'Rourke v. RKO Radio Pictures*, 44 F. Supp. 480, the Massachusetts District Court ruled against a screenwriter who alleged that a movie studio had stolen parts of his unproduced screenplay *Girls' Reformatory* for its film *Condemned Women.* The court noted that the similar plot details in both stories— prison riots, escapes, and love affairs between inmates and officials—might easily be coincidental.

CROSS-REFERENCES

Literary Property; Music Publishing; Publishing Law.

PLAIN-ERROR RULE The principle that an appeals court can reverse a JUDGMENT and order a new trial because of a serious mistake in the proceedings, even though no OBJECTION was made at the time the mistake occurred.

For example, the issuance of inconsistent INSTRUCTIONS to a JURY that would result in a miscarriage of justice can furnish the basis for a new trial, even though no timely and proper objection to the instructions was made. Although a person is entitled to a fair trial, he or she is not entitled to a flawless one; the individual does not have the right to a new trial merely because a HARMLESS ERROR has been committed.

PLAIN-MEANING RULE A principle used by courts in interpreting CONTRACTS that provides that the objective definitions of contractual terms are controlling, irrespective of whether the language comports with the actual intention of either party.

The plain meaning of the contract will be followed where the words used—whether written or oral—have a clear and unambiguous meaning. Words are given their ordinary meaning; technical terms are given their technical meaning; and local, cultural, or TRADE USAGE of terms are recognized as applicable. The circumstances surrounding the formation of the contract are also ADMISSIBLE to aid in the interpretation.

PLAINTIFF The party who sues in a CIVIL ACTION; a COMPLAINANT; the prosecution—that is, a state or the United States representing the people—in a criminal case.

PLAINTIFF IN ERROR The unsuccessful party in a lawsuit who commences proceedings for APPELLATE review of the ACTION because a mistake or "error" has been made resulting in a JUDGMENT against him or her; an APPELLANT.

PLAIN VIEW DOCTRINE In the context of SEARCHES AND SEIZURES, the principle that provides that objects perceptible by an officer who is rightfully in a position to observe them can be seized without a SEARCH WARRANT and are ADMISSIBLE as EVIDENCE.

PLAT A map of a town or a section of land that has been subdivided into lots showing the location and BOUNDARIES of individual parcels with the streets, alleys, EASEMENTS, and rights of use over the land of another.

A plat is usually drawn to scale.

PLEA A formal response by the defendant to the affirmative assertions of the plaintiff in a civil case or to the charges of the prosecutor in a criminal case.

Under the old system of COMMON-LAW PLEADING, a plea was the defendant's first PLEADING in a case, the document in which he set out reasons why the plaintiff should not win on the claim made in his or her declaration. Rather than enter a plea, a defendant could file a DEMURRER, which was a pleading in which the defendant argued that the plaintiff had not made out a legally sufficient case. If the defendant did not demur, he responded to the plaintiff's declaration with a plea.

There were two kinds of pleas, *dilatory* and *peremptory*. A DILATORY PLEA did not argue against the MERITS of the plaintiff's claim but challenged that individual's right to have the court hear the case. It was called dilatory not because it unfairly delayed the trial but simply because it postponed the time when, if ever, the court would reach the merits of the case. A PLEA IN ABATEMENT was a dilatory plea.

A peremptory plea, also called a PLEA IN BAR, did reach the merits of the case. It set out certain facts that the defendant claimed would bar the granting of relief to the plaintiff.

The plea could be a TRAVERSE, a full denial of the plaintiff's version of the facts. In that situation, the issue was defined, and the case went to trial for a determination in favor of one party or the other.

The plea could be a CONFESSION AND AVOIDANCE, by which the defendant conceded the truth of the plaintiff's ALLEGATIONS but asserted new facts by which she sought to avoid the legal effect of the plaintiff's claim. For example, the defendant could admit that she had made a bargain as claimed by the plaintiff and then add that she was a MINOR at the time that she entered into the agreement and therefore could not be bound by it. At that point, no issue would yet have been disputed by both parties, and the plaintiff would have to respond to the plea. The plaintiff had the same range of possible responses that the defendant had had when she selected the plea, but the plaintiff's responsive pleading was called a REPLICATION. If the plaintiff raised a new question, the defendant had to respond with a REJOINDER. After that, the pleading process could bounce back and forth with a SURREJOINDER, a REBUTTER, and a SURREBUTTER. Common-law pleading thus became so complex and hypertechnical that it has now been replaced by CODE PLEADING and pleading similar to that of the federal CIVIL PROCEDURE.

A defendant could also enter a plea in a case in EQUITY. This was a special kind of ANSWER to a bill in equity, that showed one or more reasons why the suit should be dismissed, delayed, or barred entirely. Since the procedures for cases AT LAW and in equity have been merged, the plea in equity has also been abolished.

A criminal defendant has some options in responding to charges made against him. The

PLEA BARGAINING: A SHORTCUT TO JUSTICE

IN FOCUS

Plea bargaining is widely used in the criminal justice system, yet seldom praised. Plea agreements are troublesome because they are something less than a victory for all involved. Prosecutors are loath to offer admitted criminals lighter sentences than those authorized by law. Likewise, most criminal defendants are less than enthusiastic over the prospect of openly admitting criminal behavior without the benefit of a trial. Despite the reservations of the parties, plea agreements resolve roughly nine out of every ten criminal cases. The sheer numbers have caused many legal observers to question the propriety of rampant plea bargaining.

Some critics of plea bargaining argue that the process is unfair to criminal defendants. These critics claim that prosecutors possess too much discretion in choosing the charges that a criminal defendant may face. When a defendant is arrested, prosecutors have the authority to level any charge if they possess enough facts to support a reasonable belief that the defendant committed the offense. This standard is called probable cause, and it is a lower standard than ability to prove a charge beyond a reasonable doubt, the standard that the prosecution must meet at trial. Thus, for leverage, a prosecutor may tack on similar, more serious charges without believing that the charges can be proved beyond a reasonable doubt at trial.

Because prosecutors are evaluated in large part on their conviction rates, they are forced to try to win at all costs. According to some critics, prosecutors use overcharging to coerce guilty pleas from defendants and deprive them of the procedural safeguards and the full investigation of the trial process.

For example, assume that a defendant is arrested for trespassing. Assume further that the trespass was an honest mistake and that the defendant was, by happenstance, on the property of a former spouse. In addition to trespassing, the prosecutor may charge the defendant, on the facts, with stalking and attempted burglary. The prospect of facing a trial on three separate criminal charges may induce the defendant to plea bargain because the potential cumulative punishment for all three crimes is severe. Ultimately the defendant may plead guilty to, and forfeit the right to a trial on, the trespassing charge, the only charge that stands a chance of being proved beyond a reasonable doubt. Such a plea bargain, claim some critics, is an illusory bargain for criminal defendants.

The practice of overcharging is impermissible, and courts may dismiss superfluous charges. However, courts are reluctant to prevent the prosecution from presenting a case on a charge that is supported by probable cause. Prosecutors have discretion in plea bargaining, and they may withdraw offers after making them. A defendant is also free to reject a plea bargain. In many cases, where a plea bargain is withdrawn or rejected and the case goes to trial, the defendant, if found guilty, receives punishment more severe than that offered by the prosecution in the plea bargain. This has been called the "trial penalty" and it is another source of criticism of the plea bargain.

A defendant who goes to trial and is found guilty of a serious felony receives,

rules of CRIMINAL PROCEDURE in the federal courts and many state courts permit a defendant to enter a plea of guilty, not guilty, or NOLO CONTENDERE, which means "I do not wish to contest it." If a defendant fails or refuses to enter any plea at all, the court will enter a plea of "not guilty" for that individual, and then the trial may begin.

PLEA BARGAINING The process whereby a criminal defendant and PROSECUTOR reach a mutually satisfactory disposition of a criminal case, subject to court approval.

Plea bargaining can conclude a criminal case without a TRIAL. When it is successful, plea bargaining results in a PLEA agreement between the prosecutor and defendant. In this agreement the defendant agrees to plead GUILTY without a trial, and in return the prosecutor agrees to dismiss certain charges or make favorable sentence recommendations to the court. Plea bargaining is expressly authorized in statutes and in court rules.

In FEDERAL COURT, for example, plea bargaining is authorized by subsection (e) of rule 11 of the Federal Rules of Criminal Procedure. Under rule 11(e), a prosecutor and defendant may enter into an agreement whereby the defendant pleads guilty and the prosecutor offers either to move for dismissal of a charge or charges, recommend to the court a particular sentence or agree not to oppose the defendant's request for a particular sentence, or agree that a specific sentence is the appropriate disposition of the case. A prosecutor can agree to take any or all of these actions in a plea agreement. Under rule 11(e), plea bargaining must take place before trial unless the parties show good cause for the delay.

Generally a judge will authorize a plea bargain if the defendant makes a knowing and voluntary WAIVER of his or her right to a trial, the defendant understands the charges, the defendant understands the maximum sentence he or she could receive after pleading guilty, and on the average, a prison sentence that is twice as long as the sentence offered in a plea bargain for the same offense. A defendant cannot be penalized for pleading not guilty and going to trial, but the U.S. Supreme Court has not held that it is impermissible to punish defendants with sentences that are longer than those offered in plea agreements. When overcharging and the trial penalty are combined in the regular practice of plea bargaining, defendants have little choice but to plead guilty, and virtually every criminal act may be disposed of without a trial. This, according to some critics, is a perversion of the criminal justice system.

Other critics focus on the benefits that plea bargaining gives to defendants. They argue that plea bargaining softens the deterrent effect of punishment because it gives criminal defendants the power to bargain for lesser punishments. These critics note that experienced criminals are more likely to receive favorable plea bargains because they are familiar with the criminal justice system. According to these critics, plea bargaining subverts the proposition that a criminal should receive a punishment suited to the crime.

Critics of plea bargaining tend to be either scholars or crime victims. Scholars complain of prosecutorial coercion, and crime victims decry the lighter sentences that plea bargaining produces. Defenders of plea bargaining tend to be the players in the system. These are judges, prosecutors, criminal defendants, and criminal defense attorneys. The majority of these persons accept plea bargaining as a necessary tool in the administration of criminal justice. They point out that critics of plea bargaining have no solution to the lack of judicial resources. Without increased funding for more courts, judges, prosecutors, and court employees, plea bargaining is a necessity in most jurisdictions.

In response to the overcharging argument, supporters of plea bargaining note that the prosecutor's discretion in charging is a concept deeply ingrained in U.S. law, and for good reason. A prosecutor is not required to decide the case before trial. Instead the prosecutor is required to press charges based on the facts and to present evidence to support the charges. If there is no reasonable interpretation of the facts to support a certain charge, the charge will be dismissed. The judge or jury makes the final decision of whether the evidence warrants conviction on a certain offense. Defendants may receive harsher sentences upon conviction at trial, but in any case the sentence must be authorized by law. Thus, procedural safeguards effectively protect criminal defendants from the perils of overcharging.

Proponents of plea bargaining also contend that both defendants and society reap benefits. Defendants benefit because both the defendant and prosecutor help to fashion an appropriate punishment. Society benefits because it is spared the cost of lengthy trials while defendants admit to crimes and still receive punishment. Although the punishment pursuant to a plea agreement is generally less severe than that imposed upon conviction after a trial, the process nevertheless produces a deterrent effect on criminal behavior because prosecutors are able to obtain more convictions. Each conviction places a defendant under the supervision of the criminal justice system, and this decreases the defendant's freedom. Moreover, subsequent convictions after a guilty plea can be punished more harshly because defendants are punished in large part according to their criminal history.

the defendant makes a voluntary CONFESSION, in court, to the alleged crime. Even if a defendant agrees to plead guilty, a judge may decline to accept the guilty plea and plea agreement if the charge or charges have no factual basis.

The judge does not participate in plea bargain discussions. Prosecutors have discretion whether to offer a plea bargain. However, a prosecutor may not base the determination of whether to negotiate on the basis of an unjustifiable standard such as race, religion, or some other arbitrary classification.

Plea bargaining can be advantageous for both prosecutors and defendants. Prosecutors may seek a plea bargain in certain cases to save valuable court time for high-priority cases. Prosecutors often are amenable to plea bargaining with a defendant who admits guilt and accepts responsibility for a crime: plea bargaining in this context is considered the defendant's reward for confessing. Prosecutors also accept plea bargains because they are evaluated in large part according to their conviction rates and all plea bargains result in a conviction because the defendant must plead guilty as part of the plea agreement.

Criminal defendants may also benefit from plea bargaining. Plea agreements provide quick relief from the anxiety of criminal prosecution because they shorten the prosecution process. Furthermore, plea agreements usually give defendants less punishment than they would receive if they were found guilty of all charges after a full trial. For example, assume that a defendant has been charged with one count of DRIVING UNDER THE INFLUENCE and one count of possession of a controlled substance with intent to sell. If the defendant goes to trial and is found guilty on both counts, he could receive a prison sentence of several years. However, if he agrees to plead guilty to the charge of possession with intent to sell, the prosecutor may drop the driving-under-the-influence charge. The net result would be a slightly shorter prison sentence than would result with inclusion of the other count. As part of the same deal, the prosecutor also may agree to reduce the remaining charge in exchange for something from the defendant. For example, the prosecutor may ask the defendant to TESTIFY against the supplier of the drugs or to build a case against the supplier by acting as an agent for the police. A reduced charge, for example down to simple possession from possession with intent to sell, would further decrease any possible prison sentence. Finally, the prosecutor may agree to recommend to the court that the defendant serve a shorter prison sentence than the maximum term allowable under the simple possession statute.

Defendants are not required to enter into plea negotiations or accept a plea agreement offer. Some defendants choose to decline a plea bargain if they believe that the risk of conviction is outweighed by the possibility of ACQUITTAL. Other defendants may disregard the risks and make a principled choice to proceed to trial. Some of these defendants seek to use trial proceedings as a forum for expressing dissent, and others merely wish to exercise their constitutional right to a trial, or to publicly declare their version of events.

Prosecutors likewise are not obliged to plea bargain. Where the alleged crime is particularly heinous or the case is highly publicized or politically charged, a prosecutor may be reluctant to offer any deals to the defendant in deference to victims or public sentiment. For example, a prosecutor may not offer a bargain to a person accused of a brutal RAPE and MURDER because such acts are widely considered to deserve the maximum allowable punishment.

The political influence on plea bargaining is more nebulous. Because prosecutors are hired by federal, state, and local governments, they often have political ties. If a case involves a prominent member of a political party, a prosecutor may refuse to offer a plea bargain to avoid the appearance of favoritism.

When a court accepts a plea agreement, the guilty plea operates as a conviction, and the defendant cannot be retried on the same offense. If the defendant breaches a plea agreement, the prosecution may reprosecute the defendant. For example, assume that Defendant A, as part of the plea agreement, must testify against Defendant B. If Defendant A pleads guilty pursuant to this agreement but later refuses to testify against Defendant B, the prosecutor may seek a revocation of the plea agreement and guilty plea.

If the government breaches a plea agreement, the defendant may seek to withdraw the guilty plea, ask the court to enforce the agreement, or ask the court for a favorable modification in the sentence. The government breaches a plea agreement when it fails to deliver its part of the plea agreement. For example, if a prosecutor agrees to dismiss a certain charge but later reneges on this promise, the defendant may withdraw her guilty plea. An unenthusiastic sentence recommendation by a prosecutor is not a breach of a plea agreement (*U.S. v. Benchimol*, 471 U.S. 453, 105 S. Ct. 2013, 85 L. Ed. 2d 462 [1985]).

When a prosecutor or defendant revokes a plea agreement, the statements made during the bargaining period are not ADMISSIBLE against the defendant in a subsequent trial. This rule is designed to foster free and open negotiations. There are, however, notable exceptions. The rule applies only to prosecutors: a defendant's statements to government agents are admissible. Furthermore, a prosecutor may use statements made by the defendant during plea negotiations at a subsequent trial to IMPEACH the defendant's credibility after the defendant testifies.

Many JURISDICTIONS maintain statutes that require victim notification of plea bargaining. In Indiana, for example, a prosecutor must notify the victim of a FELONY of negotiations with the defendant or the defendant's attorney concerning a recommendation the prosecutor may make to the court. If an agreement is reached, the prosecutor must show the agreement to the victim, and the victim may give a statement to the court at the SENTENCING hearing (Ind. Code § 35-35-3-2 [1996]).

Plea bargaining was not favored in colonial America. In fact, courts actively discouraged defendants from pleading guilty. Courts gradually accepted guilty pleas in the nineteenth century. As populations increased and court procedural safeguards increased, courts became overcrowded, and trials became more lengthy. This made trial in every case an impossibility. By the twentieth century, the vast majority of criminal cases were resolved with guilty pleas. Plea bargaining is now conducted in almost every criminal case, and roughly nine out of ten plea discussions yield plea agreements.

CROSS-REFERENCES

Beyond a Reasonable Doubt; Criminal Law; Criminal Procedure; District and Prosecuting Attorneys; Due Process of Law; Probable Cause.

PLEADING Asking a court to grant relief. The formal presentation of claims and defenses by parties to a lawsuit. The specific papers by which the ALLEGATIONS of parties to a lawsuit are presented in proper form; specifically the COMPLAINT of a plaintiff and the ANSWER of a defendant plus any additional responses to those papers that are authorized by law.

Different systems of pleading have been organized generally to serve four functions: (1) to give notice of the claim or defense; (2) to reveal the facts of the case; (3) to formulate the issues that have to be resolved; and (4) to screen the flow of cases into a particular court. Different systems may rely on the pleadings to accomplish these purposes or may use the pleadings along with other procedural devices, such as DISCOVERY, pretrial conference among the parties, or SUMMARY JUDGMENT.

Originally in ancient England, the parties simply presented themselves to a tribunal and explained their dispute. This worked well enough in the local courts and in the feudal courts where a lord heard cases involving his tenants, but the great COMMON-LAW COURTS of the king demanded more formality. From the end of the fourteenth to the middle of the sixteenth century, the royal courts began more and more to demand written pleadings that set out a party's position in a case. Predictably the shift resulted in more formality and more rigid technical requirements that were difficult to satisfy. Thus the course of COMMON-LAW PLEADING was perilous. A claim or defense that did not exactly fit the requirements of the common-law FORMS OF ACTION was thrown out with no opportunity to amend it and come back into court.

Some relief was offered by the courts of EQUITY, which were not bound by the same complex system of pleading. Beginning in the fourteenth century, the authority of such courts increased in proportion to the rigidity of the common-law pleading. Equity was the conscience of the judicial system and was charged with doing complete justice regardless of technicalities. Cases were tried before a single judge without a jury, and the judge could allow different claims and various parties all in one proceeding. Some pretrial discovery of the other party's evidence was permitted. The initial pleading by a PETITIONER in equity was the bill, but states that now have the same procedures for law and equity specify the complaint as the first pleading in all kinds of CIVIL ACTIONS today.

Despite criticism, common-law pleading endured in England and in the United States for several centuries. Beginning in 1848, some states replaced it by law with a new system called CODE PLEADING. The statutes enacting code pleading abolished the old forms of action and set out a procedure that required the plaintiff simply to state in a complaint facts that warranted legal relief. A defendant was authorized to resist the plaintiff's demand by denying the truth of the facts in the complaint or by stating new facts that defeated them. The defendant's response is called an answer.

In 1938, FEDERAL COURTS began using a modern system of pleading set out in the federal Rules of Civil Procedure. This system has been so effective that many states have enacted substantially the same rules of pleading. A pleading by a plaintiff or defendant under these rules is intended simply to give the other party adequate notice of the claim or defense. This notice must give the adversary enough information so that she can determine the evidence that she wants to uncover during pretrial discovery and then adequately prepare for trial. Because of this underlying purpose, modern federal pleading is also called notice pleading. The other objectives of earlier kinds of pleading are accomplished by different procedural devices provided for in the Federal Rules of Civil Procedure.

See also CIVIL PROCEDURE.

PLEA IN ABATEMENT In COMMON-LAW PLEADING, a response by the defendant that does not dispute the plaintiff's claim but objects to its form or the time or place where it is asserted.

A PLEA in abatement does not absolutely defeat the plaintiff's claim because, even if the plea is successful, the plaintiff may renew the lawsuit in a proper form, time, or place. For this reason, it is called a DILATORY PLEA, because it has the effect of postponing the time when a court considers the actual MERITS of the case of each party.

The plea in abatement was abolished as a particular form of response by the defendant when common-law pleading was replaced by CODE PLEADING and later by pleading rules, such as the federal Rules of Civil Procedure. Sometimes the term is still loosely used for modern procedural devices that accomplish what the old plea in abatement used to do.

See also CIVIL PROCEDURE.

PLEA IN BAR An ANSWER to a plaintiff's claim that absolutely and entirely defeats it.

A PLEA in bar sets forth matters that deny the plaintiff's right to maintain his or her lawsuit; for example, because the STATUTE OF LIMITATIONS has expired or because the claim necessarily overrides a constitutionally protected right of the defendant.

PLEBISCITE See REFERENDUM.

PLEDGE A BAILMENT or DELIVERY of PERSONAL PROPERTY to a CREDITOR as SECURITY for a DEBT or for the performance of an act.

Sometimes called *bailment*, pledges are a form of security to assure that a person will repay a debt or perform an act under CONTRACT. In a pledge one person temporarily gives POS-

SESSION of property to another party. Pledges are typically used in securing loans, pawning property for cash, and guaranteeing that contracted work will be done. Every pledge has three parts: two separate parties, a debt or obligation, and a contract of pledge. The law of pledges is quite old, but in contemporary U.S. law it is governed in most states by the provisions for secured transactions in article 9 of the UNIFORM COMMERCIAL CODE.

Pledges are different from SALES. In a sale both possession and ownership of property are permanently transferred to the buyer. In a pledge only possession passes to a second party. The first party retains ownership of the property in question, while the second party takes possession of the property until the terms of the contract are satisfied. The second party must also have a LIEN—or legal claim—upon the property in question. If the terms are not met, the second party can sell the property to satisfy the debt. Any excess profit from the sale must be paid to the DEBTOR, or first party. But if the sale does not meet the amount of the debt, legal action may be necessary.

A contract of pledge specifies what is owed, the property that shall be used as a pledge, and conditions for satisfying the debt or obligation. In a simple example, John asks to borrow $500 from Mary. Mary decides first that John will have to pledge his stereo as security that he will repay the debt by a specific time. In law John is called the *pledgor*, and Mary the *pledgee*. The stereo is referred to as *pledged property*. As in any common pledge contract, possession of the pledged property is transferred to the pledgee. At the same time, however, ownership (or TITLE) of the pledged property remains with the pledgor. John gives the stereo to Mary, but he still legally owns it. If John repays the debt under the contractual agreement, Mary must return the stereo. But if he fails to pay, she can sell it to satisfy his debt.

Pledged property must be in the possession of a pledgee. This can be accomplished in one of two ways. The property can be in the pledgee's *actual* possession, meaning physical possession (for example, Mary keeps John's stereo at her house). Otherwise, it can be in the *constructive* possession of the pledgee, meaning that the pledgee has some control over the property, which typically occurs when actual possession is impossible. For example, a pledgee has CONSTRUCTIVE possession of the contents of a pledgor's safety deposit box at a bank when the pledgor gives the pledgee the only keys to the box.

In pledges both parties have certain rights and liabilities. The contract of pledge represents only one set of these: the terms under which the debt or obligation will be fulfilled and the pledged property returned. On the one hand, the pledgor's rights extend to the safekeeping and protection of his property while it is in possession of the pledgee. The property cannot be used without permission unless use is necessary for its preservation, such as exercising a live animal. Unauthorized use of the property is called CONVERSION and may make the pledgee liable for DAMAGES; thus, Mary should not use John's stereo while in possession of it.

For the pledgee, on the other hand, there is more than the duty to care for the pledgor's property. The pledgee has the right to the possession and control of any income accruing during the period of the pledge, unless an agreement to the contrary exists. This income reduces the amount of the debt, and the pledgor must account for it to the pledgee. Additionally, the pledgee is entitled to be reimbursed for expenses incurred in retaining, caring for, and protecting the property. Finally, the pledgee need not remain a party to the contract of pledge indefinitely. She can sell or ASSIGN her interest under the contract of the pledge to a third party. However, the pledgee must notify the pledgor that the contract of pledge has been sold or reassigned; otherwise, she is guilty of conversion.

PLESSY v. FERGUSON An 1896 decision by the Supreme Court, *Plessy v. Ferguson*, 163 U.S. 537, 16 S. Ct. 1138, 41 L. Ed. 256, upheld the constitutionality of an 1890 Louisiana statute requiring white and "colored" persons to be furnished "separate but equal" accommodations on railway passenger cars.

The plaintiff, Homer Adolph Plessy, who was seven-eights Caucasian and one-eighth African, paid for a first-class seat on a Louisiana railroad. He took a seat in the coach that was reserved for white passengers, but the conductor told him to leave the "white" car and go to the "colored" coach under threat of being expelled from the train and arrested. When Plessy refused, he was ejected from the train and imprisoned. He was prosecuted for violating the law, which he asserted was unconstitutional and violated the THIRTEENTH AMENDMENT to the U.S. Constitution, which abolished SLAVERY, and the FOURTEENTH AMENDMENT to the Constitution, which prohibited certain restrictive legislative acts by the states.

The Supreme Court agreed to decide the constitutionality of the law. It reasoned that, although the Thirteenth Amendment intended to abolish slavery, it was insufficient to protect the "colored" people from certain harsh state

CORBIS-BETTMANN

In Plessy v. Ferguson *(1896), the Supreme Court maintained that the Fourteenth Amendment was not intended to enforce social equality of races, a decision that stood for 58 years.*

laws that treated them unequally. The Fourteenth Amendment was enacted "to enforce the absolute equality of the two races before the law . . . (but) it could not have been intended to abolish distinctions based upon color or to enforce social as distinguished from political equality. . . . " The Court decided that the law establishing SEPARATE BUT EQUAL public accommodations and facilities was a reasonable exercise of the POLICE POWER of a state to promote the public good. "If the two races are to meet upon terms of social equality, it must be the result of voluntary consent of the individuals."

Only Justice JOHN MARSHALL HARLAN dissented, on the ground that such a law "interferes with the personal freedom of citizens" under the guise of legal equality. He maintained that the constitutional guarantees in this country were to be color-blind.

In 1954, the Supreme Court overruled this decision and recognized that separate but equal educational facilities were inherently unequal in *Brown v. Board of Education of Topeka, Kansas,* 347 U.S. 483, 74 S. Ct. 686, 98 L. Ed. 873 (1954). Subsequent Supreme Court decisions prohibited racial segregation in any public facilities and accommodations.

CROSS-REFERENCES

Brown v. Board of Education of Topeka, Kansas; Civil Rights; Civil Rights Movement; Integration; Jim Crow Laws.

PLURALITY The opinion of an APPELLATE COURT in which more justices join than in any concurring opinion.

The excess of votes cast for one candidate over those votes cast for any other candidate.

Appellate panels are made up of three or more justices. In some cases the justices disagree over the outcome of the case to such an extent that a MAJORITY opinion cannot be achieved. (A majority opinion is one in which the number of justices who join is larger than the number of justices who do not.) To resolve such disagreements and reach a final decision, two or more justices publish opinions called concurring opinions, and the other justices decide which of these concurring opinions they will join. The concurring opinion in which more justices join than any other is called a plurality opinion. Plurality decisions can reflect a disagreement among the justices over a legal issue in a case or can reveal deeper ideological differences among the members of the court. See also COURT OPINION.

The term *plurality* is also used to describe the outcome of an ELECTION that involves more than two candidates. The candidate who receives the greatest number of votes is said to have received a plurality of the votes. In contrast, the term *majority* is used to describe the outcome of an election involving only two candidates; the winner is said to have received a majority of the votes.

A candidate who has a plurality of the votes can also have a majority of the votes, but only if she receives a number of votes greater than that cast for all the other candidates combined. Mathematically, a candidate with a plurality has a majority if she receives more than one-half of the total number of votes cast. If candidate John Doe has a plurality, he has earned more votes than any other candidate, but whether he has a majority depends on how many votes he won.

POACHING The illegal shooting, trapping, or taking of game or fish from private or public property.

The poaching of game and fish was made a crime in England in the seventeenth century, as aristocratic landowners sought to preserve their shooting and PROPERTY RIGHTS. Poor peasants did most of the poaching to supplement their diets with meat and fish.

In the United States, poaching was not considered a serious problem meriting legal measures before the twentieth century, because vast expanses of undeveloped land contained abundant sources of fish and game. The increased cultivation of land and the growth of towns and cities reduced wildlife habitats in the twentieth century. In the early 1900s, the U.S. conservation movement arose with an emphasis on preserving wildlife and managing the fish and game populations. Wildlife preserves and state and national parks were created as havens for wild animals, many of which were threatened with extinction.

Because of these changing circumstances, restrictions were placed on HUNTING and fishing. State game and fish laws now require persons to purchase LICENSES to hunt and fish. The terms of these licenses limit the kind and number of animals or fish that may be taken and restrict hunting and fishing to designated times of the year, popularly referred to as hunting and fishing seasons.

Therefore, persons who fail to purchase a license, as well as those who violate the terms of their licenses, commit acts of poaching. Most poaching in the United States is done for sport or commercial profit. Rare and endangered species, which are protected by state and federal law, are often the targets of poachers.

Poaching laws are enforced by game wardens, who patrol state and national parks and respond to violations on private property. Poachers are subject to criminal laws, ranging from MISDEMEANORS to FELONIES. Penalties may include steep fines, jail sentences, the forfeiture of any poached game or fish, the loss of hunting and fishing license privileges for several years, and the FORFEITURE of hunting or fishing equipment, boats, and vehicles used in the poaching.

CROSS-REFERENCES

Endangered Species Act; Environmental Law; Fish and Fishing.

POCKET PART An addition to many lawbooks that updates them until a new edition is published.

A pocket part is located inside the back cover of the book. A legal researcher should always consult it to ensure that the most current law is examined.

POINT A distinct proposition or question of law arising or propounded in a case. In the case of shares of STOCK, a point means $1. In the case of BONDS a point means $10, since a bond is quoted as a percentage of $1,000. In the case of market averages, the word point means merely that and no more. If, for example, the Dow-Jones Industrial Average rises from 8,349.25 to 8,350.25, it has risen a point. A point in this average, however, is not equivalent to $1.

With respect to the home MORTGAGE finance industry, a fee or charge of one percent of the PRINCIPAL of the loan that is collected by the lender at the time the loan is made and is in addition to the constant long-term stated interest rate on the face of the loan.

POISON Any substance dangerous to living organisms that if applied internally or externally, destroy the action of vital functions or prevent the continuance of life.

Economic poisons are those substances that are used to control insects, weeds, fungi, bacteria, rodents, predatory animals, or other pests. Economic poisons are useful to society but are still dangerous.

The way a poison is controlled depends on its potential for harm, its usefulness, and the reasons for its use. The law has a right and a duty pursuant to the POLICE POWER of a state to control substances that can do great harm.

In the past, an individual who was harmed by a poison that had been handled in a careless manner could institute a lawsuit for DAMAGES against the person who had mishandled the chemical. As time went on, state statutes prescribed the circumstances under which someone was legally liable for injuries caused by a poison. For example, a sale to anyone under sixteen years of age was unlawful, and a seller was required to ensure that the buyer understood that the chemical was poisonous. It was not unusual for all poisons, drugs, and narcotics to be covered by the same statutory scheme.

Specialized statutes currently regulate poisons. Pesticides must be registered with the

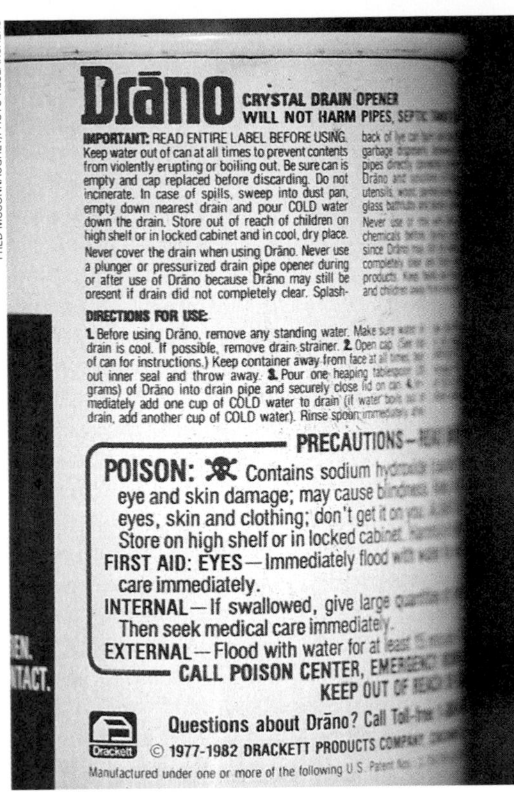

A variety of statutes regulate the labeling of poisonous substances. Household products require more detailed warnings than products intended to be handled by a specially trained person.

federal government, and those denied registration cannot be used. The ENVIRONMENTAL PROTECTION AGENCY (EPA) has issued a number of regulations governing the use of approved pesticides. Federal law also prohibits unauthorized ADULTERATION of any product with a poisonous substance and requires clear labeling for anything sold with a poisonous ingredient. It might not be sufficient to list all the chemicals in a container or even to put the word POISON on the label. The manufacturer should also warn of the injuries that are likely to occur and the conditions under which the poison will cause harm. Stricter standards are applied to household products than to poisonous products intended to be used in a factory, on a farm, or by a specially trained person. Poisonous food products are banned. Under other federal regulations, pesticide residues on foods are prohibited above certain low tolerance levels.

Certain provisions under federal law seek to protect children from poisoning. Special packaging is required for some household products so that a child will not mistake them for food or will not be able to open containers. Federal funds are available for local programs to reduce or eliminate the danger of poisoning from lead-based paint. Under the Hazardous Substances Act (15 U.S.C.A. § 1261 et seq.), toys containing poisonous substances can be banned or subjected to recall.

POISON PILL A defensive strategy based on issuing special STOCK that is used to deter aggressors in corporate TAKEOVER attempts.

The poison pill is a defensive strategy used against corporate takeovers. Popularly known as corporate raiding, takeovers are hostile mergers intended to acquire a corporation. A takeover begins when a so-called aggressor tries to buy sufficient stock in another corporation, known as the target, to seize control of it. Target CORPORATIONS use a wide range of legal options to deter takeovers, among which is the poison pill: a change in the company's stock plan or financial condition that is intended to make the corporation unattractive to the buyer. Despite its fanciful name, the poison pill does not destroy the target company. It is intended to affect the aggressor, which will be burdened with costs if it succeeds in its takeover. The strategy was widely adopted in the 1980s.

The poison pill is unique among anti-takeover strategies. At the simplest level, takeovers are about buying stock. Corporate raiders offer shareholders an inflated price for their shares. They try to buy the company for more than its stock is worth. Although this idea seems paradoxical, raiders can reap profits from their overpriced acquisition by selling off its divisions and assets. Some anti-takeover strategies try to deter the aggressor by selling off prize ASSETS first, making a counter offer to shareholders, or stipulating that the current executives will receive huge payoffs after a takeover when they are fired. These strategies can injure the company or simply benefit executives. But the poison pill involves a kind of doomsday scenario for the aggressor. If the takeover is successful, it will end up paying enormous DIVIDENDS to the company's current stockholders.

Essential to the use of such a strategy is that it is first established in the corporation's CHARTER. Among other details, these charters specify shareholders' rights. They specify that companies can issue PREFERRED STOCK—shares that give special dividends, or payments—to their holders. When a takeover bid begins, the company's BOARD OF DIRECTORS issues this preferred stock to its current shareholders. The stock is essentially worthless and is intended to scare away the aggressor. If the takeover succeeds, the stock becomes quite valuable. It can then be redeemed for a very good price or it can be converted into stock of the new controlling company—namely, the aggressor's. Both scenarios leave the aggressor with the choice of either buying the stock at a high price or paying huge dividends on it. This is the pill's poison.

Poison pill defenses are popular but somewhat controversial. The majority of large U.S. companies had adopted them by the 1990s. Part of this popularity comes from their effectiveness in delaying a corporate takeover, during which time a target company may marshal other defenses as well. Another reason is that courts have upheld their legality. One of the first important cases in this area reached the Delaware courts in 1985 (*Moran v. Household International, Inc.*, 500 A.2d 1346). However, some critics have argued that the strategy gives company directors power at the expense of shareholders. They maintain that it can limit shareholders' wealth by thwarting potentially beneficial takeovers and allowing bad corporate managers to entrench themselves. In the 1990s such arguments spurred some investors to attempt to repeal poison pill provisions in corporate charters.

See also GOLDEN PARACHUTE; MERGERS AND ACQUISITIONS.

POLICE POWER The authority conferred upon the states by the TENTH AMENDMENT to the U.S. Constitution and which the states delegate to their political subdivisions to enact measures to preserve and protect the safety, health, welfare, and morals of the community.

Police power describes the basic right of governments to make laws and regulations for the benefit of their communities. Under the system of government in the United States, only states have the right to make laws based on their police power. The lawmaking power of the federal government is limited to the specific grants of power found in the Constitution.

The right of states to make laws governing safety, health, welfare, and morals is derived from the Tenth Amendment, which states, "The powers not delegated to the United States by the Constitution, nor prohibited by it to the states, are reserved to the States respectively, or to the people." State legislatures exercise their police power by enacting statutes, and they also delegate much of their police power to counties, cities, towns, villages, and large boroughs within the state.

Police power does not specifically refer to the right of state and local government to create police forces, although the police power does include that right. Police power is also used as the basis for enacting a variety of substantive laws in such areas as ZONING, land use, fire and building codes, gambling, DISCRIMINATION, parking, crime, licensing of professionals, liquor, motor vehicles, bicycles, NUISANCES, schooling, and sanitation.

If a law enacted pursuant to the police power does not promote the health, safety, or welfare of the community, it is likely to be an unconstitutional deprivation of life, liberty, or property. The most common challenge to a statute enacted pursuant to the police power is that it constitutes a taking. A taking occurs when the government deprives a person of property or directly interferes with or substantially disturbs a person's use and enjoyment of his or her property.

The case of *Mahony v. Township of Hampton*, 539 Pa. 193, 651 A.2d 525 (1994) illustrates how a state or local JURISDICTION can exceed its police power. *Mahony* involved a zoning ORDINANCE enacted by the TOWNSHIP of Hampton in Pennsylvania. The ordinance prohibited a private party from operating a gas well in a residential district but allowed the operation of such wells by the government. Jack D. Mahony, a landowner who operated a gas well, objected to the ordinance, arguing that the disparate treatment of public and private operation of gas wells was arbitrary and not justified by any concerns related to the police power. Mahony noted that the state Department of Environmental Regulation (DER) already regulated all gas wells in the state and that there was no factual basis for distinguishing between public and private wells.

The Supreme Court of Pennsylvania agreed with Mahony that the regulation by the DER was sufficient to secure the safety of the community. The court opined that if the township wished to further ensure gas well safety, it could require the posting of a BOND with the township before granting a LICENSE to operate the well. Such a measure would ensure that the gas well was being operated by a financially secure person who would have the resources to keep the well in good repair. The court held that the total ban on private operation of gas wells in residential districts was unreasonable and that it bore no real and substantial relation to the health, safety, and welfare of the community. Therefore, the ordinance was an invalid exercise of the police power.

CROSS-REFERENCES

Eminent Domain; Land-Use Control; States' Rights.

POLICY The general principles by which a government is guided in its management of public affairs, or the legislature in its measures. A general term used to describe all CONTRACTS of INSURANCE.

As applied to a law, ordinance, or rule of law, the general purpose or tendency considered as directed to the welfare or prosperity of the state or community.

POLITICAL CAMPAIGNS See DEMOCRATIC PARTY; ELECTION CAMPAIGN FINANCING; ELECTIONS; REPUBLICAN PARTY.

MARK GODFREY/THE IMAGE WORKS

Richard Nixon's counsel argued that the president's refusal to comply with subpoenas of White House tapes was a political question because it was a dispute among members of the executive branch, namely the president and the special prosecutor. The Supreme Court compelled Nixon to produce the tapes and he resigned shortly thereafter.

POLITICAL CRIME A serious violation of law that threatens the security or existence of the government, such as TREASON or SEDITION.

POLITICAL QUESTION An issue that the FEDERAL COURTS refuse to decide because it properly belongs to the decision-making authority of elected officials.

Political questions include such areas as the conduct of foreign policy, the RATIFICATION of CONSTITUTIONAL AMENDMENTS, and the organization of each state's government as defined in its own constitution. The rule preventing federal courts from deciding such cases is called the political question doctrine. Its purpose is to distinguish the role of the federal judiciary from those of the legislature and the executive, preventing the former from encroaching on either of the latter. Under the rule, courts may choose to dismiss cases even if they have JURISDICTION over them. However, the rule has no precise formulation, and its development since the 1960s has sometimes been unpredictable.

The Supreme Court originated the idea of political questions in the early 1800s during its formative era. As with other judicial doctrines created by the Court, the rule is interpretive and self-imposed. It is neither a result of legislation nor a part of the U.S. Constitution, although it appears to emanate from the Constitution's SEPARATION OF POWERS. The Court created the political question doctrine as part of the broader concept of justiciability—the issue of whether a matter is appropriate for court review. Appropriate matters are called JUSTICIABLE controversies and may proceed to court. Political questions are not regarded as appropriate matters; they are not justiciable and, generally, will be dismissed. The political question doctrine will not be applied to every matter that arouses fierce public debate, as seen in the Court's rulings on ABORTION and AFFIRMATIVE ACTION. As the history of the Supreme Court shows, the determination of whether an issue is justiciable is at its own discretion.

Chief Justice JOHN MARSHALL first used the term political question in 1803 at a time when the Court sought to tread delicately between warring factions of politicians in Washington. Not until 1849 was the idea elaborated, in response to a crisis in the state of Rhode Island known as the Dorr Rebellion: a political uprising had resulted in the passage of two separate state constitutions, the declaration of MARTIAL LAW, and the promise of military intervention by President JOHN TYLER. The Supreme Court was asked to settle critical constitutional questions about the nature of republican government but refused (*Luther v. Borden*, 48 U.S. [7 How.] 1, 12 L. Ed. 581 [1849]). Chief Justice ROGER TANEY instead delivered the first articulation of the doctrine: federal courts should leave certain constitutional questions to the legislative and executive branches in any matter that is "a political question to be settled by the political power."

From the mid-nineteenth century until the 1960s, the political question doctrine changed very little. Then the Supreme Court began to narrow it: where previously a broad rule applied, now matters that would have been rejected as political questions became justiciable controversies. In a landmark case in 1962, the Court intervened to allow a challenge to the way in which the Tennessee legislature apportioned its voting districts (*Baker v. Carr*, 369 U.S. 186, 82 S. Ct. 691, 7 L. Ed. 2d 663). Again, in 1969, the Court took up a matter that previously would have been dismissed. This was its decision that the HOUSE OF REPRESENTATIVES could not exclude a duly elected member who met all constitutional qualifications, despite the provision in Article I of the Constitution that gives both houses of Congress the power to judge qualifications (*Powell v. McCormack*, 395 U.S. 486, 89 S. Ct. 1944, 23 L. Ed. 2d 491).

These cases cast doubt on the future of the doctrine. In 1974, the Court added further uncertainty when it ruled against President RICHARD M. NIXON's claim of EXECUTIVE PRIVILEGE in the WATERGATE scandal (*United States v. Nixon*, 418 U.S. 683, 94 S. Ct. 3090, 41 L. Ed. 2d 1039). It is well settled that the federal courts cannot supervise or control the decisions of the president or other executive official. President Nixon had relied on this fact when he defied congressional SUBPOENAS asking him to release tapes and documents made in the White House. However, the Court chose not to rigidly adhere to the rule: it held that the demands of a fair trial and criminal justice outweighed the president's claim.

CROSS-REFERENCES

Apportionment; *Baker v. Carr;* Dorr, Thomas Wilson; Judicial Review; *United States v. Nixon;* Warren Court.

POLITICAL TRIAL A trial that addresses POLITICAL QUESTIONS, involves political officials, or serves political agendas. In certain circumstances the term is used in a pejorative sense to criticize a particular trial or proceeding as unfair or unjust.

Although it is sometimes difficult to distinguish political trials from ordinary legal proceedings, political trials generally fall into one of four categories. The most familiar type of political trial is a partisan trial, which consists of criminal legal proceedings instituted by the government to solidify its power, extinguish its opposition, or flex its muscle. Such political trials, while taking place in a courtroom, have little to do with justice. Instead, partisan trials serve to promote the ideology of those holding the reins of power.

In many countries partisan trials are easy to identify because the prosecutors, judges, and defense attorneys are chosen by the government based on their allegiance to the regime's political philosophy. In other countries the government may exert subtle pressure upon judges and attorneys to influence the outcome of a case. In either situation such proceedings rarely produce a result that is fair or impartial. Some of the most notorious partisan trials took place in ADOLF HITLER's Germany and JOSEPH STALIN's Soviet Union where many of the judges, prosecutors, and defense attorneys served as instruments of terror and propaganda for their totalitarian leaders.

A second familiar type of political trial involves the prosecution of religious and political dissenters. Since time immemorial, governments have been confronted by persons who disobey the law for reasons of conscience. Such disobedience, which can take the form of active or passive resistance, presents a dilemma for most governments.

On the one hand, governments must prosecute persons who disobey the law to maintain the integrity of the legal system. Yet if the prosecution takes place in a PUBLIC FORUM, a political or religious dissenter is likely to question the propriety of a particular law or policy and challenge the legitimacy or competency of the existing government. On the other hand, if the government covertly silences a dissenter in private, the legal system exposes itself to charges of persecution, which compromises the public's respect for the law.

By prosecuting dissenters in open court before an impartial judge and an unbiased jury, the U.S. legal system attempts to strike a balance between the competing interests of the government and dissenters. Historically, many regimes have been unable to achieve this delicate balance. In ancient Greece five hundred Athenian jurors made a martyr out of Socrates when they sentenced him to death for corrupting the youth and criticizing government officials. Roman Governor Pontius Pilate sparked concerted religious opposition to his government by condemning Jesus of Nazareth for blasphemously claiming to be the Son of God and King of the Jews. In 1735 British authorities planted the seeds of rebellion in the American colonies when they unsuccessfully prosecuted journalist JOHN PETER ZENGER for seditious libel.

A third common type of political trial involves nationalists who challenge a government's authority to represent them. Nationalists speak for an identifiable group of people who share a common characteristic, such as race, religion, or ethnicity. Trials of nationalists call into question both the unity of society and the capacity of a regime to speak for the people. Governments prosecute nationalists in part to publicly affirm their ability and resolve to govern the populace. Faced with certain defeat in the short run, many nationalists still present a vigorous defense to raise political awareness and record their battle for posterity.

The 1922 trial of Mohandas K. Gandhi, for example, served as a lightening rod of nationalism in India by uniting opposition against the oppressive imperial government of Great Britain. The treason trials of Nelson Mandela in Pretoria, which took place in the late 1950s and early 1960s, similarly raised the consciousness of blacks in South Africa and focused the world's attention on the apartheid system of government. In both cases, though the nationalists were temporarily silenced by the regimes they opposed, their causes ultimately prevailed as their people were given an equal voice in the affairs of government.

The fourth type of political trial involves the trial of entire regimes, or the leading members of a particular government. When governments are overthrown by a coup or revolution, the new regime must decide how to treat members of the old regime. In some instances members of the old regime are granted CLEMENCY, and efforts are made to assimilate them into society. In other instances members of the old regime are not only expelled from office but banished from the country and deprived of their citizenship. However, in a great number of cases the old regime is put on trial by the new regime and prosecuted for every transgression, great and small.

These trials can serve at least two purposes. First, they can highlight the malignant qualities of the demised regime. Second, they can underscore the virtue of the new regime by tempering the vengeful calls for summary executions that regularly follow the cessation of hostilities in a revolution, civil war, or other type of military conflict. The Nuremberg war crimes trials, in which twenty-four of the top Nazis were tried by the Allied powers following World War II, provides a recent example where members of a vilified regime were afforded a full assortment of legal protections despite demands for summary execution.

In a limited sense all trials have a political element. As one of the three branches of government, the judiciary is an inherent part of the political system. Additionally, all trials carry with them tangible political ramifications by delineating the rights and responsibilities of civil and criminal litigants. Because many judicial decisions are considered PRECEDENT, the legal principles established in one case may be applied to other members of society in a subsequent analogous case.

However, in the United States the term *political trial* has acquired a broader meaning. A trial is generally characterized as political when it presents a question that transcends the narrow issue of guilt or innocence by implicating larger societal, cultural, or international considerations. The WATERGATE trials of the mid-1970s, for example, focused on the legal issues of breaking and entering, CONSPIRACY, and obstruction of justice. However, these trials also dramatized the fall of a president and the consequences of abusing power.

Political trials often present basic dilemmas that engage the public in a common dialogue. These trials may prompt society to examine and even reconsider its fundamental values. Certain political trials, such as the Nuremberg and Watergate trials, have helped define an era or a nation.

CROSS-REFERENCES

Black Panther Party; Chicago Eight; Civil Rights Movement; Cleaver, Eldridge; Communism; Davis, Angela Yvonne; King, Martin Luther, Jr.; Nuremberg Trials; Pacifism; Thoreau, Henry David; Tokyo Trials.

James Knox Polk

POLK, JAMES KNOX James Knox Polk, eleventh president of the United States, served just one term in office, but in that time he was extremely influential in shaping the United States' evolution into a large and politically formidable nation. Polk's primary achievements came in the area of foreign affairs, where he completed the annexation of Texas; directed the

JAMES KNOX POLK 1795–1849

1775–83 American Revolution
1795 Born, Mecklenburg County, N.C.
1812–14 War of 1812
1818 Graduated from University of North Carolina
1823 Elected to Tenn. legislature
1825 Elected to U.S. House
1836 Republic of Texas declared independence from Mexico
1939–41 Served as governor of Tenn.
1945 Texas admitted as 28th state of the Union
1946 Treaty with Great Britain set boundary of Oregon Territory at 49th parallel
1945–49 Served as 11th president
1946–48 Mexican War
1848 Peace treaty with Mexico ceded Mexican claims to territories from Texas to California; U.S. paid Mexico $15 million
1849 Died, Nashville, Tenn.

1775 1800 1825 1850

Mexican War (1846–48); and negotiated with Great Britain for the acquisition of the Oregon territory. In domestic policy, Polk was a strong advocate for lowering TARIFFS and establishing an independent treasury for the United States. Historians and presidential scholars consistently rate Polk among the most effective and important presidents of the United States.

James Polk was born on November 2, 1795, in Mecklenburg County, North Carolina. He graduated from the University of North Carolina at Chapel Hill and went on to study law, establishing a successful practice in Columbia, Tennessee.

Polk soon embarked on a political career, being elected to the Tennessee legislature in 1823 and the U.S. House of Representatives in 1825. In Congress, Polk fought to defend individual freedoms, the rights of the states against the centralizing tendencies of the national government, and a strict interpretation of the Constitution. In 1839 Polk was elected governor of Tennessee. However, his two-year term in office was undistinguished, and he was defeated in the 1841 and 1843 gubernatorial races.

After his second defeat, Polk's political career appeared to be over, but events took a surprising turn. MARTIN VAN BUREN, who had served as ANDREW JACKSON's vice president from 1833 to 1837 and as president from 1837 to 1841, was expected to be the Democratic party's presidential nominee for the 1844 election, but Van Buren's candidacy was derailed when he announced in April 1844 that he was opposed to the annexation of Texas on the grounds that it would constitute aggression against Mexico. Van Buren's support immediately eroded, because the annexation of Texas was a controversial political item widely supported by Andrew Jackson and his followers. By the time the Democrats held their nominating convention in late May, the party was in turmoil. Van Buren's supporters failed to generate the support needed for their candidate and Polk was nominated to be the presidential candidate instead.

The Whig presidential candidate in 1844 was the powerful and influential HENRY CLAY of Kentucky, who had held important positions in both the House and the Senate in addition to serving as secretary of state under JOHN QUINCY ADAMS. The campaign was hard fought and bitter. Polk eventually won with 170 electoral votes compared with Clay's 105; in the popular vote, Polk received just 38,000 more votes than Clay, out of the almost 2,700,000 votes cast.

"THE PEOPLE OF THIS CONTINENT ALONE HAVE THE RIGHT TO DECIDE THEIR OWN DESTINY."

The Polk administration added approximately 1.2 million square miles to the United States, increasing its size by fifty percent. The addition resulted from the three major foreign policy matters Polk oversaw: the annexation of Texas, the Mexican War, and negotiations with Great Britain over the Oregon territory.

Polk inherited the Texas issue from the administration of JOHN TYLER. Tyler had wrestled with Congress over methods for annexing Texas, which had existed as the independent Lone Star Republic since winning its independence from Mexico in 1836. Tyler and Congress had agreed that Texas would be given the opportunity to vote for annexation, and Polk continued this approach. The Texas congress eventually approved annexation and wrote a state constitution, which the voters approved in a general REFERENDUM. In December 1845 the U.S. Congress completed the transaction by admitting Texas as the twenty-eighth state.

The annexation led to territorial disputes that resulted in war between the United States and Mexico. For several years relations between the United States and Mexico had been rocky, primarily because the United States had made financial claims against the Mexican government. Since winning its independence from Spain in the early 1820s, Mexico had had a series of unstable governments, and foreign nationals often had lost property during the resulting revolutions. Those individuals and their governments lodged claims against the Mexican government, and by the mid-1840s, these claims amounted to millions of dollars. This dispute over claims had soured relations between the United States and Mexico, and the annexation of Texas brought matters to a crisis. As part of the annexation agreement, the United States government had consented to recognize Texas's claim to the Rio Grande boundary and to provide military protection to defend that boundary. For its part, Mexico had never given up hope of winning back Texas, and the United States' annexation, together with the assertion of the Rio Grande boundary, the placement of U.S. troops along the border, and the longstanding claims disagreement, led Mexico to break off diplomatic relations with Washington and accuse the United States of initiating war.

In response, Polk sent a representative to negotiate with the Mexican government, offering to buy California and New Mexico and relinquish U.S. claims against Mexico in return for a recognition of the Rio Grande boundary. The Mexican government refused to negotiate, and by spring of 1846, skirmishes were beginning to break out along the border. Polk requested that Congress declare war, which it did by an overwhelming margin. Though the United States lacked a powerful professional army, volunteers signed up in droves. The war lasted until September 1847, when the Mexican government agreed to enter into peace negotiations. In the resulting agreement, the Treaty of Guadalupe Hidalgo, Mexico agreed to recognize the Rio Grande as the boundary of Texas and to cede New Mexico and upper California to the United States; for its part, the United States agreed to relinquish all claims against Mexico and to pay the Mexican government $15 million.

The third major foreign policy issue requiring Polk's attention was the dispute between the United States and Great Britain over the Oregon territory, which stretched from the northern boundary of California to the Alaska panhandle, including what is now Oregon, Washington, and British Columbia. Both countries claimed the area but had agreed in 1818 to occupy it jointly, with the provision that either party could terminate the agreement with a year's notice. The United States had repeatedly requested to resolve the issue by extending the forty-ninth parallel boundary that existed between the two countries east of the Rocky Mountains, but Britain had refused, insisting on the Columbia River as the boundary.

The situation had remained unresolved, and British fur traders had continued to dominate the area into the 1830s. At that time, however, increasing numbers of U.S. settlers migrated into Oregon and pressed the United States to address their needs and defend their interests. After the 1844 presidential election, the issue became heated. As U.S. statements on the issue became more angry and aggressive, the British government grew concerned that war might break out, and it entered into earnest negotiations with the United States. In July 1845 Polk once again offered to draw the boundary at the forty-ninth parallel, but the British minister in Washington rejected the offer. Furious, Polk withdrew the offer, instead reasserting the U.S. claim to the entire territory.

In his first message to Congress in December 1845, Polk continued this hard line on Oregon, asking Congress to provide the one year's notice that the United States was terminating its joint occupancy agreement with Great Britain. In addition, he asked that jurisdiction be extended to Americans living in Oregon and that military protection be provided to emigrants along the route to Oregon. Finally, Polk reasserted the MONROE DOCTRINE, which held that North America was not open to any further colonization by European powers.

Polk's tough stance apparently spurred Great Britain to renew negotiations, and this time it agreed to the forty-ninth parallel boundary. The treaty was signed on June 15, 1846.

A principal goal of Polk's domestic agenda was to eliminate the high tariffs that had been imposed in 1842 under the Tyler administration. Polk believed that low tariffs were crucial for the success of the agricultural sector, and after strong and sustained lobbying, he was able to persuade Congress to reduce tariffs in July 1846.

A second focus of Polk's domestic efforts was the establishment of an independent treasury for the United States. Previously, the government's funds had been held in national banks or in various state banks, but Polk argued that the government's money should not be deposited in banks at all, but should be held in its own independent treasury.

Despite Polk's many successes, presidential scholars agree that he utterly failed in his ability to foresee the catastrophic consequences that the SLAVERY issue would have for the nation. A slaveholder with plantations in Tennessee and Mississippi, Polk never actively defended slavery, but he failed to see the importance that it would have, instead believing that it was an aggravating side issue that hampered the resolution of more important problems.

Polk left office when his term ended in 1849, remaining faithful to his election promise that he would serve only one term as president. Polk returned to Tennessee exhausted and in ill health. Just three months after leaving office, Polk died unexpectedly on June 15, 1849. He was fifty-four years old.

BIOGRAPHY

APWIDE WORLD PHOTOS

Milton Pollack

POLLACK, MILTON Two of the nation's great financial crises form the bookends of Milton Pollack's legal career. Pollack began his first phase of that career, as a SECURITIES lawyer, just two weeks before the 1929 stock market crash. Sixty years later, as a federal district court judge, he used his knowledge and experience to resolve a multibillion-dollar disaster left when Drexel Burnham Lambert, a powerful Wall Street investment bank, collapsed into BANKRUPTCY. The lawsuits related to Drexel were expected to drag on for decades, but under Pollack's guidance, they were resolved and completed in just over three years. Pollack considers the Drexel CLASS ACTION suit (*In re Drexel*, 960 F. 2d 285 [2d Cir. 1992]) and the resulting bankruptcy reorganization to be his "lifetime masterpieces."

Pollack was born September 29, 1906, in New York City. He attended Erasmus High School, and then Columbia College and Law

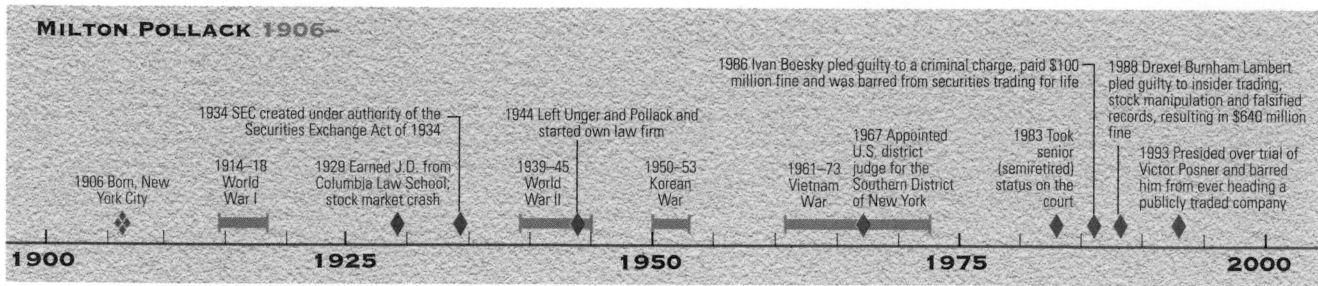

School, where he received a bachelor of arts degree in 1927 and a doctor of jurisprudence degree in 1929. He was admitted to the New York bar in 1930. Pollack married Lillian Klein on December 18, 1932.

After graduation Pollack joined the law firm of Gilman and Unger. By 1937, Gilman and Unger had become Unger and Pollack, and by 1943, Pollack had proved himself to be a force in both the legal and financial communities by winning a $4.5 million shareholder lawsuit against General Motors Corporation (*Singer v. General Motors Corp.*, 136 F. 2d 905 [2d Cir. 1943]).

In 1944 Pollack set out on his own, opening his doors as Milton Pollack. Over the next two decades, he established himself as an outstanding litigator.

On June 12, 1967, after almost forty years as a practicing attorney, Pollack was appointed U.S. district judge for the Southern District of New York by President LYNDON B. JOHNSON. Pollack authored more than 150 opinions related to securities regulation matters and opinions on many other issues.

In 1983 Pollack took senior (or semiretired) status. As a senior judge, he played a prominent role in major Wall Street disputes in the late 1980s and early 1990s, including the trials of JUNK-BOND salesmen Michael R. Milken and Ivan F. Boesky. When the Drexel bankruptcy occurred, Pollack's lifelong experience made him the logical choice to handle the resulting avalanche of complaints and actions. See also BONDS.

In 1989 Pollack approved a settlement that gave control over Drexel's continued operation to high-level SEC officials. The settlement required Drexel to cooperate in the government's investigation of former employees and to cut all ties with former Drexel executive Milken. In 1991 Pollack authorized the payment of $46.8 million to eighty thousand persons claiming losses from Boeksy's INSIDER trading and securities fraud. That same year, Pollack approved the settlement of a class action suit by Drexel creditors who had been defrauded by the firm's securities transactions.

"IN THE DAYS BEFORE THE FEDERAL RULES OF CIVIL PROCEDURE, TRIAL BY AMBUSH AND SECRECY WAS CONSIDERED NORMAL IN THE COURTS OF LAW."

Pollack also handled the 1993 trial of corporate raider Victor Posner. Because Posner had conducted illegal takeovers and had had previous criminal dealings with Milken and Boesky, Pollack barred him from ever again heading a publicly traded company. Pollack's order marked the first time a court used a 1990 law to prevent individuals from becoming directors or officers of publicly traded companies (*S.E.C. v. Drexel Burnham Lambert, Inc.*, 837 F. Supp. 587 [S.D.N.Y. 1993]).

As a senior judge, Pollack has been acknowledged as a troubleshooter who is quick to help fellow judges who have fallen behind in their work and to advise younger judges on how to handle courtroom problems. In addition to a full schedule in the Southern District of New York, Pollack also hears cases in Houston, Texas, during part of the year.

Over the course of his career, Pollack has lectured on securities law at Columbia Law School and Cornell Law School. He and his second wife, Moselle Baum Erlich Pollack, reside in New York City.

BIOGRAPHY

Walter Heilprin Pollak

POLLAK, WALTER HEILPRIN Walter Heilprin Pollak was a lawyer and civil libertarian who is credited with convincing the U.S. Supreme Court to first adopt the INCORPORATION DOCTRINE, which the Court has used to extend most of the provisions of the Bill of Rights to limit actions by state and local governments. Pollak is also remembered for his arguments for the defense in *Powell v. Alabama*, 287 U.S. 45, 53 S. Ct. 55, 77 L. Ed. 158 (1932), which extended the RIGHT TO COUNSEL in death penalty cases to state criminal trials.

Pollak was born on June 4, 1887, in Summit, New Jersey. He graduated from Harvard University in 1907 and from Harvard Law School in 1910. He joined the prominent New York City law firm of Sullivan and Cromwell, but in 1912 he left for the smaller firm of Simpson, Warren, and Cardozo. Pollak worked with BENJAMIN N. CARDOZO before Cardozo left in 1914 to become a New York Court of Appeals judge. Following Cardozo's departure and the retirement of another partner, Pollak became partner in the firm of Englehard and Pollak.

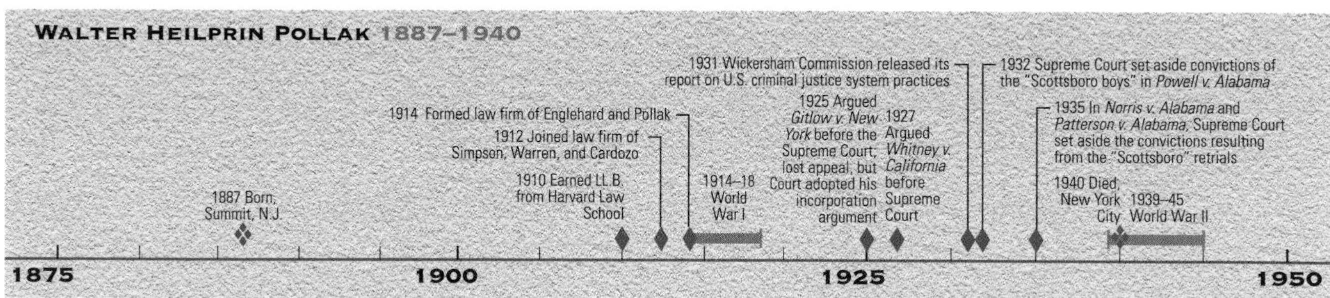

Pollak was an ardent supporter of FREEDOM OF SPEECH and the Bill of Rights. He appealed to the U.S. Supreme Court Benjamin Gitlow's conviction under New York's Criminal Anarchy Act (N.Y. Penal Law §§ 160–161 [repealed 1967]) for "advocacy of criminal anarchy," which was defined as the advocacy of "the duty, necessity or propriety of overthrowing or overturning organized government by force or violence" (*Gitlow v. New York*, 268 U.S. 652, 45 S. Ct. 625, 69 L. Ed. 1138 [1925]). Gitlow was convicted and sentenced to a prison term of five to ten years for distributing a left-wing pamphlet.

Pollak argued that the First Amendment's guarantees of freedom of speech and FREEDOM OF THE PRESS were applicable to the states because the Due Process Clause of the FOURTEENTH AMENDMENT protects "liberty" from abridgement by the states. By incorporating the FIRST AMENDMENT provisions into the Fourteenth Amendment, states could not restrain the free speech rights of persons such as Gitlow.

Though the Court did not agree with Pollak that the New York law was unconstitutional, it did adopt his incorporation argument, holding that freedom of speech and the press "are among the most fundamental personal rights and 'liberties' protected by the due process clause of the Fourteenth Amendment from impairment by the States."

In *Powell v. Alabama*, Pollak returned to the Supreme Court to argue on behalf of the "Scottsboro boys," a group of young African Americans sentenced to death for an alleged sexual assault on two white women. The defendants had not been provided effective legal counsel, and the trial had been a sham, evoking a public outcry in the North. Pollak convinced the Court that the defendants had been denied DUE PROCESS OF LAW in violation of the Fourteenth Amendment.

Pollak also served on the staff of the National Commission of Law Observance and Law Enforcement, which came to be known as the Wickersham Commission. In 1931 the commission issued its fourteen-volume report, which revealed disturbing features of the U.S. criminal justice system. It brought to public attention the use of "third-degree" interrogation methods against criminal suspects and the need for more professional police forces. Pollak helped write the report on the third degree and a staff report that demonstrated that prosecutors in a particular case had condoned and probably encouraged the giving of false testimony in convicting the defendant. The Supreme Court later agreed with Pollak's conclusion on this case. In *Mooney v. Holohan*, 294 U.S. 103, 55 S. Ct. 340, 79 L. Ed. 791 (1935), the Court ruled that a state has denied due process if it deceives the trial judge and jury by presenting evidence known to be perjured.

"MAN IS A FREE AGENT TO USE HIS TONGUE AND PEN, AS HE MAY USE HIS BRAIN AND BODY GENERALLY, FOR HIS OWN BENEFIT OR HARM IN THE CONDUCT OF HIS PRIVATE AFFAIRS."

Pollak died on October 2, 1940, in New York City.

See also GITLOW V. NEW YORK; POWELL V. ALABAMA.

POLLING THE JURY 📖 A practice whereby the jurors are asked individually whether they assented, and still assent, to the VERDICT; it consists of calling the name of each juror and requiring a declaration of his or her verdict before it is recorded. 📖

Polling can be accomplished by questioning the jurors individually or by ascertaining the fact of unanimous concurrence by general questions. Once concurrence has been determined, the polling concludes.

If unanimous concurrence, when required, does not exist upon the poll, the JURY can be either discharged or ordered to resume further deliberation.

BIOGRAPHY

POLLOCK, FREDERICK As a legal scholar and historian, Sir Frederick Pollock was a leading figure in the modernization of English legal studies in the nineteenth century. Born in London on December 10, 1845, Pollock was educated at Trinity College, Cambridge, admitted to the bar in 1871, and soon rose to eminence in his field as an author of groundbreaking histories and textbooks. He taught law in his native England and lectured briefly in the United States in 1903 and 1912. Besides his public contributions to legal scholarship, Pollock is remembered for his decades-long private correspondence with U.S. Supreme Court jus-

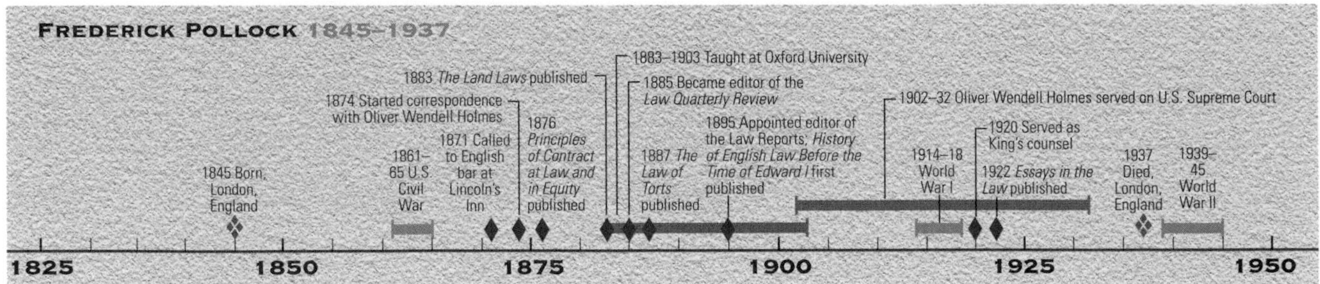

tice Oliver Wendell Holmes, Jr., which was published posthumously.

Beginning in the 1870s, Pollock wrote a series of books that marked a turning point in English legal scholarship. His approach was different from that of his predecessors, who had built their work on specific applications of the law. Pollock emphasized the law's underlying principles. Written in a direct, clear style, works such as *Principles of Contract at Law and in Equity* (1876) and a companion work *The Law of Torts* (1887) became the standard legal texts for many years; more importantly, they served as models for other textbooks and thus helped to modernize English legal education.

Pollock possessed enormous talent and energy for scholarly work. In 1883 he began teaching at Oxford University as a professor of jurisprudence. That same year he published his classic work, *The Land Laws*, and two years later he became the first editor of the *Law Quarterly Review*. Over the next three decades, he published a number of books, including *Spinoza, His Life and Philosophy* (1880); *Possession in the Common Law* (with Robert S. Wright) (1888); *A First Book of Jurisprudence* (1896); *The Expansion of the Common Law* (1904); *The Genius of the Common Law* (1912) and *The League of Nations* (1920). Many of his books were reprinted several times, and his *History of English Law Before the Time of Edward I* (with Frederic W. Maitland) (1895; rev. ed. 1898) is still often cited by legal scholars.

Contemporary law interested Pollock as much as legal history, and he played an important role in reforming the English legal system. He immersed himself in public service, variously holding positions as a member of the Privy Council, judge of the Admiralty Court of the Cinque Ports, King's Counsel, and chairman of the Royal Commission on the Public Records. In 1895 he was appointed editor of the Law Reports, charged with overseeing the production of reports on judicial opinions, and remained in that position for forty years. Such was his stature in the legal profession that even judges deferred to him.

"[THE COURTS] MAY SUPPLEMENT AND ENLARGE THE LAW AS THEY FIND IT, OR RATHER THEY MUST DO SO FROM TIME TO TIME, AS THE NOVELTY OF QUESTIONS COMING BEFORE THEM MAY REQUIRE; BUT THEY MUST NOT REVERSE WHAT HAS BEEN SETTLED."

Among Pollock's many admirers was his friend, Justice Holmes. The British law professor and the U.S. Supreme Court justice carried on a correspondence for sixty years. The letters contain discussions of the legal issues of the day, descriptions of their lives, and, at least by Holmes, mischievous portraits of their contemporaries. Each man admired the other's national legal system and his thinking: Pollock apparently borrowed ideas from Holmes for the first clear formulation of the doctrine of relative title—a concept related to ownership—in the 1880s. The correspondence was published as *The Holmes-Pollock Letters, 1874–1932* (1961). Pollock died in London on January 18, 1937.

POLLOCK v. FARMERS' LOAN & TRUST CO. A 5–4 decision of the Supreme Court, *Pollock v. Farmers' Loan & Trust Co.*, 157 U.S. 429, 15 S.Ct. 673, 39 L.Ed 759, *on rehearing*, 158 U.S. 601, 15 S. Ct. 912, 39 L. Ed. 1108 (1895), declared the Income Tax Act of 1894 unconstitutional and ultimately led to the enactment of the Sixteenth Amendment, authorizing the imposition of an income tax by the federal government.

Charles Pollock—a Massachusetts stockholder employed by the New York defendant, Farmers' Loan & Trust Co.—appealed to the U.S. Supreme Court after unsuccessfully suing the defendant in federal courts to prevent it from breaching its fiduciary duty by filing returns for and paying a federal income tax. The tax was levied upon the profits that the defendant earned, including interest it received from income-producing real estate and bonds of New York City. Pollock alleged that such a tax, authorized by the Income Tax Act of 1894, was unconstitutional because it was a direct tax upon the property itself (28 Stat. 509). Article I, Section 2, of the U.S. Constitution mandated that all direct taxes be apportioned among the several states and Section 8 of the same article required that direct taxes be uniform. Pollock argued and the Supreme Court agreed that this tax did not satisfy either requirement. The tax was levied upon the rents or income of real property held by particular corporations and

JIM WEST/IMPACT VISUALS

Workers install pollution control equipment at the city of Detroit's waste incinerator. About 16 percent of the solid waste generated in the United States is incinerated; most is buried in landfills.

businesses and was, in effect, a direct tax upon the real property itself.

Pollock also raised the issue as to the validity of the tax as levied upon New York City bonds. The Court accepted the reasoning that since states were powerless to tax the operations or property of the United States, the United States had no constitutional power to tax either state instrumentalities or property.

The Supreme Court ruled that the Income Tax Act of 1894 violated the Constitution and that the taxes imposed pursuant to it were void. It reversed the decree of the federal circuit court and remanded the case.

As a result of the decision in *Pollock v. Farmers' Loan & Trust Co.*, Congress recognized the need for a constitutional provision permitting the levy of federal income tax without apportionment among the several states. It took, however, eighteen more years before there was sufficient support for the passage of the Sixteenth Amendment.

POLLS The place where voters cast their ballots. Heads; individuals; persons singly considered.

An objection to a particular juror is called a *challenge to the poll*, as distinguished from a *challenge to the array or panel*, which is opposition to the JURY as an entity, based on a universal defect among the jurors.

POLL TAX A specified sum of money levied upon each person who votes.

Poll taxes, as a prerequisite to voting in federal ELECTIONS, are prohibited by the TWENTY-FOURTH AMENDMENT to the U.S. Constitution and have been held unconstitutional with respect to state elections.

POLLUTION The contamination of the air, water, or earth by harmful or potentially harmful substances.

The U.S. environmental movement in the 1960s emerged from concerns that air, water, and soil were being polluted by harmful chemicals and other toxic substances. During the industrial revolution of the nineteenth century, the mass production of goods created harmful wastes, much of which was dumped into rivers and streams. The twentieth century saw the popular acceptance of the AUTOMOBILE and the internal combustion engine, which led to the pollution of the air. Rapidly expanding urban centers began to use rivers and lakes as repositories for sewage.

Land pollution involves the depositing of solid wastes that are useless, unwanted, or hazardous. Types of solid waste include garbage, rubbish, ashes, sewage-treatment solids, industrial wastes, mining wastes, and agricultural wastes. Most solid waste is buried in sanitary landfills. A small percentage of municipalities incinerate their refuse, while composting is rarely employed.

Modern landfills attempt to minimize pollution of surface and groundwater. They are now located in areas that will not flood and that have the proper type of soil. Solid wastes are compacted in the landfill and are vented to eliminate the buildup of dangerous gases. Hazardous wastes, including toxic chemicals and flammable, radioactive, or biological substances, cannot be deposited in landfills, and the management of these wastes is subject to federal and state regulation. The federal government's Resource Conservation and Recovery Act (42 U.S.C.A. § 6901 et seq.) is a comprehensive regulatory statute that creates a "cradle to grave" system of controlling the entire hazardous waste life cycle.

Nuclear wastes are especially troublesome. Congress passed the Nuclear Waste Policy Act of 1982 (42 U.S.C.A. §§ 10101–226), which directed the Department of Energy to formally begin planning the disposal of nuclear wastes and imposed most of the costs of disposal on the NUCLEAR POWER industry. Since 1986 the Department of Energy has been unsuccessful in finding an acceptable site. Yucca Mountain, Nevada, is the only place earmarked for a site study.

Solid waste pollution has been reduced by recovering resources rather than burying them. Resource recovery includes massive systems that burn waste to produce steam, but it also includes the recycling of glass, metal, and paper from individual consumers and businesses. The elimination of these kinds of materials from landfills has prevented pollution and extended the period during which landfills can receive waste.

Land pollution also involves the accumulation of chemicals in the ground. Modern agriculture, which has grown dependent on chemical fertilizers and chemicals that kill insects, has introduced substances into the soil that kill more than pests. For many years the chemical DDT was routinely sprayed on crops to control pests. It was banned when scientists discovered that the chemical entered the food chain and was harming wildlife and possibly humans.

AIR POLLUTION is regulated by the federal government. The Clean Air Act was originally enacted in 1970 and was extensively amended in 1977 and again in 1990 (42 U.S.C.A. §§ 7401–7626; Pub. L. No. 95-95 [1977 amendments]; Pub. L. No. 101-549 [1990 amendments]). Under its provisions, every stationary and mobile pollution source must comply with emission standards as a means of cleaning up the ambient air quality in the area. This has meant that automobile emission control systems have been created and improved to meet more stringent air quality standards. Coal-burning electric power plants have been required to install filtration systems on their smokestacks, and manufacturing facilities have had to install equipment that "scrubs" polluted air clean.

WATER POLLUTION has existed longer than any other type of pollution. Depositing liquid and solid wastes in rivers, streams, lakes, and oceans was convenient and inexpensive for a company or municipality, but it eventually destroyed the ecosystems found in the water. Many large rivers became nothing more than sewers. Most troubling was the polluting of groundwater, creating serious health hazards for those people who drank water containing toxic substances.

The federal Clean Water Act (CWA) was originally enacted in 1972 and then amended in 1977 and 1987 (33 U.S.C.A. §§ 1251–1387; Pub. L. No. 95-217 [1977 amendments]; Pub. L. No. 100-4 [1987 amendments]). The CWA seeks to eliminate the "discharge of pollutants into navigable waters," to make water safe for people to fish and swim in, and to end the "discharges of toxic pollutants in toxic amounts." The CWA seeks to accomplish these goals through a variety of regulatory strategies.

CROSS-REFERENCES

Environmental Law; Environmental Protection Agency; Land-Use Control; Solid Wastes, Hazardous Substances, and Toxic Pollutants.

POLYGAMY The offense of having more than one wife or husband at the same time.

In every state the law allows a man or a woman to be married to only one person of the opposite sex at a time. The crime of having more than one current spouse is called polygamy. Under the law there is no difference between BIGAMY (having two spouses) and polygamy (having more than one spouse). States base their laws on the Model Penal Code § 230.1, which states that a person is guilty of the third-degree FELONY of polygamy if he or she "marries or cohabits with more than one spouse at a time in purported exercise of the right of plural marriage." The offense continues until all COHABITATION with and claim of marriage to more than one spouse terminate. Polygamy laws do not apply to ALIENS who are temporarily visiting the United States, provided that polygamy is lawful in their country of origin.

The ban on polygamy originated in English COMMON LAW. In England polygamy was repudiated because it deviated from Christian norms; MARRIAGE, it was believed, properly existed only between one man and one woman. In 1866, for example, in the seminal case of *Hyde v. Hyde*, 1 L.R.-P. & D., an English court remarked that "the law of [England was] . . . adapted to the Christian marriage, and it is wholly inapplicable to polygamy." During the nineteenth century, English and U.S. law did not recognize polygamous marriage in any form. Only in the late twentieth century has either nation given limited legal recognition to polygamous partners from other countries.

Anti-polygamy laws in the United States also sprang from religious conflict. In the mid-1800s, widespread public hostility arose toward the practice of polygamy by members of the Church of Jesus Christ of Latter-day Saints, known as Mormons. A small religious sect in the territory of Utah, the Mormons believed that their founder and prophet, Joseph Smith, had a divine revelation in 1843 that called for men to marry more than one woman; in 1852 the church announced that the practice was religiously superior to monogamy. This position angered critics throughout the country, ranging from religious leaders to novelists, editorialists, and particularly politicians. In 1856 the Republican party's first national platform denounced polygamy and SLAVERY as "those twin relics of barbarism."

These attitudes formed the basis for a full-scale legal assault on polygamy in general and on the Mormons' practice in particular. In Washington, D.C., lawmakers passed federal anti-polygamy laws that severely punished polygamists, denied them the right to vote, and ultimately repealed the legal incorporation of the Mormon Church and began proceedings to seize its property. U.S. marshals arrested hundreds of Mormons. As the church battled these measures, several cases reached the U.S. Supreme Court. The most famous case is *Reynolds v. United States*, 98 U.S. 145, 8 Otto 145, 25 L. Ed. 244 (1878), in which the Court upheld the conviction of a Mormon leader by rejecting the church's claim to protection under the FIRST AMENDMENT to the U.S. Constitution. In 1890 the Court upheld the 1887 federal statute repealing the church's incorporation (24 Stat. 635, ch. 397) in *Late Corporation of the Church of Jesus Christ of Latter-Day Saints v. United States*, 136 U.S. 1, 10 S. Ct. 792, 34 L. Ed. 478 (1890), *modified*, 140 U.S. 665, 11 S. Ct. 884, 35 L. Ed. 592 (1891). Having no further legal recourse, the MORMON CHURCH abandoned the practice of polygamy.

See also RELIGION.

POLYGRAPH An instrument used to measure physiological responses in humans when they are questioned in order to determine if their answers are truthful.

Also known as a "lie detector," the polygraph has a controversial history in U.S. law. First developed in the late nineteenth century, its modern incarnation is an electromechanical device that is attached to a subject's body during an interview. The discipline of polygraphy is based on the theory that by recording involuntary physiological changes in the subject, the polygraph yields data that can be interpreted to

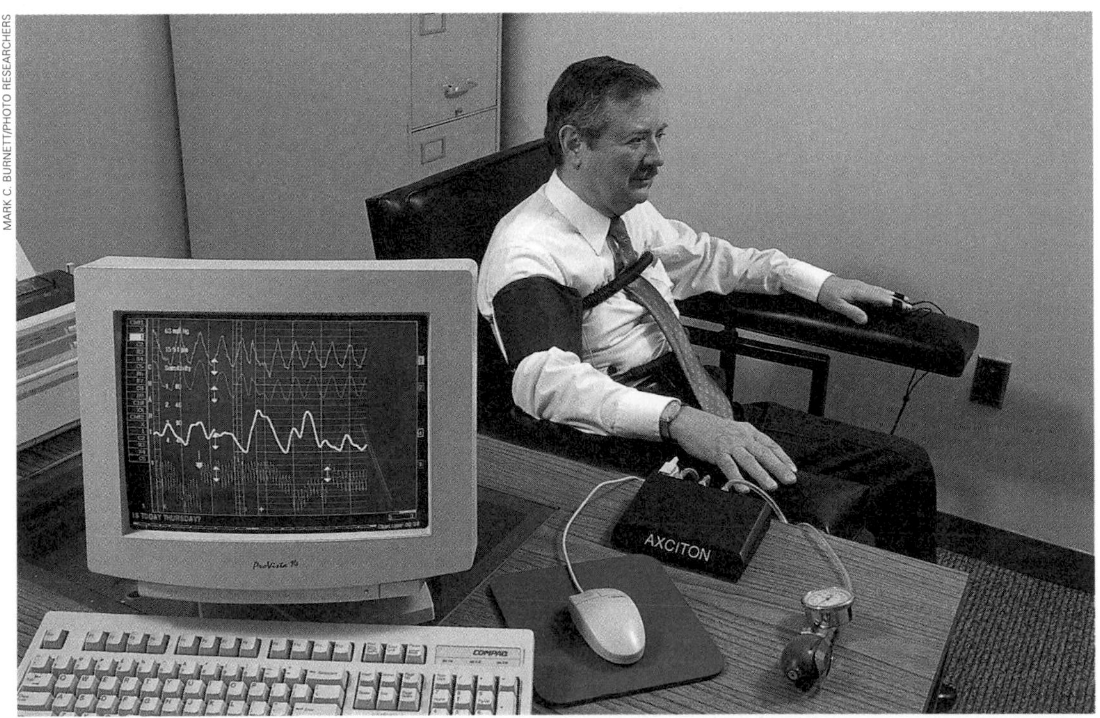

MARK C. BURNETT/PHOTO RESEARCHERS

Despite advances in polygraph technology, the courts have remained skeptical about the polygraph's trustworthiness.

determine whether the subject is telling the truth. Supporters of the scientific validity of the polygraph claim that results are approximately 90 percent accurate. For much of the twentieth century, however, polygraph EVIDENCE was INADMISSIBLE in criminal cases on grounds of unreliability. Polygraph evidence was admissible in civil cases, however, and it was also used widely in law enforcement, government, and industry.

Polygraphy uses a variety of formats. Until the 1950s the format was the relevant/irrelevant (R/I) test; it rested on the now discredited belief that a subject produces a specific identifiable physiological response when lying. The R/I test has been replaced by the control question (CQ) format, the only format routinely used in forensic tests. Typically, a trained examiner fits a subject with sensors to measure respiration, heart rate and blood pressure, and perspiration, which the polygraph records using pens on graph paper. The examiner asks a series of questions, including control questions that are designed to provoke anxiety and denial. Later, another examiner compares these answers with answers pertaining to the matter at hand. This is known as numerical CQ testing. So-called global CQ testing includes a more subjective component: one examiner scores the test while also factoring in the subject's observable physical responses, such as movement, expression, and voice.

In U.S. courts, the use of the polygraph was first addressed in 1923. In refusing to admit polygraph evidence in a MURDER case, the Court of Appeals for the District of Columbia created a legal standard that would last for nearly seventy years (*Frye v. United States*, 54 App. D.C. 46, 293 F. 1013 [1923]). This standard came to be known as the *Frye* rule, or general acceptance test. To be ADMISSIBLE in court, novel scientific evidence first must have gained general acceptance in its scientific field.

The *Frye* rule applied broadly to all scientific evidence, including polygraph evidence. Other APPELLATE COURTS followed the court's standard throughout most of the century, primarily because polygraphy never gained widespread acceptance among scientists. Nonetheless, polygraph evidence was used in civil lawsuits, and police agencies, businesses, and government offices continued to use the polygraph regularly to provide evidence, screen job applicants, and investigate security risks.

Advances in polygraphy helped spur a judicial reevaluation, but more important was the adoption of the Federal Rules of Evidence in the 1970s. Rule 702 set an important new standard for the admission of scientific evidence:

> If scientific, technical, or other specialized knowledge will assist the trier of fact to understand the evidence or to determine a fact in issue, a witness qualified as an expert by knowledge, skill, experience, training, or education, may testify thereto in the form of an opinion or otherwise.

Over the next two decades, appellate courts authorized use of polygraph evidence in a few state courts, a trend followed by the U.S. Court of Appeals for the Eleventh Circuit and the military courts. Then in 1993, in a case not specifically related to the polygraph, the U.S. Supreme Court held that rule 702 replaced the *Frye* test (*Daubert v. Merrell Dow Pharmaceuticals, Inc.*, 509 U.S. 579, 113 S. Ct. 2786, 125 L. Ed. 2d 469). In essence, the Court said that the standard of general scientific acceptance was not as important as whether expert TESTIMONY can assist jurors. Soon thereafter, several federal courts reconsidered their long-standing ban on polygraph evidence and determined that they now had the discretion to permit its introduction at trial.

Congress also reexamined the use of the polygraph in industry. In 1988 lawmakers responded to civil liberty concerns about the abuse of polygraph testing in private industry by passing the Employee Polygraph Protection Act (29 U.S.C.A. § 2001 et seq.). The law bars preemployment testing in banking, retail, and other private industries and also makes it illegal for employers to fire, discriminate against, or discipline employees who refuse to submit to polygraph tests. The act exempts government employers, private industry when an employee is under investigation for economic injury suffered by the employer, and all security services and industries that manufacture, distribute, or dispense controlled substances.

In the twentieth century, acceptance of the polygraph has been inconsistent. Even after adoption of the *Frye* rule in the 1920s, civil courts continued to allow admission of evidence that was inadmissible in the criminal courts. The standard for admissibility in criminal cases changed in the 1990s following the adoption of the Federal Rules of Evidence and the Supreme Court's decision in *Daubert.* At the same time, employers who for decades had turned to the polygraph as a credible indicator of truthfulness were barred from doing so.

PONZI SCHEME A FRAUDULENT investment plan in which the investments of later investors are used to pay earlier investors, giving the appearance that the investments of the initial participants dramatically increase in value in a short amount of time.

A Ponzi scheme is a type of investment FRAUD that promises investors exorbitant interest if they loan their money. As more investors participate, the money contributed by later investors is paid to the initial investors, purportedly as the promised interest on their loans. A Ponzi scheme works in its initial stages but inevitably collapses as more investors participate.

A Ponzi scheme is a variation of illegal pyramid sales schemes. In a pyramid sales plan, a person pays a fee to become a distributor. Once the person becomes a distributor, he receives commissions not only for the products he sells but also for products sold by individuals that he brings into the business. These new distributors are beneath the person who brought them into the pyramid scheme, so they are "under the pyramid." In illegal pyramid schemes, only the people at the top of the pyramid make substantial money because they get a commission from the products sold by everyone below them. As more people become distributors, the persons lower in the pyramid have less chance to make money.

A Ponzi scheme was once was called a "bubble," but it was renamed in 1920 after Charles Ponzi and his Boston-based company had collected almost $10 million from ten thousand investors by selling PROMISSORY NOTES that claimed to pay 50 percent profit in forty-five days. When the scheme was exposed, a Boston bank collapsed, and investors lost most of their money.

Ponzi, an Italian immigrant, thought of profiting from the widely varying currency exchange rates for International Postal Reply Coupons (IPRCs), which were redeemed for stamps. IPRCs were intended to facilitate the sending of international mail. The sender put an IPRC, rather than a stamp, on a piece of mail going to another country, and the recipient exchanged the IPRC for the appropriate stamp in her country.

Ponzi contended that he could pay a small amount for IPRCs in weak-currency countries and then redeem them at a substantial profit in the United States. He correctly noted that a stamp transaction might yield a 400 percent profit, but the amount of profit in real terms was very small. Nevertheless, he promoted his idea through his Boston-based Securities Exchange Company. In March 1920 he began soliciting funds for purchasing the IPRCs with a promised 40 percent return in ninety days. Bank interest rates at the time were just five percent. Investors started loaning Ponzi their money, and within a short time he increased the promised return on forty-five-day notes to 50 percent. He also promised a 100 percent return on funds loaned to him for ninety days. He pledged to refund money on demand to any investor before the loan period was up.

Money soon flooded Ponzi's offices. By July 1920 he was taking in $1 million a week. Ponzi made an arrangement with the Hanover Trust Company of Boston to deposit his funds. Hanover officials soon realized that Ponzi was not paying his initial investors with interest income but with the deposits of the new investors. Nevertheless, the bank eagerly sold Ponzi a large amount of its stock.

On August 2, 1920, a Boston newspaper revealed the fraud and reported that Ponzi was hopelessly insolvent. Thousands of victims immediately demanded refunds. Ponzi paid as many as he could but exhausted his funds in a week. He then declared BANKRUPTCY. In bankruptcy, the court ordered all of the persons who had been paid by Ponzi during the life of the scheme to return the proceeds to the bankruptcy TRUSTEE, who distributed the money on a PRO RATA basis to all of the other victims. Ponzi was eventually convicted of fraud in both state and federal court and imprisoned for several years.

The Ponzi scheme did not end with Charles Ponzi. It has proved to be a reliable scam in which persons are lured into giving their money to con artists who promise enormous financial returns. The early cycle of a Ponzi scheme appears to confirm the reliability of the investment, as some investors are paid the promised returns. The scheme is doomed to collapse when not enough new money exists to pay old obligations.

Gullible individuals are not the only victims of Ponzi schemes. In the early 1990s, John G. Bennett, Jr., and his Foundation for New Era Philanthropy lured many U.S. universities and nonprofit groups into investing millions of dollars in the foundation. Bennett promised these organizations that they would double their money in six months with the help of anonymous philanthropists. In May 1995 Prudential Securities, Inc., where most of the funds were deposited, discovered that New Era was under federal investigation and froze its accounts.

The action triggered New Era's bankruptcy. Bennett was later charged with eighty-two counts of fraud, MONEY LAUNDERING, and income TAX EVASION. As with the original Ponzi scheme, defrauded investors agreed to be reimbursed for up to 65 percent of their losses, with the money coming from groups that had deposited money with New Era early in the scheme and made a profit.

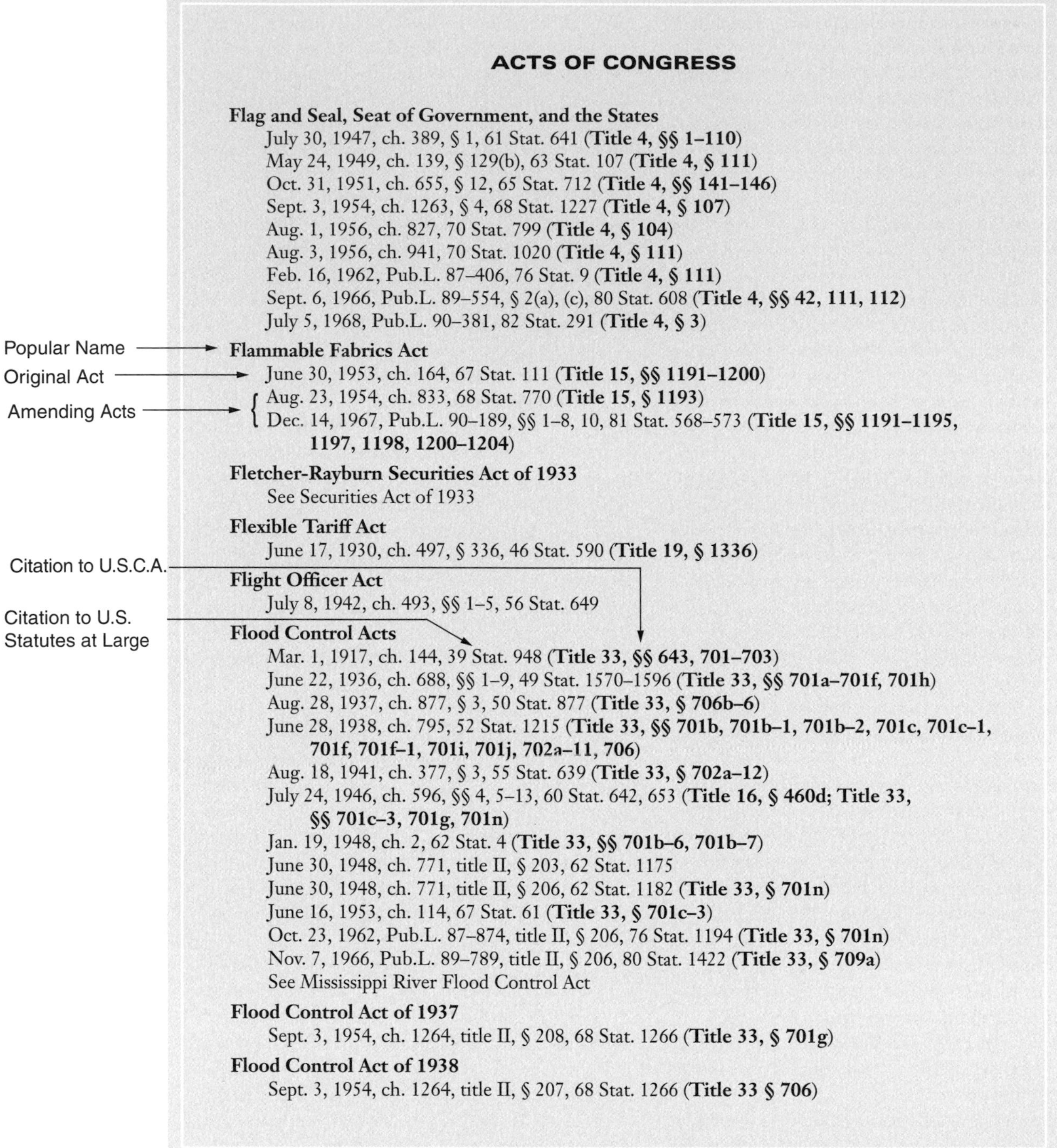

ACTS OF CONGRESS

Flag and Seal, Seat of Government, and the States
July 30, 1947, ch. 389, § 1, 61 Stat. 641 (**Title 4, §§ 1–110**)
May 24, 1949, ch. 139, § 129(b), 63 Stat. 107 (**Title 4, § 111**)
Oct. 31, 1951, ch. 655, § 12, 65 Stat. 712 (**Title 4, §§ 141–146**)
Sept. 3, 1954, ch. 1263, § 4, 68 Stat. 1227 (**Title 4, § 107**)
Aug. 1, 1956, ch. 827, 70 Stat. 799 (**Title 4, § 104**)
Aug. 3, 1956, ch. 941, 70 Stat. 1020 (**Title 4, § 111**)
Feb. 16, 1962, Pub.L. 87–406, 76 Stat. 9 (**Title 4, § 111**)
Sept. 6, 1966, Pub.L. 89–554, § 2(a), (c), 80 Stat. 608 (**Title 4, §§ 42, 111, 112**)
July 5, 1968, Pub.L. 90–381, 82 Stat. 291 (**Title 4, § 3**)

Flammable Fabrics Act
June 30, 1953, ch. 164, 67 Stat. 111 (**Title 15, §§ 1191–1200**)
Aug. 23, 1954, ch. 833, 68 Stat. 770 (**Title 15, § 1193**)
Dec. 14, 1967, Pub.L. 90–189, §§ 1–8, 10, 81 Stat. 568–573 (**Title 15, §§ 1191–1195, 1197, 1198, 1200–1204**)

Fletcher-Rayburn Securities Act of 1933
See Securities Act of 1933

Flexible Tariff Act
June 17, 1930, ch. 497, § 336, 46 Stat. 590 (**Title 19, § 1336**)

Flight Officer Act
July 8, 1942, ch. 493, §§ 1–5, 56 Stat. 649

Flood Control Acts
Mar. 1, 1917, ch. 144, 39 Stat. 948 (**Title 33, §§ 643, 701–703**)
June 22, 1936, ch. 688, §§ 1–9, 49 Stat. 1570–1596 (**Title 33, §§ 701a–701f, 701h**)
Aug. 28, 1937, ch. 877, § 3, 50 Stat. 877 (**Title 33, § 706b–6**)
June 28, 1938, ch. 795, 52 Stat. 1215 (**Title 33, §§ 701b, 701b–1, 701b–2, 701c, 701c–1, 701f, 701f–1, 701i, 701j, 702a–11, 706**)
Aug. 18, 1941, ch. 377, § 3, 55 Stat. 639 (**Title 33, § 702a–12**)
July 24, 1946, ch. 596, §§ 4, 5–13, 60 Stat. 642, 653 (**Title 16, § 460d; Title 33, §§ 701c–3, 701g, 701n**)
Jan. 19, 1948, ch. 2, 62 Stat. 4 (**Title 33, §§ 701b–6, 701b–7**)
June 30, 1948, ch. 771, title II, § 203, 62 Stat. 1175
June 30, 1948, ch. 771, title II, § 206, 62 Stat. 1182 (**Title 33, § 701n**)
June 16, 1953, ch. 114, 67 Stat. 61 (**Title 33, § 701c–3**)
Oct. 23, 1962, Pub.L. 87–874, title II, § 206, 76 Stat. 1194 (**Title 33, § 701n**)
Nov. 7, 1966, Pub.L. 89–789, title II, § 206, 80 Stat. 1422 (**Title 33, § 709a**)
See Mississippi River Flood Control Act

Flood Control Act of 1937
Sept. 3, 1954, ch. 1264, title II, § 208, 68 Stat. 1266 (**Title 33, § 701g**)

Flood Control Act of 1938
Sept. 3, 1954, ch. 1264, title II, § 207, 68 Stat. 1266 (**Title 33 § 706**)

A section from a popular name table

Internationally, the nation of Albania was plunged into civil unrest in 1997 when a multimillion-dollar Ponzi scheme collapsed. Many Albanians had invested large amounts of their savings in the scheme, which allegedly had the backing of Albanian government officials. Faced with economic ruin, citizens rioted against the government.

POPULAR NAME TABLES Reference charts that aid in locating STATUTES, if the names by which they are commonly referred to are known.

For example, one can discover the official name and location of the SHERMAN ANTI-TRUST ACT (15 U.S.C.A. § 1 et seq.) from a popular name table.

PORNOGRAPHY The representation in books, magazines, photographs, films, and other media of scenes of sexual behavior that are erotic or lewd and are designed to arouse sexual interest.

Pornography is the depiction of sexual behavior that is intended to arouse sexual excitement in its audience. During the twentieth century, Americans have debated whether pornographic material should be legally protected or legally banned. Those who believe pornography must be protected argue that the FIRST AMENDMENT to the U.S. Constitution guarantees freedom of expression, including sexual expression. Traditional opponents of pornography raise moral concerns, arguing that the First Amendment does not protect expression that corrupts people's behavior. More recently, some feminists have advocated suppressing pornography because it perpetuates gender stereotypes and promotes violence against women.

Pornography has been regulated by the legal standards that govern the concept of OBSCENITY, which refers to things society may consider disgusting, foul, or immoral, and may include material that is blasphemous. Pornography is limited to depictions of sexual behavior and may not be OBSCENE.

The U.S. Supreme Court has established that obscenity is not protected by the First Amendment. The more troublesome question has been defining what is and is not obscene. In 1957 the U.S. Supreme Court, in *Roth v. United States*, 354 U.S. 476, 77 S. Ct. 1304, 1 L. Ed. 2d 1498, stated that obscenity is "utterly without redeeming social importance" and therefore is not protected by the First Amendment. The *Roth* test for obscenity is "whether to the average person, applying contemporary community standards, the dominant theme of the material taken as a whole appeals to a prurient [lewd or lustful] interest." The *Roth* test proved difficult to use because every term in it eluded a conclusive definition.

The Supreme Court added requirements to the definition of obscenity in a 1966 case involving the bawdy English novel *Fanny Hill.* In *Memoirs v. Massachusetts*, 383 U.S. 413, 86 S. Ct. 975, 16 L. Ed. 2d 1, the Court concluded that to establish obscenity, the material must, aside from appealing to the prurient interest, be "utterly without redeeming social value" and "patently offensive because it affronts contemporary community standards relating to the description of sexual matters." The phrase "utterly without redeeming social value" allowed a loophole for pornographers. Expert witnesses testified that there was at least a shred of social value in the depiction of sexual behavior and social relations.

The Supreme Court established the basic legal standard for pornography in *Miller v. California*, 413 U.S. 15, 93 S. Ct. 2607, 37 L. Ed. 2d 419 (1973). Chief Justice WARREN E. BURGER stated in *Miller* that pornographic material would be classified as obscene if it met three criteria: (1) the work, taken as a whole by an average person applying contemporary community standards, appeals to the prurient interest; (2) the work depicts sexual conduct in a patently offensive way; and (3) the work, when taken as a whole, lacks serious literary, artistic, political, or scientific value.

Burger emphasized in *Miller* that only hard-core pornography could be designated as patently offensive. He listed examples of patently offensive descriptions or representations, including representations of "ultimate sex acts" and "masturbation, excretory functions and lewd exhibition of the genitals."

Based on *Miller*, the law distinguishes between hard-core pornography and soft-core pornography, which involves depictions of nudity and limited and simulated sexual conduct. Because it is not as graphic or explicit as hard-core pornography, soft-core pornography is protected under the First Amendment.

Child pornography, whether hard-core or soft-core, is treated severely under the law. In 1982 the Supreme Court, in *New York v. Ferber*, 458 U.S. 747, 102 S. Ct. 3348, 73 L. Ed. 2d 1113, held that child pornography is not a form of expression protected under the Constitution. It found that the state of New York had a compelling interest in protecting children from sexual abuse and found a close connection between such abuse and the use of children in the production of pornographic materials. In 1990 the Court went even further in upholding a state law prohibiting the possession and viewing of child pornography (*Osborne v. Ohio*, 495 U.S. 103, 110 S. Ct. 1691, 109 L. Ed. 2d 98).

In the 1980s some feminists began an attack on pornography and the way the Supreme Court had structured the legal debate using the First Amendment. Led by law professor CATHARINE A. MACKINNON and writer ANDREA DWORKIN, they proposed that women be permitted to sue pornographers for damages under CIVIL RIGHTS laws. In 1982, in an alliance with political conservatives opposed to pornography, MacKinnon and Dworkin convinced Indianapolis officials to pass a municipal ORDINANCE based on their civil rights approach. The ordinance described pornography as "a discriminatory practice based on sex which denies women

FEMINIST PERSPECTIVES ON PORNOGRAPHY

IN FOCUS

Pornography is a battlefield in U.S. law. For decades, courts have struggled to find a middle ground between opponents of obscenity and defenders of free speech. This debate began to shift in the 1970s as feminists introduced new theories. Obscenity and free speech were no longer the central issues, these critics argued. Their paramount concern was violence. They saw a causal link between pornographic depictions of women, and crimes ranging from harassment to rape. Beginning in the 1980s, some feminists wrote legislation that sought to control pornography in new and dramatic ways. They met strong opposition, and none of their legislation survived vetoes or court challenges. But these controversial efforts signaled a bold departure from the way U.S. citizens were accustomed to thinking about women, the law, and sexually explicit material.

Inspired by the women's liberation movement in the 1960s, many feminists began to decry pornography as sexist. In later years, a sharper critique began to emerge. To some feminist scholars, pornography made objects of women, reducing them to no more than their bodies. Other feminists regarded pornography as a deliberate means of subordinating women to men, thereby maintaining inequality. One leading feminist critic, Andrea Dworkin, took this theory even further. In books such as *Pornography: Men Possessing Women* (1979), Dworkin interpreted publications and films as training guides for committing sexual violence.

Dworkin's writings have divided feminists. Her detractors argue that because she is virtually opposed to sexual intercourse, she stands outside the mainstream of feminism. Her supporters cite high rates of sexual violence as proof that she is right. This point is frequently debated by both sides. The causal link between pornography and violence rests on anecdotal evidence. Dworkin finds this evidence sufficient, and she contends that women are not believed when they report their experience of being sexually assaulted by men who view pornography. While not denying these personal accounts, critics reply that a definite link can never be scientifically established.

One prominent feminist colleague of Dworkin's is Catharine A. MacKinnon. An author and professor of law, MacKinnon is regarded as a pioneer in providing legal recourse for victims of sexual harassment and rape. She and Dworkin created the intellectual framework for viewing pornography in a novel light: not merely as a form of speech but instead as active discrimination and violence against women. Their argument brushed aside traditional First Amendment considerations. If pornography harmed women, they claimed, then it was not deserving of legal protection as speech. This view had its first legal expression in a case they considered bringing to stop showings of the film *Deep Throat*, whose star, Linda Lovelace, contended that she was raped throughout the making of the film. Ultimately, no suit could be brought because the statute of limitations had expired, but the case served as their first step toward a practical attack on pornography.

MacKinnon and Dworkin first tried a legislative solution in Minneapolis in 1983. As coteachers of a course at the University of Minnesota Law School, they were invited to draft a law aimed at keeping adult bookstores out of residential neighborhoods. Zoning ordinances had failed in this end. They proposed amending the city's civil rights ordinance to include a new legal claim: a woman who proved that she had been harmed by pornographic material could sue its makers and distributors.

This groundbreaking approach avoided traditional definitions of obscenity. It defined pornography as the sexually explicit subordination of women in pictures or words. In the language of the proposed ordinance, subordination was images of women who

equal opportunity in society" and defined it as "the graphic sexually explicit subordination of women, whether in pictures or words," especially in a violent or degrading context. The ordinance made unlawful the production, sale, exhibition, and distribution of pornography and gave anyone injured by a person who has seen or read pornography the right to bring a civil suit against the maker or seller.

Supporters of the ordinance argued that the legislation was a civil rights measure whose purpose was to fight SEX DISCRIMINATION. In their view the ordinance regulated conduct rather than free speech and thus did not violate the First Amendment. They argued that even if pornography was viewed as speech, it should be treated as a low-value form of speech that was not entitled to First Amendment protection.

All of these arguments were rejected by the U.S. Court of Appeals for the Seventh Circuit in *Hudnut v. American Booksellers Association, Inc.*, 771 F.2d 323 (7th Cir. 1985). The court agreed that pornography affected how people view the world and their social relations but observed that the same could be said of other speech, including expressions of racial bigotry. Yet these kinds of expression are protected as speech because to do otherwise would give the government control of "all institutions of culture" and allow it to be the "great censor and director of "experience sexual pleasure in being raped" or in being "penetrated by objects or animals" (as quoted in *New York Times Magazine*, Oct. 6, 1991, at 56). Two provisions outlined the conditions under which a woman could bring suit: a plaintiff would have to prove that a pornographic work had harmed her in a specific way, or that it had harmed women in general. At hearings before the Minneapolis City Council, several women testified that they had been sexually assaulted by men who imitated scenes from pornography. The hearings galvanized debate and demonstrations. In one incident, a woman protesting pornography set herself on fire by a downtown newsstand.

The ordinance drew attacks from traditional free speech advocates, including the American Booksellers Association and the American Civil Liberties Union (ACLU). Opponents argued that the ordinance was vague, allowing too much subjectivity in deciding what material constituted subordination. Any material, they claimed, could be deemed offensive in this way. One group making this argument called itself the Feminist Anti-Censorship Task Force (FACT). Among FACT's fifty prominent members were the authors Betty N. Friedan, Kate Millett, and Adrienne Rich. They filed a legal brief attacking the ordinance on the ground that it reinforced sexist stereotypes. In a strongly worded rebuttal, MacKinnon denounced the group as being apologists for male supremacists.

The Minneapolis antipornography ordinance twice failed to pass. Mayor Donald M. Fraser vetoed it in December 1983 and in July 1984. But the ordinance served as a model for others, and in 1984, MacKinnon and Dworkin met with greater success in Indianapolis. Again, they proposed modifying existing ordinances with amendments that would allow any woman the means to seek an order prohibiting offensive pornography, as well as to seek damages. On April 23 and June 11, 1984, the Indianapolis–Marian County City Council passed General Ordinances 24 and 35, which amended chapter 16 of the Human Relations and Equal Opportunity Code. Indianapolis Mayor William H. Hudnut III signed the ordinances into law.

The law was challenged in *American Booksellers Ass'n v. Hudnut*, 598 F. Supp. 1316 (S.D. Ind. 1984). In 1985 it was declared unconstitutional (*Hudnut*, 771 F.2d 323 [7th Cir. 1985]). Judge Frank Easterbrook based his ruling on a long-standing tradition of First Amendment protection for "opinions that the government finds wrong or even hateful." However, he accepted the ordinance's central argument about pornography. He agreed that "depictions of subordination" tend to perpetuate subordination in other areas of life, causing sexual discrimination, harassment, rape, and domestic abuse. The U.S. Supreme Court affirmed Easterbrook's decision in 1986 (*Hudnut*, 475 U.S. 1001, 106 S. Ct. 1172, 89 L. Ed. 2d 291, *aff'd without comment, reh'g denied*, 475 U.S. 1132, 106 S. Ct. 1664, 90 L. Ed. 2d 206).

Following the Court's ruling, MacKinnon and Dworkin refined their approach in a proposed 1992 bill for the Massachusetts state legislature titled An Act to Protect the Civil Rights of Women and Children (H. 5194). Sponsored by Representative Barbara Hildt (D), the bill focused on individuals who could prove that they were assaulted as a result of pornography. The bill allowed victims to collect damages in civil court from publishers, filmmakers, and distributors. In testimony before the Massachusetts Legislature, MacKinnon argued that pornography enjoyed better legal protection than did women. This time, opposition came from civil rights groups as well as the New York state chapter of the National Organization for Women (NOW). NOW condemned the bill for taking the onus off criminals and placing it instead on publishers. Although considered in committee, the bill was never voted on.

The effect of feminism on the issue of pornography continues to be potent and provocative. MacKinnon and Dworkin have forced society to reevaluate what it views as worthy of its protection. Some legal scholars believe that their idea is one whose time has come. Opponents fear a new age of censorship.

See also Feminist Jurisprudence; Sex Discrimination.

which thoughts are good for us." The court, adhering to the definition of obscenity first articulated in *Miller*, ruled that the ordinance's definition of pornography would cover many works that are not obscene because it would not take the value of the work as a whole into account or consider the work as a whole. The court of appeals' decision effectively ended this approach to the regulation of pornography.

In the 1990s attention has been paid to the new ways technology can supply pornography. The use of computer bulletin boards and the INTERNET to distribute pornography nationally and internationally led to the enactment of the federal Communications Decency Act of 1996 (CDA) (47 U.S.C.A. § 223). The CDA was designed to outlaw obscene and indecent sexual material in cyberspace, including the Internet. In *Reno v. American Civil Liberties Union*, 117 S. Ct. 2329, 138 L. Ed. 2d 874 (1997), the Supreme Court overturned provisions of the CDA prohibiting transmission of obscene or indecent material by means of a telecommunications device. The Court held that the provisions represented a content-based restriction, in violation of the Free Speech Clause of the First Amendment.

CROSS-REFERENCES

Censorship; Freedom of Speech; Movie Rating; *Roth v. United States;* Telecommunications; Theaters and Shows; X Rating.

POSITIVE EVIDENCE Direct proof of the fact or point in issue, as distinguished from circumstantial proof; proof that if believed, establishes the truth or falsity of a fact in issue and does not arise from a PRESUMPTION.

See also EVIDENCE.

POSITIVE LAW Those laws that have been duly enacted by a properly instituted and popularly recognized branch of government.

Positive laws may be promulgated, passed, adopted, or otherwise "posited" by an official or entity vested with authority by the government to prescribe the rules and regulations for a particular community. In the United States, positive laws come in a variety of forms at both the state and federal levels, including legislative enactments, judicial orders, executive decrees, and administrative regulations. In short, a positive law is any express written command of the government. The belief that the only legitimate sources of law are those written rules and regulations laid down by the government is known as POSITIVISM.

POSITIVISM A school of JURISPRUDENCE whose advocates believe that the only legitimate sources of law are those written rules, regulations, and principles that have been expressly enacted, adopted, or recognized by a government body, including administrative, executive, legislative, and judicial bodies.

Positivism sharply separates law and morality. It is often contrasted with NATURAL LAW, which is based on the belief that all written laws must follow universal principles of morality, religion, and justice. Positivists concede that ethical theories of morality, religion, and justice may include aspirational principles of human conduct. However, positivists argue that such theories differ from law in that they are unenforceable and therefore should play no role in the interpretation and application of legislation. Thus, positivists conclude that as long as a written law has been duly enacted by a branch of government, it must be deemed valid and binding, regardless of whether it offends anyone's sense of right and wrong.

Positivism serves two values. First, by requiring that all law be written, positivism ensures that the government will explicitly apprise the members of society of their rights and obligations. In a legal system run in strict accordance with positivist tenets, litigants would never be unfairly surprised or burdened by the government imposition of an unwritten legal obligation that was previously unknown and nonexistent. The Due Process Clauses of the Fifth and Fourteenth Amendments incorporate this positivist value by mandating that all persons receive notice of any pending legal ACTIONS against them so that they can prepare an adequate defense.

Second, positivism curbs judicial discretion. In some cases judges are not satisfied with the outcome of a case that would be dictated by a narrow reading of existing laws. For example, some judges may not want to allow a landlord to evict an elderly and sick woman in the middle of winter, even if the law authorizes such action when rent is overdue. However, positivism requires judges to decide cases in accordance with the law. Positivists believe that the integrity of the law is maintained through a neutral and objective judiciary that is not guided by subjective notions of EQUITY.

Positivism has been criticized for its harshness. Some critics of positivism have argued that not every law enacted by a legislature should be accepted as legitimate and binding. For example, laws depriving African Americans and Native Americans of various rights have been passed by governments but later overturned as unjust or unconstitutional. Critics conclude that written law ceases to be legitimate when it offends principles of fairness, justice, and morality. The American colonists based their revolt against the tyranny of British law on this point.

Positivism still influences U.S. jurisprudence. Many judges continue to evaluate the viability of legal claims by narrowly interpreting the law. If a right asserted by a litigant is not expressly recognized by a statute, PRECEDENT, or constitutional provision, many judges will deny recovery.

BIOGRAPHY

POSNER, RICHARD A. Author, legal scholar, and federal judge, Richard A. Posner is one of the most influential and controversial figures in contemporary American law. Posner rose to prominence first in academia in the early 1970s, where he championed economic analysis of the law. With his faith in free-market capitalism and the goal of economic efficiency, he became one of the leaders of the so-called CHICAGO SCHOOL of antitrust theory, whose ideas left a broad mark on this area of law over the next decade and a half. In 1981 Posner was appointed to the U.S. Court of Appeals for the Seventh Circuit and in 1993 became its chief judge. Besides issuing more than double the national average of judicial opinions annually, Posner has continued to publish many articles and books that range across legal, social, and intellectual topics.

Posner's ascent began immediately after his graduation from Harvard Law School in 1962. First in his class, he clerked for U.S. Supreme

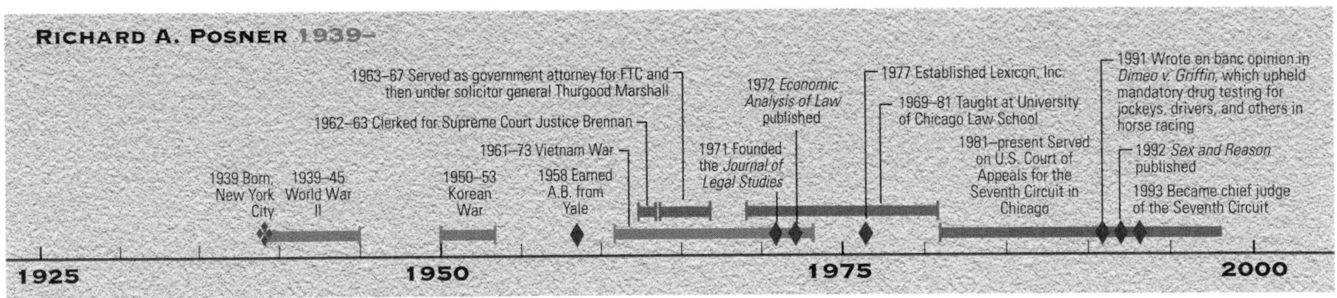

Court Justice WILLIAM J. BRENNAN, JR., who reportedly regarded him as one of the two geniuses he had known. A career as a government attorney followed, with stints on the Federal Trade Commission (FTC), in the Justice Department working for then solicitor general THURGOOD MARSHALL, and in the Johnson administration. During this time Posner also served on a highly visible AMERICAN BAR ASSOCIATION commission that evaluated the FTC, which established him as a strong supporter of free-market capitalism and a critic of federal regulation.

In 1968 Posner left government service for academia. He taught at Stanford Law School for a year before leaving for the University of Chicago, where he would soon make his mark as a leading legal theorist. Economics served as the foundation for his approach; like adherents of the nineteenth-century Utilitarian movement in English law, he believed firmly in the values of the free market and individual initiative. Many legal problems, he argued, were best approached using economic models of analysis, including those in areas that were not directly related to economics, such as criminal and constitutional law. The approach also had implications for PUBLIC POLICY. In one widely cited example, Posner argued that the system of child ADOPTION would be improved if parental rights were sold, because it would reduce the imbalance between supply and demand. Although some critics accused Posner of reducing complexities to simple matters of dollars and cents, his 1972 book *Economic Analysis of Law* became standard reading in many law schools over the next two decades.

During the 1970s Posner became a leader of the Chicago School of antitrust theory. This was a group of scholars, most of whom were associated with the University of Chicago, who, like Posner, held antiregulatory and free-market views. The Chicago School sought to turn ANTITRUST LAW—which is concerned with fair competition in business—on its head. At the heart of their arguments was the goal of economic efficiency. Posner and others urged the U.S. Supreme Court to abandon its critical view on so-called RESTRAINTS OF TRADE because business practices that had been thought to hurt competition actually helped it. Their theories had considerable impact on the Court and U.S. CORPORATIONS for the next decade and a half.

Meanwhile, Posner's visibility grew. He published a prodigious amount of writing, established a consulting firm called Lexicon, Inc., and founded the *Journal of Legal Studies*. Then political fortune smiled on him: the administration of President RONALD REAGAN saw Posner and other members of the Chicago School as its intellectual bedfellows, providing theoretical muscle to its antiregulatory politics. In 1981 Reagan nominated Posner to the U.S. Court of Appeals for the Seventh Circuit in Chicago.

"[A] PRAGMATIC APPROACH [TO LAW IS ONE] THAT IS PRACTICAL AND INSTRUMENTAL RATHER THAN ESSENTIALIST—INTERESTED IN WHAT WORKS AND WHAT IS USEFUL RATHER THAN IN WHAT 'REALLY' IS. IT IS THEREFORE FORWARD-LOOKING, VALUING CONTINUITY WITH THE PAST ONLY SO FAR AS SUCH CONTINUITY CAN HELP US COPE WITH PROBLEMS OF THE PRESENT AND THE FUTURE."

The appointment provoked debate. In a decade and a half, Posner had accumulated a number of enemies in academia, nearly all of them on the political left. Although he considered himself a classical liberal in the tradition of JOHN STUART MILL, his ideas struck opponents as crass, latter-day conservatism. Leading the attack was Ronald Dworkin, the prominent liberal professor of jurisprudence at New York University Law School and Oxford University.

Posner struck back, accusing his opponents in the professoriat of being afraid to take stands in their own work. However, he announced that he would avoid imposing his theoretical views from the bench.

As an APPELLATE judge, Posner has defied the labels his critics have applied to him. Some of his opinions have a conservative bent: in *Dimeo v. Griffin*, 943 F.2d 679 (7th Cir. 1991), Posner wrote for an EN BANC majority that upheld mandatory drug testing for jockeys, drivers, and others in horse racing, favoring the state of Illinois's interest in requiring the testing. Some of his other opinions are more liberal: in *Metzl v. Leininger*, 57 F.3d 618 (7th Cir. 1995), Posner wrote an opinion that declared unconstitutional an Illinois law requiring schools to close on Good Friday, holding that the law violated the Establishment Clause of the First Amendment. Some opinions employ his fascination for economics: in a 1986 case, *American Hospital Supply Corp. v. Hospital Products Limited*, 780 F.2d 589, he provided a mathematical formula for determining when PRELIMINARY INJUNCTIONS should be denied:

> if the harm to the plaintiff if the injunction is denied, multiplied by the probability that . . . the plaintiff . . . will win at trial, exceeds the harm to the defendant if the injunction is granted, multiplied by the probability that granting the injunction would be an error.

Most notably, he has authored a much greater number of judicial opinions than have his peers on the federal bench. By 1994 he had averaged seventy-seven opinions annually as compared with the national average of twenty-eight a year.

Throughout the 1980s and 1990s, Posner exerted a strong influence on legal thought. He has argued against popular conservative criticism that judges are too aggressive and activist, asserting that judges must be able to exercise interpretative discretion. Besides being widely read and debated in academia, he found a popular audience with his 1992 book *Sex and Reason*, a critical analysis of sexual behavior. Posner is also a leading contributor to the LAW AND LITERATURE movement, impressing both critics and supporters with his knowledge of jurisprudence and literary theory.

See also JURISPRUDENCE; UTILITARIANISM.

POSSE COMITATUS [*Latin, Power of the county.*] Referred at COMMON LAW to all males over the age of fifteen on whom a SHERIFF could call for assistance in preventing any type of civil disorder.

The notion of a *posse comitatus* has its roots in ancient English law, growing out of a citizen's traditional duty to raise a "hue and cry" whenever a serious crime occurred in a village, thus rousing the fellow villagers to assist the sheriff in pursuing the culprit. By the seventeenth century, trained MILITIA bands were expected to perform the duty of assisting the sheriff in such tasks, but all males age fifteen and older still had the duty to serve on the *posse comitatus*.

In the United States, the *posse comitatus* was an important institution on the western frontier, where it became known as the *posse*. At various times vigilante committees, often acting without legal standing, organized posses to capture wrongdoers. Such posses sharply warned first-time cattle rustlers, for instance, and usually hanged or shot second-time offenders. In 1876 a four-hundred-man posse killed one member of the infamous Jesse James gang and captured two others.

In 1878 the use of a *posse comitatus* was limited by the passage of the Posse Comitatus Act of 1878. This act, passed in response to the use of federal troops to enforce reconstruction policies in the southern states, prohibited the use of the U.S. Army to enforce laws unless the Constitution or an act of Congress explicitly authorized such use. This act was amended five times in the 1980s, largely to allow for the use of military resources to combat trafficking in illicit narcotics.

Though rarely used, the *posse comitatus* continues to be a modern legal institution. In June 1977, for example, the Aspen, Colorado, sheriff called out the *posse comitatus*—ordinary citizens with their own weapons—to hunt for escaped mass murderer Theodore ("Ted") Bundy. Many states have modern *posse comitatus* statutes; one typical example is the Kentucky statute enacted in 1962 that gives any sheriff the power to "command and take with him the power of the county or a part thereof, to aid him in the execution of the duties of his office" (Ky. Rev. Stat. Ann. § 70.060 [Baldwin 1996]).

"Posse Comitatus" is also the name taken by a right-wing, antitax extremist group founded in 1969 by Henry L. Beach, a retired dry cleaner and one-time member of the Silver Shirts, a Nazi-inspired organization that was established in the United States after ADOLF HITLER came to power in Germany. The group operated on the belief that the true intent of the founders of the United States was to establish a Christian republic where the individual was sovereign. Members of the group were united by the belief that the federal government was illegitimate, being operated by Jewish interests through the INTERNAL REVENUE SERVICE, the FEDERAL COURTS, and the Federal Reserve. The Posse Comitatus received widespread media attention in 1983 when a leader of the group, Gordon Kahl, was involved in a violent standoff with North Dakota law enforcement officers. Convicted for failure to pay taxes and then for violating the terms of his probation, Kahl shot and killed three officers and wounded three others before being shot and killed himself.

POSSESSION The ownership, control, or OCCUPANCY of a thing, most frequently land or PERSONAL PROPERTY, by a person.

The United States Supreme Court has said that "there is no word more ambiguous in its meaning than possession" (*National Safe Deposit Co. v. Stead*, 232 U.S. 58, 34 S. Ct. 209, 58 L. Ed. 504 [1914]). Depending on how and when it is used, the term *possession* has a variety of possible meanings. As a result, possession, or lack of possession, is often the subject of controversy in civil cases involving real and personal PROPERTY and criminal cases involving drugs and weapons—for example, whether a renter is entitled to possession of an apartment or whether a criminal suspect is in possession of stolen property.

The idea of possession is as old as the related concepts of private property and ownership. Our modern possession laws originated in the ancient Roman doctrines of *possessio.* English natural law inherited most of the Roman possession ideas, and later the British brought their law of possession to the American colonies. Following the War of Independence, state and federal courts continued to use and expand upon the historical notions of possession.

Possession versus Ownership Although the two terms are often confused, possession is not the same as ownership. No legal rule states that "possession is nine-tenths of the law," but this phrase is often used to suggest that someone who possesses an object is most likely its owner. Likewise, people often speak of the things they own, such as clothes and dishes, as their possessions. However, the owner of an object may not always possess the object. For example, an owner of a car could lend it to someone else to drive. That driver would then possess the car. However, the owner does not give up ownership simply by lending the car to someone else.

The myriad distinctions between possession and ownership, and the many nuances of possession, are complicated even for attorneys and judges. To avoid confusion over exactly what is meant by *possession,* the word is frequently modified by adding a term describing the type of possession. For example, possession may be actual, adverse, conscious, constructive, exclusive, illegal, joint, legal, physical, sole, superficial, or any one of several other types. Many times these modifiers are combined, as in "joint constructive possession." All these different kinds of possession, however, originate from what the law calls "actual possession."

Actual Possession "Actual possession is what most of us think of as possession—that is, having physical custody or control of an object" (*United States v. Nenadich,* 689 F.Supp. 285 [S.D. N.Y. 1988]). Actual possession, also sometimes called *possession in fact,* is used to describe immediate physical contact. For example, a person wearing a watch has actual possession of the watch. Likewise, if you have your wallet in your jacket pocket, you have actual possession of your wallet. This type of possession, however, is by necessity very limited. Frequently, a set of facts clearly indicate that an individual has

R. SIDNEY/THE IMAGE WORKS

When a parent lets a child use the family car, the parent retains ownership of the car, even though the child has possession.

possession of an object but that he or she has no physical contact with it. To properly deal with these situations, courts have broadened the scope of possession beyond actual possession.

Constructive Possession Constructive possession is a legal theory used to extend possession to situations where a person has no hands-on custody of an object. Most courts say that constructive possession, also sometimes called "possession in law," exists where a person has knowledge of an object plus the ability to control the object, even if the person has no physical contact with it (*United States v. Derose,* 74 F.3d 1177 [11th Cir. 1996]). For example, people often keep important papers and other valuable items in a bank safety deposit box. Although they do not have actual physical custody of these items, they do have knowledge of the items and the ability to exercise control over them. Thus, under the doctrine of constructive possession, they are still considered in possession of the contents of their safety deposit box. Constructive possession is frequently used in cases involving criminal possession.

Criminal Possession Both federal and state statutes make possession of many dangerous or undesirable items criminal. For example, the federal statute 26 U.S.C.A. § 5861 (1996) prohibits possession of certain firearms and other weapons. Likewise, the possession of other items considered harmful to the public, such as narcotics, burglary tools, and stolen property, is also made criminal under various laws. Criminal possession, especially of drugs, has been a major source of controversy. Making possession a crime allows for arrests and convictions without proving the use or sale of a prohibited item.

Historically, actual possession was required for a criminal possession conviction. Beginning in the 1920s, however, courts began expanding criminal possession to include constructive possession. The federal prohibition of intoxicating liquors spawned several cases involving criminal possession. In one of the first criminal cases to use constructive possession, the court found a defendant guilty of possessing illegal liquor in trunks in the actual possession of another person (*People v. Vander Heide*, 211 Mich. 1, 178 N.W. 78 [1920]). Subsequent cases, especially narcotics cases, have continued to expand the law of criminal possession.

Possession and Intent In civil cases INTENT is rarely a part of possession. However, in criminal cases possession usually requires conscious possession. In other words, the person must be conscious of the fact that the item is illegal and that he or she possesses it. A person with possession of illegal drugs may avoid conviction if he or she believed the drugs were legal. Generally, to be guilty of criminal possession, a person must either know the item is illegal when it is received or must keep possession of the object after learning it is illegal.

See also ADVERSE POSSESSION; DRUGS AND NARCOTICS.

POSSESSORY ACTION A proceeding instituted to obtain or recover the actual POSSESSION of PROPERTY, as distinguished from a proceeding that merely seeks to establish the plaintiff's title or ownership of property.

In admiralty law, a possessory action is one that is brought to recover the possession of a vessel that is had under a claim of title.

For example, an EVICTION proceeding is a possessory action to regain control of the property from a tenant.

Under old English law, a possessory action was used to regain possession of the FREEHOLD, of which the plaintiff or the plaintiff's ancestors had been wrongfully deprived by the present tenant or possessor of the property.

POSSESSORY WARRANT A rare statutory REMEDY for the recovery of PERSONAL PROPERTY that has been taken by FRAUD, violence, enticement, or seduction, or that has disappeared and is believed to be in the detention and control of the party complained against.

POSTCONVICTION REMEDIES A variety of RELIEF sought by a convicted criminal to have his or her sentence vacated, set aside, or corrected because such a sentence was based upon some violation of the U.S. Constitution.

Among the most common postconviction remedies available are the writ of HABEAS CORPUS and the writ of CORAM NOBIS.

POSTDATE To designate a written instrument, such as a CHECK, with a time or date later than that at which it is really made.

POSTHUMOUS CHILD An INFANT who is born subsequent to the death of the father or, in certain cases, the mother.

At COMMON LAW and by the laws of various states, governing DESCENT AND DISTRIBUTION, a posthumous child inherits from a deceased parent's ESTATE as an HEIR provided that the infant is born alive following a gestation period that shows that the child was conceived prior to the death of the father who has died INTESTATE. Under some statutes, it is necessary that the child be born within a ten-month period subsequent to the intestate father's death in order for the infant to be considered a posthumous child.

Laws addressing a posthumous child are rapidly becoming obsolete as medical advances extend the time period over which reproduction can occur. For example, sperm and eggs may be preserved in a frozen state past the lives of their donors. It is also possible to remove sperm or eggs, or perform a Caesarian section, after a person's death. Scholars and scientists anticipate the development of additional ways for genetic material to be preserved, and children to be born, after the death of the biological parent. These developments create new legal problems and are likely to necessitate changes for laws in several areas, including survivors' benefits, inheritance, and support.

POSTING In accounting, the act of transferring an original entry to a ledger. The act of mailing a document. A form of substituted SERVICE OF PROCESS consisting of displaying the process in a prominent place when other forms of service are unavailing.

In connection with TRESPASS statutes, the act of placing or affixing signs on private property in a manner to give notice of the trespass.

POSTMARITAL AGREEMENT An agreement made between spouses after MARRIAGE concerning the rights and responsibilities of the parties upon DIVORCE or the death of one of the spouses.

Postmarital agreements, also called postnuptial agreements, are agreements made between spouses while they are married. Postmarital agreements concern the rights and responsibilities of each spouse in the event that the other spouse dies or the couple divorces. All states allow postmarital agreements, but courts must review these agreements for procedural and substantive fairness before they can be executed.

In most states the law on postmarital agreements is similar to the law on PREMARITAL AGREEMENTS. Both parties must make full disclosure of their earnings and their property, and the agreement must be in writing and signed by both parties. If FRAUD, DURESS, or COERCION was involved in the formation of the contract, a court may declare the agreement void. Some states declare that, when creating a postmarital agreement, both parties must be represented by an attorney in order for the agreement to be valid. Courts are free to strike down provisions in postmarital CONTRACTS that violate PUBLIC POLICY.

Some states have special laws for postmarital agreements. In Minnesota, for example, the agreement may not address CHILD SUPPORT, CHILD CUSTODY, or child visitation issues, and neither party may commence an ACTION for SEPARATION or divorce within two years of the execution of the agreement. A section in Minnesota's statute also provides that no couple with a net worth of less than $1.2 million may fashion a postmarital agreement (Minn. Stat. Ann. § 519.11 [West 1996]). In Florida, if a postmarital agreement waives a spouse's rights upon the death of the other spouse, each spouse must make full and fair disclosure of ASSETS. No such disclosure is required in Florida for similar premarital agreements (Fla. Stat. Ann. § 732.702 [West 1996]).

Postmarital agreements are distinct from separation agreements. Separation agreements are intended to govern the rights and duties of the spouses upon separation and until a court orders a divorce decree or until a court recognizes the separation. Postmarital agreements, by contrast, are intended to govern the rights and duties of the spouses after a divorce.

See also HUSBAND AND WIFE.

POST MORTEM 📖 [*Latin, After death.*] Pertaining to matters occurring after death. A term generally applied to an autopsy or examination of a corpse in order to ascertain the cause of death or to the inquisition for that purpose by the CORONER. 📖

POUND, ROSCOE Roscoe Pound was one of the leading figures in twentieth-century legal thought. As a scholar, teacher, reformer, and dean of Harvard Law School, Pound strove to link law and society through his "sociological jurisprudence" and to improve the administration of the judicial system. In the early decades of the century, Pound was viewed as a radical thinker for arguing that the law is not static and must adapt to the needs of society. By the 1930s, however, he was seen as a more conservative figure, fighting the growth of federal government.

BIOGRAPHY

APWIDE WORLD PHOTOS

Roscoe Pound

Pound was born on October 27, 1870, in Lincoln, Nebraska. The son of a judge, Pound attended the University of Nebraska, earning a bachelor of arts degree in botany in 1888. His father convinced him to attend Harvard Law School, but he stayed only one year. The death of his father led Pound to return to Lincoln, where he passed the Nebraska bar examination and was admitted to the bar in 1890.

From 1890 to 1903, Pound practiced law, taught at the University of Nebraska, earned a doctorate in botany from the university, and served as the director of the state botanical survey. In addition, he helped organize the Nebraska Bar Association in 1900.

A gifted scholar, Pound could have had a distinguished career in the sciences, but his appointment in 1901 as a commissioner of appeals for the Nebraska Supreme Court permanently shifted his career to the law. As a commissioner he acted as a temporary appellate judge, helping to reduce a backlog of cases. His opinions emphasized substance over procedure and reflected a concern with the practical effect of the law.

In 1903 he was appointed dean of the Nebraska College of Law. His academic interests merged with his experience as a court commissioner in 1906 when he addressed the annual convention of the AMERICAN BAR ASSOCIATION in St. Paul. His speech, titled "The Causes of Popular Dissatisfaction with the Administration of Justice," was a call to improve court administration and a preview of his theory of law, called sociological jurisprudence. The speech, which has remained a classic statement on judicial administration, attracted the attention of John Henry Wigmore, the dean of Northwestern University School of Law. He asked Pound to join his faculty in 1907. Pound's two-year association with the school was marked by his organization of the First National Conference on Criminal Law and Criminology, which gathered participants from many professions to discuss ways to reform the CRIMINAL LAW. The

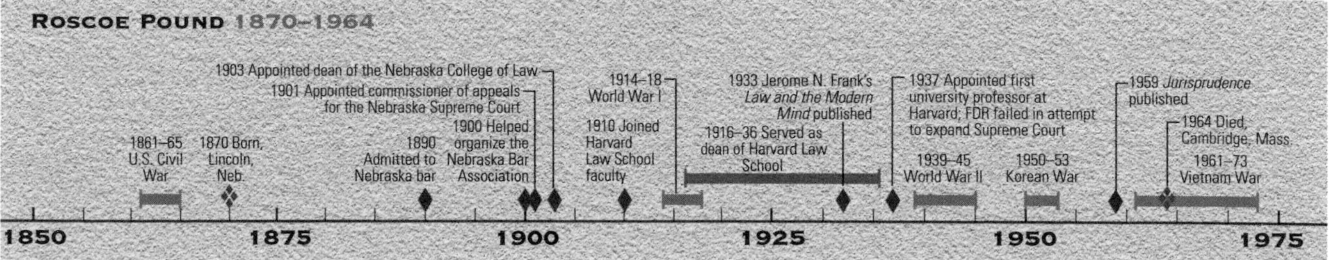

conference was one of the first of Pound's efforts to give practical application to sociological jurisprudence.

In 1910, after having spent a year at the University of Chicago, Pound joined the faculty at Harvard Law School. He was appointed dean in 1916 and served until 1936. It was during this period that Pound's views and influence were at their zenith.

Pound's contribution to U.S. jurisprudence was to further the work that OLIVER WENDELL HOLMES, JR., had begun in debunking the legal theories that had dominated during the nineteenth century. Pound fought the notion that an unchanging and inflexible "NATURAL LAW" formed the basis for the COMMON LAW. He did believe that some constant principles existed in the common law, particularly ones dealing with methods, to which he gave the name "taught legal tradition." Pound firmly believed that the implementation of the principles of the taught legal tradition by wise common-law judges resulted in substantive change, which reflected changes in society. As the interpreters of the common law, judges had a special duty to consider the practical effects of their decisions and to strive to ensure that judging facilitated rather than hindered societal growth.

Pound placed his sociological jurisprudence in opposition to what he termed "mechanical jurisprudence," which he characterized as a common but odious practice whereby judges woodenly applied precedent to the facts of cases without regard to the consequences. For Pound, the logic of previous precedent alone would not solve jurisprudential problems.

Despite his desire to see the law adapt to the needs of society, Pound believed that the common law should develop slowly and that it should only follow changes in society. Certainty in the law, especially in areas such as commercial and property law, was often more beneficial than attempts at practical alteration. He revealed a more conservative cast of mind in his distrust of legislative statutes, arguing that the slow development of judge-made law was preferable to the radical changes often brought by legislation. His study of biology led him to believe that the law, like nature, was a seamless web and that changes in one part might produce totally unexpected and undesirable results in a distant part.

Pound's sociological jurisprudence fell out of favor in the 1930s, when the "legal realist" movement attacked his philosophy. Though the legal realists and Pound had much in common, the realists, especially JEROME N. FRANK, differed over the nature of judicial decision making. Where Pound believed that judges, with the objective application of his principles of sociological jurisprudence, could logically produce the result in a given case, Frank, in his book *Law and the Modern Mind* (1933), thought otherwise. Frank maintained that not logic but the unique psychological makeup of judges was the most important factor in the resolution of a lawsuit. The realists pointed out, after analyzing many court decisions, that often a judge could support a decision for either side on a given legal issue. Therefore, they argued, judges were forced to decide cases on the basis of their subjective feelings of what was "fair" and then turn to the applicable part of the case law to furnish legal fig leaves to hide what they had actually done.

"THE LAW MUST BE STABLE, BUT IT MUST NOT STAND STILL."

Pound reacted angrily to this analysis in a series of law review articles. He believed that the rules of law, especially rules of commercial law and property, could be determined with certainty and even attain the logical coherence of propositions of Euclid. Pound conceded that it was important to study the psychology of judging, but only to prevent the aberrations the realists claimed were common. Pound thought that the realists emphasized the oddities, and not the central factors, in their analysis of the judicial system. He disliked the realists for discounting the importance of the common law and for their willingness to advocate that the law be used to change society. For Pound, the legal system worked best when the law followed society. Any attempt to make society follow the law was futile.

Pound resigned as dean of the Harvard Law School in 1936. He was appointed the first university professor of Harvard in 1937, an appointment that permitted him to teach in any of the academic units of Harvard. An opponent of much of President FRANKLIN D. ROOSEVELT's NEW DEAL legislation, Pound was actively involved in attempts to stop the great expansion of federal administrative agencies. He continued writing during his later years, publishing his monumental five-volume *Jurisprudence* in 1959. He died on July 1, 1964, in Cambridge, Massachusetts, at the age of ninety-three.

See also JURISPRUDENCE; LEGAL REALISM.

POUR-OVER A clause in a WILL or TRUST that provides that, upon the death of the creator of the trust, his or her money or property will be transferred into some other existing trust.

POWELL, ADAM CLAYTON, JR. Adam Clayton Powell, Jr., was a prominent African American congressman, serving his district in New York City's Harlem neighborhood from 1945 to 1970. A flamboyant and often controversial political figure, Powell played a key role in passing many federal education and social

BIOGRAPHY

LIBRARY OF CONGRESS

Adam Clayton Powell, Jr.

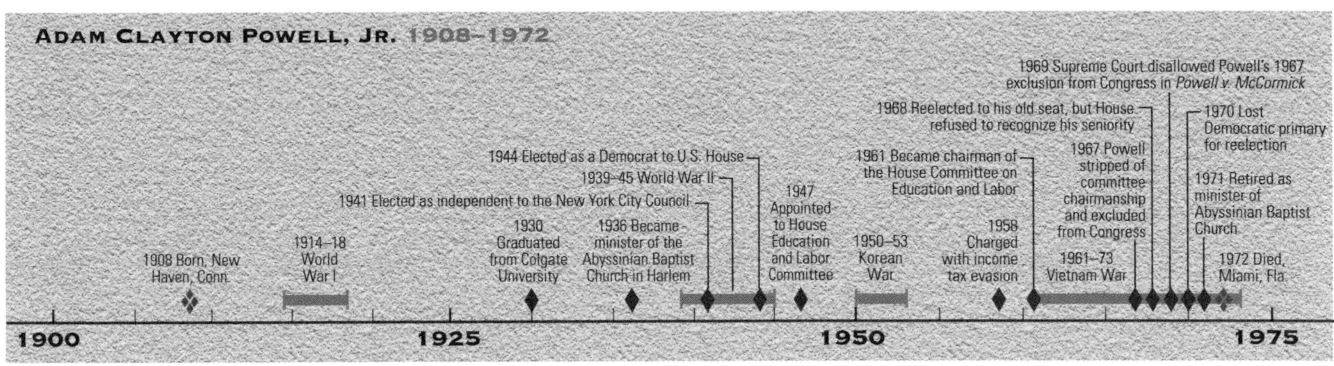

WELFARE programs in the 1960s. Near the end of his tenure, however, Powell was embroiled with the HOUSE OF REPRESENTATIVES over alleged ethical lapses.

Powell was born in New Haven, Connecticut, on November 29, 1908. When he was less than a year old, his father moved the family to New York City's Harlem neighborhood to accept the ministry at the Abyssinian Baptist Church. The church, which was a hundred years old, expanded under the elder Powell's leadership, in time becoming one of the largest congregations in the United States.

Powell graduated from Colgate University in 1930 and received a master of arts degree in religious education from Columbia University in 1931. He served as assistant minister and business manager of the Abyssinian Church in 1930 and succeeded his father as minister in 1936. He remained minister of the church for thirty-five years.

During the Great Depression of the 1930s, Powell acted aggressively to address racial and social injustice in New York City. In 1930 he organized picket lines and mass meetings to demand reform of Harlem Hospital, which had fired five African American doctors because of their race. Powell also used the church as an instrument of social welfare, distributing food, clothing, and temporary jobs to thousands of Harlem's destitute residents.

Powell soon was recognized as a charismatic CIVIL RIGHTS leader, adept at forcing restaurants, retail stores, bus companies, utilities, and phone companies either to hire or begin promoting African American employees. He transferred his efforts into the political arena in 1941, when he was elected as an independent to the New York City Council. During World War II he worked for the New York State Office of Price Administration and the Manhattan Civilian Defense, as well as publishing a weekly newspaper, *The People's Voice.*

In 1944 he was elected as a Democrat to Congress, representing the Twenty-second (later Eighteenth) District. In 1947 he took a seat on the Education and Labor Committee, which was to become the base of his power and prestige. During the 1940s and 1950s, Powell challenged racial segregation in and out of the halls of Congress. He took black constituents to the House dining room that had been informally restricted to white representatives. He introduced legislation to outlaw lynching and to ban discrimination in the armed forces, housing, transportation, and employment. He became famous for attaching an antidiscrimination amendment to many pieces of legislation. The so-called Powell Amendment was always unsuccessful, but it was a way to raise the issue of racial inequality before a House that was generally hostile to Powell's stand on civil rights.

"THESE ARE THE DAYS FOR STRONG MEN TO COURAGEOUSLY EXPOSE WRONG."

His frustration at the Democratic party's reluctance to move forward on civil rights led him in 1956 to endorse Republican President DWIGHT D. EISENHOWER for a second term. New York City Democratic party leaders were outraged at this act of disloyalty and waged a hard-fought campaign to defeat him in the 1958 primary election. Powell's loyal Harlem constituents rebuffed this effort.

In 1961 Powell became chairman of the Committee on Education and Labor. He proved to be an effective, if at times difficult, point man for the Kennedy and Johnson administrations. More than fifty pieces of major legislation were passed out of Powell's committee, including the school lunch program, education and training for the deaf, student loan programs, vocational training, and MINIMUM WAGE increases. Powell was instrumental in passing legislation to aid elementary and secondary education.

By 1966, however, Powell had alienated many House members because of his poor management of the committee budget, numerous and well-publicized government-funded trips abroad, and excessive absenteeism. These congressional problems were compounded by problems in his private life. Powell, despite being a minister, liked the high life. Married three times and attached to other women, he enjoyed his playboy image. Many members of Congress were shocked by this attitude.

More seriously, Powell had been charged with INCOME TAX evasion in 1958, but the trial ended in a HUNG JURY. In 1960 he appeared on a New York City television show and lambasted police corruption. He had previously charged on the floor of the House that a constituent, Esther James, worked for organized crime in Harlem. Statements made on the House floor are covered by congressional IMMUNITY, and Powell knew he could not be sued for slander. On the television show he repeated his charge and labeled James a Mafia "bag woman."

James proceeded to sue Powell, setting in motion a chain of legal and political misfortunes for him. After James won her slander suit and obtained DAMAGES of $46,000, Powell refused to pay the JUDGMENT. He also ignored subpoenas to appear and explain his financial records. Finally the court issued two civil contempt ARREST WARRANTS for his recalcitrance.

After the warrants were issued, Powell would only return to his Harlem district to preach on Sundays, when it was illegal to serve a civil CONTEMPT warrant. The trial court then imposed a thirty-day jail sentence for failing to appear. On appeal, the New York state APPELLATE COURT allowed Powell more time to comply with the SUBPOENA but agreed with the trial court that Powell's jail sentence was not barred by congressional immunity (*James v. Powell*, 26 A.D.2d 295, 274 N.Y.S.2d 192 [1966]). Powell was not to settle the case with James until 1969.

The James episode and allegations of congressional misconduct led the House to strip Powell of his committee chair in January 1967. In addition, the full House refused to seat him until the Judiciary Committee completed its investigation of his affairs. In February 1967 the committee recommended that Powell be censured, fined, and deprived of seniority. The full House disagreed, voting 307 to 116 to exclude him from Congress. Powell then ran in the special election to fill his vacant seat. When he won in April, he refused to take his seat. He ran again in the November 1968 election and was reelected. This time the House seated him but denied him his seniority. Powell refused to take his seat under this condition.

Following his exclusion in 1967, Powell filed a lawsuit against the House of Representatives, arguing that the House had no constitutional basis for excluding him. Typically FEDERAL COURTS do not entertain such lawsuits, because they deal with matters constitutionally delegated to the legislative branch. Although it appeared Powell's lawsuit was barred by the "POLITICAL QUESTION" doctrine, the U.S. Supreme Court ultimately decided that it could intervene. In *Powell v. McCormack*, 395 U.S. 486, 89 S. Ct. 1944, 23 L. Ed. 2d 491 (1969), the Court held that the House of Representatives could not exclude Powell, a duly elected member, who met all the constitutional qualifications of age, citizenship, and residence prescribed by the Constitution.

Powell took his House seat after the Supreme Court decision, but he lost his twenty-two years of seniority. His victory was short-lived. He lost in the June 1970 primary election and failed to get on the ballot as an independent. He retired as minister at the Abyssinian Baptist Church in 1971 and died in Miami, Florida, on April 4, 1972.

See also CONGRESS OF THE UNITED STATES.

Lewis Franklin Powell, Jr.

POWELL, LEWIS FRANKLIN, JR. Lewis Franklin Powell, Jr., served as an associate justice of the U.S. Supreme Court from 1972 to 1987. Powell, who came to the Court as one of the most distinguished lawyers in the United States, was a moderate conservative who became a key "swing" vote on a Court that became divided between conservatives and liberals.

Powell was born on November 19, 1907, in Suffolk, Virginia. A descendant of Virginia families who reached back to the settlement of Jamestown in 1607, Powell attended Washington and Lee University in Lexington, Virginia. He graduated with a bachelor's degree in 1929 and a law degree in 1931. He earned a master's degree from Harvard Law School in 1932.

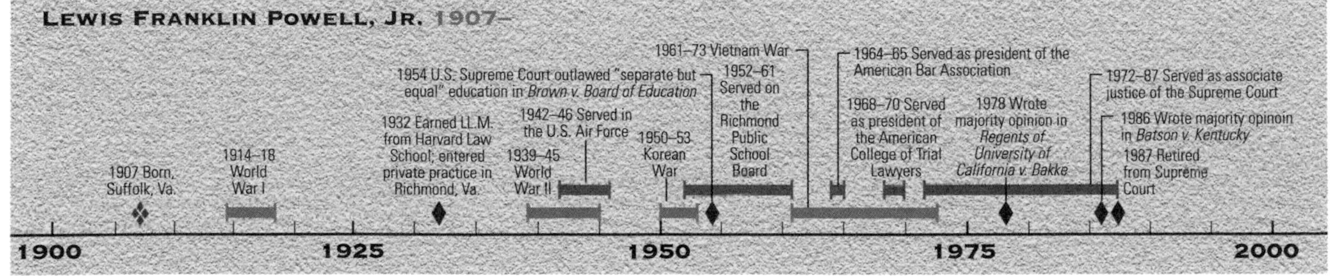

He then entered law practice in Richmond, where he remained until he was appointed to the Supreme Court in 1971. His legal career was interrupted by World War II, when he served as an Air Force intelligence officer. Powell's reputation grew nationally during the 1950s and 1960s. He was elected president of the AMERICAN BAR ASSOCIATION in 1964 and president of the American College of Trial Lawyers in 1968.

Unlike many Supreme Court appointees, Powell did not enter politics. He did, however, distinguish himself as a member and president of the Richmond Public School Board from 1952 to 1961, and later he was a member of the Virginia Board of Education. In the wake of *Brown v. Board of Education*, 347 U.S. 483, 74 S. Ct. 686, 98 L. Ed. 873 (1954), which prohibited state-imposed racial segregation in public schools, many southern communities pledged to defy or evade the Court decision. Some school boards closed the schools and encouraged attendance at white-only private schools, and others refused to integrate. Powell, as president of the Richmond Public School Board, peacefully integrated the school system and publicly called for cooperation rather than resistance to the integration of society.

President RICHARD M. NIXON nominated Powell to the Supreme Court in October 1971. Nixon had offered earlier appointments, but Powell had refused. He was easily confirmed and took his seat in January 1972. He joined a Court that was moving from a liberal majority to a more conservative makeup. Powell was a conservative on crime and law enforcement but was a strong defender of INTEGRATION and CIVIL RIGHTS. In the 1980s, as the Court grew more conservative, Powell moved to the middle and often provided the vote that broke a 4–4 deadlock.

He played a key role in *Regents of University of California v. Bakke*, 438 U.S. 265, 98 S. Ct. 2733, 57 L. Ed. 2d 750 (1978), which dealt with the legality of AFFIRMATIVE ACTION plans to remedy past racial discrimination. Powell wrote the opinion of the Court, holding that a university may consider the race of an applicant as part of its admission procedures. Powell also found, however, that the particular special admissions program at issue in the case had unlawfully discriminated against Allen Bakke, a white applicant, by denying him admission to medical school solely on the basis of his race.

Powell also wrote the majority opinion in *Batson v. Kentucky*, 476 U.S. 79, 106 S. Ct. 1712, 90 L. Ed. 2d 69 (1986), which prohibited prosecutors from excluding prospective jurors on the basis of race. Under the *Batson* test, a defendant may object to a prosecutor's PEREMPTORY CHALLENGE (a removal of a prospective juror without alleging a reason). The prosecutor then must "come forward with a neutral explanation for challenging black jurors." If a neutral explanation cannot be made, the juror will not be excused.

"THE GUARANTEE OF EQUAL PROTECTION CANNOT MEAN ONE THING WHEN APPLIED TO ONE INDIVIDUAL AND SOMETHING ELSE WHEN APPLIED TO A PERSON OF ANOTHER COLOR. IF BOTH ARE NOT ACCORDED THE SAME PROTECTION, THEN IT IS NOT EQUAL."

Powell retired from the Court in 1987.

CROSS-REFERENCES

Jury; *Regents of the University of California v. Bakke;* School Desegregation.

POWELL v. ALABAMA *Powell v. Alabama*, 287 U.S. 45, 53 S. Ct. 55, 77 L. Ed. 158 (1932), is a watershed case in CRIMINAL LAW. The *Powell* case marked the first time that the U.S. Supreme Court reversed a state court conviction because the court failed to appoint counsel or give the defendants an opportunity to obtain counsel.

On March 25, 1931, nine young black men were traveling on a freight train through Alabama. Haywood Patterson, Eugene Williams, and brothers Roy and Andy Wright were friends, having grown up together in Chattanooga, Tennessee. Ozie Powell, Olen Montgomery, Charley Weems, Willie Roberson, and Clarence Norris all hailed from different parts of Georgia. Also on the train were seven white men and two white women.

During the ride a fight broke out, and six of the seven white men were thrown off the train. The train stopped near Scottsboro, Alabama, and a sheriff's posse comprised of private citizens seized the young black men. The white females, Victoria Price and Ruby Bates, claimed that they had been raped. The bewildered black youths were roped together, herded into a truck, and driven to Scottsboro, the Jackson County seat. That night, an unruly mob demanded to lynch the youths, but Sheriff M. L. Wann declared, "If you come in here I will blow your brains out."

The youths were indicted on charges of RAPE on March 31, 1931. They were arraigned the same day in the Jackson County Circuit Court, where they entered pleas of not guilty. Although they faced rape charges, a capital offense at the time, they were held without an opportunity to communicate with the outside world, and no attorney came to see them. Most of the defendants were illiterate, and none had even the most basic knowledge of criminal law.

The court ordered that the defendants be tried in groups, with four trials in all. The trials began on April 6, 1931, just six days after the INDICTMENTS were entered and less than two weeks after the defendants were arrested. The gallery in the courtroom was packed with spectators. Outside the courtroom, a parade band supplied by the Ford Motor Company played popular tunes for the thousands who could not get a seat in the gallery.

At the beginning of the first trial Judge Alfred E. Hawkins asked the defendants if they were ready to proceed to trial. Although Hawkins previously had ordered members of the local bar to assist the defendants, no attorney answered for the defendants except Scottsboro lawyer Milo Moody, and Stephen Roddy, a lawyer from Chattanooga. Moody was seventy years old. Roddy was not a member of the Alabama bar or a criminal defense attorney, and he was unfamiliar with the court rules and laws of Alabama.

Roddy and Judge Hawkins engaged in a murky exchange that made only two things clear: the defendants had not seen an attorney until the day of trial, and they would not be receiving effective representation in their capital trials. Roddy represented the defendants in a perfunctory fashion, and the court excluded evidence helpful to the defendants. Each trial lasted less than one day, and to the noisy delight of onlookers, eight of the nine defendants were convicted and sentenced to death. Only thirteen-year-old Roy Wright was spared: his case ended in a MISTRIAL when the jury held out for the death penalty, which could not be enforced against a juvenile.

After their convictions, the youths were represented by George W. Chamlee, Sr., and Joseph R. Brodsky from the International Labor Defense, an organization dominated by Communists. On appeal to the Supreme Court of Alabama, Chamlee and Brodsky argued that the defendants had not received fair trials for various reasons. Specifically, Chamlee and Brodsky argued that the convictions should be reversed because the crowd outside the courthouse had influenced the jurors, the juries in Alabama contained no black persons, and the defendants had not received adequate legal representation. The Supreme Court of Alabama reversed the conviction of Eugene Williams on the grounds that he may have been a juvenile and should have been tried as one, but the court affirmed the other seven convictions. On March 24, 1932, the Supreme Court of Alabama ordered that the seven defendants be put to death by electrocution on August 31, 1932. The executions were postponed when the U.S. Supreme Court decided to hear the appeals.

In a 7–2 decision delivered on November 7, 1932, the Court reversed all seven convictions. Justice GEORGE SUTHERLAND, writing for the majority, began the opinion by recounting the procedural history of the case and reciting the paltry and sometimes inaccurate record of the case. Sutherland noted that the record indicated that the defendants had been represented by counsel at the arraignment, "[b]ut no counsel having been employed . . . the record does not disclose when, or under what circumstances, an appointment of counsel was made, or who was appointed." Sutherland also referred to the mob surrounding the defendants. According to Sutherland, "[I]t does not appear that the defendants were seriously threatened with . . . mob violence; but it does appear that the attitude of the community was one of great hostility." Although the intimidating atmosphere played a part in the opinion, the Supreme Court was more concerned with the procedures employed by the trial court.

Judge Hawkins had appointed the entire bar of Scottsboro to represent the defendants, but he did not require the attorneys to accept the case. Sutherland quoted the colloquy between Hawkins and Roddy that occurred just before the trial, which revealed that no attorney was prepared to take the case. Nevertheless, Hawkins allowed the trials to go forward, "and in this casual fashion," Sutherland lamented, "the matter of counsel in a capital case was disposed of."

Sutherland began the Court's legal analysis by declaring that, although the defendants may have appeared guilty, they were nonetheless presumed to be innocent. Sutherland then proceeded to frame the issue in the case as whether the defendants were denied the assistance of counsel and, if so, whether such a denial was an infringement of their rights under the FOURTEENTH AMENDMENT to the U.S. Constitution, the amendment that makes DUE PROCESS requirements applicable to the states.

Sutherland concluded that states were obliged under the Constitution to provide the right to an attorney in a criminal case and that the right had not been extended to the defendants. Sutherland cited Supreme Court precedent for the proposition that due process can be determined by ascertaining "what were the settled usages and modes of proceeding under the common and statute law of England before the Declaration of Independence." He then examined the history of the criminal defendant's right to an attorney and concluded that such a right did not exist in England until the mid-nineteenth century, that the English rule was assailed by legal analysts in England and rejected by twelve of the thirteen colonies, and that it was a necessary incident to due process of law. The denial of counsel, Sutherland declared, "is so outrageous and so obviously a perversion of all sense of proportion that the rule was constantly, vigorously and sometimes passionately assailed by English statesmen and lawyers."

Sutherland still had to make the requirement of counsel applicable to the states. The passage of the Fourteenth Amendment in 1868 forbid states to "deprive any person of life, liberty, or property, without due process of law," but it remained for the court to determine precisely what procedures constituted due process. Quoting *Hebert v. State of Louisiana,* 272 U.S. 312, 47 S. Ct. 103, 71 L. Ed. 270 (1926), Sutherland explained that due process was required if a right was "of such a character that it cannot be denied without violating those 'fundamental principles of liberty and justice which lie at the base of all our civil and political institutions.' "

Sutherland noted that it was well established that due process in a criminal case necessarily included an opportunity to be heard. Such an opportunity could not be achieved even by intelligent laypersons.

Having established that the right to an attorney was a fundamental due process right applicable to the states, Sutherland applied the law to the facts of the case. The defendants were held incommunicado and prevented from obtaining counsel of their own choice. Sutherland declared that because of

> the ignorance and illiteracy of the defendants, their youth, the circumstances of public hostility, the imprisonment; and close surveillance of the defendants by military forces, the fact that their friends and families were all in other states and communication with them necessarily difficult, and above all [because] they stood in deadly peril of losing their lives—we think the failure of the trial court to give them reasonable time and opportunity to secure counsel was a clear denial of due process.

The failure of the trial court to appoint counsel was likewise a denial of due process. Hawkins had made an attempt to appoint attorneys, but it was a feeble one. Sutherland declared that the attorneys were not "given that clear appreciation of responsibility or impressed with that individual sense of duty which should and naturally would accompany the appointment of a selected member of the bar."

The *Powell* holding declared that the Due Process Clause of the Fourteenth Amendment required that state courts give defendants an opportunity to obtain counsel. It also created the rule that due process requires state courts to appoint counsel for indigent defendants in all capital cases and that a free attorney for indigent defendants in noncapital cases is required if an unfair trial would result without the appointment. *Powell* was used as PRECEDENT for other Supreme Court decisions expanding the right to counsel, as well as decisions establishing that the legal representation defendants receive should not fall below a minimum standard of effectiveness.

The defendants were retried again and again after the Supreme Court reversed their convictions. In 1935 the High Court again intervened in the prosecutions, reversing second death sentences based on the fact that there were no blacks on the JURY rolls (*Norris v. Alabama,* 294 U.S. 587, 55 S. Ct. 579, 79 L. Ed. 1074 [1935]).

In 1937 four of the defendants were released, but the other five defendants remained in prison. Each eventually gained release through either PAROLE or escape. In 1976 Alabama officials took a new look at the case, and Governor GEORGE WALLACE pardoned Clarence Norris. Norris, the last surviving defendant, had violated his parole by fleeing Alabama and had been at large for more than thirty years.

CROSS-REFERENCES

Capital Punishment; Criminal Procedure; Incorporation Doctrine; Right to Counsel.

POWER The right, ability, or authority to perform an act. An ability to generate a change in a particular legal relationship by doing or not doing a certain act.

In a restricted sense, a liberty or authority that is reserved by, or limited to, a person to dispose of real or personal property, for his or her own benefit or for the benefit of others, or that enables one person to dispose of an interest that is VESTED in another.

POWER OF ATTORNEY A written document in which one person (the PRINCIPAL) appoints another person to act as an agent on his or her behalf, thus conferring authority on the agent to perform certain acts or functions on behalf of the principal.

Powers of attorney are routinely granted to allow the agent to take care of a variety of transactions for the principal, such as executing a stock power, handling a tax AUDIT, or maintaining a safe-deposit box. Powers of attorney can be written to be either general (full) or limited to special circumstances. A power of attorney generally is terminated when the principal dies or becomes incompetent, but the principal can revoke the power of attorney at any time.

A sample power of attorney

Power of Attorney
Know All By These Presents:

THAT

be made, constituted and appointed, and by these presents do make, constitute and appoint for and in name, place and stead true and lawful attorney

giving and granting unto said attorney full power and authority to do and perform all and every act and thing whatsoever requisite and necessary to be done in and about the premises as fully, to all intents and purposes, as might or could do if personally present, with full power of substitution and revocation, hereby ratifying and confirming all that said attorney or substitute shall lawfully do or cause to be done by virtue hereof.

IN WITNESS WHEREOF, have hereunto set hand ______ and seal ______ the day of , in the year one thousand nine-hundred and

Sealed and delivered in the presence of

____________________ } ____________________ *(Seal)*

____

State of Florida,
County of
I Hereby Certify, *that on this day of*
A.D. 19 , before me personally appeared

to me personally known, and known to me to be the same person described in and who executed the within power of attorney, and acknowledged the within power of attorney to be act and deed.

IN TESTIMONY WHEREOF, I have hereunto subscribed my name and affixed my seal of office the day and year last above written.

My Commission expires

____

____
NOTARY PUBLIC

A special type of power of attorney that is used frequently is the "durable" power of attorney. A durable power of attorney differs from a traditional power of attorney in that it continues the AGENCY relationship beyond the incapacity of the principal. The two types of durable power of attorney are immediate and "springing." The first type takes effect as soon as the durable power of attorney is executed. The second is intended to "spring" into effect when a specific event occurs, such as the disability of the principal. Most often, durable powers of attorney are created to deal with decisions involving either property management or health care.

Durable powers of attorney have become popular because they enable the principal to have her or his affairs handled easily and inexpensively after she or he has become incapacitated. Before the durable power of attorney was created, the only way to handle the affairs of an incapacitated person was to appoint a GUARDIAN, a process that frequently involves complex and costly court proceedings, as well as the often humiliating determination that the principal is wholly incapable and in need of protection. With a durable power of attorney, on the other hand, a principal can appoint someone to handle her or his affairs after she or he becomes incompetent, and the document can be crafted to confer either general power or power in certain limited circumstances. Because no judicial proceedings are necessary, the principal saves time and money and avoids the stigma of being declared incompetent.

The concept of the durable power of attorney was created in 1969 when the National Conference of Commissioners on Uniform State Laws promulgated the Uniform Probate Code (U.P.C. § 5–501). Ten years later, the provisions of the code dealing with the durable power of attorney were modified and published as the Uniform Durable Power of Attorney Act (UDPA). All fifty states recognize some version of the durable power of attorney, having adopted either the UDPA or the Uniform Probate Code, or some variation of them. Versions of the durable power of attorney vary from state to state. Certain powers cannot be delegated, including the powers to make, amend, or revoke a WILL, change INSURANCE beneficiaries, contract a MARRIAGE, and vote.

See also LIVING WILL.

POWER OF SALE A clause commonly inserted in a MORTGAGE and DEED OF TRUST that grants the creditor or trustee the right and authority, upon DEFAULT in the payment of the debt, to advertise and sell the property at public auction, without resorting to a court for authorization to do so.

Once the creditor is paid out of the net proceeds, the property is transferred by DEED to the purchaser, and the surplus, if any, is returned to the DEBTOR. The debtor is thereby completely divested of any interest in the property and has no subsequent right of REDEMPTION—recovery of property by paying the mortgage debt in full.

POWER OF TERMINATION A future interest in REAL PROPERTY whereby the GRANTOR conveys an ESTATE to another, called the GRANTEE, subject to a particular CONDITION, the breach of which forfeits the grantee's interest in the property.

For example, A, owner of Blackacre, might convey the land "To B, but if liquor is sold on the premises, then A may reenter and repossess." A has the power to terminate the interest of B in the land if the condition occurs.

A power of termination is also known as a right of reentry. See also RIGHT OF REENTRY.

PRACTICE Repeated or customary action; habitual performance; a succession of acts of similar kind; custom; USAGE. The exercise of any profession.

The form or mode or proceeding in courts of justice for the enforcement of rights or the redress of wrongs, as distinguished from the SUBSTANTIVE LAW that gives the right or denounces the wrong. The form, manner, or order of instituting and conducting an ACTION or other judicial proceeding, through its successive stages to its end, in accordance with the rules and principles laid down by law or by the regulations and PRECEDENTS of the courts.

An ATTORNEY is actually engaged in the practice of law when she maintains an office, offers to perform legal services, describes herself as an attorney on letterheads or business cards, counsels clients, negotiates with other parties or opposing counsel, and fixes and collects fees for legal work. A doctor is practicing medicine when he discovers the cause and nature of diseases, treats illnesses and injuries, or prescribes and administers medical or surgical care. Lawyers and doctors must qualify for LICENSES before they may practice their professions.

PRAECIPE [*Latin, Give an order.*] An original WRIT, one of the forms of legal process used to commence an ACTION. A praecipe was drawn up in the alternative and commanded the defendant to do what was ordered or to appear and show why he or she had not done it. An order that commands the clerk of a court to issue a formal writ of execution directing the enforcement of a JUDGMENT already rendered and commanding a public officer to seize the defendant's property in order to satisfy the DEBT.

PRAYER The request contained in a BILL in EQUITY that the court will grant the PROCESS, aid, or RELIEF that the COMPLAINANT desires.

In addition, the term *prayer* is applied to that segment of the bill that contains this request.

PREAMBLE A clause at the beginning of a CONSTITUTION or STATUTE explaining the reasons for its enactment and the objectives it seeks to attain.

Generally a preamble is a declaration by the legislature of the reasons for the passage of the statute, and it aids in the interpretation of any ambiguities within the statute to which it is prefixed. It has been held, however, that a preamble is not an essential part of an act, and it neither enlarges nor confers powers.

PRECATORY LANGUAGE Words in a WILL or a TRUST used by the TESTATOR (the person making the will) or SETTLOR (the person making a trust) to express a wish or desire to have his or her property disposed of in a certain way or to have some other task undertaken, which do not necessarily impose a mandatory obligation upon anyone to carry out the wish.

Precatory language in a will or trust usually includes such terms as the testator's "request," "hope," or "desire" that property be given to a certain person or be disposed of in a particular manner. Whether such language can be viewed as mandatory, thus creating an enforceable will or trust, or whether it merely expresses the testator's wish to have something done has been a difficult issue for the courts. The court must look to the intent of the testator to determine whether the precatory language establishes an enforceable agreement.

The court usually examines a number of factors, including other language used in the will or trust, to determine the testator's intent. For example, if in her will Anne says only that she "wishes" or "would like" her house to be sold to her cousin Bill on her death, the court may find the language to be precatory and thus unenforceable because Anne was merely expressing a wish or a recommendation. But if elsewhere in the will a definite selling price is indicated, the court may conclude that Anne, despite the precatory terms used, did intend for her cousin to be offered the house because she took the additional step of specifying the price for which the property was to be disposed of at her death.

In addition to examining other language in the will or trust for clues to the testator's intent, the court may look to the relationship of the parties involved. For instance, if Tom puts language in a trust "requesting" that his daughter receive money or a particular gift, a judge may be more apt to enforce the trust. In doing so, the court acts on the assumption that Tom and his daughter share a close personal relationship and that he would want her to be provided for following his death even if he was less than definite in the language he used in the trust.

Furthermore, language in a will or trust making a gift to CHARITY may sometimes be upheld even if it appears to be precatory. For example, if Sue states in her will that she "would like" some of her money to be used for a particular program at a university, a court may view her language as mandatory. When a charitable organization is involved, courts, as a policy matter, tend to construe language liberally to make the gift effective.

The litigation that often results from precatory language in wills and trusts can be avoided by the careful use of clear and definite language that leaves no doubt as to how the testator wishes to dispose of her or his property. Seeking legal advice when drafting a will or trust may be the best way to prevent litigation.

PRECEDENT A court decision that is cited as an example or ANALOGY to resolve similar questions of law in later cases.

The Anglo-American COMMON-LAW tradition is built on the doctrine of STARE DECISIS ("stand by decided matters"), which directs a court to look to past decisions for guidance on how to decide a case before it. This means that the legal rules applied to a prior case with facts similar to those of the case now before a court should be applied to resolve the legal dispute.

The use of precedent has been justified as providing predictability, stability, fairness, and efficiency in the law. Reliance upon precedent contributes predictability to the law because it provides notice of what a person's rights and obligations are in particular circumstances. A person contemplating an ACTION has the ability to know beforehand the legal outcome. It also means that lawyers can give legal advice to clients based on settled rules of law.

The use of precedent also stabilizes the law. Society can expect the law, which organizes social relationships in terms of rights and obligations, to remain relatively stable and coherent through the use of precedent. The need is great in society to rely on legal rules, even if persons disagree with particular ones. Justice LOUIS D. BRANDEIS emphasized the importance of this when he wrote, "*Stare decisis* is usually the wise policy, because in most matters it is more important that the applicable rule of law be settled than that it be settled right" (*Burnet v. Coronado Oil & Gas Co.*, 285 U.S. 393, 52 S. Ct. 443, 76 L. Ed. 815 [1932]).

Reliance upon precedent also promotes the expectation that the law is just. The idea that like cases should be treated alike is anchored in the assumption that one person is the legal equal of any other. Thus, persons in similar situations should not be treated differently except for legally relevant and clearly justifiable reasons. Precedent promotes judicial restraint and limits a judge's ability to determine the outcome of a case in a way that he or she might choose if there were no precedent. This function of precedent gives it its moral force.

Precedent also enhances efficiency. Reliance on the accumulation of legal rules helps guide judges in their resolution of legal disputes. If judges had to begin the law anew in each case, they would add more time to the adjudicative process and would duplicate their efforts.

The use of precedent has resulted in the publication of LAW REPORTS that contain case decisions. Lawyers and judges conduct legal research in these reports seeking precedents. They try to determine whether the facts of the present case precisely match previous cases. If so, the application of legal precedent may be clear. If, however, the facts are not exact, prior cases may be distinguished and their precedents discounted.

Though the application of precedent may appear to be mechanical, a simple means of matching facts and rules, it is a more subjective process. Legal rules, embodied in precedents, are generalizations that accentuate the importance of certain facts and discount or ignore others. The application of precedent relies on reasoning by analogy. Analogies can be neither correct nor incorrect but only more or less persuasive. REASONABLE persons may come to different yet defensible conclusions about what rule should prevail.

The judicial system maintains great fidelity to the application of precedents. There are times, however, when a court has no precedents to rely on. In these "cases of FIRST IMPRESSION," a court may have to draw analogies to other areas of the law to justify its decision. Once decided, this decision becomes precedential.

APPELLATE COURTS typically create precedent. The U.S. Supreme Court's main function is to settle conflicts over legal rules and to issue decisions that either reaffirm or create precedent. Despite the Supreme Court's reliance on precedent, it will depart from its prior decisions when either historical conditions change or the philosophy of the court undergoes a major shift. The most famous reversal of precedent is *Brown v. Board of Education*, 347 U.S. 483, 74 S. Ct. 686, 98 L. Ed. 873 (1954), in which the Supreme Court repudiated the "separate but equal" doctrine of *Plessy v. Ferguson*, 163 U.S. 537, 16 S. Ct. 1138, 41 L. Ed. 256 (1896). This doctrine had legitimated racial segregation for almost sixty years but finally gave way in *Brown*, when a unanimous court ruled that SEPARATE BUT EQUAL was a denial of EQUAL PROTECTION of the laws.

CROSS-REFERENCES

Brown v. Board of Education of Topeka, Kansas; Case Law; Court Opinion; *Plessy v. Ferguson.*

PRECEPT An order, WRIT, WARRANT, or PROCESS. An order or direction, emanating from authority, to an officer or body of officers, commanding that officer or those officers to do some act within the scope of their powers. Rule imposing a standard of conduct or action.

In English law, the direction issued by a SHERIFF to the proper returning officers of cities and boroughs within his JURISDICTION for the election of members to serve in parliament.

In old French law, a kind of letters issued by the king in subversion of the laws, being orders to the judges to do or tolerate things contrary to law.

PRECINCT A CONSTABLE's or police district. A small geographical unit of government. An election district created for convenient localization of polling places. A county or municipal subdivision for casting and counting votes in elections.

PRECIPE See PRAECIPE.

PRECLUSION ORDER A court sanction that prevents a party who has not complied with a direction to supply information in the DISCOVERY stage of a lawsuit from later supporting or challenging designated claims or defenses related to the facts that he or she withheld.

A sample preclusion order

At a Special Term, Part ______ of the ______ Court of the State of ______, held in and for the County of ______, at ______, on the ______ day of ______, 19__.

Present: Hon. ______, Justice.

______, Plaintiff,
-against-
______, Defendant,

ORDER PROHIBITING DISOBEDIENT PARTY FROM SUPPORTING CLAIM

Index No. ______

The defendant, ______, by his attorney, ______, having duly moved for an order pursuant to [*applicable law*] prohibiting the plaintiff from offering any evidence upon the trial of the above entitled action concerning [*specify claim for which support is to be prohibited*], upon the ground that the plaintiff has wilfully failed to disclose information which ought to have been disclosed, and said motion having regularly come on to be heard,

[*continued on page 132*]

A sample preclusion order (continued)

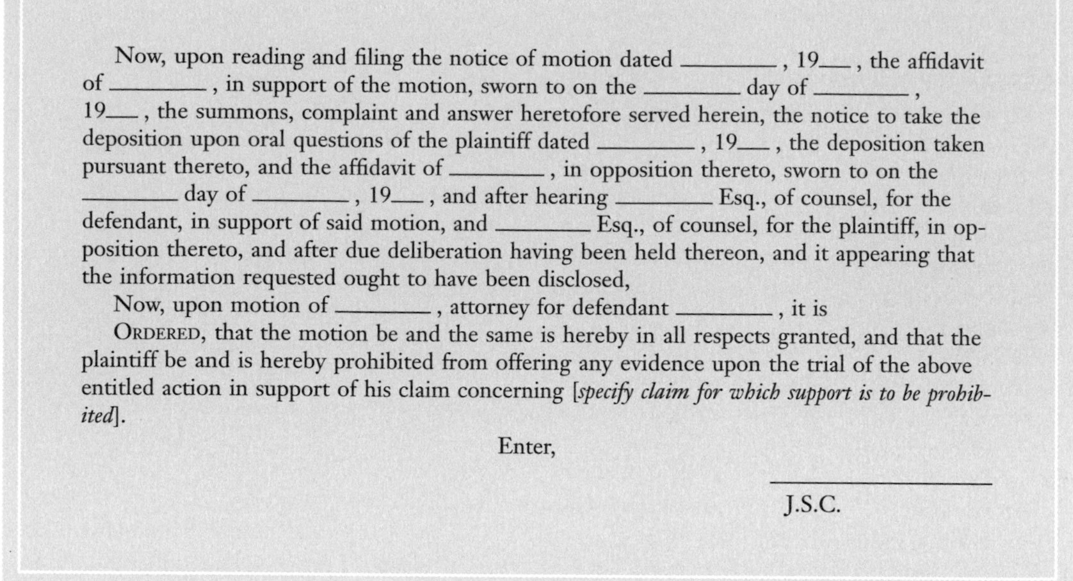

Now, upon reading and filing the notice of motion dated ________, 19___, the affidavit of ________, in support of the motion, sworn to on the ________ day of ________, 19___, the summons, complaint and answer heretofore served herein, the notice to take the deposition upon oral questions of the plaintiff dated ________, 19___, the deposition taken pursuant thereto, and the affidavit of ________, in opposition thereto, sworn to on the ________ day of ________, 19___, and after hearing ________ Esq., of counsel, for the defendant, in support of said motion, and ________ Esq., of counsel, for the plaintiff, in opposition thereto, and after due deliberation having been held thereon, and it appearing that the information requested ought to have been disclosed,

Now, upon motion of ________, attorney for defendant ________, it is

ORDERED, that the motion be and the same is hereby in all respects granted, and that the plaintiff be and is hereby prohibited from offering any evidence upon the trial of the above entitled action in support of his claim concerning [*specify claim for which support is to be prohibited*].

Enter,

____
J.S.C.

Rule 37 of the Federal Rules of Civil Procedure governs the granting of preclusion orders in actions brought in FEDERAL COURTS. See also CIVIL PROCEDURE.

PREEMPTION A doctrine based on the SUPREMACY CLAUSE of the U.S. Constitution that holds that certain matters are of such a national, as opposed to local, character that federal laws preempt or take precedence over state laws. As such, a state may not pass a law inconsistent with the federal law.

A doctrine of state law that holds that a state law displaces a local law or regulation that is in the same field and is in conflict or inconsistent with the state law.

Article VI, Section 2, of the U.S. Constitution provides that the "... Constitution, and the Laws of the United States ... shall be the supreme Law of the Land." This Supremacy Clause has come to mean that the national government, in exercising any of the powers enumerated in the Constitution, must prevail over any conflicting or inconsistent state exercise of power. The federal preemption doctrine is a judicial response to the conflict between federal and state legislation. When it is clearly established that a federal law preempts a state law, the state law must be declared invalid.

A state law may be struck down even when it does not explicitly conflict with federal law, if a court finds that Congress has legitimately occupied the field with federal legislation. Questions in this area require careful balancing of important state and federal interests. Problems arise when Congress fails to make its purpose explicit, which is often the case. The court must then draw inferences based on the presumed objectives of federal law and the supposed impact of related state action.

The federal right to regulate interstate commerce under the COMMERCE CLAUSE of the U.S. Constitution has resulted in federal preemption of state labor laws. Likewise, the Supreme Court, in *Burbank v. Lockheed Air Terminal*, 411 U.S. 624, 93 S. Ct. 1854, 36 L. Ed. 2d 547 (1973), declared that state and local laws that interfere with comprehensive federal ENVIRONMENTAL LAWS and regulations are invalid.

In *California v. Federal Energy Regulatory Commission*, 495 U.S. 490, 110 S. Ct. 2024, 109 L. Ed. 2d 474 (1990), the Supreme Court held that state regulations imposing minimum flow rates on rivers used to generate hydroelectric power were preempted by the Federal Power Act (16 U.S.C.A. § 791 et seq. [1933]). In *Mississippi Power and Light Company v. Mississippi ex rel. Moore*, 487 U.S. 354, 108 S. Ct. 2428, 101 L. Ed. 2d 322 (1988), the Court held that the Federal Energy Regulatory Commission's regulations preempted a state's authority to set electric power rates.

At the state level, preemption occurs when a state statute conflicts with a local ORDINANCE on the same subject matter. Preemption within the states varies with individual state constitutions, provisions for the powers of political subdivisions, and the decisions of state courts. For example, if a state legislature enacts gun control legislation and the intent of the legislation is to occupy the field of gun control, then a municipality is preempted from enacting its own gun control ordinance.

See also FEDERALISM; STATES' RIGHTS.

PREEMPTIVE RIGHT The privilege of a stockholder to maintain a proportionate share of the ownership of a CORPORATION by purchasing a proportionate share of any new STOCK issues.

In most JURISDICTIONS, an existing stockholder has the right to buy additional shares of a new issue to preserve equity before others have a right to purchase shares of the new issue.

PREFERENCE The act of an insolvent DEBTOR who pays one or more creditors the full amount of their claims or a larger amount than they would be entitled to receive on a PRO RATA distribution.

For example, a debtor owes three creditors five thousand dollars each. All three are equally entitled to payment, but the debtor has only twelve thousand dollars in ASSETS. Instead of paying each CREDITOR four thousand dollars, the debtor pays two creditors in full and pays the third creditor the remaining two thousand dollars.

The COMMON LAW does not condemn a preference. Some state statutes prescribe that certain transfers are void—of no legal force or binding effect—because of their preferential character. If a state antipreference provision protects any actual creditor of the debtor, the TRUSTEE in BANKRUPTCY can take advantage of it.

Bankruptcy law does condemn certain preferences. The bankruptcy trustee can void any transfer of property of the debtor if the trustee can establish the following:

1. The transfer was "to or for the benefit of a creditor."
2. The transfer was made for or on account of an "antecedent debt"—that is, a debt owed prior to the time of the transfer.
3. The debtor was insolvent at the time of the transfer.
4. The transfer was made within ninety days before the date of the filing of the bankruptcy petition or was made between ninety days and one year before the date of the filing of the petition to an INSIDER who had reasonable cause to believe that the debtor was insolvent at the time of the transfer.
5. The transfer has the effect of increasing the amount that the transferee would receive in a LIQUIDATION proceeding under chapter 7 of the bankruptcy law (11 U.S.C.A. § 701 et seq.).

11 U.S.C.A. § 547.

Other statutory provisions, however, create exceptions; if a transfer comes within an exception, the bankruptcy trustee cannot invalidate the transfer even though the aforementioned five elements exist.

See also INSOLVENCY.

PREFERRED STOCK STOCK shares that have preferential rights to dividends or to amounts distributable on LIQUIDATION, or to both, ahead of common shareholders.

Preferred stock is given preference over COMMON STOCK. Holders of preferred stock receive dividends at a fixed annual rate. The earnings of a CORPORATION are applied to this payment before common stockholders receive dividends. If corporate earnings are insufficient for the fixed annual DIVIDEND, the preferred stock will absorb the total amount of earnings, and the common stockholders will be precluded from receiving a dividend. When corporate income exceeds the amount that is needed to pay preferred stockholders, the remainder is generally paid to common stockholders. In special situations, the remainder may be distributed PRO RATA to both classes of stock, in which case the preferred stock is said to "participate" with the common stock.

Preferred stock can be cumulative or noncumulative. If it is cumulative and if the fixed dividend remains unpaid, it becomes a debit upon the surplus earnings of succeeding years. Accumulated dividends must be paid in full before common stockholders can receive dividends. When preferred stock is noncumulative, its preference is extinguished by the failure of the corporation to have sufficient earnings to pay the fixed dividend in a given year.

Corporations sometimes issue preferred stock as a defense against takeovers. If a takeover succeeds, the acquiring company is faced with the choice of buying the stock at a high price or paying dividends on it.

O.G.S., INC./THE PICTURE CUBE

PREJUDICE A forejudgment; BIAS; partiality; preconceived opinion. A leaning toward one side of a cause for some reason other than a conviction of its justice.

A juror can be disqualified from a case for being prejudiced, if his or her views on a subject or attitude toward a party will unduly influence the final decision.

When a lawsuit is dismissed WITHOUT PREJUDICE, it signifies that none of the rights or privileges of the individual involved are considered to be lost or waived. The same holds true when an ADMISSION is made or when a MOTION is denied with the designation *without prejudice*.

A DISMISSAL without prejudice permits a new lawsuit to be brought on the same grounds because no decision has been reached about the controversy on its merits. The whole subject in litigation is as much open to a subsequent suit as if no suit had ever been brought. The purpose and effect of the words *without prejudice* in a judgment, order, or decree dismissing a suit are to prohibit the defendant from using the defense of RES JUDICATA in any later action by the same plaintiff on the subject matter. A dismissal with prejudice, however, is a bar to relitigation of the subject matter.

A decision resulting in prejudicial error substantially affects an appellant's legal rights and is often the ground for a reversal of the judgment and for the granting of a new trial.

PRELAW EDUCATION A preparatory curriculum comprising introductory law courses and interdisciplinary subjects, offered to undergraduate students to instruct them in and acquaint them with the subject matter of law, thereby assisting them in deciding whether to seek admission to law school and facilitating the process of law study in law school.

Colleges and universities offer several types of prelaw education to undergraduate students who are interested in attending law school. Some institutions offer a prelaw major course of study leading to a degree, a few offer a six-year course of study that combines undergraduate and law school education, and almost all offer an informal prelaw curriculum that emphasizes skills and knowledge essential to the study and practice of law.

The AMERICAN BAR ASSOCIATION does not recommend any particular major for law school. Although political science is a popular prelaw major, there is no specific major preferred by law schools. Law students can major in anything from engineering to history to the fine arts. Some law schools state in their catalogs that they neither recommend prelaw courses nor grant an applicant any additional consideration because he or she pursued a prelaw education.

A particular major is not important to a law school admissions committee, but good grades are critical for acceptance. In addition, admissions committees seek a diverse first-year class and may look at volunteer and extracurricular activities as well as a college transcript and the results of the LAW SCHOOL ADMISSION TEST (LSAT).

Law schools have no prerequisite courses for admission. However, colleges offer courses that help hone the skills that will be important to a law student. Such "lawyering" skills include analytical thinking and problem solving, critical reading, writing, and oral communication. Courses in English, composition, and speech will enhance these means of communication. The legal profession finds its basis in the formation and operation of government institutions, and courses in political science and history help develop a better understanding of these institutions. Creative thinking is also an important skill in the legal profession. Courses in math and, specifically, logic are recommended. Because law is a social science that focuses on human behavior, courses in psychology, sociology, religion, and philosophy may also be useful.

See also CASE METHOD; LEGAL EDUCATION.

PRELIMINARY HEARING A proceeding before a judicial officer in which the officer must decide whether a CRIME was committed, whether the crime occurred within the territorial JURISDICTION of the court, and whether there is PROBABLE CAUSE to believe that the defendant committed the crime.

After the police have arrested a crime suspect, the suspect is entitled to a preliminary hearing. Designed as a safeguard against unreasonable arrest and detention, the hearing is conducted to determine whether there is sufficient EVIDENCE to hold the defendant for trial. State and federal rules of CRIMINAL PROCEDURE provide for when a hearing must be held and what issues must be raised, which depend in large part on whether the crime is a MISDEMEANOR, gross misdemeanor, or FELONY.

The most common preliminary hearing is the initial appearance, which is also called the first appearance. Various procedural steps may be taken during the initial appearance. In minor misdemeanor cases, the initial appearance may be the only one, if the defendant pleads guilty. When the charge is more serious, the accused at the initial appearance may be informed of the charges, advised of the RIGHT TO COUNSEL and the right to remain silent, warned that any statement made may be used against the suspect in court, and advised of how to seek release on bail. In some jurisdictions, including the federal courts, a PLEA may be entered and BAIL may be set at this first appearance. In other jurisdictions, the suspect will not be allowed to make a plea if the offense is a felony or gross misdemeanor, and a preliminary hearing, also called a preliminary examination, will be promptly scheduled.

The U.S. Supreme Court, in *Gerstein v. Pugh*, 420 U.S. 103, 95 S. Ct. 854, 43 L. Ed. 2d 54 (1975), mandated that persons arrested without a WARRANT and held by the police must be given a preliminary hearing to determine if there is probable cause. Probable cause means that a REASONABLE ground exists for belief in the facts, and the hearing examines whether a prudent person would believe that the suspect committed the offense in light of those facts. In *County of Riverside v. McLaughlin*, 500 U.S. 44, 111 S. Ct. 1661, 114 L. Ed. 2d 49 (1991), the Court made it a constitutional requirement that a prompt judicial determination of probable cause follow a warrantless search. It ruled that a determination must be made without unreasonable delay, and in no event later than forty-eight hours after arrest. Therefore, all state and federal warrantless arrests must comply with the holdings of *Gerstein* and *County of Riverside.*

In gross misdemeanor and felony cases there is typically a second appearance, which is known as the preliminary hearing or preliminary examination. Rule 5(c) of the Federal Rules of Criminal Procedure and state rules of criminal procedure follow essentially the same process for this type of hearing. Unlike the informality of a first appearance, the preliminary hearing is an adversarial proceeding, which includes the PROSECUTOR and the defendant's attorney. This hearing tests the existence of probable cause early in the proceedings by allowing the introduction of evidence, the examination and CROSS-EXAMINATION of WITNESSES, and limited forms of DISCOVERY (the disclosure of information). Although the features of a preliminary hearing or examination are similar to those of a trial, the hearing is confined to determining whether the defendant should stand trial or be released. A defendant may challenge the constitutionality of police actions, including searches, seizures, and CONFESSIONS. Under the federal rules, this hearing must be conducted within ten days of the initial appearance if the defendant is in police custody, and within twenty days if the defendant is not in custody.

In felony cases in states where the grand jury INDICTMENT is used to start a criminal proceeding, defendants often waive the preliminary hearing, because the GRAND JURY will make the probable cause determination. However, some defendants request a preliminary hearing because it allows them to gain information about the basis of the prosecution's case or to move for dismissal of the case. For example, O. J. Simpson requested a preliminary hearing in 1994 after being charged with two counts of first-degree murder. Although Simpson's attorney, Robert Shapiro, failed to secure a dismissal, he was able to elicit information from police and forensic witnesses that proved valuable at Simpson's 1995 murder trial, which ended in Simpson's acquittal.

PRELIMINARY INJUNCTION A temporary order made by a court at the request of one party that prevents the other party from pursuing a particular course of conduct until the conclusion of a trial on the MERITS.

A preliminary injunction is regarded as extraordinary relief. The party against whom it is sought must receive notice and an opportunity to appear at a hearing to argue that the INJUNCTION should not be granted. A preliminary injunction should be granted only when the requesting party is highly likely to be successful in a trial on the merits and there is a substantial likelihood of irreparable harm unless the injunction is granted. If a party has shown only a limited probability of success, but has raised substantial and difficult questions worthy of additional inquiry, a court will grant a preliminary injunction only if the harm to him or her outweighs the injury to others if the injunction is denied.

PREMARITAL AGREEMENT A CONTRACT made in anticipation of MARRIAGE that specifies the rights and obligations of the parties. Such an agreement typically includes terms for PROPERTY distribution in the event the marriage terminates.

A premarital agreement, also known as a prenuptial or antenuptial agreement, is a contract between two persons who intend to marry. All states recognize premarital agreements through statutes or court decisions.

A premarital agreement is an unusual contract. It is an agreement between marrying persons that, at least in part, contemplates the breakup of the marriage. The subject matter of the agreement is unique: no other contract can address such matters as CHILD CUSTODY, child education, and spousal maintenance. The relationship of the parties is special: the contract is made not by two parties operating at arm's length, but by two persons who are in love. The contract is enforceable without CONSIDERATION, or the exchange of value, whereas most contracts require consideration. Finally, the contract may not be enforced until years after it

A sample premarital agreement

Whereas, _________, of _________, herein called the Husband, and _________, of _________, herein called the Wife, contemplate entering into marriage relations; and whereas, the Husband has a large estate and has children by a former marriage; and whereas, the Wife is possessed of property in her own right and has a child by a former marriage; and whereas, the said parties desire to prescribe, limit, and determine the interest and control which each of them may have in the estate of the other party; therefore the following agreement is entered into:

Know all men by these presents: That we, _________ and _________, being about to enter into the marriage relations, do hereby agree:

Husband Releases His Rights in Wife's Estate

1. In the event of the death of the Wife during the continuance of said marriage relations, the Husband surviving her, then the Husband shall receive from the estate of the Wife the sum of five dollars; such sum when paid by the executors or administrators of the estate of the Wife to be in full for all claims and demands of every kind and character which the Husband shall have against the estate of the Wife.

Wife Limits Her Rights in Husband's Estate

2. In the event of the death of the Husband during the said marriage relations, the Wife agrees that her claim upon the estate of the Husband shall be limited to $_________, and a payment by the executors or the administrators of the estate of the Husband to the Wife, her heirs or legal representatives, of the sum of $_________ shall be in full for all claims and demands of every kind and character which the Wife shall have against the estate of the Husband.

During Marriage Each to Have Full Control of Own Property

3. During the continuance of said marriage relations, each of the parties is to have the full right to own, control, and dispose of his or her separate property the same as if the marriage relations did not exist, and each of the parties is to have the full right to dispose of and sell any and all real or personal property now or hereafter owned by each of them without the other party joining, and said transfer by either of the parties to this contract shall convey the same title that said transfer would convey had the marriage relations not existed. This contract limits the right of either party to participate in the estate of the other, whether the marriage relation is determined by death or legal proceedings.

Purpose of Contract to Limit Rights

4. The purpose of this agreement is to define and limit the claims and demands which each of the parties shall have against the estate of the other. Should either party die during the pendency of this contract, or should the contract be determined by legal proceedings, the claims herein stipulated and defined shall be the limit which either party may have against the other party or his or her estate.

Contract Made with Full Knowledge

5. This Agreement is entered into with full knowledge that each of the parties has a separate estate, and no claim or demand can be predicated upon the fact that there has been any misrepresentation or concealment as to the amount and condition of said separate estate, it being expressly agreed that each of the parties considers the amount hereinabove fixed to be sufficient participation in the estate of the other, and it being expressly stated that each of the parties has sufficient general knowledge of the condition of the estate of the other to justify making and entering into this agreement.

In witness whereof, etc.

was first formed. Although they are exceptional, premarital agreements have become increasingly popular in the United States.

The practice of making premarital agreements is ancient. Marrying Jews have made marital contracts called *ketubahs* for more than two thousand years. The secular premarital agreements that now exist in the United States can be traced back to sixteenth-century England. Many of the first premarital agreements were used by women as a way of protecting their own property. Until the nineteenth century, women were considered the property of their husbands, and what was the property of a wife became the property of her husband. A premarital agreement became the only way for a woman contemplating marriage to retain her own property.

Initially, the rights of women in premarital agreements were limited. Women had few contractual rights, and courts often struck down premarital agreements that favored women. This changed in the mid- to late nineteenth century, when states began to enact Married Women's Property Acts to protect women's rights to ownership and control of their property. Since then, the number of premarital agreements created in the United States has steadily increased.

Premarital agreements can cover a variety of topics. The most common include property and financial support rights during and after marriage, personal rights and obligations of the couple during marriage, and the education and rearing of children to be born to the couple. A typical premarital agreement is used by one spouse or both spouses to keep PERSONAL PROPERTY and income separate during the marriage or to protect certain property before one spouse embarks on a risky investment or new career.

In the absence of a premarital agreement, statutes and the courts may control the property, financial, and child-rearing issues that face a divorcing couple. Under the property distribution laws in many states, a spouse who brings a large amount of cash, property, and other financial holdings to a marriage and makes them part of the marital estate (combining them with marital ASSETS for the benefit of both parties) may lose much of that property to the other spouse upon divorce. A spouse who brings substantially more money or property to a marriage may want a premarital agreement to protect some or all of those assets in the event the marriage fails.

Marrying couples have included a wide assortment of provisions in their premarital agreements. Some agreements identify who will wash dishes, who will dispose of trash, where the couple will shop, and what will occur in the event one spouse is unable to perform sexually. Couples are free to contract on any subject, as long as the agreement does not violate PUBLIC POLICY or a criminal statute.

Some scholars and social critics argue that the premarital agreement itself is contrary to public policy. They maintain that government should promote marriage and that premarital agreements promote DIVORCE because they anticipate divorce. Supporters counter that premarital agreements actually promote marriage because they give married couples the ability to fashion their own relationship.

The supporters of premarital agreements have won the argument. Courts in all states recognize that marriage is, in part, a business relationship and that couples should be free to remain autonomous within a marriage. Many states have adopted the Uniform Premarital Agreement Act (UPAA), a set of laws on premarital agreements approved by the Commissioners on Uniform State Laws. The UPAA provides a list of property-related items on which couples may agree. It also includes a provision allowing couples to agree on any matter, including their personal rights and obligations.

Although all states recognize premarital agreements, courts tend to closely examine premarital agreements that are challenged by one of the parties. In many states the spouse seeking enforcement of a premarital agreement has the burden of proving its validity. Few courts hesitate to strike terms that are contrary to public policy or unconscionably unfair to one of the parties. A court may strike down all or part of the agreement if one of the parties agreed to the terms as a result of FRAUD or DURESS. Courts closely examine asset lists and income schedules to ensure that the parties are being forthright with each other. Couples drafting premarital agreements must be careful to explain in detail any provisions that a court might consider unfair.

Courts may strike down all or part of a premarital agreement. To be upheld, the agreement must have been procedurally and substantively fair at the time of execution, and it must be substantively fair at enforcement. Procedural fairness refers to the manner in which the contract was made. Both parties must give full and complete financial disclosure, and each party should have an opportunity to consult with his or her own lawyer. Although many JURISDICTIONS allow one attorney to represent both parties to a premarital agreement, it is generally better for the parties to have separate counsel. This prevents a later argument that the attorney for both parties was biased in favor of one side. It also gives a party who may be unsure about the agreement a chance to discuss it privately with a competent professional. Courts tend to be more comfortable with premarital agreements made by parties with separate counsel.

Substantive fairness means that the actual provisions in the agreement are fair to each party. Because a premarital agreement may be enforced many years after it was created, what seemed fair at the time of execution of the agreement may have become unfair by the time of its enforcement. Such a situation might arise where a very wealthy person and a person of very limited means married with the agreement that, in the event of a divorce, each would leave with what he or she brought to the marriage. If the marriage was brief, this arrangement may be upheld. However, if the marriage lasted many years and the spouse formerly of limited means invested substantial time and effort into advancing the couple's financial position, the agreement could now appear unfair.

Courts tend to closely scrutinize premarital agreements' provisions relating to children. Children have a special status under the law that gives them greater protection than adults receive, and many states prohibit couples from making premarital agreements that adversely affect a child's right to financial support. A court will strike down a provision that relates to any other important matter, such as a child's custody or education, if it is not in the best interests of the child.

CROSS-REFERENCES

Family Law; Husband and Wife; Postmarital Agreement.

PREMEDITATE To think of an act beforehand; to contrive and design; to plot or lay plans for the execution of a purpose.

Premeditation refers to the decision to plan to commit a crime, generally MURDER. A premeditated murder is thought out beforehand, but no specific length of time is needed for premeditation.

PREMIUM A reward for an act done.

A BOUNTY or bonus; a CONSIDERATION given to invite a loan or a bargain, as the consideration paid to the assignor by the assignee of a lease, or to the transferer by the transferee of shares of stock, etc.

In granting a lease, part of the rent is sometimes capitalized and paid in a lump sum at the time the lease is granted. This is called a *premium*.

The sum paid or agreed to be paid by an insured to the underwriter (insurer) as the consideration for the INSURANCE. The price for insurance protection for a specified period of exposure.

PREPONDERANCE OF EVIDENCE A standard of PROOF that must be met by a PLAINTIFF if he or she is to win a CIVIL ACTION.

In a civil case, the plaintiff has the burden of proving the facts and claims asserted in the COMPLAINT. If the RESPONDENT, or DEFENDANT, files a COUNTERCLAIM, the respondent will have the burden of proving that CLAIM. When a party has the burden of proof, the party must present, through TESTIMONY and EXHIBITS, enough EVIDENCE to support the claim. The amount of evidence required varies from claim to claim. For most civil claims, there are two different evidentiary standards: preponderance of the evidence, and clear and convincing evidence. A third standard, proof BEYOND A REASONABLE DOUBT, is used in criminal cases and very few civil cases.

The quantum of evidence that constitutes a preponderance cannot be reduced to a simple formula. A preponderance of evidence has been described as just enough evidence to make it more likely than not that the fact the claimant seeks to prove is true. It is difficult to translate this definition and apply it to evidence in a case, but the definition serves as a helpful guide to judges and juries in determining whether a claimant has carried his or her burden of proof.

The majority of civil claims are subjected to a preponderance of evidence standard. If a court or legislature seeks to make a civil claim more difficult to prove, it may raise the evidentiary standard to one of clear and convincing evidence.

Under some circumstances use of the low preponderance of evidence standard may be a violation of constitutional rights. For example, if a state seeks to deprive natural parents of CUSTODY of their children, requiring only proof by a preponderance of evidence is a violation of the parents' DUE PROCESS rights (*Santosky v. Kramer*, 455 U.S. 745, 102 S. Ct. 1388, 71 L. Ed. 2d 599 [1982]). Freedom in matters of family life is a fundamental liberty interest, and the government cannot take it away with only a modest evidentiary standard. However, a court may use a preponderance of evidence standard when a mother seeks to establish that a certain man is the father of her child (*Rivera v. Minnich*, 483 U.S. 574, 107 S. Ct. 3001, 97 L. Ed. 2d 473 [1987]). Most states use the preponderance of evidence standard in these cases because they have an interest in ensuring that fathers support their children.

See also CLEAR AND CONVINCING PROOF.

PREROGATIVE An exclusive privilege. The special power or peculiar right possessed by an official by virtue of his or her office. In English law, a discretionary power that exceeds and is unaffected by any other power; the special preeminence that the monarch has over and above all others, as a consequence of his or her SOVEREIGNTY.

The term *prerogative* is occasionally used by writers of law to refer to the object over which royal powers are exercised, such as fiscal prerogatives, which are the revenues of the king or queen.

PREROGATIVE WRIT Formerly a court order issued under certain circumstances on the authority of the extraordinary powers of the monarch.

The prerogative writs were procedendo, MANDAMUS, PROHIBITION, QUO WARRANTO, HABEAS CORPUS, and CERTIORARI. Today these forms of relief are also called extraordinary remedies and are issued on the strength of the inherent powers of the court to enforce its orders and to do justice. The paper granting a petition for an EXTRAORDINARY REMEDY is still called a WRIT. For example, a writ of *certiorari* grants the petitioner an opportunity to APPEAL the decision of a lower court in a case where he or she does not have a right to appeal.

PRESCRIPTION A method of acquiring a nonpossessory interest in land through the long, continuous use of the land.

Prescription refers to a type of EASEMENT—the right to use the property of another. It requires the use of the land to have been open, continuous, exclusive, and under claim of right for the appropriate statutory period. It differs from ADVERSE POSSESSION in that adverse possession entails the acquisition of TITLE to the property, whereas prescription relates to a right to use the property of another that is consistent with the rights of the owner.

PRESENT To submit for consideration or action. Immediate, not in the future.

Present ability refers to a person's immediate capacity to do an act. A *present conveyance* is made with the intention that it take effect at once.

In COMMERCIAL PAPER law, to present a CHECK means to submit it to the DRAWEE for acceptance or payment.

PRESENTENCE INVESTIGATION Research that is conducted by court services or a PROBATION officer relating to the prior criminal record, education, employment, and other information about a person convicted of a crime, for the purpose of assisting the court in passing sentence.

A presentence investigation (PSI) is prepared for persons convicted of serious crimes. In MISDEMEANOR and gross misdemeanor offenses, the court may order a PSI, whereas in FELONY cases a PSI is mandatory. State and federal statutes (18 U.S.C.A. § 3553(b) [1984]) set PSI requirements and are supplemented by federal and state rules of CRIMINAL PROCEDURE.

The presentence investigation generally consists of an interview with the defendant, a review of his or her criminal record, and a review of the specific facts of the crime. The probation or court services department prepares a report that contains all of this information and makes a recommendation to the court about the type and severity of the sentence. The court always makes the final decision about the sentence, but it may be limited by federal and state sentencing guidelines, which set standard sentences based on the seriousness of the present crime and the previous criminal history of the convicted person. A sentencing guidelines worksheet is often included in the PSI to assist the court in determining whether to depart from the guidelines and enhance or reduce the severity of the standard sentence.

If the court desires more information than is otherwise available to it as a basis for determining the mental condition of the defendant, it may order the defendant to undergo a psychiatric or psychological examination.

Since the 1980s many states have allowed the victims of a crime to participate in the presentencing stage. Some states have victim loss or victim impact forms that give crime victims an opportunity to make people in the criminal justice system aware of the impact a crime has had on their lives. Victims are also encouraged to contact the probation office and provide other relevant information for the PSI.

A PSI often contains a mix of public and confidential information. Information about juveniles and crime victims, as well as psychological reports, are confidential and must be kept out of the public record.

See also SENTENCING.

PRESENTMENT A GRAND JURY statement that a crime was committed; a written notice, initiated by a grand jury, that states that a crime occurred and that an INDICTMENT should be drawn.

In relation to COMMERCIAL PAPER, presentment is a demand for the payment or acceptance of a NEGOTIABLE INSTRUMENT, such as a CHECK. The holder of a negotiable instrument generally makes a presentment to the maker, acceptor, DRAWER, or DRAWEE.

PRESENTS The present instrument. The phrase *these presents* is used in any legal document to designate the instrument in which the phrase itself occurs.

PRESIDENTIAL POWERS The executive authority given to the PRESIDENT OF THE UNITED STATES by Article II of the Constitution to carry out the duties of the office.

APWIDE WORLD PHOTOS

The president is empowered to make treaties. The most famous signed during Bill Clinton's tenure was the North American Free Trade Agreement. Former presidents (from left) Gerald Ford, Jimmy Carter and George Bush joined Clinton (right) at the signing of the treaty.

Article II, Section 1, of the Constitution provides that the "executive power shall be vested in a President of the United States," making the president the head of the EXECUTIVE BRANCH of the federal government. Sections 2 and 3 enumerate specific powers granted to the president, which include the authority to appoint judges, ambassadors, and other high-ranking government officials, veto legislation, call Congress into special session, grant pardons, issue proclamations and orders, administer the law, and serve as commander in chief of the armed forces.

Article II gives the president authority to recommend measures for congressional consideration. Pursuant to this authority, presidents submit budgets, propose bills, and recommend other action to be taken by Congress.

Veto Power Under Article I, Section 7, of the Constitution, "every bill" and "every order, resolution or vote to which the concurrence of the SENATE and HOUSE OF REPRESENTATIVES may be necessary" must be presented to the president for approval. This "presentment" requirement does not apply to CONSTITUTIONAL AMENDMENTS, procedural rules of each house, and several other types of legislative action.

Under the Constitution, the president has ten days (not counting Sundays) in which to consider LEGISLATION presented for approval. The president has three options: sign the BILL, making it law; VETO the bill; or take no action on the bill during the ten-day period. If the president vetoes the bill, it can be overridden by a two-thirds majority of both houses of Congress. If the president takes no action, the bill automatically becomes law after ten days. However, if Congress adjourns before the ten days have expired and the president has not signed the bill, it is said to have been subjected to the pocket veto, the effect of which is the same as a veto.

In 1996 Congress gave the president the authority to select particular items from appropriation bills and individually veto them. The federal line-item veto authority (2 U.S.C.A. §§ 691 & 692) gives the president the ability to impose cuts on the FEDERAL BUDGET without vetoing a bill in its entirety. The line-item veto, like a regular veto, can be overridden by a two-thirds majority vote of both houses.

The veto gives the president enormous power to influence the writing of legislation. By threatening a veto before legislation is passed, the president can force Congress to compromise and pass amendments it would otherwise find unacceptable.

Executive Orders The president's executive powers also include the authority to issue PROCLAMATIONS and EXECUTIVE ORDERS. A proclamation is the president's official announcement that he or she is taking a particular action. Such an announcement is not the same as an executive order, which has the force and effect of law by carrying out a provision of the Constitution, a federal statute, or a treaty. The Constitution does not expressly give the president the power to promulgate executive orders. Instead, this power has been inferred from the president's obligation to faithfully execute the laws. Proclamations and executive orders are published in the *Federal Register* to notify the country of presidential actions.

Powers of Appointment The president has the power to appoint AMBASSADORS, CABINET officers, and federal JUDGES, subject to confirmation by a majority vote of the Senate. Upper-level executive branch officials, who numbered more than two thousand in 1997, are appointed solely at the discretion of the president or department head, without Senate review. The power to appoint federal judges gives a president the opportunity to place on the federal bench for lifelong terms persons who agree with the president's views on law and the role of the judicial system. A president is limited to serving eight years. A federal judge may serve for decades.

Pardon Power The president is given the power under the Constitution to "grant reprieves and pardons for offenses against the United States, except in cases of impeachment." The president may grant a full PARDON to a person accused or convicted of a federal crime, releasing the person from any punishment and restoring her or his CIVIL RIGHTS. The president may also issue conditional pardons that forgive the convicted person in part, reduce a penalty a specified number of years, or alter a penalty with conditions.

A pardon is generally a private transaction between the president and an individual. However, in 1977 President JIMMY CARTER granted an AMNESTY that was, in effect, a blanket pardon to those who were either deserters or draft evaders during the VIETNAM WAR.

Power of Impoundment Presidential IMPOUNDMENT is the refusal of the chief executive to expend funds appropriated by Congress. THOMAS JEFFERSON was the first president to impound funds, and many other presidents have followed suit. Congress has granted the president the authority not to spend funds if it has appropriated more funds than necessary to reach its goals. However, the president does not have a limitless impoundment power. The U.S. Supreme Court, in *Train v. City of New York*, 420 U.S. 35, 95 S. Ct. 839, 43 L. Ed. 2d 1 (1975), ruled that President RICHARD M. NIXON could not order the impoundment of substantial amounts of environmental protection funds for a program he vetoed, which veto was then overridden by Congress. The president cannot frustrate the will of Congress by killing a program through impoundment.

Foreign Policy Powers The president or his or her designated representative, such as the secretary of state, has the exclusive authority to communicate with other nations, recognize foreign governments, receive ambassadors, and make executive agreements. Throughout U.S. history, Congress and the courts have granted the president great deference in conducting foreign policy. This deference is based, in part, on the need for one person, rather than 535 members of Congress, to represent and speak for a national constituency.

In addition to the authority to recognize foreign governments, the president is empowered by Article II to make treaties with foreign nations, subject to the consent of the Senate. A TREATY is an agreement between two or more nations containing promises to behave in specified ways.

Executive agreements are international compacts that the president makes with foreign nations without the approval of the Senate. They do not have the same legal status as treaties unless they are subsequently ratified by the Senate. The Constitution does not expressly give the president the power to make executive agreements. However, this power has been inferred from the president's general constitutional authority over foreign affairs. At one time executive agreements involved minor matters, such as postal relations and the use of radio frequencies. Since the 1930s, however, presidents have negotiated important foreign policy issues through these agreements rather than through treaties. The Supreme Court has recognized that an executive agreement is legally equivalent to a treaty and therefore the supreme law of the land. Executive agreements enable the president to achieve results while avoiding the uncertainty of treaty ratification.

Presidential War Powers An integral part of the president's foreign policy role is the enormous power of the U.S. armed forces, over which the Constitution makes the president commander in chief. The president may threaten a foreign nation with force or actually conduct military actions to protect U.S. interests, aid U.S. allies, and maintain national security.

Although the president is commander in chief, Article I of the Constitution gives Congress the power to declare WAR. Despite this apparent constitutional impediment, presidents since Thomas Jefferson have dispatched troops to combat situations without the prior approval of Congress. The Supreme Court held in the *Prize* cases, 67 U.S. 635, 17 L. Ed. 459; 70 U.S. 451, 18 L. Ed. 197; 70 U.S. 514, 18 L. Ed. 200; 70 U.S. 559, 18 L. Ed. 220 (1863), that the president has the authority to resist force without the need for special legislative action.

In times of crisis, the president has the power to commit U.S. forces, but the Vietnam War led Congress to place limits on the presidential war power. The War Powers Resolution of 1973 (50 U.S.C.A. § 1541 et seq.) restricts the president's power to mobilize the military during undeclared war. It requires the president to make a full report to Congress when sending troops into foreign areas, limits the duration of troop commitment without congressional authorization, and provides a veto mechanism that allows Congress to force a recall of troops at any time.

The president also has broad powers over domestic policy during wartime. President ABRAHAM LINCOLN issued an order to military commanders suspending HABEAS CORPUS during the Civil War, which allowed the military to arrest and detain persons without trial for an indefinite time. Congress later passed a law suspending habeas corpus, but after the Civil War, the Supreme Court, in *Ex parte Milligan*, 71 U.S. 2, 18 L. Ed. 281 (1866), condemned Lincoln's directive establishing military jurisdiction over civilians outside the immediate war zone.

During the early days of U.S. involvement in World War II, President FRANKLIN D. ROOSE-

VELT issued orders authorizing the establishment of "military areas" from which dangerous persons could be expelled or excluded. This order was used to designate the West Coast a military area and to remove and imprison 120,000 Japanese Americans in "relocation centers" for the duration of the war. The Supreme Court upheld the relocation order in *Korematsu v. United States*, 323 U.S. 214, 65 S. Ct. 193, 89 L. Ed. 194 (1944), finding that the government had a compelling national security interest during a time of war to take such extreme measures.

CROSS-REFERENCES

Congress of the United States; Constitution of the United States; Executive Privilege; Japanese American Evacuation Cases; *Korematsu v. United States; Milligan, Ex parte;* Separation of Powers.

PRESIDENT OF THE UNITED STATES

The head of the EXECUTIVE BRANCH, one of the three branches of the federal government.

The U.S. Constitution sets relatively strict requirements about who may serve as president and for how long. Under Article II, only a natural-born CITIZEN of the United States is eligible to serve as president; a person born outside of the United States, even if he later becomes a citizen, may not serve. In addition, a person must be at least thirty-five years old to become president and must have resided in the United States for at least fourteen years. Under the TWENTY-SECOND AMENDMENT, which was added to the Constitution in 1951, no person may serve as president for more than two four-year terms. The amendment further provides that a person who succeeds to the office for more than two years of an unexpired term (for example, because a sitting president dies or resigns) may serve for only one additional four-year term.

Article II also sets the parameters of the president's authority. The article provides that the president is the commander in chief of the ARMED SERVICES. As commander in chief, the president has the power to preserve the peace by governing a captured territory until Congress establishes civil authority over it; she also may declare MARTIAL LAW, which provides for the imposition of military authority over civilians in the event of an invasion, INSURRECTION, disaster, or similar occurrence. In addition, the president can end a WAR through a TREATY or a presidential proclamation. The power to declare war, however, is vested exclusively in Congress and not the president. In a situation of an undeclared war, under the War Powers Resolution of 1973 (50 U.S.C.A. § 1541 et seq.) the president must consult with Congress before introducing armed forces into hostilities. Nevertheless, the practical effect of the statute is somewhat limited because it recognizes the power of the president to unilaterally deploy military forces when necessary.

As the head of the executive branch, the president executes the law but does not legislate, although he submits budgets, and may propose bills, to Congress. The president's legislative power is limited to approving or disapproving bills passed by Congress. If the presi-

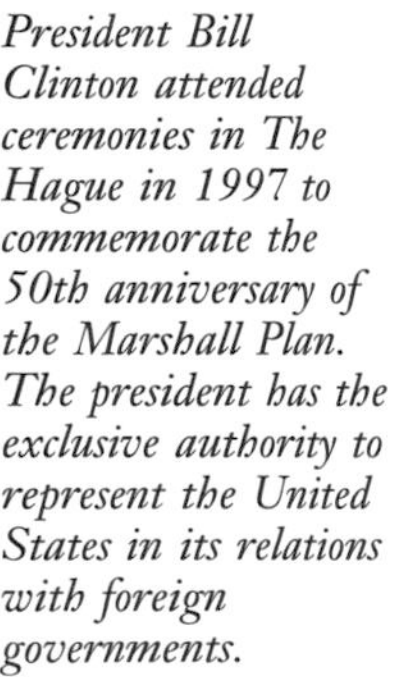

AP/WIDE WORLD PHOTOS

President Bill Clinton attended ceremonies in The Hague in 1997 to commemorate the 50th anniversary of the Marshall Plan. The president has the exclusive authority to represent the United States in its relations with foreign governments.

dent approves a measure, it becomes law. If he vetoes the bill, or refuses to approve it, it goes back to either the HOUSE OF REPRESENTATIVES or to the SENATE (wherever the bill first originated). If both bodies then pass the bill again by a two-thirds margin, the president's VETO has been overridden and she must sign it into law. Under the line-item veto law, the president may veto only a portion of a bill while leaving the remainder of the legislation intact (2 U.S.C.A. § 691 [1996]).

The president's executive powers also include the authority to issue proclamations and EXECUTIVE ORDERS. A proclamation is a general announcement of policy, whereas an executive order has the force and effect of law by carrying out a provision of the Constitution, a federal statute, or a treaty. For example, during World War II President FRANKLIN D. ROOSEVELT issued an executive order confining Japanese American citizens to camps following the bombing of Pearl Harbor.

The president has the exclusive authority to represent the United States in its relationships with governments of other countries. Through the secretary of state and other officials, the president communicates with other nations, recognizes foreign governments, and makes agreements, including the negotiation of treaties. Treaties, however, must be approved by two-thirds of the Senate before taking effect. Executive agreements with other nations do not require Senate approval but still carry the force of law. For instance, the United States, through the president, has frequently entered into executive agreements to supply economic aid to other nations.

In domestic matters the president is advised by the CABINET, which is comprised of more than a dozen executive departments covering a wide range of areas, including commerce, housing, labor, and the treasury. Each department is headed by a secretary, who is responsible for its overall administration and for reporting to the president.

Should the president be unable to serve a full term, Article II and the TWENTY-FIFTH AMENDMENT to the Constitution provide for a line of succession. If the president dies, resigns, or is removed from office through the IMPEACHMENT process, the VICE PRESIDENT becomes the acting president. This transfer of power also occurs if the president informs both houses of Congress that she is temporarily unable to discharge the duties of president. The House of Representatives can IMPEACH a president or indict her for TREASON, BRIBERY, or other HIGH CRIMES AND MISDEMEANORS. If the House votes to impeach, the president is not automatically removed from office; impeachment is instead a formal charge accusing the president of a crime. The articles, or charges, of impeachment are submitted to the Senate, where the president is tried, with the chief justice of the U.S. Supreme Court presiding over the proceeding. A two-thirds vote in the Senate is needed for a conviction, and the removal of the president from office. The only president to have been impeached was ANDREW JOHNSON, who in 1868 was acquitted by only one vote. In 1974 the House Judiciary Committee voted to impeach RICHARD M. NIXON, but he resigned from office before the entire House could vote on the matter.

In May 1997 the Supreme Court ruled that a sitting president does not have presidential IMMUNITY from suit over conduct unrelated to his official duties. The holding came in a civil suit brought by Paula Corbin Jones against President BILL CLINTON. Jones's suit was based on conduct alleged to have occurred while Clinton was governor of Arkansas.

CROSS-REFERENCES

Constitution of the United States; Electoral College; Executive Privilege; Presidential Powers; Separation of Powers; Watergate.

PRESS, FREEDOM OF See FREEDOM OF THE PRESS.

PRESUMPTION A conclusion made as to the existence or nonexistence of a fact that must be drawn from other evidence that is admitted and proven to be true. A RULE OF LAW.

If certain facts are established, a judge or jury must assume another fact that the law recognizes as a logical conclusion from the proof that has been introduced. A presumption differs from an INFERENCE, which is a conclusion that a judge or jury may draw from the proof of certain facts if such facts would lead a reasonable person of average intelligence to reach the same conclusion.

A *conclusive presumption* is one in which the proof of certain facts makes the existence of the assumed fact beyond dispute. The presumption cannot be rebutted or contradicted by evidence to the contrary. For example, a child younger than seven is presumed to be incapable of committing a FELONY. There are very few conclusive presumptions because they are considered to be a substantive rule of law, as opposed to a rule of evidence.

A REBUTTABLE PRESUMPTION is one that can be disproved by evidence to the contrary. The Federal Rules of Evidence and most state rules are concerned only with rebuttable presumptions, not conclusive presumptions.

PRESUMPTION OF INNOCENCE A principle that requires the government to prove the guilt of a criminal defendant and relieves the defendant of any burden to prove his or her innocence.

The presumption of innocence, an ancient tenet of CRIMINAL LAW, is actually a misnomer. According to the U.S. Supreme Court, the presumption of the innocence of a criminal defendant is best described as an ASSUMPTION of innocence that is indulged in the absence of contrary EVIDENCE (*Taylor v. Kentucky*, 436 U.S. 478, 98 S. Ct. 1930, 56 L. Ed. 2d 468 [1978]). It is not considered evidence of the defendant's innocence, and it does not require that a mandatory inference favorable to the defendant be drawn from any facts in evidence.

In practice the presumption of innocence is animated by the requirement that the government prove the charges against the defendant BEYOND A REASONABLE DOUBT. This DUE PROCESS requirement, a fundamental tenet of criminal law, is contained in statutes and judicial opinions. The requirement that a person suspected of a crime be presumed innocent also is mandated in statutes and court opinions. The two principles go together, but they can be separated.

The Supreme Court has ruled that, under some circumstances, a court should issue JURY instructions on the presumption of innocence in addition to INSTRUCTIONS on the requirement of PROOF beyond a reasonable doubt (*Taylor v. Kentucky*). A presumption of innocence instruction may be required if the jury is in danger of convicting the defendant on the basis of extraneous considerations rather than the facts of the case.

The presumption of innocence principle supports the practice of releasing criminal defendants from jail prior to trial. However, the government may detain some criminal defendants without BAIL through the end of trial. The EIGHTH AMENDMENT to the U.S. Constitution states that excessive bail shall not be required, but it is widely accepted that governments have the right to detain through trial a defendant of a serious crime who is a flight risk or poses a danger to the public. In such cases the presumption of innocence is largely theoretical.

Aside from the related requirement of proof beyond a reasonable doubt, the presumption of innocence is largely symbolic. The reality is that no defendant would face trial unless somebody—the crime victim, the prosecutor, a police officer—believed that the defendant was GUILTY of a crime. After the government has presented enough evidence to constitute PROBABLE CAUSE to believe that the defendant has committed a crime, the accused need not be treated as if he or she was innocent of a crime, and the defendant may be jailed with the approval of the court.

Nevertheless, the presumption of innocence is essential to the criminal process. The mere mention of the phrase *presumed innocent* keeps judges and juries focused on the ultimate issue at hand in a criminal case: whether the prosecution has proven beyond a reasonable doubt that the defendant committed the alleged acts. The people of the United States have rejected the alternative to a presumption of innocence—a presumption of guilt—as being inquisitorial and contrary to the principles of a free society.

See also CRIMINAL PROCEDURE; INQUISITORIAL SYSTEM.

PRETERMITTED HEIR A child or other descendent omitted from the WILL of a TESTATOR.

Modern laws concerning the INHERITANCE of property attempt to protect the rightful heirs. A pretermitted heir is a child or descendant of the testator—the maker of a will—who has unintentionally been omitted from the will. States have enacted "pretermitted heir statutes" that protect these heirs.

The PRESUMPTION of these statutes is that the testator must expressly DISINHERIT a child or descendant in his or her will. This presumption dates back to early ROMAN LAW. If the will does not specify intention to disinherit, the law will presume that the omission of the child or descendant was unintentional. These statutes authorize the child or descendant to take the same share of the ESTATE that he or she would have taken if the testator had died INTESTATE, without a will. All states have fixed, objective rules for dividing property when a person dies without a will, which apply to the division of an estate for pretermitted heirs.

A pretermitted heir must be a child or descendant either living at the date of the execution of the will or born thereafter. For example, if John executes a will and his son Bob is born a week later, Bob will be considered a pretermitted heir unless John changes his will to expressly disinherit Bob. If Bob has a child and dies before John, at John's death the grandchild will share in John's estate, because he or she will take Bob's share.

Some states have specific laws that deal with a child born after the making of a will. These *after-born heir* statutes are similar to pretermitted heir provisions. The presumption is that an AFTER-BORN CHILD does not revoke a will but has the effect of modifying it.

Louisiana and Puerto Rico protect children and descendants in a different way. These JURISDICTIONS, which come from a CIVIL-LAW rather than a COMMON-LAW tradition, grant heirs an

INDEFEASIBLE share. This share is a certain portion of the estate, usually expressed in a fixed dollar amount, and a percentage of the decedent's estate.

See also DESCENT AND DISTRIBUTION.

PRETRIAL CONFERENCE A meeting of the parties to an ACTION and their attorneys held before the court prior to the commencement of actual courtroom proceedings.

A pretrial conference is a meeting of the parties to a case conducted prior to TRIAL. The conference is held before the trial judge or a MAGISTRATE, a judicial officer who possesses fewer judicial powers than a judge. A pretrial conference may be held prior to trial in both civil and criminal cases. A pretrial conference may be requested by a party to a case, or it may be ordered by the court. Generally, the term *pretrial conference* is used interchangeably with the term *pretrial hearing*.

A pretrial conference may be conducted for several reasons. Pretrial conferences may be held to (1) expedite disposition of the case, (2) help the court establish managerial control over the case, (3) discourage wasteful pretrial activities, (4) improve the quality of the trial with thorough preparation, and (5) facilitate a settlement of the case.

Pretrial conferences are conducted in criminal cases to decide matters that do not inquire into the defendant's guilt or innocence. Under rule 17.1 of the Federal Rules of Criminal Procedure, pretrial conferences for criminal cases may be conducted to promote a fair and expeditious trial. In practice, federal and state courts use the pretrial conference in criminal cases to decide such preliminary matters as what EVIDENCE will be excluded from trial and what WITNESSES will be allowed to testify.

In a civil pretrial conference, the judge or magistrate, with the help of the attorneys, may (1) formulate and simplify the issues in the case, (2) eliminate FRIVOLOUS claims or defenses, (3) obtain admissions of fact and documents to avoid unnecessary proof, (4) identify witnesses and documents, (5) make schedules for the submission of pretrial BRIEFS and MOTIONS, (6) make rulings on motions submitted before the conference, (7) set dates for further conferences, (8) discuss the possibility of a settlement, and (9) discuss the consolidation or management of large, complex cases. After the conference, the judge or magistrate issues an order reflecting the results of the conference, and the order controls the future course of the case.

Generally, the substance of a pretrial conference for a criminal case is the same as that for a civil case. At the conference the judge or magistrate may make rulings on motions, eliminate repetitive evidence, and set schedules. If a preliminary issue arises after the pretrial conference, a party may request a special pretrial hearing with the court to address the issue. (This special hearing marks the distinction between pretrial hearing and pretrial conference, when such a distinction is made.) In the alternative, the parties may address such an issue in court on the first day of trial, out of the presence of the jury.

All cases are guided by procedural rules that allow parties to obtain relevant evidence from other parties. The process of turning over evidence is called DISCOVERY, and the rules that apply to obtaining evidence are called discovery rules. In civil cases, discovery refers to the right of either party to obtain evidence from the other, but in a criminal case, discovery generally refers to the right of the defendant's attorney to access information necessary to prepare a defense. Discovery issues are a common topic in pretrial conferences. Discovery orders that were issued prior to a pretrial conference may be reviewed for compliance at a pretrial conference, and new discovery orders may be issued after a pretrial conference.

Criminal defendants enjoy more procedural protections than do civil defendants, and the judge or magistrate must be careful to protect those rights. Generally, no criminal defendant who has requested assistance of counsel may be required to attend a pretrial conference without an attorney. No admissions made by the defendant or the defendant's lawyer during the conference may be used against the defendant in a trial unless the admissions are written and signed by the defendant and the defendant's attorney.

The judge or magistrate assigned to the case has the discretion whether to hold a pretrial conference, but the denial of a pretrial conference may be an unconstitutional denial of due process rights. For example, in a criminal case, a defendant has a due process right to a pretrial hearing when the defendant claims that a prosecutor has breached a plea agreement (*United States v. Ataya*, 864 F.2d 1324 [7th Cir. 1988]).

Criminal defendants must raise some issues before trial in a pretrial motion. Pretrial motions are specific requests for favorable orders from the court on particular issues. Under the Uniform Rules of Criminal Procedure, a set of model rules written by the American Law Institute and adopted by many jurisdictions, a defendant should lose the opportunity to raise the following issues if they are not raised prior to trial: defenses and objections based on defects in the INDICTMENT or formal charging instrument; requests regarding discovery, or disclosure of evidence; requests to SUPPRESS or exclude from trial potential TESTIMONY or other evidence; requests for severing the trial in cases involving codefendants; requests for the dismissal of the case; and requests for transfer of the case to another JURISDICTION.

Similar requirements are imposed on PROSECUTORS. The prosecution must tell the defendant prior to trial of its intention to use certain evidence, such as evidence obtained as a result of a search or seizure, wiretap, or other ELECTRONIC SURVEILLANCE mechanism; evidence culled from a CONFESSION, admission, or statement made by the defendant; and evidence relating to a LINEUP, show-up, picture, or voice identification of the defendant (Uniform Rules of Criminal Procedure 422(a)(1)).

Pretrial proceedings vary from jurisdiction to jurisdiction. In some jurisdictions courts have bifurcated the pretrial conference into dispositional conferences and trial management conferences. In St. Paul, Minnesota, for example, the district court schedules a trial management conference to discuss administrative aspects of the case, such as scheduling. The courts also schedule a dispositional conference in which the parties may discuss the possibility of a plea bargain or settlement. If no agreement between the parties is forthcoming at the dispositional conference, the case proceeds to trial, and the court schedules no further meetings between the parties until trial. The parties are, nonetheless, free to continue negotiating, and they also may request a special pretrial hearing if an issue arises after the conference but prior to trial.

The first pretrial conference in the United States was held in Michigan in 1929. Over the years, as courts have become more crowded, the pretrial conference has become more important. Pretrial conferences save valuable time for courts and jurors by narrowing the focus of the trial and resolving preliminary matters. They also assist the court in the fair and impartial administration of justice by facilitating discovery and reducing the element of surprise at trial. Pretrial conferences are so important in civil cases that a court may order a litigant to appear at a pretrial conference and impose fines on him if he refuses to appear (*G. Heileman Brewing Co. v. Joseph Oat Corp.*, 871 F.2d 648 [7th Cir. 1989]).

CROSS-REFERENCES

Civil Procedure; Criminal Procedure; Due Process of Law; Plea Bargaining; Right to Counsel.

PRETRIAL PUBLICITY The right of a criminal defendant to receive a fair TRIAL is guaranteed by the SIXTH AMENDMENT to the U.S. Constitution. The right of the press (print and electronic media) to publish information about the defendant and the alleged criminal acts is guaranteed by the FIRST AMENDMENT. These two constitutional safeguards come into conflict when pretrial publicity threatens to deprive the defendant of an impartial JURY.

The U.S. Supreme Court has grappled with the issue of pretrial publicity since the 1960s. In *Irvin v. Dowd*, 366 U.S. 717, 81 S. Ct. 1639, 6 L. Ed. 2d 751 (1961), the defendant, Leslie Irvin, was convicted of committing six murders in a rural area of Indiana. The crimes generated extensive media coverage. Irvin argued that the pretrial publicity prevented him from receiving a fair trial by an impartial jury. The Court agreed, noting that eight of the twelve jurors who heard the case had decided that Irvin was guilty before the trial began. Despite these admissions, the trial judge accepted as conclusive the jurors' statements that they would be able to render an impartial VERDICT. The Court held that the substantial publicity surrounding the case made the trial judge's determination of juror impartiality erroneous. It set out a basic rule that when pretrial publicity has been substantial, a trial court should not necessarily accept a juror's assertion of impartiality. In these cases a PRESUMPTION is raised that the jurors are biased.

The Supreme Court extended this concern to the trial stage in *Sheppard v. Maxwell*, 384 U.S. 333, 86 S. Ct. 1507, 16 L. Ed. 2d 600 (1966). Local officials allowed Dr. SAMUEL H. SHEPPARD's 1954 murder trial to degenerate into a media circus. The Cleveland media heavily publicized the case before trial and disrupted the control of the court during the trial. The jurors were exposed to intense media coverage of the case until the time they began their deliberations. Following deliberations, Sheppard was convicted of murder. Sheppard spent ten years in prison before the Supreme Court ruled that the publicity had deprived him of a fair trial. Sheppard was acquitted at his second trial.

The *Sheppard* case brought national attention to the problem of pretrial publicity. Trial judges attempted to address this problem by imposing gag orders on the press, preventing it from reporting pretrial information. The press resisted this approach and was supported by the Supreme Court in *Nebraska Press Association v. Stuart*, 427 U.S. 539, 96 S. Ct. 2791, 49 L. Ed. 2d 683 (1976). The Court held that the trial judge's GAG ORDER was an unconstitutional PRIOR RESTRAINT on the press.

Trial courts then attempted to close criminal trials to the public, including the press. The Supreme Court, in *Richmond Newspapers v. Virginia*, 448 U.S. 555, 100 S. Ct. 2814, 65 L. Ed.

2d 973 (1980), limited this approach, holding that the right of access to criminal trials is guaranteed by the First and Fourteenth Amendments. Closure will only be permitted if there is an overriding interest, such as ensuring a defendant's right to a fair trial. In this and subsequent cases, the Court has adopted a test that makes it very difficult to justify closure.

A troublesome issue for defense attorneys is whether a jury pool is so "contaminated" by pretrial publicity that it will be extremely difficult to seat an impartial jury. In *Mu'min v. Virginia*, 500 U.S. 415, 111 S. Ct. 1899, 114 L. Ed. 2d 493 (1991), the Supreme Court held that the Due Process Clause of the FOURTEENTH AMENDMENT does not mandate that prospective jurors be asked in VOIR DIRE examinations about specific information concerning the case that they have seen or heard in the media. The Sixth Amendment's impartial jury requirement will be satisfied when jurors do not admit during voir dire that they have been prejudiced by pretrial publicity.

Faced with court decisions that make it difficult to prevent the media from reporting pretrial information, courts have several ways of overcoming prejudicial pretrial publicity. One common tactic is for the court to issue an order prohibiting the PROSECUTOR, the defense attorney, and other trial participants from making public comments about the case. Courts often permit extensive juror questionnaires that give both sides the chance to identify persons who have been exposed to pretrial publicity and who have already made up their minds about the guilt or innocence of the defendant. A court also may sequester the jury during the course of the trial. Another tactic is to postpone the trial until publicity dies down. In rare cases a court will change the VENUE of the trial to a locale less affected by the pretrial publicity.

CROSS-REFERENCES

Criminal Law; Criminal Procedure; Due Process of Law; Freedom of the Press.

PREVAILING PARTY The litigant who successfully brings or defends an ACTION and, as a result, receives a favorable JUDGMENT or VERDICT.

PREVENTIVE DETENTION The confinement in a secure facility of a person who has not been found guilty of a crime.

Preventive detention is a special form of imprisonment. Most of the persons held in preventive detention are criminal defendants, but state and federal laws also authorize the preventive detention of persons who have not been accused of crimes, such as certain mentally ill persons.

Preventive detention is a relatively recent phenomenon. Before the 1970s the general practice in criminal courts was to set BAIL for almost all criminal defendants. For defendants accused of particularly heinous crimes, courts would set the amount of bail so high that the defendants were unlikely to be released. Defendants in MURDER cases were held in jail without bail through the end of trial.

In the early 1970s, the District of Columbia became the first JURISDICTION to experiment with preventive detention for defendants other than murder defendants. Under D.C. Code 1973, 23-1322, a defendant charged with a dangerous or violent crime could be held before trial without bail for up to sixty days. The defendant was entitled to a HEARING at which the PROSECUTOR was required to present EVIDENCE of a substantial probability that the defendant committed the alleged offense. The defendant was allowed to present evidence, cross-examine WITNESSES, and APPEAL an adverse ruling. This detention scheme was upheld by the District of Columbia Court of Appeals in *United States v. Edwards*, 430 A.2d 1321, (1981), *cert. denied*, 455 U.S. 1022 (1982).

Congress created a federal preventive detention system for criminal defendants in the Federal Bail Reform Act of 1984 (18 U.S.C.A. §§ 3141 et seq. [1996]). The act is similar to the District of Columbia law with several exceptions. Under the act, the prosecution is not required to notify a defendant that it intends to present evidence of his past crimes. The federal act allows a court to accept evidence from the prosecution without giving the defendant an opportunity to question the evidence. The federal act does not limit the defendant's detention; a defendant may be held without bail until he is found not guilty. Finally, the class of defendants eligible for preventive detention is broader in the federal act than in the District of Columbia law.

The federal act authorizes the court to conduct a preventive detention hearing upon a MOTION made by the prosecutor where the defendant is accused of (1) a crime of violence, (2) a crime for which the maximum sentence is life in prison or death, (3) an offense that is punishable by a prison term of ten years or more under the federal Controlled Substances Act or the Maritime Drug Law Enforcement Act, or (4) any FELONY if the person has been convicted of two or more violent offenses or federal drug offenses. Furthermore, a defendant may be held in preventive detention prior to trial if the court finds that she may flee or intimidate, threaten, or injure a prospective witness or juror. The court can make such a finding on its own, without a motion filed by the prosecutor.

Under the federal act, a court may consider several factors when it decides whether to detain a criminal defendant, including the nature and circumstance of the offense charged; the weight of the evidence against the defendant; the history and characteristics of the defendant, including her character, physical and mental condition, family ties, employment, financial resources, length of residence in the community, community ties, past conduct, drug and alcohol history, and criminal history; the defendant's prior attendance at court proceedings; whether the defendant was on PAROLE, PROBATION, or other conditional release at the time of the alleged offense; and the nature and seriousness of the danger to any person or the community that would be posed by the defendant's release.

Technically, a criminal defendant who is confined in jail through the end of trial is considered detained until the day of SENTENCING. Defendants sentenced to prison receive credit for the time that they serve in jail prior to the beginning of their sentence, but some defendants may go free until the day of sentencing. Under the federal act, a criminal defendant who is convicted at trial must be detained until the day of sentencing, with the following exceptions. Under 18 U.S.C.A. § 3143 (1997), a defendant who does not face a prison term may be released until the day of sentencing, and defendants who the court finds are not likely to flee and do not present a danger to the safety of any other person may also be released. If the defendant is appealing a guilty VERDICT, the court may release the defendant pending the outcome of the appeal if the court finds that the defendant is not dangerous and will not flee and that the appeal may yield a result favorable to the defendant.

The U.S. Supreme Court entertained a challenge to the federal act based on the EIGHTH AMENDMENT in 1987 in *United States v. Salerno*, 481 U.S. 739, 107 S. Ct. 2095, 95 L. Ed. 2d 697. Anthony Salerno and Vincent Cafaro, who were facing numerous federal racketeering charges, were detained without bail after a detention hearing because the court believed that they posed a danger to the community. Salerno and Cafaro appealed to the Supreme Court, arguing that the court violated their due process rights by detaining them, and therefore essentially punishing them, on the basis of potential crimes. The defendants also argued that the federal act violated the Excessive Bail Clause of the Eighth Amendment.

By a vote of six to three, the High Court rejected both arguments. According to the majority, "The mere fact that a person is detained does not inexorably lead to the conclusion that the government has imposed punishment." The Court reasoned that to determine whether detention is punishment, it must look to the legislative intent behind the act. Because Congress formulated the act to prevent danger to the community, and not as punishment for the defendant, the detention was best characterized as regulatory, and not punitive. Because the detention was not considered punishment, the defendant was due only minimal process. The Court concluded that the hearing the defendant received was sufficient process to justify the detention. The Court also rejected the defendants' excessive bail argument, noting that the Eighth Amendment prohibits only the setting of excessive bail and does not address the issue of whether bail should be available at all. All states now allow for the preventive detention of criminal defendants without bail prior to trial and for the continued detention of defendants before sentencing and during appeals.

Preventive detention may also be imposed on persons other than criminal defendants. States may detain mentally unstable individuals who present a danger to the public, including criminal defendants found not guilty by reason of insanity. In *Addington v. Texas*, 441 U.S. 418, 99 S. Ct. 1804, 60 L. Ed. 2d 323 (1979), the High Court ruled that a state may place mentally unstable persons in preventive detention for an indefinite period of time, but only after the government has shown by at least a PREPONDERANCE OF EVIDENCE that the person presents a danger to herself or to others. If the person becomes mentally stable and shows no sign of mental illness, continued confinement of the person violates due process (*Foucha v. Louisiana*, 504 U.S. 71, 112 S. Ct. 1780, 118 L. Ed. 2d 437 [1992]).

The Supreme Court has ruled that persons accused of dangerous crimes who become incompetent before trial may be placed in preventive detention until they are competent (*Jackson v. Indiana*, 406 U.S. 715, 92 S. Ct. 1845, 32 L. Ed. 2d 435 [1972]). The Court also has ruled that potentially dangerous resident ALIENS may be detained pending DEPORTATION proceedings (*Carlson v. Landon*, 342 U.S. 524, 72 S. Ct. 525, 96 L. Ed. 547 [1952]; *Wong Wing v. United States*, 163 U.S. 228, 16 S. Ct. 977, 41 L. Ed. 140 [1896]). Finally, juveniles who have been arrested on the suspicion that they have committed a crime may be placed in preventive detention if they present a danger to the community (*Schall v. Martin*, 467 U.S. 253, 104 S. Ct. 2403, 81 L. Ed. 2d 207 [1984]).

In the 1990s some states enacted laws that authorized the continued INCARCERATION of convicted child sex offenders after the offender has served his sentence. Such laws were challenged as violating several constitutional rights, including the right to due process, the right to be free from CRUEL AND UNUSUAL PUNISHMENT, the right to be free from DOUBLE JEOPARDY, and the prohibition of EX POST FACTO LAWS (laws that retroactively apply criminal sanctions).

CROSS-REFERENCES

Child Abuse; Criminal Law; Criminal Procedure; Due Process of Law; Insanity Defense.

PRICE-FIXING The organized setting of what the public will be charged for certain products or services agreed to by competitors in the marketplace in violation of the SHERMAN ANTI-TRUST ACT (15 U.S.C.A. § 1 et seq.).

Horizontal price-fixing involves agreements to set prices made among one particular class of sellers—such as producers, wholesalers, or retailers.

Vertical price-fixing occurs between different categories of the sellers of products and services, such as between a manufacturer and wholesaler, wholesaler and distributor, or distributor and retailer.

See also ANTITRUST LAW.

PRIGG v. PENNSYLVANIA A pre–Civil War case, *Prigg v. Pennsylvania*, 41 U.S. (16 Pet.) 539, 10 L. Ed. 1060 (1842), declared unconstitutional all fugitive slave laws enacted by the states on the ground that the federal law provided the exclusive remedy for the return of runaway slaves.

The national debate over slavery grew in intensity beginning in the 1840s. Many of the Northern states demonstrated their hostility to SLAVERY by enacting laws that attempted to frustrate Southern slave owners who came North in search of runaway slaves. Slave owners were outraged at these laws, arguing that the federal Fugitive Slave Act of 1793 gave them the right to reclaim their property without interference by state government. In 1842 the U.S. Supreme Court resolved the issue in *Prigg v. Pennsylvania*.

Edward Prigg, a professional slave catcher, seized Margaret Morgan, a runaway slave from Maryland living in Pennsylvania. Prigg applied to a state magistrate for certificates of removal under the federal Fugitive Slave Act of 1793 and an 1826 Pennsylvania personal liberty law. Prigg needed the certificates to legally remove Morgan and her two children to Maryland. The

Pennsylvania law had a higher standard of proof for demonstrating the slave owner applicant's TITLE to the slaves. After the magistrate refused to issue the certificates, Prigg illegally returned the slaves to Maryland. Pennsylvania indicted Prigg for KIDNAPPING under the 1826 law and extradited him from Maryland. Following his conviction, Prigg appealed to the U.S. Supreme Court.

By an 8–1 vote, the Court reversed his conviction. Writing for the Court, Justice JOSEPH STORY concluded that the Pennsylvania law was unconstitutional because it conflicted with the federal act. He based his analysis on the Fugitive Slave Clause contained in Article IV, Section 2, of the U.S. Constitution. The clause directs the return of runaway slaves to the state from where they came.

Story claimed that the clause was a "fundamental article, without the adoption of which the Union could not have been formed." His historical analysis, however, was questionable. The clause was added late in the Constitutional Convention and was not debated. Nevertheless, Story concluded that the clause was a "practical necessity." Without it, every non-slaveholding state would have been at liberty to free all runaway slaves coming within its limits. This would have "created the most bitter animosities, and engendered perpetual strife between the different states."

Having established that the Fugitive Slave Clause guaranteed the rights of slave owners to reclaim runaway slaves and to prevent non-slaveholders from interfering with such property rights, Story looked to the Fugitive Slave Act of 1793 for enforcement of these rights. Story held that the constitutional provision

Ironically, the Supreme Court's decision in Prigg v. Pennsylvania, *which appeared to favor slave owners' rights, frustrated slave owners as Northern states obliged the court by refusing to participate in fugitive slave proceedings.*

gave Congress the authority to pass the act, stating that "where the end is required, the means are given." Pennsylvania had argued that its law was based on the police powers given to it by the Constitution. Story rejected this argument, holding that because the federal law was based on a specific constitutional provision that was national in scope, the federal power on this issue was exclusive.

As an extension of this conclusion, Story ruled that states were not compelled to enforce the federal fugitive slave provisions. It would be inconsistent and without legal basis, he reasoned, for the Court to declare the preeminence of federal law and then require state courts to help carry out the law. Therefore, the federal government was "bound, through its own proper departments, legislative, judicial, or executive, as the case may require, to carry into effect all the rights and duties imposed upon it by the Constitution . . . ." Though Story wished that state judges would execute the federal law, he understood that the federal government had no power to require them to do so.

Even if there had been no federal law on runaway slaves, Story, without "the slightest hesitation," found in the Fugitive Slave Clause an implied right for a slave owner or slave owner's agent to go into any state and recapture a slave. The owner of a slave "is clothed with entire authority, in every state in the Union, to seize and recapture his slave, whenever he can do it without any breach of the peace, or any illegal violence."

Story expressly recognized the POLICE POWER of the states to arrest, detain, or exclude runaway slaves from their borders. States had as much right to protect themselves against the "depredations and evil example" of runaways as they did against "idlers, vagabonds, and paupers." These regulations, however, "can never be permitted to interfere with or to obstruct the just rights of the owner to reclaim his slave."

The *Prigg* decision angered slavery opponents. Some state judges took Story's opinion to heart and refused to participate in federal fugitive slave proceedings. In 1843 Massachusetts passed an act that forbade any state official from participating in the return of a fugitive slave under the 1793 federal law. Other Northern states passed similar acts.

Slave owners soon became aware that the withdrawal of state support curtailed their ability to return slaves to the South. There were not enough federal MAGISTRATES to process applications under the 1793 law. This led to the FUGITIVE SLAVE ACT OF 1850, which authorized the appointment of a federal commissioner in every county in the United States who could issue certificates of removal for fugitive slaves. Persons who interfered in the process were subject to criminal penalties. The 1850 act caused many runaway slaves to move to Canada.

Prigg was a crucial case because it announced that slavery was a national issue that could not be disturbed by state action. It also disclosed that the institution of slavery was woven into the Constitution.

PRIMA FACIE [*Latin, On the first appearance.*] A fact presumed to be true unless it is disproved.

In common parlance the term *prima facie* is used to describe the apparent nature of something upon initial observation. In legal practice the term generally is used to describe two things: the presentation of sufficient EVIDENCE by a civil claimant to support the legal CLAIM (a prima facie case), or a piece of evidence itself (prima facie evidence).

For most civil claims, a plaintiff must present a prima facie case to avoid DISMISSAL of the case or an unfavorable DIRECTED VERDICT. The plaintiff must produce enough evidence on all elements of the claim to support the claim and shift the burden of evidence production to the RESPONDENT. If the plaintiff fails to make a prima facie case, the respondent may move for dismissal or a favorable directed verdict without presenting any evidence to REBUT whatever evidence the plaintiff has presented. This is because the burden of persuading a judge or jury always rests with the plaintiff. See also BURDEN OF PERSUASION.

Assume that a plaintiff claims that an employer failed to promote her based on her sex. The plaintiff must produce affirmative evidence showing that the employer used illegitimate, discriminatory criteria in making employment decisions that concerned the plaintiff. The employer, as respondent, does not have a burden to produce evidence until the plaintiff has made a prima facie case of SEX DISCRIMINATION (*Texas Department of Community Affairs v. Burdine*, 450 U.S. 248, 101 S. Ct. 1089, 67 L. Ed. 2d 207 [1981]). The precise amount of evidence that constitutes a prima facie case varies from claim to claim. If the plaintiff does not present a prima facie case with sufficient evidence, the judge may dismiss the case. Or, if the case is being heard by a jury, the judge may direct the jury to return a verdict for the respondent.

Prima facie also refers to specific evidence that, if believed, supports a case or an element that needs to be proved in the case. The term *prima facie evidence* is used in both civil and criminal law. For example, if the prosecution in a murder case presents a videotape showing the defendant screaming death threats at the victim, such evidence may be prima facie evidence of intent to kill, an element that must be proved by the prosecution before the defendant may be convicted of MURDER. On its face, the evidence indicates that the defendant intended to kill the victim.

Statutes may specify that certain evidence is prima facie evidence of a certain fact. For example, a duly authenticated copy of a defendant's criminal record may be considered prima facie evidence of the defendant's prior convictions and may be used against the defendant in court (Colo. Rev. Stat. Ann. § 18-3-412 [West 1996]). A CIVIL LAW example is a statute that makes a duly certified copy or duplicate of a certificate of authority for a fraternal benefit society to transact business prima facie evidence that the society is legal and legitimate (Colo. Rev. Stat. Ann. § 10-14-603 [West 1996]).

PRIMARY AUTHORITY Law, in various forms, that a court must follow in deciding a case.

Primary authority mainly consists of statutes, decisions by the U.S. Supreme Court, and all judicial decisions handed down by the same court or a higher court within the same judicial system.

See also SECONDARY AUTHORITY.

PRIMARY EVIDENCE An authentic document or item that is offered as proof in a lawsuit, as contrasted with a copy of, or substitute for, the original.

Primary evidence, more commonly known as BEST EVIDENCE, is the best available substantiation of the existence of an object because it is the actual item. It differs from SECONDARY EVIDENCE, which is a copy of, or substitute for, the original. If primary evidence is available to a party, that person must offer it as EVIDENCE. When, however, primary evidence is unavailable—for example, through loss or destruction—through no fault of the party, he or she may present a reliable substitute for it, once its unavailability is sufficiently established.

PRIME LENDING RATE The lowest rate of interest that a financial institution, such as a bank, charges its best customers, usually large CORPORATIONS, for short-term unsecured loans.

The prime lending rate is an economic indicator and is often used as a measuring point for adjusting interest rates on other types of loans. The rate varies according to economic factors.

PRIMOGENITURE The status of being the firstborn child among several children of the same parents. A rule of INHERITANCE at COMMON LAW through which the oldest male child has the right to succeed to the ESTATE of an ancestor to the exclusion of younger siblings, both male and female, as well as other relatives.

PRINCIPAL A source of authority; a sum of a debt or obligation producing interest; the head of a school. In an AGENCY relationship, the principal is the person who gives authority to another, called an AGENT, to act on his or her behalf. In CRIMINAL LAW, the principal is the chief actor or perpetrator of a crime; those who aid, ABET, counsel, command, or induce the commission of a crime may also be principals. In investments and banking, the principal refers to the person for whom a BROKER executes an order; it may also mean the capital invested or the face amount of a loan.

A *principal in the first degree* is the chief actor or perpetrator of a crime. A *principal in the second degree* must be present at the commission of the criminal act and aid, abet, or encourage the principal in his or her criminal activity.

See also PRINCIPAL AND SURETY.

PRINCIPAL AND SURETY A contractual relationship whereby one party—the SURETY—agrees to pay the principal's DEBT or perform his or her obligation in case of the principal's DEFAULT.

The *principal* is the DEBTOR—the person who is obligated to a CREDITOR. The *surety* is the ACCOMMODATION PARTY—a third person who becomes responsible for the payment of the obligation if the principal is unable to pay or perform. The principal remains primarily liable, whereas the surety is secondarily liable. The creditor—the person to whom the obligation is owed—can enforce payment or performance by the principal or by the surety if the principal defaults. The creditor must always first seek payment from the principal before approaching the surety. If the surety must fulfill the obligation, then he can seek recovery from the principal after satisfying the creditor. An example of a principal and surety relationship occurs when a MINOR purchases a car on CREDIT and has a parent act as a surety to guarantee payment of the car loan.

A *suretyship* arises from an agreement. The parties must be competent; there must be an offer and acceptance; and valid CONSIDERATION is necessary. The parties must openly assent to the CONTRACT so that all the parties are known to each other. The surety must be identified as such so that the creditor will not hold that person primarily liable. If the face of the contract indicates a suretyship, the creditor receives sufficient notice of the three-party arrangement.

BOB DAEMMRICH/THE IMAGE WORKS

Parents often act as a surety when their minor children purchase a car. Many minors would be unable to obtain a loan without their parents' agreement to guarantee payment.

No special form of contract is needed to create a principal and surety relationship. The agreement can be consummated by written correspondence or be in the form of a BOND. No particular language is needed to identify the relationship, since courts will examine the substance and not the form of the contract to determine whether a suretyship exists. Courts will rarely imply a suretyship agreement, except when an involuntary suretyship arises out of an implied oral agreement. When joint debtors obtain a loan, each is a principal for a proportionate share of the debt and a surety for the remaining amount. In practice, however, each joint debtor is a principal and is primarily liable for the entire loan if the creditor seeks repayment. A joint debtor who pays the entire debt can, however, seek CONTRIBUTION from the other debtors.

The surety's liability is indicated by the terms of the contract. Unless otherwise provided, a surety assumes the obligation of the principal. A surety, however, can limit his LIABILITY to a certain amount since the obligations of the principal and surety do not have to be co-extensive. When a surety agrees to be accountable for a certain amount, she cannot be held responsible for a sum greater than that for which she contracted. The surety becomes liable when the principal breaches a contract with the creditor. In the absence of a contractual limitation, a surety's liability is measured by the loss or damage resulting from the default by the principal. The liability of the surety terminates when the principal's obligation is fulfilled.

PRINCIPLE A fundamental, well-settled RULE OF LAW. A basic truth or undisputed legal doctrine; a given legal proposition that is clear and does not need to be proved.

A principle provides a foundation for the development of other laws and regulations.

PRINTERS INK STATUTE Statutes enacted in a number of states making it a MISDEMEANOR to use representations that are untrue, deceptive, or misleading in advertisements.

PRIOR INCONSISTENT STATEMENTS Communications made by a WITNESS before the time he or she takes the stand to TESTIFY in an action that contradict subsequent TESTIMONY given on the same exact facts.

Prior inconsistent statements can be used in a lawsuit only to impeach (discredit) the trustworthiness of the witness' testimony. They cannot, however, be used to establish the truth of the matter they address.

The Federal Rules of Evidence govern the use of prior inconsistent statements in FEDERAL COURTS.

PRIOR RESTRAINT Government prohibition of speech in advance of publication.

One of the fundamental rights guaranteed by the FIRST AMENDMENT to the U.S. Constitution is the freedom from prior restraint. Derived from the English COMMON LAW, the rule against prior restraint prohibits government from banning expression of ideas prior to their publication. The rule against prior restraint is based on the principle that FREEDOM OF THE PRESS is essential to a free society. Attempts by government to obtain a prior restraint have largely been unsuccessful.

The rule against prior restraint was undisputed for much of U.S. history. The landmark case of *Near v. Minnesota*, 283 U.S. 697, 51 S. Ct. 625, 75 L. Ed. 1357 (1931), finally settled the issue, with the U.S. Supreme Court finding that the First Amendment imposed a heavy PRESUMPTION against the validity of a prior restraint.

In *Near*, the Court struck down a Minnesota state law that permitted public officials to seek an INJUNCTION to stop publication of any "malicious, scandalous and defamatory newspaper, magazine or other periodical." The statute was used to suppress publication of a small Minneapolis newspaper, the *Saturday Press*, which had crudely maligned local police and political officials, often in anti-Semitic terms. The law provided that once a newspaper was enjoined, further publication was punishable as CONTEMPT of court.

Chief Justice CHARLES EVANS HUGHES, in his majority opinion, called the law "the essence of censorship" and declared it unconstitutional. With its decision, the Court incorporated the First Amendment freedom of the press into the Due Process Clause of the FOURTEENTH AMEND-

MENT. This incorporation made freedom of the press fully applicable to the states.

Though Hughes agreed that a rule against prior restraint was needed, he acknowledged that this restriction was not absolute. The rule would not, for example, prevent government in time of war from prohibiting publication of "the sailing dates of transports or the number and location of troops." Threats to national security interests are almost certain to prevail over freedom of the press, but it has proved difficult to invoke the "national security" justification.

This was illustrated in the *Pentagon Papers* case of 1971 (*New York Times Co. v. United States*, 403 U.S. 713, 91 S. Ct. 2140, 29 L. Ed. 2d 822). The Nixon administration sought to prevent the *New York Times* and the *Washington Post* from publishing excerpts from a classified study (the Pentagon Papers) on the history of U.S. involvement in Vietnam, arguing that publication would hurt national security interests. The Supreme Court, by a 6–3 vote, held that the government's efforts to block publication amounted to an unconstitutional prior restraint.

The national security exception failed again in a 1979 case dealing with the publication of a magazine article that purported to explain the process of making a hydrogen bomb (*United States v. Progressive, Inc.*, 467 F. Supp. 990 [W.D. Wis. 1979]). The federal government obtained a PRELIMINARY INJUNCTION against *The Progressive*, stopping publication of the article until a HEARING on a permanent injunction could be held. Before the hearing, however, another publication printed a similar article. The government then dropped its lawsuit, and the magazine published the original article.

Prior restraint issues have arisen over prejudicial PRETRIAL PUBLICITY in sensational criminal proceedings. The defendant's right to a fair trial by an unbiased jury must be considered as well as freedom of the press. In exceptional circumstances, a court may depart from prior restraint doctrine by restricting news coverage of a criminal case. These restrictions must be narrowly tailored, and they must not unduly restrict the right of the press to inform the public. The U.S. Supreme Court, in *Nebraska Press Association v. Stuart*, 427 U.S. 539, 96 S. Ct. 2791, 49 L. Ed. 2d 683 (1976), made clear, however, that these restrictions are severely limited. The Court invalidated a GAG ORDER issued by a state trial judge that forbade the publishing or broadcasting of any confessions, admissions, or facts that strongly implicated the defendant charged with a grisly mass murder.

The rule against prior restraint does not apply to the publication of student-operated school newspapers. In *Hazelwood School District v. Kuhlmeier*, 484 U.S. 260, 108 S. Ct. 562, 98 L. Ed. 2d 592 (1988), the Supreme Court upheld a public school principal's decision to remove certain controversial material from the school newspaper. The principal based his decision on fears that the articles on teen pregnancy and divorce would allow students to identify classmates who had encountered such difficulties. Justice BYRON R. WHITE ruled that educators did not "offend the First Amendment by exercising editorial control . . . so long as their actions are reasonably related to legitimate pedagogical concerns."

See also INCORPORATION DOCTRINE; NEW YORK TIMES V. UNITED STATES.

PRISON A public building used for the confinement of people convicted of serious crimes.

Prison is a place used for confinement of convicted criminals. Aside from the death penalty, a sentence to prison is the harshest punishment imposed on criminals in the United States. On the federal level, IMPRISONMENT or INCARCERATION is managed by the Federal Bureau of Prisons, a federal agency within the Department of JUSTICE. State prisons are supervised by a state agency such as a department of corrections.

Confinement in prison, also known as a penitentiary or correctional facility, is the punishment that courts most commonly impose for serious crimes, such as felonies. For lesser crimes, courts usually impose short-term incarceration in a JAIL, detention center, or similar facility.

Confining criminals for long periods of time as the primary form of punishment is a relatively new concept. Throughout history, various countries have imprisoned criminal offenders, but imprisonment was usually reserved for pretrial detention or punishment of petty criminals with a short term of confinement.

Using long-term imprisonment as the primary punishment for convicted criminals began in the United States. In the late eighteenth century, the nonviolent Quakers in Pennsylvania proposed long-term confinement as an alternative to CAPITAL PUNISHMENT. The Quakers stressed solitude, silence, REHABILITATION, hard work, and religious faith. Confinement was originally intended not only as a punishment but as an opportunity for renewal through religion.

In 1790 the Walnut Street Jail in Philadelphia constructed a separate cell house for the sole purpose of holding convicts. This was the first prison in the United States. The concept of

Prison Life, New Hampshire State Prison

The men's prison in New Hampshire is representative of the daily life of the average prison inmate in the United States.

The New Hampshire state prison system contains three different facilities: the New Hampshire State Prison For Men in Concord, the New Hampshire State Prison For Women in Goffstown, and the Lakes Region Facility in Laconia. In 1996 the men's prison held approximately 1,600 inmates, the women's prison less than eighty, and the Lakes Region Facility around three hundred. The Lakes Region Facility is reserved for first-time offenders convicted of nonviolent crimes. The women's prison and the Lakes Region Facility are operated in much the same way as the mens' prison. Their inmates, however, are less violent than the offenders in the men's prison, and security is less stringent.

An inmate at the New Hampshire Prison For Men spends his first thirty days in Reception and Diagnostic, a separate building that houses new inmates. During the inmate's stay in Reception and Diagnostic, prison officials devise an educational and therapeutic program for him. The program is voluntary, but an inmate's participation in recommended activities can increase his chance for early parole. Officials also test the inmate to determine his personality and predict how he will be received by other inmates.

Based on the results of exams, the inmate is labelled either "predator," "prey," or "normal." These three types of prisoners are kept separate in the general prison population. Predator inmates are housed with other predators, prey inmates with other prey, and normal inmates with other normal inmates.

During the first thirty days, inmates are also classified according to a number of factors, including the inmate's conduct and his progress toward release. An inmate's classification determines the level to which he will be controlled. Classification can change if an inmate violates one of the many prison rules.

Inmates are classified either C-5, C-4, C-3, C-2, or C-1 ("C" stands for "classification"). The C-5 classification is for dangerous or problem inmates. C-4 inmates are those inmates who were C-5 but are working their way back to C-3 status, which is the general prison population. New prisoners are designated C-3 unless they break rules while in Reception and Diagnostic, in which case they may be classified as C-4 or C-5. A new inmate may also be placed in protective custody.

C-2 inmates are housed in a minimum security building just outside the prison walls, and C-1 inmates live in halfway houses in Concord and Manchester. Though they are supervised by prison officials, they live outside the prison, preparing for reentry into the community.

Daily life for a C-5 inmate is spartan. The average C-5 inmate spends all but one hour in a cell located in the Security Housing Unit (SHU) in a building separate from the rest of the prison population. A C-5 inmate has no cell mate and receives his meals in his cell. He wears slippers and a shirt and pants made of material that is thinner than the regular prison uniform. He may leave his cell for one hour of outdoor exercise a day in a cage outside the SHU. Also, for a few minutes a day, a C-5 inmate may be allowed to make collect telephone calls from a room located in the SHU.

Some C-5 inmates are allowed to work at sites located within the SHU;

long-term imprisonment became popular as the U.S. public embraced the concept of removing offenders from society and punishing them with confinement and hard labor. Before the existence of prisons, most offenders were subjected to CORPORAL PUNISHMENT or public humiliation and then released back into the community. In the nineteenth century, as the United States became more urban and industrial, poverty became widespread, and crime increased. As crime increased, the public became intolerant of even the most petty crimes, and viewed imprisonment as the best method to stop repeated criminal activity.

By the mid-nineteenth century, prisons existed throughout the United States. Prisoners were kept in unsanitary environments, forced to work at hard labor, and brutalized by guards. These conditions continued until the 1950s and 1960s, when heightened social and political discourse led to a renewed emphasis on rehabilitation.

The closing of one particular prison symbolized the change in correctional philosophy. Alcatraz Prison, located on an island off San Francisco, was used exclusively to place in solitary confinement convicts classified as either violent or disruptive. Rehabilitation was nonexistent in Alcatraz. The prison was filthy and rat-infested, and prisoners were held in dungeonlike cells, often chained to stone walls. Established in 1934, Alcatraz was closed in 1963, in part because its brutal treatment of prisoners symbolized an outdated penal philosophy.

By the mid-1960s, the stated purpose of many prisons was to educate prisoners and prepare them for life after prison. Many federal most of them make sheets, towels, or pockets for pants. C-5 inmates with work privileges are allowed to communicate with one another while they work. A C-5 inmate may keep reading materials. He may also watch his own television, but only when he has been in SHU for more than thirty days. Whenever a C-5 inmate leaves his cell, he is shackled by guards at the hands and feet and escorted until he reaches his destination.

A level of security more severe than C-5 is called "isolation." An inmate in isolation may not leave his cell except for one hour a day of outdoor exercise inside a cage. He may not watch television or listen to the radio and has one Bible for reading. An inmate may be kept in isolation only for a fifteen-day stretch, and he must be held in another setting for at least twenty-four hours before beginning another fifteen days of isolation.

Protective custody is a special classification that is similar to the C-5. Inmates in protective custody are segregated from the general population: they move about the prison in a group separate from the other inmates. Protective custody is reserved for those inmates who have requested it and have a valid fear for their safety.

C-4 inmates are held in a Close Custody Unit that is also separate from the general population. C-4 inmates may have a few more privileges than C-5 inmates, but they do not have the full number of privileges enjoyed by the general population. They may work, they are not shackled as they move outside their cells, they may eat in the dining hall with the general population, and they have cell mates. Also, the C-4 floor plan is similar to that for C-3 inmates: each cell opens into a common area where inmates may talk and play cards or other games. However, unlike C-3 inmates, C-4 inmates may not lock themselves in their cells for privacy, they may work only for a short period of time at a specific work site, and they generally have fewer privileges and are more strictly supervised than C-3 inmates.

C-3 inmates comprise the general population. They may move about the prison facility unencumbered by restraints. They work at various jobs, some building high-quality furniture. Inmates earn $1.50 a day for their work. Those who perform highly skilled work such as carpentry earn $3.00 a day. They may buy articles from the canteen, such as personal hygiene products, soda, cigarettes, tuna, candy, and chips. Inmates who attend educational classes also receive money.

Inmates on C-3 status enjoy the full range of educational and work opportunities available in the prison, and their days are often consumed by these activities. They may also use the law library for a certain amount of time a day.

C-3 inmates move from place to place at the top of the hour, and they have fifteen minutes to reach their next destination. If they are tardy for any destination, they will be reported as being out of place. Being out of place in prison is a serious infraction. If the disciplinary board finds that an inmate was out of place, the inmate may lose the privilege to watch television, listen to the radio, or talk on the telephone. Repeated violations may result in transfer to C-5 status.

An inmate may receive money from persons outside the prison, but he may not receive packages of personal items. He may not spend more than $200 per month, no matter how much money he has. He may buy items such as magazines, books, radios, and televisions, but only through the manufacturer.

Inmates may smoke cigarettes in the common area and in their cells. However, if his cell mate objects, an inmate may not smoke in his cell.

An inmate's day begins at approximately 7:00 A.M. Those inmates scheduled to begin work before 7:00 A.M. are awakened earlier. The lights are dimmed around 10:00 P.M. and sometimes 11:00 P.M. on weekend nights. Except for C-5 inmates, restless inmates may leave their cells during the night to sit in the common area.

and state courts ordered administrators to improve the conditions inside their prisons, and the quality of life for inmates greatly improved.

In 1971 a bloody, day-long riot at the Attica Correctional Facility (Attica) in New York sparked a reaction against rehabilitative ideals. More than forty people were killed in the uprising in Attica. Shortly after the Attica riot, the Federal Bureau of Prisons began to transfer unruly federal prisoners to the Federal Penitentiary at Marion, Illinois (Marion), where they were held in solitary confinement. In 1983, after three killings in the prison, the prisoners in Marion were placed on permanent lockdown, making the entire prison a solitary confinement facility virtually overnight. Marion has remained on lockdown ever since.

By the 1980s most prison administrators abandoned rehabilitation as a goal. Pressured by an increasing problem with overcrowding and the resulting increase in violence, administrators returned to punishment and security as the primary purposes of prison. Though most prisons continue to operate educational and other rehabilitative programs, the rights of prison inmates have been frozen at the minimal number recognized by courts in the 1960s and 1970s. The U.S. Supreme Court has ruled against prison guard violence, but courts have generally refused to expand the rights of prison inmates. In most cases courts have approved increased infringement of inmates' rights if prison officials declare that the restrictions are for security purposes.

Prisoners' Rights PRISONERS' RIGHTS are limited. For the most part, jail and prison inmates may demand only a "minimal civilized measure of shelter" (*Union County Jail Inmates* *v. DiBuono*, 713 F.2d 984 [3d Cir. 1983]). Generally, courts follow three basic principles when deciding whether to recognize a particular right. First, an inmate necessarily gives up many rights and privileges enjoyed by the rest of society; second, an inmate does not relinquish all constitutional rights upon placement in prison; and third, the constitutional rights retained by the prison inmate must be balanced against the security concerns of the prison.

The established rights of prison inmates include FREEDOM OF SPEECH and RELIGION; freedom from arbitrary punishment (i.e., restraints, solitary confinement) on the sole basis of beliefs, religion, or racial and ethnic origin; freedom from constant physical restraints; a small amount of space for physical movement; essentials for personal hygiene and opportunity to wash; clean bedding; adequate clothing; adequate heating, cooling, ventilation, and light; and adequate nutrition.

Prisoners' rights can be infringed for security purposes. Prisoners have the right to freedom of speech, but prison officials may search their mail, deny a wide variety of reading materials, and edit the content of prison newspapers. Prisoners have the right to adequate space, but they may be confined in isolation for long periods, even years. Prisoners have the right to freedom from restraints, but their ankles and wrists may be shackled when they are moved. They may also be temporarily strapped down or otherwise restrained if officials believe that they present a danger.

Prison inmates often attempt to establish new rights in court. Issues such as prison overcrowding, medical treatment, media access, even exposure to secondhand cigarette smoke, are among the issues courts face.

Another sensitive issue in prison is the use of prison guards of the opposite sex. Women prisoners may receive more PRIVACY in this regard than men prisoners. For example, the Ninth Circuit Court of Appeals held in 1985 that the practice of assigning female guards to conduct strip searches on nude men and watch them while showering, urinating, and defecating did not violate any constitutional rights (*Grummett v. Rushen*, 779 F.2d 491 [1985]). However, in 1993, the same court held that it was CRUEL AND UNUSUAL PUNISHMENT to allow male guards to conduct searches on female prisoners while the female prisoners were clothed (*Jordan v. Gardner*, 986 F.2d 1521 [9th Cir. 1993]).

Prisoners retain some rights aside from those concerning living conditions. Most prisons "classify" prisoners and place them in various units according to the categories. For example, violent criminals and persons suspected of gang affiliations are often housed in high-security areas of prison, separate from the rest of the general prison population. When an inmate is reclassified, he or she is entitled to notice of the reclassification and a citation of reasons for the move.

Congress and most states authorize the allowance of "good time" for prison inmates. Good time is credit for time served on good behavior, and it is used to reduce sentence length. For example, an inmate may receive one day of good time credit for every three days that he behaves well. Other states withhold recognition of good behavior until the defendant has served a certain portion of the minimum sentence imposed by the court. In New Hampshire, for example, an inmate may be released for good behavior after serving two-thirds of the minimum sentence (N.H. Rev. Stat. Ann. § 651-A:12 [1983]). When an inmate has good time credits taken away, she or he is entitled to notice, a HEARING before the prison board, and an opportunity to present EVIDENCE in her or his favor.

Inmates may also gain early release from prison through PAROLE, which is granted by the parole board. Prisoners have no right to parole, and the matter of early release is left to the graces of the parole board. Once released on parole, a parolee may be returned to prison for breaking one of the many conditions that are normally imposed. A parolee has no right to an attorney at a parole revocation hearing, nor does an inmate have the right to an attorney at a parole hearing.

Solitary confinement is used in many prisons for violent inmates and those inmates perceived as having gang-related affiliations. Some prisons are designed specifically for it. The original prisons, as envisioned by the Quakers, called for solitary confinement, but the practice was halted because of the detrimental effects it had on prisoners. However, the practice never completely ended. In the 1980s solitary confinement became a regular feature of prisons, and it has become the sole form of incarceration in so-called Security Housing Units or Supermax prisons.

In a Supermax prison, the cells are eight-by-ten feet and windowless. The cells are grouped in "pods." The cell doors are perforated with holes large enough for guards to see inside the cell, but small enough to obstruct the prisoner's vision and light. All a prisoner can see through the door is another white wall. Each cell is furnished with a built-in bunk with a toilet-sink unit. Nothing is allowed on the walls. Prisoners may be allowed television, radio, and books, but these are taken away as punishment for any rule infractions.

Prisoners in solitary confinement are kept in their cells, under surveillance, for twenty-two-and-a-half hours a day. Unlike the rest of the prison population, inmates in solitary confinement may not take advantage of educational or recreational programs. The ninety minutes outside the cell may be divided between visiting a small library, washing, and exercising in a pen connected to the pod. Prisoners are strip-searched by the guards before and after visiting any place and are placed in waist restraints and handcuffs when being escorted.

The assignment of a prisoner to solitary confinement is made by prison officials. In assigning supposed gang members to solitary confinement, it is the policy in some prisons to require that the perceived gang member "debrief" officials on his or her gang activity and renounce his or her gang affiliations before being released back into the general population.

One of the most important rights possessed by prison inmates is access to the courts through HABEAS CORPUS petitions. After an inmate has exhausted all the motions and APPEALS available to contest the conviction and prison sentence, a final round of limited JUDICIAL REVIEW is provided through the WRIT of habeas corpus. Through the ancient writ of habeas corpus, a court may order the release of a prisoner wrongly held.

Habeas corpus petitions are granted only for certain constitutional violations in the prosecution of a criminal defendant. The Anti-Terrorism and Effective Death Penalty Act of 1996, 28 U.S.C.A. § 2261 et seq., placed certain limits on this form of relief.

See also PREVENTIVE DETENTION; SENTENCING.

PRISONERS' RIGHTS The nature and extent of the privileges afforded to individuals kept in CUSTODY or confinement against their will because they were convicted of performing an unlawful act.

For most of U.S. history, the treatment of prisoners was left entirely to the discretion of PRISON administrators. In the late 1960s and early 1970s, the FEDERAL COURTS began to oversee state prison systems and develop a body of law dealing with prisoners' rights. During the 1980s, however, a more conservative Supreme Court limited prisoners' rights, and in the 1990s Congress enacted laws that severely restricted litigation and post-conviction APPEALS by prisoners.

Prisoners and Detainees A prisoner is anyone who is deprived of personal liberty against his will following his conviction of a crime. Although not afforded all the privileges of a free citizen, a prisoner is assured certain minimal rights by the U.S. Constitution and the moral standards of the community.

A detainee is an individual kept in jail even though she has not yet been convicted of a crime. A majority of detainees are individuals who are unable to obtain sufficient funds to post BAIL and therefore cannot be released from JAIL pending a trial on the criminal charges.

Historical Background Until the 1960s courts refused to set standards for the treatment of prisoners, claiming they lacked the authority and the expertise to do so. Courts deferred to experienced prison administrators to avoid interfering with their ability to respond to the varied, complex issues involved in a penal system, such as custody, security, REHABILITATION, discipline, punishment, and limited resources.

By the late 1960s, however, prison conditions in many states were clearly intolerable. Courts began to review the claims of prisoners and to intervene regularly on their behalf. Finding that even prisoners are entitled to minimum rights, federal courts in particular exhibited renewed interest in the right of access to the courts, freedom of expression and religion, the constitutional prohibition against CRUEL AND UNUSUAL PUNISHMENT, and the right to DUE PROCESS OF LAW.

Rights of Detainees A great number of persons are jailed before their trials. These persons, known as pretrial detainees, are ordinarily held because they are unable to satisfy the financial requirements for a BAIL BOND.

Important law concerning the rights of pretrial detainees emerged in the 1970s. In *Bell v. Wolfish*, 441 U.S. 520, 99 S. Ct. 1861, 60 L. Ed. 2d 447 (1979), the Supreme Court rejected the theory that pretrial detainees cannot be deprived of any right except the right to come and go as they choose. The Court criticized lower federal courts that had given detailed orders telling prison administrators how they should do their jobs. Although prisons cannot employ methods designed only to punish detainees before conviction, they can use suitable procedures for purposes of security and discipline. See also PREVENTIVE DETENTION.

Rights of Citizenship Convicted offenders are deprived of many of their CIVIL RIGHTS, both during and after their period of INCARCERATION. A majority of states deprive citizens of the right to vote in all state and federal elections upon conviction of a FELONY. Even in jurisdictions where the offender can vote after release, he ordinarily cannot obtain an absentee ballot and vote while in prison.

Conviction and incarceration for serious crimes can also lead to the total or partial loss of the right to start a lawsuit not related to imprisonment or to enter into a CONTRACT. Correction officials argue that it creates an impossible security burden to permit a prisoner the right to carry on business as usual. Most states, however, permit a prisoner to be sued.

The right of a prisoner to INHERIT property or receive a PENSION can be affected by various state laws. Most of the legal disabilities to which prisoners are subject are upheld because they do not interfere with fundamental HUMAN RIGHTS.

Personal Property Prisoners have certain rights regarding PERSONAL PROPERTY in their possession. Court decisions have established the right of a prisoner to own some personal items, such as cigarettes, stationery, a watch, cosmetics, or snack foods. In certain cases prison officials have been found to be justified in forbidding certain items because they fear that permitting inmates to accumulate some form of wealth will encourage gambling, theft, and buying favors from guards. Judges have sometimes refused to support prisoner demands for the right to own such items as radios, televisions, or personal typewriters.

Privacy Prisoners do not have the right to expect PRIVACY in a prison setting. Court decisions have established that prison officials can properly monitor and record prisoners' conversations, provided that the prisoner and her visitor are warned that this will be done. Prison officials cannot intrude upon conversations that are legally afforded confidentiality, such as those between the prisoner and the prisoner's attorney or spouse.

In *Hudson v. Palmer*, 468 U.S. 517, 104 S. Ct. 3194, 82 L. Ed. 2d 393 (1984), the Supreme Court declared that prisoners do not have a FOURTH AMENDMENT right to be free of unreasonable SEARCHES AND SEIZURES of their property because the Fourth Amendment is inapplicable to them.

Mail Throughout U.S. history, prison officials have severely restricted the mail of prisoners. For example, officials have opened incoming mail to catch plans and instruments of escape, weapons, PORNOGRAPHY, drugs, and other CONTRABAND. The threat of revoking mail privileges has also been used to enforce discipline. Courts have mandated, however, that prison officials offer good reasons for banning publications they consider inflammatory, OBSCENE, or racist. A vague allegation that a book or magazine is likely to stir up trouble has been held inadequate to justify broad CENSORSHIP.

Prison administrators cannot unreasonably restrict or censor a prisoner's outgoing mail. In 1974 the Supreme Court, in *Procunier v. Martinez*, 416 U.S. 396, 94 S. Ct. 1800, 40 L. Ed. 2d 224, ruled that the California Department of Corrections could not censor the direct personal correspondence of prisoners unless such censorship was necessary to further important interests of the government in security, order, and rehabilitation. The Court also held that a procedure must be established to determine that censorship, when appropriate, is neither arbitrary nor unduly burdensome.

Free Speech Prisoners do not have a FIRST AMENDMENT right to speak freely. Prison officials may discipline inmates who distribute circulars calling for a mass protest against mistreatment. Administrators have traditionally limited prison newspapers to issues that promote good morale.

Visitors The law has long recognized the importance of visitation rights, because such rights aid the prisoner's eventual transition back into the community by keeping the individual in touch with society.

Prisoners do not have a constitutional right to enjoy contact visits, as opposed to arrangements where prisoners are only permitted to talk to visitors over a telephone (*Block v. Rutherford*, 468 U.S. 576, 104 S. Ct. 3227, 82 L. Ed. 2d 438 [1984]). Courts have held that restrictions on visitation must be reasonable and related only to security needs and good order. Prisoners do not have a right to engage in sexual relations with a visitor.

The issue of the right of a prisoner to communicate and see visitors becomes more significant when the proposed visitor is a news reporter. Federal courts have held that a genuine need for security must be given greater weight than access to the media. Although inmates have a First Amendment right to communicate with the media, this right can be satisfied through the mail.

Before an individual interview with a reporter is approved, prison officials can require the prisoner or reporter to complete an application that discloses the names of the persons involved and the nature of the intended discussions. Officials can also limit reporters to random interviews conducted during a tour of the prison, as opposed to prearranged interviews with specific prisoners. In addition, face-to-face interviews can be banned for any prisoner who has been placed in maximum security.

Access to the Courts States cannot interfere with the right of a prisoner to PETITION a court for RELIEF. Neither a state nor a prison official can refuse, for any reason, to review a prisoner's applications and submit them to federal court. In addition, a state is not permitted to prohibit prisoners from having law books or legal papers in their cells on the basis that such materials tempt other prisoners to steal or create a fire hazard. If a prisoner is indigent, the state cannot require him to pay even a small fee to file legal papers with the court. However, a prisoner association cannot have filing fees waived. The right to proceed as an indigent party is allowed only for individual prisoners.

Prisoners have a fundamental right to legal counsel that requires special consideration. Prison officials must allow reasonable times and places for prisoners to communicate confidentially with their attorneys. Prisoners who cannot afford an attorney generally turn to fellow inmates who are experienced in arguing their own cases. Assistance from these "JAILHOUSE LAWYERS" was forbidden in most prisons until 1969, when the Supreme Court, in *Johnson v. Avery*, 393 U.S. 483, 89 S. Ct. 747, 21 L. Ed. 2d 718, held that prisons cannot completely forbid inmate assistance unless there is an alternative for prisoners. See also RIGHT TO COUNSEL.

Prisoners must be provided with writing materials and law books. Additionally, prisoners must be able to have their legal papers notarized.

Work Prisoners ordinarily receive token wages for work performed in prison. Courts have rejected prisoner lawsuits demanding fair wages for prisoner labor, concluding that prisoners do not have to be paid at all. Prisoners have no right to their own labor, or the benefits of it, while incarcerated.

Prisoners cannot refuse to work or choose the work they will do. Prison officials can punish prisoners for refusing to do work assigned to them.

Food Every prisoner is entitled to food in amounts adequate to sustain an average person. Various groups of prisoners have protested the failure of prisons to furnish them with special diets, and prisoners with special medical needs are generally accommodated. Dietary accommodations have been made for Orthodox Jews and for Muslim prisoners, though prison officials may balance the needs for prison security and economy with the religious beliefs of the inmates.

Religion A prisoner must be allowed to practice her RELIGION, obtain and keep written religious materials, see or communicate with a religious leader, and obey the rules of her religion that do not endanger order and security in the prison. In addition, wherever possible, formal religious observances for groups of inmates must be allowed on a regular basis. Prisoners can have access to religious programs broadcast on radio and television. Different religions within a particular prison must be given equal treatment.

Until 1997, when the U.S. Supreme Court overturned portions of the Religious Freedom Restoration Act (42 U.S.C.A. § 2000bb-1 (1993)), prisoners who had been denied permission to exercise their religious beliefs sought to obtain relief under this federal law. Under the law, a restriction that imposed a substantial burden on religious exercise had to further a COMPELLING STATE INTEREST in the least restrictive way to be constitutional. However, prisoners had not been successful in overturning restrictions under this law, because courts generally agreed with prison officials that compelling state interests were at stake.

Medical Care Prisoners are entitled to adequate medical treatment. A prison official's refusal to provide medical care to a seriously ill inmate violates the EIGHTH AMENDMENT's prohibition against cruel and unusual punishment (*Estelle v. Gamble*, 429 U.S. 97, 97 S. Ct. 285, 50 L. Ed. 2d 251 [1976]). In cases where the treatment is neither cruelly withheld nor intentionally mismanaged but is inept, prisoners can sue physicians in state courts for medical malpractice.

Appearance Prisons traditionally have strictly regulated the appearance of prisoners. In situations where prisoners have complained that they were denied opportunities to shower or shave, courts have insisted on minimum standards of human decency and personal hygiene. When necessary, courts have allowed prisons to force inmates to keep themselves clean for purposes of maintaining the health of the general prison population.

Discipline and Punishment The rules regarding conduct must be clearly defined and explained to inmates, and each prisoner must be provided with a written list of the rules when entering a correctional facility. Disciplinary rules must relate to the needs of security, good order, and good housekeeping.

A prisoner accused of breaking rules does not have all the rights of an accused at trial because a prison disciplinary proceeding is not the same as a criminal prosecution. Inmates are not entitled to an attorney at disciplinary hearings, nor are they entitled to confront or cross-examine the WITNESSES against them.

Prisoners must be given NOTICE of the charges against them, the particular rules they are charged with violating, and the penalties for such infractions. A HEARING can be informal for small infractions. The ordinary procedure is for the fact finder to write a statement that explains the evidence relied on and the reason for any disciplinary action taken. The punishment must reasonably relate to the seriousness of the infraction.

Prison personnel can use force in self-defense, stopping fights between inmates, compelling obedience to lawful orders where milder measures fail, and defending state property. Where guards use force without justification, a prisoner does not necessarily have the right to resist. The use of tear gas and chemical mace is justified only when an immediate danger of RIOT or serious disorder exists.

Prison officials may punish prisoners by withdrawing certain privileges, such as seeing visitors, buying items from the commissary, or earning wages. Prisoners cannot be denied fundamental human necessities.

Segregation is the most common type of punishment used in prisons for rule breaking. Prisoners can be categorized into groups and segregated from the general inmate population for a number of other reasons as well. Each prison has its own system and titles for different degrees of segregation. Separate areas may be set aside for young prisoners, repeat offenders, or prisoners who have been sentenced to death. Homosexuals and other prisoners who have or may be subjected to sexual abuse can be segregated. Segregation cannot be used, however, to separate prisoners according to race.

A number of prisons have more than one level of segregation, the most serious of which is solitary confinement. Punitive isolation is not unconstitutional in and of itself. Conditions in some prisons, however, have been found to be so strict that they constitute cruel and unusual punishment. A person in solitary confinement can be punished by the restriction of ordinary privileges, but a prisoner cannot be denied basic food, light, ventilation, or sanitation.

Unconstitutional Prisons Many federal courts have found that mere confinement in some prisons amounted to cruel and unusual punishment. The intervention of federal courts in prison reform began in the early 1970s and still continues. In 1996 eight JURISDICTIONS (Alaska, Mississippi, New Mexico, Rhode Island, South Carolina, Texas, Puerto Rico, and the Virgin Islands) were under court order or a consent decree to improve prison conditions. At the same time, major prison facilities in thirty-two jurisdictions were under court supervision. Typically, federal courts intervene when a facility has serious overcrowding or does not meet minimum standards.

Federal court intervention has forced states to improve prisons through the expenditure of money for new facilities, more staff, and improvements at existing prisons. However, many states have objected to what they perceive as unwarranted federal interference. Congress responded by passing the Prison Litigation Reform Act (PLRA) of 1995 (28 U.S.C.A. § 1932), which imposed substantive and procedural limitations on the ability of federal courts to issue INJUNCTIONS mandating prison reform. The act also restricted the courts' ability to employ special masters to assist in prison condition cases. (A special master is a person appointed by the district court to handle the day-to-day details and oversight of a case.) The law has been challenged on many fronts by those seeking reforms in prison conditions.

Remedies Available to Prisoners A prisoner who seeks to protect a constitutional or civil right is entitled to complain, but she is required to pursue whatever procedures exist within the prison before taking the case to court.

The most popular vehicle for prisoner lawsuits has been a federal civil rights statute, 42 U.S.C.A. § 1983 (1871; recodified 1979). A "section 1983 action" permits a prisoner to sue in federal court for an alleged deprivation of a federally protected or constitutional right by a person acting under the authority of state law. A prisoner may sue the warden or supervisor, a guard, or the local government that owns and runs the prison.

In the early 1980s, as many as fifteen thousand section 1983 actions were filed each year, many of them FRIVOLOUS. The Supreme Court responded by requiring many prisoners to use state tort claims acts rather than the federal statute and the federal courts. The Court also established difficult standards of proof for prisoners to meet.

In 1995 Congress sought to restrict prisoner lawsuits by devoting numerous provisions of the Prison Litigation Reform Act to this subject. The statute requires prisoners to exhaust administrative remedies before bringing a lawsuit, expands the federal courts' ability to dismiss lawsuits filed by prisoners, imposes numerous restrictions on the fees that can be awarded to a prisoner's attorney, and forbids a prisoner from filing an action for mental or emotional injury without a prior showing of physical injury. In addition, the act imposes restrictions on the ability of prisoners to proceed without paying filing fees. Another provision requires courts to prescreen lawsuits filed by prisoners and expands the grounds for dismissal of such suits. Finally, the act grants federal courts the power to revoke the good time credits of prisoners who file frivolous or harassing lawsuits or present false testimony or evidence to the court.

A prisoner's ability to file a HABEAS CORPUS action in the federal courts challenging prison conditions has also diminished. A WRIT of habeas corpus is a legal document ordering anyone who is officially holding the petitioner to bring him into court to determine whether the detention is unlawful. A federal court can hear an application for a writ of habeas corpus by a state prisoner who is being held in custody, allegedly in violation of the Constitution or the laws of the United States.

Traditionally a writ of habeas corpus was granted only for the purpose of ordering an immediate release of a prisoner from all restraints. A court would have to find that the imprisonment itself was illegal—for example, if the petitioner was convicted but his constitutional rights were violated during the trial. The scope of federal habeas corpus expanded in the 1970s and early 1980s, entitling a prisoner to the writ even if he was legally in custody but the conditions of the confinement violated his constitutional rights. The writ is rarely used in these circumstances, however, because federal courts prefer to improve prison conditions rather than set a convicted felon free.

PRIVACY In constitutional law, the right of people to make personal decisions regarding intimate matters; under the COMMON law, the right of people to lead their lives in a manner that is reasonably secluded from public scrutiny, whether such scrutiny comes from a neighbor's prying eyes, an investigator's eavesdropping ears, or a news photographer's intrusive camera; and in statutory law, the right of people to be free from unwarranted drug testing and ELECTRONIC SURVEILLANCE.

The origins of the right to privacy can be traced to the nineteenth century. In 1890 Samuel D. Warren and LOUIS D. BRANDEIS published "The Right to Privacy," an influential article that postulated a general common-law right of privacy. Before the publication of this article, no U.S. court had ever expressly recognized such a legal right. Since the publication of the article, courts have relied on it in hundreds of cases presenting a range of privacy issues.

In *Olmstead v. United States*, 277 U.S. 438, 48 S. Ct. 564, 72 L. Ed. 944 (1928), Brandeis, then a Supreme Court justice, articulated a general constitutional right "to be let alone," which he described as the most comprehensive and valued right of civilized people. For the next half century, the right to privacy gradually evolved. Today every JURISDICTION in the country recognizes some form of constitutional, common-law, or statutory right to privacy.

Constitutional Law The constitutional right to privacy protects the liberty of people to make certain crucial decisions regarding their well-being without government coercion, intimidation, or interference. Such crucial decisions may concern religious faith, moral values, political affiliation, MARRIAGE, procreation, or death. The federal Constitution guarantees the right of individuals to make these decisions according to their own conscience and beliefs. The government is not constitutionally permitted to regulate such deeply personal matters.

The right of privacy protected by the Constitution gained a foothold in *Griswold v. Connecticut*, 381 U.S. 479, 85 S. Ct. 1678, 14 L. Ed. 2d 510 (1965), in which the Supreme Court struck down a state statute forbidding married adults from using BIRTH CONTROL because the statute violated the sanctity of the marital bedroom. Acknowledging that the Constitution does not mention the word *privacy* anywhere in its text, the Court held that a general right to privacy may be inferred from the express language of the First, Third, Fourth, Fifth, and Fourteenth Amendments, as well as from the interests protected by them.

The Court said that the FIRST AMENDMENT guarantees the right to peaceably assemble, which includes the LIBERTY of any group to associate in private. The THIRD AMENDMENT prohibits the government from quartering soldiers in a private home without the consent of the owner. The FOURTH AMENDMENT forbids the government from performing warrantless and unreasonable searches of any area in which a person maintains a REASONABLE expectation of privacy. The FIFTH AMENDMENT safeguards the right of criminal suspects to keep secret any incriminating evidence that might help the government obtain a conviction against them. The FOURTEENTH AMENDMENT prevents states from denying its citizens certain fundamental rights that are deemed essential to the concepts of equality or liberty, including the right to autonomy, dignity, and self-determination.

The holding in *Griswold* was later used to strike down a Massachusetts statute that made illegal the distribution of contraceptives to unmarried persons (*Eisenstadt v. Baird*, 405 U.S. 438, 92 S. Ct. 1029, 31 L. Ed. 2d 349 [1972]). In striking down this law, the Supreme Court articulated a broader view of privacy, stating that all individuals, married or single, enjoy the liberty to make certain intimate personal decisions free from government intrusion, including the decision whether to bear or sire a child. This rationale was extended in *Roe v. Wade*, 410 U.S. 113, 93 S. Ct. 705, 35 L. Ed. 2d 147 (1973), which established the right of women to terminate their pregnancy at any time before the fetus reaches the stage of viability. *Roe* has

Protecting Your Privacy

By using computer technology, companies can legally collect information about consumers, including what they buy, what medications they take, what sites on the Internet they have visited, and their credit history. Computer software can organize this data and prepare it for sale and use by direct marketing companies, lending institutions, insurance companies, and credit bureaus.

Although it may be legal to collect this information, individuals may legitimately take steps to protect their privacy. Here are some common ways that companies collect information and some steps consumers can take to prevent this from happening:

- *Shopper's cards* Some grocery stores and other retail businesses offer discounts or premiums when a consumer uses their shopper's card. All purchases are scanned into a computer, allowing the store to compile a list of an individual's buying habits. The store may use this information to target certain customers or may sell it to companies seeking specific types of potential customers. Consumers can protect their privacy either by not using such cards or by persuading the company to limit the distribution of the information.
- *Financial data* Credit bureaus compile credit histories filled with personal information, which are sold to anyone without restriction. Although these credit reports are supposed to be sold only to those companies with a legitimate business interest, this is not always the case. Consumers are entitled to review their credit reports and correct any errors. If someone the consumer does not know has requested a report, the consumer can ask the credit bureau to investigate the legitimacy of the request.
- *Motor vehicle data* An individual's motor vehicle registration is public information in most states. In many states driver's license data (weight, age, address, driver's license number) are also public information. Automobile dealers and insurance companies collect such information. An individual can request the state motor vehicle department not to release his or her name and address to individuals or companies.

subsequently been interpreted to proscribe the government from passing regulations that unduly burden a woman's right to ABORTION.

In *Cruzan v. Missouri Department of Health*, 497 U.S. 261, 110 S. Ct. 2841, 111 L. Ed. 2d 224 (1990), the Supreme Court again enlarged the constitutional meaning of privacy by declaring that competent patients have a right to refuse life-sustaining medical treatment, including artificial nutrition and hydration. A 1997 Supreme Court case presented the issue of whether competent but terminally ill patients may hasten their death through physician-assisted suicide (*Washington v. Glucksberg*, 117 S. Ct. 2258). Representatives for the terminally ill patients argued that the right to physician-assisted suicide represents an essential liberty interest in controlling one of life's most significant decisions, whereas the state of Washington argued that this liberty interest is outweighed by the need to protect vulnerable individuals from irrational, ill-informed, and coerced decisions to end their lives. The Supreme Court held that the right to assistance in committing suicide is not a fundamental liberty interest protected by the due process clause of the Constitution, and a state's ban on assisted suicide is constitutional.

The constitutional right to privacy does not protect all forms of conduct that are pursued behind closed doors. Adults have no constitutional right to engage in homosexual SODOMY, inject intravenous drugs, solicit prostitutes, or view child PORNOGRAPHY. Nor do members of society have a right to be insulated from every potentially offensive activity. For example, the government may not forbid a movie theater from displaying nude scenes on a large outdoor screen that is visible to passing motorists. In *Erznoznik v. City of Jacksonville*, 422 U.S. 205, 95 S. Ct. 2268, 45 L. Ed. 2d 125 (1975), the Supreme Court said that the First Amendment right to show such films outweighs the privacy interests of offended passersby who can protect their sensitivity by averting their eyes.

Common Law The common law of torts recognizes five discrete rights of privacy. First, the common law affords individuals the right to sue when their seclusion or solitude has been intruded upon in an unreasonable and highly offensive manner. Second, individuals have a common-law right to sue when information concerning their private life is disclosed to the public in a highly objectionable fashion. Third, tort LIABILITY may be imposed on individuals or entities that publicize information that places someone in a false light. Fourth, the common law forbids persons from appropriating someone's name or likeness without his or her consent. Fifth, the common law prevents business competitors from engaging in unfair competition through the theft of trade secrets.

Intrusion upon Seclusion One who intentionally intrudes upon the solitude or seclusion of another is subject to liability for common-law invasion of privacy. An invasion may involve a physical intrusion into a place where a person has secluded herself, such as the nonconsensual entry into someone's home, office, apartment, or hotel room. Nonphysical intrusions may also give rise to liability when they involve the use of electronic surveillance equipment, including wiretaps, microphones, and video cameras. Alternatively, a person's seclusion may be impermissibly interrupted by persistent and unwelcome telephone calls, or by the occasional window peeper. By imposing liability in such instances, the law seeks to protect a person's tranquility and equilibrium.

Not every intrusion is actionable under this common-law TORT. The intrusion must be considered highly offensive to a reasonable person. CREDITORS are allowed to take action to collect delinquent debts but must do so in a reasonable fashion. LANDLORDS are permitted to demand late rental payments but must do so at reasonable times. A judge or jury determines what is reasonable according to the facts of each case. Individuals have no expectation of privacy in matters that are public. Thus, businesses may examine public criminal records of prospective employees without fear of liability, and photographers may take pictures of movie stars in public places.

Publicity That Discloses Private Information The common law protects individuals from publicity that discloses information about their private lives. Unlike libel, slander, and DEFAMATION actions, this common-law tort may give rise to liability for truthful publicity, as long as the information is published in a manner that is highly objectionable to a reasonable person and the information is of no legitimate concern to the public. Disclosure of private sexual relations, disgraceful family quarrels, humiliating illnesses, and most other intimate personal matters will normally give rise to liability for invasion of privacy, even if such disclosures are completely accurate. By discouraging the publication of such private and personal matters, the common law places a high value on the right of individuals to control the dissemination of information about themselves, including the right to filter out embarrassing and harmful facts that might influence the opinion of others.

Liability is not usually imposed for alleged injuries relating to matters that are intended for public consumption. A person's date of birth and military record, for example, are both matters of public record that may be disclosed without invading his or her privacy. Commercial proprietors that regularly deal with the public receive little protection from disclosures that relate to the price of their products, the quality of their services, or the manner in which they conduct business. Under the First Amendment, business proprietors receive less protection of their privacy interests because the U.S. Constitution seeks to promote the free and robust exchange of accurate information to allow consumers to make informed decisions.

False-Light Publicity The common-law tort of false-light publicity protects individuals from the public disclosure of false information about their reputation, beliefs, or activities. The information need not be of a private nature nor must it be defamatory, as must libelous and slanderous statements, before liability will be imposed. Instead, a misleading publication will give rise to liability for false-light publicity when it is placed before a large segment of the public in such a way that a reasonable person would find it highly offensive. However, publication of an inaccurate story to a single person, or a small group of people, is not considered sufficiently public to constitute publicity.

A newspaper photograph printed in close proximity to a caption suggesting criminal activity on the part of the person photographed is a classic example of false-light publicity. On the other hand, a misleading photograph, such as one that has been retouched, may not give rise to liability for false-light publicity if the photograph is accompanied by a caption that clearly explains how it has been distorted. An esteemed poet may successfully sue for false-light publicity when an inferior poem is published under her name. A war hero may assert a cognizable claim for false-light publicity if a story is aired that inaccurately portrays him as a coward.

Public officials, such as politicians, and public figures, such as professional athletes, rarely recover for false-light publicity. Before a public official or PUBLIC FIGURE can recover for false-light publicity, the First Amendment requires proof that a story or caption was published with knowledge of its falsity or in reckless disregard of its truth, a principle that has become known as the actual malice standard (*New York Times Co. v. Sullivan*, 376 U.S. 254, 84 S. Ct. 710, 11 L. Ed. 2d 686 [1964]). In most instances, public officials and public figures have thrust themselves into the public spotlight. As a condition to accepting the benefits that accompany public recognition, the law requires that such persons accept a diminished level of protection of their privacy interests. Because the First Amendment confers less protection on public persons than it does on private individuals, the Constitution encourages the media to freely disseminate information about candidates for office, government officials, and other figures who influence or shape the course of society.

Appropriation of Name or Likeness One who appropriates the name or likeness of another person is subject to liability for invasion of privacy. All individuals are vested with an exclusive PROPERTY RIGHT in their identity. No person, business, or other entity may appropriate someone's name or likeness without permission. Nonconsensual commercial APPROPRIATION of a person's name or likeness for advertising purposes is the most common type of conduct giving rise to liability under this common-law tort. By forbidding the nonconsensual use of a person's name or likeness, the law allows an individual to LICENSE her face, body, reputation, prestige, and image for remuneration.

Not every appropriation gives rise to liability for invasion of privacy. Liability will attach only when a person's name or likeness has been appropriated to obtain an immediate and direct advantage. The advantage need not yield a financial gain. However, the mere incidental use of someone's name or likeness is not a compensable appropriation.

For example, the print and electronic media may publish photographs, drawings, and other depictions of a person's name or likeness as an incidental part of their legitimate newsgathering activities without violating the common-law right to privacy. However, if a nonprofit organization uses a person's name or likeness to promote its philanthropy, it may be liable for the appropriation. The right to sue for wrongful appropriation is a personal right. Parents cannot recover damages for breach of their children's privacy, and family members cannot sue after the death of the person whose name or likeness has been misappropriated.

Theft of Trade Secrets Wrongful use, disclosure, or theft of a trade secret is actionable under the common law. Although the U.S. economy is generally governed by free-market principles, the common law requires businesses to compete fairly and forbids business rivals from improperly stealing one another's INTELLECTUAL PROPERTY for commercial advantage. Although it is difficult to formulate a comprehensive list of what constitutes the improper acquisition of a trade secret, the common law generally makes it unlawful to engage in FRAUD, MISREPRESENTATION, or other forms of deception for the purpose of obtaining confidential commercial information.

Independent analysis of publicly available products or information is not an improper means of acquisition. Through a process known as reverse engineering, a competitor may lawfully purchase a rival's product, disassemble it, and subject it to laboratory analysis for the purpose of unlocking valuable information, such as a secret formula or process. However, aerial photography of a competitor's plant constitutes tortious interference with commercial privacy. Courts have reasoned that the law should not force commercial entities to expend additional resources to conceal their interior from every possible form of exterior exposure. Conversely, commercial entities may patent many of their valuable trade secrets before placing a product on the market where it can be analyzed by a competitor. See also PATENTS.

Legislation In addition to the constitutional and common-law principles that offer protection of privacy interests, a host of statutes and regulations have been passed to define privacy in a variety of contexts. State and federal legislation regulates the circumstances under which information from financial, educational, and government records can be revealed. State and federal legislation also prescribes the conditions under which employers may subject their employees to drug testing. Federal laws strictly limit the use of electronic surveillance in both the public and private sectors.

Congress passed the FAIR CREDIT REPORTING ACT of 1970 (15 U.S.C.A. § 1681 et seq.) to prevent unreasonable and careless invasions of consumer privacy. The law permits employers, lenders, and other persons to obtain a copy of an individual's credit report for a legitimate business purpose. However, businesses may not request a credit report unless it is related to a transaction initiated by the consumer, such as a job interview or bank loan.

Commercial entities may not use credit reports for the purpose of marketing. Nor may a person or entity obtain a credit report through the use of FALSE PRETENSES, fraud, or misrepresentation. The statute authorizes consumers to review the information contained in their own credit reports and challenge inaccuracies. CREDIT BUREAUS have an obligation to correct any inaccuracies within a reasonable amount of time after learning of them.

The Privacy Act of 1974 (5 U.S.C.A. § 522a) requires the federal government to use fair practices in the collection and use of information about U.S. citizens and is designed to prevent federal agencies from disclosing certain personal information contained in their records. In general, federal agencies may not release government records without first obtaining consent from the persons who are referenced in the records. Every individual maintains the right to inspect federal agency records, correct mistakes, and add important details. In the event that an individual's right is infringed under this law, he or she can sue the federal government for money DAMAGES or a court order directing the agency to obey the law.

Similarly, the FREEDOM OF INFORMATION ACT (5 U.S.C.A. § 552 [1996]) contains limitations on the disclosure of agency information when such disclosure would constitute a "clearly unwarranted invasion of personal privacy." In most other instances, the Freedom of Information Act guarantees the right of Americans to request a copy of any reasonably identifiable record kept by a federal agency. However, the U.S. government may refuse to disclose certain sensitive information that relates to national security, foreign policy, or other classified areas. Persons whose requests for information have been denied may challenge the decision in court. The Freedom of Information Act serves the twin purposes of protecting private and classified documents from disclosure while requiring the uninhibited exchange of all other information that is consistent with an open society and a democratic government.

In 1974 Congress enacted the Family Educational Rights and Privacy Act (20 U.S.C.A. § 1232g), which gives parents the right to examine the scholastic records of their children. The act broadly defines scholastic records to include all records, files, documents, and other materials containing information directly related to a student that are maintained by an educational agency or institution. The act permits only certain individuals to have access to student records, including other institution officials who have a legitimate scholastic interest in the records, such as teachers, principals, and student loan officers. Otherwise, a school must obtain consent from the student or parent before disclosing any information contained in an educational record. The Family Educational Rights and Privacy Act applies to all public schools, including COLLEGES AND UNIVERSITIES, and to private schools that receive federal funding.

The Right to Financial Privacy Act of 1978 (12 U.S.C.A. § 3401 et seq.) entitles bank customers to a limited expectation of privacy in their financial records by requiring that law enforcement officials follow certain procedures before information can be disclosed. Unless a customer consents in writing to the disclosure of his financial records, a bank may not produce such records for government inspection unless ordered to do so by an administrative or judicial SUBPOENA or a lawfully executed search warrant. Other formal written requests for bank records may be granted if they are made for a legitimate law enforcement purpose. The Right to Financial Privacy Act applies to credit unions, trust companies, and savings and loan institutions.

The Omnibus Crime Control and Safe Streets Act of 1968 (18 U.S.C.A. § 2510 et seq.) governs the use of electronic surveillance in both the public and private sectors. In the public sector the act outlines detailed procedures the federal government must follow before conducting any form of electronic surveillance. Pursuant to authorization by the U.S. attorney general or a specially designated assistant, federal law enforcement agents must make a sworn written application to a federal judge that specifically describes the location where the communications will be intercepted, the reasons for the interception, the expected duration of the surveillance, and the identity of any persons whose conversations will be monitored. The judge must then review the surveillance application to ensure that it satisfies each of the statutory requirements and establishes probable cause to justify electronic eavesdropping.

The Omnibus Crime Control and Safe Streets Act governs the use of electronic surveillance in the private sector as well. The act prohibits any person from intentionally using or disclosing information that has been knowingly intercepted by electronic or mechanical means without the consent of the interested person. Nearly 70 percent of all reported WIRETAPPING involves DIVORCE cases and custody battles. Often, divorcing spouses, attempting to obtain embarrassing or discrediting information against one another, plant recording and listening devices throughout the marital home. Although most federal courts have ruled that the Omnibus Crime Control and Safe Streets Act applies to interspousal electronic surveillance, some courts have created a spousal immunity from civil liability under the act in an effort to preserve any remaining remnants of marital harmony.

The Omnibus Crime Control and Safe Streets Act also governs the use of electronic surveillance in the area of employment. A number of employers videotape employee movement throughout the workplace, search employees' computer files, monitor their telephone calls, and read their electronic mail. Courts have generally permitted employers to engage in such surreptitious snooping so long as it serves a legitimate and significant business purpose.

In the rest of the private sector, the Omnibus Crime Control and Safe Streets Act applies to information intercepted from telephone satellite unscrambling devices, cellular telephones, and pagers, as well as from traditional forms of electronic surveillance, such as telephone taps, microphones, and other bugging devices. However, the act does not cover information intercepted from PEN REGISTERS, which record the telephone numbers of outgoing calls, or caller identification devices, which display the telephone numbers of incoming calls, because neither captures conversations of any sort. In addition, the act does not apply to information intercepted by videotape.

Drug and ALCOHOL testing is another form of employee surveillance that raises privacy questions in both the public and private sectors. Many legislators consider drug testing by urinalysis to be intrusive, and the practice has been regulated in at least eighteen states. Three states require employers to demonstrate PROBABLE CAUSE of illegal drug use before they can compel an employee to submit to urinalysis. Six states specify that employers can instigate drug testing only if they have reason to suspect an employee of illegal drug use. In general, however, no pervasive PUBLIC POLICY against mandatory employee drug testing exists in either the public or private sector.

Drug testing in the workplace gained momentum in 1986 following a presidential commission report on drug abuse (*America's Habit: Drug Abuse, Drug Trafficking, and Organized Crime*). The commission recommended drug testing in both the public and private employment sectors. Based on this recommendation, President RONALD REAGAN ordered drug testing for federal employees in positions that require a high degree of trust and confidence (Exec. Order No. 12,564, 3 C.F.R. 224 [1986]). Guidelines promulgated by the Department of Health and Human Services established scientific and technical requirements concerning specimen collection, laboratory analysis, and interpretation of test results for the federal drug-testing program.

In response to this federal impetus, employers have dramatically increased drug testing of employees. Many state laws now encourage private employers to periodically test their employees for illegal drug use, and many private employers have asked their state legislatures to pass drug-testing laws. In the public sector, however, the U.S. Supreme Court has ruled that random drug testing of government employees constitutes a "search" that must comply with the requirements of the Fourth Amendment before it may be deemed legal (*National Treasury Employees Union v. Von Raab*, 489 U.S. 656, 109 S. Ct. 1384, 103 L. Ed. 2d 685 [1989]).

The meaning of the term *privacy* changes according to its legal context. In constitutional law, privacy means the right to make certain fundamental decisions concerning deeply personal matters free from government coercion, intimidation, or regulation. In this sense, privacy is associated with interests in autonomy, dignity, and self-determination. Under the common law, privacy generally means the right to be let alone. In this sense, privacy is associated with seclusion. Under statutory law, privacy often means the right to prevent the nonconsensual disclosure of sensitive, confidential, or discrediting information. In this sense, privacy is associated with secrecy.

CROSS-REFERENCES

Acquired Immune Deficiency Syndrome; Consumer Credit; Death and Dying; Drugs and Narcotics; E-mail; Employment Law; *Griswold v. Connecticut;* Libel and Slander; *New York Times v. Sullivan; Olmstead v. United States;* Parent and Child; Penumbra; Privileged Communication; *In re Quinlan; Roe v. Wade;* Search and Seizure.

PRIVATE That which affects, characterizes, or belongs to an individual person, as opposed to the general public.

PRIVATE ATTORNEY GENERAL A private citizen who commences a lawsuit to enforce a legal right that benefits the community as a whole.

PRIVATE BILL LEGISLATION that benefits an individual or a locality. Also called special legislation or a private act.

Many state constitutions prohibit the enactment of private bills or acts when a general law could apply. The prohibition of private bills, now more commonly known as special laws, applies to legislation that affects local governments or private individuals. Despite this constitutional language, private bills remain a part of the U.S. legislative process.

The constitutional disfavor of private bills is based on several concerns. The enactment of special legislation undermines the idea that laws apply to all persons in a state. The perception of favoritism reduces the credibility of the legislative process. The reality of special legislation is that the LEGISLATURE fails to establish responsible and uniform statewide regulation of local government units and creates preferential and prejudicial discrimination between communities. Private bills also use legislative time and energy in small amounts, leaving the legislature less able to deal with general legislative business. Nevertheless, special legislative treatment of special problems is sometimes warranted.

Legislatures can evade the constitutional provisions banning private bills by drafting laws that apply to the entire state, at least on their face. For example, a special bill for one local unit of government or person can be drawn so that it appears to apply to all units or persons meeting specific criteria. The criteria actually limit its applicability to the one community or person the sponsors intend to affect. Population is the most common "bogus" criterion since it is easy to use. Thus, a law that applies only to "a county with a population of more than 50,000 and between 350,000 and 400,000 acres" appears on its face to apply generally to all counties in the state that match the criteria. This type of legislative drafting hides special legislation and makes it appear to be general.

Courts will uphold special legislation if the classifications in the act are "open," meaning that other units of government or individuals will come under the law if at any time they meet the criteria in the law. In the example above, the population of a county given in the law was 50,000. If another county reaches that level of population and has the same amount of acreage, it will fall under the legislation, thus making the classification open. If the class is fixed by the facts as of some point in time, the class is closed, and is stripped of the PRESUMPTION that it is an honest classification related to a legitimate legislative purpose. The class is held to be descriptive of the target community or person and makes the legislation an invalid private bill.

Legislatures can limit the number of private bills either by examining them more critically or adopting statewide legislation that gives local units adequate powers to solve issues themselves, eliminating the need for private bills.

PRIVATEER A vessel that is owned, equipped, and armed by one or more private parties, that is commissioned by a hostile power to cruise the high seas to perform acts of war upon the enemy, ordinarily by attacking ships involved in commerce with the enemy. Also, the commander or a crew member of the vessel.

A privateer was commissioned by the issuance of a letter of marque to its owner to commit hostile acts at sea, generally in accordance with the laws of war. Letters of marque were formerly issued by a state to its own subjects as well as to the subjects of neutral states. The owner of a vessel who accepted letters of marque from both belligerents was, however, deemed a pirate.

Privateering was abolished by the Declaration of Paris in 1856; however, the United States, Spain, Mexico, and Venezuela did not consent to this declaration. The theory has been that the Constitution, which gives Congress the power to issue letters of marque, does not authorize it to participate in a permanent treaty abolishing privateering.

Both piracy and privateering are federal offenses that are punishable by life imprisonment.

See also MARQUE AND REPRISAL.

PRIVATE INTERNATIONAL LAW A branch of JURISPRUDENCE arising from the diverse laws of various nations that applies when private citizens of different countries interact or transact business with one another.

Private INTERNATIONAL LAW refers to that part of the law that is administered between private citizens of different countries or is concerned with the definition, regulation, and enforcement of rights in situations where both the person in whom the right inheres and the person upon whom the obligation rests are private citizens of different nations. It is a set of rules and regulations that are established or agreed upon by citizens of different nations who privately enter into a transaction and that will govern in the event of a dispute. In this respect, private international law differs from public international law, which is the set of rules entered into by the governments of various countries that determine the rights and regulate the intercourse of independent nations.

PRIVATE LAW That portion of the law that defines, regulates, enforces, and administers relationships among individuals, associations, and CORPORATIONS. As used in distinction to PUBLIC LAW, the term means that part of the law that is administered between citizen and citizen, or that is concerned with the definition, regulation, and enforcement of rights in cases where both the person in whom the right inheres and the person upon whom the obligation rests are private individuals.

PRIVATE ROADS A street or route that is designated by a public authority to accommodate a person or a group of people.

A private road is often established because an individual needs to gain access to land; such a road can cross another person's property. A private road can be used by the general public and is open to all who wish to use it, but it primarily benefits those at whose request it was established. Unlike HIGHWAYS that are cared for by the public at large, private roads are maintained at the expense of the private individuals who requested the road.

Statutory regulations must be observed when a private road is designated. An applicant can recommend a certain location for the road, but the ultimate decision rests with the highway authority, which might vary the proposed route to comply with the public interest and statutory regulations. Distance, practicality, the interests of the applicant, and the least intrusive means of utilizing private property are some considerations involved in making a road. When a private RIGHT OF WAY is requested over another person's property and the owner of the land over which the proposed route is sought provides a convenient and practical route, that passage will often be earmarked for a segment of the private road.

The authority to establish a private road is derived from the power of EMINENT DOMAIN and exists only when expressly provided by a statute. The statute must be strictly followed, especially when the private road benefits only the requesting party. Generally land is taken for the construction of a private road only in cases of necessity. The definition of necessity varies among the JURISDICTIONS and is determined on a case-by-case basis. Some jurisdictions hold that an applicant establishes necessity when she proves that a private road is absolutely indispensable as a means of reaching her land, whereas others only require proof of a reasonable and practical need for the road. Private roads are never opened merely because the applicant would find it a convenience. Before establishing one, the authority must consider all the facts and balance the benefit received by the limited number of people who use the road against the burden imposed on the owner of the land over which the proposed road will cross.

Most statutes require that an applicant file a petition with a court to commence a CIVIL ACTION for the establishment of a private road. The action is between the applicant and the owner or owners whose land will be utilized in the proposed road. The court appoints viewers, commissioners, or jurors to inspect the affected area, to decide whether the road should be established, and to suggest any needed modifications. Where statutes provide for the appointment of viewers, who subsequently find the road necessary, they will map out a route that does the least amount of damage to private property and consider the needs of the applicant. The awarding of DAMAGES to the property owner over whose land the road passes is within the exclusive discretion of the viewers. A court will review the damages award only if it is alleged that the viewers acted in a dishonest or corrupt manner.

Some statutes require the commissioners or viewers to conduct a hearing on the proposed road. Such a hearing provides for a better fact-finding procedure since the applicant and any opposing party can present arguments for or against the proposed road. If an opponent wishes to contest an application that receives a favorable report, he must file an exception, which preserves the record should the losing party decide to APPEAL. If no exceptions are filed during the hearing, a report that conforms to the law is binding on a court. A court must then enter a JUDGMENT, describing the location of the road and, if required by statute, limiting its use to a specified period or time.

The duty to maintain and repair a private road rests on the person or persons for whose benefit the road is established. If a large portion of the public utilize the road or if a statute requires its designation as a public highway, then the duty to maintain and repair falls on the public at large. Persons who are injured as a result of disrepair can seek to recover damages from the responsible party.

PRIVILEGE A particular benefit, advantage, or IMMUNITY enjoyed by a person or class of people that is not shared with others. A power of exemption against or beyond the law. It is not a right but, rather, exempts one from the performance of a DUTY, OBLIGATION, or LIABILITY.

PRIVILEGE AGAINST SELF-INCRIMINATION The right, under the FIFTH AMENDMENT to the U.S. Constitution, not to be a WITNESS against oneself in a criminal proceeding.

Generally, the parties in civil or criminal cases have the right to use all EVIDENCE relevant to the case. This general rule is considered essential to DUE PROCESS. However, there are some instances where a person may refuse to give information or answer questions concerning certain information that may be relevant to the case. One of these exceptions is the privilege against self-incrimination.

The Fifth Amendment to the U.S. Constitution states in part that no person "shall be compelled in any criminal case to be a witness against himself." The privilege stems from the concern that the Framers of the Constitution had for the rights of criminal defendants and is a defining feature of the adversarial system of justice. Under this system, the prosecution must prove the guilt of the defendant without forcing the defendant to confess or testify. By contrast, an INQUISITORIAL SYSTEM of criminal justice allows the prosecution to interrogate the defendant and extract CONFESSIONS. The founders were wary that inquisitions could lead to abuse, such as torture and intimidation in pursuit of confessions.

The privilege against self-incrimination can be divided into two categories: the rights of a witness in any case, whether civil or criminal, and the rights of a defendant in a criminal case.

A defendant in a civil case can be called to testify, although he may refuse to answer questions that incriminate him in any criminal action. Former Assemblyman Mickey Conroy of Orange County, Calif., was called to testify in a well publicized sexual harassment trial in which he was a defendant.

The privilege against self-incrimination applies only to individuals and not to CORPORATIONS or other business entities.

Witness Privilege A witness in any case can refuse to answer questions that may yield an incriminating response at any point in any civil or criminal proceeding. This includes pretrial proceedings, GRAND JURY proceedings, legislative investigations, and administrative HEARINGS. A witness called to TESTIFY at any proceeding must appear at the proceeding and be sworn in (promise to tell the truth) before the witness may claim the privilege. Failure to appear can result in a citation for CONTEMPT of court.

A witness may refuse to answer questions or give DOCUMENTARY EVIDENCE only if the answer or document would INCRIMINATE the witness. An answer is considered self-incriminating if it would lead to criminal LIABILITY in any JURISDICTION. The answer need only furnish a link in the chain of CIRCUMSTANTIAL EVIDENCE necessary for a conviction (*Blau v. United States,* 340 U.S. 159, 71 S. Ct. 223, 95 L. Ed. 170 [1950]). The answer does not have to be one that would be ADMISSIBLE as evidence in a criminal trial.

A judge must decide whether a witness declaring the privilege is entitled to it. This decision can be difficult because the judge does not know what the witness will say. The judge must consider the implications of the question in the setting in which it is asked, in determining whether the answer may incriminate the witness (*Hoffman v. United States,* 341 U.S. 479, 71 S. Ct. 814, 95 L. Ed. 1118 [1951]).

The privilege does not allow a witness to refuse to answer a question because the response may expose the witness to civil liability, social disgrace, loss of status, or loss of private employment. A witness may not claim the privilege on the grounds that an answer or document may incriminate a third party: it may be declared only by the witness for the witness.

If the STATUTE OF LIMITATIONS has expired on a crime that the witness may have committed, the witness cannot claim the privilege. Because no PROSECUTOR would be able to prosecute the witness for the crime, the witness would not be implicating herself in a crime, and the privilege would be unnecessary.

In some criminal cases, a prosecutor may grant to a witness IMMUNITY from prosecution. This immunity comes in two forms: transactional and testimonial. Transactional immunity gives the witness immunity from prosecution for the criminal acts to which the witness refers in her statements. Testimonial immunity merely prevents the prosecution from using the statements the witness makes in a subsequent prosecution of the witness. Prosecutors have the right to grant only testimonial immunity and thereby force witnesses to testify. If the witness refuses to testify after being given testimonial immunity, she could be jailed for contempt of court. Furthermore, if a witness with testimonial immunity testifies falsely, the false statements may be used against the witness in a subsequent prosecution for PERJURY.

A witness who has had incriminating documents seized from his possession pursuant to a valid search warrant cannot claim the privilege against self-incrimination. This is because the privilege is basically concerned with preventing compelled testimony. The FOURTH AMENDMENT, which applies to SEARCH WARRANTS, is concerned with PRIVACY rights, not forced testimony. Even if incriminating evidence is forcibly taken from a witness pursuant to a search, the witness cannot claim the privilege against self-incrimination because the privilege is not relevant to the law of search warrants. If incriminating evidence is found but the search warrant was invalid, the evidence may be excluded from a subsequent trial of the witness under the Fourth Amendment's EXCLUSIONARY RULE, but not under the Fifth Amendment's clause on self-incrimination.

By contrast, if police or prosecutors summon a witness to produce self-incriminating documents, the witness may claim the privilege because a SUMMONS to produce documents is similar to a demand for testimony (*Curcio v. United States,* 354 U.S. 118, 77 S. Ct. 1145, 1 L. Ed. 2d 1225 [1952]). However, police and prosecutors may force a witness to relinquish self-incriminating documents if the records pertain to a regulated public matter, such as price records kept by businesses under price regulation statutes.

A witness may waive the privilege against self-incrimination either voluntarily or unwittingly. Witnesses testifying before a grand jury or in a civil or criminal trial have no right to warnings on the privilege against self-incrimination. Moreover, a person required to appear before a PROBATION officer need not be apprised of the privilege, and any incriminating statements that the PROBATIONER makes may be used in a subsequent criminal prosecution. However, if a person is in police CUSTODY, he has the right to be informed of the right to be free from self-incrimination.

Criminal Defendant Privilege The defendant in a criminal case has all the privileges that a witness has, and more. A defendant may refuse to answer questions that may yield incriminating responses. This includes the right to remain silent upon arrest. A self-incriminating statement made by a defendant who is in police custody is not admissible in court unless the defendant made the statement voluntarily. Generally, a person is in police custody if she or he is not free to leave the presence of police officers.

Any incriminating statement that a defendant makes while in police custody is considered involuntary unless he or she has already been apprised of his or her *Miranda* rights. *Miranda* rights are the set of rights and warnings that police must read to an arrestee. One of these rights is the right to remain silent. A reading of *Miranda* rights also informs the arrestee that anything the arrestee says may be used against her in court.

Police officers must read *Miranda* rights to a criminal suspect who is in custody before asking questions because CUSTODIAL INTERROGATION is inherently coercive. The reading of *Miranda* rights ensures that a defendant who waives the privilege against self-incrimination does so voluntarily. There are some exceptions to the general rule that a police officer must read *Miranda* rights before questioning a suspect. If, for example, a police officer needs to know the location of a loaded weapon, the officer may ask a handcuffed suspect where the gun is located without reading *Miranda* rights to the suspect. The suspect's answer could later be used in court against her.

In some cases an interrogation may be so coercive that it violates the privilege against self-incrimination even if the suspect waived *Miranda* rights or was not in custody. In determining whether an interrogation was inherently coercive, a court may consider such characteristics as the suspect's age, sex, state of health, education, or level of intoxication.

For criminal defendants, the privilege against self-incrimination includes the right to refuse to testify at trial. A defendant may testify at a PRELIMINARY HEARING on the admissibility of evidence without waiving the right to not testify at trial. Incriminating statements made by a defendant in a preliminary hearing are not admissible at trial, and the prosecutor may not comment on them.

If a defendant chooses not to testify, the prosecutor may not comment about that choice during trial. If a defendant does testify in court, he loses the privilege against self-incrimination. The prosecution may cross-examine the defendant concerning the crime charged as well as other crimes, and the court will compel the defendant to answer.

The Supreme Court has held that the privilege is not compromised by laws that require persons to surrender identification to law enforcement personnel (*California v. Byers*, 402 U.S. 424, 91 S. Ct. 1535, 29 L. Ed. 2d 9 [1971]). A person who is suspected of a crime may be compelled to testify before a grand jury, a legislative body, or an administrative board. The person must appear and answer questions, but he may claim the privilege against self-incrimination when necessary.

A defendant may be ordered to submit to a pretrial psychiatric test, but most courts admit into trial only the information obtained at such examinations that relates to the competency of the defendant to stand trial. Some courts allow the information from psychiatric tests to prove or disprove a defendant's sanity. Additionally, a defendant can be compelled by court order to try on clothing to see if it fits; give samples of blood, hair, and voice; participate in an identification lineup; and provide fingerprints. Like any witness, a defendant cannot be required to produce incriminating documents. Police and prosecutors try to gain possession of such documents through the use of search warrants.

CROSS-REFERENCES

Adversary System; Criminal Law; Criminal Procedure; *Miranda v. Arizona;* Search and Seizure.

PRIVILEGED COMMUNICATION An exchange of information between two individuals in a confidential relationship.

A privileged communication is a private statement that must be kept in confidence by the recipient for the benefit of the communicator. Even if it is relevant to a case, a privileged communication cannot be used as EVIDENCE in court. Privileged communications are controversial because they exclude relevant facts from the truth-seeking process.

Generally, the laws that guide civil and criminal trials are designed to allow the admission of relevant evidence. Parties generally have access to all information that will help yield a just result in the case. Privileged communications are an exception to this rule.

Privileged communications exist because society values the PRIVACY or purpose of certain relationships. The established privileged communications are those between wife and husband, clergy and communicant, psychotherapist and patient, physician and patient, and attorney and client.

These relationships are protected for various reasons. The wife-husband and clergy-communicant privileges protect the general sanctity of MARRIAGE and RELIGION. The psychotherapist or physician and patient privilege promotes full disclosure in the interests of the patient's health. If patients were unable to keep secret communications with psychotherapists or physicians relating to treatment or diagnosis, they might give doctors incomplete information. If doctors received incomplete information, they might be unable to administer health care to the patient, which is the very purpose of the doctor-patient relationship.

The ATTORNEY-CLIENT PRIVILEGE exists for roughly the same reason as the doctor-patient privilege. In order to secure effective representation, a client must feel free to discuss all aspects of a case without the fear that her attorney will be called at trial to repeat her statements. Likewise, to retain the client's trust and do his job properly, the attorney must be allowed to withhold from the court and opposing party private communications with the client.

A communication is not confidential, and therefore not privileged, if it is overheard by a third party who is not an AGENT of the listener. Agents include secretaries and other employees of the listener. For example, a communication between a psychotherapist and patient would be privileged even if the psychotherapist's secretary happened to overhear it. In such a case, the secretary could not be forced to TESTIFY about the communication. However, a communication between a psychotherapist and a patient on a public elevator occupied by third parties would not be privileged and could be used in court.

Privileged communications are not always absolute. For instance, a criminal defendant may be able to access communications between an accuser and the accuser's doctor if the defendant's interest in the disclosure, in the opinion of the court, outweighs the interest in confidentiality. The court will consider such a request only if the defendant can establish a reasonable probability that important information exists in the communication that will be relevant to the case.

Various JURISDICTIONS may apply the concept of privilege in slightly different ways. For example, some jurisdictions distinguish between the two parties to a communication, calling one party the keeper or holder of the privilege. Other states regard the privilege as being held, and capable of being asserted, by both parties. Some states, for example, give the marital privilege to both parties, allowing either party to avoid testifying and to prevent the other from testifying as to communications made within the privacy of the marital relationship. Other states give the privilege to the testifying spouse. This gives the testifying spouse the power to waive the privilege and testify against the other spouse.

States occasionally change their laws to give the privilege to both parties or to take it from one of the parties. For example, a state may give the privilege to both clergy and communicant. Under such a law, either party to the communication could block its disclosure. In the alternative, a state could give the privilege only to the communicant, in which case the communicant could waive the privilege and obtain testimony from the cleric. These variations reflect the struggle by the courts to balance the need for information to reach a just result against the PUBLIC POLICY of encouraging free communication within certain relationships by making these communications privileged.

For federal cases, the law of privileged communications is governed by the state law in which the FEDERAL COURT sits. Within particular jurisdictions, the precise rules regarding privileged communications may be periodically redefined or adjusted as new circumstances are presented. In some states a person's relationships with sexual assault counselors, social workers, and juvenile diversion officers have been given a qualified privilege of confidentiality. In these states the court may hold a private hearing to determine whether the information is necessary to the requesting party's case or defense before ordering disclosure of the information. Many legal advocates have supported the creation of a privilege between parents and offspring, but very few courts and legislatures have recognized such a privilege.

CROSS-REFERENCES

Husband and Wife; Marital Communications Privilege; Physician-Patient Privilege.

PRIVILEGES AND IMMUNITIES Concepts contained in the U.S. Constitution that place the CITIZENS of each state on an equal basis with citizens of other states in respect to advantages resulting from citizenship in those states and citizenship in the United States.

The Privileges and Immunities Clauses are found in Article IV of the U.S. Constitution and the FOURTEENTH AMENDMENT. Both clauses apply only to citizens of the United States. ALIENS and CORPORATIONS are not citizens and, therefore, are not entitled to this protection. These clauses have proven to be of little import because other constitutional provisions have been used to settle controversies. In large part the insignificance of the clauses has been based on restrictive readings of the clauses by the U.S. Supreme Court.

Article IV provides, "The Citizens of each State shall be entitled to all Privileges and Immunities in the several states." The purpose of the clause was to facilitate the unification of the independent states into one nation so that citizens traveling throughout the country would receive the same treatment as the citizens of the states through which they passed.

The privileges and immunities that are protected under Article IV include the right to receive protection from state government; the right to acquire and possess all kinds of PROPERTY; the right to travel through or reside in any state for purposes of trade, agriculture, or professional endeavors; the right to claim the benefit of the WRIT of HABEAS CORPUS; the right to sue and defend ACTIONS in court; and the right to receive the same tax treatment as that of the citizens of the taxing state.

This clause forbids a state from unjustly depriving citizens from other states of any rights derived from state citizenship solely on the basis of nonresidence. Yet the Supreme Court has never interpreted it to preclude all deferential treatment of in-state citizens. As a result, the Privileges and Immunities Clause does not bar differential state standards governing the practice of certain professions. Out-of-state doctors, lawyers, and other professionals may be required to prove their competency based on standards that are higher than those applied to their in-state counterparts. Tuition rates at public colleges and universities are typically lower for in-state students. Out-of-state residents are charged more for hunting and fishing LICENSES than are in-state residents. Such discrepancies are generally accepted as justifiable because they advance legitimate state interests.

The Supreme Court has struck down state laws that infringed rights guaranteed by the Privileges and Immunities Clause of Article IV. In *Hicklin v. Orbeck*, 437 U.S. 518, 98 S. Ct. 2482, 57 L. Ed. 2d 397 (1978), the Court ruled that the state of Alaska failed to show a reasonable purpose for a state law that required employers to give a hiring preference to in-state residents who applied to work on the construction of oil or gas pipelines.

However, the Supreme Court has rarely used the Privileges and Immunities Clause of Article IV to invalidate discriminatory laws. The Due Process and Equal Protection Clauses of the Fourteenth Amendment are commonly applied to determine the validity of state laws that unjustly discriminate between residents and nonresidents of a state.

The Fourteenth Amendment's Privileges and Immunities Clause has virtually no significance in CIVIL RIGHTS law. The clause states, "No state shall make or enforce any law which shall abridge the privileges or immunities of citizens of the United States." This clause protects a person's rights as a citizen of the United States from unreasonable state action or interference.

The privileges and immunities of U.S. citizenship that cannot be unreasonably abridged by state laws include the right to travel from state to state; the right to vote for federal officeholders; the right to enter public lands; the right to petition Congress to redress grievances; the right to inform the national government of a violation of its laws; the right to receive protection from violence when in federal custody; the right to have free access to U.S. seaports; the right to transact business with and engage in administering the functions of the U.S. government; the right to have access to FEDERAL COURTS; and the privilege of the writ of habeas corpus.

The Supreme Court has narrowly construed the Privileges and Immunities Clause of the Fourteenth Amendment since the 1873 *Slaughter-House* cases, 83 U.S. (16 Wall.) 36, 21 L. Ed. 394 (1873). The case involved a Louisiana state law that gave one meat company the exclusive right to slaughter livestock in New Orleans. Other packing companies were required to pay a fee for using the slaughterhouses. These companies filed suit, claiming that the law violated the Privileges and Immunities Clause of the Fourteenth Amendment.

The Court upheld the Louisiana MONOPOLY law, ruling that the Privileges and Immunities Clause had limited effect because it reached only privileges and immunities guaranteed by

U.S. citizenship, not state citizenship. Because the law in question dealt with STATES' RIGHTS, the Fourteenth Amendment had no effect. The Court ruled that the Fourteenth Amendment was designed to grant former slaves legal equality, not to grant expanded rights to the general population. In addition, the Court was concerned that a broad interpretation of the Fourteenth Amendment would give too much power to the federal government and distort the concept of FEDERALISM, which grants the states a large measure of power and autonomy.

The Court has consistently followed the restrictive interpretation given the Privileges and Immunities Clause by this decision. The clause has little significance today in invalidating state statutes that present a constitutional question. When state laws infringe the fundamental rights of U.S. citizenship, the Court invokes the Equal Protection Clause to analyze the constitutionality of the state action.

See also EQUAL PROTECTION; SLAUGHTER-HOUSE CASES.

PRIVITY A close, direct, or successive relationship; having a mutual interest or right.

Privity refers to a connection or bond between parties to a particular transaction. *Privity of contract* is the relationship that exists between two or more parties to an agreement. *Privity of estate* exists between a LESSOR and a LESSEE, and *privity of possession* is the relationship between parties in successive possession of REAL PROPERTY.

PRIVY One who has a direct, successive relationship to another individual; a coparticipant; one who has an interest in a matter; private.

Privy refers to a person in PRIVITY with another—that is, someone involved in a particular transaction that results in a union, connection, or direct relationship with another. *Privies in blood* are the HEIRS of an ancestor. *Privies in* ESTATE are people who succeed or receive an ASSIGNMENT of property, such as a GRANTOR and a GRANTEE, LESSOR and LESSEE, or assignor and assignee.

PRIVY COUNCIL The Privy Council is the British Crown's private council. It is composed of more than three hundred members, including cabinet members, distinguished scholars, judges, and legislators. Once a powerful body, it has lost most of the judicial and political functions it exercised since the middle of the seventeenth century and has largely been replaced by the Cabinet.

The Privy Council derived from the King's Council, which was created during the Middle Ages. In 1540 the Privy Council came into being as a small executive committee that advised the king and administered the government. It advised the sovereign on affairs of state and the exercise of the royal prerogative. It implemented its power through royal proclamations, orders, instructions, and informal letters, and also by giving directions to and receiving reports from the judges who traveled the circuits, hearing cases in cities and towns, twice a year. It concerned itself with public order and security, the economy, public works, public authorities and corporations, local government, Ireland, the Channel Islands, the colonies, and foreign affairs.

The inner circle of advisers in the Privy Council met in the royal chamber or cabinet and was therefore called the cabinet council. In the eighteenth century, the cabinet became the council for the prime minister, the leader of Parliament. The United States adopted the cabinet idea, though its legal status is not identified in the Constitution. Cabinet members are presidential advisers who serve as executive branch department heads.

The power of the Privy Council disappeared between 1645 and 1660 during the English Civil War and the government of Oliver Cromwell. It never recovered its former position. Long policy debates shifted to Parliament, and important executive decisions went to committees. In modern days members of the Privy Council rarely meet as a group, delegating their work to committees.

The lord president of the council, who is a member of the cabinet, is the director of the Privy Council Office. The most important committee is the Judicial Committee of the Privy Council, which comprises all members of the council who have held high judicial office. Usually, however, three to five Lords of Appeal sit to hear appeals from the United Kingdom, the British Crown colonies, and members of the Commonwealth. The committee does not give a judgment but prepares a report to the sovereign, and its decision may be implemented in an Order in Council. The work of the committee has diminished because it rarely hears ecclesiastical appeals and because many Commonwealth countries have abolished the right of appeal.

See also CURIA REGIS.

PRIZE Anything offered as a reward for a contest. It is distinguished from a *bet* or *wager* in that it is known before the event who is to give either the premium or the prize, and there is but one operation until the accomplishment of the act, thing, or purpose for which it is offered.

RHODA SIDNEY/STOCK BOSTON

Lottery winners rarely see the full amount of their prizes; such money is taxed as income.

In time of war, an enemy vessel or a ship captured at sea by a belligerent power.

The fair market value of a prize or award is generally includible in GROSS INCOME. Certain exceptions are provided where the prize or award is made in recognition of religious, charitable, scientific, educational, artistic, literary, or civic achievement providing certain other requirements are met.

PRIZE COURTS Tribunals with JURISDICTION to decide disputes involving captures made upon the high seas during times of war and to declare the captured property as a PRIZE if it is lawfully subject to that sentence.

In England, admiralty courts possess jurisdiction as prize courts, in addition to their customary admiralty jurisdiction. The judge of an admiralty court receives a special commission in time of war to empower him or her to conduct such proceedings.

In the United States, federal district courts have ORIGINAL JURISDICTION to try prize cases.

See also ADMIRALTY AND MARITIME LAW.

PRIZE LAW During times of war, belligerent states may attempt to interfere with maritime commerce to prevent ships from carrying goods that will aid the war effort of an opponent. After ships are captured and brought to a friendly port, a local tribunal called a PRIZE COURT will determine the legality of the seizure, or the destruction of the vessel and cargo if the vessel cannot be sailed to a friendly port. The body of customary international law and treaties that determines the appropriateness of such actions is referred to as prize law.

Prize law has not been completely consistent in its development because the tribunals that rule on the seizure of the vessel are national tribunals and may reflect the interests of the belligerent state in interdicting the enemy war effort. The expanding scope of warfare and the concept of total war have also blurred the distinction between vessels subject to capture as a prize of war and those that are exempt. Some basic rules remain, however. All vessels of an enemy state are subject to seizure at any time by an opposing belligerent. Warships may be sunk immediately, and private merchant vessels are to be taken to a friendly port, if possible, for adjudication by a prize court. A neutral vessel on the high seas or in a belligerent's territorial sea may be stopped and searched, if it is suspected of carrying contraband, and may be condemned as a prize of war if any is found. Finally the right of coastal fishing vessels of any state to be free from seizure while plying their trade is almost universally recognized.

See also ADMIRALTY AND MARITIME LAW.

PRO *[Latin, For; in respect of; on account of; in behalf of.]*

PROBABLE CAUSE Apparent facts discovered through logical inquiry that would lead a reasonably intelligent and prudent person to believe that an accused person has committed a crime, thereby warranting his or her prosecution, or that a CAUSE OF ACTION has accrued, justifying a civil lawsuit.

Probable cause is a level of reasonable belief, based on facts that can be articulated, that is required to sue a person in civil court or to arrest and prosecute a person in criminal court. Before a person can be sued or arrested and prosecuted, the civil plaintiff or police and prosecutor must possess enough facts that would lead a REASONABLE PERSON to believe that the claim or charge is true.

The probable cause standard is more important in CRIMINAL LAW than it is in CIVIL LAW because it is used in criminal law as a basis for searching and arresting persons and depriving them of their liberty. Civil cases can deprive a person of property, but they cannot deprive a person of liberty. In civil court a plaintiff must possess probable cause to levy a claim against a defendant. If the plaintiff does not have probable cause for the claim, she may later face a MALICIOUS PROSECUTION suit brought by the defendant. Furthermore, lack of probable cause to support a claim means that the plaintiff does not have sufficient EVIDENCE to support the claim, and the court will likely dismiss it.

In the criminal arena probable cause is important in two respects. First, police must possess probable cause before they may search a person or a person's property, and they must possess it before they may arrest a person. Second, in most criminal cases the court must find that probable cause exists to believe that the defendant committed the crime before the defendant may be prosecuted.

There are some exceptions to these general rules. Police may briefly detain and conduct a limited search of a person in a public place if they have a reasonable suspicion that the person has committed a crime. Reasonable suspicion is a level of belief that is less than probable cause. A police officer possesses reasonable suspicion if he has enough knowledge to lead a reasonably cautious person to believe that criminal activity is occurring and that the individual played some part in it. In practice this requirement means that an officer need not possess the measure of knowledge that constitutes probable cause to STOP AND FRISK a person in a public place. In any case, an officer may not arrest a person until the officer possesses probable cause to believe that the person has committed a crime.

The requirement of probable cause for a SEARCH AND SEIZURE can be found in the FOURTH AMENDMENT to the U.S. Constitution, which states,

> the right of the people to be secure in their persons, houses, papers, and effects, against unreasonable searches and seizures, shall not be violated, and no Warrants shall issue, but upon probable cause, supported by Oath or affirmation, and particularly describing the place to be searched, and the persons or things to be searched.

All states have similar constitutional prohibitions against unreasonable searches and seizures.

The requirement of probable cause works in tandem with the WARRANT requirement. A warrant is a document that allows police to search a person, search a person's property, or arrest a person. A judicial MAGISTRATE or judge must approve and sign a warrant before officers may act on it. To obtain a search or ARREST WARRANT, officers must present to the magistrate or judge enough facts to constitute probable cause. A warrant is not required for all searches and all arrests. Courts have carved out exceptions that allow police to search and arrest persons without a warrant when obtaining a warrant would be impractical.

The precise amount of evidence that constitutes probable cause depends on the circumstances in the case. To illustrate, assume that a police officer has stopped a motor vehicle driver for a traffic violation. In the absence of any other facts indicating criminal activity by the driver, it would be a violation of the Fourth Amendment if the officer conducted a full-blown search of the driver and the vehicle. The mere commission of a traffic violation is not, in and of itself, a fact that supports probable cause to believe that the driver has committed a crime. However, if the officer notices that the driver's eyes are bloodshot or that the driver smells of ALCOHOL, the officer may detain and question the defendant, search him, and place him under arrest. Most courts hold that a driver's commission of a traffic violation combined with the appearance that the driver has used drugs or alcohol constitute sufficient evidence to lead a reasonable person to believe that the person is driving under the influence of drugs or alcohol.

Probable cause is not equal to absolute certainty. That is, a police officer does not have to be absolutely certain that criminal activity is taking place to perform a search or make an arrest. Probable cause can exist even when there is some doubt as to the person's guilt. Courts take care to review the actions of police in the context of everyday life, balancing the interests of law enforcement against the interests of personal liberty in determining whether probable cause existed for a search or arrest.

Legislatures may maintain statutes relating to probable cause. Many such statutes declare that a certain thing constitutes probable cause to believe that a person has committed a particular offense. For example, under federal law, a FORFEITURE judgment of a foreign court automatically constitutes probable cause to believe that the forfeited property also is subject to forfeiture under the federal racketeering law (18 U.S.C.A. § 981(i)(3) [1986]).

See also AUTOMOBILE SEARCHES; CRIMINAL PROCEDURE.

PROBATE 🕮 The court process by which a WILL is proved valid or invalid. The legal process wherein the ESTATE of a DECEDENT is administered. 🕮

When a person dies, his or her estate must go through probate, which is a process overseen by a probate court. If the decedent leaves a will directing how his or her property should be distributed after death, the probate court must determine if it should be admitted to probate and given legal effect. If the decedent dies INTESTATE—without leaving a will—the court appoints a PERSONAL REPRESENTATIVE to distribute the decedent's property according to the laws of DESCENT AND DISTRIBUTION. These laws direct the distribution of ASSETS based on hereditary succession.

In general, the probate process involves collecting the decedent's assets, liquidating liabilities, paying necessary taxes, and distributing property to HEIRS. Probate procedures are gov-

A sample order denying probate

At a Surrogate's Court held in and for the County of ________, at the Surrogate's Court Room in the Court House in the City of ________, New York, on the ________ day of ________, 19___.

Present: Hon. ________, Surrogate.
[Add title of proceeding]

DECREE
File No. ______

The alleged Last Will and Testament of ________, the above named decedent, dated the ________ day of ________, 19___, having been filed in this Court, on the ________ day of ________, 19___, and a petition for probate therefor having been on said day filed by ________, executor named therein, setting forth all the facts required by law, praying that a citation issue to all persons entitled by law to notice thereof, to show cause why a decree should not be made admitting said will to probate,

And satisfactory proof having been made that jurisdiction has been obtained of all persons entitled to notice of said proceeding,

And, ________, ________, ________, ________, ________, and ________, distributees, interested in property intended to be disposed of or affected by said alleged Last Will and Testament as aforesaid, having duly appeared herein and filed objections to the probate of said instrument containing a demand for a jury trial,

And it further appearing that due notice was given to all the parties entitled thereto of the filing of said objections and of the trial of said issues, as aforesaid, and due proof of service of such notice having been duly filed in the office of the Surrogate,

And it further appearing that the above entitled matter having duly come on to be heard on the ________ and ________ days of ________, 19___, before the Surrogate and a jury upon the said objections filed by ________, ________, ________, ________, ________, and ________ to the probate of the said alleged will, and proofs and the allegations of the respective parties having been duly heard, and after hearing ________, Esquire, attorney for the proponent, with ________, Esquire, of Counsel, and ________ and ________ for the contestants on said trial,

And the Surrogate, having heard the allegations and proofs of the parties, with the consent of the parties to this proceeding, submitted the following issues:

I. Did ________, the testatrix, subscribe the paper offered for probate bearing date the ________ day of ________, 19___, at the end thereof in the presence of each of the two subscribing witnesses, and at the time of making such subscription or acknowledgment did the testatrix declare to each of the two subscribing witnesses that the paper offered for probate was her Last Will and Testament, and were there at least two subscribing witnesses each of whom signed his name at the end of said paper at the request of the testatrix, ________?

II. At the time of the execution of said paper on the ________ day of ________, 19___, was the said ________ of sound mind and competent to dispose of her estate by will?

III. Was the execution of said paper caused or procured by the undue influence or fraud of any person or persons?

IV. Was the execution of said paper caused or procured by the duress or coercion of any person or persons?

And such aforementioned issues having been submitted to the jury by the Surrogate and the Surrogate having charged the jury as to the law thereon, and the jury, after due deliberation, having returned and rendered its verdict in favor of the contestants and against the proponent and answered the questions submitted to them as follows:

As to the instrument dated the ________ day of ________, 19___, offered for probate as the Last Will and Testament of said decedent:

I. Did ________, the testatrix, subscribe the paper offered for probate bearing date the ________ day of ________, 19___, at the end thereof in the presence of each of the two subscribing witnesses, and at the time of making such subscription or acknowledgment did the testatrix declare to each of the two subscribing witnesses that the paper of-

A sample order denying probate (continued)

fered for probate was her Last Will and Testament, and were there at least two subscribing witnesses each of whom signed his name at the end of said paper at the request of the testatrix, ________ ? (Answer yes or no) No

II. At the time of the execution of said paper on the ________ day of ________ , 19___ , was the said ________ of sound mind and competent to dispose of her estate by will? (Answer yes or no) No

III. Was the execution of said paper caused or procured by the undue influence or fraud of any person or persons? (Answer yes or no) Yes

IV. Was the execution of said paper caused or procured by the duress or coercion of any person or persons? (Answer yes or no) Yes

and a motion having been made by said counsel for proponent to set aside the verdict of the jury as to the questions and for the probate of said will and said motion having been denied by the said Surrogate.

By their verdict on the aforesaid questions the jury found that the paper purporting to be the Last Will and Testament of ________ offered for probate was not duly executed by her, that she did not have testamentary capacity, that the execution of said paper was caused or procured by the undue influence or fraud of a person or persons, and that the execution of said paper was caused or procured by the duress or coercion of a person or persons, it is hereby

ORDERED, ADJUDGED AND DECREED, that the instrument offered for probate herein bearing date the ________ day of ________ , 19___ , be and the same hereby is denied probate as the Last Will and Testament of ________ , for the reason that said paper offered for probate was not duly executed by her, that she did not have testamentary capacity, that the execution of said paper was caused or procured by the undue influence or fraud of a person or persons, and that the execution of said paper was caused or procured by the duress or coercion of a person or persons.

____
Surrogate

erned by state law and have been the subject of debate and reform since the 1960s. The Uniform Probate Code (UPC) was first proposed in 1969 by the National Conference of Commissioners on Uniform State Laws and the House of Delegates of the AMERICAN BAR ASSOCIATION. The prime focus of the UPC is to simplify the probate process. The UPC, which has been amended numerous times, has been adopted in its entirety by sixteen states: Alaska, Arizona, Colorado, Florida, Hawaii, Idaho, Maine, Michigan, Minnesota, Montana, Nebraska, New Mexico, North Dakota, South Carolina, South Dakota, and Utah. The other thirty-six states have adopted some part of the UPC but still retain distinct procedures.

Probate of a Will The probate of a will means proving its genuineness in probate court. Unless otherwise provided by statute, a will must be admitted to probate before a court will allow the distribution of a decedent's property to the heirs according to its terms.

As a general rule, a will has no legal effect until it is probated. A will should be probated immediately, and no one has the right to suppress it. The person with possession of a will, usually the executor or the decedent's attorney, must produce it. Statutes impose penalties for concealing or destroying a will or for failing to produce it within a specified time.

Probate proceedings are usually held in the state in which the decedent had domicile or permanent RESIDENCE at the time of death. If, however, the decedent owned REAL PROPERTY in a another state, the will disposing of these assets must also be probated in that state.

To qualify as a will in probate, an instrument must be of TESTAMENTARY character and comply with all statutory requirements. A document is testamentary when it does not take effect until after the death of the person making it and allows the individual to retain the property under personal control during her or his lifetime. A will that has been properly executed by a competent person—the TESTATOR—as required by law is entitled to be probated, even if some of its provisions are invalid, obscure, or cannot be implemented.

A will made as a result of FRAUD or UNDUE INFLUENCE or a will that has been altered so that all its provisions are revoked will be denied probate. If the alteration only revokes certain provisions of the will, the remaining provisions can be admitted to probate.

All separate papers, instruments, or sheets comprising the most recent of a testator's wills will be admitted to probate. Where a later will does not explicitly revoke all prior wills, two separate and distinct wills can be probated. Probate courts seek to carry out the declared intention of a testator regarding the disposition of property, and they resort to distributing property according to the law of descent and distribution only where no reasonable alternatives exist.

As a general rule, the original document must be presented for probate. Probate of a copy or duplicate of a will is not permitted unless the absence of the original is satisfactorily explained to the court. If a properly proved copy or duplicate of a will that has been lost or destroyed is presented to the court, it may be admitted to probate. Some states have special proceedings to handle such occurrences. A thorough and diligent search for the will is necessary before a copy can be probated as a lost will.

A CODICIL, which is a supplement to a will, is entitled to be probated together with the will it modifies, if it is properly executed according to statute. If it is complete in itself and can stand as a separate testamentary instrument independent of the will, the codicil alone can be admitted to probate. A codicil that has been subsequently revoked by another codicil is not entitled to probate.

A will made in a foreign language will be admitted to probate if the testator understood what it contained and it otherwise complies with other statutory requirements. A translation usually must accompany the will.

Proceedings A probate proceeding may involve either formal or informal procedures. Traditionally, probate proceedings were governed by formal procedures that required the probate court to hold hearings and issue orders involving routine matters. Consequently, the legal costs of probating an estate could be substantial. States that have adopted the UPC provisions on probate procedures allow informal probate proceedings that remove the probate court from most stages of the process, with the result that informal probate is cheaper and quicker than formal probate. Most small estates benefit from an informal probate proceeding.

The probate process begins when the executor files with the CLERK of the probate court a copy of the death certificate along with the will and a PETITION to admit the will to probate and to grant LETTERS TESTAMENTARY, which authorize him or her to distribute the estate. Although the executor usually files the probate petition, it can be filed by any person who has a pecuniary interest in the will. In states governed by the UPC, the executor must elect whether to proceed with formal or informal probate at the time of filing. However, a probate proceeding may be switched from informal to formal during the course of administration, if issues so warrant.

In a formal probate proceeding, a HEARING must be held to establish the death of the testator, the residency of the decedent, the genuineness of the will, its conformance with statutory requirements for its execution, and the competency of the testator at the time the will was made. These requirements are usually fulfilled by the attesting WITNESSES who were present at the time the will was made and who certify that it was properly executed. The number of attesting witnesses is prescribed by law. If fewer than the required number witness a will, it will be declared void, and the testator's property will pass according to the laws of descent and distribution.

When some or all of the witnesses to a will are unavailable, special steps are taken. If the required witnesses have died before the testator, the person offering the will must offer proof of death, in addition to evidence of the genuineness of the signatures and any other proof of execution available. The UPC simplifies witness issues by permitting the admission of "self-authenticating" wills. These wills contain a statement signed by the witnesses that attests to the competency of the testator and other statutory requirements. Self-authentication relieves the witnesses of the burden of appearing in court and the executor of costly procedures if the witnesses are unavailable.

If no one objects to the will at the hearing, it will be admitted to probate.

Informal probate proceedings generally do not require a hearing. The executor files the death certificate and will, along with a petition to admit the will under informal probate. The clerk of probate court reviews the submissions and recommends to the court that the will be probated. Once the court issues the order for informal probate, the executor files a series of forms that demonstrate that notice has been given to all interested parties about the probate, the decedent's creditors have been paid, and the estate's assets have been collected, appraised, and distributed to the designated heirs.

Contested Probate Proceedings The probate of a will can be opposed or contested on the ground that the instrument is void because of the testamentary INCAPACITY of the testator at the time the will was made, the failure to comply with the formalities required by law, or any matter sufficient to show the nonexistence of a valid will. When a will is contested, formal proceedings are required.

Will contests are concerned only with external validity, such as failure of due execution, fraud, MISTAKE, undue influence, lack of testamentary capacity, or lack of INTENT that the instrument be a will. Issues of internal validity, such as violation of the RULE AGAINST PERPETUITIES, must be raised in proceedings at a later stage of administration. Although a will has been probated as a genuine expression of the testator's intended distribution of property upon her or his death, the estate might be disposed of according to the laws of descent and distribution if the testamentary provisions violate the law.

Only a person having some interest that will be affected by the probate can contest it. Such persons include NEXT OF KIN who will receive property if the will is set aside and INTESTACY results, purchasers of property from the heir or heirs, administrators or executors under prior wills, and the state, if there is a possibility of ESCHEAT, which means that the government will receive the property if no living heirs can be found. CREDITORS, however, generally are not entitled to contest the will of a DEBTOR.

An executor must defend the will against attack and must employ his or her best efforts to have it sustained if he or she reasonably believes that the will is valid.

Methods by which a will can be contested generally include a CONTEST in the court having JURISDICTION over probate, an APPEAL from the order granting or denying probate, and separate actions to set aside the order granting or denying probate.

There is no constitutional right to trial by JURY in probate or will contest proceedings. Most states, however, have statutes making a trial by jury available in a will contest. Statutes usually impose time limits on the institution of will contests.

Agreement Not to Contest A testator can enter into a contract with her or his heirs in which they agree not to contest a will. If the contract is supported by CONSIDERATION—something of value—and the agreement is otherwise valid, the heirs will be prevented from contesting the will. The BENEFICIARIES under a will and the heirs can enter into a valid contract not to contest a will. States vary as to the remedies a party to an agreement not to contest a will has upon breach. These include an INJUNCTION against the prosecution of the contest, an action at law for damages, or a defense to the contest.

An agreement among heirs and beneficiaries not to contest a will is a way to avoid a costly will contest proceeding. The heirs and beneficiaries negotiate a settlement that may defeat the intention of the testator in how the assets are distributed. A settlement will be valid if all interested parties agree, but it must not exclude anyone entitled to property under the will. Under some statutes the compromise or settlement must be submitted to the probate court for approval.

Guardianship of Minor Children Wills often contain instructions on who should be appointed legal GUARDIAN of the decedent's MINOR children. The probate court may investigate the qualifications of the proposed guardian before granting an order of appointment. When a will does not contain a guardianship provision, the court itself must determine, based on the best interests of the children, who should be appointed guardian.

Right of Review A right of appeal from a probate decree is given to any person who would suffer a direct financial loss as a result of the decree. The APPELLATE COURT is restricted to a consideration of the questions presented to and determined by the lower court. An issue not presented to the probate court usually will not be considered.

See also ESTATE AND GIFT TAXES; EXECUTORS AND ADMINISTRATORS.

PROBATION A sentence whereby a convict is released from confinement but is still under court supervision; a testing or a trial period. It can be given in lieu of a prison term or can suspend a prison sentence if the convict has consistently demonstrated GOOD BEHAVIOR.

The status of a convicted person who is given some freedom on the condition that for a specified period she act in a manner approved by a special officer to whom she must report.

An initial period of employment during which a new, transferred, or promoted employee must show the ability to perform the required duties.

Probation is the period during which a person, "the probationer," is subject to critical examination and evaluation. The word *probation* is derived from *probatum*, Latin for "the act of proving." Probation is a trial period that must be completed before a person receives greater benefits or freedom.

In the criminal justice system probation is a particular type of sentence for criminal defendants. The judicial authority to order a sentence of probation is granted in statutes on the federal and state levels. Generally, probation allows a convicted defendant to go free with a suspended sentence for a specified duration during good behavior. Probationers are placed under the supervision of a probation officer and must fulfill certain conditions. If the probationer violates a condition of probation, the court may place additional restrictions on the probationer or order the probationer to serve a term of imprisonment.

A judge also may order probation in addition to a period of INCARCERATION. For example, a sentence might consist of a jail term and, after release, probation for a specified period of months or years. Probation is generally reserved for persons sentenced to short terms in jail: it is not combined with a long prison sentence. If a person is subjected to supervision after a stay in prison, the supervision is conducted by a parole officer.

Both probation and PAROLE involve the supervision of convicted criminals, but the systems are distinct. Probation is ordered by a judge; parole is granted by a parole board. Probation is an alternative to prison; parole is the early release from prison. Probation is reserved for persons convicted of less serious offenses; parole is given to persons convicted of serious offenses.

The concept of probation in the criminal law was inspired in the mid-nineteenth century by JOHN AUGUSTUS, a resident of Boston. Augustus encountered a man about to be sentenced in a Boston court and believed him to be capable of reform. Augustus posted BAIL for the man and succeeded in getting his sentence reduced. From 1841 to 1859 Massachusetts judges released approximately two thousand offenders into Augustus's custody instead of ordering incarceration.

In 1878 Massachusetts enacted the first probation statute, and Boston hired its first probation officer. In 1880 the Massachusetts legislature approved the first statewide hiring of probation officers. By 1925 all states had laws governing probation for juveniles, and by 1939 approximately thirty-nine states were maintaining laws on probation for adults. By 1967 adult probation was allowed by statute in all states.

Probation statutes generally identify the crimes available for a sentence of probation, or, conversely, they identify crimes for which probation may not be ordered. In Alaska, for example, a court may not order probation if the person has been convicted of sexual assault or if the person's conviction is his second ASSAULT or ROBBERY offense within the last ten years (Alaska Stat. § 12.55.085 [1965]).

Statutes may also identify conditions of probation. These are actions that a probationer must do or refrain from doing during probation. Though conditions may be spelled out in statutes, a sentencing judge retains wide discretion to fashion conditions according to the best interests of both the public and the defendant. In most states a probationer must not possess a firearm, commit another offense, or possess illegal drugs during the probation period. Probationers must also report regularly to a probation officer.

A judge may place additional conditions on a probationer. For example, if a defendant pleads guilty to assault, the court may order him to stay a specified distance away from the victim of the assault. In a conviction for a small amount of marijuana a judge may order the defendant to complete treatment for drug use. If a probationer violates any condition of probation, the court may order additional conditions or sentence him to a prison sentence that does not exceed the maximum term of imprisonment that could have been imposed for the crime.

Judges in state court generally have wide discretion in SENTENCING. In determining whether to sentence a defendant to probation, the court may consider a variety of factors, including the nature and circumstances of the offense and the defendant's criminal history.

Probation became a sentencing option for federal judges with the 1925 passage of the Federal Probation Act (18 U.S.C.A. § 3651). This act authorized FEDERAL COURTS to suspend imposition of a sentence, or the execution of a sentence, in favor of probation. A defendant could be placed on up to five years' probation "upon such terms and conditions as the court deemed best" when the court was satisfied that "the ends of justice and the best interest of the public as well as the defendant [would] be served thereby."

Probation as a criminal sentence was the product of a reform movement in the criminal justice system in the early twentieth century. Part of this movement was devoted to abolition of determinate sentencing, or the legislative imposition of specific sentences for specific crimes. The reform movement fought for INDETERMINATE sentencing, a method that left sentencing to the discretion of the judge and allowed the judge to fashion a sentence according to the rehabilitative needs of the criminal defendant.

Congress reversed indeterminate sentencing in federal court with the Sentencing Reform Act of 1984 (18 U.S.C.A. §§ 3551–3556). The act replaced the Federal Probation Act and established sentencing guidelines for federal judges, allowing a judge to order probation only if the offense calls for a term of imprisonment of between zero and six months. The act lists offenses for which REVOCATION of probation and imposition of imprisonment is mandatory.

The Sentencing Act also changed the role of federal probation officers in the federal criminal justice system. Under the act, probation officers must gather and present evidence on facts relevant to the sentencing guidelines. This is a shift in the focus of probation officers' work. Probation officers once worked to ensure that the sentence fit the individual offender, but now they endeavor to ensure that the defendant's sentence fits the offenses charged. In other words, the probation officer has become less like a social worker intent on the rehabilitation of the probationer and more like an informant for the court against the probationer.

Revocation of probation in federal court in conjunction with the federal sentencing guidelines have led to confusion over the application of probation. In *United States v. Granderson*, 511 U.S. 39, 114 S. Ct. 1259, 127 L. Ed. 2d 611 (1994), Ralph Stuart Granderson, Jr. was convicted of destruction of mail and sentenced to five years' probation and a fine. While on probation, Granderson tested positive for cocaine. Under 18 U.S.C.A. § 3565(a) (1984), the court was required to revoke Granderson's probation "and sentence [him] to not less than one-third of the original sentence."

At the revocation hearing the government argued that this requirement meant a term of imprisonment not less than one-third the probationary period originally ordered by the court. The court agreed and resentenced Granderson to sixty months in prison. Under the federal sentencing guidelines, Granderson could have been initially sentenced to a term of imprisonment between zero and six months.

Granderson appealed, arguing that "original sentence" did not mean a term of imprisonment equal to the length of the probationary sentence imposed but instead referred to the prison sentence that the judge initially could have ordered. The U.S. Court of Appeals for the Eleventh Circuit agreed and vacated Granderson's sentence and ordered his release from prison. According to the court of appeals, it was "legal alchemy" to convert a long-term sentence of conditional liberty into an equally long term of imprisonment (*United States v. Granderson*, 969 F.2d 980 [11th Cir. 1992]). The federal government appealed to the U.S. Supreme Court, which affirmed the ruling.

See also DETERMINATE SENTENCE; PRESENTENCE INVESTIGATION.

PROBATIONER A convict who is released from prison provided he maintains good behavior. One who is on probation whereby she is given some freedom to reenter society subject to the condition that for a specified period the individual conduct herself in a manner approved by a special officer to whom the probationer must report.

PROBATIVE Having the effect of PROOF, tending to prove, or actually proving.

When a legal controversy goes to trial, the parties seek to prove their cases by the introduction of EVIDENCE. All courts are governed by rules of evidence that describe what types of evidence are ADMISSIBLE. One key element for the admission of evidence is whether it proves or helps prove a FACT or ISSUE. If so, the evidence is deemed probative. Probative evidence establishes or contributes to proof.

Probative facts are data that have the effect of proving an issue or other information. Probative facts establish the existence of other facts. They are matters of evidence that make the existence of something more probable or less probable than it would be without them. They are admissible as evidence and aid the court in the final resolution of a disputed issue. For example, in the case of a motor vehicle accident, a witness's testimony that she saw one automobile enter the intersection on a red light is a probative fact about whether the driver was at fault.

Evidence has probative value if it tends to prove an issue. However, probative value may refer to whether the evidence is admissible. Rules of evidence generally state that relevant evidence, which tends to prove or disprove an alleged fact, may be excluded if its probative value is substantially outweighed by the danger of unfair prejudice, confusion of the issues, or misleading the jury, or by considerations of undue delay, waste of time, or needless presentation of cumulative evidence. A trial court must use a BALANCING test to make this determination, but rules of evidence generally require that relevant evidence with probative value be excluded only if it is substantially outweighed by one of the dangers described in the rule.

PRO BONO Short for *pro bono publico* [*Latin, For the public good*]. The designation given to the free legal work done by an ATTORNEY for indigent clients and religious, charitable, and other nonprofit entities.

As members of a profession, lawyers are bound by their ethical rules to charge reasonable rates for their services and to serve the PUBLIC INTEREST by providing free legal service to indigent persons or to religious, charitable, or other nonprofit groups. A lawyer's free legal service to these types of clients is designated as pro bono service.

Lawyers have always donated a portion of their time to pro bono work, but in the United States the demand for legal services from people who cannot afford to hire an attorney has grown since the 1960s. Lawyers previously donated time on an ad hoc basis. The establishment of LEGAL AID organizations to serve indigent persons in the 1960s changed the way attorneys obtained pro bono work. Legal aid attorneys, who were unable to satisfy all the legal needs of poor people, created programs to recruit private attorneys willing to donate some of their time. These programs recruit attorneys and then train them to handle common types of cases.

The AMERICAN BAR ASSOCIATION (ABA) has become a national leader in the effort to enhance pro bono legal services. The ABA Center for Pro Bono assists ABA members and the legal community in developing and supporting effective pro bono legal services in civil matters as part of the profession's effort to ensure access to legal representation and the justice system. The center helps create, design, and implement pro bono programs. It sponsors an annual conference for bar leaders, pro bono program managers, legal service staff, and others involved in the delivery of pro bono legal services to poor people.

State and local bar associations also assist in the creation and maintenance of pro bono programs. Despite these efforts, the need for legal services outstrips the pro bono services provided. State court systems have explored ways to get more lawyers involved in donating their time and skills. In Minnesota, for example, the Rules of Professional Conduct for lawyers state, "A lawyer should aspire to render at least 50 hours of pro bono publico legal services per year" (rule 6.1).

PROCEDURAL LAW The body of law that prescribes formal steps to be taken in enforcing legal rights.

Legal rights themselves are created and defined by SUBSTANTIVE LAW. Different rules generally govern civil procedure and CRIMINAL PROCEDURE, or the procedure followed in trials and in appeals. Federal Rules of Civil Procedure regulate actions in FEDERAL COURTS. Procedural law is made up of state or federal statutes, rules promulgated by individual courts, and standards established by constitutional law, particularly provisions ensuring the DUE PROCESS of law.

Procedural law is often called ADJECTIVE LAW by legal writers.

See also CIVIL PROCEDURE.

PROCEDURE The methods by which legal rights are enforced; the specific machinery for carrying on a lawsuit, including PROCESS, the PLEADINGS, rules of EVIDENCE, and rules of civil procedure or CRIMINAL PROCEDURE.

The form, manner, and order of steps taken in conducting a lawsuit are all regulated by PROCEDURAL LAW, which regulates how the law will be administered. SUBSTANTIVE LAW creates and defines rights that exist under the law.

See also CIVIL PROCEDURE.

PROCEEDING A lawsuit; all or some part of a cause heard and determined by a court, an ADMINISTRATIVE AGENCY, or other judicial authority. Any legal step or ACTION taken at the direction of, or by the authority of, a court or agency; any measures necessary to prosecute or defend an action.

The word *proceeding* may be used for all actions or it may be used for something other than the usual type of lawsuit. For example, a special proceeding may be a particular procedure for handling a certain type of dispute. Special proceedings may be commenced by a PETITION or MOTION even when no full-fledged lawsuit is pending. They usually are confined to disputes that were not recognized under the COMMON LAW or in EQUITY. For example, a proceeding to challenge decisions made by administrative agencies may be a special proceeding.

A SUMMARY PROCEEDING is governed by accelerated methods that produce a quick decision. This is done by elimination of a JURY, a PRESENTMENT, or INDICTMENT, or other elements that are allowed in regular proceedings. Summary proceedings are available only for certain types of cases, such as small claims, or in certain courts, such as a conciliation or small claims court.

An individual may represent himself in almost any type of legal proceeding. When accused murderer Colin Ferguson represented himself in his 1995 trial, he took on all the responsibilities of representation, such as questioning witnesses.

DAILY NEWS POOL PHOTO BY BILL TURNBULL

SUPPLEMENTARY PROCEEDINGS are separate from the original action. They help a successful party collect what is owed on a JUDGMENT by summoning the defendant-debtor, requiring that individual to disclose what he or she owns, and ordering that it be delivered in order to satisfy the judgment.

PROCEEDS The yield, income, money, or anything of value produced from a sale of property or a particular transaction.

Proceeds refers to whatever is received when an item is sold or to that which results or accrues from some possession or transaction. Proceeds are classified into cash and noncash categories.

PROCESS A series of actions, motions, or occurrences; a method, mode, or operation, whereby a result or effect is produced; normal or actual course of procedure; regular proceeding, as, the process of vegetation or decomposition; a chemical process; processes of nature.

In patent law, an art or method by which any particular result is produced. A definite combination of new or old elements, ingredients, operations, ways, or means to produce a new, improved, or old result, and any substantial change therein by omission, to the same or better result, or by modification or substitution, with different function, to the same or better result, is a new and patentable process.

In civil and criminal proceedings, any means used by a court to acquire or exercise its JURISDICTION over a person or over specific property. A SUMMONS or summons and COMPLAINT; sometimes, a writ.

See also SERVICE OF PROCESS.

PROCESS SERVER A person authorized by law to deliver papers, typically the COMPLAINT, to the defendant.

See also SERVICE OF PROCESS.

PROCHEIN AMI See NEXT FRIEND.

PROCLAMATION An act that formally declares to the general public that the government has acted in a particular way. A written or printed document issued by a superior government executive, such as the president or governor, which sets out such a declaration by the government.

PROCTOR A person appointed to manage the affairs of another or to represent another in a JUDGMENT.

In English law, the name formerly given to practitioners in ecclesiastical and admiralty courts who performed duties similar to those of SOLICITORS in ordinary courts.

In old English law, a proctor was an attorney who practiced in the ecclesiastical and admiralty courts. Proctors, also known as procurators, served a similar function as solicitors in the ordinary courts of England. The title of proctor was merged with that of solicitor in 1873, but it is sometimes used in the United States to designate practitioners in PROBATE and admiralty courts.

The use of proctors and procurators was an important step in English law because it signified the acceptance of legal representation. Procuration allowed one person to give power to another to act in his behalf. The proctor became the AGENT of the client, legally entitled to perform all actions that the client could have performed.

A "procuracy" was the writing or instrument that authorized a proctor or procurator to act. The document called a "power of attorney," which authorizes an attorney or agent to represent a person's interests, is based on this relationship. A POWER OF ATTORNEY may be general, giving the agent blanket authority to perform all necessary acts for the person, or specific, limiting the agent to certain actions.

The term *procuracy* was shortened to *proxy*, which has gained a more specific meaning. A PROXY is a person who is substituted or designated by another to represent her, usually in a meeting or before a public body. Shareholders in a CORPORATION commonly use a written proxy to give someone else the right to vote their shares at a shareholders' meeting.

PROCURE To cause something to happen; to find and obtain something or someone.

Procure refers to commencing a PROCEEDING; bringing about a result; persuading, inducing, or causing a person to do a particular act; obtaining possession or control over an item; or making a person available for sexual intercourse.

PRODUCE As a noun, the product of natural growth, labor, or capital. Articles produced or grown from or on the soil, or found in the soil.

As a verb, to bring forward; to show or exhibit; to bring into view or notice; as, to present a play, including its presentation in motion pictures. To produce WITNESSES or documents at trial in obedience to a SUBPOENA or to be compelled to produce materials subject to DISCOVERY rules.

To make, originate, or yield, as gasoline. To bring to the surface, as oil. To yield, as revenue. Thus, funds are *produced* by taxation, not when the tax is levied, but when the sums are collected.

PRODUCING CAUSE See PROXIMATE CAUSE.

PRODUCT LIABILITY The responsibility of a manufacturer or vendor of GOODS to compensate for injury caused by a defective good that it has provided for sale.

When a person is harmed by an unsafe product, she may have a CAUSE OF ACTION against the persons who designed, manufactured, sold, or furnished that product. In the United States, some consumers have hailed the rapid growth of product liability litigation as an effective tool for consumer protection. The law has changed from CAVEAT EMPTOR ("let the buyer beware") to strict LIABILITY for manufacturing defects that make a product unreasonably dangerous. Manufacturers and others who distribute and sell goods argue that product liability VERDICTS have enriched plaintiffs' attorneys and added to the cost of goods sold. Businesses have sought tort reform from state legislatures and Congress in hopes of reducing DAMAGE awards that sometimes number in the millions of dollars.

Theories of Liability In most JURISDICTIONS a plaintiff's cause of action may be based on one or more of four different theories: negligence, breach of warranty, misrepresentation, and strict tort liability.

NEGLIGENCE refers to the absence of, or failure to exercise, proper or ordinary CARE. It means that an individual who had a legal OBLIGATION either omitted to do what should have been done or did something that should not have been done.

A manufacturer can be held liable for negligence if lack of REASONABLE care in the production, design, or assembly of the manufacturer's product caused harm. For example, a manufacturing company might be found negligent if its employees did not perform their work properly or if management sanctioned improper procedures and an unsafe product was made.

Breach of WARRANTY refers to the failure of a seller to fulfill the terms of a PROMISE, CLAIM, or representation made concerning the quality or type of the product. The law assumes that a seller gives certain warranties concerning goods that are sold and that he must stand behind such assertions.

MISREPRESENTATION in the advertising and sales promotion of a product refers to the process of giving consumers false security about the safety of a particular product, ordinarily by drawing attention away from the hazards of its use. An action lies in the intentional concealment of potential hazards or in negligent misrepresentation. The key to recovery on the basis of misrepresentation is the plaintiff's ability to prove that he relied upon the representations that were made. Misrepresentation can be argued under a theory of breach of EXPRESS warranty or a theory of strict tort liability.

Strict liability involves extending the responsibility of the VENDOR or manufacturer to all individuals who might be injured by the product, even in the absence of FAULT. Injured guests, bystanders, or others with no direct relationship to the product may sue for damages caused by the product. An injured party must prove that the item was defective, the defect proximately caused the injury, and the defect rendered the product unreasonably dangerous.

Historical Development The history of the law of product liability is largely a history of the erosion of the doctrine of PRIVITY, which states that an injured person can sue the negligent person only if she was a party to the transaction with the injured person. In other words, a defendant's duty of reasonable care arose only from the CONTRACT, and only a party to that contract could sue for its breach. This meant that a negligent manufacturer who sold a product to a retailer, who in turn sold it to the plaintiff, was effectively insulated from liability. The plaintiff was usually without a remedy in tort, because it was the manufacturer and not the retailer whose negligence caused the harm.

The privity doctrine dominated nineteenth-century law, yet courts created exceptions to avoid denying an injured plaintiff a REMEDY. Soon privity of contract was not required where the seller fraudulently concealed the defect or where the products were inherently or imminently dangerous to human life or health, such as poisons or guns. The decisions then began to expand these exceptions. Some courts dropped the FRAUD requirement. A concealed defect coupled with some sort of "invitation" by the defendant to use the product was enough. In a few cases the term *imminently dangerous* was construed to mean especially dangerous by reason of the defect itself, and not necessarily dangerous per se. For example, products intended for human consumption, a defective scaffold, and a coffee urn that exploded would be considered imminently dangerous.

The seminal case of *MacPherson v. Buick Motor Co.*, 217 N.Y. 382, 111 N.E. 1050 (N.Y. 1916), broadened the category of "inherently" or "imminently" dangerous products so as to effectively abolish the privity requirement in negligence cases. It held that lack of privity is not a defense if it is foreseeable that the product, if negligently made, is likely to cause injury to a class of persons that includes the plaintiff. Because this is essentially the test for negligence, the exception swallowed the rule. The *MacPherson* case quickly became a leading authority, and the privity rule in negligence cases soon was ignored. Increasing public sympathy for victims of industrial negligence also contributed to the demise of the rule.

In warranty, a similar privity limitation was imposed, in part because warranties were thought to be an integral part of the sales contract. Beginning in the early twentieth century, an exception to the privity rule developed for cases involving products intended for human consumption (food, beverages, drugs) and eventually also for products intended for "intimate bodily use" (e.g., cosmetics) so that the warranty in these cases extended to the ultimate consumer. In the case of express warranties, which could be said to be made to the public generally, the privity requirement was abandoned during the 1930s. For example, a manufacturer's statement in literature distributed with an automobile that the windshield was "shatterproof" constituted an express warranty to the purchaser that the windshield would not break (*Baxter v. Ford Motor Co.*, 168 Wash. 456, 12 P.2d 409 [Wash. 1932]).

But with respect to implied warranties, exception to the privity rule did not extend beyond food, drink, and similar products until *Henningsen v. Bloomfield Motors, Inc.*, 32 N.J. 358, 161 A.2d 69 (1960). In this case the New Jersey Supreme Court abolished the privity limitation generally and held that the implied warranties run to the foreseeable ultimate user or consumer of the product. The *Henningsen* decision, which also invalidated the manufacturer's attempted DISCLAIMER of IMPLIED WARRANTY liability, has been followed in almost all jurisdictions.

From 1930 to 1960, various legal writers and a few judges discussed the creation of strict liability in tort for defective products. The best-known judicial exposition of this view was California Supreme Court Justice Roger John Traynor's concurring opinion in *Escola v. Coca Cola Bottling Co. of Fresno*, 24 Cal. 2d 453, 150 P.2d 436 (1944). A number of justifications are advanced for strict liability: negligence is often too difficult to prove; strict liability can be accomplished through a series of actions for breach of warranty; strict liability provides needed safety incentives; the manufacturer is in the best position to either prevent the harm or insure or spread the cost of the RISK; and the manufacturer of a product induces consumer reliance on the expectation of the product's safety and should be made to stand behind the product.

Finally in 1963, in *Greenman v. Yuba Power Products, Inc.*, 59 Cal. 2d 57, 377 P.2d 897, the California Supreme Court adopted strict tort liability for defective products. Within a short time, strict liability swept the country and is now the law in all but a few states.

BILL SWERSEY/THE GAMMA LIAISON NETWORK

A shopkeeper removes medication from the shelves following a recall in 1991. Prior to a series of scares involving medications that had been tampered with, drug manufacturers typically did not use safety seals in their packaging.

Negligence The duty to guard against negligence and supply a safe product applies to everyone in the chain of distribution, including a manufacturer who carelessly makes a defective product, the company that uses the product to assemble something else without discovering an obvious defect, and the vendor who should exercise greater care in offering products for sale. These individuals owe a duty of care to anyone who is likely to be injured by such a product if it is defective, including the initial buyer, her family members, bystanders, or persons who lease the item or hold it for the purchaser.

Additionally, the duty to exercise care involves all phases of getting a product to the consumers or users. The product must be designed in such a way that it is safe for its intended use. It must be inspected and tested at different stages, made from the appropriate materials, and assembled carefully. The product's container or packaging must be adequate. The manufacturer must also furnish adequate warnings and directions for use with the product. The seller is proscribed from misrepresenting the safety or character of the product and must disclose all defects.

Breach of Warranty Warranties are certain kinds of express or implied representations of fact that the law will enforce against the warrantor. Product liability law is concerned with three types of warranties involving the product's quality or fitness for use: express warranty, implied warranty of merchantability, and implied warranty of fitness for a particular purpose. These and other warranties are codified in the UNIFORM COMMERCIAL CODE (UCC), which every state has adopted.

An express warranty can be created in one of three ways: through an affirmation of fact made by the vendor of the goods to the purchaser relating to the goods, which becomes part of the bargain; by way of a description of the goods, which is made part of the basis of the bargain; and through a sample or model, which is made part of the basis of the bargain (U.C.C. § 2-313).

An express warranty can be words spoken during negotiations or written into a sales contract, a sample, an earlier purchase of the same kind of product, or claims made in publicity or on tags attached to the product. An express warranty is created when a salesperson states that the product is guaranteed to be free from defects for one year from the date of the purchase.

Implied warranties are those created and imposed by law, and accompany the transfer of title to goods unless expressly and clearly limited or excluded by the contract. However, with respect to damages for PERSONAL INJURY, the UCC states that any such contractual limitations or exclusions are "prima facie unconscionable" and cannot be enforced (U.C.C. § 2-719(3)).

The implied warranty of merchantability requires that the product and its container meet certain minimum standards of quality, chiefly that the product be fit for the ordinary purposes for which such goods are sold (U.C.C. § 2-314). This includes a standard of reasonable safety.

The implied warranty of fitness for a particular purpose imposes a similar requirement in cases where the seller knows or has reason to know of a particular purpose for which the goods are required and where the buyer is relying on the seller to select or furnish suitable goods. The seller then warrants that the goods are fit for that particular purpose (U.C.C. § 2-315). For example, assume that the buyer tells the seller, a computer supplier, that he needs a high-speed computer to manage inventory and payroll functions for his business. Once the seller recommends a particular computer to handle these requirements, she is making an implied warranty of fitness. If the computer cannot adequately process the inventory and payroll, the buyer may file suit.

The action for breach of one of these warranties has aspects of both tort and contract law. Its greatest value to the injured product user lies in the fact that liability for breach is strict. No negligence or other fault need be shown. However, in addition to the privity limitation, certain contract-related defenses have impaired the remedy's usefulness. These include the requirement that the seller receive reasonably prompt notice of the breach as a condition to his or her liability, the requirement that the buyer has relied upon the warranty, and the ability of the seller to limit or disclaim entirely the implied warranties. These defenses are most appropriate in cases where a product's failure causes economic loss. The trend has been away from strict enforcement of these defenses in personal injury cases where the action is closer to a tort action.

Strict Liability The rule of strict liability applied in product liability suits makes a seller responsible for all defective items that unreasonably threaten the personal safety of a consumer or the consumer's property. The vendor is liable if she regularly engaged in the business of selling such products, which reach the consumer without any substantial changes having been made in their condition. The vendor is liable even if she exercised care in handling the product and if the consumer bought the product somewhere else and had no direct dealings with the vendor.

Defects A critical issue in a product liability lawsuit is whether the product contains a DEFECT, which is an imperfection that renders a product unsafe for its intended use. Design defects exist when a whole class of products is inadequately planned in such a way as to pose unreasonable hazards to consumers. For example, an automobile manufacturer's design of a vehicle with the fuel tank placed in such a position that it will explode upon low-speed impact can be classified as defective. In that case, products manufactured in conformity with the intended design would be defective. A production defect arises when a product is improperly assembled. For example, frames of automobiles that are improperly welded to the body at the assembly plant would be classified as a production defect.

In addition, something other than the product itself can cause it to be defective. For example, caustic chemicals should be packaged in appropriate containers. Improper labeling, instructions, or warnings on a product or its container also make a product defective. Dangerous products should carry warning labels that explain how they should be used, under what circumstances they are likely to cause harm, and what steps can be taken in an emergency involving the product.

The principle of proper labeling includes claims made in sales brochures, product displays, and public advertising. It extends beyond

JOE POLIMENI/GAMMA LIAISON

An auto dealer holds up the parts responsible for a recall that affected thousands of Saturn owners.

warranty or negligence law, because a seller is strictly liable to users or purchasers of the product who are not in privity with the seller.

A manufacturer who creates the demand for goods through print and broadcast media has the responsibility to determine that the product has the qualities represented to the general public. Some courts allow injured consumers to sue even if they have not read a certain label or advertisement. The standard is that if the advertisement is directed toward the public at large and makes claims that a normal consumer would take into consideration when deciding to make a purchase, then the manufacturer must stand behind that claim for every member of the public.

Cause of Injuries The issue of causation of injuries can become complicated, particularly if the product involved is only an indirect or remote cause, or one of a number of causes. Regardless of the theory of liability, the plaintiff must prove that the product was defective when it left the hands of the defendant and that the defect was the cause of injury. These issues are ordinarily questions of fact to be decided by the jury.

When the EVIDENCE indicates that an injury might have been precipitated by several causes, the question becomes whether the cause for which the defendant is liable was a substantial factor in bringing about the injury. A defendant is not necessarily liable if he is responsible for the last cause or the IMMEDIATE CAUSE of the injury. For example, a person who was injured by a cooking pot that fell apart when the person removed it from the stove might not have to show that a defect in the pot handle was the only possible explanation for the accident. The jury could still properly consider whether a defect was a concurring cause of the accident, even if they found that the plaintiff misused the pot by handling it too roughly.

Risks A manufacturer has the duty to make the product as safe as possible. If the manufacturer cannot do so, he has the obligation to adequately warn users and buyers of the dangers that exist. The concept of a reasonably safe product extends to any dangers likely to arise when the product is being used normally or in a way that can be anticipated, even if it is not the purpose for which it was sold. For example, a manufacturer might foresee that someone is likely to stand on a table and might be required either to make it sufficiently strong and stable for people to do so without sustaining injury or to warn customers not to stand on it.

No liability is extended to a manufacturer if a plaintiff was disappointed because she had unreasonable hopes for a particular product. Frequently, however, a consumer's expectations are clearly reasonable but are not met. For example, no one expects to find defective brakes in a new automobile.

In some instances a defect might not be INHERENT in the product, but a consumer should be aware that care is needed. An average adult need not be warned that knives cut, that dynamite explodes, or that electrical appliances should not be used in the shower. A consumer who ignores hazards will not succeed in an action alleging product liability. However, many manufacturers print warnings about commonsense hazards to provide added protection from a lawsuit.

Traditionally, an individual must be at least as careful as a reasonably careful person. Increasing recognition has been given, however, to a more realistic standard—the occasionally careless consumer. Courts are now less interested in how obvious a danger is and more concerned with discovering how serious the risk is and how readily it could have been avoided.

A consumer who clearly misuses a product cannot recover if an injury results. For example, a person who disregards a printed warning that nail polish remover is for external use only cannot blame the manufacturer for making an imperfect product if she ingests it. In addition, the consumer is precluded from recovery if she continues to use a product that is obviously dangerous. The theory is that the consumer has assumed the risk. This rule applies, however, only to obvious defects and does not establish a duty for consumers to scrutinize every product they purchase.

Whether a consumer has assumed responsibility for using an obviously dangerous product or misused a relatively safe product depends on who the user is likely to be. The classic example is children's clothing, which generally must be at least somewhat flame-resistant, because children are less able to appreciate the danger of accidental fires.

Unavoidable Dangers Although manufacturers and sellers have a duty to take precautions and provide adequate warnings and instructions, the public can still obtain products that are unavoidably unsafe. A seller is not held strictly liable for providing the public with a product that is needed and wanted in spite of the potential risk of danger. Prescription drugs illustrate this principle, because all of them have the potential to cause serious harm if used unreasonably.

The duty to warn consumers of unavoidable dangers presents special problems if certain individuals are likely to suffer allergic reactions. The law considers an allergy to be a reaction suffered by a minority of people that is triggered by exposure to some substance. Courts used to reject claims based on allergic reactions, reasoning that the product was reasonably safe and that the injury was caused by a defect peculiar to the individual. That approach has been abandoned, with manufacturers providing careful instructions on use and clear warnings about possible symptoms that suggest an allergic reaction.

Multiparty Litigation Since the 1970s, groups of plaintiffs have filed consolidated lawsuits against the manufacturers of certain products. The makers of contraceptive devices, silicone breast implants, asbestos, and TOBACCO products have encountered this type of multiparty litigation. In many states one judge is appointed to handle all cases involving claims against such a manufacturer. The litigation process can prove costly for defendants, because they may have to defend themselves in many different states. The resulting verdicts or negotiated settlements can also be very expensive to companies.

Product Liability Reform Businesses have sought relief from state legislatures and Congress regarding product liability, contending that the shifting legal standards make them vulnerable to even the most suspect claim. Some states have passed laws that provide manufacturers with the right to defend themselves by showing that their product met generally acceptable safety standards when made. This assertion is known as the state-of-the-art defense, which relieves manufacturers of the task of attempting to make a perfect product. An injured consumer cannot recover on the theory that the product would have been safe had the manufacturer incorporated safety features that were developed after the product was made. Consumer advocates have opposed such laws because they allow manufacturers to avoid liability. The advocates argue that these laws discourage innovation because higher safety standards are set as improvements are made.

Businesses have also sought to set maximum amounts that persons can recover for PUNITIVE DAMAGES. Some states have capped awards for punitive damages. In 1996 President Bill Clinton vetoed a bill that would have limited punitive damage awards to $250,000, or two times the economic and noneconomic damages, whichever amount was greater, stating that it would deprive U.S. families of the ability to fully recover for injuries caused by defective products.

CROSS-REFERENCES

Automobiles *Sidebar: Unsafe at Any Speed;* Consumer Product Safety Commission; Consumer Protection; *MacPherson v. Buick Motor Co.*; Merchantable; Nader, Ralph; Proximate Cause; Sales Law; Tort Law.

PROFANITY Irreverence towards sacred things; particularly, an irreverent or blasphemous use of the name of God. Vulgar, irreverent, or coarse language.

The use of certain profane or OBSCENE language on the radio or television is a federal offense, but in other situations, profanity might fall within the protection of the constitutional guarantee of FREEDOM OF SPEECH.

PROFESSIO JURIS The right of contracting parties to stipulate in the document the law that will govern their agreement.

PROFESSIONAL RESPONSIBILITY The obligation of lawyers to adhere to rules of professional conduct.

As members of a profession and as officers of the court, lawyers have the responsibility of following rules of professional conduct that are mandated either by a state legislature or by the highest court in the state. Rules of professional conduct govern both the public and the private behavior of lawyers. Because lawyers are licensed to practice by the states, lawyers who violate rules of professional conduct are likewise disciplined by the states, not the federal government. The punishment for violating a state rule of professional responsibility ranges from private or public reprimand to suspension or disbarment (permanent disqualification from practicing law in the state). To the limited extent that they practice law, judges are subject to the state code of professional conduct in addition to a code of judicial conduct.

The AMERICAN BAR ASSOCIATION (ABA) formulated the Model Rules of Professional Conduct

JOHN NEUBAUER/PHOTOEDIT

A lawyer's behavior in and out of court is governed by long-standing rules of professional conduct.

in 1983 to provide uniformity and consistency in defining the professional responsibilities of lawyers. Though the ABA has no power to enforce the model rules, they serve as a guide for states in crafting rules of conduct.

History The public and the legal profession have long sought to prescribe ethical conduct for lawyers. Legal advocates existed in Greece as early as the fourth century B.C., and in first-century Rome, legal advisers and advocates began to play an active role in the formulation of systematized courts and the conduct of court operatives.

Advances in legal ethics made by legal advocates in Rome disappeared with the fall of the Holy Roman Empire and the onset of the medieval period in Europe. Legal conduct came under some scrutiny again in the twelfth century in Europe's emerging schools and universities, after William the Conqueror developed England's organized courts and jury trials. However, the ruling class dominated these medieval courts, and legal ethics remained more theoretical than practical long past the medieval period.

The emergence of ethical standards for lawyers in colonial America was gradual and local. Most colonies discouraged, and some colonies expressly prohibited, the practice of remunerated legal representation. Self-representation was the norm, and this obviated the need for a code of professional conduct.

The U.S. Constitution was an important source for the eventual formation of ethical codes for lawyers and judges. Article III of the Constitution contains substantive rules relating to law and the courts, and it establishes the JUDICIARY as an independent government power designed to check the executive and legislative branches. In addition, many of the Constitution's amendments address specific legal processes. The SIXTH AMENDMENT, for example, sets forth general rules in criminal cases, such as the requirement of representation for defendants in criminal prosecution.

Professional associations and ethical codes for lawyers and judges began to appear in the United States in the early 1800s. States formed BAR ASSOCIATIONS in the early 1800s to organize and facilitate the legal profession. The state bar associations influenced the U.S. legal system in a variety of ways and exerted control over its important players by regulating the public and private conduct of lawyers and judges.

When the Civil War ended in 1865, lawyers flooded the Southern states to take part in Reconstruction. The questionable ethics and aggressiveness of some of these lawyers caused Southern legislators to call for the regulation of lawyers. In 1887 the Alabama Bar Association adopted the first comprehensive code of ethics. Other states followed suit.

The American Bar Association was formed in Saratoga, New York, on August 21, 1878, by a group of 289 lawyers. For many years the ABA examined and debated the various state codes of ethics and in 1909 adopted and promoted the Canons of Professional Ethics. The thirty-two canons were intended to be model rules that states could adopt as regulations of legal conduct. Courts or legislatures in most states adopted this first set of standards. However, legal professionals criticized the canons as being incoherent and incomplete, and the ABA replaced them in 1969 with the Model Code of Professional Responsibility.

The model code was also criticized. An amalgam of general canons, aspirational ethical considerations, and disciplinary rules, it was sometimes contradictory and often perplexing. In 1983 the ABA replaced the code with the Model Rules of Professional Conduct.

The model rules consist only of enforceable rules and explanatory comments. The ABA periodically amends the model rules to make adjustments for evolving norms and changes in technology.

Most states have adopted the ABA Model Rules of 1983. States that have not adopted the ABA Model Rules use the ABA Model Code of Professional Responsibility of 1969 and supply their own changes.

Areas of Professional Responsibility Each of the many areas of lawyer responsibility contains a discrete category of ethical concerns. These areas can be organized as the lawyer-client relationship, the lawyer as counselor, the lawyer as advocate, transactions with persons

JEFF GREENBERG/THE IMAGE WORKS

A lawyer must communicate openly with a client, making clear the laws and processes that affect the matter at hand.

other than clients, law firms and associations, public service, information about legal services, and the integrity of the profession. The rules of conduct that govern these areas are subject to interpretation, and knowledge of what specific conduct has been found to violate a rule is often necessary for a complete understanding of the rule's meaning.

Lawyer-Client Relationship A lawyer must follow certain ethical standards when working with a client. A lawyer must be reasonably skilled in order to represent a client on a legal matter. Though a lawyer may work on legal matters unrelated to her usual practice, she may not charge the client for extra time studying to become competent in that area of the law.

A lawyer must perform lawyerly duties diligently and promptly and must openly communicate with the client. A lawyer must also abide by the client's decision regarding the scope of representation and may charge only REASONABLE fees. Several states have adopted rules that prohibit a lawyer from having a sexual relationship with a client.

One of the most critical elements of professional responsibility is keeping confidential all information regarding representation of the client. In addition, a lawyer must avoid representing others with interests that conflict with those of the client.

The issues of confidentiality and the prohibition of CONFLICTS OF INTEREST illustrate the complexity of the rules on lawyer-client relationships. Not only may a lawyer not represent interests that conflict with those of the client, but he may not represent interests that conflict with those of other clients in the law firm. For example, an attorney may not represent a defendant if another attorney in the same firm is representing the plaintiff in the same case. A firm may represent interests adverse to those of a former client if the lawyer who represented the former client is no longer with the firm. However, a firm may not represent interests adverse to those of a former client if any remaining lawyers possess confidential information regarding the particular legal matter concerning that client. But if formerly confidential information has become publicly known, the firm may represent the ADVERSE INTEREST.

Lawyer as Counselor A lawyer serves varied roles, including that of counselor. As a counselor, a lawyer renders candid advice that may refer to factors apart from the law, including moral, economic, social, and political issues relevant to the client's situation. A lawyer may act as a mediator between multiple clients but only if each client consents and the MEDIATION can be done impartially without affecting the lawyer's responsibilities to any of the clients. Finally, with the consent of the client, a lawyer may arrange an evaluation of the client for use by a third party, usually an expert trial witness.

Lawyer as Advocate A lawyer is required to be an ADVOCATE for the client. This is an important obligation because U.S. law is based on the ADVERSARY SYSTEM, which gives competing litigants the principal responsibility for gathering EVIDENCE, formulating legal theories, and presenting evidence and theories at trial to a judge and jury. However, a lawyer must not go beyond the ethical boundaries of professional responsibility in a quest for legal victory. A lawyer cannot make FRIVOLOUS claims or defenses, knowingly make false representations to a court, or falsify or obstruct access to potential evidence. Likewise, a lawyer must disclose all the material facts and legal PRECEDENT necessary to avoid misleading a court. A lawyer also has the responsibility of expediting litigation.

A lawyer must seek to preserve the integrity of the judicial process. Therefore, a lawyer cannot try to influence a judge, juror, or prospective juror through improper communications or make public comments on a case if the lawyer knows that the statements will prejudice the proceeding. If a lawyer knows that she will be a necessary witness at trial, she cannot serve as an advocate at the trial.

A PROSECUTOR in a criminal case has special responsibilities. The prosecutor may not bring legal action if he knows that the charge is not supported by PROBABLE CAUSE or seek to obtain the waiver of important pretrial rights from an unrepresented defendant. The prosecutor must make reasonable efforts to allow a defendant access to counsel and must also timely disclose exculpatory or mitigating evidence and information to the defense. (Exculpatory evidence tends to clear the defendant; mitigating evidence reduces the degree of blame or fault attributable to the defendant.) The prosecutor may not SUBPOENA a lawyer to present information on a past or present client. However, with the permission of the court after an adversarial proceeding, the prosecutor may subpoena a lawyer if the prosecutor reasonably believes that the information sought is not a privileged lawyer-client communication, the evidence is essential to the investigation or prosecution, and there is no feasible alternative way to obtain information.

Prosecutors must also refrain from making public comments that might prejudice a judicial proceeding or heighten public condemnation of the accused. However, prosecutors do not violate their professional responsibility when making public statements for legitimate purposes, such as to provide necessary public information or to aid law enforcement. For example, if an accused escapes from custody and the prosecutor believes that the accused is armed and dangerous, the prosecutor may issue a warning to that effect, even though such a warning will increase public hostility against the accused.

Transactions with Persons Other than Clients A lawyer must act ethically when communicating with persons other than his client in the course of representing the client. This means that the lawyer must communicate truthfully and fairly. Thus, a lawyer must not knowingly make a false statement or assist crime or FRAUD by failing to disclose a material fact to a third party. A lawyer is prohibited from communicating with the client of an opposing party and may not state or imply that he is disinterested. In communicating with third parties, the lawyer must make an effort to explain his role to avoid a misunderstanding and must not illegally obtain evidence from third parties. Finally, a lawyer violates his professional responsibility when using legal devices for the sole purpose of embarrassment, delay, or burden.

Law Firms and Associations With the decline of the sole practitioner and the rise of law firms, lawyers in law firms have special ethical considerations. Because a firm's senior attorneys, partners, or shareholders are responsible for the misconduct of subordinate lawyers and nonlawyer assistants, the senior members must make reasonable efforts to ensure the firm's conformity with all the rules of professional conduct.

Some practices involving the internal affairs of law firms are prohibited. For example, a lawyer cannot ethically share legal fees with nonlawyers, except to issue funds to client survivors and to pay wages to employees. A lawyer's professional judgment must not be directed or regulated by a person who employs the lawyer to perform legal services for a third party. In addition, a lawyer cannot offer to make or actually make an agreement with a client restricting his own right to practice upon termination of the agreement or base a settlement between private parties on an agreement restricting another lawyer's right to practice.

Public Service As a professional, a lawyer is expected to contribute to the community by offering legal services to those persons who cannot afford to pay regular fees. The rules of professional responsibility do not require lawyers to render PRO BONO (free) legal services, but many states set an aspirational goal of a certain number of hours of pro bono service per year. A lawyer who fails to provide such services is not subject to discipline. However, some courts may require a lawyer to accept an unpaid appointment in a certain case.

A court may also order a lawyer to represent a particular client, with the lawyer's fees paid by the government. In such a case, the lawyer may decline the appointment only for good cause. Good cause exists if the appointment would violate the rules of professional conduct or a law or would place an unreasonable financial burden on the lawyer. It also exists if the case is so repugnant to the lawyer as to impair the lawyer's relationship with the client or ability to represent the client.

A lawyer may join a legal organization apart from the lawyer's firm. Whether these organizations are concerned with administering legal

Even outside a courtroom and without the company of his client, an attorney must maintain his client's interests in all settings, such as in this informal conference with a judge and opposing counsel.

ELENA ROORAID/PHOTOEDIT

services or legal reform, the lawyer must not act in such a way as to adversely affect the interests of a client.

Information about Legal Services For many years it was considered unethical for a lawyer to advertise. The profession sought to eradicate the image of lawyers as "ambulance chasers," intent on benefiting from the suffering of others. However, in the 1970s the U.S. Supreme Court struck down rules of professional conduct that banned all lawyer advertising, ruling that absolute prohibition violated the FIRST AMENDMENT. Nevertheless, lawyer advertising may be regulated by the state, and lawyers who violate such rules may be disciplined.

Lawyers may not make unsupported comparisons to other lawyers or create unjustified expectations. Though rules of conduct expressly approve advertising, they discourage direct contact with prospective clients when a significant motive is pecuniary gain. A lawyer may contact a family member or former client but may not solicit business from anyone if the communication involves coercion or if the prospective client has indicated a desire that the solicitation cease.

Lawyers may not advertise as recognized or certified specialists unless they are patent lawyers, admiralty lawyers, or attorneys certified by an appropriate state regulatory authority. If a lawyer is certified as a specialist by an organization that is not recognized by the state, the lawyer may include the certification in advertising if it is accompanied by a statement that the jurisdiction has no procedure for approving the organization.

Integrity of the Profession Lawyers have the responsibility of maintaining the integrity of the legal profession through their personal conduct and through the monitoring of other lawyers. A lawyer or an applicant for admission to the bar is prohibited from knowingly making a false statement of material fact, or failing to disclose material facts, to the members of the admissions board or to a disciplinary authority. For example, an applicant for admission to the bar violates her professional responsibility by failing to reveal a criminal arrest or conviction.

A lawyer must preserve the integrity of the judicial system. Therefore, it is professional misconduct to make a false or reckless statement concerning the quality or integrity of a judge, adjudicative officer, or candidate for judicial or legal office.

A lawyer does have the obligation to report to the appropriate authority her knowledge of conduct that raises a substantial question as to another lawyer's honesty, trustworthiness, or fitness as a lawyer.

Professional misconduct encompasses a violation or attempted violation of the rules of professional responsibility, or the knowing assistance or inducement of a violation of the rules. Professional misconduct is also the commission of a criminal act reflecting adversely on the lawyer's fitness to practice law and any conduct involving dishonesty or prejudice to the administration of justice. For example, a lawyer who is convicted of deliberately failing to file an income tax return will likely be charged with and found guilty of professional misconduct.

Enforcement of Professional Responsibility In every state the supreme court or legislature has created a committee or board that is authorized to enforce state rules of professional conduct. This committee examines allegations of a lawyer's professional misconduct and recommends whether to reprimand him, suspend his LICENSE, place him on supervised or unsupervised PROBATION, or permanently revoke his license.

The specific procedures on professional discipline vary from state to state, but every state allows for court review of a conduct committee's recommendation to discipline a lawyer. When a lawyer's license is suspended, the lawyer may petition the supreme court for readmission to the bar, after a time specified by the state rules. The supreme court will ask the professional responsibility committee for its recommendation on reinstatement.

CROSS-REFERENCES

Attorney; Attorney-Client Privilege; Attorney Misconduct; Canons of Ethics; Confidential Communication; Ethics; Fiduciary; Legal Advertising; Malpractice; Privileged Communication; Specialization.

PROFESSIONAL SPORTS See BASEBALL; SPORTS LAW.

PROFFER To offer or TENDER, as, the production of a document and offer of the same in EVIDENCE.

PROFIT Most commonly, the gross proceeds of a business transaction less the costs of the transaction; i.e., NET proceeds. Excess of revenues over expenses for a transaction; sometimes used synonymously with net income for the period. Gain realized from business or investment over and above expenditures.

Accession of good, valuable results, useful consequences, avail, or gain. The benefit, advantage, or pecuniary gain accruing to the owner or occupant of land from its actual use; as in the familiar phrase *rents, issues and profits*, or in the expression *mesne profits*.

A sa
and

AB FURNITURE COMPANY

Statement of Profit and Loss for
Year Ending December 31, 19___

Sales	$42,700	
Cost of Sales	28,000	
GROSS PROFIT		$14,700
Other Expenses:		
Advertising	800	
Rental of Store	2,400	
Miscellaneous	1,800	
Salary of B	5,200	10,200
NET PROFIT ALLOCATED TO PARTNERS		4,500

PROFIT A PRENDRE [*French, Right of taking.*] The right of persons to share in the land owned by another.

A *profit a prendre* enables a person to take part of the soil or produce of land that someone else owns. It is a right to take from the land, as in the mining of minerals and is, therefore, distinguishable from an EASEMENT, which is a nonpossessory interest in land generally giving a person a right of way on the property of another.

See also MINE AND MINERAL LAW.

PRO FORMA As a matter of form or for the sake of form. Used to describe accounting, financial, and other statements or conclusions based upon assumed or anticipated facts.

The phrase *pro forma*, in an appealable DECREE or JUDGMENT, usually means that the decision was rendered not on a conviction that it was right, but merely to facilitate further proceedings.

PROGRESSIVE TAX A type of GRADUATED TAX that applies higher tax rates as the income of the taxpayer increases.

PRO HAC VICE For this turn; for this one particular occasion. For example, an out-of-state lawyer may be admitted to practice in a local JURISDICTION for a particular case only.

PROHIBITION The popular name for the period in U.S. history from 1920 to 1933 when the manufacture and sale of alcoholic beverages were illegal.

From 1920 to 1933 the manufacture and sale of intoxicating liquors were illegal in the United States. The EIGHTEENTH AMENDMENT to the U.S. Constitution authorized Congress to prohibit alcoholic beverages, and the TWENTY-FIRST AMENDMENT repealed this prohibition. The era of Prohibition was marked by large-scale smuggling and illegal sales of liquor, the growth of ORGANIZED CRIME, and increased restriction on personal freedom.

The prohibition movement began in the 1820s in the wake of a revival of Protestantism, which viewed the consumption of ALCOHOL as sinful and a destructive force in society. Maine passed the first state prohibition law in 1846, and other states followed in the years before the Civil War.

LIBRARY OF CONGRESS

A common sight for almost 14 years in the United States: Government agents destroying bootleg liquor seized during Prohibition.

The Prohibition party was founded in 1869, with a ban on the manufacture and sale of intoxicating liquor its only campaign goal. This party, like most temperance groups, derived its support from rural and small-town voters associated with Protestant evangelical churches. The Prohibition party reached it zenith in 1892 when its candidate for president polled 2.2 percent of the popular vote. The party soon went into decline, and though it still exists, it works mainly at the local level.

The impetus for the Eighteenth Amendment can be traced to the Anti-Saloon League, which was established in 1893. The league worked to enact state prohibition laws and had great success between 1906 and 1913. By the time national prohibition took effect in January 1920, thirty-three states (63 percent of the total population) had prohibited intoxicating liquors.

The league and other prohibition groups were opposed to the consumption of alcohol for a variety of reasons. Some associated alcohol with the rising number of ALIENS entering the country, many of whom were Roman Catholic. This anti-alien, anti-Catholic prejudice was coupled with a fear of increasingly larger urban areas by the rural-dominated prohibition supporters. Saloons and other public drinking establishments were also associated with PROSTITUTION and gambling. Finally, some employers endorsed prohibition as a means of reducing industrial accidents and increasing the efficiency of workers.

When the United States entered World War I in 1917, Congress prohibited the manufacture and importation of distilled liquor in order to aid the war effort. It also authorized the president to lower the alcoholic content of beer and wine and to restrict or forbid their manufacture.

A movement began to support elimination of intoxicating liquors by constitutional amendment. In 1917 Congress passed the Prohibition amendment and submitted it to the states for ratification. The rural-dominated state legislatures made ratification a foregone conclusion, and the Eighteenth Amendment was ratified on January 29, 1919. Congress enacted the VOLSTEAD ACT, officially known as the National Prohibition Act (41 Stat. 305 [1919]) to enforce the amendment, which became effective on January 29, 1920.

Prohibition proved most effective in small towns and rural areas. Compliance was much more difficult in urban areas, where illegal suppliers quickly found a large demand for alcohol. Cities had large immigrant populations that did not see anything morally wrong with consuming alcohol. The rise of "bootlegging" (the illegal manufacture, distribution, and sale of intoxicating liquor) by organized crime proved to be one of the unintended consequences of Prohibition.

Besides the illegal importation, manufacture, distribution, and sale of intoxicating liquors by organized crime, millions of persons evaded Prohibition by consuming "medicinal" whiskey that was sold in drugstores on real or forged prescriptions. Many U.S. industries used denatured alcohol, which was treated with noxious chemicals to make it unfit for human consumption. Nevertheless, methods were found to remove these chemicals, add water and a small amount of liquor for flavor, and sell the mixture to illegal bars, called speakeasies, or to individual customers. Finally, many persons resorted to making their own liquor from corn. This type of product could be dangerously impure and cause blindness, paralysis, and death.

The prohibition movement lost political strength in the 1920s. The stock market crash of 1929 and the resulting Great Depression of the 1930s further changed the political climate. Critics of Prohibition argued that the rise of criminal production and sale of alcohol made the legal ban ineffective. In addition, the general public's patronage of speakeasies bred disrespect for law and government. Finally, critics argued that legalizing the manufacture and sale of alcohol would stimulate the economy and provide desperately needed jobs.

In 1932 the Democratic party adopted a platform plank at its national convention calling for repeal. The landslide Democratic victory of 1932 signaled the end of Prohibition. The February 1933 resolution proposing the Twenty-first Amendment contained a provision requiring ratification by state conventions rather than state legislatures. This provision was included to prevent rural-dominated legislatures, which still supported Prohibition, from defeating the amendment.

The state ratification conventions quickly endorsed the amendment, with ratification of the Twenty-first Amendment coming on December 5, 1933. The amendment did allow prohibition by the states. A few states continued statewide prohibition, but by 1966 all states had repealed these provisions. Liquor in the United States is now controlled at the local level. Counties that prohibit the sale of alcohol are known as dry counties, and counties that allow the sale of alcohol are known as wet counties.

See also CAPONE, ALPHONSE; TEMPERANCE MOVEMENT.

PROHIBITION, WRIT OF An order from a superior court to a lower court or tribunal directing the judge and the parties to cease the litigation because the lower court does not have proper JURISDICTION to hear or determine the matters before it.

A writ of prohibition is an EXTRAORDINARY REMEDY that is rarely used.

A sample petition for a writ of prohibition

Comes now the National Labor Relations Board, by ________, Solicitor General of the United States, and ________, General Counsel of the Board, and by leave of the Court first had and obtained, files this, its petition, for a writ of prohibition and for a writ of mandamus against the Honorable ________, ________, and ________, Circuit Judges of the ________ Judicial Circuit, and the other judges and officers of the United States Court of Appeals for the ________ Circuit, and respectfully represents:

1. Pursuant to authority conferred by the Act of July 5, 1935, 49 Stat. 449, the National Labor Relations Board (hereinafter called the Board) on April 8, 1938, issued an order in a cause before the Board entitled ________, directing the Republic Steel Corporation (hereinafter called the Corporation) to cease and desist from certain unfair labor practices and to take certain affirmative action found by the Board to be necessary to effectuate the policies of the National Labor Relations Act.

2. On April 18, 1938, the Corporation filed in the United States Court of Appeals for the ________ Circuit its petition, entitled ________, for review of the aforesaid order of the Board. The Corporation in its petition alleged inter alia that the order of the Board denied to the Corporation due process of law in violation of the Fifth Amendment to the Constitution of the United States for the reason that the order had been entered without affording the Corporation an opportunity to present its case by argument, oral or upon brief. The Corporation alleged further that it had not been given a hearing in accordance with the usual and accepted rules of legal procedure and the law of the land.

[Portions omitted for the purpose of illustration.]

5. Subsequent to April 25, 1938, the Board instituted the practice of specifically calling the attention of the parties in all proceedings before it to their right to submit briefs to the Board and upon request to be heard by the Board in oral argument. The Board also determined that in cases thereafter decided which had been initiated or transferred before it (unless reasons to the contrary should appear in particular cases) an intermediate report should be prepared by a trial examiner and served upon the parties or, in the alternative, that proposed findings of fact and conclusions of law should be prepared by the Board and served upon the parties, with express notice to the parties of their right to take exceptions to the intermediate report or proposed findings and upon request to be heard by the Board in argument, oral or upon brief, upon such exceptions. With respect to certain such cases already decided, in which complaint had been made of the absence of an intermediate report or proposed findings, or of lack of argument, written or oral, the Board, although advised that its orders therein were in accordance with law, nevertheless determined to vacate the orders, to restore the cases to its docket, and to reconsider and redetermine the cases after giving full opportunities to the parties to except to proposed findings of fact and conclusions of law and after giving them express notice of their right to submit briefs to the Board and to be heard by the Board upon request in oral argument.

6. Among the cases affected by the last stated determination of the Board was ________, above referred to. On April 30, 1938, at a hearing upon a motion by the Corporation for a stay of the order of the Board in the said case, counsel for the Board, in the presence of counsel for the Corporation, advised the United States Court of Appeals for the ________ Circuit that the Board was considering vacating its order in the said case. On May 3, 1938, counsel for the Board advised the Corporation, by telegram addressed to its counsel, ________, that the Board had definitely decided to vacate its said order, and that on May 4, 1938, the said order would be so vacated.

7. Paragraph (d) of Section 10 of the Act of June 5, 1935, 49 Stat. 454, provides:

> "Until a transcript of the record in a case shall have been filed in a court, as hereinafter provided, the Board may at any time, upon reasonable notice and in such manner as it

[*continued on page 196*]

A sample petition for a writ of prohibition (continued)

shall deem proper, modify or set aside, in whole or in part, any finding or order made or issued by it."

No transcript of the record in the aforesaid case of ________, has yet been filed in the United States Court of Appeals for the ________ Circuit, or in any other court.

[Portions omitted for purpose of illustration.]

Wherefore, the said National Labor Relations Board, the aid of this honorable Court respectfully requesting, prays:

1. That a writ of mandamus be issued out of this honorable Court directing and commanding the Honorable ________, the Honorable ________, the Honorable ________, Circuit Judges of the ________ Judicial Circuit, and the other judges and officers of the United States Court of Appeals for the ________ Circuit, to vacate the order of the said court issued on May 13, 1938, restraining the National Labor Relations Board from taking any further steps or proceedings in the case of ________ and directing the Board to file in the said court a certified transcript of the record of the proceedings before the Board in the said case.

2. That a writ of prohibition be issued out of this honorable Court prohibiting the Honorable ________, ________, and ________, Circuit Judges of the ________ Judicial Circuit, and the other judges and officers of the United States Court of Appeals for the ________ Circuit, from exercising any jurisdiction upon the petition of the Republic Steel Corporation to set aside the order of April 8, 1938, entered by the National Labor Relations Board in the case of ________ without affording the Board a reasonable opportunity to vacate its said order.

3. That pending further order of the Court herein, the Honorable ________, ________, and ________, Circuit Judges of the ________ Judicial Circuit, and the other judges and officers of the United States Court of Appeals for the ________ Circuit, be stayed or restrained from enforcing the provision of the order of the said court of May 13, 1938, directing the National Labor Relations Board forthwith to file in the court a certified transcript of the record before the Board in the case of ________.

4. That the Court grant to the National Labor Relations Board such other and further relief as may be just in the premises.

____
Solicitor General of the United States

____
General Counsel, National Labor Relations Board

[Date]

________, being duly sworn, deposes that he is of counsel for the petitioner; that he has read the foregoing petition and that to the best of his information and belief the facts therein stated are true.

____

Sworn to before me this ________ day of ________, 19__.

____
Notary Public

PROMISE A written or oral declaration given in exchange for something of value that binds the maker to do, or forbear from, a certain specific act and gives to the person to whom the declaration is made the right to expect and enforce performance or forbearance. An undertaking that something will or will not occur. It is a manifestation of intent to act, or refrain from acting, in a certain manner.

In the law of COMMERCIAL PAPER, an undertaking to pay. It must be more than an acknowledgment of an obligation.

The person who makes the declaration is the *promisor*. The person to whom the declaration is made is called the *promisee*.

In CONTRACTS, a promise is essential to a binding legal agreement and is given in exchange for CONSIDERATION, which is the inducement to enter into a promise. A promise is illusory when the promisor does not bind herself to do anything and, therefore, furnishes no consideration for a valid contract.

A promise *implied in fact* is a tacit promise that can be inferred from expressions or acts of the promisor. A promise *implied by law* can arise when no express declaration is made, but the party, in EQUITY and justice, is under a legal duty as if he had in fact actually made a promise.

PROMISSORY ESTOPPEL In the law of CONTRACTS, the doctrine that provides that if a PARTY changes his or her position substantially either by acting or forbearing from acting in reliance upon a GRATUITOUS promise, then that party can enforce the PROMISE although the essential elements of a contract are not present.

Certain elements must be established to invoke promissory estoppel. A promisor—one who makes a promise—makes a gratuitous promise that he should reasonably have expected to induce action or forbearance of a definite and substantial character on the part of the promisee—one to whom a promise has been made. The promisee justifiably relies on the promise. A substantial detriment—that is, an economic loss—ensues to the promisee from action or forbearance. Injustice can be avoided only by enforcing the promise.

A majority of courts apply the doctrine to any situation in which all of these elements are present. A minority, however, still restrict its applicability to one or more specific situations from which the doctrine emanated, such as when a DONOR promises to transfer REAL PROPERTY as a GIFT and the DONEE spends money on the property in reliance on the promise.

With respect to the measure of recovery, it would be unfair to award the plaintiff the benefit of the bargain, as in the case of an express contract, since there is no bargain. In a majority of cases, however, injustice is avoided by awarding the plaintiff an amount consistent with the value of the promise. Other cases avoid injustice by awarding the plaintiff only an amount necessary to compensate her for the economic detriment actually suffered.

PROMISSORY NOTE A written, signed, unconditional PROMISE to pay a certain amount of money on demand at a specified time. A written promise to pay money that is often used as a means to borrow funds or take out a loan.

The individual who promises to pay is the *maker*, and the person to whom payment is promised is called the *payee* or *holder*. If signed by the maker, a promissory note is a NEGOTIABLE INSTRUMENT. It contains an unconditional promise to pay a certain sum to the order of a specifically named person or to BEARER—that is, to any individual presenting the note. A promissory note can be either payable on demand or at a specific time.

Certain types of promissory notes, such as corporate BONDS or retail installment loans, can be sold at a discount—an amount below their FACE VALUE. The notes can be subsequently redeemed on the date of maturity for the entire face amount or prior to the due date for an amount less than the face value. The purchaser of a discounted promissory note often receives interest in addition to the appreciated difference in the price when the note is held to maturity.

PROMOTER A person who devises a plan for a business venture; one who takes the preliminary steps necessary for the formation of a CORPORATION.

Promoters are the people, who, for themselves or on behalf of others, organize a corporation. They issue a PROSPECTUS, obtain STOCK subscriptions, and secure a CHARTER. Promoters stand in a FIDUCIARY relationship to the proposed company and must act in GOOD FAITH in all their dealings for the proposed corporation.

PROMULGATE To officially announce, to publish, to make known to the public; to formally announce a statute or a decision by a court.

PROOF The establishment of a FACT by the use of EVIDENCE. Anything that can make a person believe that a fact or proposition is true or false. It is distinguishable from evidence in that proof is a broad term comprehending everything that may be adduced at a trial, whereas evidence is a narrow term describing certain types of proof that can be admitted at trial.

The phrase *burden of proof* includes two distinct concepts, the BURDEN OF PERSUASION and the BURDEN OF GOING FORWARD. The burden of persuasion is the duty of a party to convince the trier of fact of all the elements of a CAUSE OF ACTION. The burden of going forward refers to the need of a party to refute evidence introduced at trial that damages or discredits his or her position in the ACTION. The burden of persuasion remains with the plaintiff or prosecutor throughout the action, whereas the burden of going forward can shift between the parties during the trial.

In a CIVIL ACTION, the requisite degree of proof is a preponderance of the evidence. The plaintiff must show that more probably than not the defendant violated his or her rights. In a criminal action, the prosecutor has the burden of establishing guilt BEYOND A REASONABLE DOUBT.

See also PREPONDERANCE OF EVIDENCE.

PROPER Fit; correct; reasonably sufficient. That which is well adapted or appropriate.

Proper care is the degree of care a REASONABLE, prudent person would use under similar circumstances.

A *proper party* is an individual who has an interest in the litigation. He or she can be joined—that is, brought into the ACTION—but his or her nonjoinder will not result in a dismissal. A substantial judicial decree can still be rendered in the absence of a proper party. A proper party is distinguishable from a *necessary party* in that the latter must be joined in order to give complete relief to the litigants. See also JOINDER.

PROPERTY LAW There are two types of property: REAL PROPERTY and PERSONAL PROPERTY. Most of the legal concepts and rules associated with both types of property are derived from English COMMON LAW. Modern law has incorporated many of these concepts and rules into statutes, which define the types and rights of ownership in real and personal property.

Personal property, also referred to as movable property, is anything other than land that can be the subject of ownership, including STOCKS, money, notes, PATENTS, and COPYRIGHTS, as well as intangible property.

Real property is land and ordinarily anything erected on, growing on, or affixed to it, including buildings and CROPS. The term is also used to declare any rights that issue from the ownership of land. The terms *real estate* and *real property* generally refer to land. The term *land*, in its general usage, includes not only the face of the earth but everything of a permanent nature over or under it, including minerals, oil, and gases. In modern usage, the word *premises* has come to mean the land itself or the land with all structures attached. Residential buildings and yards are commonly referred to as premises.

The difference between real property and personal property is ordinarily easily recognizable. The character of the property, however, can be altered. Property that is initially personal in nature becomes part of realty by being annexed to it, such as when rails are made into a fence on land.

In certain cases, however, the intention or agreement of the parties determines whether property that is annexed retains its character as personal property. A LANDLORD AND TENANT might agree that the new lighting fixture the tenant attaches to the ceiling of her dwelling remains the tenant's property after the expiration of the lease.

Property may be further classified as either private or public. Private property is that which belongs to one or more persons. Public property is owned by a country, state, or political subdivision, such as a MUNICIPAL CORPORATION or a school district.

Personal Property Personal property can be divided into two major categories: TANGIBLE and INTANGIBLE. Tangible property includes such items as animals, merchandise, and jewelry. Intangible property includes such rights as stock, BONDS, patents, and copyrights.

Possession Possession is a property interest under which an individual to the exclusion of all others is able to exercise power over something. It is a basic PROPERTY RIGHT that entitles the possessor to continue peaceful possession against everyone else except someone with a superior right. It also gives the possessor the right to recover personal property (often called CHATTEL) that has been wrongfully taken and the right to recover DAMAGES against wrongdoers.

To have POSSESSION an individual must have a degree of actual control over the object, coupled with an intent to possess the object and exclude others from possessing it. The law recognizes two types of possession: actual and CONSTRUCTIVE.

Actual possession exists when an individual knowingly has direct physical control over an object at a given time. For example, an individual wearing a particular piece of jewelry has actual possession of it. Constructive possession is the power and intent of an individual to control a particular item, even though it is not physically in that person's control. For example, an individual who has the key to a bank safe-deposit box, which contains a piece of jewelry that she owns, is said to be in constructive possession of the jewelry.

Lost, Mislaid, and Abandoned Property Personal property is considered to be lost if the owner has involuntarily parted with it and does not know its location. Mislaid property is that which an owner intentionally places somewhere with the idea that he will eventually be able to find it again but subsequently forgets where it has been placed. Abandoned property is property to which the owner has intentionally relinquished all rights. See also ABANDONMENT.

Lost or mislaid property continues to be owned by the person who lost or mislaid it. When finding lost goods, the finder is entitled to possession against everyone with the exception of the true owner.

The finder of lost articles on land belonging to someone else is entitled to possession against everyone but the true owner. However, if the finder of the misplaced goods is guilty of TRESPASS, she has no right to their possession. The owner of the place where an article is mislaid has a right to the article against everyone else but the true owner. Abandoned property can be possessed and owned by the first person who exercises control over it with an intent to claim it as his own. In any event, between the finder of a lost, mislaid, or abandoned article and the owner of the place where it is found, the law applies whatever rule will most likely result in the return of the article to its rightful owner.

Ordinarily when articles are found by an employee during and within the scope of her employment, they are awarded to the employer rather than to the employee who found them. See also SCOPE OF EMPLOYMENT.

Treasure trove is any gold or silver in coin, plate, or bullion that is hidden by an unknown owner in the earth or other private place for an extended period. The property is not considered treasure trove unless the identity of the owner cannot be determined. Under early common law, the finder of a treasure trove took TITLE to it against everyone but the true owner. The U.S. law governing treasure trove has been merged, for the most part, into the law governing lost property. In the absence of a contrary statutory provision, the title to treasure trove belongs to the finder against all others with the exception of the true owner. If there is a controversy as to ownership between the true owner and the state, the owner is entitled to the treasure trove.

Confusion and Accession CONFUSION and ACCESSION govern the acquisition of, or loss of title to, personal property by virtue of its being blended with, altered by, improved by, or commingled with the property of others. In confusion, the personal property of several different owners is commingled so that it cannot be separated and returned to its rightful owner, but the property retains its original characteristics. Any FUNGIBLE (interchangeable) goods, such as grain or produce, can be the subject of confusion. See also COMMINGLING.

In accession, the personal property of one owner is physically integrated with the property of another so that it becomes a constituent part of it, losing any separate identity. Accession can make the personal property of one owner become substantially more valuable chattel as a result of the work of another person. This occurs when the personal property becomes an entirely new chattel, such as when grapes are made into wine or timber is made into furniture.

Subject to the doctrine of accession, personal property can become real property through its transformation into a FIXTURE. A fixture is a movable item that was originally personal property but has become attached to, and associated with, the land and therefore is considered a part of the real property. For example, a chandelier mounted on the ceiling of a house becomes a fixture.

GRANITSAS/THE IMAGE WORKS

The items in this home that can be taken up and moved are personal property; *the house, its fixtures, and the land on which it is situated are* real property.

Bailments A BAILMENT is the rightful temporary possession of goods by an individual other than the true owner. The individual who entrusts his property into the hands of another is called the BAILOR. The person who holds the property is called the BAILEE. Ordinarily a bailment is made for a designated purpose upon which the parties have agreed. For example, when a person pawns a diamond ring, she is the bailor and the pawnshop operator is the bailee. The pawnshop owner holds the ring for an agreed period as security on the loan to the bailor. The bailor is entitled to recover possession of the ring by paying back the loan within the time period. If the bailor fails to pay back the loan in time, the bailee gains ownership of the ring and may sell it.

A bailment differs from a sale, which is an intentional transfer of ownership of personal property in exchange for something of value, because a bailment involves only a transfer of possession or CUSTODY, not ownership.

Bona Fide Purchasers The basic common-law principle is that an individual cannot pass better title than she has and a buyer can acquire no better title than that of the seller. Because a thief does not have a title in stolen goods, a person who purchases from the thief does not acquire title.

A BONA FIDE purchaser is an individual who has bought property for value with no notice of any defects in the seller's title. If a seller indicates to a buyer that she has ownership or the authority to sell a particular item, the seller is estopped (prevented) from denying such representations if the buyer resells the property to a bona fide purchaser for value without notice of the true owner's rights. At common law such an ESTOPPEL did not apply when an owner brought an item for services or repairs to a dealer and the dealer wrongfully sold the chattel. The bona fide purchaser, however, is now protected under such circumstances by the UNIFORM COMMERCIAL CODE, which has been adopted in all states.

A buyer who induces a sale through FRAUDULENT representations acquires a VOIDABLE title from the seller. A voidable title may be vacated at the seller's option, upon discovery of the buyer's FRAUD. The seller has the authority to transfer good title to a bona fide purchaser for value without notice of the outstanding equity. The voidable title rule is only applicable in situations where the owner is induced to part with title, not merely with possession, as a result of fraud or deception.

Real Property In the United States every state has exclusive JURISDICTION over the land within its borders. Each state has the power to determine the form and effect of a transfer of real property within its borders. Modern statutes have eliminated much traditional concern over the proper conveyancing of real property. In modern REAL ESTATE law, real property can be conveyed by a DEED, with the intention of the person conveying the property, the GRANTOR, that the deed take effect as a CONVEYANCE. The deed must be recorded to give notice as to who legally holds title to the property.

Estates in Real Property In real property an ESTATE is the degree, nature, and extent of an individual's ownership in real estate. Several types of estates govern interests in real property. These interests include freehold estates, nonfreehold estates, concurrent estates, specialty estates, future interests, and incorporeal interests.

Freehold Estate A FREEHOLD estate is an estate in real property that is of uncertain duration. An individual who is in possession of a freehold estate has SEISIN, which means the right to immediate possession of the land. The two basic types of freehold estates in the United States are the FEE SIMPLE absolute and the life estate. The fee simple absolute is inheritable; the LIFE ESTATE is not.

A fee simple absolute is the most extensive interest in real property that an individual can possess because it is limited completely to the individual and his HEIRS, ASSIGNS forever, and is not subject to any limitations or conditions. The person who holds real property in fee simple absolute can do whatever he wants with it, such as grow crops, remove trees, build on it, sell it, or dispose of it by WILL. The law views this type of estate as perpetual. Upon the death of the owner, if no provision has been made for its distribution, the owner's heirs will automatically inherit the land.

A life estate is an interest in property that does not amount to ownership because it is limited by a term of life, either of the individual in whom the right is VESTED or some other person, or it lasts until the occurrence or nonoccurrence of an uncertain event. A life estate *pur autre vie* is an estate that the GRANTEE holds for the life span of another person. For example, the grantor conveys the property "to grantee for the life of A."

A life estate is usually created by deed but can be created by a LEASE. No special language is required provided the grantor's intent to create such an estate is clear. The grantee of a life estate is called the life tenant.

A life tenant can use the land, take any crops from it, and dispose of his interest to another person. The life tenant cannot do anything that would injure the property or cause waste. Waste is the harmful or destructive use of real property by an individual who is in rightful possession of the property.

The life tenant has the right to exclusive possession subject to the rights of the grantor to enter the property to determine whether waste has been committed, collect any rent that is due, or make any necessary repairs.

A life estate is ALIENABLE, and therefore the life tenant can convey her estate. The grantee of a life tenant would thereby be given an estate *pur autre vie* because the death of the life tenant would extinguish the grantee's interest in the land. The life tenant is unable, however, to convey an estate that is greater than her own.

Nonfreehold Estates Nonfreehold estates are property interests of limited duration. They include tenancy for years, a tenancy at will, and a tenancy at sufferance. This type of estate arises in a landlord and tenant relationship. In such a relationship, a landlord leases land or premises to a tenant for a specific period, subject to various conditions, ordinarily in exchange for the payment of rent. Nonfreehold estates are not inheritable under the common law but are frequently assignable.

A TENANCY for years must be of a definite duration; that is, it must have a definite beginning and a definite ending. The most common example of a tenancy for years is the arrangement existing between a landlord and a tenant, where property is leased or rented for a specific amount of time.

A tenancy from year to year, also called tenancy from period to period, is of indefinite duration. The lease period is for a definite term that is renewed automatically if neither party signifies an intention to terminate the tenancy. This is a common arrangement for leasing business office space or for renting a house or apartment.

A tenancy at will is a rental relationship between two parties that is of indefinite duration because either party may end the relationship at any time. It can be created either by agreement or by failure to effectively create a tenancy for years. A tenancy at will is not assignable and is categorized as the lowest type of chattel interest in land.

A tenancy at sufferance is an estate that ordinarily arises when a tenant for years or a tenant from period to period retains possession of the premises without the landlord's consent. This type of interest is regarded as wrongful possession. In this type of estate, the tenant is essentially a trespasser except that her original entry onto the property was not wrongful. If the landlord consents, a tenant at sufferance may be transformed into a tenant from period to period, once the landlord accepts rent.

Concurrent Estates A CONCURRENT ESTATE exists when property is owned or possessed by two or more individuals simultaneously. The three basic types are JOINT TENANCY, tenancy by the entirety, and tenancy in common.

Joint tenancy is a type of concurrent relationship whereby property is acquired by two or more persons at the same time and by the same instrument. A common example is the purchase of property such as a house by two individuals. The deed conveys title to "A and B in fee absolute as joint tenants." The main feature of a joint tenancy is the RIGHT OF SURVIVORSHIP. If any one of the joint tenants dies, the remainder goes to the survivors, and the entire estate goes to the last survivor.

A tenancy by the entirety is a form of joint tenancy arising between a HUSBAND AND WIFE, whereby each spouse owns the undivided whole of the property, with the right of survivorship. It is distinguishable from a joint tenancy in that neither party can voluntarily dispose of his interest in the property.

A tenancy in common is a form of concurrent ownership in which two or more individuals possess property simultaneously. The individuals do not own an undivided interest in the property, but rather each individual has a definable share of the property. One of the tenants may have a larger share of property than the others. There is no right of survivorship, and each tenant has the right to dispose of his share by deed or will.

Specialty Estates Specialty estates are property interests in CONDOMINIUMS AND COOPERATIVES. Condominium ownership, which was introduced in the United States in 1961 and has grown in popularity, allows separate ownership of individual apartments or units in a multiunit building. The purchaser becomes the owner of a particular unit and of a proportionate share in the common elements and facilities.

In cooperative ownership, the title to a multiunit building usually is vested in a CORPORATION. The purchaser of an apartment in the building buys stock in the corporation, receiving a stock certificate and a lease to the apartment. As a stockholder, each cooperative member has an ownership interest in the corporation, which owns all the units and common areas. Each tenant pays to the corporation a fixed rent, which is applied to a single building MORTGAGE and a real estate tax bill for the entire building, as well as to INSURANCE premiums and maintenance costs.

Future Interests Future interests in real property are property rights that are not yet in existence. The privilege of possession will come into being at a designated future time. There are five basic kinds of future interests: the REVERSION, possibility of reverter, RIGHT OF REENTRY for condition broken (also known as power of termination), EXECUTORY interest, and REMAINDER. See also REVERTER, POSSIBILITY OF.

A remainder is a good example of a future interest. Remainders are subdivided into two principal categories: contingent remainders and vested remainders. A contingent remainder is based on something happening in the future. For example, Tom owns Blackacre in fee simple. While Bob and Jane are alive, Tom conveys Blackacre to Bob for life, with a remainder to the heirs of Jane. The heirs of Jane are not yet known, so they have a contingent remainder.

A vested remainder is a future interest to an ascertained person, with the certainty or possibility of becoming a present interest subject only to the expiration of the preceding property interests. If Tom owns Blackacre in fee simple and conveys Blackacre to Bob for life and then to Jane in fee simple, Jane has a vested remainder in fee that becomes a present interest upon the death of Bob. She simply has to wait for Bob's death before assuming a present interest in Blackacre.

Incorporeal Interests INCORPOREAL interests in real property are those that cannot be possessed physically because they consist of rights of a particular user or authority to enforce various agreements as to use. They include easements, COVENANTS, equitable servitudes, and LICENSES.

Easements are rights to use the property of another for particular purposes. A common type of EASEMENT in current use is the affirmative grant to a telephone company to run its line across the property of a private landowner. Easements also are now used for public objectives, such as to preserve open space and conserve land. For example, an easement might preclude someone from building on a parcel of land, which would leave such property open, thereby preserving a park for the public.

Possession Possession is a property right or interest through which one can exercise dominion or control over something to the exclusion of all others. The owner of real property has the right to exclusive possession of her land, which includes the airspace above and the space below the surface within the exterior boundaries of the property.

An owner of real property is not entitled to possess all space above her land outward to infinity but has the right to be free from those intrusions into the space that would interfere with the reasonable occupation and QUIET ENJOYMENT of the surface. A landowner, therefore, owns as much of the space above the ground as he can possess or use in connection with the land.

Possession of property adverse to the rights of the true owner results in acquisition of title by the possessor under the doctrine of ADVERSE POSSESSION. The doctrine is based upon statutes that limit the time for recovery of property, thereby operating as a bar to one's right to recover property that has been held adversely by another for a specified length of time. For example, if A builds a fence two feet inside B's property and B fails to take legal action to have the fence removed during the specified time period, A will acquire title to the property that the fence encroached.

Eminent Domain and Zoning Governments have the right to acquire privately owned land through the exercise of the power of EMINENT DOMAIN. Eminent domain is the right or power of a unit of government or a designated private individual to take private property for public use, following the payment of a fair amount of money to the owner of the property. The FIFTH AMENDMENT to the U.S. Constitution states, "nor shall private property be taken for public use, without just compensation." The theory behind eminent domain is that the local government can exercise such power to promote the general welfare in areas of public concern, such as health, safety, or morals.

Government may control how real property is used. ZONING is the regulation and restriction of real property by a local government. The most common form of land use regulation, zoning involves the division of territory based on the character of land and structures, and their fitness for particular uses. Municipalities use zoning to control and direct the development of property within their borders, according to present and potential uses of the property. Consideration is given to the conservation of property value and the most appropriate use of the land.

CROSS-REFERENCES

Land-Use Control; Sales Law; Recording of Land Titles; Registration of Land Titles; Title Insurance; Title Search.

PROPERTY RIGHT A generic term that refers to any type of right to specific PROPERTY whether it is personal or real property, tangible or intangible; e.g., a professional athlete has a valuable property right in his or her name, photograph, and image, and such right may be saleable by the athlete.

PROPERTY SETTLEMENT An agreement entered into by a HUSBAND AND WIFE in connection with a DIVORCE that provides for the division of their ASSETS between them.

Property settlements can arise through agreement of the parties, subject to approval by the court, or by court order. Once approved, the settlement functions like a contract for enforcement or modification purposes. Some states use alternate terms to describe a property settlement, such as property agreement, settlement agreement, or separation agreement.

A property settlement involves the property that the couple obtained either before marriage or during marriage. The agreement also may include such issues as MAINTENANCE (otherwise known as ALIMONY) payments to one spouse or even custody of the children.

Two types of property that must be distributed in the settlement are community or marital property, and separate property. Community or marital property consists of property that is purchased by either or both of the spouses during the time they are married. Property bought during the time the couple is married is presumed to be marital property regardless of how it was actually purchased. The assumption can be overridden only by "clear and convincing" evidence of the intent for the property to be the property of just one spouse. Separate property is property that is bought by either of the spouses before the marriage. Separate property can also be property received in exchange for other separate property, the interest on separate property, or anything that does not fall into the category of marital property.

When determining how the property will be divided, several problems may arise, including the problems of COMMINGLING and transmutation. Commingling occurs when separate and marital property are combined, or dealt with together, in a bank or financial account. When this happens, there is no distinction between separate and marital property. To prevent a finding that the commingled property is therefore marital property, the spouses need to keep separate accounts and records for each item of property. Transmutation involves separate property that the spouses have treated as marital property, making it impossible to tell what type of property the spouses had intended it to be. For example, transmutation occurs when the parties took title to property jointly but in reality only one of the spouses paid for the property. The best way to prevent commingling or transmutation from becoming an issue or hurdle in getting the settlement approved is to keep clear and accurate records.

A third problem that can arise relating to the property involved is the valuation date. The valuation date can sometimes determine which spouse receives property because a meaningful change in the value of some assets can affect their just distribution. Several dates can be applied, such as the date of trial, the date of separation, the divorce date, or the hearing date. Once the property is classified as marital or separate property and valued, the parties then must divide it between them.

The Uniform Marriage and Divorce Act (UMDA) guides spouses and courts on what to consider when distributing property. The UMDA has two provisions that deal specifically with the disposition of the couple's property. One explains that the property should be fairly divided between the parties without regard to "marital misconduct." It lists factors to consider when apportioning the property, such as the "duration of the marriage, and prior marriage of either party, antenuptial agreement of the parties, the age, health, station, occupation, amount and sources of income, vocational skills, employability, estate, liabilities, and need of each of the parties, custodial provisions, whether the apportionment is in lieu of or in addition to maintenance, and the opportunity of each for future acquisition of capital assets and income." Contribution of the spouses to the family is also a consideration. The specific facts of each case must be examined to reach a fair and just division of property.

KINDRA CLINEFF/THE PICTURE CUBE

The sometimes heavy and awkward burden of dividing possessions in connection with a divorce is often governed, if not eased, by a property settlement, which functions as a contract.

The other option given by the UMDA outlines a slightly different scheme of how property should be divided. First, each spouse's separate property is given to the appropriate spouse, then the rest of the property (the COMMUNITY PROPERTY) is divided without consideration of "marital misconduct." The factors to consider when making a division of the community property include the "contribution of each spouse to the acquisition of the marital property, including contribution of a spouse as homemaker; value of the property set aside to each spouse; duration of the marriage; and economic circumstances of each spouse when the division of property is to become effective." This option retains the distinction between property bought before the marriage (separate property) and property bought during the marriage (community property). Many states have adopted some form of these tests for their courts to use when dividing property at divorce.

Once an agreement is decided upon, the property settlement has the same enforceability as a contract.

The settlement will usually be upheld by the courts unless it is found to be invalid. A court will rule that a property settlement is invalid if it is unconscionable, which means that the agreement is so unfair to one party that it must be modified. Whether an agreement is unconscionable is determined by the facts in each case. An unconscionability finding can be based on several factors relating to property settlement. Lack of disclosure by one of the parties can be one reason to find an agreement unfair. For example, if, when the parties met to discuss and divide their assets, one spouse did not reveal the existence of a particular asset, the other spouse, who later locates or hears of the asset after the property settlement has been approved, may seek to have the settlement overturned on the basis that he or she did not know of the asset at the time of the settlement. The court may modify the settlement to avoid further injustice to one party.

Another factor that could lead a court to find a settlement unfair is whether each party had independent counsel. Independent counsel is recommended when there is a large disparity between the parties' wealth. Independent counsel means that both parties choose their own counsel; if just one party selects counsel, the court could consider counsel to be nonindependent. Lack of disclosure and lack of independent counsel are two of the most common reasons why a court will find a settlement unfair to one of the parties.

The court may also find a property settlement unenforceable because of mistake, fraud, or undue influence. If the parties make a genuine mistake about the terms of the settlement, the court can reform or modify the settlement to correct that mistake. Fraud and undue influence are also reasons to alter or modify a property settlement. If one spouse fraudulently informs the other of property or assets during the process of negotiating the settlement, that can be grounds for modifying the settlement. Undue influence means that one party used pressure or misrepresentations to force the other to sign or agree to the terms in the property settlement. When a court finds either fraud or undue influence, it modifies the property settlement to correct the unfairness.

Property settlements should be fair both in the process of reaching the settlement, avoiding any unconscionability or fraud, and in the division of the property, making an equal separation of the total marital assets. If the settlement is fair between the parties, the court is likely to enforce it.

PROPONENT One who offers or proposes.

A proponent is a person who comes forward with an a item or an idea. A proponent supports an issue or advocates a cause, such as a proponent of a WILL.

PROPOUND To offer or propose. To form or put forward an item, plan, or idea for discussion and ultimate acceptance or rejection.

PROPRIETARY As a noun, a proprietor or owner; one who has the exclusive TITLE to a thing; one who possesses or holds the title to a thing in his or her own right; one who possesses the dominion or ownership of a thing in his or her own right.

As an adjective, belonging to ownership; owned by a particular person; belonging or pertaining to a proprietor; relating to a certain owner or proprietor.

Proprietary refers to ownership or characteristics relating to ownership. It describes all the rights that the owner of property can exercise. Proprietary articles are items that are manufactured and marketed under an exclusive right.

MUNICIPAL CORPORATIONS have a proprietary function, a term describing the duty or capacity of a city to enter into business ventures or to perform discretionary acts in the best interests of the citizens. Proprietary functions differ from governmental functions, which are duties that a city performs as a political subdivision of a state.

PRO RATA [*Latin, Proportionately.*] A phrase that describes a division made according to a certain rate, percentage, or share.

In a BANKRUPTCY case, when the DEBTOR is insolvent, CREDITORS generally agree to accept a *pro rata share* of what is owed to them. If the debtor has any remaining funds, the money is divided proportionately among the creditors, according to the amount of the individual DEBTS.

A *pro rata clause* in an automobile INSURANCE policy provides that when an insured person has other insurance policies covering the same type of risk, the company issuing the policy with the pro rata clause will be liable only for a proportion of the loss represented by the ratio between its policy limit and the total limits of all the available insurance.

PRORATE To divide proportionately. To adjust, share, or distribute something or some amount on a PRO RATA basis.

PROROGATION Prolonging or putting off to another day. The discontinuation or termination of a session of the legislature, parliament, or the like. In English law, a prorogation is the continuance of the parliament from one session to another, as an adjournment is a continuation of the session from day to day. In CIVIL LAW, giving time to do a thing beyond the term previously fixed.

PRO SE For one's own behalf; in person. Appearing for oneself, as in the case of one who does not retain a lawyer and appears for himself or herself in court.

PROSECUTE To follow through; to commence and continue an action or judicial proceeding to its ultimate conclusion. To proceed against a defendant by charging that person with a crime and bringing him or her to trial.

The state, on behalf of the people, generally prosecutes a defendant accused of a crime.

See also PROSECUTOR.

PROSECUTOR One who prosecutes another for a crime in the name of the government.

State and county governments employ prosecutors to represent their local communities in COMPLAINTS against criminal defendants. On the federal level, the president appoints prosecutors to represent the United States in complaints against criminal defendants.

In some states a prosecutor must present the court with a written statement of the charges, called an INFORMATION. In other states a prosecutor is required to convene a GRAND JURY before charging a DEFENDANT with a serious crime. A grand jury is a collection of laypersons selected by the prosecutor to examine EVIDENCE and decide whether to indict the defendant and so authorize prosecution. On the federal level, the FIFTH AMENDMENT requires prosecutors to obtain an INDICTMENT for capital or "otherwise infamous" crimes, with the exception of crimes arising out of active military service.

In most criminal cases, the prosecutor must match wits with the defense attorney who represents the defendant. Almost all criminal defendants are represented by an attorney, even if they cannot afford to pay for one. If a court does not offer legal representation to a criminal defendant, the defendant may not be incarcerated upon conviction.

Prosecutors have a broad discretion in determining whether to PROSECUTE a criminal defendant. A prosecutor does not have to personally believe beyond a REASONABLE DOUBT that the defendant committed the alleged act. A prosecutor must simply possess enough evidence to support a reasonable belief that the defendant committed the crime.

There are two notable limits on the prosecutor's discretion to prosecute. First, a prosecutor may not base a prosecution on "an unjustifiable standard such as race, religion, or other arbitrary classification" (*Oyler v. Boles*, 368 U.S. 448, 82 S. Ct. 501, 7 L. Ed. 2d 446 [1962]). For example, a prosecutor may not selectively prosecute only Chinese persons who violate laws regulating laundry facilities (*Yick Wo v. Hopkins*, 118 U.S. 356, 6 S. Ct. 1064, 30 L. Ed. 220 [1886]).

Second, a prosecutor may not vindictively add charges because a defendant has pursued a constitutionally protected right (*Blackledge v. Perry*, 417 U.S. 21, 94 S. Ct. 2098, 40 L. Ed. 2d 628 [1974]). For example, assume that a defendant is convicted at TRIAL but that the conviction is reversed on APPEAL. If the prosecutor seeks to retry the defendant, the prosecutor may not, without more evidence, charge the defendant with more serious charges than the defendant faced in the first trial. A prosecutor may threaten a defendant with a more serious charge if the defendant refuses to plead guilty to a lesser criminal charge, but only if the prosecutor has evidence to support the more serious charge (*Bordenkircher v. Hayes*, 434 U.S. 357, 98 S. Ct. 663, 54 L. Ed. 2d 604 [1978]).

Prosecutors hired by the government are the only persons empowered to prosecute criminal cases. Private parties may lodge criminal complaints against persons or groups, but under state and federal statutes, only a duly authorized attorney may prosecute a criminal case. Federal and state governments can prohibit unauthorized persons from prosecuting other persons because the control of criminal prosecutions is a legitimate interest of government (*Leeke v. Timmerman*, 454 U.S. 83, 102 S. Ct. 69, 70 L. Ed. 2d 65 [1981]). This rule is sensible because it allows the government to prevent the judicial system from becoming more overburdened.

Prosecutors have many duties to perform in the course of a criminal prosecution. At the arraignment—the defendant's first appearance before the court—the prosecutor must make a BAIL recommendation. Bail is the amount of money that the defendant must pay the court to gain release from jail. Release for a fraction of bail may be obtained if a criminal defendant pays a BAIL BONDS company which promises to pay the bail if the defendant does not show for future court appearances. A prosecutor may recommend that the court deny bail to an allegedly dangerous defendant to keep the defendant in jail while the case is being processed.

The prosecutor must prepare the case against the defendant. She does this by reviewing the evidence, conducting an investigation, and communicating with police officers. The prosecutor may issue directives to law enforcement personnel to find more evidence. The prosecutor also must notify the defendant of the evidence against him and must turn over any exculpatory evidence (evidence that would tend to clear the defendant) that the prosecutor possesses.

The prosecutor usually meets with the defendant or the defendant's attorney in advance of trial to discuss the case. Considering the vast number of criminal laws passed by state and federal legislatures, defendants usually face more than one criminal charge for any given criminal episode. The ability to bring multiple charges gives prosecutors a measure of bargaining power over criminal defendants. Prosecutors often are willing to drop certain charges and recommend lesser sentences for defendants who agree to plead guilty to a certain crime. This practice is called PLEA BARGAINING.

If the defendant does not wish to plead guilty, the prosecutor usually must defend the legitimacy of the prosecution at various stages before trial. In FELONY cases the prosecutor may be required under law to obtain permission from a grand jury before she or he can prosecute the defendant. A grand jury is a panel of individuals that can reject a criminal prosecution for lack of evidence. If the grand jury returns a NO BILL, the defendant is not indicted and the case against the defendant must be dropped. If the grand jury returns a TRUE BILL, the defendant is indicted and the prosecution may proceed.

Few criminal defendants proceed to trial. More than 90 percent of all criminal prosecutions are disposed of through plea bargaining. Those criminal defendants who do proceed to trial usually mount challenges prior to trial based on the legality of evidence gathering and the sufficiency of the evidence against them. Defendants may make requests of the court. For instance, a defendant may request that the trial be moved to a different geographic location, or a defendant may ask the court to forbid the trial participants from talking to the media. The prosecutor also may challenge evidence offered by the defendant and make certain requests of the court. These challenges and requests are made in pretrial MOTIONS and HEARINGS. If the prosecutor does not rebut or respond to the defendant's arguments regarding the evidence, the court may dismiss the case before it goes to trial.

At trial the prosecutor must prove, BEYOND A REASONABLE DOUBT, that the defendant committed the alleged criminal acts. The prosecutor must make an OPENING STATEMENT, present evidence and TESTIMONY, and make a CLOSING ARGUMENT. Both the prosecutor and defense attorney have the right to cross-examine witnesses and to challenge the introduction of certain testimony and other evidence. Ultimately, the court decides what evidence will be admitted into the trial and what evidence will be excluded. If the defendant is convicted, the trial judge imposes a sentence. The prosecutor may make a SENTENCING recommendation, but the court is not obliged to follow the recommendation.

In theory, a prosecutor's job is not to convict and send to prison as many persons as possible. The basic function of a prosecutor is to seek the truth about criminal actions. Thus, if a prosecutor discovers evidence that puts the defendant's guilt in doubt or relieves the defendant of criminal liability, the prosecutor must turn that evidence over to the defendant. If a prosecutor lacks evidence of a defendant's guilt, he or she must drop the charges or decline to press charges. In practice, prosecutors find that they are judged in the court of public opinion on the number of convictions that they obtain.

In any event, a prosecutor does not decide whether to convict a defendant. That decision is made by the fact finder: either the JUDGE in a BENCH TRIAL, or the JURY in a jury trial. The prosecutor only decides whether to charge the defendant and then presents the community's case to the fact finder.

Scholars disagree on the precise historical origins of the U.S. prosecutor. The modern version of the professional prosecutor likely derives from the European practice of vesting one office with the power to conduct criminal prosecutions. In England, private parties could prosecute other private parties until the eighteenth century, but English statutes creating the office of public prosecutor existed as far back as the mid-sixteenth century. In colonial America all thirteen colonies established the office and position of attorney general. The colony's attorney general was charged with prosecuting crimes committed within the colony. Private prosecutions were carried out at times, but private prosecution ended around the beginning of the American Revolution in the 1770s. Historians have attributed the rise of the public prosecutor to the cost associated with private prosecutions. Few persons in colonial America had the time or resources to prosecute an alleged criminal.

The primacy of the public prosecutor became entrenched in the 1820s as the U.S. public began to press for the introduction of democracy into the criminal justice process. States began to allow the election of judges, and laws allowing the election of a prosecutor followed shortly thereafter. In 1832 Mississippi became the first state to include a provision in its constitution providing for the election of local prosecutors. Every state entering the Union after 1850 provided for either the election or employment of public prosecutors, and the position is now deeply rooted in the federal and state criminal justice systems.

Originally, public prosecutors were considered mere figureheads in the criminal justice system. Local SHERIFFS and even CORONERS had more say in the process than did the prosecutor. This situation changed by the mid-nineteenth century as more and more prosecutors were elected by the public rather than hired by the local government. The powers of the prosecutor gradually increased until the 1920s, when a drastic increase in crime led to heightened public scrutiny of the office and revelations that prosecutors were being corrupted by organized criminals. By the 1940s most states had enacted statutes creating licensing requirements for the office of prosecutor. Under these statutes a person who is not licensed to practice law may not perform the work of the prosecutor even if the person has won the election. Most states also created a regular office of prosecutor instead of hiring private attorneys to work as part-time prosecutors. The power of the prosecutor's office has increased ever since.

Prosecutors now have more authority than ever before. They have the authority to investigate persons, grant IMMUNITY to WITNESSES and accused criminals, and plea bargain with defendants. Prosecutors decide what criminal charges to bring and when and where a person will answer to those charges. Courts rarely second-guess the decisions of a prosecutor, and all courts presume that a prosecutor has acted appropriately. Furthermore, prosecutors enjoy immunity from suit for their official actions. They may be forced to defend against a suit for MALICIOUS PROSECUTION only if they blatantly exceed the powers of their office. A prosecutor who fabricates testimony or other evidence, for instance, may be held liable in a civil suit for malicious prosecution.

CROSS-REFERENCES

Criminal Law; Criminal Procedure; Pretrial Conference; Right to Counsel.

PROSPECTUS A document, notice, circular, advertisement, letter, or communication in written form or by radio or television that offers any security for sale, or confirms the sale of any security.

A prospectus is a document or a publication by, or on behalf of, a CORPORATION containing information on the character, nature, and purpose of an issue of shares, DEBENTURES, or other corporate securities that extends an invitation to the public to purchase the securities. The content of a prospectus is regulated by federal law. It must contain all material facts relating to the company and its operations so that a prospective investor can make an informed decision as to the merit of the investment. A prospectus must be furnished to an investor before any purchase is made.

PROSTITUTION The act of offering one's self for hire to engage in sexual relations.

Prostitution is illegal in all states except Nevada, where it is strictly regulated. Some state statutes punish the act of prostitution, and other state statutes criminalize the acts of soliciting prostitution, arranging for prostitution, and operating a house of prostitution. On the federal level, the MANN ACT (18 U.S.C.A. § 2421 [as amended 1986] makes it a crime to transport a person in interstate or foreign commerce for the purpose of prostitution or for any other immoral purpose.

Prostitution, historically and currently a trade largely practiced by women, was not a distinct offense in colonial America. A prostitute could be arrested for vagrancy if she were loitering on the streets, but generally, the act of engaging in sex for money was not itself a crime.

The first prostitution statutes were enacted during the so-called Progressive political movement of the late nineteenth and early twentieth centuries. Urban areas experienced unprecedented growth during this period. Cities became the centers of industrial manufacturing and production, and they were quickly ravaged by disease and poverty. The Progressive movement emphasized education and instituted new government controls over the activities of the general population. The movement introduced the PROHIBITION of ALCOHOL, which was banned from 1919 to 1933, vested government with increased power over the lives of poor persons, and created a host of new criminal laws, including laws on prostitution. Prostitution increased during this period, and it was seen as one of the biggest threats to public health because of its potential to spread debilitating venereal diseases such as syphilis and gonorrhea. Prostitutes were viewed as moral failures. The male customers of prostitutes were not held up to scorn, but the women who practiced prostitution were seen as responsible for increases in crime and the general decay of social morals.

Commercial Sex: Repression or Legalization?

IN FOCUS

In the United States, forty-nine of the fifty states make prostitution a crime. The only exception is Nevada, which permits brothels to operate in specific areas of the state. Since the 1970s advocates of reform have called for either the legalization or the decriminalization of prostitution. Proponents see these approaches as a way of preventing women from being punished for making a choice on how they want to earn an income. Opponents of these changes dismiss the idea that women voluntarily choose this type of work and claim that prostitution is yet another part of the U.S. commercial sex industry, which systematically subordinates women.

Proponents of decriminalization argue that it would remove the stigma associated with prostitution and increase profits. They contend that decriminalization would also relieve the police of the costly and futile effort to stop an unstoppable practice.

Legalizing prostitution would mean regulating it. Supporters contend that this would allow the government to collect millions of dollars annually in taxes, reduce collateral crime, and protect the public from sexually transmitted diseases. Proponents point to Nevada, where the use of brothels facilitates testing for diseases and reduces the number of street prostitutes.

Other supporters of decriminalization and regulation challenge what they see as the paternalistic argument that women need to be protected from sexual exploitation. This argument, they claim, is nonsensical because it means that to protect women from exploitation, society must imprison them for engaging in prostitution.

In addition, those who favor decriminalization note that the worst form of exploitation suffered by prostitutes is from pimps. If prostitution were legal, women would generally conduct business on their own, free from the parasitic and abusive conduct of pimps.

Decriminalization supporters also cite the difference between the lax policing of off-street prostitutes and the harsh treatment of street prostitutes. These observers argue that the enforcement disparity is a matter of race and class: most street prostitutes are members of historically oppressed groups, whereas off-street prostitutes generally have middle-class backgrounds. They argue that it is unfair for society to tolerate and even promote escort services while regularly jailing street prostitutes.

Opponents of legalization of prostitution have traditionally based their opposition on the immorality of commercial sex. However, modern feminist thought has developed other arguments against the removal of legal barriers to selling sex.

Many feminists have attacked the "career-choice" argument. They see it as a corruption of feminist values that otherwise favor the economic liberty of women. They contend that, from a limited range of options constrained by economics, education, sexual harassment, and abuse, the decision to sell one's body cannot be deemed a choice. Even if a woman makes a conscious decision to enter prostitution, this does not redeem the trade from being the worst form of gender-based exploitation.

The "choice" argument is also undercut, argue the opponents of legalization, by the fact that the average prostitute starts working at the age of fourteen and suffers sexual abuse, drug dependency, violence at the hands of customers, and emotional control by pimps. From this point of view, women are victims of commercial sex work.

More radical feminist critics of legalization argue that prostitution, like pornography, is an example of the unequal status of women in the United States. The right to privacy arguments advanced by legalization proponents may sound reasonable, contend critics, but they mask the systematic subordination of women. Noted feminist legal scholar Catharine A. MacKinnon has defined pornography as "the graphic sexually explicit subordination of women, whether in pictures or words," especially in a violent or degrading context. Prostitution is worse than pornography, contend these critics, because women are subjected to sex in violent and degrading contexts.

For these more radical critics of legalization and decriminalization, making commercial sex legal would legitimize the subordinated position of women in U.S. society. Just as the legalization of casino gambling has caused a dramatic increase in the number of people gambling and the amount of money wagered, the legalization of prostitution would give the commercial sex industry the opportunity to legitimately expand. Critics argue that in a consumer culture already permeated with sexual imagery, legalization is not the answer.

Legalization critics have acknowledged, however, that prostitutes are prosecuted for their acts while their male customers usually are not. In the 1980s and 1990s, many state and local governments have sought to end this double standard by enacting laws that target customers of prostitutes. This legislation has also been triggered by residents of local communities who have grown tired of enduring the presence of customers who visit their neighborhoods. These so-called anti-john laws seek to discourage customers by impounding their cars, and, in some cases, notifying their spouses of their arrest.

Many police departments have also increased their use of police decoys—officers disguised as prostitutes who lure unsuspecting customers into arrest. In addition, customers who have been arrested may find their names listed in the local newspaper or photographs broadcast on a local cable television station.

It is unlikely that prostitution will be legalized or decriminalized because few politicians would relish being associated with so morally explosive an issue as commercial sex. It is also unlikely, given prostitution's persistence throughout history, that efforts by law enforcement to prosecute prostitutes and their customers will bring an end to prostitution.

See also Feminist Jurisprudence; MacKinnon, Catharine.

Hollywood Madam

The Los Angeles prostitution prosecution and conviction of Heidi Fleiss, dubbed the Hollywood Madam by the press, raised issues that went beyond the sensational elements of the case. Feminist groups criticized Los Angeles prosecutors for continuing the familiar pattern of targeting female prostitutes while ignoring their male customers.

Heidi Fleiss, the daughter of a prominent California pediatrician and a schoolteacher, was arrested in June 1993 for running an expensive call-girl business. Fleiss was charged with pandering, or providing prostitutes to customers. It was alleged that seventy women worked for her and that her clients included Hollywood actors, U.S. politicians, and rich foreign businessmen.

The tabloid press had made Fleiss a minor celebrity before her arrest by occasionally discussing her and publishing photographs of her. Her notoriety led the Los Angeles police to conduct a "sting" operation, in which an officer posed as a customer, hiring prostitutes at a rate of $1,500 each for a supposed party. When the women arrived for the party, they and Fleiss were arrested.

In the months that followed, titillating details emerged about Fleiss and her alleged customers. At one point Fleiss offered to reveal the names of the wealthy men who used her services if she was paid $1 million. As the case neared trial, her attorney alleged that Fleiss had been selectively prosecuted and that her male customers, whose names were in her address book, would not be charged with any crimes.

The judge dismissed Fleiss's arguments, and she was convicted of pandering on December 2, 1994. The Los Angeles chapter of the National Organization of Women and some feminists charged that the failure to prosecute the rich and powerful customers demonstrated the double standard at work in the criminal justice system regarding prostitution offenses.

In the nineteenth and early twentieth centuries, states began to encourage the arrest of prostitutes for such crimes as vagrancy and loitering. Congress passed the Mann Act in 1910, which criminalized interstate prostitution, and state legislatures made prostitution a distinct criminal offense. The prostitute, not the customer, was the first to be penalized on the state and local levels; statutes that criminalized the solicitation of prostitution were passed later.

Historically, the enforcement of prostitution laws focused on apprehension of the prostitute. In the 1960s and 1970s, perhaps as a result of heightened social discourse on the issue of prostitution, police departments became more vigilant in their pursuit of customers. Local police in urban areas now regularly conduct "sting" operations designed to catch solicitors through the use of undercover agents posing as prostitutes. Many states have FORFEITURE statutes that give law enforcement agencies the power to seize and gain ownership of vehicles used by customers of prostitutes, and alleged customers may find their pictures published in the local newspaper.

All jurisdictions have made their prostitution statutes gender-neutral, but the prostitution relationship still usually consists of a man paying a woman for sex. There are occasional variations of the sexual identities of the participants in contemporary society, but, by and large, a prostitute is still more likely to be a woman or a girl. An increasing amount of prostitution occurs off the street by organized escort services, and prostitutes from these services have some measure of control over their lives. However, many prostitutes still work on the street, living a desperate, brutal, dangerous life at the mercy of a promoter, or PIMP. Because the prostitute usually is a woman or a girl, and because prostitution can wreak havoc on the life of the prostitute, the issue of prostitution has become a matter of concern for WOMEN'S RIGHTS advocates.

See also PANDER; SEX OFFENSES; VICE CRIMES.

PRO TANTO [*Latin, For so much; for as much as one is able; as far as it can go.*] A term that refers to a partial payment made on a claim.

In an EMINENT DOMAIN case, *pro tanto* describes the partial payment made by the government for the taking of land. This payment is given WITHOUT PREJUDICE, and the petitioner can maintain an ACTION for the full amount of the land.

A *pro tanto defense* is a defendant's COUNTERCLAIM against the plaintiff for one-half the requested DAMAGES.

PROTECTIONISM See IMPORT QUOTAS.

PROTECTIVE CUSTODY An arrangement whereby a person is safeguarded by law enforcement authorities in a location other than the person's home because his or her safety is seriously threatened.

When a WITNESS to a crime is intimidated not to TESTIFY because the alleged perpetrator or her associates have threatened physical violence against the witness or the witness's family, law enforcement authorities have the ability to offer the witness protective custody. Protective custody may last only until the end of a trial or it may last for several years. State and federal governments operate witness protection programs that provide assistance to those who wish to cooperate but who are afraid of physical retaliation.

Until the 1960s law enforcement used protective custody infrequently. Federal prosecution of ORGANIZED CRIME figures led to the offering of witness protection to key government informers. In 1964 Joseph Valachi became the first La Cosa Nostra member to publicly testify to the existence of the organized crime group, appearing before a congressional committee. Valachi, who was facing the death penalty, agreed to testify in return for personal protection. He was held in solitary confinement for protection and given $15 a month.

Since the 1970s the Federal Witness Security Program (18 U.S.C.A. § 3521 [1970]) has grown in size. The program is used to fight organized crime, TERRORISM, gang-related crime, and narcotics trafficking. In 1995, 141 new participants were added to the program, increasing the number to 6,580 witnesses and 14,845 total participants since the program began. Also in 1995, 257 protected witnesses testified at trials against organized crime members, resulting in a substantial number of convictions.

Under the program, the U.S. attorney general is authorized to offer security to key witnesses who have physical safety concerns. The program, which is administered by the U.S. Marshals Service, provides a new Social Security number and other documents to enable the person to establish a new identity. It also provides housing, transportation of household goods to a new residence, payments to meet basic living expenses, employment assistance, and other services necessary to assist the person in becoming self-sustaining. The witness's immediate family or a person closely associated with the witness may be provided similar assistance under the program.

In return for this assistance, the witness and family members over eighteen years of age must each sign a memorandum of agreement. The witness must agree to testify and provide information to law enforcement officials. In addition, the person must agree not to commit any crime and to take all necessary steps to avoid detection. Most witnesses remain in the program for two years before pursuing their new lives on their own.

Many states have adopted similar programs for witnesses. This type of protection, however, has come under increased scrutiny. Because witnesses who are convicted criminals are given new identities and moved to new locations, local law enforcement agencies have no knowledge that potentially dangerous persons are in their communities. Murder and other serious crimes have been committed by persons assisted through witness protection.

These programs have also been challenged because a number of high-profile criminals have received favorable treatment. Some drug dealers have been allowed to keep their narcotics-generated money and have avoided prison in return for their TESTIMONY against others involved in drug trafficking. Critics argue that it makes no sense to have the government pay to relocate drug dealers and to ensure their safety. Defenders of the program argue that this is a necessary price to pay to convict more powerful crime figures.

Witness protection programs also exist in prisons. To protect witnesses serving a PRISON sentence, the federal government has created witness protection units within federal prisons. Protected witnesses live a more comfortable life than other prisoners, which includes having free and unlimited access to telephones and cable television and the ability to use their own money to buy food, appliances, jewelry, and other items.

Aside from these witness protection programs, prisons also have protected custody units for inmates who are targets of ASSAULT or victims of SEXUAL HARASSMENT. Although conditions vary greatly in protected custody units from one institution to another, life is more restricted than in the general prison population. Some large prisons have separate protective custody facilities, but in most jails and prisons an inmate has protective custody status while housed in administrative segregation. This means that the inmate is restricted to his cell twenty-three hours a day and must take meals there as well.

PROTECTIVE ORDER A court order, direction, decree, or command to protect a person from further harassment, SERVICE OF PROCESS, or DISCOVERY.

A protective order can limit the time and place where a DEPOSITION can be taken, restrict the inspection of documents in the possession of a party, or regulate or modify the enforcement of a JUDGMENT.

PROTECTORATE A form of international guardianship that arises under INTERNATIONAL LAW when a weaker state surrenders by TREATY the management of some or all of its international affairs to a stronger state.

The extent of the reciprocal rights and duties between the protecting state and the protected state depends upon the terms of the treaty and the conditions under which other states have recognized the protectorate. Although it loses some of its independence, the protected state still exists as a state in international law and may avail itself of some of the rights of a state. Its diplomatic representatives may still enjoy normal immunities within the courts of other states, for instance, and a treaty concluded by the protecting state with a third state is not necessarily binding on the protected state.

PRO TEM [*Latin, For the time being.*] An abbreviation used for *pro tempore,* Latin for "temporary or provisional."

A person who acts as a temporary substitute serves *pro tem.* The term is often used to describe the acting head of a governing body, such as the president *pro tem* of the Senate, who presides over the Senate when the vice president is unable to do so.

PROTEST A formal declaration whereby a person expresses a personal objection or disapproval of an act. A written statement, made by a notary, at the request of a holder of a BILL or a NOTE that describes the bill or note and declares that on a certain day the instrument was presented for, and refused, payment.

A protest is generally made to save some right that would be waived unless a negative opinion was expressly voiced. Taxes are often paid under protest, an action by which a taxpayer reserves the right to recover the amount paid if he has sufficient evidence to prevail.

The document states the reasons for the refusal and provides for the notary to protest against all parties to the instrument declaring that they can be held liable for any loss or damages. A notice of protest is given by the holder of the instrument to the DRAWER or endorser of the instrument.

PROTHONOTARY A title given to the principal CLERK of a court.

PROTOCOL A brief summary; the minutes of a meeting; the etiquette of diplomacy.

Protocol refers to a summarized document or the minutes of a meeting that are initialed by the parties present to indicate the accuracy of the document or minutes.

Protocol is a section of the department of state that is responsible for advising the government, the president, the vice president, and the secretary of state on matters of diplomatic procedure governed by law or international custom and practice. Protocol is the method of officially ranking or receiving government officials.

PROVINCE The district into which a country has been divided; as, the province of Ontario in Canada. More loosely, a sphere of activity or a profession such as medicine or law.

PROVISIONAL Temporary; not permanent. Tentative, contingent, preliminary.

A provisional CIVIL SERVICE appointment is a temporary position that fills a vacancy until a test can be properly administered and statutory requirements can be fulfilled to make a permanent appointment.

BILL BURKE/IMPACT VISUALS

In a more colloquial sense, a protest is a public demonstration of disapproval of a policy of or action by an organization or individual. Here striking newspaper workers protest the hiring of replacement workers.

PROVISO A condition, stipulation, or limitation inserted in a document.

A condition or a provision in a DEED, LEASE, MORTGAGE, or CONTRACT, the performance or nonperformance of which affects the validity of the instrument. It generally begins with the word *provided.*

A proviso clause in a statute excepts something from statutory requirements, qualifies the statute, or excludes some potential area of misinterpretation.

PROVOCATION Conduct by which one induces another to do a particular deed; the act of inducing rage, anger, or resentment in another person that may cause that person to engage in an illegal act.

Provocation may be alleged as a defense to certain crimes in order to lessen the severity of the penalty normally imposed. For example, provocation that would cause a reasonable person to act in a HEAT OF PASSION—a state of mind where one acts without reflection—may result in a reduction of a charge of MURDER to a charge of voluntary MANSLAUGHTER.

PROXIMATE CAUSE An act from which an injury results as a natural, direct, uninterrupted consequence and without which the injury would not have occurred.

Proximate cause is the primary cause of an injury. It is not necessarily the closest cause in time or space nor the first event that sets in motion a sequence of events leading to an injury. Proximate cause produces particular, foreseeable consequences without the intervention of any independent or unforeseeable cause. It is also known as legal cause.

To help determine the proximate cause of an injury in NEGLIGENCE or other TORT cases, courts have devised the "but for" or "SINE QUA NON" rule, which considers whether the injury would not have occurred but for the defendant's negligent act. A finding that an injury would not have occurred but for a defendant's act establishes that the particular act or omission is the proximate cause of the harm, but it does not necessarily establish LIABILITY since a variety of other factors can come into play in tort actions.

Some JURISDICTIONS apply the "substantial factor" formula to determine proximate cause. This rule considers whether the defendant's conduct was a substantial factor in producing the harm. If the act was a substantial factor in bringing about the damage, then the defendant will be held liable unless she can raise a sufficient defense to rebut the claims.

PROXY A representative; an AGENT; a document appointing a representative.

A proxy is a person who is designated by another to represent that individual at a meet-

A sample proxy statement

__________, INC.
Smith Building
1000 Main Street
Spur, Texas 77111

NOTICE OF ANNUAL MEETING OF SHAREHOLDERS
TO BE HELD ON OCTOBER 23, 1997

September 17, 1997

To the Shareholders of
__________, INC.

The annual meeting of the shareholders of __________, Inc. will be held in the Presidential Ballroom of The Longhorn Hotel, 2000 Steer Street, Spur, Texas, on Thursday, October 23, 1997, at 9 A.M., Spur time, for the following purposes:

1. To elect a Board of Directors for the ensuing year;
2. To act upon the recommendation of the Board of Directors that __________ be elected and approved as independent public accountants to examine the Company's accounts for the current fiscal year; and

A sample proxy statement (continued)

3. To transact such other business as may properly come before the meeting or any adjournments thereof.

The Board of Directors has fixed the close of business on September 3, 1997, as the record date for determining shareholders entitled to notice of and to vote at the meeting.

You are cordially invited to attend the meeting in person. Even if you plan to attend the meeting, however, you are requested to sign, date and return the accompanying proxy as soon as possible.

By Order of the Board of Directors

S. A. JAMES, Secretary

The Company has approximately 11,500 Common Shareholders, a substantial number of whom own less than 100 shares. To insure a proper representation at the meeting if you cannot attend in person, it is important that, regardless of the amount of your holdings, you fill out, sign and return the enclosed proxy promptly. A return envelope is enclosed for your convenience.

PROXY STATEMENT

This Proxy Statement and the accompanying form of proxy are being mailed on or about September 17, 1997 in connection with the solicitation by the management of __________ Inc. (the "Company") of proxies to be used at the annual meeting of its shareholders to be held on October 23, 1997, and any and all adjournments thereof, for the purposes set forth in the accompanying notice of the meeting. When proxies are returned properly executed, the shares represented thereby will be voted. If the proxy is signed without a vote indicated in the boxes, the shares will be voted for the election as directors of the nominees named herein and in favor of the election and approval of __________ as independent public accountants to examine the Company's accounts for the current fiscal year. If a choice has been specified, however, the shares will be voted accordingly. A shareholder giving a proxy may revoke it at any time before it is voted at the meeting. In addition, a shareholder who attends the meeting may, if he wishes, vote by ballot at the meeting, thereby cancelling any proxy vote previously given.

The Company will pay the cost of soliciting proxies. In addition to the solicitation of proxies by mail, proxies may also be solicited by telephone, telegram, or personal interview by regular employees of the Company. The Company will reimburse brokerage houses and other nominees for their reasonable expenses in forwarding proxy material to beneficial owners of stock.

Whether you can attend the meeting or not, your proxy vote is important. Shares can be voted at the meeting only if the owner is present or is represented by proxy. Accordingly, it is requested that you sign and return the enclosed proxy in the envelope provided.

The principal executive offices of the Company are located in the Smith Building, 1000 Main Street, Spur, Texas 77111.

VOTING OF SHARES

Only shareholders of record at the close of business on September 3, 1997, are entitled to notice of and to vote at the meeting. At such date the Company had outstanding 4,017,281 shares of Common Stock. Each share entitles the owner of record on the record date to one vote per share on all questions submitted to shareholders.

[*continued on page 214*]

A sample proxy statement (continued)

I

ELECTION OF DIRECTORS

There are eleven directors to be elected. It is intended that the persons named in the following tabulation will be placed in nomination, and the persons named in the accompanying proxy will vote in favor of the election of such nominees, unless contrary instructions are set forth on the proxy. Each nominee is a member of the present Board of Directors. The terms of office of all directors to be elected at this annual meeting will be until the next annual meeting of shareholders and their successors are elected and qualified. The persons named in the proxy may act with discretionary authority if any nominee should become unavailable for election, although management is not aware of any circumstances likely to render any nominee unavailable. The following information has been furnished by each nominee.

Name and Principal Occupation	Served as Director Continuously Since	Shares of Common Stock Owned Beneficially at August 29, 1997
Jordy W. Evans . . . . Chairman of the boards of directors of _____ Company, _____, Inc., _____, Inc., _____, Inc., and _____ Company, subsidiaries of the Company, and Vice Chairman of the Board of the Company.	1990	69,706

[Portions omitted for purpose of illustration.]

Remuneration—The following tabulation sets forth information regarding each director and each of the three highest paid officers of the Company whose aggregate direct remuneration from the Company exceeded $180,000 during the year ended June 30, 1997, the aggregate direct remuneration paid to all persons who served as directors and officers of the Company during that period, in each case for the portion of the period in which they served as such, the estimated annual benefits to be paid upon retirement under the existing retirement plan and Company contributions under the existing stock purchase plan.

Name or Identity of Group	Capacities in Which Remuneration Was Received	Aggregate Direct Remuneration	Estimated Annual Benefits Under Retirement Plan	Annual Rate of Contributions Under Employee Stock Purchase Plan
Jackson C. Browne	Chairman of the Board, President and Chief Executive Officer, Director	$169,337	$60,242	$5,450

[Portions omitted for purpose of illustration.]

Stock Option Information—The 1993 Stock Option Plan and the 1996 Stock Option Plan (the "Plans") for officers and other key employees of the Company and its subsidiaries provide for the grant of five-year, qualified stock options, and ten-year, non-qualified stock options, to purchase Common Stock of the Company, in each case at an option price not less than the market value of the Common Stock on the date of grant.

As of August 29, 1997, there were outstanding qualified stock options covering 450 shares of the Common Stock and exercisable at an average option price of $52.66, which had been granted to officers under the Plans. The following tabulation sets forth certain information regarding the persons listed under "Remuneration," above, and all directors and officers of the Company as a group, with respect to non-qualified stock options granted to such persons under the Plans:

A sample proxy statement (continued)

Non-qualified Options:

	Granted since June 30, 1996		Exercised since June 30, 1996			Outstanding as of August 29, 1997	
	Shares	Aver. Option Price	Shares	Aggregate Purchase Price	Aggregate Market Value on Date of Purchase	Shares	Aver. Option Price
Jackson C. Browne	86,400	$12.90	—	—	—	86,400	$12.90

[Portions omitted for purpose of illustration.]

II

ELECTION AND APPROVAL OF INDEPENDENT AUDITORS

The Board of Directors has approved and recommends ________ for election and approval by the meeting as independent public accountants to examine the Company's accounts for the current fiscal year. Representatives of ________, the independent public accountants of the Company for the year ended June 30, 1997, are expected to be present at the meeting with the opportunity to make a statement, if they desire to do so, and to respond to appropriate questions. The election and approval of ________ requires the affirmative vote of a majority of the shares of Common Stock present or represented and entitled to vote at the meeting. The persons named in the accompanying proxy intend to vote the proxy in favor of such election and approval, unless contrary instructions are set forth on the proxy.

The Board of Directors is aware that there are currently pending investigations and lawsuits involving various major accounting firms and has considered the fact that several such actions are pending against ________. After such consideration, the Board recommends the continuation of this firm as independent auditors of the Company's accounts. The members of the Audit Committee of the Board of Directors are Messrs. Babe M. Carruth, J. O. Willis and R. B. Schramm.

ANNUAL REPORT

The Annual Report to shareholders, including financial statements, for the fiscal year ended June 30, 1997, has been mailed to all shareholders. The Annual Report is not a part of the proxy solicitation material.

OTHER BUSINESS

The Management does not intend to bring any business before the meeting other than the matters referred to in the accompanying notice and at this date has not been informed of any matters that may be presented to the meeting by others. However, if any other matters properly come before the meeting, it is intended that the persons named in the accompanying proxy will vote pursuant to the proxy in accordance with their best judgment on such matters.

By Order of the Board of Directors,
S. A. JAMES, Secretary

Dated: September 17, 1997

ing or before a public body. It also refers to the written authorization allowing one person to act on behalf of another.

In corporate law, a proxy is the authority to vote STOCK. This authority is generally provided by the charter and bylaws of a CORPORATION or by a state statute. If authority is not provided, a stockholder cannot vote by proxy. The record owner of the stock whose name is registered on the corporate books is the only individual who can delegate the right to vote. In the absence of an express requirement, no particular form is necessary for a proxy. It must, however, be evidenced by a sufficient written grant of authority. A proxy is not invalid if minor errors or omissions appear on the document.

Generally any power that a stockholder possesses at a corporate meeting can be delegated to a proxy. An ordinary proxy can vote on regular corporate business, such as the amendment of the bylaws. The proxy is not authorized to vote, however, on extraordinary corporate business, such as a merger, unless given special authority to do so. When a proxy acts within the scope of her authority, under AGENCY principles, the stockholder is bound as if she acted in person.

A proxy can be revoked at any time, unless it is coupled with an interest or made expressly irrevocable. The sale of a stockholder's shares automatically revokes any proxies previously given to vote those shares. A proxy can also be revoked when the stockholder gives a subsequent proxy or attends the meeting in person. A stockholder can act as a proxy for another shareholder, but it is not necessary for a proxy to be a stockholder.

PRUDENT PERSON RULE A standard that requires that a FIDUCIARY entrusted with funds for investment may invest such funds only in securities that any REASONABLE individual interested in receiving a good return of income while preserving his or her capital would purchase.

Historically known as the prudent or reasonable man rule, this standard does not mandate an individual to possess exceptional or uncanny investment skill. It requires only that a fiduciary exercise discretion and average intelligence in making investments that would be generally acceptable as sound.

PUBLIC As a noun, the whole body politic, or the aggregate of the citizens of a state, nation, or municipality. The community at large, without reference to the geographical limits of any corporation like a city, town, or county; the people.

As an adjective, open to all; notorious. Open to common use. Belonging to the people at large; relating to or affecting the whole people of a state, nation, or community; not limited or restricted to any particular class of the community.

PUBLIC ADMINISTRATIVE BODIES Agencies endowed with governmental functions.

Public administrative agencies are created by statute and only the legislature has the authority to provide for their creation. The statutory provisions that create the administrative agencies and confer functions on them determine the character of the agencies. In general, agencies represent the people and act as guardians of the PUBLIC INTEREST, not the interests of private persons. As an incident to the performance of their public functions, however, agencies can decide issues between private parties or private rights.

Administrative agencies are extensions of the legislative branch of the government and can perform acts of a legislative or quasilegislative nature. Agencies can also be part of the EXECUTIVE BRANCH of government and can be empowered to deal with matters within the scope of executive power.

Administrative agencies are continuing organizations, unaffected by changes in personnel. Ordinarily final actions of administrative officers or bodies within the scope of their authority are binding on their successors.

All persons are equally eligible to hold an administrative office unless they are excluded by some constitutional or statutory disqualification. The legislature usually establishes the qualifications of those who are to hold administrative offices. The qualifications must be reasonable in light of the functions and duties of the office. The tenure and term of administrative officers are indicated in the statute. Generally an official is entitled, and sometimes required, to hold office until a qualified successor is chosen. The power to remove an official is derived from the sovereign power of the state and is indispensable in obtaining good administration of public activities. An officer should be removed only according to law. If the office is held at the pleasure of the appointing AGENCY, the incumbent can be removed without notice or hearing.

Generally when authority is conferred on an administrative body composed of three or more members, the authority can be exercised by less than all the members, provided all had notice of the meeting and an opportunity to attend. Membership on an ADMINISTRATIVE BOARD ordinarily includes the right to vote, and statutory provisions governing the method of voting should be observed. The number of members for effective action is usually fixed by statute and action by a QUORUM is necessary. Unless provided by statute, the authority cannot be exercised by a solitary member, or less than a majority. A statutory requirement that a quorum be present is a jurisdictional one that cannot be waived; the action of less than a quorum is void in such a case.

In the interest of orderly procedure and certainty, administrative bodies keep MINUTES or written records of all proceedings and actions. Administrative agencies speak through their

AP/WIDE WORLD PHOTOS

Those whose rights are affected by administrative action are entitled to seek remedies. The operator of this dam claimed that a plan by the Federal Energy Regulatory Commission to reintroduce certain species of fish to the river would make operating the dam unprofitable.

records, and the minutes must be truthful, clear, and precise. In contested cases when an administrative agency acts in a quasi-judicial capacity, the record should contain a summary of the facts and circumstances presented and the reasons for any administrative actions.

Administrative bodies have an inherent right to amend their records. When records are incorrect, they can be changed to reflect the truth. Typographical or clerical errors can be corrected at any time.

Records should be open for inspection by persons who have some real or proper interest in them, such as the parties to a proceeding. When the records are made public, no particular reason has to be demonstrated for inspecting them, since such records can be examined out of mere curiosity. The right of inspection, however, is subject to reasonable regulation.

LIABILITY for the expenses of an ADMINISTRATIVE AGENCY is usually regulated by statute. The legislature can also grant the agency the exclusive power to fix the fees for expenses incurred in the performance of its duties.

Administrative officers and agencies have no COMMON LAW or inherent JURISDICTION of powers. Custom or USAGE cannot invest administrative officers, agencies, or bodies with authority. Their powers are wholly derived from, and limited by, the constitution, a statute, or some other legislative enactment. In addition to the express powers, the officials and agencies have whatever implied powers are reasonably necessary to effectuate the express powers and duties.

An administrative agency that originally acquires jurisdiction over a particular matter ordinarily has EXCLUSIVE jurisdiction as against an agency with CONCURRENT JURISDICTION, and no coordinate body has any right to interfere. An administrative body, however, can perform its duties in matters over which it has exclusive jurisdiction in cooperation with other public bodies and officials.

When the power and jurisdiction of federal and state agencies conflict or overlap, the federal authority is supreme and will prevail. Where Congress has preempted a particular field and has granted exclusive power over it to a federal agency, the power of a state is suspended, and a state agency has no jurisdiction, even when the particular matter sought to be administered by the state agency has not been addressed by the federal agency. The mere enactment of a federal statute authorizing a federal agency to act in a certain field does not preclude a state from enacting a statute on the same general subject and creating a state agency for its enforcement. When Congress in enacting a statute has not preempted an area, a state board or official, acting under a state statute, can assume jurisdiction and act.

As a general rule, administrative agencies or officers are not civilly liable for the consequences of their acts, when acting in GOOD FAITH within the scope of proper authority. An officer is not responsible for DAMAGES if he makes a mistake of fact in exercising discretion or an error in ascertaining and deciding on the facts of a case, or if the law is misconstrued or misapplied.

Similarly, an administrative officer is not liable for the wrongful acts or omissions of subordinates, unless she directed, authorized, or cooperated in them. Liability also results when damages occur as a result of an official acting outside her scope of jurisdiction and without legal authorization.

When exercising their powers, administrative agencies must keep within the scope of the powers granted to them. They are powerless to act contrary to the provisions of the law, and they must follow the standards established by statute. They cannot ignore or transgress the statutory limitations on their power, even to accomplish what they believe to be worthwhile goals. Acts or orders that do not fall within the powers granted are wrong and void.

Persons whose rights are affected by administrative action are entitled to an impartial action free from BIAS, PREJUDICE, or personal interest. When an individual or a group claims that an administrative act adversely affects a right, a presumption exists in favor of the legality and regularity of official acts of administrative officers and agencies. It is presumed that they act within the limits of the authority conferred on them and that facts exist that justify the administrative action.

Investigations by administrative agencies or officials are informal proceedings to obtain information to govern future action. They are not proceedings in which action is taken against anyone. An administrative investigation is comparable to a GRAND JURY investigation where WITNESSES are compelled to appear and TESTIFY.

An administrative body can be required to make certain investigations, such as when a public service commission is required to investigate the activities of a PUBLIC UTILITY. A board might also be authorized to exercise its discretion in determining when an investigation is to be made.

The form of the investigation usually depends on the nature of the question to be decided and the type of data that is needed. Investigations are ordinarily held in private, and they must be conducted so that harmful publicity will not result or influence the final outcome. In the course of its investigation, a board can review official documents and can supplement this means of inquiry by private correspondence and by conducting personal research.

Investigations by administrative agencies or officials have no parties as found in a lawsuit or criminal prosecution, and usually, there is no need to give notice of the investigation. An administrative body or official can issue a SUBPOENA requiring a witness to appear and to testify at an investigation. In addition, a subpoena can be issued for the production of any books, papers, or other documents that are relevant to the inquiry. The subpoena is void when it does not indicate that the evidence to be produced is germane to the inquiry. A person must respond to a subpoena to the best of his ability. Compliance with a subpoena is enforceable by a court order.

Although hearings can be held, as a general rule, a hearing is not an integral part of an investigation by an administrative body or official.

An administrative body or official is not bound to conduct an investigation under the strict rules of EVIDENCE required for courts, but particular evidence, such as HEARSAY evidence, has been held to be INADMISSIBLE. Witnesses can be called in an investigative proceeding and their TESTIMONY can be taken, subject to CROSS-EXAMINATION. Witnesses can even be entitled to the presence and advice of COUNSEL. The costs and expenses of an investigation can be assessed against the particular persons or CORPORATIONS involved, particularly if the complaining party receives an adverse decision.

Public administrative bodies promulgate rules and regulations. Their authority to do so and the guidelines under which the agencies perform these duties are governed by administrative law and administrative procedure.

See also ADMINISTRATIVE LAW AND PROCEDURE.

PUBLICATION Making something known to the community at large, exhibiting, displaying, disclosing, or revealing.

Publication is the act of offering something for the general public to inspect or scrutinize. It means to convey knowledge or give notice.

In COPYRIGHT law, publication is making a book or other written material available to anyone interested by distributing or offering it for sale. In the law of LIBEL AND SLANDER, publication means communicating the statement in issue to a third person other than the plaintiff (the individual whom the alleged defamatory statement concerns).

Publication of a WILL refers to the TESTATOR's informing the WITNESSES to the document of his or her intent to have the instrument operate as a will.

In the procedural rules governing the practice of law, publication of a SUMMONS is the process of publishing it in a newspaper, when required by law, in order to notify a defendant of the lawsuit.

See also PUBLISHING.

PUBLIC CONTRACT An AGREEMENT to perform a particular task to benefit the community at large that is financed by government funds.

Federal, state, and local governments enter into CONTRACTS to purchase goods and services. The construction of public buildings, HIGHWAYS, bridges, and other structures is governed by a well-defined contractual process of competitive bidding that seeks to protect the public against the squandering of public funds and prevent abuses such as FRAUD, favoritism, and extravagance.

A public contract is a legally enforceable commitment of a party to undertake the work or improvement desired by a public authority. Public contracts are largely governed by the general law of contracts. Private individuals and CORPORATIONS are held to stricter standards in their dealings with the government than in their private dealings. Conversely the government must deal fairly with those who contract with it. It can enter contracts within the limitations imposed by constitutional and statutory provisions. In addition, federal laws must be observed because most public projects receive financial aid from the federal government.

Awarding Contracts The method by which contracts are awarded is ordinarily regulated by statute or constitutional provision, and the prescribed method must be followed. For significant expenditures of public funds, government bodies usually must use a bidding process. In the awarding or letting of public contracts, the public body invites bids or makes "requests for proposals" so that it can award the contract to the bidder who qualifies under the terms of the governing statute. The submission of a bid in response to an invitation is considered an offer, and although it may not be freely withdrawn prior to acceptance, it does not become a contract unless and until such time as it is accepted by the proper public authority. A bid that does not respond to the terms contained in the invitation to bid is not within statutory requirements but is considered to be a new proposition or a counterproposal.

Competitive Bidding For major government expenditures, such as construction of public buildings and highways, government bodies require competitive bidding, which is a well-defined public process of letting a contract. Competitive bidding is a means of preventing political graft and corruption because the public nature of the process discourages favoritism and fraud. The integrity of the process is a central goal of competitive bidding. If a public official or employee is later found to have had an interest in a public contract, the agreement is void and unenforceable, and the interested parties may be subject to criminal prosecution.

To provide bidders with an opportunity to bid competitively on the same work, the appropriate public authorities must adopt plans and specifications that definitely set the extent and type of the work to be done and the materials to be furnished. The public entity itself must prepare these plans and specifications, and it must provide all prospective bidders with the same specifications from which to prepare their bids. The specifications must not be drafted so as to restrict bidding to a single bidder unless it is clearly essential to the public interest to do so.

The plans and specifications cannot be changed once an invitation for bids or the bids themselves have been made unless all bidders are notified so that they have an opportunity to bid under new conditions. In making specifications, the public authority has wide discretion concerning the particular equipment or product that it might require as part of the contract. For example, it might designate a specific product covered by a patent held or manufactured only by one bidder.

Once the plans and specifications are prepared, the public entity must publish a public notice of its intentions to receive bids. This notice does not constitute an OFFER but is merely a solicitation of offers. An invitation to bid should indicate the deadline for bids to be submitted. It must be explicit in order to facilitate intelligent bidding.

Certain conditions are required of bidders. There might be a requirement that bids be properly signed and accompanied by a financial statement of the bidder. Customary additional requirements are a certificate attesting that the bidder has not colluded with others in the submission of the bid, and a BOND or other security, which is conditioned on the making of a contract and the performance of work according to the contract.

A contractor's bond requires the contractor to pay a certain amount of money to the public authority if the obligations in the bond are not fulfilled. The bond contains two obligations: one for the faithful performance of the contract and the other for the protection of the right of laborers and material handlers to be paid.

A bid for the construction of public works must be in substantial and material conformity to the details contained in the bid specifications. All matters concerning the substance of the competitive bid, such as those that might affect price, quantity, quality, or manner of performance, must conform with the details indicated in the specifications. Failure to substantially comply will result in rejection of the bid, and a contract entered into based on such a bid is invalid.

A bid may be accepted if it contains minor or immaterial deviations from the specifications. Whether a deviation is material and substantial is determined by whether the bid limits fair competition by providing the deviating bidder with a substantial advantage or benefit not enjoyed by other bidders, a QUESTION OF FACT decided in light of all the circumstances of the case.

Once the time for filing bids expires, the bidder is bound by the bid as filed, which cannot be altered. A MATERIAL defect cannot be corrected after the bids have been opened, but a minor defect can. If necessary information is missing from a bid when it is opened, it cannot be supplied then or later by a private understanding between the bidder and the public authority.

In general, an individual who files a bid cannot withdraw it. The benefits that will accrue to a bidder under the public bidding statutes are viewed as adequate CONSIDERATION to make a bid irrevocable. Some statutes, however, permit a bidder to withdraw a bid at any time prior to its acceptance. Withdrawal is generally allowed if a bidder makes an honest and GOOD FAITH mistake in calculation that has a material effect upon the substance of the contract. A bidder can withdraw a bid only if he was reasonably prompt in providing notice of the error to the public authority or if the public authority will not suffer substantial hardship when the bid is withdrawn.

Once the public authority opens the bids, it must review them within a reasonable period to determine if one should be accepted. A bid must be accepted for the formation of a public contract to occur. An ACCEPTANCE and award of the contract to a bidder must be on the terms advertised because PUBLIC POLICY proscribes granting to a successful bidder or her subcontractor a benefit that was not extended to others who submitted bids. A public body can be granted the right by statute, or it can reserve in the advertisement of bids the right to reject any and all bids, but it cannot do so arbitrarily or without GOOD CAUSE. A typical reason for rejection of all bids is that the bid amounts exceed the public funds allocated for the project.

Ordinarily the award of a public contract under a competitive bidding statute must be to the lowest bidder unless facts establish that another bid, although higher, is the lowest one made by a responsible bidder. The lowest responsible bidder is the contractor whose bid was in substantial conformity to the plans and specifications and who is able to perform the work at the lowest cost. The dollar amount of a contractor's bid is only one factor in determining the lowest responsible bidder. The government unit must also consider a bidder's experience, prior dealings with the government body, reputation for satisfactory work, and intention to employ local labor. The fact that a low bidder has demonstrated delay, lack of cooperation, or poor performance on prior contracts supports a finding that the person is not the lowest responsible bidder.

Since the 1970s public contracts let by competitive bidding have been subject to AFFIRMATIVE ACTION requirements. The federal Public Works Employment Act (42 U.S.C.A. § 6701 et seq.), enacted in 1977, imposed certain conditions on public projects that receive financial assistance from the federal government. The most controversial provision prohibits any local public works project from being granted federal assistance unless at least 10 percent of its work goes to minority business enterprises. A minority business enterprise is a business in which minority group members own at least a 50 percent interest or, in the case of a publicly owned business, 51 percent of the stock is owned by minorities. When a bid is submitted, it must be accompanied by a statement that the bidder has taken steps to include the involvement of minorities in the project. The U.S. Supreme Court, in *Fullilove v. Klutznick*, 448 U.S. 448, 100 S. Ct. 2758, 65 L. Ed. 2d 902 (1980), upheld the constitutionality of the 10 percent requirement, holding that the set-aside provided a way for groups previously subjected to discrimination to achieve equal economic opportunity. However, in *City of Richmond v. J. A. Croson Co.*, 488 U.S. 469, 109 S. Ct. 706, 102 L. Ed. 2d 854 (1989), the Supreme Court struck down a set-aside program for minority contractors. The Court concluded that these types of affirmative action programs can only be justified to remedy prior government DISCRIMINATION instead of past societal discrimination. Thus, if it cannot be shown that a city discriminated against minorities in the past, the set-aside program is an unconstitutional preference.

Legal Challenges to Awarding of Public Contracts A low bidder is ordinarily entitled to reasonable NOTICE and a HEARING prior to rejection of the bid unless the bidder has blatantly failed to comply with a specific contract provision, such as the minority contractor requirement. Unsuccessful bidders can start lawsuits that challenge the rejection of their bids and the awarding of a public contract to another bidder. Because public contracts are matters of public interest, taxpayers can also contest the award of a contract.

The courts ordinarily will not interfere with an action of a public official or body in accepting or rejecting bids and awarding a contract, provided that the official or organization made it fairly and honestly, in good faith, and in the interest of the public. An award that was made arbitrarily or capriciously or as result of favoritism or fraud will be subjected to judicial scrutiny. There should be a reasonable time interval between the opening of the bids and the execution of a public contract to allow a disappointed bidder to bring any complaint before a court for JUDICIAL REVIEW.

Contracts executed by public officers who do not have the authority to make contracts are VOID and unenforceable. A contract is void if the bidder has failed to comply with competitive bidding requirements. A contractor has the responsibility to learn whether the contract complies with the law. In general, once the courts declare a public contract void, the contractor cannot recover unpaid claims, but the government can recover any payments it made under the contract. A public entity may be obligated to pay the REASONABLE value of the benefits received under a void contract but only in the absence of a statutory prohibition against such arrangements.

Contractual Rights of the Parties A public contract can be assigned by one contractor to another where the ASSIGNMENT is restricted to funds due under the contract. However, it is not assignable without the consent of the public body with which the contract is made. A contractor and his or her assignee are both bound by the terms of the main contract. The contractor cannot transfer by assignment anything that was not allowed under the main contract. The law can provide that no assignment is valid unless copies of the contract and the assignment are filed with the court administrator in the county where the public works project is located.

A contractor can employ SUBCONTRACTORS to perform certain portions of the work. For example, in the construction of a public building, a contractor will typically hire an electrical and a mechanical subcontractor, along with subcontractors who do cement work, roofing, and painting. A subcontractor enters an agreement with an original contractor to perform part of the work that the contractor has agreed to perform in the original contract.

A public authority has the inherent right to make reasonable and necessary changes or modifications in public contracts, according to a new agreement between the contracting parties. A public contract can also contain a provision governing its cancellation or termination under certain conditions. A public authority generally cannot lawfully RESCIND its contract without the contractor's consent, except in the case of fraud, MISTAKE, or the invalidity of the contract.

A contractor is bound to the contract as agreed, and a failure to observe it will make the contractor liable for breach of contract. The contractor is entitled to recover for work completely or substantially performed in compliance with the contract. Where a substantial performance of a contract has taken place with the use of defective materials or faulty workmanship, the defects must be corrected if practicable. If correction is not possible or practicable, the contractor will be awarded the contract price reduced by the difference between the value of the defective work and its value if completed according to the terms of the contract.

A public contractor can be compensated for additional work that results from authorized changes in the plans and specifications, as well as for extra work or materials required because conditions differ from their representation in the plans and specifications. Oftentimes contractors realize the bulk of their profit from such "change orders."

When a contractor does not complete the job within the time specified, she or he has committed a breach of the contract. Some public contracts contain penalty clauses, which assess the contractor a certain amount of money for each day past completion. On the other hand, road and bridge contracts may contain clauses that reward a contractor for finishing the project ahead of schedule.

PUBLIC DEFENDER 📖 An attorney appointed by a court or employed by the government to represent indigent defendants in criminal actions. 📖

See also RIGHT TO COUNSEL.

PUBLIC DOMAIN 📖 Land that is owned by the United States. In COPYRIGHT law, literary or creative works over which the creator no longer has an exclusive right to restrict, or receive a ROYALTY for, their reproduction or use but which can be freely copied by the public. 📖

See also PUBLIC LANDS.

PUBLIC FIGURE 📖 A description applied in LIBEL AND SLANDER actions, as well as in those alleging invasion of PRIVACY, to anyone who has gained prominence in the community as a result of his or her name or exploits, whether willingly or unwillingly. 📖

If a plaintiff in a libel or slander action qualifies as a public figure, he or she must show that the libelous or slanderous conduct of the defendant was motivated out of actual malice as required in the case of *New York Times Co. v. Sullivan*, 376 U.S. 254, 84 S.Ct. 710, 11 L.Ed.2d 686 (1964).

PUBLIC FORUM See FREEDOM OF SPEECH.

PUBLIC HEALTH SERVICE The Public Health Service is the operating division of the Department of Health and Human Services (HHS) responsible for promoting the protection and advancement of the nation's physical and mental health.

The Public Health Service was first established by Act of July 16, 1798 (ch. 77, 1 Stat. 605), which authorized the creation of hospitals to care for U.S. merchant seamen. Subsequent legislation has substantially broadened the scope of its activities, and today the Public Health Service accomplishes its goals through a number of agencies and programs. These entities coordinate and implement national health policy on the state and local levels, conduct medical and biomedical research, and enforce laws to ensure the safety of drugs and medical devices and to protect the public against impure foods and cosmetics.

M. SCHWARZ/THE IMAGE WORKS

The Centers for Disease Control and Prevention in Atlanta is the federal government's chief instrument for responding to public health emergencies, but it also develops programs to prevent and control the spread of disease.

Agency for Health Care Policy and Research The Agency for Health Care Policy and Research was established by the Omnibus Budget Reconciliation Act of 1989 (42 U.S.C.A. § 299 et seq.). As the federal government's focal point for health services research, the agency produces and disseminates information about the quality, medical effectiveness, and cost of health care. The agency's research is geared toward producing useful and accurate data concerning the design and performance of the national health care system, data that can be used to help improve health care at the federal, state, and local levels.

Centers for Disease Control and Prevention The Centers for Disease Control and Prevention (CDC) was established as an operating health agency within the Public Health Service by the secretary of health, education, and welfare (the predecessor agency of HHS) on July 1, 1973. The CDC is responsible for providing leadership in the prevention and control of diseases and for responding to public health emergencies. In consultation with state and local health care authorities, the CDC develops and administers national programs to help prevent and control the spread of communicable and preventable diseases and to prevent chronic diseases. The agency also directs and enforces foreign quarantine activities and provides consultation to other nations on the control of preventable diseases. Since the early 1980s, the CDC has been at the forefront of the federal government's efforts to control the spread of AIDS, uncovering vital information about the disease, discovering effective treatments, and working toward a cure.

Agency for Toxic Substances and Disease Registry The Agency for Toxic Substances and Disease Registry was established on April 19, 1983, by the secretary of HHS. The agency is charged with carrying out the health-related responsibilities of the Comprehensive Environmental Response, Compensation, and Liability Act of 1980 (42 U.S.C.A. § 9601 et seq.) and other federal laws concerned with the release of toxic substances into the environment. It directs programs designed to protect the public and workers from exposure to hazardous substances and their adverse health effects; collects, analyzes, and disseminates data relating to serious diseases resulting from exposure to toxic or hazardous substances; establishes and maintains listings of areas either closed to the public or restricted in use because of toxic substance contamination; and helps the ENVIRONMENTAL PROTECTION AGENCY identify hazardous waste substances requiring regulation. It also works with private and public health care organizations to provide medical care and testing to individuals who may have been exposed to hazardous substances. See also ENVIRONMENTAL LAW.

Food and Drug Administration The FOOD AND DRUG ADMINISTRATION (FDA), in existence under various other titles since 1907, is one of the oldest and most influential health-related agencies within the Public Health Service. The FDA is charged with protecting the health of the nation against unsafe foods, drugs, medical devices, and cosmetics. The FDA carries out its mission through a number of centers and offices that perform a large variety of tasks, including testing and evaluating drug products for safety and effectiveness; developing standards ensuring the quality and nutritional value of foods; and testing and labeling medical devices before they are made available for use by the public.

Health Resources and Services Administration The Health Resources and Services Administration is responsible for addressing, within the Public Health Service, issues related to the access, quality, and cost of health care. The administration works with states and communities to help deliver health care to underserved areas and groups with special needs, including migrant workers, mothers and children, homeless people, immigrant populations, and individuals living in rural areas. In addition, the administration plays a key role in the federal government's campaign against AIDS, administering provisions of the Ryan White Comprehensive AIDS Research Emergency Act of 1990 (Ryan White CARE Act) (Pub. L. No. 101-381, 104 Stat. 576 [codified in scattered sections of 42 U.S.C.A.]). Through the act, the administration funds the establishment of centers to train health service professionals caring for AIDS patients and supports the renovation of health facilities serving AIDS patients. The administration also administers the National Organ Transplant Act, 42 U.S.C.A. §§201 note, 273, 274, 274a to 274e, serving as a resource for individuals seeking information about the availability and procurement of donor organs and bone marrow.

A number of bureaus within the Health Resources and Services Administration provide additional services. The Bureau of Primary Health Care administers a variety of programs related to the recruitment and training of health professionals to work in areas traditionally underserved by doctors, nurses, and other medical personnel. For example, the bureau administers the National Health Service Corps Scholarship and Loan Repayment programs, which provide financial assistance to medical, dental, and nursing students in exchange for service in areas where there is a shortage of health professionals. The Maternal and Child Health Bureau (MCH) develops and coordinates federal policies to improve health care delivery and services for mothers and children. MCH also administers grants to implement maternal and child health service programs on the state level, as well as other programs to help reduce infant mortality.

Indian Health Service The health status of American Indians and Alaska Natives is the concern of the Indian Health Service, which is the principal federal health care advocate for these groups. The Indian Health Service administers a comprehensive health care delivery system for these groups, developing and managing programs to meet their health needs. The service also helps Native American tribes obtain and use health care through other federal, state, and local programs.

National Institutes of Health The National Institutes of Health (NIH) is the principal biomedical research agency of the federal government. Within the NIH, a number of institutes conduct research in specific areas. The National Cancer Institute was created to carry out the objectives of the National Cancer Act, 42 U.S.C.A. §§ 201 note, 218, 241, 281 note, 282 to 284, 286 note, 286a to 286g, which made the conquest of cancer a national goal. The laboratories of the Cancer Institute conduct research to find effective methods for the prevention, treatment, and eventual cure of all types of cancers. The National Heart, Lung, and Blood Institute conducts research into the uses of blood and the management of blood resources, in addition to administering programs related to the prevention and treatment of hypertension, stroke, respiratory illnesses, and sickle cell anemia. Other institutes conduct research in the areas of ALCOHOL and drug abuse, mental health, communication and neurological disorders, and aging. The National Library of Medicine is the nation's chief source of medical information. The library makes medical research databases such as MEDLINE and TOXLINE, as well as other resources, available to public and private agencies, organizations, and individuals.

CROSS-REFERENCES

Acquired Immune Deficiency Syndrome; Drugs and Narcotics; Health Care Law; Immunization Programs.

PUBLIC INTEREST Anything affecting the rights, health, or finances of the public at large.

Public interest is a common concern among citizens in the management and affairs of local, state, and national government. It does not mean mere curiosity but is a broad term that refers to the body politic and the public weal. A PUBLIC UTILITY is regulated in the public interest because private individuals rely on such a company for vital services.

PUBLIC LANDS Land that is owned by the United States government.

Public land refers to the public domain, unappropriated land belonging to the federal government that is subject to sale or other disposal under general laws and is not reserved for any particular governmental or public purpose.

Much of this land was acquired early in the history of the United States as a result of purchases, wars, or treaties made with foreign countries. The federal government used this land to encourage growth, settlement, and economic development. Land that was not developed, homesteaded, or sold remained in federal ownership as public land. Today, the federal government employs principles of land use planning and environmental protection to preserve the natural resources and scenic beauty found on public land.

PUBLIC LAW A general classification of law concerned with the political and sovereign capacity of a state.

Public law is that area of constitutional, administrative, criminal, and international law that focuses on the organization of the government, the relations between the state and its citizens, the responsibilities of government officials, and the relations between sister states. It is concerned with political matters, including the powers, rights, capacities, and duties of various levels of government and government officials.

Public law refers to an act that applies to the public at large, as opposed to a PRIVATE LAW that concerns private individual rights, duties, and liabilities.

Public law is the citation given to the original form of federal and some state laws. For example, the citation for the Economic Recovery Tax Act of 1981 is Pub. L. 97–34, Aug. 13, 1981, 95 Stat. 1720 (26 U.S.C.A. § 1 et seq.).

PUBLIC OFFERING An issue of SECURITIES offered for sale to the public.

A business can raise capital for its enterprise through the sale of securities, which include STOCKS, BONDS, notes, DEBENTURES, or other documents that represent a share in the company or a DEBT owed by the company. When a company proceeds to issue the securities, it is called an OFFERING.

There are two types of offering: private and public. A private offering is made to a limited number of persons who are so well-informed about the affairs of the company that the company does not need to file a registration statement with the state or federal government. In contrast, a public offering is made to the public at large and is governed by federal and state regulations.

Until the 1930s the public offering of securities was subject to minimal regulation. Investors had no reliable way of knowing whether the information they received about a public offering was correct and complete. Because of the lack of regulation, FRAUDULENT public offerings were common, leading to the sale of worthless stock.

The Securities Act of 1933 (15 U.S.C.A. § 77a et seq.), enacted after the stock market crash of 1929 and the resulting Great Depression, set in place rules and regulations for public offerings of securities in interstate commerce or through the mails. Before a public offering can be made, a company must file with the SECURITIES AND EXCHANGE COMMISSION a registration statement containing financial and other data, including the price at which shares will be offered to the public, commissions paid to those who underwrite the security, and any OPTIONS to purchase that have been issued.

In addition to requiring the filing of a registration statement, the Securities Act of 1933 makes it unlawful to mail or transmit in interstate commerce any security for the purpose of sale or delivery unless it is preceded or accompanied by a PROSPECTUS (a written statement of information about the public offering) that fully discloses all material facts regarding the investment, including the financial status of the enterprise. Material facts are those that are necessary to enable a purchaser to weigh the advantages and disadvantages of the investment. The BALANCE SHEET contained in the prospectus must accurately reflect the financial status of the issuing company and should include its ASSETS and LIABILITIES.

Unless a company files a registration statement that is then approved by the commission, it cannot legally make the public offering. Registration of the securities does not imply that the commission has approved the issue or that it has found the registration disclosures to be accurate. It does mean that persons filing false or incomplete information with the commission subject themselves to the risk of fine or imprisonment or both. Additionally, those persons connected with making a false or incomplete registration statement or prospectus may be liable for DAMAGES to purchasers of the securities.

Intrastate securities (those not publicly offered in interstate commerce) are governed by the laws of the state in which the stock is traded. State control of intrastate securities traffic does not conflict with federal regulation of interstate transactions. Most states have enacted BLUE SKY LAWS, which regulate public offerings in a manner similar to federal securities legislation. These state laws get their name from their attempt to stop the sale of stock in fraudulent and speculative enterprises that have nothing to offer but blue sky. Many states require registration of securities before a public offering can be made. If the business seems likely to commit fraudulent acts involving prospective purchasers of its securities, state registration will be denied, and the public offering will not be allowed to go forward.

PUBLIC POLICY A principle that no person or government official can legally perform an act that tends to injure the public.

Public policy manifests the common sense and common conscience of the CITIZENS as a whole that extends throughout the state and is applied to matters of public health, safety, and welfare. It is general, well-settled public opinion relating to the duties of citizens to their fellow citizens. It imports something that fluctuates with the changing economic needs, social customs, and moral aspirations of the people. Public policy enters into, and influences, the enactment, execution, and interpretation of legislation.

PUBLIC UTILITIES Businesses that provide the public with necessities, such as water, ELECTRICITY, natural GAS, and telephone and telegraph communication.

A public utility is a business that furnishes an everyday necessity to the public at large. Public utilities provide water, electricity, natural gas, telephone service, and other essentials. Utilities may be publicly or privately owned, but most are operated as private businesses.

Typically a public utility has a MONOPOLY on the service it provides. It is more economically efficient to have only one business provide the service because the infrastructure required to produce and deliver a product such as electricity or water is very expensive to build and maintain. A consequence of this monopoly is that federal, state, and local governments regulate public utilities to ensure that they provide a reasonable level of service at a fair price.

A public utility is entitled to charge REASONABLE rates for its product or service. Rates are generally established according to statutes and regulations. The utility usually files a proposed rate schedule with the state public utility commission for approval. The commission holds public hearings to help decide whether the proposed schedule is fair. The commission may also require increased levels of service from the utility to meet public demand.

Until the 1930s public utilities were subjected to minimal regulation. The enactment of the Public Utility Holding Company Act of 1935 (49 Stat. 803 [15 U.S.C.A. §§ 79–92z-6]) signaled a change. A HOLDING COMPANY is one that owns STOCK in, and supervises management of, other companies. The law regulates the purchase and sale of SECURITIES and ASSETS by gas and electric utility holding companies and limits holding companies to a single coordinated utility system. The law ended abuses that allowed a small number of public utilities to control large segments of the gas and electricity market and to set higher utility rates.

Public regulation of utilities has declined since the late 1970s. PUBLIC POLICY is now based on the idea that competition rather than regulation is a better way to manage this sector of the economy. AIRLINE and telephone deregulation are the most prominent examples of this shift in philosophy. Telephone deregulation was enabled by a 1982 agreement between American Telephone and Telegraph Company (AT&T) and the federal government. The federal government had sued AT&T, alleging that its monopoly on virtually all telephone service in the United States was illegal. AT&T agreed to divest itself of all local telephone companies, while retaining control of its long-distance, research, and manufacturing activities. This resulted in the creation of seven regional telephone companies with responsibility for local telephone service. Other companies now compete with AT&T for long-distance service.

At the federal level, numerous commissions oversee particular types of public utilities. These include the Federal Energy Commission, the NUCLEAR REGULATORY COMMISSION, the FEDERAL COMMUNICATIONS COMMISSION, and the SECURITIES AND EXCHANGE COMMISSION.

See also NUCLEAR POWER; TELECOMMUNICATIONS.

PUBLISH To circulate, distribute, or print information for the public at large.

In LIBEL AND SLANDER law, to utter to a third person or to make public a defamatory statement; in COMMERCIAL PAPER law, to present an instrument for payment or declare or assert that a forged instrument is genuine.

The meaning of the term *publish* differs according to the context in which it is used. In its broadest sense, the term *publishing* describes the act of making something known to the general public. A publication can be accomplished by speaking in a public place, printing information on paper and distributing it on the street, buying or otherwise securing time on television, placing information in a circulated newspaper or magazine, or other similar methods.

Laws can mandate specific forms of publication of certain information. For example, a federal statute, 41 U.S.C.A. § 416 (1997), requires that ADMINISTRATIVE AGENCIES under the EXECUTIVE BRANCH publish a notice in the *Commerce Business Daily* before entering into a CONTRACT worth more than $25,000 with a private business. The notice must contain information that is relevant to the proposed job and give all qualified private businesses an opportunity to compete for the contract with the agency. An agency may use additional sources of publication, such as trade journals, magazines, newspapers of general circulation, and other mass communication media to advertise its intention to enter into a contract with a private business.

Publication of information is required by law in other areas as well. State laws require a mortgagee who has foreclosed a MORTGAGE on REAL PROPERTY to publish a notice in a local newspaper before conducting a sale of the property. Both state and federal laws require administrative agencies to publish notices of public hearings that will be held by the agencies. Before taking action that affects legal rights, administrative agencies hold public hearings to give members of the public an opportunity to be heard.

In libel law, a defamatory statement can give rise to civil LIABILITY if the statement is made public. To be libelous, a statement must appear in print, in a picture, or in a sign. To be considered published, the statement must be received by at least one other person apart from the speaker and the defamed person. In the law of slander, the term *publish* refers to defamatory statements that are spoken in the presence of at least one other person. A transitory, humiliating gesture that is defamatory also constitutes slander if it is published, or understood, by a third party.

The term *publish* has another meaning in the law of commercial paper. Commercial paper law relates to NEGOTIABLE INSTRUMENTS such as BILLS OF EXCHANGE, PROMISSORY NOTES, bank CHECKS, and similar documents. In the law of commercial paper, publishing occurs when a check or other negotiable instrument is presented. Publication also occurs when a person vouches that a forged instrument is in fact genuine. By publishing a negotiable instrument, the publisher declares that the instrument is valid.

See also DEFAMATION.

PUBLISHING LAW The body of law relating to the publication of books, magazines, newspapers, electronic materials, and other artistic works.

Publishing law is not a discrete legal topic with its own laws. It is a collection of often disparate legal areas, such as CONTRACTS, INTELLECTUAL PROPERTY, torts, and the FIRST AMENDMENT.

Publishing is the act of distributing or otherwise making public a visual or literary work. The key players in publishing are publishers and authors. Publishers are those persons or organizations that dispense information to the public. The term *author* commonly describes writers and journalists, but where publishing is concerned, the term also describes photographers, filmmakers, video artists, and other artists whose work is published. Most publishers designate a lawyer to review a publishable work and identify its potential legal pitfalls. This person, called a legal liaison, may confer with outside legal counsel to ensure that the publication does not ensnare the publisher or author in legal conflict. A legal liaison should be familiar with the many legal issues peculiar to publishing, including COPYRIGHT and TRADEMARK infringement, sales, advertising, distribution policies, subscription agreements, special sales arrangements, INSURANCE, free speech, tax matters, and antitrust concerns stemming from the publisher's membership in trade associations. Other employees of publishers, such as editors, also should be trained to spot potential legal problems with a publishable work and bring them to the attention of the legal liaison before publication.

Publishers may be held liable for omissions, mistakes, and transgressions of their authors, as well as their own omissions, mistakes, and transgressions. One of the first and foremost concerns of publishers is copyright and trademark issues. Publishers should conduct thorough research on copyright and trademark issues before publishing a work. Among other things, publishers should ensure that copyrights are properly registered; the appropriate copyright notice is placed in each work; copyrights for work published prior to the effective date of the most recent federal Copyright Act, The Copyright Amendments Act of 1992 (2 U.S.C.A. § 179 et seq.), are renewed; the work does not violate the copyrights or trademark rights of another publisher or author; all copyrights are duly affixed to the work; all copyrights from source materials have been released or paid for; the work does not defame anyone; the work does not invade a person's right of PRIVACY; all obligations to authors, creators, and illustrators under the contract are being met; information from sources can be verified or has been confirmed; and any material derived from a dialogue between real people that is placed in quotation marks correctly sets forth the actual words spoken.

Failure to confirm quotes can lead to lengthy litigation if the quotes defame the speaker. In *Masson v. New Yorker Magazine Inc.*, 686 F. Supp. 1396 (N.D. Cal. 1987), *aff'd*, 881 F.2d 1452 (9th Cir. 1989), *and superseded*, 895 F.2d 1535 (9th Cir. 1990), *and rev'd*, 501 U.S. 496, 111 S. Ct. 2419, 115 L. Ed. 2d 447 (1991), *on remand* 832 F. Supp. 1350 (N.D. Cal. 1993), 85 F.3d 1394 (9th Cir. 1996), psychoanalyst Jeffrey M. Masson sued *New Yorker* magazine, its publisher Alfred A. Knopf, Inc., and freelance writer Janet Malcolm after Malcolm wrote a fairly unflattering article about Masson for the *New Yorker* that included quotes by Masson that Malcolm could not substantiate. The defendants ultimately prevailed but only after more than a decade of litigation.

Some publishable works run the risk of invading a person's right of privacy. A person whose privacy is invaded may recover DAMAGES for the loss of privacy, mental and emotional distress suffered as a result of the intrusion, and any specific injuries or financial losses stemming from the intrusion. The four basic types of privacy invasion are public disclosure of private and embarrassing facts, publicity that places an individual in a false light, intrusion into seclusion, and misappropriation of a per-

"I CAN'T GET NO": THE PUBLISHER SATISFACTION CLAUSE

IN FOCUS

Of all the provisions in a book contract, the satisfaction clause is the most controversial. Under the satisfaction clause, a publisher may refuse to publish an author's work and demand reimbursement for any advance payments if the publisher is not satisfied with the final product.

Publishers insist on including a satisfaction clause in book contracts to protect their own interests. A publishing company typically uses the clause when it has signed a deal with an author for a book that has not been completed. Such speculative deals are common in the world of book publishing. Many authors do not write books unless they receive an advance payment, and few publishers receive completed books that need no additional work from the author.

If a publisher is interested in a book or an idea for a book, it may seek an agreement with the author to gain the copyrights to the final product. The agreement may include an advance payment for the expected final product. When the publisher makes an advance payment, it must have a way out of the contract if the author submits a final product that is unsatisfactory. Without a satisfaction clause, authors would have less incentive to submit quality work, and publishers could be faced with manuscripts requiring an unreasonable amount of editing and rewriting.

For authors, the satisfaction clause is a potential trap. Some authors have argued that a publisher may use the clause as camouflage to reject a book for an invalid reason. For example, a publisher might reject a manuscript and claim it was unsatisfactory when the real reason for the publisher's rejection was that another publisher had beaten it to press with a book on the same subject. Such a rejection would be a bad faith rejection and would give the author a cause of action against the publisher. However, bad faith is notoriously difficult to prove in court.

For decades, courts refused to examine the motives of publishers when they invoked the satisfaction clause to terminate a book contract. The first sign of a more stringent standard of review came in 1979 in *Random House v. Gold*, 464 F. Supp. 1306 (S.D.N.Y. 1979). In *Gold*, Random House rejected author Herbert Gold's novel *Swiftie the Magician* after learning that Gold's first two books had fallen short of commercial expectations. Gold had agreed to write four books for Random House in exchange for advance payments against royalties.

When Random House offered to renegotiate Gold's contract, Gold sold *Swiftie the Magician* to McGraw-Hill. Random House sued and won back the advance payments to *Swiftie the Magician*, but in its opinion the court observed that broad discretion for publishers in their predictions of commercial success "may permit overreaching by publishers attempting to extricate themselves from bad deals."

The case of *Harcourt Brace Jovanovich v. Goldwater*, 532 F. Supp. 619 (S.D.N.Y. 1982), created a new approach to author-publisher contracts. In *Goldwater*, author Stephen Shadegg and politician Barry M. Goldwater contracted with Harcourt Brace Jovanovich to publish Goldwater's memoirs. In return for the book rights, Harcourt paid to Shadegg and Goldwater a $65,000 advance. Harcourt rejected the final manuscript nineteen months after the agreement was reached without giving the authors an opportunity to make revisions and without giving them editorial assistance. Harcourt demanded a return of the advance. Shadegg and Goldwater refused, and Harcourt sued.

The court acknowledged that the law must afford a publisher "very considerable discretion," but it also noted that a publisher does not have an "absolutely unfettered license to act or not to act in any way it wishes and to accept or reject a book for any reason whatever." The *Gold* court had said nearly as much, but the *Goldwater* court made new law when it declared that "there is an implied obligation in a contract of this kind for the publisher to engage in appropriate editorial work with the author." *Goldwater* therefore created a publisher's duty to provide editorial assistance to prevent its wanton use of the satisfaction clause. An additional duty, the duty to give an author the opportunity to make a revision, was established shortly thereafter in *Dell Publishing v. Whedon*, 577 F. Supp. 1459 (S.D.N.Y. 1984).

The satisfaction clause is likely to remain a standard provision in author-publisher contracts. Under the clause, authors will be held to their obligation to produce a satisfactory manuscript—that is, one the publisher can publish. Publishers, on the other hand, must be fair in their use of the clause against an author. Courts will no longer allow publishers to walk away from any author agreement just by reciting the word "unsatisfactory."

son's name or likeness for commercial advantage. Generally, PUBLIC FIGURES do not receive as much privacy protection as do private individuals.

Publishers also must ensure that a work does not infringe upon a person's right of publicity. The right of publicity protects a person's exclusive right to control the exploitation of his name, likeness, or persona for commercial purposes. Generally, to qualify for this protection, the person must have commercially exploited his persona. A publisher violates a person's right of publicity by publishing, without consent, the person's performance, name, or likeness for advertising or trade purposes.

Several other torts may be committed in the publication of a work. Among other torts, pub-

Starstruck Strikes Out

On September 7, 1977, actor Tony Curtis, inspired by the success of his first novel, *Kid Cody,* agreed with Doubleday & Company to write a "rags to riches story of a lascivious Hollywood starlet" called *Starstruck* (*Doubleday & Company v. Curtis,* 763 F.2d 495 [2d Cir. 1985], *rev'g,* 599 F. Supp. 779 [S.D.N.Y. 1984], and *cert. denied,* 474 U.S. 912, 106 S. Ct. 282, 88 L. Ed. 2d 247 [1985]). On the strength of negotiations by his agent, Irving Paul ("Swifty") Lazar, Curtis received an advance of $50,000, which would be offset against the future royalties expected from sales of the *Starstruck* novel. The contract specified that Curtis should submit a satisfactory manuscript by October 1, 1978, but Curtis submitted nothing until April 1980, when he delivered a partial first draft.

In August 1981, Doubleday editor Elizabeth Drew concluded that the *Starstruck* manuscript was " 'junk, pure and simple,' " and concurred with editor Adrian Zackheim, who was "appalled at the product," that Curtis's contract should be terminated under the contract's satisfaction clause *(Doubleday).* Doubleday asked Curtis to return the advance, but Curtis refused. Doubleday then sued for recovery in the Southern District of New York, and Curtis counterclaimed for third-party payments that Doubleday had received for *Kid Cody.*

At trial, Curtis argued that Doubleday had breached the contract in bad faith. According to Curtis, Doubleday had provided inadequate editorial assistance, and it had canceled the contract to avoid the terms of a related printing contract. The trial court dismissed Doubleday's claim on the theory that it had waived its right to reject the manuscript under the satisfaction clause by waiving deadlines. The trial court also dismissed Curtis's counterclaims.

On appeal, the Second Circuit Court of Appeals reversed the dismissal of Doubleday's claim. The appeals court examined the case history and found that Curtis had refused editorial assistance offered by Doubleday, including the suggestion that Curtis consult a "novel doctor." The court also held that Doubleday had not waived its rights under the satisfaction clause, that Doubleday's editors, "who were forced to harmonize an inferior manuscript, a lucrative reprint agreement and a recalcitrant author," had acted in good faith, and that Doubleday was entitled to a return of its $50,000 advance, plus interest. Curtis appealed to the United States Supreme Court, but the High Court refused to hear the appeal.

lishers should be on guard for intentional or negligent infliction of emotional distress, incitement and negligent publication, breach of confidentiality, TRESPASS, ASSAULT, and BATTERY. Trespass, assault, and battery are most common in news-gathering situations, where the competition to break stories can lead writers, photographers, and video artists to engage in questionable behavior. Battery, for example, can occur if a photographer or interviewer intentionally touches a subject in an offensive way. An assault occurs if a person puts another person in reasonable fear of a harmful or offensive physical contact, and a person commits trespass by entering on land without permission of the legal occupant.

Infliction of emotional distress is tortious conduct that causes severe emotional distress to the subject of a work. For example, a publisher could be held liable under this theory of recovery for printing a photograph in a pornographic magazine and incorrectly identifying the person in the picture if the identified person experiences work interruptions, nightmares, terror, humiliation, or other emotional distress as a result. A plaintiff in such an action may recover for both physical and mental harm resulting from the tort. A subject need not suffer physical or bodily injury to recover damages for this tort; emotional damage is sufficient. The main issue in such torts is whether the conduct by the author or publisher was so extreme and outrageous as to permit recovery for the subject's emotional distress.

The tort of incitement is speech directed to inciting or producing imminent lawless action that is likely to INCITE or produce such action. Such speech must be explicit to constitute incitement. Publishers generally will not be held liable if warnings are included in the work or the publication does not produce a CLEAR AND PRESENT DANGER of imminent injury. Negligent publication is the unintentional publication of incorrect facts that results in injury. This tort requires that the publisher owe a specific duty of care toward the injured party. This duty is difficult, but not impossible, to establish. If, for example, a publisher markets a flight manual to airplane pilots and the manual contains errors, the publisher may be liable for injuries if an airplane crashes because its pilot followed the faulty information.

Breach of confidentiality generally arises from an individual's assertion that the publisher had a duty not to disclose certain information about her. The duty may be expressed in a written or oral agreement between the parties. It also may be implied or required by law. Such statutes are designed to protect an individual's general privacy interest, protect certain sensitive information, or shield certain government information or functions from public knowledge. For example, some states maintain statutes that prohibit the publication of the full name of a juvenile accused of a crime. Another example is the federal statute that creates a CAUSE OF ACTION against persons who tape conversations without consent for criminal or tortious purposes (title III of the Omnibus Crime Control and Safe Streets Act, 18 U.S.C.A. § 2520 [1997]). If a publisher or author breaches confidentiality, she may be liable to the exposed party for injuries and financial losses stemming from the publication. In some states breach of confidentiality does not itself constitute a cause of action, but aggrieved plaintiffs may seek recovery under a breach of contract or invasion of privacy action.

The First Amendment guarantee of free speech and free press is a frequent refuge for publishers. Publishers assert the First Amendment as a defense to claims for invasion of privacy, breach of confidentiality, intentional or negligent infliction of emotional distress, incitement and negligent publication, breach of confidentiality, and right of publicity claims.

In some situations the First Amendment also provides members of the press a right of access to information. If the press has historically been granted access to a certain proceeding, and if press access would further societal interests, journalists may have a right to be present at a proceeding or to gain access to certain information (*Richmond Newspapers v. Virginia*, 448 U.S. 555, 100 S. Ct. 2814, 65 L. Ed. 2d 973 [1980]). In *Richmond*, the Supreme Court held that a First Amendment right of access prohibited trial courts from excluding journalists and the public from criminal trials.

The Supreme Court has recognized a journalist's right to access judicial documents, but it has yet to recognize a constitutional right to access all government records. However, most states, as well as the federal government, have enacted so-called SUNSHINE LAWS, which, with some exceptions, give the general public access to public records.

Most publishers maintain insurance against risks of loss. In-house or outside insurance specialists may negotiate coverage for an assortment of risks, ranging from PERSONAL INJURY and property damage to media perils such as invasion of privacy, copyright and trademark infringement, unfair competition, injuries related to faulty advertising, errors and omissions in the published product, and defamation, an intentionally false communication that injures another person's reputation or good name.

Only a handful of insurers protect against media perils because of the large potential losses involved. The few insurers that do protect against media perils do not provide coverage for all forms of media liability, and some do not offer coverage for both damage awards and legal defense costs. It is common for insurers to automatically cover authors of books in blanket policies for book publishers, but software, newspaper, and magazine publishers usually must obtain coverage for their writers by negotiating their inclusion in blanket policies.

Publishers often find that they are in legal conflict with their own authors. The conflicts between authors and publishers are usually contractual in nature, and courts use ordinary contract law principles to resolve the cases. One of the most common complaints of authors is that a publisher did not sufficiently promote their books. In deciding such a claim, a court generally looks at the facts surrounding the case to determine whether the publisher used its best efforts to market the book. Another point of conflict for authors is the satisfaction clause, a BOILERPLATE clause in book contracts that allows publishers to reject a final manuscript and demand the return of any advances if the work is not satisfactory to the publisher.

CROSS-REFERENCES

Art Law; Censorship; Entertainment Law; Evidence *Sidebar:* Journalists' Privilege; Freedom of Speech; Freedom of the Press; Gag Order; Internet; Libel and Slander; Literary Property; Music Publishing; *New York Times v. Sullivan; New York Times v. United States;* Obscenity; Pornography; Pretrial Publicity; Prior Restraint; *Roth v. United States;* Royalty; Tort Law.

PUFFING An opinion or judgment that is not made as a representation of fact.

Puffing is generally an expression or exaggeration made by a salesperson or found in an advertisement that concerns the quality of goods offered for sale. It presents opinions rather than facts and is usually not considered a legally binding promise. Such statements as "this car is in good shape" and "your wife will love this watch" constitute puffing.

PUNISHMENT The imposition of hardship in response to misconduct.

Punishments authorized in modern U.S. law include community service, monetary FINES,

LIBRARY OF CONGRESS

Debate about what constitutes "cruel and unusual punishment" continued long after ratification of the Eighth Amendment in 1791. This picture of a whipping post and pillory in Delaware dates from 1868.

forfeiture of property, restitution to victims, confinement in jail or prison, and death.

Some civil sanctions are punitive in nature. The primary aim in most civil cases is to compensate the victim. However, a judge or jury may assess punitive damages against a party in a civil case if that party's conduct was especially wicked. Punitive damages are intended to punish a party or set an example for similar wrongdoers. Though onerous, punitive damages in a civil case do not carry with them the same stigma attached to criminal punishment.

Human transgressions have been punished in various ways throughout history. The standard punishments in ancient Greek and Roman societies were death, slavery, mutilation (corporal punishment), imprisonment, or banishment. Some punishments were especially creative. In ancient Rome, for example, a person who murdered a close relative was enclosed in a sack with a cock, a viper, a dog, and a monkey, and then cast into the sea.

The ancient punishments were brought to England. Until the nineteenth century, the death penalty, or capital punishment, was imposed in England for more than two hundred different crimes. Most of these crimes were petty violations, such as pickpocketing or swindling. A defendant could be hanged, burned at the stake, or beheaded. In some cases the process of death was drawn out. A person found guilty of treason, for example, was placed on a rack and stretched, hung until not quite dead, then disemboweled, beheaded, and quartered (cut into four pieces).

Until the nineteenth century, corporal punishment in England could consist of whipping, branding, or the cutting off of a body part. Noses, ears, hands, fingers, toes, and feet were all subject to removal for criminal acts. Often the body part sliced off was the part thought responsible for the act. A pickpocket, for example, might have a hand cut off, and a spy might lose an ear, tongue, or eye. Corporal punishment could be inflicted in addition to other punishments, such as banishment, forced labor, or short-term incarceration.

The American colonies adopted and cultivated the traditional punishments of England. The most common punishments were corporal and capital. Petty criminals were often sentenced to a combination of corporal punishment and incarceration in jail for several months. The punishment for more serious crimes was usually death.

Punishment was the most comprehensive and severe in colonies founded on religious principles. In Massachusetts, controlled by the Puritans, a woman who committed adultery could be forced to wear the letter *A* in public as a punishing reminder of her conduct. Men who committed adultery were put to death, as were those who engaged in bestiality.

The witch trials in Salem, Massachusetts, illustrated the inventiveness of punishment in some of the colonies. In 1692 nineteen people were executed after children claimed that several women were practicing witchcraft. One of the alleged witnesses, who refused to participate in the trials, was slowly pressed to death under the weight of heavy rocks. See also Salem witch trials.

After the colonies won freedom from English control, enlightened social discourse led to the imposition of restraints on punishment. In 1791 the states ratified the Eighth Amendment to the U.S. Constitution to prohibit excessive bail, excessive fines, and the infliction of cruel and unusual punishments. Because the amendment did not define "cruel and unusual punishment," lawmakers and courts have had to determine what punishments are cruel and unusual. Throughout the nineteenth century, the Cruel and Unusual Punishment Clause was interpreted to prohibit only torture and barbarous punishments.

THEORIES OF PUNISHMENT

Governments have several theories to support the use of punishment to maintain order in society.

Theories of punishment can be divided into two general philosophies: utilitarian and retributive. The utilitarian theory of punishment seeks to punish offenders to discourage, or "deter," future wrongdoing. The retributive theory seeks to punish offenders because they deserve to be punished.

IN FOCUS

Under the utilitarian philosophy, laws should be used to maximize the happiness of society. Because crime and punishment are inconsistent with happiness, they should be kept to a minimum. Utilitarians understand that a crime-free society does not exist, but they endeavor to inflict only as much punishment as is required to prevent future crimes.

The utilitarian theory is "consequentialist" in nature. It recognizes that punishment has consequences for both the offender and society and holds that the total good produced by the punishment should exceed the total evil. In other words, punishment should not be unlimited. One illustration of consequentialism in punishment is the release of a prison inmate suffering from a debilitating illness. If the prisoner's death is imminent, society is not served by his continued confinement because he is no longer capable of committing crimes.

Under the utilitarian philosophy, laws that specify punishment for criminal conduct should be designed to deter future criminal conduct. Deterrence operates on a specific and a general level. General deterrence means that the punishment should prevent other people from committing criminal acts. The punishment serves as an example to the rest of society, and it puts others on notice that criminal behavior will be punished.

Specific deterrence means that the punishment should prevent the same person from committing crimes. Specific deterrence works in two ways. First, an offender may be put in jail or prison to physically prevent her from committing another crime for a specified period. Second, this incapacitation is designed to be so unpleasant that it will discourage the offender from repeating her criminal behavior.

Rehabilitation is another utilitarian rationale for punishment. The goal of rehabilitation is to prevent future crime by giving offenders the ability to succeed within the confines of the law. Rehabilitative measures for criminal offenders usually include treatment for afflictions such as mental illness, chemical dependency, and chronic violent behavior. Rehabilitation also includes the use of educational programs that give offenders the knowledge and skills needed to compete in the job market.

The counterpart to the utilitarian theory of punishment is the retributive theory. Under this theory, offenders are punished for criminal behavior because they deserve punishment. Criminal behavior upsets the peaceful balance of society, and punishment helps to restore the balance.

The retributive theory focuses on the crime itself as the reason for imposing punishment. Where the utilitarian theory looks forward by basing punishment on social benefits, the retributive theory looks backward at the transgression as the basis for punishment.

According to the retributivist, human beings have free will and are capable of making rational decisions. An offender who is insane or otherwise incompetent should not be punished. However, a person who makes a conscious choice to upset the balance of society should be punished.

There are different moral bases for retribution. To many retributivists, punishment is justified as a form of vengeance: wrongdoers should be forced to

---

After the ratification of the Eighth Amendment, corporal punishment was replaced by incarceration in jail or prison. Capital punishment, essentially the ultimate form of corporal punishment, survived into the 1970s, when it was held to be cruel and unusual (*Furman v. Georgia*, 408 U.S. 238, 92 S. Ct. 2726, 33 L. Ed. 2d 346 [1972]). That decision was overturned four years later in *Gregg v. Georgia*, 428 U.S. 153, 96 S. Ct. 2909, 49 L. Ed. 2d 859 (1976), and capital punishment was restored in many JURISDICTIONS.

The United States is the only western industrialized country to use the death penalty. Most states authorize the death penalty as a punishment for first-degree murder. Hanging, death by electrocution, and the firing squad are still used, but the most common form of capital punishment is death by lethal injection.

For more than a century after the Eighth Amendment was ratified, lawmakers and courts did not interpret its prohibition of cruel and unusual punishment to include a prohibition of disproportionate punishment. Federal and state lawmakers were free to impose punishment on convicted criminals without concern for whether the punishment fit the crime.

In 1910 the U.S. Supreme Court recognized the proportionality concept in *Weems v. United States*, 217 U.S. 349, 30 S. Ct. 544, 54 L. Ed.

THEORIES OF PUNISHMENT (CONTINUED)

suffer because they have forced others to suffer. This ancient principle was expressed succinctly in the Old Testament of the Judeo-Christian Bible: "When a man causes a disfigurement in his neighbour . . . it shall be done to him, fracture for fracture, eye for eye, tooth for tooth. . . ."

To other theorists, retribution against a wrongdoer is justified to protect the legitimate rights of both society and the offender. Society shows its respect for the free will of the wrongdoer through punishment. Punishment shows respect for the wrongdoer because it allows an offender to pay the debt to society and then return to society, theoretically free of guilt and stigma.

A third major rationale for punishment is denunciation. Under the denunciation theory, punishment should be an expression of societal condemnation. The denunciation theory is a hybrid of utilitarianism and retribution. It is utilitarian because the prospect of being publicly denounced serves as a deterrent. Denunciation is likewise retributive because it promotes the idea that offenders deserve to be punished.

The U.S. conception of punishment is a combination of the utilitarian, retributive, and denunciation theories. The most widely accepted rationale for punishment in the United States is retribution. If convicted, the sentence a defendant receives is always, at least in part, a form of retribution.

A sentence may, however, combine utilitarian ideals with retribution. For example, a defendant sentenced to prison for several years is sent there to quench the public's thirst for vengeance. At the same time, educational programs inside the prison reflect the utilitarian goal of rehabilitation.

Our legal system shows its adherence to utilitarian ideals in the creation of systems such as pretrial diversion programs, probation, and parole. These systems seek to limit punishment to the extent necessary to protect society. The utilitarian philosophy is also reflected in the assignment of different punishments for different crimes and in the notion that the amount of punishment a convicted criminal receives should be in proportion to the harm caused by the crime. For example, murder calls for imprisonment or even the death penalty. A simple assault and battery with no serious injuries is usually punished with a short jail sentence or probation and a fine.

Judges generally have the discretion to fashion punishment according to the needs of both society and the defendant. This is an expression of utilitarian tenets. However, judicial discretion in sentencing is limited. In some cases statutes require judges to impose mandatory minimum prison sentences as punishment, and these laws stand as a monument to the retributive theory.

See also Utilitarianism.

793. In *Weems*, Paul A. Weems was convicted of falsifying a single item of a public record and sentenced to hard labor for twelve to twenty years while chained at the wrists and ankles. The Court in *Weems* examined the nature of the crime, compared Weems's sentence with punishment in other jurisdictions for the same offense, and looked at the punishment for more serious crimes within the same jurisdiction.

In light of the comparisons, the Court found that the punishment of Weems was too harsh. According to the Court, the Eighth Amendment was designed to protect against such disproportionate punishment, and it ordered the case against Weems dismissed. Since the *Weems* decision, courts and lawmakers in the United States have attempted to find the right amount of punishment for various criminal acts.

Both legislators and judges determine punishment. Legislators identify the range of punishments that a court may impose for a certain crime. Punishment for crimes is listed in federal, state, and local laws. In most cases statutes name a variety of punishments appropriate for the crime, and courts have discretion in determining the precise punishment. However, many federal and state laws on narcotics identify a mandatory minimum prison sentence that must be imposed, and this takes sentencing discretion away from the judge.

In *Harmelin v. Michigan*, 501 U.S. 957, 111 S. Ct. 2680, 115 L. Ed. 2d 836 (1990), Ronald Harmelin challenged the punishment he received for possession of more than 650 grams of cocaine. Though he had no prior FELONIES, Harmelin was convicted in Michigan state court and sentenced to spend the rest of his life in prison. On appeal the U.S. Supreme Court upheld the sentence, ruling that "severe, mandatory penalties may be cruel, but they are not unusual in the constitutional sense, having been employed in various forms throughout our Nation's history."

Critics argue that the *Harmelin* opinion sidestepped the proportionality requirement created in earlier High Court cases and threw into doubt the standard for cruel and unusual punishment. Under *Harmelin*, proportionality is not required; what is relevant is whether the punishment has been used in the United States in the past. If it has been used, it is not unusual, and therefore not violative of the Cruel and Unusual Punishment Clause.

Because lawmakers can change laws, the list of acts that warrant punishment is not static. Before the twentieth century, many acts, such as SODOMY, adultery, and premarital sex were punished with prison terms. In most states either these acts are no longer illegal or the laws prohibiting them are no longer enforced. Possession of most psychotropic substances was not punished until the late nineteenth and early twentieth centuries. The manufacture, sale, and transportation of ALCOHOL was punished in the United States from 1919 to 1933 (Prohibition). Debtors used to be punished with imprisonment, but this practice was discontinued in the 1830s.

Some acts have always been illegal, but the level of punishment inflicted for the crime has fluctuated. Drunk driving, for example, is punished more severely now than it was before the 1970s. The possession of a small amount of marijuana used to warrant a long prison term in most jurisdictions, but modern statutes limit the punishment for this crime to monetary fines and PROBATION.

In assigning punishment for drug offenses, most laws differentiate between distribution and possession. State and federal statutes generally punish the selling or distribution of drugs more severely than possession. Repeat possession violators may receive short-term incarceration, but long prison terms are usually reserved for purveyors of illicit drugs. Lawmakers may vary the punishment within the same offense for different forms of the same drug. Possession of crack cocaine in most states and in the federal system, for example, is punished more harshly than possession of powder cocaine.

Before the Civil War, many states in the South had separate statutory codes for slaves, which imposed more severe punishment on slaves than on free persons. For example, any attempt by a slave to commit a crime punishable by death was punished with death, but free persons were not put to death for attempts. Also, the range of acts punished under slave codes was wider than that punished under the statutory codes for free persons. See also SLAVERY.

Since the end of the Civil War, statutory codes in all states have purported to punish all persons equally. However, the issue of fairness concerning who gets punished has not disappeared. Many analysts of punishment in the United States cite the disproportionate number of African Americans in prisons as proof of selective prosecution and punishment. Scholars and others have also questioned a system that punishes drug offenses more harshly than violent offenses.

Critics also note disparities between punishment of impoverished persons and punishment of wealthy persons, noting that poor defendants are punished more harshly because they do not have the resources necessary to mount a vigorous defense to criminal charges.

The United States relies primarily on incarceration as punishment. However, many states have sought alternatives to incarceration. Many states use short-term boot camps to rehabilitate first-time offenders. These highly regimented camps are intended to give offenders the discipline and respect for authority necessary to succeed in society. Other states and localities are experimenting with alternatives to imprisonment for drug offenders, such as treatment, probation, and work requirements. Others have supplanted long periods of confinement with a small dose of public humiliation and a variety of deprivations.

In Nevada, for example, a person convicted of one drunk driving offense may be ordered to perform forty-eight hours of community service dressed in clothing that identifies the person as a drunk driving offender. Additionally, the defendant is deprived of his or her driver's license for ninety days; ordered to pay a fine ranging from $200 to $1,000; and required to attend, at the defendant's own expense, an alcohol abuse education course.

CROSS-REFERENCES

Criminal Law; Drugs and Narcotics; Racketeer Influenced and Corrupt Organizations Act; Sentencing.

As an alternative to incarceration, lawbreakers in some states are sentenced to do community service, such as cleaning up public lands.

GILLES MINGASSON/GAMMA-LIAISON

SENDING A MESSAGE OR A PLAINTIFF'S WINDFALL?

IN FOCUS

Punitive damages are a controversial issue in tort and product liability law. Injured plaintiffs and their attorneys often seek punitive damages from companies that have made allegedly defective or unsafe products and have known about the defects or safety problems. Plaintiffs view punitive damages as a way of sending a message to the manufacturer and to business, in general, that it is financially unwise to cut corners or ignore safety concerns. On the other hand, defendants in these actions contend that punitive damages are unfair, unpredictable, and often excessive. In their view, the plaintiff receives a financial windfall unrelated to the actual damages in the lawsuit.

Proponents of punitive damages believe that this type of award serves a number of important societal functions, including retribution, deterrence, compensation, and law enforcement.

Supporters of punitive damages contend that one function for such an award is to provide retribution to the victim of the defendant's reckless or wanton conduct. When a person is injured by the wanton misconduct of another, the plaintiff has the right to express her outrage by extracting a judicial fine from the wrongdoer. Seeking retribution allows the plaintiff to punish an intentional lawbreaker in much the same way as the criminal justice system punishes him.

Proponents believe that the most important function that punitive damages serve is that of deterrence. As in criminal law, the predominant purpose of punitive damages is to prevent similar misconduct in the future. Because the law does not catch and punish all persons who wantonly violate the rights of others, supporters argue that punitive damages help deter misconduct by publicizing, and at times sensationalizing, the punishment of those persons found guilty of egregious misconduct. Punitive damages tell manufacturers and other businesses that financial penalties will follow if companies sell products known to be defective.

Advocates of punitive damage awards also contend that these awards serve a compensation function. Although a plaintiff may receive actual damages for the injuries suffered, many of the plaintiff's actual losses, including those involving intangible harm, are not compensable under the rules of compensatory damage liability. Punitive damages help the plaintiff to be made whole again.

Another function of punitive damages articulated by supporters is law enforcement. Without the prospect of a large punitive damage windfall, many persons would not be willing to make their claims. Punitive damages act as a law enforcement vehicle, energizing prospective plaintiffs and motivating them to enforce the rules of law and to promote the functions of retribution, deterrence, and compensation.

Critics of punitive damages believe that large monetary awards are unfair, unreasonable, and not productive for society. One of their central criticisms goes to the idea of punitive damages as "quasi-criminal" punishments. Noting that proponents talk of retribution and

PUNITIVE DAMAGES Monetary compensation awarded to an injured party that goes beyond that which is necessary to compensate the individual for losses and that is intended to punish the wrongdoer.

Punitive damages, also known as exemplary damages, may be awarded by the trier of fact (a JURY or a judge, if a jury trial was waived) in addition to actual DAMAGES, which compensate a plaintiff for the losses suffered due to the harm caused by the defendant. Punitive damages are a way of punishing the defendant in a civil lawsuit and are based on the theory that the interests of society and the individual harmed can be met by imposing additional damages on the defendant. Since the 1970s punitive damages have been criticized by U.S. business and insurance groups which allege that exorbitant punitive damage awards have driven up the cost of doing business.

Punitive damages have been characterized as "quasi-criminal," because they stand halfway between the criminal and civil law. Though they are awarded to a plaintiff in a private civil lawsuit, they are noncompensatory and in the nature of a criminal fine.

Punitive damages were first recognized in England in 1763 and were recognized by the American colonies almost immediately. By 1850 punitive damages had become a well-established part of CIVIL LAW.

The purposes of punitive damages are to punish the defendant for outrageous misconduct and to deter the defendant and others from similar misbehavior in the future. The nature of the wrongdoing that justifies punitive damages is variable and imprecise. The usual terms that characterize conduct justifying these damages include *bad faith*, *fraud*, *malice*, *oppression*, *outrageous*, *violent*, *wanton*, *wicked*, and *reckless*. These aggravating circumstances typically refer to situations where the defendant acted intentionally, maliciously, or with utter disregard for the rights and interests of the plaintiff.

deterrence, these critics argue that it is unfair to impose these "criminal" fines on defendants who do not have the usual safeguards of criminal procedure. They note that a plaintiff should satisfy a higher burden of proof than a mere "preponderance of the evidence," the usual standard in a civil trial. Some states have agreed, mandating that "clear and convincing evidence," a higher burden of proof, be used by the jury in determining whether to award punitive damages.

Critics also charge that the vagueness of standards for determining the defendant's liability for punitive damages and for calculating the award itself causes juries to make decisions based on passion, bias, and prejudice rather than on the law. The vagueness in such terms as *reckless*, *willful*, or *wanton* leads critics to conclude that juries have no meaningful, objective way to make an informed decision. Many states have recognized this criticism and developed a variety of procedures to instruct the jury fully and precisely and to require the trial court to assess the sufficiency of the evidence before awarding punitive damages and to issue written reasons why the award was or was not deserved in light of the legal standards.

The U.S. Supreme Court, in *BMW of North America v. Gore*, ___U.S.___, 116 S. Ct. 1589, 134 L. Ed. 2d 809 (1996), also developed guidelines for assessing punitive damages. The Court held that the "degree of reprehensibility of defendant's conduct" is the most important indication of reasonableness in measuring punitive damages. The Court also measured the possible excessiveness of a punitive damage award by applying a ratio between the plaintiff's compensatory damages and the amount of the punitive damages.

Critics also note that the deterrence rationale is undercut when defendants are insured against punitive damage awards. In addition, when a government employee is found liable for misconduct and punitive damages are awarded, the taxpayers must pay for the award. Taxpayers are innocent parties, making it unreasonable for them to bear the punishment for the actions of a government employee.

Critics argue that because punitive damages are noncompensatory, they provide the plaintiff with an undeserved financial windfall. The public gains no benefit when an individual receives a multimillion dollar punitive damage verdict. Some states have responded to this criticism by requiring that part of a punitive damage award be paid to the state for some type of public good.

Finally, in mass disaster cases, involving products like asbestos, a manufacturer may have to pay multiple punitive damage awards. Critics contend that allowing punitive damages to early plaintiffs may bankrupt defendants, thereby depriving later plaintiffs of compensatory damages.

For these and other reasons, the critics see punitive damages as counterproductive to the public good. Large awards result in increased costs of products and services and even discourage companies from producing products or providing services out of fear of litigation.

The controversy over punitive damages is likely to continue because it involves fundamental issues of justice, fairness, and the public good.

See also Clear and Convincing Proof; Preponderance of Evidence.

Unless otherwise required by statute, the award of punitive damages is left to the discretion of the trier of fact. A small number of states refuse to award punitive damages in any action, and the remainder have instituted various ways of determining when and how they are to be awarded. In some states an award of NOMINAL DAMAGES, which acknowledges that a legal right has been violated but little harm has been done, is an adequate foundation for the recovery of punitive damages. In other states the plaintiff must be awarded COMPENSATORY DAMAGES before punitive damages are allowed.

In the absence of statutory authorization, punitive damages usually cannot be recovered in breach-of-contract actions. Punitive damages are sometimes recoverable in tort actions in which breach of CONTRACT is tangentially involved.

Punitive damages will not be awarded in tort actions based on the defendant's NEGLIGENCE alone. The conduct must have been WILLFUL, WANTON, or reckless to constitute an intentional offense. Willfulness implies a plan, purpose, or intent to commit a wrongdoing and cause an injury. For example, if an automobile manufacturer knows that the gas tank in its car will likely explode on impact but does not change the design because it does not wish to incur additional costs, the behavior could be classified as willful. Conduct is considered wanton if the individual performing the act is cognizant that it is likely to cause an injury, even though specific intent to harm someone does not exist, such as when an individual shoots a gun into a crowd. Although the individual does not have the intent to injure anyone in particular, injury is a natural and probable consequence of the act. RECKLESSNESS is an act performed with total disregard of its foreseeable harmful consequences. Punitive damages can be awarded on the basis of an injurious act done with ill will, a wrongful or illegal motive, or without any legal justification, but a wrongful act performed in

GOOD FAITH is an inadequate basis for such an award. For example, if a grocery sold canned goods that later turned out to be tainted, and the store did not know of the problem before selling the canned goods, it would be liable for compensatory damages to the victims who ate the food, but would not be liable for punitive damages.

The measurement of punitive damages has been controversial because traditionally the amount to be awarded is, for the most part, within the discretion of the trier of fact. To determine the amount, the jury or court must consider the nature of the wrongdoer's behavior, the extent of the plaintiff's loss or injury, and the degree to which the defendant's conduct is repugnant to a societal sense of justice and decency. In some states the financial worth of the defendant can properly be considered.

Ordinarily, an award of punitive damages by a jury will not be upset as excessive or inadequate. If the trial court believes that the jury award is excessive or unwarranted by the facts, it can remove punitive damages from the final judgment, or it can reduce the amount through a procedural process called REMITTITUR.

Since the 1980s APPELLATE COURTS have been called on to review punitive damage awards and to assess the procedural fairness involved in awarding such damages. State legislatures and the courts have attempted to craft ways of ensuring REASONABLE punitive damage awards, but there is no uniform approach.

The U.S. Supreme Court, in *Pacific Mutual Life Insurance v. Haslip*, 499 U.S. 1, 111 S. Ct. 1032, 113 L. Ed. 2d 1 (1991), upheld a large punitive damage award on the grounds that the Alabama jury had received adequate jury instructions and the Alabama Supreme Court had applied a seven-factor test to assess the reasonableness of the award.

Two years later the U.S. Supreme Court shifted its stance on how it would assess whether a punitive damage award was excessive. In *TXO Productions Corp. v. Alliance Resources Corp.*, 509 U.S. 443, 113 S. Ct. 2711, 125 L. Ed. 2d 366 (1993), the Court stated that the Due Process Clause of the FOURTEENTH AMENDMENT to the U.S. Constitution prohibits a state from imposing a "grossly excessive" punishment on a person held liable in tort. Whether a VERDICT is grossly excessive must be based on an identification of the state interests that a punitive award is designed to serve. If the award is disproportionate to the interests served, it violates due process.

The Court further defined the issues surrounding excessive awards in *BMW of North America v. Gore*, __U.S.__, 116 S. Ct. 1589, 134 L. Ed. 2d 809 (1996). In this case the plaintiff, Ira Gore, was sold a purportedly new automobile. In fact, the car had been repainted because of damage during shipping. When Gore found out, he sued BMW. During the litigation he discovered that for many years BMW had routinely repainted cars and sold them as new. The jury awarded Gore $4,000 in compensatory damages and punitive damages of $4 million. The Alabama Supreme Court reduced the punitive damages to $2 million but upheld the reduced award.

On appeal, the U.S. Supreme Court overturned the punitive damage award. First, the Court identified the "degree of reprehensibility of defendant's conduct" as the most important indication of reasonableness in measuring a punitive damage award under the Due Process Clause. In the Court's view, the damages imposed should reflect the enormity of the defendant's offense and may not be grossly out of proportion to the severity of the offense. In Gore's case the award was excessive because BMW's conduct did not demonstrate indifference or reckless disregard for the health and safety of others. The minor repairs it made to the cars did not affect their performance, safety features, or appearance.

Second, the Court applied the most commonly used indicator of excessiveness, the ratio between the plaintiff's compensatory damages and the amount of the punitive damages. Even though the state court reduced the punitive damages by half, the Court found the ratio of five hundred to one to be outside the acceptable range.

Finally, the Court examined the difference between the punitive damage award and the civil or criminal sanctions that Alabama could impose for comparable misconduct. The fact that the $2 million verdict was substantially greater than Alabama's $2,000 civil fine for deceptive trade practices was another ground for finding the punitive damages excessive, according to the Court.

CROSS-REFERENCES

Due Process of Law; Product Liability; Tort Law.

PURCHASE To buy; the transfer of property from one person to another by an agreement. Under the UNIFORM COMMERCIAL CODE (UCC), taking by sale, discount, negotiation, MORTGAGE, PLEDGE, LIEN, issue, reissue, GIFT, or any voluntary transaction.

PURCHASE MONEY MORTGAGE A security device entered into when the seller of property, as opposed to a bank or financial institution, advances a sum of money or credit to the purchaser in return for holding the MORTGAGE on the property.

The seller of the property, rather than a lending institution, is the mortgagee. These mortgages are given concurrently with the CONVEYANCE of the land or the transfer of the items sold.

PURCHASE ORDER A document authorizing a seller to deliver goods, with payment to be made at a later date.

A purchase order is a written authorization requesting a vendor to furnish goods to a purchaser. It is an offer from the purchaser to buy certain articles. The offer is accepted by the seller when she supplies the requested items. A CONTRACT is formed and the seller can expect payment in return for the delivered goods.

PURE FOOD AND DRUG ACT OF 1906 The first federal law (34 Stat. 768) prohibiting the interstate transportation and sale of adulterated food enacted by Congress pursuant to its power under the COMMERCE CLAUSE.

Scandals concerning the purity and quality of food sold to the U.S. public became widespread as the unsanitary methods used by the food industry were disclosed.

Dr. Harvey W. Wiley was instrumental in the passage of the Pure Food and Drug Act, which was subsequently amended in 1912, 1913, and 1919. The act defined adulterated food as that which is combined or packaged with another substance that adversely affects the quality or strength of the food; is substituted in whole or part by another substance; has had any essential component removed in whole or part; has been blended, coated, colored, or stained to conceal damage or inferiority; has had poisonous or harmful additions made to it; is composed of filthy or decomposed animal or vegetable matter; or is the product of a diseased animal or an animal that has died other than by slaughtering.

In 1938, Congress enacted the more stringent Federal Food, Drug, and Cosmetic Act (21 U.S.C.A. § 301 et seq.), which superseded the provisions of the Pure Food and Drug Act of 1906.

See also FOOD AND DRUG ADMINISTRATION.

PURE SPEECH Written and spoken words that fall within the scope of protection provided by the FIRST AMENDMENT to the Constitution.

Pure speech and other types of communication, such as PICKETING and SYMBOLIC SPEECH or SPEECH PLUS, that involve conveying an idea or message through behavior, are safeguarded by the Constitution against arbitrary and unreasonable interference by the government. This right of freedom of expression is not, however, absolute. Pure speech and other communications are not protected if they present a CLEAR AND PRESENT DANGER to society or if they constitute libel, obscenity, or slander.

See also FREEDOM OF SPEECH.

PURGE To exonerate someone; to clear someone of guilt, charges, or accusations.

Purging CONTEMPT is to clear an individual of contempt of court. This is generally accomplished by a formal apology to the court and the payment of a fine.

PURPORT To convey, imply, or profess; to have an appearance or effect.

The purport of an instrument generally refers to its facial appearance or import, as distinguished from the TENOR of an instrument, which means an exact copy or duplicate.

PURSUANT According to a prescribed method or some authority. To follow after or follow out; to execute or carry out by reason of something.

To do an act pursuant to the law is to conform to the requirements of a statute.

PURVIEW The part of a statute or a law that delineates its purpose and scope.

Purview refers to the enacting part of a statute. It generally begins with the words *be it enacted* and continues as far as the repealing clause. The purview is distinguished from other parts of a statute, such as the title, PREAMBLE, and SAVINGS CLAUSES.

PUT An option—a right that operates as a continuing proposal—given in exchange for CONSIDERATION—something of value—permitting its holder to sell a particular STOCK or COMMODITY at a fixed price for a stated quantity and within a limited time period.

A put is purchased for a fee paid to the person who agrees to accept the stock or goods if they are offered. The purchaser of this right to sell expects the price of the stock or commodity to decrease so that he can deliver the stock or commodity at a profit. If the price rises, the option need not be exercised. The reverse transaction is a CALL.

PUTATIVE Alleged; supposed; reputed.

A *putative father* is the individual who is alleged to be the father of an illegitimate child.

A *putative marriage* is one that has been contracted in good faith and pursuant to ignorance, by one or both parties, that certain impediments exist to render it null and void.

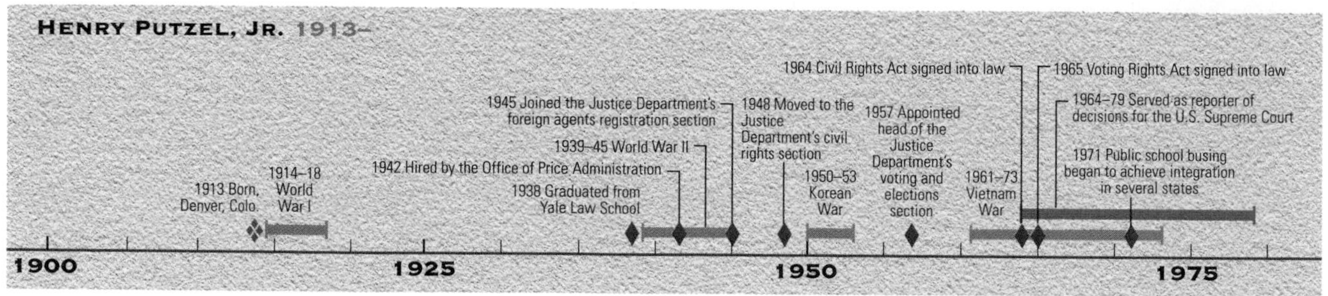

PUTZEL, HENRY, JR. Henry Putzel, Jr., served as the REPORTER of decisions of the U.S. Supreme Court from 1964 to 1979. Before becoming reporter, Putzel practiced law and served in a variety of important positions in the federal government. As an attorney with the Justice Department's civil rights division, Putzel dealt with racially discriminatory voting practices.

BIOGRAPHY

Putzel was born on October 8, 1913, in Denver, Colorado. He graduated from Yale University in 1935 and earned a law degree from Yale in 1938. He entered private law practice in St. Louis but left in 1942 for a position in Washington, D.C., as an attorney in the federal Office of Price Administration. In 1945 Putzel transferred to the Justice Department, where he worked in the foreign agents registration section. He moved to the department's civil rights section in 1948. Following the Supreme Court's decision in *Brown v. Board of Education*, 347 U.S. 483, 74 S. Ct. 686, 98 L. Ed. 873 (1954), which overturned the SEPARATE-BUT-EQUAL doctrine and struck down state-mandated segregation of public schools, Putzel worked on enforcing SCHOOL DESEGREGATION. He also prosecuted individuals who had violated federal criminal CIVIL RIGHTS laws. In 1957 he was named to head the voting and ELECTIONS section of the Justice Department's civil rights division. He investigated allegations of racial discrimination in voting and election fraud.

The Supreme Court appointed Putzel its reporter of decisions in 1964, the thirteenth person to hold the position. As reporter, Putzel was responsible for the accuracy of each opinion, the preparation of HEADNOTES and a SYLLABUS that summarizes the decisions, and the actual publication of each volume of decisions. During his fifteen-year tenure, he edited or coedited sixty-four volumes (volumes 376 through 440) of the *United States Reports*. A major change in reporting procedure occurred while Putzel was reporter. The Court ordered the preparation of headnotes before the announcement of the decision, rather than after the release of the opinion, as had been the practice.

Putzel retired from his position in 1979.

PYRAMID SALES SCHEME See REFERRAL SALES SCHEME.

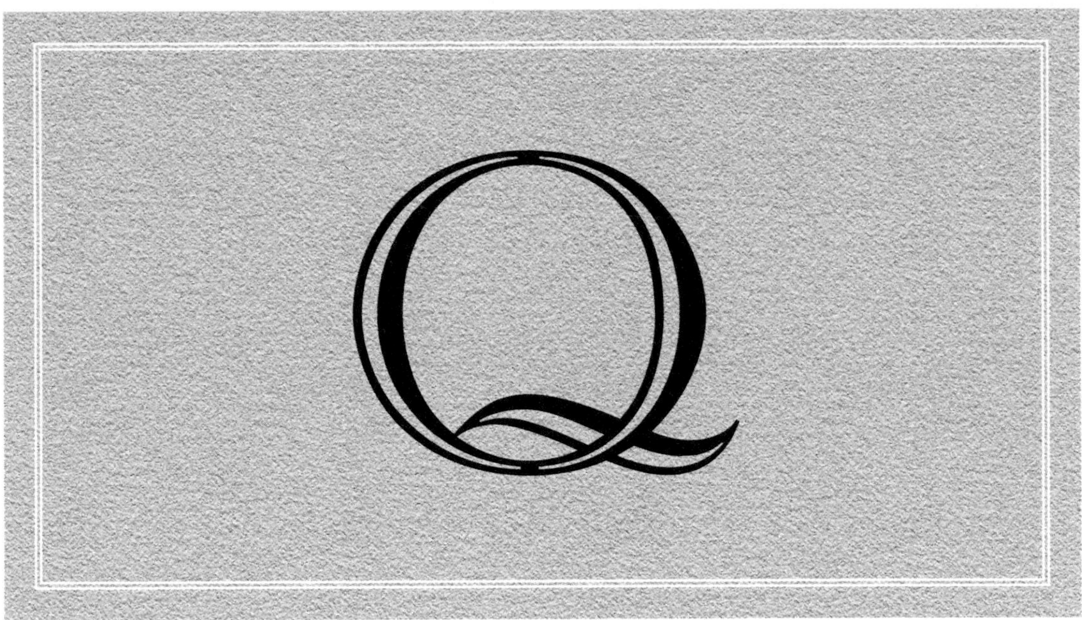

QUA [*Latin, Considered as; in the character or capacity of.*] For example, "the trustee *qua* trustee [that is, in his or her role as trustee] is not liable."

QUALIFICATION A particular attribute, quality, property, or possession that an individual must have in order to be eligible to fill an office or perform a public duty or function.

For example, attaining the AGE OF MAJORITY is a qualification that must be met before an individual has the CAPACITY to enter into a CONTRACT.

The term *qualification* also refers to a limitation or restriction that narrows the scope of language (such as that contained in a statute) that would otherwise carry a broader meaning.

QUALIFIED ACCEPTANCE In CONTRACT law, an assent to an offer that is either conditional or partial and alters the offer by changing the time, amount, mode, or place of payment.

In order for a contract to be valid, an ACCEPTANCE of an offer must not be subject to any conditions; therefore, a qualified acceptance is tantamount to a COUNTEROFFER.

QUANTUM MERUIT [*Latin, As much as is deserved.*] In the law of CONTRACTS, a doctrine by which the law infers a PROMISE to pay a REASONABLE amount for labor and materials furnished, even in the absence of a specific legally enforceable AGREEMENT between the parties.

A party who performs a valuable service for another party usually enters into a written contract or agreement before performing the service, particularly when the party is in the business of performing that service. For instance, most professional roofers hired to repair a roof insist on having a formal agreement with the owner of the house before beginning the repairs. In the absence of an agreement or formal contract, the roofer may be unable to recover losses in court if the transaction goes awry. Quantum meruit is a judicial doctrine that allows a party to recover losses in the absence of an agreement or binding contract.

By allowing the recovery of the value of labor and materials, quantum meruit prevents the unjust enrichment of the other party. A person would be unjustly enriched if she received a benefit and did not pay for it when fairness required that payment be made. Quantum meruit can be used to address situations where no contract exists or where a contract exists but for some reason is unenforceable. In such cases courts imply a contract to avoid an unjust result. Such contracts are called QUASI CONTRACTS.

Quantum meruit also describes a method used to determine the exact amount owed to a person. A court may measure this amount either by determining how much the defendant has benefited from the transaction or by determining how much the plaintiff has expended in materials and services.

The doctrine of quantum meruit was developed in the seventeenth century by the royal Court of CHANCERY in England. This court worked apart from the COMMON-LAW courts to grant relief that was due under general principles of fairness but could not be obtained under the strict legal PRECEDENTS of the common-law courts. The system of basing decisions on basic principles of fairness became known as EQUITY. The Chancery Court devel-

APWIDE WORLD PHOTOS

In the absence of a binding contract, these builders may still be able to extract payment from a recalcitrant homeowner under the doctrine of quantum meruit.

oped quantum meruit along with other equitable doctrines that allowed a person to recover or collect for other valuable acts performed without a contract, such as the delivery of goods or money. Some of the first cases of quantum meruit involved recovery by persons in so-called trades of common calling, such as innkeepers, tailors, blacksmiths, and tanners.

As service industries increased, so did claims for recovery under quantum meruit, and the doctrine was adopted by colonial courts. U.S. courts now apply quantum meruit principles in a wide variety of cases, including cases involving attorneys' fees, physicians' fees, construction work, government contracts, and even domestic relations suits for "palimony." PALIMONY is a form of financial support that is similar to ALIMONY but arises out of a nonmarital relationship.

Courts have crafted four basic elements that the plaintiff must prove before she may recover under the doctrine of quantum meruit: (1) that valuable services were rendered; (2) that the services were rendered to the defendant; (3) that the services were accepted, used, and enjoyed by the defendant; and (4) that the defendant was aware that the plaintiff, in performing the services, expected to be paid by the defendant.

The case of *Montes v. Naismith and Trevino Construction Co.*, 459 S.W.2d 691 (Tex. Civ. App. 1970), illustrates how quantum meruit works. In August 1968 Abraham Montes began oral negotiations with Abdon Perez regarding improvements Montes sought for his homestead. Perez testified that Montes brought a contract to him more than once, but that the contract was never complete, and no contract was ever signed. Despite the lack of a contract, Perez arranged for the Naismith and Trevino Construction Company to do the work on Montes's house. Montes paid $1,800 to Perez, and Perez withdrew from the transaction.

Naismith and Trevino made improvements on Montes's homestead for a total value of $3,835.36, but Montes refused to pay for the improvements. Naismith and Trevino brought suit against Montes, arguing that even though they did not have a contract with Montes, they should be paid for their labor and the materials they used in making improvements to his house. The court agreed and entered JUDGMENT for Naismith and Trevino in the amount of $1,760, the amount of the services and materials provided by Naismith and Trevino less the amount Montes had paid to Perez. The court based its ruling on the theory of quantum meruit.

The doctrine of quantum meruit is contained in court decisions and, to a lesser extent, in statutes. It can be a confusing doctrine: many courts mix quantum meruit with the similar principles of RESTITUTION and unjust enrichment. Restitution is a broad term that describes measures taken by a civil or criminal defendant to restore a victim to the status that he enjoyed before the defendant caused a loss or injury. Unjust enrichment is an equitable approach to civil relationships that covers more than just contractual situations. A civil plaintiff may recover under the doctrine of unjust enrichment by showing (1) that the plaintiff conferred a benefit on the defendant; (2) that the defendant appreciated or knew of the benefit; and (3) that, under the circumstances, it was unfair for the defendant to accept or retain the benefit without paying for it. Most courts consider quantum meruit a particular form of legal restitution that follows the basic restitutionary principle of preventing unjust enrichment.

QUANTUM VALEBANT [*Latin, As much as they were worth.*] An archaic form of PLEADING a lawsuit to recover payment for goods that have been sold and delivered.

QUARE [*Latin, Wherefore; for what reason; on what account.*] The introductory term used in the Latin form of a number of common-law WRITS at the beginning of the statement of the reason for the dispute.

Quare is more commonly used in its English form, *query*.

QUASH To overthrow; to annul; to make void or declare invalid; e.g., "quash a SUBPOENA."

Unreasonable, obviously irregular, or oppressive subpoenas, INJUNCTIONS, indictments, and orders can be quashed by a court. For example, if jurors have been selected improperly, the court can quash the proceedings.

In criminal cases, if an INDICTMENT is defective to such a degree that no judgment could be made if the defendant were to be convicted, the court typically will quash the indictment. In criminal cases, a motion made by the prosecution to quash an indictment is much more likely to succeed than one made by the defense, whose motion would appear self-serving.

QUASI [*Latin, Almost as it were; as if; analogous to.*] In the legal sense, the term denotes that one subject has certain characteristics in common with another subject but that intrinsic and material differences exist between them.

A quasi contract is an obligation invoked by law in the absence of an agreement. Its purpose is to create a legal duty where, in fact, no promise or agreement was entered into by the parties.

When an ADMINISTRATIVE AGENCY makes rules and regulations, it is acting in a quasi-legislative capacity.

QUASI CONTRACT An obligation that the law creates in the absence of an AGREEMENT between the parties. It is invoked by the courts where unjust enrichment, which occurs when a person retains money or benefits that in all fairness belong to another, would exist without judicial relief.

A quasi contract is a contract that exists by order of a court, not by agreement of the parties. Courts create quasi contracts to avoid the unjust enrichment of a party in a dispute over payment for a good or service. In some cases a party who has suffered a loss in a business relationship may not be able to recover for the loss without EVIDENCE of a CONTRACT or some legally recognized agreement. To avoid this unjust result, courts create a fictitious agreement where no legally enforceable agreement exists.

To illustrate, assume that a homebuilder has built a house on Alicia's property. However, the homebuilder signed a contract with Bobby, who claimed to be Alicia's AGENT but, in fact, was not. Although there is no binding contract between Alicia and the homebuilder, most courts would allow the homebuilder to recover the cost of the services and materials from Alicia to avoid an unjust result. A court would accomplish this by creating a fictitious agreement between the homebuilder and Alicia and holding Alicia responsible for the cost of the builder's services and materials.

Quasi contracts sometimes are called implied-in-law contracts to distinguish them from implied-in-fact contracts. An implied-in-law contract is one that at least one of the parties did not intend to create but that should, in all fairness, be created by a court. An implied-in-fact contract is simply an unwritten, nonexplicit contract that courts treat as an express written contract because the words and actions of the parties reflect a consensual transaction. The difference is subtle but not without practical effect.

One notable difference between the two implied contracts is that courts have no JURISDICTION over quasi-contract claims against the federal government. Under the doctrine of SOVEREIGN IMMUNITY, the federal government cannot be sued without its consent. An implied-in-fact contract arises from an actual agreement that was not memorialized in writing, and if an agent of the government entered into an agreement, a court could find consent to suit on the part of the government. A quasi-contract claim, by contrast, does not allege that an agreement existed, only that one should be imposed by the court to avoid an unjust result. Because a quasi-contract claim does not allege any consent on the part of the government, it would fail under the doctrine of sovereign immunity.

A quasi contract may afford less recovery than an implied-in-fact contract. A contract implied in fact will construct the whole agreement as the parties intended, so the party seeking the creation of an implied contract may be entitled to expected profits as well as the cost of labor and materials. A quasi contract will be created only to the extent necessary to prevent unjust enrichment. As one court has put it, contracts implied in law are "merely remedies granted by the court to enforce equitable or

State long-arm statutes have almost completely eliminated the need for quasi in rem jurisdiction as a basis for personal jurisdiction.

APWIDE WORLD PHOTOS

moral obligations in spite of the lack of assent of the party to be charged" (*Gray v. Rankin*, 721 F. Supp 115 [S.D. Miss. 1989]). The amount of recovery for an implied-in-law contract usually is limited to the cost of labor and materials because it would be unfair to force a person who did not intend to enter into a contract to pay for profits.

Quasi contracts are made possible by the doctrine of QUANTUM MERUIT (Latin for "as much as is deserved"), which allows courts to imply a contract where none exists. Quantum meruit includes implied-in-fact contracts as well as quasi contracts. Courts also use the term *quantum meruit* to describe the process of determining how much money the charging party may recover in an implied contract.

QUASI IN REM JURISDICTION The power of a court to hear a case and enforce a JUDGMENT against a party, even if the party is not personally before the court, solely because the party has an interest in REAL PROPERTY or PERSONAL PROPERTY within the geographical limits of the court.

Quasi in rem is a type of PERSONAL JURISDICTION exercised by a court over a party who owns property within the jurisdictional boundaries of the court. A court must have personal jurisdiction over the parties to a case before it can bind them with its decision. A court can gain personal jurisdiction over a party who resides in the court's home state; a court can also gain JURISDICTION over an out-of-state party who has made some contact with the state or who owns property within the court's geographical limits. There are two types of jurisdiction based on property: quasi in rem and IN REM.

Both in rem and quasi in rem jurisdiction are based on the presence of the party's property within the court's territorial authority. In each instance the court may exercise jurisdiction without the actual presence of the party in court. The distinction between the two types of jurisdiction involves the nature of the dispute to which each applies and the extent of the authority each conveys. In rem (Latin for "against the thing") jurisdiction applies where the dispute involves the property itself. A court exercising in rem jurisdiction has the authority to make a decision as to the property's ownership that will be binding on all the world. Quasi in rem (Latin for "sort of against the thing") jurisdiction applies to personal suits against the defendant, where the property is not the source of the conflict but is sought as compensation by the plaintiff. The authority of a court exercising quasi in rem jurisdiction is limited to a determination of the respondent's interest in the property.

A RESPONDENT in a quasi in rem proceeding is entitled to receive NOTICE of the proceeding. If the respondent makes an appearance to defend against a quasi in rem claim, he may be forced to defend against all the claims made by the plaintiff. In many states a respondent may avoid this by making a limited appearance to defend the case on the MERITS with only the property located in the area at stake.

The concept of quasi in rem jurisdiction has become all but obsolete. It is no longer acceptable for a state court to gain personal jurisdiction over a defendant merely because the defendant owns property in the state. In *Shaffer v. Heitner*, 433 U.S. 186, 97 S. Ct. 2569, 53 L. Ed. 2d 683 (1977), the U.S. Supreme Court ruled that a respondent must have a minimum level of purposeful contacts with the FORUM state before a state court may gain jurisdiction over the respondent. With enough contacts a respondent is deemed to have consented to the jurisdiction of the state and its courts. The *Shaffer* Court also held that courts should consider fair play and substantial justice in determining whether to require the appearance of an out-of-state respondent. These considerations should be applied to all forms of personal jurisdiction: in personam, in rem, and quasi in rem.

The practical effect of the *Shaffer* decision is to limit the number of cases based on in rem and quasi in rem jurisdiction. Due to the increasingly interstate nature of commerce in modern society, the average person may have contacts with, or own property in, several faraway states without even knowing it. Without a narrowed treatment of quasi in rem jurisdiction, potential civil respondents would be open to suit in any number of states with which they have no real connection. To guard against the abuse of quasi in rem jurisdiction, courts tend to closely examine intangible, movable property such as money and other NEGOTIABLE INSTRUMENTS, such as STOCKS, BONDS, and INSURANCE policies. To exercise quasi in rem jurisdiction over money or other negotiable instruments, a court will examine the nature of the respondent's contacts with the state and the relation of the property to the underlying dispute.

Quasi in rem jurisdiction as a basis for personal jurisdiction has been almost completely absorbed by LONG-ARM STATUTES. These statutes help plaintiffs gain in personam jurisdiction, so quasi in rem jurisdiction, with its limited relief, is frequently unnecessary. However, if the plaintiff's home state does not have a long-arm statute and an out-of-state respondent owns property in the state, the plaintiff may seek an ATTACHMENT of the property by asking the court to exercise quasi in rem jurisdiction over the property.

QUASI-JUDICIAL The action taken and discretion exercised by public administrative agencies or bodies that are obliged to investigate or ascertain facts and draw conclusions from them as the foundation for official actions.

As a general rule, only courts of law have the authority to decide controversies that affect individual rights. One major exception to this general rule is the power of an ADMINISTRATIVE AGENCY to make decisions concerning the rights of parties. An administrative agency is a body of government created by a legislature and charged with supervision and regulation of a particular area of governmental concern. Part of the regulatory power given to an administrative agency is the power of ADJUDICATION. Under the Administrative Procedure Act (60 Stat. 237 [5 U.S.C.A. § 551 et seq.]), an agency engages in adjudication when it follows a process for the formulation of an order. With the exception of rule making, any decision by an agency that has a legal effect is a quasi-judicial action.

Complaints against administrative agencies often arise when an agent denies benefits or places restrictions on an individual. For example, a homeowner who seeks to build another structure on her property must obtain approval from a number of administrative agencies. If the local conservation agency refuses to issue a permit for the building of a new structure, the homeowner may appeal this decision in a hearing before the agency's administrative board. The board may hear TESTIMONY and examine EVIDENCE at the hearing, and then it will decide whether to issue the permit or uphold the agency's refusal.

Quasi-judicial activity is limited to the issues that concern the particular administrative agency. For example, the Social Security Administration may resolve disputes on issues concerning Social Security contributions and benefits, but it may not decide any other issues, even those related to Social Security benefits such as tax, estate, and probate questions.

An administrative agency must hold a formal hearing only when required by statute. A formal HEARING is a complete hearing with the presentation of testimony, evidence, and arguments. An informal hearing usually is a simple meeting and discussion between an agent of the agency and the individual affected by the agency's actions. As a general rule, the scope of a hearing depends on the importance of the right at issue. If the Internal Revenue Service attempts to take away a person's homestead, for example, a full hearing would be required. By contrast, when an agent of the Department of Safety issues a small fine for illegal parking, the agency needs to provide only a brief, one-to-one meeting with a hearing officer regarding the issuance of the fine.

Quasi-judicial action by an administrative agency may be appealed to a court of law. With a few exceptions, a plaintiff generally must exhaust all remedies available through an agency before appealing the agency's decision in a case. One notable exception is that a person may appeal directly to a court of law and bypass the quasi-judicial activity of an administrative agency if the agency's remedies would be inadequate. For instance, if the CREDITORS of a failed bank are suing the Federal Savings and Loan Insurance Corporation, they need not go through the agency's hearings before filing suit in a court of law because the agency has ADVERSE INTERESTS to the creditors (*Coit Indep. Joint Venture v. FSLIC*, 489 U.S. 561, 109 S. Ct. 1361, 103 L. Ed. 2d 602 [1989]).

CROSS-REFERENCES

Administrative Law and Procedure; Bureaucracy; Public Administrative Bodies; Regulation.

QUASI-LEGISLATIVE The capacity in which a PUBLIC ADMINISTRATIVE AGENCY or body acts when it makes RULES and REGULATIONS.

When an administrative agency exercises its rule-making authority, it is said to act in a quasi-legislative manner. Administrative agencies acquire this authority to make rules and regulations that affect legal rights through statutes. This authority is an exception to the general principle that laws affecting rights should be passed only by elected lawmakers.

Administrative agency rules are made only with the permission of elected lawmakers, and elected lawmakers may strike down an administrative rule or even eliminate an agency. In this sense quasi-legislative activity occurs at the discretion of elected officials. Nevertheless, administrative agencies create and enforce many legal rules on their own, often without the advice of lawmakers, and the rules have the force of law. This means they have a binding effect on the general public.

Examples of quasi-legislative actions abound. Dozens of administrative agencies exist on the federal level, and dozens more exist on the state and local levels, and most of them have the authority to make rules that affect substantive rights. Agencies with authority over environmental matters may pass rules that restrict the rights of property owners to alter or build on their land; departments of revenue may pass rules that affect how much tax a person pays; and local housing agencies may set and enforce standards on health and safety in housing. These are just a few of the myriad rules passed by administrative agencies.

Except where prohibited by statute or judicial precedent, quasi-legislative activity may be challenged in a court of law. Generally, a person challenging quasi-legislative activity must wait until the rule-making process is complete and the rule or regulation is set before challenging it. Moreover, a challenge to an agency's rule or regulation usually must be made first to the agency itself. If no satisfaction is received from the agency, the complainant can then challenge the rule or regulation in a court of law.

Another distinctive feature of quasi-legislative activity is the provision of NOTICE and a HEARING. When an administrative agency intends to pass or change a rule that affects substantive legal rights, it usually must provide notice of this intent and hold a public hearing. This gives members of the public a voice in the quasi-legislative activity.

CROSS-REFERENCES

Administrative Law and Procedure; Bureaucracy; Public Administrative Bodies.

QUEEN'S BENCH See KING'S BENCH OR QUEEN'S BENCH.

QUESTION OF FACT An issue that involves the resolution of a factual dispute or controversy and is within the sphere of the decisions to be made by a jury.

A question of fact is a factual dispute between litigants that must be resolved by the JURY at TRIAL. It is an issue that is MATERIAL to the outcome of the case and requires an interpretation of conflicting views on the factual circumstances surrounding the case.

A question of fact is best understood by comparing it to a QUESTION OF LAW. Whether a particular issue in a civil case is a question of fact or law is significant because it can determine whether a party wins the case on summary judgment. Summary judgment is a JUDGMENT on the MERITS of the case without a trial. A civil RESPONDENT may move for summary judgment at any time after the suit has been filed, but a PLAINTIFF generally must wait a short period after filing the suit (for the DEFENDANT to respond) before moving for summary judgment. In determining whether to grant a MOTION for summary judgment, a court may consider admissions by the parties in their PLEADINGS, ANSWERS to INTERROGATORIES and DEPOSITIONS, and AFFIDAVITS of personal knowledge of facts.

A court will order summary judgment in a civil case if there is no genuine issue of fact and, based on the undisputed facts, the moving party is entitled to summary judgment as a matter of law. If a case does not involve any questions of fact, the only issues are questions of law, so the fact-finding process of a trial is not needed.

To illustrate, suppose that a plaintiff files suit to enforce an agreement to buy a plot of real estate. The respondent declares in her answer that the agreement was oral, and the plaintiff does not deny that the agreement was oral. The court could then order summary judgment in favor of the respondent because a CONTRACT for the sale of land must be in writing to be enforceable. Assuming that no other issues are involved, the admission that the agreement was oral eliminates the only material question of fact in the case. The only issue the court would have to decide would be a question of law: whether an oral agreement for the sale of land is enforceable. It is not, so the plaintiff would lose the case without the benefit of a trial because there are no material facts for a fact finder to decide.

Even if a plaintiff challenges a respondent's answer, a respondent may still win summary judgment by proving before trial that no question of fact exists in the case. To do this, the respondent must prove that no question of fact exists by the evidentiary standard that would be used at trial. In civil trials, this standard is either a preponderance of the evidence or the slightly higher standard of clear and convincing evidence. See also CLEAR AND CONVINCING PROOF; PREPONDERANCE OF EVIDENCE.

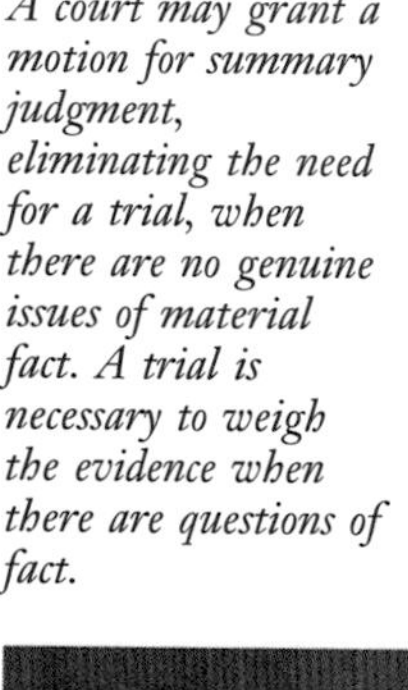

A court may grant a motion for summary judgment, eliminating the need for a trial, when there are no genuine issues of material fact. A trial is necessary to weigh the evidence when there are questions of fact.

Whether an issue is a question of fact or law is not always clear. In *Cruse v. Coldwell Banker*,

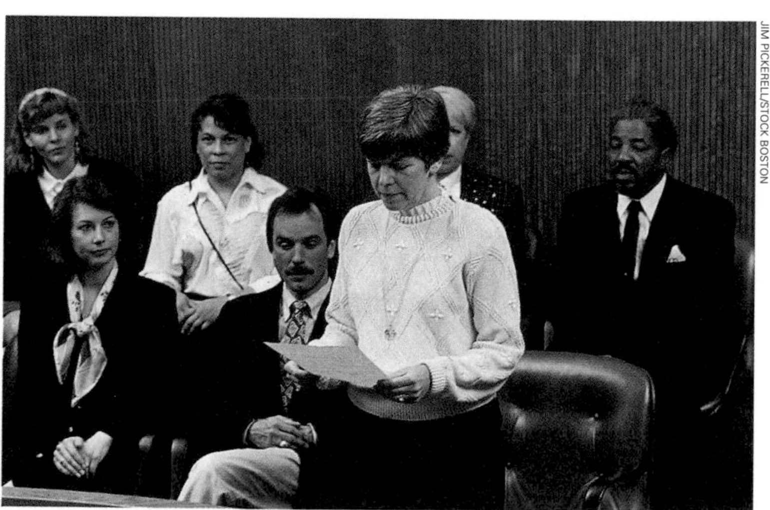

JIM PICKERELL/STOCK BOSTON

667 So. 2d 714 (Ala. 1995), Gary and Venita Cruse were shown a house advertised as new, although the sellers, Randy and Brenda Harris, were living in the house. The Cruses bought the house before making a complete inspection. Upon further inspection they discovered numerous defects, and sued the seller and the brokerage firm for FRAUD. The respondents moved for summary judgment on the grounds that the Cruses knew that the sellers were living in the house and that the Cruses signed a contract that stated that they took the house as it was, without WARRANTIES. The trial court granted the motion, ruling that no question of fact existed in the case and that the respondents were entitled to summary judgment as a matter of law. On appeal, the Alabama Supreme Court reversed the judgment. Regardless of the contract and the Cruses' knowledge of previous inhabitants, the description of the house as new carried with it an IMPLIED WARRANTY of HABITABILITY. Because no determination had been made as to whether the house was actually new, a material question of fact remained and summary judgment was inappropriate.

A question of fact receives the same treatment in a bench (non-jury) trial as it does in a jury trial. The only difference is that in a BENCH TRIAL the same person resolves both questions of law and fact because the fact finder is the judge. Nevertheless, in a bench trial, a judge may not decide material questions of fact without first affording the parties the process of a trial.

On APPEAL, a question of fact is treated differently than a question of law. If an APPELLANT alleges that the fact finder incorrectly decided questions of fact, an appeals court will give deference to the fact finder's decisions. The fact finder gets to see and hear all the EVIDENCE and thus is in a better position to make factual determinations than is the appeals court. If an appellant claims that the trial judge incorrectly decided a question of law, however, the appeals court will examine the trial judge's ruling more carefully. Essentially, it is more difficult to overturn a VERDICT based on a question of fact than a verdict based on a question of law.

QUESTION OF LAW An issue that is within the province of the JUDGE, as opposed to the JURY, because it involves the application or interpretation of legal principles or statutes.

At any stage in a proceeding, before or during TRIAL, a judge may have to determine whether to let a jury decide a particular issue. In making this determination, the judge considers whether the issue is a question of law or a QUESTION OF FACT. If the question is one of fact, it should be decided by the jury at trial. If the question is one of law, the judge may decide it without affording the parties the opportunity to present EVIDENCE and WITNESSES to the jury.

A question of law involves the interpretation of principles that are potentially applicable to other cases. In contrast, a question of fact requires an interpretation of circumstances surrounding the case at hand. Resolving questions of fact is the chief function of the jury. Resolving questions of law is a chief function of the judge.

If the PLEADINGS and initial evidence in a case show that there are no factual disputes between the parties, a court may grant summary judgment to a party. Summary judgment is a final JUDGMENT in the case made by the court before trial. A court may grant summary judgment in a case that contains no factual disputes because such a case presents only a question, or questions, of law, so the fact-finding function of the jury is not needed.

On APPEAL, the trial court's ruling on a question of law generally receives closer scrutiny than a jury's findings of fact. Being present at the trial, the fact finder is in a better position than the appeals court to evaluate evidence and TESTIMONY.

An issue may be characterized on appeal as a mixed question of law and fact. A mixed question occurs when the facts surrounding the case are admitted and the rule of the applicable law is undisputed; the issue then is whether the rule of law was correctly applied to the established facts. In a criminal case, for example, assume that a trial court, over the objection of the defendant, allows the prosecution to present evidence that the defendant was identified as the perpetrator. If the defendant is found guilty and challenges the identification procedure on appeal, the question is one of both law and fact. The appeals court must decide whether the trial court correctly applied the law on DUE PROCESS in identification procedures to the particular identification procedure used in the case. In such a case, the appeals court will scrutinize both the facts and the trial judge's rulings on questions of law.

QUICK ASSETS PERSONAL PROPERTY that is readily marketable.

Quick ASSETS are items, such as jewelry, that can be easily converted to cash for immediate use.

QUID PRO QUO [*Latin, What for what or Something for something.*] The mutual CONSIDERATION that passes between two parties to a contractual AGREEMENT, thereby rendering the agreement valid and binding.

In common usage, quid pro quo refers to the giving of one valuable thing for another. Quid pro quo has the same meaning in the law but with varying implications in different contexts.

Quid pro quo, or the exchange of valuable consideration, is required for the formation of a valid CONTRACT between individuals who are not merchants. This requirement of mutual consideration, or the exchange of something of value, indicates the sincerity of the parties' intent to adhere to the contract between them.

The term *quid pro quo* is also used in the contexts of politics and SEXUAL HARASSMENT. In politics quid quo pro can refer to the use of political office for personal benefit. For instance, an elected official might promise favorable governmental treatment to a person in exchange for something of value. This form of quid pro quo would be a violation of the law. On the federal level, the Hobbs Act (18 U.S.C.A. § 1951 [1994]) makes it a FELONY for a public official to EXTORT property under COLOR OF OFFICE. Trading campaign contributions for promises of official actions or inactions are also prohibited under the act.

In the area of sexual harassment, quid pro quo describes a form of sexual blackmail. Quid pro quo sexual harassment is the conditioning of employment benefits on an employee's submission to unwelcome sexual conduct. Title VII of the Civil Rights Act (42 U.S.C.A. § 2000 (e)-2 [1988]) provides a remedy for quid pro quo sexual harassment. Most courts follow the EQUAL EMPLOYMENT OPPORTUNITY COMMISSION's guidelines and hold that the necessary quid pro quo exists if submission to unwelcome sexual advances "is made either explicitly or implicitly a term or condition of an individual's employment" or if submission to unwelcome sexual advances "is used as the basis for employment decisions affecting such individual" (29 C.F.R. § 1604.11(a)(1)-(2) [1997]).

QUIET ENJOYMENT A COVENANT that promises that the GRANTEE or TENANT of an ESTATE in REAL PROPERTY will be able to possess the premises in peace, without disturbance by hostile claimants.

Quiet enjoyment is a right to the undisturbed use and enjoyment of real property by a tenant or landowner. The right to quiet enjoyment is contained in covenants concerning real estate. Generally a covenant is an agreement between two parties to do or refrain from doing something.

Courts read a covenant of quiet enjoyment between the LANDLORD AND TENANT into every rental agreement, or TENANCY. Thus a renter, or tenant, has the right to quiet enjoyment of the leased premises regardless of whether the rental agreement contains such a covenant.

In the covenant of quiet enjoyment, the landlord promises that during the term of the tenancy no one will disturb the tenant in the tenant's use and enjoyment of the premises. Quiet enjoyment includes the right to exclude others from the premises, the right to peace and quiet, the right to clean premises, and the right to basic services such as heat and hot water and, for high-rise buildings, elevator service. In many respects the implied covenant of quiet enjoyment is similar to an IMPLIED WARRANTY of HABITABILITY, which warrants that the landlord will keep the leased premises in good repair. For example, the failure to provide heat would be a breach of the implied covenant of quiet enjoyment because the lack of heat would interfere with the tenant's use of the premises and would also make the premises uninhabitable, especially in a cold climate.

Other rights related to quiet enjoyment may be tailored to specific situations. For example, at least one court has found that the ringing of smoke alarms for more than a day is an interference with a tenant's quiet enjoyment of leased premises (*Manzaro v. McCann*, 401 Mass. 880, 519 N.E.2d 1337 [1988]).

Tenants have at least two remedies for a landlord's breach of the covenant of quiet enjoyment: the tenant can cease to pay rent until the problem is solved, or the tenant can move out. A tenant who moves out may be liable for any rent owing under the agreement if a court decides that the landlord did not breach the covenant of quiet enjoyment.

A covenant of quiet enjoyment may be included in an exchange, or CONVEYANCE, of land ownership at the option of the parties to the deed. Quiet enjoyment has a slightly different scope in the context of land ownership than it has in the context of a tenancy. When a seller gives a DEED to the land to another party, the seller no longer has control over the property. The covenant of quiet enjoyment, when contained in a deed to real estate, warrants that the TITLE to the land is clear, meaning that it has no ENCUMBRANCES, or claims against it by other persons.

A warranty deed includes a covenant of quiet enjoyment. By contrast, a QUITCLAIM DEED makes no warranties regarding the title and contains no covenant of quiet enjoyment.

QUIET TITLE ACTION A proceeding to establish an individual's right to ownership of REAL PROPERTY against one or more adverse claimants.

An ACTION to quiet TITLE is a lawsuit filed to

establish ownership of real property (land and buildings affixed to land). The PLAINTIFF in a quiet title action seeks a court order that prevents the RESPONDENT from making any subsequent CLAIM to the property. Quiet title actions are necessary because REAL ESTATE may change hands often, and it is not always easy to determine who has title to the property.

A quiet title suit is also called a suit to remove a cloud. A cloud is any claim or potential claim to ownership of the property. The cloud can be a claim of full ownership of the property or a claim of partial ownership, such as a LIEN in an amount that does not exceed the value of the property. A title to real property is clouded if the plaintiff, as the buyer or recipient of real estate, might have to defend her full ownership of the property in court against some party in the future. A landowner may bring a quiet title action regardless of whether the respondent is asserting a present right to gain POSSESSION of the premises.

For example, assume that the seller of the property agreed to sell but died before the sale was finalized. Assume further that the seller also gave the property to a nephew in a WILL. In such a situation, both the nephew and the buyer have valid grounds for filing a suit to quiet title because each has a valid claim to the property.

The law on quiet title actions varies from state to state. Some states have quiet title statutes. Other states allow courts to fashion most of the laws regarding quiet title actions. Under the COMMON LAW, a plaintiff must be in possession of the property to bring a quiet title action, but many state statutes do not require actual possession by the plaintiff. In other states possession is not relevant. In some states only the person who holds LEGAL TITLE to the real estate may file a quiet title action, but in other states anyone with sufficient interest in the property may bring a quiet title action. Generally, a person who has sold the property does not have sufficient interest. When a landowner owns property subject to a MORTGAGE, the landowner may bring a quiet title action in states where the mortgagor retains title to the property. If the mortgagee keeps the title until the mortgage is paid, the mortgagee, not the landowner, would have to bring the action.

The general rule in a quiet title action is that the plaintiff may succeed only on the strength of his own claim to the real estate, and not on the weakness of the respondent's claim. The plaintiff bears the burden of proving that he owns the title to the property. A plaintiff may have less than a FEE SIMPLE, or less than full ownership, and maintain an action to quiet title. So long as the plaintiff's interest is valid and the respondent's interest is not, the plaintiff will succeed in removing the cloud (the respondent's claim) from the title to the property.

See also CLOUD ON TITLE.

IN RE QUINLAN *In Re Quinlan*, 70 N.J. 10, 355 A.2d 647 (1976), was the first major judicial decision to hold that life-sustaining medical treatments may be discontinued in appropriate circumstances, even if the patient is unable or incompetent to make the decision. The New Jersey Supreme Court's decision has been followed by nearly every state APPELLATE COURT to consider the issue. In addition to establishing a patient's right to refuse life-sustaining medical treatments, the *Quinlan* decision also made clear that a decision to remove or withhold life support systems from an incompetent patient would not constitute HOMICIDE or medical MALPRACTICE.

In 1975, Karen Ann Quinlan, age twenty-two, stopped breathing and lapsed into a coma. Quinlan's treating physicians determined that in addition to being comatose, Quinlan was in a "chronic persistent vegetative state" and could not survive without the assistance of a respirator. Further, the physicians believed that Quinlan had no chance of recovery and could not survive for more than a year even with the assistance of the respirator. Although Quinlan was not dead by any legal standard, her family wished to disconnect the respirator. The treating physicians, however, refused. Quinlan's father then sought judicial approval to act as Quinlan's legal GUARDIAN and to have the respirator removed.

After a lower court refused to order physicians to remove the respirator, Quinlan's father appealed to the New Jersey Supreme Court. First the court determined that a patient's decision regarding whether to continue with life-sustaining medical treatments implicates the patient's right to privacy, much as a woman's decision to terminate a pregnancy implicates the right to PRIVACY, as established in *Roe v. Wade*, 410 U.S. 113, 93 S. Ct. 705, 35 L. Ed. 2d 147 (1973).

The court then proceeded to weigh Quinlan's right to privacy against the state's interest in preserving human life and defending the right of a physician to administer medical treatment according to his or her best judgment. The court found that as the degree of bodily invasion increases and the prognosis for the patient's recovery dims, the patient's right to privacy increases and the state's interest weakens. In Quinlan's case, where the medical procedures were extremely invasive and Quinlan

APWIDE WORLD PHOTOS

Nearly every state appellate court followed the New Jersey Supreme Court ruling that allowed Karen Quinlan's parents (shown here holding her photograph) to withhold life-sustaining medical treatment from their comatose daughter.

had virtually no chance of recovering from a permanent vegetative state, the court concluded that Quinlan could choose to have the respirator discontinued, even if it meant she would die.

However, Quinlan was unable to make this decision. Thus, the court was faced with the issue of whether Quinlan's father could make the decision on her behalf. The court concluded that Quinlan's father and the rest of her family could decide whether to disconnect the respirator, stating that the "decision should be accepted by a society the overwhelming majority of whose members would, we think, in similar circumstances, exercise such a choice in the same way for themselves or for those closest to them." The court stated that Quinlan's father should act in accordance with his understanding of his daughter's best interests and not necessarily upon what his daughter would have done had she been able to express her wishes.

Although the *Quinlan* decision is most often cited as the decision that recognized the "right to die," commentators have stated that the decision's most important legacy was offering the medical profession freedom from criminal prosecution and civil LIABILITY when removing life support from patients in a chronically vegetative state. The *Quinlan* court stated that it believed the TESTIMONY of Quinlan's doctors who testified that the fear of criminal prosecution or civil liability had nothing to do with their refusal to disconnect Quinlan's respirator at her father's request and that their decision comported with standard medical practices. However, the court also believed that the fear of criminal sanctions and civil liability must have had some bearing on medical standards and practices as they then existed.

Thus, the *Quinlan* court was faced with the conflict between the patient's right to refuse invasive, life-sustaining medical procedures and the doctors' right to treat their patient as they saw fit. The court believed that the focal point in balancing these rights ought to be the possibility of the patient's returning to a cognitive and fulfilling life, as opposed to the "forced continuance of that biological vegetative existence" to which Quinlan was doomed. In resolving Quinlan's case, the court concluded that if her attending physicians, after consulting with the hospital's ethics committee, concluded that Quinlan had no reasonable possibility of ever emerging from her comatose condition to a cognitive, sapient state, the respirator that was believed to be sustaining her life ought to be removed in accordance with her family's wishes. The physicians could not be subject to criminal or civil liability for that decision.

Ironically, the New Jersey Supreme Court's decision had little impact on Quinlan's fate. Almost six weeks after the Court's ruling, Quinlan was still attached to a respirator and more medical technology was being employed to keep her alive. Eventually Quinlan was weaned off the respirator in accordance with her family's wishes, but she still survived another nine years, although she never emerged from a comatose state.

The *Quinlan* case has influenced U.S. law by providing the framework for deciding the difficult legal issues that continue to arise as advances in medical technology allow doctors to keep patients alive, even when they have little or no chance of returning to normal life. Nearly every judicial decision since *Quinlan* has recognized a patient's right to refuse life-sustaining medical treatments. Finally, the courts have agreed with *Quinlan* that where a patient is incompetent, the right to refuse such treatments may be asserted by the patient's family or guardian.

CROSS-REFERENCES

Death and Dying; Patients' Rights; Physicians and Surgeons.

QUIT To vacate; remove from; surrender possession.

When a TENANT leaves premises that he or she has been renting, the tenant is said to quit such premises.

A *notice to quit* is written notification given by a LANDLORD to a tenant that indicates that the landlord wants to repossess the premises and that the tenant must vacate them at a certain designated time.

QUI TAM ACTIONS CIVIL ACTIONS maintained by private persons on behalf of both themselves and the government to recover damages or to enforce penalties available under a statute prohibiting specified conduct. The term *qui tam* is short for the Latin *qui tam pro domino rege quam pro se ipso in hac parte sequitur*, which means "who brings the action for the king as well as for himself."

Qui tam actions are unusual in that the plaintiffs do not ALLEGE injuries to themselves but rather claim injuries to the government. In a successful qui tam action, the plaintiff, who is known as a *relator* or *informer*, shares any monetary recovery with the sovereign (the government).

Qui tam actions are created solely by statute. Legislatures authorize qui tam actions to encourage private citizens to assist the government in enforcing its statutes. By authorizing a qui tam action, the legislature creates a dual enforcement scheme where both private citizens and the EXECUTIVE BRANCH may redress violations of the statute creating the ACTION. In some respects a qui tam action is similar to the more common citizens' suit, which allows a private citizen to sue to redress injuries to the public. For example, environmental statutes often authorize citizens' suits as a means for members of the public to redress injuries to the environment. In a citizens' suit, however, the plaintiff citizen alleges an injury to herself as a member of the public at large, whereas a plaintiff in a qui tam action alleges a specific injury to the government.

Although qui tam actions are relatively unknown, they have existed in England for hundreds of years and in the United States since the foundation of the government. And although qui tam actions were authorized by the very first Congress, the most important statute creating qui tam actions was the False Claims Act of 1863. During the Civil War, defense contractors frequently defrauded the Union government. In response, Congress enacted the False Claims Act, which sought to encourage private citizens who had information concerning corrupt defense contractors to come forward.

Under the original False Claims Act, a successful relator in a qui tam action was entitled to one-half of the DAMAGES and FORFEITURES recovered and collected from the defendant, while the other half went to the federal treasury. This procedure was frequently abused, however, as plaintiffs brought qui tam actions when the government had already instituted criminal investigations against defense contractors. Thus, private citizens profited from the government's efforts to stop FRAUD by defense contractors. In response, Congress barred qui tam actions based on information already known to the government at the time the civil suit was filed, even if the government had taken no action on the information. Because of this restriction and the repeal of many qui tam statutes, the qui tam action was almost extinct until 1986.

In 1986 Congress revitalized qui tam actions under the False Claims Act in response to the widespread procurement abuses by defense contractors during President RONALD REAGAN'S defense buildup. The 1986 amendments to the False Claims Act (31 U.S.C.A. §§ 3729 et seq.) increased the financial incentives for bringing a qui tam action while easing the jurisdictional requirements for instituting a suit. Specifically the 1986 amendments permit relators to bring qui tam actions even if the government is aware of the information on which the action is based, unless the RELATOR obtained the information from public disclosures by the government. As a result of the amendments, the number of companies sued in qui tam actions under the False Claims Act has greatly increased. In addition to defense contractors, MEDICARE and MEDICAID providers have frequently been the target of qui tam actions. The False Claims Act is currently the only widely used statute authorizing qui tam actions.

The 1986 amendments to the False Claims Act have been challenged by defendants and other critics who assert that qui tam actions unconstitutionally delegate the executive branch's obligation to enforce statutes to unaccountable and self-interested citizens. In addition, defendants have argued that relators in qui tam actions lack legal STANDING to bring a lawsuit. The U.S. Constitution requires a plaintiff in a lawsuit to allege a distinct injury to himself; when a plaintiff fails to allege such an injury, he lacks standing to sue. Critics of qui tam actions point out that qui tam relators are alleging an injury to the government rather than themselves.

Despite these challenges, no court has held the qui tam provisions of the False Claims Act unconstitutional. In early 1997 the Supreme Court agreed to hear an appeal of a qui tam action under the False Claims Act but declined to review the Ninth Circuit's determination that the act's qui tam provisions are constitutional (*Hughes Aircraft Co. v. United States*, __U.S. __, 117 S. Ct. 1871, 138 L. Ed. 2d 135 [1997]). Defenders of qui tam actions point out that the individual members of the public are, at least indirectly, hurt by fraud against the government because the government is financially supported by the public. The courts have also repeatedly recognized Congress's authority to legislate the means for implementing its policy objectives. By authorizing qui tam actions, Congress has determined that allowing citizens to sue on behalf of the government is a valid and effective means for enforcing statutes. Thus, the qui tam action remains an important weapon in redressing fraud against the government. In 1996 qui tam actions led to nearly $1.5 billion in recoveries.

QUITCLAIM DEED An instrument of CONVEYANCE of REAL PROPERTY that passes any TITLE, CLAIM, or interest that the grantor has in the premises but does not make any representations as to the validity of such title.

A quitclaim deed is a release by the GRANTOR, or conveyor of the deed, of any interest the grantor may have in the property described in the DEED. Generally a quitclaim deed relieves the grantor of LIABILITY regarding the ownership of the property. Thus, the grantor of a quitclaim deed will not be liable to the GRANTEE, or recipient of the deed, if a competing claim to the property is later discovered. A quitclaim deed is not a guarantee that the grantor has CLEAR TITLE to the property; rather it is a relinquishment of the grantor's rights, if any, in the property. By contrast, in a warranty deed the grantor promises that she owns the property with no cloud on the title (that is, no competing claims).

The holder of a quitclaim deed receives only the interest owned by the person conveying the deed. If the grantee of a quitclaim deed learns after accepting the deed that the grantor did not own the property, the grantee may lose the property to the true owner. If it turns out that the grantor had only a partial interest in the property, the quitclaim deedholder holds only that partial interest.

In some states a quitclaim deed does not relieve the grantor of liability for all ENCUMBRANCES, or clouds, on the title. In these states a grantor must warrant that neither the grantor nor anyone associated with the grantor has a claim to the title. The grantor must defend the title for the grantee if a cloud on the title arose under or through the grantor. For example, if a CONTRACT made by the grantor resulted in a LIEN being placed on the property, the grantor would have to defend against that claim for the grantee, even under a quitclaim deed. If the property has changed hands several times after the cloud first appeared, however, the grantor may not be liable to the grantee.

See also CLOUD ON TITLE.

QUO ANIMO [*Latin, With what intention or motive.*] A term sometimes used instead of the word *animus*, which means design or MOTIVE.

QUORUM A majority of an entire body; e.g., a quorum of a legislative assembly.

A quorum is the minimum number of people who must be present to pass a law, make a judgment, or conduct business. Quorum requirements typically are found in a court, legislative assembly, or corporation (where those attending might be directors or stockholders). In some cases, the law requires more people than a simple majority to form a quorum. If no such defining number is determined, a quorum is a simple majority.

A quorum also might mean the number of members of a body defined as competent to transact business in the absence of the other members. The purpose of a quorum rule is to give decisions made by a quorum enough authority to allow binding action to be conducted.

In both houses of Congress, a quorum consists of a simple majority of members.

QUO WARRANTO A legal proceeding during which an individual's right to hold an office or governmental privilege is challenged.

In old English practice, the WRIT of quo warranto—an order issued by authority of the king—was one of the most ancient and important writs. It has not, however, been used for centuries, since the procedure and effect of the judgment were so impractical.

Currently the former procedure has been replaced by an *information in the nature of a quo warranto*, an EXTRAORDINARY REMEDY by which a prosecuting attorney, who represents the public at large, challenges someone who has usurped a public office or someone who, through abuse or neglect, has forfeited an office to which she was entitled. In spite of the fact that the remedy of quo warranto is pursued by a prosecuting attorney in a majority of JURISDICTIONS, it is ordinarily regarded as a civil rather than criminal action. Quo warranto is often the only proper legal remedy; however, the legislature can enact legislation or provide other forms of relief.

Statutes describing quo warranto usually indicate where it is appropriate. Ordinarily it is proper to try the issue of whether a public office or authority is being abused. For example, it might be used to challenge the unauthorized practice of a profession, such as law or medicine. In such situations, the challenge is an assertion that the defendant is not qualified to hold the position she claims—a medical doctor, for example.

In some quo warranto proceedings, the issue is whether the defendant is entitled to hold the office he claims, or to exercise the authority he presumes to have from the government. In addition, proceedings have challenged the right to the position of county commissioner, treasurer, school board member, district attorney, judge, or tax commissioner. In certain jurisdictions, quo warranto is a proper proceeding to challenge individuals who are acting as officers or directors of business CORPORATIONS.

A prosecuting attorney ordinarily commences quo warranto proceedings; however, a statute may authorize a private person to do so without the consent of the prosecutor. Unless otherwise provided by statute, a court permits the filing of an information in the nature of quo warranto after an exercise of sound discretion, since quo warranto is an extraordinary exercise of power and is not to be invoked lightly. Quo warranto is not a right available merely because the appropriate legal documents are filed. Valid reason must be indicated to justify governmental interference with the individual holding the challenged office, privilege, or license.

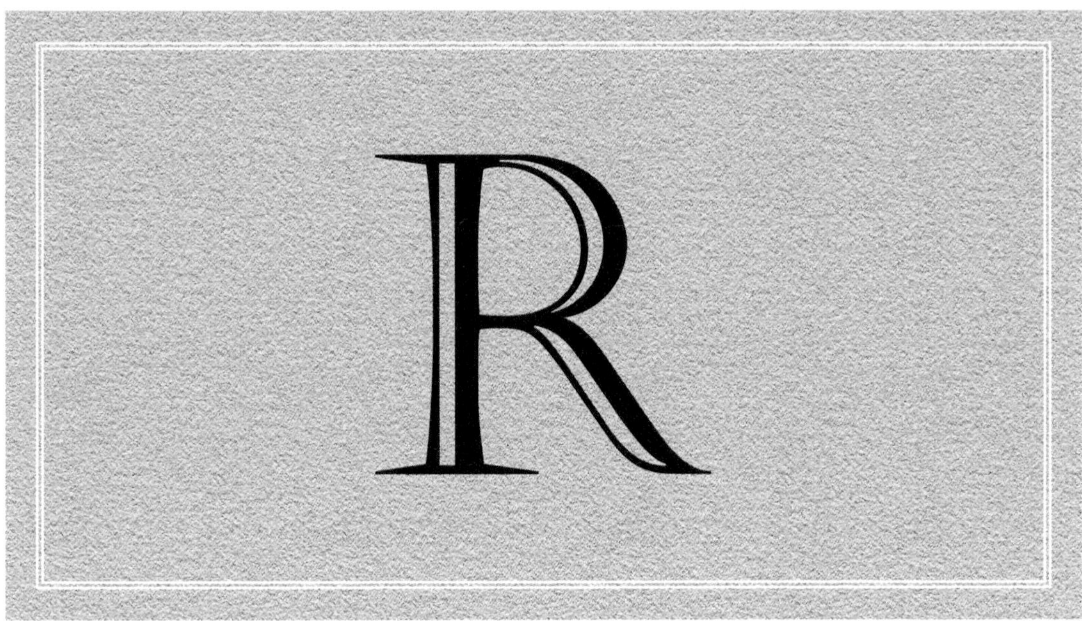

RACKETEER INFLUENCED AND CORRUPT ORGANIZATIONS ACT A set of federal laws (18 U.S.C.A. § 1961 et seq. [1970]) specifically designed to punish criminal activity by business enterprises.

Congress passed the Racketeer Influenced and Corrupt Organizations Act (RICO) as part of the Organized Crime Control Act of 1970. ORGANIZED CRIME in the United States had been increasing since the TWENTY-FIRST AMENDMENT's prohibition of ALCOHOL was repealed in 1933. Crime groups and families that had been bootlegging moved on to other moneymaking crimes by controlling legitimate businesses and using some of them as fronts for criminal activity. Over the years Congress had enacted several statutes authorizing increased punishment for typical organized crimes such as gambling, loan sharking, transportation of stolen goods, and EXTORTION. However, it had not passed legislation specifically punishing the very act of committing organized crime.

Organized crime continued to proliferate in the 1960s. Congress responded by passing legislation specifically dealing with organized crime. After investigating and debating organized crime legislation for approximately twenty years, beginning with Senate committee hearings conducted in 1951 by Tennessee Senator Estes Kefauver, Congress finally passed RICO.

The specific goal of RICO is to punish the use of an enterprise to engage in certain criminal activity. A person who uses an enterprise to engage in a pattern of racketeering activity may be convicted under the RICO criminal statute (18 U.S.C.A. § 1963). An enterprise is defined as "any individual, partnership, corporation, association, or other legal entity, and any union or group of individuals associated in fact although not a legal entity." A pattern is defined as "at least two acts of racketeering activity, one of which occurred after the effective date of [RICO's passage] and the last of which occurred within ten years . . . after commission of a prior act of racketeering activity." Racketeering activity includes a number of discrete criminal offenses, such as gambling, BRIBERY, extortion, BANKRUPTCY fraud, MAIL FRAUD, securities FRAUD, PROSTITUTION, narcotics trafficking, loan sharking, and MURDER.

RICO outlaws every manner in which an enterprise can be used for long-term racketeering activity. Under the law no person may invest racketeering proceeds to acquire any interest in an enterprise; no person may acquire or maintain an interest in an enterprise through a pattern of racketeering activity; and no person associated with or employed by an enterprise may conduct that enterprise's affairs through a pattern of racketeering activity.

The punishment for violating the criminal provisions of RICO is exceptionally harsh. If convicted, a defendant is fined and sentenced to not more than twenty years in prison for each RICO violation. Furthermore, the defendant must forfeit any interest, claim against, or property or contractual right over the criminal enterprise, as well as any property that constitutes the racketeering activity or was derived from the racketeering activity. Finally, RICO contains civil provisions that allow a party injured by a RICO defendant to recover from the defendant in civil court. A successful civil RICO

RICO IN NEED OF REFORM?

When Congress passed the Racketeer Influenced and Corrupt Organizations (RICO) Act (18 U.S.C.A. § 1961 et seq.) in 1970, its intent was to mount an all-fronts attack on the infiltration of legitimate businesses by organized criminal enterprises. The RICO Act provides criminal and civil remedies, which are designed to imprison racketeers and to destroy the financial base of organized crime. Since the act's passage, however, its civil provisions have been applied more often than its criminal provisions and have generally been used against businesses and other organizations that are not dominated by organized crime. Plaintiffs have discovered that the act's broad language allows its use in cases involving malpractice and "garden variety commercial fraud." Critics of this use of civil RICO have called for congressional reform.

IN FOCUS

The U.S. Supreme Court, in *Sedima S.P.R.L. v. Imrex Co.*, 473 U.S. 479, 105 S. Ct. 3275, 87 L. Ed. 2d 346 (1985), upheld the constitutionality of the RICO Act and made clear that, unless amended by Congress, the statute must be interpreted broadly. The *Sedima* decision removed a number of judicially created barriers to using civil RICO against legitimate businesses.

Despite congressional attempts to limit the scope of civil RICO, only one major area of law has been removed from the RICO Act. The Private Securities Litigation Reform Act of 1995 (15 U.S.C.A. § 77 et seq.) eliminated liability for RICO claims based on securities fraud, unless the defendant has already been criminally convicted of securities fraud. The act thus removed the threat of treble (triple) damages in such cases. Congress concluded that federal securities laws generally provide adequate remedies for victims of securities fraud. Therefore, it was unnecessary and unfair to expose defendants in securities cases to the threat of treble damages and other extraordinary remedies provided by the RICO Act.

Critics of the RICO Act applaud this congressional action but argue that the same reasoning can and should be applied to other areas of civil law. These critics maintain that the act's broad scope has given plaintiffs an unfair advantage in civil litigation.

One criticism of civil RICO is that no criminal convictions are necessary to win a civil case under the act. The plaintiff need only show by a preponderance of evidence that it is more likely than not that the on-going criminal enterprise occurred. By contrast, a criminal RICO case must be proved beyond a reasonable doubt.

In addition, the judge and jury in a criminal RICO case are prohibited from drawing an adverse inference from a defendant's invocation of the Fifth Amendment privilege against self-incrimination. No such ban exists, however, in a civil RICO case. Critics contend that it is unfair for a party in a civil RICO case who has concerns about potential criminal liability to be forced to waive her Fifth Amendment privilege in order to mount an effective defense in the civil action. Once testimony is given in the civil case, the party has effectively waived the privilege against self-incrimination, and the testimony may be used in a subsequent criminal prosecution. Critics contend that the RICO Act should be amended to stay (delay) a civil RICO proceeding until a criminal RICO proceeding has been concluded.

The critics of civil RICO also believe that its use has given plaintiffs an unfair tool that often serves to coerce a party to settle out of fear of a treble damages award. These critics believe that no civil RICO action should be allowed unless the party has been convicted under criminal RICO.

Critics also contend that criminal RICO has been an almost total failure in stopping the infiltration of legitimate businesses by organized crime. Not only have very few criminal RICO cases been brought to trial, but most of the defendants in those cases were not the targets Congress originally intended. According to the critics, most criminal uses of the RICO Act are redundant. Other laws exist to punish government corruption and white-collar crimes. The RICO Act merely enhances their penalties.

Despite these criticisms, the RICO Act has many supporters. While agreeing that the statute is broad in scope and imprecise in language, they contend that Congress wanted the act to read just this way. Congress recognized that private enforcement of the act through civil lawsuits would supplement the government's inadequate prosecution resources.

Supporters of civil RICO also point out that parties can be protected from waiving the privilege of self-incrimination. A trial court has the authority to stay a civil RICO proceeding until a criminal RICO prosecution has been concluded or the government announces that a criminal action will be commenced. In addition, a trial court may enter a protective order that keeps the information revealed by the party confidential or sealed. Finally, as in a criminal case a judge in a civil RICO action may advise a jury not to draw an adverse inference if the defendant does not testify.

Finally, supporters believe RICO actions should not be limited to organized crime. They argue that as a matter of public policy, it is reasonable to award treble damages to victims of commercial fraud and other illegal behavior that comes within the language of the act. According to civil RICO's defenders, these damage awards act as a deterrent to businesses and organizations that have created social harm by conducting business in a distinctly criminal way.

See also Beyond a Reasonable Doubt; Preponderance of Evidence; Securities; Self-Incrimination.

plaintiff may collect TREBLE DAMAGES, or three times the amount lost to the defendant, as well as attorney's fees and other costs associated with the litigation. The intent of the many and various sanctions is to cripple and ultimately eradicate organized crime enterprises.

RICO employs broad definitions to sweep a wide variety of enterprise criminal activity into its purview. One of the original goals of RICO was to eliminate organized crime families, such as the loose collection of crime families that comprised the Mafia. However, because Congress could not legislate against specific persons or families, it was forced to use broad language to define racketeering and organized crime. The far-reaching language of the statute has subjected a wide range of criminal defendants to RICO's penalties. The typical RICO defendant is far from the stereotypical violent mobster. A RICO defendant can be anyone who uses a business in any way to commit two or more of the many racketeering offenses.

RICO has proved to be a powerful tool in the federal government's fight against organized crime. Many states also have enacted RICO-style statutes designed to apprehend organized crime that somehow escapes the provisions of RICO. Prosecutors have used RICO against a variety of criminals and obtained lengthy sentences for them. According to many critics, RICO has been expanded beyond its original purpose of eradicating traditional organized crime groups to convict petty, nonviolent criminals and sentence them to unduly long prison terms. Supporters of RICO counter that the act was intended to reach all organized crime, not just traditional organized crime groups. Advocates of RICO argue further that the act is not unduly harsh because the use of a business enterprise to conduct criminal activity is more dangerous and more difficult to eradicate than individual, freelance criminal activity and that therefore the defendants who commit acts that bring them under RICO's provisions deserve the punishment they receive.

Most observers have agreed that the civil provisions of RICO have been abused. Beginning in the late 1970s, civil attorneys began to realize the enormous moneymaking potential of RICO's civil provisions allowing payment of treble damages, fees, and costs to successful RICO plaintiffs. It became common for supposed victims to bring CIVIL ACTIONS against anyone who was remotely and indirectly associated with a criminal enterprise and financially solvent enough to pay a RICO JUDGMENT. Some of the targets of civil RICO claims have included accountants, bankers, insurance companies, securities firms, and major corporations such as General Motors and MCI Communications. In many cases defendants in civil RICO cases have denied any wrongdoing but have been forced to settle because they were afraid of losing and being forced to pay a huge judgment.

In 1993 the Supreme Court limited the scope of civil RICO claims with its decision in the case of *Reves v. Ernst & Young*, 507 U.S. 170, 113 S. Ct. 1163, 122 L. Ed. 2d 525. In *Reves*, an accounting firm performed three AUDITS of a farmers' cooperative to determine its financial health after its general manager and accountant were convicted of tax fraud. When the cooperative went bankrupt, note holders on the cooperative filed suit against forty individuals and entities associated with the cooperative. One of the claims was a civil RICO claim against the accounting firm. The note holders claimed that the accountants participated in a scheme to inflate the value of the cooperative above its actual value, that this scheme constituted fraud, and that the accountants had participated in the operation or management of the cooperative's affairs. The Supreme Court disagreed, holding that the accounting firm's level of participation in the cooperative did not rise to the level of operation or management of the cooperative's affairs and that therefore it was beyond the reach of RICO LIABILITY.

See also GAMING; LOAN SHARK; MONEY LAUNDERING.

RAILROAD The idea of using rails for transportation was first conceived as early as the sixteenth century. The first railroads used wooden rails to guide horse-drawn wagons. In the eighteenth century, cast-iron wheels and rails were used in Europe and England, and by the nineteenth century, horses had been replaced by steam-driven engines as the source of power. The first public railroad equipped for steam-powered engines was a twenty-mile track built in England in the 1820s.

In the United States, the first commercial steam-powered railroad service was provided in South Carolina. On December 25, 1830, the South Carolina Railroad pulled a short passenger train from Charleston. Compared with the trains and lines today, the first trains were small and the lines were short. But the technology continued to improve, and railroads increased in number, size, and strength throughout the first half of the nineteenth century. In 1830 only twenty-three miles of rail existed in the United States. By the mid-1830s, more than one thousand miles of railroad tracks had been laid, and by 1850 more than nine thousand miles of rails existed.

At first, most of the railroads were constructed in the eastern states. As the United States bought, acquired, and conquered land to the west of the colonies in the first half of the nineteenth century, many industrialists came to see the railroad as the perfect vehicle for access to the natural resources and growing markets of the West. The idea of a transcontinental railroad was born in the early 1840s. The discovery of gold in California in 1848 accelerated the plans, but the most important event that inspired the creation of a transcontinental railroad was the Civil War.

The federal government was eager to assume control over California to gain a strategic advantage over the Confederacy. Passage to California by rail was the best way to secure a link to the West. In May 1862 Congress passed the Pacific Railroad Act, 43 U.S.C.A. § 942-3, which granted public land to the Union Pacific Railroad for each mile of track that it laid from Nebraska to California. The LAND GRANTS were designed to encourage private investment in the railroads. Shortly thereafter, the Central Pacific Railroad began to compete with the Union Pacific for government land grants.

The construction of a transcontinental rail system was an enormous task. It was difficult for the private sector to find the resources to fund such an endeavor, and it became apparent to all concerned that a railroad system that spanned the entire country would not be developed without some help from the government. From 1862 to 1871, the federal government granted more than one hundred million acres of land to private railroad companies to promote the construction of railroads. As the country moved westward, construction increased. As construction increased, the need to move materials and goods increased, and this created a dependency on the railroads.

The railroads became the most important service in the country from the late nineteenth century through the first part of the twentieth century. They largely supplanted the use of canals and other waterways for shipping large loads because they were faster than watercraft, operated on more direct routes, and were capable of carrying larger loads. As the public dependency on railroads increased, the railroad business became extremely profitable. Railroad companies consolidated and integrated the rail lines but maintained a vast system connecting all of the continental United States.

In 1920 the Transportation Act, 40 U.S.C.A. § 316, allowed railroads to abandon certain routes that were not profitable. As the railroads consolidated, they were forced to cut costs by laying off workers. Congress addressed the problem by freezing railroad employment levels for three years in the Emergency Railroad Transportation Act of 1933. Shortly thereafter, the INTERSTATE COMMERCE COMMISSION mandated protections for dismissed or displaced railroad workers. Today, dismissed or laid-off railroad workers are entitled to compensation, fringe benefits, moving and housing expenses, and training for new employment.

Class I Railroads: 1980 to 1995

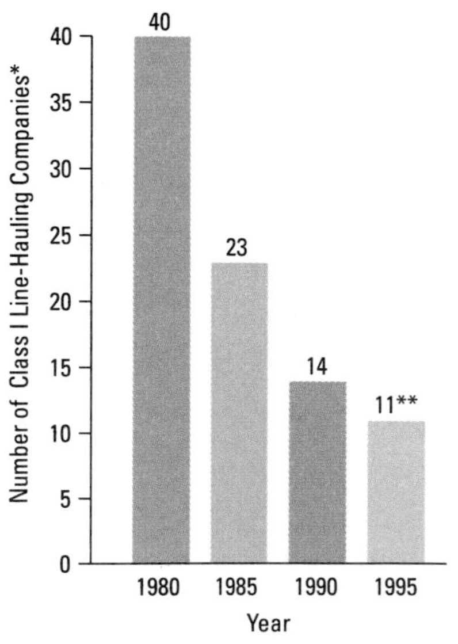

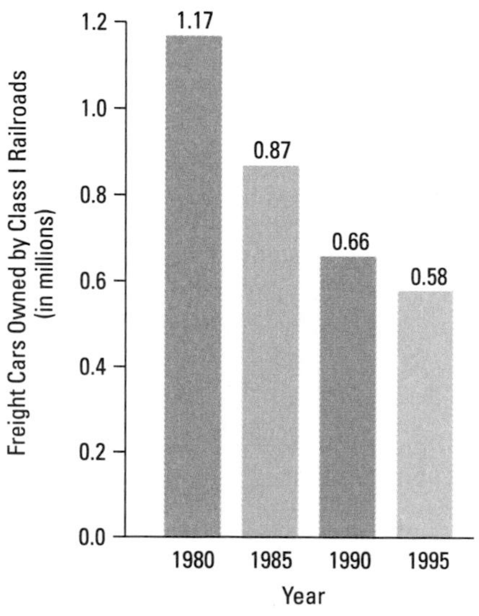

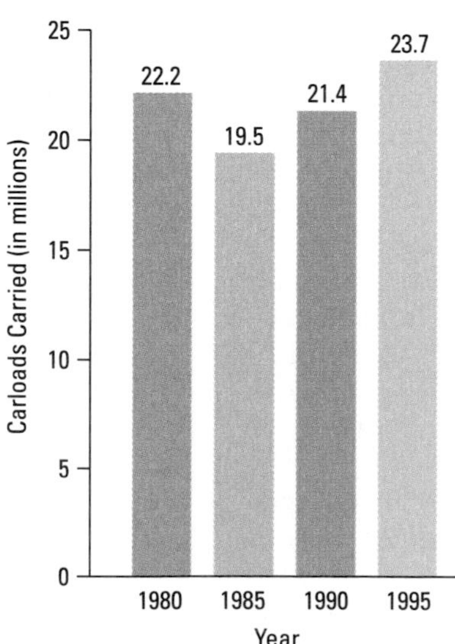

* Class I railroads are those that reported revenues of at least $255.9 million annually (1995 statistics).
** As of 1997, company mergers dropped the number of Class I railroads to nine. They include: Burlington Northern Santa Fe Railway, Conrail, Canadian National, Canadian Pacific Railway, CSX Transportation, Illinois Central, Kansas City Southern Lines, Norfolk Southern, and Union Pacific.

Source: Association of American Railroads, Washington, DC, *Railroad Facts, Statistics of Railroads of Class I,* annual.

The railroad boom of the late nineteenth century not only made moguls of railroad owners but also led to monopolies in other markets, such as the coal, iron, and steel markets. Large railroad companies were able to offer lower prices to buyers than could smaller companies. Unlike other producers, the railroads did not have to pay for shipping costs. The public outcry over these unfair trade practices, and the inability of states to deal with an essentially interstate problem, forced Congress to regulate the railroad industry. Around the same time, the existing railroad companies began to support regulation of railroad prices to keep rates from dropping due to increased competition within the railroad industry itself.

Congress passed the SHERMAN ANTI-TRUST ACT of 1890 (15 U.S.C.A. § 1 et seq.) to prevent monopolization, or the unreasonable interference with the ordinary and usual competitive pricing or distribution system of the open market in interstate trade. In 1887 Congress passed the INTERSTATE COMMERCE ACT (24 Stat. 379), which established the Interstate Commerce Commission to regulate, in large part, the railroad industry. The commission was granted the power to set railroad rates. However, the Supreme Court struck down this grant of power, and the commission was relegated to an information-gathering agency. In 1906 Congress again granted to the Interstate Commerce Commission the power to set railroad service rates, and this grant of power survived JUDICIAL REVIEW (*Delaware, Lackawanna, & Western Railroad Co. v. United States*, 231 U.S. 363, 34 S. Ct. 65, 58 L. Ed. 269 [1913]).

Another important concern about railroads was price discrimination in railroad service. Railroads are COMMON CARRIERS, which describes a transportation business that offers service to the general public. The rates charged by common carriers are regulated under the theory that their service has an effect on interstate commerce, which is within the regulatory power of the federal government under Article I, Section 8, Clause 3, of the U.S. Constitution. Under its power to regulate interstate commerce, Congress prevents rate discrimination on the public railways because rate discrimination is a patently unfair trade practice that has a detrimental effect on interstate commerce and the economic health of the country. For instance, a railroad cannot charge some customers one rate for shipping on the railroad and charge a subsidiary of the railroad company a lesser rate. Passenger trains also may not discriminate in rates or service because they offer carrier service to the general public.

Congress and the states have enacted numerous statutes and regulations to address the extraordinary number of issues presented by railroads. The subject matter of these statutes and administrative regulations ranges from safety regulations to local speed limits to rate controls. In 1966 Congress created the Federal Railroad Administration along with the Department of Transportation to give special attention to railroad concerns.

The success of the railroad system was not without costs. Railroad work proved to be among the most dangerous occupations in existence. Freight car derailments, undependable brakes, and the challenging task of switching heavy, rolling cars from one track to another in railroad yards all took their toll on railroad workers. Approximately 3,500 railroad workers were killed each year between 1903 and 1907, and the death toll continued at approximately one a day for several years after that.

States began to enact safety measures to protect railroad employees, but the state laws varied and did not always provide protection for workers. In 1970 Congress passed the Federal Railroad Safety Act, 49 U.S.C.A. § 20101 et seq., to achieve uniformity in railroad safety regulations. The act provides for safety enforcement procedures, track safety standards, freight car safety standards, emergency order procedures, train-marking regulations, accident report procedures, locomotive safety and inspection standards, safety appliance standards, power brake and drawbar specifications, and regulations on signal systems and train control systems.

Railroad work is still a relatively taxing occupation, but it is nowhere near as dangerous as it once was. The quality of freight equipment has improved, and due to the creation of single-unit trains, freight cars do not have to be switched from track to track as often as they once were. Most railroad-related accidents and deaths now occur at grade crossings, where railroad tracks cross roadways.

Railroad labor, management, and executive unions have been responsible for many of the gains in railroad safety. Railroad unions were some of the first unions created, and they quickly evolved to be among the most powerful. The railroad labor unions are still among the most influential LABOR UNIONS in the country.

Under the law, railroads are a special form of transportation. Railroad companies must pay taxes on their land and pay for the maintenance of their rights of way. This is not the case for other transporters. Trucking companies do not have to pay their own separate taxes for road-

The Robber Barons

The U.S. railroad barons of the mid- to late nineteenth century loomed over the nation's economy. Unfettered by rules and unrestrained by lawmakers and judges, the handful of railroad owners and executives could do virtually whatever they wanted. The vast fortunes they built and control they exercised not only helped to expand national frontiers but also ushered in the market controls that now limit the creation of trusts and monopolies.

The railroad barons were colorful men. Probably the most notorious was Jay Gould (1836–92). A one-time tannery operator from New York with little education, Gould gained control of the Erie Railroad while still in his early thirties. His methods included a number of unlawful or unethical practices: issuing fraudulent stock, bribing legislators, starting price wars against competitors, betraying associates, using his newspaper to cause financial ruin, and manipulating the gold market. Gould even managed to dupe the U.S. Treasury, causing the 1869 stock market panic. At the time of his death, he was worth $77 million.

The barons were passionately monopolistic. As a director of the Union Pacific Railroad, Edward Henry Harriman (1849–1909) gobbled up western competitors until he controlled the entire Pacific Coast. But he could not out-gobble James J. Hill (1838–1916), the immensely successful Canadian immigrant whose Great Northern Railway linked the North to the West. Harriman's vicious stock battle with Hill led to a mutually satisfying truce: a short-lived monopoly called the Northern Securities Company, which the U.S. Supreme Court dissolved in 1904.

The barons' heyday began to decline at the turn of the century with increasing public outrage over unpredictable ticket prices and fluctuations in the stock market tied to the railroads. Increasing federal pressure, through laws, regulation, and court orders, ended their reign. By 1907, when the Interstate Commerce Commission denounced Harriman and other financiers for trying to destroy rival railroads, the age of the "robber barons" was over.

ways, and they do not have to pay to maintain them. Barge companies do not have to pay taxes on or maintain the waterways that they use, and airlines use airports and airways built in large part with public funds. Railroad companies must pay to build and maintain their tracks because they are for their exclusive use. However, railroad companies have received some assistance from government because railroads are important to the nation's economy and because they have needed it.

In the 1930s the trucking industry made technological strides that put it in direct competition with the railroads. Pneumatic tires were created to support heavier freights, hydraulic brakes were devised to safely increase the weight of a load, and a network of paved intercity HIGHWAYS provided easy access and direct routes. The market advantages of trucking became apparent immediately, and the golden age of railroading came to an end after World War II. Railroads abandoned thousands of miles of tracks and laid off workers. The radical shift in transportation reshaped the map of the United States as small towns that depended on railroads for business turned into ghost towns.

The Regional Rail Reorganization Act of 1973 (45 U.S.C.A. §§ 701–797) consolidated the bankrupt northeastern railroads into a single railroad called ConRail, a for-profit corporation comprised of the bankrupt railroads. The consolidation resulted in some abandonments, but it eliminated duplicate mileage and helped save and maintain the most popular routes. In March 1997 Conrail was bought by CSX Corp. and Norfolk Southern Corp. It will be divided between the two companies.

Congress gave railroad companies federal funds to upgrade the railroad system in the Railroad Revitalization and Regulatory Reform Act of 1976 (45 U.S.C.A. § 801 et seq.). This act also shortened the length of time that railroads had to wait before abandoning a track.

President JIMMY CARTER proved to be a champion of railroad deregulation. Under Carter's watch, the Interstate Commerce Commission dropped the government controls on shipping rates for coal, eliminated regulations regarding the shipping of produce, and made it easier for railroads to abandon unprofitable lines. Congress topped off several years of railroad legislation with the Staggers Rail Act of 1980 (codified in scattered sections of titles 11, 45, and 49 of the U.S.C.A.). The Staggers Act eliminated government rate controls and made it still easier for railroads to abandon lines. Although the deregulation resulted in many layoffs, the changes lowered prices, made railroads more profitable, and allowed railroad companies to increase expenditures on safety measures.

The railroad system in the United States reached its peak in 1920, when approximately 272,000 miles of rails existed. Today, less than 150,000 miles of rails exist. Railroads do not dominate the transportation market like they once did, but the railroad system has been pared down and stabilized. The rails remain necessary for large, bulky loads of heavy cargo. For personal transportation, the passenger service Amtrak was established in 1970 and subsidized by Congress to provide nationwide railroad passenger service at reduced rates. Amtrak and a few shorter, private lines offer passenger service in many parts of the country.

CROSS-REFERENCES

Antitrust Law; Carriers; Commerce Clause; Monopoly.

RAILROAD RETIREMENT ACT The Railroad Retirement Act is a federal law (45 U.S.C.A. § 231 et seq.) enacted by Congress in 1937 that provides a special system of ANNUITY, PENSION, and death benefits to RAILROAD workers.

Congress first passed the Railroad Retirement Act in 1934 to reward the hard work done by railroad workers, recognize the national benefits conferred by railroad work, and encourage the retirement of older railroad workers. By offering the means for railroad workers "to enjoy the closing days of their lives with peace of mind and physical comfort," Congress intended to provide jobs to younger workers and generally improve the operation of the railroads with stronger, more able bodies (H.R. Rep. No. 1711, 74th Cong., 1st Sess. 10 [1935]).

The U.S. Supreme Court rejected the first version of the act. In 1935 the Court ruled that the act violated the U.S. Constitution because it deprived the railroads of PROPERTY without DUE PROCESS under the FIFTH AMENDMENT and because it exceeded Congress's power to regulate interstate commerce (*Railroad Retirement Board v. Alton R.R. Co.*, 295 U.S. 330, 55 S. Ct. 758, 79 L. Ed. 1468 [1935]). Congress passed a similar law the following year based on its power to tax and spend for the GENERAL WELFARE (49 Stat. 967 and 974). That act was put on hold by judicial order (*Alton R.R. Co. v. Railroad Retirement Board*, 16 F. Supp. 955 [D.C. 1936]). President FRANKLIN D. ROOSEVELT worked with Congress to reformulate the act, and in 1937 the Railroad Retirement Act emerged.

The act established the Railroad Retirement Board to administer the benefits program. The Railroad Retirement Board also administers the benefits programs under the Railroad Unemployment Insurance Act (45 U.S.C.A. §§ 351 et seq.) and manages other railroad-related issues.

The Railroad Retirement Act was amended several times to make it similar to the benefits scheme of the SOCIAL SECURITY ACT (42 U.S.C.A. § 301 et seq.). In 1970 Congress established a Commission on Railroad Retirement to thoroughly analyze the structure of the act. The commission recommended changes, Congress negotiated with the railroad industry, and the act was overhauled in 1974.

The Railroad Retirement Act of 1974 is a complex set of requirements for benefits that essentially provides two tiers of benefits. One level is similar to a private pension plan. The benefits received on this level are determined according to earnings and career service. To qualify for these benefits, the employee must have worked in the railroad industry for at least ten years. For seasonal workers, it may take several more years of railroad work to qualify. No benefits are paid until the employee either reaches the normal retirement age under the Social Security Act (age sixty-five), or age sixty with thirty years of service.

The second and larger tier of benefits under the act provides annuities that are similar to, and a replacement of, Social Security benefits. Under the act, that portion of earnings that would normally go into a worker's Social Security account instead goes into a railroad retirement account. This account provides slightly higher returns than the average Social Security account. To qualify for this benefit, a railroad worker must work in the industry a total of ten years.

The act also provides disability benefits to disabled workers and the children or parents of deceased railroad workers. A spouse of an employee who worked in the railroad industry for ten years or more also receives individual annuities. These benefits to the spouse cease if the couple divorces.

Under the act, an employee is considered any person who received remuneration to work for any railroad company or carrier or for any railroad association that was owned by at least two businesses engaged in the railroad business.

BIOGRAPHY

APWIDE WORLD PHOTOS

Roberta Cooper Ramo

RAMO, ROBERTA COOPER Roberta Cooper Ramo, the first woman elected president of the AMERICAN BAR ASSOCIATION (ABA), was a pathbreaker in many ways. Ramo was also the first ABA president with a technological bent, proselytizing for decades about the need for

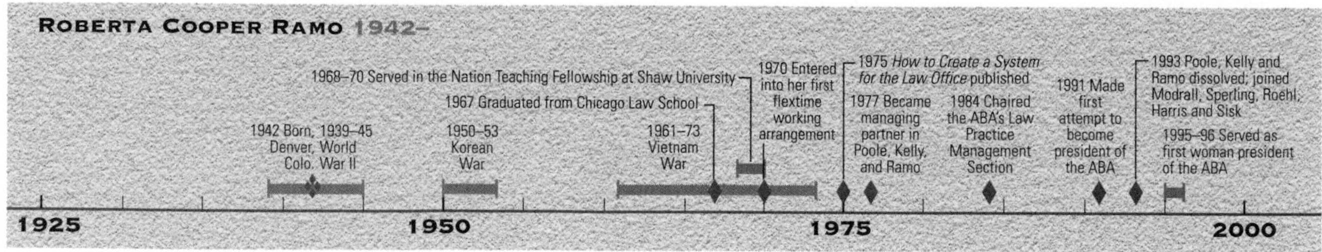

modern management techniques and computerization in running law firms.

Ramo was born August 8, 1942, in Denver. The daughter of a Western clothing retailer, she graduated from the University of Colorado magna cum laude in 1964. She then entered the University of Chicago Law School, and received a juris doctorate in 1967.

Already Ramo and her husband, Barry W. Ramo, were pursuing their careers in tandem to balance work and family. They had married while both were attending the University of Colorado, she as an undergraduate and he studying to be a cardiologist. When she went to law school in Chicago, he took an internship there. When he took a position at a teaching hospital at Duke University, in North Carolina, she ran into a professional wall as a new woman lawyer at a time when the number of woman lawyers was still small. "I was unable even to get an interview with a law firm in Durham, Raleigh or Chapel Hill," she said. "I was the only one from my law school class without a job." Ramo's law school dean called a friend in North Carolina, the state's former governor Terry Sanford, to ask for help in finding her a job. As governor, Sanford had convinced the Ford Foundation that it ought to try developing a state foundation for distributing its grants, which led to the creation of the North Carolina Fund. In 1968, Ramo took a Nation Teaching Fellowship at Shaw University in Raleigh. After graduation Ramo moved with her husband, Barry W. Ramo, to North Carolina where she spent a year distributing Ford Foundation grants through a state foundation.

In 1970, Ramo moved to San Antonio, where she began working part-time with the twelve-lawyer firm of Sawtelle, Goode, Davidson, and Troilo. She had an eighteen-month-old child and was seven months pregnant when she interviewed for the job. Ramo and the law firm entered into an agreement that now is so common that it has a name—flextime. She would come in earlier than most of the other lawyers, about 7:00 A.M., and leave earlier, about 2:00 P.M., taking work home with her. The agreement called for her to be paid two-thirds of what others in the firm were getting.

"JUSTICE IS NOT SIMPLY ANOTHER GOVERNMENT ENTITLEMENT, BUT THE HISTORIC MANDATE OF A FREE SOCIETY."

In 1972, the Ramos moved to Albuquerque, where she had grown up, and Ramo made a similar arrangement with another law firm, where she worked for two years. Then she spent three years as a sole practitioner, from 1974 until 1977, before becoming a managing partner in Poole, Kelly, and Ramo, still working in a part-time, flextime arrangement. That kind of setup continued until the late 1980s, until her last child graduated from high school. In 1993, Ramo's firm dissolved, and she went with the Albuquerque firm of Modrall, Sperling, Roehl, Harris, and Sisk. Her practice has primarily been in real estate, health, probate, estate planning, and commercial real estate leasing.

Over the years, despite the demands of her family and her own desire to do more than her agreed share of work, Ramo was heavily involved in community activities. She spent six years as a regent for the University of New Mexico, served on the board and executive committee of the Greater Albuquerque Chamber of Commerce, was a director of the New Mexico Symphony Orchestra, and was a board member with numerous other professional and civic organizations. At the same time, Ramo was active in the state bar of New Mexico, chairing its Section of Business, Banking, and Corporations, and was on the board of directors of the Albuquerque Bar Association.

In the early 1970s, Ramo took her proselytizing about the need for automation and modern management techniques in law firms nationwide, and she wrote what one member of the ABA's board of governors later described as "a revolutionary book," titled *How to Create a System for the Law Office*. The 1975 book became a best-seller year after year and proved to be the most popular book ever published by the ABA. That work brought Ramo together with Miami lawyer Samuel S. Smith, who had been lecturing around the United States on the same themes. They, along with others, began traveling and lecturing together, doing so for seven years. Eventually, they cofounded the ABA's Law Practice Management Section.

Having worked her way to prominence within the organization, Ramo made her first run for ABA president in 1991. Only one other woman had run for that office, in 1986, only to pull out of the race very early when she failed to gain significant support. Ramo's bid became legend in ABA politics, where it is not unusual for someone to run unopposed for president and where the vote usually is very quick when it concerns two candidates. For the first time, three contenders were left at the time of the election, and the voting dragged throughout the day to an unprecedented eighty-eight ballots before she finally lost.

Ramo ran again and won in 1995, serving from August of that year to August 1996. The perception and reality of the old guard tradition in ABA leadership were so strong that when she was elected, the *New York Times* noted that even with two women on the U.S. Supreme Court and two women at the highest level of the Justice Department, a "perhaps even more formidable barrier has fallen." (Feb. 4, 1994).

RANDOLPH, ASA PHILIP A. Philip Randolph played a central role in the drive for CIVIL RIGHTS for African Americans from the 1920s to the 1970s. He was the most prominent African American labor leader during his lifetime, but his leadership went well beyond the struggle to integrate labor unions. As the founder of the Brotherhood of Sleeping Car Porters, he confronted U.S. presidents from FRANKLIN D. ROOSEVELT to JOHN F. KENNEDY over the slow pace of civil rights reform.

Randolph was born April 15, 1889, in Crescent City, Florida. He moved to New York City as a young man, where he attended City College of New York. He joined the Socialist party and campaigned against U.S. involvement in World War I, going so far as to attack W. E. B. DU BOIS, one of the founders of the NATIONAL ASSOCIATION FOR THE ADVANCEMENT OF COLORED PEOPLE, for urging African Americans to serve in the armed forces.

His life's work grew out of a request by Pullman car porters to help them organize a union. In the 1920s railroads dominated U.S. transportation. The dining cars, club cars, and sleeping cars of passenger trains were staffed by African American porters, who earned their money primarily from the tips of passengers. Ignored by the American Federation of Labor (AFL), the porters turned to Randolph for assistance.

Randolph sought from the Pullman Company recognition of the union, improved working conditions, and a MINIMUM WAGE. The struggle took twelve years, but Randolph finally achieved these goals. Despite his success the AFL continued to refuse to allow black members.

World War II thrust Randolph into the national spotlight when, in 1941, he demanded that President Roosevelt ban racial discrimination in defense industries. Randolph informed the president that if his demand was not met, he would organize a mass march on Washington, D.C. Roosevelt capitulated, signing an order that integrated industries accepting federal defense contracts and which established the Fair Employment Practices Commission.

The membership of the Brotherhood of Sleeping Car Porters (now part of the Brotherhood of Railway and Airline Clerks) declined in the 1950s, as airlines and automobiles became the dominant modes of long-distance transportation. Randolph continued to ascend, however, as he became vice president of the American Federation of Labor and Congress of Industrial Organizations (AFL-CIO) in 1957.

The only prominent African American to head a union, Randolph refused to act as a mere symbol of racial INTEGRATION. He repeatedly urged the AFL-CIO to integrate its unions, earning the displeasure of the organization's leadership, including President George Meany.

Randolph again achieved national prominence for promoting a march on Washington, D.C. In 1963 he called for a march to protest racial discrimination and to demand jobs for

"I HAVE SPENT ALL OF MY LIFE IN THE LABOR AND CIVIL RIGHTS MOVEMENTS, WHICH IS TO SAY THAT I HAVE SPENT A LIFETIME IN SEARCH OF SOLUTIONS TO THE PROBLEM OF RACE AND THE PROBLEM OF JOBS."

BIOGRAPHY

AP/WIDE WORLD PHOTOS

Asa Philip Randolph

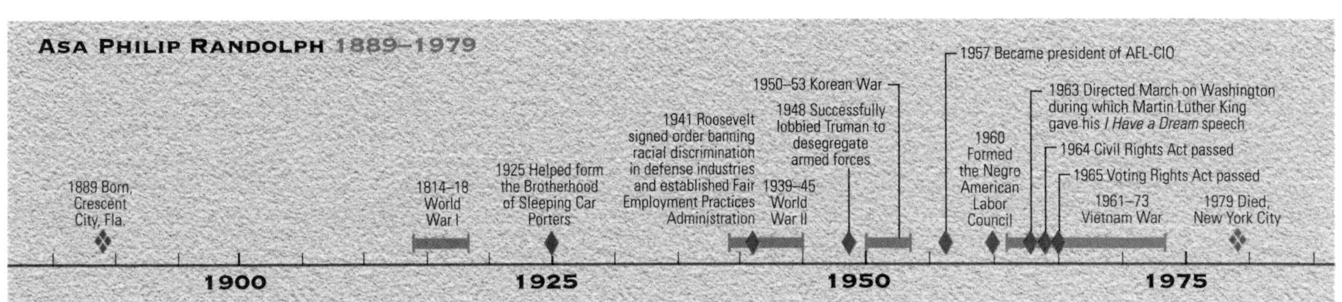

African Americans. He later agreed to join forces with other civil rights leaders, including Dr. Martin Luther King, Jr., who had called separately for a march on Washington that would focus on the need for civil rights legislation. Randolph was given the job of organizing the march. On August 28, 1963, the March on Washington for Jobs and Freedom took place in front of the Lincoln Memorial. More than 200,000 people heard King's *I Have a Dream* speech, and many millions watched on television. Randolph played a central role in this important event.

Randolph continued in the 1960s and 1970s to lobby for civil rights legislation and jobs for African Americans. He died May 16, 1979, in New York City.

See also civil rights movement; labor union.

BIOGRAPHY

RANDOLPH, EDMUND JENNINGS Edmund Jennings Randolph served as U.S. attorney general and secretary of state during the administration of President George Washington. Randolph previously had played a central role in the drafting of the U.S. Constitution.

Randolph was born on August 10, 1753, in Williamsburg, Virginia. He attended William and Mary College and then studied law with his father, who was a prominent lawyer and the king's attorney in the colony of Virginia. As the American Revolution approached, Randolph sided with the independence movement, while his father remained loyal to the crown. In 1775 Randolph's father, mother, and sisters left for England.

In 1775 Randolph briefly served in the Virginia militia as an aide to George Washington before returning to manage his uncle's estate. Randolph's friendship with Washington continued, and soon Randolph was handling Washington's personal legal affairs.

Randolph's political career began in 1776 when he served in the Virginia Constitutional Convention. He helped draft a bill of rights and a state constitution. That same year he was appointed state attorney general, a post he held for ten years. During this period he also briefly served as mayor of Williamsburg. From 1779 to 1782, Randolph was a member of the Continental Congress. In 1786 he was elected governor of Virginia.

Randolph was a prominent member of the Constitutional Convention of 1787. A key issue before the convention was the structure and representation of a national legislature. Delegates from small states opposed those from large states. Randolph offered the Virginia Plan on behalf of the large states, which provided for a two-house legislature with representation of each state based on its population or wealth. William Paterson of New Jersey proposed the New Jersey Plan on behalf of the smaller states, which provided for equal representation in Congress. The matter was resolved by the Connecticut Compromise, which created a bicameral legislature with proportional representation in the lower house and equal representation of the states in the upper house.

Randolph refused to sign the final draft of the Constitution because he believed that it did not protect the rights of states and individuals. In 1788 he did, however, urge Virginia to ratify the Constitution, proclaiming the need for national unity.

From 1789 to 1794, he served as U.S. attorney general for the new national government. Following Thomas Jefferson's resignation as secretary of state, President Washington appointed Randolph to the post. France and Great Britain were at war at the time, and both countries had supporters within the United States. Randolph attempted to carry out Washington's policy of neutrality in the conflict but earned enemies on both sides.

"THE PREROGATIVE OF [A PRESIDENTIAL] PARDON . . . IS TOO GREAT A TRUST. THE PRESIDENT HIMSELF MAY BE GUILTY. THE TRAITORS MAY BE HIS OWN INSTRUMENTS."

Randolph's public career ended in a cloud of scandal in 1795, after the British minister to the United States claimed that Randolph had expressed a willingness to accept money from France to create U.S. policy favorable to that country. Though the charges were eventually shown to be untrue, Randolph resigned.

Randolph returned to Virginia and practiced law for the remainder of his life. In 1807 he served as chief defense counsel for Aaron Burr, who was on trial for treason. Burr was acquit-

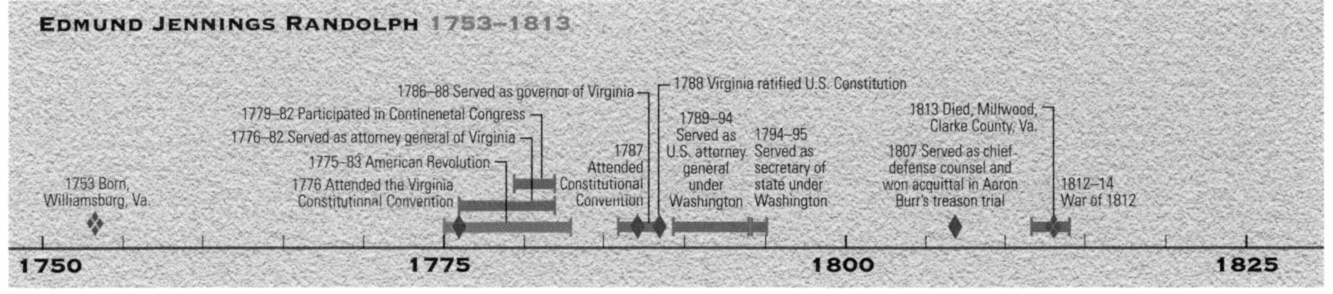

ted after it became clear that the charges were groundless and politically motivated.

Randolph died on September 12, 1813, at his estate in Clarke County, Virginia.

See also Bill of Rights; Constitution of the United States.

RANKIN, JEANNETTE Jeannette Rankin of Montana was the first woman in U.S. history to be elected to the U.S. House of Representatives. A nonconformist Republican, she served two nonconsecutive terms in the House. Rankin is best remembered for her opposition to war. In 1917 she voted against the entry of the United States into World War I, and in 1941 she took the same position against U.S. involvement in World War II. During the 1960s Rankin protested U.S. military action in Southeast Asia.

Biography

Jeannette Rankin

Rankin was born on June 11, 1880, on a ranch near Missoula, Montana. The oldest of seven children, Rankin was first among a family of high achievers. One of Rankin's sisters became dean of women at the University of Montana, and another taught in the English department there. Rankin's only brother and another sister became well-known, politically connected attorneys.

Rankin was an intelligent but undistinguished student. She graduated from the University of Montana in 1902 with a bachelor's degree in biology and then taught school for six years. In 1908 she left Montana to seek other challenges.

Earlier Rankin had visited Boston where she saw urban slums for the first time. She vowed to help improve the living and working conditions of poor Americans. In 1908 Rankin entered the New York School of Philanthropy in New York City (renamed the Columbia School of Social Work) and became a social worker.

In 1910 Rankin moved to Spokane, Washington, to work in a children's home. Inspired by the supporters of women's suffrage, Rankin concluded that good legislation was more effective than social work in solving society's problems. She joined the suffrage movement in Washington and campaigned successfully for an amendment to the state constitution that gave women the right to vote.

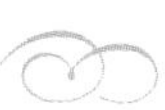

"We're half the people; we should be half the Congress."

After victory in Washington, Rankin returned to her native Montana to work for women's suffrage. In what was a bold move at the time, Rankin addressed the state legislature on the issue, reminding lawmakers that all citizens in a democracy deserved a voice. Her lobbying and organizing efforts paid off, and Montana gave women the right to vote.

Rankin continued to spread her message by traveling across the country, giving pro-suffrage speeches. She became a prominent member of the National American Woman Suffrage Association. At the same time, Rankin also became involved in the turn-of-the-century peace movement, helping establish the Women's Peace Party.

In 1917 Rankin decided to run for election to the U.S. House of Representatives. Montana had only one congressional district at the time because of its small population. Rankin campaigned for a federal suffrage amendment, stricter employment laws to protect women and children, and continued neutrality in the war being waged in Europe. She won the election by a very narrow margin, and at age thirty-six became the first woman to serve in the U.S. House of Representatives.

Soon after she took office, Rankin's position on U.S. neutrality was tested. President Woodrow Wilson sought a U.S. declaration of war against Germany. On April 6, 1917, Rankin voted against U.S. involvement in World War I. Although forty-nine other representatives cast negative votes, Rankin's vote was widely publicized— and criticized—because she was the only female member of Congress.

Rankin was not reelected to Congress in 1918, in part because of her antiwar vote but also because she had antagonized powerful mining interests in Montana.

After her defeat Rankin resumed her work with the peace movement. She was a delegate to the Women's International Conference on Permanent Peace in Zurich where women analyzed the Versailles Peace Treaty of World War I.

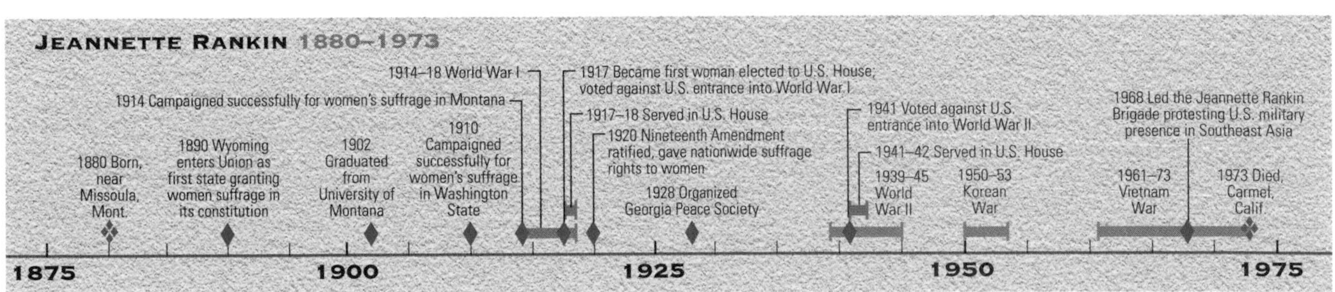

This process led to the formation of the Women's International League for Peace and Freedom. In 1928 Rankin organized the Georgia Peace Society and in the 1930s she was a lobbyist for the National Council for the Prevention of War.

When war erupted again in Europe in 1939, Rankin was convinced that most U.S. citizens shared her views on neutrality. She returned to Montana to run for the House of Representatives. Rankin was reelected and reentered Congress in 1941.

The bombing of Pearl Harbor by Japan on December 7, 1941, shattered widespread support for U.S. neutrality. This time when President FRANKLIN D. ROOSEVELT sought a declaration of war against Japan, Rankin was the only legislator to vote against it. Her vote, although consistent with her two decades of work in the international peace movement, was roundly criticized as unpatriotic. Rankin's political career was irreparably damaged, and she did not run for reelection.

During the 1950s and early 1960s, Rankin traveled abroad and lived modestly in Georgia. The VIETNAM WAR drew her back into the public spotlight. In 1968 she led the Jeannette Rankin Brigade, a half-million women demonstrating in Washington, D.C., against U.S. military presence in Southeast Asia. In 1969 she took part in antiwar protests in South Carolina and Georgia.

Rankin died on May 18, 1973, in Carmel, California.

See also NINETEENTH AMENDMENT; WOMEN'S RIGHTS.

RANTOUL, ROBERT, JR. Robert Rantoul, Jr., was a Massachusetts attorney who served in various state and federal offices during his brief life. He is best remembered, however, for his denunciations of the common-law tradition, for his leadership in the CODIFICATION movement, and for his defense of LABOR UNIONS.

Rantoul was born on August 13, 1805, in Beverly, Massachusetts. He attended private schools before enrolling at Harvard University.

"JUDGE-MADE LAW IS EX POST FACTO LAW, AND THEREFORE UNJUST. AN ACT IS NOT FORBIDDEN BY THE STATUTE LAW, BUT IT BECOMES BY JUDICIAL DECISION A CRIME. THE JUDICIARY . . . RUNS RIOT BEYOND THE CONFINES OF LEGISLATIVE POWER."

BIOGRAPHY

LIBRARY OF CONGRESS

Robert Rantoul, Jr.

He was admitted to the Massachusetts bar and practiced law in Salem.

Rantoul served in the Massachusetts legislature for several terms before becoming U.S. attorney for the district of Massachusetts. He was briefly a Democratic member of the U.S. House of Representatives in the late 1840s. In 1851 he was elected to serve the last year of a term as U.S. senator.

Rantoul's congressional service was short but distinguished. He opposed the FUGITIVE SLAVE ACT OF 1850 and supported the expansion of railroads to the western territories. The town of Rantoul, Illinois, was named in his honor for his RAILROAD legislation.

Nevertheless, Rantoul's importance lies in his critique of the common-law tradition and his call for the codification of all law by the legislature. The codification movement, of which Rantoul was a prominent spokesperson, attacked the COMMON LAW as unsuitable for a democratic republic. Randolph believed that allowing judges to interpret and adapt the law led to decisions about issues that were properly within the province of the legislature. Rantoul advocated that the legislature write a set of laws, to be contained in a CODE book, that judges would apply to the cases before them.

Rantoul presented his ideas about the common law and codification in their fullest form in a two-hour Fourth of July address at Scituate, Massachusetts, in 1836. Rantoul stated that "the Common Law is but the glimmering taper by which [English] men groped their way through the palpable midnight in which learning, wit, and reason were almost extinguished." "The Common Law," he continued, "had its origin in folly, barbarism, and feudality."

Rantoul believed that the problem in the common-law method was the discretion permitted the judge. He claimed that judge-made law is EX POST FACTO LAW and therefore unjust. Persons could not know the law because "no one knows what the law is before [the judge] lays it down." Moreover, a judge was able to rule differently from case to case.

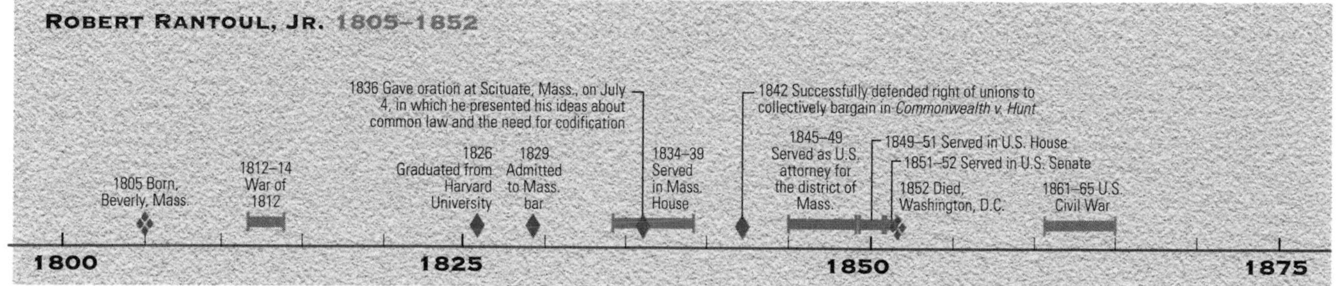

Because the poor could not afford legal counsel, they were at a disadvantage when they entered a courtroom. Without an attorney, a person was at the mercy of the court. The only solution, Rantoul argued, was to abandon the common-law system and codify all laws into one book that everyone could read and understand.

The codification movement had limited success during the nineteenth century. Rantoul advocated a code but never tried to write one. DAVID DUDLEY FIELD, a New York attorney, wrote what became known as the Field Code of Civil Procedure. His code was enacted in twenty-four states, most of them in the West. California adopted it in 1872. See also FIELD CODE OF NEW YORK.

Rantoul also distinguished himself as an advocate for labor unions in the landmark Massachusetts case of *Commonwealth v. Hunt*, 45 Mass. (4 Met.) 111, 38 Am. Dec. 346 (1842). Rantoul defended members of the bootmakers union who had been indicted for criminal CONSPIRACY because they sought to bargain collectively. The charge of criminal conspiracy had been a potent weapon in preventing the formation of unions. Rantoul persuaded Chief Justice LEMUEL SHAW and the Supreme Judicial Court of Massachusetts to set aside the INDICTMENTS. In his opinion, Shaw agreed with employers that competition was vital to the economy but concluded that unions stimulated competition. Shaw stated that, as long as the unions used legal methods, they were free to seek concessions from employers.

Rantoul died at age forty-seven on August 7, 1852, in Washington, D.C.

RAPE A criminal offense defined in most states as forcible sexual relations with a person against that person's will.

Rape is the commission of unlawful sexual intercourse or unlawful sexual intrusion. Rape laws in the United States have been revised over the years, and they vary from state to state.

Historically, rape was defined as unlawful sexual intercourse with a woman against her will. The essential elements of the crime were sexual penetration, force, and lack of CONSENT. Women who were raped were expected to have physically resisted to the utmost of their powers or the man would not be convicted of rape. Additionally, a husband could have sex with his wife against her will without being charged with rape. Beginning in the 1970s, state legislatures and courts expanded and redefined the crime of rape to reflect modern notions of equality and legal propriety.

All states now define rape without reference to the sex of the victim and the perpetrator. However, the overwhelming majority of rape victims are women. A woman may be convicted of raping a man, a man may be convicted of raping a man, and a woman may be convicted of raping another woman. Furthermore, a spouse may be convicted of rape if he forces the other spouse to have nonconsensual sex. Many states do not punish the rape of a spouse as severely as the rape of a non-spouse.

Many states also have redefined lack of consent. Before the 1970s many courts viewed the element of force from the standpoint of the victim. A man would not be convicted of rape of a COMPETENT woman unless she had demonstrated some physical resistance. In the absence of physical resistance, courts usually held that the sex was consensual. Today, in many states, the prosecution can prove lack of consent by presenting evidence that the victim objected verbally to the sexual penetration or sexual intrusion.

Lack of consent is a necessary element in every rape. This does not mean that a person may make sexual contact with a MINOR or incapacitated person who actually consented. Lack of consent results from either forcible compulsion by the perpetrator or an incapacity to consent on the part of the victim. Persons who are physically or mentally helpless or who are under a certain age in relation to the perpetrator are deemed legally incapable of consenting to sex.

Most states choose to label the crime of rape as sexual assault. Sexual assault is divided into degrees, such as first-, second-, third-, and fourth-degree sexual assault. West Virginia provides a good illustration of how rape laws are written. In West Virginia a person is guilty of sexual assault in the first degree when that person engages in sexual intercourse or sexual intrusion with another person and either inflicts serious bodily injury upon anyone or employs a deadly weapon in the commission of the act (W. Va. Code § 61-8B-3 [1996]). Additionally, a person age fourteen years or older who engages in sexual intercourse or sexual intrusion with another person who is eleven years old or less is guilty of first-degree sexual assault. A person convicted of the crime of first-degree sexual assault in West Virginia faces imprisonment for at least fifteen years and not more than thirty-five years and may be fined from $1,000 to $10,000.

In West Virginia a person commits sexual assault in the second degree by engaging in

New Approach to Treating Rape Victims

A woman who has been raped often encounters painful and humiliating procedures when she reports her sexual assault. She is sent to a hospital emergency room where she waits indefinitely for a medical examination and the collection of evidence that is needed to convict a suspect. She often has little privacy while she waits. In addition, she is asked to tell her story of sexual assault several times.

The National Victim Center estimates that only 16 percent of rapes in the United States are reported each year. This low reporting rate can be attributed in part to the cold, impersonal reporting process and the rape victim's fear of appearing at the trial of the suspect.

A program called SANE (Sexual Assault Nurse Examiners) has been established in Tulsa and several other U.S. cities, which seeks to treat the emotional, physical, and legal needs of rape victims with greater consideration and sensitivity. In the SANE program, female nurses are trained to handle the physical examination of the victim and to obtain physical evidence using a sexual offense collection kit. In addition, the nurses are taught to interview the victim about the assault and to keep good records, which are critical to a successful criminal prosecution of the suspect.

Victims are seen in private rooms that are decorated to avoid the look of a sterile, hospital waiting room. The nurse examiner allows the victim to complete the examination at her own pace, in from one to five hours. A police officer is available to transport the evidence to headquarters but is not allowed in the examining room.

Prosecutors have lauded the SANE program because its nurse examiners are better than emergency-room staff at confirming sexual contact and collecting evidence that shows the encounter was forcible rather than consensual.

SANE also gets credit for encouraging rape victims to agree to testify at the criminal trial of the suspect. It is believed that women who receive insensitive treatment during the initial stages of reporting a sexual assault do not want to proceed with prosecution. Because the SANE program treats victims with sympathy, care, and respect, women who have been examined through the program are more likely to agree to cooperate.

sexual intercourse or sexual intrusion with another person without that person's consent and the lack of consent results from forcible compulsion. Forcible compulsion is (1) physical force that overcomes such earnest resistance as might reasonably be expected under the circumstances; (2) threat or intimidation, either EXPRESS or IMPLIED, placing the victim or another person in fear of death, bodily injury, or kidnapping; or (3) fear by a person under sixteen years of age caused by intimidation by another person who is at least four years older than the victim.

Another way to commit second-degree sexual assault in West Virginia is to engage in sexual intercourse or sexual intrusion with someone who is physically helpless. The punishment for second-degree sexual assault is imprisonment for at least ten years but not more than twenty-five years and may include a fine of from $1,000 to $10,000.

Third-degree sexual assault is committed when a person engages in sexual intercourse or sexual intrusion with another person who is mentally defective or mentally incapacitated, or when a person age sixteen years or older has sex with a person who is less than sixteen years old and is at least four years younger than the defendant. Third-degree sexual assault is punishable in West Virginia by at least one, but no more than five, years in prison and may include a fine of not more than $10,000.

The provisions that refer to the age of the victim and the perpetrator are called statutory rape provisions. Statutory rape sections punish the perpetrator without regard to the consent of the victim. Such laws are in place in all states to enforce the generally accepted notions that children are incapable of consenting to sex because of their youth and innocence, and that sexual intercourse or intrusion of a child by an older person is socially unacceptable and harmful to the child. The term *statutory rape* also refers to the sections that punish sex with physically and mentally incapacitated persons, who are similarly unable to consent to sex.

Rape or sexual assault statutes carefully define the type of contact that constitutes rape. In Hawaii, for example, the term *sexual penetration* is defined as "vaginal intercourse, anal intercourse, fellatio, cunnilingus, analingus, deviate sexual intercourse, or any intrusion of any part of a person's body or of any object into the genital or anal opening of another person's

Rape Shield Laws: Can They Be Fair?

Introduced in the 1970s, shield laws sought to revolutionize rape trials. By prohibiting the introduction of a rape victim's reputation or sexual history at trial, lawmakers removed one of the age-old stigmas that had prevented the successful prosecution of rapists and had kept women from bringing cases to court. Originally, the laws met with widespread acceptance. Two decades after their adoption by most states and the federal government, however, they have given rise to a debate in which neither side is satisfied with them. Advocates say they have not worked as well as desired. Opponents argue that their effect has been to deny defendants a fair trial. The legal future of these revolutionary laws hinges on a difficult question: how can courts protect victims without curtailing the rights of defendants?

IN FOCUS

The origin of shield laws is a response to the historical prosecution of rape. Most accusations of rape assert that the victim did not give sexual consent. At common law and in the present, the vast majority of rape cases have been tried in state courts before a jury. Traditionally, convictions have been notoriously hard to win. There is usually no evidence on the consent question other than the claims of the parties, making it difficult to prove lack of consent "beyond a reasonable doubt" as required in a criminal case. Hence, at trial, credibility is everything: if the accuser is not believable, the defendant is likely to be acquitted.

Defense attorneys typically challenge the accuser's credibility. For centuries, there was one effective path to such an end: to present evidence of the victim's past sexual behavior to undermine the present allegation. At common law, the victim's past sexual behavior was always considered relevant and admissible at trial. In this way, the law embodied social and moral values that put a high premium on a woman's sexuality. Conventional views of chastity regarded the sexually active woman as being promiscuous, and, in turn, promiscuity was thought to connote dishonesty. To cast doubt on the accuser's word and to show the likelihood of her having consented to sex with the defendant, defense attorneys commonly pursued evidence about her sexual life. If she had sex with men, or so the underlying belief went, how could she have been raped?

To combat these antiquated notions, rape shield laws arose through two significant developments. The sexual revolution of the 1960s dramatically changed social values regarding premarital sexual activity, and feminist legal theory became highly influential a decade later. Feminist critics attacked the premises on which the common-law origins of rape defenses were based. Their argument posed a question that only a generation earlier would have been widely dismissed: why should a woman's sexual history matter at all in relation to her claim of rape? Not only was such evidence irrelevant, they asserted, but harmful. Its use in court discouraged a woman from bringing a charge of rape because, in effect, *she* would be put on trial. Fearing a public assault on her reputation, a victim had a strong incentive not to report a rape. And when women were willing to undergo a barrage of intrusive questions, they often saw their claims mocked and their violators allowed to go free.

But for political success, passage of the laws required political support. Proponents won this support from conservative lawmakers. Although not generally known for embracing either the sexual revolution or feminist legal theory, these lawmakers backed the laws in state legislatures because they represented a solid law-and-order position. The idea that criminals sometimes improperly escape prosecution through the legal maneuvering of defense attorneys, and that the law should close such loopholes, had become a centerpiece of the conservative legal reform agenda by the 1970s. With this backing, rape shield laws were easily adopted. By the 1990s, all but two states had them.

By the late 1980s, however, some proponents were troubled. Shield laws had not lived up to expectations. Merely providing protections to victims had not been enough to change longstanding social and legal habits. In 1987 the National Organization for Women and twenty-five other groups reported that gender bias against women litigants was still pervasive in courtrooms. As a result, women's testimony was accorded less credibility by judges and attorneys. Also, defense attorneys continued to introduce evidence that the shield laws were designed to bar. They could succeed if the evidence was introduced creatively, chiefly because state laws left judges wide discretion and unclear direction on what to admit as evidence. While seeking to tighten the admission of evidence in general, some shield law proponents wanted the laws strengthened to exclude even more kinds of evidence, such as the type of clothing a victim was wearing at the time of an assault.

In addition to such obstacles, various exceptions weakened rape shield laws. In particular, they provided little or no protection if the victim knew her assailant. Most state statutes allowed the admission of evidence about a past sexual relationship between the accuser and the defendant, and therefore defense attorneys often attempted to persuade juries that there had been such a relationship. Behavior by a woman that was even slightly indicative of a past sexual relationship with her assailant would work against her at trial.

By the 1990s a backlash against the laws developed. Defense attorneys, law professors, and civil liberties activists maintained that the laws were unfair to criminal defendants. They had two main arguments: restrictions on the admission of evidence undermined the defense attorney's goal of providing the best defense, and more significantly, such restrictions deprived the defendant of his Sixth Amendment right to a full

(continued on next page)

RAPE SHIELD LAWS: CAN THEY BE FAIR? (CONTINUED)

defense, including confronting his accuser and presenting witnesses in his favor. Many opponents of shield laws acknowledged that women face traditional obstacles in rape prosecutions but saw the laws as a poor remedy if they denied defendants due process and sent the innocent to jail.

Among leading opponents of shield laws was Alan M. Dershowitz, the celebrated Harvard law professor and criminal appellate lawyer. Dershowitz unsuccessfully appealed the 1991 rape conviction of former boxing champion Mike Tyson to the U.S. Supreme Court, which refused to hear the case. Dershowitz argued that the trial court had unconstitutionally barred admission of evidence that would have acquitted Tyson: allegations that his accuser, a nineteen-year-old woman, had previously falsely accused another man of rape to avoid angering her father about her sexual activity. Because such evidence related to the victim's past sexual history, it was ruled inadmissible. In the view of Dershowitz and other opponents, such evidence should be allowed because it can reveal an accuser's motive to lie about consensual sex with a defendant. Frustrating these critics is the fact that appellate courts have consistently upheld shield laws, despite finding that some trial courts have applied the laws unconstitutionally.

From early enthusiasm to increasing skepticism, rape shield laws have endured a difficult quarter century since their passage. Their intention was to remove barriers that prevented women from reporting rape and winning convictions. Both proponents and opponents believe reform is needed, yet they disagree on what form it should take. Proponents want to strengthen shield laws to increase protections for women. But opponents counter that the laws are already strongly biased against defendants, depriving them of fundamental liberties.

See also Dershowitz, Alan Morton; Due Process of Law; Sixth Amendment.

body . . . however slight." Sexual contact is "any touching of the sexual or other intimate parts of a person . . . or of the sexual or other intimate parts of the actor by the person, whether directly or through the clothing or other material intended to cover the sexual or other intimate parts" (Haw. Rev. Stat. § 707-700 [1996]).

Most states punish lesser sexual intrusions with statutes on SEXUAL ABUSE. Like sexual assault statutes, sexual abuse statutes are divided into degrees based on the nature of the contact. Sexual abuse consists of nonconsensual sexual contact with another person. Lack of consent is present if the victim is a minor or physically helpless, or if the victim was forcibly compelled to consent to the contact. A person convicted of sexual abuse may be fined and sentenced to a term in jail or prison. Because the crime does not involve penetration, the punishment for sexual abuse is less than that authorized for persons convicted of sexual assault.

A few states have eliminated the requirement that a competent adult rape victim physically resist the attacker. Physical resistance in some rape situations presents a greater danger to the victim. The states that have eliminated the

Age of Rape Victims and Relationship Between Victim and Offender

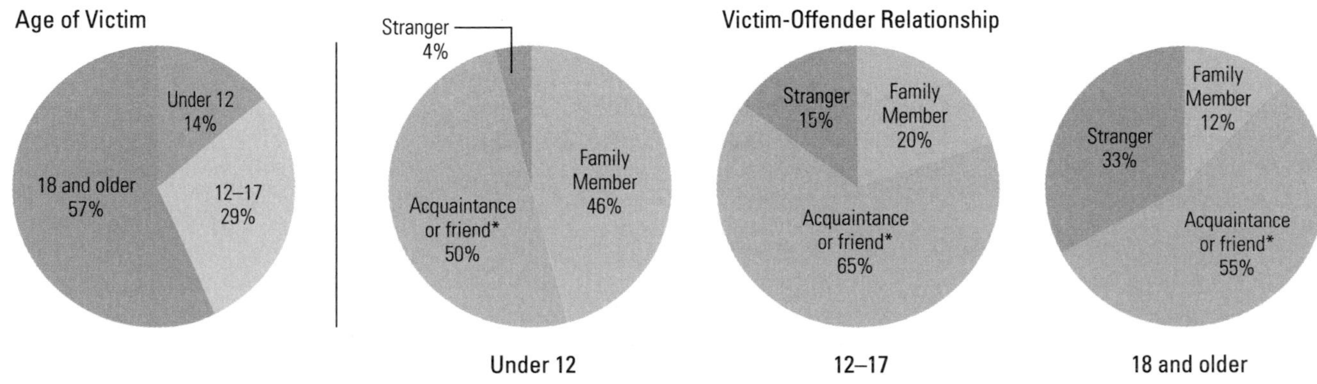

* Includes other nonfamily relationships.

Source: Data based on interviews with rape victims reported to law enforcement agencies in 1991 in three states (Alabama, North Dakota, and South Carolina). *Using NIBRS Data to Analyze Violent Crime,* BJS Technical Report, NCJ-144785, October 1993.

physical requirement have found it to be unfair to require physical resistance on the part of the victim if such resistance risks greater injury. In Michigan, for example, force or COERCION "includes but is not limited to" several situations, including where the actor coerces the victim through threats of force or violence and the victim believes that the actor can carry out the threats, and where the actor physically overcomes the victim through the actual application of physical force (Mich. Comp. Laws Ann. § 750.520a [West 1996]). Nowhere in Michigan's rape statutes is consent based on an analysis of the victim's physical resistance.

The states that have not eliminated physical resistance as a test for lack of consent have declined to do so for fear of convicting an adult who has sex with another adult without the knowledge that he or she is not consenting. Nevertheless, even in a state that has not eliminated the physical resistance requirement for competent adults, if the victim says "No" or otherwise verbally indicates lack of consent, the perpetrator still may be convicted of rape. This is because prosecutors have argued, and appeals courts have agreed, that some amount of force, no matter how slight, should be sufficient to fulfill the forcible compulsion element. The sexual penetration of a competent adult, for example, may be enough force to meet a forcible compulsion requirement, if the victim indicated a lack of consent.

Most states have so-called rape shield laws. These laws restrict or prohibit the use of evidence respecting the sexual history of rape victims and the victims of other sexual offenses. Before the enactment of rape shield laws in the 1970s and 1980s, rape trials often focused on the chastity of the victim to determine whether the victim was actually raped. Rape shield laws keep the focus of a rape prosecution on the actions of the defendant rather than the prior actions of the alleged victim.

CROSS-REFERENCES

Child Abuse; Domestic Violence; Feminist Jurisprudence; Husband and Wife; Pornography; Statutory Rape.

RATABLE That which can be appraised, assessed, or adjusted through the application of a formula or percentage.

Ratable property is that which is taxable or capable of being appraised or assessed.

RATE Value, measure, or degree; a charge, payment, or price determined through the application of a mathematical formula or based upon a scale or standard.

For example, an interest rate is determined by the ratio between the principal and interest.

Rate is also used synonymously with *tax*.

RATIFICATION The confirmation or adoption of an act that has already been performed.

A principal can, for example, ratify something that has been done on his or her behalf by another individual who assumed the authority to act in the capacity of an agent. In addition, proposed amendments to the U.S. Constitution must be ratified by three-quarters of the state legislatures or by conventions in three-quarters of the states.

See also CONSTITUTIONAL AMENDMENT.

RATIO DECIDENDI [*Latin, The ground or reason of decision.*] The legal principle upon which the decision in a specific case is founded.

The *ratio decidendi* is also known as the rationale for a decision.

RATIONAL BASIS TEST A judicial standard of review that examines whether a legislature had a reasonable and not an arbitrary basis for enacting a particular statute.

Courts employ various standards of review to assess whether legislative acts violate constitutionally protected interests. The U.S. Supreme Court has articulated the rational basis test for those cases where a plaintiff alleges that the legislature has made an arbitrary or irrational decision. When a court employs the rational basis test, it usually upholds the constitutionality of the law, because the test gives great deference to the legislative branch.

A law that touches on a constitutionally protected interest must be rationally related to furthering a legitimate government interest. In applying the rational basis test, courts begin with a strong PRESUMPTION that the law or policy under review is valid. The burden of proof is on the party making the challenge to show that the law or policy is unconstitutional. To meet this burden, the party must demonstrate that the law or policy does not have a rational basis. This is difficult to prove, because a court can usually find some reasonable ground for sustaining the constitutionality of the challenged law or policy.

For example, a state law that prohibits performing dentistry without a LICENSE deprives laypersons of their constitutionally protected rights to make CONTRACTS freely and discriminates against those unable or unwilling to obtain a license. But a court would undoubtedly uphold the constitutionality of the law because the license requirement is a rational means of advancing the state's legitimate interests in public health and safety.

For a hundred years, the rational basis test has been part of the U.S. Supreme Court's review of cases that alleged denial of EQUAL

PROTECTION of the laws. State and federal laws arc filled with discriminations, or classifications, of various kinds. A law that would apply universally and treat all persons equally is virtually impossible to craft. Because all laws classify by imposing special burdens or by conferring special benefits on some people and not others, there are always persons who are displeased. For example, when a state limits the privilege to purchase and consume intoxicating liquor to persons twenty-one and older, it is engaging in AGE DISCRIMINATION. But a court would find this was not a denial of equal protection because the legislature has a legitimate interest in restricting the drinking age and the law advances that interest in a rational way.

Under the Fifth and Fourteenth Amendments to the U.S. Constitution, persons are entitled to equal protection of the laws. The Supreme Court, in *Gulf, Colorado & Santa Fe Railway Co. v. Ellis*, 165 U.S. 150, 17 S. Ct. 255, 41 L. Ed. 666 (1897), first articulated the rational basis test under equal protection. The Court stated that "it is not within the scope of the Fourteenth Amendment to withhold from States the power of classification." However, the Court continued, "it must appear" that a classification is "based upon some reasonable ground—some difference which bears a just and proper relation to the attempted classification—and is not a mere arbitrary selection."

A person challenging a law on equal protection grounds has a very difficult task. The Supreme Court has used the rational basis standard to practice judicial restraint and to limit its ability to overturn legislation. In areas of social and economic policy, where constitutionally suspect classifications (race, religion, alienage, or national origin) are not at issue, nor are any fundamental constitutional rights at stake, a law must be upheld if there is any "reasonably conceivable state of facts that could provide a rational basis for the classification" (*United States Railroad Retirement Bd. v. Fritz*, 449 U.S. 166, 101 S. Ct. 453, 66 L. Ed. 2d 368 [1980]).

In addition, the Court does not require a legislature to articulate its reasons for enacting a statute, holding that "[i]t is entirely irrelevant for constitutional purposes whether the conceived reason for the challenged distinction actually motivated the legislature" (*FCC v. Beach Communications, Inc.*, 508 U.S. 307, 113 S. Ct. 2096, 124 L. Ed. 2d 211 [1993]). Thus, the Court stated, a "legislative choice is not subject to courtroom fact-finding and may be based on rational speculation unsupported by evidence or empirical data" (*FCC v. Beach Communications*). This means that a court is permitted to find a rational basis for a law, even if it is one that was not articulated by the legislature.

Because of these factors, application of the rational basis test usually results in the upholding of the law. Nevertheless, it remains the primary test for determining the constitutionality of classifications that encroach on economic interests.

CROSS-REFERENCES

Fifth Amendment; Fourteenth Amendment; Judicial Review.

RAVISHMENT Unlawful CARNAL KNOWLEDGE of a female by a male by force, against her will and without her consent.

Ravishment is the same as RAPE, a criminal offense defined by most statutes as unlawful sexual intercourse with a female by a male with force and without her consent.

RAWLS, JOHN John Rawls is one of the major moral and political philosophers of the twentieth century. His work embraces liberalism and egalitarianism, while rejecting UTILITARIANISM and more radical political ideas. His most important work, *A Theory of Justice* (1971), discusses the idea of "justice as fairness."

Rawls was born on February 21, 1921, in Baltimore, Maryland. He earned his bachelor's degree from Princeton University in 1943 and his doctorate from Princeton in 1950. Rawls was an instructor at Princeton between 1950 and 1952, before attending Oxford University in England as a Fulbright Fellow. Upon his return to the United States in 1953, he was a

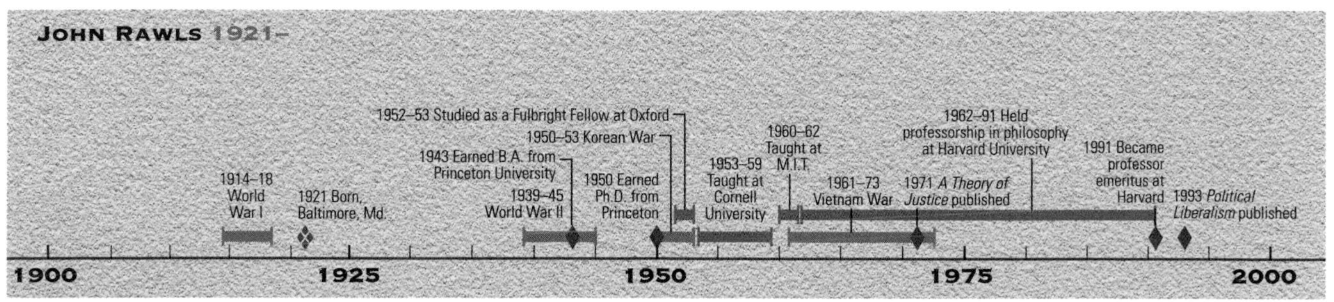

professor at Cornell University (1953–59) and the Massachusetts Institute of Technology (1960–62).

In 1962 Rawls was appointed professor of philosophy at Harvard University, an institution he served until his retirement in 1991. He continues as a professor emeritus at Harvard.

Rawls developed his ideas on JUSTICE in scholarly articles in the 1950s and 1960s. The publication of *A Theory of Justice* in 1971 was the culmination of this work. The book received widespread praise for its application of analytic techniques to the substantive (rather than the methodological) issues in morality.

Rawls's theory of justice is premised on two fundamental principles of justice that, he believes, would guarantee a just and morally acceptable society. The first principle guarantees the right of each person to have the most extensive basic LIBERTY compatible with the liberty of others. The second principle states that social and economic positions are to be to everyone's advantage and open to all.

A central concern for Rawls is to show how such principles would be universally adopted. Working from these principles, Rawls develops in detail a simple but powerful idea that he calls "justice as fairness." This idea proposes that the rules of a group are fair to the extent that a person would agree to be bound by them when ignorant ("the veil of ignorance") of his own possession of characteristics that the rules of the system reward or penalize. In this "original position," a person would not agree to unfair rules because there would be the possibility that she would be disadvantaged by them. Thus, the original position forces a person to make moral conclusions and to adopt a generalized point of view in making a social contract.

Rawls published *Political Liberalism* in 1993.

See also JURISPRUDENCE; MORAL LAW.

RE 🕮 [*Latin, In the matter of; in the case of.*] 🕮

A term of frequent use in designating judicial proceedings, in which there is only one party. Thus, "*Re* Vivian" signifies "In the matter of Vivian," or "in Vivian's Case."

See also IN RE.

BIOGRAPHY

LIBRARY OF CONGRESS

Ronald Wilson Reagan

"I BELIEVE THAT GOVERNMENT IS THE PROBLEM, NOT THE ANSWER."

REAGAN, RONALD WILSON Ronald Wilson Reagan served as president of the United States from 1981 to 1989. A former radio announcer, screen actor, and governor of California, Reagan's conservative political philosophy challenged the role the federal government played in U.S. society. An avowed opponent of big government, he proposed to return power to the states and to strip the federal government of many of its regulatory functions. Although he was not successful on all fronts, Reagan changed the political landscape that had remained virtually untouched since the presidency of FRANKLIN D. ROOSEVELT.

Reagan was born on February 6, 1911, in Tampico, Illinois. When he was nine, his family moved to Dixon, Illinois. He attended nearby Eureka College and graduated in 1932. He worked as a radio and sports announcer at several stations in Iowa before being discovered by a Hollywood talent scout and signed to an acting contract by Warner Brothers motion picture studio in 1937.

Reagan appeared in more than fifty movies between 1937 and the early 1950s. His most famous role was that of Notre Dame University football player George Gipp in *Knute Rockne—All American.* From 1942 to 1945 he served in the U.S. Army, making training films for World War II soldiers. It was after the war that Reagan became interested in politics, initially from his work with the Screen Actors Guild, a union representing Hollywood film actors. Elected president of the union in 1947, Reagan was a vigorous supporter of the labor movement as well as an able negotiator with the major movie studios.

Originally a Democrat and an admirer of President Roosevelt, he became concerned about Communist influence in the Hollywood LABOR UNIONS. During the late 1940s and early 1950s Hollywood was caught up in a RED SCARE. The House Un-American Activities Committee held highly publicized hearings where screen actors, screenwriters, producers, and directors

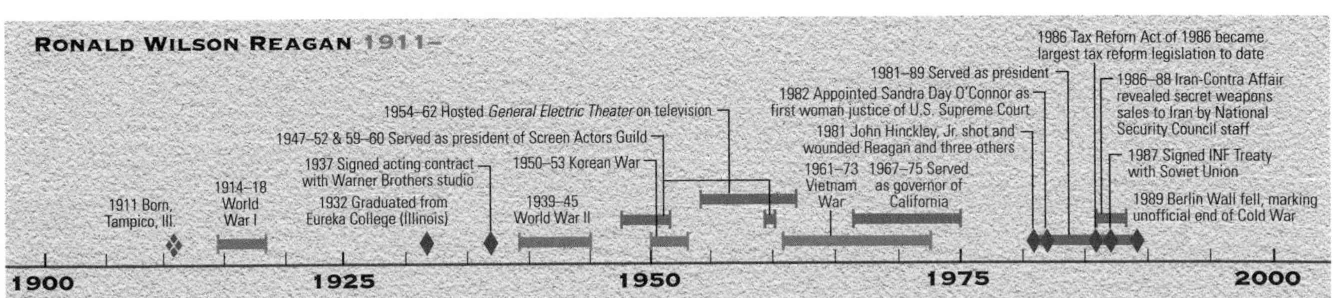

were interrogated about their participation in Communist organizations. Reagan initially defended his Hollywood brethren but soon backed away.

His divorce from actress Jane Wyman in 1949 and his remarriage to actress Nancy Davis also had an effect on Reagan's politics. His new wife's father was a political conservative who helped steer him toward the Republican party. As his movie career declined, his interest in politics increased. He was hired by the General Electric Company to be its traveling spokesperson and host of the *General Electric Theater* on television. From 1954 to 1962, Reagan maintained this relationship with General Electric. His conservative ideology deepened as he gave speeches around the country supporting U.S. business, criticizing government regulation, and attacking COMMUNISM.

Reagan became a national political figure during the 1964 presidential campaign. An ardent supporter of Arizona Senator BARRY M. GOLDWATER, who espoused the same conservative philosophy, Reagan gave a televised speech that tried to revitalize Goldwater's sagging campaign against President LYNDON B. JOHNSON. Goldwater lost the election, but Reagan gained the attention of Republican political leaders.

At the urging of a group of prominent California businessmen, Reagan ran as the Republican candidate for governor of California in 1966. Democratic Governor Edmund ("Pat") Brown, who had defeated RICHARD M. NIXON in 1962, dismissed Reagan as a television actor and took him lightly. Reagan proved, however, to be a formidable opponent. A polished and effective public speaker, he spoke out against welfare cheaters and antiwar radicals on college campuses. He won the election by nearly one million votes, the most convincing victory ever achieved against an incumbent governor in U.S. history.

Reagan's two terms as governor (he was reelected in 1970) were marked by conflict with a Democratic-controlled legislature. He raised state income taxes, contrary to his political platform, but justified the increase as the means of paying for a reduction in local property taxes. He implemented some reforms in WELFARE programs and improved the state's higher education system.

In 1974 he decided not to run for a third term as governor, setting his sights instead on the White House. In 1976 he challenged President GERALD R. FORD for the Republican party nomination. Ford, who became president in 1974 when Richard M. Nixon resigned, was a moderate Republican who had been severely damaged by his PARDON of Nixon. Reagan fell only sixty votes short of defeating Ford for the nomination.

From 1976 to 1980, Reagan prepared himself for another presidential race. He kept in public view through a newspaper column and a radio show where he commented on public affairs. In 1980 he defeated his Republican rivals and was nominated for president, with GEORGE BUSH as his vice-presidential running mate.

Reagan easily defeated President JIMMY CARTER, whose popularity plummeted when the national economy suffered from high inflation and unemployment. Carter also was damaged by the Iranian hostage crisis, in which fifty-two Americans were held hostage by Iran. His inability to resolve the hostage crisis, which included a failed military rescue mission, contributed to his overwhelming defeat in November 1980. In 1984 Reagan won the largest victory in U.S. presidential history, when he defeated former Vice President Walter F. Mondale.

On January 21, 1981, as Reagan was being inaugurated president, Iran released the fifty-two hostages. With that crisis resolved, Reagan set out to cut income taxes, reduce the federal budget, increase defense spending, and deregulate U.S. business. On March 31, 1981, his efforts were temporarily sidetracked when John W. Hinckley, Jr., shot and wounded Reagan and his press secretary, James S. Brady. Reagan made a quick and complete recovery. In the aftermath his popularity rose even higher.

Reagan's economic plans were built on a theory called supply-side economics. This theory asserts that when taxes are cut, the money put back into the economy stimulates the production of more goods and services, thereby increasing jobs, with the result that more taxes are generated than were cut at the beginning of the process. Reagan persuaded Congress in 1981 to reduce taxes over a three-year period and to impose severe budget cuts on nondefense spending.

The results of "Reaganomics" proved mixed. The economy entered a recession in 1982 before rebounding in 1983. Inflation dropped, but government spending was not reduced sufficiently to make up for the revenue lost through tax cuts. The problem was exacerbated when Congress passed Reagan's tax reform package in 1986. Tax rates were reduced, and millions of low-income persons were removed from the tax rolls. Consequently, the federal government borrowed money to pay for the tax cuts. The national debt doubled in size between 1981 and 1986. By the time Reagan left office, the United

States had gone from a creditor nation to the world's largest debtor nation, owing half a trillion dollars to foreign investors.

Pressure on the FEDERAL BUDGET also came from Reagan's determination to begin the largest peacetime military buildup in U.S. history. Many new weapons systems were proposed, but the cornerstone of his defense system proposal was the Strategic Defense Initiative. Dubbed "Star Wars" by the media and his critics, Reagan proposed to build an antiballistic missile defense system that would shoot down Soviet missiles from space. Billions of dollars were committed to research, but actual systems proved hard to devise.

In foreign affairs, Reagan came into office maintaining his strong anti-Communist position, calling the Soviet Union an "evil empire." Reagan sought to negotiate ARMS CONTROL with the Soviet Union. In 1987 he negotiated the INTERMEDIATE-RANGE NUCLEAR FORCES TREATY (INF Treaty). The INF Treaty was the first agreement where both sides destroyed existing weapons. Relations between the superpowers improved during Reagan's second term, mainly because the new Soviet premier, Mikhail Gorbachev, sought to change the COLD WAR climate.

Reagan made a dramatic change in the FEDERAL COURTS through his appointment power. During his two terms he filled 372 of the 736 judgeships in the federal courts. Attorneys General WILLIAM FRENCH SMITH and EDWIN MEESE III set up a screening process that assured Reagan that he would be appointing judges who were in agreement with his conservative philosophy. In 1982 he appointed SANDRA DAY O'CONNOR to the Supreme Court, the first woman to sit on the Court. He elevated Justice WILLIAM H. REHNQUIST to chief justice of the Court in 1986 and appointed Judge ANTONIN SCALIA to the seat vacated by Rehnquist.

Reagan ran into problems with two of his other nominees. When he nominated Judge ROBERT H. BORK in 1987 to succeed Justice LEWIS F. POWELL, JR., the nomination met a firestorm of criticism. Bork was an outspoken jurist, the best-known conservative judge in the country. When the Senate defeated his nomination, Reagan appointed Judge DOUGLAS H. GINSBURG. Ginsburg withdrew his nomination after he disclosed that he had smoked marijuana. On his third attempt, Reagan successfully appointed Judge ANTHONY M. KENNEDY to the Court.

The last two years of the Reagan administration were consumed with the political damage caused by the IRAN-CONTRA Affair. Members of the NATIONAL SECURITY COUNCIL staff secretly sold weapons to Iran, a terrorist state that was forbidden to purchase armaments under U.S. law. One goal of the weapons sales was to facilitate the release of U.S. hostages held in Lebanon, but another goal was to use some of the proceeds to support the Nicaraguan anti-Communist Contra rebels against the Marxist Sandinista government. Because Congress had forbidden U.S. support of the rebels, the actions of Reagan's staff were illegal.

In late 1986 the details of these actions began to emerge. Reagan denied any knowledge of the actions taken by his advisers, but Senate hearings on the matter in 1987 cast doubt on the president's statements. The hearings damaged Reagan's administration because they revealed that the president apparently was out of touch with the conduct of national affairs.

Despite Iran-Contra, Reagan left office a popular president. After leaving office in 1989, he retired to California.

See also TAX REFORM ACT OF 1986.

REAL In CIVIL LAW, relating to a *thing* (whether movable or immovable), as distinguished from a person. Relating to *land*, as distinguished from PERSONAL PROPERTY. This term is applied to lands, TENEMENTS, and HEREDITAMENTS.

REAL ACTIONS Lawsuits concerning REAL PROPERTY, or land. Under the COMMON LAW, one of three categories of FORMS OF ACTIONS, the procedures by which a lawsuit was begun.

The categories of forms of actions were real actions, for lawsuits for the recovery of land; MIXED ACTIONS, for lawsuits for the recovery of land and of monetary damages for harm done to it; and PERSONAL ACTIONS, for lawsuits to recover items of PERSONAL PROPERTY or monetary damages.

REAL ESTATE Land, buildings, and things permanently attached to land and buildings. Also called realty and REAL PROPERTY.

Real estate is the modern term for land and anything that is permanently affixed to it. FIXTURES include buildings, fences, and things attached to buildings, such as plumbing, heating, and light fixtures. Property that is not affixed is regarded as PERSONAL PROPERTY. For example, furniture and draperies are items of personal property.

The sale and LEASE of real estate in the United States are major economic activities and are regulated by state and federal laws. The two major types of real estate are commercial and residential real estate. Commercial real estate involves the sale and lease of property for

New and Existing One-Family Houses Sold, 1970 to 1994

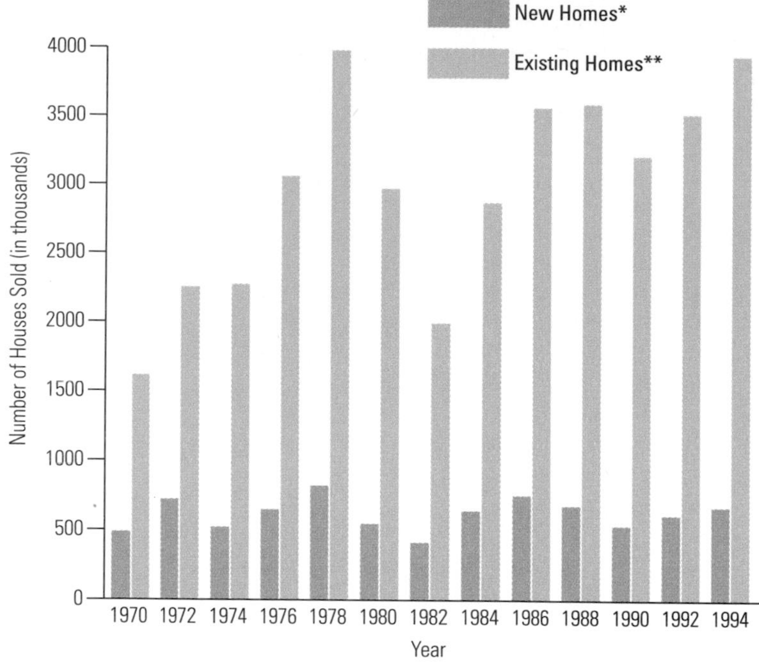

* Based on monthly interviews with builders or owners of one-family houses for which building permits have been issued or, for nonpermit areas, on which construction has started.
** Based on data reported by participating real estate multiple listing services.

Sources: U.S. Bureau of the Census and U.S. Department of Housing and Urban Development, *Current Construction Reports,* series C25, and *New One-Family Houses Sold,* monthly; National Association of REALTORS, Washington, DC, *Real Estate Outlook: Market Trends & Insights* (copyright).

business purposes. Residential real estate involves the sale and rental of land and houses to individuals and families for daily living.

The sale of residential property is heavily regulated. All states require real estate AGENTS and BROKERS, who earn a commission from the owner of real estate for selling the property, to be licensed. To get a LICENSE, a person must have a high school diploma, be at least eighteen years old, and pass a written test on real estate principles and law.

Since the 1970s, home buyers have been given additional protection under the law. Many states and municipalities require a seller of real estate to file a truth-in-housing statement. A seller must disclose any problems with the home, such as a wet basement or the presence of termites, on the form. Failure to disclose this information can result in the revocation of the purchase agreement or a lawsuit by the buyers against the seller for FRAUD. In addition, some laws require an inspector to visit the property to determine if there are any problems.

Most purchases of residential real estate require the buyer to obtain a MORTGAGE from a bank or other lending institution. The lending institution receives a SECURITY interest on the real estate, which means that if the borrower DEFAULTS in paying back the mortgage, the institution can obtain TITLE to the property and resell it to pay off the mortgage debt.

The federal government enacted the Real Estate Settlement Procedure Act of 1974 (RESPA) (12 U.S.C.A. § 2601 et seq.) to ensure that the buyer of residential real estate is made aware of the many costs associated with the sale. RESPA mandates that a federally insured lending institution give the buyer advance notice of all the costs to be paid on the date of closing the transactions. These costs typically include the cost of property surveys, APPRAISALS, TITLE SEARCHES, brokers' fees, and administrative and processing charges.

See also SALES LAW.

REAL EVIDENCE Probative matter furnished by items that are actually on view, as opposed to a verbal description of them by a WITNESS.

For example, a weapon used in the commission of a crime would be classified as real EVIDENCE.

REALIZED Actual; converted into cash.

A realized profit, for example, is a cash-in-hand gain as opposed to a paper profit, such as the increase in value of a particular STOCK, which could potentially be lost prior to the time it is sold.

REAL PROPERTY See LAND-USE CONTROL; PROPERTY LAW; ZONING.

REASONABLE Suitable; just; proper; ordinary; fair; usual.

The term *reasonable* is a generic and relative one and applies to that which is appropriate for a particular situation.

In the law of NEGLIGENCE, the REASONABLE PERSON standard is the standard of care that a reasonably prudent person would observe under a given set of circumstances. An individual who subscribes to such standards can avoid LIABILITY for negligence. Similarly a reasonable act is that which might fairly and properly be required of an individual.

REASONABLE DOUBT A standard of proof that must be surpassed to convict an accused in a criminal proceeding.

Reasonable doubt is a standard of PROOF used in criminal trials. When a criminal defendant is prosecuted, the prosecutor must prove the defendant's guilt BEYOND A REASONABLE DOUBT. If the JURY—or the judge in a BENCH TRIAL—has a reasonable doubt as to the defendant's guilt, the jury or judge should pronounce the defendant not guilty. Conversely, if the jurors or judge have no doubt as to the defendant's guilt, or if their only doubts are unreasonable doubts, then the prosecutor has proven the defendant's guilt beyond a reasonable doubt and the defendant should be pronounced GUILTY.

Reasonable doubt has been described a number of ways. One popular description, from the federal jury instructions, holds that proof beyond a reasonable doubt is "proof of such a convincing character that a reasonable person would not hesitate to rely and act upon it in the most important of his own affairs." A judge or juror has reasonable doubt as to a defendant's guilt if, based on all the EVIDENCE in the case, the judge or juror would be uncomfortable with a criminal conviction. A criminal conviction imposes public humiliation on the defendant, as well as various hardships such as INCARCERATION, monetary FINES, and, in many cases, FORFEITURE of property.

Reasonable doubt is the highest standard of proof used in court. In civil litigation the standard of proof is either proof by a preponderance of the evidence or proof by clear and convincing evidence. These are lower burdens of proof. A preponderance of the evidence simply means that one side has more evidence in its favor than the other, even by the smallest degree. Clear and convincing evidence is evidence that establishes a high probability that the fact sought to be proved is true. The main reason that the high proof standard of reasonable doubt is used in criminal trials is that criminal trials can result in the deprivation of a defendant's liberty or in the defendant's death, outcomes far more severe than occur in civil trials where money DAMAGES is the common remedy.

Reasonable doubt is required in criminal proceedings under the Due Process Clause of the FIFTH AMENDMENT to the U.S. Constitution. In *In re Winship*, 397 U.S. 358, 90 S. Ct. 1068, 25 L. Ed. 2d 368 (1970), the U.S. Supreme Court ruled that the highest standard of proof is grounded on "a fundamental value determination of our society that it is far worse to convict an innocent man than to let a guilty man go free."

The reasonable doubt standard is not used in every stage of a criminal prosecution. The prosecution and defense need not prove beyond a reasonable doubt that every piece of evidence offered into trial is authentic and relevant. If a prosecutor or defendant objects to a piece of evidence, the objecting party must come forward with evidence showing that the disputed evidence should be excluded from trial. Then the trial judge decides to admit or exclude it based on a preponderance of the evidence presented. A similar procedure employing a preponderance standard is used when a party challenges a variety of evidence, such as coerced CONFESSIONS, illegally seized evidence, and statements extracted without the furnishing of the so-called *Miranda* warning.

The reasonable doubt standard is inapplicable to still other phases of a criminal prosecution. Lower standards of proof are permissible in PAROLE revocation proceedings, proceedings to revoke PROBATION, and PRISON inmate disciplinary proceedings.

CROSS-REFERENCES

Clear and Convincing Proof; Criminal Law; Criminal Procedure; Due Process of Law; Preponderance of Evidence.

REASONABLE PERSON A phrase frequently used in TORT and CRIMINAL LAW to denote a hypothetical person in society who exercises average care, skill, and judgment in conduct and who serves as a comparative standard for determining LIABILITY.

The decision whether an accused is guilty of a given offense might involve the application of an objective test in which the conduct of the accused is compared to that of a reasonable person under similar circumstances. In most cases, persons with greater than average skills, or with special duties to society, are held to a higher standard of care. For example, a physician who aids a person in distress is held to a higher standard of care than is an ordinary person.

See also NEGLIGENCE.

REASONABLE WOMAN A standard used by fact finders in SEXUAL HARASSMENT litigation to determine whether sexual harassment has occurred.

Under title VII of the CIVIL RIGHTS ACT of 1964 (42 U.S.C.A. §§ 2000e–2000e-2 [1988]), it is illegal for an employer to discriminate against employees on the basis of sex. Under sexual harassment guidelines set forth by the EQUAL EMPLOYMENT OPPORTUNITY COMMISSION, the two basic types of sexual harassment are quid pro quo sexual harassment and hostile environment harassment (29 C.F.R. § 1604 [1993]). Quid pro quo harassment occurs when an employer conditions employment opportunities on an employee's submission to unwelcome sexual advances. Hostile environment harassment is unwelcome sexual conduct that interferes with an individual's employment or creates an intimidating, hostile, or offensive work environment. The standard that is used in evaluating whether a person has been subjected to sexual harassment varies from JURISDICTION to jurisdiction: some use a REASONABLE PERSON standard, and some use a reasonable woman standard.

In evaluating alleged sexual harassment, the reasonable person standard is an objective standard of perception based on a fictitious, reasonable person. Using this standard in a sexual harassment case, the fact finder would ask whether a reasonable person in the plaintiff's position would have felt that the respondent's actions constituted grounds for a sexual harassment claim. By contrast, a reasonable woman standard allows the fact finder to ask whether a reasonable woman in the plaintiff's position would have felt that the respondent's actions constituted sexual harassment. The difference is that the reasonable woman standard accounts for the different perceptions between men and women regarding words or actions of a sexual nature.

The courts that use the reasonable woman standard recognize a difference between men and women regarding the effect of unwanted sexual interaction. Because women historically have been more vulnerable to rape and sex-related violence than have men, these courts believe that the proper perspective for evaluating a claim of sexual harassment is that of the reasonable woman.

See also SEX DISCRIMINATION; WOMEN'S RIGHTS.

REBATE Discount; diminution of interest on capital lent in consideration of prompt repayment thereof; reduction of a stipulated charge that is not credited in advance but is returned subsequent to payment in full.

A *tax rebate* is a sum of money refunded to a taxpayer after full payment of the tax has been made.

REBUS SIC STANTIBUS [*Latin, At this point of affairs; in these circumstances.*] A tacit condition attached to all TREATIES to the effect that they will no longer be binding as soon as the state of facts and conditions upon which they were based changes to a substantial degree.

REBUT To defeat, dispute, or remove the effect of the other side's facts or arguments in a particular case or controversy.

When a defendant in a lawsuit proves that the plaintiff's ALLEGATIONS are not true, the defendant has thereby rebutted them.

REBUTTABLE PRESUMPTION A conclusion as to the existence or nonexistence of a fact that a judge or jury must draw when certain EVIDENCE has been introduced and admitted as true in a lawsuit but that can be contradicted by evidence to the contrary.

A rebuttable presumption can be overturned only if the evidence contradicting it is true and if a REASONABLE PERSON of average intelligence could logically conclude from the evidence that the presumption is no longer valid. For example, a person who has been judicially declared incompetent is presumed incompetent unless there is sufficient proof, usually in the form of medical testimony, that the person has regained competency.

Rather than simply reducing retail prices, many automobile manufacturers choose to offer rebates to new car buyers.

JEFF GREENBERG/PHOTOEDIT

CULVER PICTURES

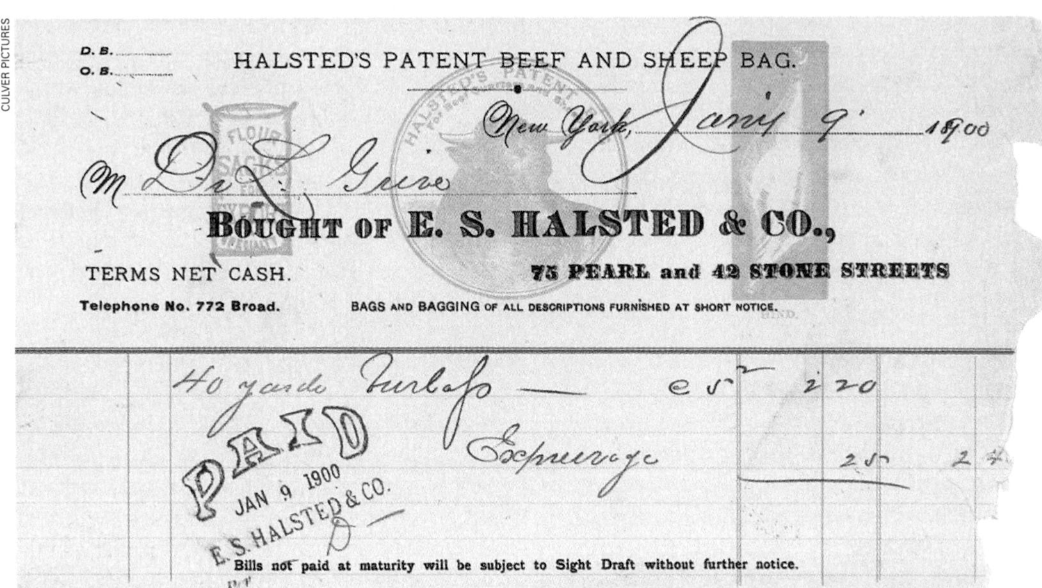

D. B.

O. B.

HALSTED'S PATENT BEEF AND SHEEP BAG.

New York, Jan'y 9' 1900

BOUGHT OF E. S. HALSTED & CO.,

TERMS NET CASH.

75 PEARL and 42 STONE STREETS

Telephone No. 772 Broad.

BAGS AND BAGGING OF ALL DESCRIPTIONS FURNISHED AT SHORT NOTICE.

40 yards burlap — 2 20

Expressage 25

PAID JAN 9 1900 E. S. HALSTED & CO.

Bills not paid at maturity will be subject to Sight Draft without further notice.

This receipt (dated 1900) confirms both receipt of goods by the buyer and receipt of payment by the seller.

In CRIMINAL LAW, there is a presumption of innocence in favor of the accused. The prosecution must establish BEYOND A REASONABLE DOUBT that the accused committed the crime charged.

REBUTTER In COMMON-LAW PLEADING, the response made by a defendant to a plaintiff's SURREJOINDER, which rebuts earlier denials made by the defendant.

The making of a rebutter occurs in the third round of the series of PLEADINGS made by the parties. First, there is the plaintiff's declaration which is countered by the defendant's PLEA. Next, the plaintiff makes a REPLICATION which is answered by the defendant in his or her REJOINDER. In the third stage of pleading, the plaintiff makes a surrejoinder to which the defendant responds by use of the rebutter.

RECALL The right or procedure by which a public official may be removed from a position by a vote of the people prior to the end of the term of office.

Recall is the retiring of an elected officer by a vote of the electorate. Some state constitutions prescribe the procedure that must be followed in a recall—for example, requiring the filing of a petition containing the signatures of a specific number of qualified voters.

RECAPTION Regaining POSSESSION of; taking back.

Recaption is a COMMON LAW remedy exercised by an individual who has been wrongfully deprived of GOODS. Through recaption, the owner may lawfully claim and retake goods whenever he or she finds them, as long as this is done in an orderly and legal manner. An individual who removes his borrowed car that was not returned to him from his neighbor's driveway is exercising recaption.

RECEIPT Acknowledgment in writing that something of value, or cash, has been placed into an individual's POSSESSION; written confirmation of payment rendered. *Receipt of goods* refers to the act of taking physical possession of them.

RECEIVER An archaic term, used in COMMON LAW and CIVIL LAW countries, to designate an individual who holds and conceals stolen goods for thieves. Currently an independent individual appointed by a court to handle money or property during a lawsuit.

Courts appoint receivers to take custody, manage, and preserve money or property that is subject to litigation so that when the final JUDGMENT is rendered, the property remains available to accomplish what has been ordered. The power to appoint a receiver is rarely utilized by the courts, and only upon a showing that it is required to preserve the property. RECEIVERSHIP cannot properly be used to coerce a party or to gain control of a business from someone who is capable of managing it. Receivership is an EXTRAORDINARY REMEDY, designed to benefit everyone involved. It is, however, a harsh remedy, since it involves restraining an individual's property, removing it from his control, and causing additional legal expenses.

The appointment of a receiver, which is a PROVISIONAL remedy to be exercised while litigation is pending, is ordinarily prescribed by statute, as are a receiver's powers. Ordinarily a receiver can be appointed only after a lawsuit is initiated.

According to the statutes of different states, receivers have been appointed in ACTIONS for DIVORCE, the removal of a TRUSTEE, or the FORECLOSURE of a MORTGAGE and in proceedings for the DISSOLUTION of a CORPORATION, for an ACCOUNTING of PARTNERSHIP money, or for a creditor's suit. The appointment of a receiver is justified when property in dispute is allowed to deteriorate to the extent where emergency repairs are necessary, and where there is good reason to suspect that the property is going to be sold, wasted, taken out of state, misused, or destroyed if the court does not act to preserve it. A receiver can also be appointed in situations where it appears that no one with a legal right to manage certain property is present, or no mentally competent adult is entitled to hold it. A receiver is sometimes appointed to preserve property during litigation between two parties who appear to have an equal right to use the property but who are unwilling to acknowledge each other's interest.

A judge can appoint a receiver following the filing of an application, or petition, with the court. In certain instances, all those who are interested in a case join together, and in the event that the court has JURISDICTION over the property and the parties, an appointment can proceed upon their consent.

An application for the appointment of a receiver is often submitted by a CREDITOR. It might be FRAUD or COLLUSION for a DEBTOR to have a friendly creditor nominate an individual the debtor chooses. A receiver generally should not be appointed unless notice is served on all interested parties and a hearing is conducted where a judge determines the MERITS of the case. On good evidence that an emergency exists, however, a judge can grant the petition for a receivership and hold a hearing as soon as possible thereafter.

Obligations A receiver assumes control of all the property subject to the receivership but does not take TITLE to the property and cannot exercise control over property outside the territorial authority of the court. Any property that has already been transferred in a fraudulent sale designed to cheat creditors is beyond the reach of the receiver; however, the receiver has the power to initiate a lawsuit, requesting that the court set aside the transfer. Any rights, such as LIENS or mortgages, that others have in the property remain valid. Anyone in possession of property listed in the receivership order can be compelled to turn it over to the receiver. A refusal to comply, or interference with the receivership, is punishable as a CONTEMPT of court.

A receiver does not represent the individual whose property is being administered, since the receiver is an officer of the court and is responsible to the court for protecting the interests of all opposing parties fairly. Where it is not clear how the receiver must perform his or her duty, he or she may properly apply to the court for instructions. He or she can be removed and held financially liable for failure to obey orders of the court, for neglect of duties, or for abuse of authority. The receiver must exercise judgment in fulfilling the duties, and her decisions must be reasonable. The receiver might be required to post a BOND to ensure faithful performance of the duties and is required to account to the court at regular intervals for all the property entrusted to her during, and at the termination of, the appointment.

Compensation A receiver has a right to be compensated for services and to be reimbursed for costs or traveling expenses. In cases where it is necessary for the receiver to hire an attorney, counsel fees are allowed. To obtain compensation, the receiver submits an itemized report of services to the court. The amount of payment depends upon the extent and value of the property, the difficulties encountered, and the time spent, as well as upon the receiver's skill, experience, and diligence and the success of his efforts. The time and manner of payment are, for the most part, left to the discretion of the court; unless authorized by the court, it is illegal for the receiver to take payment money out of the property being managed.

RECEIVERSHIP A court order whereby all the property subject to dispute in a legal ACTION is placed under the dominion and control of an independent person known as a RECEIVER.

Receivership is an EXTRAORDINARY REMEDY, the purpose of which is to preserve property during the time needed to prosecute a lawsuit, if a danger is present that such property will be dissipated or removed from the jurisdiction of the court if a receiver is not appointed. Receivership takes place through a court order and is utilized only in exceptional circumstances and with or without the consent of the owner of the property.

RECEIVING STOLEN PROPERTY The offense of acquiring goods with the knowledge that they have been stolen, extorted, embezzled, or unlawfully taken in any manner.

The earliest statute that made receiving stolen property a crime was enacted in England in 1692. It provided that the receiver—the person who accepts the property—should be deemed an ACCESSORY after the fact to the THEFT. The crime became a separate substantive offense in 1827, and it has been similarly treated in a majority of U.S. JURISDICTIONS.

Elements Receiving stolen property is defined by statute in most states. Generally it consists of four elements: (1) the property must

JONATHAN NOURAK/PHOTOEDIT

If they knew its source, anyone taking possession of this furniture stolen during the 1994 Los Angeles riots would be guilty of receiving stolen property.

be received; (2) it must have been previously stolen; (3) the person receiving the property must know it was stolen; and (4) the receiver must intend to deprive the owner of his or her property.

A person receives stolen property by acquiring or taking manual possession of it. Physical possession, however, is not always required. Under some statutes, it is sufficient if the accused has exercised control over the property. For example, a statute may declare that paying for the property constitutes control, regardless of whether the accused has handled it.

In many jurisdictions a belief that the property is stolen satisfies the knowledge element. It has been held that a mere suspicion does not constitute knowledge. Some statutes provide that a person has knowledge if he knows, or has reason to know, that goods are stolen. Another test is whether a REASONABLE PERSON would suspect that the property was stolen. Knowledge is commonly proved by the circumstances surrounding the receipt of the property. For example, unexplained possession of goods that were recently stolen raises a PRESUMPTION that the possessor received them illegally.

In order to be guilty, the receiver must intend to deprive the owner of the property. The crime is committed even if the receiver intends to obtain a reward for returning the property because she has gained a benefit from depriving the owner of possession, even temporarily.

Defenses An honest, although mistaken, belief that property is not stolen is a defense to the crime of receiving stolen property. Intoxication is another defense, but the intoxication must be severe enough to prevent any knowledge that the property was stolen. INFANCY and insanity are also good defenses.

See also INSANITY DEFENSE.

Punishment The punishment for receiving stolen property is a fine or imprisonment. The term of years imposed varies from state to state. In jurisdictions where value is an element of the offense, the severity of the penalty is commensurate with the value of the goods. Where value is not an element, it might still be significant in determining the severity of the punishment.

Civil Remedies In a majority of states, the person whose property was stolen may bring a CONVERSION action against the receiver of stolen property. If the accused is found to have converted the property, the victim has a choice of remedies. The victim may demand that the accused return the stolen property or may require the accused to pay the full value of the property at the time it was converted.

Federal Law Receiving stolen property is proscribed by federal statute (18 U.S.C.A. § 662) when it occurs within the maritime or territorial jurisdiction of the United States or when such property has moved in interstate commerce.

RECESS In the practice of courts, a brief interval during which all business is suspended without an ADJOURNMENT.

A recess in legislative practice is an interval of time between sessions of the same continuous body, as opposed to the period between the final adjournment of one legislative body and the convening of another at the next regular session.

RECIDIVISM The behavior of a repeat or habitual criminal. A measurement of the rate at which offenders commit other crimes, either by arrest or conviction baselines, after being released from incarceration.

Both state and federal laws have been enacted in an attempt to reduce the number of repeat or habitual offenses. For example, Washington's habitual criminal statute imposes a minimum sentence of ten years imprisonment for persons convicted of a second FELONY, third MISDEMEANOR, or third PETIT LARCENY. Furthermore, in the event that a person is convicted of a third felony, fifth misdemeanor, or a fifth petit larceny, the statute imposes a life sentence (Wash. Rev. Code § 9.92.090 [1996]).

Another state that has enacted a recidivism statute is California. California's recidivism statute, more commonly known as the three-strikes law, increases SENTENCING when the recidivist commits additional crimes. If convicted of a second felony, the criminal's sentence doubles the sentence of the first-time felon, and if convicted of a third violent crime or serious felony, the person will be sentenced to triple the sentence of a first-time felon, or twenty-five years imprisonment, whichever is greater (Cal. Penal Code § 667 [West 1996]).

Congress also responded to the recidivism rates in the United States by enacting the Violent Crime Control and Law Enforcement Act of 1994 (Pub. L. No. 103-322, 108 Stat. 1796). This act mandates life imprisonment for the commission of a serious violent felony, or a combination of two or more serious felonies or drug offenses.

There are many ideas on how to solve the problem of recidivism. Some of these include requiring literacy programs in penal institutions, electronic monitoring of home confinement, greater use of halfway houses, and "boot camp" programs consisting of military marching, discipline, physical training, work, classes, and drug and alcohol treatment for young, first-time offenders.

RECIPROCAL Bilateral; two-sided; mutual; interchanged.

Reciprocal obligations are duties owed by one individual to another and vice versa. A reciprocal CONTRACT is one in which the parties enter into mutual agreements.

Reciprocal laws are statutes of one state that give rights and privileges to the citizens of another state if that state extends similar privileges to the citizens of the first state. A common example is the Reciprocal Enforcement of Support Act, which is a uniform law adopted in a majority of JURISDICTIONS, by which a tribunal in the state where a wife or mother resides is able to commence proceedings for CHILD SUPPORT against a husband or father who resides in another state.

RECITAL A formal statement appearing in a legal document such as a DEED that is preliminary in nature and provides an explanation of the reasons for the transaction.

The recital in a deed, for example, might indicate the reasons why the owner is selling the property.

In PLEADING, a recital is the statement of matter that is introductory to a positive ALLEGATION; it begins with the words, "For that whereas . . ." and is followed by the claim of the party.

RECKLESSNESS Rashness; heedlessness; wanton conduct. The state of mind accompanying an act that either pays no regard to its probably or possibly injurious consequences, or which, though foreseeing such consequences, persists in spite of such knowledge.

Recklessness transcends ordinary NEGLIGENCE. To be reckless, conduct must demonstrate indifference to consequences under circumstances involving peril to the life or safety of others, although no harm is intended.

RECOGNITION The confirmation or acknowledgment of the existence of an act performed, of an event that transpired, or of a person who is authorized by another to act in a particular manner.

In tax law, a capital gain is *recognized* when a taxpayer has actually received payment. Such gain must then be reported on INCOME TAX forms, and capital gains tax must be paid on it.

In INTERNATIONAL LAW, the term *recognition* refers to the formal acknowledgment by one state that another state exists as a separate and independent government. Recognition is not a mere technicality. A state has no status among nations until it is recognized by other states, in spite of the fact that it might possess all other attributes of a state, including a definable territory and population, a recognizable government, and a certain amount of continuity or stability.

The decision to recognize a new national government is a political act that is in the discretion of the officials who are responsible for foreign policy. In the United States, the president makes the decision to recognize a country and can do so by making a formal announcement or by having another official, such as the secretary of state, make the announcement for him. Recognition can also be informal, such as by opening negotiations with a new state or exchanging diplomats with it.

A nation is not truly sovereign and independent unless other nations recognize its SOVEREIGNTY. Formal recognition operates to assure a new state that it will be permitted to hold its place and rank as an independent political body among the nations.

Recognition takes effect from the time it is given as if the state had always existed, and a new government can carry forward international projects initiated by the old government it replaces.

Many difficulties come into play when a government is not recognized. For example, an unrecognized government is not entitled to participate in diplomatic negotiations or to have its laws applied in lawsuits or in JURISDICTIONS.

The term *recognition* is also used in relation to armed conflicts. If a state of belligerency is recognized, then the law of WAR applies with all of its protections for prisoners of war and noncombatants. Recognition of a state of belligerency ordinarily comes from an uninvolved state that declares itself neutral. A neutral country is able to recognize a state of belligerency and carry on trade and diplomatic relations with both sides of the conflict.

RECOGNIZANCE A recorded obligation, entered into before a tribunal, in which an individual pledges to perform a specific act or to subscribe to a certain course of conduct.

For example, an individual who owes money might enter into a recognizance whereby she agrees to satisfy the DEBT.

In CRIMINAL LAW, an individual who has been found guilty of an offense can be mandated to enter into a recognizance whereby she agrees to keep the peace in the future. An individual who has been accused but not yet convicted of a criminal offense may be allowed to go free prior to the trial without being required to post a BAIL BOND. The accused individual provides the court with a formal written statement, which declares that his failure to appear will precipitate payment to the court of a specifically indicated sum of money. This is known as a release on one's own recognizance, or personal recognizance.

RECONCILIATION The restoration of peaceful or amicable relations between two individuals who were previously in conflict with one another.

Reconciliation ordinarily implies forgiveness for injuries on either or both sides. The term is often applied to the parties to a DIVORCE who cease proceedings for the dissolution of their marriage upon a resolution of their differences. *Reconciliation* is used interchangeably with *conciliation.*

RECONVEYANCE The transfer of REAL PROPERTY that takes place when a MORTGAGE is fully paid off and the land is returned to the owner free from the former DEBT.

RECORDING OF LAND TITLES A process by which proof of ownership of REAL PROPERTY is filed in the appropriate county office or court to allow purchasers, creditors, and other interested parties to determine the status of the property interests therein.

The process of recording begins when a duly executed, acknowledged, and delivered document is brought to the recorder's office for filing in the record books in the county where the property is located. The recorder's office also keeps a set of indexes containing information about each document so that the document can be discovered by a TITLE SEARCH. A majority of states have a "GRANTOR-GRANTEE INDEX," a set of volumes containing an alphabetical reference to the surname of the GRANTOR followed by the name of the GRANTEE, a brief description of the document and the property, and the location of the filed document in the official record books. The same information is contained in the "grantee-grantor index," which is organized alphabetically by surname of the grantee. A few states use a "tract index," which organizes all of the documents according to the location of the property.

An individual planning to purchase land commissions a title search, which involves examining the list of successive conveyances, from original owner to the present holder, that affect a parcel of land. The person conducting the title examination, usually a lawyer or TITLE INSURANCE examiner, prepares an "abstract of title," summarizing the CHAIN OF TITLE and listing any LIENS, charges, or liabilities to which the land may be subject. The ABSTRACT OF TITLE is EVIDENCE of the marketability of the record title; a purchaser of an interest in real property will take title subject to all interests constructively disclosed or implied by the record, and subject to any interests of which the purchaser has actual notice.

In nearly every state the validity of a CONVEYANCE, as between grantor (seller) and grantee (purchaser), is not affected by whether the DEED is filed in the public records or not; the question is not who has possession of the deed but who owns TITLE to the land. Before the enactment of state recording acts, the question of priority of title was generally a question of time. For example, if O, owner in FEE SIMPLE of land, sells to A, giving A a deed to the land, but O later decides to sell the same land to B, B takes nothing because A was first to purchase the land, leaving O nothing to convey to B. Under state recording acts, however, if A fails to record the deed before B buys and B meets certain criteria with respect to B's status and behavior, B still receives good title from O and A takes nothing. B is considered a "bona fide purchaser" or a "purchaser in good faith," if he or she gives "valuable consideration without actual, implied or constructive notice of inconsistent outstanding rights of others . . . " (*Miller v. Hennen*, 438 N.W.2d 366, 369 [Minn. 1989]).

Three general categories of state recording acts are in use in the United States: "notice," "race," and "race-notice" recording statutes, the least common of which are the race recording acts. Under a race recording statute, if A fails to record title, B must record his or her title before A records. (It is therefore a "race" to the recorder's office where the first person to file has title to the property.) To prevail against an unrecorded conveyance, B must have paid value, yet there is no requirement that B be without notice of A's conveyance at the time of B's recording in order to prevail.

Unlike the race recording statute, the notice and race-notice recording statutes prevent B from prevailing if B is first to record but does so with notice of the prior unrecorded conveyance. Under a notice recording statute, if B is a BONA FIDE purchaser and is therefore without notice of A's prior unrecorded conveyance, B will prevail regardless of whether A records before B. On the other hand, under a race-notice recording statute, B will not prevail, despite her or his bona fide purchaser status, if B does not record before A.

The recording statutes only work to the detriment of the holders of unrecorded instruments. A properly recorded document will prevail over subsequent claims, regardless of whether those claimants actually search for or find the recorded instrument. Courts often use the term "constructive notice" to describe this imputation of knowledge if a proper and reasonable investigation would have revealed the recorded instrument. Because the recording system was designed to encourage and protect reliance on the public records, no legal protection is afforded those individuals who have not significantly relied upon such records.

A purchaser with "ACTUAL NOTICE" of a prior unrecorded interest in the premises will take title subject to that interest even though it may be unrecorded. Rumor or gossip usually are insufficient to provide notice, but if a purchaser has heard more reliable information about a possible adverse claim to the land, he or she is expected to make a reasonable investigation. In such cases, an individual might be charged with "inquiry notice" in addition to actual or CONSTRUCTIVE notice of previous claims. Inquiry notice is not applied in the same manner as constructive notice, which is applied automatically; it must first be shown that a suspicious fact existed to originate the duty to conduct an inquiry.

One of the most litigated aspects of notice is the universally accepted rule that a purchaser of an interest in land is deemed to have actually viewed the land before buying. The purchaser is held to inquiry notice of the facts that an inspection, or a conversation with those in possession of the land, would disclose. The problem occurs in determining what is possession—for example, when the holder of the unrecorded interest only uses the property for a limited purpose, such as for camping or cutting timber.

Not every instrument that has been delivered to the recorder's office and copied into the records is held to be recorded or to have provided sufficient notice within the meaning of the recording acts. The recorder's office makes no representation that the instruments it preserves are authentic and reliable, and in many cases one cannot detect the defects by solely examining the document itself. For example, the instrument may contain a forged SIGNATURE, have a defective ACKNOWLEDGMENT, never have been delivered to the buyer, have been issued by a seller who is without CAPACITY, and so on. Some states have enacted curative statutes which provide that after the passage of a certain number of years, instruments that lack SEALS or acknowledgments or other technical requirements are deemed to have been properly recorded.

In some cases, documents can be located only with difficulty, such as with "wild deeds"—recorded deeds not appearing in the chain of title. Most of these difficulties do not occur in tract-index systems in which all conveyances affecting a given parcel will be indexed on a single page. There are situations, however, in which the tract index shows conveyances by parties who are not in the chain of the record title. Such conveyances do not impart constructive notice of an interest. However, they may not be disregarded, and they put the purchaser to the burden of an inquiry.

The more problematic and common error occurs when the instrument has been misindexed at the recorder's office. In this situation courts generally hold that the instrument was not recorded because it was not indexed in a manner sufficient to provide constructive notice to any individual searching the record. Some states, however, provide that an instrument is deemed recorded upon its deposit in the recorder's office. In either case, the careful purchaser or grantee should return to the recorder's office a few days after recording his or her deed to ensure that it has been properly recorded.

Not all written instruments affecting real property interests are recordable. Recording statutes may explicitly provide that certain documents need not be recorded to protect the individuals in whom a property interest is created, such as with short-term leases and executory sales contracts. On the other hand, not all interests in land derive from written instruments. These types of adverse claims to title fall entirely outside the coverage of the recording acts and include the following property interests: ADVERSE POSSESSION, prescriptive EASEMENTS, implied easements, easements by necessity, and oral boundary line agreements.

See also REGISTRATION OF LAND TITLES.

RECORDS Written accounts of acts, transactions, or instruments that are drawn up pursuant to legal authority by an appropriate officer and appointed to be retained as memorials or permanent evidence of matters to which they are related.

A *public record* is a document that has been filed with, or furnished by, a governmental agency and is available to the public for inspection. For example, *title of record* to property is an ownership interest that has been duly filed in the office of public land records.

BOB DAEMMRICH/STOCK BOSTON

Abstracts of title are among the most commonly searched public records.

The term *record* also applies to the formal, written account of a case, which contains the history of actions taken, papers filed, rulings made, and all written opinions.

RECOUPMENT To recover a loss by a subsequent gain. In PLEADING, to set forth a CLAIM against the plaintiff when an ACTION is brought against one as a defendant. Keeping back of something that is due, because there is an equitable reason to withhold it. A right of the defendant to have a deduction from the amount of the plaintiff's DAMAGES, for the reason that the plaintiff has not complied with the cross-obligations or independent COVENANTS arising under the same CONTRACT.

RECOURSE The right of an individual who is holding a COMMERCIAL PAPER, such as a CHECK or PROMISSORY NOTE, to receive payment on it from anyone who has signed it if the individual who originally made it is unable, or refuses, to tender payment.

Recourse is the right of the holder to recover against a prior endorser, who is secondarily liable. When a check is endorsed *without recourse*, it signifies that the endorser will not be liable to pay in the event that payment is refused.

RECOVERED MEMORY The remembrance of traumatic childhood events, usually involving SEXUAL ABUSE, many years after the events occurred.

The heightened awareness of child sexual abuse that developed in the 1980s also brought with it the controversial topic of recovered memory. Some mental health therapists contended that children repress memories of abuse so completely that years later they have no memory of the abuse. These therapists believed that, through the use of recovered memory therapy, victims are able to recover the memories of the traumatic events and begin dealing with their psychological effects. Others in the medical community, however, held deep reservations about the idea of repressed memory and the therapy techniques that purported to recover them. These critics argued that, without established standards or procedures, a psychotherapist faced the danger of implanting false memories in a patient. By the mid-1990s these fears were justified, as patients won multimillion dollar verdicts against their therapists based on claims that they created false and destructive memories.

During the 1980s many adults who recovered memories of child sexual abuse through therapy sought to hold their abusers accountable in a court of law. However, under STATUTE OF LIMITATIONS provisions, the time for a lawsuit had expired. Courts and legislators responded by changing these laws. Typically, these laws provide that the ACTION must be filed within a certain number of years after the plaintiff either reaches the AGE OF MAJORITY or knew or had reason to know that sexual abuse caused the injury.

Once the statute of limitations problem was resolved, a number of civil lawsuits were filed alleging sexual abuse that happened many years before. Lawsuits against Catholic priests using recovered memories as EVIDENCE resulted in large damage awards in several cases. Criminal charges were also successfully brought against alleged abusers on the basis of recovered memory. Apart from the award of DAMAGES, some therapists believe that a trial and a confrontation between the abuser and the abused is essential to restoring the victim's mental health. In the 1980s courts allowed recovered memory testimony into evidence, despite objections by defendants that there was no scientific basis for believing memories could be recovered. In addition, defendants contended that the memories were untrue, implanted in the patient through a mixture of drug therapy and suggestive questioning.

By the early 1990s, there was a backlash against recovered memory and its use in the law. The False Memory Syndrome Foundation was established as a support group by members of families who claimed they had been falsely accused of abuse by their children through recovered memory. Mental health professionals also contested the validity of recovered memory. Some argued that it is never reliable, whereas others believed it is sometimes reliable but only when elicited by a properly trained professional. In 1994 the American Medical Association (AMA) adopted a policy statement that proclaimed that recovered memories of childhood sexual abuse are often unreliable and should not be assumed to be true. The AMA statement concluded that few cases in which adults make accusations of abuse can be proved or disproved using recovered memories because there is no way to distinguish true memories from imagined events. That same year the American Psychiatric Association also expressed similar misgivings about recovered memory.

In 1994 a California jury awarded $500,000 in a MALPRACTICE case brought against two therapists by Gary Ramona, a father who claimed that the therapists had implanted false memories of childhood sexual abuse in his daughter. In 1996 a Minnesota jury awarded David and Lisa Carlson $2.5 million after the longest psychiatric malpractice trial in U.S. history. The Carlsons sued Lisa Carlson's therapist, charging that she used hypnosis, drugs, coercion, and pressure to implant false memories.

By 1995 a number of state courts had issued decisions that attacked the validity of recovered memories and held that these memories were insufficient to sustain a lawsuit unless supported by independent evidence.

See also CHILD ABUSE.

RECOVERY 📖 The acquisition of something of value through the JUDGMENT of a court, as the result of a lawsuit initiated for that purpose. 📖

For example, an individual might obtain recovery in the form of DAMAGES for an injury.

The term *recovery* is also used to describe the amount ultimately collected, or the amount of the judgment itself.

RECRIMINATION 📖 A charge made by an individual who is being accused of some act against the accuser. 📖

Recrimination is sometimes used as a defense in ACTIONS for DIVORCE. Traditionally the underlying theory was that a divorce could be granted only when one individual was innocent and the other guilty, and the defense of recrimination allowed the party accused of misconduct to terminate divorce proceedings by asserting guilt against the other party. As grounds for divorce were expanded, however, recrimination became more and more readily provable.

Recrimination has been limited or eliminated as a defense in some states, and others allow it only where one spouse accuses the other of ADULTERY and the defendant wants to prove that the plaintiff was also guilty of that offense. In some JURISDICTIONS, the courts have attempted to counterbalance the plaintiff's accusation with the defendant's defense by allowing only comparable grounds to be offset by recrimination.

RECUSE 📖 To disqualify or remove oneself as a JUDGE over a particular proceeding because of one's CONFLICT OF INTEREST. Recusal, or the judge's act of disqualifying himself or herself from presiding over a proceeding, is based on the maxim that judges are charged with a duty of impartiality in administering justice. 📖

When a judge is assigned to a case, she reviews the general facts of the case and determines whether she has any conflict of interest concerning the case. If a conflict of interest exists, the judge may recuse herself on her own initiative. In addition, any party in a case may make a motion to require the judge to recuse herself from hearing the case. The initial presiding judge usually determines whether or not the apparent conflict requires her recusal, and the judge's decision is given considerable deference. Some jurisdictions, however, require another judge to decide whether or not the presiding judge should be disqualified. If a judge fails to recuse himself when a direct conflict of interest exists, the judge may later be reprimanded, suspended, or disciplined by the body that oversees judicial administration. In addition, in some cases where a judge presides over a matter in which he has a direct conflict of interest, any criminal conviction or civil damage award in the case may be reversed or set aside.

Generally, a judge must recuse himself if he has a personal BIAS or PREJUDICE concerning a PARTY to the lawsuit or has personal knowledge of the facts that are disputed in the proceeding. The CODE OF JUDICIAL CONDUCT, a judicial ethics code drafted by the AMERICAN BAR ASSOCIATION in 1972 and adopted by most states and the federal government, outlines situations in which a judge should disqualify himself from presiding over a matter. Canon 3C of the Judicial Code outlines these situations, including the judge's personal bias or prejudice toward a matter or its participants, personal knowledge of the facts that are disputed in a case, a professional or familial relationship with a party or an attorney, or a financial interest in the outcome of the matter. Most interpretations of the code mandate a judge's disqualification or recusal if any of these factors are present.

In some cases the parties to a proceeding may waive the judge's disqualification and allow the judge to preside over the case. The judge's disqualification is waived when both parties agree to the WAIVER or when one or more of the parties continues to participate in the proceedings.

The term recusation was at one time considered an exception to JURISDICTION, the effect of which was to disqualify the particular judge by reason of the judge's interest or prejudice in the proceeding.

See also CANONS OF JUDICIAL ETHICS; JUDICIAL CONDUCT.

REDEMPTION The liberation of an ESTATE in REAL PROPERTY from a MORTGAGE.

Redemption is the process by which land that has been mortgaged or pledged is bought back or reclaimed. It is accomplished through a payment of the DEBT owed or a fulfillment of the other conditions.

REDLINING A discriminatory practice whereby lending institutions refuse to make MORTGAGE loans, regardless of an applicant's CREDIT history, on properties in particular areas in which conditions are allegedly deteriorating.

The term *redlining* stems from some lenders' practice of using a red pencil to outline such areas. Redlining violates CIVIL RIGHTS statutes.

REDRESS Compensation for injuries sustained; recovery or RESTITUTION for harm or injury; DAMAGES or equitable relief. Access to the courts to gain REPARATION for a wrong.

RED SCARE Throughout much of the twentieth century, the United States worried about Communist activities within its borders. This concern led to sweeping federal action against ALIENS and CITIZENS alike during periods known today as Red scares. Using the derogatory term *Red* for Communist, the phrase is a form of criticism: it implies overreaction resulting from excessive suspicion, unfounded accusation, and disregard for constitutional law.

The first Red scare followed the Bolshevik revolution in Russia in November 1917, and lasted until 1920. It was marked by antiradical legislation in U.S. immigration law, extensive federal probes of suspected radicals and their organizations, and mass arrests and deportations of aliens. The second Red scare arose prior to World War II, and reached new heights during the COLD WAR years.

The origins of the first Red scare lay in the Russian Revolution and the horrendous experience of World War I. COMMUNISM was not yet perceived as the only enemy; ANARCHISM (the advocacy of violent overthrow of government and law) also caused fear. In the United States, no great effort was made to separate these two political philosophies, for they both seemed to represent a single threat: foreign attempts to undermine the nation's government and institutions. Congress responded by putting new antiradical protections in the Immigration Act of 1918 (§§ 1–3, as amended, 8 U.S.C.A. § 137 (c, e–g)). Although antagonism toward different races and beliefs had marked immigration law for decades, this change introduced political limits: it allowed for the deportation of aliens on the grounds of anarchist beliefs or membership in anarchist organizations. Riding a wave of anti-immigrant sentiment, lawmakers frequently grumbled about "foreign troublemakers."

Early in 1919, Congress began pressuring the Justice Department to take action against radicals. It had a receptive audience in Attorney General A. MITCHELL PALMER. A self-styled enemy of foreign subversion who hoped to become president, Palmer was given to making public statements like "fully 90% of the communist and anarchist agitation is traceable to aliens." Then, on June 2, 1919, a bomb exploded outside Palmer's Washington, D.C., home. Found among the remains of the dead bomber was a pamphlet signed by "the anarchist fighters," warning of more violence to come. The attack set in motion changes that would leave a lasting mark on federal law enforcement: Palmer created the Radical Division of the Justice Department, and assigned a promising young bureaucrat named J. EDGAR HOOVER to head it. Within a few months, Hoover had compiled thousands of names of suspected radicals and their organizations; later, as director of the FEDERAL BUREAU OF INVESTIGATION (FBI), he would compile more.

Although many people associate the term "Red Scare" with 1950s McCarthyism, America has endured more than one such period. This cartoon showing a Bolshevik creeping under the American flag dates from 1919.

Spurred by public expectations, the Justice Department acted in November 1919 and January 1920 by launching massive raids. More than ten thousand people were arrested—some for membership in Communist or left-wing groups, others on no greater pretext than that they looked or sounded foreign—and then jailed and interrogated with little regard for their right to due process. Hundreds were subsequently deported, some aboard a U.S. Navy troop transport. But the raids backfired: Congress was scandalized by the disregard shown for constitutional rights. Along with the newly formed AMERICAN CIVIL LIBERTIES UNION (ACLU) and the AMERICAN BAR ASSOCIATION, lawmakers denounced the attorney general. The raids had two unforeseen consequences for Palmer: first, they ended his presidential aspirations, and second, they dashed his hopes of seeing new federal legislation that would allow for the arrest of subversive *citizens*, much as the 1918 Immigration Act permitted deportation of subversive *aliens*. Hoover, who had overseen the execution of the raids and some deportations, escaped reproach.

The backlash against the first Red scare did nothing to prevent a recurrence. Fears of anarchism subsided, but the onset of World War II produced new worries about fascism, Nazism, and Communism. The instigators of the second Red scare turned their gaze inward: not foreigners but U.S. citizens now seemed dangerous. These concerns led to the creation of the House Un-American Activities Committee (HUAC) in 1938. Lasting until 1969, this panel of the House of Representatives held many hearings into alleged subversion by private citizens, unions, and Hollywood. The cold war years also saw another dramatic manifestation of Red scare tactics: the Communist witch-hunts of Senator JOSEPH R. MCCARTHY, who brought unfounded accusations of Communist infiltration of the State Department and the military. Both HUAC and McCarthy benefited substantially from the cooperation of the FBI, whose durable director, Hoover, fed them information.

HUAC represented the last gasp of the Red scares. In the late 1960s and early 1970s, the cold war still had important geopolitical implications. However, federal interest in hunting down radicals had waned: a backlash against McCarthyism was one reason, as was the divisive experience of the VIETNAM WAR. Although the cold war continued until the breakup of the Soviet Union in 1991, its effects were felt primarily in foreign policy and military expansion. Today, the legacy of the Red scares to U.S. law can be measured in several ways: a greater interest in civil liberties; a decline of Congress's role as a forum for interrogating private citizens; federal reform that has curtailed the power of the FBI; and a 1990 reform of immigration law that removed anarchism and Communism as grounds for deportation (Immigration and Nationality Act of 1990, U.S.C.A. § 1101 et seq.).

See also GOLDMAN, EMMA; SMITH ACT.

REDUCTIO AD ABSURDUM [*Latin, Reduction to absurdity.*] In logic, a method employed to disprove an argument by illustrating how it leads to an absurd consequence.

REED, STANLEY FORMAN Stanley Forman Reed served as associate justice of the U.S. Supreme Court from 1938 to 1957. Before his appointment to the Court, Reed served as U.S. solicitor general. Reed was a strong supporter of congressional power to regulate the U.S. economy but was more moderate in his support of civil liberties.

Reed was born on December 31, 1884, in Macon County, Kentucky. Educated at private schools, he graduated from Kentucky Wesleyan College in 1902. He earned a second bachelor's degree at Yale University. Reed attended law school at both the University of Virginia and Columbia University but never completed his law degree. In 1908 he went to Paris and studied for a year at the Sorbonne.

He returned from Europe and studied for the Kentucky bar exam. He was admitted in 1910 and began a law practice as a solo practitioner in Macon County. From 1912 to 1916, he served in the Kentucky General Assembly but left to serve in the Army during World War I. After the war he joined a large law firm.

President HERBERT HOOVER appointed Reed general counsel of the Federal Farm Board in 1929. Though Reed was a Democrat, the Republican Hoover promoted him to general counsel of the Reconstruction Finance Corporation (RFC) in 1932. The RFC was Hoover's belated attempt to use the power of the federal government to lift the U.S. economy out of the economic depression that had begun in November 1929. When FRANKLIN D. ROOSEVELT succeeded Hoover as president in 1933, he kept Reed in this position.

Reed continued to impress his superiors. In 1935 he was appointed U.S. solicitor general, whose duty it is to argue cases before the U.S. Supreme Court. In this position Reed was called on to defend the constitutionality of NEW DEAL economic programs that empowered the federal government to regulate the national economy. He met a conservative Supreme Court, with the majority of the justices opposed to these new programs. The centerpiece of the New Deal was the NATIONAL INDUSTRIAL RECOVERY ACT of 1933 (NIRA), 48 Stat. 195, which was designed to bolster the national economy through the enforcement of "codes of fair competition." Reed's arguments in the 1935 case that challenged the constitutionality of the NIRA (*A.L.A. Schechter Poultry Corp. v. United States*, 295 U.S. 495, 55 S. Ct. 837, 79 L. Ed. 1570) were unsuccessful, and the act was declared unconstitutional.

BIOGRAPHY

ARTIST: CHARLES HOPKINSON. COLLECTION OF THE SUPREME COURT OF THE UNITED STATES.

Stanley Forman Reed

"THE UNITED STATES . . . GRANTS TO ALL CITIZENS A RIGHT TO PARTICIPATE IN THE CHOICE OF ELECTED OFFICIALS . . . [A] CHOICE WHICH CANNOT BE NULLIFIED BY A STATE THROUGH CASTING ITS ELECTORAL PROCESS IN A FORM WHICH PERMITS . . . RACIAL DISCRIMINATION IN THE ELECTION. CONSTITUTIONAL RIGHTS WOULD BE OF LITTLE VALUE IF THEY COULD BE THUS INDIRECTLY DENIED."

Reed had mixed success defending New Deal programs before the Court. President Roosevelt, knowing that Reed believed in the New Deal, appointed him to the Supreme Court in 1938. The appointment marked the decline of conservative economic thought on the Court and helped pave the way for sustaining federal programs and policies in the future. Reed consistently upheld the right of Congress, under the power of the COMMERCE CLAUSE of the U.S. Constitution, to regulate the national economy.

Apart from economic issues, Reed was a moderate. He wrote the majority opinion in *Smith v. Allwright*, 321 U.S. 649, 64 S. Ct. 757, 88 L. Ed. 987 (1944), that struck down the "white primary" in the southern states. The device effectively kept African Americans from exercising their right to vote in any meaningful sense. At that time the South was a virtual one-party system dominated by the Democratic party. State Democratic parties excluded African Americans from party membership, and state legislatures closed the primaries to everyone but party members. African Americans were thus barred from voting in the primary. The general election was a mere formality for the primary winner because there was at most token Republican opposition. Reed declared the practice unconstitutional, because it violated the FIFTEENTH AMENDMENT's prohibition against denying the right to vote to citizens because of their race. Reed also voted to end the SEPARATE-BUT-EQUAL doctrine of racial segregation in *Brown v. Board of Education*, 347 U.S. 483, 74 S. Ct. 686, 98 L. Ed. 874 (1954).

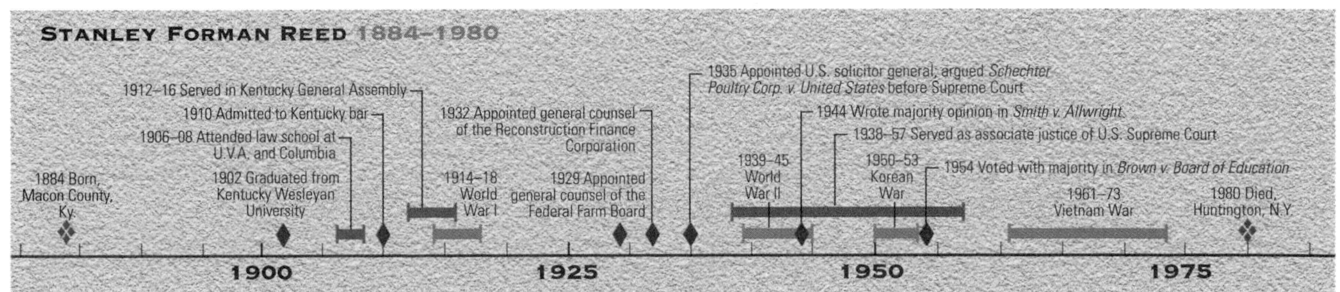

Reed was more conservative regarding civil liberties. He supported the admission of illegally obtained evidence in criminal trials in *Wolf v. Colorado*, 338 U.S. 25, 69 S. Ct. 1359, 93 L. Ed. 1782 (1949), and wrote the opinion in *Adamson v. California*, 332 U.S. 46, 67 S. Ct. 1672, 91 L. Ed. 1903 (1947), that declined to apply the FIFTH AMENDMENT's guarantee against SELF-INCRIMINATION to state court proceedings.

Reed retired from the Court in 1957. He died on April 2, 1980, in Huntington, New York.

REENTRY See RIGHT OF REENTRY.

REFEREE A judicial officer who presides over civil HEARINGS but usually does not have the authority or power to render JUDGMENT.

Referees are usually appointed by a judge in the district in which the judge presides. Referees aid the judge by hearing certain matters and by making recommendations concerning special or complicated issues. Judges generally delegate a portion of their judicial power to referees, who then report their recommendations to the judge concerning the issue.

The English chancery master was the forerunner of the present-day referee. In eighteenth-century England, the chancellor courts used special masters to aid the CHANCERY in handling its expanding EQUITY jurisdiction. Accordingly, the chancery master aided the CHANCELLOR only in equitable matters, such as marriage dissolutions, TRUST matters, and financial accountings. U.S. jurisdictions adopted the use of special masters or referees modeled on the English chancery master.

In most JURISDICTIONS a referee must be an attorney. Nevertheless, in some complex property or financial matters, a judge may appoint a person who is not an attorney to preside over a dispute and to make recommendations. The term *reference* usually refers to the trial and determination of issues arising in a CIVIL ACTION by a person appointed for that purpose by the court. An order of reference, which is also called a referral order, is the court order that appoints the referee to hear and recommend action on the issues that are specified in the order.

Judges generally appoint a referee to hear complicated matters, such as financial accountings, property LIEN issues, or business valuation disputes. Many jurisdictions also have referees who are appointed to hear specified special-jurisdiction matters, such as FAMILY LAW, trust and PROBATE, and pretrial DISCOVERY disputes. Parties to an action may agree to have a matter heard by a referee. In some jurisdictions the parties' consent to the appointment of a referee to hear the matter may result in the parties' waiver of any right to a jury trial.

A referee makes recommendations to the judge or court that appoints the referee but generally does not issue enforceable orders. A referee generally cannot render judgment in a case. The referee's general duty is to provide a report to the appointing judge on the issues of fact or law that prompted the referee's appointment. It has been said that "nothing can originate before a referee, and nothing can terminate with or by the decision of a referee." Referees generally serve at the pleasure of the judge and accordingly hold less judicial authority than the appointing judge. As a judicial officer, a referee is subject to the CODE OF JUDICIAL CONDUCT.

In some jurisdictions a referee may be called a special master, COURT COMMISSIONER, or a MAGISTRATE. The Federal Rules of Civil Procedure, for example, allow for the appointment of a "master," who can be a referee, an auditor, an examiner, or an assessor. Generally, however, the duties of a master are the same as those of a referee, and the appointing judge may limit the master's powers to report only on specified issues or to perform only particular acts. The federal judiciary also uses magistrate judges—judicial officers who perform a broad range of delegated or statutory duties, such as presiding over initial hearings in criminal cases, MISDEMEANOR trials, pretrial proceedings, and the trial of civil cases. The Federal Magistrate Act of 1968 (Pub. L. No. 90-578, 82 Stat. 1107 [codified at 28 U.S.C.A. §§ 604, 631–639]) created the current system of federal magistrate judges and governs the duties of such magistrates.

REFERENCE The process by which a tribunal sends a CIVIL ACTION, or a particular issue in the action, to an individual who has been appointed by the tribunal to hear and decide upon it, or to obtain evidence, and make a report to the court.

See also REFEREE.

REFERENDUM The right reserved to the people to approve or reject an act of the LEGISLATURE, or the right of the people to approve or reject LEGISLATION that has been referred to them by the legislature.

The referendum power is created by state constitutions and is conferred on the citizens of a state or a local subdivision of the state. Referendum provides the people with a means of expressing their opinion on proposed legislation before it becomes operative as a law. The power of referendum does not permit the people to invalidate a law that is already operative but suspends or annuls a law that has not yet gone into effect. In this sense, referendum is similar to a governor's VETO power. Also, by referendum the people may reinstate an act that the legislature has expressly repealed.

The referendum, along with the *initiative*, are the two forms of direct legislation adopted by many states during the direct democracy movement of the early twentieth century. Referendum allows the people to state their opinion on laws that have been enacted by the legislature, and the INITIATIVE allows the people to propose their own laws. Thus, in the states that have adopted the initiative and referendum, the people essentially form another branch of the legislature, having the ability both to enact laws and to overturn laws passed by the elected legislature but not yet in effect. An initiative or a referendum passed by the people has the same force and effect as any act of the legislature. A referendum may be challenged on constitutional grounds, on grounds that proper procedures were not followed in the referendum process and election, or on grounds that the referendum or initiative was outside the scope of authority granted by the state constitution. Also, in some states the governor may veto an initiative or referendum.

The general initiative and referendum were first adopted in the United States in South Dakota in 1898, and many states soon followed. The movement toward direct legislation did not grow from a desire of the people to exercise the legislative function directly. Rather, many people distrusted their legislative bodies, believing that large CORPORATIONS and powerful groups of individuals were corrupting legislation. The power of referendum made most legislation subject to the will of the people.

The referendum power is derived solely from a state's constitution and applies to that state's laws; people do not have the right to challenge federal legislation by referendum. The right of referendum and the procedure to be followed in exercising the referendum right are set forth in the state's constitution and statutes. The referendum process is essentially the same in every state. First, there must be a petition for referendum that states, among other things, the title and nature of the legislative act the petition seeks to have submitted for referendum. The petition is then circulated for signatures. Generally, anyone eligible to vote may sign a petition for referendum, even if he or she is not registered to vote. When the required number of signatures is collected, the petition is filed. If the petition is certified as sufficient, the referendum measure is placed on the election ballot for approval or rejection by the people. If the required number of votes, usually a majority of the votes cast, are in favor of the referendum, it passes. Usually, the people vote on a referendum measure during the general election, but special referendum ELECTIONS also may be held.

In some states there is no limit on the referendum power, and any law may be challenged by referendum. In many states, however, the constitution creates exceptions to the referendum power for certain types of legislation. Commonly, constitutional provisions regarding referendums create an exception for laws necessary for the support of the state government and state or public institutions, because a referendum on any such measure might cause a branch of the government to cease to function. This exception applies mainly to tax and appropriation measures. Also, most states create an exception to the referendum power for laws necessary for the immediate preservation of the public peace, health, or safety, thereby allowing the legislature to exercise the police power unimpaired. Finally, measures declared by the legislature to be emergency measures are usually not subject to referendum.

REFORMATION A remedy utilized by the courts to correct a written instrument so that it conforms to the original intent of the parties to such an instrument.

Legal documents, such as CONTRACTS, DEEDS, MORTGAGES, and TRUSTS, are all proper subjects for reformation. Since the original intent of the parties must control, however, a totally new agreement cannot be created through reformation.

The court, in the exercise of its EQUITY powers to do justice, will reform a document only in the event that FRAUD or MUTUAL MISTAKE occurred in its execution.

Reformation is a remedy that is granted at the discretion of the court only where the facts and circumstances of a particular case warrant it. It will not be granted where an entirely new agreement would result between the parties or where unwarranted hardships would be imposed upon them. Only an individual who has acted in GOOD FAITH can apply to the court to have an instrument reformed.

Reformation is not available as a remedy to correct every minor error, such as typographical errors; rather, it is granted where there has been a mutual mistake that substantially affects the parties' rights and obligations. The MISTAKE must have been in existence at the time the instrument was drawn up. A mistake in the description of land and its boundaries ordinarily justifies reformation of an agreement where the purchaser and seller intended that all the seller's property be sold to the purchaser. In addition, a mistake of law by which both parties to the instrument have incorrectly comprehended the legal effect of the facts and the document might also result in reformation.

REFORMATORIES State institutions for the confinement of juvenile delinquents.

Any MINOR under a certain specified age, generally sixteen, who is guilty of having violated the law or has failed to obey the reasonable directive of his or her parent, GUARDIAN, or the court is ordinarily treated as a delinquent under state statute. The purpose of reformatories is to impose punishment for crimes committed by INFANTS while concurrently rehabilitating the offenders through educational and vocational training so that they will become law-abiding citizens.

The powers of a state to establish and maintain reformatories, as well as the authority of its agencies to do so, are ordinarily contained in constitutional or statutory provisions. Such authority is based upon the sovereign power of the state as PARENS PATRIAE to safeguard the welfare of children within its borders by removing them from harmful environments and putting them in institutions where their development will be supervised.

Reformatories—which are also known as houses of refuge, state vocational institutions, reform schools, juvenile correction centers, and industrial or training schools—are generally not considered PRISONS. In some states, however, they are part of the prison system with adult inmates.

See also JUVENILE LAW.

REFORM PARTY H. Ross Perot, founder of Electronic Data Systems, Inc., ran for president in 1992 as an independent candidate and received nineteen percent of the popular vote. In September 1995 Perot organized the Reform party and was the party's 1996 presidential candidate. The Reform party's ticket, which included Perot's running mate, Pat Choate, appeared on the ballot in every state and won eight percent of the vote.

Perot entered the 1992 presidential race in February 1992 and gradually gained substantial widespread support with a well-financed campaign and straight talk about government. Perot made campaign finance reform, national trade deficits, and the balancing of the FEDERAL BUDGET the main issues in his campaign. In July Perot withdrew from the race when he received critical media coverage and lost his campaign manager, Edward J. Rollins. However, public support for his candidacy persisted, and Perot reentered the race in October with former Navy admiral James B. Stockdale as his running mate.

After running for president as an independent in 1992, Ross Perot organized the Reform Party in 1995 and ran a second time.

In 1996 the Reform party fielded several candidates in ELECTIONS across the country. At the party's national convention, University of Denver professor and former Colorado governor Richard D. Lamm challenged Perot's nomination, but Perot won handily.

The Reform party is devoted to thrifty, accessible government and Perot has vowed that, although he may not again run for president, the party will not fold.

See also ELECTION CAMPAIGN FINANCING; INDEPENDENT PARTIES.

REFRESHING MEMORY The process of aiding a witness's recollection of certain details during a trial by allowing him or her to consult documents, memoranda, or books in order to better remember past transactions or events about which he or she is testifying.

A WITNESS is not permitted to rely completely upon such materials, nor may the witness read from them directly while giving TESTIMONY. The witness must be capable of testifying to the facts from a present, independent recollection.

REFUGEES Individuals who leave their native country for social, political, or religious reasons, or who are forced to leave, as a result of any type of disaster, including WAR, political upheaval, and famine.

Often refugees are unwilling to return to their country of citizenship because they fear political, social, or cultural persecution. The refugees turn to other countries for protection and support. A related problem is statelessness, which occurs when one's country of citizenship has been absorbed by another nation through war or political change. The United States has promulgated policies to aid refugees and stateless persons both internationally, through various international organizations and treaties, and domestically, through national IMMIGRATION policies.

International Refugee Policies There have always been refugees, but their plight was first recognized as a major international problem after World War I when the number of refugees in Europe and Asia Minor totaled in the millions. The first world institution to come to the aid of refugees was the League of Nations Office of High Commissioner for Refugees, established in 1921. Although U.S. President WOODROW WILSON was a principal founder of the LEAGUE OF NATIONS, the U.S. Senate refused to ratify the TREATY on which it was based, and the United States never joined the League. This office was later called the Nansen Office in honor of the Norwegian scholar who first headed it. The Nansen Office provided assistance to one-and-a-half million Greeks who were resettling from Asia Minor to Greece, and to the half million Turks resettling from Greece to Turkey.

The rise of Nazi Germany led to another flood of international refugees in 1933. Because Germany would not permit the Nansen Office to assist those individuals, the League of Nations created the Office of the High Commissioner for the Refugees from Germany. By 1938 the office was expanded to help Austrian refugees fleeing the Nazis as well. The two League of Nations offices were later combined into the Office of the High Commissioner for Refugees. In 1938 thirty-two countries met to establish the Intergovernmental Committee for Refugees, at the urging of U.S. President FRANKLIN D. ROOSEVELT. This time the United States was a member of the organization. These organizations helped European political and social refugees in a variety of ways, including by giving them identity and travel documents.

By 1944 all of the functions of the Office of the High Commissioner for Refugees and the Intergovernmental Committee for Refugees were assumed by the UNITED NATIONS in an office that was later called the International Refugees Organization (IRO). The United States was a member of the United Nations and participated in this international front as well. The IRO helped one-and-a-half million European and Asian refugees. It was dismantled in 1951, and its duties were taken over by a new Office of the United Nations High Commissioner for Refugees (UNHCR).

The UNHCR is responsible for protecting international refugees and assisting with the problems created by mass movements of people resulting from civil disturbance or military conflict. The high commissioner follows policy directives handed down by the U.N. General Assembly. The United Nations encourages countries to admit refugees and stateless persons and provide resettlement opportunities for them. The U.N. also seeks to help refugees achieve self-sufficiency and family security in their new homes. Members of the United Nations agree to help refugees and stateless persons by giving them the same civil liberties afforded their nationals and the same economic rights afforded other foreign nationals.

In 1948 the United Nations also addressed the Palestinian refugee situation in the Middle East by creating a new organization, the United Nations Relief for Palestinian Refugees, later called the United Nations Relief and Works Agency for Palestine Refugees in the Near East (UNRWA). The UNRWA assisted more than one-and-a-half million Palestinian refugees through the early 1970s.

In 1982 the UNHCR turned its attention to the 1.2 million African refugees in Somalia, Sudan, Djibouti, Kenya, and the horn of Africa. The majority of refugees were escaping conditions of famine in the underdeveloped African countries. Also in the early 1980s, the UNHCR assisted more than 36,000 Vietnamese boat people in the South China Sea. During the 1980s, the UNHCR helped 2.9 million refugees leave Afghanistan and resettle in Pakistan.

The United Nations also helps refugees by assisting in their voluntary repatriation, or return to their home country. By 1988 the UNHCR helped at least 150,000 refugees return to their countries of origin, mostly in Africa and Central America. The U.N. General Assembly declared in 1988 that voluntary repatriation is the ideal solution to the problems faced by refugees.

In the late 1980s and early 1990s, the UNHCR began to study the particular problems faced by women and children refugees and called for further efforts to protect these special groups.

In addition to the United Nations and the League of Nations, various international charitable organizations, such as Amnesty International, strive to aid refugees and stateless persons. Religious relief organizations also have aided refugees by providing food, clothing, shelter, and resettlement assistance.

Domestic Refugee Policies In the early years of the United States, the states were responsible for the naturalization of ALIENS, and the only requirement to be naturalized was a pledge of loyalty. Now the federal government closely regulates the entry of all aliens, including refugees, through the Immigration and Naturalization Service. The standards for naturalization have become more demanding and exacting.

Before the twentieth century, the U.S. approach to admitting refugees was no different from the admission of general immigrants, which was based on quotas for each country. During World War II, the insensitivity of this policy became evident as the United States turned away Jewish refugees because its quota for German immigrants had been met, and the refugees were forced to return to Nazi Germany.

In 1945 President HARRY S. TRUMAN signed an EXECUTIVE ORDER that gave displaced persons, or refugees, priority over other immigrants. Congress passed the War Brides Act, 59 Stat. 659, in 1945 and the Displaced Persons Act, 62 Stat. 1009, in 1948 to make the United States more responsive to international immigration and refugee situations. The War Brides Act permitted the immigration of 120,000 alien wives and children of U.S. soldiers. The Displaced Persons Act allowed for more than the normal quota of refugees from Poland, Germany, Latvia, Russia, and Yugoslavia to be admitted.

The Refugee Relief Act of 1953, 67 Stat. 400, allowed for the entry of 214,000 refugees during a limited period on a non-quota basis. Many Hungarian "freedom fighters" were admitted under the act in 1956. President DWIGHT D. EISENHOWER invited another 30,000 Hungarian refugees to come to the United States following their country's revolution on a "parole" status, meaning they were not granted immigrant visas.

The Fair-Share Refugee Act of 1960, 74 Stat. 504, permitted the Department of Justice to admit even more refugees under parole status. Under this act, many refugees from Communist and Middle Eastern countries resettled in the United States.

In the late 1970s and early 1980s, a flood of refugees from Vietnam, Cambodia, and Laos came to the United States. In 1975, 200,000 Indochinese refugees arrived, and by 1985 nearly 400,000 Southeast Asians came to the United States. Throughout this period, Jewish refugees from Russia continued to be admitted to the United States.

The Refugee Act of 1980, 8 U.S.C.A. § 1525, raised the number of annual immigrants permitted from 290,000 to 320,000, of which 50,000 could be refugees. Mass admittance of refugees pursuant to the president's parole authority was not permitted, but the president was allowed to admit refugees over the 50,000 annual limit with congressional consultation.

Cuban and Haitian refugees in the early 1980s tested the ability of the United States to accommodate and assimilate refugees. The Cubans were seen as fleeing from the Communist regime of Fidel Castro and therefore were permitted entry into the United States. Flight from a Communist country was a long-standing accepted qualifying basis for refugee status. The sheer numbers of Cuban refugees who came to the United States by boat made their entry difficult, but not impossible, to process.

Unlike the Cubans, the Haitian refugees claimed that they were fleeing poverty, a condition not recognized by the United States as qualifying one for refugee status. However, the Haitians asserted that once they left Haiti they could not return or else they would face political persecution for having left. The U.S. government did not accept the Haitians' fear of persecution as sufficient to admit them as refugees and concluded that they were economic immigrants. The Haitians were detained in large relocation camps and then deported. In 1981 President RONALD REAGAN signed an executive order authorizing the U.S. Coast Guard to stop boats leaving Haiti and turn them around if they were transporting economic immigrants.

See also HUMAN RIGHTS; INTERNATIONAL LAW.

REFUNDING Reimbursing funds in RESTITUTION or repayment. The process of refinancing or borrowing money, ordinarily through the sale of BONDS, to pay off an existing DEBT with the proceeds derived therefrom.

REGENTS OF UNIVERSITY OF CALIFORNIA v. BAKKE A 1978 decision by the Supreme Court, *Regents of the University of California v. Bakke*, 438 U.S. 265, 98 S. Ct. 2733, 57 L. Ed. 2d 750, commonly referred to as *Bakke*, held that although the university unlawfully discriminated against a white applicant by denying him admission to its medical school solely on the basis of his race, the university may consider the race of an applicant in its admission procedure in order to attain ethnic diversity in its student body.

In 1972, Allan Bakke, a thirty-three-year-old white male engineer, applied for admission to the medical school of the University of California, Davis, and was not accepted. Bakke was one of 2,664 applicants that year for one hundred places. He applied again the next year and was again rejected. This second year, minority applicants with grade point averages, *Medical College Admission Test* scores, and other qualifications that were lower than Bakke's were accepted under a special minority admission program. This program set aside sixteen of the one hundred places in the entering class for minority groups titled blacks, Chicanos, Asians, and American Indians.

Following his second rejection, in 1974, Bakke instituted a lawsuit in the Superior Court of California against the university on the grounds that his rights had been violated under the Equal Protection Clause of the FOURTEENTH AMENDMENT of the U.S. Constitution; the California Constitution; and title VI of the CIVIL RIGHTS ACT of 1964 (42 U.S.C.A. § 2000d et seq.), which proscribed the exclusion of any person from a federally funded program on the basis of race.

The California lower court ruled that the school's admission program was in violation of the state and federal constitutions and title VI, but it would not order the university to admit Bakke to the medical school, because Bakke had not shown that he would have won admission had there been no special minority program. Bakke then appealed to the California Supreme Court, which ruled that it was incumbent upon the university, not Bakke, to prove that he would not have been admitted if the special program had not been in effect. The school acknowledged that it could not satisfy the requirement, and the court ordered the university to admit Bakke. The university appealed to the U.S. Supreme Court, which granted CERTIORARI (agreed to review the case), and the court order requiring Bakke's admission was suspended pending a decision by the High Court.

The *Bakke* case aroused intense controversy. CIVIL RIGHTS supporters feared that the Court might hold that specific policies could not be employed to remedy past discrimination. On the other side of the issue stood Bakke and his supporters, charging that Bakke's civil rights were being violated simply because of his race, which happened to be white. A great deal of weight hung over the *Bakke* case as it moved through the courts, and, with enormous publicity surrounding their decision, the Supreme Court justices were keenly aware of the case's importance.

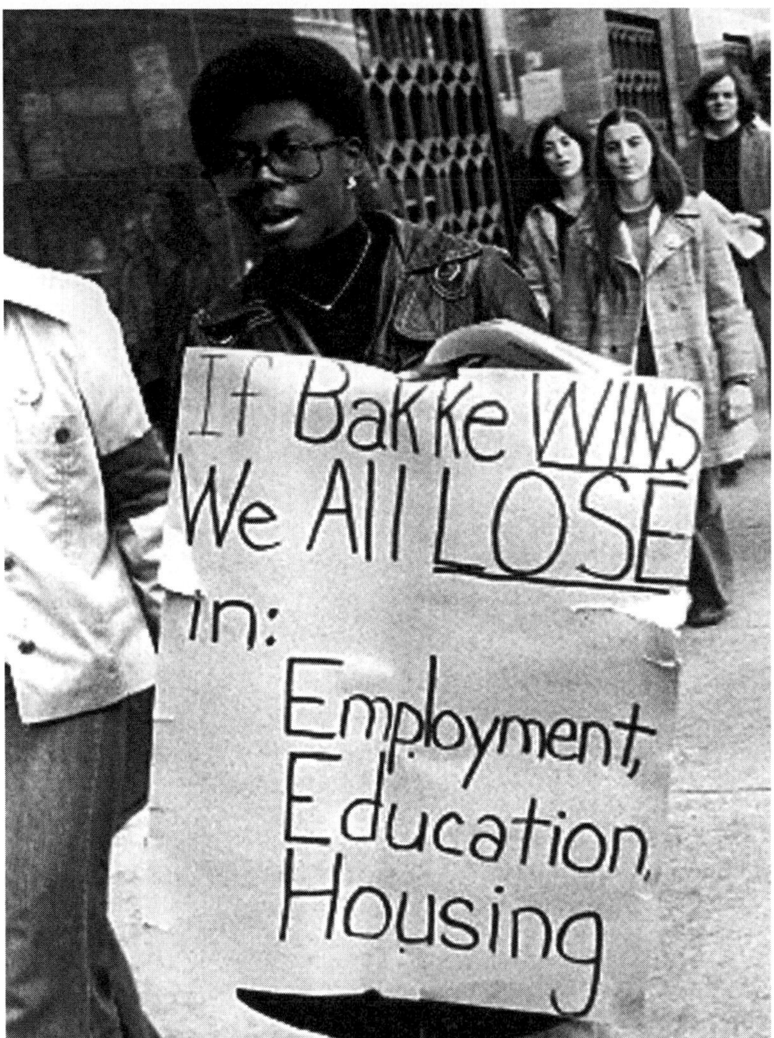

UPI/CORBIS-BETTMANN

During the U.S. Supreme Court's deliberation in Regents of University of California v. Bakke, picketers surrounded Detroit's Federal Building to protest Bakke's discrimination claim.

On June 27, 1978, the Court divided sharply in its decision, presenting six separate opinions. Four justices chose to address only the statutory issue of title VI and found for Bakke, including his admission to the medical school, because the quota in the university's admission plan had clearly excluded Bakke on the basis of his race. Four justices addressed the larger constitutional issue of the Equal Protection Clause and found for the medical school because its intent was not to exclude Bakke but only to include individuals of other races for compelling government reasons. The deciding swing vote was cast by Justice LEWIS F. POWELL, JR., who found for both. Powell's contention was that the title VI plurality was correct in that the university had violated the "plain meaning" of the Civil Rights Act, which proscribed discrimination based on race, and ordered Bakke admitted to the medical school. But Powell also found that the university could use "race-conscious" factors in selecting its applicants in order to achieve the benefits of a "diverse student body."

This divided decision settled the *Bakke* case, but it left the legal issue muddled: what actions, if any, could the state take to protect minorities in the marketplace? Subsequent court decisions struggled repeatedly over this primary civil rights question.

CROSS-REFERENCES

Colleges and Universities; Equal Protection; Strict Scrutiny; *United Steelworkers v. Weber*.

REGISTER To record, or enter precisely in a designated place, certain information in the public records as is mandated by statute. A book of public records.

A register contains various types of information that is available to the public, such as births, dates, and marriages.

The term *register* is also used as a designation for the public official charged with the duty of maintaining such records.

REGISTER OF DEEDS The designation, in certain JURISDICTIONS, of the public officers who record documents that establish ownership of property, MORTGAGES, and other instruments that relate to REAL PROPERTY in official record books provided and maintained for such purpose.

Registers of deeds are also known as recorders of deeds.

See also RECORDING OF LAND TITLES.

REGISTRAR The public official charged with the duty of making and maintaining public records.

Common examples are the registrars of voters and deeds.

REGISTRATION Enrollment; the process of recording entries in an official book.

For example, the names of stockholders might be registered in the official books of a CORPORATION. Similarly motor vehicles are ordinarily registered with the state motor vehicle department, and voters are registered so that they may participate in elections. In some jurisdictions, statutes establish systems by which land TITLES can be registered so that the ownership of REAL PROPERTY can always be readily ascertained through a consultation of public records. See also REGISTRATION OF LAND TITLES.

REGISTRATION OF LAND TITLES A system by which ownership of REAL PROPERTY is established through the issuance of an official CERTIFICATE indicating the name of the individual in whom such ownership is vested.

Land titles are registered through a statutory process called the *Torrens title system*, in somewhat the same way that automobile titles are now registered in most states. Under current Torrens acts, land ownership can be readily ascertained without any need for repeated examinations of voluminous public records, and the resulting titles are generally secure and marketable.

The TORRENS TITLE SYSTEM takes its name from Sir Robert R. Torrens, a native of Ireland who later became the first premier of South Australia. It is said that in 1850 Torrens first thought of applying to land the same method of registering and transferring ownership used for ships. In 1858 the first Torrens Title Act went into effect in South Australia, largely through Torrens's efforts. Although the system is known by his name, Torrens was by no means the inventor of the statutory system for land registration now in place in the United States.

Under Torrens statutes, an individual who registers TITLE to land is required to first file an application with the appropriate court. All those who have or claim to have any interest in the property must be given notice of the proceedings so that they have an opportunity to make their claims to the land. Anyone seeking to be the registered owner of the land must show that he or she has good title "as against the world." The person need not be in actual possession of the land, however.

When title to land is established to the satisfaction of the court, it will issue a decree to settle and declare title. The decree must be entered on the records of the court and is conclusive of the rights of the parties, such as the fact of ownership and the area and boundary lines of the land. Upon registration of the decree, a designated officer, ordinarily called the *registrar of titles*, makes and files the original certificate of title in the proper register. A duplicate of the certificate must be delivered to the registered owner. Once this procedure has been completed, the land becomes registered land. Any subsequent transfers and dealings regarding it must be made according to statute.

Torrens acts were adopted in twenty states and territories between 1895 and 1917, but only eleven states now have title registration statutes in effect. Moreover, in those eleven states, the use of the Torrens title system remains optional and is confined to certain localities wherein only a relatively small proportion of the land is registered. Among several factors that may account for the lack of widespread acceptance of a title registration system are structural defects in some of the acts that have left numerous interests unaccounted for on the title certificate and have resulted in procedural problems in filing claims. Some people in states in which the system remains optional also have cited the high cost of initial registration as being prohibitive. Finally, TITLE INSURANCE companies, ABSTRACT companies, and title lawyers in general have vigorously opposed the Torrens title system because universal adoption of the system would decrease the demand for title insurance and would in effect render the need for these services obsolete.

See also RECORDING OF LAND TITLES.

REGRESSIVE TAX A tax with a rate that decreases as the taxpayer's income increases.

The result of a regressive tax is that the lower-income taxpayer pays a larger percentage of his or her income in taxes than does the higher-income taxpayer. The opposite of the regressive tax is the PROGRESSIVE TAX. With progressive taxes, such as the federal INCOME TAX, the effective tax rates increase as the taxpayer's income increases. The proportionate tax rate, also referred to as a flat tax rate, remains constant as income rises. Under a proportionate tax system, higher-income individuals pay a greater amount of taxes than lower-income individuals pay, but the ratio is identical.

Consumption taxes, which are taxes on consumer goods and services, are usually regressive because individuals with lower incomes spend a larger portion of their income on these goods and services than higher-income individuals do. Some examples of these consumption taxes are the taxes on ALCOHOL and TOBACCO, also referred to as "sin taxes."

Some taxes can be a combination of the different tax rates. For example, the SOCIAL SECURITY tax is proportional until the taxpayer reaches the maximum income level. However, once the taxpayer's income reaches the maximum cap, all income earned over the cap is not taxed. The result is a regressive tax because the individual earning in excess of the maximum income level is paying a lower percentage of her or his income in taxes than the lower-income individual is paying.

See also TAXATION.

REGULAR Customary; usual; with no unexpected or unusual variations; in conformity with ordinary practice.

An individual's regular course of business, for example, is the occupation in which that person is normally engaged to gain a livelihood.

REGULATION A rule of order having the force of law, prescribed by a superior or competent authority, relating to the actions of those under the authority's control.

Regulations are issued by various federal government departments and agencies to carry out the intent of LEGISLATION enacted by Congress. Administrative agencies, often called "the BUREAUCRACY," perform a number of different government functions, including rule making. The rules issued by these agencies are called regulations and are designed to guide the activity of those regulated by the AGENCY and also the activity of the agency's employees. Regulations also function to ensure uniform application of the law.

Administrative agencies began as part of the EXECUTIVE BRANCH of government and were designed to carry out the law and the president's policies. Congress, however, retains primary control over the organization of the bureaucracy, including the power to create and eliminate agencies and confirm presidential nominations for staffing the agencies. Congress has also created administrative agencies that exist outside of the executive branch and are independent of presidential control. President FRANKLIN D. ROOSEVELT and the NEW DEAL plan he implemented created many new administrative agencies. Over the years administrative agencies have become more powerful participants in the overall federal government structure as Congress and the president have delegated more legislative and executive duties to them. Administrative agencies have also become responsible for many judicial functions.

The judicial and legislative functions of administrative agencies are not exactly like those of the courts or the legislature, but they are similar. Because regulations are not the work of the legislature, they do not have the effect of law in theory; but in practice, regulations can have an important effect in determining the outcome of cases involving regulatory activity. Much of the legislative power vested in administrative agencies comes from the fact that Congress can only go so far in enacting legislation or establishing guidelines for the agencies to follow. Language that is intrinsically vague and cannot speak for every factual situation to which it is applied, as well as political factors, dictate that the agencies have much to interpret and decide in enforcing legislation. For example, SECURITIES laws prohibit INSIDERS from profiting against the PUBLIC INTEREST, but it is left to the applicable administrative agency, the SECURITIES AND EXCHANGE COMMISSION, to define "public interest." The FOOD AND DRUG ADMINISTRATION, another administrative agency, must keep unsafe food and ineffective drug products off the market, but further administrative refinement and interpretation is necessary for the agency to determine what products are "unsafe" or "ineffective." The FEDERAL COMMUNICATIONS COMMISSION must interpret laws regulating BROADCASTING; the TREASURY DEPARTMENT issues regulations interpreting the INTERNAL REVENUE CODE; and the Board of Governors of the Federal Reserve System issues regulations governing the actions of Federal Reserve banks. The many other administrative agencies and departments make regulations to provide clarity and guidance in their respective areas of the law.

Administrative agencies carry out legislation in several ways, including enacting regulations to carry out what the agency believes is the legislative intent. Agencies generally formulate proposed regulations and then open up rule-making proceedings in which interested parties can testify and comment on them. The agency then issues a rule or policy that binds the agency in future cases just as statutory law does.

The Administrative Procedure Act of 1946, 5 U.S.C.A. § 551 et seq., with its subsequent amendments, was designed to make administrative agencies accountable for their rule making and other government functions. It imposed a number of procedural requirements designed to make procedures among agencies more uniform. In administrative rule-making proceedings formal HEARINGS must be held, interested parties must be given the opportunity to comment on proposed rules, and the adopted formal rules must be published in the *Federal Register*. After being published in the *Federal Register*, the regulations are subsequently arranged by subject in the *Code of Federal Regulations*. The Administrative Procedure Act has been criticized, however, because it contains a number of exemptions that allow the agencies discretion in whether or not they strictly adhere to the guidelines established in the act. Organizations such as the AMERICAN BAR ASSOCIATION are working toward eliminating such discretion in administrative agencies.

CROSS-REFERENCES

Administrative Agency; Administrative Law and Procedure; Code of Federal Regulations; Federal Register; Public Administrative Bodies; Quasi-Legislative.

REHABILITATION The restoration of former rights, authority, or abilities.

The process of rehabilitating a WITNESS involves restoring the CREDIBILITY of the witness following IMPEACHMENT by the opposing party. Rehabilitating a prisoner refers to preparing him or her for a productive life upon release from prison.

PHOTOGRAPHER: DANE PENLAND COLLECTION OF THE SUPREME COURT OF THE UNITED STATES.

William Hubbs Rehnquist

REHNQUIST, WILLIAM HUBBS William Hubbs Rehnquist was appointed to the U.S. Supreme Court in 1972 and was elevated to the position of chief justice in 1986. A political and judicial conservative, Rehnquist has consistently sought to limit the power of the federal government to intervene in matters traditionally left to the states.

Rehnquist was born on October 1, 1924, in Milwaukee, Wisconsin. In 1943 he joined the U.S. Army Air Corps and served until 1946. He then took advantage of the GI Bill to attend college at Stanford University. After graduating in 1948 with both a bachelor's and a master's degree, Rehnquist earned a second master's degree in political science from Harvard University in 1949. He then attended Stanford University Law School, where he finished first in his 1952 graduating class.

Rehnquist then served as a law clerk for U.S. Supreme Court Justice ROBERT H. JACKSON. It was during the 1952 term that the Court first heard arguments on the constitutionality of state-segregated public education. In a memorandum to Jackson that would come back to haunt him at his judicial confirmation hearings, Rehnquist argued for upholding the SEPARATE-BUT-EQUAL doctrine contained in *Plessy v. Ferguson*, 163 U.S. 537, 16 S. Ct. 1138, 41 L. Ed. 256 (1896).

Leaving his judicial clerkship in 1953, Rehnquist relocated to Phoenix, where he joined the

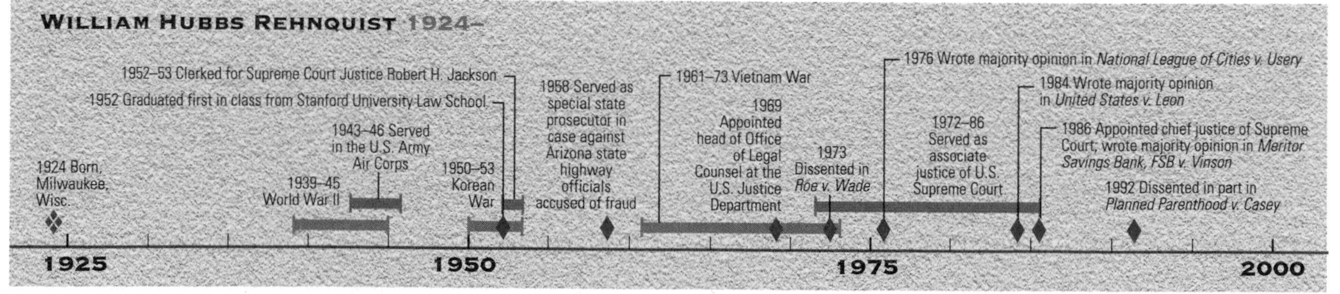

state bar and entered private practice. In 1958 he served as a special state prosecutor, bringing charges against several state highway officials who were accused of FRAUD. During his years of practice, he specialized in civil litigation.

Rehnquist's path to the Supreme Court began in Arizona Republican party politics of the 1950s. Under the leadership of U.S. Senator BARRY M. GOLDWATER, the party became the dominant force in Arizona government, espousing a political view that was more rigid and doctrinaire than that of the national Republican party. Rehnquist became active in the party and made the acquaintance of RICHARD G. KLEINDIENST, an attorney who chaired the state Republican party and who was a close adviser to Goldwater. Kleindienst served as Rehnquist's political mentor and involved him in the 1964 presidential election that Goldwater lost to President LYNDON B. JOHNSON.

In 1968 Kleindienst worked on RICHARD M. NIXON's presidential campaign. After Nixon was elected, he appointed Kleindienst deputy attorney general. Kleindienst in turn recommended Rehnquist for the position of assistant attorney general in charge of the Office of Legal Counsel in the U.S. Justice Department. Attorney General JOHN N. MITCHELL was initially reluctant to hire Rehnquist, but after interviewing Rehnquist, Mitchell became convinced that he was the right person for the job.

As head of the Office of Legal Counsel, Rehnquist supplied legal advice to all the departments of the federal government. He also became one of the most stalwart defenders of the Nixon administration's policies. He supported PREVENTIVE DETENTION and the administration's authority to order WIRETAPPING and surveillance without a court order. He also agreed that the EXCLUSIONARY RULE in criminal cases should be abolished. This rule excludes evidence that the police have illegally seized.

In 1971 President Nixon nominated Rehnquist to the U.S. Supreme Court. Senate Democrats, concerned about Rehnquist's conservative philosophy and his actions as a member of the Nixon administration, sought to defeat the nomination. They used Rehnquist's memorandum supporting the upholding of *Plessy* as evidence that he was hostile to CIVIL RIGHTS. Despite these efforts, Rehnquist was easily confirmed.

Rehnquist joined a Court headed by Chief Justice WARREN E. BURGER. At the time of his appointment, the Court still had a liberal majority. Rehnquist immediately became the most conservative member of the Court. When the Court ruled in *Roe v. Wade*, 410 U.S. 113, 93 S. Ct. 705, 35 L. Ed. 2d 147 (1973), that a woman had the right to an ABORTION, Rehnquist dissented. He has remained consistently opposed to abortion but has never found enough votes to overturn the decision.

As justices retired or died during the 1970s and early 1980s, more conservative justices were appointed to the Court. Rehnquist's views on FEDERALISM began to be adopted by his colleagues. The concept of federalism concerns the distribution of power to the states and the federal government. Until the coming of FRANKLIN D. ROOSEVELT'S NEW DEAL in the 1930s, states had much more power over regulating day-to-day life than the federal government did. The liberal WARREN COURT of the 1960s greatly expanded the right of Congress to regulate economic and other societal activities.

"JUSTICE IS TOO IMPORTANT A MATTER TO BE LEFT TO THE JUDGES, OR EVEN TO THE LAWYERS: THE AMERICAN PEOPLE MUST THINK ABOUT, DISCUSS, AND CONTRIBUTE TO THE FUTURE OF THEIR COURTS."

By the late 1970s, Rehnquist convinced a majority of the Court to begin to pull back from the idea that the federal government, which included the federal courts, could intrude into areas traditionally left to the states. In *National League of Cities v. Usery*, 426 U.S. 833, 96 S. Ct. 2465, 49 L. Ed. 2d 245 (1976), Rehnquist held that the COMMERCE CLAUSE of the U.S. Constitution did not give Congress the power to extend federal MINIMUM WAGE and overtime standards to state and local governments.

Rehnquist wrote decisions that restricted the power of a federal court to oversee the reform of a police department (*Rizzo v. Goode*, 423 U.S. 362, 96 S. Ct. 598, 46 L. Ed. 2d 561 [1976]), prohibited construing nineteenth-century federal civil rights laws to allow AFFIRMATIVE ACTION (*General Building Contractors v. Pennsylvania*, 458 U.S. 375, 102 S. Ct. 3141, 73 L. Ed. 2d 835 [1982]), and prevented plaintiffs from collecting government benefits wrongfully withheld by state governments (*Edelman v. Jordan*, 415 U.S. 651, 94 S. Ct. 1347, 39 L. Ed. 2d 662 [1974]).

In cases involving CRIMINAL LAW and procedure, Rehnquist has consistently sided with law enforcement. In *Illinois v. Gates*, 462 U.S. 213, 103 S. Ct. 2317, 76 L. Ed. 2d 527 (1983), he crafted a new rule that made it easier for police to obtain a WARRANT on the basis of an informant's tip. He supported the creation of a "good faith" exception to the exclusionary rule (*United States v. Leon*, 468 U.S. 897, 104 S. Ct. 3405, 82 L. Ed. 2d 677 [1984]) and has upheld the constitutionality of pretrial detention (*United States v. Salerno*, 481 U.S. 739, 107 S. Ct. 2095, 95 L. Ed. 2d 697 [1987]). Rehnquist has also been a consistent defender of the constitutionality of the death penalty and a consistent critic of lengthy and repetitive death penalty appeals based on the writ of HABEAS CORPUS.

In civil rights cases, Rehnquist has sought to tie affirmative action to specific discriminatory conduct against the plaintiffs rather than to past societal wrongs. He did, however, write the majority opinion in *Meritor Savings Bank, Federal Savings Bank v. Vinson*, 477 U.S. 57, 106 S. Ct. 2399, 91 L. Ed. 2d 49 (1986), which applied title VII of the CIVIL RIGHTS ACT of 1964 (42 U.S.C.A. § 2000a et seq.) to SEXUAL HARASSMENT on the job. An employer may be held liable if a "hostile work environment" is created where sexual harassment takes place.

In recognition of Rehnquist's record on the Court, President RONALD REAGAN nominated him in 1986 to succeed Chief Justice Burger. Again there was opposition to his nomination, but he was easily confirmed.

Though President Reagan and President GEORGE BUSH appointed conservatives to the Court after Rehnquist became chief justice, the Rehnquist Court has maintained a moderate course. Justices SANDRA DAY O'CONNOR, DAVID H. SOUTER, and ANTHONY M. KENNEDY, who have moderately conservative views, have resisted calls from Rehnquist and Justices ANTONIN SCALIA and CLARENCE THOMAS to overturn Court precedents, including *Roe v. Wade.*

See also PLESSY V. FERGUSON; ROE V. WADE.

REINSTATE To restore to a condition that has terminated or been lost; to reestablish.

To reinstate a case, for example, means to restore it to the same position it had before dismissal.

REINSURANCE The CONTRACT made between an INSURANCE company and a third party to protect the insurance company from losses. The contract provides for the third party to pay for the loss sustained by the insurance company when the company makes a payment on the original contract.

A reinsurance contract is a contract of INDEMNITY, meaning that it becomes effective only when the insurance company has made a payment to the original policyholder. Reinsurance provides a way for the insurance company to protect itself from financial disaster and ruin by passing on the risk to other companies. Reinsurance redistributes or diversifies the risk or threat associated with the business of issuing policies by allowing the reinsured to show more ASSETS by reducing its reserve requirements. The reinsurance industry has become more popular over the last decade because natural disasters and mass tort litigation have resulted in large payouts by insurance companies. Because of the large size of the payments, some insurance companies have become insolvent.

The parties to the reinsurance contract are the reinsurer, the reinsured, and the original policyholder. The reinsurer is the third party or the company issuing the reinsurance POLICY. Typically, reinsurers engage solely in the business of issuing reinsurance policies; however any company that meets the requirements and is authorized to issue insurance may issue such policies. The reinsured is the insurance company that issued the first policy and is now applying for reinsurance. The original policyholder or original INSURED is the party who purchased the original policy. When the reinsurance contract is between just the two insurance companies (the reinsured and the reinsurer), the original policyholder usually has no rights against the reinsurer.

The reinsurance policy covers the risk or LIABILITY associated with the original policy issued. The reinsurance policy must be for a specific insurable interest. The interest to be insured must exist at the time the reinsurance policy is issued; it cannot be created later. All or part of the liability of the original policy can be covered by the reinsurance, but nothing greater. The reinsurance policy cannot cover a period longer than the original policy. Generally, because the reinsurance is not a PROMISE to pay the DEBT of another but to INDEMNIFY a potential liability, the STATUTE OF FRAUDS does not require the agreement to be in writing. Most often in practice, however, reinsurance policies are written to avoid problems later.

The two basic types of reinsurance are facultative reinsurance and treaty reinsurance. Facultative reinsurance is issued on an individual analysis of the situation and facts of the underlying policy. It may cover all or a part of the underlying policy. By deciding coverage case by case, the reinsurer can determine if it wants the RISK associated with that particular policy. Facultative reinsurance is used by the reinsured to reduce the chance of loss or risk associated with a certain policy.

Treaty reinsurance, on the other hand, is written to cover a particular class of policies issued by the reinsured. Examples of classes covered by treaty reinsurance are all property insurance policies or all CASUALTY insurance policies written by the reinsured. Treaty reinsurance automatically passes the risk to the reinsurer for all policies that are covered by the treaty, not just one particular policy. Treaty policies are more general than facultative policies because the reinsurance decision is based on general potential liability rather than on a specific enumerated risk.

In addition to the two types of reinsurance issued, there are two ways that coverage can be allotted between the parties: either proportionally or non-proportionally. Proportional reinsurance is where the reinsured obtains coverage for only a portion or percentage of the loss or risk from the reinsurer. The proportion of coverage is typically based on the percentage of PREMIUMS paid to the reinsurer. For example, if the reinsured pays 40 percent of the premiums to the reinsurer, then the reinsured recovers 40 percent of its losses when it pays the original policyholder according to the original policy terms. The reinsured can only recover a portion of its total loss, not the entire amount. The amount actually paid by the reinsurer is not figured into the reinsurance contract, only the percentage of loss the policy will cover.

In contrast, non-proportional reinsurance covers a set amount of loss. A base or deductible amount is set in the reinsurance policy, and any loss exceeding that amount is paid by the reinsurer. The amount being paid by the reinsurer has no relationship to the premiums received. The reinsured, in effect, is reimbursed for all payments made under the original policy that exceed the deductible amount. The deductible amount can be figured either by each event or in the aggregate. Either type of coverage can be used in either facultative or treaty insurance contracts. The terms of the policy depend on the situation and the relationship the reinsured and the reinsurer have had in the past. Reinsurance policy terms can be made to be flexible for the appropriate facts at the time.

Although the terms of the policies can be flexible, several doctrines help to define the nature of the reinsurer and reinsured relationship. These doctrines are the duty of utmost good faith and the doctrine of "follow the fortunes." The duty of utmost good faith has several facets, including the requirement that both parties to the reinsurance contract deal with each other with candor and honesty. The duty assumes that both parties are sophisticated and knowledgeable in the insurance industry. As a result, they should be aware of what is relevant and necessary for the other party to know. The reinsured must follow the duty by disclosing all material facts to the reinsurer that relate to or affect the original policy and its calculated risk. The reinsured must essentially put the reinsurer in the same position as it would be in when deciding about the risks and the possibility of coverage on the original policy.

In addition, the duty requires that the reinsured act with honesty in negotiating any settlement with the original policyholder. If the settlement is not handled by following the appropriate business procedures, the reinsurer may not be bound by its terms and then does not have to pay under the policy coverage.

Lastly, the duty of utmost good faith requires the reinsured to provide adequate NOTICE of any CLAIM or potential claim to the reinsurer. For notice to be adequate, it should be given as soon as the reinsured becomes aware of a potential claim. To be aware, the reinsured must investigate with diligence to discover these possible claims. Notice is required to make the reinsured aware of the possible need for available funds in case a claim is filed. Notice also allows the reinsured to participate, if desired, in the defense of the underlying claim. Practically, reinsurers may also use the notice of potential claims to determine renewal of, or change in, premiums under the reinsurance contract. The duty of utmost good faith that is part of reinsurance policies requires the reinsured and reinsurer to deal with each other in an honest, sophisticated manner.

Also implicit to reinsurance policies is the follow-the-fortunes doctrine. "Follow the fortunes" means the reinsurer should follow along with the reinsured's payment to the original policyholder. Provided the reinsured makes a GOOD FAITH payment that reasonably falls within the terms of the original policy to the policyholder, the reinsurer is then required to make payment according to the terms of the reinsurance policy. The reinsurer should make the payment even if payment is not specifically mandated under the terms of the policy but is arguably within the meaning of its terms. The doctrine is meant to encourage coverage by reinsurers and discourage unnecessary litigation by the parties over interpretation of the policy.

The follow-the-fortunes doctrine does have limits to protect the reinsurer from excessive payments. The reinsurer is not obligated to cover payments made by the reinsured that are clearly outside of the policy language. Also, the reinsurer is not obligated to follow the business fortune of the reinsured, only the insurance-related fortune of the company. The reinsurer need only indemnify for the type of loss intended by the policy, not losses due to uncollectible premiums. Losses clearly related to the business decision and not the policy are not within the scope of the doctrine. The follow-the-fortunes doctrine implies a duty by the reinsurer to indemnify reasonable payments made by the reinsured under the underlying insurance policy.

Once the policy terms and the parties' relationship are defined, several defenses are available to the parties to avoid liability. Defenses that may be available include normal contract defenses, inadequate notice and failure to disclose, or MISREPRESENTATION. Usually any defense available to either party to a contract would be available to either the reinsurer or the reinsured. Those defenses can include impossibility of PERFORMANCE, an act outside the parties' authority, actions by a party that are inconsistent with the policy, actions by a party that unreasonably increase the risk, or misconduct by the parties. Any defense that would be an option for a party under the original insurance policy is available for the parties to the reinsurance policy.

The defense of inadequate notice is available to the reinsurer. If the reinsured has violated its duty to give prompt and REASONABLE notice to the reinsurer, the reinsurer may be able to reduce or refuse payment under the policy. Because of the relationship between the parties, the reinsured is required to comply fully with all the terms of the policy or the reinsurer is not necessarily obligated. However, the reinsurer must often show that it has been prejudiced or hurt by the lack of notice in order to avoid liability on the policy.

The most common defense available to the parties is the failure to disclose (also referred to as FRAUD, misrepresentation, or concealment). This defense is tied heavily to the duty of utmost good faith because both deal with the disclosure of MATERIAL facts. For the reinsurer to assert the defense of failure to disclose, the reinsured must have concealed some relevant or important information. Relevant information would include facts such as a claim previously filed under the original policy or an unusually high risk related to the original policy. The failure to disclose need not be an intentional statement known to be false; it could also be the reinsured's failure to investigate and determine the truth of a fact. When deciding if a fact or information is material or relevant, the courts ask if the misrepresented or withheld information, if disclosed, would have changed the reinsurer's decision to issue the policy. Just the false statement is not enough to avoid liability; the reinsurer must have acted upon that misrepresentation in such a way that it was prejudiced. If the reinsurer's decision or action would have been different regarding the risk, it may be relieved of liability.

Generally, the original policyholder has no rights against the reinsurer. Because the original policyholder has no contract with the reinsurer, they have no obligations to each other. This can be altered by inserting language into the reinsurance policy allowing the original policyholder to obtain payment directly from the reinsurer. Such language often is effective only when the reinsured becomes insolvent or unable to pay. These clauses are not often used because a reinsured can view such clauses as a lack of confidence in its ability to pay. The clause may be used in the case of a reassignment or sale of the policy to another insurance company to protect the original insured.

Without specific language in the policy, the original policyholder has few rights with the reinsured. If the reinsured becomes overly active in the claim process and defense, it could open itself to a direct claim. The original insured can bring an action against the reinsurer if the reinsurance policy requires the reinsurer to pay any claim directly to the original policyholder. The original policyholder is considered a third-party beneficiary and can sue either the reinsured or the reinsurer. The recovery obtained by the original policyholder cannot be more than the total loss.

REJOINDER The answer made by a defendant in the second stage of COMMON-LAW PLEADING that rebuts or denies the assertions made in the plaintiff's REPLICATION.

The rejoinder allows a defendant to present a more responsive and specific statement challenging the ALLEGATIONS made against him or her by the plaintiff.

RELATION KIN; relative. The connection of two individuals, or their situation with respect to each other, who are associated, either by law, agreement, or kinship in a social status or union for purposes of domestic life, such as PARENT AND CHILD or HUSBAND AND WIFE.

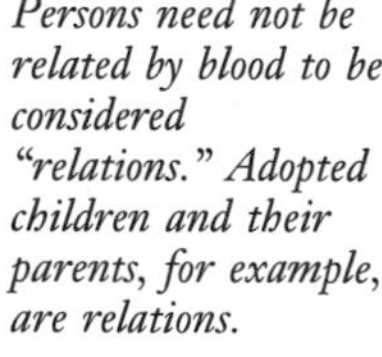

Persons need not be related by blood to be considered "relations." Adopted children and their parents, for example, are relations.

CREWS/THE IMAGE WORKS

The doctrine of *relation* is the principle by which an act performed at one time is deemed, through a LEGAL FICTION, to have been performed at a prior time. For example, in the CONVEYANCE of REAL PROPERTY, the final proceeding that completes the transfer of property is considered, for certain purposes, to have become effective by relation as of the day when the first proceeding took place. Relation, in essence, is the legal term for retroactive effect.

RELATOR The individual in whose name a legal ACTION is brought by a state; the individual who relates the facts on which an action is based.

The relator is the individual upon whose COMPLAINT certain WRITS are issued. The relator is the party of interest in a proceeding, who is allowed to institute such proceeding in the name of the people, or in the name of the attorney general when such official has the sole right to sue. For example, if A was the relator and B was the defendant, the CITATION of the case would read, *State ex rel. A v. B.*

RELEASE A contractual agreement by which one individual assents to relinquish a CLAIM or right under the law to another individual against whom such claim or right is enforceable.

The right or claim given up in a release ordinarily involves CONTRACTS or TORTS. A *general release* encompasses all claims that are in existence between the parties and are within their contemplation when the release is executed. A *specific release* is generally limited to the particular claims specified therein.

No particular form or language is required for a release, provided the contract is complete and clearly indicates the releasor's intention. In the absence of a specific statutory provision, releases need not be in writing.

In order for it to take effect, a release must be supported by adequate CONSIDERATION. Provided something of value is received, the consideration will be deemed adequate. The consideration can take various forms—such as payment to an employee for time lost due to an injury, in exchange for a release of the employee's damage claim; or REPOSSESSION of a particular item in exchange for the release or DISCHARGE of a DEBT.

Validity Since it is a contract, a release is subject to the same validity requirements as a contract. A voluntary release that is obtained in exchange for valuable consideration from an individual who is capable of totally understanding its legal effect is valid. An individual who signs a release has the obligation to read its contents prior to executing it; the person cannot have the release set aside because he or she has not become familiar with its contents. A release is not void merely because the bargain was unwise.

In situations where a release has been executed as a result of a MUTUAL MISTAKE that significantly affects the parties' rights, it can be set aside. In order to ascertain whether a release was executed under mutual mistake, all of the circumstances regarding the signing of the release must be taken into consideration, including the sum paid for release and whether the issue of LIABILITY was in dispute at the time the settlement was made.

An innocent misrepresentation that is relied upon by the releasor justifies setting aside a release induced by it. For example, by relying on a medical diagnosis for an injury sustained, an individual might sign a release in exchange for a particular sum of money. If, subsequently, the individual discovers that the injury is more serious than was indicated by the initial diagnosis, the release can be set aside, since the claims were released based on misrepresentation.

FRAUDULENT representations made by the releasee and relied on by the individual who gives up the claim for injury will also invalidate a release.

Torts Under the COMMON LAW, when an individual who had been injured by the wrongful acts of two or more persons acting in concert—known as JOINT TORTFEASORS—executed a release to one of the defendants, the releasor was regarded as having relinquished the claim against all the defendants, unless rights against them were clearly and specifically reserved in the release.

This rule proved to be unfair, however, because it forced the injured party to give up an entire claim against all TORTFEASORS without necessarily being totally compensated. Few JURISDICTIONS still apply this rule. Most states currently permit a plaintiff to continue an ACTION against the remaining joint tortfeasors after one of them has been released from liability unless the plaintiff has made an intentional surrender of the claim or has been totally compensated. An agreement of this type is called a COVENANT not to sue—the plaintiff does not give up the lawsuit but agrees not to enforce the claim against a particular joint tortfeasor although the others are still liable.

RELEASE TIME PROGRAM The name of the arrangement by which local public school boards permit students to be dismissed from classes prior to the completion of the regular school day for purposes of religious instruction.

The FIRST AMENDMENT to the Constitution guarantees freedom of RELIGION in both belief and practice under the Free Exercise Clause but prohibits the government from aiding and recognizing any religion under the Establishment Clause. Such constitutional mandates are binding upon the states through the Due Process Clause of the FOURTEENTH AMENDMENT. The state must remain neutral in its treatment of religion; at the same time, it must refrain from infringing upon a person's right to practice his or her faith. Since their creation in 1914 in Gary, Indiana, release time programs have provided a means by which students who would otherwise be deprived of an opportunity to receive religious instruction can learn about their religion. Such programs have, however, come under judicial scrutiny because of the claim that the involvement of public school boards in religious concerns violates the Establishment Clause.

In the 1948 case of *People of State of Illinois ex rel. McCollum v. Board of Education*, 333 U.S. 203, 68 S. Ct. 461, 92 L. Ed. 649, a release time program provided by the Champaign, Illinois, public schools was alleged to be unconstitutional. The schools offered classroom space once a week for one period of thirty to forty-five minutes during the school day to private teachers to instruct interested students in religion. The students who were "released" for religious training had to present signed parental request forms in order to attend such courses. All other students were sent to other parts of the school building to finish the school day while this religious instruction took place. Both the "release time" students and the other students had to satisfy attendance requirements to comply with compulsory education laws of the state. A taxpayer named Vashti McCollum, the parent of a student, sought MANDAMUS to compel the school board to adopt and enforce regulations prohibiting all religious instruction in public schools. The state trial and appellate courts denied the WRIT, and the plaintiff appealed to the U.S. Supreme Court. The Court ruled that the involvement of the public school in the program of religious education was so great that it violated the First Amendment. The Court based its reasoning on the facts that public classrooms financed by taxpayers were used for religious purposes and that, furthermore, the public system of compulsory education was used to disseminate religion.

Another challenge was brought concerning a release time program in the New York City

AP/WIDE WORLD PHOTOS

Vashti McCollum smiles while reading a newspaper account of her successful 1948 challenge of an Illinois public school release time program. The U.S. Supreme Court found the program unconstitutional.

public schools in the 1952 case of *Zorach v. Clauson*, 343 U.S. 306, 72 S. Ct. 679, 96 L. Ed. 954. In this instance, students participated in the program only upon the written requests of their parents. Such pupils were "released," or permitted to leave school, for one hour of regular class time once a week to attend religious instruction at sectarian centers. All other students remained in school. Church officials were responsible for making weekly attendance reports to the schools. The plaintiff, Tessim Zorach, a taxpayer and the parent of a student, brought an action in state court to review the action of the school board in permitting such a program. The case was brought on appeal to the Supreme Court by the plaintiff, who was unsuccessful at the state court level. The Court affirmed the decision of the state courts, finding that the program did not violate the Constitution. It distinguished the facts of this case from those in *McCollum*. Here the only thing provided by the school was an accommodation of schedules to enable its students to participate in a program of religious instruction. To deny the children the time to attend such instruction off the school premises would implicitly convey a government attitude of hostility toward religion that might be violative of the constitutional guarantee of freedom of religion.

School boards possess discretion in the creation of release time programs for their students, subject to the safeguards of religious freedom. Although some cooperation between public schools and sectarian officials is essential to develop mutually agreeable arrangements, those programs that involve an excessive and complex interaction of church and state will not pass constitutional muster.

See also SCHOOLS AND SCHOOL DISTRICTS.

RELEVANCY The tendency of a fact offered as EVIDENCE in a lawsuit to prove or disprove the truth of a point in issue.

A fact offered as evidence must bear a logical relationship to a point in issue for the court to permit its admission as evidence. In addition to such relevancy, evidence must also be MATERIAL; it must strongly establish the truth or falsity of a point in issue if it is to be used as proof of a particular issue.

RELIEF Financial assistance provided to the indigent by the government. The redress, or benefit, given by a court to an individual who brings a legal ACTION.

The relief sought in a lawsuit might, for example, be the return of PROPERTY wrongfully taken by another, compensation for an injury in the form of DAMAGES, or enforcement of a CONTRACT.

RELIGION The FIRST AMENDMENT to the U.S. Constitution provides that "Congress shall make no law respecting an establishment of religion, or prohibiting the free exercise thereof." The first part of this provision is known as the Establishment Clause, and the second part is known as the Free Exercise Clause. Although the First Amendment only refers to Congress, the U.S. Supreme Court has held that the FOURTEENTH AMENDMENT makes the Free Exercise and Establishment Clauses also binding on states (*Cantwell v. Connecticut*, 310 U.S. 296, 60 S. Ct. 900, 84 L. Ed. 1213 [1940], and *Everson v. Board of Education*, 330 U.S. 1, 67 S. Ct. 504, 91 L. Ed. 711 [1947], respectively). Since that incorporation, an extensive body of law has developed in the United States around both the Establishment Clause and the Free Exercise Clause.

To determine whether an action of the federal or state government infringes upon a person's right to freedom of religion, the court must decide what qualifies as religion or religious activities for purposes of the First Amendment. The Supreme Court has interpreted religion to mean a sincere and meaningful belief that occupies in the life of its possessor a place parallel to the place held by God in the lives of other persons. The religion or religious concept need not include belief in the existence of God or a supreme being to be within the scope of the First Amendment.

As the case of *United States v. Ballard*, 322 U.S. 78, 64 S. Ct. 882, 88 L. Ed. 1148 (1944), demonstrates, the Supreme Court must look to the sincerity of a person's beliefs to help decide if those beliefs constitute a religion that deserves constitutional protection. The *Ballard* case involved the conviction of organizers of the I Am movement on grounds that they defrauded people by falsely representing that their members had supernatural powers to heal people with incurable illnesses. The Supreme Court held that the JURY, in determining the line between the free exercise of religion and the punishable offense of obtaining PROPERTY under FALSE PRETENSES, should not decide whether the claims of the I Am members were actually true, only whether the members honestly believed them to be true, thus qualifying the group as a religion under the Supreme Court's broad definition.

In addition, a belief does not need to be stated in traditional terms to fall within First Amendment protection. For example, Scientology—a system of beliefs that a human being is essentially a free and immortal spirit who merely inhabits a body—does not propound the existence of a supreme being, but it qualifies as a religion under the broad definition propounded by the Supreme Court. The Supreme Court has deliberately avoided establishing an exact or a narrow definition of religion because freedom of religion is a dynamic guarantee that was written in a manner to ensure flexibility and responsiveness to the passage of time and the development of the United States. Thus, religion is not limited to traditional denominations.

The First Amendment guarantee of freedom of religion has deeply rooted historical significance. Many of the colonists who founded the United States came to this continent to escape religious persecution and government oppression. This country's founders advocated religious freedom and sought to prevent any one religion or group of religious organizations from dominating the government or imposing its will or beliefs on society as a whole. The revolutionary philosophy encompassed the principle that the interests of society are best served if individuals are free to form their own opinions and beliefs.

When the colonies and states were first established, however, most declared a particular religion to be the religion of that region. But by the end of the American Revolution, most state-supported churches had been disestablished, with the exceptions of the state churches of Connecticut and Massachusetts, which were disestablished in 1818 and 1833, respectively. Still, religion was undoubtedly an important element in the lives of the American colonists, and U.S. culture remains greatly influenced by religion.

Establishment Clause The Establishment Clause prohibits the government from interfering with individual religious beliefs. The government cannot enact laws aiding any religion or establishing an official state religion. The courts have interpreted the Establishment Clause to accomplish the separation of church and state on both the national and state levels of government.

The authors of the First Amendment drafted the Establishment Clause to address the problem of government sponsorship and support of religious activity. The Supreme Court has defined the meaning of the Establishment Clause in cases dealing with public financial assistance to church-related institutions, primarily parochial schools, and religious practices in the public schools. The Court has developed a three-pronged test to determine whether a statute violates the Establishment Clause. According to that test, a statute is valid as long as it has a secular purpose; its primary effect neither advances nor inhibits religion; and it is not excessively entangled with religion. Because this three-pronged test was established in *Lemon v. Kurtzman*, 403 U.S. 602, 91 S. Ct. 2105, 29 L. Ed. 2d 745 (1971), it has come to be known as the *Lemon* test. Although the Supreme Court adhered to the *Lemon* test for several decades, since the 1990s it has been slowly moving away from that test, without having expressly rejected it.

The Court has stated that the Establishment Clause means that neither a state nor the federal government can organize a church. The government cannot enact legislation that aids one religion, aids all religions, or prefers one religion over another. It cannot force or influence a person to participate in, or avoid, religion or force a person to profess a particular religious belief. No tax in any amount can be levied to support any religious activities or organizations. Neither a state nor the federal government can participate, whether openly or secretly, in the affairs of any religious groups.

Federal and state governments have accepted and implemented the doctrine of the separation of church and state by minimizing contact with religious institutions. Although the government cannot aid religions, it can acknowledge their role as a stabilizing force in society. For example, religious institutions, along with other charitable or nonprofit organizations, have traditionally been given tax exemptions. This practice, even when applied to religious organizations, has been deemed constitutional because the legislative aim of a property tax exemption is not to advance religion but to ensure that the activities of groups that enhance the moral and mental attitudes of the community will not be inhibited by TAXATION. The organizations lose the tax exemption if they undertake activities that do not serve the beneficial interests of society. Thus, in 1983 the Supreme Court decided in *Bob Jones University v. United States*, 461 U.S. 574, 103 S. Ct. 2017, 76 L. Ed. 2d 157, that nonprofit private schools that discriminated against their students or prospective students on the basis of race could not claim tax-exempt status as a charitable organization for the purposes of federal tax laws.

It is also believed that the elimination of such tax exemptions would lead the government into excessive entanglements with religious institutions. The exemption, therefore, is believed to create only a minimal and remote involvement between church and state—less than would result from taxation. The restricted fiscal relationship, therefore, enhances the desired separation.

Religion and Education The many situations where religion and education overlap are a source of great controversy. In the early nineteenth century, the vast majority of Americans were Protestant, and Protestant-based religious exercises were common in the public schools. Legal challenges to these practices began in the state courts when a substantial number of Roman Catholics arrived in the United States. Until 1962 when the U.S. Supreme Court began to directly address some of these issues, most states upheld the constitutionality of prayer and Bible reading in the public schools.

In the 1962 case of *Engel v. Vitale*, 370 U.S. 421, 82 S. Ct. 1261, 8 L. Ed. 2d 601, the Supreme Court struck down as unconstitutional a prayer that was a recommended part of the public school curriculum in the state of New York. The prayer had been approved by Protestant, Catholic, and Jewish leaders in the state. Although the prayer was nondenominational and student participation in it was strictly vol-

UPI/CORBIS-BETTMANN

In 1954, children say a prayer to open the first day of classes in the newly desegregated Washington, D.C., schools. Prayer continued to be a part of the daily routine in some schools for many years.

untary, it was struck down as violative of the Establishment Clause.

In 1963 the Supreme Court heard the related issues of whether voluntary Bible readings or recitation of the Lord's Prayer were constitutionally appropriate exercises in the public schools (*Abington School District v. Schempp*, 374 U.S. 203, 83 S. Ct. 1560, 10 L. Ed. 2d 844). It was in these cases that the Supreme Court first formulated the three-pronged test for constitutionality. In applying the new test, the Court concluded that the exercises did not pass the first prong of the test: they were not secular in nature, but religious, and thus they violated the Establishment Clause because they violated state neutrality requirements.

Although students in public schools are not permitted to recite prayers, the practice of a state legislature opening its sessions with a nondenominational prayer recited by a chaplain receiving public funds has withstood constitutional challenge. In *Marsh v. Chambers*, 463 U.S. 783, 103 S. Ct. 3330, 77 L. Ed. 2d 1019 (1983), the Supreme Court ruled that such a practice did not violate the Establishment Clause. In making its decision, the Court noted that this was a customary practice and that the proponents of the BILL OF RIGHTS also approved of the government appointment of paid chaplains.

The Supreme Court has also held that a religious invocation, instituted by school officials, at a public school graduation violates the Establishment Clause (*Lee v. Weisman*, 505 U.S. 577, 112 S. Ct. 2649, 120 L. Ed. 2d 467 [1992]).

In 1980 the Supreme Court overturned a Kentucky statute requiring the posting of the Ten Commandments, copies of which were purchased with private contributions, in every public school classroom (*Stone v. Graham*, 449 U.S. 39, 101 S. Ct. 192, 66 L. Ed. 2d 199). Although the state argued that the postings served a secular purpose, the Court held that they were plainly religious. Four of the Supreme Court's nine justices dissented from the Court's opinion and were prepared to conclude that the postings were proper based on their secular purpose.

Because the Establishment Clause calls for government neutrality in matters involving religion, the government need not be hostile or unfriendly toward religions because such an approach would favor those who do not believe in religion over those who do. In addition, if the government denies religious speakers the ability to speak or punishes them for their speech, it violates the First Amendment's right to FREEDOM OF SPEECH. The Supreme Court held in 1981 that it was unconstitutional for a state university to prohibit a religious group from using its facilities when the facilities were open for use by organizations of all other kinds (*Widmar v. Vincent*, 454 U.S. 263, 102 S. Ct. 269, 70 L. Ed. 2d 440). The principles established in *Widmar* were unanimously reaffirmed by the Supreme Court in *Lamb's Chapel v. Center Moriches Union Free School District*, 508 U.S. 384, 113 S. Ct. 2141, 124 L. Ed. 2d 352 (1993). In 1995 the Supreme Court held that a state university violates the Free Speech Clause when it refuses to pay for a religious organization's publication under a program in which it pays for other student organization publications (*Rosenberger v. Rector and Visitors of the University of Virginia*, 515 U.S. 819, 115 S. Ct. 2510, 132 L. Ed. 2d 700).

Facing another education and religion issue, the Supreme Court declared in *McCollum v. Board of Education*, 333 U.S. 203, 68 S. Ct. 461, 92 L. Ed. 649 (1948), that public school buildings could not be used for a program that allowed pupils to leave classes early to receive religious instruction. The Court found that this program violated the Establishment Clause because the tax-supported public school buildings were being used for the teaching of religious doctrines, which constituted direct government assistance to religion.

However, the Court held that a release-time program that took place outside the public school buildings was constitutional because it involved neither religious instruction in public school classrooms nor the expenditure of public funds (*Zorach v. Clauson*, 343 U.S. 306, 72 S. Ct. 679, 96 L. Ed. 954 [1952]). All costs in that case were paid by the religious organization conducting the program.

The U.S. Supreme Court has also held that states may not restrict the teaching of ideas on the grounds that they conflict with religious teachings where those ideas are part of normal classroom subjects. In *Epperson v. Arkansas*, 393 U.S. 97, 89 S. Ct. 266, 21 L. Ed. 2d 228 (1968), the Court struck down a state statute that forbade the teaching of evolutionary theory in public schools. The Court held that the statute violated the Establishment Clause because its purpose was to protect religious theories of creationism from inconsistent secular theories.

In a 1993 case, the Supreme Court held that the Establishment Clause did not prevent a public school from providing a sign language interpreter for a deaf student who attended a religiously affiliated school within the school district (*Zobrest v. Catalina Foothills School District*, 509 U.S. 1, 113 S. Ct. 2462, 125 L. Ed. 2d 1). Commentators have noted that this case demonstrates the Court's willingness to uphold religiously neutral government aid to all school children, regardless of whether they attend a religiously affiliated school, where the aid is designed to help the children overcome a physical or learning disability. It is not clear, however, whether the Court will extend this holding to more general forms of aid to children in religious and public schools alike.

Government and Religion The closing of government offices on particular religious holidays is unconstitutional if no secular purpose is served (*Mandel v. Hodges*, 54 Cal. App. 3d 596, 127 Cal. Rptr. 244 [1976]). But if employees won the closing through COLLECTIVE BARGAINING, it is permissible even without a secular purpose (*Americans United for Separation of Church and State v. Kent County*, 97 Mich. App. 72, 293 N.W.2d 723 [1980]).

Government display of symbols with religious significance raises Establishment Clause issues. In the 1984 case of *Lynch v. Donnelly*, 465 U.S. 668, 104 S. Ct. 1355, 79 L. Ed. 2d 604, the Supreme Court upheld the right of a city to erect in a park a Christmas display that included colored lights, reindeer, candy canes, a Santa's house, a Christmas tree, a "SEASONS GREETINGS" banner, and a nativity scene. The Court decided the inclusion of the nativity scene along with traditional secular Christmas symbols did not promote religion to an extent prohibited by the First Amendment.

Free Exercise Clause The Free Exercise Clause guarantees a person the right to practice a religion and propagate it without government interference. This right is a liberty interest that cannot be deprived without DUE PROCESS OF LAW. Although the government cannot restrict a person's religious beliefs, it can limit the practice of faith when a substantial and COMPELLING STATE INTEREST exists. The courts have found that a substantial and compelling state interest exists where the religious practice poses a threat to the health, safety, or welfare of the public. For example, the government could legitimately outlaw the practice of POLYGAMY that was formerly mandated by the doctrines of

JESUS, MEET SANTA

IN FOCUS

Christmas and the First Amendment have had a rocky relationship. A decades-long battle over the place of worship and tradition in public life has erupted nearly every year when local governments sponsor holiday displays on public property. Lawsuits against towns and cities often, but not always, end with the courts ordering the removal of religious symbols whose government sponsorship violates the First Amendment. Since the 1980s, however, the outcome of such cases has become less predictable as deep divisions on the Supreme Court have resulted in new precedents that take a more nuanced view of the law. In such cases, context determines everything. Placing a nativity scene with the infant Jesus outside a town hall may be unconstitutional, for example, but the display may be acceptable if Santa Claus stands nearby.

On the question of religious displays, the First Amendment has two broad answers depending on the sponsor. Any private citizen can put up a nativity scene on private property at Christmas time: citizens and churches commonly exercise their First Amendment right to freedom of speech to do so. But when a government sets up a similar display on public property, a different aspect of the amendment comes into play. Governments do not enjoy freedom of speech, but, instead, are controlled by the second half of the First Amendment—the Establishment Clause, which forbids any official establishment of religion. All lawsuits demanding that a crèche, cross, menorah, or other religious symbol be removed from public property allege that the government that put it there has violated the Establishment Clause.

The Supreme Court has reviewed challenges to government sponsored displays of religious symbols under the *Lemon* test. Based on criteria from several earlier decisions and named after the case *Lemon v. Kurtzman*, 403 U.S. 602, 91 S. Ct. 2105, 29 L. Ed. 2d 745 (1973), the test recognizes that government must accommodate religion but forbids it to support religion. To survive constitutional review, a display must meet all three requirements or "prongs" of the test: it must have a secular (nonreligious) purpose, it must have the primary effect of neither advancing nor inhibiting religion, and it must avoid excessive entanglement between government and religion. Failing any of the three parts of the test constitutes a violation of the Establishment Clause.

Starting in the 1980s, the test began to divide the Supreme Court. Conservative justices objected because it blocked what they saw as a valid acknowledgment of the role of religion in public life; opposing them were justices who believed in maintaining a firm line between government and religion. In significant cases concerning holiday displays, the Court continued to use the *Lemon* test but with new emphasis on the question of whether the display has the effect of advancing or endorsing a particular religion.

This shift in emphasis first emerged in 1984 in a case involving a Christmas display owned and erected by the City of Pawtucket, Rhode Island, in a private park. The display included both a life-sized nativity scene with the infant Jesus, Mary, and Joseph and secular symbols such as Santa's house, a Christmas tree, striped poles, animals, and lights. Pawtucket residents successfully sued for removal of the nativity scene in federal district court, where it was found to have failed all three prongs of the *Lemon* test (*Donnelly v. Lynch*, 525 F. Supp. 1150 [D.R.I. 1981]). The decision was upheld on appeal, but, surprisingly, in *Lynch v. Donnelly*, 465 U.S. 668, 104 S. Ct. 1355, 79 L. Ed. 2d 604 (1984), the Supreme Court narrowly reversed in a 5–4 vote and found the entire display constitutional.

The majority in *Lynch* stressed historical context, emphasizing that the crèche belonged to a tradition "acknowledged in the Western World for 20 centuries, and in this country by the people, by the Executive Branch, by the Congress, and the courts for two centuries." The display, ruled the Court, passed each prong of the *Lemon* test. First, the city had a secular purpose in celebrating a national holiday by using religious symbols that "depicted the historical origins" of the holiday. Second, the display did not primarily benefit religion. Third, no excessive entanglement between government and religion existed. Perhaps most significantly, the Court saw the crèche as a "passive symbol": although it derived from religion, over time it had come to represent a secular message of celebration.

Lynch laid bare the deep divisions on the Court. By emphasizing context, the majority appeared to suggest that the ruling was limited to circumstances similar to those in the case at hand: religious symbols could be acceptable in a holiday display if used with secular symbols. The majority did not enunciate any broad new protections for governments eager to sponsor crèches. Nonetheless, the opinion did not satisfy the dissenters, who sharply criticized the majority for failing to vigorously apply the *Lemon* test. They noted that the city could easily have celebrated the holiday without using religious symbols, and they saw the crèche as nothing less than government endorsement of religion.

The emphasis on context became even more pronounced in a 1989 case, *County of Allegheny v. American Civil Liberties Union*, 492 U.S. 573, 109 S. Ct. 3086, 106 L. Ed. 2d 472. In *Allegheny*, a Pennsylvania county appealed a lower court ruling that had banned its two separate holiday displays: a crèche situated next to poinsettia plants inside the county courthouse, and an eighteen-foot menorah (a commemorative candelabrum in the Jewish faith) standing next to a Christmas tree and a sign outside a city-county office building. Each religious symbol was owned by a religious group—the crèche by the

(continued on next page)

JESUS, MEET SANTA (CONTINUED)

Catholic Holy Name Society and the menorah by Chabad, a Jewish organization. Viewing the displays in context, the Court permitted one but not the other, and its reasoning turned on subtle distinctions.

The Court deemed the crèche an unconstitutional endorsement of religion for two reasons. First, the presence of a few flowers around the crèche did not mediate its religious symbolism in the way that the secular symbols had done for the crèche in *Lynch*. Second, the prominent location doomed the display. By choosing the courthouse, a vital center of government, the Court said the county has sent "an unmistakable message" that it endorsed Christianity.

But the menorah passed constitutional review. Like the crèche in *Lynch*, its religious significance was transformed by the presence of secular symbols: the forty-five-foot Christmas tree and a sign from the city's mayor that read, "During this holiday season, the city of Pittsburgh salutes liberty. Let these festive lights remind us that we are keepers of the flame of liberty and our legacy of liberty." Even so, members of the majority disagreed on precisely what message was sent by the display. Justice Harry A. Blackmun read it as a secular message of holiday celebration. In a more complicated view, Justice Sandra Day O'Connor said it "acknowledg[ed] the cultural diversity of our country and convey[ed] tolerance of different choice in matters of religious belief or non-belief by recognizing that the winter holiday season is celebrated in diverse ways by our citizens." Whatever the exact message, the majority agreed that it did not endorse religion.

Since the 1980s the thrust of Supreme Court doctrine has been to allow publicly sponsored holiday displays to include religious symbols. This expansive view of the First Amendment grew out of the Court's acknowledgment that local governments can accommodate civic tradition. Religious symbols on their own are unconstitutional. A display including such symbols may pass review, however, if it features secular symbols as well. Context is the determinant: to avoid violating the Establishment Clause, a crèche or menorah may need a boost from Santa Claus.

the Church of Jesus Christ of Latter-day Saints (Mormons) but could not outlaw the religion or belief in Mormonism itself (*Reynolds v. United States*, 98 U.S. 145, 25 L. Ed. 244 [1878]). The Supreme Court has invalidated very few actions of the government on the basis of this clause.

Religious practices are not the only method by which a violation of the Free Exercise Clause can occur. In *West Virginia State Board of Education v. Barnette*, 319 U.S. 624, 63 S. Ct. 1178, 87 L. Ed. 1628 (1943), the Supreme Court held that a public school could not expel children because they refused on religious grounds to comply with a requirement of saluting the U.S. flag and reciting the pledge of allegiance. In that case the children were Jehovah's Witnesses, and they believed that saluting the flag fell within the scope of the biblical command against worshipping false gods.

In *Wisconsin v. Yoder*, 406 U.S. 205, 92 S. Ct. 1526, 32 L. Ed. 2d 15 (1972), the Supreme Court held that state laws requiring children to receive education up to a certain age impinged upon the religious freedom of the Amish who refused to send their children to school beyond the eighth grade because they believed that it would impermissibly expose the children to worldly influences that conflicted with their religious beliefs.

In 1993 Congress passed the controversial Religious Freedom Restoration Act (RFRA), which provides that "[g]overnment shall not substantially burden a person's exercise of religion even if the burden results from a rule of general applicability," unless the government can demonstrate that the burden furthers a compelling governmental interest in the least restrictive way. This statute was enacted in response to the Supreme Court's 1990 decision in *Employment Division v. Smith*, 494 U.S. 872, 110 S. Ct. 1595, 108 L. Ed. 2d 876. The *Smith* case involved a state law that denied UNEMPLOYMENT COMPENSATION benefits to anyone who had been fired from his or her job for job-related misconduct. This case involved two individuals who had been fired from their jobs for ingesting peyote, which was forbidden by state law. The individuals argued that their ingestion of peyote was related to a religious ceremony in which they participated. The Supreme Court ruled that the Free Exercise Clause did not require an exemption from the state law banning peyote use and that unemployment compensation could therefore lawfully be denied.

RFRA directly superseded the *Smith* decision. However, soon after it was enacted, many courts ruled that RFRA violated either the Establishment Clause or the SEPARATION OF POW-

ERS doctrine. In the 1997 case of *City of Boerne v. P. F. Flores*, 1997 WL 345322, the U.S. Supreme Court voted 6–3 to invalidate RFRA on the grounds that Congress had exceeded the scope of its enforcement power under section 5 of the Fourteenth Amendment in enacting RFRA. Section 5 of the Fourteenth Amendment permits Congress to enact legislation enforcing the Constitutional right to free exercise of religion. However, the Court held that this power is limited to only preventative or remedial measures. The court found that RFRA went beyond that and actually made substantive changes in the governing law. Because Congress exceeded its power under the Fourteenth Amendment in enacting RFRA, it contradicted vital principles necessary to maintain separation of powers and the federal-state balance, and thus was unconstitutional.

Although the Free Exercise Clause protects against government action, it does not restrict the conduct of private individuals. For example, the courts generally will uphold a testator's requirement that a BENEFICIARY attend a specified church to receive a TESTAMENTARY gift, because the courts refuse to question the religious views of a TESTATOR in the interest of PUBLIC POLICY. Similarly, the Free Exercise Clause does not protect a person's religious beliefs from infringement by the actions of private CORPORATIONS or businesses, although federal and state CIVIL RIGHTS laws may make such private conduct unlawful.

The government cannot enact a statute that wholly denies the right to preach or to disseminate religious views, but a state can constitutionally regulate the time, place, and manner of soliciting upon the streets and of conducting meetings in order to safeguard the peace, order, and comfort of the community. It can also protect the public against FRAUDS perpetrated under the cloak of religion, as long as the law does not use a process amounting to a PRIOR RESTRAINT, which inhibits the free exercise of religion. In a 1951 case, the Supreme Court held that it was unconstitutional for a city to deny a Baptist preacher the renewal of a permit for evangelical street meetings, even though his previous meetings included attacks on Roman Catholicism and Judaism that led to disorder in the streets, because it constituted a prior restraint (*Kunz v. New York*, 340 U.S. 290, 71 S. Ct. 312, 95 L. Ed. 280).

State laws known as Sunday closing laws, which prohibit the sale of certain goods on Sundays, have been declared constitutional against the challenge of Orthodox Jews who claimed that the laws created an economic hardship for them because their faith requires them to close their businesses on Saturdays and who therefore wanted to do business on Sundays (*Braunfield v. Brown*, 366 U.S. 599, 81 S. Ct. 1144, 6 L. Ed. 2d 563 [1961]). The Supreme Court held that although the law imposed an indirect burden on religion, it did not make any religious practice itself unlawful.

In *United States v. Lee*, 455 U.S. 252, 102 S. Ct. 1051, 71 L. Ed. 2d 127 (1982), the Supreme Court upheld the requirement that Amish employers withhold SOCIAL SECURITY and unemployment insurance contributions from their employees, despite the Amish argument that this violated their rights under the Free Exercise Clause. The Court found that compulsory contributions were necessary to accomplish the overriding government interest in the proper functioning of the Social Security and unemployment systems.

The Supreme Court has also upheld the assignment and use of Social Security numbers by the government to be a legitimate government action that does not violate the Free Exercise Clause (*Bowen v. Roy*, 476 U.S. 693, 106 S. Ct. 2147, 90 L. Ed. 2d 735 [1986]).

In the 1989 case of *Hernandez v. Commissioner of Internal Revenue*, 490 U.S. 680, 109 S. Ct. 2136, 104 L. Ed. 2d 766, the Supreme Court held that the government's denial of a taxpayer's deduction from gross income of "fixed donations" to the Church of Scientology for certain religious services was constitutional. These fees were paid for certain classes required by the Church of Scientology, and the Court held that they did not classify as charitable contributions because a good or service was received in exchange for the fee paid.

The Supreme Court has held that employers operating as part of a religious community, such as the Amish, are required to withhold Social Security and unemployment insurance contributions from their employees.

BLAIR SEITZ/PHOTO RESEARCHERS

In *Jimmy Swaggart Ministries v. Board of Equalization*, 493 U.S. 378, 110 S. Ct. 688, 107 L. Ed. 2d 796 (1990), the Court ruled that a religious organization is not exempt from paying a state's general sales and use taxes on the sale of religious products and religious literature.

Similarly, the Court decided in *Heffron v. International Society for Krishna Consciousness (ISKCON)*, 452 U.S. 640, 101 S. Ct. 2559, 69 L. Ed. 2d 298 (1981), that a state rule limiting the sale or distribution of merchandise to specific booths was lawful, even when applied to ISKCON members whose beliefs mandated them to distribute or sell religious literature and solicit donations in public places.

Military regulations have also been challenged under the Free Exercise Clause. In *Goldman v. Weinberger*, 475 U.S. 503, 106 S. Ct. 1310, 89 L. Ed. 2d 478 (1986), the Supreme Court held that the Free Exercise Clause did not require the Air Force to permit an Orthodox Jewish serviceman to wear his yarmulke

Designated Denomination of Americans in 1996

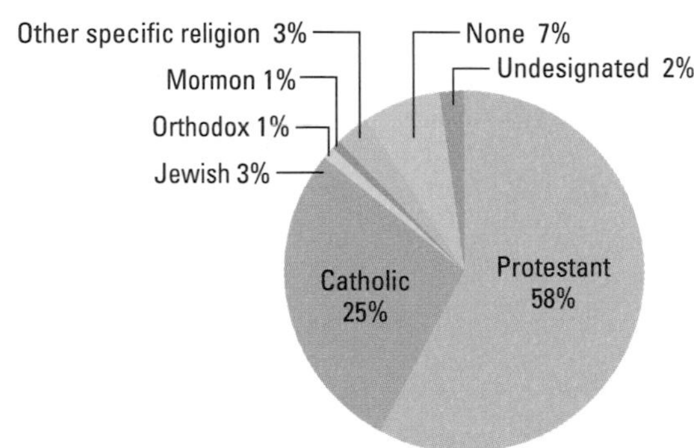

Church/Synagogue Membership, by Region, 1992–93

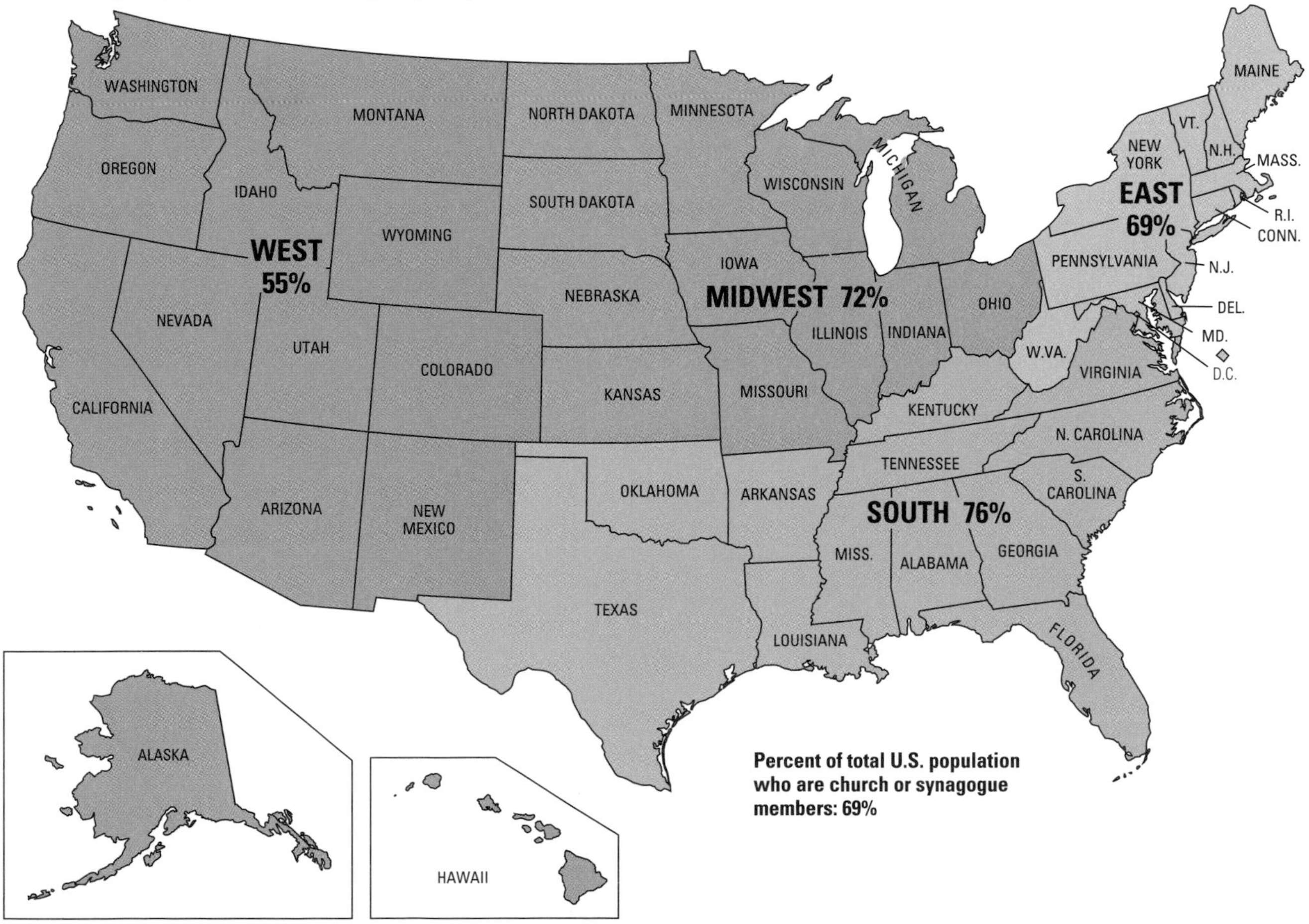

WEST 55%
MIDWEST 72%
EAST 69%
SOUTH 76%

Percent of total U.S. population who are church or synagogue members: 69%

Source: Web site of Princeton Religion Research Center, Princeton, NJ. Based on surveys conducted by the Gallup Organization, Inc.

Agostini v. Felton

In June 1997 the U.S. Supreme Court rolled back restrictions that it had imposed twelve years earlier on federal aid to religious schools. In a 5–4 decision in *Agostini v. Felton,* 117 S. Ct. 1997 (1997), the Court ruled that public school teachers can teach remedial education classes to disadvantaged students on the premises of parochial schools—a dramatic reversal of the Court's earlier hard line.

Federal law provides funds for such services to all children of low-income families under title I of the Elementary and Secondary Education Act of 1965 (20 U.S.C.A. § 6301 et seq.). But in 1985 the Court barred public school instructors from teaching title I classes on parochial school premises. In *Aguilar v. Felton* (473 U.S. 402, 105 S. Ct. 3232, 87 L. Ed. 2d 290), the majority ruled that the mere presence of public employees at these schools had the effect of unconstitutionally advancing religion. To comply with the order, New York parked vans outside of parochial school property to deliver the services, a system that cost taxpayers $100 million between 1985 and 1997.

In a 1995 challenge, New York City argued that intervening cases had invalidated the Supreme Court's earlier ruling. Upon accepting the case on appeal in 1997, the Court agreed. In her majority opinion, Justice Sandra Day O'Connor held that *Aguilar* had been overruled by two more recent cases based on the Establishment Clause of the U.S. Constitution, *Witters v. Washington Department of Services for the Blind,* 474 U.S. 481, 106 S. Ct. 748, 88 L. Ed. 2d 846 (1986), and *Zobrest v. Catalina Foothills School District,* 509 U.S. 1, 113 S. Ct. 2462, 125 L. Ed. 2d (1993). O'Connor said that the two cases—permitting a state tuition grant to a blind person who attended a Christian college, and allowing a state-employed sign language interpreter to accompany a deaf student to a Catholic school, respectively—made it clear that the premises in *Aguilar* were no longer valid.

Although limited specifically to title I programs, the decision added fuel to another long-standing controversy. Proponents and opponents of school vouchers—a system under which parents would be able to allocate their tax dollars to their children's private school education—disputed whether the case indicated that the Court was moving toward embracing the voucher idea.

while in uniform and on duty. The Court found that the military's interest in discipline was sufficiently important to outweigh the incidental burden the rule had on the serviceman's religious beliefs.

However, a law that places an indirect burden on the practice of religion so as to impede the observance of religion, or a law that discriminates between religions, is unconstitutional. Thus, the Supreme Court has held that the denial of unemployment compensation to a Seventh Day Adventist who was fired from her job and could not obtain any other work because of her refusal to work on Saturdays for religious reasons was unconstitutional (*Sherbert v. Verner,* 374 U.S. 398, 83 S. Ct. 1790, 10 L. Ed. 2d 965 [1963]). The *Sherbert* case was reaffirmed and applied in the 1987 case of *Hobbie v. Unemployment Appeals Commission of Florida,* 480 U.S. 136, 107 S. Ct. 1046, 94 L. Ed. 2d 190.

In the 1993 case of *Church of the Lukumi Babalu Aye, Inc. v. Hialeah,* 508 U.S. 520, 113 S. Ct. 2217, 124 L. Ed. 2d 472, remanded on other grounds, the High Court overturned a city law that forbade animal slaughter insofar as the law banned the ritual animal slaughter by a particular religious sect. The Court found that the law was not a religiously neutral law of general applicability but was specifically designed to prevent a religious sect from carrying out its religious rituals.

In *Cruz v. Beto,* 405 U.S. 319, 92 S. Ct. 1079, 31 L. Ed. 2d 263 (1972), the Supreme Court affirmed that prisoners are entitled to their rights under the Free Exercise Clause, subject only to the requirements of PRISON security and discipline. Thus, the Court held that a Texas prison must permit a Buddhist prisoner to use the prison chapel and share his religious materials with other prisoners, just as any other prisoner would be permitted to so act.

States have been allowed to deny DISABILITY benefits, however, to applicants who refuse to submit to medical examinations for religious reasons. Courts have held that this is constitutional because the state has a compelling interest in verifying that the intended recipients of the tax-produced assistance are people who are legitimately entitled to receive the benefit. Likewise, states can regulate religious practices to protect the public health. Thus, state laws requiring the vaccination of all children before they are allowed to attend school are constitutional because the laws are designed to prevent the widespread epidemic of contagious diseases. Public health protection has been deemed to outweigh any competing interest in the exercise of religious beliefs that oppose any forms of medication or immunization.

A number of cases have involved the issue of whether there is a compelling state interest to require that a blood transfusion be given to a patient whose religion prohibits such treatment. In these cases the courts look to the specific facts of the case, such as whether the patient is a MINOR or a mentally incompetent individual, and whether the patient came to the hospital voluntarily seeking help. The courts have generally authorized the transfusions in cases of minors or mentally incompetent patients in recognition of the compelling government interest to protect the health and safety of people. However, the courts are divided as to whether they should order transfusions where the patient is a COMPETENT adult who steadfastly refuses to accept such treatment on religious grounds despite the understanding that her or his refusal could result in death. The Supreme Court has not ruled on this issue yet, and therefore there is no final judicial opinion on the propriety of such orders.

The use of secular courts to determine intra-church disputes has raised issues under both the Free Exercise Clause and the Establishment Clause. The Supreme Court decided in the 1871 case of *Watson v. Jones*, 80 U.S. 679, 20 L. Ed. 666, that judicial intervention in cases involving ownership and control of church ASSETS necessarily had to be limited to determining and enforcing the decision of the highest judicatory body within the particular religious group. For congregational religious groups, such as Baptists and Jews, the majority of the congregation was considered the highest judicatory body. In hierarchical religions, such as the Roman Catholic Church and the Russian Orthodox Church, the diocesan bishop was considered the highest judicatory authority. The Supreme Court consistently applied that principle until its 1979 decision in *Jones v. Wolf*, 443 U.S. 595, 99 S. Ct. 3020, 61 L. Ed. 2d 775. In that case the Court held that the "neutral principles of law developed for use in all property disputes" could be constitutionally applied in intra-church litigation. Under this case courts can examine the language of the church charters, real and personal property DEEDS, and state statutes relating to the control of property generally.

Religious Oaths Prohibited The Constitution also refers to religion in Article VI, Clause 3, where it provides, "No religious test shall ever be required as a qualification to any office or public trust under the United States." The provision is binding only on the federal government.

In early American history, individual states commonly required religious oaths for public officers. But after the Revolutionary War, most of these religious tests were eliminated. Today, the individual states, through their constitutions or statutes, have restrictions similar to that of the U.S. Constitution, on imposing a religious OATH as a condition to holding a government position.

Freedom to express religious beliefs is entwined with the First Amendment guarantee of freedom of expression. The federal or state governments cannot require an individual to declare a belief in the existence of God as a qualification for holding office (*Torcaso v. Watkins*, 367 U.S. 488, 81 S. Ct. 1680, 6 L. Ed. 2d 982 [1961]).

CROSS-REFERENCES

Abington School District v. Schempp; Charities; Ecclestiastical Courts; *Engel v. Vitale;* Flag; Immunization Programs; Parent and Child; Schools and School Districts; Scopes, John T.

REMAINDER

A future interest held by one person in the REAL PROPERTY of another that will take effect upon the expiration of the other property interests created at the same time as the future interest.

The law of real property permits a person who owns REAL ESTATE to convey all or part of her rights in the property to another person or persons. Legal conveyances of property become more complicated when the person who owns the property, the GRANTOR, gives a present interest (the right to the possession and use of the property) in the property to one person for either life or a set period of time, and also gives a future interest (also called a nonpossessory interest) in the property to another person. The future interest is called a remainder, and the holder of this interest is called the remainderman.

Remainders are subdivided into two principal categories: CONTINGENT remainders and VESTED remainders. A contingent remainder can be created in two different ways. First, it can be a remainder to a person not ascertained at the time the interest is created. For example, Tom owns Blackacre in FEE SIMPLE, which means he owns it with no ownership limitations. While Bob and Jane are alive, Tom conveys Blackacre to Bob for life, with a remainder to the HEIRS of Jane. The heirs of Jane are not yet known, so they have a contingent remainder.

LIAISON INTERNATIONAL

A remainder can be an effective way to ensure the desired disposition of real property. Parents may convey property to a child for life, with a remainder to another person.

A remainder also will be classified as contingent, whether or not the remainderman is ascertained, where the possibility of becoming a present interest is subject not only to the expiration of the preceding property interest but also to some specific event occurring before the expiration of the preceding interest. This event is called a special condition precedent. For example, if Tom owns Blackacre in fee and conveys Blackacre to Bob for life and then to Jane if she marries Bill, then Jane has a contingent remainder in fee, conditioned on the death of Bob and the marriage to Bill.

A vested remainder is a future interest to an ascertained person, with the certainty or possibility of becoming a present interest subject only to the expiration of the preceding property interests. If Tom owns Blackacre in fee simple and conveys Blackacre to Bob for life and to Jane in fee simple, Jane has a vested remainder in fee that becomes a present interest upon the death of Bob. As a remainderman, she simply has to wait for Bob's death before assuming a present interest in Blackacre.

For a remainder to be effective, it must be contained in the same instrument of CONVEYANCE (document, such as a DEED) that grants the present interest to another person.

See also ESTATE.

REMAND To send back.

A higher court may remand a case to a lower court so that the lower court will take a certain action ordered by the higher court. A prisoner who is remanded into custody is sent back to prison subsequent to a preliminary hearing before a tribunal or magistrate until the hearing is resumed, or the trial is commenced.

REMEDIAL STATUTE A law enacted for the purpose of correcting a defect in a prior law, or in order to provide a REMEDY where none previously existed.

REMEDY The manner in which a right is enforced or satisfied by a court when some harm or injury, recognized by society as a wrongful act, is inflicted upon an individual.

The law of remedies is concerned with the character and extent of relief to which an individual who has brought a legal ACTION is entitled once the appropriate court procedure has been followed, and the individual has established that he or she has a substantive right that has been infringed by the defendant.

Categorized according to their purpose, the four basic types of judicial remedies are (1) DAMAGES; (2) RESTITUTION; (3) coercive remedies; and (4) declaratory remedies.

The remedy of damages is generally intended to compensate the injured party for any harm he or she has suffered. This kind of damages is ordinarily known as COMPENSATORY DAMAGES. Money is substituted for that which the plaintiff has lost or suffered. NOMINAL DAMAGES, generally a few cents or one dollar, are awarded to protect a right of a plaintiff even though he or she has suffered no actual harm. The theory underlying the award of punitive damages is different since they are imposed upon the defendant in order to deter or punish him or her, rather than to compensate the plaintiff.

The remedy of restitution is designed to restore the plaintiff to the position he or she occupied before his or her rights were violated. It is ordinarily measured by the defendant's gains, as opposed to the plaintiff's losses, in order to prevent the defendant from being unjustly enriched by the wrong. The remedy of restitution can result in either a pecuniary recovery or in the recovery of property.

Coercive remedies are orders by the court to force the defendant to do, or to refrain from doing, something to the plaintiff. An INJUNCTION backed by the CONTEMPT power is one kind of coercive remedy. When issuing this type of remedy, the court commands the defendant to act, or to refrain from acting, in a certain way. In the event that the defendant willfully disobeys, he or she might be jailed, fined, or otherwise punished for contempt. A decree for SPECIFIC PERFORMANCE commands the defendant to perform his or her part of a CONTRACT after a breach thereof has been established. It is issued only in cases where the subject matter of a contract is unique.

Declaratory remedies are sought when a plaintiff wishes to be made aware of what the law is, what it means, or whether or not it is constitutional, so that he or she will be able to take appropriate action. The main purpose of this kind of remedy is to determine an individual's rights in a particular situation.

Nature of Remedies Remedies are also categorized as equitable or legal in nature.

Monetary damages awarded to a plaintiff because they adequately compensate him or her for the loss are considered a legal remedy. An equitable remedy is one in which a recovery of money would be an inadequate form of relief.

Courts design equitable remedies to do justice in specific situations where money does not provide complete relief to individuals who have been injured. Injunctions, decrees of specific performance, DECLARATORY JUDGMENTS, and CONSTRUCTIVE TRUSTS are typical examples of some kinds of equitable remedies. Restitution is regarded as either a legal or equitable remedy, depending upon the nature of the property restored.

The distinction between legal and equitable remedies originally came about because courts of law only had the power to grant legal remedies, whereas courts of EQUITY granted equitable remedies to do justice in situations where money would be inadequate relief. The courts of law and the courts of equity have merged, but the distinction still has some importance because in a number of courts, a trial by jury is either granted or refused, according to whether the remedy sought is legal or equitable. When a legal remedy is sought, the plaintiff is entitled to a jury trial, but this is not true when an equitable remedy is requested.

Sometimes a plaintiff might have both legal and equitable remedies available for the redress of personal grievances. In such a case, a plaintiff might have to exercise an ELECTION OF REMEDIES.

Provisional Remedies A provisional remedy is one that is adapted to meet a specific emergency. It is the temporary PROCESS available to the plaintiff in a CIVIL ACTION that protects him or her against loss, irreparable injury, or dissipation of the property while the action is pending. Some types of provisional remedies are injunction, RECEIVERSHIP, arrest, ATTACHMENT, and GARNISHMENT.

REMISSION Extinguishment or release of a DEBT.

A remission is conventional when it comes about through an express grant to the DEBTOR by a CREDITOR. It is tacit when the creditor makes a voluntary surrender of the original TITLE to the debtor under private signature constituting the obligation.

The term *remission* is also used in reference to the forgiveness or condonation of an injury or offense, or the act through which a FORFEITURE or PENALTY is forgiven.

REMIT To transmit or send. To relinquish or surrender, such as in the case of a FINE, punishment, or sentence.

An individual, for example, might remit money to pay bills.

REMITTANCE Money sent from one individual to another in the form of cash, CHECK, or some other manner.

Financial statements sent by a CREDITOR to a DEBTOR frequently refer to the process of submitting a monthly remittance.

REMITTITUR The procedural process by which an excessive VERDICT of the JURY is reduced. If money damages awarded by a jury are grossly excessive as a matter of law, the judge may order the plaintiff to REMIT a portion of the award.

The remedy of remittitur is designed to cure an award of damages that is grossly excessive without the necessity of a new trial or an APPEAL. In some cases, an award by a jury is so completely out of line with the damages proven in the case that it is UNCONSCIONABLE.

Ordinarily, however, an award of punitive damages will not be upset as excessive in the absence of gross error or prejudice on the part of the jury.

Remittitur frequently occurs when a defendant requests a new trial because he or she regards the verdict for the plaintiff as excessive.

REMOVAL The transfer of a person or thing from one place to another. The transfer of a case from one COURT to another. In this sense, removal generally refers to a transfer from a court in one JURISDICTION to a court in another, whereas a change of VENUE may be granted simply to move a case to another location within the same jurisdiction.

Normally a plaintiff has the right to choose the court where he or she will commence an action. An important exception to this rule is the defendant's right, in some circumstances, to have a case removed from a state court to a FEDERAL COURT. Federal law explains this right of removal in detail. It is available only when the federal court has jurisdiction, or authority, to hear such a case. The right may be claimed only by a defendant; plaintiff cannot petition for removal of a case he or she has commenced in state court, even after the defendant asserts a COUNTERCLAIM against the plaintiff that would justify the exercise of federal jurisdiction.

If a plaintiff has more than one claim against a defendant, and not all of the claims qualify for removal, it is not clear whether the whole case should be sent to the applicable federal court. Sometimes the individual claims that support federal jurisdiction can be severed and heard in federal court individually. This can be done if the removable claims are sufficiently distinct that they can be determined on their own. Otherwise they must be tried together. A federal court has discretion to weigh the circumstances and decide each case on its own facts. The right of the plaintiff to pick the court must be balanced with the right of the defendant to use a federal court when there is federal jurisdiction. The same considerations apply when there are multiple defendants, and some are entitled to removal of the case but others are not. If there are multiple defendants and multiple claims, the reasoning can become rather confusing.

The process of removal raises serious questions concerning FEDERALISM, the relationship of the states and the federal government. The idea of a federal court ousting a state court from a lawsuit already pending in the state is somewhat unsettling. The removal procedure itself emphasizes the potential for conflict. A person who is sued in a state court files a petition in the nearest federal court asking for removal of the ACTION, which has the effect of removing the action to the federal court. A copy of that petition is then filed in the state court. The state court can take no further action whatsoever unless, and until, the federal court remands, or sends, the case back to it. The procedure generally works well because federal judges are careful to recognize the legitimate interests of the states in determining causes that are not necessarily federal in nature.

See also FEDERAL QUESTION.

RENDER Return; yield; pay or perform, as in charges or services.

To *render judgment* means to pronounce, declare, or state the decision of the court in a particular case. To *render a verdict* means that a jury agrees upon and returns a written decision into court and hands the decision to the judge sitting at the trial.

RENEWAL Rehabilitation; reestablishment; substitution of a new right or obligation for another of the same or similar nature.

In regard to BONDS, renewal signifies an extension of time for maturity. A stipulation for the renewal of a LEASE requires the making of a new lease, as opposed to an extension, which involves adding time to a LEASEHOLD agreement already in existence without executing a new instrument.

Janet Reno

RENO, JANET President BILL CLINTON appointed Janet Reno U.S. attorney general on February 11, 1993. The first woman to serve as attorney general, Reno previously served as the state attorney for Florida's Dade County, which includes Miami. During her first term as attorney general, Reno sought stricter GUN CONTROL laws, lobbied for funding for more local police officers, and worked with communities to develop better methods of crime prevention.

Reno was born on July 21, 1938, in Miami, Florida. Her parents were journalists who worked for Miami daily newspapers. Reno attended public schools in Dade County and enrolled at Cornell University in 1956. After her graduation in 1960, she attended Harvard Law School, one of only sixteen women in a class of more than five hundred students. She graduated in 1963 but found that her gender made it difficult to find work as a lawyer in Miami.

In 1971 Reno was named staff director of the Florida House Judiciary Committee. In this position she oversaw the revision of the Florida court system. In 1973 she was named counsel for the state senate's committee responsible for revising the Florida Criminal Code. That same year she accepted a position in the Dade

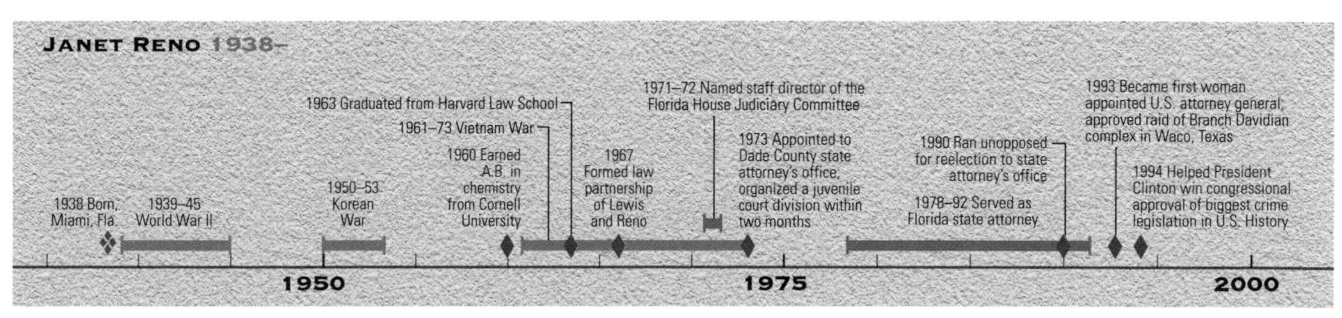

County state attorney's office, which has jurisdiction over the Greater Miami area. She quickly succeeded in organizing a juvenile division within the office.

Reno left the state attorney's office in 1976 to become a partner in a private Miami law firm. She was drawn back into government service in 1978 when the Dade County state attorney stepped down before the end of his term. Appointed state attorney, Reno was elected to a full term in November 1978, and the voters returned her to office four more times.

As state attorney Reno managed an office of 940 employees, with an annual budget of $30 million and a yearly docket of 120,000 cases. She established a career criminal unit that worked with federal officials and local law enforcement to arrest and convict career criminals and sentence them to substantial prison time. Reno also helped establish the Miami drug court, which has been a model for courts in the United States. The drug court provides alternative punishment for nonviolent offenders who have a drug abuse problem. More than half of those offenders who have completed the program have remained free of drugs.

Reno also focused attention on prevention programs that enabled children to grow in a safe, constructive environment. She helped reform the juvenile justice system and pursued delinquent fathers for CHILD SUPPORT payments.

As U.S. attorney general, Reno entered the public spotlight almost immediately. On February 28, 1993, approximately one hundred agents from the Bureau of ALCOHOL, TOBACCO AND FIREARMS (ATF) raided the Waco, Texas, compound of the members of the Branch Davidian religious cult, who were led by David Koresh. The agents and cult members exchanged gunfire. Four ATF agents died, six cult members were killed, and sixteen people were wounded.

After the unsuccessful raid, a long standoff ensued. Reno oversaw the negotiations between Koresh and agents of the FEDERAL BUREAU OF INVESTIGATION (FBI). For fifty-one days negotiations continued, but in April the FBI alerted Reno that cult members were planning a mass suicide. Though Koresh had released some children, many remained in the compound.

Reno ordered an assault on the compound, which took place on April 19, 1993. Cult members started fires in three locations, which soon engulfed the wooden buildings. Eighty-six cult members, including seventeen children, died that day. Reno, expressing anguish over the loss of life, particularly the children's lives, took full responsibility for the decision to storm the compound. She came under heavy attack for having approved the plan, which she defended as having been based on the information known at the time. She conceded, however, that based on the results, it had obviously been the wrong decision.

"NOTHING CAN MAKE ME MADDER THAN LAWYERS WHO DON'T CARE ABOUT OTHERS."

Reno's greatest achievement during the first Clinton administration was helping the president win congressional approval of the 1994 crime bill, the biggest crime legislation in U.S. history (Pub. L. No. 103-322, 108 Stat. 1796). The $30.2 billion measure was a complex mixture of government spending and changes to previous criminal law. It authorized the funding of social programs, the hiring of one hundred thousand police officers nationwide, and the building of new prisons. Reno applauded the increased legal protections afforded women and children under the Violence Against Women Act of 1994 contained in the bill. The National Rifle Association had protested Reno's efforts to ban nineteen assault-style firearms, yet Congress included this controversial measure in the final bill. The bill also prohibits gun purchases by people who are subject to a court restraining order because of DOMESTIC VIOLENCE.

Reno has traveled throughout the United States, visiting with local officials to encourage crime prevention programs and law enforcement methods such as community policing.

Reno was reappointed attorney general in January 1997.

RENT STRIKE An organized protest on the part of tenants in which they withhold the payment of CONSIDERATION for the use or occupation of PROPERTY from their LANDLORD until their grievances are settled.

A rent strike is ordinarily unlawful since a TENANT who occupies LEASEHOLD premises has a

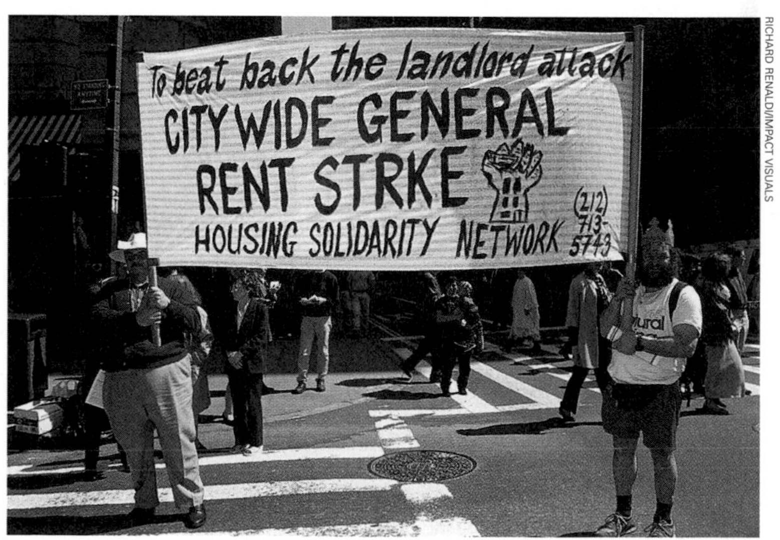

RICHARD RENALD/IMPACT VISUALS

During the city's annual Easter parade in 1997, New York City renters advocated a rent strike to protest rent increases.

legal obligation to pay rent. Even if a landlord does not make needed repairs or provide necessary services, a tenant ordinarily is not released from the obligation to pay rent unless he or she leaves the premises and can show that they were uninhabitable, or unless the tenant can demonstrate that the landlord was attempting to force him or her to move out.

Certain courts refuse to recognize rent strikes as lawful on the grounds that any failure to pay rent constitutes a breach of the tenant's obligation and legally makes the tenant subject to eviction. A rent strike, however, is distinguishable from other failures to pay rent because its purpose is to coerce the landlord to take a particular action. Increasingly the courts have recognized that a rent strike is not an ordinary failure to pay rent. Some JURISDICTIONS have developed procedures through which tenants are able to pay their rent into the court, or to a court-appointed RECEIVER. The landlord receives the money only after essential repairs have been made, or the receiver can use the funds to contract for such repairs.

See also LANDLORD AND TENANT.

RENUNCIATION The abandonment of a right; repudiation; rejection.

The renunciation of a right, power, or privilege involves a total divestment thereof; the right, power, or privilege cannot be transferred to anyone else. For example, when an individual becomes a citizen of a new country, that individual must ordinarily renounce his or her citizenship in the old country.

RENUNCIATION OF WAR Although INTERNATIONAL law makes some distinction between a just and an unjust war, state practice until the conclusion of World War I had generally disregarded that distinction and maintained WAR as a legitimate means of resolving disputes or increasing the power of the state. Recognized methods for resolving disputes peacefully did exist, however; under the Covenant of the LEAGUE OF NATIONS, for example, member states promised to utilize such methods before resorting to war.

Formal rejection of war as a means of national policy for settling controversies came in 1928 with the conclusion of the KELLOGG-BRIAND PACT. Titled the General Treaty for the Renunciation of War, the Kellogg-Briand Pact obligated signatories to abandon force in favor of negotiation, ARBITRATION, MEDIATION, or other methods of settling disputes peacefully. Although the signatories renounced war with each other, the Kellogg-Briand Pact still permitted war for self-defense, for collective enforcement of international obligations, between signatories and nonparty states, and against a signatory that had derogated its obligations under the treaty by going to war.

The UNITED NATIONS Charter, which has had broader acceptance than the Kellogg-Briand Pact, carries the aims of the pact further by prohibiting the use of force or even the threat of force. The charter also attempts to impose these obligations on nonmembers in Article 2(6).

See also MEDIATION, INTERNATIONAL LAW.

RENVOI The process by which a court adopts the rules of a forcign JURISDICTION with respect to any conflict of laws that arises.

President Calvin Coolidge (seated at table, left) and Secretary of State Frank B. Kellogg sign the Kellogg-Briand Pact, a formal renunciation of war. Sixty-three nations eventually signed the pact, although the treaty was silent on what would be done if anyone violated the agreement.

In some instances, the rules of the foreign state might refer the court back to the law of the forum where the case is being heard.

The term *renvoi* also refers to the rules that, in a lawsuit by a nonresident upon a cause arising locally, the capacity to sue is determined by the law of the nonresident's domicile, rather than by local law.

The doctrine of renvoi is seldom followed in the United States and has also been rejected by a number of foreign legal scholars.

REORGANIZATION The process of carrying out, through agreements and legal proceedings, a business plan for winding up the affairs of, or foreclosing a MORTGAGE upon, the property of a CORPORATION that has become insolvent.

Reorganization is ordinarily accomplished by way of a JUDICIAL SALE of the property of the corporation. The purchasers then often form a new corporation to which substantially all assets of the old are transferred.

See also BANKRUPTCY.

REORGANIZATION PLAN A scheme authorized by federal law and promulgated by the PRESIDENT whereby he or she alters the structure of federal agencies to promote government efficiency and economy through a transfer, consolidation, coordination, authorization, or abolition of functions.

A reorganization plan must specify the reorganizations that the president deems to be necessary after making an investigation. A plan may provide for

(1) the transfer of the whole or a part of an agency, or of the whole or a part of the functions thereof, to the jurisdiction and control of another agency;

(2) the abolition of all or a part of the functions of an agency, except that no enforcement function or statutory program shall be abolished by the plan;

(3) the consolidation or coordination of the whole or a part of an agency, or of the whole or a part of the functions thereof, with the whole or a part of another agency or the functions thereof;

(4) the consolidation or coordination of a part of an agency or the functions thereof with another part of the same agency or the functions thereof;

(5) the authorization of an officer to delegate any of his or her functions;

(6) or the abolition of the whole or a part of an agency that does not have, or on the taking effect of the reorganization plan will not have, any functions.

No more than three plans may be pending before Congress at one time. In the message conveying a reorganization plan, the president must specify, with respect to each abolition of a function encompassed in the plan, the statutory authority for the exercise of the function. The message must also estimate any reduction or increase in expenditures, itemized where practicable, and describe in detail any improvements in management, delivery of federal services, execution of the laws, and increases in efficiency of government operations that, it is expected, will ensue from the reorganization plan.

The president can withdraw the plan at any time prior to the conclusion of sixty calendar days of a continuous session of Congress, following the date on which the plan is submitted to Congress.

Additional contents of a reorganization plan are permitted by federal law. A reorganization plan submitted by the president

(1) may change, in such cases as the president considers necessary, the name of an agency affected by a reorganization and the title of its head and shall designate the name of an agency resulting from a reorganization and the title of its head;

(2) may provide for the appointment and pay of the head and one or more officers of any agency (including an agency resulting from a consolidation or other type of reorganization), if the president finds and, in the message transmitting the plan, declares that by reason of a reorganization made by the plan, the provisions are necessary;

(3) shall provide for the transfer or other disposition of the records, property, and personnel affected by a reorganization;

(4) shall provide for the transfer of such unexpended balances of APPROPRIATIONS, and of other funds, available for use in connection with a function or agency affected by a reorganization, as the president considers necessary by reason of the reorganization for use in connection with the functions affected by the reorganization, or for the use of the agency that shall have the functions after the reorganization plan is effective; and

(5) shall provide for terminating the affairs of an abolished agency.

A reorganization plan can neither provide for, nor have the effect of

(1) creating a new executive department, abolishing or transferring an executive department or independent regulatory agency,

An example of a reorganization plan

REORGANIZATION PLAN NO. 1 OF 1980

45 F.R. 40561, 94 Stat. 3585

Prepared by the President and submitted to the Senate and the House of Representatives in Congress assembled March 27, 1980, [as amended May 5, 1980] pursuant to the provisions of Chapter 9 of Title 5 of the United States Code [Chapter 9 of this title].

NUCLEAR REGULATORY COMMISSION

Section 1. (a) Those functions of the Nuclear Regulatory Commission, hereinafter referred to as the "Commission", concerned with:

(1) policy formulation;

(2) rulemaking, as defined in section 553 of Title 5 of the United States Code [section 553 of this title], except that those matters set forth in 553(a) (2) and (b) which do not pertain to policy formulation orders or adjudications shall be reserved to the Chairman of the Commission;

(3) orders and adjudications, as defined in section 551(6) and (7) of Title 5 of the United States Code [section 551(6) and (7) of this title];

shall remain vested in the Commission. The Commission may determine by majority vote, in an area of doubt, whether any matter, action, question or area of inquiry pertains to one of these functions. The performance of any portion of these functions may be delegated by the Commission to a member of the Commission, including the Chairman of the Nuclear Regulatory Commission, hereinafter referred to as the "Chairman," and to the staff through the Chairman.

(b) (1) With respect to the following officers or successor officers duly established by statute or by the Commission, the Chairman shall initiate the appointment, subject to the approval of the Commission; and the Chairman or a member of the Commission may initiate an action for removal, subject to the approval of the Commission:

(i) Executive Director for Operations,

(ii) General Counsel,

(iii) Secretary of the Commission,

(iv) Director of the Office of Policy Evaluation,

(v) Director of the Office of Inspector and Auditor,

(vi) Chairman, Vice Chairman, Executive Secretary, and Members of the Atomic Safety and Licensing Board Panel,

(vii) Chairman, Vice Chairman and Members of the Atomic Safety and Licensing Appeal Panel.

[Balance is omitted for purpose of illustration.]

JIMMY CARTER

THE WHITE HOUSE,
March 27, 1980.

or all the functions thereof, or consolidating two or more executive departments or two or more independent regulatory agencies, or all the functions thereof;

(2) continuing an agency beyond the period authorized by law for its existence or beyond the time when it would have terminated if the reorganization had not been made;

(3) continuing a function beyond the period authorized by law for its exercise or beyond the time when it would have terminated if the reorganization had not been made;

(4) authorizing an agency to exercise a function that is not expressly authorized by law at the time the plan is transmitted to Congress;

(5) increasing the term of an office beyond that provided by law for the office; or

(6) dealing with more than one logically consistent subject matter.

A reorganization plan ordinarily is effective at the conclusion of the first period of sixty calendar days of continuous session of Congress after the date on which the plan is transmitted to it, unless, between the transmittal date and the end of the sixty-day period, either house passes a resolution declaring that the house does not favor the reorganization plan. A reorganization plan can prescribe that its provisions will be effective at a time later than the date on which the plan otherwise would be effective. In addition, if both Houses of Congress have defeated a resolution of disapproval, the provisions can be effective at a time earlier than the expiration of the sixty-day period.

An effective reorganization plan is published in the STATUTES AT LARGE, in the same volume as the PUBLIC LAWS, and in the FEDERAL REGISTER.

If a statute is enacted, an action taken, a regulation promulgated by an agency, or a function affected by a reorganization before the effective date of the reorganization, it has, except to the extent rescinded, modified, superseded, or made inapplicable by or under authority of law, or by the abolition of a function, the same effect as if the reorganization had not been made. If, however, the statute, regulation, or other action has vested the functions in the agency from which it is removed under the reorganization plan, the function, insofar as it is to be exercised after the plan becomes effective, is regarded as vested in the agency under which the function is placed by the plan.

A suit, ACTION, or other proceeding lawfully instituted by or against the head of an agency or other officer of the United States, in his or her official capacity, or in relation to the performance of his or her official duties, does not abate because a reorganization plan becomes effective. If a MOTION, an application for a court order, or a supplemental petition showing a necessity for a survival of the suit, action, or proceeding is filed at any time within twelve months after the reorganization plan takes effect, the court may allow the suit, action, or proceeding to be maintained by or against the successor of the head or officer under the reorganization achieved by the plan or, if there is no successor, against such agency or officer as the president designates.

The appropriations or portions thereof unexpended because of the operation of the reorganization plan revert to the Department of the TREASURY.

CROSS-REFERENCES

Administrative Agency; Administrative Law and Procedure; Bureaucracy; Executive Branch.

REPARABLE INJURY A TORT, or civil wrong, that can be compensated through the payment of pecuniary DAMAGES, as distinguished from IRREPARABLE INJURY or harm that is not compensable through the payment of money.

REPARATION COMPENSATION for an injury; REDRESS for a wrong inflicted.

The losing countries in a WAR often must pay DAMAGES to the victors for the economic harm that the losing countries inflicted during wartime. These damages are commonly called military reparations. The term *reparation* may also be applied to other situations where one party must pay for damages inflicted upon another party.

In the twentieth century, military reparations have been extracted from Germany twice. After Germany's defeat in World War I, the Allies conducted a peace conference in Paris at which they drafted the Treaty of Versailles (225 Consol. T. S. 188 [June 28, 1919]) which was extremely harsh toward Germany. Germany was compelled to deliver to the Allies one–eighth of its livestock and provide ships, railroad cars, locomotives, and other materials to replace those it had destroyed during the war. Germany also had to provide France with large quantities of coal as reparations.

The treaty required Germany to pay large yearly sums of money to the Allies, but it did not set the total amount due. A reparations commission, which was created to determine the amount, decided in 1921 to set total cash reparations at about $33 billion.

Efforts to collect the reparations failed, primarily because the German economy was in dire straits in the 1920s. U.S. financier Charles G. Dawes presided over a committee of experts to deal with this problem. In 1924 the Allies and Germany adopted the Dawes Plan, which reorganized the German national bank, placed stringent economic controls on Germany, and provided for loans to Germany, all to improve the German economy so that the country could make reparations. In 1929 Germany renegotiated its reparations requirements with the Allies. A committee headed by U.S. representative OWEN D. YOUNG reduced the amount Germany owed and ended foreign controls over the German economy. Even this reduced amount of reparations was not paid. When ADOLF HITLER came to power in 1933, he repudiated the Treaty of Versailles and the reparations provisions.

In the twentieth century, the term *reparation* has come to imply FAULT. However, in some circumstances nations may pay for damages inflicted by their armed forces without admitting fault or legal LIABILITY, by offering compensation ex gratia, which is Latin for "out of

A woman held in an Idaho internment camp during World War II sits among camp artifacts on display in a museum. Most surviving internees of the camps have received reparations from the U.S. government.

grace." Such payments are usually made for humanitarian or political reasons.

For example, the United States paid Switzerland $4 million for the accidental bombing of the town of Schaffhausen during World War II and paid Japan $2 million in the mid–1950s after an atomic bomb test that the United States conducted in the Pacific showered a Japanese fishing boat and its crew with radiation.

The U.S. government has granted reparations to the Japanese Americans who were interned during World War II as a result of Executive Order No. 9066 signed by President FRANKLIN D. ROOSEVELT in February 1942. The order led to the incarceration of approximately 120,000 persons of Japanese ancestry; 77,000 were U.S. citizens and the rest legal and illegal resident ALIENS. The president was reacting to wartime hysteria that gripped the West Coast immediately after the Japanese attack on Pearl Harbor. Rumors about treasonous Japanese residents either communicating vital war secrets to the Japanese government or actively aiding the enemy abounded as U.S. citizens began to fear a Japanese invasion of the mainland. Though these rumors proved false, Japanese Americans suffered because of their nationality. Those interned were forced to sell their homes, furnishings, and businesses at low, distressed prices because they were only allowed to take what they could carry. Families were uprooted and spent time in relocation camps, the last of which did not close until 1946, six months after the end of the war.

During the war Japanese Americans sought restoration of their rights through the courts, but to no avail. In 1942 Fred Toyosaburo Korematsu was convicted for failing to report for relocation. In 1944 the U.S. Supreme Court, in *Korematsu v. United States*, 323 U.S. 214, 65 S. Ct. 193, 89 L. Ed. 194, upheld the constitutionality of the relocation orders.

For forty years Japanese Americans sought reparations for their wartime imprisonment and loss of property. The Civil Liberties Act of 1988 (50 App. U.S.C.A. § 1989b) amounted to an apology from the U.S. government for the wartime internment of Japanese Americans. The act established a $1.25 billion trust fund to pay reparations. Each of the approximately sixty thousand surviving internees received $20,000 tax free.

Reparations are also awarded to some crime victims. Several states have enacted the Uniform Crime Victims Reparation Act, which awards reparations to persons who have been victims of crimes involving physical violence. Reparations may be granted for medical and hospital costs not covered by medical insurance, lost wages, and other costs associated with a crime.

In addition, some federal statutes provide for reparations for violations of law. For example, persons suffering losses because of violations of the Commodity Futures Trading Act (7 U.S.C.A. § 18) may use the act to seek reparation against the violator.

See also JAPANESE AMERICAN EVACUATION CASES; VICTIMS OF CRIME.

REPEAL The ANNULMENT or ABROGATION of a previously existing statute by the enactment of a later law that revokes the former law.

The revocation of the law can either be done through an *express repeal*, whereby a statute specifically indicates that the former law shall be revoked and abrogated, or through an *implied repeal*, which arises when the later statute contains provisions that are so contrary or irreconcilable with those of the prior law that only one can remain in force.

The repeal of a law differs from the AMENDMENT thereof, because the amendment of a law involves making a change in a law that already exists, leaving a portion of the original still standing. When a law is repealed, however, it is completely abrogated.

REPLEVIN A legal ACTION to recover the POSSESSION of items of personal property.

Replevin is one of the oldest FORMS OF ACTION known to COMMON LAW, first appearing about the beginning of the thirteenth century. It was a legal procedure for claiming the right to have personal property returned from the possession of one who had less right to hold it than the plaintiff. Originally the action may have been available only for the recovery of GOODS that were illegally held past the time the defendant had the right to their possession, but soon the right was extended to cover every situation, whether the defendant wrongfully took or just withheld another's property. As time passed, if the goods themselves could not be recovered, the courts sometimes gave judgment for an amount of money representing the value of the goods. Generally, however, replevin aimed at restoring the property itself to the person entitled to possess it. The defendant could not claim as an excuse that the property belonged to someone not involved in the lawsuit because the only issue before the court was rightful possession, not TITLE. For example, an executor of an estate could seek replevy of racehorses boarded by the decedent if the owner of the stable refused to release them. It would be no defense that the executor was not the owner of the horses.

Replevin differed from the actions of TRESPASS and TROVER in that it sought recovery of the specific items of property in dispute rather than monetary damages. Unlike trover, the plaintiff was not bound to prove that the defendant had converted the goods to his or her own use, only that the defendant wrongfully refused to give them up. Unlike trespass, the defendant in an action to replevy goods was not claiming that he or she owned the property, only that he or she was entitled to hold on to it rather than give it to the plaintiff. The action of DETINUE was available to recover property that the defendant acquired lawfully and then unlawfully refused to return, such as in an ordinary BAILMENT situation.

Like other forms of action, replevin was wrapped up in technicalities that made it unwieldy for many plaintiffs. Modern statutes have replaced the old forms with more efficient laws of civil procedure; in most states, these include a particular statute regulating the recovery of personal property wrongfully withheld. These procedures generally incorporate elements of the COMMON-LAW ACTIONS of detinue and replevin. The plaintiff usually initiates proceedings by serving papers showing why he or she claims the property and by posting a BOND equal to double the value of the property. Then the SHERIFF seizes the property and, after a short period, delivers it to the plaintiff to hold until a hearing can be had on the claim. Most statutes allow the defendant to regain the property before the hearing by posting a bond of his or her own and filing an AFFIDAVIT stating that he or she is entitled to possession of the property. In some states, it is possible to punish a defendant who secretes, destroys, or disposes of the property by citing him or her for CONTEMPT of court. An uncooperative defendant or the losing party can be ordered to pay monetary damages to the other party. The bond posted by either party is a source of money to pay any costs or damages assessed against that party.

REPLICATION In COMMON-LAW PLEADING, the response of a plaintiff to the defendant's PLEA in an action AT LAW, or to the defendant's ANSWER in a suit in EQUITY.

Common-law pleading required the plaintiff to set out the claim in a DECLARATION or, in equity, in a BILL. The defendant responded with a plea or answer. When the defendant raised a new point in his or her response, the plaintiff was required to introduce an additional fact that defeated this new point. The plaintiff had an opportunity to respond in a paper called a replication. The modern equivalent is known as the REPLY.

REPLY The PLEADING in which a plaintiff responds to the defendant's demand for relief asserted in a SET-OFF or COUNTERCLAIM.

In most states and in the FEDERAL COURTS, a reply is permitted only when the defendant has specifically made a properly labeled counterclaim or when the court orders the plaintiff to file a formal response to an ANSWER.

REPORT An official or formal statement of facts or proceedings. To give an account of; to relate; to tell or convey information; the written statement of such an account.

For example, one kind of report is the formal statement in writing made to a court by a *master*, a CLERK, or a referee who has been appointed to inquire into a particular matter for the court. Sometimes the report of a public official is distinguished from a RETURN. A return typically discloses something done or observed by the official, whereas a report shows the results of an investigation into matters outside the personal knowledge of the official.

Regularly published volumes of books containing accounts of decisions and opinions of various courts are sometimes referred to as reports, but more often they are called REPORTERS.

The annual report for stockholders is prepared by a CORPORATION, a consumer report describes the qualities of a manufactured product, and a credit report assesses the creditworthiness of a business or consumer for a bank or other lender.

REPORTER One who prepares a summary or gives an account. A court reporter is a person who records court proceedings as they take place and then later transcribes the account. A published volume of the decisions of a court or a group of courts.

JAMES SCHAFFER/PHOTOEDIT

A court reporter's transcript of court proceedings will be relied upon if any testimony requires repeating, or if a party or a higher court must later review the proceedings.

REPOSSESSION The taking back of an item that has been sold on CREDIT and delivered to the purchaser because the payments have not been made on it.

For example, if an individual fails to render prompt payments on a new car, the car might be subject to repossession by the finance company, which has extended the credit.

REPRESENT To exhibit or expose; to appear in the character of.

When an item is represented, it is produced publicly. To represent an individual means to stand in his or her place, acting as his or her substitute or attorney.

REPRESENTATION Any action or conduct that can be turned into a statement of fact.

For example, displaying a car with an odometer reading of ten miles constitutes a representation to a prospective buyer that the car has only been driven ten miles.

The term *representation* is used in reference to any express or implied statement made by one of the parties to a CONTRACT to another, regarding a particular fact or circumstance that serves to influence the consummation of the deal.

As applied to the law of DESCENT AND DISTRIBUTION, representation is the principle by which the ISSUE of an individual who has died inherits the portion of an ESTATE that such person would have taken if he or she had lived.

REPRESENTATIVE An individual who stands in the place of another.

With respect to constitutional law, a representative is an individual chosen by the electorate to serve as its spokesperson in a legislative body, such as the SENATE or HOUSE OF REPRESENTATIVES.

A PERSONAL REPRESENTATIVE is an individual who is named in a WILL, or appointed by a PROBATE court, to supervise the distribution of property remaining after another individual's death.

REPRESENTATIVE ACTION A legal action in which one or a few members of a class sue on behalf of themselves and other members of the same class; a lawsuit brought by the stockholders of a CORPORATION, on its behalf, for the enforcement of a corporate right.

See also CLASS ACTION.

REPRIEVE The suspension of the execution of the death penalty for a period of time.

Reprieve is generally an act of CLEMENCY that is extended to a prisoner in order to give him or her an opportunity to find a means or reason for reducing the sentence imposed.

The term *reprieve* is also used generally in reference to the withdrawal of any sentence for a period of time.

REPRODUCTION A woman's right to determine whether she will give birth was not legally recognized until the 1960s and 1970s, when U.S. Supreme Court decisions established that right. Until that time, women in the United States were denied access to BIRTH CONTROL and to legal abortions by state criminal laws. Since the 1970s there has been ongoing controversy over legalized ABORTION, with the Supreme Court allowing states to impose restrictions on obtaining the procedure. In addition, medical science has developed techniques of ARTIFICIAL INSEMINATION and in vitro fertilization that enable pregnancy. These advances, in turn, have created opportunities for SURROGATE MOTHERHOOD, opening up even more legal issues dealing with reproductive rights. Because of the cultural importance placed on motherhood and the intersection of religious beliefs and public policy, the debate over reproductive rights has been contentious.

Historical Background In the nineteenth century, the average size of the U.S. family declined dramatically. A white woman in 1800 gave birth to an average of seven children. By the end of the century, the average was three-and-a-half children. In part the decline was caused by the dissemination of scientific information on birth control. Many of the nineteenth-century proponents of family planning were radical social reformers, who offended church and community leaders with their graphic descriptions of human reproduction.

Conservatives sought to curtail this information on birth control and abortion. The most prominent conservative watchdog was Anthony Comstock, a New York businessman who led a national reform effort against OBSCENE materials. His work resulted in the federal Comstock Law of 1873, which criminalized the transmission and receipt of "obscene," "lewd," or "lascivious" publications through the U.S. mail. The law specified that materials designed, adapted, or intended "for preventing conception or producing abortion" were included in the list of banned items. Some states passed "little Comstock laws" that prohibited the use of contraceptives.

Until the second half of the nineteenth century, few states had criminal laws against abortion. Women in colonial times had used abortion to dispose of the offspring of RAPE or SEDUCTION. Abortion was not illegal under the COMMON LAW as long as it was performed before "quickening," the period at about four or five months when the fetus begins to move in the womb.

State legislatures passed laws in the first half of the nineteenth century that adopted the quickening rule, and a few states allowed abortion after quickening to save the life of the mother. Abortions increased markedly in the 1850s and 1860s, especially among middle-class white women.

Religious leaders began to denounce abortion, but the American Medical Association (AMA) proved to be the most successful in ending legalized abortion. The AMA was formed in 1847, and the all-male professional group (women were not allowed to become doctors) made abortion law reform one of its top priorities. The AMA saw abortion reform as a way to increase its influence and to drive out unlicensed practitioners of abortion. By the 1880s medical and religious leaders had convinced all-male state legislatures (women were not allowed to vote) to impose criminal penalties on persons performing abortions and, in some states, on the women who had abortions. The laws were based on the states' POLICE POWER to regulate public health and safety. This had some justification because abortion procedures of the time were dangerous, subjecting women to sterility and, in many cases, death. In response, women turned to birth control and to illegal abortions. The legal restrictions on birth control and abortion that were created in the late nineteenth century would not be removed until the 1960s and 1970s.

Birth Control In the early twentieth century, a group of reformers sought to legally provide birth control information. The most prominent of these reformers was MARGARET SANGER, who coined the term *birth control.* Sanger challenged state laws restricting birth control information, seeking to draw public support. Though the courts generally rebuffed her efforts, Sanger helped build a national movement. In 1921 she founded the American Birth Control League, which in 1942 became the Planned Parenthood Federation of America.

Renewed legal challenges to restrictive state laws began in the 1950s. By 1960 almost every state had legalized birth control. Nevertheless, laws remained on the books that prevented the distribution of birth control information and contraceptives. A specific target was the 1879 Connecticut little Comstock law that made the sale and possession of birth control devices a misdemeanor. The law also prohibited anyone from assisting, abetting, or counseling another in the use of birth control devices.

The Supreme Court reviewed the Connecticut law in *Griswold v. State of Connecticut,* 381 U.S. 479, 85 S. Ct. 1678, 14 L. Ed. 2d 510 (1965). Estelle Griswold was the director of Planned Parenthood in Connecticut. Just three days after Planned Parenthood opened a clinic in New Haven, Griswold was arrested. She was convicted and fined $100. The Connecticut courts upheld her conviction, rejecting the contention that the state law was unconstitutional.

The Supreme Court struck down the Connecticut birth control law on a vote of 7 to 2. In his majority opinion, Justice WILLIAM O. DOUGLAS announced that the law was unconstitutional because it violated an individual's right to PRIVACY. Douglas asserted that "specific guarantees in the Bill of Rights have penumbras, formed by emanations from those guarantees that help give them life and substance. Various guarantees create zones of privacy." Thus, these "penumbras" (things on the fringe of a major region) and "emanations" added up to a general, independent right of privacy. In Douglas's view this general right was infringed by the state of Connecticut when it outlawed birth control. He said that the state cannot be permitted "to search the sacred precincts of marital bedrooms for telltale signs of the use of contraceptives."

The *Griswold* decision invalidated the Connecticut law only insofar as it invaded marital privacy, leaving open the question of whether states could prohibit the use of birth control devices by unmarried persons. In *Eisenstadt v. Baird*, 405 U.S. 438, 92 S. Ct. 1029, 31 L. Ed. 2d 349 (1972), the Court reviewed a Massachusetts law that prohibited unmarried persons from obtaining and using contraceptives. William Baird was arrested after giving a lecture on birth control to a college group and providing contraceptive foam to a female student. The Court struck down the law, establishing that the right of privacy is an individual right, not a right enjoyed only by married couples. Justice William J. Brennan, Jr., in his majority opinion, stated, "If the right of privacy means anything, it is the right of the individual, married or single, to be free from unwarranted governmental intrusion into matters so fundamentally affecting a person as the decision whether or not to beget a child."

With *Griswold* and *Eisenstadt*, state prohibition of birth control information and devices came to an end. These decisions also enabled schools to give more information to students concerning sex education. Some schools even dispense contraceptives.

Abortion The establishment in *Eisenstadt* of an individual's right to privacy soon had dramatic implications for state laws that criminalized abortions. Until the 1960s abortion was illegal in every state, except to save the mother's life. The growth of the modern feminist movement in the 1960s led to calls for the legalization of abortion, and many state legislatures began to amend their laws to permit abortion when the pregnancy resulted from a rape or when the child was likely to suffer from a serious birth defect. However, these laws generally required a committee of doctors to approve the abortion.

State legislation was swept away with the Supreme Court's controversial decision in *Roe v. Wade*, 410 U.S. 113, 93 S. Ct. 705, 35 L. Ed. 2d 147 (1973). A class action lawsuit challenged the state of Texas's abortion law. Sarah Weddington, the attorney for "Jane Roe," argued that the Constitution allows a woman to control her own body, including the decision to terminate an unwanted pregnancy.

The Supreme Court, on a 7–2 vote, struck down the Texas law. Justice Harry A. Blackmun, in his majority opinion, relied on the prior right to privacy decisions to justify the Court's action. Blackmun concluded that the right to privacy "is broad enough to encompass a woman's decision whether or not to terminate her pregnancy." More importantly, he stated that the right of privacy is a fundamental right. This meant that the state of Texas had to meet the strict scrutiny test of constitutional review.

Contraceptive Use in the United States, 1995

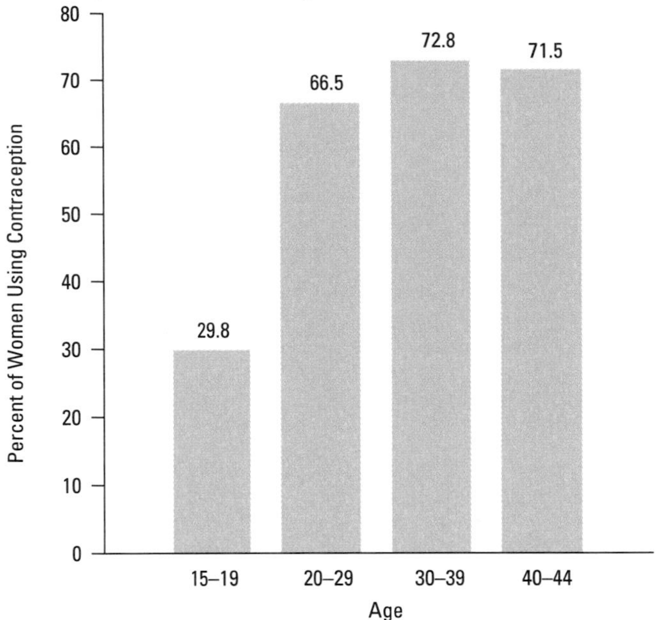

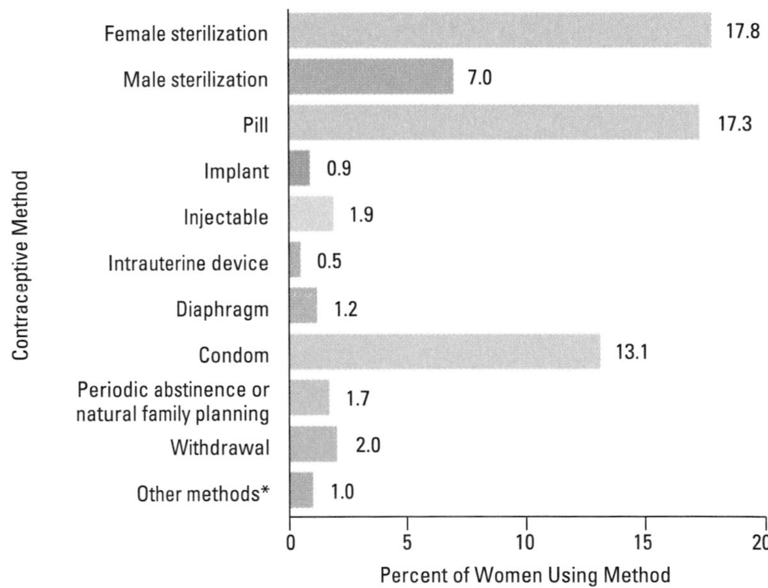

*Includes morning-after pill, foam, cervical cap, Today sponge, suppository, jelly or cream (without diaphragm), and other methods not shown separately.

Source: "Fertility, Family Planning, and Women's Health: New Data from the 1995 National Survey of Family Growth," *Vital Health Statistics*, vol. 23, no 19, 1997, U.S. National Center for Health Statistics.

Restricting Antiabortion Protests

The legalization of abortion resulted in the creation of many groups opposed to the medical procedure. Some groups have sought to take away this reproductive right by lobbying Congress and state legislatures, and others have picketed outside clinics that offer abortion services. In the 1990s groups such as Operation Rescue sought to prevent abortions by organizing mass demonstrations outside clinics and blockading their entrances, as well as confronting and impeding women seeking to enter the clinics.

Clinics responded by obtaining court injunctions that restricted how close abortion protestors could get to clinic property. Abortion protestors claimed that these court orders violated their First Amendment rights of assembly and free speech.

The U.S. Supreme Court, in *Schenck v. Pro-Choice Network of Western New York,* __U.S. __, 117 S. Ct. 855, 137 L. Ed. 2d 1 (1997), clarified what types of restrictions a judge could impose on abortion clinic protests. The Court upheld an injunction provision that imposed a fixed buffer zone around the abortion clinic. In this case the buffer zone affected protests within fifteen feet from either side or edge of, or in front of, doorways or doorway entrances, parking lot entrances, and driveways and driveway entrances. Chief Justice William H. Rehnquist ruled that the government had an interest in ensuring public safety and order, promoting free flow of traffic, protecting property rights, and protecting a woman's freedom to seek pregnancy-related services.

However, the Court did strike down a provision concerning floating buffer zones. These zones, which prohibited demonstrations within fifteen feet of any person or vehicle seeking access to or leaving abortion facilities, "burdened more speech than was necessary" to serve the government interests cited in support of fixed zones. Thus, protestors were free to approach persons outside the fifteen-foot fixed buffer zone.

Texas showed a COMPELLING STATE INTEREST because it had a strong interest in protecting maternal health that justified reasonable state regulation of abortions performed after the first trimester (three months) of pregnancy. However, Texas also sought to proscribe all abortions and claimed a compelling state interest in protecting unborn human life. Though the Court acknowledged that this was a legitimate interest, it held that it does not become compelling until that point in pregnancy when the fetus becomes "viable," capable of "meaningful life outside the mother's womb." Beyond the point of viability, the Court held that the state may prohibit abortion, except in cases where it is necessary to preserve the life or health of the mother.

The Court rejected the argument that a fetus is a "person" as that term is used in the Constitution and thus possesses a right to life. To find a fetus to be a person would make any abortion a HOMICIDE, which would prevent a state from allowing abortions in cases of rape or where the pregnancy endangers the life of the mother.

The *Roe* decision elicited a hostile reaction from opponents of abortion. The creation of a "pro-life" movement that sought to overturn *Roe* was immediate, becoming a new fixture in U.S. politics. Pro-life forces sought a constitutional amendment to undo the decision, but it fell one vote short in the U.S. Senate in 1983. Over time, as the composition of the Supreme Court has changed, the Court has modified its views, without overturning *Roe.*

In the 1970s a majority of the Court resisted efforts by some states to put restrictions on a woman's right to have an abortion. In *Planned Parenthood of Central Missouri v. Danforth,* 428 U.S. 52, 96 S. Ct. 2831, 49 L. Ed. 2d 788 (1976), the Court struck down a Missouri law that required MINORS to obtain the consent of their husbands or parents before obtaining an abortion. In 1979, in *Bellotti v. Baird,* 443 U.S. 622, 99 S. Ct. 3035, 61 L. Ed. 2d 797, the Court invalidated a similar Massachusetts law. Both opinions emphasized the personal nature of abortion decisions and the fact that the state cannot give someone else a veto over the exercise of one's constitutional rights.

In *Akron v. Akron Center for Reproductive Health,* 462 U.S. 416, 103 S. Ct. 2481, 76 L. Ed. 2d 687 (1983), the Court struck down a city ORDINANCE that required that all abortions be performed in hospitals; a twenty-four-hour waiting period pass before an abortion could be performed; certain specified statements be made by a doctor to a woman seeking an abortion to ensure that she made a truly informed decision; and all fetal remains be disposed in a humane and sanitary manner. The

Court held that these requirements imposed significant burdens on a woman's exercise of her constitutional right without substantially furthering the state's legitimate interests.

Opponents of abortion were successful, however, in preventing the payment of public funds for abortions not deemed medically necessary. In *Maher v. Roe*, 432 U.S. 464, 97 S. Ct. 2376, 53 L. Ed. 2d 484 (1977), the Court upheld a Connecticut state regulation that denied MEDICAID benefits to indigent women seeking to have abortions, unless their physicians certified that their abortions were medically necessary. The Court found the law permissible because poor women were not a "suspect class" entitled to strict scrutiny review and because the regulation did not unduly burden the exercise of fundamental rights. In 1980 the Court upheld a provision of federal law, commonly known as the Hyde amendment, forbidding federal funds to support nontherapeutic abortions (*Harris v. McRae*, 448 U.S. 297, 100 S. Ct. 2671, 65 L. Ed. 2d 784).

During the 1980s and 1990s, the conservative majority on the Court showed more deference to state regulation of abortions. In *Webster v. Reproductive Health Services*, 492 U.S. 490, 109 S. Ct. 3040, 106 L. Ed. 2d 410 (1989), the Court upheld a Missouri law restricting abortions that contained the statement, "the life of each human being begins at conception." On a 5–4 vote, the Court upheld a law that forbids state employees from performing, assisting in, or counseling women to have abortions. It also prohibited the use of any state facilities for these purposes and required all doctors who would perform abortions to conduct viability tests on fetuses at or beyond twenty weeks' gestation.

In 1991 the Court upheld federal regulations imposed by the Reagan administration that barred birth control clinics that received federal funds from providing information about abortion services to their clients (*Rust v. Sullivan*, 500 U.S. 173, 111 S. Ct. 1759, 114 L. Ed. 2d 233). The Supreme Court found the regulation to be a legitimate condition imposed on the receipt of federal financial assistance.

The Court appeared to be ready to overturn the *Roe* precedent, but it surprised observers when it upheld *Roe* in *Planned Parenthood v. Casey*, 505 U.S. 833, 112 S. Ct. 2791, 120 L. Ed. 2d 674 (1992). The Pennsylvania law restricting abortions required spousal notification, parental consent in cases of minors, and a twenty-four-hour waiting period before the abortion could be performed. Similar requirements had been struck down by the Court before.

On a 5–4 vote, the Court reaffirmed the essential holding of *Roe* that the constitutional right of privacy is broad enough to include a woman's decision to terminate her pregnancy. Though there was no majority opinion, the controlling opinion by Justice ANTHONY M. KENNEDY, joined by Justices SANDRA DAY O'CONNOR and DAVID H. SOUTER, defended the reasoning of *Roe* and the line of cases that followed it. However, the joint opinion abandoned the trimester framework and declared a new "undue burden" test for judging regulations of abortion. Using this test, the joint opinion upheld the parental consent, waiting period, and record-keeping and reporting provisions, but invalidated the spousal notification requirement.

Pregnancy and Medical Developments Artificial insemination, in vitro fertilization, and embryo transplants have created new opportunities for conceiving children. With artificial insemination, sperm from a donor is introduced into the vagina or cervix of a woman by any method other than sexual intercourse. Originally this technique was used when a husband was sterile or impotent, but it is now available to women regardless of whether they are married. For example, a lesbian couple could use artificial insemination to start a biological family.

The technique of in vitro fertilization gained international attention with the birth of Louise Brown, the first child conceived by in vitro fertilization, in England in 1978. This technique involves the fertilization of the egg outside the womb. The embryo is then transferred to a woman's uterus.

Pregnancies, Number and Outcome: 1992

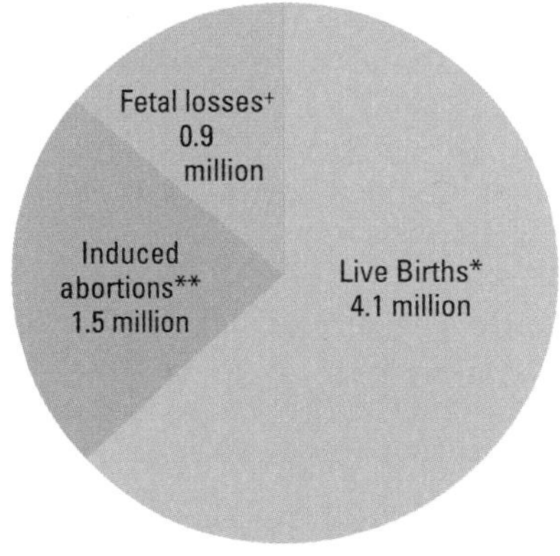

*Live births: based on registered births published annually by the National Center for Health Statistics.
**Induced abortions: derived from published reports by the Allan Guttmacher Institute.
+Fetal losses: based on National Survey of Family Growth conducted by NCHS.

Source: U.S. National Center for Health Statistics, *Monthly Vital Statistics Report*, vol. 41, No. 6, Supplement.

Because sperm and eggs can be frozen and stored indefinitely, there are occasional legal disputes over the rights to these genetic materials when a husband and wife divorce.

These techniques have led to surrogate motherhood. In these cases a woman agrees to be either artificially inseminated by a sperm-donor father or have a fertilized ovum inserted into her uterus. After giving birth, the surrogate mother legally surrenders the infant to the person or couple who will adopt and rear the child. The idea of surrogate motherhood is attractive to some couples because a child born of a surrogate mother will share half or all the genetic material of the parents who will raise the child.

Many surrogate mothers are close friends or relatives of the childless couple. However, the practice of commercial surrogate arrangements has increased greatly since the late 1980s. Many major cities have surrogate agencies, which are often run by doctors and lawyers, that maintain lists of potential surrogate mothers and help match a woman with a couple wanting to have a baby. Commercial surrogate agencies typically charge a fee of $10,000 or more to make the arrangements, which is in addition to the surrogate mother's expenses and fees, which may range from $10,000 to $100,000.

Commercial surrogate arrangements are not legal in all states, and there is little case law on the subject. Some states declare surrogacy CONTRACTS null, void, and unenforceable because they are against PUBLIC POLICY. Opponents of commercial surrogacy believe that such arrangements exploit the surrogate mother and turn children into a commodity. They also are concerned that if a child is born with a disability, the adoptive parents may decline to take the child. Finally, there is the issue of the surrogate mother who does not wish to surrender the child after birth.

The so-called *Baby M* case illustrates the legal complications that accompany an attempt by a surrogate mother to assert the right to keep the child. In 1987 Mary Beth Whitehead agreed to be the surrogate mother for the sperm-donor father, William Stern. Whitehead signed a contract agreeing to turn over the child to Stern and his wife, in return for a payment of $10,000. When Whitehead refused to turn over the baby, whom she called Melissa, Stern went to court seeking custody of the girl to whom he referred as Sara. The New Jersey Supreme Court held that the surrogate contract was against public policy and that the right of procreation did not entitle Stern and his wife to custody of the child (*In the Matter of Baby M*, 109 N.J. 396, 537 A.2d 1227 [1988]). Nevertheless, based on the best interests of the child, the court awarded custody to the Sterns and granted Whitehead visitation rights.

Reproductive Hazards in the Workplace Legal disputes have arisen when employers have barred pregnant women and women of childbearing age from jobs that pose potential hazards to the fetus. The Supreme Court, in *United Auto Workers v. Johnson Controls*, 499 U.S. 187, 111 S. Ct. 1196, 113 L. Ed. 2d 158 (1991), ruled that a female employee cannot be excluded from jobs that expose her to health risks that may harm her fetus. The Court found that the exclusion of the women violated title VII of the CIVIL RIGHTS ACT of 1964 (42 U.S.C.A. § 2000e et seq.) because the company policy only applied to fertile women, not fertile men. Justice Blackmun, in his majority opinion, noted that the policy singled out women on the basis of gender and childbearing capacity rather than on the basis of fertility alone. Concerns about the health of a child born to a worker at the plant were to be left "to the parents who conceive, bear, support, and raise them [the children] rather than to the employers who hire those parents."

CROSS-REFERENCES

Adoption; Fetal Rights; Fetal Tissue Research; Genetic Engineering; *Griswold v. Connecticut;* Husband and Wife; Penumbra; *Roe v. Wade;* Sex Discrimination; Wattleton, Faye; Women's Rights.

REPUBLIC That form of government in which the administration of affairs is open to all the CITIZENS. A political unit or "state," independent of its form of government.

The word *republic*, derived from the Latin *res publica*, or "public thing," refers to a form of government where the citizens conduct their affairs for their own benefit rather than for the benefit of a ruler. Historically republics have not always been democratic in character, however. For example, the ancient Republic of Venice was ruled by an aristocratic elite.

In the U.S. historical tradition, the belief in republicanism shaped the U.S. Revolution and Constitution. Before the revolution, leaders developed many political theories to justify independence from Great Britain. THOMAS PAINE, in his book *Common Sense* (1775), called for a representative government for the colonies and for a written constitution. Paine rejected the legitimacy of the monarchy to have a part in government. This attack on the king was echoed the following year in the DECLARATION OF

James Madison, chief architect of the Constitution and champion of republicanism.

INDEPENDENCE, where THOMAS JEFFERSON proposed that colonists reject the monarchy and become republican citizens.

Framers of the U.S. Constitution intended to create a republican government. Article IV, Section 4, states "The United States shall guarantee to every State in this Union a Republican Form of Government. . . ." Though the language was vague, the authors of the Constitution clearly intended to prevent the rise to power of either a monarchy or a hereditary aristocracy. Article I, Section 9, states, "No Title of Nobility shall be granted by the United States," and most state constitutions have similar provisions.

The guarantee of republican government was designed to provide a national remedy for domestic insurrection threatening the state governments and to prevent the rise of a monarchy, about which there was some talk at the time.

JAMES MADISON, the author of many of the essays included in *The Federalist Papers* (1787–88), put forward a sophisticated concept of republican government. He explained in Number 10 that a republic must be contrasted with a democracy. In the eighteenth century the term "democracy" meant what is now called a pure or direct democracy, wherein legislation is made by a primary assembly of citizens, as existed in several rural Swiss cantons and in New England towns. In a pure democracy, Madison argued, there is no check on the majority to protect the weaker party or individuals and therefore such democracies "have ever been spectacles of turbulence and contention," where rights of personal security and property are always in jeopardy.

By a republic, Madison meant a system in which REPRESENTATIVES are chosen by the citizens to exercise the powers of government. In Number 39 of *The Federalist Papers*, he returned to this theme, saying that a republic "is a government which derives all its powers directly or indirectly from the great body of the people; and is administered by persons holding their offices during pleasure, for a limited period, or during good behavior." Generally, such leaders as Madison and JOHN ADAMS believed that republicanism rests on the foundation of a balanced constitution, involving a SEPARATION OF POWERS and checks and balances.

The republican form of government has remained a constant in U.S. politics. State constitutions follow the federal constitution in dividing powers among the legislative, executive, and judicial branches. Likewise, states have adopted the various checks and balances that exist between the three branches, including the executive VETO power and JUDICIAL REVIEW.

The U.S. Supreme Court has stayed out of controversies that involve whether the government of a state is republican in character. For example, in *Pacific States Telephone and Telegraph Co. v. Oregon*, 223 U.S. 118, 32 S. Ct. 224, 56 L. Ed. 377 (1912), the Court declined to rule whether state legislation by INITIATIVE and REFERENDUM (legislation approved directly by the people through the ballot) was inconsistent with republicanism. The Court refused to rule because it considered this issue a POLITICAL QUESTION outside its JURISDICTION. It is now well established that it is the province of Congress and the president, not the courts, to decide whether the government of a state is republican in character.

CROSS-REFERENCES

Constitution of the United States; *Federalist Papers*; Locke, John.

MILESTONES IN THE LAW

LEE V. WEISMAN

ISSUE

Religion

MATERIALS

Opinion of the District Court for the District of Rhode Island, January 9, 1990
Opinion of the Court of Appeals for the First Circuit, July 23, 1990
Briefs to the Supreme Court
Opinion of the Supreme Court, June 24, 1992

HOW TO USE MILESTONES IN THE LAW

In this section, the reader is invited to study the court opinions and the briefs of the parties in a case addressing the vitality of religious tradition in the ceremonies of public institutions. As you read these materials, you may wish to consider the following questions:

- How much significance should courts place on tradition (other than legal precedent) when interpreting present day constitutional issues?
- Should courts consider the beliefs of the Founders of the United States, apart from those expressed in the Constitution, in rendering opinions?
- How did the Supreme Court's approach to Establishment Clause cases change with this opinion?
- After reading the Supreme Court's opinion, can you see a way that a prayer could be offered at a public school graduation ceremony without violating *Lee v. Weisman?*

THIS CASE IN HISTORY

The proper relationship between religion and government is a question that has divided society and the courts, and fueled contentious political battles, since before the founding of the United States. Often this question surfaces in the context of schools, where tradition can have as much significance as religion in the lives of parents, students, and school personnel. In *Lee v. Weisman*, the Court was asked to decide whether a school-sponsored nondenominational prayer given at a high school graduation ceremony violated the Establishment Clause of the First Amendment. By a decision of 5–4, the Supreme Court ruled that such a prayer was unconstitutional. The division of opinion on the Court was mirrored in public schools, where parents, students, and school officials either praised, or sought to circumvent, the decision.

Daniel WEISMAN, etc.,
Plaintiff, Appellee,

v.

Robert E. LEE, et al.,
Defendants, Appellants.

No. 90–1151.

United States Court of Appeals,
First Circuit.

Heard May 10, 1990.

Decided July 23, 1990.

Public school student and her father brought suit seeking permanent injunction to prevent inclusion of invocations and benedictions in form of prayer in promotion and graduation ceremonies of city public schools. The United States District Court for the District of Rhode Island, 728 F.Supp. 68, Francis J. Boyle, Chief Judge, granted relief, and appeal was taken. The Court of Appeals, Torruella, Circuit Judge, held that benediction invoking deity delivered by member of clergy at annual public school graduation violated establishment clause of the First Amendment.

Affirmed.

Bownes, Senior Circuit Judge, concurred and filed opinion.

Levin H. Campbell, Circuit Judge, dissented and filed opinion.

Constitutional Law ⇐84.5(3)
Schools ⇐165

Benediction invoking deity delivered by member of clergy at annual public school graduation violated establishment clause of the First Amendment. U.S.C.A. Const. Amend. 1.

Joseph A. Rotella, Providence, R.I., for defendants, appellants.

Sandra A. Blanding, Warwick, R.I., for plaintiff, appellee.

Before CAMPBELL and TORRUELLA, Circuit Judges, and BOWNES, Senior Circuit Judge.

TORRUELLA, Circuit Judge.

This is an appeal from the United States District Court for the District of Rhode Island. The issue presented for review is whether a benediction invoking a deity delivered by a member of the clergy at an annual public school graduation violates the Establishment Clause of the First Amendment of the Constitution as construed by the Supreme Court under the second prong of the *Lemon* test. *See Lemon v. Kurtzman,* 403 U.S. 602, 612–13, 91 S.Ct. 2105, 2111–12, 29 L.Ed.2d 745 (1971). The district court held that it did. 728 F.Supp. 68 (D.R.I.1990).

We are in agreement with the sound and pellucid opinion of the district court and see no reason to elaborate further.

Affirmed.

BOWNES, Senior Circuit Judge (concurring).

Although the district court wrote a very good opinion, which I join in affirming, I am compelled to make some additional comments of my own because of the significance of this case and the strong emotions that it and other Establishment Clause cases generate.[1]

1. I am troubled by a report in The Boston Globe that officials at a school in Rhode Island have intentionally violated Judge Boyle's ruling by having a prayer at graduation. Boston Globe, June 10, 1990 at 67. This blatant disregard for the law drew "howls of approval[,] applause, and cheers" at the graduation. Similar disobedience of the law has followed decisions in other recent prayer cases. See N.Y. Times, Sept. 2, 1989 at 1 (*Football Prayer Ban stirring Anger in South*) (disobedience of *Jager v. Douglas County School District,* 862 F.2d 824 (11th Cir.1989)).

I point out that there is formidable religious authority condemning prayer in public:

> And when thou prayest, thou shall not be as the hypocrites are: for they love to pray standing in the synagogues and in the corners of the streets, that they may be seen of men.... when thou prayest, enter into thy closet, and when thou has shut the door, pray to thy Father in secret. But when ye pray, use not vain repetitions, as the heathen do: for they think they shall be heard for their much speaking.

Over three hundred and fifty years ago, Roger Williams was banished from the Massachusetts Bay Colony for, among other "heresies," arguing that the civil government should be completely separate from religion.[2] He travelled south and founded what became the state of Rhode Island, which was the first colony to require the separation of church and state.[3] Since that time the people of Rhode Island have been sporadically involved in probing the permissible intersections between religion and government. *See, e.g., Lynch v. Donnelly,* 465 U.S. 668, 104 S.Ct. 1355, 79 L.Ed.2d 604 (1984); *Lemon v. Kurtzman,* 403 U.S. 602, 91 S.Ct. 2105, 29 L.Ed.2d 745 (1971) (deciding *Robinson v. DiCenso*). Once again this volatile and troublesome issue is before us.

We are asked to determine whether the Establishment Clause prohibits public prayer at a public middle school[4] graduation ceremony. Broadly, this requires us to examine the text of the Constitution and interpret its meaning based on the various tools of constitutional analysis. In its narrowest aspect, we must examine Supreme Court Establishment Clause precedent to determine whether a prayer at a middle school graduation ceremony is similar enough to prayer in the classroom to be controlled by the Court's cases prohibiting school prayer. *Wallace v. Jaffree,* 472 U.S. 38, 105 S.Ct. 2479, 86 L.Ed.2d 29 (1985) (daily moment of silence expressly for prayer); *Stone v. Graham,* 449 U.S. 39, 101 S.Ct. 192, 66 L.Ed.2d 199 (1980) (posting of ten commandments in school rooms); *Abington School District v. Schempp,* 374 U.S. 203, 83 S.Ct. 1560, 10 L.Ed.2d 844 (1963) (daily Bible reading); *Engel v. Vitale,* 370 U.S. 421, 82 S.Ct. 1261, 8 L.Ed.2d 601 (1962) (daily prayer). Appellants claim that a graduation benediction is more like the legislative prayer approved in *Marsh v. Chambers,* 463 U.S. 783, 103 S.Ct. 3330, 77 L.Ed.2d 1019 (1983), and therefore the school prayer cases are not controlling.

1. THE TEXT OF THE CONSTITUTION.

I begin my discussion with an examination of the text of the Constitution. Unlike earlier political documents, such as the Declaration of Independence,[5] the Constitution is completely secular, neither invoking nor referring to "God" or any deity.[6] The First Amendment prohibits "laws respecting the establishment of religion." U.S. Const. amend. I.[7]

The scope of that prohibition has proven extremely difficult to delineate and implement in contemporary society. The words

Matthew 6: 5–7 (King James).

2. A contributing factor in his exile was his controversial interpretation of the Bible, which was the political as well as religious guide for the Puritans. Similarly, this case raises the subsidiary question of how to read the Constitution.

3. Charter of Rhode Island and Providence Plantations, July 8, 1663, *reprinted in Sources of Our Liberties* 162 (R. Perry ed. 1978).

4. A middle school, as the name implies, is the school that children attend after grade school and before high school.

5. *Amicus Curie* National Legal Foundation would have us read the religious imagery of the Declaration into the Constitution. There is no justification for such a reading. The omission of a reference to a Deity in the Constitution was not inadvertent; nor did it remain unnoticed. *Marsh,* 463 U.S. at 807, 103 S.Ct. at 3344 (Brennan, J., dissenting) (*quoting* Pfeffer, *The Deity in American Constitutional History,* 23 J. Church & State 215, 217 (1981)). In fact, it is a striking affirmation of the Establishment Clause.

6. In the Constitution of 1787, "religion" only appears in Article VI ("no religious test shall be required").

7. The Amendment has been applied to the states through the Fourteenth Amendment in *Cantwell v. Connecticut,* 310 U.S. 296, 60 S.Ct. 900, 84 L.Ed. 1213 (1940). The Establishment Clause was applied to the states in *Everson v. Board of Education,* 330 U.S. 1, 67 S.Ct. 504, 91 L.Ed. 711 (1947). There was a dispute over whether the Congress that passed the Fourteenth Amendment thought that it would incorporate the Bill of Rights. This dispute focused on the weight that should be given to Congress's consideration of the "Blaine Amendment" after the Fourteenth Amendment had been enacted. The Amendment would have expressly applied language similar to the First Amendment to the states. *See also Abington,* 374 U.S. at 254–59, 83 S.Ct. at 1588–91 (Brennan, J., concurring) (discussing the incorporation of the Amendment). *See generally,* A. Meyer, *The Blaine Amendment and the Bill of Rights,* 64 Harv.L.Rev. 939 (1951).

of the Amendment give us some indication of its meaning. The use of the word "respecting" indicates that a broader sweep should be given to "establishment," thus prohibiting many actions that could lead to the establishment of religion. *County of Allegheny v. ACLU,* — U.S. —, 109 S.Ct. 3086, 3130, 106 L.Ed.2d 472 (1989) (Stevens, J., concurring in part, dissenting in part) ("'Respecting' means concerning or with reference to. But it also means with respect—that is 'reverence,' 'goodwill,'.... Taking into account this richer meaning, the Establishment Clause, in banning laws that concern religion, especially prohibits those that pay homage to religion."); *see also Lemon,* 403 U.S. at 612, 91 S.Ct. at 2111; *Engel,* 370 U.S. at 436, 82 S.Ct. at 1269. In addition, the use of "religion" rather than "church" implies a prohibition against more than merely an established national church. *See, e.g., Everson,* 330 U.S. at 31, 67 S.Ct. at 519 ("Madison could not have confused 'church' and 'religion' or 'an established church' and an establishment of religion.'"). Beyond these preliminary inquiries, the "plain meaning" of the text is of little help in determining results in this case, so we must turn to the interpretation and practice that has evolved throughout the past two hundred years.

In trying to create meaning from the Establishment Clause, courts and commentators have constructed various historical arguments. But historians have decidedly mixed views about what "establishment" meant to the framers. Judges and historians have been unable to agree about what ideas informed the writing of the Constitution,[8] what exactly occurred in the debates surrounding ratification (the specific intent of the framers),[9] or what impact the "religious character" of various post-ratification practices should have on the meaning we give to the Constitution.[10]

The Court has spent considerable time considering and debating the history of the religion clauses, and each time the results have been inconclusive. *Compare Wallace,* 472 U.S. at 79–84, 105 S.Ct. at 2501–04 (O'Connor, J., concurring) ("The primary issue raised by Justice Rehnquist's dissent

8. Extensive debate surrounds what exactly "the" framers of the Constitution meant or intended. At least three distinct major strands have been isolated, each identified with an individual: Jefferson, Williams and Madison. Jefferson focused on a "wall of separation between church and state" to protect the state from the church. *See, e.g., Reynolds v. United States,* 98 U.S. 145, 164, 25 L.Ed. 244 (1879); Letter from Thomas Jefferson to Nehemiah Dodge and others, A Committee of the Danbury Baptist Association (Jan. 1, 1802) *reprinted in* 5 P. Kurland, *The Founders' Constitution* 96 (1987); *see also Everson,* 330 U.S. at 28, 67 S.Ct. at 517; *But cf. Wallace,* 472 U.S. at 92, 105 S.Ct. at 2508 (Rehnquist, J., dissenting) ("The Establishment Clause has been expressly freighted of Jefferson's misleading metaphor for nearly 40 years.... He would seem to any detached observer as a less than ideal source of contemporary history as to the meaning of the religion clauses of the First Amendment."). Williams thought that a "hedge or wall of separation [should exist] between the garden of the church and the wilderness of the world" in order to protect religion from the corruption of the world. *See generally,* P. Miller, *Roger Williams: His Contribution to the American Tradition* 99 (1953). Madison's view was that competition among sects both religious and political was in everyone's best interest. Justice Rehnquist has tried to distinguish between Madison "as an advocate of sensible legislative compromise and not as an advocate of incorporating the Virginia Statute of Religious Liberty" to support the proposition that Madison believed the single intent of the amendment was to prevent the establishment of a national church (such as the Church of England). *Wallace,* 472 U.S. at 98, 105 S.Ct. at 2511 (Rehnquist, J., dissenting). This approach has been criticized. *See, e.g., Wallace,* 472 U.S. at 79, 105 S.Ct. at 2501 (O'Connor, J., concurring).

9. Legislative history is virtually non-existent for this provision. *Marsh,* 463 U.S. at 814, 103 S.Ct. at 3347 (Brennan, J., dissenting). *But see County of Allegheny,* 109 S.Ct. at 3129–30 (Stevens, J., concurring in part, dissenting in part); *Wallace,* 472 U.S. at 91–100, 105 S.Ct. at 2507–12 (Rehnquist, J., dissenting).

10. Religious practice in the nineteenth century is not a persuasive argument about the meaning of the Constitution because historians have noted that the various religious practices of the government in the nineteenth century were more expansive than at the time of ratification. Christmas and Thanksgiving became national holidays at that time, for example. *See generally* Botein, *Religious Dimensions of the Early American State reprinted in* R. Beeman, S. Botein and E. Carter, *Beyond Confederation: Origins of the Constitution and American National Identity* 315 (1987) (discussing the increase in religious practice by the government in the nineteenth century).

is whether the historical fact that our Presidents have long called for public prayers of thanks should be dispositive on the constitutionality of prayers in the public schools. I think not.") *with Wallace* 472 U.S. at 91–114, 105 S.Ct. at 2507–19 (Rehnquist, J., dissenting); *compare Marsh,* 463 U.S. at 786–92, 103 S.Ct. at 3333–36 *with Marsh,* 463 U.S. at 813–17, 103 S.Ct. at 3347–49 (Brennan, J., dissenting) (discussing the extent to which the practices of the First Congress reveal the intent behind and support interpretations of the Constitution); *compare Everson,* 330 U.S. at 8–16, 507–12 *with Everson,* 330 U.S. at 28–43, 67 S.Ct. at 517–25 (Rutledge, J., dissenting); *see also Engel,* 370 U.S. at 425–30, 82 S.Ct. at 1264–67. *See generally Abington,* 374 U.S. at 232–65, 83 S.Ct. at 1576–94 (Brennan, J., concurring) (scholarly discussion of the role of the history in interpreting the Establishment Clause). It is useless to rehash this continuing debate. The ground has been trodden so much that it is barren of meaning and persuasive power. The "historical record" is inconclusive on the various cross-currents in the minds of the framers. Because of the tangled and often conflicting historical record, it is unlikely that, as an empirical matter, we can ever know the original intention of the authors of the Constitution.[11] Even if we could reconstruct the framers' intent, that would not necessarily be determinative in this case, given our two hundred years of experience with the Constitution and changing circumstances. *See, e.g., County of Allegheny,* 109 S.Ct. at 3099 ("Perhaps in the early days of the republic [the prohibitions of the Establishment Clause] were understood to protect only the diversity within Christianity, but today they are recognized as guaranteeing religious liberty and equality to the infidel, the atheist, or the adherent of a non-Christian faith such as Islam or Judaism" (quotation and citation omitted)). *See generally Abington,* 374 U.S. at 232–65, 83 S.Ct. at 1576–94 (Brennan, J., concurring); T. Jefferson, *Autobiography reprinted in The Founders' Constitution* 85 ("The bill for establishing religious freedom ... meant to [include] within the mantle of its protection, the Jew and the Gentile, the Christian and the Mahometan, the Hindoo and Infidel of every denomination."). An additional facet of the problem of framers' intent is what was the framers' intention about their intent. Scholars have argued that the original intention of the framers was that their intentions were irrelevant to interpreting the Constitution. *See, e.g.,* H.J. Powell, *The Original Understanding of Original Intention,* 98 Harv.L.Rev. 885 (1985).

2. THE SCHOOL PRAYER CASES.

Although the Court may have sent confusing signals on the theoretical or historical underpinnings of the Establishment Clause, it has strictly and consistently interpreted the prohibitions of the Establishment Clause in cases involving prayer in the public schools. The Court

> has been particularly vigilant in monitoring compliance with the Establishment Clause in elementary and secondary schools. Families entrust public schools with the education of their children, but condition their trust on the understanding that the classroom will not purposely be used to advance religious views that may conflict with the private beliefs of the student or his or her family.

Edwards v. Aguillard, 482 U.S. 578, 585, 107 S.Ct. 2573, 2578, 96 L.Ed.2d 510 (1987). The Court has consistently struck down laws or practices that allow or mandate forms of prayer in the schools,[12] and it has

11. The debate about the history of the Establishment Clause highlights problems of historical theory in the Court's opinions. Historians recover "facts" and, through selecting certain facts from the universe of available facts, construct narratives that explain a historical problem. Historical interpretations are not "facts" but rather are narratives drawn from the facts selected by the historian. *See generally,* H. White, *Interpretation in History, reprinted in* H. White, *Tropics of Discourse* (1978); H. White, *Metahistory: The Historical Imagination in Nineteenth-Century Europe* (1973).

12. *Wallace v. Jaffree,* 472 U.S. 38, 105 S.Ct. 2479, 86 L.Ed.2d 29 (1985) (daily moment of silence expressly for prayer); *Stone v. Graham,* 449 U.S. 39, 101 S.Ct. 192, 66 L.Ed.2d 199 (1980) (posting of ten commandments in school rooms); *Abington School District v. Schempp,*

never allowed a prayer at a formal school function. *But see Board of Education v. Mergens,* — U.S. —, 110 S.Ct. 2356, 110 L.Ed.2d 191 (1990) (allowing Christian club as voluntary extracurricular activity at public school).

The appellants argue that this case is not controlled by the school prayer cases because graduation attendance is voluntary, graduation sometimes takes place off-campus, and it occurs only once a year. They contend that the prayers are acceptable under either the prevailing *Lemon* test or under the exception to that standard delineated in *Marsh v. Chambers.* Such arguments have been rejected by other courts. *See, e.g., Jager v. Douglas County School District,* 862 F.2d 824 (11th Cir.1989) (prohibiting prayer before high school football game and rejecting the use of *Marsh*), *cert. denied,* — U.S. —, 109 S.Ct. 2431, 104 L.Ed.2d 988 (1989); *Graham v. Central Community School Dist.,* 608 F.Supp. 531 (D.Iowa 1985) (prohibiting prayer at high school graduation and rejecting application of *Marsh*); *see also Schempp,* 374 U.S. at 224–25, 83 S.Ct. at 1572–73 ("[T]he fact that individual students may absent themselves ... furnishes no defense to a claim of unconstitutionality under the Establishment Clause."); *Engel,* 370 U.S. at 430, 82 S.Ct. at 1266 ("[T]he fact that the [prayer] on the part of students is voluntary can[not] serve to free it from the limitations of the Establishment clause.").

3. THE LEMON TEST.

In evaluating the acceptability of practices under the Establishment Clause, the Court has generally applied a derivative of the three-pronged "*Lemon*" test:

> First, the [practice] must have a secular purpose; second, its principal or primary effect must be one that neither advances nor inhibits religion; finally, [it] must not foster 'an excessive government entanglement with religion.'

Lemon v. Kurtzman, 403 U.S. 602, 612–13, 91 S.Ct. 2105, 2111–12, 29 L.Ed.2d 745 (1971) (citations omitted). A practice or statute that fails to meet any of these requirements violates the Establishment Clause. *See Edwards,* 482 U.S. at 583, 107 S.Ct. at 2577. Only one Establishment Clause case since *Lemon* has not applied some form of this test. *Edwards v. Aguillard,* 482 U.S. 578, 583 n. 4, 107 S.Ct. 2573, 2577 n. 4, 96 L.Ed.2d 510 (1987) (referring to *Marsh v. Chambers,* 463 U.S. 783, 103 S.Ct. 3330, 77 L.Ed.2d 1019 (1983), which did not involve public schools); *see also County of Allegheny v. ACLU,* — U.S. —, 109 S.Ct. 3086, 3100 n. 4, 106 L.Ed.2d 472 (1989) (collecting cases that have used *Lemon* test); *Grand Rapids School Dist. v. Ball,* 473 U.S. 373, 383, 105 S.Ct. 3216, 3222, 87 L.Ed.2d 267 (1985) ("We have particularly relied on *Lemon* in every case involving the sensitive relationship between government and religion in the education of our children.").

The district court properly and carefully applied this test and determined that the practice of invocations and benedictions at school graduations ran afoul of the second, "effect," prong of the *Lemon* test.

A. Secular Purpose

The secular purpose prong of *Lemon* requires us to determine whether the predominant purpose of the practice in question is secular. The question is not whether there is or could be any secular purpose, but rather whether the actual predominant purpose is to endorse religion. *Wallace,* 472 U.S. at 56, 105 S.Ct. at 2489; *see also Lynch,* 465 U.S. at 690, 104 S.Ct. at 1368 ("The purpose prong ... asks whether the government's actual purpose is to endorse or disapprove of religion."). That requirement "is precisely tailored to the Establishment Clause's purpose of assuring that Government not intentionally endorse religion or religious practice." *Wallace,* 472 U.S. at 75, 105 S.Ct. at 2499 (O'Connor, J., concurring). In examining the secular purpose, the Court has examined whether the stated purpose is "sincere and not a sham." *See, e.g., Edwards,* 482 U.S. at 587, 107 S.Ct. at 2579 (Louisiana's creation science

374 U.S. 203, 83 S.Ct. 1560, 10 L.Ed.2d 844 (1963) (daily bible reading); *Engel v. Vitale,* 370 U.S. 421, 82 S.Ct. 1261, 8 L.Ed.2d 601 (1962) (daily prayer).

act, although purporting to foster "academic freedom," in fact did not have a secular purpose); *Stone*, 449 U.S. at 41, 101 S.Ct. at 193 ("[T]he Ten Commandments are undeniably a sacred text in the Jewish and Christian Faiths, and no legislative recitation of a supposed secular purpose can blind us to that fact.").

Although reciting a prayer before a graduation ceremony might, as appellants argue, have the residual sectarian effects of solemnizing the occasion,[13] the primary purpose is religious. Specifically invoking the name and the blessing of "God" on the graduation ceremony is a supplication and thanks to "God" for the academic achievement represented by the graduation and a hope for the continuation of such good fortune. It does not serve a purely or predominantly solemnizing function. A graduation ceremony does not need a prayer to solemnize it.

B. Secular Effect

Justice O'Connor has tried to focus the secular effect discussion on the government's endorsement of religion: "What is crucial is that a government practice not have the effect of communicating a message of government endorsement or disapproval of religion." *Lynch*, 465 U.S. at 692, 104 S.Ct. at 1369 (O'Connor, J., concurring). As the district court held, it is self-evident that a prayer given by a religious person chosen by public school teachers communicates a message of government endorsement of religion.

C. Excessive Entanglement

The excessive entanglement prong prohibits actions that "may interfere with the independence of institutions." *Lynch*, 465 U.S. at 667, 104 S.Ct. at 1355 (O'Connor, J., concurring). In particular, this prong is concerned with the state impermissibly monitoring or overseeing religious affairs. *Marsh*, 463 U.S. at 798–99, 103 S.Ct. at 3339–40 (*citing Lemon*, 403 U.S. at 614–22, 91 S.Ct. at 2112–16). For example, the Court struck down a provision of a zoning ordinance that allowed churches "veto" power over liquor licenses within 500 feet of the church. *Larkin v. Grendel's Den*, 459 U.S. 116, 103 S.Ct. 505, 74 L.Ed.2d 297 (1982). Implicit in this prong, and central to any understanding of the First Amendment, is the belief that the government should not become involved with the determination of religious practice.

Although neither party strongly advances arguments on this prong, I am struck by the instances of entanglement in this case. In *Jager*, the court found no entanglement problem because the school did not monitor the content of the prayers or choose the speaker. *Jager*, 862 F.2d at 831. Here school officials did both. Appellants make much of the fact that the school has chosen to give a suitably non-denominational prayer because school officials distributed a pamphlet entitled "Guidelines for Civic Occasions." These guidelines suggest what kind of prayers should be written. This supervision of the content of the prayers by the school officials implicates the entanglement prong. The school is impermissibly involved in regulating the content of the prayer. In addition, unlike both *Stein* and *Jager*, school teachers chose the speaker who gave the prayer at graduation. This has the effect of involving those teachers in choosing among various religious groups, an activity that is surely prohibited by the Establishment Clause.

4. MARSH.

Recognizing the strictness of the *Lemon* test, the appellants urge that we follow the limited exception to the application of the test delineated in *Marsh v. Chambers*, 463 U.S. 783, 103 S.Ct. 3330, 77 L.Ed.2d 1019

13. It is ironic that many groups that advocate prayer (or "religious liberty"), argue that prayer has no religious intent or effect. They emphasize the "solemnizing function" of an invocation or benediction at graduation and other ceremonies. Inevitably, they analogize prayer to public situations where religion is a dead letter, such as the use of "God" on coins or the "under God" language in the Pledge of Allegiance, to support their position. I am surprised that religious groups would support an argument that explicitly relegates the value of religion in our society to the merely ceremonial.

(1983). In *Marsh,* the Supreme Court upheld the practice of the Nebraska Legislature to begin each legislative session with a prayer. *Marsh* was based on the "unique" and specific historical argument that the framers did not find legislative prayers offensive to the Constitution because the first Congress approved of legislative prayers. *Marsh,* 463 U.S. at 791, 103 S.Ct. at 3335.

That history and those special circumstances are not present at middle school graduations. The Court has specifically stated that "[s]uch a historical approach is not useful in determining the proper roles of church and state in public schools, since free public schools were virtually non-existent at the time the Constitution was adopted." *Edwards,* 482 U.S. at 583 n. 4, 107 S.Ct. at 2577 n. 4; *Grand Rapids School Dist. v. Ball,* 473 U.S. 373, 390 n. 9, 105 S.Ct. 3216, 3226 n. 9, 87 L.Ed.2d 267 (1985) (the Court has "never indulged a similar assumption [to *Marsh*] with respect to prayers conducted at the opening of the school day."); *see also Jager v. Douglas County School Dist.*, 862 F.2d 824 (11th Cir.1989) (recognizing that *Marsh* is inapplicable to school invocations); *Graham v. Central Community School,* 608 F.Supp. 531, 535 (D.Iowa) (same); *but see Stein v. Plainwell Community Schools,* 822 F.2d 1406 (6th Cir.1987) (apparently applying *Marsh* exception in the context of school invocations/benedictions but still finding Establishment Clause violation).

A number of differences between this case and *Marsh* reinforce my view that *Marsh* is inapplicable to school prayer cases. Middle school students are at a very different stage in their development and relationship to prayers than state legislators. The legislators are able to debate and vote on whether and where to have prayers; students have the prayers imposed upon them. Appellants argue that because this is only a once-a-year occurrence it does not implicate the Establishment Clause the way daily prayers do. I disagree. Because graduation represents the culmination of years of schooling and is the school's final word to the students, the prayer is highlighted and takes on special significance at graduation.

The *Stein* decision does not help the appellants. In *Stein,* a Sixth Circuit panel struck down a school invocation and benediction as violating the Establishment Clause. *Stein,* 822 F.2d 1406 (6th Cir. 1987). Each judge wrote an opinion. Judge Merritt, in the court's opinion, thought that the *Marsh* exception applied to school prayer but held that the content of the prayer in question violated the Establishment Clause because it was not sufficiently non-denominational. Judge Milburn concurred in result but added that the *Lemon* test should be applied in examining the invocations and benedictions. Judge Wellford dissented, stating that the *Lemon* test should be applied and that under that test the prayer before the court was acceptable. Such a split in the panel, particularly when the result is contrary to what the appellants seek, is not persuasive authority.

In addition, the analysis of the judges in the majority, in which they parse through the content of the prayers to determine if they are not too offensive, is troubling. The court prohibited the specific prayer because "the language says to some parents and students: we do not recognize your religious beliefs, our beliefs are superior to yours." *Stein,* 822 F.2d at 1410. But the judges imply that some prayers are denominationally neutral enough to offend no one. Such a prayer would be acceptable, under the court's view in *Stein,* under the Establishment Clause. This, I suggest, would be contrary to the teachings of the Court. *See Engel v. Vitale,* 370 U.S. 421, 430, 82 S.Ct. 1261, 1266, 8 L.Ed.2d 601 ("[T]he fact that the prayer may be denominationally neutral ... can [not] serve to free it from the limitations of the Establishment Clause"). Such a prayer would also be extremely difficult, if not impossible, to compose. *See Marsh,* 463 U.S. at 819–21, 103 S.Ct. at 3350–51 (Brennan, J., dissenting) (cataloguing the problems with creating a non-denominational prayer).

Judges should not be passing on the acceptability of specific passages in prayers.

See, e.g., Marsh, 463 U.S. at 794, 103 S.Ct. at 3337 ("The content of the prayer is not of concern to judges."). The ruling in *Stein* invites parents and students to review prayers to determine if the content is sufficiently neutral. That creates more rather than less religious friction by encouraging individuals to debate the content of prayers.

5. THE USE OF A DEITY.

The district court made some statements in the course of its opinion that were in the same vein as the *Stein* court's discussion of non-denominational prayer. Relying on the fact that the invocation and benediction referred to a deity, the court stated that if "God" "had been left out of the benediction ... the Establishment Clause would not be implicated." *Weisman v. Lee,* 728 F.Supp. 68, 74 (D.R.I.1990). This, in my opinion, is too literal and narrow an interpretation of prayer and of what is acceptable under the Constitution. The Constitution prohibits prayer in public schools and not merely references to a deity. An invocation (literally invoking the name of God over the proceedings) and a benediction (blessing the proceedings) are by their very terms prayers and religious. A benediction or invocation offends the First Amendment even if the words of the invocation or benediction are somehow manipulated so that a deity is not mentioned. *See, e.g., Karen B. v. Treen,* 653 F.2d 897, 901 (5th Cir.1981), *aff'd.,* 455 U.S. 913, 102 S.Ct. 1267, 71 L.Ed.2d 455 (1982) ("[P]rayer is perhaps the quintessential religious practice for many of the world's faiths ... [it is] an address of entreaty, supplication, praise, or thanksgiving directed toward some sacred or divine spirit, being or object."). Although I think it is probably impossible to pray without invoking a deity directly or indirectly,[14] the direct reference to a deity should not be the constitutional touchstone for our analysis.

In sum, as Justice Black stated long ago, the 'establishment of religion' clause of the First Amendment means at least this: neither a state nor the federal government can set up a church. Neither can pass laws which aid one religion, aid all religions, or prefer one religion to another.

Everson, 330 U.S. at 15, 67 S.Ct. at 511. By having benedictions and invocations at school graduations, the Providence School District has violated the Establishment Clause. I concur in affirming the opinion of the district court.

CAMPBELL, Circuit Judge (dissenting).

As Judge Torruella states, Chief Judge Boyle's opinion for the district court is indeed "sound and pellucid," in that it expresses well what may be the Supreme Court's ultimate view in this confused area of the law. I say "may." As indicated below, I prefer another view but am aware that the district court's position may be more in keeping with Supreme Court consensus.

I am less amenable to Judge Bownes' reasoning. His seems to me an extreme position, especially his view that a benediction would offend the First Amendment even if a deity were not even mentioned. Judge Bownes would apparently strike down the benediction suggested by the district court (which uses the same words as the challenged prayer, but omits all references to God). That version reads in part, as follows: "For the legacy of America where diversity is celebrated and the rights of minorities are protected we are thankful.... May our aspirations for our country and for these young people, who are our hope for the future, be richly fulfilled." *See Weisman v. Lee,* 728 F.Supp. at 74–75, n. 10. It is difficult to see why this would violate the Establishment Clause. The First Amendment prohibits the making of a law "respecting an establishment of religion, or prohibiting the free exercise thereof." What is there so religious about expressing thanks for diversity and for the protection of minority rights? Is Thanksgiving a forbidden rite? Must courts outlaw the public reading of Walt Whitman or Keats's "Ode on a Grecian Urn"?

14. Even the "Guidelines for Civic Occasions" recognize that public prayer must "remain faithful to the purposes of acknowledging divine presence and seeking blessing."

These extreme views of my colleague suggest the problems that inhere in banning invocations—including those that mention a deity. By so doing we deprive people of an uplifting message that seems especially suitable for a rite of passage like a graduation, where those present wish to give deeply felt thanks. Our First Amendment jurisprudence normally protects speech rather than suppressing it. It seems anomalous to outlaw Rabbi Gutterman's tolerant, benign, nonsectarian supplication—a message so entirely appropriate in that setting, and surely inoffensive to virtually all of those present.*

If one were to ask people what are the problems of our time, they would hardly respond that our youth and their parents are being corrupted by over-exposure to noble aspirations of this character. The common complaints are that 13 year old children are selling crack; that instead of doing homework, students are watching violent TV; that the tolerant ideals mentioned by the rabbi are being rejected in favor of destructive habits of mind and character. So what good, one might ask, is accomplished by preventing an invocation like this?

The answer, of course, is that we are also concerned to preserve the separation of church and state—a fundamental tenet of our Constitution, the benefits of which are undisputed. One need only look at Lebanon, Iran, and Northern Ireland to see what evils this tenet seeks to avoid.

Yet the question remains, is it necessary—to preserve separation of church and state—to prevent benedictions and invocations of this generous, inclusive sort? There is a tradition of such remarks at public functions going back to the Founders. *See Marsh v. Chambers,* 463 U.S. 783, 103 S.Ct. 3330, 77 L.Ed.2d 1019 (1983) (sustaining prayer at opening of state legislature's session). It seems unreasonable to say that *Marsh* applies only to state legislative sessions. One would expect it to cover other public meetings. If so, it may extend to a graduation ceremony like this. *See Stein v. Plainwell Community Schools,* 822 F.2d 1406 (6th Cir.1987) (upholding nonsectarian prayers at a public school graduation). Chief Judge Boyle, nonetheless rejected the *Stein* and the *Marsh* analogy. He not only felt that *Marsh* was strictly limited to a *legislative* session, he also believed that prayer at a graduation ceremony was more analogous to prohibited school prayer than to prayer at a legislative session. He further feared church-state entanglement if courts must determine what prayers are nonsectarian enough to pass muster.

I am troubled most by Chief Judge Boyle's last point. Still, it seems reasonably simple to separate out sectarian from nonsectarian utterances. I suspect that most Americans of all persuasions—including the increasing numbers who adhere to religions or ethical systems outside the Judeo–Christian framework—find it is appro-

* Rabbi Gutterman's invocation reads, in its entirety, as follows:

God of the Free, Hope of the Brave:

For the legacy of America where diversity is celebrated and the rights of minorities are protected, we thank You. May these young men and women grow up to enrich it.

For the liberty of America, we thank You. May these new graduates grow up to guard it.

For the political process of America in which all its citizens may participate, for its court system where all can seek justice we thank You. May those we honor this morning always turn to it in trust.

For the destiny of America we thank You. May the graduates of Nathan Bishop Middle School so live that they help to share it.

May our aspirations for our country and for these young people, who are our hope for the future, be richly fulfilled. AMEN.

The Rabbi's benediction reads as follows:

O God, we are grateful to You for having endowed us with the capacity for learning which we have celebrated on this joyous commencement.

Happy families give thanks for seeing their children achieve an important milestone. Send Your blessings upon the teachers and administrators who helped prepare them.

The graduates now need strength and guidance for the future. Help them to understand that we are not complete with academic knowledge alone. We must each strive to fulfill what You require of us all: To do justly, to love mercy, to walk humbly.

We give thanks to You, Lord, for keeping us alive, sustaining us and allowing us to reach this special, happy occasion. AMEN.

1099

priate and meaningful for public speakers to invoke the deity not as an expression of a particular sectarian belief but as an expression of transcendent values and of the mystery and idealism so absent from much of modern culture.

I think that *Marsh* and *Stein* provide a reasonable basis for a rule allowing invocations and benedictions on public, ceremonial occasions, provided authorities have a well-defined program for ensuring, on a rotating basis, that persons representative of a wide range of beliefs *and ethical systems* are invited to give the invocation. The rule should make provision not only for representatives of the Judeo–Christian religions to give the invocation, but for representatives of other religions and of nonreligious ethical philosophies to do so. In some years, lay persons who do not represent any organized religion or philosophy might be asked to give a nonreligious invocation. The possibility exists, of course, that a particular audience might occasionally be exposed to a prayer redolent of a particular religious tradition, but the next year a different invocation would be given—perhaps by an agnostic. In brief, I think the First Amendment values are more richly and satisfactorily served by inclusiveness than by barring altogether a practice most people wish to have preserved.

It appears, both from the sensitivity of the delivered prayer and the nonsectarian guidelines drawn up by the Assistant Superintendent, that the Providence School Committee went some distance to ensure that different faiths were included and that prayers were nonsectarian. It may be, however, that even more needs to be done, to ensure not only that the state does not identify itself with a particular religion but with religion generally. If so, I would simply require the Committee to broaden its rules as above suggested, and, otherwise, to continue to permit invocations and benedictions of diverse character at high school and middle school graduations.

Daniel WEISMAN, personally and as next friend of Deborah Weisman

v.

Robert E. LEE, individually and as principal of the Nathan Bishop Middle School; Thomas Mezzanotte, individually and as principal of Classical High School; Joseph Almagno, individually and as Superintendent of the Providence School Department; Vincent McWilliams; Robert DeRobbio; Mary Batastini; Albert Lepore; Roosevelt Benton; Mary Smith Anthony Caprio; Bruce Sundlun and Roberto Gonzalez, individually and as members of the Providence School Committee.

Civ. A. No. 89-0377B.

United States District Court, D. Rhode Island.

Jan. 9, 1990.

Public school student and her father brought suit seeking a permanent injunction to prevent the inclusion of invocations and benedictions in the form of prayer in the promotion and graduation ceremonies of city public schools. The District Court, Francis J. Boyle, Chief Judge, held that benediction or invocation delivered by clergy at an annual public school graduation ceremony violates the establishment clause of the First Amendment, if the benediction or invocation invokes a deity.

So ordered.

Constitutional Law ⚩84.5(3)
Schools ⚩165

Benediction or invocation delivered by clergy at an annual public school graduation ceremony violates the establishment clause of the First Amendment, if the benediction or invocation invokes a deity; practice of having such a benediction or invocation delivered at public school graduation ceremonies has the effect of advancing religion. U.S.C.A. Const.Amend. 1.

Sandra A. Blanding, Revens & DeLuca, Ltd., Warwick, R.I., for plaintiffs.

Joseph A. Rotella, Providence, R.I., for defendants.

Amy Adelson, Lois Waldman, Marc D. Stern, Jeremy S. Garber, New York City, amicus curiae for American Jewish Congress.

OPINION

FRANCIS J. BOYLE, Chief Judge.

The issue presented is whether a benediction or invocation which invokes a deity delivered by clergy at an annual public school graduation ceremony violates the first amendment of the United States constitution. This Court finds that because a deity is invoked, the practice is unconstitutional under the Establishment Clause of the first amendment as construed by the United States Supreme Court.

I. FACTS [1]

Each June, the Providence School Committee and Superintendent of Schools for the City of Providence sponsor graduation or promotion ceremonies in the city's public middle and high schools. The graduation ceremonies for high school students are generally held off school grounds, usually at Veterans Memorial Auditorium, which the Providence School Department rents for the occasion. Other sites have also been used. Middle school promotion ceremonies usually take place on school property, at the schools themselves.

The Providence School Committee and the Superintendent permit public school principals to include invocations and benedictions, delivered by clergy, in the graduation and promotion ceremonies. Over the past five or six years, most, but not all, of the public school graduation and promotion ceremonies have included invocations and benedictions. The practice has in fact been followed for many years.

The Assistant Superintendent of Schools has distributed to school principals a pamphlet entitled "Guidelines for Civic Occasions" as a guideline for the type of prayers to be used at the ceremonies. The pamphlet is prepared by the National Conference of Christians and Jews, a national organization with an office in Providence. The guidelines suggest methods of composing "public prayer in a pluralistic society," stressing "inclusiveness and sensitivity" in the structuring of non-sectarian prayer. The guidelines do not suggest the elimination of reference to a deity as appropriate.

Plaintiff Daniel Weisman's daughter, Deborah, was to graduate from Nathan Bishop Middle School, a public junior high school in Providence, in June of 1989. The ceremony was planned by two teachers from the school, and was to be held on the school grounds. Part of the program for that day included an invocation and benediction delivered by Rabbi Leslie Gutterman of the Temple Beth El of Providence. Four days before the ceremony was to take place, Plaintiff filed a motion for a temporary restraining order seeking to prevent the inclusion of prayer to a deity in the form of an invocation and benediction in the Providence public schools' graduation ceremonies. The day before the ceremony, this Court denied the Plaintiff's motion, essentially because the Court was not afforded adequate time to consider the important issues of the case.

On June 20, 1989, Deborah Weisman and her family attended the graduation ceremony for Deborah's class at Bishop Middle School. The principal of the school, Robert E. Lee, had received the "Guidelines for Civic Occasions" pamphlet from the Assistant Superintendent of Schools, and provided Rabbi Gutterman with a copy of the guidelines. Mr. Lee also spoke to Rabbi Gutterman to advise him that any prayers delivered at the ceremonies should be non-sectarian. Rabbi Gutterman was not told that he could not appeal to a deity.

Rabbi Gutterman began his invocation by addressing a deity in the first line of his text, and concluded with "Amen." [2] The benediction similarly opened with an appeal to a God, asked God's blessings, gave thanks to a Lord, and concluded with

1. The parties have filed an agreed statement of facts.

2. Both the invocation and benediction are examples of elegant simplicity, thoughtful content, and sincere citizenship. The full text of Rabbi Gutterman's invocation is as follows:

God of the Free, Hope of the Brave:

For the legacy of America where diversity is celebrated and the rights of minorities are protected, we thank You. May these young men and women grow up to enrich it.

For the liberty of America, we thank You. May these new graduates grow up to guard it.

For the political process of America in which all its citizens may participate, for its court system where all can seek justice we thank You. May those we honor this morning always turn to it in trust.

For the destiny of America we thank You. May the graduates of Nathan Bishop Middle School so live that they might help to share it.

May our aspirations for our country and for these young people, who are our hope for the future, be richly fulfilled.

AMEN

"Amen."[3] The parties agree that Rabbi Gutterman's invocation and benediction were prayers.[4]

Deborah Weisman continues to attend public school in the city of Providence. She is now a freshman at Classical High School in Providence. Plaintiff now seeks a permanent injunction to prevent the inclusion of invocations and benedictions in the form of prayer in the promotion and graduation ceremonies of the Providence public schools. Plaintiff's amended complaint names Principal Lee, the superintendent of Providence public schools, the principal of Classical High School, and the members of the Providence School Committee as defendants.

The parties agree resolution of the case is governed by the first amendment of the United States Constitution, specifically the Establishment Clause.[5] It is to that law that we now turn.

II. THE ESTABLISHMENT CLAUSE

"The [Supreme] Court has been particularly vigilant in monitoring compliance with the Establishment Clause in elementary and secondary schools." *Edwards v. Aguillard,* 482 U.S. 578, 583–84, 107 S.Ct. 2573, 2577, 96 L.Ed.2d 510 (1987). Since the landmark 1962 decision of *Engel v. Vitale,* 370 U.S. 421, 82 S.Ct. 1261, 8 L.Ed.2d 601 (1962), the Supreme Court has steadfastly required that the schoolchildren of America not be compelled, coerced, or subtly pressured to engage in activities whose predominant purpose or effect was to advance one set of religious beliefs over another, or to prefer a set of religious beliefs over no religion at all.[6] God has been ruled out of public education as an instrument of inspiration or consolation.

This vigilance is based upon the perceived sensitive nature of the school environment and the apprehended effect of state-led religious activity on young, impressionable minds. *Grand Rapids School District v. Ball,* 473 U.S. 373, 383, 105 S.Ct. 3216, 3222, 87 L.Ed.2d 267 (1985); *Edwards,* 482 U.S. at 584, 107 S.Ct. at 2577. "Families entrust public schools with the education of their children, but condition their trust on the understanding that the classroom will not purposely be used to advance religious views that may conflict with the private beliefs of the stu-

3. The following is the full text of Rabbi Gutterman's benediction:

> O God, we are grateful to You for having endowed us with the capacity for learning which we have celebrated on this joyous commencement.
>
> Happy families give thanks for seeing their children achieve an important milestone. Send Your blessings upon the teachers and administrators who helped prepare them.
>
> The graduates now need strength and guidance for the future. Help them to understand that we are not complete with academic knowledge alone. We must each strive to fulfill what You require of us all: To do justly, to love mercy, to walk humbly.
>
> We give thanks to You, Lord, for keeping us alive, sustaining us and allowing us to reach this special, happy occasion.
>
> AMEN

4. Webster's Dictionary defines prayer as "a solemn and humble approach to Divinity in word or thought usu[ally] involving petition, confession, praise or thanksgiving." A benediction is defined as "the invocation of a blessing on persons or things being dedicated to God." An invocation is "a prayer of entreaty that is usu[ally] a call for the divine presence and is offered at the beginning of a meeting or service of worship." Webster's Third New International Dictionary (unabridged), G & L Merriam Co., Springfield, Massachusetts (1981).

5. The first amendment provides in relevant part, "Congress shall make no law respecting an establishment of religion, or prohibiting the free exercise thereof...." U.S. Const. amend. I.

6. In *Everson v. Board of Education,* 330 U.S. 1, 67 S.Ct. 504, 91 L.Ed. 711 (1947), the Court summarized the Establishment Clause in these oft-repeated words:

> The "establishment of religion" clause of the First Amendment means at least this: Neither a state nor the Federal Government can set up a church. Neither can pass laws which aid one religion, aid all religions, or prefer one religion over another. Neither can force nor influence a person to go to or remain away from church against his will or force him to profess a belief or disbelief in any religion ... Neither a state nor the Federal Government can, openly or secretly, participate in the affairs of any religious organizations, or groups, and vice versa.

330 U.S. at 15–16, 67 S.Ct. at 511–12.

dent and his or her family." *Edwards,* 482 U.S. at 584, 107 S.Ct. at 2577.

Under the Establishment Clause, the Court has struck down state statutes that required a daily Bible reading before class (*Abington School District v. Schempp,* 374 U.S. 203, 83 S.Ct. 1560, 10 L.Ed.2d 844 (1963)), or required that a copy of the Ten Commandments be posted in every classroom (*Stone v. Graham,* 449 U.S. 39, 101 S.Ct. 192, 66 L.Ed.2d 199 (1980)), or required the recitation of a "denominationally neutral" prayer at the beginning of the school day (*Engel v. Vitale,* 370 U.S. 421, 82 S.Ct. 1261, 8 L.Ed.2d 601 (1962)), or statutes which authorized a daily moment of silence expressly for prayer (*Wallace v. Jaffree,* 472 U.S. 38, 105 S.Ct. 2479, 86 L.Ed.2d 29 (1985)). In virtually all of these cases, the Court acknowledged that while "[w]e are a religious people whose institutions presuppose a Supreme Being," (*Zorach v. Clauson,* 343 U.S. 306, 313, 72 S.Ct. 679, 684, 96 L.Ed. 954 (1952)), the Establishment Clause of the first amendment was intended to prevent a State from becoming involved in leading its citizens, however young, in appeals to or adoration of a deity.

The Supreme Court "consistently has applied the three-pronged test of *Lemon v. Kurtzman,* 403 U.S. 602, 91 S.Ct. 2105, 29 L.Ed.2d 745 (1971) to determine whether a particular state action violates the Establishment Clause of the Constitution." *Edwards,* 482 U.S. at 597, 107 S.Ct. at 2584 (Powell, J. concurring); *Grand Rapids School District,* 473 U.S. at 383, 105 S.Ct. at 3222 (1985) ("We have particularly relied on *Lemon* in every case involving the sensitive relationship between government and religion in the education of our children"). An evaluation of the authorized practice of the Providence School Committee under the *Lemon* test is necessary, "mindful of the particular concerns that arise in the context of public elementary and secondary schools." *Edwards,* 482 U.S. at 585, 107 S.Ct. at 2578.

III. THE LEMON TEST

The *Lemon* test reviews governmental actions using three prongs: "First, the [practice] must have a secular ... purpose; second, its principal or primary effect must be one that neither advances nor inhibits religion; [third], the [practice] must not foster 'an excessive entanglement with religion.'" *Lemon v. Kurtzman,* 403 U.S. 602, 612–13, 91 S.Ct. 2105, 2111, 29 L.Ed.2d 745 (1971) (citations omitted). "State action violates the Establishment Clause if it fails to satisfy any of these prongs." *Edwards,* 482 U.S. at 583, 107 S.Ct. at 2577.

The second prong of the *Lemon* analysis examines whether the effect of the action violates the Establishment Clause. It is here that the invocation and benediction practice runs afoul of the first amendment. Because this Court finds that the Providence School Committee's practice fails to meet constitutional scrutiny under the second prong of the *Lemon* test, it is not necessary to discuss the first and third parts of the test.

The Second Lemon Prong: Principal Effect Must Neither Advance Nor Inhibit Religion

One method of determining whether a state action advances or inhibits religion is to determine whether the action creates an identification of the state with a religion, or with religion in general. "Government promotes religion as effectively when it fosters a close identification of its powers and responsibilities with those of any—or all—religious denominations as when it attempts to inculcate specific religious doctrines." *Grand Rapids School District,* 473 U.S. at 389, 105 S.Ct. at 3225.

The particular circumstances of each government action are critical in the examination of the effect that any church-state identification may have on its audience. For example, in *Grand Rapids School District v. Ball,* the Court distinguished between two of its earlier precedents. In *McCollum v. Board of Education,* 333 U.S. 203, 68 S.Ct. 461, 92 L.Ed. 649 (1948), the Court held that religious instruction could not be held on public school premises as a part of the school program, even though the instruction was conducted by non-public school personnel and participation was voluntary. In *Zorach v. Clauson,* however, the Court held that a similar program that was conducted off school premises passed constitutional scrutiny. 343 U.S. 306, 72 S.Ct. 679, 96 L.Ed. 954 (1952). As the Court explained in *Grand Rapids,* "[t]he difference in symbolic impact helps to explain the difference between the cases. The symbolic connection of church and state in the *McCollum* program presented the students with a graphic symbol of the 'concert or union or dependency' of church and state ... This very symbolic union was conspicuously absent in the *Zorach* program." *Grand Rapids School District,* 473 U.S. at 391, 105 S.Ct. at 3226.

Similarly, in *Grand Rapids School District v. Ball,* 473 U.S. 373, 105 S.Ct. 3216, 87 L.Ed.2d 267 (1985), the Court invalidated a "Shared Time" program in which a school district provided classes to nonpublic school students at public expense in classrooms located in and leased from the nonpublic schools. The Court emphasized that students attending both public and nonpublic school classes within the same building "would be unlikely to discern the crucial difference between the religious school classes and the 'public school' classes...." 473 U.S. at 391, 105 S.Ct. at 3226. The Court pointed out that even the students who were able to recognize the difference between the two classes "would have before [them] a powerful symbol of state endorsement and encouragement of the religious beliefs taught in the same class at some other time during the day." *Id.* at 392, 105 S.Ct. at 3227.

In this case, the benediction and invocation advance religion by creating an identification of school with a deity, and therefore religion. The invocation and benediction present a "symbolic union" of the state and schools with religion and religious practices. While the fact that graduation is a special occasion distinguishes this school day from all others, the uniqueness of the day could highlight the particular effect that the benediction and invocation may have on the students. The presence of clerics is not by itself determinative. It is the union of prayer, school, and important occasion that creates an identification of religion with the school function. The special nature of the graduation ceremonies underscores the identification that Providence public school students can make.[7] "This effect—the symbolic union of government and religion in one sectarian enterprise—is an impermissible effect under the Establishment Clause." *Id.*

Closely related to the identification analysis is examination which determines whether the effect of the governmental action is to endorse one religion over another, or to endorse religion in general. The response is a foregone conclusion; that is, the reference to a deity necessarily implicates religion. *See Grand Rapids School District,* 473 U.S. at 389, 105 S.Ct. at 3225 ("If this identification conveys a message of government endorsement or disapproval of religion, a core purpose of the Establishment Clause is violated"). In recent cases, the "endorsement" inquiry has come to the fore of *Lemon* analysis. *County of Allegheny v. American Civil Liberties Union,* — U.S. —, 109 S.Ct. 3086, 3100, 106 L.Ed.2d 472 (1989). Therefore, "an important concern of the effects test is whether the symbolic union of church and state effected by the challenged governmental action is sufficiently likely to be perceived by adherents of the controlling denominations as an endorsement, and by the nonadherents as a disapproval, of their individual religious choices. The inquiry into this kind of effect must be conducted with particular care when many of the citizens perceiving the governmental message are children in their formative years." *Grand Rapids School District,* 473 U.S. at 390, 105 S.Ct. at 3226. In this case, the Providence School Committee has in effect endorsed religion in general by authorizing an appeal to a deity in public school graduation ceremonies. The invocations and benedictions convey a tacit preference for

7. Of course, the reverse might also be true. Students might conclude that a deity is not an important part of their lives. This Court is not permitted to ruminate concerning the aptness of this possible result as the Establishment Clause is currently construed.

some religions, or for religion in general over no religion at all. Schoolchildren who are not members of the religions sponsored, or children whose families are nonbelievers, may feel as though the school and government prefer beliefs other than their own.

It is of no significance that the invocation and benediction are supposed to be nondenominational, or that participation or even recognition of the prayers is voluntary. In *Engel v. Vitale*, 370 U.S. 421, 82 S.Ct. 1261, 8 L.Ed.2d 601 (1962), the Court invalidated a New York statute which required a short, nondenominational prayer to be recited at the beginning of each school day. "Neither the fact that the prayer may be denominationally neutral," the Court wrote, "nor the fact that its observance on the part of the students is voluntary can serve to free it from the limitations of the Establishment Clause, as it might from the Free Exercise Clause, of the First Amendment...." 370 U.S. at 430, 82 S.Ct. at 1266–67.

In summary, the practice of having a benediction and invocation delivered at public school graduation ceremonies has the effect of advancing religion. The special occasion of graduation coupled with the presence of prayer creates an identification of governmental power with religious practice. Finally, the practice of including prayer may have the effect of either endorsing one religion over others, or of endorsing religion in general. For these reasons, the practice of providing guidelines for "non-sectarian" prayer fails to withstand constitutional scrutiny.

Defendants rely heavily on *Marsh v. Chambers*, 463 U.S. 783, 103 S.Ct. 3330, 77 L.Ed.2d 1019 (1983). In that opinion, the Supreme Court upheld the Nebraska state legislature's opening of each session with a prayer led by a chaplain who was paid by the State. The Court noted that "[t]he opening of sessions of legislative and other deliberative public bodies with prayer is deeply embedded in the history and tradition of this country." 463 U.S. at 786, 103 S.Ct. at 3333. The Court noted the long history, dating back to the Continental Congress, of opening legislative sessions with a prayer offered by a chaplain who was paid by the state. This unique "unambiguous and unbroken history" led the Court to hold that the drafters of the Constitution did not intend the first amendment to bar such legislative prayers.[8]

Defendant argues that this court should follow the reasoning of the Sixth Circuit Court of Appeals in *Stein v. Plainwell Community Schools*, 822 F.2d 1406 (6th Cir.1987), in which the court extended *Marsh* to include benediction and invocations at public school commencement ceremonies. In *Stein*, the Court of Appeals held that annual high school graduation exercises were analogous to the legislative and judicial sessions in *Marsh*. The Court of Appeals found that the invocations and benedictions at graduation provided less opportunity for religious indoctrination or peer pressure than did classroom prayer for two reasons: first, the public nature of the ceremonies and the usual presence of parents acted as a buffer from religious coercion; second, the prayers were not led by a teacher or school official, thus they did not implicate the teacher-student relationship. 822 F.2d at 1409. The Court of Appeals did, however, find that the particu-

8. Like legislative prayer, religious involvement in American education has a long history. Beginning in colonial times, the first schools in this country were religiously motivated. *See generally Lemon v. Kurtzman*, 403 U.S. at 645, 91 S.Ct. at 2127 (opinion of Brennan, J.) Public school education was not begun until about 1840, nearly seventy years after the Declaration of Independence, and a half century after the adoption of the Constitution. The purpose of colonial schools was to ensure that children could read and understand the principles of Biblical faith. H.G. Good, *A History of American Education*, 40–41 (1975). Many of the charters of America's oldest colleges and universities expressly state that the institutions' purpose was to spread the Christian faith. For example, Dartmouth College was founded to "spread[ ] Christian knowledge among" American Indians "with a view to their carrying the gospel in their own language." Charter of Dartmouth College, (1769). The point is that at the time the Constitution was adopted, there really was no public education except that intimately connected with religious purpose. There is no factual basis for an historical argument that the first amendment was intended by the drafters to isolate religion from education.

lar benediction and invocation challenged in *Stein* were unacceptable under the *Marsh* holding because they contained language that was based on Christian theology and thus were not nonsectarian. *Id.* at 1410. As the Supreme Court did in *Marsh,* the *Stein* court did not apply the *Lemon* test.[9]

Stein's extension of the *Marsh* rationale is not persuasive. The *Marsh* holding was narrowly limited to the unique situation of legislative prayer. The clearest indication of this fact is that the *Marsh* decision did not use the *Lemon* test in its review of legislative benedictions. Since the *Lemon* test was first developed in 1971, every case involving the issue of prayer in school has used its analysis. *Edwards v. Aguillard,* 482 U.S. 578, 583 n. 4, 107 S.Ct. 2573, 2577 n. 4, 96 L.Ed.2d 510 ("The *Lemon* test has been applied in all cases since its adoption in 1971, except in *Marsh v. Chambers*"); *Grand Rapids School District v. Ball,* 473 U.S. 373, 383, 105 S.Ct. 3216, 3222, 87 L.Ed.2d 267 (1985) ("We have particularly relied on *Lemon* in every case involving the sensitive relationship between government and religion in the education of our children"). *Marsh's* unique exception to the *Lemon* test would most likely not be applied to school prayer cases, which on the basis of existing precedent requires use of the *Lemon* analysis. When the practice of the Providence School Committee is reviewed under *Lemon,* it fails to withstand Establishment Clause scrutiny, *supra.*

Extending the *Marsh* analysis to school benedictions is arguably unworkable because it results in courts reviewing the content of prayers to judicially approve what are acceptable invocations to a deity. *See Stein,* 822 F.2d at 1410 (reviewing language of invocation and benediction). What must follow is gradual judicial development of what is acceptable public prayer. This result is as contrary to the requirements of the Establishment Clause as is legislative composition of an official state prayer. *See Engel,* 370 U.S. at 425, 430, 82 S.Ct. at 1264, 1266.

Finally, the non-sectarian guidelines used by the School Committee are not a means of rescue. They are useful in environments where prayer is permitted. Here, it is not the particular nature or wording of the prayers which implicates the first amendment—it is prayer at the ceremony which transgresses the Establishment Clause.

On every other school day, at every other school function, the Establishment Clause prohibits school-sponsored prayer. If the students cannot be led in prayer on all of those other days, prayer on graduation day is also inappropriate under the doctrine currently embraced by the Supreme Court.

It is necessary to explain what this decision does not do. First, "[n]othing in the United States Constitution as interpreted by this Court ... prohibits public school children from voluntar[y] [private] pray[er] at any time before, during, or after the school day," or anytime during the graduation ceremonies. *Wallace v. Jaffree,* 472 U.S. 38, 67, 105 S.Ct. 2479, 2495, 86 L.Ed.2d 29 (1985) (O'Connor, J. concurring). Second, nothing in this decision prevents a cleric of any denomination or anyone else from giving a secular inspirational message at the opening and closing of the graduation ceremonies. Counsel for plaintiff conceded at argument, as she must, that if Rabbi Gutterman had given the exact same invocation as he delivered at the Bishop Middle School on June 20, 1989 with one change—God would be left out—the Establishment Clause would not be implicated.[10]

9. The rationale of the *Stein* decision is far from clear precedent. The case was heard by three judges of the sixth circuit, and each judge wrote an opinion in the case. The opinion for the court adopted *Marsh,* did not apply *Lemon,* but found that language of the challenged prayers did not meet *Marsh's* requirement of nonsectarian prayer. The concurring opinion applied not only the *Marsh* standard, but also applied the *Lemon* test and found that while commencement prayer in general survived *Lemon* scrutiny, the language of the particular prayers in the case did not. The dissenting opinion agreed with much of the two majority opinions, but argued that all commencement prayers passed the *Lemon* test, including those in the *Stein* case.

10. Rabbi Gutterman could have delivered the following benediction:

For the legacy of America where diversity is celebrated and the rights of minorities are

75

The plaintiff here is contesting only an invocation or benediction which invokes a deity or praise of a God.

Finally, in the words of Justice Kennedy, "The case before [the court] illustrates better than most that the judicial power is often difficult in its exercise ... The hard fact is that sometimes we must make decisions we do not like. We make them because they are right, right in the sense that the law and the Constitution, as we see them, compel the result." *Texas v. Johnson*, — U.S. —, 109 S.Ct. 2533, 2548, 105 L.Ed.2d 342 (1989) (Kennedy, J. concurring). The fact is that an unacceptably high number of citizens who are undergoing difficult times in this country are children and young people. School-sponsored prayer might provide hope to sustain them, and principles to guide them in the difficult choices they confront today. But the Constitution as the Supreme Court views it does not permit it. Choices are made in order to protect the interests of all citizens.[11] Unfortunately, in this instance there is no satisfactory middle ground. Neither the legislative, nor the executive, nor the judicial branch may define acceptable prayer. Those who are anti-prayer thus have been deemed the victors. That is the difficult but obligatory choice this Court makes today.

Plaintiff may prepare and present a form of judgment within ten days declaring that the inclusion of prayer in the form of invocations or benedictions at public school promotion or graduation exercises in the City of Providence is unconstitutional in violation of the first amendment and permanently enjoining the School Committee of the City of Providence, its agents or employees from authorizing or encouraging the use of prayer in connection with school graduation or promotion exercises.

SO ORDERED.

> protected, we are thankful. May these young men and women grow up to enrich it.
>
> For the liberty of America, we are thankful. May these new graduates grow up to guard it.
>
> For the political process of America in which its citizens may participate, for its court system where all can seek justice we are thankful. May those we honor this morning always turn to it in trust.
>
> For the destiny of America we are thankful. May the graduates of Nathan Bishop Middle School so live that they might help to share it.
>
> May our aspirations for our country and for these young people, who are our hope for the future, be richly fulfilled.

11. Justice Brennan described the effect of the first amendment in his opinion for the Court in *Grand Rapids School District v. Ball:*

> ... For just as religion throughout history has provided spiritual comfort, guidance, and inspiration to many, it can also serve power-

THE SUPREME COURT OF THE UNITED STATES

OCTOBER TERM, 1991

No. 90-1014

ROBERT E. LEE, ET AL., PETITIONERS,

V.

DANIEL WEISMAN, ETC., RESPONDENT

ON WRIT OF CERTIORARI TO THE UNITED STATES COURT OF APPEALS FOR THE FIRST CIRCUIT

REPLY BRIEF FOR THE PETITIONERS

JOSEPH A. ROTELLA
622 Charles Street
Providence, RI 02904
(401) 861-0012

JAY ALAN SEKULOW
1000 Thomas Jefferson Street, N.W.
Suite 520
Washington, D.C. 20007
(202) 337-2273

CHARLES J. COOPER*
MICHAEL A. CARVIN
PETER J. FERRARA
ROBERT J. CYNKAR
SHAW, PITTMAN, POTTS & TROWBRIDGE
2300 N Street, N.W.
Washington, D.C. 20037
Counsel for Petitioners
**Counsel of Record*

TABLE OF CONTENTS

THE SUPREME COURT OF THE UNITED STATES OCTOBER TERM, 1991 No. 90-1014

ROBERT E. LEE, ET AL., PETITIONERS,
v.
DANIEL WEISMAN, ETC., RESPONDENT

ON WRIT OF CERTIORARI TO THE UNITED STATES COURT OF APPEALS FOR THE FIRST CIRCUIT

REPLY BRIEF FOR THE PETITIONERS

ARGUMENT

I. RESPONDENT'S "NEUTRALITY" TEST IS UNWORKABLE AS A JURIDICAL TOOL, PRODUCING RESULTS UNFAITHFUL TO THE PRINCIPLE EMBODIED IN THE ESTABLISHMENT CLAUSE

A. Respondent's construction of the Establishment Clause requires an exclusively secular civic life for this nation

Respondent argues that *Lemon v. Kurtzman*, 403 U.S. 602 (1971), is the "distillation" of a body of precedent teaching judges to use government "neutrality" toward religion as a standard with which to measure the bounds of the Establishment Clause. Resp. Br. at 16-17. This test, according to Respondent, includes the notion that government is not to act so as to communicate a "message of endorsement" of religion. Resp. Br. at 22-23. Since, in Respondent's mind, the reference to God in Rabbi Gutterman's graduation invocation and benediction constitutes such an endorsement, it is unconstitutional. Resp. Br. at 28-30. The rabbi's reference to God was not "neutral" toward God, and thus was an establishment of religion. Respondent's understanding of the Establishment Clause's requirements punctuates the point advanced in our opening brief: If the familiar and venerable tradition of graduation invocations and benedictions violates the Establishment Clause, what civic expression of religious belief does not?

Respondent, obviously aware of the startling sweep of his vision of the Establishment Clause, opens his argument with an attempt at reassurance. This case, Respondent says, is not about "prayer during presidential inaugurations, congressional sessions, and proclamations of National Days of Thanksgiving." Resp. Br. at 11. But nowhere in his brief can Respondent bring himself to say that those cases, no doubt soon to follow if Respondent prevails here, would or could come out differently under his analysis. Surely our national motto—"In God We Trust"—and our Pledge of Allegiance must be forbidden government "endorsements" of religion under Respondent's view of the "neutrality" required by the Establishment Clause.

Respondent fails to articulate any principled limits on his analysis because his analysis is logically not susceptible to any limit short of its goal: The complete elimination from American civic life of all expressions of religious sentiment. Counsel for one of Respondent's amici has explained elsewhere the logic of Respondent's notion of government "neutrality" toward religion: [The Supreme Court] should not have held that chaplains can open each meeting of a state legislature with prayer, or that municipalities can erect Christmas displays. These decisions are wholly unprincipled and indefensible. A little bit of government support for religion may be only a little bit of establishment, but it is still an establishment. The government should not put "In God We Trust" on coins; it should not open court sessions with "God save the United States and this honorable Court"; and it should not name a city or a naval vessel for the Body of Christ or the Queen of the Angels. Laycock, "Equal Access and Moments of Silence: The Equal Status of Religious Speech by Private Speakers," 81 *Nw. U.L. Rev.* 1, 8 (1986).[1]

---

[1] Prof. Laycock's conclusions concerning the results of the "neutrality" or "no-endorsement" test are shared by some other commentators. See, e.g., Jones, "In God We Trust" and the Establishment Clause, 31 *J. of Church & State* 381, 382 (1989) ("God-references fail the Supreme Court's Establishment Clause doctrines. . . ."); Smith, "Symbols, Perceptions, and Doctrinal Illusions: Establishment Neutrality and the 'No Endorsement' Test," 86 *Mich. L. Rev.* 266, 307 (1987) ("The No-Endorsement Test") ("Ceremonial uses of prayer, such as the invocation given before a legislative session, or public religious allusions such as the motto on coins confessing 'In God We Trust,' may communicate support or approval for religious beliefs."); Loewy, "Rethinking Government Neutrality Towards Religion Under the Establishment Clause: The Untapped Potential of Justice O'Connor's Insight," 69 *N.C.L. Rev.* 1049, 1055–58 (1986) ("Rethinking Government Neutrality") (concluding that the Pledge of Allegiance and the opening of Supreme Court sessions violate the Establishment Clause); Choper, "The Free Exercise Clause: A Structural Overview and an Appraisal of Recent Developments," 27 *Wm. & Mary L. Rev.* 943, 947 (1986) ("The placement of 'In God We Trust' on coins and currency . . . seems to have no real

Some lower courts have embraced this logic of the "neutrality" or "no-endorsement" standard, as can be seen in cases such as those invalidating city seals with religious imagery,[2] as well as in the district court's conclusion below that "God has been ruled out of public education." App. 21a.[3]

The arguments of Respondent and his amici underscore how the secularizing principle they espouse, if indeed embraced by the Constitution, would be amplified in modern American society. They take pains to point out that public schools came along decades after the founding generation. Resp. Br. at 37-38; American Jewish Cong. Br. at 25-32. That is true; indeed, modern American government is no doubt far more pervasively involved in the lives of Americans—both individually and as communities—than the Framers ever contemplated. If Respondent's view of "neutrality" is the rule courts are to apply under the Establishment Clause, the innumerable ways the modern state touches our lives means that a sweeping purge of religious expression from broad ranges of our social intercourse must be in order. See Pet. Br. at 8-9.[4]

Though Respondent's amici claim that their analysis of the Establishment Clause "is a helpful way of explaining that it is not a forbidden benefit to religion to exempt conscientious objectors or otherwise remove burdens from religious practice," American Jewish Cong. Br. at 45, this conclusory statement reveals more their appreciation of the reach of their thinking than some principled way to limit it. As a logical matter, "accommodation" and "endorsement" are not so readily distinguished,[5] and, as a practical matter, commonly spring from the same motivation.[6] This weakness of their "no-endorsement" test as a doctrinal tool is illustrated by criticism from supporters of that test directed at *Lynch v. Donnelly*, 465 U.S. 668 (1984), upholding a town's sponsorship of a nativity scene in a Christmas display, criticism based on the conclusion that the creche constituted an unconstitutional endorsement of religion.[7]

Trying to circumscribe the broad implications of his position for all manner of public acknowledgments of religious values, Respondent seeks to emphasize the "public school setting" as a "crucial" distinction for reaching what he urges as the proper outcome here. Resp. Br. at 11. Yet Respondent's theory that the Establishment Clause mandates government "neutrality" toward religion surely undermines his notion that the "public school setting" is distinct from other civic ceremonies under the Establishment Clause as he understands it. Neutrality is a goal obviously not dependent on a setting nor made more constitutionally endangered in a local public school, as opposed to the chamber of the national legislature or the supreme judicial body of the land. In short, nothing about the graduation setting logically identifies what Respondent advances as "the essential nature of this case," Resp. Br. at 11, in terms of the very analysis

---

purpose other than a religious one. Moreover, the proclamations by almost all our Presidents of national days of Thanksgiving to 'Almighty God' only seem fairly characterized as having a religious purpose."); Lupu, "Keeping the Faith: Religion, Equality and Speech in the U.S. Constitution," 18 *Conn. L. Rev.* 739, 746 n.30 (1986) (urging the elimination of "all references to God in public life").

[2] See, e.g., *Harris v. City of Zion*, 927 F.2d 1401 (7th Cir.), petition for cert. filed, 60 U.S.L.W. 3083 (U.S. July 19, 1991) (No. 91-141); *Friedman v. Board of County Commissioners*, 781 F.2d 777 (10th Cir. 1985), cert. denied, 476 U.S. 1169 (1986). See also *Roberts v. Madigan*, 921 F.2d 1047 (10th Cir. 1990), petition for cert. filed, 59 U.S.L.W. 3654 (U.S. Mar. 15, 1991) (No. 90-1448).

[3] "App." denotes the Appendix to the Petition for a Writ of Certiorari.

[4] See also McConnell, Book Review, 6 *Const. Commentary* 123, 124-25 (1989) (reviewing T. Curry, *The First Freedoms: Church and State in America to the Passage of the First Amendment* (1986)) ("As the scope of government expands into areas that formerly were private and often religious (such as education and social welfare), excluding religion from the governmental sphere becomes a powerful engine of secularization.").

[5] See, e.g., The No-Endorsement Test at 282 ("Far from being mutually exclusive, 'accommodation' and 'endorsement' of religion are much more likely to coincide. Asking whether a law beneficial to religion is an 'endorsement' or an 'accommodation,' therefore, is no more sensible than asking whether a lemon is yellow or sour; the answer in each case is, 'Both.' "). Under Respondent's analysis, providing a government benefit, such as unemployment compensation, solely on account of an individual's religious practices must be seen as a forbidden government endorsement of religion, suggesting that cases like *Thomas v. Review Board*, 450 U.S. 707 (1981), and *Sherbert v. Verner*, 374 U.S. 398 (1963), must be discarded if Respondent prevails here.

[6] See, e.g., McConnell, "Accommodation of Religion," 1985 *Sup. Ct. Rev.* 1, 47 ("Legislative history in an accommodation case is quite likely to reveal that the legislators who cared enough to sponsor the legislation were those who approved of the religious practice in question.").

[7] See, e.g., Rethinking Government Neutrality at 1065. In *Lynch*, Justice O'Connor's understanding of "endorsement" did not extend so far as to render Thanksgiving proclamations, the national motto, judicial ceremonies, and the like unconstitutional, id. at 692-93 (O'Connor, J., concurring), as would Respondent's theory. Indeed, we submit that under the endorsement analysis articulated by Justice O'Connor, the graduation prayers here do not constitute an Establishment Clause violation. See Pet. Br. at 44 nn. 42-43.

Respondent wishes this Court to adopt. That setting thus cannot serve to cabin the expansive implications of Respondent's interpretation of the Establishment Clause.

Close and candid examination of the "no-endorsement" standard thus brings to mind the observation made by Justice Kennedy, joined by the Chief Justice and Justices White and Scalia: Either the endorsement test must invalidate scores of traditional practices recognizing the place religion holds in our culture, or it must be twisted and stretched to avoid inconsistency with practices we know to have been permitted in the past, while condemning similar practices with no greater endorsement effect simply by reason of their lack of historical antecedent. Neither result is acceptable. *County of Allegheny v. American Civil Liberties Union*, 492 U.S. 573, 674 (1989) (Kennedy, J., concurring in the judgment in part and dissenting in part). Strikingly, almost 30 years ago Justice Goldberg warned—while invalidating Bible reading and prayer in public classrooms—that "untutored devotion to the concept of neutrality" could lead to the exact result now sought by Respondent and achieved by the vision of the Establishment Clause he advances;[8] "a brooding and pervasive devotion to the secular and a passive, or even active, hostility to the religious." *Abington School Dist. v. Schempp*, 374 U.S. 203, 306 (1963) (Goldberg, J., concurring).[9] A doctrinal tool that leads lower courts on this drive towards the secular is at war with "the central role religion plays in our society," *Allegheny County*, 492 U.S. at 657 (Kennedy, J., concurring in the judgment in part and dissenting in part), and with the rule of law established by the Framers of the First Amendment.

[8] By their discussion of *Lemon* and the cases that preceded it, Respondent and his amici seem to imply that these precedents have produced workable doctrine with which courts can faithfully and consistently apply the Establishment Clause. See, e.g., Resp. Br. at 16-23; American Jewish Cong. Br. at 32-48; Council on Religious Freedom Br. at 4-12. In so doing, Respondent and his amici have simply ignored the substantial criticism directed at *Lemon* and related cases by members of this Court and by respected scholars. See Pet. Br. at 12 and nn. 10-11. "Although the *Lemon* test has survived for over a decade and a half, few have found the formulation satisfactory." The No-Endorsement Test at 269.

[9] Exclusively secular criteria for all sphere of government activity produce results far from "neutral." See, e.g., McConnell, "Neutrality Under the Religion Clauses," 81 *Nw. U.L. Rev.* 146, 162 (1986) ("If the public school day and all its teaching is strictly secular, the child is likely to learn the lesson that religion is irrelevant to the significant things of this world, or at least that the spiritual realm is radically separate and distinct from the temporal. However unintended, these are lessons about religion. They are not 'neutral.' Studious silence on a subject that parents may say touches all of life is an eloquent refutation.").

B. The Framers' disestablishment decision sought to protect religious choice from government coercion, not to exclude religious expression from civic life

The constitutional analysis of Respondent and his amici rests on a fundamentally confused interpretive methodology, particularly with respect to the use and significance of historical evidence of the Establishment Clause's intended meaning. In short, Respondent and his amici seek to dismiss altogether the direct evidence of what the Framers meant—the statements and conduct of the Framers themselves. Instead, they urge us to look to the history of certain public school controversies that occurred almost a century after the Establishment Clause was framed and adopted, and to what the states did in implementing their own disestablishment policies at the time of the Founding.

In his effort to draw this Court's attention away from the voluminous contemporaneous statements and practices of the Framers, Respondent first caricatures our reliance upon this direct and compelling evidence of the Framers' understanding of the Establishment Clause. According to Respondent, our historical analysis reduces to "anything the Founders did is OK." American Jewish Cong. Br. at 21.[10] We make no such claim. After all, as Respondent correctly suggests, Congress adopted the Sedition Act of 1798, when memories of the framing and ratification of the First Amendment were still fresh. But the Sedition Act provoked a "great controversy" and was "vigorously condemned as unconstitutional." *New York Times Co. v. Sullivan*, 376 U.S. 254, 273-74 (1964). Jefferson (who, along with Madison, led the attack) denounced the Act as "a nullity, as absolute and palpable as if Congress had ordered us to fall down and worship a golden image." Id. at 276.

In contrast, the historical examples of official religious activity described in our opening brief were uncontroversial, inspiring no constitutional crisis, no storm of protest, not even reported litigation. Thus while we grant that it is theoretically possible that the Framers of a constitutional provision could contemporaneously and openly engage in a wide range of practices that they understood to violate that provision, we find it highly unlikely, to say the least, that such dishonorable conduct could pass

[10] Respondent's brief discusses historical evidence only briefly, Resp. Br. at 34-40, but "fully endorses" the "more extensive historical analysis" of amici American Jewish Congress, et al. Id. at 40 n.17. We will therefore attribute to Respondent all historical arguments made by those amici.

without exciting substantial public controversy and constitutional challenge.

Respondent, however, advances precisely the opposite proposition—that this Court should dismiss as irrelevant the Framers' contemporaneous religious statements and practices because they were not controversial. Resp. Br. at 37-38; American Jewish Cong. Br. at 20-25. According to Respondent, "[g]overnment prayer and religious proclamations" were not controversial in the Founders' time because "the nation was overwhelmingly Protestant, and no significant group of Protestants was victimized by these practices." American Jewish Cong. Br. at 25-26. See Resp. Br. at 37-38. This "unexamined Protestant consensus," broke down in the latter half of the nineteenth century, when Catholic complaints about Protestant instruction and Bible reading in the schools led to political turmoil.[11] Only then, says Respondent, did it become clear that government prayer and religious proclamations violate the Establishment Clause. From this premise, Respondent invites this Court to adopt the following interpretive reasoning:

"The [constitutional] principle was the same in both generations: government should not support or endorse religion.... The framers adopted the principle, and they applied it to all issues that were controversial among Protestants. They did not see its application to practices that substantially all Protestants could accept. But they put the principle in the Constitution, ready to be applied to new examples of the same evil." Resp. Br. at 37-38. See American Jewish Cong. Br. at 29-32; Laycock, " 'Nonpreferential' Aid to Religion: A False Claim About Original Intent," 27 *Wm. & Mary L. Rev.* 875, 913-14 (1986).

Adoption of Respondent's interpretive theory requires acceptance of one of two conclusions, neither of which is tenable. Either the Founders knowingly engaged in unconstitutional practices—"[g]overnment prayer and religious proclamations"—because no one complained, or the practices that they engaged in were constitutional until someone complained. The first conclusion follows from Respondent's notions that the principle of the Establishment Clause was clear—no "endorsement" of religion—and that an "avowal of divine faith," such as prayer, is a clear "endorsement" of religion. Resp. Br. at 27; see American Jewish Cong. Br. at 51-52. It follows that the Founders' frequent and official avowals of faith were intentional and knowing constitutional violations.[12] We submit that the more plausible reading of the history surrounding the framing of the First Amendment is that the Framers' religious statements and conduct as government officials were not controversial because they were viewed as clearly consistent with the principle embodied in the Establishment Clause.

The alternative conclusion that could flow from Respondent's argument—that official expressions of religious values were constitutional until they became controversial almost a century after ratification of the First Amendment—obviously represents a novel approach to constitutional adjudication. No one would dispute, certainly not Petitioners, that a constitutional safeguard applies to "new examples of the same evil." Resp. Br. at 38. As we put it in our opening brief, "the First Amendment prohibits modern methods of establishing a religion no less than it prohibits ancient ones." Pet. Br. at 31 n.32 (emphasis omitted). But governmental expressions of religious values are not new. And a practice that was so plainly understood by the Framers to be outside the Establishment Clause's prohibitions does not come within it, ipso facto, simply because the practice, in a different age, becomes "controversial."

In sum, we reiterate our opening brief's point that this case is governed by thc *Marsh* Court's common sense observation that, "[i]n this context, historical evidence sheds light not only on what the draftsmen intended the Establishment Clause to mean, but also on how they thought that Clause applied to the practice authorized by the First Congress—their actions reveal their intent." *Marsh v. Chambers*, 463 U.S. 783, 790 (1983); Pet. Br. at 30. The only rational conclusion that can be drawn from the historical record is not that the religious statements and conduct of the Framers were constitutionally invalid because they were not controversial, but rather that they were not controversial because they were not constitutionally invalid.

[11] These practices apparently continued in one form or another until they were definitively declared unconstitutional in *Engel v. Vitale*, 370 U.S. 421 (1962), and *Abington School Dist. v. Schempp*, 374 U.S. 203 (1967). As we noted in our opening brief, classroom prayer and Bible reading do implicate the principle of the Establishment Clause: the protection of individual religious choice from government coercion. Pet. Br. at 35-44.

[12] Nor can the Founders' religious practices be viewed as some kind of ubiquitous constitutional mistake. The Founders and their intellectual forbears repeatedly explain their establishment philosophy in terms that indicate that they had given the proper relationship of government and religion much careful thought. See Pet. Br. at 14-18; Smith, "Separation and the 'Secular': Reconstructing the Disestablishment Decision," 67 *Tex. L. Rev.* 955, 962–75 (1989) ("Separation").

The only historical evidence offered by Respondent that relates to the relevant time frame—the founding period—focuses exclusively on the legislative development of disestablishment within the states. The Establishment Clause, however, did not even apply to the states at that time; indeed, it had been specifically framed to ensure that Congress would be disabled from interfering with state establishments. See note 22, infra. Quite apart from the doubtful relevance of the state practices cited by Respondent, see *Allegheny County*, 492 U.S. at 670 n.7 (Kennedy, J., concurring in the judgment in part, and dissenting in part) ("[T]he relevant historical practices are those conducted by governmental units which were subject to the constraints of the Establishment Clause."),[13] the substance of those state practices has been seriously mischaracterized by Respondent.

For example, Respondent contends that the South Carolina Constitution of 1778 contained only "a bare endorsement" of the Christian Protestant religion as the established religion of the state, but that it was nevertheless found to be an unacceptable establishment of religion, despite the lack of coercion, and was repealed in the Constitution of 1790. See Resp. Br. at 36; American Jewish Cong. Br. at 3, 14-16. Far from articulating "a bare endorsement of religion," the 1778 South Carolina Constitution mandated numerous coercive requirements.[14] Indeed, widely noted historian Anson Phelps Stokes concluded that the 1778 Constitution included "detailed provisions to insure a Protestant state probably . . . without parallel in our national history." A. Stokes, *Church and State in the United States* 432 (1950) ("Church and State").

Respondent and his amici similarly claim that Virginia created "a bare endorsement" of the Episcopal Church, without any coercion, through the 1784 statute "for incorporating the Protestant Episcopal Church." They again argue that this "bare endorsement" without coercion was found to be an unacceptable establishment of religion and was subsequently repealed. See Resp. Br. at 36-37; American Jewish Cong. Br. at 3, 12-14, 16. But the incorporation statute nowhere stated that the Episcopal Church was to be the established, official church of the state. T. Buckley, *Church and State in Revolutionary Virginia 1776–1787* 106-07 (1977) ("Revolutionary Virginia"); Church and State at 384-87. Indeed, Respondent's amici admits that the "state's endorsement was implicit rather than explicit." American Jewish Cong. Br. at 13. Yet even the characterization of the Act as an "implicit endorsement" does not withstand scrutiny.

The Act transferred authority over the organization and operation of the church, which had been the established church, from the state to the church. To execute this disestablishment, the Act transferred the formerly state-owned property used by the church, including church buildings, surrounding land, and "glebes" farmed for the support of ministers, to church ownership. Church and State at 384–87; Revolutionary Virginia at 106–07. The statute incorporated the church, not to implicitly endorse it as the established church, but because the church now needed a legal form or entity

---

[13] One of Respondent's amici offers a quotation from Jefferson which it contends supports the relevance of early state practice in construing the Establishment Clause. National PEARL Br. at 13 n.21. Examination of the full letter from which the quotation is drawn, however, shows the opposite to be the case. In this letter, Jefferson discusses the practice of the preceding Presidents in issuing Presidential Proclamations of Prayer, in explaining why he, virtually alone among the Presidents, refused to do so on Establishment Clause grounds, believing such proclamations to have a coercive effect. See Pet. Br. at 33-34. Jefferson believed he was so constrained not only because of the Establishment Clause, but also because of the Constitution's provision "which reserves to the states the powers not delegated to the U.S." T. Jefferson, Letter to Rev. Samuel Miller, in 5 *The Founders' Constitution* 98 (P. Kurland & R. Lerner eds. 1987) ("The Founders' Constitution"). He then goes on: "I am aware that the practice of my predecessors may be quoted. But I have ever believed that the example of state executives led to the assumption of that authority by the general government, without due examination, which would have discovered that what might be a right in a state government, was a violation of that right when assumed by another." Id. at 99. Based on this evidence, at least, Jefferson clearly believed that the states may engage in practices that are not prohibited by the Establishment Clause, and, consequently, understood that such state practices are not evidence of what was prohibited by the Clause.

[14] Articles 3, 12, and 13 provided that only members of the Protestant religion could serve in state offices. Under Article 13, only persons who acknowledged a belief in God and in a future state of rewards and punishments could vote. These coercive features of the South Carolina Constitution of 1778 are pointed out by one of Respondent's other amici. See National PEARL Br. at 14. Article 38 of the 1778 Constitution stated that religious toleration would be granted only to persons and religious societies that acknowledge a belief in one God, and a future state of rewards and punishments, and that God is to be publicly worshipped. "Equal religious and civil privileges" were guaranteed only to "denominations of Christian Protestants." In order to "be, and be constituted a church," and become incorporated, a church organization had to subscribe to five designated articles of faith. In addition, no one was allowed to be a minister of a legally recognized church unless they subscribed to the five specified articles of faith, and several additional beliefs. See 6 F. Thorpe, *The Federal and State Constitutions* 3248–57 (1906) ("Federal and State Constitutions").

distinct from that of the state to hold that property and to otherwise go about its affairs. James Madison himself, as a member of the Virginia Assembly, voted for the bill, explaining: "The necessity of some sort of incorporation for the purpose of holding and managing the property of the church could not well be denied, nor a more harmless modification of it now obtained." Church and State at 386. See also Revolutionary Virginia at 106-07. Indeed, the support of Madison and his allies in the Assembly created the majority in favor of the bill.[15]

Respondent argues that the Virginia general assessment bill proposed by Patrick Henry in 1785 did not involve coercion, but was nevertheless rejected as an establishment of religion. Resp. Br. at 35-36; American Jewish Cong. Br. at 16-17. The bill, however, clearly was coercive. Each taxpayer's funds were to be distributed to the Christian denomination designated by that taxpayer, or to a general state fund that would be used to support the local schools in each county. All schooling at the time was private and inextricably intertwined with religious values and teachings.[16] Thus, whether directed to a denomination of the taxpayer, or distributed to a school by a state fund, such assessments unavoidably compelled taxpayers to contribute to certain religious activities.[17]

Notably, parties on both sides of the assessment debate did not question the compulsion involved in an assessment. Proponents of assessments expressly acknowledged their coercive effects, arguing that since all received the civil benefits of a religious citizenry, all should be compelled to contribute to religion.[18] Madison, the leading opponent of the Virginia assessment, opposed the bill precisely because of its coercive quality, as he eloquently set out in his historic Memorial and Remonstrance. Pet. Br. at 21-22.[19] While the assessment bill provoked debate over many issues, the permissibility of a "bare endorsement" of religion was not among them.[20]

The arguments of Respondent and his amici that purport to draw on history fail not only because they do not seriously challenge the conclusion that coercion of religious choice was the focus of the Framers,[21] but because they

[15] Church and State at 386. Moreover, the controversy regarding repeal of the Act arose out of the grant of the formerly state property to the church, not that the bill provided an "endorsement" of the Episcopal Church. Revolutionary Virginia at 65-72, 140, 167, 171. While the legislature had originally viewed the grant of state property in the incorporation act as clarifying the effective current property rights of the Episcopal Church, id. at 166-69, the repeal forces viewed the Act as effectively granting a large amount of state financial aid, raised by coercive general taxation, to the Church. The motivating concern behind the repeal movement was, therefore, a coercive practice that from the dissenters' perspective hardly amounted to a "bare endorsement." Indeed, because the 1787 repeal of the incorporation act left the property in church hands, the controversy continued after repeal of the incorporation act, until 1802, when the legislature authorized the seizure and sale of all the property granted to the Episcopal Church in the 1784 act, except the church buildings and their immediate surrounding land. Id. at 170-72.

[16] See, e.g., J. Whitehead, *The Rights of Religious Persons in Public Education* 41–42 (1991); R. Michaelsen, *Piety in the Public School* 80–81, 85 (1970); F. Eby and C. Arrowood, *The Development of Modern Education in Theory, Organization and Practice* 538–39, 548–49 (1934).

[17] The fact that ministers and church organizations led the fight for state-mandated assessments further indicates that the practical effect of an assessment was to compel contributions to denominations that might not have been made voluntarily.

[18] See Church and State at 388 (The first petition asking for the general assessment bill complained that without it the people were "left without the smallest coercion to contribute to" religion, and asked for an act "to compel every one to contribute something . . . to the support of religion."); First Freedoms at 138-140, 145.

[19] See also J. Curry, *The First Freedoms: Church and State in America to the Passage of the First Amendment* 136, 144–45, 147 (1990) ("First Freedoms"); Church and State at 389-391; Revolutionary Virginia at 138, 140, 149-51.

[20] Respondent and his amici attempt to use the Maryland assessment bill, also rejected in 1785, to the same effect. Resp. Br. at 35-36; American Jewish Cong. Br. at 17-19. This tax was again effectively coercive for those not exempt, for the same reasons as the Virginia bill. Moreover, the Maryland bill was not rejected because it was an establishment of religion, since Maryland maintained a religious establishment throughout this period. Christianity was declared the official state religion, public office was limited to Christians, and the constitutional protection for religious liberty was limited to "all persons professing the Christian religion." First Freedoms at 153-54, 157-58. The legislature also continued to exercise organizational control in minute detail over the Anglican church. Id. at 153-54. Indeed, for many years after the assessment bill was rejected, the state constitution retained a provision empowering the legislature to "lay a general and equal tax for the support of the Christian religion." Id. at 154, 157.

[21] Respondent's amici believes the coercion of religious choice could not be the vice at which the Establishment Clause is targeted because such a conclusion would leave no "independent meaning" to the Clause. American Jewish Cong. Br. at 9. Such an argument creates an artificial distinction, for both of the Religion Clauses seek to preserve religious choice from interference by government power, proceeding from a common fundamental philosophical premise that such interference is beyond the jurisdiction of civil government. See Pet. Br. at 14-18. Applications of the Free Exercise and Establishment Clauses may overlap, but they are directed at different types of government action, the first a government prohibition of religious belief or practice, the second the exercise of government power in favor of a religious belief. For example, an ordinance prohibiting all religions from owning property would be a burden on the free exercise of religion; a religiously-motivated statute bestowing direct financial aid only to religions would be an impermissible establishment of religion; and a regulation making members of only one religious

also do not establish that the secularizing results of their "no-endorsement" test could have been a serious goal of the Framers, and so be the animating principle of the Establishment Clause.[22] As demonstrated in our opening submission, the architects of our tradition of religious liberty premised their cause on explicitly religious philosophical principles, arguing that the reforms they sought were Divinely inspired. Pet. Br. at 14-22, 30-34. That they did without hesitation or embarrassment, underscores the pervasiveness of religious values and assumptions in the thinking of that time and hence the unlikelihood that citizens of that generation could have viewed a secular political culture purged of religious content as a live alternative. Separation at 969.

In the historical circumstances of the Framers, the coercive power of the state was able to constrain religious liberty due to the institutional integration of church and state. "[G]overnments controlled or directly intervened in the internal affairs of churches, and churches claimed and were formally endowed with governmental powers."[23] By undoing this institutional integration, the Framers freed religious choice from the specter of government's coercive powers. Thus, faithful application of the Framers' disestablishment decision, and of the rule of law they intended to embody in the Establishment Clause, yields the conclusion that the First Amendment can be violated only by the governmental coercion of religious choice, whether directly or indirectly, but not by the expression of religious values in our civic life.

denomination or sect eligible for a government benefit would be both. Moreover, even a neutral law prohibiting religious practice implicates free exercise rights, but raises no establishment concerns.

[22] Respondent tries to tease such an expansive, secular goal out of the Establishment Clause by arguing that the word "respecting" means the Clause was designed to address any action touching religion. See Resp. Br. at 39-40. But the word "respecting" was used in the Clause to prohibit the federal government from enacting laws "respecting" or "concerning" the many state establishments existing at the time, as well as to prohibit it from creating its own establishment. See R. Cord, *Separation of Church and State: Historical Fact and Current Fiction* 5, 9, 12–15, 49, 127 (1982); M. Malbin, *Religion and Politics: The Intentions of the Authors of the First Amendment* 4, 9–15 (1978); Note, "Jefferson and the Church-State Wall: A Historical Examination of the Man and the Metaphor," 1978 *B.Y.U.L. Rev.* 645, 651-53; Kruse, "The Historical Meaning and Judicial Construction of the Establishment of Religion Clause of the First Amendment," 2 *Washburn L.J.* 65, 85, 89 (1962). Even the use of the word "touching," as proposed by Rep. Livermore, did not embrace a secularizing goal, but, consistent with Livermore's anti-Federalist views, was designed to bar federal power from affecting state establishments. See id.

[23] Id. at 963.

II. NO ONE'S RELIGIOUS BELIEFS WERE SUBJECTED TO GOVERNMENT COERCION DURING THE GRADUATION CEREMONY

Respondent claims that we have employed a "limited definition of coercion," failing to appreciate "the subtle pressures . . . in the school setting." Resp. Br. at 10. Quite the contrary, in our opening brief, we recognized the importance of sensitivity to subtle forms of coercion. Pet. Br. at 36; see also *Allegheny County*, 492 U.S. at 659-60 (Kennedy, J., concurring in the judgment in part and dissenting in part). In that brief, Pet. Br. at 39-44, we went on to point out that the classroom setting, due to compulsory attendance,[24] the role of the teacher as an authority figure, and the fundamental pedagogical premise of the environment, may render young students "susceptible to unwilling religious indoctrination." *Wallace v. Jaffree*, 472 U.S. 38, 81 (1985) (O'Connor, J., concurring in the judgment). See also *Edwards v. Aguillard*, 482 U.S. 578, 584 (1987) ("The State exerts great authority and coercive power through mandatory attendance requirements. . . .").

While underscoring the supposed importance for Establishment Clause analysis of some generic "public school setting," Respondent seeks to depreciate the precise attributes of the actual setting of the graduation invocation and benediction here, Resp. Br. at 28-30, attributes which reveal these graduation exercises to be a "noncoercive setting" devoid of those elements of subtle coercion that have been of concern to this Court in the past.[25] As this Court put it recently, "there is little if any risk of official state endorsement or coercion where no formal classroom activities are involved." *Board of Educ. v. Mergens*, 110 S. Ct. at 2372. Respondent simply overlooks the complete absence in the

[24] Once it is determined that attendance at a public event is not compulsory, as was the case here, the coercion inquiry logically is at an end. See Pet. Br. at 39-41. Even if attendance is compulsory, the other features of the event, as in the graduation exercises here, may nevertheless lead to the conclusion that no coercion, even indirect, of religious choice is evident. See Pet. Br. at 41-44.

[25] The "heightened vigilance" in all this Court's cases applying the Establishment Clause in the public school context arises from coercive features, intrinsic to the classroom, such as mandatory attendance requirements and the like. Yet Respondent has embraced the very passages from *Wallace* and *Edwards* (quoted in text) that make this apparent, ignoring the obvious point of the Court's analysis. See Resp. Br. at 14-16. Indeed, where mandatory attendance requirements are not involved in a public school setting, this Court has found no Establishment Clause violation. *Widmar v. Vincent*, 454 U.S. 263 (1981); *Board of Educ. v. Mergens*, 110 S. Ct. 2356 (1990).

graduation setting of those facts that make the classroom so distinctive for Establishment Clause analysis. See, e.g., *Abington School Dist. v. Schempp*, supra (Bible readings part of prescribed curriculum; conducted under supervision of teachers; children may be excused during reading); *Engel v. Vitale*, supra (state-drafted school prayer).

The graduation ceremonies at issue here are not held during class; they are not necessarily even held at a public school. J.A. 12-17. Students choose to be present; the ceremony is short, occurs only once in a student's career, and does not involve teaching; and virtually all of the students who choose to attend are in the company of their parents.[26]

Thus, the potentially coercive aspects of the classroom setting are not present at graduation exercises.[27] As for the importance of the occasion and the other attributes noted by Respondent, Resp. Br. at 28-30, they simply do not distinguish a public school graduation ceremony from many other civic ceremonies. If the desire of Respondent to attend his daughter's graduation requires the censorship of Rabbi Gutterman's prayers here, surely George Bush should have been barred at his inaugural from making a prayer his "first act as President."[28]

Respondent's complaint, after all, is that he "is opposed to and offended by the inclusion of prayer in the public school graduation ceremony." J.A. 5. He does not contend that he or his daughter were subjected to unwanted efforts at indoctrination in Judaism, that they were penalized for not subscribing to Rabbi Gutterman's expression of religious values, or even that they were subject to pressure, ostracism, or embarrassment as a result of their views of the rabbi's prayers. J.A. 2-7 (Complaint); J.A. 10-19, 24 (Agreed Statement of Facts). Nor do the facts here reveal the indirect coercion that can result from compelling a student to attend class and to opt out of a classroom religious activity. "No one was compelled to observe or participate in any religious ceremony or activity." *Allegheny County*, 492 U.S. at 664 (Kennedy, J., concurring in the judgment in part and dissenting in part).

Respondent has simply been unable to point to any feature of the graduation invocation and benediction here that poses a "realistic risk" that these prayers "represent an effort to proselytize or are otherwise the first step down the road to an establishment of religion." Id. Failing to employ governmental power to directly or indirectly coerce the religious choice of the graduating students, Rabbi Gutterman's invocation and benediction did not violate the Establishment Clause.

CONCLUSION

For the foregoing reasons, and for the reasons stated in our opening brief, the judgment of the court of appeals should be reversed.

---

[26] It is precisely these kinds of characteristics that have led lower courts to conclude that a graduation ceremony is quite different from "a classroom setting, where the prospect of subtle official and peer coercion warrants stricter separation of the state from things religious." *Jones v. Clear Creek Indep. School Dist.*, 930 F.2d 416, 422 (5th Cir. 1991). See *Albright v. Board of Educ.*, No. 90-C-639G, slip op. at 16 (D. Utah May 15, 1991) (secondary school graduation invocations and benedictions delivered in "voluntary and non-coercive circumstances"); Pet. Br. at 42 & n.4.

[27] Obviously aware of this distinction, Respondent is reduced to a transparent exaggeration to link graduation with normal classroom activities, arguing that "[p]romotional and graduation ceremonies are as integral to a child's school career as is daily class attendance." Resp. Br. at 16.

[28] George Bush, Inaugural Address, January 20 1989 in *Inaugural Addresses of the Presidents of the United States from George Washington, 1789 to George Bush, 1989* at 346 (Bicentennial ed. 1989).

THE SUPREME COURT OF THE UNITED STATES

OCTOBER TERM, 1991

NO. 90-1014

ROBERT E. LEE, ET AL., PETITIONERS,
v.
DANIEL WEISMAN, ETC., RESPONDENT

ON WRIT OF CERTIORARI TO THE UNITED STATES COURT OF APPEALS FOR THE FIRST CIRCUIT

RESPONDENT'S BRIEF

SANDRA A. BLANDING (Counsel of Record)
REVENS BLANDING
Revens & St. Pierre
946 Centerville Road
Warwick, Rhode Island 02886
(401) 822-2900

STEVEN R. SHAPIRO
JOHN A. POWELL
American Civil Liberties Union Foundation
132 West 43 Street
New York, New York 10036
(212) 944-9800

TABLE OF CONTENTS

THE SUPREME COURT OF THE UNITED STATES OCTOBER TERM, 1991 NO. 90-1014

ROBERT E. LEE, ET AL., PETITIONERS,
V.
DANIEL WEISMAN, ETC., RESPONDENT

ON WRIT OF CERTIORARI TO THE UNITED STATES COURT OF APPEALS FOR THE FIRST CIRCUIT

RESPONDENT'S BRIEF

STATEMENT OF THE CASE

Respondent Daniel Weisman, whose daughter Deborah attends a public school in the City of Providence, Rhode Island, initiated this action in June 1989, in order to prevent the inclusion of prayer in Deborah's eighth grade promotional ceremony from the Nathan Bishop Middle School. The district court allowed the ceremony to proceed as scheduled.[1] The parties then submitted the case to the district court upon an Agreed Statement of Facts, which is summarized below.

At the close of each school year, the Members of the Providence School Committee and the Superintendent of Schools sponsor a promotional ceremony in each of the City's public middle schools and a graduation ceremony in each of the City's public high schools. (J.A.12, P11).[2] Eighth grade promotional ceremonies for the public middle schools are routinely conducted on school premises; high school graduation ceremonies are generally conducted in auditoriums which petitioners rent for the occasion. (J.A.13-16, PP19-29; J.A.17, P34). Petitioners supervise and authorize the content of the public school promotional and graduation ceremonies. (J.A.12, P12). Their practice has been to allow the principal of each middle school and each high school to include, in the school's ceremony, an invocation and benediction in the form of prayer, delivered by clergy who are selected by school department employees. (J.A.12, P13; J.A.18, P40).

In June 1989, when respondent initiated this action, his daughter Deborah was an eighth grade student in the Nathan Bishop Middle School, a public school in the City of Providence. (J.A.10, P3). Teachers at the Nathan Bishop Middle School had planned a promotional ceremony for eighth grade students and had suggested to the principal, petitioner Robert E. Lee, that Rabbi Leslie Gutterman be asked to deliver an invocation and benediction at the ceremony. (J.A.12-13, P16). Petitioner Lee conveyed the invitation to Rabbi Gutterman, who accepted. (J.A.17, P36).

Prior to the actual ceremony, petitioner Lee provided to Rabbi Gutterman a pamphlet entitled "Guidelines for Civic Occasions," published by the National Conference of Christians and Jews. (J.A.13, P17). This pamphlet specifies the type of "public prayer" which should be composed for civic occasions. (J.A.20-21). Petitioners had distributed this pamphlet to all of the principals of Providence's middle schools and high schools as a guideline for the type of prayer to be included in the promotional and graduation ceremonies conducted in Providence's public schools. (J.A.12, PP14-15). Petitioner Lee also instructed Rabbi Gutterman personally that the prayers he delivered at Nathan Bishop's promotional ceremony should be nonsectarian. (J.A.13, P17).

The parties agree that the invocation and benediction delivered by Rabbi Gutterman are prayers. (J.A. 17, P36). For his invocation, Rabbi Gutterman prayed, as follows: God of the Free, Hope of the Brave: For the legacy of America where diversity is celebrated and the rights of minorities are protected, we thank You. May these young men and women grow up to enrich it. For the liberty of America, we thank You. May these new graduates grow up to guard it. For the political process of America in which all its citizens may participate, for its court system where all can seek justice we thank You. May those we honor this morning always turn to it in trust. For the destiny of America we thank You. May the graduates of Nathan Bishop Middle School so live that they might help to share it. May our aspirations for our country and for these young people, who are our hope for the future, be richly fulfilled.

AMEN

---

[1] Daniel Weisman filed his initial complaint four days before the Nathan Bishop Middle School's promotional ceremony was scheduled to be held. The district court judge denied his Motion for a Temporary Restraining Order on the ground that the court did not have sufficient time, prior to the scheduled ceremony, to adequately address the issues presented. Deborah Weisman now attends Classical High School, a public high school in the City of Providence whose graduation ceremonies generally include prayer. (J.A.10, P3; J.A.13-14, P20).

[2] References to the joint appendix are preceded by letters "J.A." The decisions below, which were included in the appendix to the petition for certiorari, are cited at "App.A" or "App.B."

(J.A.22). For his benediction, Rabbi Gutterman offered the following prayer: O God, we are grateful to You for having endowed us with the capacity for learning which we have celebrated on this joyous commencement. Happy families give thanks for seeing their children achieve an important milestone. Send Your blessings upon the teachers and administrators who helped prepare them. The graduates now need strength and guidance for the future, help them to understand that we are not complete with academic knowledge alone. We must each strive to fulfill what You require of us all: To do justly, to love mercy, to walk humbly. We give thanks to You, Lord, for keeping us alive, sustaining us and allowing us to reach this special, happy occasion.

AMEN

(J.A.23).

From 1985 through 1989, many, but not all, graduation ceremonies conducted by the City of Providence's public high schools included invocations and benedictions in the form of prayer, delivered by clergy.[3] (J.A.13, P18). In each case in which prayers were included, the respective high school produced and distributed a program that identified the name and institutional affiliation of the clergy who delivered the prayers. (J.A.13-14, PP19-22). During the same time period, Providence's six public middle schools conducted annual promotional ceremonies for eighth grade students. All of these ceremonies took place on the premises of the respective school. (J.A.15-16, PP23-28). Two of the six public middle schools included invocations and benedictions in the form of prayer in their ceremonies; the remaining four schools did not include prayer in their promotional ceremonies. Like the high schools, each middle school produced programs that identified the clergy delivering the invocation and benediction. (J.A.15, PP23-24). Parents and friends of students are invited to attend Providence public schools' promotional and/or graduation ceremonies. (J.A.18, P42). Attendance at the ceremony is not mandatory for students. (J.A.18, P41).

In holding that the practice of including prayer in public school graduation and promotional ceremonies violates the Establishment Clause of the United States Constitution, the district court noted: "The [Supreme] Court has been particularly vigilant in monitoring compliance with the Establishment Clause in elementary and secondary schools." *Edwards v. Aquillard* [sic], 482 U.S. 578, 583-84 (1987).... This vigilance is based upon the perceived sensitive nature of the school environment and the apprehended effect of State-led religious activity on young, impressionable minds. App.B at 21a-22a (citation omitted).

Relying on established precedent, the district court analyzed the facts before it under the three-pronged test set forth in *Lemon v. Kurtzman*, 403 U.S. 602 (1971). Specifically, the district court held that "the benediction and invocation advance religion by creating an identification of school with a deity, and therefore religion." App.B at 24a (footnote omitted). This prohibited effect was heightened, according to the district court, by the fact that the challenged prayers were offered at graduation ceremonies. "It is the union of prayer, school, and important occasion that creates an identification of religion with a school function. The special nature of the graduation ceremonies underscores the identification that Providence public school students can make." App.B at 24a. The court then evaluated whether or not the identification of school with religion conveyed a message endorsing a particular religion or religion in general. After reviewing the facts in the record, the court concluded that petitioners' practice did convey such a message. App.B at 25a.[4]

Petitioners argued before the district court that the constitutionality of their policy concerning prayer at middle school promotional ceremonies and at high school graduation ceremonies should be analyzed under *Marsh v. Chambers*, 463 U.S. 783 (1983). The court rejected *Marsh* as inapplicable to prayer in a public school setting. App.B at 27a. Furthermore, the district court held "[e]xtending the Marsh analysis to school benedictions is arguably unworkable because it results in courts reviewing the content of prayers to judicially approve what are acceptable invocations to a deity.... What must follow is a gradual judicial development of what is acceptable public prayer." Id. (citations omitted).

The United States Court of Appeals for the First Circuit affirmed the district court's decision, with Judge Campbell dissenting. App.A at 1a-17a. The majority opinion simply adopted the reasoning of the lower court; however, Judge Bownes' concurring opinion elaborated on the purpose and entanglement prongs of the

[3] Of five public high schools located in the City of Providence, only one high school never included prayer in its graduation ceremonies during the five year period reviewed in the record. (J.A.16, P29).

[4] Because the court found that the challenged practice has the effect of advancing and endorsing religion, its analysis does not address issues of purpose and entanglement. App.B at 2a.

Lemon test, which were not addressed by the district court. App.A at 2a, 9a-11a. Judge Bownes found that the primary purpose of prayer at a graduation ceremony is religious and that "a prayer given by a religious person chosen by public school teachers communicates a message of government endorsement of religion." App.A at 9a-10a. Judge Bownes also found that the specific facts of this case raise entanglement concerns for two reasons. First, school teachers choose speakers among various religious groups. Second, school officials engage in the supervision and regulation of the content of the prayers offered by clergy. App.A at 10a.

Judge Campbell's dissenting opinion tacitly concedes that petitioners' practice is unconstitutional under existing precedent. Consequently, he is forced to articulate a new rule that would provide for the allowance of invocations and benedictions at ceremonial occasions, provided that speakers are rotated among "representatives of the Judeo-Christian religion . . . representatives of other religions and of nonreligious ethical philosophies. . . ." App.A at 16a. As Judge Campbell himself recognizes, however, "[i]t may be . . . that even more needs to be done, to insure not only that the state does not identify itself with a particular religion but with religion generally." Id.

SUMMARY OF ARGUMENT

The issue in this case is whether public school officials violate the Establishment Clause when they include prayer as an integral part of promotional or graduation ceremonies, choose the clergy who appear at each ceremony, and monitor the content of prayers that are delivered to the assembled students. The court below found that such practices cannot be sustained under any interpretation of the Establishment Clause ever adopted by this Court. That decision is correct and should be affirmed.

Petitioners do not seriously quarrel with the decision below. Instead, they have seized upon this case as a vehicle to ask the Court to overturn more than four decades of well-settled law and rule, for the first time, that there can be no "establishment" of religion in the absence of coercion. It is an old and discredited argument that has been rejected by this Court on numerous occasions including, most recently, only two years ago. See *County of Allegheny v. ACLU*, 492 U.S. 573 (1989). If it is even reached in this case (since it was not raised below), it can and should be rejected again.

Because petitioners' attack is focused more on this Court's Establishment Clause jurisprudence than the decision below, their brief continuously refers to practices that are not at issue in this case, such as Thanksgiving Day proclamations. In so doing, petitioners distort the issues before this Court and ignore the Court's historic awareness of "the sensitive relationship between government and religion and the education of our children." *Grand Rapids School District v. Ball*, 473 U.S. 373, 383 (1985).

By focusing exclusively on the *Lemon* test, petitioners also ignore this Court's explicit recognition that *Lemon* did not create a new test but merely distilled the principles articulated in previous decisions. Before and after *Lemon*, this Court has consistently stressed that the Establishment Clause requires government neutrality toward religion in order to preserve the integrity of both. See, e.g., *Abington v. Schempp*, 374 U.S. 203, 226 (1963). It is that principle, not just *Lemon*, that petitioners have violated.

This is not a case where the religious significance of the challenged practice is questionable or marginal. Petitioners have stipulated that this is a case about prayer, and this Court has consistently described prayer as an inherently religious activity. By incorporating prayer into a major public school ceremony, petitioners have violated every prong of the *Lemon* test. The unavoidable message delivered to the school children is that school officials support and encourage participation in a religious exercise. Efforts to dilute that message by reviewing the prayer before it is delivered only entangle school officials with religious practices that should remain the domain of the clergy.

Citing *Marsh v. Chambers*, 463 U.S. 783, petitioners contend that the use of prayer at public school promotional and graduation ceremonies is consistent with other historical practices of the framers and, therefore, must be consistent with the Establishment Clause. Confronted with similar arguments in the past, this Court has noted that "a historical approach is not useful in determining the proper roles of church and state in public schools. . . ." *Edwards v. Aguillard*, 482 U.S. 578, 583 n.4 (1987). Moreover, *Marsh* itself carefully distinguished between religious practices aimed at adults and those directed at children who are more susceptible to "religious indoctrination." 463 U.S. at 792.

Petitioners' use of history to support their proposed coercion test is equally flawed. It is true that the founding generation opposed the coercion of religious beliefs. However, it is also true that the founding generation opposed the noncoercive endorsement of religion, and repealed a variety of provisions providing for such endorsement during the very years that the Constitution was being debated and adopted. Respecting that history, this Court has squarely and repeatedly rejected any claim that coercion is a necessary element of the Establishment Clause. See, e.g., *Engel v. Vitale*, 370 U.S. 421, 431 (1962); *Abington v. Schempp*, 374 U.S. at 224-25; *Committee for Public Education v. Nyquist*, 413 U.S. 756, 786 (1973).

Finally, petitioners' definition of coercion disregards the subtle pressures that the Court has always recognized as coercive, especially in the school setting. Indeed, no member of this Court has ever adopted the limited definition of coercion that petitioners now embrace. The pressure upon public school children to conform to their classmates' behavior and their teachers' expectations and instructions does not vanish when the classroom door closes and the graduation march begins. Petitioners' unwillingness to recognize that fact highlights the unsuitability of their proposed coercion test.

ARGUMENT

I. PETITIONERS' PRACTICE OF INVITING CLERGY TO OFFER PRAYERS AT THE PROMOTIONAL AND GRADUATION CEREMONIES HELD BY PUBLIC MIDDLE SCHOOLS AND HIGH SCHOOLS VIOLATES THE ESTABLISHMENT CLAUSE UNDER ANY CRITERIA EVER ADOPTED BY THIS COURT

A. Any analysis of the constitutionality of petitioners' practice of including prayer in public school promotional and graduation ceremonies must begin with recognition of the special nature of the public school setting

Petitioners' global analogies which liken prayer in public school promotional and graduation ceremonies to prayer during presidential inaugurations, congressional sessions, and proclamations of National Days of Thanksgiving, are a thinly disguised attempt to escape the essential nature of this case. Unlike petitioners' analogies, this case is about the constitutionality of prayer in a public school setting. That distinction is crucial, moreover. This Court has consistently recognized that the introduction of religion into the public schools raises special and severe problems under the Establishment Clause. Thus, while acknowledging the value of prayer " 'based on our spiritual heritage,' " *Engel v. Vitale*, 370 U.S. at 425 (citation omitted), and posting of the Ten Commandments " 'as the fundamental legal code of Western Civilization and the Common Law of the United States,' " *Stone v. Graham*, 449 U.S. 39, 41 (1980) (citations omitted), this Court has never hesitated to strike down such practices when undertaken as part of public education.

Because of this Court's enhanced sensitivity towards Establishment Clause violations within the public schools, a constitutional analysis of prayer at public school functions is intrinsically distinct and segregable from considerations applicable to other public arenas. Justice Frankfurter eloquently traced the roots of this special concern in a concurring opinion in Ill. ex rel. *McCollum v. Board of Education*, 333 U.S. 203, 212 (1948), in which he took note of the fierce struggles for state support among conflicting denominations that led to a burgeoning public school system, removed from the divisiveness of competing religious groups: Zealous watchfulness against fusion of secular and religious activities by Government itself, through any of its instruments but especially through its educational agencies, was the democratic response of the American community to the particular needs of a young and growing nation, unique in the composition of its people. . . . The sharp confinement of the public schools to secular education was a recognition of the need of a democratic society to educate its children, insofar as the State undertook to do so, in an atmosphere free from pressures in a realm in which pressures are most resisted and where conflicts are most easily and most bitterly engendered. Designed to serve as perhaps the most powerful agency for promoting cohesion among a heterogeneous democratic people, the public school must keep scrupulously free from entanglement in the strife of sects. Id. at 215–17 (footnote omitted).

The importance of maintaining strict neutrality toward religion within the public education system is a thread that weaves together all modern Establishment Clause decisions of this Court addressing the juxtaposition of religion and public schools. Since this Court first began to grapple with the meaning and intent of the Establishment Clause, it has decreed both advocacy for religion and hostility towards religion out of bounds within this nation's public schools. In his lengthy concurrence in *Abington v. Schempp*, 374 U.S. 203, Justice Brennan summarized the Court's views on religion in the public schools: [T]he American experiment in free public education available to all children has been guided in large measure by the dramatic evolution of the religious diversity among the population which our public schools serve. The interaction of these two important forces in our national life has placed in bold relief certain positive values in the consistent application to public institutions generally, and public schools particularly, of the constitutional decree against official involvements of religion which might produce the evils the Framers meant the Establishment Clause to forestall.... It is implicit in the history and character of American public education that the public schools serve a uniquely public function: the training of American citizens in an atmosphere free of parochial, divisive, or separatist influences of any sort—an atmosphere in which children may assimilate a heritage common to all American groups and religions.... [T]his is a heritage neither theistic nor atheistic, but simply civic and patriotic. Id. at 241-42 (citations omitted).

Like Justice Frankfurter, Justice Brennan recognized the unique role filled by public education in a country that, over time, has become extraordinarily diverse in the religious beliefs of its citizens.[5] In *Epperson v. Arkansas*, 393 U.S. 97, 104-05 (1968), the Court reaffirmed its special concern for religious practices in the public schools, citing with approval *Shelton v. Tucker*, 364 U.S. 479, 487 (1960)(" '[T]he vigilant protection of constitutional freedoms is nowhere more vital than in the community of American schools' "), and *Keyishian v. Board of Regents*, 385 U.S. 589, 603 (1967)("[T]he First Amendment 'does not tolerate laws that cast a pall of orthodoxy over the classroom' ").

Recent decisions of this Court continue to recognize the special role of the public education system in our society, coupled with the understanding that public school children are more susceptible than adults to religious messages. Rejecting a comparison between presidential proclamations celebrating Thanksgiving and a period of silence for the purpose of prayer in the public schools, Justice O'Connor has observed: At the very least, Presidential Proclamations are distinguishable from school prayer in that they are received in a non-coercive setting and are primarily directed at adults, who presumably are not readily susceptible to unwilling religious indoctrination. This Court's decisions have recognized a distinction when government-sponsored religious exercises are directed at impressionable children who are required to attend school, for then government endorsement is much more likely to result in coerced religious beliefs. *Wallace v. Jaffree*, 472 U.S. 38, 81 (1985) (O'Connor, J., concurring) (citations omitted). See also *Grand Rapids School District v. Ball*, 473 U.S. at 383 ("We have particularly relied on *Lemon* in every case involving the sensitive relationship between government and religion in the education of our children. The government's activities in this area can have a magnified impact on impressionable young minds...."); *Edwards v. Aguillard*, 482 U.S. at 583–84 ("The Court has been particularly vigilant in monitoring compliance with the Establishment Clause in elementary and secondary schools.... The State exerts great authority and coercive power through mandatory attendance requirements, and because of the students' emulation of teachers as role models and the children's susceptibility to peer pressure") (footnote omitted) (citation omitted).[6]

Petitioners choose to ignore the consistent recognition by this Court, spanning more than forty years, that the public education system in this country fills a unique and vital role in the lives of our children and in the continued vitality of constitutional principles upon which this country is founded. This case is not about presidential proclamations, inaugural ceremonies, or the opening of legislative or judicial sessions. Rather, this case is about prayer in a public school sponsored event, delivered by a member of the clergy chosen by a public school official, and both planned and supervised by school officials as the culmination of a child's progress through the public school system. To suggest that the special vigilance which this Court has long accorded in evaluating religious practices within the public schools is inapplicable here is to blink at reality. Promotional and

[5] In *Edwards v. Aguillard*, 482 U.S. at 607 n.6, Justice Powell in his concurrence noted that "The Encyclopedia of American Religions (2d ed. 1987) describes 1,347 religious organizations."

[6] This Court reaffirmed, just one year ago, its deep concern with the intermingling of public school officials, religion, and school children. *Board of Education v. Mergens*, ___U.S. ___, 110 S.Ct. 2356 (1990). Applying the *Lemon* test to an Establishment Clause challenge to the Equal Access Act, the *Mergens* Court carefully reviewed the limitations imposed by the Act on any involvement of school officials in voluntary, student-organized and student-led groups. Because the Act on its face prohibited the school from sponsoring religious groups or their meetings, limited school official involvement to custodial, "non-participatory" attendance, and forbade any state influence of any religious activity, the Court's plurality held that the purpose of the Act was to "prevent discrimination against religious and other types of speech," and that no message of school endorsement was conveyed by the mere allowance of a wide variety of student-initiated and student-led clubs. Id. at 2370–73. The basic thesis underlying the Court's analysis in *Mergens* was the creation of a limited public forum for student groups. The facts in this case are not remotely comparable—here, public school teachers chose a member of the clergy to deliver prayers at an event run by and organized by public school officials. Those same officials directed the clergy they chose regarding the content of the prayers he or she was to deliver.

graduation ceremonies are as integral to a child's school career as is daily class attendance.[7] Any analysis of a school policy pertaining to these ceremonies which implicates Establishment Clause concerns must begin with the heightened vigilance accorded to religious practices in the public schools.

B. The *Lemon* test reflects the concept that the Establishment Clause mandates neutrality and autonomy between public schools and religion

For the past twenty years, this Court and the lower courts have consistently relied on the so-called *Lemon* test in evaluating Establishment Clause claims. As Justice Powell has observed, *Lemon* "identifies standards that have proved useful in analyzing case after case both in our decisions and in those of other courts. It is the only coherent test a majority of the Court has ever adopted." *Wallace v. Jaffree*, 472 U.S. at 63 (Powell, J., concurring).

Petitioners' singleminded focus on *Lemon*, however, disregards the fact that *Lemon* itself is merely a distillation of this Court's other Establishment Clause holdings. Indeed, *Lemon*'s formulation of secular purpose and effect flows directly from *Schempp*'s explanation of "wholesome neutrality." 374 U.S. at 222. Thus, in asking the Court to reconsider *Lemon*, petitioners are effectively asking the Court to reconsider its entire Establishment Clause jurisprudence covering nearly half a century. See, e.g., *Everson v. Board of Education*, 330 U.S. 1, 18 (1947) ("[The First] Amendment requires the State to be a neutral in its relations with groups of religious believers and non-believers. . . ."); *Zorach v. Clausen*, 343 U.S. 306, 314 (1952) ("The government must be neutral when it comes to competition between sects"); *Abington v. Schempp*, 374 U.S. at 226 ("In the relationship between man and religion, the State is firmly committed to a position of neutrality"); *Epperson v. Arkansas*, 393 U.S. at 103–104 ("Government in our democracy, state and national, must be neutral in matters of religious theory, doctrine, and practice"); *Roemer v. Board of Public Works of Maryland*, 426 U.S. 736, 741 (1976) ("Neutrality is what is required"); *Wallace v. Jaffree*, 472 U.S. at 60 ("[G]overnment must pursue a course of complete neutrality toward religion").

To discard the concepts embodied in *Lemon* and expounded upon in numerous decisions by this Court is to invite havoc in both the lower courts and in the administration of the public schools. To discard *Lemon* is to discard the rationale of *Schempp*, and all of this Court's decisions that teach that prayer cannot be incorporated into the public schools. To discard *Lemon* is to solicit renewed litigation of all of the practices which this Court has already determined impermissibly mix religion and public education.[8]

The basic concepts enunciated in the *Lemon* test were not newly devised in *Lemon*, but developed gradually, founded on the premise that the Establishment Clause requires government to maintain neutrality towards competing religious sects and towards religion generally. " 'The government is neutral, and, while protecting all, it prefers none, and it discharges none.' " *Abington v. Schempp*, 374 U.S. at 215, citing with approval *Minor v. Board of Education in Cincinnati* (Super.Ct. Cincinnati, Ohio, 1870) (Taft, J., dissenting). Government, in short, is prohibited both from inhibiting the free exercise of religion and from allowing "a majority" to use "the machinery of the State to practice its beliefs." *Abington v. Schempp*, 374 U.S. at 226.

In discussing the genesis of the Establishment Clause, this Court observed in 1947, long before *Lemon*, that, [t]he people [in Virginia], as elsewhere, reached the conviction that individual religious liberty could be achieved best under a government which was stripped of all power to tax, to support, or otherwise to assist any or all religions. . . . *Everson v. Board of Education*, 330 U.S. at 11. The Court employed similar language in holding, during the following year, that religious instruction within the public schools, taught by private religious groups, violates the Establishment Clause: This is beyond all question a utilization of the tax-established and tax-supported public school system to aid religious groups to spread their faith. And it falls squarely under the ban of the First Amendment. . . . *Ill. ex rel. McCollum v. Board of Education*, 333 U.S. at 210.

---

[7] Indeed, as the district court aptly observed, "The special nature of the graduation ceremonies underscores the identification that Providence public school students can make." App.B at 24a.

[8] Indeed, the National School Boards Association (NSBA) has filed a brief amicus curiae in this case which, although nominally in support of petitioners, is actually an argument in support of the continued "viability of the *Lemon* test." NSBA Brief at 3. The Association's brief takes no position on the merits of this case; however, it vividly describes the chaos which would result were the Court to discard *Lemon:* However difficult the *Lemon* test may sometimes be to apply, it has been the test for 20 years and school people, students and parents have relied on it. If the Court in this case develops a "new test," assuredly that action will send out a message to schools, students, parents and communities throughout this country that all of the religion in the schools' cases are no longer "good law" or at least are questionable. NSBA Brief at 20.

The next Establishment Clause case decided by this Court and related to practices within the public schools was *Zorach v. Clausen*, 343 U.S. 306. While the Court in *Zorach* did not refer to government actions "supporting," "aiding" or "assisting" religion, it employed other terms equally familiar in modern Establishment Clause jurisprudence. Thus, the Court held, the First Amendment "studiously defines the manner, the specific ways, in which there shall be no concert or union or dependency one on the other [i.e. church on state, or vice versa]." Id. at 312. In particular, "[g]overnment may not finance religious groups nor undertake religious instruction nor blend secular and sectarian education. . . ." Id. at 314 (emphasis added).

Three decades ago, in *McGowan v. Maryland*, 366 U.S. 420, 449 (1961), the Court employed the terms "purpose and effect" in its analysis of the constitutionality of Sunday closing laws: After engaging in the close scrutiny demanded of us when First Amendment liberties are at issue, we accept the State Supreme Court's determination that the statute's present purpose and effect is not to aid religion but to set aside a day of rest and recreation. These terms began to be referred to as the Establishment Clause "test" several years later, when the Court considered the constitutionality of daily recitation of the Bible and Lord's Prayer in public school classrooms: The test may be stated as follows: what are the purpose and the primary effect of the enactment? If either is the advancement or inhibition of religion then the enactment exceeds the scope of legislative power as circumscribed by the Constitution. That is to say that to withstand the strictures of the Establishment Clause there must be a secular legislative purpose and a primary effect that neither advances nor inhibits religion. *Abington v. Schempp*, 374 U.S. at 222 (citations omitted), cited with approval in *Epperson v. Arkansas*, 393 U.S. at 107.

In *Walz v. Tax Commission of the City of New York*, 397 U.S. 664 (1970), this Court began to further develop the concepts of "purpose" and "effect" as they pertain to Establishment Clause issues: Determining that the legislative purpose of tax exemption is not aimed at establishing, sponsoring, or supporting religion does not end the inquiry, however. We must also be sure that the end result—the effect—is not an excessive government entanglement with religion. Id. at 674.

The Court relied on its analysis in *Schempp* and *Walz* when it devised the now familiar *Lemon* test: First, the statute must have a secular legislative purpose; second, its principal or primary effect must be one that neither advances nor inhibits religion; finally, the statute must not foster "an excessive government entanglement with religion." *Lemon v. Kurtzman*, 403 U.S. at 612-13 (citations omitted).

In sum, *Lemon* simply coalesced concepts which the Court had been applying in Establishment Clause cases for over twenty years. Indeed, the Court itself has recognized this to be true: [T]hese tests or criteria should be "viewed as guidelines" within which to consider "the cumulative criteria developed over many years and applying to a wide range of governmental action challenged as violative of the Establishment Clause." *Committee for Public Education v. Nyquist*, 413 U.S. at 773 n.31, quoting *Tilton v. Richardson*, 403 U.S. 672, 677-78 (1971). See also *Meek v. Pittenger*, 421 U.S. 349, 358 (1975) ("These tests constitute a convenient, accurate distillation of this Court's efforts over the past decades. . . ."). Since *Lemon*, its familiar three-prong test has been accepted by this Court as a logical and comprehensible starting point for constitutional analysis in Establishment Clause cases.[9]

While consistently reaffirming the *Lemon* framework as a viable means of analyzing Establishment Clause issues, this Court recently clarified and refined its meaning and substance. In her concurrence in *Lynch v. Donnelly*, 465 U.S. 668, 690 (1984), Justice O'Connor restated the heart of the *Lemon* test: The purpose prong of the *Lemon* test asks whether government's actual purpose is to endorse or disapprove of religion. The effect prong asks whether, irrespective of government's actual purpose, the practice under review in fact conveys a message of endorsement or disapproval. An affirmative answer to either question should render the challenged practice invalid.

---

[9] The one exception, of course, is this Court's decision in *Marsh v. Chambers*, 463 U.S. at 791, in which the Court adopted a historical analysis, centered upon the "unique history" of legislative chaplains. The *Marsh* Court was squarely presented with a practice identical to one authorized and adopted by the Congress which drafted the First Amendment. The *Marsh* rationale, however, does not "fit" the facts before the Court here. As the Court has previously noted in *Edwards v. Aguillard*, 482 U.S. at 583 n.4, such an approach "is not useful in determining the proper roles of church and state in public schools, since free public education was virtually nonexistent at the time the Constitution was adopted" (citations omitted). See also *Wallace v. Jaffree*, 472 U.S. at 80 (O'Connor, J., concurring) (noting that since free public education was "virtually nonexistent" when the framers adopted the First Amendment "it is unlikely that [they] anticipated the problems of interaction of church and state in the public schools"). Indeed, the natural evolution of our culture, together with astounding technological progress, guarantee that innumerable practices not even imagined by the framers may collide with constitutional principles. It is the everyday work of the Court to apply constitutional principles to facts and circumstances beyond the ken of the framers.

The "purpose" and "effect" prongs of the *Lemon* test are thus addressed by an evaluation of both the objective and subjective "components of the message" conveyed by the challenged government action. A secular purpose which is a mere sham is not enough to save a challenged practice from constitutional infirmity. See *Stone v. Graham*, 449 U.S. 39. Rather, it is the actual intent of the government which is critical under the "purpose" prong. This approach was endorsed by six Justices of the Court in *Wallace v. Jaffree*, 472 U.S. at 56, and by seven Justices in *Grand Rapids School District v. Ball*, 473 U.S. at 389 (noting further that if a symbolic "link" or "identification" of government with religion conveys a message of endorsement, the Establishment Clause is violated). See also *Edwards v. Aguillard*, 482 U.S. at 583 n.4.

Most recently, in *County of Allegheny v. ACLU*, 492 U.S. at 600–01, this Court has explained the reach of the term "endorsement" as follows: [T]he very concept of "endorsement" conveys the sense of promoting someone else's message. Thus, by prohibiting government endorsement of religion, the Establishment Clause prohibits . . . the government's lending its support to the communication of a religious organization's religious message.

Petitioners propose no less than a total reconstruction of modern Establishment Clause jurisprudence, developed painstakingly and carefully by this Court over the past four decades. They propose the abandonment of the very cornerstone of what the Establishment Clause is understood to mean. In the process, they disregard the notion of stare decisis, which this Court described only a few weeks ago as "the preferred course because it promotes the evenhanded, predictable, and consistent development of legal principles, fosters reliance on judicial decisions, and contributes to the actual and perceived integrity of the judicial process." *Payne v. Tennessee*, __U.S. __, 59 U.S.L.W. 4814, 4819 (June 27, 1991).

It is true that *Payne* precipitated a debate among the members of the Court over the scope and meaning of stare decisis in constitutional cases. Yet, every member of the *Payne* Court agreed that allegiance to stare decisis is most compelling when the challenged principle of law reflects the accumulated wisdom of a body of precedents stretching back over many years and many courts.[10] That is precisely the situation here. Under these circumstances, this Court has continued to adhere to the proposition that "the doctrine of stare decisis is of fundamental importance to the rule of law." *Payne v. Tennessee*, 59 U.S.L.W. at 4823 (Souter, J., concurring), quoting *Welch v. Texas Dep't of Highways and Public Transportation*, 483 U.S. 468, 494 (1987). Petitioners have offered no persuasive reason why the doctrine of stare decisis should be abandoned in this case.

C. Prayers at public middle school promotional ceremonies and at public high school graduation ceremonies fail each prong of the three-part *Lemon* test

1. The purpose of including prayer in public middle and high school promotional and graduation ceremonies is to endorse religion The only evidence submitted to the district court in this case was contained in the parties' Agreed Statement of Facts. (J.A. 10-19, 24).[11] The Agreed Statement of Facts contains no evidence of any secular purpose for the inclusion of prayer in the promotional and graduation ceremonies of Providence's public schools. Moreover, this Court has often recognized the essential religious nature and manifest religious purpose of prayer. *Wallace v. Jaffree*, 472 U.S. at 72 (O'Connor, J., concurring) (contrasting the "inherently religious" nature of vocal prayer, which is "a religious exercise," to a moment of silence, which may be neither); *Stone v. Graham*, 449 U.S. at 41 (holding that the Ten Commandments is "undeniably a sacred text in the Jewish and Christian faiths"); *Abington v. Schempp*, 374 U.S. at 225 (noting that reading the Bible and recitation of the Lord's Prayer are "religious exercises"); *Engel v. Vitale*, 370 U.S. at 424-25 ("the nature of . . . prayer has always been religious").

Indeed, this Court has never found a valid secular purpose for any type of government sponsored prayer in a public school setting. Rather, in each of the foregoing cases, the Court has firmly and unequivocally rejected any alleged secular purpose for school sponsored prayer and even for school encouragement of prayer: The addition of "or voluntary prayer" [in the Alabama statute authorizing a period of silence in public schools] indicates that the State intended to characterize prayer as a fa-

---

[10] For example, Chief Justice Rehnquist's opinion for the majority in *Payne* stressed that the overruled holding in *Booth v. Maryland*, 482 U.S. 496 (1987), was not "mandated" by any "prior decisions of this Court." 59 U.S.L.W. at 4816. Similarly, Justice Scalia's concurring opinion (joined by Justices O'Connor and Kennedy) described the holding in *Booth* as "a novel rule." Id. at 4821.

[11] Petitioners have devoted a mere six pages of their brief to a discussion of *Lemon* as applied to the facts of this case.

vored practice. Such an endorsement is not consistent with the established principle that the government must pursue a course of complete neutrality toward religion. The importance of that principle does not permit us to treat this as an inconsequential case involving nothing more than a few words of symbolic speech on behalf of the political majority. For whenever the State itself speaks on a religious subject, one of the questions that we must ask is "whether the government intends to convey a message of endorsement or disapproval of religion".... Keeping in mind, as we must, "both the fundamental place held by the Establishment Clause in our constitutional scheme and the myriad, subtle ways in which Establishment Clause values can be eroded," we conclude that Section 16-1-20.1 violates the First Amendment. *Wallace v. Jaffree*, 472 U.S. at 60-61 (footnotes omitted). See also *Edwards v. Aguillard*, 482 U.S. 578 (holding that the preeminent purpose of a Louisiana statute requiring "Creation Science" to be taught in conjunction with evolution was religious).[12]

Petitioners argue that their practice of including prayer in public school promotional and graduation ceremonies is to "solemnize the occasion" and to provide "recognition and acknowledgment of the role of religion in the lives of our citizens." Pet.Br. at 44 n.43. Petitioners' pretensions to a secular purpose must fail on the facts of this case. It is undisputed that more than half of Providence's middle schools and one of its five high schools have repeatedly succeeded in producing promotional and/or graduation ceremonies without the use of prayer. Apparently, the officials of those schools have fostered secular means to solemnize and dignify their ceremonies. On these facts, one can only conclude that the officials who chose to include prayer did so because they wished to encourage or endorse prayer itself. *County of Allegheny v. ACLU*, 492 U.S. at 618 ("Where the government's secular message can be conveyed by two symbols, only one of which carries a religious meaning, an observer might reasonably infer from the fact that the government has chosen to use the religious symbol that the government means to promote religious faith").

Petitioners' second asserted secular purpose—a recognition and acknowledgment of religion—denies the essential nature of prayer. Prayer is not passive; it is active. Prayer does not merely "recognize" and "acknowledge" religion; "[i]t is a solemn avowal of divine faith and supplication for the blessings of the Almighty." *Engel v. Vitale*, 370 U.S. at 424. If it is not permissible for government to induce and encourage public school children to meditate on the Ten Commandments, if it is not permissible for government to encourage or endorse silent prayer in the classroom, then it is assuredly not permissible for government to choose a clergy who will pray at an important public school function and to choose what kind of prayer that clergy will be allowed to deliver. "[I]t is no part of the business of government to compose ... prayers for any group of the American people to recite." Id. at 425. A government that advises chosen clergy regarding the form of prayer that is acceptable to government officials is in the business of composing prayer. Can there be any doubt that a government that engages in such activities is intending to endorse not only the religion itself, but a particular type of neutered, generic religion? Can there be any doubt that a government that engages in such activities is not maintaining the neutrality towards religion and between religious beliefs that the Establishment Clause demands? As this Court has stated, "[h]owever desirable ... [the government's purpose] might be as a matter of private devotion, it is not a permissible state objective under the Establishment Clause." *Stone v. Graham*, 449 U.S. at 42.

2. The effect of including prayer in the promotional and graduation ceremonies of public middle schools and high schools is to convey a message of endorsement of religion Petitioners do not explain how the inclusion of prayer in the promotional and graduation ceremonies organized, supervised, and run by public school officials can do anything but convey the message that those officials endorse religion as one of the values they are

[12] A number of lower courts have likewise concluded that prayer in various public school gatherings, such as football games, school assemblies, commencement exercises, pep rallies, and athletic contests serve no secular purpose. See *Jager v. Douglas County School District*, 862 F.2d 824 (11th Cir.), cert. denied, 109 S. Ct. 2431 (1989)(striking down invocations delivered prior to public high school football games); *Collins v. Chandler Unified School District*, 644 F.2d 759 (9th Cir.), cert. denied, 454 U.S. 863 (1981) (striking down opening prayers delivered by a student at voluntary school assemblies); *Graham v. Central Community School District of Decatur*, 608 F.Supp. 531 (S.D. Iowa 1985) (holding that invocations and benedictions during commencement exercises serve a Christian religious purpose); *Doe v. Aldine Independent School District*, 563 F.Supp. 883 (S.D. Texas 1982) (holding that a prayer posted over the entrance of a public school gymnasium, sung at athletic contests, pep rallies, and graduation ceremonies has no secular purpose); *Sands v. Morongo Unified School District*, 809 P.2d 809 (Cal.Sup.Ct. 1991) (striking down prayer at commencement). But see *Jones v. Clear Creek Middle School District*, 930 F.2d 416 (5th Cir. 1991) (upholding prayer at commencement).

responsible for inculcating. Petitioners simply state these facts: (1) the prayers are delivered and prepared by clergy, rather than by school officials; (2) the ceremony occurs only once in each student's career; (3) the prayers are brief; (4) the prayers do not take place in a classroom; (5) attendance is not mandatory; and (6) parents and friends are present. Pet.Br. at 47-48. Petitioners make no attempt to explain, however, how these facts diminish the religious message of endorsement conveyed by prayer at public school ceremonies. Indeed, they do not.

Consider, from a child's view, the importance of his or her promotional or graduation ceremony. This one day is the culmination and the reward of years of effort. This one day is his or her day to be recognized, applauded, congratulated for his or her achievements. The importance of graduation day for an eighth grade or twelfth grade student cannot be minimized. As the district court recognized: While the fact that graduation is a special occasion distinguishes this school day from all others, the uniqueness of the day could highlight the particular effect that the benediction and invocation may have on the students. The presence of clerics is not by itself determinative. It is the union of prayer, school, and important occasion that creates an identification of religion with a school function. The special nature of the graduation ceremonies underscores the identification that Providence public school students can make. App.B at 24a (footnote omitted).

Consider, from a child's point of view, the planning for his or her graduation ceremony. Teachers have selected the format and the program. Teachers have chosen who will deliver speeches, who will sing, who will hand out diplomas. Teachers have decided who will open and close the ceremony and, in this case, teachers have decided that the person who will do this is a member of the clergy. Teachers "practice" the ceremonies with the children who are graduating. They tell the children how to line up, where to walk, where to sit, when to sit and stand, and generally how they should behave. Teachers, in short, are running this show.[13]

Consider, as well, the graduation ceremony itself. It is typical for the children who are being promoted or who are graduating to be seated together, for family and friends to be seated apart. When the ceremony begins, when, in this case, the clergy rises to deliver the invocation—what will the child see? He will see school officials and teachers standing and adopting stances appropriate to prayer. He will have been told to stand himself. Indeed, he will have no choice but to stand himself, for to adopt a stance different from the rest of his classmates and from his teachers will be to cause a disruption in the ceremony. He will hear a prayer being offered. And he will have, inescapably, the sense that teachers and school officials are endorsing and supporting the message being delivered. Moreover, in choosing the clergy, by making him or her part of this important public school ceremony, petitioners have unequivocally lent the support of government "to the communication of a religious organization's religious message." *County of Allegheny v. ACLU*, 492 U.S. at 601.[14]

Petitioners have used the machinery of government to encourage participation in a religious exercise. *Wallace v. Jaffree*, 472 U.S. at 73 n.2 (O'Connor, J., concurring). This is a violation of the Establishment Clause.[15]

3. Petitioners' practice impermissibly entangles government with religion Petitioners argue that their practices avoid the pitfalls of government entanglement with religion because school officials merely distributed, but did not formulate, the "Guidelines for Civic Occasions," and because school officials do not write or monitor the officiating clergy's prayers. Pet.Br. at 44 n.43. Petitioners do not accurately state the pertinent facts. According to the parties' Agreed Statement of Facts: Defendant Robert E. Lee, principal of the Nathan Bishop Middle School, received, from Assistant Superintendent of Schools Arthur Zarrella, a document entitled "Guidelines for Civic Occasions" as a guideline for the type of prayer to be included in the graduation ceremony of the

---

[13] This Court has recognized the importance of "students' emulation of teachers as role models" as well as "children's susceptibility to peer pressure." *Edwards v. Aguillard*, 482 U.S. at 584.

[14] It is useful to consider the differences between the manner in which graduation ceremonies are conducted and the manner in which legislative sessions are conducted—legislators are free to, and frequently do, enter and leave the legislative chambers at will; they do so, not in a processional, but individually; legislators may enter a legislative session in the middle of the session and leave before it is over; legislators are not compelled to remain quiet during the session, but engage in discussion among themselves; legislators are adults, and have not been told how to behave by others holding a position of authority over them; the progress of a legislative session is much less controlled and more variable than a graduation ceremony.

[15] The brevity of the prayers offered and the fact that attendance at the ceremony is not required of the child are inconsequential. These issues have already been addressed and dismissed as irrelevant by this Court. See *Wallace v. Jaffree*, 472 U.S. 38; *Abington v. Schempp*, 374 U.S. at 224-25; *Engel v. Vitale*, 370 U.S. at 430, 436.

Nathan Bishop Middle School . . . Defendant Robert E. Lee, provided to Rabbi Gutterman a copy of the "Guidelines for Civic Occasions" . . . and, in addition, spoke personally to Rabbi Gutterman to advise him that prayers that he gave at the invocation and benediction should be non-sectarian in nature. (J.A.12-13, PP14, 17). The guidelines in question, published by the National Conference of Christians and Jews, include, among other suggestions, "appropriate" opening ascriptions to be used for the deity in public prayer. (J.A.21). The guidelines also suggest that public prayer should "remain faithful to the purposes of acknowledging divine presence and seeking blessing, not as opportunity to preach, argue or testify." Id.

Clearly, petitioners not only choose which religious sects will be represented and will be allowed to pray at public school ceremonies, they also monitor the types of prayers that are offered and "advise" the clergy chosen as to what types of prayers are acceptable. By so doing, petitioners interfere with the way that the chosen clergy practice their respective religious beliefs. See *Larkin v. Grendel's Den*, 459 U.S. 116, 122 (1982) (state interference with the practice of religious faith violates the First Amendment). This is an impermissible entanglement of government with religion.

D. The historical analysis adopted by the Court in *Marsh v. Chambers* does not save petitioners' practice of including prayer in public school promotional and graduation ceremonies from constitutional infirmity

Petitioners attempt to broaden the Court's analysis of the constitutionality of legislative prayer set forth in *Marsh v. Chambers*, 463 U.S. at 791, to encompass the practice of inviting clergy to deliver prayers at public school promotional and graduation ceremonies. The proposition petitioners advance is that "any interpretation of the Establishment Clause faithful to its intended meaning 'must permit not only legitimate practices two centuries old but also any other practices with no greater potential for an establishment of religion.' " Pet.Br. at 30 n.31, quoting *County of Allegheny v. ACLU*, 492 U.S. at 670 (Kennedy, J., concurring in the judgment in part and dissenting in part).

This Court has squarely rejected both *Marsh*'s applicability to practices with impact on the relationship between religion and public education and blind validation of all practices arguably acceptable to the framers' generation. See *Schad v. Arizona*, __U.S. __, 59 U.S.L.W. 4761, 4767 (June 21, 1991). Indeed, the *Marsh* Court itself cautioned that "[s]tanding alone, historical patterns cannot justify contemporary violations of constitutional guarantees." *Marsh v. Chambers*, 463 U.S. at 790. Were historical acceptance alone sufficient to assure the constitutional validity of any given action, the Court would be compelled to uphold such practices as public whipping and racial segregation of schools. Id. at 814 n.30 (Brennan, J., dissenting). See also *Committee for Public Education v. Nyquist*, 413 U.S. at 792. Discrimination against non-Christians would also be acceptable. *County of Allegheny v. ACLU*, 492 U.S. at 604–05. Clearly, *Marsh* was not intended to produce such intolerable results.

Nor can *Marsh* be read as validating practices which bring religion into the public education system. This Court first recognized in *Schempp* that historical analyses are misplaced in constitutional inquiries relating to the public schools: [T]he structure of American education has greatly changed since the First Amendment was adopted. In the context of our modern emphasis upon public education available to all citizens, any views of the eighteenth century as to whether the exercises at bar are an "establishment" offer little aid to decision. Education, as the Framers knew it, was in the main confined to private schools more often than not under strictly sectarian supervision. Only gradually did control of education pass largely to public officials. It would, therefore, hardly be significant if the fact was that the nearly universal devotional exercises in the schools of the young Republic did not provoke criticism; even today religious ceremonies in church-supported private schools are constitutionally unobjectionable. 374 U.S. at 238–39 (footnote omitted). See also *Wallace v. Jaffree*, 472 U.S. at 80 (O'Connor, J, concurring) ("Since there then existed few government run schools, it is unlikely that the persons who drafted the First Amendment, and the state legislators who ratified it, anticipated the problems of interaction of church and state in the public schools"). In *Edwards v. Aguillard*, 482 U.S. at 583 n.4, this Court specifically stated that "a historical approach is not useful in determining the proper roles of church and state in public schools, since free public education was virtually nonexistent at the time the Constitution was adopted." Finally, the *Marsh* Court itself observed that legislative prayers are primarily directed to adults, who are not as readily susceptible to "religious indoctrination" or peer pressure as children. *Marsh v. Chambers*, 463 U.S. at 792.

Thus, petitioners can produce no precedent whatsoever from this Court which supports the extension of *Marsh* to religious practices within the public schools. In fact, each time this Court has addressed the issue, it has flatly rejected petitioner's argument.

II. GOVERNMENT COERCION HAS NEVER BEEN ACCEPTED AS A NECESSARY ELEMENT OF AN ESTABLISHMENT CLAUSE VIOLATION

A. Historically, the meaning of the Establishment Clause was not limited to a prohibition of government coercion of religion

Petitioner's principal argument is not that this Court has ever adopted their coercion test, but rather that nearly every modern Justice has fundamentally misunderstood the Establishment Clause. Petitioners urge the Court to throw out all its precedents and start over on the basis of petitioners' version of history.

Petitioners' history is not based on any particular practice of the framers with regard to public schools; public schools barely existed. Nor is petitioners' history based on any principle articulated by the framers. Petitioners quote the framers denouncing religious coercion, but the invalidity of religious coercion is not at issue. The dispute is over petitioners' further claim that government can aid religion if it does not coerce. Petitioners do not quote the framers saying that. Nor do petitioners discuss the only eighteenth century debates that would have posed the issue.

Both then and now, the essence of establishment was the designation or endorsement of a preferred religion. Indeed, the leading historical dictionary defines establishment in terms of recognition, and does not even mention coercion: Establishment 2. esp. The "establishing" by law (a church, religion, form of worship). (See ESTABLISH v. 7) Establish 7. From 16th c. often used with reference to ecclesiastical ceremonies or organization, and to the recognized national church or its religion. 3 *Oxford English Dictionary* 298 (1933).

This definition is fully consistent with American usage in the period of the framing. Coercion to attend the established church had been abandoned well before the Revolution. T. Curry, *The First Freedoms* 78-104 (1986). Tax support for the established church continued in the southern colonies only up to independence. Id. at 136 (Virginia), 150 (South Carolina), 151-52 (North Carolina), 153 (Georgia), 154-57 (Maryland). In New England, tax support continued into the early national period. But in both regions, defenders of establishment tried to save tax support by letting all denominations participate, by letting each taxpayer choose the church or clergyman to receive his payments and, in Virginia and Maryland, by exempting some citizens entirely. Id. at 141, 145 (Virginia), 155-57 (Maryland), 164 (Massachusetts), 180-81 (Connecticut), 185-86 (New Hampshire), 188-89 (Vermont). These efforts to make establishment nonpreferential and noncoercive did not save it. The most important political battle over disestablishment was fought over precisely this issue in Virginia in 1785, and the nonpreferential general assessment was rejected. Id. at 140-47. By 1833, the last of these laws had been repealed as inconsistent with the American principle of disestablishment. L. Levy, *The Establishment Clause* 38 (1986).

As tax support and compelled attendance were abandoned, there remained the core of establishment, the endorsement of a state religion. The endorsement issue was most cleanly separated from more coercive forms of establishment in South Carolina and Virginia. The South Carolina Constitution of 1778 declared that "The Christian Protestant religion shall be deemed, and is hereby constituted and declared to be, the established religion of this State." S.C. Const. art. 38 (1778), reprinted in 6 F. Thorpe, ed., *The Federal and State Constitutions* 3255 (1906).

No one was required to support this religion in any way. No citizen was required to attend services or contribute financial support. The Constitution guaranteed religious toleration and forbade tax support for churches. Id. at 3255-56. The established religion in South Carolina consisted of a simple declaration that the state endorsed Protestantism. That violated the contemporary understanding of disestablishment, and the provision was repealed in 1790. See S.C. Const. art. 8 (1790), reprinted in Thorpe at 3264. Petitioner's theory implies that the South Carolina Constitution of 1778 could be validly reenacted today.

In Virginia, the last vestige of establishment was a simple act of incorporation for the Protestant Episcopal Church. The act had no coercive effect on the opponents of establishment, but they objected to it because it singled out Episcopalians for "peculiar distinctions" and "particular sanction." T. Buckley, *Church and State in Revolutionary Virginia, 1776-1787* at 165 (1977). The legislature repealed the act in 1787. Id. at 170.

In these two instances, Americans of the founding generation actually debated and voted on the question whether government could endorse religion if it did so noncoercively. The answer was no. These debates show how the framers understood disestablishment when they attended to the issue. The dissenting churches, focused on the task of eliminating the former Anglican establishment, insisted on eliminating mere endorsements.

Petitioners ignore this history of real debate over the meaning of disestablishment, and rely instead on a practice that was not debated: prayers and religious declarations among adults in civil ceremonies. These practices were not debated because they were not controversial among Protestants, and there were no other religious minorities with sufficient political strength to raise the issue.

This unexamined Protestant consensus broke down in the face of two developments in the nineteenth century: the emergence of public schools, and large-scale Catholic and Jewish immigration. Catholic complaints about Protestant instruction and Bible reading in the public schools led to political conflict and physical violence. A. Stokes, *Church and State in the United States* 830–35 (1950). It then became clear that in a more pluralistic society, religious observances in public schools caused the same evils that tax support for churches, and endorsements of Episcopalians, had caused in the time of the framers.

The principle was the same in both generations: government should not support or endorse religion. Such endorsements cause religious strife if they disadvantage any significant group in the community. The framers adopted the principle, and they applied it to all issues that were controversial among Protestants. They did not see its application to practices that substantially all Protestants could accept. But they put the principle in the Constitution, ready to be applied to new examples of the same evil. Protestant-Catholic and Christian-Jewish conflict revealed that government sponsored religious observances, especially among children, caused the very evils that the Establishment Clause had been intended to prevent. American understanding of the reach of the disestablishment principle has expanded with the steady increase in religious pluralism, and the constitutional tradition is reflected in this Court's decisions prohibiting religious observances in public schools.

Petitioners also rely on James Madison's comment that the Establishment Clause meant that "Congress should not establish a religion, and enforce the legal observation of it by law, nor compel men to worship God in any manner contrary to their conscience." Pet.Br. at 24. This comment does not help petitioners. It does not state petitioners' position, and it does not describe the version of the Establishment Clause ultimately adopted.

Madison's statement has three clauses: Congress may not (1) establish a religion, (2) enforce observation, or (3) compel worship. Petitioners rely on clauses (2) and (3) and treat them as exclusive. But clause (1) is as broad as the meaning of establishment. If to establish a religion meant to recognize or endorse a religion in the vocabulary of the late eighteenth century, then Madison said that Congress cannot recognize or endorse a religion. Whatever establishment meant, Madison repeated it; he did not define it or limit it.

Madison cannot have meant for his listeners to ignore clause (1) and consider only clauses (2) and (3). Those two clauses alone would not even prevent tax support for churches. Congress could collect taxes for all religions or a particular religion without compelling anyone to observe that religion or to worship in a particular manner. So with clause (1) included, Madison's statement is entirely consistent with this Court's cases. With clause (1) excluded, Madison's statement is obviously incomplete, even narrower than petitioners' position.

Whatever Madison meant in this isolated comment is of little moment.[16] The House promptly rejected the draft Madison had paraphrased, and adopted Mr. Livermore's sweeping substitute: "Congress shall make no laws touching religion, or infringing the rights of conscience." 1 Annals of Cong. 731 (J. Gales ed. 1834). Any law referring to religion in any way would "touch" religion; adoption of the Livermore amendment is inconsistent with the claim that this discussion in the House confined the Establishment Clause to coercion.

The clause was further redrafted in the Senate and the Conference Committee. Those debates were not recorded, but votes in the Senate Journal reveal an unsuccessful attempt to narrow the clause to forbid only those establishments that preferred a particular sect, society, or denomination. Four such drafts were ultimately rejected. 3 L. de Pauw, ed., *Documentary*

[16] Indeed, Madison himself would have denied the legitimacy of considering this statement. Madison and the other framers believed that the Constitution should be construed in light of the text adopted and the evils to be eliminated, without reference to legislative history. See Baade, " 'Original Intent' in Historical Perspective: Some Critical Glosses," 69 *Tex.L.Rev.* 1001 (1991); Powell, "The Original Understanding of Original Intent," 98 *Harv.L.Rev.* 885 (1985).

History of the First Federal Congress of the United States of America 151, 166, 220 (1972). The draft that was finally ratified is one of the most sweeping considered by either House. It forbids not just the establishment of religion, but any law respecting an establishment. It does not merely forbid establishment of a church or even of "a" religion; it forbids "establishment of religion" generally. See Laycock, " 'Nonpreferential' Aid to Religion: A False Claim about Original Intent," 27 *Wm. & Mary L.Rev.* 875, 881-82, 886 (1986).

There is no reason to believe that this sweeping clause used "establishment" in less than the full sense accorded to the phrase by the opponents of established religion. Historical usage as reflected in the dictionary, and contemporary political debates over disestablishment in the states, both show that the word included recognition and endorsement. That is what the Establishment Clause prohibits. That is what this Court has always said the Establishment Clause prohibits. Petitioners' attempt to rewrite history ignores the most important evidence.[17]

B. This Court has consistently rejected coercion as a necessary element of an Establishment Clause violation

Not only does history fail to support petitioners' thesis that coercion is a necessary element of an Establishment Clause violation, but this Court has repeatedly rejected such a proposition, both specifically and by inference. Beginning with *Everson v. Board of Education*, 330 U.S. 1, this Court has clearly understood the Establishment Clause to reach beyond a prohibition of government coerced participation in religion: The "establishment of religion" clause of the First Amendment means at least this: Neither a State nor Federal Government can set up a church. Neither can pass laws which aid one religion, aid all religions, or prefer one religion over another. Neither can force nor influence a person to go to or to remain away from church against his will or force him to prefer a belief or disbelief in any religion. . . . Neither a state nor the Federal Government can, openly or secretly, participate in the affairs of any religious organizations or groups and vice versa. Id. at 15-16. The *Everson* Court clearly envisaged constitutional protection against noncoercive governmental involvement in religion.

In *Engel v. Vitale*, 370 U.S. at 430, the Court, specifically held that "[t]he Establishment Clause, unlike the Free Exercise Clause, does not depend upon any showing of direct governmental compulsion and is violated by the enactment of laws which establish an official religion whether those laws operate directly to coerce nonobserving individuals or not." This Court has consistently and unconditionally adhered to this principle whenever presented with a "coercion" argument. See *Abington v. Schempp*, 374 U.S. at 224-25 ("Nor are these required exercises mitigated by the fact that individual students may absent themselves upon parental request, for that fact furnishes no defense to a claim of unconstitutionality under the Establishment Clause"); *Committee for Public Education v. Nyquist*, 413 U.S. at 786 ("[W]hile proof of coercion might provide a basis for a claim under the Free Exercise Clause, it was not a necessary element of any claim under the Establishment Clause"); *Wallace v. Jaffree*, 472 U.S. at 60 n.51.

Most recently, Justice O'Connor addressed this issue in her concurrence in *County of Allegheny v. ACLU*, 492 U.S. at 627–28 (citations omitted): An Establishment Clause standard that prohibits only "coercive" practices or overt efforts at government proselytization . . . but fails to take account of the numerous more subtle ways that government can show favoritism to particular beliefs or convey a message of disapproval to others, would not, in my view, adequately protect the religious liberty or respect the religious diversity of the members of our pluralistic political community. Thus, this Court has never relied on coercion alone as the touchstone of Establishment Clause analysis. . . . To require a showing of coercion, even indirect coercion, as an essential element of an Establishment Clause violation would make the Free Exercise Clause a redundancy. . . . Moreover, as even Justice Kennedy recognizes, any Establishment Clause test limited to "direct coercion" clearly would fail to account for forms of "[S]ymbolic recognition or accommodation of religious faith" that may violate the Establishment Clause.

The core of the doctrine which petitioners exhort the Court to adopt is summarized in one sentence—"Religious speech alone cannot amount to the kind of government coercion of religious choice that implicates the Establishment Clause." Pet.Br. at 36. Petitioners openly suggest that government may participate in religious debates, may encourage religion, and may criticize religious expression. Id. at 37. The government need not be neutral towards reli-

---

[17] A far more extensive historical analysis appears in the Brief Amicus Curiae of the American Jewish Committee, et al. Respondent fully endorses that analysis.

gion generally or towards particular religious sects so long as it does not force or fund the practice of religion. Id. The breadth of government practices which would be constitutionally acceptable under petitioners' doctrine is startling—government officials would be allowed to exhort citizens to join a favored sect; conversely, the same officials would be free to publicly condemn a disfavored sect. Government would be able to sponsor a Roman Catholic mass, an evangelical prayer meeting, or any other type of religious service the officials in power happen to favor. Indeed, under petitioners' doctrine, joined by the Solicitor General, government would actually be allowed to sponsor a church, so long as no one was forced to join and no tax funds were used to support it. Petitioners cannot possibly invoke historical precedent in support of this argument, for the genesis of the Establishment Clause arose from the religious persecution borne of such sponsorship. See *Engel v. Vitale*, 470 U.S. at 431 ("The history of governmentally established religion, both in England and in this country, showed that whenever government had allied itself with one particular form of religion, the inevitable result had been that it had incurred the hatred, disrespect and even contempt of those who held contrary beliefs").

In interpreting the meaning of the Establishment Clause, this Court has recognized, as it must, that the religious complexion of the country today is vastly different than it was at the time the First Amendment was ratified. *Abington v. Schempp*, 374 U.S. at 240-41 (Brennan, J., concurring); *Edwards v. Aguillard*, 482 U.S. at 607 n.6 (Powell, J., concurring). While many government practices favoring Christianity may have been acceptable to the framers' generation, they are no longer acceptable if we are to honor the spirit of both the Free Exercise and the Establishment Clause. *County of Allegheny v. ACLU*, 492 U.S. at 630 (O'Connor, J., concurring). This Court has always so held. *Wallace v. Jaffree*, 472 U.S. at 52. To accept petitioners' doctrine would destroy the concept of government neutrality towards religion and would open the door for the very evils the Establishment Clause was intended to prevent.

C. Although coercion has never been held to be a necessary element of an Establishment Clause violation, petitioners' practice is nonetheless coercive

Petitioners advocate an extraordinarily narrow definition of coercion. In so doing, they suggest that this Court eliminate common sense from judicial decision-making.

In case after case, the Court has acknowledged and considered the coercive effect of subtle actions of government officials, especially when those actions impact on children within the public education system. Even Justice Stewart, who advocated an interpretation of the Establishment Clause restricted to government coercion of religious beliefs, recognized the indirect coercive pressures operating on public school children: [A] law which provided for religious exercises during the school day and which contained no excusal provision would obviously be unconstitutionally coercive upon those who did not wish to participate. And even under a law containing an excusal provision, if the exercises were held during the school day, and no equally desirable alternative were provided by the school authorities, the likelihood that children might be under at least some psychological compulsion to participate would be great. *Abington v. Schempp*, 374 U.S. at 318 (Stewart, J., dissenting).

The subtle pressure upon children to conform to their peers and to emulate teachers has been recognized and acknowledged in every modern decision of this Court involving religion in the public schools. See, e.g., *Engel v. Vitale*, 370 U.S. at 431 ("When the power, prestige and financial support of government is placed behind a particular religious belief, the indirect coercive pressure upon religious minorities to conform to the prevailing officially approved religion is plain"); *Grand Rapids School District v. Ball*, 473 U.S. at 390 ("The symbolism of a union between church and state is most likely to influence children of tender years, whose experience is limited and whose beliefs consequently are the function of environment as much as a free and voluntary choice"); *Wallace v. Jaffree*, 472 U.S. at 60 n.51, 71 (O'Connor, J., concurring); *Edwards v. Aguillard*, 482 U.S. at 584 ("The State exerts great authority and coercive power through mandatory attendance requirements, and because of the students' emulation of teachers as role models and the children's susceptibility to peer pressure"); *Board of Education v. Mergens*, 110 S.Ct. at 2378 (Kennedy, J., concurring) ("This inquiry [with respect to coercion] must be undertaken with sensitivity to the special circumstances that exist in a secondary school where the line between voluntary and coerced participation may be difficult to draw").

The very type of subtle pressure which the Court has previously described as coercive operates in this case on children who are being promoted from middle school or are graduating from high school in the Providence school system. Because coercion was not raised as an issue before the district court, no facts were developed by either party with regard to coercion, other than the mere acknowledgment that attendance at graduation and promotional ceremonies is not mandatory for students. (J.A.18, P41). However, this Court need not blind itself to the realities of how promotional and graduation ceremonies are conducted, nor to the importance of those ceremonies to the children involved, nor to the coercion inherent in government proselytizing on behalf of religion. No choice is offered to a child who is offended by the inclusion of prayers in the ceremony except to forego attendance altogether. Graduation ceremonies are organized and formal affairs. The children who are to be recognized enter and leave the room together, after family and friends have already been seated. They enter in a processional, anxiously and proudly watched by their families. In the unlikely event that the child were allowed to avoid coerced participation in prayer by leaving the room, there is overwhelming pressure not to take such obvious nonconforming action. Imagine the embarrassment and humiliation of a nonadhering child who attempts to withdraw from the room as all of his or her classmates are standing to begin an opening prayer. To deny that a child who wished to take such action is not coerced into conformity is nonsensical. As Justice O'Connor observed when discussing voluntary school prayer: Under all of these statutes, a student who did not share the religious beliefs expressed in the course of the exercise was left with the choice of participating, thereby compromising the nonadherent's beliefs, or withdrawing, thereby calling attention to his or her nonconformity. The decisions acknowledged the coercion implicit under the statutory schemes. *Wallace v. Jaffree*, 472 U.S. at 72 (O'Connor, J., concurring) (citations omitted). Withdrawing from part of a graduation ceremony is clearly even more disruptive than withdrawing from a classroom, and there is a concomitant increase in the coercive pressure on a student not to take such action, even if it were allowed.

If the nonadhering child chooses to be present during his or her promotional or graduation ceremony and not to withdraw during periods of prayer, he or she is subject to the additional subtle coercion inherent in proselytizing. The Court found in *Stone v. Graham* that the mere posting of religious texts on a schoolroom wall may have the effect of inducing school children "to read, meditate upon, perhaps to venerate and obey, the Commandments." 449 U.S. at 42. If the mere posting of a religious text may have such an effect, how much more of an effect will be realized from group prayer, spoken out loud.

The child who objects to prayer is thus left with only one choice—not to attend his or her promotional or graduation ceremony. No "equally desirable alternatives" are available. *Abington v. Schempp*, 374 U.S. at 318 (Stewart, J., dissenting). It is difficult to imagine how anyone could seriously argue that the child faced with such a choice is under no pressure to conform to the majority's notion of acceptable behavior. The message which the school and its teachers are delivering to the nonadhering child is clear: We have chosen to include in this all-important ceremony a prayer delivered by a religious person whom we have also chosen. This is your graduation; however, if your beliefs are offended by our choice of religion, you are free to miss your graduation. We will mail you a diploma.

Such a choice, delivered by teachers and government, is nothing short of cruel. It is surely not voluntary in any judicially cognizable sense, and cannot be constitutional under the First Amendment.

CONCLUSION

For the reasons stated above, the decision of the United States Court of Appeals for the First Circuit should be affirmed.

THE SUPREME COURT OF THE UNITED STATES

OCTOBER TERM, 1991

No. 90-1014

ROBERT E. LEE, ET AL., PETITIONERS,

v.

DANIEL WEISMAN, ETC., RESPONDENT

ON WRIT OF CERTIORARI TO THE UNITED STATES CIRCUIT COURT OF APPEALS FOR THE FIRST CIRCUIT

BRIEF FOR THE PETITIONERS

JOSEPH A. ROTELLA
622 Charles Street
Providence, RI 02904
(401) 861-0012

JAY ALAN SEKULOW
1000 Thomas Jefferson Street, N.W.
Suite 520
Washington, DC 20007
(202) 337-2273

CHARLES J. COOPER*
MICHAEL A. CARVIN
PETER J. FERRARA
ROBERT J. CYNKAR
SHAW, PITTMAN, POTTS & TROWBRIDGE
2300 N Street, N.W.
Washington, DC 20037
(202) 663-8000
Counsel for Petitioners
**Counsel of Record*

TABLE OF CONTENTS

QUESTIONS PRESENTED

I. Do school authorities violate the Establishment Clause by allowing a speaker at a public junior high or high school graduation ceremony to offer an invocation and a benediction that acknowledge a deity?

II. Whether direct or indirect government coercion of religious conformity is a necessary element of an Establishment Clause violation?

THE PARTIES

I. The petitioners in this case, who were the appellants in the court of appeals, are Robert E. Lee, individually and as principal of Nathan Bishop Middle School of Providence, Rhode Island; Thomas Mezzanotte, individually and as principal of Classical High School of Providence, Rhode Island: Robert F. Roberti, individually and as superintendent of the Providence School Department; and Vincent P. McWilliams, Mary Bastastini, Roosevelt Benton, Roberto Gonzalez, Donald Lopes, Jintana Pond, Lisa Powers, Mary Smith, and Julia Steiny individually and as members of the Providence School Committee.

II. The respondent in this case, who was the appellee in the court of appeals, is Daniel Weisman, personally and as next friend of Deborah Weisman.

THE SUPREME COURT OF THE UNITED STATES OCTOBER TERM, 1991 NO. 90-1014

ROBERT E. LEE, ET AL., PETITIONERS,
v.
DANIEL WEISMAN, ETC., RESPONDENT

ON WRIT OF CERTIORARI TO THE UNITED STATES CIRCUIT COURT OF APPEALS FOR THE FIRST CIRCUIT

BRIEF FOR THE PETITIONERS

OPINIONS BELOW

The opinion of the Court of Appeals for the First Circuit is reported at 908 F.2d 1090, and is reproduced in the Appendix to the Petition for a Writ of Certiorari at App. 1a.

The opinion of the United States District Court for the District of Rhode Island is reported at 728 F.Supp. 68, and is reproduced in the Appendix to the Petition for a Writ of Certiorari at App. 18a.

JURISDICTION

The judgment of the United States Court of Appeals for the First Circuit was entered on July 23, 1990. No petitions for rehearing were filed. The Petition for a Writ of Certiorari was timely filed on December 21, 1990, and was granted on March 18, 1991. The jurisdiction of this Court is invoked under 28 U.S.C. § 1254(1).

CONSTITUTIONAL PROVISION INVOLVED

This case involves the Establishment Clause of the First Amendment to the United States Constitution, which provides: "Congress shall make no law respecting an establishment of religion."

STATEMENT OF THE CASE

A. The graduation ceremony

For many years the Providence School Committee and Superintendent have permitted, but not directed, school principals to include invocations and benedictions in the graduation ceremonies of the city's public junior high and high schools. J.A. 12, 24; App. 19a.[1] As a result, some, but not all, public middle and high schools in Providence have included invocations and benedictions in their graduation ceremonies. J.A. 4, 12-16, 18; App. 19a. Such invocations and benedictions are not written or delivered by city employees, but by members of the clergy invited to participate in these ceremonies for that purpose. J.A. 12-13, 18. The schools provide the clergy with guidelines for the ceremonies prepared by the National Conference of Christians and Jews, which stress inclusiveness and sensitivity in authorizing nonsectarian prayer for public civic ceremonies. J.A. 13, 20-21; App. 19a. The clergy who have delivered these prayers in recent years have included Jewish rabbis and ministers of various Christian denominations. J.A. 12-15.

As the parties have stipulated, attendance at these ceremonies is voluntary, J.A. 18, with parents and friends of the students invited to attend. J.A. 18. The high school graduation ceremonies are usually held off school grounds, while middle school promotion ceremonies usually take place on the premises of the school. J.A. 12-16, 18; App. 19a.

Respondent Daniel Weisman's daughter, Deborah, was graduated from Nathan Bishop Middle School, a public junior high school in Providence, in June 1989. J.A. 4-5, 10; App. 19a. Rabbi Leslie Gutterman of the Temple Beth El of Providence delivered the invocation and benediction at the ceremony. J.A. 17; App. 19a.

Four days before the ceremony, respondent sought a temporary restraining order to prevent the inclusion of invocations and benedictions in the graduation ceremonies of the Providence public junior high and high schools.[2] App. 19a. The district court denied the motion the day before the ceremony, due to lack of time to consider it adequately before the scheduled event. App. 19a-20a.

On June 20, 1989, Deborah Weisman and her family attended the scheduled graduation ceremony at Nathan Bishop Middle School. App. 20a. Rabbi Gutterman's invocation addressed a deity at the beginning, and concluded with "Amen."[3] App. 20a. The benedic-

---

[1] "J.A." denotes the Joint Appendix. "App." denotes the Appendix to the Petition for a Writ of Certiorari.

[2] Respondent invoked the jurisdiction of the district court under 28 U.S.C. ss 1331, 1343, 2201, and 2202 (1988), as well as the court's pendant and ancillary jurisdiction, J.A. 2.

[3] The invocation, in its entirety, read as follows: God of the Free, Hope of the Brave: For the legacy of America where diversity is celebrated and the rights of minorities

tion opened with a reference to God, asked God's blessing, gave thanks to the Lord, and concluded with "Amen."[4] The district court characterized both the invocation and the benediction as "examples of elegant simplicity, thoughtful content, and sincere citizenship." App. 20a.

Deborah Weisman entered Classical High School in Providence in September 1989, and she has continued to attend that school since then. J.A. 10; App. 21a. In July 1989, respondent filed an amended complaint in this action, seeking a permanent injunction against invocations and benedictions in future graduation ceremonies of the Providence public junior high and high schools. App. 21a. The district court ruled in favor of respondent and granted the requested relief.

B. The district court decision

The district court's Establishment Clause analysis, which the court of appeals majority characterized as "sound and pellucid" and adopted as its own, App. 2a, opened with the observation that under this Court's precedents "God has been ruled out of public education as an instrument of inspiration or consolation" because of "the perceived sensitive nature of the school environment and the apprehended effect of state-led religious activity on young, impressionable minds." App. 21a-22a. The district court determined that the invocation and benediction failed under the second prong of the three-prong test established in *Lemon v. Kurtzman*, 403 U.S. 602 (1971). The practice impermissibly advanced religion "by creating an identification of school with a deity." App. 24a. According to the district court, "the Providence School Committee ha[d] in effect endorsed religion in general by authorizing an appeal to a deity in public school graduation ceremonies." App. 25a. The district court did not reach the other inquiries under *Lemon*—whether the practice had a secular purpose and whether it fostered an excessive entanglement with religion.

The district court expressly declined to follow the Sixth Circuit's reasoning in *Stein v. Plainwell Community Schools*, 822 F.2d 1406 (6th Cir. 1987), which held that nondenominational invocations and benedictions in public school graduation ceremonies are not per se unconstitutional. The *Stein* court had relied upon *Marsh v. Chambers*, 463 U.S. 783 (1983), in which this Court rejected an Establishment Clause challenge to the Nebraska Legislature's practice of opening each day's session with a prayer offered by a paid chaplain. The district court here, however, concluded that the "*Marsh* holding was narrowly limited to the unique situation of legislative prayer." App. 27a. As proof of this point, the district court noted that *Marsh* was the only case since 1971 in which the Court did not apply the *Lemon* test. The district court also noted that application of the *Marsh* analysis in the context of graduation invocations and benedictions would result in courts "reviewing the content of prayers to judicially approve what are acceptable invocations to a deity." App. 27a.

Finally, the district court made clear that Rabbi Gutterman's invocation and benediction were unconstitutional solely because they made reference to a deity: [N]othing in this decision prevents a cleric of any denomination or anyone else from giving a secular inspirational message at the opening and closing of the graduation ceremonies. Counsel for plaintiff conceded at argument, as she must, that if Rabbi Gutterman had given the exact same invocation as he delivered at the Bishop Middle School on June 29, 1989 with one change—God would be left out—the Establishment Clause would not be implicated. App. 28a. To punctuate the point, the court recast a new version of Rabbi Gutterman's invocation, one cleansed of its references to God and, thus, of its perceived constitutional infirmity. App. 28a.

C. The court of appeals decision

A majority of the Court of Appeals for the First Circuit affirmed, over a dissenting opinion by Judge Campbell. The panel majority simply

---

are protected, we thank You. May these young men and women grow up to enrich it. For the liberty of America, we thank You. May these new graduates grow up to guard it. For the political process of America in which all its citizens may participate, for its court system where all can seek justice we thank You. May those we honor this morning always turn to it in trust. For the destiny of America we thank You. May the graduates of Nathan Bishop Middle School so live that they might help to share it. May our aspirations for our country and for these young people, who are our hope for the future, be richly fulfilled. AMEN App. 20a.

[4] The benediction, in its entirety, read as follows: O God, we are grateful to You for having endowed us with the capacity for learning which we have celebrated on this joyous commencement. Happy families give thanks for seeing their children achieve an important milestone. Send Your blessings upon the teachers and administrators who helped prepare them. The graduates now need strength and guidance for the future. Help them to understand that we are not complete with academic knowledge alone. We must each strive to fulfill what You require of us all: To do justly, to love mercy, to walk humbly. We give thanks to You, Lord, for keeping us alive, sustaining us and allowing us to reach this special, happy occasion. AMEN App. 20a-21a.

endorsed the district court's opinion and did not elaborate further. App. 2a.

Judge Bownes concurred separately, concluding that the invocation and benediction violated all three prongs of the *Lemon* test. Noting that "[a] graduation ceremony does not need a prayer to solemnize it," Judge Bownes concluded that the primary purpose of the practice is religious. App. 9a-10a. He also believed that "it is self-evident that a prayer given by a religious person chosen by public school teachers communicates a message of government endorsement of religion." App. 10a. The practice fostered an excessive entanglement with religion by virtue of the School Committee's policies of providing guidelines for the composition of nondenominational invocations and of permitting school authorities to select the speakers. App. 10a-11a.

Judge Bownes also found this Court's decision in *Marsh* inapposite. *Marsh*, according to Judge Bownes, "was based on the 'unique' and specific historical argument that the framers did not find legislative prayers offensive to the Constitution because the first Congress approved of legislative prayers." App. 11a. *Marsh* did not apply here "since free public schools were virtually nonexistent at the time the Constitution was adopted." App. 11a (quoting *Edwards v. Aguillard*, 482 U.S. 578, 583 n.4 (1987)). Thus, Judge Bownes rejected the Sixth Circuit's analysis in *Stein*, and also criticized that court's "troubling" inquiry into the nondenominational content of the challenged invocation. App. 12a. Finally, Judge Bownes stated that the Establishment Clause would have been offended by Rabbi Gutterman's invocation and benediction even if cleansed of their references to a deity. Noting that invocations and benedictions "are by their very terms prayers and religious," Judge Bownes concluded that the practice "offends the First Amendment even if the words of the invocation or benediction are somehow manipulated so that a deity is not mentioned." App. 13a.

In dissent, Judge Campbell believed that "*Marsh* and *Stein* provide a reasonable basis for a rule allowing invocations and benedictions on public, ceremonial occasions," so long as school authorities take care to invite speakers representing a wide range of religious beliefs and nonreligious ethical philosophies. App. 16a.

INTRODUCTION AND SUMMARY OF ARGUMENT

When this Court invalidated state-mandated prayer in the classroom almost 30 years ago in *Engel v. Vitale*, 370 U.S. 421 (1962), it peered down the road to this case, and, contrary to the lower courts here, denied that the constitutional compass it was setting would put the Establishment Clause at odds with the "many manifestations in our public life of belief in God." Id. at 435 n.21. The *Engel* Court thus rebuffed Justice Stewart's concern, expressed in dissent, that beginning the school day with prayer is indistinguishable from opening sessions of Congress and this Court with prayer, or from invoking God's blessing at presidential inaugural ceremonies, or from countless other "official expressions of religious faith in and reliance upon a supreme Being" by institutions and officials of the federal government. Id. at 450 n.9. According to the *Engel* majority, "[s]uch patriotic or ceremonial occasions bear no true resemblance to the unquestioned religious exercise that the State of New York has sponsored in this instance." Id. at 435 n.21.

Notwithstanding the *Engel* majority's confident assessment of the validity of official ceremonial references to a deity, the courts below prohibited any reference to a deity in public school graduation ceremonies on the basis of the "effects" prong of the *Lemon* tripartite test. Both the court of appeals majority and the district court equated official reference to a deity with endorsement of religion. Because "reference to a deity necessarily implicates religion," the courts below believed that it was a "forgone conclusion" that the "Providence School Committee ha[d] in effect endorsed religion in general by authorizing an appeal to a deity in public school graduation ceremonies." App. 25a. At the same time, the courts below dismissed *Marsh* as a narrow exception to *Lemon*, extending only to official religious practices, such as legislative prayer, that were well known and broadly accepted when the First Amendment was framed in 1791—an exception inapplicable here because the origins of public schooling in this country can be traced back only a century and a half.

Under the reasoning of the lower courts in this case, it is clear that all references to a deity, not just invocations and benedictions, must be cleansed from public school graduation ceremonies. Recitations of the Pledge of Allegiance, for example, would be forbidden. Similarly, commencement speakers would have to take care to avoid references to a deity in their remarks to the graduates. The Rev. Martin Luther King's well-known commencement address to the 1961 graduating class of Lincoln University could not, consistent with the ruling below, be delivered at the 1991 graduation ceremony of a Providence public high school.[5]

But this is not all. For the reasoning of the courts below cannot be confined to public school graduation ceremonies. The invocation and benediction at issue in this case are but a single and unremarkable manifestation of the venerable and broad tradition of official expression of religious values in the public life of the Nation. If the courts below have correctly stated the law, then a staggering variety of ceremonial and familiar practices in our public life must be censored to exclude forbidden references to a deity, just as the district court below revised Rabbi Gutterman's invocation. Indeed, if governmental expression of religious belief is what the First Amendment forbids, Rabbi Gutterman's manifestly nonsectarian prayers at Nathan Bishop Middle School's graduation ceremony surely pale as a constitutional threat when compared to the Reverend Billy Graham's distinctly sectarian prayer to the Holy Trinity at President Bush's inauguration, a ceremony attended by the constitutional officers of all three branches of the federal government and witnessed by millions of people throughout this country and the world. *County of Allegheny v. American Civil Liberties Union*, 492 U.S. 573, 671–72 n.9 (1989) (Kennedy, J., concurring in the judgment in part and dissenting in part).

By striking down a practice that is as old as American public education itself[6] and that traditionally has been and is now incorporated in the commencement exercises of the vast bulk of schools and colleges throughout the country,[7] the lower courts' ruling forces the candid mind to question the legitimacy of the constitutional doctrine that yields so startling a result. To be sure, we argue in Part II below that the *Lemon* test does not require invalidation of graduation invocations and benedictions. But we cannot conscientiously argue that the lower courts' application of *Lemon* was unreasonable. Indeed, since the granting of the Petition for Certiorari in this case, both the California Supreme Court and the Court of Appeals for the Fifth Circuit have decided the precise issue raised here, one upholding graduation invocations and benedictions under *Lemon* and the other striking them down.[8]

---

[5] King's speech contained a number of references to the deity, and he concluded his commencement address with the same stirring words later made famous in his "I Have A Dream" speech delivered from the steps of the Lincoln Memorial on August 28, 1963: That will be the day when all of God's children, black men and white men, Jews and Gentiles, Catholics and Protestants, will be able to join hands and sing in the words of the old Negro spiritual, "Free at last! Free at last! Thank God Almighty, we are free at last!" Martin Luther King, Jr., Commencement Address, Lincoln University, June 6, 1961 in 31 *Negro History Bulletin* 10, 15.

[6] At least as early as May 31, 1804, at the first graduation ceremony of one of the nation's first public universities—the University of Georgia—The Reverend Mr. Marshall offered an invocation, and The Reverend Hope Hull concluded the proceedings with a prayer. A. Hull. *A Historical Sketch of the University of Georgia* 17-19 (1894); *Augusta [Ga] Chronicle*, June 23, 1804. At the University of Virginia, founded by Thomas Jefferson, an "Order of Exercises" dated June 26, 1850, began with prayer. J. Whitehead, *The Rights of Religious Persons in Public Education* 210 (1991). Indeed, the academic ceremonies of graduation, dating back before the founding of our country, are largely drawn from religious ceremonies. DuPuy, "Religion, Graduation and the First Amendment: A Threat or a Shadow?", 35 *Drake L. Rev.* 323, 358 (1985–1986). In *Stein*, Judge Milburn observed that the courts "can take judicial notice that invocations and benedictions at public school commencements have been a traditional practice since the beginning of public schools in this country." 822 F.2d at 1410 (Milburn, J., concurring).

[7] Today invocations and benedictions are recognized as standard elements of graduation ceremonies. K. Sheard, *Academic Heraldry in America* 71 (1962) ("The commencement program today consists primarily of an invocation, a commencement address, the awarding of earned degrees, the awarding of honorary degrees, and the benediction."). *The Commencement Manual of the National Association of Secondary School Principals*, at 2 (1975) states that "nearly every program includes an invocation and a benediction."

[8] Compare *Jones v. Clear Creek Indep. School Dist.*, No. 89-2638 (5th Cir. April 18, 1991) (Lexis U.S. App. 6746) (upholding graduation invocations and benedictions) with *Sands v. Morongo Unified School Dist.*, No. SO12721 (Cal. May 6, 1991) (Lexis 1724) (invalidating graduation invocations and benedictions). A number of other federal and state courts have considered the issue, and their conclusions have been mixed. Cases upholding graduation invocations and similar practices are: *Stein*, 822 F.2d 1406 (6th Cir. 1987); *Albright v. Board of Educ.*, No. 90-C-639G (D. Utah May 15, 1991); *Grossberg v. Deusebio*, 380 F.Supp. 285, 289 E.D.Va. 1974); *Wood v. Mt. Lebanon Township School Dist.*, 342 F.Supp. 1293, 1294-95 (W.D. Pa. 1972); *Wiest v. Mt. Lebanon School Dist.*, 457 Pa. 166, 320 A.2d 362, 365-66, cert. denied, 419 U.S. 967 (1974). See also *Florey, v. Sioux Falls School Dist.*, 619 F.2d 1311 (8th Cir.), cert. denied, 449 U.S. 987 (1980) upholding school board rules outlining school activities during Christmas assemblies); *Brandon v. Board of Educ.*, 635 F.2d 971, 979 (2d Cir. 1980), cert. denied, 454 U.S. 1123 (1981) ("[W]here a clergyman briefly appears at a yearly high school graduation ceremony, no image of official state approval is created."); *Bogen v. Doty*, 598 F.2d 1110, 1111 (8th Cir. 1979) (upholding invocations at meetings of county board); *Lincoln v. Page*, 109 N.H. 30, 241 A.2d 799 (1968) (upholding invocations at town meetings); *Anderson v. Salt Lake City Corp.*, 475 F.2d 29, 34 (10th Cir.), cert. denied, 414 U.S. 879 (1973) (upholding posting of Ten Commandments in public building); Opinion of the Justices, 108 N.H. 97, 228 A.2d 161 (1967) (bill requiring the posting of "In God We Trust" in public school classrooms would be constitutional). Cases invalidating graduation invocations and similar practices are: *Lundberg v. West Monona Community School Dist.*, 731 F.Supp. 331 (N.D. Iowa 1989); *Graham v.*

The division among the lower courts on the issue of graduation prayer, however, is far from atypical in the jurisprudence that has developed under *Lemon*'s tripartite test. Since its inception, the *Lemon* test has spawned a cacophony of conflicting decisions in the lower federal courts, particularly in cases involving practices with historical sanction.[9] And candor requires us to add, respectfully, that the anomalies spawned by *Lemon* have not been limited to the inferior federal courts.[10] Not surprisingly, a majority of the Justices of this Court have expressed dissatisfaction with aspects of the *Lemon* test.[11]

More telling, however, is the dissatisfaction with *Lemon* implied in the Court's decision in *Marsh*. In upholding the Nebraska Legislature's practice of opening its sessions with a prayer offered by a paid chaplain, the *Marsh* Court did not attempt the exceedingly difficult task of justifying the practice at issue under the *Lemon* test. Indeed, Justice Brennan observed in dissent that, "if the Court were to judge legislative prayer through the unsentimental eyes of our settled doctrine [i.e., the *Lemon* test], it would have to strike it down as a clear violation of the Establishment Clause." *Marsh*, 463 U.S. at 796 (Brennan, J., dissenting). But the *Lemon* test not only is unsentimental, it is indifferent to our Nation's heritage of official ceremonial acknowledgments of religious faith, and woodenly applying its formulaic prescription would have required the *Marsh* majority to ignore the common-sense proposition on which its decision was largely premised:

> It can hardly be thought that in the same week Members of the First Congress voted to appoint and to pay a chaplain [to deliver opening prayers] for each House and also voted to approve the draft of the First Amendment for submission to the states, they intended the

---

Central Community School Dist., 608 F.Supp. 531 (S.D. Iowa 1985); *Doe v. Aldine Indep. School Dist.*, 563 F.Supp. 883 (S.D. Tex. 1982); *Bennett v. Livermore Unified School Dist.*, 193 Cal. App.3d, 1012, 238 Cal. Rptr. 819 (1987); *Kay v. David Douglas School Dist.*, 79 Or. App. 384, 719 P.2d 875 (1986), rev'd on other grounds, 303 Or. 574, 738 P.2d 1389 (1987), cert. denied, 484 U.S. 1032; see also *North Carolina Civil Liberties Union v. Constangy*, 751 F.Supp. 552 (W.D.N.C. 1990) (judge's practice of opening daily sessions with recitation of brief prayer was unconstitutional).

[9] Challenges to religious imagery included in city seals illustrate this point, for such seals commonly are designed near in time to a city's founding and reflect the distinctive social, cultural, geographic, or historical roots of the community. For example, in *Johnson v. Board of County Commissioners*, 528 F.Supp. 919 (D.N.M. 1981), rev'd sub non. *Friedman v. Board of County Commissioners of Bernalillo County*, 781 F.2d 777 (10th Cir. 1985) (en banc), the district court rejected an Establishment Clause challenge to a city seal, concluding that it did not have the effect of impermissibly advancing religion because it was "an iconographic illustration of the rich cultural heritage of Bernalillo County." 528 F.Supp. at 924. The Tenth Circuit nevertheless found the district court's analysis to be clearly erroneous, driven by its understanding of the Lemon "effects" test to observe that a "person approached by officers leaving a patrol car emblazoned with this seal could reasonably assume that the officers were the Christian police. . . ." 781 F.2d at 782. See also *Harris v. City of Zion*, 927 F.2d 1401, 1403-04 (7th Cir. 1991) (holding unconstitutional Zion's nearly century-old seal); id. at 1423 (Easterbrook, J., dissenting) ("Zion's seal has been in use for 89 years without stifling religious diversity. . . . Not one resident of Zion other than Harris has expressed concern."); Brief for Liberty Counsel as Amicus Curiae 2-18 (reviewing "chaotic, conflicting decisions in the lower courts" under the *Lemon* test).

[10] This Court has itself admitted to the "considerable internal inconsistency" in its opinions involving the Religion Clauses, *Walz v. Tax Comm'n*, 397 U.S. 664, 668 (1970), and confessed that under *Lemon* it has "sacrifice[d] clarity and predictability for flexibility." *Committee for Public Educ. v. Regan*, 444 U.S. 646, 662 (1980). See, e.g., *Wallace v. Jaffree*, 472 U.S. 38, 110-11 (1985) (Rehnquist, J., dissenting) (setting out examples of the difficulty the Court has had in "making the *Lemon* test yield principled results"). Paulsen, "Religion, Equality, and the Constitution: An Equal Protection Approach to Establishment Clause Adjudication," 61 *Notre Dame L. Rev.* 311, 316-17 (1986) ("This scatter-pattern of decisions is the combined product of the tripartite *Lemon* test and the Court's occasional desire to provide an escape from the straitjacket that an honest application of *Lemon* would force upon society. . . ."); Choper, "The Religion Clauses of the First Amendment: Reconciling the Conflict," 41 *U. Pitt. L. Rev.* 673, 681 (1980) (noting "the absence of any principled rationale" in the Court's Religion Clause jurisprudence); Kurland, "The Irrelevance of the Constitution: The Religion Clauses of the First Amendment and the Supreme Court," 24 *Vill. L. Rev.* 3, 20 (1978) ("Judicial discretion, rather than constitutional mandate, controls the results."). In particular, a literal application of *Lemon* would seem plainly to invalidate a number of practices which this Court has held are required by the Free Exercise Clause. Compare *Sherbert v. Verner*, 374 U.S. 398 (1963) (government may not burden an employee's free exercise rights by failing to accommodate his Sabbath observance) with *Estate of Thornton v. Caldor, Inc.*, 472 U.S. 703 (1985) (statute that provides employees with unqualified right not to work on their Sabbath violates the Establishment Clause).

[11] See *County of Allegheny v. American Civil Liberties Union*, 492 U.S. at 656 (Kennedy, J., concurring in the judgment and dissenting in part) ("Substantial revision of our Establishment Clause doctrine may be in order."); *Wallace v. Jaffree*, 472 U.S. 38, 112 (1985) (Rehnquist, J., dissenting) (*Lemon* test is "a constitutional theory [that] has no basis in the history of the amendment it seeks to interpret, is difficult to apply and yields unprincipled results."); *Aguilar v. Felton*, 473 U.S. 402, 429 (1985) (O'Connor, J., dissenting) (expressing "doubts about the entanglement test"); *Roemer v. Board of Public Works*, 426 U.S. 736, 768 (1976) (White, J., concurring in the judgment) ("I am no more reconciled now to *Lemon* than I was when it was decided. . . . The threefold test of *Lemon* imposes unnecessary, and . . . superfluous tests for establishing [a First Amendment violation]."); *Edwards v. Aguillard*, 482 U.S. 578, 636 (1987) (Scalia, J., dissenting) ("pessimistic evaluation . . . of the totality of *Lemon* is particularly applicable to the 'purpose' prong").

> Establishment Clause of the Amendment to forbid what they had just declared acceptable.

Marsh, 463 U.S. at 790. Thus, in *Marsh*, and we submit, in this case, the *Lemon* test was ill-suited to assist the Court in its essential task, which Justice Brennan well described in *Abington School Dist. v. Schempp*, 374 U.S. 203, 294 (1963) (Brennan, J., concurring): "[T]he line we must draw between the permissible and the impermissible is one which accords with history and faithfully reflects the understanding of the Founding Fathers."

In the pages that follow, we demonstrate that the history surrounding the framing and ratification of the Establishment Clause reveals two points of controlling significance in this case. First, by making particular provision for religious liberty within the otherwise general First Amendment protection of expression, the Framers did not intend to deprecate or restrain religious expression in the life of the nation. The Establishment Clause was not intended to operate as some sort of constitutional gag order, enjoining public officials and their invitees to omit any reference to God from civic ceremonies. To the contrary, public ceremonial acknowledgments of faith in God were welcomed and encouraged by the Founders; they, certainly no less than contemporary Americans, were "a religious people whose institutions presuppose[d] a Supreme Being." *Zorach v. Clauson*, 343 U.S. 306, 313 (1952).

Second, the history of the First Amendment reveals why the Founders engaged in and encouraged official ceremonial expressions of religious faith: such references did not involve the government's coercive powers. The struggle for religious freedom in this country was animated by an overriding philosophical premise—that matters of conscience can be influenced only by reason, not force, and that in appealing to reason, "all men [should] be free to profess, and by argument to maintain, their opinion in matters of religion." Virginia, Act for Establishing Religious Freedom (1785), in 5 *The Founders' Constitution* 84, 85 (P. Kurland & R. Lerner eds. 1987) (hereinafter "Kurland"). The Founders did not fear expression of religious values by public officials; they feared coercion of religious values by public officials. The First Amendment was designed by the Framers to protect only against the latter.

ARGUMENT

I. THE GRADUATION PRAYERS HERE DID NOT VIOLATE THE ESTABLISHMENT CLAUSE BECAUSE THEY DID NOT INVOLVE GOVERNMENT COERCION OF RELIGIOUS CONFORMITY

A. Government coercion of religious conformity is a necessary element of an Establishment Clause violation

1. The philosophy of the Founders Among the Founders, Madison and Jefferson were "the architects of our principles of religious liberty." *American Jewish Congress v. City of Chicago*, 827 F.2d 120, 132 (7th Cir. 1987) (Easterbrook, J., dissenting). The blueprint, however, was in large part provided by John Locke, probably the foremost exponent of the classical liberal philosophy of government that animated the Framers generally, and Jefferson particularly. In his Letter Concerning Toleration, Locke distinguishes between government coercion relating to religion, which he deemed unjustifiable, and government expression or persuasion concerning religion, which he deemed unobjectionable. Locke wrote: The care of souls cannot belong to the civil magistrate, because his power consists only in outward force; but true and saving religion consists in the inward persuasion of the mind. . . . Confiscation of estate, imprisonment, torments, nothing of that nature can have any such efficacy as to make men change the inward judgment that they have framed of things. It may indeed be alleged that the magistrate may make use of arguments, and thereby draw the heterodox into the way of truth, and procure their salvation. I grant it; but this is common to him with other men. . . . Every man has commission to admonish, exhort, convince another of error, and, by reasoning, to draw him into truth; but to give laws, receive obedience, and compel with the sword, belongs to none but the magistrate. And upon this ground, I affirm that the magistrate's power extends not to the establishing of any articles of faith, or forms of worship, by the force of his laws. For laws are of no force at all without penalties, and penalties in this case are absolutely impertinent, because they are not proper to convince the mind.[12]

These views on religious liberty form a common thread running throughout Madison's and Jefferson's writings on the subject, and are

---

[12] Locke, "A Letter Concerning Toleration" (1684), in Kurland, supra p. 14, at 52, 53. St. George Tucker in *Blackstone's Commentaries* (1803), in Kurland, supra p. 14, at 96, later recognized a similar distinction between unjustifiable religious coercion and unobjectionable official persuasion or recognition of religion. Tucker cites as "an axiom, concerning the human mind," that "religion, or the duty we owe to our Creator, and the manner of discharging it, can be dictated only by reason and conviction, not by force or violence." He elaborated: In

reflected perhaps nowhere more distinctly than in Jefferson's Notes on the State of Virginia. Jefferson, Notes on the State of Virginia, Query 17, 157-61 (1784) (hereinafter "Notes"), in Kurland, supra p. 14, at 79-80. Jefferson opened by recounting that this country was settled largely by immigrants fleeing the coercion, indeed persecution, of English laws demanding their conformity to and support of the established Anglican Church. Many of those settlers, however, including those who established Virginia, "shewed equal intolerance" of differing religious faiths once they became "[p]ossessed . . . of the powers of making, administering, and executing the laws. . . ." Id.[13]

In 1776, Jefferson noted, the newly independent Commonwealth of Virginia adopted a Constitution containing a Declaration of Rights with a clause guaranteeing religious liberty.[14] Jefferson complained that in obedience to the Virginia Constitution's guaranty of religious freedom, the legislature had repealed only the prior acts of the English parliament compelling observance of and support for the established English church.[15] The legislature did not repeal prior acts of the colonial assembly that coerced conformity to the Christian religion by, inter alia, disqualifying dissenters from holding public office and imposing criminal penalties. Jefferson made clear that the freedom to profess one's religious opinions publicly is integral to the freedom to have religious opinions. And the free exercise of the right to form and profess one's religious sentiments causes no injury, while subjecting that right to government coercion causes no good. As Jefferson put it:

> The error seems not sufficiently eradicated, that the operations of the mind, as well as the acts of the body, are subject to the coercion of the laws. . . . The legitimate powers of government extend to such acts only as are injurious to others. But it does me no injury for my neighbor to say there are twenty gods, or no god. It neither picks my pocket nor breaks my leg. . . . Constraint may make him worse by making him a hypocrite, but it will never make him a truer man. . . . Reason and free inquiry are the only effectual agents against error. . . . It is error alone which needs the support of government. Truth can stand by itself. Subject opinion to coercion: Whom will you make your inquisitors? Fallible men; men governed by bad passions, by private as well as public reasons. And why subject it to coercion? To produce uniformity. But is uniformity of opinion desirable? . . . Difference of opinion is advantageous in religion. The several sects perform the office of a Censor morum over each other. . . . What has been the effect of coercion? To make one half the world fools, and the other half hypocrites. . . . [W]e cannot effect [truth] by force. Reason and persuasion are the only practicable instruments. Notes, in Kurland, supra p. 14, at 79-80.

2. The fight for religious liberty in Virginia

In 1779, Jefferson drafted an "Act for Establishing Religious Freedom." This Court has often recognized that the history surrounding the Virginia General Assembly's enactment in 1786

---

vain, therefore, may the civil magistrate interpose the authority of human laws, to prescribe that belief, or produce that conviction, which human reason rejects. . . . The martyr at the stake, glories in his tortures, and proves that human law may punish, but cannot convince. . . . Id. at 96. Tucker further noted, however: Statesmen should countenance [genuine religion] only by exhibiting, in their own example, a conscientious regard to it in those forms which are most agreeable to their own judgments, and by encouraging their fellow citizens in doing the same. Id. at 97.

[13] Legal compulsion was the hallmark of establishments in the American colonies, the colonists having adopted many of the practices that inspired their own flights from England and elsewhere in Europe. See 6 W. & A. Durant, *The Story of Civilization* 208–20, 501–506, 523–601, 631–41 (1957); L. Pfeffer, *Church, State and Freedom*, 20-30 (rev. 1st ed. 1967). Professor Joseph Brady, in a seminal historical work on the Establishment Clause, quotes historian Marcus W. Jernegan's description of the typical laws establishing state religions: The general rule in those colonies having an established church was to require dissenters to support it by paying tithes or taxes, and also to attend the official church services under penalty. They were also frequently required to submit to various tests or oaths, and to subscribe to the creeds and catechisms of the established church. Sometimes the right to settle in a colony, or the privilege of naturalization, or citizenship, or the right to vote and hold office, depended on submission to religious tests. J. Brady, *Confusion Twice Confounded: The First Amendment and the Supreme Court* 6–7 (1954). See also L. Levy, *The Establishment Clause: Religion and the First Amendment* 4 (1987).

[14] The religious freedom clause of Virginia's Declaration of Rights reads as follows: That religion, or the duty we owe to our Creator, and the manner of discharging it can be directed only by reason and conviction, not by force or violence; and therefore all men are equally entitled to the free exercise of religion, according to the dictates of conscience; and that it is the mutual duty of all to practice Christian forbearance, love, and charity toward each other. Virginia Declaration of Rights, Section 16 (June 12, 1776), Va. Const. art. I, s 16, in Kurland, supra p. 14, at 70.

[15] The Anglican Church of England was established in Virginia's original charter in 1606, which required all ministers in the Colony to preach Christianity according to Anglican doctrines. L. Levy, supra n.13, at 3. In 1611, the Colony required all citizens to attend church and observe the Sabbath, and enacted severe punishments for blasphemy, sacrilege, and criticism of the doctrine of the Trinity. Id. The law also required all to embrace Anglican doctrine, and to pay for the maintenance of Anglican churches and ministers. Id. at 3–4. Every clergyman was required to accept the Anglican Thirty-Nine Articles of Faith, and every church was required to follow the liturgy of the Church of England according to the Anglican Book of Common Prayer. Id. at 4.

of Jefferson's bill accurately reflect "the long and intensive struggle for religious freedom in America" and is "particularly relevant in the search for the First Amendment's meaning." *McGowan v. Maryland*, 366 U.S. 420, 437 (1961). The Religious Freedom Act was aimed specifically at government coercion in the form of (1) taxation for the support of religion; (2) religious tests for holding public office; and (3) government restraints on the propagation of religious beliefs. The Act's substantive provision reads as follows: [N]o man shall be compelled to frequent or support any religious worship, place, or ministry whatsoever, nor shall be enforced, restrained, molested, or burthened in his body or goods, nor shall otherwise suffer, on account of his religious opinions or beliefs; but that all men shall be free to profess, and by argument to maintain, their opinion in matters of religion, and that the same shall in no wise diminish, enlarge, or affect their civil capacities. Virginia, Act for Establishing Religious Freedom, in Kurland, supra p. 14 at 85.

As Judge Easterbrook has noted, the Act "does not protest government use of persuasion on matters religious; it is concerned with compulsion alone." American Jewish Congress, 827 F.2d at 135 (Easterbrook, J., dissenting). Indeed, far from protesting government use of persuasion on religious matters, the Act guarantees to "all men" freedom of religious expression. "All men" clearly includes those holding public office, for an essential purpose of the Act was to render religious belief and expression irrelevant to one's "civil capacities," such as the ability to seek and hold public office.[16] That government and government officials are no less free than ordinary citizens to express religious opinions is thus clear from the Act's substantive protections. But if any doubt persists on this point, it is foreclosed by the Act's preamble, which itself contains a full-bodied expression of religious belief, arguing in effect that the principles reflected in the Act were Divinely inspired. The preamble provides in pertinent part:

> Whereas Almighty God hath created the mind free; that all attempts to influence it by temporal punishments or burthens, or by civil incapacitations, tend only to beget habits of hypocrisy and meanness, and are a departure from the plan of the Holy author of our religion, who being Lord both of body and mind, yet chose not to propagate it by coercions on either, as was in his Almighty power to do.... Virginia, Act for Establishing Religious Freedom, in Kurland, supra p. 14, at 84.

If Rabbi Gutterman's invocation in this case violated the Establishment Clause, then Virginia's enactment of the Act for Establishing Religious Freedom was itself an establishment of religion, and if reenacted today, Jefferson's preamble would have to be deleted. See American Jewish Congress, 827 F.2d at 136 (Easterbrook, J., dissenting).

Jefferson's Religious Freedom Act was not enacted until 1786, in the aftermath of Patrick Henry's unsuccessful attempt to pass "A Bill Establishing A Provision for Teachers of the Christian Religion" ("Assessment Bill").[17] Henry's bill was "nothing more nor less than a taxing measure for the support of religion, designed to revive the payment of tithes suspended since 1777." *Everson v. Board of Educ.*, 330 U.S. 1, 36 (1947) (Rutledge, J., dissenting). The Assessment Bill permitted each taxpayer to designate which Christian church would receive his payment, and in default of a designation, the taxes were paid into a public fund to aid "seminaries of learning." Id.

Madison led the opposition to the Assessment Bill, briefing the arguments against it in his famed Memorial and Remonstrance Against Religious Assessments.[18] Madison, Memorial and Remonstrance Against Religious Assessments (1785) in Kurland, supra p. 14, at 82–84. The Memorial and Remonstrance is a bill of particulars against the use of government power to coerce support of religion. Madison's main arguments against the Assessment Bill sprang from a common theme, stated in his preamble: that the Bill, "if finally armed with the sanctions of a law, will be a dangerous abuse of power . . ." Id. at 82.

---

[16] While the language of the Act's substantive provision admits of no doubt on this point, the preamble speaks directly to the issue as well: [O]ur civil rights have no dependence on our religious opinions, any more than our opinions in physics or geometry; . . . therefore the proscribing any citizen as unworthy the public confidence by laying upon him an incapacity of being called to offices of trust and emolument, unless he profess or renounce this or that religious opinion, is depriving him injuriously of those privileges and advantages to which in common with his fellow citizens he has a natural right; . . . it tends only to corrupt the principles of that religion it is meant to encourage, by bribing with a monopoly of worldly honours and emoluments, those who will externally profess and conform to it.... Virginia, Act for Establishing Religious Freedom, in Kurland, supra p. 14, at 84.

[17] The Bill appears in *Everson v. Board of Educ.*, 330 U.S. 1, 72-74 (1947) (Appendix to Opinion of Rutledge, J., dissenting).

[18] Justice Rutledge characterized the Memorial and Remonstrance as "the most concise and the most accurate statement of the views of the First Amendment's author concerning what is 'an establishment of religion.' " *Everson*, 330 U.S. at 37 (Rutledge, J., dissenting).

In his lead argument against the measure, Madison invoked the Lockean postulate, enshrined in Virginia's Declaration of Rights, " 'that Religion or the duty which we owe to our Creator and the manner of discharging it, can be directed only by reason and conviction, not by force or violence.' " Id. p 1. Freedom of religion, being "in its nature an unalienable right," wrote Madison, is not abridged by one's membership in "Civil Society," and thus is subject neither to "the will of the majority" or "to that of the Legislative Body." Id. pp 1, 2. Madison warned that a government "which can force a citizen to contribute three pence only of his property for the support of any one establishment, may force him to conform to any other establishment in all cases whatsoever." Id. p 3. He argued further that "compulsive support" of religion frustrates rather than maintains "the purity and efficacy of Religion," noting that historically religion had flourished "without the support of human laws," while "ecclesiastical establishments" had led to religious "superstition, bigotry and persecution." Id. at 82-83 pp 4, 6, 7. Finally, Madison warned against arming the proposed Bill "with the force of a law," and argued that "attempts to enforce by legal sanctions" measures as widely unpopular as the Assessment Bill would "tend to enervate the laws in general." Id. at 83–84 pp 11, 13.

For Madison, the evil of the Assessment Bill was its proposed use of government power to coerce support of religion, which he saw as the sine qua non of an "establishment." Nowhere in his Memorial and Remonstrance did he voice concern about expression of religious beliefs by government or its officials. To the contrary, not only did he extol the "freedom to embrace, to profess and to observe" religious beliefs (id. at 82 P 4), he exercised that freedom in the Memorial and Remonstrance itself, closing it with a prayer to "the Supreme Lawgiver of the Universe."[19]

The Memorial and Remonstrance not only brought about the defeat of the Assessment Bill, it also generated popular support for Jefferson's Religious Freedom Bill, which passed in January 1786. Many years later, Madison praised the Religious Freedom Bill as "a true standard of Religious liberty," describing it as follows: "Here the separation between the authority of human laws, and the natural rights of Man excepted from the grant on which all political authority is founded, is traced as distinctively as words can admit, and the limits to this authority established with as much solemnity as the forms of legislation can express." Madison, Detached Memoranda (1817) (hereinafter "Detached Memoranda"), in Kurland, supra p. 14, at 103.

3. The framing of the Establishment Clause Following hard on the heels of this experience in Virginia were the debates in the First Congress over the Establishment Clause of the First Amendment. Madison, a member of the House of Representatives from Virginia, again played the leading role. The debate in the States over ratification of the Constitution had centered on the Constitutional Convention's failure to include a bill of rights. Opposition to the Constitution was led by the Anti-Federalists, who believed that a bill of rights was essential to preserving individual liberties against encroachment by the national government. Supporters of ratification, the Federalists, argued that a bill of rights was unnecessary because the national government lacked the delegated power to act in a manner that would violate their religious and other civil liberties. Still, two states—Rhode Island and North Carolina—refused to ratify the Constitution in the absence of amendments in the nature of a bill of rights, and three of the ratifying states—New Hampshire, New York, and Virginia—proposed that an amendment guaranteeing religious freedom be offered by the First Congress.[20] J. Elliot, *Debates on the Federal Constitution* 659 (1891); 1 id. at 328.

Madison took the lead in introducing a set of proposed amendments in the House of Representatives, including the following proposal concerning religious freedom: "The Civil Rights of none shall be abridged on account of religious belief or worship, nor shall any na-

[19] Madison prayed [t]hat the Supreme Lawgiver of the Universe, by illuminating those to whom it is addressed, may on the one hand, turn their Councils from every act which would affront his holy prerogative, or violate the trust committed to them: and on the other guide them into every measure which may be worthy of his blessing, may redound to their own praise and may establish more firmly the liberties, the prosperity, and the happiness of the Commonwealth. Id. P 15.

[20] The Virginia proposal was typical: That religion, or the duty which we owe to our Creator, and the manner of discharging it can be directed only by reason and conviction, not by force and violence and therefore all men have an equal, natural and inalienable right to the free exercise of religion, according to the dictates of conscience, and that no particular religious sect or society ought to be favored or established by law in preference to others. Virginia Ratifying Convention, Proposed Amendments (1788), in Kurland, supra p. 14, at 89. North Carolina proposed an identical amendment, and New York and Rhode Island quite similar ones. See J. Elliot, *Debates on the Federal Constitution* 244, 334 (1891). New Hampshire proposed an amendment stating: "Congress shall make no laws touching religion or to infringe the rights of conscience." 1 id. at 362.

tional religion be established, nor shall the full and equal rights of conscience be in any manner, or on any pretext, infringed." 1 *Annals of Cong.* 451 (J. Gales ed. 1834). Madison's proposals were referred to a Select Committee consisting of Madison and ten others. The Committee ultimately reported out the following language: "[N]o religion shall be established by law, nor shall the equal rights of conscience be infringed." Id. at 729.

The debate over this proposal in the House was not extensive. Madison's comments make clear, however, that the purpose of the proposed amendment was to protect against government coercion of religious observance or support. Madison advised his colleagues that "he apprehended the meaning of the words to be, that Congress should not establish a religion, and enforce the legal observation of it by law, nor compel men to worship God in any manner contrary to their conscience." Id. at 730, in Kurland, supra p. 14, at 93. Representative Benjamin Huntington agreed with Madison's understanding of the amendment's meaning, but feared that "others might find it convenient to put another construction upon it." He suggested that it might be construed to prevent enforcement in federal court of private pledges to contribute to the support of a minister or a church building. See id. at 730-31, in Kurland, supra p. 14, at 93. Madison answered that insertion of the word "national" before the word "religion" in the proposal would "point the amendment directly to the object it was intended to prevent." Id. at 731, in Kurland, supra p. 14, at 93. That object, according to Madison, was that "one sect might obtain a preeminence, or two combine together, and establish a religion to which they would compel others to conform." Id., in Kurland, supra p. 14, at 93.[21]

The debates in the Senate were secret, and there is no record of any further debate on the Religion Clauses in the House. *Wallace v. Jaffree*, 472 U.S. at 97 (Rehnquist, J., dissenting). And while the proposed amendment was revised several times before the House and Senate finally agreed on the language that ultimately became the First Amendment (see id.), none of the changes affected Madison's points about the intended meaning of the Establishment Clause. American Jewish Congress, 827 F.2d at 136 (Easterbrook, J., dissenting).

Thus according to the chief architect and sponsor of the First Amendment in the First Congress, the Establishment Clause was designed to protect against laws[22] compelling conformity in matters of religion. No one disagreed with Madison's statements concerning the intended meaning of the provision. Indeed, the debate in the House over the wording of the amendment did not question the intended meaning of the amendment—on that issue Madison's view was accepted as common ground. Rather, the debate over the Establishment Clause focused on the concern that the proposed language might be construed to go beyond the meaning ascribed to it by Madison.

But whatever else may be said about the views of the First Congress concerning the meaning of the Establishment Clause, this much is clear: the Framers of the First Amendment did not conceive that constitutional protection against government establishments of religion would forbid the expression of religious opinions by government or its officials. While there was no discussion on this issue among the Founders at the time of the framing of the First Amendment, evidence of their views on it abounds nonetheless. For "their actions reveal their intent." *Marsh*, 463 U.S. at 790.

4. The conduct of the Founders As this Court has often recognized, our Nation's tradition of official ceremonial expressions of religious beliefs dates back to its inception. See, e.g., *March v. Chambers*, 463 U.S. at 787-88; *Lynch v. Donnelly*, 465 U.S. 668, 673-74 (1984). America was founded on an appeal "to the Supreme Judge of the world" and to "the laws of nature and of nature's God." The Declaration of Independence also proclaimed that all men "are endowed by their Creator with cer-

[21] Representative Elbridge Gerry attacked Madison's suggested insertion of the word "national" as supporting the claim of the Anti-Federalists, made in state ratifying conventions, that the Federalists favored a "national" government rather than a federal one. Madison withdrew his suggestion. 1 *Annals of Congress* 731, in Kurland, supra p. 14, at 93. Representative Samuel Livermore of New Hampshire moved that the proposed language be altered to echo that proposed by his state's ratifying convention: "Congress shall make no laws touching religion, or infringing the rights of conscience." Id. Livermore's motion carried. Id.

[22] Indeed, the use of the word "law" in the Establishment Clause underscores the Framers' intent to prohibit coercive practices. ("Congress shall make no law. . . ."). A law by definition involves a binding obligation backed by compulsion. *Zwerling v. Reagan*, 576 F. Supp. 1373, 1376-78 (C.D. Cal. 1983) ("Fundamental to the existence of a law is the obligation it creates and the sanction it imposes. It is a matter of compulsion and does not take the nature of a plea, suggestion or request."). See also *American Banana Co. v. United Fruit Co.*, 213 U.S. 347, 356 (1909) ("Law is a statement of the circumstances in which the public force will be brought to bear upon men through the courts."); *United States Fidelity & Guaranty Co. v. Guenther*, 281 U.S. 34, 37 (1930) (defining law "as meaning the rules of action or conduct duly prescribed by controlling authority, and having binding legal force.").

tain inalienable rights," and relied on "the protection of Divine Providence." George Washington, in his first inaugural address, sought the blessings of God, "that Almighty Being" and "the Great Author of every public and private good." Indeed, Washington thought "it would be peculiarly improper to omit in [his] first official act [his] fervent supplications to that Almighty Being who rules over the universe. . . ."[23] Almost without exception, Washington's successors in office, up to and including President Bush,[24] have included in their inaugural addresses statements of religious sentiment and supplications for God's assistance in discharging their official obligations. Indeed, the inaugural addresses of both Thomas Jefferson (at both his first[25] and second[26] inaugural ceremonies) and James Madison[27] contain moving expressions of religious faith.

At the conclusion of Washington's inauguration ceremony, the new President and both Houses of Congress attended a religious service conducted by the First Episcopal Bishop of New York at St. Paul's Chapel in New York City, in accordance with a joint congressional resolution providing for the service. See A. Stokes & L. Pfeffer, *Church and State in the United States* 87 (rev. 1st ed. 1964).

On the day after the House of Representatives of the First Congress voted to adopt the Establishment Clause, the House adopted a resolution requesting President Washington to proclaim "a day of public thanksgiving and prayer, to be observed by acknowledging with grateful hearts the many and signal favours of Almighty God." *Lynch*, 465 U.S. at 675 n.2. Washington responded by proclaiming November 26, 1789, as a day of thanksgiving in which to offer "our prayers and supplications to the Great Lord and Ruler of Nations, and beseech Him to pardon our national and other transgressions." Id. Washington issued a similar proclamation of thanksgiving in 1795, and this practice was followed by President John Adams, who issued two such proclamations, and President Madison, who issued four.[28] R. Cord, *Separation of Church and State: Historical Fact and Current Fiction* 53 (1982). This tradition has been continued throughout our history by virtually every President, with the exception of Jefferson.[29] *Lynch*, 465 U.S. at 675 n.2; 3 A. Stokes, *Church and State in the United States* 180–93 (1950).

The First Congress also adopted the policy, followed ever since, of opening daily sessions of the House and Senate with prayers by an official chaplain. *Marsh*, 463 U.S. at 787–88. Madison was a member of the House Committee that proposed the policy, and he voted in favor of the bill authorizing it. Id. at 788 n.8.[30]

---

[23] George Washington, First Inaugural Address, April 30, 1789, in *Inaugural Addresses of the Presidents of the United States from George Washington, 1789 to George Bush, 1989* at 1, 2 (Bicentennial ed. 1989) (hereinafter cited as "Inaugural Addresses of the Presidents").

[24] And my first act as President is a prayer. I ask you to bow your heads: Heavenly Father, we bow our heads and thank You for Your love. Accept our thanks for the peace that yields this day and the shared faith that makes its continuance likely. Make us strong to do Your work, willing to heed and hear Your will, and write on our hearts these words: "Use power to help people." For we are given power not to advance our own purposes, nor to make a great show in the world, nor a name. There is but one just use of power, and it is to serve people. Help us remember it, Lord. Amen. George Bush, Inaugural Address, January 20, 1989, in *Inaugural Addresses of the Presidents*, supra n.23, at 345, 346.

[25] Kindly . . . enlightened by a benign religion, professed, indeed, and practiced in various forms, yet all of them inculcating honesty, truth, temperance, gratitude, and the love of man: acknowledging and adoring an overruling Providence, which by all its dispensations provides that it delights in the happiness of man here and his greater happiness hereafter. . . . And may that Infinite Power which rules the destinies of the universe lead our councils to what is best, and give them a favorable issue of your peace and prosperity. Thomas Jefferson, First Inaugural Address, March 4, 1801, in *Inaugural Addresses of the Presidents*, supra n.23, at 13, 15, 17.

[26] I shall need, too, the favor of that Being in whose hands we are, who led our fathers, as Israel of old, from their native land and planted them in a country flowing with all the necessaries and comforts of life; who has covered our infancy with His providence and our riper years with His wisdom and power, and to whose goodness I ask you to join in supplications with me that He will so enlighten the minds of your servants, guide their councils, and prosper their measures that whatsoever they do shall result in your good, and shall secure to you the peace, friendship, and approbation of all nations. Thomas Jefferson, Second Inaugural Address, March 4, 1805, in *Inaugural Addresses of the Presidents*, supra n.23, at 18, 22-23.

[27] In these my confidence will under every difficulty be best placed, next to that which we have all been encouraged to feel in the guardianship and guidance of that Almighty Being whose power regulates the destiny of nations, whose blessings have been so conspicuously dispensed to this rising Republic, and to whom we are bound to address our devout gratitude for the past, as well as our fervent supplications and best hopes for the future. James Madison, First Inaugural Address, March 4, 1809, in *Inaugural Addresses of the Presidents*, supra n.23, at 25, 28.

[28] Madison later questioned the wisdom, not the constitutionality, of his practice as President of issuing Thanksgiving proclamations. See Detached Memoranda, in Kurland, supra p. 14, at 105; American Jewish Congress, 827 F.2d at 136 (Easterbrook, J., dissenting).

[29] We discuss Jefferson's refusal to issue such proclamations at pp. 32–34, infra.

[30] Madison subsequently came to the view that paying congressional chaplains out of taxpayer funds violated the Establishment Clause. See Detached Memoranda, in Kurland, supra p. 14, at 104. Madison's constitutional objection to the chaplaincy system was apparently limited to the issue of tax support, although he also criticized the practice of opening Congress's sessions with a prayer by a chaplain as a violation of "equal rights." See id.

The chaplaincy practice was also followed by the Continental Congress from its inception in 1774. *Marsh*, 463 U.S. at 786-87.

Congress's early chaplains not only opened daily sessions with prayer, they conducted Sunday worship services in the hall of the House of Representatives. Beginning around 1800, the House of Representatives authorized the use of its hall for regular Sunday religious services performed by congressional chaplains or by visiting ministers. 1 Stokes, *Church and State in the United States* 499–507 (1st ed. 1950). Both Jefferson and Madison often attended these services while serving as President. Id. at 499, 501.

Nor did the First Congress hesitate to reenact the Northwest Ordinance of 1787, which provided that "[r]eligion, morality, and knowledge, being necessary to good government and the happiness of mankind, schools and the means of education shall forever be encouraged." *Wallace v. Jaffree*, 472 U.S. at 100 (Rehnquist, J., dissenting).

Ceremonial references to God have not been limited to the political branches of the federal government. This Court's own sessions have been opened by the Crier with the invocation "God save the United States and this Honorable Court" at least since the time of Chief Justice Marshall. See *Engel v. Vitale*, 370 U.S. 421, 446 (1962) (Stewart, J., dissenting). It is also noteworthy that Chief Justice John Jay, in March 1790 advised district court Judge Richard Law that the custom in New England courts of having a clergyman attend court sessions as chaplain "should in my opinion be observed and continued" during sessions held by Chief Justice Jay as circuit justice. 2 *The Documentary History of the Supreme Court of the United States*, 1799–1800 13 (1990).

5. The Founders' understanding of the Establishment Clause What this Court said in *Marsh* is equally apt here: "In this context, historical evidence sheds light not only on what the draftsmen intended the Establishment Clause to mean, but also on how they thought that Clause applied to the practice authorized by the First Congress—their actions reveal their intent." *Marsh*, 463 U.S. at 790.[31] Against the historical backdrop described above, it cannot reasonably be maintained that the Framers of the First Amendment intended the Establishment Clause to prohibit official expressions of religious sentiments—a practice that they freely engaged in and encouraged as public officials before, during, and after the framing of the Amendment itself.[32] To the contrary, this conduct of the Founders reflected their intentions concerning the Establishment Clause, which in turn reflected their philosophical beliefs concerning the proper relationship between religion and government.

As previously discussed, those who led the fight for religious freedom that culminated in ratification of the First Amendment valued truth above all else, in spiritual no less than political matters. "Truth can stand by itself," said Jefferson, "error alone . . . needs the support of government." Notes, in Kurland, supra

[31] The courts below evaded the lessons of the framing of the First Amendment by denying the relevance of that history to this case. They dismissed *Marsh* as a narrow exception to *Lemon* for official religious practices, such as legislative prayer, that were common in 1791 and were specifically approved by the First Congress. Thus, because public education did not become a part of our accepted traditions until the mid-19th Century, the *Marsh* case, according to the courts below, is inapposite here. But the history of legislative prayer not only reveals that the Framers of the Establishment Clause likely did not intend the Clause to forbid that specific practice; it also provides broader insight into what the First Congress intended the words "an establishment of religion" to mean. See *County of Allegheny*, 492 U.S. at 670 (Kennedy, J., concurring in the judgment in part and dissenting in part). In other words, the history surrounding the framing of the Establishment Clause (or any other constitutional provision) has both a retail and a wholesale significance. And any interpretation of the Clause faithful to its intended meaning "must permit not only legitimate practices two centuries old but also any other practices with no greater potential for an establishment of religion." Id. The contrary view advanced in this case by the courts below is on the order of saying that the Fourth Amendment does not reach electronic surveillance, that the Commerce Clause does not embrace interstate motor carriage, or that the First Amendment does not extend to the electronic media.

[32] Contrary to Judge Bownes' suggestion, App. 11a, this Court did not hold in *Edwards v. Aguillard*, 482 U.S. 583 n.4, that the "historical approach" taken in *Marsh* is inapplicable in the public schooling context. After noting that legislative prayer was upheld in *Marsh* on the basis of "historical acceptance of the practice," the *Edwards* Court stated: "Such a historical approach is not useful in determining the proper roles of church and state in public schools, since free public education was virtually nonexistent at the time the constitution was adopted." Id. This observation means only that because public education did not exist at the time of the Founding, there can be no historical acceptance of a practice relating to public education that would support the constitutionality of the practice. The observation in *Edwards* surely does not stand for the remarkable proposition that the constitutional history surrounding practices common in 1791 is without significance to the resolution of constitutional challenges to closely analogous innovations in 1991. In addition, it seems doubtful that the courts below would find that the historical circumstances surrounding the framing of the Establishment Clause limit the practices prohibited by the Clause in the same manner that the courts below believe those historical circumstances limit the practices permitted under the Clause. In other words, the courts below no doubt would agree that the First Amendment prohibits modern methods of establishing a religion no less than it prohibits ancient ones.

p. 14, at 80. The Founders knew that an "establishment" of religion could neither arise nor survive without government coercion, and that it would perish wherever men were "free to profess, and by argument to maintain, their opinion in matters of religion." Virginia, Act for Establishing Religious Freedom, in Kurland, supra p. 14, at 85. A simple statement of religious belief cannot coerce adherence by others. In Jefferson's vivid formulation, "[i]t neither picks my pocket nor breaks my leg." Notes, in Kurland, supra p. 14, at 80. This is no less true of the religious expressions of government and its officials, so long as neither employs the state's coercive powers.

In none of the historical examples discussed above did the religious expressive activities involve an attempt to use government power to coerce religious conformity. No one was required to attend the inaugural ceremonies of Presidents Washington, Jefferson, or Madison, and those who chose to attend were in no way required to accept or support the religious sentiments expressed by the speakers. No one was required to give thanks on the day designated for that purpose in the proclamations of President Washington and his successors, and those who chose to do so were in no way required to accept or support the religious beliefs professed by the proclamation's author. No one, legislator or citizen, was required to attend the chaplain's invocations opening sessions of Congress, nor to accept or support the religious beliefs expressed by the chaplain.[33] Because these expressive activities did not coerce religious conformity, the Founders engaged in them without fear that they violated the Establishment Clause.

Thus, the history surrounding the proposal, framing, and ratification of the Establishment Clause leads to this conclusion: the "wall of separation" between religion and government erected in the First Amendment was not understood or intended by the Framers to be a quarantine, so thoroughly isolating God from civic life that even acknowledgments of His existence were forbidden. Rather, the Establishment Clause was intended to separate, and thus to protect, religion from the coercive power of government.

6. Jefferson's "Wall of Separation" None of the Founders disagreed with this understanding of the Establishment Clause, including the author of the famous "wall of separation" metaphor. Indeed, Jefferson's letter to the Danbury Baptist Association is a concise summary of the central philosophical precepts on which he had elaborated at greater length in his earlier Notes on the State of Virginia, see supra at 16-18.[34]

The nature of Jefferson's "wall of separation between Church and State" is illuminated by the following statement appearing earlier in the same sentence of his Danbury letter: "the legislative powers of government reach actions only, and not opinions. . . ." Danbury Letter, in Kurland, supra p. 14, at 96. This statement, versions of which recur throughout Jefferson's writings on this subject, makes clear his view that the evil from which the church was constitutionally separated was not the State qua state, but rather the State's "legislative powers"—its powers to coerce. One cannot read Jefferson's other, more elaborate writings on the relationship between religion and government and fail to grasp this essential distinction.

While Jefferson's refusal to issue Thanksgiving proclamations as President would, at first blush, appear inconsistent with this point, he explained his decision precisely in terms of coercion. In a letter to Rev. Samuel Miller, President Jefferson stated that he had no authority "to prescribe" or "to direct" the "religious exercises of his constituents." Letter from Thomas Jefferson to Rev. S. Miller (Jan. 23, 1808) (hereinafter "Letter to Miller"), in Kurland, supra p. 14, at 98, 98–99. Jefferson disagreed with the argument that a Thanksgiving proclamation would be merely recommendatory: "It must be meant too that this recommendation is to carry some authority, and to be sanctioned by some penalty on those who disregard it; not indeed of fine and imprisonment, but of some degree of proscription perhaps in public opinion." Id. at 99. Jefferson made a similar point in his second inaugural address: "In matters of religion I have considered that its free exercise is placed by the Constitution independent of the powers of the General Government. I have therefore undertaken on no occasion, to prescribe the religious exercises suited to it. . . ." *Inaugural Addresses of the Presidents*, supra n.23, at 20. Elsewhere in his second inaugural address, as previously discussed, supra n.26, Jefferson expressed his own religious sentiments and movingly sought God's blessings.

[33] Indeed, Madison noted that the "daily devotions" opening congressional sessions had "degenerat[ed] into a scanty attendance, and a tiresome formality." Detached Memoranda, in Kurland, supra p. 14, at 104.

[34] The letter opens with the statement "that religion is a matter which lies solely between man and his God, that he owes account to none other for his faith or his worship, that the legislative powers of government reach actions only, and not opinions. . . ." Letter from Thomas Jefferson to Danbury Baptist Association (Jan. 1, 1892) (hereinafter "Danbury Letter"), in Kurland, supra p. 14, at 96.

These statements make clear that Jefferson refrained from issuing Presidential Thanksgiving proclamations because he viewed them as coercive and thus "interdicted by the Constitution." Letter to Miller, in Kurland, supra p. 14, at 98. He obviously entertained no such objection to presidential expressions of personal religious belief, such as that contained in his second inaugural address. Thus, while one may disagree with Jefferson's view that a recommendatory Thanksgiving proclamation would nonetheless be coercive (as did the other Founders, and as we do below), one cannot disagree that Jefferson believed coercion to be a necessary element of a First Amendment violation.[35]

7. This Court's decisions prior to *Engel*

That government coercion of religious conformity was understood by the Framers to be a necessary element of an Establishment Clause violation should not startle the modern legal mind. Rather, until this Court's decision in *Engel*, the question of government coercion had been central to this Court's Establishment Clause jurisprudence. See, e.g., *McGowan v. Maryland*, 366 U.S. 420, 453 (1961) ("We do not hold that Sunday legislation may not be a violation of the 'Establishment' Clause if it can be demonstrated that its purpose . . . or its operative effect—is to use the State's coercive power to aid religion."); *Zorach v. Clauson*, 343 U.S. 306, 311 (1952) ("If in fact coercion were used, if it were established that any one or more teachers were using their office to persuade or force students to take religious instruction, a wholly different case would be presented."); *Illinois ex rel. McCollum v. Board of Educ.*, 333 U.S. 203, 209 (1948) ("The operation of the state's compulsory education system thus assists and is integrated with the program of religious instruction carried on by separate religious sects."); *Cantwell v. Connecticut*, 310 U.S. 296, 303 (1940) (The Establishment Clause "forestalls compulsion by law of the acceptance of any creed or the practice of any form of worship.").

Though *Engel* itself involved government coercion, 370 U.S. at 430–31, the Court's dictum that the purposes underlying the Establishment Clause "go much further" than prohibiting official coercive influence on religious belief, id. at 431, severed the key principle to which prior caselaw had been anchored. As we noted at the outset, the *Engel* Court did not intend to place the Establishment Clause on a collision course with the "many manifestations in our public life of belief in God." Id. at 435 n.21. But by breaking the link to coercion, *Engel* set the Establishment Clause on a path not imagined by that Court, to *Lemon* and judicial supervision over the location and relative size of creches, candy canes, talking wishing wells, Christmas trees, etc., etc., in official Christmas holiday displays.

As we will show below, *Lemon* and its progeny do not require invalidation of the graduation prayers challenged here. We turn first, however, to the question whether the Establishment Clause's safeguard against government coercion of religious conformity was violated by the invocation and benediction offered by Rabbi Gutterman.

B. There was no government coercion in this case

We do not doubt that "[s]peech may coerce in some circumstances. . . ." *County of Allegheny*, 492 U.S. at 661 (Kennedy, J., concurring in the judgment in part and dissenting in part). But this case discloses no government action coercing religious conformity. Neither respondent nor his daughter were required to attend the graduation ceremony at Nathan Bishop Middle School, and, once there, they were in no way compelled, or even encouraged, to conform to the religious beliefs expressed by Rabbi Gutterman. Indeed, respondent has never claimed otherwise. Rather, his complaint is that he "is opposed to and offended by the inclusion of prayer in the public school graduation ceremony of his child both at the middle school and the high school level." J.A. 5. See also J.A. 18. Moreover, neither the district court nor the court of appeals suggested, much less found, that Providence school officials had engaged in even indirect coercion of anyone's religious beliefs. See App. 1a-30a.

Thus, this case came before the district court with no evidence even of "subtle coercion, be it in the form of taxation to supply the substantial benefits that would sustain a state-established faith, direct compulsion to observance, or governmental exhortation to religiosity that amounts in fact to proselytizing." *County of Allegheny*, 492 U.S. at 659-60 (Kennedy, J., concurring the judgment in part and dissenting in part). Nevertheless, in the eyes of the district court, the simple "union of prayer, school, and important occasion" yielded an identification of

---

[35] Jefferson, in his second inaugural address, asked his countrymen to join him in "supplications" to God, which seems puzzling in light of his refusal to make similar requests in presidential Thanksgiving proclamations. Additionally, Jefferson had a federalism reason for refusing to issue Thanksgiving proclamations. He believed that authority to "prescribe" religious exercises was reserved to the states. See Letter to Miller, in Kurland, supra p. 14, at 98–99; *Inaugural Addresses of the Presidents*, supra n.23, at 20.

religion with the public school, and so an Establishment Clause violation. App. 24a. As we show below, however, the combination of religious expression and the particular setting here cannot result in any government infringement of religious liberty prohibited by the Constitution. Religious speech alone cannot amount to the kind of government coercion of religious choice that implicates the Establishment Clause. And the setting here, a public secondary school commencement ceremony, does not add any of the coercive elements that could realistically turn Rabbi Gutterman's expressions of religious sentiment into instruments of religious compulsion.

1. Speech alone cannot coerce religious choice It bears repeating that the Framers themselves freely engaged in religious speech at the same time they were disabling government from using its power to coerce religious choice. Indeed, the Framers often used religious speech in the very instruments by which they disabled government's power to interfere with religious liberty. See, e.g., Virginia Act for Establishing Religious Freedom, in Kurland, supra p. 14, at 84. Clearly, the Framers were animated by the proposition, in Judge Easterbrook's modern phrasing, that "[s]peech is not coercive; the listener may do as he likes." American Jewish Congress, 827 F.2d at 132 (Easterbrook, J., dissenting). Though the Constitution may "prevent the government from using force or funds to aid or inhibit the practice of religion," at the same time "the government may participate as a speaker in moral debates, including religious ones." Id. Consistent with this notion, this Court has held that the government may encourage what it may not compel. *Harris v. McRae*, 448 U.S. 297 (1980), and may critically label expression that it may not otherwise burden, *Meese v. Keene*, 481 U.S. 465 (1987). See also *Block v. Meese*, 793 F.2d 1303, 1314 (D.C. Cir. 1986) (quoting L. Tribe, *American Constitutional Law* 588, 590 (1978)) ("[T]he guarantee of freedom of speech 'does not mean that government must be ideologically' neutral," or 'silence government's affirmation of national values,' or prevent government from 'add[ing] its own voice to the many that it must tolerate.' ").

Respondent's effort to silence speech that "offends" him is limited by no principle save each listener's unique sensibilities. It reduces to a rule that all "government speech about religion is per se suspect." *County of Allegheny*, 492 U.S. at 661 (Kennedy, J., concurring in the judgment in part and dissenting in part). If that is the operative principle of the Establishment Clause, all references to God and to religion will have to be removed from civic life. "The holidays, the chaplains, the proclamations, the slogans, the oath, the pledge, and the creche alike give offense—to those of other faiths (or no faith) who feel slighted, to those of the same faith who believe that governmental involvement with religion diminishes both institutions, to those who see the camel's nose." American Jewish Congress, 827 F.2d at 133 (Easterbrook, J., dissenting).[36]

Again, we do not deny that "[s]peech may coerce in some circumstances," *County of Allegheny*, 492 U.S. at 661 (Kennedy, J., concurring in the judgment in part and dissenting in part), but it is only by virtue of the particular circumstances surrounding speech that government expression may be transformed into a power to interfere unconstitutionally with religious choice. Thus, in *Abington School Dist.*, 374 U.S. at 223, Bible reading was "prescribed as part of the curricular activities of students who are required by law to attend school." In *Illinois ex rel. McCollum*, 333 U.S. at 209–10, students "compelled by law to go to school for secular education [were] released in part from their legal duty upon condition that they attend the religious classes." And in *Engel*, 370 U.S. at 430, children were similarly compelled by law to attend class, presented with a state-composed prayer, and given an option to be excused from its recitation—an option available in the circumstances only at the price of the "ridicule and ostracism of their peers for nonconformity." American Jewish Congress, 827 F.2d at 134 (Easterbrook, J., dissenting).[37]

---

[36] Moreover, grounding a restraint of religious expression on the offense that may be taken by a listener is radically alien to this Court's First Amendment jurisprudence protecting other forms of speech. See, e.g., *Boos v. Barry*, 485 U.S. 312, 322 (1988) ("[I]n public debate our own citizens must tolerate insulting, even outrageous, speech. . . ."); *Hustler Magazine v. Falwell*, 485 U.S. 46, 51 (1988) (noting the Court's "longstanding refusal to allow damages to be awarded because the speech in question may have an adverse emotional impact on the audience"). As Justice Harlan noted, "It is firmly settled that under our Constitution the public expression of ideas may not be prohibited merely because the ideas are themselves offensive to some of their hearers." *Street v. New York*, 394 U.S. 576 (1969). Given that the First Amendment singles out a particular form of speech, religious expression, for special protection, it would be an odd result indeed to exclude religious speech from the scope of this principle that safeguards all other forms of expression.

[37] Looking to context to evaluate unconstitutional coercion is a familiar approach of this Court in many other areas outside of Establishment Clause jurisprudence. In *Bantam Books v. Sullivan*, 372 U.S. 58 (1963), for example, the availability of criminal sanctions for distribution of allegedly pornographic material and government officials' threats to institute criminal proceedings resulted, in "a scheme of state censorship effectuated by

In short, the facts that religious speech occurred on a government platform, was uttered by a government-sponsored speaker, and offended one (at least) member of the audience cannot by itself work a violation of the Establishment Clause.

2. Attendance at the graduation ceremony was voluntary The setting in which the religious speech occurred here reveals no government "pressure upon a student to participate in a religious activity." *Board of Educ. v. Mergens*, 110 S.Ct. 2356, 2378 (Kennedy, J., concurring in part and concurring in the judgment). Attendance at the Nathan Bishop Middle School's graduation ceremony was entirely voluntary. J.A. 18.[38]

This case is thus unlike the classroom prayer context at issue in *Engel.* There, the state used its coercive power to compel attendance of students in the classroom. To be sure, nonattendance for religious reasons was excused if the student was willing to endure the stigma of nonconformity associated with leaving the class. The student was put to this difficult choice by virtue of the state's mandatory attendance requirement, because the student was required to be present in the classroom in the first instance. In other words, the costs to the student of leaving the classroom during the morning prayer (e.g., stigma, embarrassment, ostracism) were directly attributable to the state's law requiring the student's presence in the classroom in the first place. Absent the mandatory attendance requirement, there would be no government coercion. See *Mergens*, 110 S.Ct. at 2372 ("[T]here is little if any risk of official state . . . coercion where no formal classroom activities are involved.").

In contrast, graduates of the Nathan Bishop Middle School, as well as other schools in the Providence school district, were entirely free to stay away from the graduation ceremony; attendance was wholly voluntary. The coercive power of the state was not implicated at all.

Of course, graduates and their parents typically have a strong desire to attend their commencement exercises.[39] But a personal desire, no matter how strong or understandable, to attend some civic ceremony or function—whether it be a public school graduation ceremony, an inauguration ceremony or investiture, a legislative or judicial session, or whatever—simply does not amount to government compulsion to attend the event. Many people came from all over the country, some at great expense and personal sacrifice, to attend President Bush's inauguration ceremony. Still, no one was compelled by the government to attend the event. Those who did, did so voluntarily, despite the fact that the newly elected President would likely continue the inaugural tradition of seeking God's blessing. The strength of respondent's desire to attend his daughter's graduation ceremony does not entitle him to exclude from the proceedings any religious speech that he may find objectionable. A contrary rule would essentially accord editorial privileges over the ceremony to any person desiring to attend it.[40]

3. The religious beliefs of those who attended the ceremony were not coerced Quite apart from the voluntary nature of attendance at public school graduation ceremonies in Providence, it is clear that those who attended Nathan Bishop Middle School's graduation ceremony in 1989 were in no way coerced to accept or support the religious beliefs expressed by Rabbi Gutterman. "No one was compelled to . . . participate in any religious ceremony or

---

extralegal sanctions." Id. at 72. To determine when official action constitutes a Fourth Amendment seizure, courts must "assess the coercive effect of police conduct." *Michigan v. Chesternut*, 486 U.S. 567, 573 (1988). A seizure occurs "only if, in view of all the circumstances surrounding the incident, a reasonable person would have believed that he was not free to leave." Id., quoting *United States v. Mendenhall*, 446 U.S. 544, 554 (1980).

[38] This fact has figured prominently in lower court decisions rejecting Establishment Clause challenges to public school graduation prayers. See, e.g., *Albright*, slip op. at 16 (secondary school graduation invocations and benedictions delivered in "voluntary and non-coercive circumstances"); *Wood*, 342 F.Supp. at 1295 ("[T]he fact that the graduation ceremony is not compulsory strips the function of any semblance of governmental establishment or even condonation.").

[39] In *Smith v. Board of Educ.*, 844 F.2d 90 (2d Cir. 1988), an Orthodox Jewish senior, unable to attend his high school's Saturday commencement exercises due to religious strictures, sought to compel a change in the day of the event. Noting that attending graduation was not a prerequisite to a student receiving a diploma, the Second Circuit rejected the student's claim with the observation that the "exercises are merely a social occasion on which students and their families and friends gather to mark an event." Id. at 94.

[40] In addition, as the *Albright* Court pointed out, though respondent and his daughter can speak of their desire to attend graduation without any invocation or benediction, the "same can be said in reverse as to graduating seniors who want such prayer." Slip op. at 9. One commentator elaborated: A student raised in a religious tradition who is taught the importance of prayer, who is exposed to public prayer at weddings, funerals, major governmental functions, and other significant transitional moments of life, may well be as firmly convinced that prayer at graduation, one of the most significant events in his or her life to date, is as essential as the non-believing student thinks it is not. Such a student may find a graduation without prayer incomplete, unfulfilling or downright offensive. The "believing" student's choice of foregoing graduation or "participating in a ceremony with which they have fundamental disagreement" is no less "odious" than that of the "unbelieving" student. DuPuy, supra n.6, at 353.

activity." *County of Allegheny*, 492 U.S. at 664 (Kennedy, J., concurring in the judgment in part and dissenting in part). Unlike *Abington School Dist.*, in which the students were asked to stand and recite a prayer in unison, no one was required to join in, agree with, or even listen to Rabbi Gutterman's invocation and benediction.

That students and other children are in attendance at graduation ceremonies does not alter this analysis. Children also attend presidential inauguration ceremonies, legislative and court sessions, and countless other civic ceremonies and events in which religious values are expressed. That fact, standing alone, does not render all religious speech at such occasions coercive. Nor can graduation ceremonies be aptly analogized to the potentially coercive classroom context. The Sixth Circuit in Stein elaborated on the distinctions between graduation ceremonies and classroom instruction: Although children are obviously attending the ceremony, the public nature of the proceeding and the usual presence of parents acts as a buffer against religious coercion. In addition, the graduation context does not implicate the special nature of the teacher-student relationship—a relationship that focuses on the transmission of knowledge and values by an authority figure. 822 F.2d at 1409.[41]

To the *Stein* court's points we should add that graduation invocations and benedictions are but brief segments of a much longer, otherwise entirely secular, ceremony. In addition, school authorities do not themselves deliver these ceremonial acknowledgments of religion. They merely invite a private citizen to offer the invocation, authored by the speaker himself, just as they invite other speakers with different secular views to address the audience during the ceremony. Furthermore, though graduation exercises may be held on the premises of a school, J.A. 12-18; App. 19a, they are not part of the pedagogical activities of the school.

Underscoring the lack of coercive influences in the graduation ceremony setting is this Court's acknowledgment in *Mergens* that secondary school students understand "that schools do not endorse everything they fail to censor." 110 S.Ct. at 2372. See also *Jones*, slip op. at 12 ("The graduation ceremony lies on the threshold of high school students' transitions into adulthood, when religious sensibilities hardly constitute impressionable blank slates."); *Albright*, slip op. at 21 ("[H]igh school students are not 'babes in arms' and . . . are mature enough to understand that a school does not endorse or promote a religion by permitting prayer. . . .").

Just as attendees at Nathan Bishop Middle School's 1989 graduation need not accept or support the religious beliefs expressed in Rabbi Gutterman's invocation and benediction, so also [t]he holder of a nickel need not trust in God, no matter what the coin says, and need not contribute the nickel (or even three pence) to a church. He may labor on Christmas if he likes—though Ebenezer Scrooge had to give Bob Cratchit that day off without governmental compulsion. He may "affirm" rather than "swear" when giving testimony and be silent while others say the Pledge of Allegiance. . . . He need not study or even own a Bible during the "Year of the Bible." And he may turn his back on the creche. American Jewish Congress, 827 F.2d at 133 (Easterbrook, J., dissenting). If Rabbi Gutterman's prayers are held to coerce religious conformity among members of his audience, and thus to be unconstitutional, a staggering variety of traditional and venerable acknowledgments of religion must be extirpated from our public life. It must follow, for example, that this Court's Crier coerces religious conformity when he opens oral argument sessions. There is no principled distinction.

In sum, the religious speech challenged here is devoid of any element of government coercion that could interfere with the religious liberty of the audience. Accordingly, petitioners have committed no offense against "the great object" of the Religion Clauses: the "freedom to worship as one pleases without government interference or oppression." *County of Allegheny*, 492 U.S. at 660 (Kennedy, J., concurring in the judgment in part and dissenting in part).[42]

---

[41] See also *Jones*, slip op. at 13 (Graduation is "an assembly where many parents are present rather than a classroom setting, where the prospect of subtle official and peer coercion warrants stricter separation of the state from things religious."); *Grossberg*, 380 F.Supp. at 288 (In graduation exercises, "[t]here is none of the repetitive or pedagogical function of the exercises which characterized the school prayer cases."); *Wood*, 342 F.Supp. at 1294 ([G]raduation ceremonies . . . are ceremonial and are in fact not a part of the formal, day-to-day routine of the school curriculum to which is attached compulsory attendance."); *Wiest*, 320 A.2d at 367 (Roberts, J., concurring) (noting "the public and ceremonial nature of the occasion and the presence of students and adults of all persuasions").

[42] Since inclusion of a traditional, brief invocation and benediction in commencement exercises does not effect an unconstitutional coercion of religious choice, exclusion of speech because of its religious content would seem to violate the free speech and free exercise rights of the speaker and his audience. See, e.g., *Widmar v. Vincent*, 454 U.S. 263, 276 (1981). Similarly, depriving students who are religious of this kind of expression at their graduation solely because it is religious signals a government disapproval of religion that is also contrary

II. *LEMON V. KURTZMAN* DOES NOT REQUIRE INVALIDATION OF THE VENERABLE TRADITION OF GRADUATION INVOCATIONS AND BENEDICTIONS

The courts below held that the graduation invocations and benedictions at issue here had the principal effect of advancing religion—the second prong of the *Lemon* analysis—and so violated the Establishment Clause. App. 23a. As a result, they did not address the other two components of *Lemon*.[43]

The holding below rested on the conclusion that "[t]he special occasion of graduation coupled with the presence of prayer creates an identification of governmental power with religious practice." App. 25a. As we have candidly admitted above, we cannot in good conscience urge that this application of *Lemon* was wholly unfaithful to that precedent. Yet examination of the subsequent development of *Lemon*—notably this Court's warnings concerning its limits—suggests that a more accurate vision of the Establishment Clause as seen through the lens of *Lemon* would approve of the kind of graduation prayers at issue in this case.

The courts below were certainly correct that one iteration of the "effects" prong of *Lemon* focuses on whether a governmental practice appears to endorse or sponsor religion through "a close identification" of government power with religious activities. *Grand Rapids School Dist. v. Ball*, 473 U.S. 373, 389 (1985). Yet they then went on to apply the *Grand Rapids* "close identification" notion untempered by this Court's Establishment Clause teaching in other major precedents. Thus the courts below were able to follow a rather simple recipe for their judgment in this case. As the district court put it, "It is the union of prayer, school, and important occasion that creates an identification of religion with the school function." App. 24a. In other words, add religious expression to an important civic event and you have a violation of the Establishment Clause.

In contrast, this Court has never embraced such an absolute analysis. *Lemon* itself did "not call for total separation between church and state." 403 U.S. at 614. See also *Committee for Public Educ. & Religious Liberty v. Nyquist*, 413 U.S. 756, 760 (1973) ("It has never been thought either possible or desirable to enforce a regime of total separation. . . ."); *Wallace*, 472 U.S. at 69 (O'Connor, J., concurring in the judgment) (noting that "[c]haos would ensue" if every statute that promotes a secular goal but also has "a primary effect of helping or hindering a sectarian belief" were invalidated under the Establishment Clause). To the contrary, the Constitution "affirmatively mandates accommodation, not merely tolerance, of all religions, and forbids hostility toward any." *Lynch v. Donnelly*, 465 U.S. 668, 673 (1984). As a result, this Court has warned that "[f]ocus exclusively on the religious component of any activity would inevitably lead to its invalidation under the Establishment Clause." Id. at 680.

This is the warning ignored, and the error made, by the courts below. The district court forthrightly observed that, in its view, "the Establishment Clause would not be implicated" by the "exact same invocation" if "God would be left out." App. 28a. To underscore this point, the court then recast Rabbi Gutterman's invocation into a court-approved version, deleting only references to God. App. 28a n.10.

---

to the Establishment Clause. See *County of Allegheny*, 492 U.S. at 660 (O'Connor, J., concurring in part and concurring in the judgment). Accordingly, it is well to recall here Justice Brennan's admonition: "Religionists no less than members of any other group enjoy the full measure of protection afforded speech, association, and political activity generally. The Establishment Clause . . . may not be used as a sword to justify repression of religion or its adherents from any aspect of public life." *McDaniel v. Paty*, 435 U.S. 618, 641 (1978) (Brennan, J., concurring in the judgment).

[43] The graduation prayers in this case pass muster under the other two elements of the *Lemon* test. First, these prayers have "the secular purpose of solemnizing the occasion." *Albright*, slip op. at 17. See also *Jones*, slip op. at 8 (Graduation "invocations addressing a deity" are "as consistent with the secular solemnizing purpose as any religious purpose."); *Stein*, 822 F.2d at 1409 ("The invocation and benediction at a graduation ceremony serves the 'solemnizing' function. . . ."). In addition, they serve the legitimate and important purpose of providing "recognition and acknowledgment of the role of religion in the lives of our citizens." *County of Allegheny*, 492 U.S. at 623 (O'Connor, J., concurring in part and concurring in the judgment). Second, no government action threatens excessive entanglement with religion. Neither the Providence School Committee nor the Superintendent requires prayer to be included in graduation ceremonies in the school district. J.A. 18. Though guidelines for such prayer are distributed to the schools, those guidelines are not formulated by government officials, the prayers are prepared by outside clergy, and no government review or monitoring of the prayers is involved. See *Jones*, slip op. at 15 (noting that even review by school officials of invocations for sectarianism and proselytization does not constitute excessive entanglement). Far from being the kind of "comprehensive, discriminating, and continuing state surveillance" prohibited by *Lemon*, 403 U.S. at 619, the guidelines distributed here are akin to the guidelines for public schools' Christmas assemblies upheld in *Florey v. Sioux Falls School Dist.* 49-5, 619 F.2d 1311 (8th Cir.), cert. denied, 449 U.S. 987 (1980), which the court concluded served to avoid, rather than create, excessive entanglement with religion. Id. at 1318. Moreover, ongoing government surveillance of graduation speakers to censor any reference to the deity necessarily involves an equal or greater degree of religious entanglement.

With such narrow reasoning, the courts below failed to employ the broader analysis mandated by this Court for application of the *Lemon* standards. "Every government practice must be judged in its unique circumstances to determine whether it constitutes an endorsement or disapproval of religion." *Lynch*, 465 U.S. at 694 (O'Connor, J., concurring). It is true that God could be "left out" of the invocation and benediction at issue here. So too could God be left out of the invocation that has traditionally opened this Court's sessions. But the availability of a more secular alternative has never been deemed relevant to the Establishment Clause inquiry. *Lynch*, 465 U.S. at 681 n.7. See also *County of Allegheny*, 492 U.S. at 636 (O'Connor, J., concurring in part and concurring in the judgment) (observing that a "more secular alternative" test "is too blunt an instrument for Establishment Clause analysis, which depends on sensitivity to the context and circumstances presented by each case").

Examination of the circumstances of the graduation prayer here does not support the conclusion that such ceremonies produce a "close identification" of government with religion. Including such invocations and benedictions in commencement ceremonies vastly predates the existence of American public schools, and a format for such proceedings was well established by the time government entered education.[44] Clearly, communal traditions, not government action, have been the impetus for including such elements in graduation ceremonies.

In Providence, the School Committee and Superintendent have left the decision to each school whether to include an invocation and benediction in graduation exercises, with the result that some ceremonies have included such prayers, while others have not. J.A. 4, 12-16, 18, 24; App. 19a. No government official prepares or delivers these prayers, though guidelines for prayer at public civic ceremonies from the National Conference of Christians and Jews are provided to the clergy invited to deliver them. J.A. 12-15; App. 19a. In addition to this passive government role, graduation or promotion ceremonies obviously occur only once in a student's career at a school, and an invocation or benediction is merely a brief part of each ceremony.[45] Moreover, the ceremonies are removed from the usual pedagogical setting of the classroom, where attendance is compulsory and authoritative instruction is the normal order of the day. Graduation ceremonies take place rather in a voluntary assembly in which family and friends may accompany the student in this traditional coming-of-age celebration.

This context bears little similarity to those situations in which this Court has invalidated government action under *Lemon* for conferring an "imprimatur of state approval on religious sects or practices." *Widmar v. Vincent*, 454 U.S. 263, 274 (1981). See, e.g., *Grand Rapids School Dist.*, 473 U.S. 389–392 (1985) ("symbolic union" between church and state where students move back and forth between religious and "public school" classes in the same private school building, and public school teachers may appear to be "regular adjunct [s]" to the religious school); *Abington School Dist.*, (Bible readings part of prescribed curriculum; conducted under supervision of teachers; children may be excused from classroom during reading); *Engel* (state-drafted school prayer); *Illinois ex rel. McCollum v. Board of Educ.*, 333 U.S. 203 (1948) ("release time" program for religious instruction on public school grounds; nonparticipating students kept at school for secular work.).

The extremely limited role of religion in graduation exercise in the form of this invocation and benediction does not constitute a government endorsement of religion as understood in this Court's cases. Neither the texts of the invocation and benediction—in the district court's words, "examples of elegant simplicity, thoughtful content, and sincere citizenship" App. 20a—nor the circumstances of their delivery should be construed as "making adherence to a religion relevant in any way to a person's standing in the political community." *County of Allegheny*, 492 U.S. at 594, quoting *Lynch*, 465 U.S. at 687 (O'Connor, J., concurring). The courts below found government endorsement here simply by virtue of the school's failure to censor references to the deity, as its revision of the invocation so unmistakably demonstrates. Such a notion cannot be squared with this Court's contrary view that "schools do not endorse everything they fail to censor." *Mergens*, 110 S.Ct. at 2372.

In sum, in our constitutional order, such acknowledgements of religion achieve the completely legitimate ends of "solemnizing public

[44] K. Sheard, supra n.7, at 71; DuPuy, supra n.6, at 358.

[45] See *Jones*, slip op. at 13 (noting the brief duration of commencement prayers as part of the Fifth Circuit's conclusion that they do not constitute government endorsement of religion); *Grossberg v. Deusebio*, 380 F.Supp. 285, 289 (E.D. Va. 1974) ("The event, in short, is so fleeting that no significant transfer of government prestige can be anticipated.").

occasions, expressing confidence in the future, and encouraging the recognition of what is worthy of appreciation in society." *Lynch*, 465 U.S. at 693 (O'Connor, J., concurring). *Lemon* should not be read, as did the courts below, to prevent Americans from choosing, as they have for two centuries, to use religious expression in such a role.

CONCLUSION

For the foregoing reasons, the judgment of the court of appeals should be reversed.

505 U.S. 577, 120 L.Ed.2d 467

⊥577Robert E. LEE, Individually and as Principal of Nathan Bishop Middle School, et al., Petitioners

v.

Daniel WEISMAN etc.

No. 90–1014.

Argued Nov. 6, 1991.

Decided June 24, 1992.

Public school student and her father brought suit seeking permanent injunction to prevent inclusion of invocations and benedictions in form of prayer in graduation ceremonies of city public schools. The United States District Court for the District of Rhode Island, Francis J. Boyle, Chief Judge, 728 F.Supp. 68, granted relief. Appeal was taken. The Court of Appeals for the First Circuit, 908 F.2d 1090, affirmed. Petition for certiorari was granted. The Supreme Court, Justice Kennedy, held that school could not provide for "nonsectarian" prayer to be given by clergyman selected by school.

Affirmed.

Justice Blackmun concurred and filed opinion with which Justice Stevens and Justice O'Connor joined.

Justice Souter concurred and filed opinion, with which Justice Stevens and Justice O'Connor joined.

Justice Scalia dissented and filed opinion with which Chief Justice Rehnquist, Justice White, and Justice Thomas joined.

1. Constitutional Law ⚷84.5(3)

Reassessment of decision in *Lemon v. Kurtzman*, which set forth standards for evaluation of establishment clause cases, was not required in order to determine whether "nonsectarian" prayer could be offered at school graduation; "pervasive" degree of government involvement with religious activity in present case, to point of creating state-sponsored and state-directed religious exercise in public school, was sufficient to determine constitutionality without reference to *Lemon* test. U.S.C.A. Const.Amends. 1, 14.

2. Constitutional Law ⚷84.1

Principle that government may accommodate free exercise of religion does not supercede fundamental limitations imposed by establishment clause. U.S.C.A. Const. Amends. 1, 14.

3. Constitutional Law ⚷84.1

It is beyond dispute that, at minimum, Constitution guarantees that government may not coerce anyone to support or participate in religion or its exercise, or otherwise act in way which establishes state religion or religious faith or tends to do so. U.S.C.A. Const.Amends. 1, 14.

4. Constitutional Law ⚷84.5(3)
Schools ⚷165, 178

Public school's activities in connection with the offering of prayer at graduation ceremony constituted government involvement prohibited by establishment clause; school officials decided that there would be prayer at ceremony, selected clergyman to give prayer, and dictated content of prayer by presenting to clergyman pamphlet setting forth guidelines for "nonsectarian" prayer at school graduations. U.S.C.A. Const.Amends. 1, 14.

5. Constitutional Law ⟹84.5(3)

Schools ⟹165, 178

Establishment clause prohibited public school students from being exposed to religion in form of "nonsectarian" prayer given by school-selected clergyman at graduation ceremony, even though students were subjected to variety of ideas in courses, with freedom of communication being protected by First Amendment; under free speech portion of First Amendment it was contemplated that government would be participant in expression of ideas, while under establishment clause it was provided that government would remain separate from religious affairs. U.S.C.A. Const.Amends. 1, 14.

6. Constitutional Law ⟹84.5(3)

Schools ⟹165, 178

Public school's inclusion of "nonsectarian" prayer in school graduation ceremony constituted impermissible establishment of religion under establishment clause, by coercing student to stand and remain silent during giving of prayer, even though student was not required to join in message in any way and could meditate on own religion or let mind wander, and even though prayer and closing benediction involved approximately two minutes of total ceremony. U.S.C.A. Const.Amends. 1, 14.

7. Constitutional Law ⟹84.5(3)

Schools ⟹165, 178

A requirement that student stand and remain silent during giving of "nonsectarian" prayer at graduation ceremony in public school violated establishment clause, even though attendance at ceremony was completely voluntary; student would not be required to give up attendance at ceremony, an important event in her life, in order to avoid unwanted exposure to religion. U.S.C.A. Const.Amends. 1, 14.

Syllabus *

Principals of public middle and high schools in Providence, Rhode Island, are permitted to invite members of the clergy to give invocations and benedictions at their schools' graduation ceremonies. Petitioner Lee, a middle school principal, invited a rabbi to offer such prayers at the graduation ceremony for Deborah Weisman's class, gave the rabbi a pamphlet containing guidelines for the composition of public prayers at civic ceremonies, and advised him that the prayers should be nonsectarian. Shortly before the ceremony, the District Court denied the motion of respondent Weisman, Deborah's father, for a temporary restraining order to prohibit school officials from including the prayers in the ceremony. Deborah and her family attended the ceremony, and the prayers were recited. Subsequently, Weisman sought a permanent injunction barring Lee and other petitioners, various Providence public school officials, from inviting clergy to deliver invocations and benedictions at future graduations. It appears likely that such prayers will be conducted at Deborah's high school graduation. The District Court enjoined petitioners from continuing the practice at issue on the ground that it violated the Establishment Clause of the First Amendment. The Court of Appeals affirmed.

Held: Including clergy who offer prayers as part of an official public school graduation ceremony is forbidden by the Establishment Clause. Pp. 2655–2661.

(a) This Court need not revisit the questions of the definition and scope of the principles governing the extent of permitted accommodation by the State for its citizens' religious beliefs and practices, for the controlling precedents as they relate to prayer and religious exercise in primary and second-

* The syllabus constitutes no part of the opinion of the Court but has been prepared by the Reporter of Decisions for the convenience of the reader. See *United States v. Detroit Lumber Co.*, 200 U.S. 321, 337, 26 S.Ct. 282, 287, 50 L.Ed. 499.

ary public schools compel the holding here. Thus, the Court will not reconsider its decision in *Lemon v. Kurtzman,* 403 U.S. 602, 91 S.Ct. 2105, 29 L.Ed.2d 745. The principle that government may accommodate the free exercise of religion does not supersede the fundamental limitations imposed by the Establishment Clause, which guarantees at a minimum that a government may not coerce anyone to support or participate in religion or its exercise, or otherwise act in a way which "establishes a ⌊578[state] religion or religious faith, or tends to do so." *Lynch v. Donnelly,* 465 U.S. 668, 678, 104 S.Ct. 1355, 1361, 79 L.Ed.2d 604. P. 2655.

(b) State officials here direct the performance of a formal religious exercise at secondary schools' promotional and graduation ceremonies. Lee's decision that prayers should be given and his selection of the religious participant are choices attributable to the State. Moreover, through the pamphlet and his advice that the prayers be nonsectarian, he directed and controlled the prayers' content. That the directions may have been given in a good-faith attempt to make the prayers acceptable to most persons does not resolve the dilemma caused by the school's involvement, since the government may not establish an official or civic religion as a means of avoiding the establishment of a religion with more specific creeds. Pp. 2655–2657.

(c) The Establishment Clause was inspired by the lesson that in the hands of government what might begin as a tolerant expression of religious views may end in a policy to indoctrinate and coerce. Prayer exercises in elementary and secondary schools carry a particular risk of indirect coercion. *Engel v. Vitale,* 370 U.S. 421, 82 S.Ct. 1261, 8 L.Ed.2d 601; *School Dist. Abington v. Schempp,* 374 U.S. 203, 83 S.Ct. 1560, 10 L.Ed.2d 844. The school district's supervision and control of a high school graduation ceremony places subtle and indirect public and peer pressure on attending students to stand as a group or maintain respectful silence during the invocation and benediction. A reasonable dissenter of high school age could believe that standing or remaining silent signified her own participation in, or approval of, the group exercise, rather than her respect for it. And the State may not place the student dissenter in the dilemma of participating or protesting. Since adolescents are often susceptible to peer pressure, especially in matters of social convention, the State may no more use social pressure to enforce orthodoxy than it may use direct means. The embarrassment and intrusion of the religious exercise cannot be refuted by arguing that the prayers are of a *de minimis* character, since that is an affront to the rabbi and those for whom the prayers have meaning, and since any intrusion was both real and a violation of the objectors' rights. Pp. 2657–2659.

(d) Petitioners' argument that the option of not attending the ceremony excuses any inducement or coercion in the ceremony itself is rejected. In this society, high school graduation is one of life's most significant occasions, and a student is not free to absent herself from the exercise in any real sense of the term "voluntary." Also not dispositive is the contention that prayers are an essential part of these ceremonies because for many persons the occasion would lack meaning without the recognition that human achievements cannot be understood apart from their spiritual essence. This position fails to acknowledge that what ⌊579for many was a spiritual imperative was for the Weismans religious conformance compelled by the State. It also gives insufficient recognition to the real conflict of conscience faced by a student who would have to choose whether to miss graduation or conform to the state-sponsored practice, in an environment where the risk of compulsion is especially high. Pp. 2659–2660.

(e) Inherent differences between the public school system and a session of a state legislature distinguish this case from *Marsh v. Chambers,* 463 U.S. 783, 103 S.Ct. 3330, 77

L.Ed.2d 1019, which condoned a prayer exercise. The atmosphere at a state legislature's opening, where adults are free to enter and leave with little comment and for any number of reasons, cannot compare with the constraining potential of the one school event most important for the student to attend. Pp. 2660–2661.

908 F.2d 1090 (CA1 1990), affirmed.

KENNEDY, J., delivered the opinion of the Court, in which BLACKMUN, STEVENS, O'CONNOR, and SOUTER, JJ., joined. BLACKMUN, J., *post*, p. 2661, and SOUTER, J., *post*, p. 2667, filed concurring opinions, in which STEVENS and O'CONNOR, JJ., joined. SCALIA, J., filed a dissenting opinion, in which REHNQUIST, C.J., and WHITE and THOMAS, JJ., joined, *post*, p. 2678.

Charles J. Cooper, for petitioners.

Kenneth W. Starr, as amicus curiae, in support of petitioners.

Sandra A. Blanding, for respondent.

⊥580 Justice KENNEDY delivered the opinion of the Court.

School principals in the public school system of the city of Providence, Rhode Island, are permitted to invite members of the clergy to offer invocation and benediction prayers as part of the formal graduation ceremonies for middle schools and for high schools. The question before us is whether including clerical members who offer prayers as part of the official school graduation ceremony is consistent with the Religion Clauses of the First Amendment, provisions the Fourteenth Amendment makes applicable with full force to the States and their school districts.

⊥581 I

A

Deborah Weisman graduated from Nathan Bishop Middle School, a public school in Providence, at a formal ceremony in June 1989. She was about 14 years old. For many years it has been the policy of the Providence School Committee and the Superintendent of Schools to permit principals to invite members of the clergy to give invocations and benedictions at middle school and high school graduations. Many, but not all, of the principals elected to include prayers as part of the graduation ceremonies. Acting for himself and his daughter, Deborah's father, Daniel Weisman, objected to any prayers at Deborah's middle school graduation, but to no avail. The school principal, petitioner Robert E. Lee, invited a rabbi to deliver prayers at the graduation exercises for Deborah's class. Rabbi Leslie Gutterman, of the Temple Beth El in Providence, accepted.

It has been the custom of Providence school officials to provide invited clergy with a pamphlet entitled "Guidelines for Civic Occasions," prepared by the National Conference of Christians and Jews. The Guidelines recommend that public prayers at nonsectarian civic ceremonies be composed with "inclusiveness and sensitivity," though they acknowledge that "[p]rayer of any kind may be inappropriate on some civic occasions." App. 20–21. The principal gave Rabbi Gutterman the pamphlet before the graduation and advised him the invocation and benediction should be nonsectarian. Agreed Statement of Facts ¶ 17, *id.*, at 13.

Rabbi Gutterman's prayers were as follows:

"INVOCATION

"God of the Free, Hope of the Brave:

"For the legacy of America where diversity is celebrated and the rights of minorities are protected, we ⊥582 thank You. May these young men and women grow up to enrich it.

"For the liberty of America, we thank You. May these new graduates grow up to guard it.

"For the political process of America in which all its citizens may participate, for its court system where all may seek justice we thank You. May those we honor this morning always turn to it in trust.

"For the destiny of America we thank You. May the graduates of Nathan Bishop Middle School so live that they might help to share it.

"May our aspirations for our country and for these young people, who are our hope for the future, be richly fulfilled.

AMEN"

"BENEDICTION

"O God, we are grateful to You for having endowed us with the capacity for learning which we have celebrated on this joyous commencement.

"Happy families give thanks for seeing their children achieve an important milestone. Send Your blessings upon the teachers and administrators who helped prepare them.

"The graduates now need strength and guidance for the future, help them to understand that we are not complete with academic knowledge alone. We must each strive to fulfill what You require of us all: To do justly, to love mercy, to walk humbly.

"We give thanks to You, Lord, for keeping us alive, sustaining us and allowing us to reach this special, happy occasion.

AMEN"

Id., at 22–23.

⊥583 The record in this case is sparse in many respects, and we are unfamiliar with any fixed custom or practice at middle school graduations, referred to by the school district as "promotional exercises." We are not so constrained with reference to high schools, however. High school graduations are such an integral part of American cultural life that we can with confidence describe their customary features, confirmed by aspects of the record and by the parties' representations at oral argument. In the Providence school system, most high school graduation ceremonies are conducted away from the school, while most middle school ceremonies are held on school premises. Classical High School, which Deborah now attends, has conducted its graduation ceremonies on school premises. Agreed Statement of Facts ¶ 37, *id.,* at 17. The parties stipulate that attendance at graduation ceremonies is voluntary. Agreed Statement of Facts ¶ 41, *id.,* at 18. The graduating students enter as a group in a processional, subject to the direction of teachers and school officials, and sit together, apart from their families. We assume the clergy's participation in any high school graduation exercise would be about what it was at Deborah's middle school ceremony. There the students stood for the Pledge of Allegiance and remained standing during the rabbi's prayers. Tr. of Oral Arg. 38. Even on the assumption that there was a respectful moment of silence both before and after the prayers, the rabbi's two presentations must not have extended much beyond a minute each, if that. We do not know whether he remained on stage during the whole ceremony, or whether the students received individual diplomas on stage, or if he helped to congratulate them.

The school board (and the United States, which supports it as *amicus curiae*) argued that these short prayers and others like them at graduation exercises are of profound meaning to many students and parents throughout this country who consider that due respect and acknowledgment for divine guidance and for the deepest spiritual aspirations of ⊥584 our people ought to be expressed at an event as important in life as a graduation. We assume this to be so in addressing the difficult case now before us, for the significance of the prayers lies also at the heart of Daniel and Deborah Weisman's case.

B

Deborah's graduation was held on the premises of Nathan Bishop Middle School on June 29, 1989. Four days before the ceremony, Daniel Weisman, in his individual capacity as a Providence taxpayer and as next friend of Deborah, sought a temporary restraining order in the United States District Court for the District of Rhode Island to prohibit school officials from including an invocation or benediction in the graduation ceremony. The court denied the motion for lack of adequate time to consider it. Deborah and her family attended the graduation, where the prayers were recited. In July 1989, Daniel Weisman filed an amended complaint seeking a permanent injunction barring petitioners, various officials of the Providence public schools, from inviting the clergy to deliver invocations and benedictions at future graduations. We find it unnecessary to address Daniel Weisman's taxpayer standing, for a live and justiciable controversy is before us. Deborah Weisman is enrolled as a student at Classical High School in Providence and from the record it appears likely, if not certain, that an invocation and benediction will be conducted at her high school graduation. Agreed Statement of Facts ¶ 38, App. 17.

The case was submitted on stipulated facts. The District Court held that petitioners' practice of including invocations and benedictions in public school graduations violated the Establishment Clause of the First Amendment, and it enjoined petitioners from continuing the practice. 728 F.Supp. 68 (1990). The court applied the three-part Establishment Clause test set forth in *Lemon v. Kurtzman,* 403 U.S. 602, 91 S.Ct. 2105, 29 L.Ed.2d 745 (1971). Under that test as described in our past cases, to satisfy the Establishment Clause a governmental [585] practice must (1) reflect a clearly secular purpose; (2) have a primary effect that neither advances nor inhibits religion; and (3) avoid excessive government entanglement with religion. *Committee for Public Ed. & Religious Liberty v. Nyquist,* 413 U.S. 756, 773, 93 S.Ct. 2955, 2965, 37 L.Ed.2d 948 (1973). The District Court held that petitioners' actions violated the second part of the test, and so did not address either the first or the third. The court decided, based on its reading of our precedents, that the effects test of *Lemon* is violated whenever government action "creates an identification of the state with a religion, or with religion in general," 728 F.Supp., at 71, or when "the effect of the governmental action is to endorse one religion over another, or to endorse religion in general." *Id.,* at 72. The court determined that the practice of including invocations and benedictions, even so-called nonsectarian ones, in public school graduations creates an identification of governmental power with religious practice, endorses religion, and violates the Establishment Clause. In so holding the court expressed the determination not to follow *Stein v. Plainwell Community Schools,* 822 F.2d 1406 (1987), in which the Court of Appeals for the Sixth Circuit, relying on our decision in *Marsh v. Chambers,* 463 U.S. 783, 103 S.Ct. 3330, 77 L.Ed.2d 1019 (1983), held that benedictions and invocations at public school graduations are not always unconstitutional. In *Marsh* we upheld the constitutionality of the Nebraska State Legislature's practice of opening each of its sessions with a prayer offered by a chaplain paid out of public funds. The District Court in this case disagreed with the Sixth Circuit's reasoning because it believed that *Marsh* was a narrow decision, "limited to the unique situation of legislative prayer," and did not have any relevance to school prayer cases. 728 F.Supp., at 74.

On appeal, the United States Court of Appeals for the First Circuit affirmed. The majority opinion by Judge Torruella adopted the opinion of the District Court. 908 F.2d 1090 (1990). Judge Bownes joined the majority, but wrote a separate concurring opinion in which he decided that the [586] practices challenged here violated all three parts of the *Lemon* test. Judge Bownes went on to agree with the District Court that *Marsh* had no application to school prayer cases and that the *Stein* decision was flawed. He concluded by suggesting that under Establishment Clause rules no prayer, even one excluding any mention of the Deity, could be offered at a public school graduation ceremony. 908

F.2d, at 1090–1097. Judge Campbell dissented, on the basis of *Marsh* and *Stein*. He reasoned that if the prayers delivered were nonsectarian, and if school officials ensured that persons representing a variety of beliefs and ethical systems were invited to present invocations and benedictions, there was no violation of the Establishment Clause. 908 F.2d, at 1099. We granted certiorari, 499 U.S. 918, 111 S.Ct. 1305, 113 L.Ed.2d 240 (1991), and now affirm.

II

These dominant facts mark and control the confines of our decision: State officials direct the performance of a formal religious exercise at promotional and graduation ceremonies for secondary schools. Even for those students who object to the religious exercise, their attendance and participation in the state-sponsored religious activity are in a fair and real sense obligatory, though the school district does not require attendance as a condition for receipt of the diploma.

[1] This case does not require us to revisit the difficult questions dividing us in recent cases, questions of the definition and full scope of the principles governing the extent of permitted accommodation by the State for the religious beliefs and practices of many of its citizens. See *County of Allegheny v. American Civil Liberties Union, Greater Pittsburgh Chapter,* 492 U.S. 573, 109 S.Ct. 3086, 106 L.Ed.2d 472 (1989); *Wallace v. Jaffree,* 472 U.S. 38, 105 S.Ct. 2479, 86 L.Ed.2d 29 (1985); *Lynch v. Donnelly,* 465 U.S. 668, 104 S.Ct. 1355, 79 L.Ed.2d 604 (1984). For without reference to those principles in other contexts, the controlling precedents as they relate to prayer and religious exercise in primary and secondary public schools compel the holding here that the policy of the city of Providence is an ⌊587unconstitutional one. We can decide the case without reconsidering the general constitutional framework by which public schools' efforts to accommodate religion are measured. Thus we do not accept the invitation of petitioners and *amicus* the United States to reconsider our decision in *Lemon v. Kurtzman, supra.* The government involvement with religious activity in this case is pervasive, to the point of creating a state-sponsored and state-directed religious exercise in a public school. Conducting this formal religious observance conflicts with settled rules pertaining to prayer exercises for students, and that suffices to determine the question before us.

[2, 3] The principle that government may accommodate the free exercise of religion does not supersede the fundamental limitations imposed by the Establishment Clause. It is beyond dispute that, at a minimum, the Constitution guarantees that government may not coerce anyone to support or participate in religion or its exercise, or otherwise act in a way which "establishes a [state] religion or religious faith, or tends to do so." *Lynch, supra,* at 678, 104 S.Ct., at 1361; see also *County of Allegheny, supra,* 492 U.S., at 591, 109 S.Ct., at 3100, quoting *Everson v. Board of Ed. of Ewing,* 330 U.S. 1, 15–16, 67 S.Ct. 504, 511–512, 91 L.Ed. 711 (1947). The State's involvement in the school prayers challenged today violates these central principles.

[4] That involvement is as troubling as it is undenied. A school official, the principal, decided that an invocation and a benediction should be given; this is a choice attributable to the State, and from a constitutional perspective it is as if a state statute decreed that the prayers must occur. The principal chose the religious participant, here a rabbi, and that choice is also attributable to the State. The reason for the choice of a rabbi is not disclosed by the record, but the potential for divisiveness over the choice of a particular member of the clergy to conduct the ceremony is apparent.

Divisiveness, of course, can attend any state decision respecting religions, and neither its existence nor its potential ⌊588necessarily invalidates the State's attempts to accommodate religion in all cases. The potential for divisiveness is of particular relevance here though, because it centers around an overt religious exercise in a secondary school environment where, as we discuss below, see *infra*, at 2659, subtle coercive pressures exist and where the student had no real alternative which would have allowed her to avoid the fact or appearance of participation.

The State's role did not end with the decision to include a prayer and with the choice of a clergyman. Principal Lee provided Rabbi Gutterman with a copy of the "Guidelines for Civic Occasions," and advised him that his prayers should be nonsectarian. Through these means the principal directed and controlled the content of the prayers. Even if the only sanction for ignoring the instructions were that the rabbi would not be invited back, we think no religious representative who valued his or her continued reputation and effectiveness in the community would incur the State's displeasure in this regard. It is a cornerstone principle of our Establishment Clause jurisprudence that "it is no part of the business of government to compose official prayers for any group of the American people to recite as a part of a religious program carried on by government," *Engel v. Vitale*, 370 U.S. 421, 425, 82 S.Ct. 1261, 1264, 8 L.Ed.2d 601 (1962), and that is what the school officials attempted to do.

Petitioners argue, and we find nothing in the case to refute it, that the directions for the content of the prayers were a good-faith attempt by the school to ensure that the sectarianism which is so often the flashpoint for religious animosity be removed from the graduation ceremony. The concern is understandable, as a prayer which uses ideas or images identified with a particular religion may foster a different sort of sectarian rivalry than an invocation or benediction in terms more neutral. The school's explanation, however, does not resolve the dilemma caused by its participation. The question is not the good faith of the school in attempting to make ⊥589 the prayer acceptable to most persons, but the legitimacy of its undertaking that enterprise at all when the object is to produce a prayer to be used in a formal religious exercise which students, for all practical purposes, are obliged to attend.

We are asked to recognize the existence of a practice of nonsectarian prayer, prayer within the embrace of what is known as the Judeo–Christian tradition, prayer which is more acceptable than one which, for example, makes explicit references to the God of Israel, or to Jesus Christ, or to a patron saint. There may be some support, as an empirical observation, to the statement of the Court of Appeals for the Sixth Circuit, picked up by Judge Campbell's dissent in the Court of Appeals in this case, that there has emerged in this country a civic religion, one which is tolerated when sectarian exercises are not. *Stein*, 822 F.2d, at 1409; 908 F.2d 1090, 1098–1099 (CA1 1990) (Campbell, J., dissenting) (case below); see also Note, Civil Religion and the Establishment Clause, 95 Yale L.J. 1237 (1986). If common ground can be defined which permits once conflicting faiths to express the shared conviction that there is an ethic and a morality which transcend human invention, the sense of community and purpose sought by all decent societies might be advanced. But though the First Amendment does not allow the government to stifle prayers which aspire to these ends, neither does it permit the government to undertake that task for itself.

The First Amendment's Religion Clauses mean that religious beliefs and religious expression are too precious to be either proscribed or prescribed by the State. The design of the Constitution is that preservation and transmission of religious beliefs and worship is a responsibility and a choice committed to the private sphere, which itself is promised freedom to pursue that mission. It must not be forgotten then, that while concern must be given to define the protection granted to an objector or a dissenting nonbeliever, these same Clauses exist to protect religion from government in⊥terference.590

James Madison, the principal author of the Bill of Rights, did not rest his opposition to a religious establishment on the sole ground of its effect on the minority. A principal ground for his view was: "[E]xperience witnesseth that ecclesiastical establishments, instead of maintaining the purity and efficacy of Religion, have had a contrary operation." Memorial and Remonstrance Against Religious Assessments (1785), in 8 Papers of James Madison 301 (W. Rachal, R. Rutland, B. Ripel, & F. Teute eds. 1973).

These concerns have particular application in the case of school officials, whose effort to monitor prayer will be perceived by the students as inducing a participation they might otherwise reject. Though the efforts of the school officials in this case to find common ground appear to have been a good-faith attempt to recognize the common aspects of religions and not the divisive ones, our precedents do not permit school officials to assist in composing prayers as an incident to a formal exercise for their students. *Engel v. Vitale, supra,* 370 U.S., at 425, 82 S.Ct., at 1264. And these same precedents caution us to measure the idea of a civic religion against the central meaning of the Religion Clauses of the First Amendment, which is that all creeds must be tolerated and none favored. The suggestion that government may establish an official or civic religion as a means of avoiding the establishment of a religion with more specific creeds strikes us as a contradiction that cannot be accepted.

The degree of school involvement here made it clear that the graduation prayers bore the imprint of the State and thus put school-age children who objected in an untenable position. We turn our attention now to consider the position of the students, both those who desired the prayer and she who did not.

[5] To endure the speech of false ideas or offensive content and then to counter it is part of learning how to live in a pluralistic society, a society which insists upon open discourse towards the end of a tolerant citizenry. And tolerance₅₉₁ presupposes some mutuality of obligation. It is argued that our constitutional vision of a free society requires confidence in our own ability to accept or reject ideas of which we do not approve, and that prayer at a high school graduation does nothing more than offer a choice. By the time they are seniors, high school students no doubt have been required to attend classes and assemblies and to complete assignments exposing them to ideas they find distasteful or immoral or absurd or all of these. Against this background, students may consider it an odd measure of justice to be subjected during the course of their educations to ideas deemed offensive and irreligious, but to be denied a brief, formal prayer ceremony that the school offers in return. This argument cannot prevail, however. It overlooks a fundamental dynamic of the Constitution.

The First Amendment protects speech and religion by quite different mechanisms. Speech is protected by ensuring its full expression even when the government participates, for the very object of some of our most important speech is to persuade the government to adopt an idea as its own. *Meese v. Keene,* 481 U.S. 465, 480–481, 107 S.Ct. 1862, 1870–1871, 95 L.Ed.2d 415 (1987); see also *Keller v. State Bar of California,* 496 U.S. 1, 10–11, 110 S.Ct. 2228, 2234–2235, 110 L.Ed.2d 1 (1990); *Abood v. Detroit Bd. of Ed.,* 431 U.S. 209, 97 S.Ct. 1782, 52 L.Ed.2d 261 (1977). The method for protecting freedom of worship and freedom of conscience in religious matters is quite the reverse. In religious debate or expression the government is not a prime participant, for the Framers deemed religious establishment antithetical to the freedom of all. The Free Exercise Clause embraces a freedom of conscience and worship that has close parallels in the speech provisions of the First Amendment, but the Establishment Clause is a specific prohibition on forms of state intervention in religious affairs with no precise counterpart in the speech provisions. *Buckley v. Valeo,* 424 U.S. 1, 92–93, and n. 127, 96

S.Ct. 612, 669–670, and n. 127, 46 L.Ed.2d 659 (1976) (*per curiam*). The explanation lies in the lesson of history that was and is the inspiration for the Establishment Clause, the lesson that in ⌊592the hands of government what might begin as a tolerant expression of religious views may end in a policy to indoctrinate and coerce. A state-created orthodoxy puts at grave risk that freedom of belief and conscience which are the sole assurance that religious faith is real, not imposed.

The lessons of the First Amendment are as urgent in the modern world as in the 18th century when it was written. One timeless lesson is that if citizens are subjected to state-sponsored religious exercises, the State disavows its own duty to guard and respect that sphere of inviolable conscience and belief which is the mark of a free people. To compromise that principle today would be to deny our own tradition and forfeit our standing to urge others to secure the protections of that tradition for themselves.

[6] As we have observed before, there are heightened concerns with protecting freedom of conscience from subtle coercive pressure in the elementary and secondary public schools. See, *e.g., School Dist. of Abington v. Schempp,* 374 U.S. 203, 307, 83 S.Ct. 1560, 1616, 10 L.Ed.2d 844 (1963) (Goldberg, J., concurring); *Edwards v. Aguillard,* 482 U.S. 578, 584, 107 S.Ct. 2573, 2578, 96 L.Ed.2d 510 (1987); *Board of Ed. of Westside Community Schools (Dist. 66) v. Mergens,* 496 U.S. 226, 261–262, 110 S.Ct. 2356, 2377–2378, 110 L.Ed.2d 191 (1990) (KENNEDY, J., concurring). Our decisions in *Engel v. Vitale,* 370 U.S. 421, 82 S.Ct. 1261, 8 L.Ed.2d 601 (1962), and *School Dist. of Abington, supra,* recognize, among other things, that prayer exercises in public schools carry a particular risk of indirect coercion. The concern may not be limited to the context of schools, but it is most pronounced there. See *County of Allegheny v. American Civil Liberties Union, Greater Pittsburgh Chapter,* 492 U.S., at 661, 109 S.Ct., at 3137 (KENNEDY, J., concurring in judgment in part and dissenting in part). What to most believers may seem nothing more than a reasonable request that the nonbeliever respect their religious practices, in a school context may appear to the nonbeliever or dissenter to be an attempt to employ the machinery of the State to enforce a religious orthodoxy.

⌊593We need not look beyond the circumstances of this case to see the phenomenon at work. The undeniable fact is that the school district's supervision and control of a high school graduation ceremony places public pressure, as well as peer pressure, on attending students to stand as a group or, at least, maintain respectful silence during the invocation and benediction. This pressure, though subtle and indirect, can be as real as any overt compulsion. Of course, in our culture standing or remaining silent can signify adherence to a view or simple respect for the views of others. And no doubt some persons who have no desire to join a prayer have little objection to standing as a sign of respect for those who do. But for the dissenter of high school age, who has a reasonable perception that she is being forced by the State to pray in a manner her conscience will not allow, the injury is no less real. There can be no doubt that for many, if not most, of the students at the graduation, the act of standing or remaining silent was an expression of participation in the rabbi's prayer. That was the very point of the religious exercise. It is of little comfort to a dissenter, then, to be told that for her the act of standing or remaining in silence signifies mere respect, rather than participation. What matters is that, given our social conventions, a reasonable dissenter in this milieu could believe that the group exercise signified her own participation or approval of it.

Finding no violation under these circumstances would place objectors in the dilemma of participating, with all that implies, or protesting. We do not address whether that choice is acceptable if the affected citizens are mature adults, but we think the State may not, consistent with the Establishment Clause, place primary and secondary school children in this position. Research in psychology supports the common assumption that adolescents are often susceptible to pressure from their peers towards conformity, and that the influence is strongest in matters of social convention. Brittain, Adolescent Choices and Parent–Peer Cross–Pressures, 594 28 Am.Sociological Rev. 385 (June 1963); Clasen & Brown, The Multidimensionality of Peer Pressure in Adolescence, 14 J. of Youth and Adolescence 451 (Dec.1985); Brown, Clasen, & Eicher, Perceptions of Peer Pressure, Peer Conformity Dispositions, and Self–Reported Behavior Among Adolescents, 22 Developmental Psychology 521 (July 1986). To recognize that the choice imposed by the State constitutes an unacceptable constraint only acknowledges that the government may no more use social pressure to enforce orthodoxy than it may use more direct means.

The injury caused by the government's action, and the reason why Daniel and Deborah Weisman object to it, is that the State, in a school setting, in effect required participation in a religious exercise. It is, we concede, a brief exercise during which the individual can concentrate on joining its message, meditate on her own religion, or let her mind wander. But the embarrassment and the intrusion of the religious exercise cannot be refuted by arguing that these prayers, and similar ones to be said in the future, are of a *de minimis* character. To do so would be an affront to the rabbi who offered them and to all those for whom the prayers were an essential and profound recognition of divine authority. And for the same reason, we think that the intrusion is greater than the two minutes or so of time consumed for prayers like these. Assuming, as we must, that the prayers were offensive to the student and the parent who now object, the intrusion was both real and, in the context of a secondary school, a violation of the objectors' rights. That the intrusion was in the course of promulgating religion that sought to be civic or nonsectarian rather than pertaining to one sect does not lessen the offense or isolation to the objectors. At best it narrows their number, at worst increases their sense of isolation and affront. See *supra*, at 2658.

[7] There was a stipulation in the District Court that attendance at graduation and promotional ceremonies is voluntary. Agreed Statement of Facts ¶ 41, App. 18. Petitioners and 595 the United States, as *amicus*, made this a center point of the case, arguing that the option of not attending the graduation excuses any inducement or coercion in the ceremony itself. The argument lacks all persuasion. Law reaches past formalism. And to say a teenage student has a real choice not to attend her high school graduation is formalistic in the extreme. True, Deborah could elect not to attend commencement without renouncing her diploma; but we shall not allow the case to turn on this point. Everyone knows that in our society and in our culture high school graduation is one of life's most significant occasions. A school rule which excuses attendance is beside the point. Attendance may not be required by official decree, yet it is apparent that a student is not free to absent herself from the graduation exercise in any real sense of the term "voluntary," for absence would require forfeiture of those intangible benefits which have motivated the student through youth and all her high school years. Graduation is a time for family and those closest to the student to celebrate success and express mutual wishes of gratitude and respect, all to the end of impressing upon the young person the role that it is his or her right and duty to assume in the community and all of its diverse parts.

The importance of the event is the point the school district and the United States rely upon to argue that a formal prayer ought to be permitted, but it becomes one of the principal reasons why their argument must fail. Their contention, one of considerable force were it not for the constitutional constraints applied to state action, is that the prayers are an essential part of these ceremonies because for many persons an occasion of this significance lacks meaning if there is no recognition, however brief, that human achievements cannot be understood apart from their spiritual essence. We think the Government's position that this interest suffices to force students to choose between compliance or forfeiture demonstrates fundamental inconsistency in its argumentation. It fails to acknowledge that what for many of $\lfloor_{596}$Deborah's classmates and their parents was a spiritual imperative was for Daniel and Deborah Weisman religious conformance compelled by the State. While in some societies the wishes of the majority might prevail, the Establishment Clause of the First Amendment is addressed to this contingency and rejects the balance urged upon us. The Constitution forbids the State to exact religious conformity from a student as the price of attending her own high school graduation. This is the calculus the Constitution commands.

The Government's argument gives insufficient recognition to the real conflict of conscience faced by the young student. The essence of the Government's position is that with regard to a civic, social occasion of this importance it is the objector, not the majority, who must take unilateral and private action to avoid compromising religious scruples, hereby electing to miss the graduation exercise. This turns conventional First Amendment analysis on its head. It is a tenet of the First Amendment that the State cannot require one of its citizens to forfeit his or her rights and benefits as the price of resisting conformance to state-sponsored religious practice. To say that a student must remain apart from the ceremony at the opening invocation and closing benediction is to risk compelling conformity in an environment analogous to the classroom setting, where we have said the risk of compulsion is especially high. See *supra*, at 2658–2659. Just as in *Engel v. Vitale*, 370 U.S., at 430, 82 S.Ct., at 1266, and *School Dist. of Abington v. Schempp*, 374 U.S., at 224–225, 83 S.Ct., at 1572–1573, where we found that provisions within the challenged legislation permitting a student to be voluntarily excused from attendance or participation in the daily prayers did not shield those practices from invalidation, the fact that attendance at the graduation ceremonies is voluntary in a legal sense does not save the religious exercise.

Inherent differences between the public school system and a session of a state legislature distinguish this case from *Marsh v. Chambers*, 463 U.S. 783, 103 S.Ct. 3330, 77 L.Ed.2d 1019 (1983). The considerations$_{597}$ we have raised in objection to the invocation and benediction are in many respects similar to the arguments we considered in *Marsh*. But there are also obvious differences. The atmosphere at the opening of a session of a state legislature where adults are free to enter and leave with little comment and for any number of reasons cannot compare with the constraining potential of the one school event most important for the student to attend. The influence and force of a formal exercise in a school graduation are far greater than the prayer exercise we condoned in *Marsh*. The *Marsh* majority in fact gave specific recognition to this distinction and placed particular reliance on it in upholding the prayers at issue there. 463 U.S., at 792, 103 S.Ct., at 3336. Today's case is different. At a high school graduation, teachers and principals must and do retain a high degree of control over the precise contents of the program, the speeches, the timing, the movements, the dress, and the decorum of the students. *Bethel School Dist. No. 403 v. Fraser*, 478 U.S. 675, 106 S.Ct. 3159, 92 L.Ed.2d 549 (1986). In this atmosphere the state-imposed character of an invocation and benediction by clergy selected by the school combine to make the prayer a state-sanctioned religious exercise in which the student was left with no alternative but to submit. This is different from *Marsh* and suffices to make the religious exercise a First Amendment violation. Our Establishment Clause jurisprudence remains a delicate and fact-sensitive one, and we cannot accept the parallel relied upon by petitioners and the United States between the facts of *Marsh* and the case now before us. Our decisions in *Engel v. Vitale, supra,* and *School Dist. of Abington v. Schempp, supra,* require us to distinguish the public school context.

We do not hold that every state action implicating religion is invalid if one or a few citizens find it offensive. People may take offense at all manner of religious as well as nonreligious messages, but offense alone does not in every case show a violation. We know too that sometimes to endure ⌊598social isolation or even anger may be the price of conscience or nonconformity. But, by any reading of our cases, the conformity required of the student in this case was too high an exaction to withstand the test of the Establishment Clause. The prayer exercises in this case are especially improper because the State has in every practical sense compelled attendance and participation in an explicit religious exercise at an event of singular importance to every student, one the objecting student had no real alternative to avoid.

Our jurisprudence in this area is of necessity one of line-drawing, of determining at what point a dissenter's rights of religious freedom are infringed by the State.

> "The First Amendment does not prohibit practices which by any realistic measure create none of the dangers which it is designed to prevent and which do not so directly or substantially involve the state in religious exercises or in the favoring of religion as to have meaningful and practical impact. It is of course true that great consequences can grow from small beginnings, but the measure of constitutional adjudication is the ability and willingness to distinguish between real threat and mere shadow." *School Dist. of Abington v. Schempp, supra,* 374 U.S., at 308, 83 S.Ct., at 1616 (Goldberg, J., concurring).

Our society would be less than true to its heritage if it lacked abiding concern for the values of its young people, and we acknowledge the profound belief of adherents to many faiths that there must be a place in the student's life for precepts of a morality higher even than the law we today enforce. We express no hostility to those aspirations, nor would our oath permit us to do so. A relentless and all-pervasive attempt to exclude religion from every aspect of public life could itself become inconsistent with the Constitution. See *School Dist. of Abington, supra,* at 306, 83 S.Ct., at 1615 (Goldberg, J., concurring). We recognize that, at graduation time and throughout the course of the educational process, there will ⌊599be instances when religious values, religious practices, and religious persons will have some interaction with the public schools and their students. See *Board of Ed. of Westside Community Schools (Dist. 66) v. Mergens,* 496 U.S. 226, 110 S.Ct. 2356, 110 L.Ed.2d 191 (1990). But these matters, often questions of accommodation of religion, are not before us. The sole question presented is whether a religious exercise may be conducted at a graduation ceremony in circumstances where, as we have found, young graduates who object are induced to conform. No holding by this Court suggests that a school can persuade or compel a student to participate in a religious exercise. That is being done here, and it is forbidden by the Establishment Clause of the First Amendment.

For the reasons we have stated, the judgment of the Court of Appeals is

Affirmed.

Justice BLACKMUN, with whom Justice STEVENS and Justice O'CONNOR join, concurring.

Nearly half a century of review and refinement of Establishment Clause jurisprudence has distilled one clear understanding: Government may neither promote nor affiliate itself with any religious doctrine or organization, nor may it obtrude itself in the internal affairs of any religious institution. The application of these principles to the present case mandates the decision reached today by the Court.

I

This Court first reviewed a challenge to state law under the Establishment Clause in *Everson v. Board of Ed. of Ewing,* 330 U.S. 1, 67 S.Ct. 504, 91 L.Ed. 711 (1947).[1] Relying on the history of the ⌊600Clause, and the Court's prior analysis, Justice Black outlined the considerations that have become the touchstone of Establishment Clause jurisprudence: Neither a State nor the Federal Government can pass laws which aid one religion, aid all religions, or prefer one religion over another. Neither a State nor the Federal Government, openly or secretly, can participate in the affairs of any religious organization and vice versa.[2] "In the words of Jefferson, the clause ⌊601against establishment of religion by law was intended to erect 'a wall of separation between church and State.'" *Everson,* 330 U.S., at 16, 67 S.Ct., at 511 (quoting *Reynolds v. United States,* 98 U.S. 145, 164, 25 L.Ed. 244 (1879)). The dissenters agreed: "The Amendment's purpose ... was to create a complete and permanent separation of the spheres of religious activity and civil authority by comprehensively forbidding every form of public aid or support for religion." 330 U.S., at 31–32, 67 S.Ct., at 519–520 (Rutledge, J., dissenting, joined by Frankfurter, Jackson, and Burton, JJ.).

In *Engel v. Vitale,* 370 U.S. 421, 82 S.Ct. 1261, 8 L.Ed.2d 601 (1962), the Court considered for the first time the constitutionality of prayer in a public school. Students said aloud a short prayer selected by the State Board of Regents: "'Almighty God, we acknowledge our dependence upon Thee, and we beg Thy blessings upon us, our parents, our teachers and our Country.'" *Id.,* at 422, 82 S.Ct., at 1262. Justice Black, writing for the Court, again made clear that the First Amendment forbids the use of the power or prestige of the government to control, support, or influence the religious beliefs and

1. A few earlier cases involving federal laws touched on interpretation of the Establishment Clause. In *Reynolds v. United States,* 98 U.S. 145, 25 L.Ed. 244 (1879), and *Davis v. Beason,* 133 U.S. 333, 10 S.Ct. 299, 33 L.Ed. 637 (1890), the Court considered the Clause in the context of federal laws prohibiting bigamy. The Court in *Reynolds* accepted Thomas Jefferson's letter to the Danbury Baptist Association "almost as an authoritative declaration of the scope and effect" of the First Amendment. 98 U.S., at 164. In that letter Jefferson penned his famous lines that the Establishment Clause built "a wall of separation between church and State." *Ibid. Davis* considered that "[t]he first amendment to the Constitution ... was intended ... to prohibit legislation for the support of any religious tenets, or the modes of worship of any sect." 133 U.S., at 342, 10 S.Ct., at 300. In another case, *Bradfield v. Roberts,* 175 U.S. 291, 20 S.Ct. 121, 44 L.Ed. 168 (1899), the Court held that it did not violate the Establishment Clause for Congress to construct a hospital building for caring for poor patients, although the hospital was managed by sisters of the Roman Catholic Church. The Court reasoned: "That the influence of any particular church may be powerful over the members of a non-sectarian and secular corporation, incorporated for a certain defined purpose and with clearly stated powers, is surely not sufficient to convert such a corporation into a religious or sectarian body." *Id.,* at 298, 20 S.Ct., at 124. Finally, in 1908 the Court held that "the spirit of the Constitution" did not prohibit the Indians from using their money, held by the United States Government, for religious education. See *Quick Bear v. Leupp,* 210 U.S. 50, 81, 28 S.Ct. 690, 700, 52 L.Ed. 954.

2. The Court articulated six examples of paradigmatic practices that the Establishment Clause prohibits: "The 'establishment of religion' clause of the First Amendment means at least this: Neither a state nor the Federal Government can set up a church. Neither can pass laws which aid one religion, aid all religions, or prefer one religion over another. Neither can force nor influence a person to go to or to remain away from church against his will or force him to profess a belief or disbelief in any religion. No person can be punished for entertaining or professing religious beliefs or disbeliefs, for church attendance or non-attendance. No tax in any amount, large or small, can be levied to support any religious activities or institutions, whatever they may be called, or whatever form they may adopt to teach or practice religion. Neither a state nor the Federal Government can, openly or secretly, participate in the affairs of any religious organizations or groups and *vice versa.*" *Everson v. Board of Ed. of Ewing,* 330 U.S., at 15, 67 S.Ct., at 511–512.

practices of the American people. Although the prayer was "denominationally neutral" and "its observance on the part of the students [was] voluntary," *id.*, at 430, 82 S.Ct., at 1266, the Court found that it violated this essential precept of the Establishment Clause.

A year later, the Court again invalidated government-sponsored prayer in public schools in *School Dist. of Abington v. Schempp,* 374 U.S. 203, 83 S.Ct. 1560, 10 L.Ed.2d 844 (1963). In *Schempp,* the school day for Baltimore, Maryland, and Abington Township, Pennsylvania, students began with a reading from the Bible, or a recitation of the Lord's Prayer, or both. After a thorough review of the Court's prior Establishment Clause cases, the Court concluded:

> ⌊602"[T]he Establishment Clause has been directly considered by this Court eight times in the past score of years and, with only one Justice dissenting on the point, it has consistently held that the clause withdrew all legislative power respecting religious belief or the expression thereof. The test may be stated as follows: what are the purpose and the primary effect of the enactment? If either is the advancement or inhibition of religion, then the enactment exceeds the scope of legislative power as circumscribed by the Constitution." *Id.*, at 222, 83 S.Ct., at 1571.

Because the schools' opening exercises were government-sponsored religious ceremonies, the Court found that the primary effect was the advancement of religion and held, therefore, that the activity violated the Establishment Clause. *Id.*, at 223–224, 83 S.Ct., at 1572–1573.

Five years later, the next time the Court considered whether religious activity in public schools violated the Establishment Clause, it reiterated the principle that government "may not aid, foster, or promote one religion or religious theory against another or even against the militant opposite." *Epperson v. Arkansas,* 393 U.S. 97, 104, 89 S.Ct. 266, 270, 21 L.Ed.2d 228 (1968). " 'If [the purpose or primary effect] is the advancement or inhibition of religion then the enactment exceeds the scope of legislative power as circumscribed by the Constitution.' " *Id.*, at 107, 89 S.Ct., at 272 (quoting *Schempp,* 374 U.S., at 222, 83 S.Ct., at 1571). Finding that the Arkansas law aided religion by preventing the teaching of evolution, the Court invalidated it.

In 1971, Chief Justice Burger reviewed the Court's past decisions and found: "Three ... tests may be gleaned from our cases." *Lemon v. Kurtzman,* 403 U.S. 602, 612, 91 S.Ct. 2105, 2111. In order for a statute to survive an Establishment Clause challenge, "[f]irst, the statute must have a secular legislative purpose; second, its principal or primary effect must be one that neither advances nor inhibits religion; finally the statute must not foster an excessive government entanglement with ⌊603religion." *Id.*, at 612–613, 91 S.Ct., at 2111 (internal quotation marks and citations omitted).[3] After *Lemon,* the Court continued to rely on these basic principles in resolving Establishment Clause disputes.[4]

3. The final prong, excessive entanglement, was a focus of *Walz v. Tax Comm'n of New York City,* 397 U.S. 664, 674, 90 S.Ct. 1409, 1414, 25 L.Ed.2d 697 (1970), but harkens back to the final example in *Everson:* "Neither a state nor the Federal Government can, openly or secretly, participate in the affairs of any religious organizations or groups and *vice versa.*" *Everson,* 330 U.S., at 16, 67 S.Ct., at 511. The discussion in *Everson* reflected the Madisonian concern that secular and religious authorities must not interfere with each other's respective spheres of choice and influence. See generally The Complete Madison 298–312 (S. Padover ed. 1953).

4. Since 1971, the Court has decided 31 Establishment Clause cases. In only one instance, the decision of *Marsh v. Chambers,* 463 U.S. 783, 103 S.Ct. 3330, 77 L.Ed.2d 1019 (1983), has the Court not rested its decision on the basic principles described in *Lemon.* For example, in the most recent Establishment Clause case, *Board of Ed. of Westside Community Schools (Dist. 66) v. Mergens,* 496 U.S. 226, 110 S.Ct. 2356, 110 L.Ed.2d 191 (1990), the Court applied the three-part *Lemon* analysis to the Equal Access Act, which made it unlawful for public secondary schools to deny equal access to any student wishing to hold religious meetings. *Id.*, at 248–253,

Application of these principles to the facts of this case is straightforward. There can be "no doubt" that the "invocation of God's blessings" delivered at Nathan Bishop Middle School "is a religious activity." *Engel,* 370 U.S., at 424, 82 S.Ct., at 1263. In the words of *Engel,* the Rabbi's prayer "is a solemn avowal of divine faith and supplication for the blessings of the Almighty. The nature of such a prayer has always been religious." *Ibid.* The question then is whether the government has "plac[ed] its official stamp of approval" on the prayer. *Id.,* at 429, 82 S.Ct., at 1266. As the Court ably demonstrates, when the government "compose[s] official prayers," *id.,* at 425, 82 S.Ct., at 1264, selects the member of the clergy to deliver the prayer, has the prayer delivered at a public school event that is planned, supervised and given by school officials, and pressures604 students to attend and participate in the prayer, there can be no doubt that the government is advancing and promoting religion.[5] As our prior decisions teach us, it is this that the Constitution prohibits.

II

I join the Court's opinion today because I find nothing in it inconsistent with the essential precepts of the Establishment Clause developed in our precedents. The Court holds that the graduation prayer is unconstitutional because the State "in effect required participation in a religious exercise." *Ante,* at 2659. Although our precedents make clear that proof of government coercion is not necessary to prove an Establishment Clause violation, it is sufficient. Government pressure to participate in a religious activity is an obvious indication that the government is endorsing or promoting religion.

But it is not enough that the government restrain from compelling religious practices: It must not engage in them either. See *Schempp,* 374 U.S., at 305, 83 S.Ct., at 1615 (Goldberg, J., concurring). The Court repeatedly has recognized that a violation of the Establishment Clause is not predicated on coercion. See, *e.g., id.,* at 223, 83 S.Ct., at 1572; *id.,* at 229, 83 S.Ct., at 1575 (Douglas, J., concurring); *Wallace v. Jaffree,* 472 U.S. 38, 72, 105 S.Ct. 2479, 2498, 86 L.Ed.2d 29 (1985) (O'CONNOR, J., concurring in judgment) ("The decisions [in *Engel* and *Schempp*] acknowledged the coercion implicit under the statutory schemes, but they expressly turned only on the fact that the government was sponsoring a manifestly religious exercise" (citation omitted)); *Committee for Public Ed. & Religious Liberty v. Nyquist,* 413 U.S. 756, 786, 93 S.Ct. 2955, 2972, 37 L.Ed.2d 948 (1973) ("[P]roof of coercion ... [is] not a necessary element of any claim under the Establishment Clause"). The Establishment Clause proscribes public schools from "conveying or attempting to convey605 a message that religion or a particular religious belief is *favored* or *preferred,*" *County of Allegheny v. American Civil Liberties Union, Greater Pittsburgh Chapter,* 492 U.S. 573, 593, 109 S.Ct. 3086, 3101, 106 L.Ed.2d 472 (1989) (internal quotation marks omitted; emphasis in original), even if the schools do not actually "impos[e] pressure upon a student to participate in a religious activity."[6] *Board of Ed. of Westside Com-*

110 S.Ct., at 2370–2373 (plurality opinion); *id.,* at 262, 110 S.Ct., at 2378 (Marshall, J., concurring in judgment). In no case involving religious activities in public schools has the Court failed to apply vigorously the *Lemon* factors.

5. In this case, the religious message it promotes is specifically Judeo–Christian. The phrase in the benediction: "We must each strive to fulfill what you require of us all, to do justly, to love mercy, to walk humbly" obviously was taken from the Book of the Prophet Micah, ch. 6, v. 8.

6. As a practical matter, of course, anytime the government endorses a religious belief there will almost always be some pressure to conform. "When the power, prestige and financial support of government is placed behind a particular religious belief, the indirect coercive pressure upon religious minorities to conform to the prevailing officially approved religion is plain." *Engel v. Vitale,* 370 U.S. 421, 431, 82 S.Ct. 1261, 1267, 8 L.Ed.2d 601 (1962).

munity Schools (Dist. 66) v. Mergens, 496 U.S. 226, 261, 110 S.Ct. 2356, 2378, 110 L.Ed.2d 191 (1990) (KENNEDY, J., concurring in part and concurring in judgment).

The scope of the Establishment Clause's prohibitions developed in our case law derives from the Clause's purposes. The First Amendment encompasses two distinct guarantees—the government shall make no law respecting an establishment of religion or prohibiting the free exercise thereof—both with the common purpose of securing religious liberty.[7] Through vigorous enforcement of both Clauses, we "promote and assure the fullest possible scope of religious liberty and tolerance for all and ... nurture the conditions which secure the best hope of attainment of that end." *Schempp,* 374 U.S., at 305, 83 S.Ct., at 1615 (Goldberg, J., concurring).

There is no doubt that attempts to aid religion through government coercion jeopardize freedom of conscience. Even subtle pressure diminishes the right of each individual to choose voluntarily what to believe. Representative Carroll explained during congressional debate over the Estab|606lishment Clause: "[T]he rights of conscience are, in their nature, of peculiar delicacy, and will little bear the gentlest touch of governmental hand." 1 Annals of Cong. 757 (1789).

Our decisions have gone beyond prohibiting coercion, however, because the Court has recognized that "the fullest possible scope of religious liberty," *Schempp,* 374 U.S., at 305, 83 S.Ct., at 1615 (Goldberg, J., concurring), entails more than freedom from coercion. The Establishment Clause protects religious liberty on a grand scale; it is a social compact that guarantees for generations a democracy and a strong religious community—both essential to safeguarding religious liberty. "Our fathers seem to have been perfectly sincere in their belief that the members of the Church would be more patriotic, and the citizens of the State more religious, by keeping their respective functions entirely separate." Religious Liberty, in Essays and Speeches of Jeremiah S. Black 53 (C. Black ed. 1885) (Chief Justice of the Commonwealth of Pennsylvania).[8]

The mixing of government and religion can be a threat to free government, even if no one is forced to participate. When the government puts its *imprimatur* on a particular religion, it conveys a message of exclusion to all those who do not adhere to the favored beliefs.[9] A government cannot |607be premised on the belief that all persons are created equal when it asserts that God prefers some. Only "[a]nguish, hardship and bitter strife" result "when zealous religious groups struggl[e] with one another to obtain the Government's stamp of approval." *Engel,* 370 U.S., at 429, 82 S.Ct., at 1266; see also *Lemon,* 403 U.S., at 622–623, 91 S.Ct., at 2115–2116; *Aguilar v. Felton,* 473 U.S. 402, 416, 105 S.Ct. 3232, 3239, 87 L.Ed.2d 290

7. See, *e.g., Everson,* 330 U.S., at 40, 67 S.Ct., at 523 (Rutledge, J., dissenting) (" 'Establishment' and 'free exercise' were correlative and coextensive ideas, representing only different facets of the single great and fundamental freedom"); *School Dist. of Abington v. Schempp,* 374 U.S. 203, 227, 83 S.Ct. 1560, 1574, 10 L.Ed.2d 844 (1963) (Douglas, J., concurring); *id.,* at 305, 83 S.Ct., at 1615 (Goldberg, J., concurring); *Wallace v. Jaffree,* 472 U.S. 38, 50, 105 S.Ct. 2479, 2486, 86 L.Ed.2d 29 (1985).

8. See also *Engel,* 370 U.S., at 431, 82 S.Ct., at 1267 (The Clause's "first and most immediate purpose rested on the belief that a union of government and religion tends to destroy government and to degrade religion"); *Illinois ex rel. McCollum v. Board of Ed. of School Dist. No. 71, Champaign Cty.,* 333 U.S. 203, 212, 68 S.Ct. 461, 465, 92 L.Ed. 649 (1948) ("[T]he First Amendment rests upon the premise that both religion and government can best work to achieve their lofty aims if each is left free from the other within its respective sphere").

9. "[T]he Establishment Clause is infringed when the government makes adherence to religion relevant to a person's standing in the political community. Direct government action endorsing religion or a particular religious practice is invalid under this approach because it sends a message to nonadherents that they are outsiders, not full members of the political community, and an accompanying message to adherents that they are insiders, favored members of the political community." *Wallace v. Jaffree,* 472 U.S., at 69, 105 S.Ct., at 2496 (O'CONNOR, J., concurring in judgment) (internal quotation marks omitted).

(1985) (Powell, J., concurring).[10] Such a struggle can "strain a political system to the breaking point." *Walz v. Tax Comm'n of New York City,* 397 U.S. 664, 694, 90 S.Ct. 1409, 1424, 25 L.Ed.2d 697 (1970) (opinion of Harlan, J.).

When the government arrogates to itself a role in religious affairs, it abandons its obligation as guarantor of democracy. Democracy requires the nourishment of dialog and dissent, while religious faith puts its trust in an ultimate divine authority above all human deliberation. When the government appropriates religious truth, it "transforms rational debate into theological decree." Nuechterlein, Note, The Free Exercise Boundaries of Permissible Accommodation Under the Establishment Clause, 99 Yale L.J. 1127, 1131 (1990). Those who disagree no longer are questioning the policy judgment of the elected but the rules of a higher authority who is beyond reproach.

⊥608 Madison warned that government officials who would use religious authority to pursue secular ends "exceed the commission from which they derive their authority and are Tyrants. The People who submit to it are governed by laws made neither by themselves, nor by an authority derived from them, and are slaves." Memorial and Remonstrance against Religious Assessments (1785), in The Complete Madison 300 (S. Padover ed. 1953). Democratic government will not last long when proclamation replaces persuasion as the medium of political exchange.

Likewise, we have recognized that "[r]eligion flourishes in greater purity, without than with the aid of Gov[ernment]." [11] *Id.,* at 309. To "make room for as wide a variety of beliefs and creeds as the spiritual needs of man deem necessary," *Zorach v. Clauson,* 343 U.S. 306, 313, 72 S.Ct. 679, 683, 96 L.Ed. 954 (1952), the government must not align itself with any one of them. When the government favors a particular religion or sect, the disadvantage to all others is obvious, but even the favored religion may fear being "taint[ed] . . . with a corrosive secularism." *School Dist. of Grand Rapids v. Ball,* 473 U.S. 373, 385, 105 S.Ct. 3216, 3223, 87 L.Ed.2d 267 (1985). The favored religion may be compromised as political figures reshape the religion's beliefs for their own purposes; it may be reformed as government largesse brings government regulation.[12] Keeping religion in the hands of private groups minimizes state intrusion on religious choice and best enables each religion to "flourish according to the ⊥609 zeal of its adherents and the appeal of its dogma." *Zorach,* 343 U.S., at 313, 72 S.Ct., at 683.

It is these understandings and fears that underlie our Establishment Clause jurispru-

10. Sigmund Freud expressed it this way: "a religion, even if it calls itself the religion of love, must be hard and unloving to those who do not belong to it." S. Freud, Group Psychology and the Analysis of the Ego 51 (1922). James Madison stated the theory even more strongly in his "Memorial and Remonstrance" against a bill providing tax funds to religious teachers: "It degrades from the equal rank of Citizens all those whose opinions in Religion do not bend to those of the Legislative authority. Distant as it may be, in its present form, from the Inquisition it differs from it only in degree. The one is the first step, the other the last in the career of intolerance." The Complete Madison, at 303. Religion has not lost its power to engender divisiveness. "Of all the issues the ACLU takes on—reproductive rights, discrimination, jail and prison conditions, abuse of kids in the public schools, police brutality, to name a few—by far the most volatile issue is that of school prayer. Aside from our efforts to abolish the death penalty, it is the only issue that elicits death threats." Parish, Graduation Prayer Violates the Bill of Rights, 4 Utah Bar J. 19 (June/July 1991).

11. The view that the Establishment Clause was primarily a vehicle for protecting churches was expounded initially by Roger Williams. "[W]ordly corruptions . . . might consume the churches if sturdy fences against the wilderness were not maintained." M. Howe, The Garden and the Wilderness 6 (1965).

12. "[B]ut when a religion contracts an alliance of this nature, I do not hesitate to affirm that it commits the same error as a man who should sacrifice his future to his present welfare; and in obtaining a power to which it has no claim, it risks that authority which is rightfully its own." 1 A. de Tocqueville, Democracy in America 315 (H. Reeve transl. 1900).

dence. We have believed that religious freedom cannot exist in the absence of a free democratic government, and that such a government cannot endure when there is fusion between religion and the political regime. We have believed that religious freedom cannot thrive in the absence of a vibrant religious community and that such a community cannot prosper when it is bound to the secular. And we have believed that these were the animating principles behind the adoption of the Establishment Clause. To that end, our cases have prohibited government endorsement of religion, its sponsorship, and active involvement in religion, whether or not citizens were coerced to conform.

I remain convinced that our jurisprudence is not misguided, and that it requires the decision reached by the Court today. Accordingly, I join the Court in affirming the judgment of the Court of Appeals.

Justice SOUTER, with whom Justice STEVENS and Justice O'CONNOR join, concurring.

I join the whole of the Court's opinion, and fully agree that prayers at public school graduation ceremonies indirectly coerce religious observance. I write separately nonetheless on two issues of Establishment Clause analysis that underlie my independent resolution of this case: whether the Clause applies to governmental practices that do not favor one religion or denomination over others, and whether state coercion of religious conformity, over and above state endorsement of religious exercise or belief, is a necessary element of an Establishment Clause violation.

I

Forty-five years ago, this Court announced a basic principle of constitutional law from which it has not strayed: the ⌊610Establishment Clause forbids not only state practices that "aid one religion ... or prefer one religion over another," but also those that "aid all religions." *Everson v. Board of Ed. of Ewing,* 330 U.S. 1, 15, 67 S.Ct. 504, 511, 91 L.Ed. 711 (1947). Today we reaffirm that principle, holding that the Establishment Clause forbids state-sponsored prayers in public school settings no matter how nondenominational the prayers may be. In barring the State from sponsoring generically theistic prayers where it could not sponsor sectarian ones, we hold true to a line of precedent from which there is no adequate historical case to depart.

A

Since *Everson,* we have consistently held the Clause applicable no less to governmental acts favoring religion generally than to acts favoring one religion over others.[1] Thus, in *Engel v. Vitale,* 370 U.S. 421, 82 S.Ct. 1261, 8 L.Ed.2d 601 (1962), we held that the public schools may not subject their students to readings of any prayer, however "denominationally neutral." *Id.,* at 430, 82 S.Ct., at 1266. More recently, in *Wallace v. Jaffree,* 472 U.S. 38, 105 S.Ct. 2479, 86 L.Ed.2d 29 (1985), we held that an Alabama moment-of-silence statute passed for the sole purpose of "returning voluntary prayer to public schools," *id.,* at 57, 105 S.Ct., at 2490, violated the Establishment Clause even though it did not encourage students to pray to any particular deity. We said that "when the underlying principle has been examined in the crucible of litigation, the Court has unambiguously concluded that the individual freedom of conscience protected by the First Amendment embraces the right to select any religious faith or none at all." *Id.,* at 52–53, 105 S.Ct., at 2487–2488. This conclusion, we held,

> "derives support not only from the interest in respecting the individual's freedom of conscience, but also from the conviction that religious beliefs worthy of respect are the product of free and voluntary choice by

1. Cf. *Larson v. Valente,* 456 U.S. 228, 102 S.Ct. 1673, 72 L.Ed.2d 33 (1982) (subjecting discrimination against certain religious organizations to test of strict scrutiny).

the faithful, ⌊611and from recognition of the fact that the political interest in forestalling intolerance extends beyond intolerance among Christian sects—or even intolerance among 'religions'—to encompass intolerance of the disbeliever and the uncertain." *Id.*, at 53–54, 105 S.Ct., at 2488 (footnotes omitted).

Likewise, in *Texas Monthly, Inc. v. Bullock*, 489 U.S. 1, 109 S.Ct. 890, 103 L.Ed.2d 1 (1989), we struck down a state tax exemption benefiting only religious periodicals; even though the statute in question worked no discrimination among sects, a majority of the Court found that its preference for religious publications over all other kinds "effectively endorses religious belief." *Id.*, at 17, 109 S.Ct., at 901 (plurality opinion); see *id.*, at 28, 109 S.Ct., at 907 (BLACKMUN, J., concurring in judgment) ("A statutory preference for the dissemination of religious ideas offends our most basic understanding of what the Establishment Clause is all about and hence is constitutionally intolerable"). And in *Torcaso v. Watkins*, 367 U.S. 488, 81 S.Ct. 1680, 6 L.Ed.2d 982 (1961), we struck down a provision of the Maryland Constitution requiring public officials to declare a " 'belief in the existence of God,' " *id.*, at 489, 81 S.Ct., at 1680, reasoning that, under the Religion Clauses of the First Amendment, "neither a State nor the Federal Government ... can constitutionally pass laws or impose requirements which aid all religions as against non-believers ...," *id.*, at 495, 81 S.Ct., at 1683. See also *Epperson v. Arkansas*, 393 U.S. 97, 104, 89 S.Ct. 266, 270, 21 L.Ed.2d 228 (1968) ("The First Amendment mandates governmental neutrality between religion and religion, and between religion and nonreligion"); *School Dist. of Abington v. Schempp*, 374 U.S. 203, 216, 83 S.Ct. 1560, 1568, 10 L.Ed.2d 844 (1963) ("this Court has rejected unequivocally the contention that the Establishment Clause forbids only governmental preference of one religion over another"); *id.*, at 319–320, 83 S.Ct., at 1622 (Stewart, J., dissenting) (the Clause applies "to each of us, be he Jew or Agnostic, Christian or Atheist, Buddhist or Freethinker").

Such is the settled law. Here, as elsewhere, we should stick to it absent some compelling reason to discard it. See ⌊612*Arizona v. Rumsey*, 467 U.S. 203, 212, 104 S.Ct. 2305, 2311, 81 L.Ed.2d 164 (1984); *Payne v. Tennessee*, 501 U.S. 808, 842, 111 S.Ct. 2597, 2617–2618, 115 L.Ed.2d 720 (1991) (SOUTER, J., concurring).

B

Some have challenged this precedent by reading the Establishment Clause to permit "nonpreferential" state promotion of religion. The challengers argue that, as originally understood by the Framers, "[t]he Establishment Clause did not require government neutrality between religion and irreligion nor did it prohibit the Federal Government from providing nondiscriminatory aid to religion." *Wallace, supra*, at 106, 105 S.Ct., at 2515 (REHNQUIST, J., dissenting); see also R. Cord, Separation of Church and State: Historical Fact and Current Fiction (1988). While a case has been made for this position, it is not so convincing as to warrant reconsideration of our settled law; indeed, I find in the history of the Clause's textual development a more powerful argument supporting the Court's jurisprudence following *Everson*.

When James Madison arrived at the First Congress with a series of proposals to amend the National Constitution, one of the provisions read that "[t]he civil rights of none shall be abridged on account of religious belief or worship, nor shall any national religion be established, nor shall the full and equal rights of conscience be in any manner, or on any pretext, infringed." 1 Annals of Cong. 434 (1789). Madison's language did not last long. It was sent to a Select Committee of the House, which, without explanation, changed it to read that "no religion shall be established by law, nor shall the equal rights of conscience be infringed." *Id.*, at 729. Thence the proposal went to the Committee of the Whole, which was in turn dissatisfied with the Select Committee's language and adopted an alternative proposed by Samuel Livermore of New Hampshire: "Congress shall make no laws touching religion, or infringing the rights of conscience." See *id.*, at 731. Livermore's proposal would have forbidden laws having anything to do with religion and was thus not ⊥613only far broader than Madison's version, but broader even than the scope of the Establishment Clause as we now understand it. See, *e.g.*, *Corporation of Presiding Bishop of Church of Jesus Christ of Latter-day Saints v. Amos*, 483 U.S. 327, 107 S.Ct. 2862, 97 L.Ed.2d 273 (1987) (upholding legislative exemption of religious groups from certain obligations under civil rights laws).

The House rewrote the amendment once more before sending it to the Senate, this time adopting, without recorded debate, language derived from a proposal by Fisher Ames of Massachusetts: "Congress shall make no law establishing Religion, or prohibiting the free exercise thereof, nor shall the rights of conscience be infringed." 1 Documentary History of the First Federal Congress of the United States of America 136 (Senate Journal) (L. de Pauw ed. 1972); see 1 Annals of Cong. 765 (1789). Perhaps, on further reflection, the Representatives had thought Livermore's proposal too expansive, or perhaps, as one historian has suggested, they had simply worried that his language would not "satisfy the demands of those who wanted something said specifically against establishments of religion." L. Levy, The Establishment Clause 81 (1986) (hereinafter Levy). We do not know; what we do know is that the House rejected the Select Committee's version, which arguably ensured only that "no religion" enjoyed an official preference over others, and deliberately chose instead a prohibition extending to laws establishing "religion" in general.

The sequence of the Senate's treatment of this House proposal, and the House's response to the Senate, confirm that the Framers meant the Establishment Clause's prohibition to encompass nonpreferential aid to religion. In September 1789, the Senate considered a number of provisions that would have permitted such aid, and ultimately it adopted one of them. First, it briefly entertained this language: "Congress shall make no law establishing One Religious Sect or Society in preference to others, nor shall the rights of conscience be infringed." See 1 Documentary History, *supra*, at 151 ⊥614(Senate Journal); *id.*, at 136. After rejecting two minor amendments to that proposal, see *ibid.*, the Senate dropped it altogether and chose a provision identical to the House's proposal, but without the clause protecting the "rights of conscience," *ibid.* With no record of the Senate debates, we cannot know what prompted these changes, but the record does tell us that, six days later, the Senate went half circle and adopted its narrowest language yet: "Congress shall make no law establishing articles of faith or a mode of worship, or prohibiting the free exercise of religion." *Id.*, at 166. The Senate sent this proposal to the House along with its versions of the other constitutional amendments proposed.

Though it accepted much of the Senate's work on the Bill of Rights, the House rejected the Senate's version of the Establishment Clause and called for a joint conference committee, to which the Senate agreed. The House conferees ultimately won out, persuading the Senate to accept this as the final text of the Religion Clauses: "Congress shall make no law respecting an establishment of religion, or prohibiting the free exercise thereof." What is remarkable is that, unlike the earliest House drafts or the final Senate proposal, the prevailing language is not limited to laws respecting an establishment of "a religion," "a national religion," "one religious sect," or specific "articles of faith."[2] The Framers re⊥615peatedly considered and delib-

2. Some commentators have suggested that by targeting laws respecting "an" establishment of religion, the Framers adopted the very nonpreferentialist position whose much clearer articulation they repeatedly rejected. See, *e.g.*, R. Cord, Separation of Church and State 11–12 (1988).

erately rejected such narrow language and instead extended their prohibition to state support for "religion" in general.

Implicit in their choice is the distinction between preferential and nonpreferential establishments, which the weight of evidence suggests the Framers appreciated. See, *e.g.*, Laycock, "Nonpreferential" Aid 902–906; Levy 91–119. But cf. T. Curry, The First Freedoms 208–222 (1986). Of particular note, the Framers were vividly familiar with efforts in the Colonies and, later, the States to impose general, nondenominational assessments and other incidents of ostensibly ecumenical establishments. See generally Levy 1–62. The Virginia statute for religious freedom, written by Jefferson and sponsored by Madison, captured the separationist response to such measures. Condemning all establishments, however nonpreferentialist, the statute broadly guaranteed that "no man shall be compelled to frequent or support any religious worship, place, or ministry whatsoever," including his own. Act for Establishing Religious Freedom (1785), in 5 The Founders' Constitution 84, 85 (P. Kurland & R. Lerner eds. 1987). Forcing a citizen to support even his own church would, among other things, deny "the ministry those temporary rewards, which proceeding from an approbation of their personal conduct, are an additional incitement to earnest and unremitting labours for the instruction of mankind." *Id.*, at 84. In general, Madison later added, "religion & Govt. will both exist in greater purity, the less they are mixed together." Letter from J. Madison to E. Livingston (July 10, 1822), in 5 The Founders' Constitution, at 105, 106.

What we thus know of the Framers' experience underscores the observation of one prominent commentator, that confining the Establishment Clause to a prohibition on preferential aid "requires a premise that the Framers were extraordinarily bad drafters—that they believed one thing but adopted language that said something substantially different, and that they did so after repeatedly attending to the ⌊616choice of language." Laycock, "Nonpreferential" Aid 882–883; see also *County of Allegheny v. American Civil Liberties Union, Greater Pittsburgh Chapter*, 492 U.S. 573, 647–648, 109 S.Ct. 3086, 3129–3130, 106 L.Ed.2d 472 (1989) (opinion of STEVENS, J.). We must presume, since there is no conclusive evidence to the contrary, that the Framers embraced the significance of their textual judgment.[3] Thus, on balance, history neither contradicts nor warrants reconsideration of the settled principle that the Establishment Clause forbids support for religion in general no less than support for one religion or some.

Yet the indefinite article before the word "establishment" is better seen as evidence that the Clause forbids any kind of establishment, including a nonpreferential one. If the Framers had wished, for some reason, to use the indefinite term to achieve a narrow meaning for the Clause, they could far more aptly have placed it before the word "religion." See Laycock, "Nonpreferential" Aid to Religion: A False Claim About Original Intent, 27 Wm. & Mary L.Rev. 875, 884–885 (1986) (hereinafter Laycock, "Nonpreferential" Aid).

3. In his dissent in *Wallace v. Jaffree*, 472 U.S. 38, 105 S.Ct. 2479, 86 L.Ed.2d 29 (1985), THE CHIEF JUSTICE rested his nonpreferentialist interpretation partly on the post-ratification actions of the early National Government. Aside from the willingness of some (but not all) early Presidents to issue ceremonial religious proclamations, which were at worst trivial breaches of the Establishment Clause, see *infra*, at 2678, he cited such seemingly preferential aid as a treaty provision, signed by Jefferson, authorizing federal subsidization of a Roman Catholic priest and church for the Kaskaskia Indians. 472 U.S., at 103, 105 S.Ct., at 2514. But this proves too much, for if the Establishment Clause permits a special appropriation of tax money for the religious activities of a particular sect, it forbids virtually nothing. See Laycock, "Nonpreferential" Aid 915. Although evidence of historical practice can indeed furnish valuable aid in the interpretation of contemporary language, acts like the one in question prove only that public officials, no matter when they serve, can turn a blind eye to constitutional principle. See *infra*, at 2675.

C

While these considerations are, for me, sufficient to reject the nonpreferentialist position, one further concern animates my judgment. In many contexts, including this one, nonpreferentialism requires some distinction between "sectarian" religious practices and those that would be, by some measure, ecumenical enough to pass Establishment Clause muster. Simply by requiring the enquiry, nonpreferentialists invite the courts to engage in comparative theology. I can hardly imagine a subject less amenable to the compe⊥617tence of the federal judiciary, or more deliberately to be avoided where possible.

This case is nicely in point. Since the nonpreferentiality of a prayer must be judged by its text, Justice BLACKMUN pertinently observes, *ante,* at 2664, n. 5, that Rabbi Gutterman drew his exhortation " '[t]o do justly, to love mercy, to walk humbly' " straight from the King James version of Micah, ch. 6, v. 8. At some undefinable point, the similarities between a state-sponsored prayer and the sacred text of a specific religion would so closely identify the former with the latter that even a nonpreferentialist would have to concede a breach of the Establishment Clause. And even if Micah's thought is sufficiently generic for most believers, it still embodies a straightforwardly theistic premise, and so does the rabbi's prayer. Many Americans who consider themselves religious are not theistic; some, like several of the Framers, are deists who would question Rabbi Gutterman's plea for divine advancement of the country's political and moral good. Thus, a nonpreferentialist who would condemn subjecting public school graduates to, say, the Anglican liturgy would still need to explain why the government's preference for theistic over nontheistic religion is constitutional.

Nor does it solve the problem to say that the State should promote a "diversity" of religious views; that position would necessarily compel the government and, inevitably, the courts to make wholly inappropriate judgments about the number of religions the State should sponsor and the relative frequency with which it should sponsor each. In fact, the prospect would be even worse than that. As Madison observed in criticizing religious Presidential proclamations, the practice of sponsoring religious messages tends, over time, "to narrow the recommendation to the standard of the predominant sect." Madison's "Detached Memoranda," 3 Wm. & Mary Q. 534, 561 (E. Fleet ed. 1946) (hereinafter Madison's "Detached Memoranda"). We have not changed much since the days of Madison, and the judiciary should not ⊥618willingly enter the political arena to battle the centripetal force leading from religious pluralism to official preference for the faith with the most votes.

II

Petitioners rest most of their argument on a theory that, whether or not the Establishment Clause permits extensive nonsectarian support for religion, it does not forbid the state to sponsor affirmations of religious belief that coerce neither support for religion nor participation in religious observance. I appreciate the force of some of the arguments supporting a "coercion" analysis of the Clause. See generally *County of Allegheny, supra,* 492 U.S., at 655–679, 109 S.Ct., at 3134–3146 (opinion of KENNEDY, J.); McConnell, Coercion: The Lost Element of Establishment, 27 Wm. & Mary L.Rev. 933 (1986). But we could not adopt that reading without abandoning our settled law, a course that, in my view, the text of the Clause would not readily permit. Nor does the extratextual evidence of original meaning stand so unequivocally at odds with the textual premise inherent in existing precedent that we should fundamentally reconsider our course.

A

Over the years, this Court has declared the invalidity of many noncoercive state laws and practices conveying a message of religious endorsement. For example, in *County of*

Allegheny, supra, we forbade the prominent display of a nativity scene on public property; without contesting the dissent's observation that the crèche coerced no one into accepting or supporting whatever message it proclaimed, five Members of the Court found its display unconstitutional as a state endorsement of Christianity. *Id.,* at 589–594, 598–602, 109 S.Ct., at 3098–3101, 3103–3105. Likewise, in *Wallace v. Jaffree,* 472 U.S. 38, 105 S.Ct. 2479, 86 L.Ed.2d 29 (1985), we struck down a state law requiring a moment of silence in public classrooms not because the statute coerced students to participate in prayer (for it did not), but because the manner of ⊥619 its enactment "convey[ed] a message of state approval of prayer activities in the public schools." *Id.,* at 61, 105 S.Ct., at 2492; see also *id.,* at 67–84, 105 S.Ct., at 2495–2504 (O'CONNOR, J., concurring in judgment). Cf. *Engel v. Vitale,* 370 U.S., at 431, 82 S.Ct., at 1267 ("When the power, prestige and financial support of government is placed behind a particular religious belief, the indirect coercive pressure upon religious minorities to conform to the prevailing officially approved religion is plain. But the purposes underlying the Establishment Clause go much further than that").

In *Epperson v. Arkansas,* 393 U.S. 97, 89 S.Ct. 266, 21 L.Ed.2d 228 (1968), we invalidated a state law that barred the teaching of Darwin's theory of evolution because, even though the statute obviously did not coerce anyone to support religion or participate in any religious practice, it was enacted for a singularly religious purpose. See also *Edwards v. Aguillard,* 482 U.S. 578, 593, 107 S.Ct. 2573, 2583, 96 L.Ed.2d 510 (1987) (statute requiring instruction in "creation science" "endorses religion in violation of the First Amendment"). And in *School Dist. of Grand Rapids v. Ball,* 473 U.S. 373, 105 S.Ct. 3216, 87 L.Ed.2d 267 (1985), we invalidated a program whereby the State sent public school teachers to parochial schools to instruct students on ostensibly nonreligious matters; while the scheme clearly did not coerce anyone to receive or subsidize religious instruction, we held it invalid because, among other things, "[t]he symbolic union of church and state inherent in the [program] threatens to convey a message of state support for religion to students and to the general public." *Id.,* at 397, 105 S.Ct., at 3230; see also *Texas Monthly, Inc. v. Bullock,* 489 U.S., at 17, 109 S.Ct., at 901 (plurality opinion) (tax exemption benefiting only religious publications "effectively endorses religious belief"); *id.,* at 28, 109 S.Ct., at 907 (BLACKMUN, J., concurring in judgment) (exemption unconstitutional because State "engaged in preferential support for the communication of religious messages").

Our precedents may not always have drawn perfectly straight lines. They simply cannot, however, support the position that a showing of coercion is necessary to a successful Establishment Clause claim.

⊥620 B

Like the provisions about "due" process and "unreasonable" searches and seizures, the constitutional language forbidding laws "respecting an establishment of religion" is not pellucid. But virtually everyone acknowledges that the Clause bans more than formal establishments of religion in the traditional sense, that is, massive state support for religion through, among other means, comprehensive schemes of taxation. See generally Levy 1–62 (discussing such establishments in the Colonies and early States). This much follows from the Framers' explicit rejection of simpler provisions prohibiting either the establishment of a religion or laws "establishing religion" in favor of the broader ban on laws "respecting an establishment of religion." See *supra,* at 2668–2669.

While some argue that the Framers added the word "respecting" simply to foreclose federal interference with state establishments of religion, see, *e.g.,* Amar, The Bill of Rights as a Constitution, 100 Yale L.J. 1131, 1157 (1991), the language sweeps more broadly than that. In Madison's words, the Clause in its final form forbids "everything like" a national religious establishment, see Madison's "Detached Memoranda" 558, and, after incorporation, it forbids "everything like" a state religious establishment.[4] Cf. *County of Allegheny,* 492 U.S., at 649, 109 S.Ct., at 3130 (opinion of STEVENS, J.). The sweep is broad enough that Madison himself characterized congressional provisions for legislative and military chaplains as unconstitutional "establishments." Madison's "Detached Memoranda" 558–559; see *infra,* at 2675, and n. 6.

⌊621While petitioners insist that the prohibition extends only to the "coercive" features and incidents of establishment, they cannot easily square that claim with the constitutional text. The First Amendment forbids not just laws "respecting an establishment of religion," but also those "prohibiting the free exercise thereof." Yet laws that coerce nonadherents to "support or participate in any religion or its exercise," *County of Allegheny, supra,* at 659–660, 109 S.Ct., at 3136 (opinion of KENNEDY, J.), would virtually by definition violate their right to religious free exercise. See *Employment Div., Dept. of Human Resources of Ore. v. Smith,* 494 U.S. 872, 877, 110 S.Ct. 1595, 1599, 108 L.Ed.2d 876 (1990) (under Free Exercise Clause, "government may not compel affirmation of religious belief"), citing *Torcaso v. Watkins,* 367 U.S. 488 (1961); see also J. Madison, Memorial and Remonstrance Against Religious Assessments (1785) (compelling support for religious establishments violates "free exercise of Religion"), quoted in 5 The Founders' Constitution, at 82, 84. Thus, a literal application of the coercion test would render the Establishment Clause a virtual nullity, as petitioners' counsel essentially conceded at oral argument. Tr. of Oral Arg. 18.

Our cases presuppose as much; as we said in *School Dist. of Abington,* "[t]he distinction between the two clauses is apparent—a violation of the Free Exercise Clause is predicated on coercion while the Establishment Clause violation need not be so attended." 374 U.S., at 223, 83 S.Ct., at 1572; see also Laycock, "Nonpreferential" Aid 922 ("If coercion is . . . an element of the establishment clause, establishment adds nothing to free exercise"). While one may argue that the Framers meant the Establishment Clause simply to ornament the First Amendment, cf. T. Curry, The First Freedoms 216–217 (1986), that must be a reading of last resort. Without compelling evidence to the contrary, we should presume that the Framers meant the Clause to stand for something more than petitioners attribute to it.

⌊622C

Petitioners argue from the political setting in which the Establishment Clause was framed, and from the Framers' own political practices following ratification, that government may constitutionally endorse religion so long as it does not coerce religious conformity. The setting and the practices warrant canvassing, but while they yield some evidence for petitioners' argument, they do not reveal the degree of consensus in early constitutional thought that would raise a threat to *stare decisis* by challenging the presumption that the Establishment Clause adds something to the Free Exercise Clause that follows it.

The Framers adopted the Religion Clauses in response to a long tradition of coercive state support for religion, particularly in the form of tax assessments, but their special antipathy to religious coercion did not exhaust their hostility to the features and incidents of establishment. Indeed, Jefferson and Madison opposed any political appropria-

4. In *Everson v. Board of Ed. of Ewing,* 330 U.S. 1, 67 S.Ct. 504, 91 L.Ed. 711 (1947), we unanimously incorporated the Establishment Clause into the Due Process Clause of the Fourteenth Amendment and, by so doing, extended its reach to the actions of States. *Id.,* at 14–15, 67 S.Ct., at 511; see also *Cantwell v. Connecticut,* 310 U.S. 296, 303, 60 S.Ct. 900, 903, 84 L.Ed. 1213 (1940) (dictum). Since then, not one Member of this Court has proposed disincorporating the Clause.

tion of religion, see *infra,* at 2674–2676, and, even when challenging the hated assessments, they did not always temper their rhetoric with distinctions between coercive and noncoercive state action. When, for example, Madison criticized Virginia's general assessment bill, he invoked principles antithetical to all state efforts to promote religion. An assessment, he wrote, is improper not simply because it forces people to donate "three pence" to religion, but, more broadly, because "it is itself a signal of persecution. It degrades from the equal rank of Citizens all those whose opinions in Religion do not bend to those of the Legislative authority." J. Madison, Memorial and Remonstrance Against Religious Assessments (1785), in 5 The Founders' Constitution, at 83. Madison saw that, even without the tax collector's participation, an official endorsement of religion can impair religious liberty.

Petitioners contend that because the early Presidents included religious messages in their inaugural and Thanksgiving Day addresses, the Framers could not have meant the ⌊623Establishment Clause to forbid noncoercive state endorsement of religion. The argument ignores the fact, however, that Americans today find such proclamations less controversial than did the founding generation, whose published thoughts on the matter belie petitioners' claim. President Jefferson, for example, steadfastly refused to issue Thanksgiving proclamations of any kind, in part because he thought they violated the Religion Clauses. Letter from Thomas Jefferson to Rev. S. Miller (Jan. 23, 1808), in 5 The Founders' Constitution, at 98. In explaining his views to the Reverend Samuel Miller, Jefferson effectively anticipated, and rejected, petitioners' position:

> "[I]t is only proposed that I should *recommend,* not prescribe a day of fasting & prayer. That is, that I should *indirectly* assume to the U.S. an authority over religious exercises which the Constitution has directly precluded from them. It must be meant too that this recommendation is to carry some authority, and to be sanctioned by some penalty on those who disregard it; not indeed of fine and imprisonment, but of some degree of proscription perhaps in public opinion." *Id.,* at 98–99 (emphasis in original).

By condemning such noncoercive state practices that, in "recommending" the majority faith, demean religious dissenters "in public opinion," Jefferson necessarily condemned what, in modern terms, we call official endorsement of religion. He accordingly construed the Establishment Clause to forbid not simply state coercion, but also state endorsement, of religious belief and observance.[5] And if he opposed ⌊624impersonal

5. Petitioners claim that the quoted passage shows that Jefferson regarded Thanksgiving proclamations as "coercive": "Thus, while one may disagree with Jefferson's view that a recommendatory Thanksgiving proclamation would nonetheless be coercive . . . one cannot disagree that Jefferson believed coercion to be a necessary element of a First Amendment violation." Brief for Petitioners 34. But this is wordplay. The "proscription" to which Jefferson referred was, of course, by the public and not the government, whose only action was a noncoercive recommendation. And one can call any act of endorsement a form of coercion, but only if one is willing to dilute the meaning of "coercion" until there is no meaning left. Jefferson's position straightforwardly contradicts the claim that a showing of "coercion," under any normal definition, is prerequisite to a successful Establishment Clause claim. At the same time, Jefferson's practice, like Madison's, see *infra,* at 2675, sometimes diverged from principle, for he did include religious references in his inaugural speeches. See Inaugural Addresses of the Presidents of the United States 17, 22–23 (1989); see also n. 3, *supra.*

Petitioners also seek comfort in a different passage of the same letter. Jefferson argued that Presidential religious proclamations violate not just the Establishment Clause, but also the Tenth Amendment, for "what might be a right in a state government, was a violation of that right when assumed by another." Letter from Thomas Jefferson to Rev. S. Miller (Jan. 23, 1808), in 5 The Founders' Constitution 99 (P. Kurland & R. Lerner eds. 1987). Jefferson did not, however, restrict himself to the Tenth Amendment in condemning such proclamations by a national officer. I do not, in any event, understand petitioners to be arguing that the Establishment Clause

Presidential addresses for inflicting "proscription in public opinion," all the more would he have condemned less diffuse expressions of official endorsement.

During his first three years in office, James Madison also refused to call for days of thanksgiving and prayer, though later, amid the political turmoil of the War of 1812, he did so on four separate occasions. See Madison's "Detached Memoranda" 562, and n. 54. Upon retirement, in an essay condemning as an unconstitutional "establishment" the use of public money to support congressional and military chaplains, *id.*, at 558–560,[6] he concluded that "[r]eligious proclamations625 by the Executive recommending thanksgivings & fasts are shoots from the same root with the legislative acts reviewed. Altho' recommendations only, they imply a religious agency, making no part of the trust delegated to political rulers." *Id.*, at 560. Explaining that "[t]he members of a Govt . . . can in no sense, be regarded as possessing an advisory trust from their Constituents in their religious capacities," *ibid.*, he further observed that the state necessarily freights all of its religious messages with political ones: "the idea of policy [is] associated with religion, whatever be the mode or the occasion, when a function of the latter is assumed by those in power." *Id.*, at 562 (footnote omitted).

Madison's failure to keep pace with his principles in the face of congressional pressure cannot erase the principles. He admitted to backsliding, and explained that he had made the content of his wartime proclamations inconsequential enough to mitigate much of their impropriety. See *ibid.*; see also Letter from J. Madison to E. Livingston (July 10, 1822), in 5 The Founders' Constitution, at 105. While his writings suggest mild variations in his interpretation of the Establishment Clause, Madison was no different in that respect from the rest of his political generation. That he expressed so much doubt about the constitutionality of religious proclamations, however, suggests a brand of separationism stronger even than that embodied in our traditional jurisprudence. So too does his characterization of public subsidies for legislative and military chaplains as unconstitutional "establishments," see *supra*, at 2675, and n. 6, for the federal courts, however expansive their general view of the Establishment Clause, have upheld both practices. See *Marsh v. Chambers*, 463 U.S. 783, 103 S.Ct. 3330, 77 L.Ed.2d 1019 (1983) (legislative chaplains);626 *Katcoff v. Marsh*, 755 F.2d 223 (CA2 1985) (military chaplains).

To be sure, the leaders of the young Republic engaged in some of the practices that separationists like Jefferson and Madison criticized. The First Congress did hire institutional chaplains, see *Marsh v. Chambers*, *supra*, at 788, 103 S.Ct., at 3334, and Presidents Washington and Adams unapologetically marked days of " 'public thanksgiving and prayer,' " see R. Cord, Separation of Church and State 53 (1988). Yet in the face of the separationist dissent, those practices prove, at best, that the Framers simply did not share a common understanding of the Establishment Clause, and, at worst, that they, like other politicians, could raise constitutional ideals one day and turn their backs on them the next. "Indeed, by 1787 the provisions of

is exclusively a structural provision mediating the respective powers of the State and National Governments. Such a position would entail the argument, which petitioners do not make, and which we would almost certainly reject, that incorporation of the Establishment Clause under the Fourteenth Amendment was erroneous.

6. Madison found this practice "a palpable violation of . . . Constitutional principles." Madison's "Detached Memoranda" 558. Although he sat on the committee recommending the congressional chaplainship, see R. Cord, Separation of Church and State: Historical Fact and Current Fiction 23 (1988), he later insisted that "it was not with my approbation, that the deviation from [the immunity of religion from civil jurisdiction] took place in Congs., when they appointed Chaplains, to be paid from the Natl. Treasury." Letter from J. Madison to E. Livingston (July 10, 1822), in 5 The Founders' Constitution, at 105.

the state bills of rights had become what Madison called mere 'paper parchments'—expressions of the most laudable sentiments, observed as much in the breach as in practice." Kurland, The Origins of the Religion Clauses of the Constitution, 27 Wm. & Mary L.Rev. 839, 852 (1986) (footnote omitted). Sometimes the National Constitution fared no better. Ten years after proposing the First Amendment, Congress passed the Alien and Sedition Acts, measures patently unconstitutional by modern standards. If the early Congress's political actions were determinative, and not merely relevant, evidence of constitutional meaning, we would have to gut our current First Amendment doctrine to make room for political censorship.

While we may be unable to know for certain what the Framers meant by the Clause, we do know that, around the time of its ratification, a respectable body of opinion supported a considerably broader reading than petitioners urge upon us. This consistency with the textual considerations is enough to preclude fundamentally reexamining our settled law, and I am accordingly left with the task of considering whether the state practice at issue here violates our traditional understanding of the Clause's proscriptions.

⌊627III

While the Establishment Clause's concept of neutrality is not self-revealing, our recent cases have invested it with specific content: the State may not favor or endorse either religion generally over nonreligion or one religion over others. See, *e.g., County of Allegheny,* 492 U.S., at 589–594, 598–602, 109 S.Ct., at 3098–3101, 3103–3105; *Texas Monthly,* 489 U.S., at 17, 109 S.Ct., at 901 (plurality opinion); *id.,* at 28, 109 S.Ct., at 907 (BLACKMUN, J., concurring in judgment); *Edwards v. Aguillard,* 482 U.S., at 593, 107 S.Ct., at 2582–2583; *School Dist. of Grand Rapids,* 473 U.S., at 389–392, 105 S.Ct., at 3225–3227; *Wallace v. Jaffree,* 472 U.S., at 61, 105 S.Ct., at 2492; see also Laycock, Formal, Substantive, and Disaggregated Neutrality Toward Religion, 39 DePaul L.Rev. 993 (1990); cf. *Lemon v. Kurtzman,* 403 U.S. 602, 612–613, 91 S.Ct. 2105, 2111, 29 L.Ed.2d 745 (1971). This principle against favoritism and endorsement has become the foundation of Establishment Clause jurisprudence, ensuring that religious belief is irrelevant to every citizen's standing in the political community, see *County of Allegheny, supra,* 492 U.S., at 594, 109 S.Ct., at 3101; J. Madison, Memorial and Remonstrance Against Religious Assessments (1785), in 5 The Founders' Constitution, at 82–83, and protecting religion from the demeaning effects of any governmental embrace, see *id.,* at 83. Now, as in the early Republic, "religion & Govt. will both exist in greater purity, the less they are mixed together." Letter from J. Madison to E. Livingston (July 10, 1822), in 5 The Founders' Constitution, at 106. Our aspiration to religious liberty, embodied in the First Amendment, permits no other standard.

A

That government must remain neutral in matters of religion does not foreclose it from ever taking religion into account. The State may "accommodate" the free exercise of religion by relieving people from generally applicable rules that interfere with their religious callings. See, *e.g., Corporation of Presiding Bishop of Church of Jesus Christ of Latter-day Saints v. Amos,* 483 U.S. 327, 107 S.Ct. 2862, 97 L.Ed.2d 273 (1987); see also *Sherbert v. Verner,* 374 U.S. 398, 83 S.Ct. 1790, 10 L.Ed.2d 965 (1963). Contrary to the ⌊628views of some,[7] such accommodation does

7. See, *e.g., Thomas v. Review Bd. of Indiana Employment Security Div.,* 450 U.S. 707, 726, 101 S.Ct. 1425, 1436, 67 L.Ed.2d 624 (1981) (REHNQUIST, J., dissenting); Choper, The Religion Clauses of the First Amendment: Reconciling the Conflict, 41 U.Pitt.L.Rev. 673, 685–686 (1980); see also *Walz v. Tax Comm'n of New York City,* 397 U.S. 664, 668–669, 90 S.Ct. 1409, 1411, 25 L.Ed.2d 697 (1970); *Sherbert v. Verner,* 374 U.S. 398, 414, 416, 83 S.Ct. 1790, 1799, 1800, 10

not necessarily signify an official endorsement of religious observance over disbelief.

In everyday life, we routinely accommodate religious beliefs that we do not share. A Christian inviting an Orthodox Jew to lunch might take pains to choose a kosher restaurant; an atheist in a hurry might yield the right of way to an Amish man steering a horse-drawn carriage. In so acting, we express respect for, but not endorsement of, the fundamental values of others. We act without expressing a position on the theological merit of those values or of religious belief in general, and no one perceives us to have taken such a position.

The government may act likewise. Most religions encourage devotional practices that are at once crucial to the lives of believers and idiosyncratic in the eyes of nonadherents. By definition, secular rules of general application are drawn from the nonadherent's vantage and, consequently, fail to take such practices into account. Yet when enforcement of such rules cuts across religious sensibilities, as it often does, it puts those affected to the choice of taking sides between God and government. In such circumstances, accommodating religion reveals nothing beyond a recognition that general rules can unnecessarily offend the religious conscience when they offend the conscience of secular society not at all. Cf. *Welsh v. United States,* 398 U.S. 333, 340, 90 S.Ct. 1792, 1796, 26 L.Ed.2d 308 (1970) (plurality opinion). Thus, in freeing the Native American Church from federal laws forbidding peyote use, see Drug Enforcement Administration Miscellaneous Exemptions, 21 CFR ⌊629§ 1307.31 (1991), the government conveys no endorsement of peyote rituals, the Church, or religion as such; it simply respects the centrality of peyote to the lives of certain Americans. See Note, The Free Exercise Boundaries of Permissible Accommodation Under the Establishment Clause, 99 Yale L.J. 1127, 1135–1136 (1990).

B

Whatever else may define the scope of accommodation permissible under the Establishment Clause, one requirement is clear: accommodation must lift a discernible burden on the free exercise of religion. See *County of Allegheny, supra,* 492 U.S., at 601, n. 51, 109 S.Ct., 3105, n. 51; *id.,* at 631–632, 109 S.Ct., at 3121–3122 (O'CONNOR, J., concurring in part and concurring in judgment); *Corporation of Presiding Bishop, supra,* 483 U.S., at 348, 107 S.Ct., at 2875 (O'CONNOR, J., concurring in judgment); see also *Texas Monthly, supra,* 489 U.S., at 18, 18–19, n. 8, 109 S.Ct., at 901, 901–902, n. 8 (plurality opinion); *Wallace v. Jaffree, supra,* 472 U.S., at 57–58, n. 45, 105 S.Ct., at 2490, n. 45. But see *County of Allegheny, supra,* 492 U.S., at 663, n. 2, 109 S.Ct., at 3138, n. 2 (KENNEDY, J., concurring in judgment in part and dissenting in part). Concern for the position of religious individuals in the modern regulatory State cannot justify official solicitude for a religious practice unburdened by general rules; such gratuitous largesse would effectively favor religion over disbelief. By these lights one easily sees that, in sponsoring the graduation prayers at issue here, the State has crossed the line from permissible accommodation to unconstitutional establishment.

Religious students cannot complain that omitting prayers from their graduation ceremony would, in any realistic sense, "burden" their spiritual callings. To be sure, many of them invest this rite of passage with spiritual significance, but they may express their religious feelings about it before and after the ceremony. They may even organize a privately sponsored baccalaureate if they desire the company of likeminded students. Because they accordingly have no need for the machinery of the State to affirm their beliefs, the ⌊630government's sponsorship of prayer at the graduation ceremony is most reasonably understood as an official endorsement of religion and, in this instance, of theistic religion.

L.Ed.2d 965 (1963) (Stewart, J., concurring in result); cf. *Wallace v. Jaffree,* 472 U.S., at 83, 105 S.Ct., at 2504 (O'CONNOR, J., concurring in judgment).

One may fairly say, as one commentator has suggested, that the government brought prayer into the ceremony "precisely because some people want a symbolic affirmation that government approves and endorses their religion, and because many of the people who want this affirmation place little or no value on the costs to religious minorities." Laycock, Summary and Synthesis: The Crisis in Religious Liberty, 60 Geo. Wash.L.Rev. 841, 844 (1992).[8]

Petitioners would deflect this conclusion by arguing that graduation prayers are no different from Presidential religious proclamations and similar official "acknowledgments" of religion in public life. But religious invocations in Thanksgiving Day addresses and the like, rarely noticed, ignored without effort, conveyed over an impersonal medium, and directed at no one in particular, inhabit a pallid zone worlds apart from official prayers delivered to a captive audience of public school students and their families. Madison himself respected the difference between the trivial and the serious in constitutional practice. Realizing that his con|631temporaries were unlikely to take the Establishment Clause seriously enough to forgo a legislative chaplainship, he suggested that "[r]ather than let this step beyond the landmarks of power have the effect of a legitimate precedent, it will be better to apply to it the legal aphorism de minimis non curat lex...." Madison's "Detached Memoranda" 559; see also Letter from J. Madison to E. Livingston (July 10, 1822), in 5 The Founders' Constitution, at 105. But that logic permits no winking at the practice in question here. When public school officials, armed with the State's authority, convey an endorsement of religion to their students, they strike near the core of the Establishment Clause. However "ceremonial" their messages may be, they are flatly unconstitutional.

Justice SCALIA, with whom THE CHIEF JUSTICE, Justice WHITE, and Justice THOMAS join, dissenting.

Three Terms ago, I joined an opinion recognizing that the Establishment Clause must be construed in light of the "[g]overnment policies of accommodation, acknowledgment, and support for religion [that] are an accepted part of our political and cultural heritage." That opinion affirmed that "the meaning of the Clause is to be determined by reference to historical practices and understandings." It said that "[a] test for implementing the protections of the Establishment Clause that, if applied with consistency, would invalidate longstanding traditions cannot be a proper reading of the Clause." *County of Allegheny v. American Civil Liberties Union, Greater Pittsburgh Chapter,* 492 U.S. 573, 657, 670, 109 S.Ct. 3086, 3135, 3142, 106 L.Ed.2d 472 (1989) (KENNEDY, J., concurring in judgment in part and dissenting in part).

These views of course prevent me from joining today's opinion, which is conspicuously bereft of any reference to history. In holding that the Establishment Clause prohibits invocations and benedictions at public-school graduation ceremonies, the Court—with nary a mention that it is doing |632so—

8. If the State had chosen its graduation day speakers according to wholly secular criteria, and if one of those speakers (not a state actor) had individually chosen to deliver a religious message, it would have been harder to attribute an endorsement of religion to the State. Cf. *Witters v. Washington Dept. of Services for Blind,* 474 U.S. 481, 106 S.Ct. 748, 88 L.Ed.2d 846 (1986). But that is not our case. Nor is this a case where the State has, without singling out religious groups or individuals, extended benefits to them as members of a broad class of beneficiaries defined by clearly secular criteria. See *Widmar v. Vincent,* 454 U.S. 263, 274–275, 102 S.Ct. 269, 277, 70 L.Ed.2d 440 (1981); *Walz, supra,* 397 U.S., at 696, 90 S.Ct., at 1425 (opinion of Harlan, J.) ("In any particular case the critical question is whether the circumference of legislation encircles a class so broad that it can be fairly concluded that religious institutions could be thought to fall within the natural perimeter"). Finally, this is not a case like *Marsh v. Chambers,* 463 U.S. 783, 103 S.Ct. 3330, 77 L.Ed.2d 1019 (1983), in which government officials invoke spiritual inspiration entirely for their own benefit without directing any religious message at the citizens they lead.

lays waste a tradition that is as old as public-school graduation ceremonies themselves, and that is a component of an even more longstanding American tradition of nonsectarian prayer to God at public celebrations generally. As its instrument of destruction, the bulldozer of its social engineering, the Court invents a boundless, and boundlessly manipulable, test of psychological coercion, which promises to do for the Establishment Clause what the *Durham* rule did for the insanity defense. See *Durham v. United States,* 94 U.S.App.D.C. 228, 214 F.2d 862 (1954). Today's opinion shows more forcefully than volumes of argumentation why our Nation's protection, that fortress which is our Constitution, cannot possibly rest upon the changeable philosophical predilections of the Justices of this Court, but must have deep foundations in the historic practices of our people.

I

Justice Holmes' aphorism that "a page of history is worth a volume of logic," *New York Trust Co. v. Eisner,* 256 U.S. 345, 349, 41 S.Ct. 506, 507, 65 L.Ed. 963 (1921), applies with particular force to our Establishment Clause jurisprudence. As we have recognized, our interpretation of the Establishment Clause should "compor[t] with what history reveals was the contemporaneous understanding of its guarantees." *Lynch v. Donnelly,* 465 U.S. 668, 673, 104 S.Ct. 1355, 1359, 79 L.Ed.2d 604 (1984). "[T]he line we must draw between the permissible and the impermissible is one which accords with history and faithfully reflects the understanding of the Founding Fathers." *School Dist. of Abington v. Schempp,* 374 U.S. 203, 294, 83 S.Ct. 1560, 1609, 10 L.Ed.2d 844 (1963) (Brennan, J., concurring). "[H]istorical evidence sheds light not only on what the draftsmen intended the Establishment Clause to mean, but also on how they thought that Clause applied" to contemporaneous practices. *Marsh v. Chambers,* 463 U.S. 783, 790, 103 S.Ct. 3330, 3335, 77 L.Ed.2d 1019 (1983). Thus, "[t]he existence from the beginning of the Nation's life of a practice, [while] not conclusive of its constitutionality ...[,] is a fact of considerable import in the interpretation" of the ⌊633Establishment Clause. *Walz v. Tax Comm'n of New York City,* 397 U.S. 664, 681, 90 S.Ct. 1409, 1417–1418, 25 L.Ed.2d 697 (1970) (Brennan, J., concurring).

The history and tradition of our Nation are replete with public ceremonies featuring prayers of thanksgiving and petition. Illustrations of this point have been amply provided in our prior opinions, see, *e.g., Lynch, supra,* 465 U.S., at 674–678, 104 S.Ct., at 1359–1361; *Marsh, supra,* 463 U.S., at 786–788, 103 S.Ct., at 3333–3334; see also *Wallace v. Jaffree,* 472 U.S. 38, 100–103, 105 S.Ct. 2479, 2512–2514, 86 L.Ed.2d 29 (1985) (REHNQUIST, J., dissenting); *Engel v. Vitale,* 370 U.S. 421, 446–450, and n. 3, 82 S.Ct. 1261, 1275–1277, and n. 3, 8 L.Ed.2d 601 (1962) (Stewart, J., dissenting), but since the Court is so oblivious to our history as to suggest that the Constitution restricts "preservation and transmission of religious beliefs ... to the private sphere," *ante,* at 2656, it appears necessary to provide another brief account.

From our Nation's origin, prayer has been a prominent part of governmental ceremonies and proclamations. The Declaration of Independence, the document marking our birth as a separate people, "appeal[ed] to the Supreme Judge of the world for the rectitude of our intentions" and avowed "a firm reliance on the protection of divine Providence." In his first inaugural address, after swearing his oath of office on a Bible, George Washington deliberately made a prayer a part of his first official act as President:

> "[I]t would be peculiarly improper to omit in this first official act my fervent supplications to that Almighty Being who rules over the universe, who presides in the councils of nations, and whose providential aids can supply every human defect, that His benediction may consecrate to the liberties and happiness of the people of the United States a Government instituted by

themselves for these essential purposes." Inaugural Addresses of the Presidents of the United States, S.Doc. 101–10, p. 2 (1989).

Such supplications have been a characteristic feature of inaugural addresses ever since. Thomas Jefferson, for example, ⌊634prayed in his first inaugural address: "[M]ay that Infinite Power which rules the destinies of the universe lead our councils to what is best, and give them a favorable issue for your peace and prosperity." *Id.*, at 17. In his second inaugural address, Jefferson acknowledged his need for divine guidance and invited his audience to join his prayer:

> "I shall need, too, the favor of that Being in whose hands we are, who led our fathers, as Israel of old, from their native land and planted them in a country flowing with all the necessaries and comforts of life; who has covered our infancy with His providence and our riper years with His wisdom and power, and to whose goodness I ask you to join in supplications with me that He will so enlighten the minds of your servants, guide their councils, and prosper their measures that whatsoever they do shall result in your good, and shall secure to you the peace, friendship, and approbation of all nations." *Id.*, at 22–23.

Similarly, James Madison, in his first inaugural address, placed his confidence

> "in the guardianship and guidance of that Almighty Being whose power regulates the destiny of nations, whose blessings have been so conspicuously dispensed to this rising Republic, and to whom we are bound to address our devout gratitude for the past, as well as our fervent supplications and best hopes for the future." *Id.*, at 28.

Most recently, President Bush, continuing the tradition established by President Washington, asked those attending his inauguration to bow their heads, and made a prayer his first official act as President. *Id.*, at 346.

Our national celebration of Thanksgiving likewise dates back to President Washington. As we recounted in *Lynch:*

> ⌊635"The day after the First Amendment was proposed, Congress urged President Washington to proclaim 'a day of public thanksgiving and prayer, to be observed by acknowledging with grateful hearts the many and signal favours of Almighty God.' President Washington proclaimed November 26, 1789, a day of thanksgiving to 'offe[r] our prayers and supplications to the Great Lord and Ruler of Nations, and beseech Him to pardon our national and other transgressions....'" 465 U.S., at 675, n. 2, 104 S.Ct., at 1360, n. 2 (citations omitted).

This tradition of Thanksgiving Proclamations—with their religious theme of prayerful gratitude to God—has been adhered to by almost every President. *Id.*, at 675, and nn. 2 and 3, 104 S.Ct., at 1360, and nn. 2 and 3; *Wallace v. Jaffree, supra,* 472 U.S., at 100–103, 105 S.Ct. at 2512–2514 (REHNQUIST, J., dissenting).

The other two branches of the Federal Government also have a long-established practice of prayer at public events. As we detailed in *Marsh,* congressional sessions have opened with a chaplain's prayer ever since the First Congress. 463 U.S., at 787–788, 103 S.Ct., at 3334. And this Court's own sessions have opened with the invocation "God save the United States and this Honorable Court" since the days of Chief Justice Marshall. 1 C. Warren, The Supreme Court in United States History 469 (1922).

In addition to this general tradition of prayer at public ceremonies, there exists a more specific tradition of invocations and benedictions at public school graduation exercises. By one account, the first public high school graduation ceremony took place in Connecticut in July 1868—the very month, as it happens, that the Fourteenth Amendment (the vehicle by which the Establishment Clause has been applied against the States) was ratified—when "15 seniors from the

Norwich Free Academy marched in their best Sunday suits and dresses into a church hall and waited through majestic music and long prayers." Brodinsky, Commencement Rites Obsolete? Not At All, A 10–Week Study Shows, 10 Updating636 School Board Policies, No. 4, p. 3 (Apr. 1979). As the Court obliquely acknowledges in describing the "customary features" of high school graduations, *ante*, at 2653, and as respondents do not contest, the invocation and benediction have long been recognized to be "as traditional as any other parts of the [school] graduation program and are widely established." H. McKown, Commencement Activities 56 (1931); see also Brodinsky, *supra*, at 5.

II

The Court presumably would separate graduation invocations and benedictions from other instances of public "preservation and transmission of religious beliefs" on the ground that they involve "psychological coercion." I find it a sufficient embarrassment that our Establishment Clause jurisprudence regarding holiday displays, see *County of Allegheny v. American Civil Liberties Union, Greater Pittsburgh Chapter*, 492 U.S. 573, 109 S.Ct. 3086, 106 L.Ed.2d 472 (1989), has come to "requir[e] scrutiny more commonly associated with interior decorators than with the judiciary." *American Jewish Congress v. Chicago*, 827 F.2d 120, 129 (CA7 1987) (Easterbrook, J., dissenting). But interior decorating is a rock-hard science compared to psychology practiced by amateurs. A few citations of "[r]esearch in psychology" that have no particular bearing upon the precise issue here, *ante*, at 2659, cannot disguise the fact that the Court has gone beyond the realm where judges know what they are doing. The Court's argument that state officials have "coerced" students to take part in the invocation and benediction at graduation ceremonies is, not to put too fine a point on it, incoherent.

The Court identifies two "dominant facts" that it says dictate its ruling that invocations and benedictions at public school graduation ceremonies violate the Establishment Clause. *Ante*, at 2655. Neither of them is in any relevant sense true.

637A

The Court declares that students' "attendance and participation in the [invocation and benediction] are in a fair and real sense obligatory." *Ibid.* But what exactly is this "fair and real sense"? According to the Court, students at graduation who want "to avoid the fact or appearance of participation," *ante*, at 2656, in the invocation and benediction are *psychologically* obligated by "public pressure, as well as peer pressure, . . . to stand as a group or, at least, maintain respectful silence" during those prayers. *Ante*, at 2658. This assertion—*the very linchpin of the Court's opinion* —is almost as intriguing for what it does not say as for what it says. It does not say, for example, that students are psychologically coerced to bow their heads, place their hands in a Dürer-like prayer position, pay attention to the prayers, utter "Amen," or in fact pray. (Perhaps further intensive psychological research remains to be done on these matters.) It claims only that students are psychologically coerced "to stand . . . *or*, at least, maintain respectful silence." *Ibid.* (emphasis added). Both halves of this disjunctive (*both* of which must amount to the fact or appearance of participation in prayer if the Court's analysis is to survive on its own terms) merit particular attention.

To begin with the latter: The Court's notion that a student who simply *sits* in "respectful silence" during the invocation and benediction (when all others are standing) has somehow joined—or would somehow be perceived as having joined—in the prayers is nothing short of ludicrous. We indeed live in a vulgar age. But surely "our social conventions," *ibid.*, have not coarsened to the point that anyone who does not stand on his chair and shout obscenities can reasonably be deemed to have assented to everything said in his presence. Since the Court does not dispute that students exposed to prayer at graduation ceremonies retain (despite "subtle coercive pressures," *ante,* at 2656) the free will to sit, cf. *ante,* at 2658, there is absolutely no basis for the Court's |638decision. It is fanciful enough to say that "a reasonable dissenter," standing head erect in a class of bowed heads, "could believe that the group exercise signified her own participation or approval of it," *ibid.* It is beyond the absurd to say that she could entertain such a belief while pointedly declining to rise.

But let us assume the very worst, that the nonparticipating graduate is "subtly coerced" . . . to stand! Even that half of the disjunctive does not remotely establish a "participation" (or an "appearance of participation") in a religious exercise. The Court acknowledges that "in our culture standing . . . can signify adherence to a view or simple respect for the views of others." *Ibid.* (Much more often the latter than the former, I think, except perhaps in the proverbial town meeting, where one votes by standing.) But if it is a permissible inference that one who is standing is doing so simply out of respect for the prayers of others that are in progress, then how can it possibly be said that a "reasonable dissenter . . . could believe that the group exercise signified her own participation or approval"? Quite obviously, it cannot. I may add, moreover, that maintaining respect for the religious observances of others is a fundamental civic virtue that government (including the public schools) can and should cultivate—so that even if it were the case that the displaying of such respect might be mistaken for taking part in the prayer, I would deny that the dissenter's interest in avoiding *even the false appearance of participation* constitutionally trumps the government's interest in fostering respect for religion generally.

The opinion manifests that the Court itself has not given careful consideration to its test of psychological coercion. For if it had, how could it observe, with no hint of concern or disapproval, that students stood for the Pledge of Allegiance, which immediately preceded Rabbi Gutterman's invocation? *Ante,* at 2653. The government can, of course, no more coerce political orthodoxy than religious orthodoxy. *West |639Virginia Bd. of Ed. v. Barnette,* 319 U.S. 624, 642, 63 S.Ct. 1178, 1187, 87 L.Ed. 1628 (1943). Moreover, since the Pledge of Allegiance has been revised since *Barnette* to include the phrase "under God," recital of the Pledge would appear to raise the same Establishment Clause issue as the invocation and benediction. If students were psychologically coerced to remain standing during the invocation, they must also have been psychologically coerced, moments before, to stand for (and thereby, in the Court's view, take part in or appear to take part in) the Pledge. Must the Pledge therefore be barred from the public schools (both from graduation ceremonies and from the classroom)? In *Barnette* we held that a public school student could not be compelled to *recite* the Pledge; we did not even hint that she could not be compelled to observe respectful silence—indeed, even to *stand* in respectful silence—when those who wished to recite it did so. Logically, that ought to be the next project for the Court's bulldozer.

I also find it odd that the Court concludes that high school graduates may not be subjected to this supposed psychological coercion, yet refrains from addressing whether "mature adults" may. *Ante,* at 2658. I had thought that the reason graduation from high school is regarded as so significant an event is that it is generally associated with transition from adolescence to young adulthood. Many graduating seniors, of course, are old enough to vote. Why, then, does the Court treat them as though they were first-graders? Will we soon have a jurisprudence that distinguishes between mature and immature adults?

B

The other "dominant fac[t]" identified by the Court is that "[s]tate officials direct the performance of a formal religious exercise" at school graduation ceremonies. *Ante,* at 2655. "Direct[ing] the performance of a formal religious exercise" has a sound of liturgy to it, summoning up images of the principal directing acolytes where to carry the cross, or showing the rabbi where to unroll the Torah. A Court professing to be ⌊640engaged in a "delicate and fact-sensitive" line-drawing, *ante,* at 2661, would better describe what it means as "prescribing the content of an invocation and benediction." But even that would be false. All the record shows is that principals of the Providence public schools, acting within their delegated authority, have invited clergy to deliver invocations and benedictions at graduations; and that Principal Lee invited Rabbi Gutterman, provided him a two-page pamphlet, prepared by the National Conference of Christians and Jews, giving general advice on inclusive prayer for civic occasions, and advised him that his prayers at graduation should be nonsectarian. How these facts can fairly be transformed into the charges that Principal Lee "directed and controlled the content of [Rabbi Gutterman's] prayer," *ante,* at 2656, that school officials "monitor prayer," *ante,* at 2657, and attempted to " 'compose official prayers,' " *ante,* at 2656, and that the "government involvement with religious activity in this case is pervasive," *ante,* at 2655, is difficult to fathom. The Court identifies nothing in the record remotely suggesting that school officials have ever drafted, edited, screened, or censored graduation prayers, or that Rabbi Gutterman was a mouthpiece of the school officials.

These distortions of the record are, of course, not harmless error: without them the Court's solemn assertion that the school officials could reasonably be perceived to be "enforc[ing] a religious orthodoxy," *ante,* at 2658, would ring as hollow as it ought.

III

The deeper flaw in the Court's opinion does not lie in its wrong answer to the question whether there was state-induced "peer-pressure" coercion; it lies, rather, in the Court's making violation of the Establishment Clause hinge on such a precious question. The coercion that was a hallmark of historical establishments of religion was coercion of religious orthodoxy and of financial support *by force of law and threat of penalty.* Typically, attendance at the state ⌊641church was required; only clergy of the official church could lawfully perform sacraments; and dissenters, if tolerated, faced an array of civil disabilities. L. Levy, The Establishment Clause 4 (1986). Thus, for example, in the Colony of Virginia, where the Church of England had been established, ministers were required by law to conform to the doctrine and rites of the Church of England; and all persons were required to attend church and observe the Sabbath, were tithed for the public support of Anglican ministers, and were taxed for the costs of building and repairing churches. *Id.,* at 3–4.

The Establishment Clause was adopted to prohibit such an establishment of religion at the federal level (and to protect state establishments of religion from federal interference). I will further acknowledge for the sake of argument that, as some scholars have argued, by 1790 the term "establishment" had acquired an additional meaning—"financial support of religion generally, by public taxation"—that reflected the development of "general or multiple" establishments, not limited to a single church. *Id.,* at 8–9. But that would still be an establishment coerced *by force of law.* And I will further concede that our constitutional tradition, from the Declaration of Independence and the first inaugural address of Washington, quoted earlier, down to the present day, has, with a few aberrations, see *Church of Holy Trinity v. United States,* 143 U.S. 457, 12 S.Ct. 511, 36 L.Ed. 226 (1892), ruled out of order government-sponsored endorsement of religion—even when no legal coercion is present, and indeed even when no ersatz, "peer-pressure" psycho-coercion is present—where the endorsement is sectarian, in the sense of specifying details upon which men and women who believe in a benevolent, omnipotent Creator and Ruler of the world are known to differ (for example, the divinity of Christ). But there is simply no support for the proposition that the officially sponsored nondenominational invocation and benediction read by Rabbi Gutterman—with no one legally coerced to recite ⊥642them—violated the Constitution of the United States. To the contrary, they are so characteristically American they could have come from the pen of George Washington or Abraham Lincoln himself.

Thus, while I have no quarrel with the Court's general proposition that the Establishment Clause "guarantees that government may not coerce anyone to support or participate in religion or its exercise," *ante*, at 2655, I see no warrant for expanding the concept of coercion beyond acts backed by threat of penalty—a brand of coercion that, happily, is readily discernible to those of us who have made a career of reading the disciples of Blackstone rather than of Freud. The Framers were indeed opposed to coercion of religious worship by the National Government; but, as their own sponsorship of nonsectarian prayer in public events demonstrates, they understood that "[s]peech is not coercive; the listener may do as he likes." *American Jewish Congress v. Chicago*, 827 F.2d, at 132 (Easterbrook, J., dissenting).

This historical discussion places in revealing perspective the Court's extravagant claim that the State has "for all practical purposes," *ante*, at 2656, and "in every practical sense," *ante*, at 2661, compelled students to participate in prayers at graduation. Beyond the fact, stipulated to by the parties, that attendance at graduation is voluntary, there is nothing in the record to indicate that failure of attending students to take part in the invocation or benediction was subject to any penalty or discipline. Contrast this with, for example, the facts of *Barnette*: Schoolchildren were required by law to recite the Pledge of Allegiance; failure to do so resulted in expulsion, threatened the expelled child with the prospect of being sent to a reformatory for criminally inclined juveniles, and subjected his parents to prosecution (and incarceration) for causing delinquency. 319 U.S., at 629–630, 63 S.Ct., at 1181. To characterize the "subtle coercive pressures," *ante*, at 2656, allegedly present here as the "practical" equiva⊥643lent of the legal sanctions in *Barnette* is . . . well, let me just say it is not a "delicate and fact-sensitive" analysis.

The Court relies on our "school prayer" cases, *Engel v. Vitale*, 370 U.S. 421, 82 S.Ct. 1261, 8 L.Ed.2d 601 (1962), and *School Dist. of Abington v. Schempp*, 374 U.S. 203, 83 S.Ct. 1560, 10 L.Ed.2d 844 (1963). *Ante*, at 2658. But whatever the merit of those cases, they do not support, much less compel, the Court's psycho-journey. In the first place, *Engel* and *Schempp* do not constitute an exception to the rule, distilled from historical practice, that public ceremonies may include prayer, see *supra*, at 2679–2681; rather, they simply do not fall within the scope of the rule (for the obvious reason that school instruction is not a public ceremony). Second, we have made clear our understanding that school prayer occurs within a framework in which legal coercion to attend school (*i.e.*, coercion under threat of penalty) provides the ultimate backdrop. In *Schempp*, for example, we emphasized that the prayers were "prescribed as part of the curricular activities of students who are *required by law* to attend school." 374 U.S., at 223, 83 S.Ct., at 1572 (emphasis added). *Engel*'s suggestion that the school prayer program at issue there—which permitted students "to remain silent or be excused from the room," 370 U.S., at 430, 82 S.Ct., at 1266—involved "indirect coercive pressure," *id.*, at 431, 82 S.Ct., at 1267, should be understood against this backdrop of legal coercion. The question whether the opt-out procedure in *Engel* sufficed to dispel the coercion resulting from the mandatory attendance requirement is quite different from the question whether forbidden coercion exists in an environment *utterly devoid of legal compulsion.* And finally, our school prayer cases turn in part on the fact that the classroom is inherently an instructional setting, and daily prayer there—where parents are not present to counter "the students' emulation of teachers as role models and the children's susceptibility to peer pressure," *Edwards v. Aguillard,* 482 U.S. 578, 584, 107 S.Ct. 2573, 2578, 96 L.Ed.2d 510 (1987)—might be thought to raise special concerns regarding state interference with the liberty of parents to direct the religious upbringing of their children: "Families entrust public₆₄₄ schools with the education of their children, but condition their trust on the understanding that the classroom will not purposely be used to advance religious views that may conflict with the private beliefs of the student and his or her family." *Ibid.;* see *Pierce v. Society of Sisters,* 268 U.S. 510, 534–535, 45 S.Ct. 571, 573, 69 L.Ed. 1070 (1925). Voluntary prayer at graduation—a one-time ceremony at which parents, friends, and relatives are present—can hardly be thought to raise the same concerns.

IV

Our Religion Clause jurisprudence has become bedeviled (so to speak) by reliance on formulaic abstractions that are not derived from, but positively conflict with, our long-accepted constitutional traditions. Foremost among these has been the so-called *Lemon* test, see *Lemon v. Kurtzman,* 403 U.S. 602, 612–613, 91 S.Ct. 2105, 2111, 29 L.Ed.2d 745 (1971), which has received well-earned criticism from many Members of this Court. See, *e.g., County of Allegheny,* 492 U.S., at 655–656, 109 S.Ct., at 3134 (opinion of KENNEDY, J.); *Edwards v. Aguillard, supra,* 482 U.S., at 636–640, 107 S.Ct., at 2605–2607 (SCALIA, J., dissenting); *Wallace v. Jaffree,* 472 U.S., at 108–112, 105 S.Ct., at 2516–2518 (REHNQUIST, J., dissenting); *Aguilar v. Felton,* 473 U.S. 402, 426–430, 105 S.Ct. 3232, 3245–3247, 87 L.Ed.2d 290 (1985) (O'CONNOR, J., dissenting); *Roemer v. Board of Pub. Works of Md.,* 426 U.S. 736, 768–769, 96 S.Ct. 2337, 2355, 49 L.Ed.2d 179 (1976) (WHITE, J., concurring in judgment). The Court today demonstrates the irrelevance of *Lemon* by essentially ignoring it, see *ante,* at 2655, and the interment of that case may be the one happy byproduct of the Court's otherwise lamentable decision. Unfortunately, however, the Court has replaced *Lemon* with its psycho-coercion test, which suffers the double disability of having no roots whatever in our people's historic practice, and being as infinitely expandable as the reasons for psychotherapy itself.

Another happy aspect of the case is that it is only a jurisprudential disaster and not a practical one. Given the odd basis for the Court's decision, invocations and benedictions will be able to be given at public school graduations next ₆₄₅June, as they have for the past century and a half, so long as school authorities make clear that anyone who abstains from screaming in protest does not necessarily participate in the prayers. All that is seemingly needed is an announcement, or perhaps a written insertion at the beginning of the graduation program, to the effect that, while all are asked to rise for the invocation and benediction, none is compelled to join in them, nor will be assumed, by rising, to have done so. That obvious fact recited, the graduates and their parents may proceed to thank God, as Americans have always done, for the blessings He has generously bestowed on them and on their country.

* * *

The reader has been told much in this case about the personal interest of Mr. Weisman and his daughter, and very little about the personal interests on the other side. They are not inconsequential. Church and state would not be such a difficult subject if religion were, as the Court apparently thinks it to be, some purely personal avocation that can be indulged entirely in secret, like pornography, in the privacy of one's room. For most believers it is *not* that, and has never been. Religious men and women of almost all denominations have felt it necessary to acknowledge and beseech the blessing of God as a people, and not just as individuals, because they believe in the "protection of divine Providence," as the Declaration of Independence put it, not just for individuals but for societies; because they believe God to be, as Washington's first Thanksgiving Proclamation put it, the "Great Lord and Ruler of Nations." One can believe in the effectiveness of such public worship, or one can deprecate and deride it. But the longstanding American tradition of prayer at official ceremonies displays with unmistakable clarity that the Establishment Clause does not forbid the government to accommodate it.

The narrow context of the present case involves a community's celebration of one of the milestones in its young citizens'646 lives, and it is a bold step for this Court to seek to banish from that occasion, and from thousands of similar celebrations throughout this land, the expression of gratitude to God that a majority of the community wishes to make. The issue before us today is not the abstract philosophical question whether the alternative of frustrating this desire of a religious majority is to be preferred over the alternative of imposing "psychological coercion," or a feeling of exclusion, upon nonbelievers. Rather, the question is *whether a mandatory choice in favor of the former has been imposed by the United States Constitution.* As the age-old practices of our people show, the answer to that question is not at all in doubt.

I must add one final observation: The Founders of our Republic knew the fearsome potential of sectarian religious belief to generate civil dissension and civil strife. And they also knew that nothing, absolutely nothing, is so inclined to foster among religious believers of various faiths a toleration—no, an affection—for one another than voluntarily joining in prayer together, to the God whom they all worship and seek. Needless to say, no one should be compelled to do that, but it is a shame to deprive our public culture of the opportunity, and indeed the encouragement, for people to do it voluntarily. The Baptist or Catholic who heard and joined in the simple and inspiring prayers of Rabbi Gutterman on this official and patriotic occasion was inoculated from religious bigotry and prejudice in a manner that cannot be replicated. To deprive our society of that important unifying mechanism, in order to spare the nonbeliever what seems to me the minimal inconvenience of standing or even sitting in respectful nonparticipation, is as senseless in policy as it is unsupported in law.

For the foregoing reasons, I dissent.

ABBREVIATIONS

A.	Atlantic Reporter
A. 2d	Atlantic Reporter, Second Series
AAA	American Arbitration Association; Agricultural Adjustment Act of 1933
AAPRP	All African People's Revolutionary Party
ABA	American Bar Association; Architectural Barriers Act, 1968
ABM Treaty	Anti-Ballistic Missile Treaty of 1972; antiballistic missile
ABVP	Anti-Biased Violence Project
A/C	Account
A.C.	Appeal Cases
ACAA	Air Carrier Access Act
ACF	Administration for Children and Families
ACLU	American Civil Liberties Union
ACS	Agricultural Cooperative Service
Act'g Legal Adv.	Acting Legal Advisor
ACUS	Administrative Conference of the United States
ACYF	Administration on Children, Youth, and Families
A.D. 2d	Appellate Division, Second Series, N.Y.
ADA	Americans with Disabilities Act of 1990
ADAMHA	Alcohol, Drug Abuse, and Mental Health Administration
ADC	Aid to Dependent Children
ADD	Administration on Developmental Disabilities
ADEA	Age Discrimination in Employment Act of 1967
ADR	alternative dispute resolution
AEC	Atomic Energy Commission
AECB	Arms Export Control Board
A.E.R.	All England Law Reports
AFDC	Aid to Families with Dependent Children
aff'd per cur.	affirmed by the court
AFIS	automated fingerprint identification system
AFL	American Federation of Labor
AFL-CIO	American Federation of Labor and Congress of Industrial Organizations
AFRes	Air Force Reserve
AFSCME	American Federation of State, County, and Municipal Employees
AGRICOLA	Agricultural Online Access
AIA	Association of Insurance Attorneys
AID	artificial insemination using a third-party donor's sperm; Agency for International Development

AIDS	acquired immune deficiency syndrome
AIH	artificial insemination using the husband's sperm
AIM	American Indian Movement
AIUSA	Amnesty International, U.S.A. Affiliate
AJS	American Judicature Society
ALEC	American Legislative Exchange Council
ALF	Animal Liberation Front
ALI	American Law Institute
ALJ	administrative law judge
All E.R.	All England Law Reports
ALO	Agency Liaison
A.L.R.	American Law Reports
AMA	American Medical Association
Am. Dec.	American Decisions
amdt.	amendment
Amer. St. Papers, For. Rels.	American State Papers, Legislative and Executive Documents of the Congress of the U.S., Class I, Foreign Relations, 1832–1859
AMVETS	American Veterans (of World War II)
ANA	Administration for Native Americans
Ann. Dig.	Annual Digest of Public International Law Cases
ANZUS	Australia–New Zealand–United States Security Treaty Organization
AOA	Administration on Aging
APA	Administrative Procedure Act of 1946
APHIS	Animal and Plant Health Inspection Service
App. Div.	Appellate Division Reports, N.Y. Supreme Court
Arb. Trib., U.S.-British Convention of 1853	Arbitration Tribunal, Claim Convention of 1853, United States and Great Britain
ARS	Advanced Record System
Art.	article
ASCS	Agriculture Stabilization and Conservation Service
ASM	available seatmile
ASPCA	American Society for the Prevention of Cruelty to Animals
Asst. Att. Gen.	Assistant Attorney General
AT&T	American Telephone and Telegraph
ATFD	Alcohol, Tobacco and Firearms Division
ATLA	Association of Trial Lawyers of America
ATTD	Alcohol and Tobacco Tax Division
ATU	Alcohol Tax Unit
AZT	azidothymidine
BALSA	Black-American Law Student Association
BATF	Bureau of Alcohol, Tobacco and Firearms
BCCI	Bank of Credit and Commerce International
BEA	Bureau of Economic Analysis
Bell's Cr. C.	Bell's English Crown Cases
Bevans	United States Treaties, etc. *Treaties and Other International Agreements of the United States of America, 1776–1949* (compiled under the direction of Charles I. Bevans) (1968–76)
BFOQ	bona fide occupational qualification
BI	Bureau of Investigation
BIA	Bureau of Indian Affairs; Board of Immigration Appeals
BJS	Bureau of Justice Statistics
Black.	Black's United States Supreme Court Reports
Blatchf.	Blatchford's United States Circuit Court Reports
BLM	Bureau of Land Management
BLS	Bureau of Labor Statistics
BMD	ballistic missile defense
BOCA	Building Officials and Code Administrators International
BPP	Black Panther Party for Self-Defense

Brit. and For.	British and Foreign State Papers
Burr.	James Burrows, *Report of Cases Argued and Determined in the Court of King's Bench during the Time of Lord Mansfield* (1766–1780)
BVA	Board of Veterans Appeals
c.	Chapter
C^3I	Command, Control, Communications, and Intelligence
C.A.	Court of Appeals
CAA	Clean Air Act
CAB	Civil Aeronautics Board
CAFE	corporate average fuel economy
Cal. 2d	California Reports, Second Series
Cal. 3d	California Reports, Third Series
CALR	computer-assisted legal research
Cal. Rptr.	California Reporter
CAP	Common Agricultural Policy
CATV	community antenna television
CBO	Congressional Budget Office
CCC	Commodity Credit Corporation
CCDBG	Child Care and Development Block Grant of 1990
C.C.D. Pa.	Circuit Court Decisions, Pennsylvania
C.C.D. Va.	Circuit Court Decisions, Virginia
CCEA	Cabinet Council on Economic Affairs
CCR	Center for Constitutional Rights
C.C.R.I.	Circuit Court, Rhode Island
CD	certificate of deposit
CDA	Communications Decency Act
CDBG	Community Development Block Grant Program
CDC	Centers for Disease Control and Prevention; Community Development Corporation
CDF	Children's Defense Fund
CDL	Citizens for Decency through Law
CD-ROM	compact disc read-only memory
CDS	Community Dispute Services
CDW	collision damage waiver
CENTO	Central Treaty Organization
CEQ	Council on Environmental Quality
CERCLA	Comprehensive Environmental Response, Compensation, and Liability Act of 1980
cert.	*certiorari*
CETA	Comprehensive Employment and Training Act
C & F	cost and freight
CFC	chlorofluorocarbon
CFE Treaty	Conventional Forces in Europe Treaty of 1990
C.F. & I.	Cost, freight, and insurance
CFNP	Community Food and Nutrition Program
C.F.R.	Code of Federal Regulations
CFTC	Commodity Futures Trading Commission
Ch.	Chancery Division, English Law Reports
CHAMPVA	Civilian Health and Medical Program at the Veterans Administration
CHEP	Cuban/Haitian Entrant Program
CHINS	children in need of supervision
CHIPS	child in need of protective services
Ch.N.Y.	Chancery Reports, New York
Chr. Rob.	Christopher Robinson, *Reports of Cases Argued and Determined in the High Court of Admiralty* (1801–1808)
CIA	Central Intelligence Agency
CID	Commercial Item Descriptions
C.I.F.	Cost, insurance, and freight
CINCNORAD	Commander in Chief, North American Air Defense Command
C.I.O.	Congress of Industrial Organizations

C.J.	chief justice
CJIS	Criminal Justice Information Services
C.J.S.	Corpus Juris Secundum
Claims Arb. under Spec. Conv., Nielsen's Rept.	Frederick Kenelm Nielsen, *American and British Claims Arbitration under the Special Agreement Concluded between the United States and Great Britain, August 18, 1910* (1926)
CLE	Center for Law and Education
CLEO	Council on Legal Education Opportunity
CLP	Communist Labor Party of America
CLS	Christian Legal Society; critical legal studies (movement), Critical Legal Studies (membership organization)
C.M.A.	Court of Military Appeals
CMEA	Council for Mutual Economic Assistance
CMHS	Center for Mental Health Services
C.M.R.	Court of Military Review
CNN	Cable News Network
CNO	Chief of Naval Operations
C.O.D.	cash on delivery
COGP	Commission on Government Procurement
COINTELPRO	Counterintelligence Program
Coke Rep.	Coke's English King's Bench Reports
COLA	cost-of-living adjustment
COMCEN	Federal Communications Center
Comp.	Compilation
Conn.	Connecticut Reports
CONTU	National Commission on New Technological Uses of Copyrighted Works
Conv.	Convention
Corbin	Arthur L. Corbin, *Corbin on Contracts: A Comprehensive Treatise on the Rules of Contract Law* (1950)
CORE	Congress of Racial Equality
Cox's Crim. Cases	Cox's Criminal Cases (England)
CPA	certified public accountant
CPB	Corporation for Public Broadcasting, the
CPI	Consumer Price Index
CPSC	Consumer Product Safety Commission
Cranch	Cranch's United States Supreme Court Reports
CRF	Constitutional Rights Foundation
CRS	Congressional Research Service; Community Relations Service
CRT	critical race theory
CSA	Community Services Administration
CSAP	Center for Substance Abuse Prevention
CSAT	Center for Substance Abuse Treatment
CSC	Civil Service Commission
CSCE	Conference on Security and Cooperation in Europe
CSG	Council of State Governments
CSO	Community Service Organization
CSP	Center for the Study of the Presidency
C-SPAN	Cable-Satellite Public Affairs Network
CSRS	Cooperative State Research Service
CSWPL	Center on Social Welfare Policy and Law
CTA	*cum testamento annexo* (with the will attached)
Ct. Ap. D.C.	Court of Appeals, District of Columbia
Ct. App. No. Ireland	Court of Appeals, Northern Ireland
Ct. Cl.	Court of Claims, United States
Ct. Crim. Apps.	Court of Criminal Appeals (England)
Ct. of Sess., Scot.	Court of Sessions, Scotland
CU	credit union

CUNY	City University of New York
Cush.	Cushing's Massachusetts Reports
CWA	Civil Works Administration; Clean Water Act
Dall.	Dallas' Pennsylvania and United States Reports
DAR	Daughter of the American Revolution
DARPA	Defense Advanced Research Projects Agency
DAVA	Defense Audiovisual Agency
D.C.	United States District Court
D.C. Del.	United States District Court, Delaware
D.C. Mass.	United States District Court, Massachusetts
D.C. Md.	United States District Court, Maryland
D.C.N.D.Cal.	United States District Court, Northern District, California
D.C.N.Y.	United States District Court, New York
D.C.Pa.	United States District Court, Pennsylvania
DCS	Deputy Chiefs of Staff
DCZ	District of the Canal Zone
DDT	dichlorodiphenyltricloroethane
DEA	Drug Enforcement Administration
Decl. Lond.	Declaration of London, February 26, 1909
Dev. & B.	Devereux & Battle's North Carolina Reports
Dig. U.S. Practice in Intl. Law	Digest of U.S. Practice in International Law
Dist. Ct. D.C.	United States District Court, District of Columbia
D.L.R.	Dominion Law Reports (Canada)
DNA	deoxyribonucleic acid
DNase	deoxyribonuclease
DNC	Democratic National Committee
DOC	Department of Commerce
DOD	Department of Defense
Dodson	Dodson's Reports, English Admiralty Courts
DOE	Department of Energy
DOER	Department of Employee Relations
DOJ	Department of Justice
DOS	disk operating system
DOT	Department of Transportation
DPT	diphtheria, pertussis, and tetanus
DRI	Defense Research Institute
DSAA	Defense Security Assistance Agency
DUI	driving under the influence; driving under intoxication
DWI	driving while intoxicated
EAHCA	Education for All Handicapped Children Act of 1975
EBT	examination before trial
ECPA	Electronic Communications Privacy Act of 1986
ECSC	Treaty of the European Coal and Steel Community
EDA	Economic Development Administration
EDF	Environmental Defense Fund
E.D.N.Y.	Eastern District, New York
EDP	electronic data processing
E.D. Pa.	Eastern District, Pennsylvania
EDSC	Eastern District, South Carolina
E.D. Va.	Eastern District, Virginia
EEC	European Economic Community; European Economic Community Treaty
EEOC	Equal Employment Opportunity Commission
EFF	Electronic Frontier Foundation
EFT	electronic funds transfer
Eliz.	Queen Elizabeth (Great Britain)
Em. App.	Temporary Emergency Court of Appeals

ENE	early neutral evaluation
Eng. Rep.	English Reports
EOP	Executive Office of the President
EPA	Environmental Protection Agency; Equal Pay Act of 1963
ERA	Equal Rights Amendment
ERISA	Employee Retirement Income Security Act of 1974
ERS	Economic Research Service
ESF	emergency support function; Economic Support Fund
ESRD	End-Stage Renal Disease Program
ETA	Employment and Training Administration
ETS	environmental tobacco smoke
et seq.	*et sequentes* or *et sequentia;* "and the following"
EU	European Union
Euratom	European Atomic Energy Community
Eur. Ct. H.R.	European Court of Human Rights
Ex.	English Exchequer Reports, Welsby, Hurlstone & Gordon
Exch.	Exchequer Reports (Welsby, Hurlstone & Gordon)
Eximbank	Export-Import Bank of the United States
F.	Federal Reporter
F. 2d	Federal Reporter, Second Series
FAA	Federal Aviation Administration; Federal Arbitration Act
FAAA	Federal Alcohol Administration Act
FACE	Freedom of Access to Clinic Entrances Act of 1994
FACT	Feminist Anti-Censorship Task Force
FAO	Food and Agriculture Organization of the United Nations
FAR	Federal Acquisition Regulations
FAS	Foreign Agricultural Service
FBA	Federal Bar Association
FBI	Federal Bureau of Investigation
FCA	Farm Credit Administration
F. Cas.	Federal Cases
FCC	Federal Communications Commission
FCIA	Foreign Credit Insurance Association
FCIC	Federal Crop Insurance Corporation
FCRA	Fair Credit Reporting Act
FCU	Federal credit unions
FDA	Food and Drug Administration
FDIC	Federal Deposit Insurance Corporation
FDPC	Federal Data Processing Center
FEC	Federal Election Commission
Fed. Cas.	Federal Cases
FEMA	Federal Emergency Management Agency
FFB	Federal Financing Bank
FGIS	Federal Grain Inspection Service
FHA	Federal Housing Authority
FHWA	Federal Highway Administration
FIA	Federal Insurance Administration
FIC	Federal Information Centers; Federation of Insurance Counsel
FICA	Federal Insurance Contributions Act
FIFRA	Federal Insecticide, Fungicide, and Rodenticide Act
FIP	Forestry Incentives Program
FIRREA	Financial Institutions Reform, Recovery, and Enforcement Act
FISA	Foreign Intelligence Surveillance Act of 1978
FMCS	Federal Mediation and Conciliation Service
FmHA	Farmers Home Administration
FMLA	Family and Medical Leave Act of 1993
FNMA	Federal National Mortgage Association, "Fannie Mae"
F.O.B.	free on board

FOIA	Freedom of Information Act
FPC	Federal Power Commission
FPMR	Federal Property Management Regulations
FPRS	Federal Property Resources Service
FR	Federal Register
FRA	Federal Railroad Administration
FRB	Federal Reserve Board
FRC	Federal Radio Commission
F.R.D.	Federal Rules Decisions
FSA	Family Support Act
FSLIC	Federal Savings and Loan Insurance Corporation
FSQS	Food Safety and Quality Service
FSS	Federal Supply Service
F. Supp.	Federal Supplement
FTA	U.S.-Canada Free Trade Agreement, 1988
FTC	Federal Trade Commission
FTS	Federal Telecommunications System
FUTA	Federal Unemployment Tax Act
FWPCA	Federal Water Pollution Control Act of 1948
GAO	General Accounting Office; Governmental Affairs Office
GAOR	General Assembly Official Records, United Nations
GA Res.	General Assembly Resolution (United Nations)
GATT	General Agreement on Tariffs and Trade
Gen. Cls. Comm.	General Claims Commission, United States and Panama; General Claims Commission, United States and Mexico
Geo. II	King George II (Great Britain)
Geo. III	King George III (Great Britain)
GM	General Motors
GNMA	Government National Mortgage Association, "Ginnie Mae"
GNP	gross national product
GOP	Grand Old Party (Republican)
GOPAC	Grand Old Party Action Committee
GPA	Office of Governmental and Public Affairs
GPO	Government Printing Office
GRAS	generally recognized as safe
Gr. Br., Crim. Ct. App.	Great Britain, Court of Criminal Appeals
GRNL	Gay Rights National Lobby
GSA	General Services Administration
Hackworth	Green Haywood Hackworth, *Digest of International Law* (1940–44)
Hay and Marriott	Great Britain. High Court of Admiralty, *Decisions in the High Court of Admiralty during the Time of Sir George Hay and of Sir James Marriott, Late Judges of That Court* (1801)
HBO	Home Box Office
HCFA	Health Care Financing Administration
H.Ct.	High Court
HDS	Office of Human Development Services
Hen. & M.	Hening & Munford's Virginia Reports
HEW	Department of Health, Education, and Welfare
HHS	Department of Health and Human Services
Hill	Hill's New York Reports
HIRE	Help through Industry Retraining and Employment
HIV	human immunodeficiency virus
H.L.	House of Lords Cases (England)
H. Lords	House of Lords (England)
HNIS	Human Nutrition Information Service
Hong Kong L.R.	Hong Kong Law Reports
How.	Howard's United States Supreme Court Reports
How. St. Trials	Howell's English State Trials
HUAC	House Un-American Activities Committee

HUD	Department of Housing and Urban Development
Hudson, Internatl. Legis.	Manley O. Hudson, ed., *International Legislation: A Collection of the Texts of Multipartite International Instruments of General Interest Beginning with the Covenant of the League of Nations* (1931)
Hudson, World Court Reps.	Manley Ottmer Hudson, ed., *World Court Reports* (1934–)
Hun	Hun's New York Supreme Court Reports
Hunt's Rept.	Bert L. Hunt, *Report of the American and Panamanian General Claims Arbitration* (1934)
IAEA	International Atomic Energy Agency
IALL	International Association of Law Libraries
IBA	International Bar Association
IBM	International Business Machines
ICBM	intercontinental ballistic missile
ICC	Interstate Commerce Commission
ICJ	International Court of Justice
IDEA	Individuals with Disabilities Education Act, 1975
IEP	individualized educational program
IFC	International Finance Corporation
IGRA	Indian Gaming Regulatory Act, 1988
IJA	Institute of Judicial Administration
IJC	International Joint Commission
ILC	International Law Commission
ILD	International Labor Defense
Ill. Dec.	Illinois Decisions
ILO	International Labor Organization
IMF	International Monetary Fund
INA	Immigration and Nationality Act
IND	investigational new drug
INF Treaty	Intermediate-Range Nuclear Forces Treaty of 1987
INS	Immigration and Naturalization Service
INTELSAT	International Telecommunications Satellite Organization
Interpol	International Criminal Police Organization
Int'l. Law Reps.	International Law Reports
Intl. Legal Mats.	International Legal Materials
IPDC	International Program for the Development of Communication
IPO	Intellectual Property Owners
IPP	independent power producer
IQ	intelligence quotient
I.R.	Irish Reports
IRA	individual retirement account; Irish Republican Army
IRCA	Immigration Reform and Control Act of 1986
IRS	Internal Revenue Service
ISO	independent service organization
ISSN	International Standard Serial Numbers
ITA	International Trade Administration
ITI	Information Technology Integration
ITO	International Trade Organization
ITS	Information Technology Service
ITU	International Telecommunication Union
IUD	intrauterine device
IWC	International Whaling Commission
IWW	Industrial Workers of the World
JCS	Joint Chiefs of Staff
JDL	Jewish Defense League
JOBS	Jobs Opportunity and Basic Skills
John. Ch.	Johnson's New York Chancery Reports
Johns.	Johnson's Reports (New York)
JP	justice of the peace

K.B.	King's Bench Reports (England)
KGB	Komitet Gosudarstvennoi Bezopasnosti (the State Security Committee for countries in the former Soviet Union)
KKK	Ku Klux Klan
KMT	Kuomintang
LAPD	Los Angeles Police Department
LC	Library of Congress
LD50	lethal dose 50
LDEF	Legal Defense and Education Fund (NOW)
LDF	Legal Defense Fund, Legal Defense and Educational Fund of the NAACP
LEAA	Law Enforcement Assistance Administration
L.Ed.	Lawyers' Edition Supreme Court Reports
LMSA	Labor-Management Services Administration
LNTS	League of Nations Treaty Series
Lofft's Rep.	Lofft's English King's Bench Reports
L.R.	Law Reports (English)
LSAS	Law School Admission Service
LSAT	Law School Aptitude Test
LSC	Legal Services Corporation; Legal Services for Children
LSD	lysergic acid diethylamide
LSDAS	Law School Data Assembly Service
LTBT	Limited Test Ban Treaty
LTC	Long Term Care
MAD	mutual assured destruction
MADD	Mothers against Drunk Driving
MALDEF	Mexican American Legal Defense and Educational Fund
Malloy	William M. Malloy, ed., *Treaties, Conventions, International Acts, Protocols, and Agreements between the United States of America and Other Powers* (1910–38)
Martens	Georg Friedrich von Martens, ed., *Noveau recueil général de traités et autres act es relatifs aux rapports de droit international* (Series I, 20 vols. [1843–75]; Series II, 35 vols. [1876–1908]; Series III [1909–])
Mass.	Massachusetts Reports
MCH	Maternal and Child Health Bureau
Md. App.	Maryland, Appeal Cases
M.D. Ga.	Middle District, Georgia
Mercy	Movement Ensuring the Right to Choose for Yourself
Metc.	Metcalf's Massachusetts Reports
MFDP	Mississippi Freedom Democratic party
MGT	Management
MHSS	Military Health Services System
Miller	David Hunter Miller, ed., *Treaties and Other International Acts of the United States of America* (1931–1948)
Minn.	Minnesota Reports
MINS	minors in need of supervision
MIRV	multiple independently targetable reentry vehicle
Misc.	Miscellaneous Reports, New York
Mixed Claims Comm., Report of Decs.	Mixed Claims Commission, United States and Germany, Report of Decisions
M.J.	Military Justice Reporter
MLAP	Migrant Legal Action Program
MLB	major league baseball
MLDP	Mississippi Loyalist Democratic party
Mo.	Missouri Reports
Mod.	Modern Reports, English King's Bench, etc.
Moore, Dig. Intl. Law	John Bassett Moore, *A Digest of International Law*, 8 vols. (1906)
Moore, Intl. Arbs.	John Bassett Moore, *History and Digest of the International Arbitrations to Which the United States Has Been a Party*, 6 vols. (1898)

Morison	William Maxwell Morison, *The Scots Revised Report: Morison's Dictionary of Decisions* (1908–09)
M.P.	member of Parliament
MPAA	Motion Picture Association of America
mpg	miles per gallon
MPRSA	Marine Protection, Research, and Sanctuaries Act of 1972
M.R.	Master of the Rolls
MS-DOS	Microsoft Disk Operating System
MSHA	Mine Safety and Health Administration
NAACP	National Association for the Advancement of Colored People
NAAQS	National Ambient Air Quality Standards
NABSW	National Association of Black Social Workers
NAFTA	North American Free Trade Agreement, 1993
NARAL	National Abortion Rights Action League
NARF	Native American Rights Fund
NARS	National Archives and Record Service
NASA	National Aeronautics and Space Administration
NASD	National Association of Securities Dealers
NATO	North Atlantic Treaty Organization
NAVINFO	Navy Information Offices
NAWSA	National American Woman's Suffrage Association
NBA	National Bar Association
NBC	National Broadcasting Company
NBLSA	National Black Law Student Association
NBS	National Bureau of Standards
NCA	Noise Control Act; National Command Authorities
NCAA	National Collegiate Athletic Association
NCAC	National Coalition against Censorship
NCCB	National Consumer Cooperative Bank
NCE	Northwest Community Exchange
NCJA	National Criminal Justice Association
NCLB	National Civil Liberties Bureau
NCP	national contingency plan
NCSC	National Center for State Courts
NCUA	National Credit Union Administration
NDA	new drug application
N.D. Ill.	Northern District, Illinois
NDU	National Defense University
N.D. Wash.	Northern District, Washington
N.E.	North Eastern Reporter
N.E. 2d	North Eastern Reporter, Second Series
NEA	National Endowment for the Arts
NEH	National Endowment for the Humanities
NEPA	National Environmental Protection Act; National Endowment Policy Act
NFIP	National Flood Insurance Program
NGTF	National Gay Task Force
NHRA	Nursing Home Reform Act, 1987
NHTSA	National Highway Traffic Safety Administration
Nielsen's Rept.	Frederick Kenelm Nielsen, *American and British Claims Arbitration under the Special Agreement Concluded between the United States and Great Britain, August 18, 1910* (1926)
NIEO	New International Economic Order
NIH	National Institutes of Health, the NIH
NIJ	National Institute of Justice
NIRA	National Industrial Recovery Act; National Industrial Recovery Administration
NIST	National Institute of Standards and Technology, the NIST
NITA	National Telecommunications and Information Administration
N.J.	New Jersey Reports

N.J. Super.	New Jersey Superior Court Reports
NLRA	National Labor Relations Act
NLRB	National Labor Relations Board
No.	Number
NOAA	National Oceanic and Atmospheric Administration
NOW	National Organization for Women
NOW LDEF	National Organization for Women Legal Defense and Education Fund
NOW/PAC	National Organization for Women Political Action Committee
NPDES	National Pollutant Discharge Elimination System
NPL	national priorities list
NPR	National Public Radio
NPT	Non-Proliferation Treaty
NRA	National Rifle Association; National Recovery Act
NRC	Nuclear Regulatory Commission
NSC	National Security Council
NSCLC	National Senior Citizens Law Center
NSF	National Science Foundation
NSFNET	National Science Foundation Network
NTIA	National Telecommunications and Information Administration
NTID	National Technical Institute for the Deaf
NTIS	National Technical Information Service
NTS	Naval Telecommunications System
NTSB	National Transportation Safety Board
N.W.	North Western Reporter
N.W. 2d	North Western Reporter, Second Series
NWSA	National Woman Suffrage Association
N.Y.	New York Court of Appeals Reports
N.Y. 2d	New York Court of Appeals Reports, Second Series
N.Y.S.	New York Supplement Reporter
N.Y.S. 2d	New York Supplement Reporter, Second Series
NYSE	New York Stock Exchange
N.Y. Sup.	New York Supreme Court Reports
NYU	New York University
OAAU	Organization of Afro American Unity
OAP	Office of Administrative Procedure
OAS	Organization of American States
OASDI	Old-age, Survivors, and Disability Insurance Benefits
OASHDS	Office of the Assistant Secretary for Human Development Services
OCED	Office of Comprehensive Employment Development
OCHAMPUS	Office of Civilian Health and Medical Program of the Uniformed Services
OCSE	Office of Child Support Enforcement
OEA	Organización de los Estados Americanos
OFCCP	Office of Federal Contract Compliance Programs
OFPP	Office of Federal Procurement Policy
OICD	Office of International Cooperation and Development
OIG	Office of the Inspector General
OJARS	Office of Justice Assistance, Research, and Statistics
OMB	Office of Management and Budget
OMPC	Office of Management, Planning, and Communications
ONP	Office of National Programs
OPD	Office of Policy Development
OPEC	Organization of Petroleum Exporting Countries
OPIC	Overseas Private Investment Corporation
Ops. Atts. Gen.	Opinions of the Attorneys-General of the United States
Ops. Comms.	Opinions of the Commissioners
OPSP	Office of Product Standards Policy
O.R.	Ontario Reports
OR	Official Records

OSHA	Occupational Safety and Health Administration
OSHRC	Occupational Safety and Health Review Commission
OSM	Office of Surface Mining
OSS	Office of Strategic Services
OST	Office of the Secretary
OT	Office of Transportation
OTA	Office of Technology Assessment
OTC	over-the-counter
OUI	operating under the influence
OWBPA	Older Workers Benefit Protection Act
OWRT	Office of Water Research and Technology
P.	Pacific Reporter
P. 2d	Pacific Reporter, Second Series
PAC	political action committee
Pa. Oyer and Terminer	Pennsylvania Oyer and Terminer Reports
PATCO	Professional Air Traffic Controllers Organization
PBGC	Pension Benefit Guaranty Corporation
PBS	Public Broadcasting Service; Public Buildings Service
P.C.	Privy Council (English Law Reports); personal computer
PCIJ	Permanent Court of International Justice Series A—Judgments and Orders (1922–30) Series B—Advisory Opinions (1922–30) Series A/B—Judgments, Orders, and Advisory Opinions (1931–40) Series C—Pleadings, Oral Statements, and Documents relating to Judgments and Advisory Opinions (1923–42) Series D—Acts and Documents concerning the Organization of the World Court (1922–47) Series E—Annual Reports (1925–45)
PCP	phencyclidine (no need to spell out)
P.D.	Probate Division, English Law Reports (1876–1890)
PDA	Pregnancy Discrimination Act of 1978
PD & R	Policy Development and Research
Perm. Ct. of Arb.	Permanent Court of Arbitration
Pet.	Peters' United States Supreme Court Reports
PETA	People for the Ethical Treatment of Animals
PGM	Program
PHA	Public Housing Agency
Phila. Ct. of Oyer and Terminer	Philadelphia Court of Oyer and Terminer
PHS	Public Health Service
PIC	Private Industry Council
Pick.	Pickering's Massachusetts Reports
PIK	Payment in Kind
PINS	persons in need of supervision
PIRG	Public Interest Research Group
P.L.	Public Laws
PLAN	Pro-Life Action Network
PLI	Practicing Law Institute
PLO	Palestine Liberation Organization
PNET	Peaceful Nuclear Explosions Treaty
POW-MIA	prisoner of war–missing in action
Pratt	Frederic Thomas Pratt, *Law of Contraband of War, with a Selection of Cases from the Papers of the Right Honourable Sir George Lee* (1856)
Proc.	Proceedings
PRP	potentially responsible party
PSRO	Professional Standards Review Organization
PTO	Patents and Trademark Office
PURPA	Public Utilities Regulatory Policies Act

PUSH	People United to Serve Humanity
PWA	Public Works Administration
PWSA	Ports and Waterways Safety Act of 1972
Q.B.	Queen's Bench (England)
Ralston's Rept.	Jackson Harvey Ralston, ed., *Venezuelan Arbitrations of 1903* (1904)
RC	Regional Commissioner
RCRA	Resource Conservation and Recovery Act
RCWP	Rural Clean Water Program
RDA	Rural Development Administration
REA	Rural Electrification Administration
Rec. des Decs. des Trib. Arb. Mixtes	G. Gidel, ed., *Recueil des décisions des tribunaux arbitraux mixtes, institués par les traités de paix* (1922–30)
Redmond	Vol. 3 of Charles I. Bevans, *Treaties and Other International Agreements of the United States of America, 1776–1949* (compiled by C. F. Redmond) (1969)
RESPA	Real Estate Settlement Procedure Act of 1974
RFRA	Religious Freedom Restoration Act
RICO	Racketeer Influenced and Corrupt Organizations
RNC	Republican National Committee
Roscoe	Edward Stanley Roscoe, ed., *Reports of Prize Cases Determined in the High Court of Admiralty before the Lords Commissioners of Appeals in Prize Causes and before the Judicial Committee of the Privy Council from 1745 to 1859* (1905)
ROTC	Reserve Officers' Training Corps
RPP	Representative Payee Program
R.S.	Revised Statutes
RTC	Resolution Trust Company
Ryan White CARE Act	Ryan White Comprehensive AIDS Research Emergency Act of 1990
SAC	Strategic Air Command
SACB	Subversive Activities Control Board
SADD	Students against Drunk Driving
SAF	Student Activities Fund
SAIF	Savings Association Insurance Fund
SALT I	Strategic Arms Limitation Talks of 1969–72
SAMHSA	Substance Abuse and Mental Health Services Administration
Sandf.	Sandford's New York Superior Court Reports
S and L	savings and loan
SARA	Superfund Amendment and Reauthorization Act
Sawy.	Sawyer's United States Circuit Court Reports
SBA	Small Business Administration
SCLC	Southern Christian Leadership Conference
Scott's Repts.	James Brown Scott, ed., *The Hague Court Reports*, 2 vols. (1916–32)
SCS	Soil Conservation Service
SCSEP	Senior Community Service Employment Program
S.Ct.	Supreme Court Reporter
S.D. Cal.	Southern District, California
S.D. Fla.	Southern District, Florida
S.D. Ga.	Southern District, Georgia
SDI	Strategic Defense Initiative
S.D. Me.	Southern District, Maine
S.D.N.Y.	Southern District, New York
SDS	Students for a Democratic Society
S.E.	South Eastern Reporter
S.E. 2d	South Eastern Reporter, Second Series
SEA	Science and Education Administration
SEATO	Southeast Asia Treaty Organization
SEC	Securities and Exchange Commission
Sec.	Section
SEEK	Search for Elevation, Education and Knowledge
SEOO	State Economic Opportunity Office

SEP	simplified employee pension plan
Ser.	Series
Sess.	Session
SGLI	Servicemen's Group Life Insurance
SIP	state implementation plan
SLA	Symbionese Liberation Army
SLBM	submarine-launched ballistic missile
SNCC	Student Nonviolent Coordinating Committee
So.	Southern Reporter
So. 2d	Southern Reporter, Second Series
SPA	Software Publisher's Association
Spec. Sess.	Special Session
SRA	Sentencing Reform Act of 1984
SS	Schutzstaffel (German for Protection Echelon)
SSA	Social Security Administration
SSI	Supplemental Security Income
START I	Strategic Arms Reduction Treaty of 1991
START II	Strategic Arms Reduction Treaty of 1993
Stat.	United States Statutes at Large
STS	Space Transportation Systems
St. Tr.	State Trials, English
STURAA	Surface Transportation and Uniform Relocation Assistance Act of 1987
Sup. Ct. of Justice, Mexico	Supreme Court of Justice, Mexico
Supp.	Supplement
S.W.	South Western Reporter
S.W. 2d	South Western Reporter, Second Series
SWAPO	South-West Africa People's Organization
SWAT	Special Weapons and Tactics
SWP	Socialist Workers party
TDP	Trade and Development Program
Tex. Sup.	Texas Supreme Court Reports
THAAD	Theater High-Altitude Area Defense System
TIA	Trust Indenture Act of 1939
TIAS	Treaties and Other International Acts Series (United States)
TNT	trinitrotoluene
TOP	Targeted Outreach Program
TPUS	Transportation and Public Utilities Service
Tripartite Claims Comm., Decs. and Ops.	Tripartite Claims Commission (United States, Austria, and Hungary), Decisions and Opinions
TRI-TAC	Joint Tactical Communications
TRO	temporary restraining order
TS	Treaty Series, United States
TSCA	Toxic Substance Control Act
TSDs	transporters, storers, and disposers
TTBT	Threshold Test Ban Treaty
TVA	Tennessee Valley Authority
UAW	United Auto Workers; United Automobile, Aerospace, and Agricultural Implements Workers of America
U.C.C.	Uniform Commercial Code; Universal Copyright Convention
U.C.C.C.	Uniform Consumer Credit Code
UCCJA	Uniform Child Custody Jurisdiction Act
UCMJ	Uniform Code of Military Justice
UCPP	Urban Crime Prevention Program
UCS	United Counseling Service
UDC	United Daughters of the Confederacy
UFW	United Farm Workers
UHF	ultrahigh frequency
UIFSA	Uniform Interstate Family Support Act

UIS	Unemployment Insurance Service
UMDA	Uniform Marriage and Divorce Act
UMTA	Urban Mass Transportation Administration
UNCITRAL	United Nations Commission on International Trade Law
UNCTAD	United Nations Conference on Trade and Development
UN Doc.	United Nations Documents
UNDP	United Nations Development Program
UNEF	United Nations Emergency Force
UNESCO	United Nations Educational, Scientific, and Cultural Organization
UNICEF	United Nations Children's Fund
UNIDO	United Nations Industrial and Development Organization
Unif. L. Ann.	Uniform Laws Annotated
UN Repts. Intl. Arb. Awards	United Nations Reports of International Arbitral Awards
UNTS	United Nations Treaty Series
UPI	United Press International
URESA	Uniform Reciprocal Enforcement of Support Act
U.S.	United States Reports
USAF	United States Air Force
U.S. App. D.C.	United States Court of Appeals for the District of Columbia
U.S.C.	United States Code
U.S.C.A.	United States Code Annotated
U.S.C.C.A.N.	United States Code Congressional and Administrative News
USCMA	United States Court of Military Appeals
USDA	U.S. Department of Agriculture
USES	United States Employment Service
USFA	United States Fire Administration
USICA	International Communication Agency, United States
USSC	U.S. Sentencing Commission
U.S.S.R.	Union of Soviet Socialist Republics
UST	United States Treaties
USTS	United States Travel Service
v.	*versus*
VA	Veterans Administration, the VA
VGLI	Veterans Group Life Insurance
Vict.	Queen Victoria (Great Britain)
VIN	vehicle identification number
VISTA	Volunteers in Service to America
VJRA	Veterans Judicial Review Act of 1988
V.L.A.	Volunteer Lawyers for the Arts
VMI	Virginia Military Institute
VMLI	Veterans Mortgage Life Insurance
VOCAL	Victims of Child Abuse Laws
WAC	Women's Army Corps
Wall.	Wallace's United States Supreme Court Reports
Wash. 2d	Washington Reports, Second Series
WAVES	Women Accepted for Volunteer Service
WCTU	Women's Christian Temperance Union
W.D. Wash.	Western District, Washington
W.D. Wis.	Western District, Wisconsin
WEAL	West's Encyclopedia of American Law, Women's Equity Action League
Wend.	Wendell's New York Reports
WFSE	Washington Federation of State Employees
Wheat.	Wheaton's United States Supreme Court Reports
Wheel. Cr. Cases	Wheeler's New York Criminal Cases
Whiteman	Marjorie Millace Whiteman, *Digest of International Law,* 15 vols. (1963–73)
WHO	World Health Organization
WIC	Women, Infants, and Children program
Will. and Mar.	King William and Queen Mary (Great Britain)

WIN	WESTLAW Is Natural; Whip Inflation Now; Work Incentive Program
WIU	Workers' Industrial Union
W.L.R.	Weekly Law Reports, England
WPA	Works Progress Administration
WPPDA	Welfare and Pension Plans Disclosure Act
WWI	World War I
WWII	World War II
Yates Sel. Cas.	Yates' New York Select Cases

BIBLIOGRAPHY

PACIFISM

Kellett, Christine Hunter. 1984. "Draft Registration and the Conscientious Objector: A Proposal to Accommodate Constitutional Values." *Columbia Human Rights Law Review* 15.

PAINE, THOMAS

Aldridge, Alfred Owen. 1959. *Man of Reason: The Life of Thomas Paine.* Philadelphia: Lippincott.

Ayer, A. J. 1988. *Thomas Paine.* New York: Macmillan.

PALMER, ALEXANDER MITCHELL

Hall, Kermit L. 1989. *The Magic Mirror: Law in American History.* New York: Oxford Univ. Press.

Justice Department. 1985. *Attorneys General of the United States, 1789–1985.* Washington, D.C.: Justice Department.

Stephens, Otis H., Jr., and John M. Scheb II. 1993. *American Constitutional Law.* St. Paul: West.

PARDON

Stephens, Otis H., Jr., and John M. Scheb II. 1993. *American Constitutional Law.* St. Paul: West.

PARENS PATRIAE

Hall, Kermit L. 1989. *The Magic Mirror: Law in American History.* New York: Oxford Univ. Press.

PARENT AND CHILD

"Children's Legal Rights." 1993. *CQ Researcher* (April 23).

Hall, Kermit L. 1989. *The Magic Mirror: Law in American History.* New York: Oxford Univ. Press.

Postman, Neil. 1982. *The Disappearance of Childhood.* New York: Delacorte.

Purdy, Laura M. 1992. *In Their Best Interest?* Ithaca, N.Y.: Cornell Univ. Press.

Stephens, Otis H., Jr., and John M. Scheb II. 1993. *American Constitutional Law.* St. Paul: West.

PARKS, ROSA LOUISE MCCAULEY

Celsi, Teresa. 1991. *Rosa Parks and the Montgomery Bus Boycott.* Brookfield, Conn.: Millbrook Press. 1992.

Parks, Rosa, with Jim Haskins. 1992. *Rosa Parks: My Story.* New York: Dial.

Robinson, Jo Ann Gibson. 1987. *The Montgomery Bus Boycott and the Women Who Started It.* Knoxville, Tenn.: Univ. of Tennessee Press.

PAROLE

Bamonte, Thomas J. 1993. "The Viability of *Morrissey v. Brewer* and the Due Process Rights of Parolees and Other Conditional Releasees." *Southern Illinois University Law Journal* 18.

"Forum: Parole and Sentencing Reform in Virginia." 1995. *Virginia Journal of Social Policy and the Law* 2.

Zechman, Joseph A. 1988. "Constitutional Law—Due Process in Federal Parole Rescission Hearings—*Green v. McCall,* 822 F.2d 284 (2d Cir. 1987)." *Temple Law Review* 61.

PAROL EVIDENCE

Mann, Richard A., and Barry S. Roberts. 1995. *Essentials of Business Law and the Legal Environment.* 5th ed. St. Paul: West.

PARSONS, THEOPHILUS

Osgood, Russell K., ed. 1992. *The History of the Law in Massachusetts: The Supreme Judicial Court 1692–1992.* Boston: Supreme Judicial Court Historical Society.

PARTIES

Stephens, Otis H., Jr., and John M. Scheb II. 1993. *American Constitutional Law.* St. Paul: West.

PARTITION

Thomas, David A., ed. 1994. *Thompson on Real Property.* Charlottesville, Va.: Michie.

PARTNERSHIP

Bromberg, Alan, and Larry Ribstein. 1995. *Limited Liability Partnerships and the Revised Uniform Partnership Act.* Boston: Little, Brown.

Callison, J. William. 1995. *Partnership Law and Practice.* New York: McGraw-Hill.

Dickerson, Claire Moore. 1991. *Partnership Law Adviser.* New York: Practising Law Institute.

Partnerships, LLCs, and LLPs: Uniform Acts, Taxation, Drafting, Securities, and Bankruptcy. 12th ed. Vol. 1. 1996. Philadelphia: American Law Institute–American Bar Association Committee on Continuing Professional Education.

Patent and Trademark Office

United States Government Manual, 1995–1996. Washington, D.C.: U.S. Government Printing Office.

Patents

Mann, Richard A., and Barry S. Roberts. 1995. *Essentials of Business Law and the Legal Environment.* 5th ed. St. Paul: West.

Walterscheid, Edward C. 1996. "The Early Evolution of the U.S. Patent Law: Antecedents." *Journal of the Patent and Trademark Office Society* 78 (October).

Paternity

McDuff, Lawrence J. 1994. "The 'Inconceivable' Case of *Tierce v. Ellis.*" *Alabama Law Review* 46.

Patients' Rights

Annas, George J. 1989. *The Rights of Patients.* 2d ed. Carbondale and Edwardsville, Ill.: Southern Illinois Univ. Press.

"Dying Wishes Are Ignored by Hospitals, Doctors." 1996. *Trial* (February).

Hoffmann, Diane E., Sheryl Itkin Zimmerman, and Catherine J. Tompkins. 1996. "The Dangers of Directives or the False Security of Forms." *Journal of Law, Medicine, and Ethics* (spring).

"Living Wills." *West's Legal Forms (Elder Law).* 1994 and 1996 Supps. St. Paul: West.

Oberman, Michelle. 1996. "Minor Rights and Wrongs." *Journal of Law, Medicine, and Ethics* (summer).

Rodwin, Marc A. 1994. "Patient Accountability and Quality of Care: Lessons from Medical Consumerism and the Patients' Rights, Women's Health and Disability Rights Movements." *American Journal of Law and Medicine* 20.

Peckham, Rufus Wheeler

Hall, Kermit L. 1989. *The Magic Mirror: Law in American History.* New York: Oxford Univ. Press.

Pennsylvania Constitution of 1776

Williams, Robert F. 1989. "The State Constitutions of the Founding Decade: Pennsylvania's Radical Constitution and Its Influences on American Constitutionalism." *Temple Law Review* 62 (summer).

Witte, Harry L. 1995. "Judicial Selection in the People's Democratic Republic of Pennsylvania: Here the People Rule?" *Temple Law Review* 68.

Pen Register

Mason, Geoffrey C. 1996. "Electronic Surveillance." *Georgetown Law Journal* 84.

Lee, Laurie Thomas. 1993. "U.S. Telecommunications Privacy Policy and Caller ID." *California Western Law Review* 30.

Zitter, Jay M. 1993. "Caller ID System, Allowing Telephone Call Recipient to Ascertain Number of Telephone from Which Call Originated, as Violation of Right to Privacy, Wiretapping Statute, or Similar Protections." *American Law Reports* 9.

Pension

Driggers, Martin S., Jr. 1996. "Minister's Pension Contract Is an 'Ecclesiastical Matter' Not Reviewable by the Court." *South Carolina Law Review* 48 (autumn).

Gregory, David. 1987. "The Scope of ERISA Preemption of State Law: A Study in Effective Federalism." *University of Pittsburgh Law Review* 48 (winter).

Lantry, Terry L. 1996. "Retirees' Pensions Insulated from State Income Tax." *Taxation for Lawyers* 25 (November–December).

Penumbra

Greely, Henry T. 1989. "A Footnote to 'Penumbra' in *Griswold v. Connecticut.*" *Constitutional Commentary* 6.

Helscher, David. 1994. "*Griswold v. Connecticut* and the Unenumerated Right of Privacy." *Northern Illinois University Law Review* 15.

Henly, Burr. 1987. " 'Penumbra': The Roots of a Legal Metaphor." *Hastings Constitutional Law Quarterly* 15.

Peremptory Challenge

Stephens, Otis H., Jr., and John M. Scheb II. 1993. *American Constitutional Law.* St. Paul: West.

Perjury

Aycock, George W. III. 1993. "Nothing But The Truth: A Solution to the Current Inadequacies of the Federal Perjury Statutes." *Valparaiso Law Review* 28.

Curriden, Mark. 1995. "The Lies Have It." *ABA Journal* 81 (May).

Feinstein, Ami L. 1993. "*United States v. Dunnigan* and Sentence Enhancements for Perjury: Constitutional Perhaps, but Unnecessary in Fact." *American Criminal Law Review* 31.

Perkins, Frances

Davis, Kenneth S. 1979. *FDR: The New Deal Years, 1933–1937.* New York: Random House.

Freedman, Russell. 1990. *Franklin Delano Roosevelt.* New York: Clarion Books.

Morgan, Ted. 1985. *F.D.R.: A Biography.* New York: Simon & Schuster.

Whitney, Sharon, and Tom Raynor. 1986. *Women in Politics.* New York: Franklin Watts.

Personal Representative

Ross, Bruce S., and Henry T. Moore, Jr. 1986–1996. *California Practice Guide: Probate.* The Rutter Group.

Physicians and Surgeons

Appleby, Kristyn S., and Joane Tarver. 1994. "Confidentiality of Medical Records." *Trial Diplomacy Journal* (September–October).

Borzo, Greg. 1996. "Liability Records Going On Line in Massachusetts." *American Medical News* (July 1).

Guglielmo, Wayne J. 1996. "Are Doctors Evading the Malpractice Data Bank?" *Medical Economics* (May 28).

Jackson, Anthony. 1995. "Action for Wrongful Life, Wrongful Pregnancy, and Wrongful Birth in the United States and England." *Loyola of Los Angeles International and Comparative Law Journal* (April).

"The National Practitioner's Data Bank." 1996. *Trauma* (April).

PIERCE, FRANKLIN

Stephens, Otis H., Jr., and John M. Scheb II. 1993. *American Constitutional Law*. St. Paul: West.

PINKERTON, ALLAN

Hall, Kermit L. 1989. *The Magic Mirror: Law in American History*. New York: Oxford Univ. Press.

PINKERTON AGENTS

Hall, Kermit L. 1989. *The Magic Mirror: Law in American History*. New York: Oxford Univ. Press.

"History: Pinkerton National Detective Agency." 1997. Pinkerton site. World Wide Web (May 30).

PINKNEY, WILLIAM

Baade, Hans W. 1991. " 'Original Intent' in Historical Perspective: Some Critical Glosses." *Texas Law Review* 69 (April).

Forte, David F. 1996. "Marbury's Travail: Federalist Politics and William Marbury's Appointment as Justice of the Peace." *Catholic University Law Review* 45 (winter).

Hickey, Donald R. 1987. "The Monroe-Pinkney Treaty of 1806: A Reappraisal." *William and Mary Quarterly* 44.

Ireland, Robert M. 1970. "William Pinkney: A Revision and Re-emphasis." *American Journal of Legal History* 14.

Jay, Stewart. 1985. "Origins of Federal Common Law: Part One." *University of Pennsylvania Law Review* 133 (June).

Joyce, Craig. 1986. Review of *Supreme Court Justice Joseph Story: Statement of the Old Republic*, by R. Kent Newmeyer. *Michigan Law Review* 84 (February/April).

Rowe, Gary D. 1992. "The Sound of Silence: United States v. Hudson & Goodwin, the Jeffersonian Ascendancy, and the Abolition of Federal Common Law Crimes." *Yale Law Journal* 101 (January).

PIRACY

Menefee, Samuel Pyeatt. 1990/1991. " 'Yo Heave Ho!': Updating America's Piracy Laws." *California Western International Law Journal* 21.

Short, Greg. 1994. "Combatting Software Piracy: Can Felony Penalties for Copyright Infringement Curtail the Copying of Computer Software?" *Santa Clara Computer and High Technology Law Journal* 10 (June).

PLAGIARISM

Keyt, Aaron. 1988. "An Improved Framework for Music Plagiarism Litigation." *California Law Review* 76 (March).

PLEA BARGAINING

Alschuler, Albert W., and Andrew G. Deiss. 1994. "A Brief History of Criminal Jury in the United States." *University of Chicago Law Review* 61.

Gifford, Donald G. 1983. "Meaningful Reform of Plea Bargaining: The Control of Prosecutorial Discretion." *University of Illinois Law Review* 37.

Jackson, Nick. 1990. "Internal Exile: A Proposal for a Federal System." *Detroit College of Law Review*.

Meares, Tracey L. 1995. "Rewards for Good Behavior: Influencing Prosecutorial Discretion and Conduct with Financial Incentives." *Fordham Law Review* 64 (December).

Odiaga, Ursula. 1989. "The Ethics of Judicial Discretion in Plea Bargaining." *Georgetown Journal of Legal Ethics* 2.

Scott, Robert E., and William J. Stuntz. 1992. "Plea Bargaining as Contract." *Yale Law Journal* 101.

Soni, Anjili, and Michael E. McCann. 1996. "Guilty Pleas." *Georgetown Law Journal* 84.

POISON PILL

Animashaun, Babatunde M. 1991. "Poison Pill: Corporate Antitakeover Defensive Plan and the Directors' Responsibilities in Responding to Takeover Bids." *Southern University Law Review* 18 (fall).

Wingerson, Mark R., and Christopher H. Dorn. 1992. "Institutional Investors in the U.S. and the Repeal of Poison Pills: A Practitioner's Perspective." *Columbia Business Law Review*.

POLITICAL TRIAL

Christenson, Ron. 1986. *Political Trials: Gordian Knots in the Law*. New Brunswick, N.J.: Transaction Press.

POLK, JAMES KNOX

Bergeron, Paul H. 1987. *The Presidency of James K. Polk*. Lawrence, Kan.: Univ. Press of Kansas.

______. 1994. "James K. Polk." In *Encyclopedia of the American Presidency*, edited by Leonard W. Levy and Louis Fisher. New York: Simon & Schuster.

Johannsen, Robert W. 1986. "James K. Polk." In *The American Presidents*. Vol. 1, *Washington to Buchanan*, edited by Frank N. Magill. Pasadena: Salem Press.

Pletcher, David M. 1996. "James K. Polk." In *The Presidents*, 2d ed., edited by Henry F. Graff. New York: Scribner.

POLLACK, MILTON

Arkin, Stanley S., and Kenneth P. Coleman. 1991. "Judicial Activism as an Art: Drexel Case." *New York Times* (June 7): 2.

Feerick, John D., and Milton Pollack. 1994. "Remarks Delivered on the Occasion of the Presentation of the Fordham-Stein Prize to the Honorable Milton Pollack on October 26, 1994." *Fordham Urban Law Journal* 22 (fall).

Oakes, James L. 1989. "Grace Notes on 'Grace Under Pressure.' " *Ohio State Law Journal* 50.

Riencke, Mary, and Nancy Lichterman, eds. 1979. *The American Bench: Judges of the Nation*. 2d ed. Minneapolis: Reginald Bishop Forster.

Robbins, David E., and Michael H. Stone, panelists. 1995. New York Stock Exchange, Inc. Symposium on Arbitration in the Securities Industry. "Discovery." *Fordham Law Review* 63 (April).

Robbins, Ira P. 1987. "Judicial Sabbaticals." Federal Judicial Center Staff Paper.

POLLAK, WALTER HEILPRIN

Hall, Kermit L. 1989. *The Magic Mirror: Law in American History*. New York: Oxford Univ. Press.

Pollak, Louis H. 1982. "Advocating Civil Liberties: A Young Lawyer before the Old Court." *Harvard Civil Rights–Civil Liberties Law Review* 17.

______. 1991. "Thomas I. Emerson: Pillar of the Bill of Rights." *Yale Law Journal* 101.

Stephens, Otis H., Jr., and John M. Scheb II. 1993. *American Constitutional Law.* St. Paul: West.

POLLOCK, FREDERICK

Gordley, James, and Mattei, Ugo. 1996. "Protecting Possession." *American Journal of Comparative Law* 44 (spring).

POLYGAMY

Dane, Perry. 1996. "The Public, the Private, and the Sacred: Variations on a Theme of Nomos." *Cardozo Studies in Law and Literature* 8 (spring–summer).

Gordon, Sarah Barringer. 1996. " 'Our National Hearthstone: Anti-polygamy Fiction and the Sentimental Campaign against Moral Diversity in Antebellum America." *Yale Journal of Law and the Humanities* 8 (summer).

POLYGRAPH

Arendell, Robert L., and Stephen C. Peters. 1996. "Revisiting the Admissibility of Polygraph Evidence after *Daubert*." *Colorado Lawyer* 25 (February).

McCall, James R. 1996. "Misconceptions and Reevaluation—Polygraph Admissibility after *Rock* and *Daubert*." *University of Illinois Law Review.*

PONZI SCHEME

"Head of New Era Indicted." 1997. National Association of College and University Business Offices site. World Wide Web (April 15).

"The Renaissance of Ponzi Schemes." 1997. National Better Business Bureau site. World Wide Web (April 15).

PORNOGRAPHY

Stephens, Otis H., Jr., and John M. Scheb II. 1993. *American Constitutional Law.* St. Paul: West.

POSITIVISM

Sebok, Anthony J. 1995. "Misunderstanding Positivism." *Michigan Law Review* 93.

Soper, Philip. 1996. "Searching for Positivism." *Michigan Law Review* 94.

POSNER, RICHARD A.

Margolick, David M. 1981. "Ally and Foe Admire Bench Nominee." *New York Times* (November 20).

Posner, Richard. 1987. "What Am I? A Potted Plant?" *The New Republic* (September 28).

Rosen, Jeffrey. 1995. "Overcoming Posner." *Yale Law Journal* (November).

POSSE COMITATUS

Corcoran, James. 1990. *Bitter Harvest.* New York: Viking.

Hasday, Jill Elaine. 1996. "Civil War as Paradigm: Reestablishing the Rule of Law at the End of the Cold War." *Kansas Journal of Law and Public Policy* 5.

Malcolm, Joyce Lee. 1994. *To Keep and Bear Arms.* Cambridge: Harvard Univ. Press.

POSSESSION

Lafave, Wayne R., and Austin W. Scott, Jr. 1995. *Substantive Criminal Law.* St. Paul: West.

Singer, George H. 1992. "Constructive Possession of Controlled Substances: A North Dakota Look at a Nationwide Problem." *North Dakota Law Review* 68.

Snyder, David V. 1992. "Symposium: Relationships among Roman Law, Common Law, and Modern Civil Law: Possession: A Brief for Louisiana's Rights of Succession to the Legacy of Roman Law." *Tulane Law Review* 66 (June).

POSTMARITAL AGREEMENT

Mercing, Christine S. 1990. "The Uniform Premarital Agreement Act: Survey of Its Impact in Texas and across the Nation." *Baylor Law Review* 42 (fall).

Mullin, William E., and Judith T. Younger. 1994. "Premarital and Postmarital Agreements." *Bench and Bar* (December).

Practising Law Institute (PLI). 1989. *Tax Aspects of Spousal Rights: Pre- and Post- Mortem*, by Ronald S. Kochman. Tax Law and Estate Planning Course Handbook series, PLI order no. D4-5206.

POUND, ROSCOE

Hall, Kermit L. 1989. *The Magic Mirror: Law in American History.* New York: Oxford Univ. Press.

POWELL, ADAM CLAYTON, JR.

Hamilton, Charles V. 1991. *Adam Clayton Powell.* New York: Atheneum.

POWELL, LEWIS FRANKLIN, JR.

Stephens, Otis H., Jr., and John M. Scheb II. 1993. *American Constitutional Law.* St. Paul: West.

POWELL V. ALABAMA

Geimer, William S. 1995. "A Decade of Strickland's Tin Horn: Doctrinal and Practical Undermining of the Right to Counsel." *William and Mary Law Review* 4.

Goodman, James. 1994. *Stories of Scottsboro: The Rape Case That Shocked 1930's America and Revived the Struggle for Equality.* New York: Pantheon Books.

Haskins, James. 1994. *The Scottsboro Boys.* New York: Holt.

POWER OF ATTORNEY

Brennan, Daniel S. 1990. "Durable Power of Attorney: An Ethical Option When Planning for Elderly Clients." *Georgetown Journal of Legal Ethics* 3 (spring).

Insel, Michael S. 1995. "Durable Power Can Alleviate Effects of Client's Incapacity." *Estate Planning* 22 (February).

Rains, Ramona C. 1996. "Planning Tools Available to the Elderly Client." *American Journal of Trial Advocacy* 19 (spring).

Schmitt, Michael N., and Steven A. Hatfield. 1991. "The Durable Power of Attorney: Applications and Limitations." *Military Law Review* 132 (spring).

PRECATORY LANGUAGE

McElwee, L. A. 1992. "Precatory Language in Wills: Mere Utterances of the Sibyl?" *Probate Law Journal* 11.

PRECEDENT

Stephens, Otis H., Jr., and John M. Scheb II. 1993. *American Constitutional Law.* St. Paul: West.

Preemption

Mellinkoff, David. 1992. *Mellinkoff's Dictionary of American Legal Usage.* St. Paul: West.

Stephens, Otis H., Jr., and John M. Scheb II. 1993. *American Constitutional Law.* St. Paul: West.

Prelaw Education

"Prelaw FAQs." 1997. University of Florida Academic Advising Services site. World Wide Web (May 7).

Premarital Agreement

Aspen Law & Business, a Division of Aspen Publishers. 1996. *The Effect of Pregnancy on Validity of Prenuptial Agreements,* by Victoria M. Ho and Laura W. Morgan. Fair$hare series no. 4.

Graham, Laura P. 1993. "The Uniform Premarital Agreement Act and Modern Social Policy: The Enforceability of Premarital Agreements Regulating the Ongoing Marriage." *Wake Forest Law Review* 28 (winter).

Preponderance of Evidence

Kaas, Carolyn Wilkes. 1996. "Breaking Up a Family or Putting It Back Together Again: Refining the Preference in Favor of the Parent in Third-Party Custody Cases." *William and Mary Law Review* 37.

Presentence Investigation

Minnesota Statutes and Rules of Criminal Procedure. 1997. Federal Sentencing Guidelines Commission site. World Wide Web (May 6).

Presidential Powers

Stephens, Otis H., Jr., and John M. Scheb II. 1993. *American Constitutional Law.* St. Paul: West.

President of the United States

Nelson, Michael, ed. 1996. *The Presidency A to Z.* Washington, D.C.: Congressional Quarterly.

Pretrial Conference

Carlson, Elaine A. 1992. "Rule 166 Pretrial Conferences, Masters and Private Agreements: Revitalizing Old Tools to Meet Today's Needs." *South Texas Law Review* 33.

Masciopinto, Tony J. 1990. "*G. Heileman Brewing Co. v. Joseph Oat Corp.*: Expanding Rule 16's Scope to Compel Represented Parties with Full Settlement Authority to Attend Pretrial Conferences." *DePaul Law Review* 39.

Miller, Frank W., Robert O. Dawson, George E. Dix, and Raymond I. Parnas. 1991. *Prosecution and Adjudication.* 4th ed. Westbury, N.Y.: Foundation Press.

Shands, Cean. 1997. Telephone interview.

Pretrial Publicity

Stephens, Otis H., Jr., and John M. Scheb II. 1993. *American Constitutional Law.* St. Paul: West.

Preventive Detention

Miller, Frank W., Robert O. Dawson, George E. Dix, and Raymond I. Parnas. 1991. *Prosecution and Adjudication,* 4th ed. Westbury, N.Y.: Foundation Press.

Miller, Marc, and Martin Guggenheim. 1990. "Pretrial Detention and Punishment." *Minnesota Law Review* 75.

Prigg v. Pennsylvania

Hall, Kermit L. 1989. *The Magic Mirror: Law in American History.* New York: Oxford Univ. Press.

Prima Facie

Herlitz, Georg Nils. 1994. "The Meaning of the Term 'Prima Facie.'" *Louisiana Law Review* 55.

Prior Restraint

Stephens, Otis H., Jr., and John M. Scheb II. 1993. *American Constitutional Law.* St. Paul: West.

Prison

Bennett, Steven C. 1983. "The Privacy and Procedural Due Process Rights of Hunger Striking Prisoners." *New York University Law Review* 58.

Burger, Warren E. 1986. "The High Cost of Prison Tuition." *University of Miami Law Review* 40.

Call, Jack E. 1995. "The Supreme Court and Prisoner's Rights." *Federal Probation* 59 (March).

Carter, Rubin "Hurricane." 1995. "Death Penalty Symposium Keynote Address." *Santa Clara Law Review* 35.

Fallone, Edward A. 1988. "Preserving the Public Health: A Proposal to Quarantine Recalcitrant AIDS Carriers." *Boston University Law Review* 68.

Gifford, John, public information officer, New Hampshire Department of Corrections. 1996. Interview, July 11.

Miller, Nan D. 1995. "International Protection of Prisoners: Is Solitary Confinement in the United States a Violation of International Standards?" *California Western International Law Journal* 26.

New Hampshire Department of Corrections. 1994. *Biennial Report for the Biennium Ending June 30, 1994.*

Pillsbury, Samuel H. 1982. "Creatures, Persons, and Prisoners: Evaluating Prison Conditions under the Eighth Amendment." *Southern California Law Review* 55.

Potts, Jeff. 1993. "American Penal Institutions and Two Alternative Proposals for Punishment." *South Texas Law Review* 34.

Robbins, Ira P. 1993. "The Prisoners' Mail Box and the Evolution of Federal Inmate Rights." *Federal Rules Decisions* 144.

Rudovsky, David, Alvin J. Bronstein, Edward I. Koren, and Julia D. Cade. 1988. *The Rights of Prisoners.* 4th ed. Carbondale, Ill.: Southern Illinois University Press.

Sowle, Stephen D. 1995. "A Regime of Social Death: Criminal Punishment in the Age of Prisons." *New York University Review of Law and Social Change* 21.

Tachiki, Scott N. 1995. "Indeterminate Sentences in Supermax Prisons Based upon Alleged Gang Affiliations: A Reexamination of Procedural Protection and a Proposal for Greater Procedural Requirements." *California Law Review* 83.

Willens, Jonathan A. 1987. "Structure, Content and the Exigencies of War: American Prison Law after Twenty-five Years 1962–1987." *American University Law Review* 37.

Prisoners' Rights

Stephens, Otis H., Jr., and John M. Scheb II. 1993. *American Constitutional Law.* St. Paul: West.

PRIVACY

Dworkin, Ronald. 1996. *Freedom's Law: The Moral Reading of the American Constitution.* Cambridge: Harvard Univ. Press.

Posner, Richard. 1981. *The Economics of Justice.* Cambridge: Harvard Univ. Press.

Restatement of Torts. 2d ed. 1977. New York: American Law Institute.

Warren, Samuel D., and Louis D. Brandeis. 1890. "The Right to Privacy." *Harvard Law Review* 4.

PRIVILEGE AGAINST SELF-INCRIMINATION

"Criminal Law and Procedure; Privilege against Compelled Self-Incrimination." 1994. *SMH Bar Review.*

"Evidence; Self-Incriminating Testimony." 1994. *SMH Bar Review.*

PRIVILEGED COMMUNICATION

Chaikin, Lisa A. 1995. "Privileged Communications Act Violates an Individual's Constitutional Right to Litigate and the Separation of Powers." *Suffolk University Law Review* 29.

"Evidence." 1994. SMH Bar Review.

"1994 Legislative Update." 1994. *Colorado Law* 23 (August).

"Parent-Child Loyalty and Testimonial Privilege." 1987. *Harvard Law Review* 100.

"Revised Proposed Alabama Rules of Evidence." 1994. *Alabama Law Review* 46 (fall).

Turfe, Edward M. 1995. "Constitutional Law—Due Process—A Trial Judge Must Conduct an In Camera Review of a Complainant's Privileged Communications when the Defendant Can Establish a Reasonable Probability That Material Information Exists in Such Communications; *People v. Stanaway,* 521 N.W.2d 557 (Mich. 1994), *cert. denied,* 115 S. Ct. 923 (1995)." *University of Detroit Mercy Law Review* 72.

Wallace, Lianne K. 1994. "Privileged Communications in Sexual Assault Cases: Rhode Island's Treatment of Clergyman-Parishioner and Psychotherapist-Patient Communications." *Suffolk University Law Review* 28.

PRIVILEGES AND IMMUNITIES

Hall, Kermit L. 1989. *The Magic Mirror: Law in American History.* New York: Oxford Univ. Press.

Stephens, Otis H., Jr., and John M. Scheb II. 1993. *American Constitutional Law.* St. Paul: West.

PROBATE

Averill, Lawrence H., Jr. 1992. "An Eclectic History and Analysis of the 1990 Uniform Probate Code." *Albany Law Review* 55.

PROBATION

Bunzel, Sharon M. 1995. "The Probation Officer and the Federal Sentencing Guidelines: Strange Philosophical Bedfellows." *Yale Law Journal* 104.

MacIsaac, Mary C. 1995. "Probation." *Georgetown Law Journal* 83.

Smith, Michael George. 1995. "The Propriety and Usefulness of Geographical Restrictions Imposed as Conditions of Probation." *Baylor Law Review* 47.

PRO BONO

"ABA Center for Pro Bono." 1997. American Bar Association site. World Wide Web (January 24).

Minnesota Rules of Court. 1996. St. Paul: West.

PROHIBITION

Stephens, Otis H., Jr., and John M. Scheb II. 1993. *American Constitutional Law.* St. Paul: West.

PROPERTY SETTLEMENT

Clark, Homer H., Jr. 1987. *The Law of Domestic Relations in the United States.* 2d. ed. St. Paul: West.

Dougherty, Francis M. 1987. "Divorce: Excessiveness or Adequacy of Combined Property Division and Spousal Support Awards—Modern Cases." *American Law Reports* 55.

Elrod, Linda D. 1996. "Family Law in the Fifty States 1994–1995: Case Digests." *Family Law Quarterly* 29.

Practising Law Institute (PLI). 1989. *Marital Agreements* by Glenda A. Fowler. Tax Law and Estate Planning Course Handbook series no. 184. PLI order no. D4-5206.

Practising Law Institute (PLI). 1990. *Overview of Matrimonial Law in the State of New York and the Role of Matrimonial Agreements* by Stanley Plesent. New York Law Course Handbook series no. 62. PLI order no. F4-3714.

PROSECUTOR

Chattin, Rebecca M. 1996. "Prosecutorial Discretion." *Georgetown Law Journal* 84 (April).

Miller, Frank W., Robert O. Dawson, George E. Dix, and Raymond I. Parnas. 1991. *Prosecution and Adjudication.* 4th ed. Westbury, N.Y.: Foundation Press.

Misner, Robert L. 1996. "Recasting Prosecutorial Discretion." *Journal of Criminal Law and Criminology* 86 (spring).

PROSTITUTION

Clements, Tracy M. 1996. "Prostitution and the American Health Care System: Denying Access to a Group of Women in Need." *Berkeley Women's Law Journal* 11.

Conant, Michael. 1996. "Federalism: The Mann Act, and the Imperative to Decriminalize Prostitution." *Cornell Journal of Law and Public Policy* 5 (winter).

Hauge, Carol H. 1995. "Prostitution of Women and International Human Rights Law: Transforming Exploitation into Equality." *New York International Law Review* 8 (summer).

Lucas, Ann M. 1995. "Race, Class, Gender, and Deviancy: The Criminalization of Prostitution." *Berkeley Women's Law Journal* 10.

PROTECTIVE CUSTODY

Moushey, Bill. 1996. "Protected Witness." Pittsburgh Post Gazette site. World Wide Web (May 26–31).

United States Government Manual, 1996–1997. Washington, D.C.: U.S. Government Printing Office.

PUBLIC CONTRACT

Stephens, Otis H., Jr., and John M. Scheb II. 1993. *American Constitutional Law.* St. Paul: West.

PUBLIC HEALTH SERVICE

United States Government Manual 1995–1996. Washington, D.C.: U.S. Government Printing Office.

PUBLISHING LAW

Perle, E. Gabriel, and John Taylor Williams. 1997. *The Publishing Law Handbook.* 2d ed. Vol. 1. New York: Aspen Law & Business.

Punishment

Bowman, Frank O., III. 1995. "Playing '21' with Narcotics Enforcement: A Response to Professor Carrington." *Washington and Lee Law Review* 52.

Denno, Deborah W. 1994. "Is Electrocution an Unconstitutional Method of Execution? The Engineering of Death over the Century." *William and Mary Law Review* 35.

Dressler, Joshua. 1987. *Understanding Criminal Law.* New York: Bender.

Ewald, William. 1995. "Comparative Jurisprudence (I): What Was It Like To Try a Rat?" *University of Pennsylvania Law Review* 143.

Fletcher, Betty B. 1995. "The Death Penalty in America: Can Justice Be Done?" *New York University Law Review* 70.

Gutterman, Melvin. 1993. "Prison Objectives and Human Dignity: Reaching a Mutual Accommodation." *1992 Brigham Young University Law Review.*

Halley, Janet E. 1993. "Reasoning about Sodomy: Act and Identity in and after *Bowers v. Hardwick.*" *Virginia Law Review* 79.

Jackson, Bernard S. 1995. "Modelling Biblical Law: The Covenant Code." *Chicago-Kent Law Review* 70.

Johnson, Paula C. 1995. "At the Intersection of Injustice: Experiences of African American Women in Crime and Sentencing." *American University Journal of Gender and Law* 4.

Massey, Calvin R. 1987. "The Excessive Fines Clause and Punitive Damages: Some Lessons from History." *Vanderbilt Law Review* 40.

Petersen, Scott K. 1993. "The Punishment Need Not Fit the Crime: *Harmelin v. Michigan,* and the Eighth Amendment." *Pepperdine Law Review* 20.

Practising Law Institute (PLI). 1994. *Sheltering Assets in 1994,* by Thomas Moers Mayer. Real Estate Law Planning Course Handbook series.

Sendor, Benjamin B. 1996. "The Relevance of Conduct and Character to Guilt and Punishment." *Notre Dame Journal of Law, Ethics and Public Policy* 10.

Punitive Damages

Owen, David G. 1994. "Punitive Damages Overview: Functions, Problems and Reform." *Villanova Law Review* 39.

Putzel, Henry, Jr.

Stephens, Otis H., Jr., and John M. Scheb II. 1993. *American Constitutional Law.* St. Paul: West.

Quantum Meruit

Sloan, Judy Beckner. 1996. "Quantum Meruit: Residual Equity In Law." *DePaul Law Review* 42.

Quasi Contract

Knapp, Charles L., and Nathan M. Crystal. 1987. *Problems In Contract Law: Cases and Materials.* 2d ed. Boston and Toronto: Little, Brown.

Sloan, Judy Beckner. 1996. "Quantum Meruit: Residual Equity In Law." *DePaul Law Review* 42.

Quasi-Judicial

Mashaw, Jerry L., Richard A. Merrill, and Peter M. Shane. 1992. *Administrative Law: The American Public Law System; Cases and Materials.* 3d ed. St. Paul: West.

Question of Fact

Arnold, Alvin L., and Marshall E. Tracht. 1996. "Fraud: Whether a House Is New Is Question of Fact." *Real Estate Law Report* 26 (November).

Louisell, David W., Geoffrey C. Hazard, Jr., and Colin C. Tait. 1989. *Pleading and Procedure: State and Federal; Cases and Materials.* 6th ed. Westbury, N.Y.: Foundation Press.

Meslar, Roger W., ed. 1990. *Legalines Civil Procedure.* 3d ed. Chicago: Harcourt Brace Jovanovich Legal and Professional Publications.

Question of Law

Thomas, Janet Shiffler. 1984. "Likelihood of Confusion under the Lanham Act: A Question of Fact, a Question of Law, or Both?" *Kentucky Law Journal* 73.

Quid Pro Quo

Dickinson, Lynn T. 1995. "Quid Pro Quo Sexual Harassment: A New Standard." *William and Mary Journal of Women and the Law* 2 (fall).

Yarbrough, Steven C. 1996. "The Hobbs Act in the Nineties: Confusion of the Quid Pro Quo Standard in Extortion Cases Involving Public Officials." *Tulsa Law Journal* 31 (summer).

Quiet Enjoyment

"Real Property." 1994. *SMH Bar Review.*

"Real Property." 1994. *SMH Bar Review.*

In Re Quinlan

Risley, Robert L. 1994. "Ethical and Legal Issues in the Individual's Right to Die." *Ohio Northern University Law Review* 20.

Stevens, M. L. Tina. 1996. "The Quinlan Case Revisited: A History of the Cultural Politics of Medicine and the Law." *Journal of Health Politics, Policy and Law* 21 (spring).

Weinberg, Joanna K. 1988. "Whose Right Is It Anyway? Individualism, Community, and the Right to Die: A Commentary on the New Jersey Experience." *Hastings Law Journal* 40 (November).

Qui Tam Actions

Brody, Kenneth D. 1990. "Recent Developments in the Area of 'Qui Tam' Lawsuits." *Federal Bar News and Journal* 37 (December).

Cahoy, James. 1996. "U.S. Supreme Court to Review Scope of Qui Tam Lawsuits under Federal False Claims Act." *West's Legal News* (October 17).

Caminker, Evan. 1989. "The Constitutionality of Qui Tam Actions." *Yale Law Journal* 99 (November).

Quitclaim Deed

"Real Property." 1994. *SMH Bar Review.*

Racketeer Influenced and Corrupt Organizations Act

Clarkin, Catherine M. 1994. "*Reves v. Ernst & Young:* The Elimination of Professional Liability under RICO." *Catholic University Law Review* 43 (spring).

Disanto, Carrie J. 1996. "*Reves v. Ernst & Young:* The Supreme Court's Engimatic Attempt to Limit Outsider Liability under 18 U.S.C. § 1962(c)." *Notre Dame Law Review* 71.

Goldsmith, Michael. 1993. "Judicial Immunity for White-Collar Crime: The Ironic Demise of Civil RICO." *Harvard Journal on Legislation* 30 (winter).

Vizera, Diane Lynne. 1993. "Redirecting the Debate on 'Garden Variety' Abuses of Civil RICO." *Columbia Journal of Law and Social Problems* 26.

RAILROAD

American Law Institute (ALI). 1996. *Drug and Alcohol Testing Issues in the Airline and Railroad Industries*, by Robert J. DeLucia. Airline and Railroad Labor and Employment Law series, ALI order no. ABA CLE, SA31.

Ballam, Deborah A. 1994. "The Evolution of the Government-Business Relationship in the United States: Colonial Times to Present." *American Business Law Journal* 31 (February).

Bergene, John, assistant director of communication and public affairs, United States, Canadian Pacific Railroad. 1997. Telephone interview, February 28.

MacDonald, James M., and Linda C. Cavalluzzo. 1996. "Railroad Deregulation: Pricing Reforms, Shipper Responses, and the Effect on Labor." *Industrial and Labor Relations Review* 50 (October).

Malz, Wayne, principal inspector, Federal Railroad Administration, Fort Snelling, St. Paul. 1997. Telephone interview, March 3.

Phillips, Theodore G. 1991. "Beyond 16 U.S.C. sec. 1247 (D): The Scope of Congress's Power to Preserve Railroad Rights-of-Way." *Hastings Constitutional Law Quarterly* 18 (summer).

Price, W. Joseph. 1995. "Video Dialtone: Concentration or Competition." *CommLaw Conspectus* 3 (winter).

Sinozich, Paula A., et al. 1993. "Project: The Role of Preemption in Administrative Law." *Administrative Law Review* 45 (spring).

Smolinsky, Paul. 1995. "Railroad Labor Law." *George Washington Law Review* 63 (June).

Wild, Steven R. 1995. "A History of Railroad Abandonments." *Transportation Law Journal* 23 (summer).

Zawacki, Deanna M. 1995. "Workers' Compensation in the Sixth Circuit: The Evolution from Physical to Mental Disability Claims." *Detroit College of Law at Michigan State University Law Review* (fall).

RANDOLPH, ASA PHILIP

Branch, Taylor. 1988. *Parting the Waters: America in the King Years 1954–63.* New York: Simon & Schuster.

Kluger, Richard. 1976. *Simple Justice.* New York: Knopf.

O'Neill, William L. 1971. *Coming Apart: An Informal History of America in the 1960s.* New York: Quadrangle Books.

RANKIN, JEANNETTE

Berson, Robin Kadison. 1994. *Marching to a Different Drummer: Unrecognized Heroes of American History.* Westport, Conn.: Greenwood Press.

Stineman, Esther. 1980. *American Political Women: Contemporary and Historical Profiles.* Littleton, Colo.: Libraries Unlimited.

RANTOUL, ROBERT, JR.

Hall, Kermit L. 1989. *The Magic Mirror: Law in American History:* New York: Oxford Univ. Press.

RAPE

Bachman, Ronet, and Raymond Paternoster. 1993. "A Contemporary Look at the Effects of Rape Law Reform: How Far Have We Really Come?" *Journal of Criminal Law and Criminology* 84 (fall).

Morgan, Jack M. 1993. "*Michigan v. Lucas:* Rape Shields, Criminal Discovery Rules, and the Price We Pay in Pursuit of the Truth." *Utah Law Review.*

Scalo, Rosemary J. 1995. "What Does 'No' Mean in Pennsylvania?—The Pennsylvania Supreme Court's Interpretation of Rape and the Effectiveness of the Legislature's Response." *Villanova Law Review* 40.

Wallach, Shawn J. 1997. "Rape Shield Laws: Protecting the Victim at the Expense of the Defendant's Constitutional Rights." *New York Law School Journal of Human Rights* 97 (winter).

RATIONAL BASIS TEST

Stephens, Otis H., Jr., and John M. Scheb. 1993. *American Constitutional Law.* St. Paul: West.

RAWLS, JOHN

Bullock, Alan, and R. B. Woodings, eds. 1983. *20th Century Culture: A Biographical Companion.* New York: Harper & Row.

Rawls, John. 1971. *A Theory of Justice.* Cambridge: Harvard Univ. Press.

REAL ESTATE

Oran, Daniel. 1991. *Oran's Dictionary of the Law.* 2d ed. St. Paul: West.

REASONABLE DOUBT

Devitt, Edward James, and Charles B. Blackmar. 1977. *Federal Jury Practice and Instructions.* 3d ed. Vol. 1.

REASONABLE WOMAN

Goldberg, Deborah B. 1995. "The Road to Equality: The Application of the Reasonable Woman Standard in Sexual Harrassment Cases." *Cardozo Women's Law Journal* 2.

RECIDIVISM

Brooks, Justin. 1994. "Keeping the Jailhouse Lawyer Out of Jail." *Criminal Justice* 9 (summer).

Burns, Jerald C., and Gennaro F. Vito. 1995. "An Impact Analysis of the Alabama Boot Camp Program." *Federal Probation* 59 (March).

McClain, Meredith. 1996. " 'Three Strikes and You're Out': The Solution to the Repeat Offender Problem?" *Seton Hall Legislative Journal* 20.

Potts, Jeff. 1993. "American Penal Institutions and Two Alternative Proposals for Punishment." *South Texas Law Review* 34.

RECORDING OF LAND TITLES

Browder, Olin L., et al. 1989. *Basic Property Law.* 5th ed.

Thorson. 1994. "Fundamentals of Title Examination." *MSBA Continuing Legal Education* 1 (April).

RECOVERED MEMORY

Lazo, Joy. 1995. "True or False: Expert Testimony on Repressed Memory." *Loyola of Los Angeles Law Review* 28.

Mason, Mary Ann. 1995. "The Child Sex Abuse Syndrome." *Psychology, Public Policy, and Law* 1.

Recuse

Abramson, Leslie W. 1992. *Studies of the Justice System: Judicial Disqualification under Canon 3 of the Code of Judicial Conduct.* 2d ed. Chicago, Ill.: American Judicature Society.

Comisky, Morvin, and Philip C. Patterson. 1987. *The Judiciary—Selection, Compensation, Ethics and Discipline.* New York: Quorum Books.

Red Scare

Gentry, Curt. 1991. *J. Edgar Hoover: The Man and His Secrets.* New York: Norton.

Powers, Richard G. 1987. *Secrecy and Power: The Life of J. Edgar Hoover.* New York: Free Press.

Reed, Stanley Forman

Stephens, Otis H., Jr., and John M. Scheb II. 1993. *American Constitutional Law.* St. Paul: West.

Referee

Sinclair, Kent, Jr. 1996. *Practice before Federal Magistrates.* New York: Bender.

Referendum

Coury, Christopher A. 1994. "Direct Democracy through Initiative and Referendum." *Notre Dame Journal of Law, Ethics and Public Policy* 8.

Warner, Daniel M. 1995. "Direct Democracy: The Right of the People to Make Fools of Themselves; The Use and Abuse of Initiative and Referendum, A Local Government Perspective." *Seattle Law Review* 19 (fall).

Reform Party

Williams, Victor, and Alison M. Macdonald. 1994. "Rethinking Article II, Section 1 and Its Twelfth Amendment Restatement: Challenging Our Nation's Malapportioned, Undemocratic Presidential Election Systems." *Marquette Law Review* 77.

Refugees

Janosik, Robert J., ed. 1987. *Encyclopedia of the American Judicial System.* Vol. III. New York: Scribner.

Lawson, Edward. 1991. *Encyclopedia of Human Rights.* New York: Taylor & Francis.

Osmanczyk, Edmund Jan. 1990. *Encyclopedia of the United Nations.* 2d ed. New York: Taylor & Francis.

Registration of Land Titles

Browder, Olin L., et al. 1989. *Basic Property Law.* 5th ed.

Regressive Tax

Congressional Research Service. 1990. *Would a Social Security Tax Cut Increase Progressivity?* CRS 90-235 RCO. Washington, D.C.: Congressional Research Service.

Howard, Jay M. 1992. "When Two Tax Theories Collide: A Look at the History and Future of Progressive and Proportionate Personal Income Taxation. *Washburn Law Journal* 32.

Samuels, Leslie B. 1995. "Remarks of Leslie B. Samuels." *Federal Bar Association Section of Taxation Report* 11.

Regulation

Janosik, Robert J., ed. 1987. *Encyclopedia of the American Judicial System.* Vol. II. New York: Scribner.

Reinsurance

Appleman's Insurance Law & Practice. 1976.

Bank, Jonathan F., and Kenneth R. Pierce. 1995. "Reinsurance: Overview and Discussion of Current Problems." *Litigation and Administrative Practice Course Handbook Series* 518.

Couch on Insurance. 1996. St. Paul: West.

Diaconis, John S., and Douglas W. Hammond. 1996. "Introductory Comments and Basic Overview of Reinsurance Terms." *Litigation and Administrative Practice Course Handbook Series* 546.

Ostrager, Barry R., and Thomas R. Newman. 1994. *Handbook on Insurance Coverage Disputes.*

Religion

Harvard Law Review Association. 1984. "Government-Sponsored Nativity Scenes." *Harvard Law Review* 98 (November).

Janosik, Robert J., ed. 1987. *Encyclopedia of the American Judicial System.* Vol. III. New York: Scribner.

Levy, Leonard W., Kenneth L. Karst, and Dennis J. Mahoney, eds. 1986. *Encyclopedia of the American Constitution.* Vol. 3. New York: Macmillan.

Rotunda, Ronald D., and John E. Nowak. 1992. *Treatise on Constitutional Law: Substance and Procedure.* 2d ed. Vol. 4. St. Paul: West.

Spiropoulos, Andrew C. 1997. "The Constitutionality of Holiday Displays on Public Property (Or How the Court Stole Christmas)." *Oklahoma Bar Journal* 68 (May 31).

Swanson, James L., and Christian L. Castle, ed. 1990. *First Amendment Law Handbook.* New York: Boardman.

Reno, Janet

Department of Justice site. 1997. World Wide Web.

Reproduction

Hall, Kermit L. 1989. *The Magic Mirror: Law in American History* New York: Oxford Univ. Press.

Stephens, Otis H., Jr., and John M. Scheb II. 1993. *American Constitutional Law.* St. Paul: West.

Republic

Hall, Kermit L. 1989. *The Magic Mirror: Law in American History.* New York: Oxford Univ. Press.

Stephens, Otis H., Jr., and John M. Scheb II. 1993. *American Constitutional Law.* St. Paul: West.

TABLE OF CASES CITED

U

W

Y

Z

INDEX

BY NAME

Index

By Subject

References that include photos or exhibits are printed in *italic* type.

S